THE ROMAN
EMPIRE AT BAY
AD 180–395

At the outset of the period covered by this book, Rome was the greatest power in the world. By its end, it had fallen conclusively from this dominant position. David Potter's comprehensive survey of two critical and eventful centuries traces the course of imperial decline, skilfully weaving together cultural, intellectual, and political history.

Particular attention is paid throughout to the structures of government, the rise of Persia as a rival, and the diverse intellectual movements in the empire. There is also a strong focus on Christianity, transformed in this period from a fringe sect to the leading religion.

Against this detailed background, Professor Potter argues that the loss of power can mainly be attributed to the failure in the imperial elite to respond to changes inside and outside the empire, and to internal struggles for control between different elements in the government, resulting in an inefficient centralization of power at court.

A striking achievement of historical synthesis combined with a compelling interpretative line, *The Roman Empire at Bay* enables students of all periods to understand the dynamics of great imperial powers.

David S. Potter is Professor of Greek and Latin at the University of Michigan. His previous publications include *Literary Texts and the Roman Historian* (Routledge 1999) and (with David Mattingly) *Life, Death and Entertainment in the Roman Empire* (1999).

D1571547

ROUTLEDGE HISTORY
OF THE ANCIENT WORLD
General editor: Fergus Millar

THE ANCIENT NEAR EAST
c. 3000–330 BC
Amélie Kuhrt

GREECE IN THE MAKING
1200–479 BC
Robin Osborne

THE GREEK WORLD 479–323 BC
Third edition
Simon Hornblower

THE GREEK WORLD AFTER ALEXANDER
323–30 BC
Graham Shipley

THE BEGINNINGS OF ROME:
ITALY AND ROME FROM THE BRONZE AGE
TO THE PUNIC WARS (*c.* 1000–264 BC)
Tim Cornell

THE ROMAN WORLD 44 BC–AD 180
Martin Goodman

THE ROMAN EMPIRE AT BAY AD 180–395
David Potter

THE MEDITERRANEAN WORLD IN
LATE ANTIQUITY AD 395–600
Averil Cameron

THE ROMAN EMPIRE AT BAY
AD 180–395

David S. Potter

LONDON AND NEW YORK

FOR ELLEN,
WITH LOVE

First published 2004
by Routledge
2 Park Square, Milton Park, Abingdon, Oxon OX14 4RN

Simultaneously published in the USA and Canada
by Routledge
270 Madison Avenue, New York, NY 10016

Reprinted 2005, 2007 (twice), 2008

Routledge is an imprint of the Taylor & Francis Group, an informa business

© 2004 David S. Potter

Typeset in Garamond by
Florence Production Ltd, Stoodleigh, Devon
Printed and bound in Great Britain by
MPG Books Ltd, Bodmin

British Library Cataloguing in Publication Data
A catalogue record for this book is available from the British Library

Library of Congress Cataloging in Publication Data
A catalog record for this book has been requested

ISBN 10: 0–415–10057–7 (hbk)
ISBN 10: 0–415–10058–5 (pbk)
ISBN 13: 978–0–415–10057–1 (hbk)
ISBN 13: 978–0–415–10058–8 (pbk)

CONTENTS

ILLUSTRATIONS

Maps

Plates

PREFACE

This book is about the way that an empire changed in the course of two hundred years. I would say evolved, were it not that the metaphor implies improvement, and whatever else one may conclude from the pages that follow, the Roman Empire was a less powerful state at the end of the period that I am covering than it was at the beginning. In the pages that follow, I shall argue that the strength of the Roman Empire derived from the way that the empire was formed. At the height of its power the Roman Empire was an ad hoc collection of acquisitions brought together at various times that, because there never was any grand plan of empire, were governed in ways that suited them. The geographical diversity of the empire was mirrored in its administrative diversity.

The equilibrium of the first and second centuries was impossible to maintain because governments must change; no large institution can exist in a steady state. The way that the institution will change may be affected by the nature of the managerial class – is the management open to new ideas and new perspectives? Does it have a decent strategic plan? Can it understand the capabilities of its rivals? What sort of people rise to the top? In talking about the government of the Roman Empire we are often talking about what constitutes its corporate culture, and how well that corporate culture is in tune with factors that may determine the success or failure of the institution. In the case of the Roman Empire I argue that the rise of the court bureaucracy in the early third century was at odds with earlier traditions of decentralization. Decentralized power strengthened the hands of emperors who were able to negotiate between different interest groups, avoiding, if they were successful, excessive dependence on any one class. The difficulty that inhered in the earlier tradition of government was that it made tremendous demands on the emperor himself, a fact that was implicitly recognized by claims that the emperor was the "best man" in the state, ruling because he alone had the qualities necessary to govern. Behind this rhetoric lay the unfortunate reality, not just of monarchies, but of all systems of government including a chief executive officer, that some who obtain these positions are unequal to the demands of the job.

The consequence of inadequacy at the top was that effective control of the state would fall into the hands of those physically closest to the emperor, members of the palace staff. While the traditions of republican government promoted a diversity of approaches, the tradition of palace government tended to promote a more centralized approach to government. In the early third century, the result was to concentrate authority in the hands of equestrian officials, whose experience was largely in the sectors of imperial finance and law. The men who held these posts tended to deeply conservative patterns of thought, which, while characteristic of the upper classes in general, were in many ways badly suited to understanding a world in which the interests of an external power, the recently emergent Sasanian dynasty in Persia, drove the agenda of foreign affairs.

To those who dominated the government in the early third century, recalling the reigns of Severus and Caracalla – who set the diverse bodies of government against each other as ways of securing the centrality of the emperor in decision-making – dynamic leadership was to be dreaded. At the same time the concentration of power in the palace eliminated safety valves of early centuries that enabled emperors to distance themselves from points of crisis. While an Augustus, a Tiberius, or even a Marcus Aurelius could govern extensive military operations through their subordinates, the emperors of the third century, even when they were adolescents, were expected to take personal command of their armies, and to pay for failure with their lives. An important consequence of centralization was therefore the increased instability of the imperial office itself.

The lessons of the mid-third century were not lost upon Diocletian, who, with great success, strove to establish a system of government wherein the emperor could govern without having to place himself at personal risk on the battlefield. He created a collegial style of government wherein responsibility for failure (and there were some notable failures) could be diffused, while credit for success was shared. Diocletian's experiment was the most radical change in the style of administration since the reign of Augustus, and made it possible for the empire to recover its position in the world.

The ability to control narrative had always been crucial to establishing the legitimacy of government. Like all large states the Roman Empire was an "imagined community", depending upon shared myths for its coherence. From the time of Augustus onwards, the emperor needed to create a congenial story that would justify his position – for Augustus the centerpiece would be that he had ended the civil wars (never mind his role in the events), for the emperors of the second century it was the stability of a government that they ensured through their family relationships, for Diocletian it was that he had saved the state from imminent collapse. Despite this success, his experiment in government was too radical, and could not survive the ambitions of the younger generation. New narratives were shaped to compete with that imposed by Diocletian in his last years, the most powerful being that of the young Constantine, who reasserted the claims of hereditary monarchy against collegial control. It was also Constantine who would confirm the trend already evident of aligning the imperial capital to the emperor rather than the emperor to the capital as had been the case prior to the emergence of the Diocletianic regime. This represented the ultimate triumph of court-centered government over other styles of administration, and led to the reassertion of bureaucratic control over imperial prerogative. Although Constantine, Constantius II, and Julian were all very strong personalities, capable of dominating their officials, the experience of strong government by the emperor led to a powerful reaction after Julian's death. By the end of the fourth century, the emperor had difficulty making himself heard over the interests of diverse groups that flocked to the court to obtain a stamp of legitimacy for their desires. Government for and by committee was reasserted, once again at a time when the empire was faced with new challenges from outside, and had limited internal resources with which to meet those threats.

The emperors of the second century juggled the interests of many groups within imperial society – ranging from their freedmen to members of the senate, from equestrians and municipal aristocrats to the urban population of Rome and various groups within the army. Competition encouraged these groups to identify the interest of the emperor (the preservation of ordered society with himself at the top) with their own. The result of the concentration of power in the hands of court bureaucrats and the leaders of the military bureaucracy was to create a divergence of interest between the emperor and the governing class, whereby the more general interest inherent in the imperial office was subordinated to the parochial interest of imperial officials (principally the security of their status and that of their associates). The result was that the administration of the empire as a whole lost direction, and the state as a whole became less powerful. The threats to the security of the empire that arose in the course of the third and fourth centuries may have been more severe than those of the first and second centuries; imperial powers have a tendency to increase the efficiency of their rivals, but this is not a sufficient explanation for the shift in the balance of power between the empire and its neighbors. Complacency, a sense that internal objectives mattered more than the good of the whole, and government, as it were, by special interest, are among the reasons that these external rivals could become what they did – in the case of Germanic tribes, the successors to the Roman Empire in the west.

The most dramatic transformation in these centuries was not, however, in the structure of imperial government, or even in the relationship between Rome and its neighbors. The most dramatic transformation in the fourth century was the establishment of Christianity as the dominant religion in the empire. This was largely the result of Constantine's decision to support Christian interests, and of the devotion of his son, Constantius II. Constantine and Constantius II created a momentum for growth in the number of

Christians, while, at the same time, vastly complicating the definition of what it meant to be a Christian. There had never been a single definition of belief to which all Christians had subscribed before the Council of Nicaea in 325 AD. There had, however, long been a variety of Christianities defined both by choices of books that were regarded as holy and lifestyles that were considered appropriate. The battles over Christian doctrine that raged in the course of the fourth century, given fresh intensity by the involvement of the court, mask what may be the more important point – that the diversity of the Christian movement was strengthened in the course of the fourth century. The fact that Christianity remained a highly flexible system of thought, despite all efforts by those in the established church hierarchy to make it otherwise, perhaps ensured that diverse legacies of classical antiquity would be preserved in the Byzantine Empire, as well as in western Europe and the later Islamic states.

This book was a long time in the writing, and it is a pleasure to acknowledge many debts that made completion possible. Glen Bowersock and John Matthews taught me how to study the Roman world, and their friendship has sustained my efforts over many years. Whatever good there may be in what follows owes a great deal to their inspiration and kindness. I likewise owe a debt that cannot be expressed in words to the four great historians of the ancient world with whom I worked in the early 1980s at New College, Oxford: Robin Lane Fox, Geoffrey de Ste. Croix, Antony Andrewes, and George Forrest. At the same time I had the pleasure of knowing two historians of more recent times, Erich Christianson and Penry Williams, while Michael Dummett taught me (over lunch) something about the structure of philosophical thought. In my years at Michigan, Rudi Lindner and Brian Schmidt have been ready guides to areas of history before and after the period of Roman power. My students have tolerated any amount of guff as my thoughts have evolved over time, and made me rethink a very great deal. Traianos Gagos and Bob Caldwell have been called upon, countless times, for help with papyri – and they have given more freely of their time than anyone could reasonably ask. Sara Rappe has given generously of herself in helping me to understand the history of thought in the Roman world; Bill Metcalf answered countless questions on numismatics; Benjamin Acosta-Hughes and Ralph Williams have tried to make me a better reader of literature; David Ross taught me a lot about Latin; and Sabine MacCormack never ceased to help me think about a broader picture. Ludwig Koenen has always set a standard of intellectual integrity to which I can only aspire.

This book, which may be read not only as a history of Rome, but as a more general study of management and management styles, was written after I had undertaken to be faculty director of the Lloyd Hall Scholars Program at the University of Michigan. The experience of being a lower-level bureaucratic functionary has influenced the way that I have understood the history of Roman institutions. At the same time, Rachael Weisz taught me how institutional structures worked, while, in the last year, Charlotte Whitney took upon herself so much of the burden of administration that I could actually finish this book, while she, Kim Haynes, and Felicia Kleinberg made it a pleasure to come to work. Mark Tucker, an artist and teacher of extraordinary ability, helped me think about the way that people can see the world without texts.

I would never have written this book without the encouragement of Fergus Millar. He has answered countless inquiries and provided enormous help. That he should ask someone who he knew would not agree with him to write this book is a sign of his extraordinary integrity. His willingness to read work that was hardly complete, and make it better, has sustained the project from the beginning. Where I have been obstinate, he has been understanding; where I have been ignorant, he has been a guide.

Richard Stoneman and Catherine Bousfield at Routledge have been astonishingly patient as deadline after deadline passed for this book with vague assurances that something was happening. Richard Isomaki undertook to edit the manuscript with great skill and efficiency before it went to press, Miranda Chaytor copyedited the book once it was in production, Richard Wilson delivered a meticulous proofread and Catherine Gulick also provided much help with the proofs. The coins used to illustrate this volume were largely obtained through the Classical Numismatic Group, Forum Ancient Coins, Guy Clark Ancient Coins and Antiquities, and Ancient Treasure Coins. Robin Meador-Woodruff guided me through the Kelsey's coin collection, and collection of photographs, locating the splendid picture of the Arch of Constantine that is plate 13. I am also grateful to the Princeton University Press for providing permission to use maps from Richard Talbert's magnificent *Barrington Atlas of the Classical World*. I am also grateful to Professor Talbert for guiding me through the process of obtaining this permission.

Books like this take time to write, in the evenings and on weekends. My family has paid the price for this. Our daughter Natalie even decided that she should not have to go to bed unless "Daddy does his computer." Our daughter Claire had a variety of things to say, while noting that my study was scarcely an example to inspire order. My father read much of the book and made many improvements, and my mother has helped in countless other ways. My greatest debt, however, reflected in the dedication, is to Ellen, *uxor carissima*.

ABBREVIATIONS

For works not found here the reader is referred to the list of secondary works in *L'Année philologique* and, for classical texts, to the lists in Liddell and Scott.

A. Arch. Hung	*Acta Archaeologica Academiae Scientiarum Hungaricae*
AAS	*Les annales archéologiques de Syrie*
AJN	*American Journal of Numismatics*
AJP	*The American Journal of Philology*
ANRW	*Aufstieg und Niedergang der römischen Welt*, ed. H. Temporini *et al.* (Berlin, 1972–)
Ant. af.	*Antiquités africains*
AS	*Anatolian Studies*
BAR	*British Archaeological Reports*
BASP	*Bulletin of the American Society of Papyrologists*
BCH	*Bulletin de correspondance hellénique*
BHAC	*Bonner Historia-Augusta-Colloquium*
BICS	*Bulletin of the Institute of Classical Studies*
BMCR	*The Bryn Mawr Classical Review*
BSOAS	*Bulletin of the School of Oriental and African Studies*
BzZ	*Byzantinische Zeitschrift*
CPh	*Classical Philology*
CQ	*Classical Quarterly*
CRAI	*Comptes rendus de l'Académie des Inscriptions et Belles-Lettres*
CSEL	*Corpus Scriptorum Ecclesiasticorum Latinorum*
Damaszener Mitt.	*Damaszener Mitteilungen*
DOP	*Dumbarton Oaks Papers*
GCS	*Die griechischen christlichen Schriftsteller der erstern Jahrhunderte*
GRBS	*Greek, Roman and Byzantine Studies*
HSCP	*Harvard Studies in Classical Philology*
HTR	*Harvard Theological Review*
JAC	*Jahrbuch für Antike und Christentum*
JECS	*Journal of Early Christian Studies*

JEH	*Journal of Ecclesiastical History*
JHS	*The Journal of Hellenic Studies*
JQR	*Jewish Quarterly Review*
JRA	*The Journal of Roman Archaeology*
JRS	*The Journal of Roman Studies*
LSJ	Liddell and Scott, *Greek–English Lexicon*, 9th edn., rev. H. Stuart Jones (1925–40); Suppl. by E. A. Barber and others (1968)
MAAR	*Memoirs of the American Academy at Rome*
MEFR	*Mélanges de l'École Française de Rome*
NAC	*Numismatica e antichità classiche*
NC	*Numismatic Chronicle*
NZ	*Numismatische Zeitschrift*
OCD³	S. Hornblower and A. J. Spawforth, *The Oxford Classical Dictionary*, 3rd edn. (Oxford, 1996)
OLD	P. G. W. Glare, *Oxford Latin Dictionary* (Oxford, 1982)
OMS	L. Robert, *Opera Minora Selecta*, 7 vols. (Amsterdam)
Opitz, *Urkunden*	H. G. Opitz, *Urkunden zur Geschichte des arianischen Streites 318–328* (Berlin, 1934)
PAPS	*Proceedings of the American Philosophical Society*
PEQ	*Palestine Exploration Quarterly*
PIR	*Prosopographia Imperii Romani* ed. Klebs and Dessau (1897–98)
PIR²	*Prosopographia Imperii Romani*, 2nd edn., ed. E. Groag, A. Stein *et al.* (1930–)
PLRE	A. H. M. Jones, J. R. Martindale and J. Morris, *The Prosopography of the Later Roman Empire* 1 (Cambridge, 1971)
RB	*Revue biblique*
RE	*Real-Encyclopädie der classischen Altertumswissenschaft*, ed. A. Fr. von Pauly, rev. G. Wissowa *et al.* (Stuttgart, 1894–1980)
REA	*Revue des études anciennes*
Rev. Num.	*Revue numismatique*
RIC	*The Roman Imperial Coinage*
RIDA	*Revue internationale des droits de l'antiquité*
Riv. Stor. Ant.	*Rivista storica dell'antichità*
SDHI	*Studia et Documenta Historiae et Iuris*
Suppl. Hell.	H. Lloyd-Jones and P. Parsons, *Supplementum Hellenisticum*
TAPA	*Transactions of the American Philological Association*
Turner, *EOMIA*	C. H. Turner, *Ecclesiae Occidentalis monumenta iuris antiquissima* (Oxford, 1899–1939)
W. Arch.	*World Archaeology*
ZfN	*Zeitschrift für Numismatik*
ZPE	*Zeitschrift für Papyrologie und Epigraphik*

Classical texts

Acta Ab.	*Passio sanctorum Dativi, Saturnini presbyteri et aliorum* (*Acta of the Abitinean Martyrs*)
Acta Proc.	*Acta Proconsularia Sancti Cypriani*
A. G.	Aulus Gellius
Agath.	Agathias
Amb. *De fide*	Ambrose, *De fide*
Amb. *Ep.*	Ambrose, *Epistulae*
Amb. *Ep. extra coll.*	Ambrose, *Epistulae extra collationem*
Amm. Marc.	Ammianus Marcellinus
Anon. post Dionem	The Anonymous Continuator of Dio (fragments in *FHG* 4)
Arist. *Or.*	Aelius Aristides, *Orationes*
Arles can.	*Concilium Arelatense anno 314 habitum* in Jonkers, *Acta et Symbola conciliorum*
Arr. *Perip. M. Eux.*	Arrian, *Periplus Maris Euxini*
Arr. *Tactica*	Arrian, *Tactica*
Ath. *Apol. contra Ar.*	Athenaeus, *Apologia contra Arianos*
Ath. *Deip*	Athenaeus, *Deipnosophistae*
Ath. *De syn.*	Athenaeus, *De synodis*
Ath. *Hist. Ar. ad mon.*	Athenaeus, *Historia Arianorum ad monachos*
Ath. *V. Ant.*	Athenaeus, *Vita Antonii*
Aug. *Breviculus*	Augustinus, *Breviculus collationis cum Donatistis*
Aug. *Civ. Dei*	Augustinus, *Civitas Dei*
Aug. *Conf.*	Augustinus, *Confessiones*
Aug. *Contra Cresc.*	Augustinus, *Contra Cresconium*
Aug. *C. litt. Petil.*	Augustinus, *Contra litteras Petiliani*
Aug. *C. Parm.*	Augustinus, *Contra epistulam Parmeniani*
Aug. *Contra partem Don.*	Augustinus, *Contra partem Donati post gesta*
Aug. *Ep.*	Augustinus, *Epistulae*
Aur. Vict. *De Caes.*	Aurelius Victor, *Liber de Caesaribus*
[Aur. Vict.] *Epit. de Caes.*	Anon., *Epitome de Caesaribus*
Aus. *Act. grat.*	Ausonius, *Gratiarum actio*
Aus. *Mos.*	Ausonius, *Mosella*
CH	*Corpus Hermeticum*
Chron. Pasch.	*Chronicon Paschale*

CJ	*Codex Justiniauns*
Claud. *De VI cons. Hon.*	Claudian, *Panegyricus de sexto consulatu Honorii Augusti*
CMC	L. Koenen and C. Römer, *Der Kölner Mani-Kodex. Über das Werden seines Leibes* (Opladen, 1988)
Coll. Avell.	*Collectio Avellana*
Corpus Agr. Rom.	*Corpus Agrimensorum Romanorum*
C. Th.	*Codex Theodosianus*
Cyp. *Ep.*	Cyprian, *Epistulae*
D	*Digesta*
Dio	Cassius Dio
Dio Chrys. *Or.*	Dio Chrysostom, *Orationes*
Elvira can.	*Concilium Eliberitanum anno 305 habitum* in Jonkers, *Acta et Symbola conciliorum*
Epict.	Epictetus
Epiph. *Pan*	Epiphanius, *Panarion*
Eunap.	Eunapius, *Historae*, fragments in R. C. Blockley, *The Classicizing Historians of Late Antiquity*, vol. 2
Eunap. *VS*	Eunapius, *Vitae sophistarum*
Euseb. *Hist. eccl.*	Eusebius, *Historia ecclesiastica*
Euseb. *Mart. Pal.*	Eusebius, *De Martyribus Palestinae*
Euseb. *Praep. evang.*	Eusebius, *Praeparatio Evangelica*
Euseb. *Vit. Const.*	Eusebius, *Vita Constantini*
Eutrop. *Brev.*	Eutropius, *Breviarum*
Evag. *HE*	Evagrius, *Historia ecclesiastica*
Fast. Hydat.	*Fasti Hydatiani*
Festus, *Brev.*	Festus, *Breviarum*
FGrH	F. Jacoby, *Die Fragmente der griechischen Historiker*
FHG	*Fragmenta Historicorum Graecorum*
FIRA³	E. Riccobono *et al.*, *Fontes Iuris Romani Ante Justiniani*, 3rd edn.
FIRA⁷	Bruns *et al.*, *Fontes Iuris Romani Antiqui*, 7th edn.
Firm. Mat. Math.	Firmicus Maternus, *Mathesis*
Flor.	Florus
Frag. Vat.	*Fragmenta Vaticana* in *FIRA³*, 461–540
Fronto, *Ep.*	Fronto, *Epistulae*
Gai. *Inst.*	Gaius, *Institutes*
George	George Syncellus, *Ecologa Chronographia*
Gesta. Con. Carth.	S. Lancel, *Gesta conlationis Carthaginiensis anno 411*
Greg. Naz. *Or.*	Gregory Nazianzus, *Orationes*
HA	*Historia Augusta*
Herod.	Herodian

Hipp. *Dan.*	Hippolytus, *Commentaria in Danielem*
Hipp. *Ref.*	Hippolytus, *Refutatio omnium haeresium*
Iam. *De myst.*	Iamblichus, *De mysteriis*
Jer. *Chron.*	Jerome, *Chronica*
John Ant.	John of Antioch, fragments in *FHG* 4
Jord. *Get.*	Jordanes, *Getica*
Jul. *Caes.*	Julian, *Caesares*
Jul. *Ep.*	Julian, *Epistulae*
Jul. *Mis.*	Julian, *Misopogon*
Jul. *Or.*	Julian, *Orationes*
Lact. *DI*	Lactantius, *Institutes Divinae*
Lact. *DMP*	Lactantius, *De mortibus persecutorum*
Lucian, *Alex.*	Lucian, *Alexander*
Lucian, *Syr. D.*	Lucian, *De Syriae dea*
Macarius, *Apocr.*	Macarius, *Apocriticus*
Mal.	John Malalas, *Chronographia*
M. Pol.	*Martyrium Polycarpis*
M. Theod.	*Martyrium Theodoti*
Nicaea can.	*Concilium Nicaenum anno 325 habitum* in Jonkers, *Acta et Symbola conciliorum*
Num.	Numenius
Optatus, *Tract.*	Optatus, *Tractatus*
Orac. Sib.	*Oracula Sibyllina*
Origen, *C. Cels.*	Origen, *Contra Celsum*
Origen, *Exhort.*	Origen, *Exhortatio ad Martyrium*
Origen, *Princ.*	Origen, *De Principalibus*
Origo	*Origo Constantini imperatoris*
Oros.	Orosius, *Historia contra paganos*
Pan.	*XII Panegyrici Latini*
P. Ath.	P. Maraval, *La passion inédite de S. Athénogène de Pédachthoé en Cappadoce* (*BHG* 197b), Subsidia Hagiographica 75 (Brussels, 1990)
P. Perp.	*Passio Perpetuae et Felicitatis*
P. Pion.	*Passio Pionii*
Pap. *Resp.*	Papinian, *Fragmenta ex libris responsarum et quaestionum* in *FIRA*[3], 432–46
Paulinus, *V. Amb.*	Paulinus, *Vita Ambrosii*
Phil. *Her.*	Philostratus, *Heroicus*
Phil. *V. Apoll.*	Philostratus, *Vita Apollonii*
Phil. *V. Soph.*	Philostratus, *Vitae sophistarum*
Philost. *HE*	Philostorgius, *Historia Ecclesiastica*
Plin. *HN*	C. Plinius, *Historia Naturalis*
Plot. *Enn.*	Plotinus, *Enneads*
Plut. *Mor.*	Plutarch, *Moralia*
Porph.	Publius Optatianus Porphyrius

Porph. *Abst.*	Porphyry, *De abstinentia*
Porph. *In Christ*	A. von Harnack, *Porphyrius "Gegen die Christen,"* 15 *Bücher: Zeugnisse, Fragmente und Referate, Abhandlungen der königlich preussischen Akademie der Wissenschaften*, Phil-Hist. Kl. 1916, vol. 1 (Berlin, 1916)
Porph. *Plot.*	Porphyry, *Vita Plotini*
Ruf. *Hist. eccl.*	Rufinus, *Historia ecclesiastica*
SC	*Constitutiones Sirmondianae*
Socrates, *Hist. eccl.*	Socrates, *Historia ecclestiastica*
Soz. *Hist. eccl.*	Sozomon, *Historia ecclestiastica*
Suet.	Suetonius
Sulp. Sev. *Chron.*	Sulpicius Severus, *Chronicon*
Symm. *Ep.*	Symmachus, *Epistulae*
Symm. *Or.*	Symmachus, *Orationes*
Symm. *Rel.*	Symmachus, *Relationes*
Tac.	Tacitus
Tert. *Ad Scap.*	Tertullian, *Ad Scapulam*
Tert. *Apol.*	Tertullian, *Apologeticus*
Them.	Themistius, *Orationes*
Theod. *Hist. eccl.*	Theodoret, *Historia ecclesiastica*
Theoph. *Chron.*	Theophanes, *Chronicon*
Zon.	Zonaras, *Epitome Historiarum*
Zos.	Zosimus, *Historia Nova*

Inscriptions and papyri

AE	*L'Année épigraphique*
Aphrodisias and Rome	J. Reynolds, *Aphrodisias and Rome*, Journal of Roman Studies Monograph 1 (London, 1982)
Aphrodisias in Late Antiquity	C. Roueché, *Aphrodisias in Late Antiquity*, Journal of Roman Studies Monograph 5 (London, 1989)
BE	*Bulletin épigraphique*
CIL	*Corpus Inscriptionum Latinarum*
CIS	*Corpus Inscriptionum Semiticarum*
HS	H. Desseau, *Inscriptiones Latinae Selectae*
IG	*Inscriptiones Graecae*
IGBR	G. Mihailov, *Inscriptiones Graecae in Bulgaria Repertae*
IGLS	*Inscriptions grecques et latines de la Syrie*
IGR	R. Cagnet, *Inscriptiones Graecae ad Res Romanas Pertinentes*
ILS	H. Dessau, *Inscriptiones Latinae Selectae*
ILCV	E. Diehl, *Inscriptiones Latinae Christianae Veteres*
Inschr. V. Eph.	*Die Inschriften von Ephesos*
IRT	*Inscriptions of Roman Tripolitania*
I. Strat.	*Die Inschriften von Stratonikeia*

LW	Le Bas-Waddington, *Inscriptions grecques et latines recuilles en Grèce et en Asie Mineure*
MAMA	*Monumenta Asiae Minoris Antiqua*
OGIS	W. Dittenberger, *Orientis Graeci Inscriptiones Selectae*
Oliver, *Greek Constitutions*	J. H. Oliver, *Greek Constitutions of Early Roman Emperors from Inscriptions and Papyri*
P. Bingen	R. De Smet, H. Melaerts, and C. Saerens, *Papyri in honorem Johannis Bingen Octogenarii*
P. Cairo Isid.	A. E. R. Boak and H. C. Youtie, *The Archive of Aurelius Isidorus in the Egyptian Museum, Cairo and the University of Michigan*
PE	S. Lauffer, *Diokletians Preisedikt*
P. Dura	*The Excavations at Dura-Europos Conducted by Yale University and the French Academy of Inscriptions and Letters Final Report*, vol. 5, pt. 1, *The Parchments and Papyri*
P. Flor.	*Papiri greco-egizii, Papiri Fiorentini*
P. Geiss	*Griechische Papyri im Museum des oberhessischen Geschichtsvereins zu Geissen*
PGM	K. Preisendanz, *Papyri Graecae Magicae*
P. Herm.	B. R. Rees, *Papyri from Hermopolis*
P. Lond.	*Greek Papyri in the British Museum*
P. Neph.	B. Kramer and J. C. Skelton (with G. M. Browne), *Das Archiv des Nepheros und verwandte Texte*
P. Oslo	*Papyri Osloensis* (1925–36)
P. Oxy.	*Oxyrhynchus Papyri*
P. Ryl.	*Catalogue of the Greek Papyri in the John Rylands Library at Manchester*
PSI	*Papiri Greci et Latini, Pubblicazioni della Società italiana per la recerca dei papiri greci et latini in Egitto* (1912–)
P. Teb.	*Tebtunis Papyri*
RGDS	*Res Gestae Divi Saporis*
SEG	*Supplementum Epigraphicum Graecum*
Sel. Pap.	*Select Papryi*
TAM	E. Kalinka *et al.*, *Tituli Asiae Minoris* (1901–)

Part I

THE SHAPE OF THE ROMAN EMPIRE

1

CULTURE, ECOLOGY, AND POWER

Power

"After the Greek empire, no other will be raised up except that which possesses the domination in our own day and is solidly established: this is a fact evident to all. It has teeth of iron, because it kills and tears to pieces the entire world by its own force, just like iron. . . . [It] is not one nation, but an assemblage of all languages and all the races of man, it is a levy of recruits with a view to war." The author of these lines was a Christian named Hippolytus, and the images that he was explaining were those of the beast in chapter 4 of the Book of Daniel.[1] Although he may not now be a household name, and although he wrote a very long time ago – toward the beginning of the third century AD – Hippolytus' influence is still very much with us today. It was Hippolytus who asserted that Christ was born on December 25 in the forty-second year of Augustus, a date that was to become enshrined in Christian tradition and forms the basis of the common era by which so much of the world now measures time.[2]

The fate of Hippolytus is not dissimilar to the fate of many others who will pass through the pages of this book. He is little remembered in part because he does not fall within the periods that define the notion of the "classic."

Our image of classical antiquity stems from two cities at two very different times. One is Athens of the fifth and fourth centuries BC; the other is Rome, three hundred years later. The earlier period is that in which the classical form of narrative history took shape, and the period in which the western tradition of drama was formed. It was the period in which standards of rhetoric and art were created, and the great Athenian experiment of democracy took shape, flourished, and fell. Rome in the last century BC was the time of Cicero, of Catullus, and of Virgil, the giants of Latin literature. It too was a time of incredible chaos, the period in which the republican form of government that had enabled Rome to rise to unparalleled power in the Mediterranean world failed to withstand the pressures that accompanied the acquisition of empire, degenerating into civil war. It was the Rome of Caesar,

3

of Pompey, of Antony, Cleopatra, and Augustus. Our view of these two great periods in antiquity was formed, in large part, by the imperial culture of the succeeding centuries, whose inhabitants accorded the status of "classic" to works of earlier generations.

Hippolytus, then, could not be a "classical" thinker because he was part of a generation that defined "classical" as something other than itself. He remains important precisely because imperial definitions of the "classic" helped shape the way that the memory of the ancient world was transmitted. The Rome that helped shape the future direction of European and Mediterranean history was less that of Cicero than that of Hippolytus; it was less that of Augustus than that of Constantine.

The Roman Empire that defined the "classic" may be seen as a dictatorship, supported by military force, or as the catalyst for both modern Europe and the Middle East, facilitated by a system of government that allowed countless peoples to communicate through a shared culture. Rome failed as the Mediterranean world's sole superpower, and the shared culture derived from the study of the "classics" gave way, with increasing rapidity, to new cultures, shaped from the amalgam of "classics" with the reformed style of Judaism that became Christianity. How and why these things happened will be the story of this book. This story will take its shape from the interaction of groups that were formed by, and supported through, the institutions of the Roman state, and the way that classical culture served both to enable, and complicate, communication between these groups. It will be the story of how the diversity of power structures, supported by the diversity of the empire's population, coalesced into fewer and fewer structures that ultimately failed of their purpose.

To begin again with Hippolytus, his primary concern in the commentary on Daniel, as it was in a closely related work on the coming of the Antichrist, was to show that the end of the world was a long way off.[3] His intention was to show that teaching by rival Christian groups to the effect that the end of the world was imminent was false. He tells of a group in Syria that had set off into the countryside in the expectation of meeting Christ, only to find that they were assailed by beasts and brigands. They had to be rescued by the provincial governor.[4] Thus, while his view of the Roman Empire is bleak – he admits that the empire is like the kingdom of Satan because it is all-powerful – he makes it clear that there is worse to come.[5] It is, in his view, the Roman Empire that restrains the coming of the end; the sign that the actual kingdom of Satan was at hand would be the fall of the empire and its dissolution into ten democracies – symbolized, in Hippolytus' view, by the ten toes of the beast in chapter 4 of Daniel.[6]

Hippolytus saw his world as the creation of Rome. The paramount power of its military force was all that could bind the diverse peoples of the empire together. Other contemporaries would praise the empire as a great fort that protected the countless cities that constituted the civilized world within its figurative (and, in places, actual) walls.[7] An empire that could degenerate into ten democracies, or be described as a conglomeration of cities, might also be described as one constituted of diverse power structures wherein people defined their position in terms of their relationship to the ultimate power of the emperor.[8] In an empire of nearly sixty million people, these power structures were extraordinarily varied.

About the time that Hippolytus was writing about Daniel, a group of tenant farmers who lived on an imperial estate in the Bagradas valley of modern Tunisia (then the Roman province of Numidia) wrote to Commodus (AD 180–92) to complain that their rights were being violated.[9] The tenants claimed that the person to whom the estate had been leased by the imperial agent (procurator) who oversaw the lands belonging to the emperor in this region was demanding services to which he was not entitled. The tenants could appeal to a law passed in the time of the emperor Hadrian (AD 117–38) that gave them the right to own marginal land that they cultivated, and to pass this land on to their heirs.[10] The lessee could appeal to the self-interest of the procurator who may have been interested in maximizing the possible revenue from the estate (or in supporting a comparatively important man against his social inferiors). The procurator sent in troops who beat and imprisoned tenants who stood up to him. Somehow a man named Lurius Lucullus, who could write an eloquent petition and had familiarity with the law, came forward to represent the tenants.[11]

The clash between tenant farmers trying to maintain traditional rights and the lessee, backed by the emperor's official, could only be adjudicated at the imperial court. In this case, the emperor's decision favored the tenants against his own officials. We know this because the grateful tenants inscribed the dossier of letters on stone so that all might know that the highest authority had been drawn into their valley and done justice.

The tale of the tenants in the Bagradas valley might serve as a paradigm for the way in which disputes between different groups could be decided, and of the overarching authority of the emperor. And so it should, but it was only one paradigm for the exercise of power. Five years before these tenants launched their appeal to Rome, a group of Christians was imprisoned at Lyons in France on charges that included incest and cannibalism. The governor arrived to hear the case, and in the face of what was a well-organized lynch mob, temporized by writing to the emperor, asking him what to do with regard to individual defendants who were Roman citizens. He sent those who were not citizens to perish in the amphitheater. The emperor upheld his decision to maintain the distinction between the two groups of Christians when he responded that citizens should be decapitated. The decision was based on the principle that Roman citizens should have superior rights to those of the emperor's subjects who had not attained such a status. Unfortunately the person primarily affected by this decree, a man named Attalus, appears to have been the main object of local displeasure. The governor gave in to the crowd, and the emperor's order notwithstanding, Attalus met a horrific fate on the sand of Lyons's amphitheater.[12]

The foregoing examples suggest that the Roman Empire was too complex and large for general laws to be universally applicable. Despite the outward image of uniformity and power that is often evoked by the mention of Rome, the tale of the Roman Empire is more often than not one of radical change. The second century AD was highly unusual.[13] Five emperors succeeded each other without violence between AD 98 and 180. This length of time without assassination or civil strife was unparalleled between the time that Rome achieved its paramount position in the Mediterranean world and the fifth century AD when the western provinces of the empire ceased to be ruled by a Roman emperor.

The periodic upheavals that struck the Roman world may perhaps be taken as a sign of the strength rather than the weakness of the system. For many centuries the source of Rome's power, its unmatched military potential, remained unchallenged despite chaos at the top. The accomplishment of the Roman state, despite its instability, still knows no parallel in the history of the Mediterranean world and surrounding lands.

Perhaps the most remarkable fact about the Roman Empire is that it was a geographic monstrosity. Tertullian, a Christian writer of the late second and early third centuries who lived in Carthage, the principal city in the Roman province of Africa, took it as a sign of the falsity of pagan gods that a priest of Serapis (a god of Egyptian origin) should have offered sacrifice for the health and well-being of the emperor Marcus Aurelius when Marcus had been dead for several weeks.[14] In Tertullian's view, if Serapis was a god, he would have notified his priest that the sacrifice was redundant. What is perhaps more significant is that an event, the death of Marcus, that occurred in the Balkans should be personally relevant to a person living in North Africa. And it was also relevant to a person living in Britain, in France, in Syria, and in Turkey. It was the emperor's position as referee between the diverse hierarchies that constituted the civil society of the Roman Empire that made it so. Even if his word might be ignored, decisions of all sorts were his to make. His physical presence was invoked throughout these lands by countless temples, innumerable milestones marking the roads that bound the empire together, by monuments at the mouths of harbors, and at public events of all sorts. When news came of a missive from the emperor, those assembled in public places were supposed to listen, with heads bowed as his words were read out. They might then choose to forget those words, try to twist them to some personal advantage, or read between the lines to find some hidden meaning, but they would still have heard them.[15] Whenever a person engaged in a financial transaction, the coin that was used would bear the emperor's image. Whenever a person dated a document, the date would bear the imprint of the imperial government. When he wanted to honor the emperor, he would often use the language that he had learned from the emperor's pronouncements to do so.[16]

If we may return to Hippolytus' interpretation of the ten toes on the beast as ten democracies, we may see in this statement the notion that the imperial government was the institution that linked these groups together. In his view, the peoples of the empire had little in common other than the opportunity to serve in the army, which is another way of defining power in terms of overarching imperial institutions. If we were to expand and refine Hippolytus' view further, it might be to move in the direction of a view that structures such as that of the imperial system of taxation created a series of interrelated economic zones whose character and, consequently, whose existences were enabled by the imperial government.[17] Studies of the circulation of coinage in the empire would seem to dictate precisely such a view.[18] It has, for instance, been conclusively demonstrated that local coinages of Greek cities in the east circulated within relatively limited areas around their point of issuance.[19] Bankers, as we now know, tended to specialize in local transactions. They did not transfer large quantities of coin from place to place, but they could engage in local financial transactions for absentee investors.[20] The engines that drove these financial systems were extremely wealthy individuals who held properties around the Mediterranean, and the imperial government. It was the imperial government that could provide either bullion to be minted into coinage or, in other cases, the coinage itself, to ensure that the money supply of individual areas was adequate to what the state regarded as its needs.[21]

The fate of Britain as the imperial power was withdrawn in the fourth and fifth centuries AD offers, perhaps, the greatest testimony to the importance of the order imposed by the imperial government. The reason for this is that Britain is unusual in that another authority did not fill the vacuum created by the departure of Roman government.[22]

The ending of Roman Britain was a process that was already well in train during the last decades covered by this book, and a radically different social structure would emerge within thirty years of the death of Theodosius in AD 395. Indeed, many people who had grown to maturity in Theodosius' lifetime might sense that the world was not what it once was before they left it. On December 31, 406, the Rhine frontier would be irreparably breached, and a new Germanic nation, the Visigoths, would be in the process of formation within the frontiers. The Visigoths, and some of the tribes that crossed the Rhine, would carve out new kingdoms by adapting and reforming existing governmental structures. But this would not happen in Britain because those structures would have vanished before the Saxon peoples began to settle on British soil. It is this that makes the case of Britain so important for broader understanding of what made the Roman Empire work.

As early as the 380s there were signs that there was something wrong with life, as it had been lived, in Britain. Towns were beginning to fall into disrepair, as were some villas, the houses of the elite. By AD 403 coin hoards that had been buried by landholders in fear of their safety and never recovered are beginning to show signs of significant change.[23] The clipping of bits of metal off coins, which was banned by the imperial government, begins to be widespread, and, interestingly, the forging of bronze coins appears to have become notably less common. The copying of bronze coins was connected with their use in day-to-day economic exchange, suggesting that a monetary economy was ceasing to function. After 402 it appears that silver coins ceased being shipped to the island, suggesting that the local imperial authorities were having trouble getting paid.[24] In 407, the governor of Britain was proclaimed emperor and set out for Gaul, where he was killed four years later. No effort was made to restore central authority or, consequently, to collect taxes. It has been argued that the tax structure of the imperial government created a mechanism of exchange between towns and the countryside that created a unified local economy, and it was the connec-

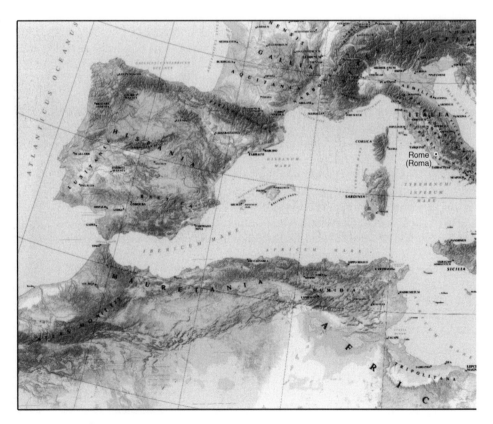

Map 1 The Mediterranean

Source: *Barrington Atlas of the Classical World*, courtesy of the Princeton University Press.

8

tion of this local economy with other local economies that was facilitated by Rome. If the broader connection was eliminated, there was little to keep a local economy running as it had before. In Britain the removal of the bulk of the garrison to fight in Gaul, and subsequent collapse of provincial administration, destroyed the basic mechanisms through which local hierarchies were linked together, and through which local economies were joined. By about AD 430 town life that had been nurtured on the island for more than 300 years had ended, while in the countryside many villas, once the rural bases for the civic aristocracy, were in decline. Mosaic floors were covered in dirt, hearths were built inside rooms that had once been for display, imports ceased.[25] Connection with the broader culture of the Roman world that had been mediated by the elites who had once lived in these houses was so diminished in significance that it cannot be traced.

The fate of Britain raises the question of what besides participation in the hierarchical structure of Roman imperial government made a person Roman?

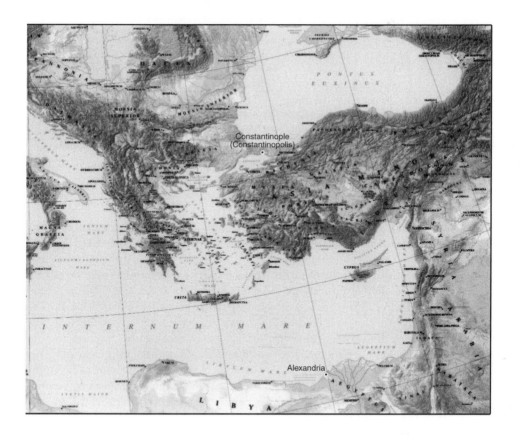

To what extent was there a shared culture in the Roman Empire, and, to the extent that there was such a culture, how deeply did it penetrate into the peasant societies that constituted the bulk of the population of the empire? Some 80 percent of the people who lived in the empire were peasants. What did a peasant who lived in France have in common with one who lived in North Africa? There are no easy answers to these questions, and to some extent the answers will vary according to the structure of the hierarchies that were predominant at any given period.[26]

The fate of Britain raises questions that may be no less significant than the first. Why did Romano-British society dissolve in the fourth to fifth centuries, while in the third century the weakening of Roman central government gave rise to a variety of alternative Romes? How did the balance of power between Rome and the lands it ruled change in the course of the fourth century? Did the increasing centralization of political and intellectual control in the imperial court have the effect of depressing allegiance to the central government and erasing critical space within which local societies could forge relationships with the central government?

Ecology

No account of the cultural complexities of the Roman world can ignore the diversity imposed by geography. The three central geological formations of the empire are mountains, rivers, and the Mediterranean Sea. These features define the zones of human habitation and interaction, but they do not prescribe the course that these interactions might take. The Mediterranean might act as a gigantic moat, or as a gigantic highway; rivers might be roadblocks, or they might be avenues; and a mountain range may be a lesser obstacle if one could be sure of what was to be found on the other side.

In any consideration of Roman history, it is the Mediterranean that must come first, for the Roman Empire was a Mediterranean phenomenon before it became a continental one in Europe, Africa, and the Near East. The sea itself was formed around a hundred million years ago when the African landmass collided with the Eurasian. Around twenty million years ago the eastern outlet of the Mediterranean was closed off by the Arabian landmass, and about six million years ago, it dried up when glaciation lowered the level of the Atlantic so that a land bridge emerged between Europe and Africa. The retreat of the glaciers raised sea levels again, enabling the Atlantic to pour over this land bridge into the enormous valley that had been created by the former evaporation. The new sea thereby created occupies an area of roughly 1,143,000 square miles (if the Black Sea is included). From the Strait of Gibraltar, where the sea is only twelve hundred feet deep, to the coast of Lebanon, where the Mediterranean narrows, it is 2,300 miles long with an average width of 500 miles. Its average depth is five thousand feet, and its water level is sustained by the influx of the Atlantic. Two characteristics

10

of the sea that stem from its surroundings are that it has very low tides and a rapid rate of evaporation, increasing its salinity.[27]

The collision of continents left the Mediterranean ringed with high mountain ranges: the Atlas mountains of North Africa, the Pyrenees, and the Alps. The Alps, along with the Carpathian mountains, create a watershed that separates western Europe, effectively a peninsula bounded by the Atlantic and its two wings, the Baltic and Mediterranean seas, from the bulk of the Eurasian plain. In addition to the mountains, the principal features of this peninsula are three great rivers: the Rhine, the Danube, and the Rhône. The valley of the Rhône offers a line of communication from the Mediterranean coast to the interior, while the lateral lines of the Rhine and Danube defined, ideologically, if not actually, the northern limits that a Mediterranean power could hope to control. On the Spanish peninsula, the great valley of the Guadalquivir opened the heartland to the broader world of the sea.

On the northeastern end of the Mediterranean, the mountains that define the Anatolian plateau continue a geological formation that ends in the west with the Alps and with the Himalayas in the east. On the Mediterranean end the ascent to the plateau is gradual as the result of four great rivers that flow down into the sea. On the northern and southern edges of Anatolia, bounded by the Pontic outcropping of the Caucasus mountains and the Taurus, the division between the ecology of the upland and coastal regions is pronounced. South of the Taurus mountains, a line of mountain ranges – the Amanus, Jebel Ansariyah (Mount Casius in antiquity), the Lebanon and the anti-Lebanon – divides a thin coastal region from the semidesert of the Syrian plain, which extends to the banks of the Euphrates River in the east and gives way to the desert plateau of the Hauran in the south. There are three rivers that rise in the Lebanon: the Orontes, the Litani, and the Jordan. The Orontes flows north, emptying in the Mediterranean on the northern edge of the Jebel Ansariyah; the Litani, rising a few miles from the Orontes, flows south to the sea near the modern city of Tyre. The Jordan flows south through Galilee to its termination in the Dead Sea on the eastern edge of the mountainous ridge that extends north out of the Sinai. Another river, the Nile, flowing out from the mountains of Uganda and Ethiopia in east-central Africa, enters the Mediterranean through an enormous delta whose apex lies around 125 miles south of the sea coast.

The diverse geology of the Roman Empire supported, as it does now, a wide variety of ecologies ranging from northern Britain to the edge of the Atlas mountains. Variation of rainfall and temperature may indicate the extremes that a person who traveled across the empire would encounter. Let us assume the case of an army officer, on the move from the city of Dura on the Euphrates to the camp at Vindolanda in Britain. At Dura average rainfall was around seven inches a year and average temperature around 73 degrees, while at Vindolanda average rainfall was around twenty-eight inches and average temperature around 48 degrees.[28] Our putative traveler would probably come to the Mediterranean at Seleucia, one of the great ports of Syria that enabled the passage of men and material from the west to the army on the eastern frontier (if this traveler was following another branch of the trade route, he might go to Caesarea in Palestine or Alexandria in Egypt). The journey by sea would enable the traveler to bypass the Alps and sail either out into the Atlantic (a very unlikely scenario) or to go directly to Marseilles at the mouth of the Rhône. Our traveler would leave the Rhône near Autun, to reach the Seine, which would take him to the great port city of Boulogne. It would then be a short trip across the English Channel to Richborough. From that point onwards the journey would probably be by land, following the roads built by the legions of Rome to London, and thence northwards through York to the region of Hadrian's Wall. Assuming a rapid and trouble-free journey, this traveler, who would have left the banks of the Euphrates in the winter so as to take advantage of the best sailing times, would now be cold and wet, winter having arrived at the point of destination just short of a year later.[29]

Although the Mediterranean facilitated this journey, our hypothetical traveler is not a "Mediterranean" person, and it is arguable that no such class of person existed.[30] Our traveler moved from the Semitic environment of Mesopotamia to the Celtic of Britain. In so doing this person passed through several other ecological and cultural zones, for the mountains that ring the sea create sixty-four microclimates. With storms that move from west to east, average rainfall varies by as much as twenty inches – from fifteen to thirty-five inches – a year.

Rainfall affects the production of food, which is to some degree dependent upon local plant life. There are three characteristic types of vegetation throughout the region: scrub woodland, maquis, and garigue. Scrub woodland is typically rather open with low-crowned trees standing individually or in clumps, with an average height of between thirty and forty feet. The three primary species that make up this tree cover are the olive, evergreen oak, and Aleppo pine.[31] Maquis, consisting of dense, scrubby evergreens standing between six and twelve feet tall, is characteristic of the upland regions. The most common species are heath, the strawberry tree, and rockrose, with oleander, the chaste tree, and sweet bay also being well represented. Thickets of maquis are integrated into a regime of garigue, an open association of shrubs, often rich in fragrant oils, that ordinarily stand three to four feet high. These ecological regimes are ordinarily restricted to the zone below 2,500 feet, though this average disguises a tendency for the upper limit to increase as one passes from north to south. The mean upper limit in northern Spain is 1,600 feet, while in the Sierra Nevada of southern Spain it is 3,300 feet, and around 4,000 feet in the Atlas mountains. Along the extremely wet coast of Croatia, the range is around 650 feet, while on the Albanian coast it reaches only 200 feet. A few hundred miles further south, on the west coast of the Peloponnese, it reaches about 2,200 feet, and about 2,600 feet on the Cyrenaican coast of North Africa (modern Libya). Moving from east to west, the mean elevation of the Mediterranean regime of vegetation increases around 1,600 feet along the coast of Turkey, 1,900 feet in southern Italy, and 2,500 outside the range of the Sierra Nevada in southern Spain.[32]

The line of Mediterranean vegetation extends inland along the coast of western Europe to the southern edge of the Massif Central, the Jura, and the Alps. There it is replaced by a regime of mid-latitude mixed forest in which the primary species are oak and beech, with the exceptions of coastal ever-green forests along the Bay of Biscay and the Atlantic coast of Britain. Coniferous forest predominates in the mountainous zones. From northern France and the Low Countries the mixed forest runs in a continuous and ever-widening spread to the Urals. This forest dominates the Balkan peninsula, with the exception of the coastal zones, until it merges with the treeless steppe of Moravia and the Ukraine.

Within the Mediterranean basin the essential components of the diet were the olive, wheat, beans, and grapes, though there were some notable exceptions.[33] The olive tree does not grow in Egypt, which may have contained somewhere between 7 and 8 percent of the population of the empire.[34] Nor will the olive tree grow above eight hundred meters or in regions that experience frost. The inland regions of France, Spain, the Balkans, Anatolia, the Po valley of northern Italy, and, of course, the island of Britain did not support olive cultivation. When these regions are taken together with Egypt, it is possible that some 30 percent of the population did not have olive oil as a staple of its diet. In Egypt, sesame oil was substituted; in western Europe and Anatolia, butter was used instead. Cows and goats were the predominant source of dairy products, and a substantial question subsists as to how important these animals were as sources of meat in the overall diet. It has been asserted that pigs alone were kept basically for meat. This view is based largely on the literary evidence for the consumption of pork products in Italy and the use of young pigs as sacrificial animals in Greek cult.[35] It is further suggested that the short Mediterranean growing season, along with a shortage of grass and other fodder, meant that there was little meat available on a day-to-day basis. Consumption of meat on a regular basis was an elite activity in which the less well off joined on rare occasions. This may be true, but recent work has called some of these assumptions into question. While there is no doubt that the wealthy had more access to meat than the poor, the assumption that pigs were the only animals kept for consumption is very dubious, as is the assumption that the poor lived as involuntary vegetarians.[36]

West-central Italy was the great region of pig consumption in the Roman Empire: from the period of the late republic on through the period covered by this book some two-thirds of all animal remains are porcine. This reflects a cultural preference among the inhabitants of Rome and surrounding regions. It is not true of the rest of Italy. In Campania, for instance, pre-Roman sites show a greater concentration of bovine remains until the first century BC, when this region finally joined the Latin pattern of pork-eating. In south Italy there is evidence for much higher consumption of sheep and goats, which conforms with other regions that were influenced by the western Greeks. Northern Italy reveals a greater taste in beef (though still less than that for sheep and pigs) which may reflect the tastes of the pre-Roman, Celtic, population. Even more interesting is that a much higher proportion of pig remains appears in urban contexts (roughly 54 percent) than in rural (circa 49 percent). The increase in the consumption of pork throughout Italy may reasonably be taken as a sign of the predominance of west-central Italian tastes that stemmed from the preeminence of the city of Rome. When attention is shifted to Spain, a similar pattern emerges, though with one significant variation. Here cattle predominate in the early period (circa 46–63 percent), while the sheep and goat remains drop from approximately 39 percent to approximately 21 percent with a corresponding increase in the percentage of pig. A very different dietary pattern took hold north of the Pyrenees and Alps. In the Gallic provinces cattle and pigs predominate, both before and after the coming of Rome (we are told of a Gallic tradition of pig-rearing that predates Caesar's conquest in the 50s BC), while Provence in the south appears to have had a significantly higher proportion of sheep and goat in the diet. Cattle are clearly the preferred source of meat in Britain and Germany, though there is an interesting regional difference in that sheep far outnumber pigs in Britain, while the reverse is true along the Rhine.

The significance of pork as a source of nutrition declines radically in the east. On rural sites in Greece up to 74 percent of remains are of sheep, 10 percent are of cattle, and 15 percent are of pigs. The proportions change in urban sites, where cattle remains may amount to as much as 21 percent, and the proportions of sheep to pig are roughly 46 percent to 32 percent (with wide variation from site to site). This would suggest that pork might have been seen, as the evidence of cult suggests, as a prestigious food to be consumed, along with beef, on public occasions. In Asia Minor bovine and sheep remains (in roughly equal proportions – 38 percent and 40 percent respectively) predominate over pigs. The absence of pigs is far more striking in the Semitic provinces and Egypt, where the overwhelming proportion of remains are of sheep (72 percent urban and 67 percent rural) with cattle coming in a distant second (circa 22 percent urban and 27 percent rural) and pigs an even more distant third (circa 6 percent urban and 7 percent rural). In North Africa, sheep are a clear majority at all periods, with an unusual variation in the fourth and fifth centuries whereby cattle remains decline from approximately 24 percent to 4 percent and pigs increase from 18 percent to 31 percent. Perhaps remains from military contexts provide the most interesting control on these numbers, since in those places consumption patterns mirror those of civilian communities. Far from being a force for dietary

14

change, the army's diet changed according to the habits of the peoples upon whom they were quartered.

The proportions of animal remains across the empire suggest that the Latin taste in pork was a highly localized phenomenon. The one area where the Roman army may have effected some change in dietary patterns was Britain, where the proportion of beef increased, possibly reflecting the tastes of soldiers recruited from the Gallic and German provinces. No influence can be detected in the east.

The ratios of animal remains cannot tell us how much meat the average person consumed. Nor can evidence for animal size – evidence from medieval records leads to the conclusion that the animals were comparatively small by modern standards – tell us all that much about consumption.[37] What we need to know is not how big the animals were, but rather what the ratio was of human to beast. Thus, while there is reason to think that cereals and legumes provided the bulk of the rural diet because of the poor quality of meat, we cannot begin to estimate how high this proportion actually was. An assumption that cereals and legumes constituted as much as 75 percent might well be wrong, since it is based upon assumptions about regional meat production that are not borne out by the archaeological evidence.[38] Assumptions about the absence of meat are also problematic, as they neglect the place of fish in the diet. In this case the evidence is yet to be assembled in the way that it has been for animal flesh. What we do know, on the notoriously unreliable evidence from our literary texts, is that fish tended to be regarded as a luxury food for the rich, and that the fisherman was notoriously poor. The Mediterranean as a whole is less productive of aquatic life than other oceans (a feature of its relatively high temperature and high salinity), and it was harder to fish with the technologies available in the premodern period because of its steep continental shelves. But this is not true of every region: we know of cities such as Tarentum in southern Italy where the sea seems to have been a source of prosperity, and fish-farming was practiced in the Roman period.[39] One product of this industry was a form of fish sauce (garum) that seems to have been widely consumed in urban areas throughout the empire.[40]

Fish, lamb, bread, cheese, olive oil, beans, and the like were consumed in different proportions depending on where a person lived. Location would also determine other additions to the diet. The corpses of animals slaughtered in the amphitheater at Rome appear to have been offered as a supplement to the inhabitants of Rome (given the unusual scale of these entertainments, this is unlikely to have been of similar significance in any other city).[41] Galen, the great doctor of the second century AD, gives a list of cereals that were characteristic of colder regions, and every region produced its own variety of wine.[42] Most were more fortunate than the people of Caunus on the western coast of Turkey, who found that their product should be mixed with seawater. In the northern provinces beer was a significant alternative to wine, even after the introduction of the vine to France in the first century AD (one of the few genuine ecological improvements in Roman history). It was also an important beverage in Egypt and, perhaps, at locations on the Euphrates.[43] One of the oldest and most revered divinities in the Mesopotamian tradition was Tammuz, who numbered among his functions the fermentation of grain.[44] Milk is a nutrient with an interesting history as well. In the Greek world it seems that its consumption was taken as a sign of barbarism.[45] Civilized people, it seems, turned milk into cheese. Milk-drinking was especially associated with pastoralists. This may be true, but it is sometimes hard to be sure just what this means – taken at face value this topos would suggest that it was not consumed in "civilized" areas. This may be true, but the most obvious pastoralist was the local shepherd. It might be that the notion that milk consumption was for barbarians masked a class bias as well as a cultural one. We simply cannot know for certain.

Diet is intimately connected with the physical well-being of the population. In much of the Mediterranean the low average rainfall masks a high degree of interannual variation (both too much and too little could be a problem). Although peasant farmers might pursue strategies to reduce the risk, a couple of bad years in a row could all but eliminate their reserves. In Greece and western Turkey, at least one year in three could be problematic, leading to crop failure and consequent food shortages, a fact of life that was complicated by the fact that "wheat's unpardonable fault was its low yield."[46] A portion of the Roman province of Africa Proconsularis (in modern Tunisia) was regarded as exceptionally fertile because grains planted there yielded a 5:1 return.[47] The area around Leontini in Sicily, benefiting from the rich volcanic soils around Mount Aetna, is said to have produced wheat with a yield of 10:1, above the average of 8:1 in a good year and 6:1 for a more typical year, in southern Italy.[48] These figures, derived from ancient authors, are in line with figures for southern Italy derived from studies of the early modern period.[49] There is no reason to think that figures from medieval France are not on the same scale as those from the Roman period, showing substantial interregional variation in accordance with local ecological conditions. Thus the 1338 yield figures from Provence are on the order of 4 or 5:1, a ratio that remained reasonably constant into the early eighteenth century, and are comparable with those of other Mediterranean regions.[50] In the alluvial regions of Artois, the figures are much higher, ranging from roughly 8–12:1 (or even 14–15:1 at one fertile estate).[51] Across the channel, at Winchester between 1200 and 1499, the average yield was 4:1 (with a high of 6.1:1 and a low of 2.5:1). At Merton College, Oxford, yields between 1333 and 1336 averaged 4.3:1.[52] Low yield rates such as these are especially interesting, as Britain and North Africa had reputations as grain exporters, suggesting that this renown was due to relatively low population density and, possibly, to the ability of absentee landlords to extract what they needed even to the point of causing local food shortages.[53] The overall picture that may be derived of farming in the Roman Empire is that conditions were similar to those in the Middle Ages, with its patterns of good and bad years. The insecurity of the food supply in the premodern world suggests that the inhabitants of the countryside lived under the perpetual threat of shortage. Even if the diet was less heavily dependent on wheat as is sometimes suggested, shortages of grain translate into the death of animals, and loss of fertilizer and seed for the future. What is more, conditions of premodern agriculture suggest that a majority of the rural inhabitants of the Roman world suffered from a diet that lacked sufficient vitamins to be nourishing. Incorrect feeding over generations can have disastrous effects, and these problems are heightened in periods when the population is expanding.[54] There is some reason to think that the population of the Roman Empire did just this in the century and a half after Augustus.

It has been estimated that the population of the Roman Empire increased from a near historical low in the first century BC to a near historical high in the second century AD. A low estimate for the earlier period is not unreasonable. Extraordinary chaos struck the entire area of the Roman world from the beginning of the great wars of conquest in the late republic and the even greater civil wars that accompanied them in the first three quarters of the first century BC. The arrival of the peace established by Augustus may have allowed the population of the empire to expand from somewhere around 45 million people to somewhere in the vicinity of 64 million people by the time of Marcus Aurelius. A population that is nearing the limits of the carrying capacity of the land that supports it may suffer more seriously from malnutrition than a smaller one.[55] The impact of the so-called Antonine plague, a series of epidemics that raged from 165 into the mid-180s and killed off some 10 percent of the empire's population, may be a reflection of the inherent bad health. The plague's devastation was perhaps all the more severe in that the response of a rural population to such a disaster is often an increase in the birthrate. Such an effect is demonstrable in premodern China and England, and strongly suggested by the evidence of Egyptian census returns from the later half of the second century AD.[56] These records reveal sudden, catastrophic falls in population, followed by a rapid recovery with a population that was slightly younger than the one prior to the catastrophe. The population may thus have recovered to its preplague size within fifty years – and continued to place extreme pressure on the land that supported it.

The Antonine plague is not the only indication that life was harsh and short in the Roman world. Life expectancy at birth is a useful measure of social welfare, and evidence from the Roman world reveals patterns that are, once again, commensurate with that of a preindustrial population. The Egyptian evidence suggests an average life expectancy at birth of between twenty-two and twenty-five years.[57] This evidence is of value not because it represents an absolutely reliable guide to the Egyptian experience; rather it is important because it provides some empirical support to comparative studies based on somewhat later premodern societies (whose records are better preserved). Such comparison makes it reasonable to assume that there were not substantial differences between the life-cycle in the Roman Empire and in other states occupying the same ecological niche prior to the demographic transition that began, in Europe, in the eighteenth century. But there may be more to it than that. While, as a consequence of both the empirical approach to the Egyptian evidence and the comparative approach, it is reasonable to think that average life expectancy at birth in some parts of the empire was around twenty-five years, evidence connected with other parts of the empire suggests a rather longer life-span. An analysis of magistrates from the Italian city of Canusium suggests that their life expectancy was nearly thirty-two years at birth, and the career pattern of Roman senators – who had to be over forty if they were (except under unusual circumstances) to hold the highest office (consul) – might again assume a life expectancy at birth that is closer to thirty than twenty-five.[58] Comparison with other premodern societies suggests that location had a greater impact on longevity than status – meaning that people in overpopulated areas like Rome or the Nile valley likely lived shorter lives than did people living in other climates and under other conditions.[59]

Although he might not necessarily have lived longer, the elite Roman male was better nourished, better exercised, and better cared for than the average peasant. The result was likely to have been physiologically noticeable. In ideological terms, the point was enshrined in the earliest surviving Greek literature, the Homeric poems, which formed the core of an educated person's learning in those parts of the empire where Greek was the dominant language of the upper class. The story of Thersites, the common soldier who ventured to oppose the will of Agamemnon, leader of the Greeks at Troy, appears to have been a popular one. One thing that made Thersites so notable was that he was

> the ugliest man who came beneath Ilion. He was bandy-legged and went lame of one foot, with shoulders stooped and drawn together over his chest, and above this his skull went up to a point with the wool grown sparsely upon it.
>
> (*Iliad* 2.16–19, trans. Lattimore)

When Odysseus returned home to Ithaca in disguise, it took the intervention of the goddess Athena to make him look insignificant enough to pass for a beggar. The intrinsic interest of the upper classes in both the Latin- and Greek-speaking sections of the empire in physiognomy, in the outer person and mirror of the inner, may stem, in part, from the quite different dietary experiences of the dominant and dominated classes of the empire.[60]

Across this vast expanse of ecologies the fundamental practices of rural life were necessarily diverse, as were relationships between urban centers and the land around them. Rome, the imperial capital, to take the most obvious example, transformed the rural economy of Italy, creating, in place of the distinct regions of early Italy, an integrated series of urban systems ranging from "regional central places to centers of local marketing and administration."[61] Beyond its impact on the Italian economy, the demands of feeding a city of some one million people facilitated the growth of an imperial network of great regional centers, which, though not as large as Rome, were not utterly overshadowed by it. Carthage, Alexandria, and Antioch were as ecologically distinct from Rome as they were from each other, but, functionally, their existence helped spur the development of local networks of cities. The study of the olive tree suggests that it was precisely the demands of the great centers that spurred an enormous increase in the cultivation of the tree.[62] Moreover, as it has likewise been estimated that the bulk of agricultural production from Egypt, Africa, and Syria remained inside the province, it is arguable that the vastness of Rome was only possible because its growth had spurred developments needed to provide the surplus that supported it. The existence of regional centers likewise appears to have spurred diversification of secondary agricultural produce. As the authors of a recent study of the Mediterranean have observed:

> Two places growing barley or almonds; two places cultivating fragmented lots with irrigation; two places using unfree labour . . . may be wildly different from each other because of their respective contexts in the wider ecology of connectivity. Excessive concentration on the traditional classification by crop-type or regime will obscure and render unintelligible much of their economic and social history.[63]

To return to the earlier question of what it meant to be Roman, one answer is simply that it was to be resident in a region whose economy was given direction by the grand cities of the Mediterranean rim. Such an answer is perhaps excessively minimalist, for it is to say little more than that one was born, lived, and died in an administrative entity known as the Roman Empire. As such it would also be misleading, since the impact of Rome extended well beyond the administrative boundaries of the Roman state. Studies of the Germanic lands to the north of the Rhine and Danube suggest that a taste in Roman goods may have helped shape political structures.[64] The transfer of such goods to the north was, from the first century AD onwards, under administrative control, ideally passing through certain defined customs posts.[65] The manipulation of the flow of these goods could be used to shore up or undermine chieftains whose position depended, in part, upon their ability to reward their followers with prestige items imported

19

from the empire. But such goods also may have come north with men who had served in the Roman army. No longer members of the imperial establishment, they nonetheless brought with them tastes that were formed south of the border. The Runes with which texts were inscribed in northern lands appear to have developed in southern Denmark as a result of contact with Rome. Members of elite society appear to have desired to mark their goods in imitation of habits they had learned of in the south.[66]

A survey of those influenced by the structures of Roman government would necessarily include also those who were involved in the transshipment of goods, by land and sea, to the Far East. We know a good deal less than we would like about the organization of this trade, but it is worth noting that the trade with India appears to have passed through a series of discrete economic zones, with the personnel changing at various points along the way. In this regard it is perhaps significant that Chinese information about major cities of trade from India through the Persian Gulf and the Red Sea in the second century AD appears to have been derived from traders of Semitic background.[67] In the same vein, it is notable that a freedman who reached Ceylon from Egypt was lost, while members of the embassy from An-Tun, the king of Ta-ch'in (a Roman emperor named Antoninus) to the emperor of China, were evidently merchants from Vietnam.[68] Whatever the ethnic identity of the traders, the forms that they used were still those of the Roman world. The fascinating text of a loan agreement for the delivery of a gigantic cargo that had arrived in Egypt from India refers to an earlier loan agreement that appears to have been drawn up in a style compatible with the Roman world at Muziris in India.[69] The Seleucid dynasty had taken over a developed network of trade with India from the Achaemenids; the Ptolemies had taken over the western and northern ends of other trade routes with central Africa, southern Arabia, and India. Both continued to flourish under Roman rule, and, at least on the Egyptian end, with a substantial degree of control being exercised from Rome once products reached the empire.[70] In India itself there seems to have been a colony of merchants who erected a temple of Augustus at Muziris on the southeastern coast, and that grain was shipped out for the use of "those concerned with shipping," who are distinct from the "merchants who do not use it" – Indians who ate rice.[71] Palmyra, albeit a city that fell within the borders of the province of Syria, controlled much of the trade with the east that passed up through Mesopotamia, in its own right, and Palmyrene merchants are attested as being involved with the trade through Egypt as well. Their appearance here suggests that they were connected with a broad network of traders, professionals in the "eastern trade" wherever it landed.[72] Inscriptions from South Arabia that commemorate ceremonies conducted by the Hadramawt king 'Il'add Yalut mention representatives from Palmyra, Babylonia, and India.[73] The Palmyrenes, like the Indians, are here because their interests are specifically involved.

The answer proposed above does not really help very much, nor would it be viable to say that being Roman meant nothing at all. At the very least it meant that even the inhabitants of rural areas were in contact with the broad structure of elite culture that bound different parts of the empire together. We know, for instance, of numerous villages throughout the provinces of Syria and Arabia, like "the village of Rêsô" near Petra, or Sekla near Apamaea, that derived their names from important landholders.[74] Villages like that at Kefr-Laha in Arabia, or Umm ez-Zitoum in Syria, possessed a corporate body, or *koinon*, with which, it appears, local worthies would associate. In the case of Umm ez-Zitoum a man identified as a town councilor, *bouleutes*, joined with the sons of two veterans to aid "the *koinon* of the village and of the God" in erecting a building "on behalf of the safety and victory of our Lord Marcus Aurelius Probus Augustus" in 282.[75] At Kefr-Laha three veterans joined with the *koinon* in erecting a shrine to the emperor Maximinus in 236.[76] In these cases we need not suppose that the veterans were themselves villagers. Rather, having retired on the generous pensions granted soldiers, they had become landowners in the region, and they provided a link between the village and the greater world of the empire. In the Hauran, a region of modern Jordan, where there were no significant cities at the time that the province of Arabia was created in AD 106, we see other developments, inspired by the central government, whereby villages were awarded the status of *metrokomai*, or "mother villages" in the later second and early third centuries. The places of which we know appear to have had small garrisons, which contributed to their elevation, since these places developed the infrastructure of small cities to support the troops.[77]

Moving north and west to the region of Karamanli in modern Turkey, we can watch the initiates of Zeus Sabasios, making dedications on behalf of "their salvation, and the salvation of the village of the Hormêleoi and the salvation of Annia Faustina and of Tiberius Claudius."[78] Annia Faustina was the grandniece of Marcus Aurelius, and Tiberius Claudius was Tiberius Claudius Severus Proculus, her husband and the consul of 210. It is likely that the village was part of an estate that they owned in the area. In the region of Cavurbeleni in southern Turkey, when we find a wealthy woman erecting statues of herself and her husband, and giving a dinner for the people of the village, we may assume that they owned much land in the area.[79] So too may have Gaius Julius Julianus Tatianus, a wealthy man of Thyateira in Lydia (western Turkey) have owned land in or around the village Tabeirnoi, whose people erected a statue in his honor.[80] In the first part of the second century AD, the Roman Asinius Rufus wrote to the civic magistrates of Sardis asking them to recognize the right of the village of Arillenoi to hold a fair, pointing out that he was doing this as a courtesy to them since he could easily have written straight to the emperor instead.[81] While we do not know what happened in the end, the letter itself is a remarkable piece of diplomacy, revealing that all power did not lie with the cities in their dealings with the villages in their territory. Asinius, who says that he was asked to act because his ancestors had been patrons of the place, did not want to insult the magistrates of Sardis by having the emperor give them an order in a matter where they could preserve their dignity by acting on their own. In another case, we find the governor of Asia asking the civic authorities at Philadelphia in western Turkey to allow a monthly market at a village called Tetrapyrgia (probably owned by the man who had asked him to intervene) on a day that would not clash with other local markets.[82] These markets enabled villagers to exchange their surplus produce, acquire goods from traders, and, in some cases, to grow and acquire an identity of their own.[83]

Turning to another part of the empire, where the evidence is of a different sort, we come to North Africa, which is worth a look even though the best of the evidence for the interpenetration of urban and rural life will not appear until the fourth century AD in the context of church controversy and conflicts between settled and nomadic peoples. When we do get this evidence, it helps provide a context for appeal of the tenant farmers of the Bagradas valley, and the appearance of their champion. The area will be filled with large estates, described variously as *fundi* and *castella*, owned by members of elite families. These *castella* are the architectural descendants of the "towers" that were the central buildings of estates owned by major urban landholders as far back as the third century BC – it was in such an estate that the great Carthaginian general Hannibal hid himself after his defeat at the hands of Scipio Africanus in 201 BC.[84] Around these estates, and often supported by the estate owners themselves (who, in Africa, were less likely to be constrained by civic governments), were markets. These markets were, it seems, sponsored by the landholders as benefactions, a way of supporting existing structures in the countryside, and, in a sense integrating the value system of the urban aristocracy with the needs of the rural population.[85] Such markets could help bring peasants into contact with people like Lurius Lucullus.

The form of Lurius' appeal reflects another aspect of the connection between peasants and the imperial government – there is remarkable similarity across time and space in the form of petitions to emperors from the countryside, opening with lengthy summaries of the injustice they wish corrected and concluding with prayers for salvation.[86] It may be that the authors of these petitions were guided by handbooks, or had their pleas shaped for them by an imperial official – we have drafts of a petition from a grammarian who wished to complain to the emperor that he was not being paid by the town in Egypt that owed him his salary, along with the draft of a letter to an official whom he hoped would help get his petition a favorable response.[87] In one case we can identify the person who brought the petition before the emperor as a soldier with connections to the village that he seeks to help.[88] People from an imperial estate in Lydia complained that ten people had been kidnapped by imperial policemen and held for ransom – though by the time that this appeal was written one man had managed to come up with the equivalent of the 16,000 Roman sesterces that the kidnappers demanded.[89] The fact that they inscribed the tale of their woes suggests that they received help. These people may be oppressed, but they are not poor, and they are not isolated from means of redress.

In economic terms, while there is no reason to suppose that the peasant in North Africa learned new agricultural techniques from peasants in Italy, there is every reason to think that these peasants planted more acres of grain and more olive trees than they would have had the Roman Empire not existed.[90] The peasant in Syria still spoke Aramaic and farmed in much the same way that his ancestors did, but his landlord likely spoke Greek; and the enormous expansion of farming in north-central Syria is at best explained as a direct consequence of the development of Antioch as a major administrative center.[91] The fact that the landlord of our putative Syrian peasant spoke Greek was perhaps nothing new, given that the area around Antioch and the inland cities that grew up on the inland lines of communication toward the Euphrates were largely Seleucid foundations. But the ability of this landlord to communicate with the landlord of our putative North African peasant was a function of Roman government.

To return again to the question of what it meant to be Roman, it might, perhaps, be better to admit that there can be no single answer, no lowest common denominator that is very useful. Rather it may be better to see varying degrees of Roman-ness depending on a person's location and status. Just as the Roman Empire could not change the way peasants farmed, it could not dictate a single model of participation in the system of government. What it could do was offer ways for people, however they participated, to communicate. The cities of the Roman Empire were linked by a shared cultural idiom, and their wealthier inhabitants who set the tone of urban life through their buildings and benefactions may have had more in common with one another than with the peasants who farmed their land. But the very fact of this link might transform the way that the peasant understood the world.

Cult and culture

When he read much of the evidence presented in the last few pages, Michael Rostovtzeff, the great Russian historian of antiquity, saw a great distinction between the peasant of the countryside and what he referred to as the bourgeoisie that dominated life in the cities.[92] His language was that of a member of the Russian intelligentsia of the turn of the twentieth century, and his views were plainly influenced by the world that he had seen destroyed in 1917–18. But to be able to explain his views in light of his personal experience (something that Rostovtzeff himself was prone to do) should not be to invalidate them.[93] The distinction between town and country life that he perceived was real. What is at issue is whether or not the relationship was symbiotic, or, as he saw it, hostile.[94] I have suggested that the situation may not have been as bleak as Rostovtzeff thought it was, though it must be admitted that the more positive picture is connected with what I take to be evidence for village elites who had access to urban patrons, and may not reflect the lot of those living at the subsistence level; and it cannot tell us much about how contact with urban culture might have changed the way people saw the world around them. To understand this it is necessary to examine the mental stratigraphy of rural areas.[95] The lives of rural peoples, closely tied though they are to the earth, are not simply defined by agricultural technologies. The inhabitants of the countryside had brains; they had emotional lives, aspirations, and beliefs that did not continue unchanged from the Stone Age to the advent of modern technologies. The rhythms of everyday life were not simply those of sowing, reaping, and reproduction. Every age left its imprint. The study of the mentalities of rural peoples as well as of their bodies is akin to the study of the earth. Just as different geological ages have left their imprint on the earth's crust, so too the study of rural life is, in a sense, stratigraphic. Just as rock formations may reveal the course of regional evolution, so too may the physical remains of cult sites supplement the uneven written record to suggest phases of human development. One crucial issue in the period covered by this book is the rise of Christianity, and the rise of Christianity is unthinkable if the peasants of the empire were immune to external influences. The adaptation of local cults to the common culture of the aristocratic city also suggests something of the intellectual effects of the Roman Empire.

The geologist has one obvious advantage in describing the stratigraphy of the earth as opposed to that of the collective mind: a mutually agreed vocabulary. A second advantage may also be cheerfully conceded to the geologist. The geologist is talking about something that demonstrably exists. The historian who makes simple assertions about the collective *mentalité* of a people whose expressions are largely lost may rapidly run out of things to say. The historian may be on safer ground when talking about behaviors. It is plain, for instance, that swords were thrown into bodies of water at cult sites in northern Gaul. In the pre-Roman period these swords were largely of Celtic design. In the first century AD the pattern of deposition shifts suddenly and irretrievably to swords of Roman design.[96] There are two reasonable conclusions about the deposition of swords in pre-Roman contexts. One is that they are trophies of war being offered to a divinity that was thought to have helped in the victory. The other is that the sword was offered to a divinity at a point of transition in a warrior's life, the most likely being when he reached the end of his effective fighting career. If the pattern in the Roman period is a continuation of the pattern in the pre-Roman period, then it is reasonable to think that the sword was sunk when it was no longer to be used; and that the Roman swords of the first century were offered up when men were mustered out of the *auxilia*. The person who offered his sword in this way also carried with him a bronze diploma certifying that he had completed his service according to Roman regulations. The loyal servant of Rome may thus be seen to exist either between two radically different worlds, those of his Celtic heritage and of his Roman employers, or to have forged a new, coherent existence that accommodated the demands of both. To see in this practice a stratum in the human geology of Gaul may permit one to avoid the necessity of choosing either answer, and that may be preferable. It marks the addition of a new element in the lives of Gallic warriors, who now were able to channel the warlike traditions of their ancestors into a new direction; Roman rule did not rob such people of their capacity for self-definition through combat. It plainly did not require that such people abandon traditions that were important to them, but rather it enabled them to forge a form of participation in a new order.

At some point, probably in the third century, a man named Aurelius Diphilianus erected an altar at Dura-Europos to "the ancestral God, Zeus Betylos, of those by the Orontes."[97] Aside from the fact that he identifies himself as a soldier in the Roman Legion IV Scythica Antoniniana, we know nothing about this man. We do not know if he was a native of Syria, and thus we do not know if the ancestral God, Zeus Betylos of those by the Orontes, was his ancestral god, or a god whom he had encountered in his service. However he had encountered Zeus Betylos, Diphilianus clearly thought that he was important enough to pray to, and that his prayers had obtained the desired result. The name of the god combines two significant elements, the name of the Greek god Zeus with a name derived from a Semitic style of representing divinities as objects, in this case as stones or betyls. In the Semitic tradition, betyls were stones that were inhabited by gods, and so Diphilianus may be saying that his god is the Zeus that inhabits the betyl. Otherwise, if he is using Betylos as an adjective, he may be saying that this particular Zeus is the betyl. If that is so, then his understanding of the god would probably have struck "those by the Orontes" as rather peculiar.

However Diphilianus understood his god, he is illustrative of a process. His name, Aurelius, suggests that he, or, possibly his father – we cannot take it back much further than that because Dura was destroyed in 256/57 – obtained citizenship from the emperor Caracalla (whose proper name was Marcus Aurelius Antoninus). The name Diphilianus is a hybridization of the common Greek name Diphilus, with the Latin *-anus* ending indicating attachment (or, to be more precise, since he spelled his name in Greek, the ending is *-anos*, whose usage to indicate attachment is modeled on the Latin usage). The appearance of a man with such names in the Syrian desert is unthinkable without the institutions of Rome, which have, quite literally in this case, helped define his identity. As a polytheist, he presumably felt that it was a good idea to betake himself, for assistance when stressed, to a divinity who appears to be the local version of the ruler of the gods.

It might be argued that the similar processes of divine redefinition connected with the offering of swords in Gaul and the creation of the altar of Diphilianus stem not from generalized patterns of cultural adjustment, but rather from attachment to the institutions of Rome.[98] In both cases soldiers are involved, but that is not the case with many other such dedications. No such intervention, for instance, can be detected behind a three-word dedication at Ksar Lemsa in Libya: *Maragzu Aug(usto) sac(rum)*, or "dedicated to Maragzu Augustus."[99] Maragzu is the chief god of the region; his importance in the Roman context is emphasized by the addition of the title Augustus, which signifies the concept of supreme power. Maragzu, as the name suggests, was a divinity of the local Berber population who, rather than being effaced by the new regime, is assimilated to a generalized conception of importance. Similarly, at Sidi Amor Jedidi, also in Libya, two local magistrates, P. Cornelius Viator and Justus son of Bithies, repaired the shrine *(aedes)* dedicated to the *mibilis Cererum* in the reign of Antoninus Pius (AD 138–61). *Mibilis* is a western Phoenician word, used here as an equivalent for the Latin *numen* (divine power). Its usage in this way appears to be a development from its original meaning, which was "holy place," or, better, the place where the spirit of a divinity resides; as with a betyl, the place where the divinity resided was filled with the spirit. The cult that they celebrated was perhaps as mixed as the language that they used to celebrate it. The "Cereses" *(Cererum)* are evidently a Phoenician adaptation of the Greek cult of Demeter and Kore (or Persephone).[100] According to a tradition reported by the historian Diodorus, writing in the first century BC, the Carthaginians had destroyed a shrine to these goddesses in 396 BC.[101] All manner of disasters then struck them, including a devastating plague, the destruction of their army, and a mutiny by their mercenaries. They then created this new cult, which led to the preservation of their state (as they saw it). In this sense the Phoenician Cereses became not so much symbols of fertility, as was the Greek Demeter who had been assimilated in Roman tradition to the Italian goddess Ceres (hence the title in this text), as of salvation.

In a case like this, or Maragzu Augustus, a term like *Romanization* fails to do justice to the process, for what is suggested is not the formulation of "Romanized" conceptions of the gods, but rather the formulation of new identities that were neither Roman nor traditional. The conception of the Cereses was not opposed to that of Ceres; the men who reconstructed the shrine, commemorating the emperor as they did so, do not appear to be asserting a local tradition against the cultural imperatives of the governing power. Rather, their action reveals a moment of evolution in an ongoing effort to understand the workings of the divine within their community. Similarly, divinities such as Dii Mauri, or Dii Macni and Dii Magifae Augusti, attested at various points in modern Algeria, represent a combination of idioms to express concepts that are at once both local and universal.[102] To describe the combination of idioms as a form of syncretism, whereby gods of one tradition are assimilated to those of another, may be as misleading as a term such as *Romanization*, for the Dii Mauri remain, quintessentially, the gods of their region, not divinities who have become something different.[103] The polytheist traditions of the ancient world were in constant flux, able to update themselves to new situations and demands, and knowledge of the gods was potentially increasing with new revelations at all times.[104] If divinities were to continue to be worshipped, they had to be updated to meet the needs of their worshippers.[105]

Perhaps the most striking example of one way in which existing divinities could be reinterpreted through new circumstances is offered by a story that was composed with a view to debunking the whole process. According to Luke the evangelist, the apostle Paul and his companion Barnabas arrived at the city of Lystra on the northern slopes of the Taurus mountains of southern Turkey, in a district known as Lycaonia, where they met a cripple:

> This man listened while Paul was speaking. Paul fixed his eyes on him and saw that he had faith to be cured, so he said to him in a loud voice, "stand up straight on your feet"; and he sprang up and started to walk. When the crowds saw what Paul had done, they shouted in their native Lycaonian, "The gods have come down to us in human form." They called Barnabas Jupiter, and Paul they called Mercury because he was the spokesman. And the priest of Zeus, whose temple was just outside the city, brought oxen and garlands to the gates.
>
> (Acts 14:9–13)

Paul and Barnabas dissuaded them from offering sacrifice, but interestingly, Luke does not say that the crowd then converted to the faith.[106] The inhabitants of Lystra, disappointed though they may have been by the disclaimer, had been prepared to sacrifice the ox that their priest had brought because, in their understanding, Zeus was a god of oxen, and he was, at times, depicted in the company of a young man. This Zeus is known to us from a series of reliefs as Zeus Ampelitês, a divinity who specialized in the protection of horses and cows. A pair of reliefs depicts him in the company of a young man, his messenger.[107] We do not know the origin of this Zeus, but he was one of a series of manifestations of the god that were worshipped in the Upper Tembris valley of Phrygia. They may all go back to gods in the period prior to the rise of the great post-Alexandrine Greek kingdoms in Asia Minor who were associated with Zeus as a mark of their primacy. A spectacular event such as that narrated by Luke could then lead to further development in understanding of how they might function on earth. In this way they provide a vehicle for reifying novel events in a traditional context.

Greek and Latin, as the dominant tongues of the urban elite, could not only enable the reinterpretation of existing cult in response to an external stimulus, they could also permit new claims to be put forward. Thus at Turda in Libya (probably the ancient site of Zugal) a dedication was made to the *numen* of King Saturn, the father of the gods, and to Latona, mother of Apollo and Diana.[108] The description of Saturn as king *(rex)* and father of the gods is unique to this text, as is the pairing of Saturn with Latona. The cult of Saturn in North Africa descends from the Phoenician cult of Baal, but Latona is a distinctively Greco-Roman entity. In an area rich in olive trees, commemoration of Latona might have seemed particularly appropriate since she had given birth to Apollo and Diana under one. The assertion that this Saturn was king of all the gods may look back to an original Phoenician understanding of the divinity, but that is less certain than the obvious point that the novel assertion here is made possible by the permeable boundaries of local and supraregional culture.

It is possible that developments in one area could promote those in another – at least that is a possible reading of the odd dedication to "Jupiter and Juno, Dracco and Draccena, and Alexander" made by a slave named Epitynchanus at some point in the third century near Stobi, in what is now the former Yugoslav republic of Macedonia.[109] It appears that Dracco and Draccena are best understood as local divinities, reflecting a badly attested cult of dragons. To pair them with Jupiter and Juno, leading divinities of the Roman pantheon, suggests that they should be understood as being on the same level. The Alexander mentioned here is very probably the Alexander who invented and promoted the cult of a snake named Glycon at Abonuteichos in northwestern Turkey during the reign of Antoninus Pius.

Glycon, who gave oracles from his shrine, was said by Alexander (who staged his birth using an ostrich egg and a small snake) to have been the son of Asclepius; his serpentine form was intended to evoke the serpents of his putative father. In addition to his oracles, it was alleged that Glycon would perform cures for those who slept in his temple, just as Asclepius did in his great sanctuaries at Epidauros in Greece and Pergamon in western Turkey. He was not presented as the chief of all the gods, but he does seem to have found a consort (who slept with Alexander), which may have led to the reinterpretation of the Balkan Dracco by Epitynchanus.[110] What little we know of dragon cults in the area suggests that dragons were not ordinarily visualized as having mates. A first-century dedication in Paeonia was made by a retired member of the Praetorian Guard to "the dragon who is honored here," and an eighth-century text describing polytheist monuments in the area of Constantinople mentions only "a big bronze dragon."[111] One North African text is dedicated to Dragon Augustus (another example of the process described above whereby imperial titles were adopted into local conceptions of divine power).[112] Another commemorates "Divine Hand of Dragon."[113] It is a little hard to visualize just what the dragon with the divine hand would have looked like; but we do know that divine hands,

28

more generally (and in human form) were worshipped as angels in Semitic contexts.[114] "Divine Hand of Dragon" probably marks the continuation of Phoenician worship in the area, the divine hand being the messenger of the god Dragon.

Dragons then had a history of worship in both Semitic and Balkan contexts. Glycon, while not, strictly speaking, a dragon, could thus be brought into line with those traditions if a person thought that this was reasonable. The movement of concepts from one region to another, and their reinterpretation, was a function of the shared languages of the urban elites, and this process does permit the evolution of ideas outside of the immediate urban, elite context. The shrines of the gods were public places, and the celebration of the gods at public festivals enabled the transmission of information, new or old, about them. At Abonuteichos, for instance, Alexander celebrated a three-day festival where the life history of Glycon was reenacted.[115] At the city of Oenoanda in Lycia (southwestern Turkey) we know of a grand festival instituted by one Gaius Julius Demosthenes in honor of himself at which the villagers who farmed the civic territory would assemble to offer sacrifice. One of the crucial features of the dossier that describes the process of auto-immortalization that Demosthenes set in motion is that it reveals a mechanism through which elite values were communicated into the countryside. A decree emanating from the town council lists all the surrounding villages and the sacrifices that they should offer. A representative section is as follows:

> The *agonothete* (official in charge of the festival) himself, one bull; the civic priest of the emperors and the priestess of the emperors, one bull; the priest of Zeus, one bull; the three *panegyriarchs* (officials in charge of other festivals), one bull; the secretary of the council and the five *prytaneis* (the executive officials of the town council), two bulls; the two market supervisors, one bull . . . of the villages, Thersenos with Armadu, Arissos, Merlakanda, Mego Oros, [. . .]lai, Kirbus, Euporoi, Oroata, [. . .]rake Valo and Yskapha, with their associated farmsteads, two bulls.[116]

The procession thus joins together people from the countryside, living in villages with distinctively non-Greek names, with the leaders of the civic community. These villagers were there to see, and to hear, to learn about Demosthenes and the wider world, just as were the inhabitants of Abonuteichos and its surrounding countryside present to learn about Glycon. Temples were storehouses of local knowledge, and it was at the annual festivals that these storehouses of learning were opened to the public.

The festival of Demosthenes, like countless other festivals in the Greek world, was not simply for the local folk. It was well advertised in the hope of bringing visitors from other parts of the region to town. It was the commonality of elite culture that made this possible in a way that it had not been prior to the rise of supraregional states after Alexander the Great's conquests (335–323 BC); and it may be that the cult of Glycon offers one of the best examples of the way that a skilled entrepreneur could exploit the mobility that the Roman state enabled. Glycon offered two services that were greatly valued, healing and information about the future. Within twenty years of the foundation of the cult, Glycon had acquired clients from among the governing aristocracy of Rome. One of these clients was the governor of Cappadocia at the eastern edge of the Anatolian plateau in AD 161. Another was the governor of Asia at the same period.[117] The result was that Glycon gained access to the capital, and Alexander spread the word of his accomplishments far and wide. The oracle was even consulted by the emperor Marcus Aurelius, who had acquiesced in the renaming of Abonuteichos as Ionopolis in the first years of his reign, in AD 170.[118] The new name of the city disguised its Pontic origins by providing a fictitious link to the Greek world. This was not a move that appears to have aroused protest from the local inhabitants, who are said to have enjoyed the publicity (and money) that the famous cult brought in.

Marcus Aurelius, like other Roman emperors, was aware of the importance that attached to cult. The favor that he showed by consulting Glycon marked him as a man in touch with developments in the world of the divine. This was important, as the gods alone were free of his control. His predecessors can likewise be seen consulting oracles and publicizing the results as a way of proving that the gods took direct interest in their doings.[119] But it is with Marcus himself that we can see the exploitation of the fluidity with which divine actions could be viewed. On a relatively straightforward level, he advertised the story that his prayers had called fire from the sky to destroy an enemy siege engine in AD 172.[120] In the same year (probably) he spread the story of the salvation of his army by another miracle. In this case, when the army was cut off and under pressure from a force of Germanic barbarians, an enormous storm burst over the battlefield, enabling the Romans to win the day. In a visual depiction of the event, a watery divinity pours himself forth over the fighting men, barbarians collapse, and Romans advance. According to a version of the story that is preserved in a contemporary oracular text, Marcus was personally responsible for the miracle.[121] According to a somewhat later account, provided by Cassius Dio in the early third century, the miracle was the work of the Egyptian Harnouphis, who accompanied the emperor, and the god in question was Hermes Aerios, a Hellenized version of the Egyptian god Thoth–Shou.[122]

We will probably never know what actually happened, but, even if we did, that knowledge would be less significant than what we already know. People understood what they were told in ways that made sense to them. Hence the attribution of the miracle to "the heavenly god" in one text, and to Harnouphis in another. The account was sufficiently powerful to influence later imperial propaganda (see p. 109 below) and was appropriated both by Christians before the end of the third century, and by the emergent theurgist strain of Platonism in the later third or early fourth.[123] It is the version that includes Harnouphis and Thoth–Shou that is most interesting in the present context.

Cassius Dio called Harnouphis a *magos*. The word *magos* was originally applied to a representative of the Zoroastrian priestly hierarchy. His wisdom could be translated into *mageia*, or the ability to command divine powers. The use of the word to describe an Egyptian holy man reflects an ongoing process by which the wisdom of non-Greek peoples was homogenized into a generic form of "eastern wisdom."[124] As Aelian, a collector of marvels who wrote in the early third century AD, put it,

> Who could fail to admire the wisdom of the barbarians? None of them lapsed into atheism, and none argue about the gods – whether they exist or do not exist, and whether they have any concern for us or not. . . . The barbarians I have just mentioned (Celts, Indians, and Egyptians) say that gods exist, that they provide for us, that they indicate the future by omens and signs, by entrails and by other forms of instruction and teachings. These indeed are a lesson for men which derives from the gods' forethought on their behalf. They also say that much is revealed in advance by dreams and by the stars themselves. In these matters their faith is strong. They sacrifice with purity, they piously avoid pollution, performing rites and preserving custom in ceremony, and have other practices as a result of which it is agreed that they respect and worship the gods with conviction.
>
> (*Misc.* 2.31, trans. Wilson)

On this model, indeed, the "barbarian" is the best guide to proper worship for the contemporary inhabitant of the empire. Aelian's view was scarcely idiosyncratic.

Priests of Egypt, initially the representatives of specific local cults in the Nile valley, could thus become *magi*, detached from their local context.[125] Harnouphis was one of a number of Egyptians to be found in the company of emperors during the second century AD. Hadrian seems to have had a particularly interesting encounter with a man named Pancrates, who showed him powerful spells.[126] More than that, Pancrates was a poet in Greek, and, in giving Hadrian a tour of Alexandria, showed him a red lotus, which he claimed should be called the "Antinoeios" in honor of Hadrian's favorite, Antinous since he alleged that it had sprung from the blood of a lion Hadrian had recently killed while hunting in North Africa.[127] Hadrian rewarded him with a large payment for his spells and perpetual maintenance in the museum at Alexandria for his poem. Like Harnouphis, he was a man who bridged

31

Greek and Egyptian cultural traditions. Another such person may have been the less fortunate Serapion who made ill-advised use of "face time" with the emperor Caracalla (AD 211–17) by telling him that he would die. He was immediately executed.[128]

The international reputation of Egyptian holy men, who had begun to spread about the Mediterranean in the wake of Alexander's conquests, bringing Hellenized versions of local wisdom with them, had an impact on Egypt itself. The image of the traveling priest who could instruct kings was a powerful one in the literature of Pharaonic Egypt, and it was the continuation of this indigenous tradition that fed the desire of Greeks or Romans for "barbarian learning." The wise Egyptian who traveled around the Mediterranean might still have a place in his native district, and the reputation of Egyptian wisdom would also draw outsiders into the Egyptian countryside. Harnouphis and Pancrates existed at one end of a continuum of information that stretched from the banks of the Nile to Rome. The "international performer," as these two clearly were, could flourish by appropriating a Greco-Roman stereotype of the eastern wise man while functioning in a non-Egyptian context.[129] The person who came from abroad to Egypt would be seeking people who were recognizable in terms of this same stereotype. It is under the influence of this interest that the Egyptian holy man who stayed at home, and served primarily the Egyptians who sought him out in his temple, might change the services that he offered to both foreigner and native.

The traveler who came to Egypt looking for wisdom did so in the expectation that he would meet a *magos* who had direct access both to the divine and to books of ancient wisdom. The ideal type is perhaps best revealed by the fictions created by outsiders. Thus Lucian of Samosata created a Pancrates (the name plainly taken from the famous magician whom Hadrian dealt with).[130] He had lived in temples for twenty-three years while taking instruction directly from the goddess Isis. In Lucian's story he met a young man who had been sent to Egypt by his father in order to learn wisdom. Intercepting him on a journey up the Nile, where he hoped to obtain an oracle from the talking statue of Memnon – the fictional traveler had a lot of company in this, as we shall see in later chapters – he promised him instruction in magic. After witnessing Pancrates' performance of marvelous acts (riding crocodiles and swimming with other beasts) the traveler left his servants behind and wandered off with him. As they traveled he watched Pancrates perform various wonders, and then, after overhearing his spell, he tried to use it himself. The result was a disaster, and Pancrates ceased his instruction. More fortunate was a man named Thessalus who likewise had come to Egypt to further his education. He succeeded in obtaining a "book of Nectanebus" containing twenty-four ways to cure the body according to signs of the zodiac with the aid of stones and plants.[131] Feeling that something was missing, he decided to seek a vision of the god Asclepius to gain better knowledge. He duly found a magician who, after a three-day wait, enabled him to receive the word of God. The experience, which took place in an underground room, looks as if it occurred in a temple that had been redesigned to accommodate Greek tourists who were used to underground oracular chambers such as those of Apollo at Claros in Turkey or Trophonius in Lebadeia, and, later, that of Glycon.[132]

Thessalus' search began with the discovery of a book. Such books had an important place in mediating the transition from older traditions of Egyptian learning to those more accessible to a broader Mediterranean audience. Thus a papyrus, dating from the reign of Augustus, which contains magical recipes opens with the statement that it is a copy of one found "in Heliopolis in the sacred book said to be of Hermes in the *adyton* in Egyptian writing, translated into Greek."[133] The phrase reflects the language of Pharaonic texts, and the practice, in Pharaonic times, of keeping libraries of sacred books within temples. It was the use of Greek that enabled this wisdom to pass from a local context into regional, and thence Mediterranean circulation.

The process of translation led to changes within the indigenous Egyptian setting. A hoard of texts found near Thebes in Egypt that date to the third century AD mingle Greek, Old Coptic, and Demotic spells. The mixture of languages, sometimes in the same scribal hand, represents the evolution of the priestly practice, and of the services that the priests expected to perform.[134] On another level, books of the so-called Hermetic corpus are primarily in the form of revelations made by Hermes Trismegistos, a Hellenized form of the god Thoth who was, in ancient Egyptian religion, the teacher of crafts. In many of these books Hermes appears to a disciple and gives him a lesson based on the tenets of Greek philosophy. While the philosophy may be Greek, the form of the book may be traced back to the wisdom literature of the Middle Kingdom, which offered its audiences the revelation of great sages.

The admixture of Greek, Demotic, and Coptic may represent local evolution, and should have been comprehensible to those who collected the books. But the fact remains that this was still a local development. It remains to wonder just what an outsider would have made of it. The Demotic and Coptic would have been meaningless to a man like Thessalus, who would simply see it as "Egyptian" without being able to see what it may have meant locally. So too we may wonder what a traveler from Gaul would have made out of "Divine Hand of Dragon." To say that something is a local response to shared culture is not the same thing as saying that the response would have been comprehensible to another participant in that same shared culture who lacked the local knowledge needed to see what was really happening. So long as diverse responses could remain embedded in their indigenous context, there was no cause for conflict.

Not all gods stayed at home. In the centuries after Alexander the Great's conquest of Persia, eastern peoples appear to have been drawn west in greater numbers, possibly because new centers of power such as Alexandria and Pergamon made the Aegean lands far more important than they had been in the past.[135] They brought with them their gods, who, while taking on Greek names such as Zeus Hadad, remained, at heart, very much gods of Syria, Egypt, or Anatolia. Zeus Hadad, for instance, was originally from northern Syria and was understood not as a local manifestation of the Greek god, but rather as the supreme god to whom the closest Greek approximation was Zeus. So too were divinities like the "Syrian Goddess," Atargatis, and the "Great Mother," Cybele, of Anatolia thought to be greater than others.[136] Similar claims were made for Isis of Egypt, whose cult, linked with the cult of Serapis, was perhaps the most widespread of non-Greek cults prior to the time of Augustus. In all cases these cults were essentially henotheistic, meaning that their worshippers asserted that the god was the most powerful of all the divinities, that other gods were subordinate to him or her. In that their priests were professionals, these cults also differed from civic cults in the Greco-Roman world, where priests were, with a very few exceptions, not professionals. The priests of Atargatis, for instance, were notable because they traveled in groups seeking converts and gifts for their god. Yahweh, another decidedly henotheistic divinity, imposed strict dietary and behavioral standards on his followers, who were also expected to remit a portion of their annual earnings to his temple at Jerusalem.[137] Isis, whose cult began to attract Greek converts in the Aegean from the third century BC onwards, likewise had professional priests; even as the texts that proclaimed her power to the world acquired an overlay of Greek thought, they retained some of the flavor of the Egyptian original.[138]

Although it is more than a bit misleading to refer to cults such as those of Isis, Yahweh, Zeus Hadad, or Atargatis as "eastern" insofar as that term implies that they came from outside the territory of the Roman Empire, it is important to recognize that cults from Syria, Egypt, and Anatolia injected a henotheistic element into the religious life of the empire. The first two centuries AD would see the further expansion of interest in such gods, albeit in a variety of forms. One of these was the worship of the "Highest God."[139] Worship of the Highest God took a number of different forms that shaded into each other from time to time and place to place. In some areas we find dedications to Zeus the Highest, "Dios Hypsistos"; in others worship of Theos Hypsistos – Highest God – and in others, more simply Highest, Hypsistos. At Stratoniceia in Caria, for instance, there are dedications to Zeus the Highest and another divinity whose name is rendered variously as "the Divine," or "The Divine Messenger," "the Divine Heavenly Messenger," "the Divine Good" or even "the Divine Royal." In other places – places as widely separated geographically as Palmyra in Syria and Tanais on the Black Sea – we meet "Highest God the Hearer," or "Zeus the Highest and the Hearer," while in Jewish context we often find only "Highest" or "Highest God."[140] The diversity of appellations and companions in these dedications makes it impossible to assume that there is a single conception of this god, or that there was a single form of worship. But this is what is perhaps most important, for it shows that there was a general interest in identifying a henotheistic divinity who was above all others. It may not be pushing the evidence too far to see in this desire to find a highest god some projection of the rise of monarchies in the post-Alexandrine world, a desire to equate the existence of an all-powerful individual on the human plane with some all-powerful divinity who governed the universe.

An imprecise conception of the "Highest God" may have allowed room for discussion. Certainly it does appear that the spread of Judaism may have been assisted by the fact that Yahweh was a "highest god," and non-Jews seem to have been drawn into associate membership with Jewish groups through the similarity between their conceptions of the Highest God.[141] It is particularly in Asia Minor that we find significant groups of God-fearers who were Greeks associated with, but not fully part of, a synagogue.[142] Indeed the spread of the use of the language of "highness" in the imperial period is perhaps best seen as a reflection of the sort of behavior whereby one divinity could be identified with another. It is a form of behavior that should be seen as distinct from that connected with cults such as that of Isis or Atargatis, where a single priesthood established basic conceptions of the god for others to follow. It did not, however, preclude the continued formation and spread of other cults whose inception may be traced to a single religious figure who inspired others with a passion to preach some new way of dealing with the divine, as was the case with the cult of Glycon.

The success of Alexander suggests a model for understanding the spread of cults for which we lack even the evidence offered by a hostile narrative. In the case of the cult of Mithras, which gained a greater following, over a much wider area, than did that of Glycon, we cannot even be certain where the impulse came from – plausible cases have been made for areas as diverse as Rome, the Black Sea, and Commagene – but the evidence, largely archaeological in this case, reveals the foundational activity of a very well organized group.[143] The evidence for this group is provided by the remarkable consistency in the way that the story of Mithras was made the basis of a cult that required its members to be initiated into the "mysteries" of the god. Throughout the empire we find representations of Mithras' birth from a stone, his capture of a bull, his creation of the cosmos after he slaughtered this bull, and of his miraculous creation of a spring by shooting at a rock with one of his arrows.[144] The conception of the god, who was originally a member of the Iranian pantheon, seems similar to that of other Near Eastern divinities in that he was now seen as the savior of mankind from evil. The astrological symbolism associated with his cult suggests that the founders of the movement had drawn upon Greek astrology as part of their effort to explain what the god had done, and used it to contextualize their vision of the god as the sun.[145] Their cult was thus neither Greek nor Iranian nor

Anatolian. It was rather the product of the fusion of traditions to create a divinity who would be comprehensible because he partook of the multi-culturalism of the empire. The fact that evidence for his worship should be found so often in military contexts suggests that the message of the god was what counted. The army, as Hippolytus said, drew from all parts of the empire, and was thus a natural place for a god whose myth looked to the salvation of all to be celebrated. The message was reinforced by the ranking of initiates to the mysteries in accord with their station in life – officers tended to hold the highest positions, and so forth. In this way the cult served to help strengthen the sense of order within society, which may have made it all the more popular with members of the imperial establishment.[146]

Although a very different sort of cult from that of Mithras, Christianity likewise owed its early spread to the efforts of a small, but deeply convinced, group of people in one part of the empire.[147] Its rise was assisted by the prior spread of Judaism and may have owed to its Jewish ancestry the notion that it should have a history recorded in books. Dependence upon literary narrative, which became pronounced after the composition of the gospels in the second half of the first century AD, helped set the non-Jewish version of the faith preached by Paul and his associates apart from other versions of Christianity that would continue to exist on the fringes of Judaism – we shall meet one of these groups in a later chapter.[148] As Christianity developed its own literature, it also developed its capacity to generate a distinctive message that was a potent counterweight to the dominant system of values. A religion that took as its founder a man who had been crucified by a Roman magistrate, a man who was quoted as saying that salvation was dependent upon faith in the will of God no matter what one's social status, was plainly at variance with cults that were integrated with existing social groups. Owing something, perhaps, to the overt hostility of the emperor Nero, who blamed Christians for the fire that ravaged the city of Rome in AD 64, the emergent cult might attract those who felt dissatisfied with the world around them. It offered a venue within which adherents could define a society that was dependent upon behaviors that were often at odds with others.[149] These behaviors were given a universal significance by the central role of texts.

The centrality of texts to the Christian experience is perhaps best illustrated by the fact that so many battles within the church, so many efforts to define new forms of Christianity, were, in the early centuries, connected with books. The rise of one brand of alternative Christianity, Montanism, which spread outwards from Phrygia and took as its central tenet the notion that the Holy Spirit remained active in the world, was facilitated by the circulation of new books of prophecy.[150] Another alternative brand of Christianity, Marcionism, which spread from Rome at the same period, was based upon a thorough rejection of the Jewish heritage.[151] It too depended upon texts, in this case a revised version of the gospel of Luke. The emergence of both groups may be associated with an increasingly strong sense of canon based upon the four gospels that form the core of the New Testament along with the epistles and the Book of Revelation. The spread of the cult, and the ability to translate the teaching of a Palestinian teacher to a pan-Mediterranean audience were, as Christians themselves came to recognize, only made possible by the existence of the Roman Empire.

Taken in isolation, these various religious phenomena may allow for a variety of interpretation; taken as whole, they may be seen as a visible record of the process through which corporate identities evolved. The path of evolution is obviously dependent upon the starting point. An infusion of Latin was not going to make a Berber or Phoenician cult in North Africa look like a Celtic cult in Britain; an infusion of Greek was not going to make a rural Zeus in central Anatolia look like Amon in Egypt. But these infusions of Greek and Latin, like a layer of volcanic ash, will leave their imprint upon the intellectual stratigraphy of each region where they were a feature of the dominant political discourse. It was also a process that gave rise to very different forms of religious practice that could, to a degree, transcend local differences. In this way it begins to be possible to gain some impression of what it was that the empire enabled.

2

GOVERNMENT

The divisions of the land

The simple mention of the Roman Empire is sometimes enough to conjure up an image of something that is immensely stable. Hadrian's Wall or a fort in the Jordanian desert may stand as images of all-encompassing power. The grandeur of the Colosseum, triumphal arches, or marble streets suggest stability and coherence. Such structures were intended to do precisely that. As early as the time of Tiberius we find monumental arches being placed so as to symbolize the capacity of Roman rule and the ability of Rome's rulers to command respect all across the known world.[1] There is little or no reason to think that either the rulers of the empire or the subjects with whom they communicated thought differently about this. The rhetoric deployed by a Roman senator, a Jewish historian, a Greek orator and the authors of oracular texts all offer views of what the empire looked like that accord with the monumentalized images of power that were constructed both by Rome's rulers and by Rome's subjects.[2] On a personal level, the images of self-definition presented in sculpture, painting, and the other plastic arts suggest an ideology of aristocratic homogenization that spanned the empire.[3] Such an ideology produced and reinforced the common cultural idiom that we saw at the end of the last chapter, an idiom that permitted the linking of local trains of thought to broader cultural patterns.

The homogenization of outward forms of discourse, the creation of an authorized discourse of unity could (and can) be somewhat misleading. The ability to communicate with their neighbors did not make Christians any more "normal" than it made African peasants into cultural twins of Gauls. It also occluded, both to later eyes and, at times, I think, to the eyes of contemporaries, the extraordinary diversity of governmental practice. While all might agree on the dominant position of the emperor, there was nowhere articulated a clear theory of government beyond the most banal notions that officials should be honest, and that they should be able. What theory there was tended to hark back to the period of the republic, to the notion that the Roman state was actually the *Res publica populi Romani*, the public possession

38

of the Roman people, and that one's role in controlling the *res publica* depended upon one's status.[4] This totalitarian model of the city-state, one in which a citizen body owed services and received benefits in accordance with one's capacity to serve, was hopelessly outmoded when the emperor had replaced the corporate body of Roman citizens as the determinant of service and reward. But the third-century jurist Ulpian could still theorize that the emperor's power derived from the people:

> What the emperor decides has the force of law because the *populus* confers its power in him and to him all of its own *imperium* and power with a *lex regia*, which is passed concerning his own power.[5]

Ulpian's statement is interesting not only because of its use of archaic terminology – a *lex regia* is a legal fiction constructed to explain the power of Rome's archaic kings – but also because it bore no actual relationship to practice in his own day. An emperor's decrees had the effect of law as soon as he acceded to the throne, and his accession was not dependent upon the passage of a law. Indeed, the passage of the law tended to follow prior acclamation by either an army or the imperial guard, and was essentially contingent upon a display of military support. It was this first acclamation, from AD 69 onwards, that gave the emperor the praenomen *imperator* that signified his claim to rule.[6]

Ulpian's statement reveals a fundamental disjuncture between a theory based on historical reconstruction and a practice dictated by the rhythms of an absolute monarchy. It is a disjuncture illustrated elsewhere in his writings. For he could write in a book on law that "the governor in a province has greater authority in that province than anyone other than the emperor" and in a book on the governor's duties that "if there should be a case involving money which pertains to the emperor's procurator, he would do better to avoid it."[7] In his view "whatever things are done by the procurator of Caesar, if they are ratified by him, are as if they are done by Caesar."[8]

The failure to arrive at a coherent reconciliation between the traditions of republican government and the habits of the monarchy is perhaps nowhere so clear as in the structure of provincial government. There were, in all, thirty-seven provinces when Commodus became emperor. Each province consisted of a patchwork of territories that fell into three basic categories: the land of cities, of the emperor, and of the Roman people. The proportions of land in each province depended upon the time at which the territory that formed it had come under Roman rule. Those areas that had become Roman before Augustus contained high proportions of public land, or land that had been confiscated from political units existing at the time of annexation or later restructuring of internal organization. Those regions that had fallen to Rome from the time of Augustus onwards contained little or no public land, as all conquered territory had fallen to the emperor for his disposition.

The coexistence of civic and imperial land reflects the coexistence of two quite different practices of government. In broader terms, the division reflects the uneasy combination of a retrospective style of administration that depended upon precedent, and a prospective style of government that took its direction from the court. The crucial theory that underlay civic administration was that the Roman state, or *Res publica*, could enter into different relationships with the people whom it controlled. For some their relationship with the *Res publica* was governed by treaty; for others it involved varying degrees of admission to the *Res publica* itself. The theory that underlay the administration of imperial properties is that the only authority that mattered was that of the emperor himself.

Cities

The republican roots of the relationship between cities and the provinces to which they were assigned is perhaps most obvious in the multiple statuses to which a city might aspire. The diversity of these statuses appears to have been determined by practices at different times in Roman history, practices that were determined by political concerns rather than any coherent theory of government. There is otherwise no logical way to reconstruct a clear hierarchy of civic statuses, or to reconcile what was done at one period with what was done at another. The history of each city's relationship to the *Res publica* appears to have been determined on an ad hoc basis. What appeared reasonable at one point in the case of one city was not necessarily a precedent for another city.

The bulk of cities were stipendiary, which meant that they had to pay taxes to Rome and were subject to the oversight of the provincial governor. Within a province they were divided into judicial districts whose chief cities the governor would visit in the course of his annual tour of the province.[9] Identification as a *conventus* center, as these cities were known, was a mark of distinction that was avidly sought.[10] To be a *conventus* center was to be favored above one's neighbors, since it meant that people from the rest of the district would assemble there once a year, and that the governor would be personally accessible to leading citizens.

Past status and connections (albeit connections that were often the result of mythological invention) continued to be crucial in defining city status under Roman rule, as Ulpian reminded the prospective governor:

> If he (the governor) should come to some famous city or the leading city of the province, he ought to tolerate the city's commendation of itself to him and ought not to look bored when hearing its praise of itself since provincials hold that as a point of honor for themselves.
>
> (*D*. 1.7.1)

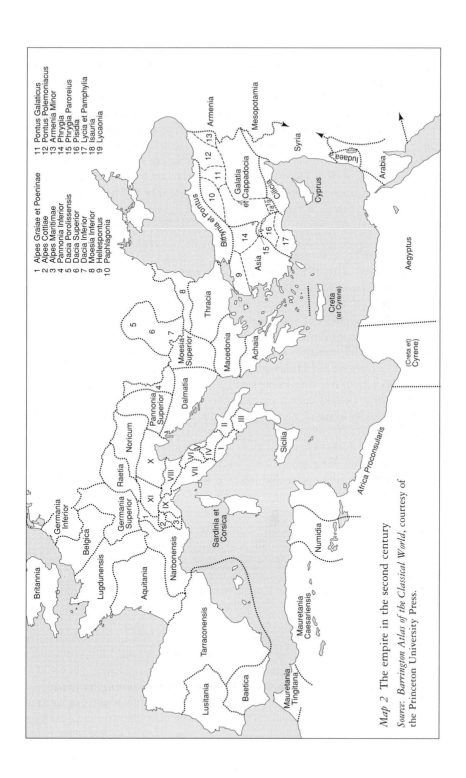

1 Alpes Graiae et Poeninae
2 Alpes Cottiae
3 Alpes Maritimae
4 Pannonia Inferior
5 Dacia Porolissensis
6 Dacia Superior
7 Dacia Inferior
8 Moesia Inferior
9 Hellespontus
10 Paphlagonia
11 Pontus Galaticus
12 Pontus Polemoniacus
13 Armenia Minor
14 Phrygia
15 Phrygia Paroreius
16 Pisidia
17 Lycia et Pamphylia
18 Isauria
19 Lycaonia

Map 2 The empire in the second century

Source: *Barrington Atlas of the Classical World*, courtesy of the Princeton University Press.

These stories were a significant feature of the intellectual matrix that we examined at the end of the last chapter, another way in which traditional cult offered a vehicle of communication. Thus when Antinous, from Bithynium-Claudiopolis in northern Turkey, was identified as the favorite of Hadrian, the city of Mantinea in Greece was able to claim favors for itself on the grounds that Bithynium was its colony. The genealogy of Bithynium was a fiction, but it was a fiction that had benefited the inhabitants of Bithynium because it gave the city a respectable Greek pedigree. Needless to say, it also helped Mantinea when Hadrian awarded the city games in honor of Antinous.[11] Hadrian himself had actively promoted interest in mythological kinships when he permitted the foundation of the league of the Hellenes at Athens in 132 to celebrate his completion of the temple of Olympian Zeus, and himself. To be admitted to this league a city had to prove its "true" Greek credentials.[12]

The ultimate mark of favor was imperial recognition of a city's rights. In some cases this might be recognition that its temple had the right of sanctuary *(asylia)*, in other cases the importance of its local myths. If these rights were recognized, then the city might feel safe in its title as a *conventus* center, or, in the Greek-speaking provinces, aspire to the greater dignity of being recognized as the *metropolis* of the province.[13] The importance of this title had been enhanced by Hadrian, who began the process of awarding the title to more than one city in a province.

The concept behind the title of metropolis goes back to the earliest days of the Greek city-state. A city that sent out a colony, or *apoikia*, became, de facto, the "mother" to that place, and to any cities founded by it. The specific terminology is probably a result of the common use of kinship terms to describe political units of all sorts in archaic Greece.[14] As children owed reverence to their parents, so too would *apoikiai* retain certain obligations to their metropolis. When Athens rose to power in the course of the fifth century, it attempted to assert that all Ionian Greeks were in fact settlers from Athens, and thus that all Ionian cities should regard Athens as their metropolis.[15] The status could then be asserted by cities in their dealings with one another, and the process of doing so was plainly well developed in the period after Alexander the Great's conquests of the Persian Empire. This was a period that saw a flowering of fictive kinships as a way of binding together the diverse communities of the Greek kingdoms that emerged from Alexander's empire.[16]

Recognition as a *conventus* center, or as a metropolis, were the pinnacles to which stipendiary cities could aspire. But there were other statuses beyond that, statuses that were determined by historical circumstance. A city that had performed some great service for Rome at the time when a province was created, or in a subsequent war, might have been given freedom. Such cities, known as *civitates liberae*, were technically outside of the province, though in practice most free cities had come under some sort of supervision in the course of the second century AD.[17] But even then this supervision was less than that of the stipendiary cities. What it chiefly seems to have involved was either the appointment of imperial officials (curators) who would oversee a city's finances, or regulation of the city's contact with the surrounding province by the governor, who might enter it in the course of his annual tour of that province, or both.[18] The city itself would remain free of taxes, and its citizens were exempt from service in provincial organizations if they wished to be. What both free and stipendiary cities had in common was that a contractual relationship theoretically governed their relationship with Rome. In addition to the *civitates liberae*, we also hear of cities with treaties and cities with immunity (*civitates foederatae* and *civitates immunes* respectively). The immunity in question appears primarily to have been from taxation, while the treaty rights might specify some unusual privileges as compared to other stipendiary cities, but ones falling short of freedom or immunity.

Perhaps the most important thing that *civitates liberae, foederatae,* and *immunes* had in common with stipendiary cities was that they were not formally part of the *Res publica* – their connections with the *Res publica* made them *socii*, or allies, of Rome. Individual inhabitants of these cities might (and some would) have the Roman citizenship, but the community as a whole would not, and it was citizenship that, at least notionally, set the possessors of empire apart from the subjects of empire. As Ulpian's archaic formula put it, the *populus* granted *imperium* to the emperor. Although this was a fiction, it nonetheless points to what was still an important distinction between citizen and noncitizen, for citizens still had the theoretical power to determine the course of events in ways that subjects did not. In more practical terms, Roman citizens had notional protections from the arbitrary actions of magistrates that noncitizens lacked.[19] Perhaps the best illustration of this distinction comes from a late first-century text, the Acts of the Apostles, in the description of Paul's arrest at Jerusalem. Jews from Asia had seen Paul and begun to riot. The commanding officer of the garrison had sent in some troops to investigate the cause of the riot and had been directed to Paul by the crowd. As they arrested him, asking him if he were the Egyptian who had caused the trouble, Paul said that he was "A Jew, a Tarsian from Cilicia, a citizen of no mean city."[20] The officer who had come to arrest him appears to have been convinced by this claim that he was a reputable person and thus one who should be allowed to speak. After he spoke, again claiming to be a Tarsian and a person of good Jewish education, a further riot broke out, leading to Paul's arrest and detention at the garrison's barracks. The commanding officer then ordered him to be flogged, at which point he identified himself as a Roman citizen, and thus immune to the flogging that he would have been liable to as a Tarsian.[21] Paul's claim to be a Tarsian and a Jew in the public context established his right to speak within the Jewish community. He may well have thought that claiming to be Roman at this point would have turned his Jewish audience away immediately. To speak to Jews, he depended upon his status as a Jew. In a Roman context, he removed himself from the category of Jew and placed himself in a category that gave him specific rights that were otherwise denied to him. In doing so he was moving from one form of hierarchy to another, and the personal story of Paul may stand as a paradigm for the status of communities as well as for individuals. The rules governing communities of Roman citizens were different from those governing communities of *socii*, but these rules were not necessarily consistent, and the variation between types of Roman community will offer further evidence for the proposition that there was no coherent pattern in the evolution of civic statuses.

There were two basic types of Roman community, the *municipium* (pl. *municipia*) and the *colonia* (pl. *coloniae*).[22] In the republic the title *municipium* was granted to cities that were awarded partial rights within the *Res publica*. While officials within the *municipium* might gain Roman citizenship by virtue of the fact that they had held office, the bulk of the free male and female inhabitants were citizens only of the *municipium*. The creation of municipal communities dates to the end of the fourth century BC. The notion of partial citizenship that was entailed in their creation goes back even further, to the time when Rome was but one of a number of Latin communities in the Tiber valley. Members of the Latin league, of which Rome was a part, had special rights in that they could move to Rome, that they could do business there, and they could marry Roman citizens. But they remained full citizens of their native towns. These rights were known as Latin rights.[23] With the creation of *municipia*, Latin rights were extended beyond the original Latin community to other parts of Italy, and they were altered by the addition of the right to claim Roman citizenship if one held office in the *municipium*. The fact that Roman citizenship was gained by holding local office is the most important distinction between *municipia* and stipendiary cities.

The mid-republican rationale for Latin rights within Italy had become irrelevant by the middle of the first century BC, when all cities in Italy south of the Po river were given citizenship. But, by that time, it seems that municipal status had taken on a new importance within the provinces. Since the decision to grant citizenship to all of Italy was a purely political one, taken to end the war between Rome and its Latin allies in the early eighties BC, there was no pressure to rationalize the status of provincial communities, and there remained, it seems, a genuine prejudice against them. Similarly, when citizen rights were extended to Sicily and northern Italy in the forties BC, these were political decisions, taken for short-term political advantage with no concern for rationalizing statuses elsewhere. Thus by the second century AD we find not only the descendants of earlier decisions about civic status in the provinces (*municipia* with Latin rights) but also the anomaly of *municipia* with citizen rights, and *municipia* with "greater Latin rights."[24]

There is no logical explanation for either of the later categories. The one, a *municipium* with citizen rights, is, in terms of republican theory, a plain contradiction in terms, but the city of Utica became such a place through the dispensation of Augustus in the triumviral period.[25] The other, "greater Latin rights," appears to have involved grants of citizenship not only to magistrates but also to members of the town council.[26] The purpose of this status appears to have been to distinguish one *municipium* from another as being more or less favored. The creation of such a status should perhaps not surprise us, as decisions about civic status were not based on administrative theory, but rather involved the adaptation of administrative theory to suit specific political concerns.

The same confusion, stemming from the same way of doing business, affects the other form of communal relationship with the *Res publica*, the *colonia*. In republican theory, which again dates to the late fourth century BC, a *colonia* was a community of Roman citizens. *Coloniae* tended to be planted in existing cities.[27] When this happened, inhabitants of the pre-existing community could become Roman citizens if they were admitted to full citizenship within the colony. In practice this tended to mean that members of the local elite were included and members of the lower classes continued to exist as a subordinate group.[28]

A colony was a new foundation by the *Res publica* whose citizens were, by definition, transplanted Roman citizens. As Roman communities, albeit ones separated by some great distance from Rome, they retained autonomy in the administration of their laws. A period of massive colonial foundation took place under Augustus, who used colonies to settle veterans from the huge armies that were enrolled to fight in the civil wars, and who followed earlier republican practice of easing the population pressure on Rome itself by moving people into colonies.[29] After that colonies tended to be founded in areas that were newly brought under the control of the state as a way of creating outposts of Roman power in zones that were still considered insecure. Often these settlements consisted of retired soldiers.

The meaning of colonial status varied from region to region within the empire and began to change in the course of the first century. As early as the year AD 19 a decree of the senate mentions *coloniae* of Latins. In theory this should have been impossible, as Latin rights ought to have been a feature of *municipia* rather than *coloniae*.[30] But it does no good to claim that the members of the senate who drafted this decree did not know what they were talking about. The existence of *coloniae* of Latins suggests that a process of ad hoc redefinition of city status, similar to that which was occurring in the case of *municipia*, was already under way.[31] The picture is further complicated in the third century, when Ulpian wrote,

> It must be recognized that there are certain *coloniae* with *ius Italicum*, as is the most splendid *colonia* of the Tyrians in Syria Phoenice, from

whence I come. It is outstanding in its territory, most ancient of foundation, powerful in war, most tenacious of the treaty which it struck with the Romans; for the deified Severus and our emperor granted it *ius Italicum* because of its great and conspicuous loyalty to the Roman *Res publica* and *imperium*.

(*D*. 50.15.1.1)

He goes on to list other cities in the east that have the same *ius Italicum*, a status that is attested as early as the first century AD in the context of *coloniae*, and there it appears to imply that the community so designated consisted entirely of Roman citizens.[32] If this is correct, then it appears that the simple definition of republican times had broken down. A *colonia* could either have a dual community of Romans and indigenous peoples, or it could consist entirely of Roman citizens, wherein the indigenous community had been granted citizenship as a result of a corporate grant of *ius Italicum* to their city.[33]

In the western provinces *coloniae* were crucial centers of Roman culture, and desire to attain their status led to the progressive spread of Roman institutions into stipendiary communities. The title of *colonia* was taken as a mark of communal *humanitas*, or the quality of civilization that Rome represented.[34] In the east, where the title originally designated a place that had received an infusion of Italian settlers (often of veterans) the title obviously had a somewhat different implication. In a region already marked by strong traditions of civic life, the title remained a valuable mark of favor, equivalent to that of a free city, but the cities themselves did not play the same role in spreading specifically Roman ideals. Their Latinity gradually eroded as their inhabitants assimilated themselves to local customs, but the status remained important, since it conveyed recognition that the city had a special place within the hierarchy of locations within a province.[35] It was perhaps this progressive disjuncture between status and culture that made colonial status even more desirable, until, by the third century, it was aspired to by distinctively non-Latin and non-Greek cities in the Semitic regions of the empire. It would be in the generation after Marcus Aurelius' death, with Septimius Severus on the throne, that colonial status was bestowed as a way of upgrading the status of cities that had earned his particular favor. In the case of Tyre, which Ulpian refers to with such pride, the suggestion is that the city deserved the title because of its ancient distinction. The reality was something different, for the fortunes of Tyre were connected with those of the emperor who conferred the status. It became a *colonia* because it sided with Severus in the civil war of 193.[36]

Civic status within a province, while ostensibly based upon republican theory, was thus in constant flux. The evolution of terms shows no coherent rhyme or reason over the centuries. Rather it reflects the constantly changing structure of the central government's relations with the diverse communities that it controlled. The lack of consistency may be the most reasonable feature of this system. As cities differed from one another, as areas of the empire differed so much from one another, the language of status was like the cultural veneer of *humanitas* in that it created a common ground for discussion without assuming a specific resolution. The central role of the emperor in distributing those statuses gave him a place in local politics.

The emperor's land

When the emperor dealt with cities he did so by virtue of his position as the leader of the *Res publica*. His own land, independent of any civic control, was distinguished from the *Res publica* as either his "private account" *(ratio privata)* or his *patrimonium* (inheritance). This land was administered not by agents of the *Res publica*, but rather by his own personal agents; the agents of the *Res publica*, including provincial governors, were advised to steer clear of them unless a serious crime was involved.[37]

By a legal fiction that has yet to be fully explained, the totality of the imperial estates passed from one emperor to the next even if an emperor succeeded to the throne through the murder of his predecessor. Thus, while the notion, so important in medieval western thought, of the "emperor's two bodies" was never coherently enunciated, it was clearly present in the notion that property passed with the position independently of the individual. Thus the hereditary lands attached to the throne are referred to as the *patrimonium Caesaris*, or estate of Caesar, rather than as the *patrimonium* of a specific Caesar. Antoninus Pius went one step further when he subdivided the imperial properties between the *patrimonium* generally and the *ratio privata*, or the property that was for his personal use. Ulpian distinguished these properties as being alienable and inalienable – lands that were part of the *ratio privata* could be given away, while other properties could no more be given away than could the Roman Forum.[38] In the second century, the administration of both kinds of property was placed under the *fiscus*, or personal treasury of the emperor, a distinct entity from the treasury of Saturn and other state treasuries, which were ordinarily supported by tax revenues that belonged to the state.

It is impossible now to get a clear picture of the scope of the *patrimonium* or *ratio privata* for every region of the empire. But we do know, for instance, that roughly 40 percent of the Fayum in Lower Egypt fell into this category, as did vast tracts of land in the interior of Asia Minor. The emperor owned silver mines in Spain, he owned mines in the Balkans, he owned much of the productive land in North Africa, forests in Italy, and all the royal land in kingdoms that had been integrated into the empire from the time of Augustus onwards.[39] His lands effectively constituted a state within the state.

In addition to the emperor's lands there were also broad territories that belonged to the *Res publica*, acquired during the conquests of the republican period. The proportion of this land to the total land in any given region varied depending upon the point at which a territory had come under Roman control. It was far more prevalent in Italy and provinces such as Asia, Cyrene, or Cyprus where royal lands had been annexed prior to Augustus.

The administration of both imperial and public land was given over to officials known as procurators. Procurators were of two sorts, depending on their specific function, praesidial and personal. Praesidial procurators were charged with the administration of small provinces, while personal procurators administered lands belonging to the emperor within a province. We shall return to praesidial procurators below, but personal procurators require some discussion now, as they are directly relevant to the issue of the emperor's land.

Personal procurators replaced civic authorities and the governors who oversaw their activities on imperial lands – this is why the tenants of imperial estates had to appeal to the emperor and other procurators rather than governors when they felt that they were being oppressed. It is a situation that is well reflected in a passage from the text discussed in chapter 1 in which villagers complained that ten of their fellows had been kidnapped and held for ransom by imperial officials. In making their appeal they tell the emperor,

> We, therefore, did what was possible for pitiable people bereft of life and relatives, what was possible for us: we informed your procurator of the administrative region, Aurelius Marcianus, and your equestrian procurators in Asia.
>
> (Keil and von Premerstein, "Bericht,"
> n. 55, 16–21, trans. Hauken)

Likewise the peasants who appealed to Commodus through Lurius Licinius said:

> Help us! We are weak farmers, sustaining life by the work of our hands and we are unequal to the lessee who, as a result of his lavish bribes, is most influential with your procurators.
>
> (*ILS* 6870 3.18–22)

Where the procurator ruled, as Ulpian suggests, the governor was not involved, there were no civil authorities, and the occupants of imperial estates were not considered citizens of any city.[40] The regulation for the imperial mine at Vipasca in Portugal supplements the "bottom-up" view of government offered by these texts by revealing the range of authority a local procurator could have.[41] In addition to setting the rents, which he collected, the procurator had full authority to administer such institutions as baths, barbers' shops, and shoemakers. In cases of minor offenses he could flog slaves or exclude free men from the territory of the mines. Similarly, in the case of the North African estates, when the tenants tried to assert their rights against the man to whom he had leased the land, the procurator was able to send in troops to beat the recalcitrant.[42] It appears that governors would regularly place troops under the control of a procurator if he needed them. Thus when Prasutagus, king of the Iceni, a British tribe, died in AD 61, the procurator Decianus Catus showed up with an armed guard to claim the portion of his estate that was left to the emperor. So too, in 111, when the procurators of the imperial estates in Bithynia set off to collect rents from upland properties, the governor gave them a number of men from his escort.[43]

The government of stipendiary cities was founded upon the principle that the civic authorities would maintain order themselves, only calling in the governor if serious trouble erupted. They could flog or imprison people whom they regarded as malefactors, and they had their own police forces. Virtually by definition, the regions governed by procurators were without the institutions of civic government, which is why they needed to have direct access to imperial soldiers to enforce their will. Troops placed at their disposal were under the direct control of the procurator for so long as he needed them. Like civic magistrates, the procurator could also judge cases that arose between individuals who were entirely within his jurisdiction. If a case arose where his interests were contested by individuals who were under another jurisdiction, or where his claims were contested by another entity (e.g. a case where an estate had been left partially to the emperor and partially to a city), he might not be the judge, but would rather sit as part of the governor's council in deciding the case (governors were given sole authority to make a decision, but they were expected to take advice while doing so).[44]

The parallel between procurators and civic magistrates works only so far. The fiscal interests of the emperor could extend well beyond the confines of his estates. There were, for instance, procurators who were charged with the oversight of troupes of gladiators, whose duty it was to make sure that the officials in charge of the day-to-day administration of these troupes collected the money that they were supposed to get when they rented them out. They would presumably also adjudicate disputes over payment.[45] Other procurators were placed in charge of acquiring new estates that came to the emperor either because no other owner could be found or because a will was invalid (*bona vacantia* and *bona caduca*).[46] There is no obvious reason why the emperor should have had a claim to this land, but it has reasonably been proposed that this was an extension of the rights of kings in the Greek world that was adopted by the imperial government as early as the time of Augustus and extended throughout the empire.[47] The importance of these developments, and of the practice by which procurators came to be judges in cases involving disputes over taxation, is that they illustrate the way that the private bureaucracy that was developed to serve solely the emperor's interest could be expanded throughout a province.

If one simply examines the duties of a provincial governor, with his small staff, who rode from city to city holding court, it would appear that even stipendiary cities were essentially self-governing as far as their day-to-day administration was concerned. When the activities of procurators and their staffs are taken into account, the picture changes rather substantially, and it appears that the government was considerably more present.[48] Procuratorial administration supplemented that of both civic authorities and the governor in the emperor's interest, and it rarely respected the boundaries of individual provinces. Zones of individual procuratorial authority might extend to include several provinces (as for instance was true of the procurators charged with gladiatorial administration), or it might be limited to districts within provinces. Under Marcus' rule some larger provinces were subdivided into smaller units along the lines of procuratorial districts – it was a sign of things to come.[49] The centralizing nature of the government of the *patrimonium* was, in time, to replace the older laissez-faire style of republican government, but, as we shall see, that process was to accompany other substantial changes in the nature of the empire.

The revenues of the state

The divisions of the land are directly connected not only with the style of administration, but also with the way that revenue was derived from the land to support the activities deemed important by the state. The wealth of the emperor depended upon rents paid on the imperial estates, income from mines that he owned, and certain other revenue streams such as the highly lucrative supply of first-class gladiators whom private individuals were often compelled to employ as an indirect cost of holding office.[50] The revenues of the *Res publica* on the other hand were derived from a variety of taxes. These fall into three basic categories: the land tax, the head tax, and direct imposts on a wide variety of economic activities.[51] Liability for the land tax and the head tax was established by censuses that were conducted in each province on a regular cycle that was set at different lengths for each province. This same census cycle established liability for the head tax. The census established the total amount from each source that a community was to pay each year. Responsibility for collection of the tax assessed rested with local authorities. Other monetary taxes, including the 5 percent taxes on inheritances and on goods sold at auction, as well as export and import taxes and taxes on other activities were "farmed out" to corporations of tax collectors, the *publicani*. In each census period corporations bid for the right to collect certain of these taxes.[52] The corporation was responsible for payment of the tax to the state from its own resources. It expected to make up these resources from collection of the tax. If the corporation collected more than it bid, it kept the money. If it collected less than its bid, it swallowed the loss unless it could negotiate relief for itself from the state. We shall look at the component features of this process in turn, starting with the census.

The census

The provincial census was a product of the age of Augustus.[53] Prior to Augustus, the census, consisting of an enumeration of Roman citizens conducted by the censors, occurred every five years (until the chaos of the first century BC). In addition to counting citizens, the censors had been charged with letting out contracts for taxes and for other public services, as well as scrutinizing the morals of members of the two leading orders. Provincial tax assessments, and individual forms of taxation, which varied enormously from province to province, were originally taken over from the entities that had previously controlled the areas that were transformed into provinces. In Augustus' reign censuses were taken, in many cases more than once, to determine liability for payment, and to provide a mechanism for control of the population. After the initial census, different cycles appear to have been set for reassessments. A fourteen-year cycle, for instance, was set for Egypt, a twelve-year cycle seems to have been imposed on Syria, and ten-year cycles seem to have been standard for much of the rest of the empire.[54] In areas that came under the control of the *Res publica* during his reign and later, a census was one of the first acts of provincialization and appears to have resulted in some rationalization of existing tax structures to fit the basic pattern of land, head, and transit taxes.

The best evidence for the way that the census actually worked comes from Egypt, from whose sands have come some three hundred census declarations and several registers of taxable property.[55] Many declarations from 89 AD onwards refer at the beginning to an edict of the prefect of Egypt ordering that people register. We do not know how long people had to do this, but it stands to reason that some time-frame was set. The unit of declaration was the household, and the technical term for the census in Egypt was the "house-by-house register," with the consequence that returns also list places in which no one was registered, either because the property was vacant or the owner had moved away. The head of each household was responsible for enumerating all residents in the house and all property that belonged to them. In order to do so they were required to make the declaration in their home-town, as the edict of Vibius Maximus in 104 AD makes clear:

> The house-to-house census having started, it is compulsory for all people who are, for whatever reason, absent from their nomes (districts), to be summoned to return to their own hearths so that they may complete the customary business of registration and apply themselves to the cultivation that concerns them.[56]

Some Egyptians, however, owned property in more than one nome, and for practical purposes the nome of one's registration was simply the one in which one had been registered during the last census. If a person wished to change official domicile, that person had to apply to the authorities to do so, and file a census return in other places where he or she owned property. The act of registration took place before the local scribe who used a standard form to record the declaration. What the scribe then did with the returns varied from place to place and time to time, but it seems to have been common to glue the declarations together in order to make up a scroll that listed all the property that had been registered (in larger places it would require more than one). A copy then seems to have been made to send to the nome capital, the original being retained locally.

The comprehensive nature of the returns (they included people not liable for the head tax) made them a valuable resource for solving problems that arose outside of tax issues. They provided basic evidence that could be used to determine inheritance and social status, such as whether one was freeborn or a freed slave, an important point since freed slaves were barred from certain roles in society. Likewise, if an inheritance was disputed, the census returns enabled officials to gain a picture of what was likely to be the truth. They also enabled the state to gain a picture of the distribution of land within a community, thus supplementing the surveys that determined the land tax.

Those who took the census were also responsible for drawing the survey that was the basis for the land tax, a process that is described in some detail by Ulpian:

> It is laid down in the list of rules for the census that land must be entered in the census in this way: the name of each property, the community, and the district to which it belongs, its nearest two neighbors; then how many *iugera* of land have been sown for the last ten years, how many vines vineyards have, how many *iugera* are olive plantations and with how many trees, how many *iugera* have been used for hay for the last ten years, how many *iugera* of pasture there are, likewise of wood for felling. The man who declares anything must value it. A census-taker should respect equity in that it is appropriate to his office for a man to be relieved who for particular reasons is unable to enjoy the extent of land declared in public records. So if part of his land has been lost in an abyss, he should be relieved by the census-taker. If his vines are dead or his trees are dead of drought, it is unjust for their number to be listed in the census; but if he has cut down trees or vines, nonetheless he is commanded to declare their number as it was at the time of the census, unless he has shown good reason for cutting them down to the census-taker.
>
> (*D.* 50.15–15.1)[57]

No system of registration is foolproof: the system described by Ulpian manifestly depends upon the honesty of individuals making declarations and the energy of those who checked them. People lied in their census declaration in antiquity just as they lie on their tax forms today. This could lead to some quite extraordinary records, such as the one in which a woman is identified, one year, as the wife and daughter of the head of household, and in another identified by her brother as a spouse by the same mother but not the same father. She was the offspring of a moment of indiscretion on her mother's part in a world that lacked adequate birth control. Not all lies, of course, were intended to shield members of the family. The regulations of the official in charge of the Egyptian tax office, the *idios logos*, state,

> Persons who do not register themselves or those whom they ought to register in the house-by-house register ought to be fined a quarter of their property, and if they are reported as not registering in two house-by-house registers, they are fined two quarters.
>
> Romans and Alexandrians who have not registered those whom they ought, whether one or more, are fined one quarter.
>
> Those who do not register slaves suffer confiscation of the slaves only.
>
> (*Sel. Pap.* 2.206)

The distinction that appears here between Romans, Alexandrians, and ordinary Egyptians relates to the fact that Romans and Alexandrians were not subject to paying the land and head taxes. Alexandrians were exempted by dispensation of Augustus, continuing Ptolemaic privileges for citizens of the capital, and people who were admitted to the metropolitan (ruling) classes of Egyptian towns were taxed at a lower rate. The fact of the registration of Alexandrians and Romans underlines the importance attached to the census for giving the state a view of its total population. The issue of nonreportage that is raised here reflects the all-intrusive nature of the census procedure. People were there to check, and the fines were very heavy. It is perhaps no surprise then that the first census in a province was often accompanied by a revolt, for it was through the census that people were most obviously brought under the control of the state.

The land tax and the head tax

In the case of people who were not Roman citizens, and that included the overwhelming majority of people within the empire prior to the year 212, the census determined liability to the head tax and the land tax.[58] Roman citizens in Italy had been exempted from these forms of taxation in the second century BC and would remain exempt until the act of Galerius made all who were not inhabitants of Italy liable to the head tax. The exemption of Italy, like the exemption of Romans and Alexandrians in Egypt, stems from a tradition of government similar to that which we saw in the manipulation of city statuses. It was a feature of the construction of diverse hierarchies that depended for their existence upon the will of the emperor. Those of higher status and greater local influence tended to be treated with greater consideration precisely because it was their loyalty that was felt to be most important. But what if one was not exempt?

The land tax, or *tributum soli*, was based on the registration of land as being of a certain quality. Land of different quality was assessed at different rates, though there was no consistency in how this land was described from one province to another. The categories described by Ulpian in the passage quoted on p. 52 above are not the same as those listed by an authority on the measurement of land, who wrote:

> Fields subject to tax have many statuses. In some provinces they pay a definite portion of the yield, some [paying] a fifth, some [paying] a seventh. In other provinces the taxes are paid in money figured on an estimation of the value of the land. Definite values have been established for lands, as in Pannonia (where there are) fields of first value, fields of second value, meadows, acorn-bearing woods, ordinary woods, and pastures. The tax assessment for all of these fields is set to the limit of their fertility, *iugum* by *iugum*. In the valuation of these lands great care must be displayed in the survey so that no claims should be established through false declarations. For in Phrygia and all of Asia, disputes arising from this source are as common as they are in Pannonia.
>
> (*Corpus Agr. Rom.*, pp. 168–69)[59]

The author of these lines is, of course, being somewhat disingenuous in his assertion that an accurate survey would eliminate the problem of false declarations, but that is to be expected in a book on land measurement. People moved boundary stones, and no amount of legislation on the evils of that practice was going to stop it. One recourse was to the album that was made at the time of the survey that recorded where each boundary stone had been placed. Another was to define a taxable unit for the land tax, or *iugum*, not an area, but rather by the amount sown, the amount produced, or by the area that could be sowed.[60] According to an inscription of the first century AD from southern Turkey, a governor simply stated that a *iugum* was an area that produced a certain amount of grain (in this case seventy-five *modii*).[61]

Just as there may have been no consistency in the way the land in a province was described, so too there were discrepancies from place to place in the rate at which different categories of land were assessed, and even in what constituted a taxable unit. In the passage quoted above we can see that lower rates were applied to the worst land. The variation in these rates, like the *Lex Mancia*, which granted to the cultivator free use of marginal land that was brought under cultivation, reveals that the Roman state was capable of encouraging certain economic activities through the manipulation of the tax code. In these cases it did so not by commanding that some pattern of behavior be followed. Rather it sought to enable it by granting concessions.

Elsewhere we find land (on an imperial estate) taxed at 12.5 percent, and we are told that peasants who farmed land around the city of Nicaea in north-western Turkey paid 10 percent.[62] In all of these cases it appears that the tax was collected in kind. So too was it collected in kind, right off the threshing floor, in Egypt, at rates that varied substantially from one variety of land to another. For the purpose of these taxes the basic unit of land was the *aroura*, just over two-thirds of an acre, and the unit of taxation was the *artaba*, a unit of measure that was equivalent to about forty liters.[63] As a general practice it appears that roughly one *artaba* of seed was planted for each *aroura* of land, and that the expected return was around ten to one.[64] Taxes on private land (for which rent would also be paid) tended to hover around 15 percent, though there is evidence for rates lower than 10 percent on some land and as high as 20 on other.[65] Tenants on public land paid rather higher rates, possibly on the (false) assumption that they were paying lower rents. Their rates averaged around 30 percent, though again there was enormous variation according to the quality of the land.[66]

While payment in kind appears to have been widespread, as may be seen from the range of places that have produced evidence for the practice, it was by no means universal. As Hyginus observed, monetary taxes ranging from 14 to 20 percent were collected from a number of provinces; Syria is attested as being one of these provinces, as is the region of southern Turkey known as Cilicia.[67] An inscription from the city of Nakrasa in Lydia reveals that the land tax was assessed at 144 *drachmai* per *iugum*. The latter, a staggeringly high rate, may only be explained by the fact that the land in question was a vineyard, which may not reflect the nature of payment of other taxes. In Egypt, also, the tax on vineyards was in money.[68]

There is no clear pattern that can be discerned behind the nature of assessments for the land tax. The decision as to whether it should be in cash or kind was made on an ad hoc basis; it may have reflected the needs of the government at the moment, and these could change. There is clear testimony to the assessment of a money tax on North Africa in the late republic, while there is equally clear (and plentiful) evidence for its collection in grain under the emperors when Africa came to be one of the major regions supplying food to Rome. The initial assessment of money taxes in Syria dates to the time of Julius Caesar, who had to pay his troops, and it may have been left that way because a major army remained based there.[69] While there is ample evidence for Augustan censuses in Gaul, there is little evidence of what form they were to take. What there is, however, may tend to suggest that they were assessed in kind, despite the fact that the Gallic provinces supported a vast concentration of forces on the Rhine.[70] Unlike Syria, Gaul did not have a long history of civic life and had not been a central administrative zone for a highly organized state prior to the Roman conquest. In this matter, as in so much else, administrative practice was shaped by local needs and possibilities rather than by some centralizing genius at Rome.

The head tax *(tributum capitis)* was nearly as diverse in its application as the land tax, though it was always collected in money.[71] Like the land tax, a total assessment was made for each community, and the civic authorities were responsible for its collection. In ordinary circumstances these authorities would collect the amount due from each household, though in extraordinary circumstances a wealthy person might pay the entire sum for his city for a year. As a result of such acts of civic generosity we know that the total assessment for the island of Tenos was 18,500 drachmai.[72] Likewise another wealthy individual left an endowment to the island of Ibiza of 90,000 sesterces "so that the annual tribute to Rome would be paid from it, so that the citizens would not be compelled to pay tribute in difficult times."[73]

The decision on whom to count varied from province to province. Thus we know from the Tenian inscription mentioned above that the city counted all free men, women, and children. In the province of Macedonia the tax appears to have included not only all free persons, but also slaves who were not kept for "personal use."[74] A similar provision appears to have been imposed on the province of Asia in the late republic, and not to have been changed later.[75] The elder Pliny gives numbers of "free persons" for a trio of districts in northwestern Spain, which suggests that there too the tax was imposed on men and women.[76] Appian, a historian of the age of Antoninus Pius who was deeply interested in the revenues of Rome (the loss of his book on the subject is to be much regretted), says that in North Africa the head tax was likewise imposed on both sexes.[77] Only free males over the age of fourteen paid the Egyptian head tax, known as the *laographia*. In Syria, as we have seen, those liable included girls over twelve and boys over fourteen. The cutoff for liability may have been set generally at sixty-five in the second century AD (which might explain why the age was raised from sixty-two in Egypt).

Just as the count of those liable to the head tax varied from place to place, so too, it appears, did the amount that each person was assessed. The only direct evidence comes from Egypt, where figures run from a high of forty drachmai per year in the Fayum to sixteen drachmai in other places. Some of this variation may be explained by the wealth of the district in question. Other variations (which include mild variations over a series of years in the late first to early second centuries at one location) suggest that the state could raise or lower the payment from year to year as need dictated.[78]

56

The head tax did not apply to Roman citizens, making it, in the words of a late third-century Christian, a mark of captivity.[79] Likewise Roman citizens may have been exempt from a variety of other taxes that were collected on a local level. No one, however, was exempt from transport taxes, and Romans had to pay certain other taxes that provincials did not (albeit not ones that appear to be anything like as onerous).

Transport taxes, known as *portoria*, were levied on behalf of the imperial government at fixed entry points into every province. Cities also levied similar taxes on goods that entered their territories. Indeed, some of our best evidence for the goods that were transported around the empire comes from the local tariffs preserved on inscriptions from Palmyra in the Syrian desert in the second century AD, from the city of Zarai in North Africa, and, from a much later period, the tariff of Anazarbus in southern Turkey.[80] In Palmyra, there are taxes on unguents transported in goatskins taxed at the rate of thirteen denarii per camel-load, while unguents transported in alabaster containers are charged twenty-five denarii a load (presumably the stuff in the alabaster vessels was a lot better). Olive oil is likewise assessed at thirteen denarii for each four-goatskin camel-load, while a donkey-load of olive oil will rate a tax of only seven denarii, and so it seems is animal fat.[81] At Anazarbus, items that were found crossing the border range from *garum* and heavy cordage, to gourds, lead, and slaves. In each case the reckoning of the tax appears to be straightforward. The assessor could look at the camel and see that it had four goatskins of animal fat on it and exact his fourteen denarii, while the tax collector at Anazarbus could see (and perhaps scent) a load of *garum* and exact his money. Only in the case of slaves does it appear that the importer has much chance to lie, for there is a significant distinction in the charge for importing slaves who have already lived in Palmyra for a year and new slaves (ten denarii versus twenty-two). The tax on these "veteran" slaves would appear to be a form of transit tax exacted from people who took slaves with them on their travels.

The situation with imperial *portoria* was very different, as is now revealed by the inscription, found at Ephesus, containing the import regulations for the province of Asia, assembled through the work of an imperial commission in AD 62.[82] In this case the method of exaction, which descends from the practice of the Attalid kings who ruled Asia prior to the formation of the Roman province, places the burden on the person transporting the goods. This person must make a declaration at the first tax office he encounters on arriving in the province. The tax collector might then, it seems, make an inspection of his goods to see if he was telling the truth, and, if not, he could confiscate half of the load. If he was satisfied with the accuracy of the declaration he would then issue a document certifying that the person had paid his customs duty and would not have to pay again while in the province. To judge from another imperial tariff, this one from Coptos in Egypt, at the entrance to the zone of desert that lay under imperial control between the Nile valley and Ptolemais on the Red Sea, through which a major portion of the trade with India flowed, the procedure in Asia did not reflect a universal practice. Concerns at Coptos were quite different from those in the province of Asia, for the trade through Coptos was not open to everyone, and the bulk of the surviving text is concerned with the status of individuals entering the restricted zone.[83] While it may be presumed that individuals had to declare who they were, the tax on loads going east is simply assessed by the animal. There was presumably some other procedure, possibly at Ptolemais to govern the extraction of duties on the fabulously valuable luxuries that were being landed there. The elder Pliny suggests that, in the reign of Claudius, the right to collect a tax that amounted to something like twenty-five million sesterces a year was purchased by a man named Annius Plocamus.[84]

The official in charge of the exaction of the taxes at Coptos was the prefect in charge of the *mons Berenicis*, an agent of *patrimonium*, who controlled that area. While there is no direct proof on this point, it is likely that the *portoria* that he exacted was paid into the imperial *fiscus*, rather than the *aerarium*. The people collecting taxes in Ephesus were servants of the corporation of *publicani* who had negotiated the collection of the *portoria* for the province. Some question arises as to whether they were still in business in the late second century, but the limited evidence available suggests that they were.[85] So too they were still collecting *portoria* in Syria, Egypt, Spain, and Syria Palaestina. This was not, however, the case everywhere. The collection of *portoria* in Illyricum had been transferred from corporations of *publicani* to imperial officials in the reign of Marcus, and a similar shift, at roughly the same period, had occurred in Gaul. We have no idea why this happened, though in the case of Illyricum it may be suggested that it had something to do with proximity to a war zone (albeit with some circumspection, since the same could be said of Syria, though there the war was both shorter and more successful).[86] What is significant about the evidence for a gradual transformation in the collection of revenue is that it suggests that the state might have been compelled to make changes because it could not find suitable people to purchase the taxes. A letter dating to the first century AD from Egypt suggests that even then there could be problems:

At the sale of taxes held by me and you with the usual officials present, the contractors for the stamp tax and the market tax were recalcitrant on the ground that they had lost enough already and were in danger of going bankrupt. So we decided that we should inspect earlier contracts and, as far as possible, relieve the contractors, in case they should run away if force is applied to them.

(Wilcken, *Chrest.* 275)[87]

Some years later Hadrian stated,

> It is a truly inhumane practice by which people who have contracted
> for the public revenues and lands are retained, if these properties
> cannot be leased again, for lessees will not easily be found, unless
> they know that, once the five-year period of their lease is completed,
> they will not be kept on against their will.
>
> (D. 49.14.3.6)

The substitute for the individual contractor was an imperial official who
would oversee local collection of the tax. The downside for the imperial
government was that, while the tax farmer had to pay in advance to collect
the tax, the community did not.

The principle behind both the land tax and the head tax was that the state
should be able to know in advance how much revenue it could expect to
receive in each year. Given that the land tax was reassessed over a relatively
long cycle (ordinarily every ten years) and that contracts to tax farmers were
for a five-year period, the system was remarkably inelastic. There was little
room in the basic structure to raise new revenues in case of a sudden emergency, and there was a sense that the state, through granting tax relief, could
encourage behaviors it thought to be generally beneficial. The same pattern
is evident with a small group of monetary taxes that were assessed upon
Roman citizens (and also farmed out on five-year contracts). These were
chiefly the 5 percent tax on inheritances, which was established by Augustus
to fund the *aerarium militare*, or the treasury set aside to pay retirement
benefits to retiring soldiers, the 5 percent tax on the manumission of slaves,
and the 1 percent tax on goods sold at auction.[88] The 4 percent tax on the
sale of slaves, introduced by Nero, may also have survived his reign, though
the evidence for it is highly circumstantial.[89]

Another theme that runs not only through these comments, but through
many others as well, was a sense of equity. The state did not set arbitrary
rates of taxation; rather it determined rates on the basis of what had been
paid in the past. The state presented the system as one that was fair, and
seems to have been concerned that its subjects understood its view on this
point. To some degree it is also fair to say that this view is not completely
unreasonable. There is some reason to think that Roman tax rates were somewhat lower than those of the states that it succeeded in the eastern
Mediterranean and that the state tried to limit abuses of the system by the
very individuals upon whom it depended. This is not to say that people liked
paying taxes; the evidence for informers and stiff penalties for noncompliance
is enough to show that people would try to avoid them if possible. It is also
not to say that the system was particularly fair. The burden of the land tax
and the head tax was regressive: you did not pay at a lower rate if you were
poor. The wealthiest man in Ephesus paid the same head tax as the poorest

laborer. But it is to suggest that, as far as the interests of the state went, the traditional tax system was not designed to maximize revenue, and, as we shall see, it was not sufficient to pay for the government of the empire.

The insufficiency of the tax system was recognized as early as the reign of Augustus, who paid enormous sums from his personal fortune into the state treasury. The vast estates of the emperor provided him with the discretionary revenues that were needed to meet exceptional expenses, and there were avenues open to the emperor that were not open to the *Res publica* to maximize his income in time of need. Two of these have already been mentioned, these being the right of succession to estates to which there was no heir, and the right to claim vacant land (p. 49 above). Another, and this was a serious issue in aristocratic society, was to seize the estates of persons convicted of serious crimes. Emperors would often swear an oath to the senate that they would sentence no senator to death, which was one way of saying that the emperor would not regard their estates as a potential source of revenue. But even emperors who had sworn this oath would not keep it, and there was a long history of confiscation as a method of raising ready cash. The triumvirs had justified the proscriptions, in part, by the need to pay their armies, and Suetonius suggested that the cruelty of Caligula was, in part, motivated by his need for money.[90] Tacitus remarked that Tiberius was restrained toward the property of those condemned in the lawcourts, which was surprising given that he was a cruel man.[91] Whatever the truth of the observations by Tacitus or Suetonius, the significance of their observations lies in the fact that two intellectuals of the early second century should assume that one way to raise money would be, in the words of the fourth-century historian Ammianus Marcellinus, "to fall upon the rich like a torrent."[92] Other methods, which include two employed by Marcus Aurelius to raise the money necessary for the German wars of the 170s, were to auction off palace property and impose an extraordinary sales tax on gladiators. Under Marcus the tax was set at 25 to 33 percent and yielded between two and three million sesterces a year.[93]

The revenues of the *fiscus* were particularly important in the emperor's dealings with two key constituencies: the population of Rome and the army. Many public entertainments were funded directly from the emperor's *fiscus*. It was also from the *fiscus* that other rewards were paid to the troops, and it was the use of his personal money to pay these rewards that helped forge his relationship with the armies in the field.[94]

The emperor and his officials

The emperor had two bodies, and thus he also had two faces, the one being institutional, the other personal. The reconciliation of these two faces was dependent upon the personality of the individual ruler: a weak man or an imbecile (the empire had its share of both) might be subsumed within his position, leaving most of the acts of government to his subordinates. His personal idiosyncrasy would often be a greater concern to those charged with the oversight of affairs than to the bulk of his subjects, who would still see that the basic functions of government occurred. It is with the good or strong emperor that the potential strengths and weaknesses of the system become most clear, and it is perhaps fortunate that we have a description of what such an emperor might be like from the pen of an emperor himself; Marcus Aurelius says that he had observed in his adoptive father and predecessor

> Gentleness and unshaken resolution in judgements taken after full examination; no vainglory about external honors; love of work and perseverance; readiness to hear those who had anything to contribute to the public advantage; the desire to award every man according to his desert without partiality; the experience that knew where to tighten the rein, where to relax. Prohibition of unnatural practices, social tact and permission to his suite not invariably to be present at his banquets nor attend his progress from Rome as a matter of obligation, and always to be found the same by those who had failed to attend him through engagements. Exact scrutiny in council and patience; not that he was avoiding investigation, satisfied with first impressions. An inclination to keep his friends, and nowhere fastidious or the victim of his manias but his own master in everything, and cheerful in his outward disposition. His long foresight and ordering of the merest trifle without making scenes . . . his unceasing watch over the needs of the empire and his stewardship of its resources; his patience under criticism by individuals of such conduct . . . temperance in all things and firmness, nowhere want of taste or search for novelty.
>
> (*Med.* 1.16, trans. Farquharson, adapted)

The work in which Marcus recorded these thoughts was a private diary. Never intending to publish his innermost thoughts, Marcus has given us a unique insight into his mind. That Marcus was a good man cannot be doubted, and there is nothing in the diary that would lead one to question a contemporary's statement that "he did everything from innate excellence rather than artifice."[95] He valued truth, feared the gods, and ever reminded himself that he, like other mortals, would die and be forgotten. His personal qualities evoked the admiration of contemporaries and created an image of the ideal emperor that would endure for a half century after his death.

The *Meditations*, as Marcus' diary came to be called, is also a disturbing document.[96] It chronicled his struggle to remember, above all else, that he was only one man, a mortal like any other, his need to remember that he would die and be forgotten as others had been before him. The character of the emperor mattered:

> In these two ways you must always be prepared: the one, only to act as the principle of the royal and lawgiving art prescribes for the benefit of mankind; the second, to change your purpose, if some one is there to correct and guide you away from some fancy of yours.
>
> (*Med.* 3.12)

Marcus realized that, if he were not careful, even the very forces that he struggled to control could overwhelm him. Marcus himself may have coined the verb that he employs in a passage where he urges modesty upon himself: *apokaisarizô*, to become a Caesar. The phrase in which it is included, "beware that you do not become a Caesar, that you are not dipped in the purple, it can happen," betrays a deeply held fear of his role.[97] A "Caesar" is a tyrant, given to pomposity and an excessive valuation of the outward trappings of power. Marcus viewed himself as a philosopher and regretted that he had no time to read even his own *Meditations* back to himself, or to review collections of improving sayings that he had made.[98] Even though he had so little time, the capacity to adhere to philosophic principles gave him his identity: "let the God within be the guardian of a real man, a man of ripe years, a statesman, a Roman, a magistrate, who has taken his post like one waiting for the retreat to sound, ready to depart, needing no oath, nor any man as witness."[99]

He seems to have needed to remind himself that he had to listen, and that he had to accept criticism of his ideas without giving the impression that he was angry. "In ten days you will seem to be a god to those whom you appear to be a beast or a baboon, if you return to your principles and reverence for the word."[100] Although the phrase is concocted from standard Stoic doctrine, it takes on new meaning when it appears in the memoirs of an emperor. The immense power inherent in his position made it impossible to act or react without acute consciousness of the effect that his every mood might have on those around him: "a scowl on the face is eminently against nature."[101] And those who were around him could trouble him deeply. "Most important of all," he wrote:

> Turn inward to your own self, whenever you blame the traitor or the ungrateful, for the fault is plainly yours, whether you trusted a man with such a disposition to keep faith or whether, when you bestowed a favor, you did not give it unreservedly or so that you received the whole fruit from your act then and there. For when you have done good, what more oh man do you wish.
>
> (*Med.* 9.42)

The character of those who stood closest to him seems to have disappointed him.[102] He recalled the teachers of his youth with fondness, thanking them for what they had given him, but he rarely seems so happy with the contemporaries of the last decade of his life, the period to which the bulk of the *Meditations* seem to belong. Death seems often better than putting up with them.[103]

The ideal of Marcus, and Antoninus before him, was rarely reached, or even remotely approached, in subsequent centuries. But how important were these qualities, and what difference did it make if the emperor were a saint, a tyrant, or a fool? Students of all eras of human history confront precisely the problem of the interaction between individual and institutions. Thus while it might be arguable that World War II was the inevitable consequence of the Treaty of Versailles, the particular form of the postwar German revival and the horrors that followed are unthinkable without Hitler. Russia in the 1930s might have been a very different place if Trotsky had triumphed rather than Stalin, and millions of lives might have been saved. The human catastrophes that were caused by China's Great Leap Forward in the 1950s or the Khmer Rouge in the 1970s are likewise inexplicable as the inevitable course of events.

Not all individual interventions in human history need be catastrophic: the fall of the Roman republic might have been the inevitable result of the disjuncture between the fossilized political institutions of a city-state and the demands of ruling an empire. But the particular form of the Roman monarchy was anything but inevitable. It was very much the product of one man's political skill, and his ability to mold existing institutions to suit his needs, those of the people of Rome, of Italy, and the provinces, as well as of the governing classes and army. Augustus drew upon traditions of administration that had emerged in previous generations, regularized ad hoc arrangements, and redefined the role of central government. More importantly, he forged, as Sulla and Caesar had not, a position that did not depend upon his peculiar abilities in order to survive. Despicable an individual as in many ways he was, Augustus had the wisdom to see that he would not live forever, and that effective government depended upon a viable interaction of an executive officer with the institutions that enabled him to function. In some ways he may have also benefited from the fact that he was a demographic freak. As we have seen, most people in the Roman Empire did not live to the age of seventy-seven, as he did. In commenting upon the rise of the monarchy, Tacitus observed that by the time Augustus died, there were none who could remember the free republic, and if they did, they had been taught to remember that it collapsed into civil war.[104] *Bellum civile* was the bogeyman of the Julio-Claudian era. In official dogma its evils had been buried by the wisdom of Augustus, who had forged a new era of consensus. The threat of chaos, of a return to the bad old days of unbridled aristocratic government, was so powerful that when Augustus' insane great-grandson, Caligula, was murdered in AD 41, the people of Rome rose to protest the possibility that a new ruler not be chosen.[105] By that time, there had also developed a sufficiently powerful interest among the governing class to ensure that a chief executive officer would be needed as at least the nominal head of state.

Two issues that recur in the history of the Roman Empire are the nature of change, and the power of the central government to influence social evolution. Two factors that will remain wild cards are the personality of the monarch and the length of time that he will rule. Marcus saw himself as the guardian of stability, as had his predecessor, and so for a period of more than forty years the central government remained essentially passive, seeking to preserve a status quo. In doing so, Marcus' reign may be seen as a classic example of the "petition and response" style of government in that the emperor ordinarily acted in response to requests for action, rarely setting general policies himself.[106]

Government by petition may place a great deal of power in the hands of the subjects, since the central authority tends not to act without prior action on the part of the governed. That said, it may be the case that even the ostensibly passive act of responding to petitions is a more active form of government than it appears on the surface to be. The vast bulk of petitions that are recorded had positive answers – no one was interested in recording moments when the emperor said no to him, no community wanted a record of its failures of negotiation inscribed in the heart of its downtown. The bulk of negative responses to cities are found in cities other than the one to which they were addressed.[107] But it was through the decision to answer one petition favorably and another unfavorably that an emperor could influence the structures of local hierarchies, on both the provincial and the civic levels, and influence the sort of petitions that places would make. Furthermore, many petitions are addressed to an emperor in response to some earlier decision, and as such they represent only one feature of an ongoing discourse. The essentially conservative approach to government that is favored by the petition-and-response style may be coincidentally activist in the most damaging sense: by predetermining the nature of correspondence, it can act as a retardant to change.

Perhaps as important as the ability granted the emperor to influence local situations, if he chose to, was the fact that this system allowed his subjects to think that he might care. Perhaps the strongest illustration of this principle appears in Apuleius' novel about the adventures of Lucius, transformed by magic into an ass.[108] At a time that he was being beaten by one of his owners, he tried to call upon Caesar for aid. Statues of the emperor were a place of refuge for slaves fleeing their masters, or unfortunate local dignitaries trying to escape an angered crowd. If, as we have seen, tenant farmers were being mistreated, it was to the emperor to whom they would turn.[109] If a person contracted to collect a tax tried to do so in violation of civic rights, it was again to the emperor that a city such as Aphrodisias would complain, hoping to receive a message couched politely, as was this one from Hadrian:

[The imperat]or Caesar son of the divine Trajan Parthicus, grandson of the divine Nero, Trajan [Hadria]n Augustus, pontifex maximus, having the tribunician power for the third time, [cons]ul for the third time: [gree]tings to the Magistrates, Council and People of the Aphrodisians. Your freedom, autonomy and other rights grants to you by the senate and emperors before me, I have previously confirmed. Having been petitioned by the embassy concerning the use of iron and the tax on nails, although the matter is controversial since this is not now the first time that the tax collectors have attempted to collect it from you, knowing that the city is worthy of the other privileges, and is removed from the list of cities in the province, I release it from the tax, and I have written to Claudius Agrippinus, my procurator, to order the contractor for the tax on iron in Asia to stay away from your city. Farewell.[110]

Here again, the emperor is acting against what is, strictly speaking, his own financial interest and, it seems, overturning an earlier decision, possibly by his predecessor, to let the matter stand. In doing so he is expressly admitting that his subjects have rights that he should not infringe. The ability to rescind a local action lent the emperor an aura of power beyond that of all other officials, an aura of superior justice, that was complemented by that of legitimacy and military power that he advertised through his titles and letters.

While there can be no question but that a central feature of the emperor's role was to listen to the complaints of his subjects, and little to suggest that this did not establish the imperial office as a potential "force for justice" within the empire, it was up to the individual emperor to determine if he should use this role to reshape or preserve the status quo. Likewise, a failure by the emperor to respond, or to maintain the aura of legitimacy and military omnipotence, might have serious consequences for the capacity of the imperial office to provide a unifying point for the empire as a whole. He could be a force for justice only if he could be seen to be strong.

Few leaders, ancient or modern, have the vision and capacity to reshape their societies. Marcus, for instance, may have had the capacity, but he lacked the inclination, and he sought to leave the empire that he left after nineteen years on the throne very much as he had found it. Constantine, on the other hand, had both the inclination and ability to do otherwise. In a mere thirty-one years, from 306 to 337, he set changes in motion that would forever alter the intellectual structure of European history, in part because he exploited institutions that were formed under his immediate predecessors, and in part because he shaped new institutions that depended upon his vision for their success. If he had not had twelve years of sole rule before his death, and if he had not been succeeded by sons who, to the best of their limited abilities, shared his vision for the next thirty-one years, we cannot be certain that Christianity would have become the force that it did.

The question of the emperor's role in giving direction to the society that he ruled is inextricably connected to the problem of time in history. The great strength of Fernand Braudel's vision of history, as adumbrated in his classic account of the Mediterranean world in the sixteenth century, is the recognition that the history of events and the history of social structures are not the same thing.[111] The problem that Braudel confronted, that of how precisely to describe the interaction between social structures and the history of events, is perhaps easier to describe than it is to solve. I cannot pretend to have done so, but I may suggest that the tension between two sorts of time is critical to the understanding of imperial history. The history of events by definition moves within the everyday time of human existence. The collective time within which social structures exist may proceed at a very different rate. The stronger the emperor, the closer the speed in the two areas of time might be; the weaker the emperor, the greater the disjunction.

The governing classes

The governmental institutions of the Roman state were intensely hierarchical, giving the chief executive officer the potential to effect significant change, for good or ill. But they were also based on patronage, making it possible for them to function with a weak executive, and also for officeholders to prefer weak central leadership that would enable them to function with less oversight, and to advance the cause of their dependants. The immense size of the empire meant that the emperor was reliant upon his ministers and their servants for day-to-day administration. It was often up to his officials to decide just how to interpret his instructions. Thus the procurator in charge of estates in the Bagradas valley placed his interest in supporting a chief tenant above his obligation to observe the terms of the Hadrianic *lex Manciana* until ordered to do otherwise by the emperor; the governor of Gallia Lugdunenis ignored Marcus' order to decapitate Roman citizens rather than send one to his death in the amphitheater.[112]

The governor of Gallia Lugdenensis and the procurator in North Africa represent what, in the age of Marcus, were two quite distinct career paths in the imperial service, the senatorial and the equestrian. These are paths that we have already glimpsed in our survey of the administrative divisions of the state, and some further examination of what they meant is now in order.

The senatorial career was centered on the traditional offices inherited from the republic. Admission to the rank resulted from tenure of the quaestorship, a post that involved providing budgetary and secretarial assistance to a more senior official, or admission to the status of a magistrate (a process known as adlection) by the emperor. First-time membership required free birth, a large estate (valued under Augustus at one million sesterces), and imperial favor.[113] In the language of Roman law, one sought the *latus clavus*, the purple stripe that marked senatorial status, from the emperor himself.[114] Once obtained, senatorial status could be inherited for at least three generations even if no member of the family held an office in the intervening period.[115]

Perhaps because the status was inheritable, a high proportion of actual officeholders in each generation consisted of first-time members.[116] Few families seem to have remained in the senate for more than the three generations won by the first holder of senatorial office. It is hard to know precisely why this should be so, though it does appear that both the financial and personal demands that office-holding placed upon individuals were high. We know, for example, that there was an exemption from the general rule that wives could not bestow property upon their husbands in the case of those who sought to win the "broad stripe."[117] This exemption is best explained as recognition that families had difficulty maintaining the fortune required of senators. The job also required extended periods of service abroad, and the ability to deal with the emperor. Of all the aspects of senatorial life, it was pressure to remain in favor that was perhaps the most intense. Promotion from one rank to another depended upon it, and upon it also depended a community of taste with the emperor and the ability to deal with his favorites. Failure in this area, or, even more spectacularly, the decision to join a conspiracy, could be ruinous. Conspiracy was not simply a sign of imperial irrationality; it might also be a function of imperial longevity, as years passed and hope of joining the charmed circle evaporated.

The consequence of turnover was the transformation of the imperial elite, in the course of the second century, from one that was primarily Italian, to one whose membership was split fairly evenly between men of Italian and provincial background.[118] It is one of the remarkable features of Roman history that the relatively stable aristocracy that had gained the empire in the republic gave way to a new aristocracy that was drawn from Rome's former subjects under the monarchy.

The process by which the senate was transformed from the preserve of hereditary aristocrats, whose origins lay in west-central Italy, to one that encompassed the entire empire, was set in motion by the civil wars of the first century BC. The result of the Social War (90–88 BC), fought between Rome and a number of Italian states with which it had previously been allied, was the opening of the senate to the wealthy classes of all Italy. The process was accelerated by the civil wars of Marius and Sulla, which saw wholesale executions of the scions of aristocratic families and the confiscation of their properties. It was Sulla, in the wake of his victory, who increased the size of the senate from its traditional level of three hundred to six hundred, enrolling three hundred members of the equestrian order in its ranks.[119] These three hundred new senators represent the beginning of a new, pan-Italian senate.

Admission to the ranks of this body was accelerated in the civil wars of the forties and thirties BC as Caesar, Antony, and Augustus rewarded supporters with this status, so much so that the senate had grown to nearly one thousand by the time that Augustus returned to Italy after the capture of Alexandria in 30 BC, the last event of the civil wars. Augustus reduced the senate back to six hundred through a series of deeply unpopular *lectiones* (expulsions) in the course of the next decade. And it was, by the time that he was through, a very different senate. Drawn heavily from peninsular Italy, it was no longer dominated, as it once was, by the great consular families of the Latin plain.[120] It also had its first provincial members. The earliest of these people, Balbus, was a millionaire supporter of Julius Caesar from Spain, while the first easterner, who shows up at the same time as Balbus (he was his adopted father), was Gnaeus Pompeius Theophanes. His name proclaims the fact that Caesar's great rival, Gnaeus Pompey, for whom he was both historian and chief of staff, gave him the citizenship. Theophanes' son was governor of Asia in AD 5.[121]

Augustus continued a process of unifying the local aristocracies of the empire through admission to the senate that had begun to take shape in the two generations before his victory. Members of the traditional aristocracy continued to hold influential positions for the next several generations, supported as they were by the enormous wealth that had accrued to them in the course of the conquest of empire, and through adroit maneuvering in the civil wars.[122] But their days were numbered. Tacitus, himself a senator of provincial ancestry, observed that a passion for high living was to be the downfall of many who beggared themselves by trying to maintain the magnificence either of their establishment or of their pretensions.[123] They tended to involve themselves in conspiracies against reigning emperors. The last member of a great republican family to rise to prominence was Sulpicius Galba, who was responsible for the overthrow of Nero, himself the last male representative of three great late republican families, in AD 68. Galba was murdered in 69, to be replaced by Salvius Otho, of Ferentium, whose father had entered the senate through the favor of Livia, the wife of Augustus.[124] He was replaced in turn by Aulus Vitellius, who owed his prominence to the favor that his father had gained from the emperor Claudius. Vitellius' grandfather had been an equestrian official of Augustus. Vitellius was in turn overthrown, still in AD 69, by Flavius Vespasianus, the son of an auctioneer from Reate.

In the age of Vespasian and his sons, Titus and Domitian, who ruled from AD 69 to 96, the senate was still largely Italian; about three-quarters of known senators in this period came from the peninsula, but those from abroad were gaining influence. Domitian would be succeeded, briefly, by another Italian, Nerva – whose family owed its importance to the favor of Tiberius – but he selected the son of one of Vespasian's leading generals, Ulpius Traianus, to succeed him. Traianus, or Trajan, as he is commonly known, was from Spain, the descendant of an Italian family that had emigrated in the first century BC. Under Trajan and his successor, Hadrian, his nephew, the senate was recruited even more heavily from the provinces; the proportion with non-Italian roots climbed to just under 50 percent. The transformation continued to be reflected in the palace by Antoninus Pius and Marcus himself, descended from families that had entered the senate from southern Gaul and Spain respectively.

What did senators do? The accomplishment of Augustus was largely to transform the senate from a highly politicized body whose membership might be characterized by a devotion to seeking the domination of the state (or attachment to those who could achieve this aim) to a body of more professionalized administrators. While it is impossible to write a history of the expansion of bureaucratic roles filled by senators, several trends are evident in the first two centuries AD. Perhaps the two most interesting of these are, first, the growth of positions connected with civic administration outside of Rome and, second – not unconnected with the first – the enormous expansion in the number of jobs for ex-praetors. Under the republic, a man could hold the praetorship, in ordinary circumstances, when he was thirty-nine years old, the consulship when he was forty-one. At least one of the succeeding two years would usually be filled with a provincial governorship. As there were ten praetors and only two consuls, the average career would end at that point unless a person had a friend who went on to the consulship and required his advice while governing his own province, or needed someone to command his troops. Several of the legionary commanders of Caesar and Pompey were, for example, ex-praetors (some were even ex-consuls), and Cicero used his brother Quintus (who had been praetor years earlier and had served under Caesar) as his assistant when he governed the province of Cilicia (southern Turkey) in 51 BC.[125] The examples of Caesar, Pompey, and Cicero point to a crucial failing in the republican system of government. There was no institutional way to enlist the services of experienced administrators, and, as there was rarely a future for an ex-praetor, there was little to constrain his behavior as a governor.

Augustus began a process of expanding the number of consulships by making more regular use of the republican institution of the "replacement" or "suffect" consulship. This form of consulship was instituted to ensure that there would be two consuls if one died in office. The surviving consul or a designated official would hold an election to fill the empty spot.[126] Augustus changed the traditional system by moving the election of suffect consuls into the context of the election of the consuls who would take office on January 1 (the *consules ordinarii*).[127] At a set point in their year of office, one or both *consules ordinarii* would resign and be replaced by the suffect or suffects, depending on how many had been elected. The institution proved so popular that, before the end of the Julio-Claudian period, six or more suffect consuls might be elected for each year. The practice was expanded

Table 1

At Rome	In Italy	In the provinces
2 prefects for grain distribution	9 overseers of the roads	24 commanders of legions, some simultaneously as governors
3 prefects of the military treasury	4–5 judges	3 judges
2 prefects of the state treasury	an indeterminate number of prefects to oversee the distribution of food for child support (a post sometimes combined with that of an overseer of roads)	14 assistants to governors (*legati pro praetore*)
		8 proconsuls (provincial governors)

under the Flavians and into the second century, though by 100 the election of suffects had been separated from that of the *ordinarii* and placed at a meeting of the senate on January 12 of the year that they would hold office.[128] Each pair of consuls would hold office for about three months.[129]

The institution of the suffect consulship, by creating more offices to which one could aspire, enabled the creation of a series of offices to be held after the praetorship and before the consulship. The new office also had the effect of elevating the importance of the "ordinary consulship" as a mark of special imperial favor to which a person might aspire after a period of further service to the state. The offices available for ex-praetors and ex-consuls were many and varied. The offices for ex-praetors at the time of Marcus' death in AD 180 are shown on table 1.[130] The offices for ex-consuls are shown on table 2.[131]

In addition to these regular posts there was an indeterminate number of civic curators (appointed to oversee the fiscal administration of a city) and other special posts that were created on an ad hoc basis as the need arose that might be filled by either ex-consuls (consulars) or ex-praetors (praetorians). The distribution of regular offices is a good indicator of the concerns of government. Thus the majority of offices at both the consular and praetorian level are in the provinces, and they involve military commands – the consular *legati Augusti pro praetore* governed provinces in which there were legions. In sum, there were ninety to ninety-five senators holding office in the provinces each year, and many senators spent about ten of the twenty-five years of their active careers in a variety of provincial posts.[132]

One of the most striking features of the Roman conception of provincial administration is that there was no division between specialized civilian and

Table 2

At Rome	In Italy	In the provinces
1 curator of the banks of the Tiber	1 prefect to oversee support systems for children	13 *legati Augusti pro praetore* (provincial governors)
2 curators of public works		2 proconsuls (Africa and Asia)
1 curator of the water supply		
1 prefect of the city		

military officials. The man who commanded a legion in one year might be assigned in the next to be prefect of the state treasury, overseer of a road, or even to serve as a civic curator. The office of civic curator is an especially interesting one, as it reflects a recognition that most local civic authorities were incapable of the reasonable management of their fiscal resources, and that the governor, whose duty it was to inspect the finances of cities in his province, was simply too busy to do so effectively. Since the city was the basic taxable unit in the empire, this failure might have a direct impact on imperial revenues. At Rome, central concerns were with the food supply (we will see further aspects of this when we turn to equestrian careers), flood control (the task of the curator of the Tiber bank), fresh water, and the maintenance of public buildings. The office of city prefect, which involved the administration of justice, was an immensely prestigious one that was often held prior to obtaining the ultimate mark of imperial favor, a second consulship.

Given the range of offices that senators might be expected to hold, the question that quite naturally arises is their actual competence to manage any of them. Was the Roman Empire administered by a group of glorified amateurs? The answer to this question is probably no, and the reason for this may emerge from an examination of a few careers that have come down to us, either through inscriptions or through the work of Lucius Cassius Dio, the senatorial historian who will himself provide our first case. It is indeed to Dio himself that we owe an enunciation of the theory behind the accumulation of official posts between magistracies:

As for those who have served as praetors, let them hold some office amongst the subject nations (before they have been praetors I do not think that they should have this privilege, but they ought first to serve for one or two terms as lieutenants to the ex-praetors just mentioned); then they should next hold office as consuls, provided that they have proved satisfactory officials to the end of their terms, and after that they should receive the more important governorships.[133]

Implicit in Dio's statement is not only that men rose to higher office because they demonstrated ability in lower offices, but also the notion that the emperor ought to respect the accomplishments of his subordinates. Mutual respect was the key to the system. Just as the emperor should receive honor from his subjects, so too should he bestow honor upon those who deserved it. For Dio, and others, a good senator was a man of upright character who deserved the respect implicit in promotion.[134]

Dio was born at Nicaea in the province of Bithynia (a portion of northern Turkey) in AD 163 or 164.[135] His father, Cassius Apronianus, had risen to a suffect consulship in 184, and he had brought his son to Rome by 180 at the latest. As a senator, Apronianus was required to own an estate in Italy, which is most likely the same estate near Capua in the region of Campania at which Dio himself would later spend much time when he was in Italy.[136] Despite the move to Campania, which may have been made easier by the resilient Hellenism of that part of Italy, Dio appears to have retained close connections with the region of his birth. He calls Nicaea "my homeland," whereas Capua is described as "the place where I spend my time whenever I am in Italy."[137] There is no reason to think that he was exceptional in this attitude. We know, for instance, that the younger Pliny, whose heavily edited correspondence provides much valuable information about the attitudes of the senatorial class during the early second century, remained closely tied to his home city of Comum in northern Italy. It was at Comum that he spent his money and where young men from the area sought him as a patron for their advancement in Rome, and it was in the region of Comum that he found his wives. The homeland was the source of wealth and support, and it was where a man who might struggle to compete on the highest stage, who might obtain the praetorship but never a consulship, could still border on divinity.[138]

The senator would not forget his homeland, or wish to be forgotten. So L. Octavius Aur[elianus?] Didasus was thanked by the people of his city, Ureu in North Africa, for his singular faith in looking after the interests of the citizens, and for rebuilding the city baths and probably its water supply as well from his own pocket.[139] At Patara in southern Turkey, Tiberius Claudius Dryantianus Antoninus, a contemporary of Marcus Aurelius, is known to us only because he improved his city's theater.[140] Senators might also, on occasion, hold a local office.[141] But even if they did hold this local office, they would still remain somewhat apart from local society – one would not expect to see them on a regular basis, and if one did, they might be extraordinarily grand. A senator from Smyrna, noted for his wealth and oratorical skill, once came home to find that the provincial governor was staying in his house, and threw him out into the street.[142] No local magistrate would have dared such a thing, and this man's act might be seen not only as an assertion of his prominence, but also as a reminder to the whole community that it was a great place because he had been born there. He was also very lucky, because the man whom he evicted was outstanding for his forgiving nature and allowed Hadrian to reconcile him with the house-holder at the time that he was promoted to higher office. The higher office was that of emperor, for the evictee was none other than Antoninus Pius. This incident may serve as a paradigm for the way that the senatorial class mediated between local hierarchies and central power. As an aspirant to membership in this class would say to Antoninus,

> You have divided into two parts all the men in your empire – with this expression I have indicated the whole inhabited world – and everywhere you have made citizens all who are the more accomplished, noble, and powerful people, even if they retain their local affinities, while the remainder you have made subjects and the governed.[143]

Cassius Dio would have approved these sentiments. He would have added that, through the integration of leading men from the senate into the provinces, the emperor would ensure that there were no obvious leaders of revolts. In his view the government of the empire needed to be entrusted to men such as himself who were well educated and, by virtue of their education, capable of understanding complex situations.[144] Dio's observation about the importance of integrating dynastic families from the provinces into the central government is an important one, and one that had been underscored in the later years of Marcus' reign by a short-lived revolt led by Avidius Cassius, governor of Syria, and the emperor's deputy for administration in the east. Avidius was a native of the province of Syria, and, after his death, Marcus established the rule that no person should govern the province in which he had been born.[145] It is a unique and significant feature of the Roman Empire that, with the exception of a period in the 260s, local dynasts were not in a position to dictate policy to the central government. In this regard the efficiency of Roman government compares favorably with that of other great preindustrial empires such as those of Achaemenid Persia, the Ummayad Caliphate, or Han China. On the other hand, the existence of a large cadre of central administrators meant that when revolts did break out, they did so from within the central government itself, and that the leaders of these revolts could exploit a wide range of connections that they had built up over the years.

Dio's admiration for well-educated administrators masks two issues, one that may be directly relevant to his own career, the other to the changing nature of the senate in the time that he lived. Dio brought himself to the attention of the emperor Septimius Severus in the mid-190s by writing a

book about the portents that preceded Severus' seizure of power in 193.
While Severus appears to have appreciated this work, he does not seem to
have been impressed with Dio's own administrative capacity. Dio would not
receive a major governorship until the decade after Severus' death, when he
received three in quick succession from Alexander Severus before being
awarded a second consulship in 229. The only prior provincial post that we
know of in his case was that of civic curator in his home province during
the reign of Elagabalus (218–22). The rapid promotion of Dio in old age
may, as we shall see, be a sign more of a problem with the government of
Alexander than with that of Severus.

In Dio's lifetime a different sort of man had been rising to high position.
It is arguable that Antoninus Pius and Hadrian before him had been lulled
into an excessive sense of security, had ignored developments beyond the
borders of the frontier, and tended to favor excessively men who shared their
specific cultural tastes.[146] Such men might make decent provincial governors
and reasonable commanders of the legions in peacetime, and it is a little
hard to see how Pius, who never left Italy while emperor and had limited
military experience, could evaluate potential commanders after a long period
of peace. Before Pius had died there were signs of trouble on the eastern
frontier, as the power of the Parthian kingdom, humbled by Trajan in the
last years of his life, began to revive. As part of the settlement of the eastern
provinces arranged by Hadrian in AD 117, the kingdom of Mesene, key to
the trade with India through the Persian Gulf, had been left independent.[147]
Its independence was crushed in the late 150s, which might have served
as a warning. It did not, and the empire seemed to have been woefully unpre-
pared for the Parthian invasion that was launched into Syria and Anatolia as
Marcus came to the throne. Enough generals were found to help stem the
tide, but they were not of the traditional aristocracy.

The careers of Marcus' leading generals are marked by rapid movement
from province to province, as they were needed to quell some crisis, and even
the command of more than one province at a time. None of the eight such
men who are known, Statius Priscus, M. Iallus Bassus, M. Servilius Fabianus,
M. Claudius Fronto, P. Helvius Pertinax, C. Arrius Antoninus, C. Vettius
Sabinianus, and Claudius Pompeianus, had a father who had been consul.[148]
In six of these eight cases it is not easy to trace other aspects of their backgrounds. We do not know where Statius Priscus came from, Iallus Bassus
seems to have come from southern France, the evidence tying Servilius
Fabianus to northern Italy is slight (but all that there is), and Claudius Fronto
may have been the son of a dignitary from the province of Asia.[149] Arrius
Antoninus and Vettius Sabinianus came from North Africa.[150] Claudius
Pompeianus and Pertinax are better known, the result of the former's
marriage to one of Marcus' daughters, and of the latter's brief reign as emperor
in AD 193.

Claudius Pompeianus was the son of an equestrian from Antioch in Syria. We know nothing of the early stages of his career, prior to his appearance as a governor of one of the Danubian provinces in 167 but he must have impressed Marcus mightily, because in 169, he betrothed him to his daughter Lucilla, recently widowed by the death of Marcus' adoptive brother (and co-emperor) Lucius Verus. Neither Lucilla nor her mother Faustina seems to have been pleased by the match, which makes it seem all the more clear that Marcus admired Claudius. In the next few years, he made him his virtual deputy in the conduct of the wars in the Balkans.[151]

Pertinax was the son of a freedman.[152] He had begun his adult life as a professional interpreter of texts. His father had made enough money in the wool trade to be able to send his son to study with a significant grammarian, which gave the future emperor the connections to set himself up in the business.[153] It did not pay very well, so he sought a commission as a centurion in the army from his father's patron, L. Hedius Rufus Lollianus Avitus.[154] Lollianus came from the upper echelon of the senatorial aristocracy. His father had been suffect consul under Trajan in AD 114 and had gone on to the prestigious governorship of Asia under Hadrian.[155] His father's prominence may have helped Lollianus obtain the rank of *consul ordinarius* in 144 (a mark of high favor). A combination of ability and longevity had made him a valued servant of Marcus Aurelius, who had dispatched him to the east during the Parthian crisis of the early 160s. His elder son had been consul in AD 155, and his younger (probably much younger) son would rise to the consulship in AD 193.

Lollianus' patronage of Pertinax is an excellent example of the way in which the senatorial aristocracy could mediate the passage of a person from local to imperial prominence. After a rough start, Pertinax proved himself a first-rate small-unit commander in the war with the Parthians, which resulted in his transfer to a command in Britain.[156] From there he moved to a cavalry command in the Balkans, and then to a post in the administration of the child-welfare scheme in Italy. He did not remain long in this post before he was elevated to command of the fleet on the Rhine, and then to a senior command in the Balkans under the eye of Marcus himself. For some reason, now lost to us, Marcus became suspicious of him, possibly the result of some senior officers who felt that he had risen too far, too fast.[157]

That may have been so, but in achieving what he had already achieved he had come now to the attention of Claudius Pompeianus, and Claudius, who may have heard similar complaints about himself, convinced Marcus to employ him yet again in a military capacity.[158] Now Marcus was impressed, adlecting him into the senate and, to make amends for further complaining, giving him the rank of praetor.[159] Pertinax continued to impress, rising to the consulship in 175 and a series of extremely important commands, including the administration of three Balkan provinces during the revolt of Avidius Cassius.

The career of Pertinax to this point (and we shall pick it up again later) is immensely suggestive of the stresses upon the senatorial order in Marcus' time. The repeated whispering campaigns that are recorded in his biography, and Marcus' response to them, are unlikely to have been unique. The fact that Marcus could be convinced that Pertinax was the victim of conspiracy suggests that he was familiar enough with the problem. There were people who plainly resented his presence, just as there were others who benefited from helping him. An able client reflected well upon the patron, and Pertinax was plainly lucky in having very important people behind him as he rose through the ranks. He recognized the debt that he owed to Pompeianus by seating him on the bench next to him when the latter ended a long absence from meetings of that body to support his former client.[160]

The arrival of Pertinax in the senate, and the success of other military men who rose to high rank under Marcus, are signs that the governing class remained open to talent. Likewise these careers illustrate the crucial point that much of the burden of government was shouldered, in the years prior to 180, by men who had achieved the praetorship, and that the praetorian career provided the testing ground for higher office. But this was not the only route to power, and the senatorial order was not alone in providing administrators. Up to the point that he was adlected into praetorian status, Pertinax was still an equestrian, and the commands that he held were characteristic of the equestrian military career.

Even more than the senatorial career, the equestrian provided a link between local hierarchies and those immediately surrounding the emperor. The equestrian order was one of the fundamental structures in the civil, social, and political hierarchies of Rome.[161] To be an equestrian one had to be of free birth. If a person were a freed slave, he could enter the order through a legal fiction that bestowed a fictive paternity upon him, a sign of the importance placed upon birth as a criterion for entry into the order. An equestrian also needed to have a minimum amount of property, defined at least under Augustus, if not much earlier, as being 400,000 sesterces. Finally, an equestrian had to be a person of good moral standing. Admission to the order depended finally upon public recognition of a person's birth, wealth, and character through award of the "public horse," a legal act that had been restored to prominence by Augustus, and that resulted in the registration of a man within the equestrian centuries. It had the further benefit of giving a person preferred seating first in the theater (under Augustus) and then in other places of public spectacle. It was thus possible to be of equestrian standing in terms of birth and wealth without being, strictly speaking, an equestrian. Recognition by the emperor that one belonged among the equestrians was the crucial distinguishing feature between a wealthy man and a wealthy equestrian man.

The relatively strict criteria for membership in the order disguise vast social differences among equestrians. Some were former slaves whose financial status was sufficient for them to hope that a son might become a centurion; others were freedmen rich enough to enter the order themselves and hope that their descendants could enter the senate (as some did).[162] Many were leaders of local communities whose prominence was marked by the ability to get a job "away from home" in the lower echelons of imperial service. Others were multimillionaires who had avoided a senatorial career either because they were not interested, or because they felt that they could obtain greater influence through a series of posts that were closed to senators. The equestrian order thus consisted, unofficially, of numerous strata bridging the gap between municipalities and the imperial court.[163] These strata were permeable, as people might hope to ascend from one level to the next within the order itself – and the mechanism for this transition was often the imperial service. Rank within the emperor's service marked the clearest distinctions, and, as was the case with the senate, imperial favor was a crucial factor in determining the shape of a career. It was even possible, as the case of Pertinax shows, for a man of exceptional talent to rise out of the equestrian order altogether.

The sheer size of the equestrian order when compared to the senate, limited as it was to around six hundred, is another important factor in considering the role of equestrians in government. There were posts at the upper end of the equestrian ladder that were fully as important as any to which a senator could aspire. These included the office of praetorian prefect, prefect of the grain supply for Rome, prefect of Egypt, prefect of the watch at Rome, and a group of imperial secretaries whose titles denote their specific areas of competence. Chief among the secretaries were the *ab epistulis latinis*, responsible for the emperor's letters in Latin, the *ab epistulis graecis*, who had similar responsibility for imperial communications in Greek, and the *a libellis*, who drafted legislation.[164] A further secretary, the *a patrimonio*, oversaw the administration of the imperial estates. The posts of *ab epistulis latinis* and *ab epistulis graecis* were often reserved for men of letters, while that of the *a libellis* was often held by an experienced lawyer. Taken as a group, these three positions represent both the reactive and proactive aspects of the court, for the job of the *ab epistulis* was to respond to requests, while that of the *a libellis* appears to have been to draft legislation. Additional lawyers are found as *consiliarii*, or advisers to the emperor's *consilium*, which consisted of his leading confidants, both senatorial and equestrian.

There was no single path to these high posts. In the case of the *ab epistulis graecis* it appears that specialized knowledge of government was not a prerequisite. Thus Marcus Aurelius appointed a man named Alexander the "Clay Plato" as his *ab epistulis graecis* in the 170s because he was one of the leading rhetoricians of his time.[165] So too Marcus was impressed by the orator Hadrian of Tyre when in 176 he heard him declaim at Athens, where he held the chair in rhetoric with spectacular ostentation, wearing the most expensive clothes and precious gems and being carried to his lectures in a carriage drawn by horses with silver bridles. Marcus offered him the chair of Greek at Rome, which he held into his eighties when Commodus offered him the job of *ab epistulis graecis* as recognition of his excellence.[166] Aspasius of Ravenna, despite his Italian origin, became so prominent as a Greek orator that he too held the chair of Greek in the capital. Sometime between AD 211 and 216 he was appointed *ab epistulis graecis*.[167]

In describing one of his *ab epistulis graecis*, Aelius Antipater, the emperor Caracalla called him "my friend and teacher, entrusted with the composition of Greek letters."[168] The phrasing is significant, for the word "friend" in this context identifies him as a member of the court; the role of teacher states the obvious point that a man raised to such a position had distinguished himself as an educator. But the final phrase, "entrusted with the composition of Greek letters," is one of the few explicit statements that we have of the role of the *ab epistulis* in actually crafting the way that the emperor sounded to his subjects. Caracalla, though much given to military display, nonetheless fancied himself an intellectual. He could certainly read and write Greek, but here he is making it clear that the *ab epistulis* wrote his letters, a point that is supported by the statement of a contemporary who said that Antipater made the emperor sound the way that he should.[169] The point is reinforced by another document of the same period, this one being an attack on Aspasius of Ravenna for a prose style inappropriate to imperial communications. Again the precise wording is significant:

> When he became imperial secretary, he wrote letters that were more controversial than was suitable, and others that were not clear, neither of which is appropriate to an emperor; for whenever an emperor writes a letter, it is necessary that he be neither given to rhetorical syllogism or to trains of reasoning, but to dignity, and he should not be obscure, since he gives voice to law, and lucidity is the interpreter of law.
>
> (Phil. *V. Soph.* 628)

What the author of these lines is saying is that the emperor is the persona behind the letters, and that this persona is the creation of the secretary.[170] Senior academics did not enter government to take dictation. But what of the actual decision? Who made that? In this case the answer is less obvious. An emperor like Marcus may well have made the bulk of them himself, or approved decisions taken by his officials. Cassius Dio, in a speech that he places in Marcus' mouth, manages to include a number of sentiments that are paralleled in the *Meditations*, which there is no reason to think that he had read. Dio's ability to do this may be taken as confirmation of a statement in another historian of the period, Herodian, that Marcus had a distinctive prose style.[171] Those accustomed to reading imperial communications, like Philostratus of Lemnos, were not themselves necessarily members of the inner circle, and they would have been able to notice significant changes in prose style.[172] An emperor like Marcus' son Commodus may not have had the time to do it, for in the early part of his reign he appears to have been drinking quite heavily. In the last year of his life he was busy training to be a public combatant in the amphitheater, even taking up residence in the barracks of the *secutores* (a variety of gladiator to whose style he aspired). There is little reason to think that many of his senior officials accompanied him to dinner with the gladiators or discussed policy with him as he trained. The result was that actual decision-making was left to his senior officials, and that he tended to rely very heavily on the advice of certain favorites. People noticed this too, and Marius Maximus, who wrote biographies of the emperors from Nerva to Elagabalus, specifically said that Commodus was so careless in the handling of communication that he answered many petitions with the same formula and would simply conclude letters with the word *vale*, or "farewell."[173] Marius' observation suggests that the emperor would be expected to comment on a completed letter, presumably to confirm its content. Marcus, it may be presumed, did more than this. The evidence for a recognizable style suggests that at the very least he would make sure that something that went out over his name sounded like he had written it. Commodus would not.

If the secretaries were amateur administrators who were drawn into government to lend it the appropriate public aura of *humanitas*, the same cannot be said of the other major officers of court. The chief of these officers was ordinarily the praetorian prefect. Ever since the Praetorian Guard was established by Augustus, its commander, or prefect, had been an equestrian. As early as Tiberius, the praetorian prefect had surpassed the prefect of Egypt, also an equestrian in rank, as Augustus did not feel that a senator could be allowed to govern the province from which so much of the grain for the city of Rome was drawn. Tiberius' two prefects, Sejanus and Macro – the one who ultimately aspired to the throne, the other of whom succeeded in becoming a kingmaker (and smothering Tiberius on his deathbed) – owed their preeminence to Tiberius' increasing lack of interest in government as his reign progressed. Sejanus had owed his position to the close links between his family and court, which had enabled him to form a close attachment with Tiberius before the latter became emperor. Macro owed his prominence to the fact that he was the prefect of the city watch at Rome when Tiberius decided to eliminate Sejanus. Other peculiar circumstances explain a character like Tigellinus, the evil genius behind the last years of Nero, who came to the prefecture because he did a good business in chariot horses, and Nero liked racing chariots.

The peculiarities of the Julio-Claudian appointments to high office disappear under the Flavian dynasty that succeeded it. Before the end of the Julio-Claudian period it had become standard practice to have two prefects. This was continued in subsequent centuries, though from time to time we find only one man in office. But only very rarely were these men (or was this man) lacking in significant previous experience.[174] There were under Marcus some 127 procuratorial positions filled by equestrians. Before holding a procuratorial post a man would ordinarily hold several minor military commands. Thus Marcus Bassaeus Rufus, a long-serving prefect under Marcus, had entered government as Pertinax did (or had tried to), by holding the rank of chief centurion. After two postings in this rank, he had risen to prefect of a cohort of the city watch, tribune (commander) of a cohort of the garrison of Rome, and tribune of a praetorian cohort. He had then served as procurator for three different provinces before moving up to serve as *a rationibus*, the secretary who oversaw the accounts of the *patrimonium*. His next office was prefect of the city watch, followed by a stint as prefect of Egypt before being appointed praetorian prefect in 169.[175] He remained in office until the middle of the next decade. His colleague of his first three years in office, Macrinius Vindex, is less well known – though we do know that he was governor of one of the provinces of Dacia some fifteen years prior to becoming prefect, a fact that suggests he too had long experience in administration.[176] The man whom Rufus succeeded in office, T. Furius Victorinus, had been prefect for eight years before his death of the plague. He too had begun his service with three military commands before advancing to a provincial procuratorship in Spain, followed by an appointment to the *ludus magnus*, in which he oversaw the imperial gladiators in Rome. He moved on from the *ludus magnus* to command of first the fleet based at Misenum and then of the one at Ravenna. His next appointment was as *a rationibus*, followed by the prefectures of the watch and of Egypt.[177] Rufus' colleague after the death of Macrinius in 172, Tarrutenus Paternus, had rather a different background. He had entered the highest echelon of government as *ab epistulis latinis*, before demonstrating a degree of military competence that is not ordinarily to be expected of academics. In 171 he campaigned successfully against the Marcomani, a tribe that resided in the area of modern Hungary, and as prefect in 179 he won a spectacular victory over other northern tribesmen. In this case it may be that his close attendance upon the emperor had revealed his talents, and his interests had changed. He was the author of a four-book treatise on military matters.[178] The final prefect to be appointed by Marcus was Tigidius Perennis, about whose early career we know nothing save that it involved military commands.[179]

The careers of the praetorian prefects of Marcus are to some degree parallel to those of the generals who rose to prominence in the 170s. The military demands of these years put the ability to command men in battle at a premium, and the Marcus whom we see in the *Meditations* was plainly surrounded by men who may have had little in common with his philosophic interests. Bassaeus Rufus was little impressed by at least one grand intellectual who appeared in court, Herodes Atticus, the wealthiest man in Greece. Bassaeus seems to have wanted to kill him.[180]

How did a man rise to a position where he might be selected to be prefect of the watch, of Egypt and of the praetorians? And how did promotion through the equestrian ranks compare with that of senators? We do not have certain answers for these questions. The regularity with which certain posts appear in the careers of prefects may suggest that there was a pattern of promotion within the equestrian bureaucracy, and this is to some degree true.[181] Some posts were clearly more important than others, and carried higher salaries – the fact that these posts were salaried sets them apart from senatorial offices, which were "honors," for which a man received a generous expense account but no official salary.[182] On the lowest levels of procuratorial administration there were posts that paid 60,000 sesterces a year, the next level paid 100,000, and the highest 200,000 and 300,000 respectively. But we do not know how a man moved from one post to another, though we do know that a man did not move from a higher-paying to a lower-paying position, which shows that ranking of posts was fixed. Although there were no exams, and, as far as we know, there was nothing that approximated a formal performance review, it does appear that emperors reviewed the credentials of people who were recommended to them at specific times of the year unless there was some crisis.[183] In all probability, if a man did not foul up a job, he might expect another, so long as he retained friends who were higher up the ladder of offices than he was. Just as promotion in senatorial ranks was dependent upon a combination of imperial favor and performance, so too was it in equestrian. The careers of the *ab epistulis* may stand out as exceptions to the general rule in that they gained their reputations as orators well before they came within the purview of the court. On the other hand, it was the demonstration of competence that led to their promotion, and it is unlikely that this was an exception to the rule. Rather, as we can see in the case of Marcus' regime, it was the definition of what constituted competence that might change with circumstances.

These figures for equestrian salaries are also significant because they represent very high incomes, the lowest of them being on a par with the annual income of a poorer senator, the highest of them being among the higher senatorial incomes. It is really not possible then to separate procuratorial administrators from senatorial in terms of economic status, or, often, in terms of the functions that they served. Nor can we say that equestrian administrators were more professional than senators, since the typical consul would have held more posts, on average, than the typical equestrian. Most equestrian administrators held no more than one or two senior posts before they retired (or died). Indeed, many procurators would return to their home communities as major figures on the local scene rather than scale the heights of the praetorian prefecture.

While it would be incorrect to suggest that senators and equestrian administrators necessarily had different interests, it would also be incorrect to suggest that there was a complete community of interest either.[184]

81

Membership in the senate did carry with it a social status that was lacking for equestrians: the emperor was, after all, a senator rather than an equestrian. The major military commands remained, under Marcus, the preserve of senators, and the gap was only bridged in the case of the praetorian prefects. So too, major provincial governorships were senatorial rather equestrian. It would be wrong to suggest that this did not make a difference to members of the senate. There remained a sense of class solidarity among senators that would influence the way that they reacted to developments at court. For senators, their status as senators, as the ideological heirs of those senators who had conquered the empire before Augustus, was important, as was the notion that the emperors must be drawn from their ranks.

In the case of both senatorial and equestrian careers, admission to the highest levels of office depended upon the emperor. He was the source of honor and respect, which remained key aspects of aristocratic ideology.[185] The exercise of patronage at this level was the essence of court politics, and it is in this context that the personality of the emperor once again comes to the fore. Marcus clearly took pains to know his officials; thus he was able to recognize slanders about Pertinax when he heard them, and he decided to elevate Claudius Pompeianus against the will of those who were closest to him. So too he personally appreciated the rhetorical accomplishments of Alexander the "Clay Plato," and appreciated Herodes Atticus enough to allow him to live when his praetorian prefect thought that he should die. Not all emperors were so careful. Just as Commodus would not pay attention to the content of correspondence that went out in his name, so too he allowed his favorites to be the source of patronage within his court. At this level there can be no hard-and-fast rules of conduct, but rather there are tendencies and patterns of behavior that repeat themselves with greater or lesser degrees of significance. It may be that a radical change in style, as between Marcus and Commodus, was a more serious problem than continuity in style, even if it concentrated power within a group of courtiers. Officials might well adjust their behavior according to the familiar patterns of conduct. But when those rules changed suddenly, not all might be able to change with them.

One final point needs to be made, and this is that while the number of equestrian posts certainly outnumbered those available to senators, it did not do so by a very wide margin. If most equestrian posts were a function of the needs of the *patrimonium*, it is fair to say that the weight of government at the time of Marcus' death in 180 was still balanced relatively evenly between the emperor's household and the senate. This will change in the course of the next century, and with it will change the whole style of government.

Part II

RESHAPING
THE OLD ORDER

3

CRISES IN GOVERNMENT

The reign of Commodus

Marcus thanked the gods that his children were not deficient of mind or deformed in body, that his wife was who she was: obedient, affectionate, and simple. He likewise thanked the gods that his adoptive brother was such a good man, able to encourage him through respect and natural affection.[1] His judgment of those closest to him was not shared by all. Many seem to have felt that his brother was a lightweight, that his wife was a slut, and that his son was an idiot.[2] Rumor also had it that his wife was a better judge of their son's character than he was. When Marcus fell seriously ill in 175, she is said to have sparked the encouraged Avidius Cassius to seize the throne so that her son would not become emperor.[3]

One of the inherent weaknesses of monarchy is that it is so difficult to control the succession. An emperor with mature male descendants had little choice but to allow them to succeed him. Tiberius did so in the case of Caligula with great reluctance, and he is said to have thought that Caligula was a menace. He may even have tried to prevent Caligula's accession by launching a covert campaign to undermine him, being dissuaded only when his own reading of the stars convinced him that there was no point.[4] By the end, even if Marcus may have begun to entertain some doubts about the wisdom of his choice, there was nothing that he could do, short of killing Commodus. Weighing against any change of heart were powerful sentiments in Roman society in favor of the dynastic principle. The so-called adoptive principle that had resulted in the accession of Hadrian, Antoninus, and Marcus himself had actually served to keep the throne within the family of Trajan: Hadrian was Trajan's principal heir, and Antoninus, who may have been a distant relative, was adopted because he would adopt Lucius Verus and Marcus, who was Hadrian's nephew.[5] Thus it was that, on November 27, 176, Marcus had made Commodus his co-ruler so that, in effect, his death meant that, instead of there being two emperors, there was now only one.[6] What he did, or tried to do, was to surround Commodus with a large body of experienced advisers in the hope that they would be able to educate him in the responsibilities of government. He failed, and so, in the long run, did Commodus.

According to Dio, the problem with Commodus was not that he was inherently evil. It was rather that he was stupid. Marius Maximus seems to have been less charitable. He appears to have thought that Commodus was thoroughly wicked, given to debauchery at an early age, and prone to cruelty. Herodian said that Marcus feared lest his son become addicted to his pleasures (with good reason, as it turned out).[7] Whatever explanation one chooses for the reign that followed, the basic problem was that Commodus lacked the ability to govern as his father had governed, and the system that he inherited placed an enormous burden on the emperor himself. If the emperor could not govern, then there were two options: rule by committee or rule by a regent. Marcus attempted to direct matters to the former end, but the character of Commodus and tensions within Marcus' own governing circle led rapidly to the other.

Marcus died at Sirmium on the Danube because the northern wars that he had proclaimed to be at an end in 176 had flared up again in 178, necessitating his presence with the army.[8] According to Dio and Marius Maximus, Marcus was determined, in the last years of his life, to incorporate the lands of the tribes that had bedeviled his reign into two new provinces north of the Danube.[9] If this is so, then it represents a significant change from his former imperial policy, which was to maintain the borders as they were. The defeat of Parthia in AD 165 had resulted in some minor readjustment of the frontier in Syria, but no effort at the sort of massive annexation that Trajan had set in motion before his death in 117 by which northern Mesopotamia, the region north of the Taurus line known as Armenia, and most of Iraq had briefly been added to the empire.[10] Hadrian had abandoned these provinces immediately upon his accession, and Antoninus Pius had made it a tenet of his policy that when tribes outside of the empire offered themselves to Rome, they would be refused if their lands could not support the cost of occupation.[11] Aside from an advance into southern Scotland, which appears to have been given up by Marcus, he had added no significant territory.[12] A series of treaties that Dio detailed in his history preserve terms that Marcus had offered northern tribes in the course of the 170s. None of these involved the annexation of new lands. Rather, they established strict limitations on the ability of the tribes to assemble within striking distance of the frontier, and observation points in tribal land that was not to be annexed.[13] With the state emerging from serious financial woes occasioned by the earlier wars, there is no reason to think that Marcus had changed his mind about the advisability of adding new land that would need to be garrisoned directly.

What may have led to the charge that Commodus abandoned Marcus' plans, influenced by a faction at court and a desire for relaxation at Rome, was the haste with which Commodus brought the ongoing wars to an end. He returned to Rome in triumph on October 22, 180, a little bit over six

Plate 1 Lucilla Augusta, widow of Lucius Verus and sister of Commodus. *Credit: RIC* Marcus Aurelius no. 781, author's collection, photo by Ivory Photo, Ann Arbor, MI.

months after his father's death.[14] He was never again to leave the area of the city despite the fact that war continued to flare up in the Balkans for the next several years, resulting in major Roman victories in 185 and 188/9.[15] If the notion that Commodus abandoned the policy of his father may be seen as a fiction invented later to discredit him, the rapid rise to power of a particular faction at court led by persons who took advantage of his inherent laziness is not. The large council of advisers that Marcus had left behind him would have required Commodus to think, and there is every reason to believe that he found the effort of weighing contradictory opinions difficult. He was, after all, eighteen years old when his father died.

Tensions latent in the latter years of Marcus' reign soon burst out.[16] Commodus evidently relied heavily upon the advice of his *cubicularius*, Saoterus, who had accompanied him in the triumphal chariot when he had returned to Rome (they kissed as they passed through the street).[17] He also appears to have shown some senior members of the senate less respect than they thought they deserved.[18] Relations between the court and members of the high aristocracy degenerated. Those who felt that they had been extruded from their proper places in the councils of the emperor gathered around Lucilla.[19] Considerably older than her brother (she was nineteen when he was born), and retaining the privileges that she had gained as the wife of Lucius Verus (including her own seat in the imperial box at public entertainments), she was an obvious focal point for the discontented.[20] Toward the end of 182 a conspiracy was formed that included Claudius Pompeianus Quintianus, nephew of Lucilla's husband and the betrothed of her daughter by Lucius Verus; Lucilla's nephew, Ummidius Quadratus; two other young men, Norbanus and Paralius; Norbanus' sister; and Paralius' mother.[21] It is entirely likely that they were supported by Paternus, who seems to have wanted to eliminate Saoterus.[22] Close acquaintance with Commodus (and, possibly, the assurance that some guards would be inattentive) made it feasible. A sense of imperial ceremonial may have dictated the time and place for the attempt, but an exaggerated sense of theater was their undoing. As Commodus entered the imperial box in the Colosseum, the young Pompeianus, with a dagger concealed within his clothing, decided to announce his intentions with the words, "Behold! The senate sends you this."[23] He would have done better to strike first and speak second.

The aftermath of the conspiracy was bloody. The four male conspirators and Norbanus' sister were executed. Lucilla was exiled to Capri, where she was later murdered. Paralius' mother was exiled. The botched assassination gave Perennis an opening to eliminate other rivals, including a number of senior advisers to Marcus and his colleague, Paternus.[24] Dio is scathing on the nature of the charges. He argued that one of the victims, Salvius Julianus, who had recently commanded a major army, could have marched on Rome if he had really wanted to remove the emperor, and that Paternus could have killed the emperor at any time when he was commander of the guard.[25] Marius Maximus, who may have been present at the trials, gives further details, saying that Paternus had plotted with Julianus to make Julianus' son emperor, and provides the circumstantial details surrounding the murder of Saoterus, suggesting that Dio's outrage on Paternus' part was misplaced.[26] It is more than likely that Paternus was responsible.

After eliminating Paternus (who had been promoted out of his position through adlection to the senate to remove him from the protection of the guard), Perennis laid charges against Sextus Quintilius Condianus, whose father and uncle had shared numerous high commands under Marcus.[27] Sextus escaped into hiding, but his father and uncle were killed. Vitruvius Secundus, a former *ab epistulis*, was executed because of his friendship with Paternus.[28] The elder Pompeianus, though cleared of complicity in the designs of his wife, withdrew from Rome, while Pertinax, then governor of Syria, was dismissed.[29] There can be little doubt but that the execution of so many senior officials sent shock waves throughout the senatorial aristocracy. Dio gives a sense of the tension felt by senior officials when he tells of a response that Sextus Quintilius Condianus had obtained from a dream oracle in Cilicia, where Dio was assisting his father, who was governor of the province. The dream included the image of a youth strangling two serpents connected with that of a lion pursuing a fawn. After the fact they realized that the youth must be Hercules, whom Commodus would soon take to imitating, and the serpents were his senatorial victims.[30] Sextus was clearly a friend of theirs; his flight and the death of his father and uncle along with that of Julianus eliminated men who had been patrons to others. Through these murders Perennis had established himself as the sole power behind the throne, or so he thought, and the power of Marcus' senior staff was broken.[31]

In his account of the murders that followed the conspiracy of 182, Dio places the blame squarely on the shoulders of Commodus, exculpating Perennis, whom others, reasonably, make the central figure.[32] So too, when he recounts how Perennis fell victim to a conspiracy in 185:

> He did not deserve to suffer this, both on his own account and on that of the whole Roman empire, except insofar as his desire for power was the cause of the destruction of his colleague Paternus; in private he never strove in the least for fame or wealth, but he lived an incorruptible and temperate life, and he was wholly responsible for the security of both Commodus and his reign.
>
> (Dio 72.10.1, trans. Cary)

It would be wrong to speculate on the reasons for Dio's attitude. He wrote his history long after Perennis died, and there is no reason to think that he necessarily took this view to obscure some favor that had been done him while he was young.[33] He wrote what he did in response to a view reflected by Marius Maximus that Perennis was the evil genius behind all the executions, and in the face of a version of the story of the reign known to Herodian that was as negative as that told by Maximus.[34] Dio seems genuinely to have thought that Perennis tried his best, and to some degree his view might make some sense. If Perennis had been desperate to gain power, he must also have been smart enough to know that he could only keep it if he promoted able men to high position underneath him.

Dio's view, misguided or not, makes some sense insofar as the record of provincial command and military success in the mid-180s was good. But it neglects the impact of simple hatred on the ability to govern, and there can be no doubt that there were people who hated Perennis very deeply indeed, both in the senate and at court. The conflict within the senate between members of older families and recent appointees was evident enough in Marcus' time; less obvious was that between members of the professional aristocracies, both senatorial and equestrian and that of the palace. This may have been a function of the fact that Marcus was so rarely at Rome, for with an emperor who resided almost exclusively in Rome, the staff charged with his personal care assumed a much greater role. This staff was derived from a very different source from that of the senior administration. The staff of the palace largely consisted of slaves; its overseers were freedmen and freedwomen. By the second century, reasonably consistent career patterns had become established within the household, culminating, for men, with the office of the *a cubiculo* who administered the emperor's bedchamber.[35] More than a valet, the *a cubiculo* controlled access to the emperor in his private moments and had to manage personalities neither concordant nor weak. For women the path to power lay rather more directly through the emperor's bedroom. Commodus kept numerous concubines (not unusual, for many of his predecessors had maintained close sexual relationships with people other than their wives), and they could play a role in determining whom he would hear. The next three political revolutions in the court of Commodus all revolve to some degree around the issue of who could have access to Commodus, and when. The first of these, which led to the fall of Perennis, may well have stemmed from conflicts between the praetorian prefect and the *a cubiculo*, a man named Cleander, who had succeeded Saoterus in office.[36]

Cleander, who gets a uniformly bad press from the surviving sources, perhaps because he, and his colleagues, represented a threat to the social hierarchy, may have owed his rise in part to the fact that he had been the emperor's companion in youth, and was close enough to him to be allowed to marry one of his concubines, a woman named Damostratia.[37] His influence was sufficiently great prior to Perennis' death that Commodus listed him ahead of the *ab epistulis graecis* and *a rationibus* in a letter to Athens.[38] What was so upsetting about this to members of the traditional governing classes was that the *a cubiculo* was a freedman. While we may, or may not, believe the story that Dio tells about his sale in the public slave market, his rise to a position ahead of senior equestrian officials signals again the importance of access in determining actual rank.[39] This is underlined by a (false) story of the way that Cleander arranged Perennis' ouster told by Herodian. The tale includes a performance at the theater where a "philosopher" had appeared on stage to denounce Perennis, and then soldiers who had been introduced into the palace to show the emperor a coin with Perennis' portrait on it, a clear sign that he aspired to the throne. Bogus though this tale may be, it reveals the general perception that the palace staff could let whomever they wanted in to see the emperor, and that they were perfectly capable of fabricating whatever evidence they needed to support their case.

The actual story of Perennis' fall appears to begin in 184–85 with a mutiny in Britain, leading Perennis to dispatch a man named Ulpius Marcellus as the new governor.[40] Marcellus was a good general, but a stern disciplinarian, and the result of his command was both victory and mutiny. We do not know what happened to Marcellus when the mutiny broke out (or even if he was still in the province), but the legionary legates appear to have brought some order by dispatching fifteen hundred men to Italy to lay their complaints before the emperor in person.[41] Dio then says that Cleander had made Commodus suspicious of Perennis and thus that when the soldiers complained that Perennis was trying to make himself emperor, Commodus believed them and turned his prefect over to them to be killed.[42]

While the account of Perennis' fall in Dio, the main source for the last paragraph, may be more accurate, it is still worth returning for a moment to Herodian's story. Taken together, the two tales represent three crucial aspects of the exercise of power. Dio's story plainly puts the main stress on the emperor's relationship with the army. As we shall see, over and over again, this relationship was maintained with a dynamic that was far different from any other. Soldiers swore their oath to the emperor in person, and assumed a privileged relationship with the throne. It was expected that the emperor would meet with them in person to hear their complaints. The tale of Herodian assumes not only the power of the personal relationship between the emperor and his palace staff in determining events, but also the use of public entertainments as a venue for the public exposition of policies that were worked out behind closed doors. The thrust of Herodian's account is that Commodus was prepared for later revelations in private by the public revelation of the actor who spoke to him from the stage. Various public entertainments were crucial to the emperor's relationship with the people of his capital, and he was expected to pay attention to what they said there. The crowd's response to government ordinarily took the form of rhythmic acclamations, and the chants of the crowd became an essential part of the business of government.[43] The emperor, or his representative, ignored the shouted will of the people at his peril — as one adviser to Marcus put it, "Everywhere the people dominate and prevail."[44] As another, earlier, observer commented:

> The Romans are fanatically keen on this type of show [chariot racing] and eagerly assemble in the Circus Maximus to watch it. The crowds there petition the emperor for what they want, and the emperors who decide not to resist their requests are particularly popular.[45]

No issue so consumed the people of Rome as that of their feeding. The organization of a subsidized grain supply for the people had been a major political issue in the republic, and one of the crucial acts of Augustus had been to put it on a much better-organized footing.[46] The simple threat of a food shortage was enough to cause a riot of major proportions, and it was this, taken with the habit of communicating with the government through acclamations at the Circus, that would bring down Cleander.

Cleander had emerged from the destruction of Perennis as the leading figure at court, and with his success the balance of power swung from traditional administrators to the palace staff. He began to build a faction of subordinates in the senate, if that is the correct interpretation of the remarkable appointment of twenty-five consuls in the year, and disrupted the command of the guard while assuming the position of *a pugione* in addition to that of *cubicularius*.[47] The anomalous title, which means "at the dagger," implied that he was personally responsible for the emperor's safety — an obvious dig at the equestrian hierarchy, which had proven less than loyal. Within the palace itself, it appears that the ebb and flow of influence led to the demise of the empress, Bruttia Crispina, who was exiled to Capri and executed on a charge of adultery.[48]

The vigor of Cleander's action led to a reaction two years later. The agents of his destruction were Papirius Dionysius, the prefect of the grain supply, and, according to Dio, the concubine Marcia.[49] Marcia was a remarkable woman: the daughter of a freedman named Marcus Aurelius Sabinianus Euhodius from Anagnina in Italy, she first appears in the historical record as the concubine of Quadratus.[50] It appears she brought her own staff with her when she moved into the palace. Her *a cubiculo*, the former *a cubiculo* of her deceased lover, was a man named Eclectus, who would rise to the position of *a cubiculo* to Commodus himself.[51]

Of the sundry entertainments available in Rome, circus chariot-racing drew the largest crowds; the Circus Maximus, where the races were held, could seat 150,000 people.[52] These races lasted all day, and the intervals between them were given over to a variety of entertainments, including beast hunts, athletic events, and dramatic performances. It was an entertainment between races that Papirius Dionysius exploited to start a riot. According to Dio,

> As the seventh race was about to begin, a crowd of children ran into the Circus, and a large woman of frightening appearance led them, who was thought, on account of what happened next, to have been a demon. The children shouted many frightening acclamations, and the crowd, taking them up shouted all manner of insult. Finally they leapt down and went off to find Commodus, who was in the Quintilian suburb, shouting his praises and curses at Cleander.
>
> (72.13.3–4)

Cleander sent in troops to quell the riot, but they failed to stem the tide. Marcia, who was with Commodus, told the emperor what was happening, and he responded by ordering Cleander's death.[53] Papirius had circumvented Cleander's dominance of both the court bureaucracy and the guard just as effectively as Cleander had once circumvented that of Perennis, by appealing to the one group whom Cleander could not frighten into submission. It was an object lesson in the complexity of politics in the capital, and of the impossibility of controlling the government by fear alone. With or without the emperor's active involvement, the consensus of the diverse interest groups at Rome had to be won if an administration was to succeed.

Cleander had no immediate successor in government, though much of the power that he once had appears to have passed to Marcia and Eclectus.[54] They soon had to contend with a new problem: the increasing eccentricity of Commodus himself. In 192 he declared that he was the god Hercules on earth, and renamed the city of Rome after himself.[55] His interest in public performance became ever stronger, and he began to spend ever more time training with both gladiators and beast hunters. At the end of 192 he appeared in the Colosseum, slaughtering beasts in the morning and fighting as a gladiator in the afternoon. His prowess as a beast hunter was evidently substantial, as was his increasing hostility to the governing classes. After killing an ostrich he is said to have waved its head at the seats occupied by the senators with an odd expression on his face. Cassius Dio says that he had to start chewing on the wreath that was part of the attire of a senator at the games to keep from laughing (which would have been an insult punishable by death).[56]

Erratic as he now was in public, Commodus' conduct in the palace became even more so. Marcia and Eclectus decided that they had to kill him, and they were joined in their determination by Quintus Aemilius Laetus, the recently appointed praetorian prefect.[57] On New Year's Eve 192 they administered a large dose of poison in some beef. When it appeared that Commodus might survive (he had begun vomiting heavily and went to his bath), they sent a professional athlete who was residing in the palace to strangle him.

The new emperor

The first of January was a day of great solemnity at Rome. It was the day that new consuls, praetors, and aediles took office, and at dawn the new consuls would be escorted from their houses to the Capitoline. After the completion of sacrifices to the gods, the consuls would preside over a meeting of the senate. The first act of this meeting was the swearing of an oath to obey the decrees of the Caesars.[58] The devotions of the senate were mirrored in all the military camps, where soldiers would assemble before the sanctuary of the standards to swear their own oath. Thus it was on January 1, 193, that Commodus duly received the oaths of his legions. He had already been dead for several hours.

The early morning hours of January 1 were ones of intense activity for the assassins of Commodus. Together they determined to place Pertinax on the throne. Laetus and Eclectus went to his house, telling him that Commodus had died of overindulgence, and brought him to the praetorian camp, where Laetus promised the guard an enormous bribe to secure its support. The guard duly proclaimed Pertinax emperor, despite some unfortunate remarks from Pertinax himself that caused them to suspect that he would withdraw privileges granted by Commodus.[59]

The selection of Pertinax is said to have been dictated by the fact that he was the last of the trusted advisers of Marcus Aurelius to be left alive.[60] This may be true. The choice suggests that the conspirators thought that it was important to offer the senate a ruler to whom they could not reasonably object. The order of events on January 1, however, underlines the fact that the guard had assumed a critical role in the accession of a new emperor. Without the prior approval of the guard, there was simply no point in presenting a candidate to the senate, as such an action would be taken as a slight by the most powerful single-interest group in the capital.

After his proclamation by the guard, Pertinax tried to enter the senate house so that he could greet the senate in the morning. But the attendant who kept the keys could not be found, so he went instead to the temple of

Concord, just off the Forum, to await the coming of dawn.[61] There the magistrates joined him, and when the doors of the senate house were finally opened, he went there to greet his former colleagues. When they assembled, Pertinax is said to have addressed the members as follows:

> I have been named emperor by the soldiers, but I really do not want the office, but I will resign it this very day because of my age, ill health and sad state of affairs.[62]

His language implies that his claim to office was legitimated solely by the action of the guard, and that the guard's action was recognized as decisive. The offer to resign was a formulaic one. Ever since the time of Augustus the emperor was expected to present a show of unwillingness to take up its burdens, and the offer to quit was, in a sense, a highly rhetorical assertion of power: you cannot resign an office that you do not have. The senate recognized the signal that it was being sent and duly added its acclamation to that of the guard. On the ideological side, it was recognized that the good man did not want power. He waited to be called, and thus by seeking to refuse power, Pertinax staked a moral claim to the office.[63]

Commodus remained popular in some significant quarters: the guard appears to have liked him, and the soldiery in general may have felt a deep-seated loyalty to the old dynasty.[64] Much as a senator like Cassius Dio or Marius Maximus might profess horror at Commodus' displays in the amphitheater and the delight that he took in racing chariots, and at the speed with which he ordered executions of senior senators and fired prefects of the guard, these were not activities that impacted on the average inhabitant of Rome or of the empire at large. References to Commodus in what may be the most important work of intellectual history to survive from the early third century, Philostratus' *Lives of the Sophists*, are remarkably neutral.[65] Commodus was the emperor, and a mark of imperial favor was a mark of imperial favor, something to be valued even if the emperor drank a lot and liked decapitating ostriches in public. To the average inhabitant of the empire the institutional face of the emperor was more important than the personal. This made the task with which Pertinax was confronted all the more difficult. If he was to survive, he needed somehow to establish his own profile, to place his own stamp on affairs, and to build a personal base of support from within the diverse constituencies that surrounded the throne.

The most obvious way in which an emperor could establish his public persona was through legislation. People listened to the communications of the emperor, and they read them. Commodus' "style" was clearly distinct from that of Marcus, but that was not all.[66] There was a long tradition of prefacing legislation with an explanation of why it was necessary. The "motivation" clauses of senatorial decrees, in which these explanations were provided, had expanded throughout the first century BC and into the age of

Augustus, as a way of explaining state policy.[67] The senate could order that the record of its proceedings be published in a highly public place in prominent cities, and the accounts of its proceedings were evidently circulated. A speech of the emperor to the senate would very likely be sent out to all the provinces with instructions that it be read out and posted so that it could be seen. The degree of permanence accorded to these publications obviously varied from place to place and in accordance with the general interest that accrued to them. Thus the speech of Marcus eliminating the tax on the purchase of gladiators, and the extensive response to it offered by a member of the senate, was regarded as significant enough to be recorded at length in at least two cities.[68] Other pronouncements might be recorded in abbreviated form, so that only their local application has survived, but even then, the decision to publish a part of the document reflects public interest in what the emperor said.[69]

Pertinax seems to have spoken early and often on the subject of the empire's finances. We cannot know how serious the situation that he addressed actually was, but there can be no doubt that imperial pronouncements on matters connected with revenues commanded especially close attention.[70] This was a point that could not have been lost on him, and he evidently wanted to give the impression that he was bringing a new sense of responsibility to the job. As Herodian puts it, "Report of his gentle rule spread throughout all nations, both those subject to Rome and those that were allied to it, and all the camps of the legions, so that people thought that his reign was divinely established."[71] Shortly after assuming the throne, he delivered a speech to the guard in which he claimed that he had made good on his promise to pay them the donative offered by Laetus, despite the fact that there had been a mere one million sesterces in the treasury when Commodus died. The gift itself was some twelve million sesterces, and he paid it after a highly public auction of Commodus' property in the palace that was designed to reveal that his predecessor had spent the resources of the state on himself.[72] So too he published the names of imperial freedmen who had received large sums of money from his predecessor with the amounts they had received.[73] And he reprised the policy of former emperors who had begun their reigns by assailing those who were thought to have profited by bringing false charges against their personal enemies or people whom the emperor was known to dislike, as well as by restoring the reputation of those who were said to have been unjustly convicted.[74] On the broader stage, he limited the ability of the *patrimonium* to claim *bona vacantia*, and stated that it was better "to rule a state that was poor than to pile up wealth through paths of peril and dishonor."[75] Likewise he appears to have restated the Hadrianic law that gave people who cultivated empty land, even on imperial estates, rights of ownership over that land.[76] This was plainly a political pronouncement since, as the case of the Bagradas tenants shows, that law was still regarded as operative at court.[77] He is also said to have stated that the *patrimonium* was not his, but rather the property of the state. As a demonstration of this point he undertook to pay nine years of arrears to funds for child support in Italy, and to make good on salaries that had been unpaid.[78]

Murder

Pertinax moved quickly to establish an image of himself as a conscientious administrator in the wake of the follies of Commodus. To judge from contemporary accounts, he succeeded, at least to a degree, in convincing his fellow senators that he was on the right track, and the people of Rome seemed to have been impressed by his denunciation of Commodus' luxury.[79] But he failed utterly with the guard and with the palace staff. No matter the lengths that Pertinax had gone to pay their donative, the guard still remembered the mass executions that followed his accession in connection with a bizarre effort to place one of the consuls of 193 on the throne in his place.[80] The palace staff may not have been much enthused by the open contempt that Pertinax displayed toward the lifestyle that had been led under Commodus. As Cassius Dio put it, "He had failed to understand . . . that one cannot with safety reform everything at once."[81]

On the morning of March 28, two hundred members of the guard left the barracks, in close formation, and made their way to the palace.[82] The servants made no effort to resist them as they went in search of the emperor. One source alleges that when he heard them coming, Pertinax ordered Laetus to speak to them, and that, instead of doing his duty, Laetus covered his head and fled to the camp. In what Dio calls an act of folly, Pertinax, accompanied by Eclectus and several other *cubicularii*, met with them and gave a long speech. The troops hesitated; perhaps Pertinax would succeed as other generals, as Caesar, Augustus, and Germanicus had done, in suppressing the mutiny by the sheer force of his presence. But it was not to be. We may visualize Pertinax standing before his killers, a deep silence in the room, the soldiers replacing their swords in their scabbards, until one man stepped forward and hurled his spear at the emperor's chest.[83] The spell was broken and the assassins rushed forward to complete the slaughter. Eclectus tried to defend his emperor, and died with him. The other *cubicularii* fled.

The murderers cut Pertinax's head from his body and returned to the camp, where they found Pertinax's father-in-law, who had been dispatched by the emperor to find out what was happening, negotiating to take the throne himself.[84] Flavius Sulpicianus, for this is the man in question, had been elevated to the post of prefect of the city by his son-in-law, and was thus in theoretical charge of the civil administration of Rome. He may well have felt that he was in a position to command the allegiance of the guard, especially as Laetus seems to have gone into hiding. But it was not to be so.

News of Pertinax's end would naturally have spread fast, and one man, Didius Julianus, who had been Pertinax's colleague in the consulship, went down to the senate house to see what was happening.[85] He found the doors locked, but as he was standing there, he encountered two tribunes of the guard who urged him to come immediately to the camp and make himself emperor.

Julianus arrived at the camp as Sulpicianus was holding an assembly of the soldiers.[86] The gates were locked, so Julianus stood there yelling over the wall that he, not Sulpicianus, should be their candidate, that they should not choose a man who would avenge Pertinax. Being a man of standing, he would not have stood before the camp alone. He would have had members of his entourage about him, and they set to work making placards that could be read from the wall. On them was written the promise that he would restore the memory of Commodus.[87] What happened next is somewhat obscure, but it appears that the guard was concerned lest Sulpicianus try to avenge Pertinax's murder and was impressed by Julianus' promise to restore Commodus' memory. Julianus backed his promise concerning Commodus with a further promise that he could immediately pay a donative of twenty-five thousand sesterces a man.[88]

The soldiers were impressed enough by his representations to admit Julianus. It appears that the two contestants for the throne were then conducted to different locations within the camp where they negotiated through representatives of the guard. When Julianus finally offered his massive donative, it was agreed by those running the proceedings that he had won. An assembly of the guard was convened, and Julianus was proclaimed emperor after he promised not to execute Sulpicianus.[89] This later promise was perhaps taken as a sign that he would also make good on his promise not to take vengeance upon the assassins. That evening, surrounded by the soldiers, he summoned a meeting of the senate, and, enacting the formula of renunciation, he said that he was at the senate's disposal without conditions, while making a speech in which he suggested that he was the best man for the job. A decree was duly passed conferring upon him all the authority of a ruler.[90]

The circumstances of Julianus' election shocked contemporaries, though perhaps more so after the event, when a false tradition was circulated in which the praetorians were said to have auctioned the empire to the highest bidder. But, when the auction is removed from the story, the events of the day appear to be more thoroughly grounded in the behaviors of aristocratic life. Sulpicianus was doing no more than Pertinax had done by asking the guard for its approval, and Julianus' conduct resembles nothing so much as that of a man who had presided over a public entertainment. Placards with simple slogans on them had been features of entertainments for centuries, perhaps none so famously as one borne at the triumph of Julius Caesar with the words *veni, vidi, vici* ("I came, I saw, I conquered") written on it.[91] The placards of Julianus need have said nothing more than *memoria Commodi restituenda est* ("The reputation of Commodus must be restored"), a phrase that, like Caesar's, could easily be taken up by a crowd. The training of an aristocrat in rhetoric prepared him for public disputation, and that would involve the speedy assemblage of a claque to shout the right things as the principal spoke.[92] The stages upon which the drama was played out were three: the palace, Forum, and praetorian camp, which were separated from one another by less than a mile.

What is astonishing about the events of March 28, 193 is not so much that they took place, but rather that they had not taken place more frequently, for they are not dissimilar to events in the course of the first century. When Caligula was murdered in 41, the senate had met to decide the future of the empire while Claudius was proclaimed in the camp, his final succession being negotiated by Herod Agrippa, who moved back and forth between the two loci of power.[93] So too in 68, Nero was driven from power when the senate declared him a public enemy, and the prefect of the guard convinced his men to proclaim Galba emperor on the same day.[94] When Galba was murdered in 69, it was Otho, masterminding the plot from the camp, who was able to move into the Forum and take power.[95]

The security of the emperor rested upon his ability to control events in the Forum and the camp from the palace. If he failed to maintain control of events in either location, there were no institutional safeguards to prevent anything from happening. Perhaps the lesson that Pertinax really failed to learn was that preeminence in one locus of power meant nothing if it was not accompanied by equal preeminence in the other two.

Revolution

Julianus controlled the guard, especially beholden to him because he had promised not to punish the murderers of Pertinax, and because he actually seems to have been able to pay the donative that he promised. But something had snapped. The mystique that surrounded the office of emperor seems to have been shattered by the events in the praetorian camp in a way that perhaps no one could have predicted. Pertinax had some claim to the throne because of his connections with the house of Marcus: he was plainly beloved of his old patron Claudius Pompeianus, and he had a great record as a soldier. Julianus had no such record, his well-advertised affection for Commodus won him no friends among members of the senate who seem to have genuinely loathed Commodus, and the people of Rome despised him.

The guard that was Julianus' chief prop was deeply unpopular with the average Roman. Living in a self-contained community in their camp, they had to remain separate from the populus at large if they were to function as the riot police in the capital. When called out to quell a popular disturbance, they did so in full battle order, killing indiscriminately as they went. Indeed, the formation adopted by the men who proceeded to the palace to kill Pertinax may have been precisely that which they used when attacking a crowd. An emperor who was as closely linked with the interests of the guard as Julianus could expect trouble, and he got it on the first full day of his reign.

On that first morning he went down to the Forum to offer sacrifice to Janus, the two-faced god whose temple was located there. A crowd gathered and began to curse him. After he had gone from the temple of Janus to the senate house, making a placatory speech, he tried to ascend the Capitoline, and there he was attacked.[96] He attempted to quell the riot by offering money and invoking the memory of Commodus. This only increased the frenzy, as people seem to have felt that he was confusing them with the despised praetorians. They began to stone him, and he ordered the guard to attack. Rioting continued throughout the day, and the people occupied the Circus Maximus, a symbolic act that shows how significant that spot had become as a focal point of communication between the emperor and his subjects.[97] In occupying the circus the people took over the seats ordinarily reserved for members of the upper classes. The regular seating arrangement was intended to reify the ideological order of society; its rejection signified the degeneration of civil society.[98]

The riots in the circus allegedly precipitated a fatal error on Julianus' part. He began to fear the commanders of the major armies, especially, it seems, those of the Danube and Syria. It is alleged that he sent a centurion to murder Niger, the governor of Syria, and it is certain that he sent men of consular rank to remove the governor of Pannonia Inferior from office.[99] He may have done something similar with regard to Clodius Albinus, who commanded the notoriously mutinous legions in Britain. None of them was amused, or so the story goes.

According to a tradition popularized later by the governor of Pannonia Inferior, Pescennius Niger was the first to raise the standard of rebellion.[100] This is the sort of lie that the governor of Pannonia Inferior, one Septimius Severus, was quite capable of telling. There is no reason to doubt that it was Severus who engineered his own proclamation as emperor first, and that the governors of Britain and Syria followed suit as soon as they found out what he had done.[101] The only question that remains is whether or not Julianus actually plotted against these gentlemen first; that, as we shall see, is a dubious proposition.

There was little in Severus' early life to suggest that he would prove to be the particularly dynamic figure that he would become. Born on April 11, 145, at Lepcis Magna in Tripolitania (modern Libya), Severus was descended from a long line of local notables who could trace their roots to the period of Punic domination. Indeed, it appears that he grew up in a household where Punic was the first language – we are told that he still spoke with a pronounced Punic accent in his adult years, which made it difficult for him to enunciate an unaspirated "s." The result was that he would tend to pronounce his own name as Sheptimiush Sheverush.[102] His grandfather had moved to Italy, where he enjoyed exalted literary company. There still exists a poem in his honor by Statius, the preeminent poet of the late Flavian era. Interestingly, given Septimius' difficulty with Latin, his grandfather seems to have conquered his own linguistic challenges, passing as an Italian among Italians. One reason for the difference in Latinity between the two men may be that Septimius' father did not move to Italy, preferring to stay at home while two relatives entered upon senatorial careers. One, P. Septimius Aper, was suffect consul in 153, and another, C. Septimius Severus, was suffect consul in 160.[103]

Two consular relatives made entry into a senatorial career a viable option for the young Septimius and, indeed, for his elder brother, Septimius Geta, as well.[104] It may have been in 164 that he held his first office, one of the twenty junior positions reserved for aspiring senators who had received the "broad stripe" that marked imperial recognition of his designs. In 169 Septimius was quaestor. He held the office again in 170, this time in Spain (we do not know where he served during his first term). In 173 he served on the staff of his relative, C. Septimius Severus, when the latter was governor of Tripolitania, and there he married a woman from Lepcis named Paccia Marciana.[105] In 175 he was tribune of the plebs, and in 177 he became praetor. Three years later he was given command of a legion in Syria. The governor under whom he served was Pertinax. In 182, Pertinax was fired in the wake of the conspiracy against Commodus.[106] A year later Septimius was dismissed as well, but Perennis was not to last long, and in the wake of his murder, Cleander recalled Severus to public life.[107]

Paccia Marciana had died at some point in the interim, possibly around 183, and Septimius now sought a new wife. He had heard of Julia Domna, daughter of the Sampsiceramid line, which descended from the kings of Emesa in Syria, perhaps while stationed in that province. He now sought her hand in marriage, obtaining her assent in 187, while he was governor of one of the Gallic provinces.[108] Three years later he held the consulship, again through the patronage of Cleander, one of the twenty-five men to do so in that year.[109] Severus' connections with the Semitic side of the empire, the fact that he spoke Punic, was married first to a woman from his own Punic background, and then to a woman from another Semitic city, stand as stunning reminders of the fluidity of classical culture. Severus was no less a senator by virtue of his Punic background than Pertinax was by virtue of his servile ancestry.

The relative stability of the Antonine age permitted, and indeed, encouraged the assimilation of local nobles of all sorts into the Mediterranean governing class. The study of modern immigrant communities has identified two central forms of interaction with the dominant culture of the host state. These are multicultural and bicultural. An individual may be described as multicultural if that person lives within a community that retains a strong identity with the home country while at the same time functioning within the community of the host country. A bicultural person will retain a sense of his or her roots within an immigrant society, while at the same time pursuing a life that removes him or her from that community. A man like Severus offers a virtual paradigm for the bicultural individual.

The three rivals of Severus offer different models for assimilation into the ruling class. Two of them also had connections with Africa. Julianus' mother was from Hadrumentum, and Clodius Albinus was descended from an Italian family that had settled in North Africa.[110] Julianus' family was connected with that of the jurist Salvius Julianus, who achieved considerable age and prominence from the time of Hadrian to the time of Marcus, while that of Clodius is described by Dio as noble (which may indicate a senatorial ancestor or simply that it was wealthy).[111] Pescennius Niger appears to have been from Italy, and to have been the first person in his family to enter the senate.[112] Including Pertinax, it is striking that all five men who aspired to or held the throne in 193 were the first members of their immediate families to achieve the consulship. Only Severus had consular relatives, but after the first stages of his career, they cannot be said to have helped him much, and he does not seem to have made much of an impression on the population of Rome. The person whom the crowds called upon as a savior was Niger, not him.

Civil war

Severus may not have stood out in the years before 193, but from January onwards he proved himself to be a master of the arts of revolution. We cannot now know when he began to aspire to the throne, but there is reason to think that news of the abortive attempt by Falco upon the life of Pertinax suggested the possibility that Pertinax would not last. It would have been folly to move against Pertinax while he was alive. Long experience of command in the Balkans under Marcus had left him with a good reputation among the senior soldiers who had served under him, but it also meant that, if Pertinax were to die, these same soldiers might wish to avenge him. According to an account that may be heavily based upon Severus' autobiography, he began to explore the possibility of taking the throne through conversations with small groups of officers, testing out the will of the men as soon as he heard that Pertinax was dead.[113] There is no reason to believe his version of the chronology: he was proclaimed emperor on April 9, just about the earliest possible day after he could have received news of the events at Rome on March 28.[114] The meeting must have occurred earlier – which makes the story that Julianus tried to kill him very dubious indeed – but this point aside, the process is a familiar one. Generals communicated with their men in three ways: through their officers, through large mass meetings, and through addresses to individual units.[115] A serious matter for which the response of the soldiers at a public meeting needed to be managed in advance would always begin with the junior officers, those who were most closely in touch with the men. The name of Pertinax evidently did carry some weight, and so might jealousy of the guard, receiving huge donatives that were not given to the ordinary rank and file.

Having tested the will of the troops, Severus had also to test that of his colleagues in surrounding provinces. He derived a further advantage from the fact that his older brother, P. Septimius Geta, was governor of another of the Danubian provinces, Moesia Inferior.[116] He may also have had some personal connection with the governor of Dacia, Q. Aurelius Polus Terentianus, who was a member of the same priestly college to which Severus had been admitted a few years before.[117] The odd men out were the governors of Pannonia Superior and Moesia Superior. We have now no information about the latter of these men, but the former, C. Valerius Pudens, appears to have supported Severus immediately.[118] There is no reason to think that the governor of Moesia Inferior did otherwise. A series of coins minted at Severus' behest later in the year commemorates fifteen of the sixteen legions encamped in the Danubian provinces. The ceremony of proclamation was duly enacted, with an appropriate display of reluctance by Severus, on April 9.[119]

As his troops prepared to march, Severus entered into negotiations with Clodius Albinus, offering to adopt him and make him his heir, a position that was signified by offering him the title of Caesar. Albinus accepted the offer, perhaps as Severus' armies were already moving into Italy. Severus had evidently presented himself as a man with children too young to succeed him, and as a man who was too old to remain very long on the throne.[120]

At the time that Severus wrote to Albinus, the question of the children was all the more significant in that Severus, like all other provincial governors, had been compelled to leave his at Rome, a policy instituted by Commodus. Severus, though, appears to have arranged for his children to be spirited out of the capital before Julianus could take any action against them.[121] The escape of the children may be the first clue that Julianus had of what turned out to be an extraordinarily well-organized group of supporters for Severus in Rome. Julianus' own preparations for defense stalled through the ill discipline of the praetorians, the inexperience of troops recruited from the fleet, and the ability of elephants brought in from the imperial elephant farm at Larentum to destroy the fighting towers with which they were equipped.[122] Letters from Severus appear to have been delivered to many quarters, troops sent to occupy key points deserted, and Julianus lost heart. On June 1 he summoned a meeting of the senate to ask that Severus be named co-ruler with himself, but it was too late. The praetorians had received letters promising that they would suffer no harm if they surrendered the murderers of Pertinax. They did so, and announced the fact to the consul Silius Messalla, who then convened a meeting of the senate on his own authority. Julianus had now lost two of the three power points in the capital, and that sealed his fate. The senate passed three motions, one sentencing Julianus to death, the second naming Severus emperor, and the third conferring divine honors on Pertinax.[123] A soldier was sent to the palace, where he found Julianus, abandoned by his supporters, and killed him.

Severus' advance on the capital had demonstrated a thorough command of the political structure of the city, and he took immediate steps to ensure that he would remain in control. He summoned the praetorians, without arms, to a meeting with him outside of the city and dismissed them.[124] He replaced them with a new guard drawn from the soldiers who had marched from the Balkans, and the prefects appointed by Julianus, who had changed sides at an opportune moment, were retained in office.[125] There was, however, a new prefect of the watch, appointed by Severus, who distinguished himself by rounding up the children of Niger. His name was Fulvius Plautianus.[126]

Severus not only understood the structure of power in the capital; he also understood the importance of spectacle in legitimating that power. His entry into Rome was, according to Dio,

> The most brilliant of any that I have witnessed; for the whole city had been decked out with garlands of flowers and laurel and adorned with richly colored stuffs, and it was ablaze with torches and burning incense; the citizens wearing white robes and with radiant countenances, uttered many shouts of good omen; the soldiers, too, stood out conspicuous in their armor as they moved about like participants in some holiday procession; and finally we (senators) were walking about in state.
>
> (Dio 75.1.4, trans. Cary)

The procession, with the distinct elements of the power structure of Rome marked out by their dress, gave visual confirmation of the social order. It was supplemented a few days later by another spectacle, the formal funeral of Pertinax, which culminated in the release of an eagle from a box atop the funeral pyre that symbolized his soul's ascent to join the gods.[127] The two spectacles, triumphal entry and deification, the latter being especially significant as Severus had adopted himself into the family of Pertinax when he was proclaimed, and included the name of his predecessor in his own.[128] His right to rule was confirmed by the diverse groups upon whom it had to depend, and by appeal to divine sanction. It all had also to be done fast, for Pescennius Niger was already on the march from Syria.

Niger's effort was doomed to fail. Severus could muster the sixteen legions of the Danube against a mere six in the eastern provinces, three as part of the garrison of Syria, two in the province of Arabia, and the sixth at Melitene in Commagene.[129] To have any chance of success, Niger recognized that he would have to move fast enough to win some success that could cause support for Severus to falter. Before Severus had completed arrangements in Rome, a force had crossed the Dardanelles and advanced as far as Perinthus, defeating a portion of Severus' army under Fabius Cilo.[130] That was not enough to convince people to desert Severus, and it was the last success Niger would win. An army group assembled from the Pannonian legions and placed under the command of Claudius Candidus drove Niger's forces back into western Turkey.[131] A fleet arrived from Italy to take Candidus' army across the Bosphorus, in sufficient force that he was able to pursue Niger while still leaving enough troops behind to initiate a long and bloody siege of Byzantium, which remained loyal to Niger, who had made the city his head-quarters.[132] This siege would last for three years.

Despite later traditions (owing much, if not all, to the pen of Severus) concerning the sloth of Niger, and the equally unmilitary qualities of his men, the eastern army plainly fought hard and well; its retreat, the most difficult of all military operations, was conducted with skill.[133] Despite two defeats, one near Cyzicus, the other outside of Nicaea, the bulk of Niger's troops were able to withdraw to the Taurus, where they conducted a fierce defense of the passes. Perhaps as a result of his failure to prevent Niger's withdrawal, Candidus was replaced by Cornelius Anullinus, an old associate of Severus, who now advanced into Syria.[134] The final battle was fought in May 194 near Issus, the scene of Alexander's great victory over Darius III in 332 BC, and later the site of a triumphal arch commemorating Severus' victory.[135] It is testimony to Niger's ability to motivate his men that they showed up to fight at all. Long before the battle, Severus had been able to exploit his control of the children of provincial governors who had remained at Rome and the rivalries between cities throughout the region. The governor of Arabia changed sides, presumably taking with him the legion under his command; another legion, stationed in Palestine, deserted, and various cities rose up in revolt.[136] Nonetheless, the battle at Issus is said to have been hard fought, and Niger only fled the scene when the result was no longer in doubt.[137] He was captured a few days later and killed. His head was displayed throughout the principal cities of his province before being sent for further display at Rome.[138]

The two most significant features of this conflict (at least as they can now be recovered) are not directly connected with the military encounters in the field. They are rather with the way in which Severus described those encounters and the way that local communities involved themselves in the struggle. Byzantium, of course, was remarkable in that it was able to withstand a siege that lasted for years, but its allegiance may have been determined simply by the fact that Niger had gotten there first. In other cases long-standing rivalries between cities moved from the status of rhetorical contests for imperial favor to actual bloodshed. The cities of Nicomedia and Nicaea in northern Turkey had long contended for imperial favor, and now they chose opposite sides in the war. Immediately after learning of the victory at Cyzicus, Nicomedia had sent an embassy to Severus proclaiming its adherence to his cause. As a consequence, so Herodian tells us,

> The people of Nicaea . . . because of their rivalry with Nicomedia, joined the other side, by opening their gates to Niger's army and taking in any fugitives that came their way, as well as the garrison that Niger sent for Bithynia. The two cities were like army camps and provided the bases from which the forces clashed.[139]

The further consequence of the devotion of Nicaea to the cause of Niger was that Nicomedia's position as metropolis of Bithynia was confirmed. It may be a mark of the attention that people were paying to the progress of the war that the defections of Tyre and Laodicea both took place as Niger was preparing his position south of the Taurus. What is significant is that the leading citizens of these places were willing to take extreme risks to further the position of their cities (and, coincidentally, of themselves). The individual civic hierarchies of the empire could not see themselves in isolation from the power of the central government, and regional politics, of necessity, took their direction from those of the imperial government. The nexus of relationships could not be made clearer than it was by Herodian:

> While these events (the retreat of Niger) were taking place in Cappadocia, there was an outbreak of civil war, the Laodicians in Syria through hatred of Antioch, the Tyrians in Phoenicia through enmity with Beirut. Learning of Niger's defeat, they ventured to tear down his honors and proclaim Severus.
>
> (Herod. 3.3.3)[140]

Laodicea and Antioch were leading cities of Syria, though Antioch had always been the more important place, as it had once been a primary seat of the Seleucid kings. The penalties inflicted on Antioch were remarkable: it was reduced from the rank of a city to that of a village and attached to Laodicea, which was awarded the status of a *colonia*. Antioch's own Olympic games were transferred to Antioch in Cilicia, where they would henceforth be held in association with games commemorating Severus' victory.[141]

The situation between the two cities of Phoenicia was somewhat different. Tyre was one of the most ancient cities of the region, while Beirut owed its prominence to its foundation as a veteran colony by Augustus in 15 BC.[142] In culture and background the two places could not have been more distinct.[143] Tyre preserved the memory of the ancient Phoenician kings, minting coins with Phoenician legends, celebrating the ancient Phoenician divinities Melquart and Astarte, and claiming primacy among the cities of Phoenicia. It was thoroughly bicultural, mixing elements of its Phoenician past with the Greek needed to make its uniqueness comprehensible on the imperial stage. The strong sense of the past that is exuded by Tyre is perhaps expressed most clearly in the work of a second-century author from a neighboring Phoenician city, Byblos, in his account of the ancient myths of his people. This author, who went by the Greek name of Philo, wrote:

> It is necessary for the sake of clarity below and for the determination of particulars to state explicitly that the most ancient of the barbarians, especially the Phoenicians and the Egyptians, from whom the remainder of mankind received their ideas, considered as the greatest gods those who discovered things useful for life or who, in some way, benefited other nations.[144]

It was Philo who used the Greek word *barbaros* in its sense of foreigner (non-Greek) to express the superiority of the wisdom of his people in terms that were borrowed from the Greek philosopher Euhemerus. This seamless mingling of traditions may be taken as characteristic of Phoenician culture, and that was opposed to the inherent Roman-ness of Beirut. At Beirut the gods who were commemorated were not Melquart and Astarte, but rather those of the Roman pantheon. The coins of Beirut were minted with Latin rather than Phoenician, or even Greek, legends. Instead of respecting the ancient authority of Tyre, Beirut asserted its independence of neighboring cities by flaunting the title of *colonia*. No wonder there was tension between the two places, but they were able to coexist so long as there was unity in the imperial administration. With that unity shattered, the terms of coexistence changed as well. And there was more to the civil war than that. After Severus had proved victorious, we are told that he punished the supporters of Niger in all the cities of the east.[145] He had his own supporters in these places as well, and in each place we may imagine desperate efforts to exploit division for personal advantage. It is impossible to see the civil war as an isolated event involving only the armies of Rome.

It is arguable that, as a man who himself united the culture of his homeland with that of the capital, Severus was particularly conscious of the empire-wide impact of his conduct. He appears to have been determined to leave his mark upon the provinces. The old province of Syria was itself divided into two new provinces, Syria Coele, "hollow Syria," encompassing the regions whose urban culture had been fundamentally reshaped by the Seleucid kingdom, and Syria Phoenice, "Phoenician Syria," encompassing those regions that retained a more strongly Semitic urban character.[146] His own wife, Julia Domna, was, of course, another product of this region, and her homeland of Emesa defected from Niger, as did Heliopolis, another city in the region, which was rewarded with the title of *colonia* with the *ius Italicum*.[147] Tyre was similarly entitled a *colonia* as a reward for what it had done.[148]

Severus' actions may be seen as recognizing the integration of the Semitic portions of the empire into the center of government. It may even be that his ability to convey his personal biculturalism to these places had contributed to the decision of their diverse ruling classes to back him against his rival. We cannot now know if this is true. But we do know that Severus took a particular interest both in his North African homeland and in the development of the Semitic provinces, an interest that resulted in the most significant alteration of the shape of the eastern frontier since the time of Augustus.

Before exploring the further restructuring of the east, we must, however, pay some attention to a second aspect of the reportage of the war. That is Severus' interest in providing evidence of divine favor. Given that Severus was the first man to successfully seize power in a civil war since Vespasian over a century earlier, extensive reportage should perhaps not be surprising. Even Pertinax had had some time to provide an account of astonishing coincidences portending his future glory, and Didius Julianus could point to the curious coincidence that he had been Pertinax's colleague as consul and had succeeded him as governor of Africa in 189 or 190.[149]

Appeal to divine confirmation had a long history in the struggle for power at Rome. As early as the late third century BC Scipio Africanus claimed divine aid at crucial moments of the campaign that drove the Carthaginians from Spain, and, in the first century BC, Marius, Sulla, and Caesar had all offered numerous signs of the divine plans that had resulted in their prominence. Augustus had gone even further, advertising his horoscope as proof that his supremacy was inevitable. Throughout the next two centuries a distinctive pattern emerged in the circulation of portents outwards from the palace at points of crisis.[150] So too did various patterns of disruption, involving the same media. Vespasian proved himself the master of such techniques in AD 69. His supporters waged a clandestine campaign of divine disruption in Italy while he advertised oracles proclaiming his right to rule from his base in Palestine, a campaign that was supplemented by reports of miracles that he performed at Alexandria as his armies advanced in Italy.[151]

Severus' campaign to establish his divine credentials was equally powerful.[152] It is alleged that he had received the first glimmerings of future greatness from an astrologer who cast a horoscope for him. When the astrologer perceived its significance, he asked Severus for his "own nativity, and not that of another man." When Severus assured him that he had given accurate information, the astrologer "revealed to him all the things that later came to pass." The story is not unlike one told about the emperor Augustus in 44 BC, which is probably no accident.[153] Likewise, Severus is the most probable source for the tale that he selected Julia Domna as his second wife because he discovered that her horoscope indicated that she would marry a monarch.[154] He also probably told the world about a consultation of Zeus Belus, whose shrine was at Apamea in Syria, while still a private citizen. The god is said to have pointed to a passage of Homer that could be interpreted as a sign that he would rule.[155] One sign of the reaction to this sort of direct imperial indication of taste is Cassius Dio's first historical work, an account of the portents that inspired Severus to take the throne.[156] In later years this taste was graphically illustrated: Severus had a picture of the stars painted on the ceiling of the palace. On public display there was a version that was accurate in all respects save for the actual position of the stars at the moment of his birth, so that people would not know exactly when he would die. The fully accurate version was depicted in his private apartments.[157]

Information of the sort mentioned in the last paragraph tended to be circulated out from the palace through court favorites, or, as is quite obvious in the case of the horoscope, when a person entered the palace.[158] But Severus needed to reach more people, more quickly, if he were to establish his claim as forcefully as he wished. His view of the job of emperor did not restrict itself to influencing the members of the ruling elite at Rome, or simply the urban population. Just as the ruling classes of the cities of the empire could be expected to divide along party lines, so too did all of them need to know why it was that Severus was destined to rule. Herodian reports that he described the dreams, oracles, and signs that encouraged him to take the throne not only in his autobiography, but also in his public dedications of statues.[159] He would also have done so through painted images, which, along with Severus' autobiography, seem to have informed Herodian's understanding of events.[160] They will almost certainly have informed Dio as well. They may even have helped form Dio's evident conviction that Severus was, to some degree, the agent of Fortune.[161]

It was, in Dio's view, a divinity that strengthened Severus' forces at the battle of Issus, and he tells of a miraculous wind that blew in the face of Niger's army, securing victory for Severus:

> They (Niger's soldiers) would have been completely victorious had it not been for the fact that clouds gathered out of a clear sky, a wind sprang up after a calm, and there followed heavy thunderclaps, sharp lightnings, and a violent rain-storm, all of which they had to face. This did not trouble Severus' troops as it was at their backs; but it caused great confusion to Niger's men, since it was directly in their faces. Most of all the opportune coming of the storm inspired courage in the one side, which believed it was being aided by the divine, and fear in the other, which felt that the divine force was fighting against it.
>
> (Dio 74.7.6–7, trans. Cary, adapted)

Herodian leaves the divine wind out of his account of Issus but does record it in the battle that enabled Severus' army to breach the defenses of the Taurus, saying that

> Severus' soldiers had reached a state of exhaustion by now and the defenders believed that they had nothing to worry about over the fortifications. Then suddenly one night there were a series of enormous cloudbursts accompanied by heavy snow. (It must be remembered that the whole of Cappadocia has hard winters, particularly in the Taurus mountains.) As a result, a large, rushing mountain stream came pouring down and was built up into an enormously powerful torrent because the normal channel was dammed up and was holding back the flow of water . . . when the garrison on the blockade saw what had happened, they were afraid that now the mountain torrent had swept away the wall and there was no further obstacle, they would be surrounded by an enemy flanking action. So, leaving their post, they fled. Severus' army was delighted at the event and their spirits rose because they believed they were being guided by divine providence.
>
> (Herod. 3.3.7–8, trans. Whittaker)

The similarity between the descriptions of these two events suggests very strongly that these two authors are not in fact describing two events, but rather offering their readings of the same event. Herodian, who thought that the battle was fought on the site of Alexander's victory over Darius (and had been there) recognized that an account that included mountains and torrents could not be connected with the place that he had seen, so he transferred it to a mountainous region north of the area.[162] Dio knew of no battle in the Taurus, but thought that the final encounter was in a mountainous terrain.[163] Rather than multiplying battles, the most economical hypothesis is that the two authors are giving us separate reactions to an elaborate description of a single event. They both get the main point of the story very clearly: that Severus' victory stemmed from a divine storm. Their reading of the event is presumably just what Severus desired, and it is quite likely in Herodian's case that he was basing his description on a picture.

The divine storm itself had important overtones, for it evoked the memory of one of the most dramatic stories connected with Marcus' wars on the northern frontier. This was a divine storm that arose and overwhelmed a barbarian force that threatened to annihilate one of his armies. In one version of this event, it is even stated that Pertinax was the commander of the troops. By advertising his own weather miracle, Severus was not only reinforcing his claim to be the agent of fortune, but also what was to become his claim to be the true heir of Pertinax and Marcus.[164] He had already adopted himself into the family of Pertinax and would soon declare Commodus his brother.

In some way the ground for this transformation was already well laid. Not only had he asserted that Pertinax had tried to restore the empire to the standards of Marcus, but he, like Pertinax, Didius, Pescennius, and Albinus, had adopted a public appearance that recalled the memory of the bearded, curly-haired Marcus. He thus had the signs of divine favor that marked him as Marcus' true heir, and he had the "Marcus look."

The solidification of power

With Niger defeated, Severus made his way to the east. Claiming (with what degree of truth it is impossible to know) that Niger had sought aid from the kingdoms east of the frontier and that they had violated their treaty with Rome by attacking the city of Nisibis, he resolved to invade northern Mesopotamia. Moreover, and this was no doubt a consideration, as the aspiring heir of Marcus, a success in the east would recall the successes won by Marcus' armies in the 160s. The invasion of northern Mesopotamia involved the annexation of a new province (called Osrhoena) that bordered, somehow, on the reduced kingdom of Osrhoene.[165] The conquest was completed by the end of 195, and Severus further received a submissive embassy from the kingdom of Adiabene, which abutted the Tigris across from Osrhoene. It was enough to claim victory, and with news that the army of Marius Maximus had finally completed the conquest of Byzantium, Severus returned to Rome by the end of 196.

By the time that he returned, war with Albinus was already under way. It appears that Severus had raised his eldest son, Caracalla, to the rank of Caesar before the end of 195, thus breaking the arrangement that he had made with Albinus in 193.[166] Additionally, he formally adopted himself into the family of Marcus, restoring the reputation of Commodus (who was now deified as Severus' "brother").[167] This piece of dynastic legerdemain left no room at all for any claims that Albinus may have had on the basis of their earlier agreement. It also made plain to the senate that he was not chary of attacking its privileges, one of which remained the formal ability to cast posthumous judgment on a ruler by deciding whether or not he should be deified. Antoninus Pius, for instance, had argued with the senate that it should deify Hadrian, admitting that the senate had the power to decide. Severus' action made it clear that the Antonine tradition of formal respect for the senate's role would be severely truncated.[168]

Severus may have hoped to take Albinus by surprise by launching an attack while he was still away from Rome. Success was virtually guaranteed when the German legions remained loyal to Severus, and fresh forces came to their aid from the Danube. The disparity in numbers between the forces of the two sides was enormous, roughly four to one in Severus' favor, and, as was the case with Niger, there was dissension in the rear. In this case Dio tells of a schoolteacher from Rome who took off for Gaul, pretending to be a

(a)

(b)

(c)

Plate 2 The dynastic look: Marcus, Commodus, and Severus. (a) Marcus Aurelius. *Credit*: KM 1991.2.564. Photo courtesy of the Kelsey Museum of Archaeology, University of Michigan. (b) Commodus. *Credit*: *RIC* Commodus no. 97 (Rome 184); author's collection, photo courtesy of Forum Ancient Coins. (c) Septimius Severus. *Credit*: *RIC* Severus no. 308 (Rome 209); author's collection, photo courtesy of Ancient Treasure Coins.

senator (his background as an educator may have enabled him to sound the part), and raised a band of men with whom he raided Albinus' supply lines.[169]

The early successes may not have had the impact that Severus desired on the people of Rome, who were perhaps quite tired of civil war. There was a serious demonstration in the Circus Maximus, during the chariot races that were held on December 15.[170] Dio, who was there, says that the crowd sat through a specialty race in which six horses were yoked to each chariot instead of the usual four without applauding, and then, in the interval between races they suddenly acclaimed the city of Rome as "Immortal Queen" and then asked, "How long are we to suffer such things?" and "How long are we to be waging war?" Then they cried, "So much for that" and returned to watching the races. Dio, as was his wont, interpreted this as the result of divine action, though he should have known better. The acclamation of Rome was based on a standard acclamation type, and the other two are much simpler in Latin than in English translation, both being three words, e.g. *quo usque* plus verb.[171] Severus may have read it differently, as an act of subversion prompted by supporters of Albinus in the city, and we cannot know how he would have taken two other phenomena that Dio took as omens of the future. One was a "fire" burning in the northern sky at night, the other a "fine rain like silver" that fell out of the clear sky in the Forum of Augustus. Dio says that he recovered some of the substance that had fallen and plated some bronze coins with it, and that it stuck for three days.[172] There is no way of knowing what Dio had or did, though the simple solution that he is merely embellishing Severan propaganda in these cases goes too far. It seems rather to be the case that Dio was, once again, seeking confirmation for what was unfolding around him.

The events in question unfolded very fast. Albinus was in an impossible situation unless he could force a decisive battle quickly and defeat Severus in person. The decisive battle was fought at Lyons on February 19. Accounts of what happened varied significantly – Dio says explicitly that he would not repeat the lies that Severus had told about it, and Herodian gives some details as to just what some of those lies might have been. The situation seems to have been complicated by the fact that Severus was fleeing the field when one of his generals, Julius Laetus, won the day.[173]

The war with Albinus was no more limited to Gaul than the war with Niger had been to the regions in which it was fought. Herodian reports that Severus had captured the correspondence of Albinus, and that the senate awaited his return with trepidation as a result. Sixty-four members of the senate were under arrest when he returned to Rome; twenty-nine of them would be executed for treason and their property confiscated to the *fiscus*.[174] Dio says that members of the senate were dismayed to find that Severus continued to publicize his reevaluation of Commodus, and criticized them for their dislike.[175] Tertullian in Carthage suggests that a commission of inquiry was sent there to round up other supporters of Albinus.[176] Africa may have been particularly targeted because of Albinus' roots in the province, but it is unlikely to have been the only place where lives were lost or ruined in the aftermath of the battle of Lyons.

For Rome, at least, we can gain some sense of the impact of Severus' triumph from Dio's tales of the fear with which senators greeted one another in the streets:

> All pretended to be on the side of Severus, but they were confuted as often as any sudden tidings arrived, being unable to conceal the feelings hidden in their hearts. For when off their guard they started at reports that came without warning, and in such ways, as well as by their countenances and behavior, the feelings of each one became manifest.
>
> (Dio 75.8.5, trans. Cary)

Severus too may have felt some discomfort there, for, after offering lavish celebration of his success to the people of the city, he left again on campaign before the end of the summer and would not return until five more years had passed.[177] The excuse was that the Parthians had taken advantage of his distraction in the west to attack the fortress city of Nisibis by the Euphrates.[178]

It is likely that the new war was the direct result of Severus' previous campaign in northern Mesopotamia. The Parthian king had every reason to regard Adiabene, whose submission Severus had demanded, as being within his sphere of influence and the increased Roman presence at Nisibis as an infringement upon his traditional territory. Severus, on the other hand, may have seen the conflict as an opportunity to win easy glory by defeating a weak, but traditional, foe.[179] The internal divisions within the Parthian kingdom were underlined by the fact that the brother of the Parthian king accompanied Severus.[180]

The occupation of Nisibis in force would become the defining issue between Rome and Persia for the next century and a half. From Pompey to Severus the Roman frontier had stopped at the Euphrates. Trajan's brief annexation of Mesopotamia had been abandoned as soon as he died, and Marcus had simply extended Roman power south along the Euphrates after his victories. The world into which Severus now moved would be transformed by the operations of the 190s, and so too would Rome's relationship with Parthia now that the buffer states between the two powers were to be removed.

Although Osrhoene had some things in common with Commagene, the former kingdom, now part of a Roman province that abutted it on the west bank of the Euphrates, its differences are of genuine significance.[181] Although the kingdom of Osrhoene was a product of the collapse of Seleucid power, Edessa, Carrhae, and Nisibis were three of the oldest continuously occupied cities on earth. In Commagene, which had emerged as an independent kingdom during the breakup of Alexander's empire, there were still reminiscences of the mixed Persian and Aramaic past, perhaps none so striking as the massive shrine on Nemrud Dag and the rock-cut inscriptions of its former kings. Lucian, the great satirist of the second century AD who was from Samosata, the chief city of the region, says that he knew both Greek and Aramaic in his youth.[182] But the crucial point here is that they were both drawn to Rome and toward the Mediterranean. Although Greek was certainly spoken in Edessa, it was not the primary language of expression. This language was Syriac, the local Aramaic dialect, written in a local script.[183] The most famous writer produced by Edessa in the second century was Bardaisan, but his work only became known in the west because it was translated from the Syriac in which he wrote it.[184] And while the people of Commagene might look at the memorials of kings who were descended from the Achaemenid dynasty, the kings of Edessa had intermarried with the Arsacid royal house of Parthia. The inhabitants of Commagene worshipped divinities with a Semitic past, but they did so in Greek, and they were in many ways quite similar in this to the Punic community of North Africa from which Severus had emerged. The gods of Edessa were Bel, Nebo, and Atargatis, ancient divinities of Mesopotamia.[185] The temples in which they were worshipped were built on the Mesopotamian pattern, and the habits of worship (which included auto-emasculation by the male priests of Atargatis) were distinctly non-Roman. Carrhae, to the south, was in the unusual position of administering two very ancient temples that were located several miles outside its walls, one to the moon goddess, the other to Sin, the moon god. A third temple, also to a moon goddess, may have occupied a prominent position within its walls. The extraurban temples to the moon goddess and moon god were both of great antiquity; the latter still housed the memorials of the last king of independent Babylon, Nabonidus, who had resided there for many years.[186]

To the southeast of Osrhoene was a kingdom of relatively recent date, centered on the relatively new city of Hatra.[187] Hatra was a city of the Arab population of northern Mesopotamia. The culture of Hatra, as it has emerged from excavations, mingles elements of the Semitic, Mesopotamian, and Iranian worlds. The temple at which Šamaš, the sun god who was the principal divinity of the local pantheon, was worshipped had been built on the Iranian pattern, while the art that decorated it is characteristic of the Semitic world with its stress on frontality and symmetry.[188] The titulature of its rulers is derived from that of the Parthian kings, and their nomenclature suggests that they intermarried with the Parthian royal family. So long as the city remained within the orbit of Parthian power, it enabled the kings of Parthia to exert influence over the nomadic tribes that controlled the frontier zone between the two empires. The annexation of Osrhoene thus brought Rome directly into a contest with Hatra.

The plan of Severus' campaign, insofar as it can be reconstructed from the fragmentary account in Cassius Dio, appears to have been to eliminate Parthian influence in northern Mesopotamia.[189] Roman armies advanced rapidly on the Parthian capital of Ctesiphon (just south of modern Baghdad) and sacked it.[190] They turned then on Hatra, which withstood the siege.[191] Despite the operational success represented by the sack of Ctesiphon, the campaign of Severus was thus a strategic draw, at best. It failed to overturn the balance of power in northern Mesopotamia, and it left Roman power in what was now a new province of Mesopotamia dangerously exposed in a world that was very different from that which it controlled east of the Euphrates.[192] As Dio put it,

> Severus said that he had acquired a great country and provided a bulwark for Syria. The facts proclaim otherwise, that it has been for us the cause of constant wars and of enormous expense. It yields very little, it costs a very great deal, and, reaching out to people who are closer to the Medes and Persians, we are always, in some way, fighting their wars.
>
> (75.3.2–3)

If Dio had been inclined to think in terms of a map (which he was not), he might have noted that the new province was a geopolitical nightmare. It was designed to control the road system that stretched from Edessa to Nisibis and south from there to Singara.[193] Severus did not extend direct control to the north of the Tur Abdin, which dominates the landscape of the region, leaving his new province exposed on the northern flank, and the Parthians in control of the best route into Armenia from the south, a route that ran along the east bank of the Tigris.[194]

Success or failure, depending on how one sees it, the campaign in Mesopotamia was the last offensive conducted by Severus in person for more than a decade, but it was not enough to take him back to Rome for an immediate celebration. Instead he returned to Antioch, where his son, Caracalla, assumed the *toga virilis*, marking the fact that he had come of age, and was designated consul. Antioch itself was made again into a city, with the rank of a *colonia*, perhaps in recognition of the fact that it was a major staging ground for the campaign against Persia, and was simply too important a place to be left seething at its former treatment.[195] It was then that Severus visited Egypt before returning overland to Rome, where he arrived at the end of 202.

Upon entering Egypt, Severus' first stop was the tomb of Pompey at Pelusium. Hadrian had rebuilt the tomb, and Severus may have been concerned to eradicate any sense of a curse that may have descended from the fact that the murderer of Pompey was a Lucius Septimius.[196] But there may have been more to it than that. Pompey was a tangential ancestor of

Marcus Aurelius, and thus, now, of Severus himself. And Severus seems to have had an interest in the civil wars of the republic – he had told the senate that Caesar and Pompey had perished because they were too merciful. The young Augustus, Marius, and Sulla were, in his view, more rational examples for a man beset with strife to follow.[197] In celebrating Pompey he could be reminding others of just what the consequences of Pompey's actions were. History was certainly on his mind as he passed through Alexandria, viewing the tomb of Alexander and walling it up so that others could not. And so too he was fascinated by the antiquities. Marius Maximus noted that he was interested in the god Serapis and wanted to honor him, and to see the other great sites. Dio says that he was fascinated by the antiquities of the land, inquiring into all hidden secrets and taking from the sanctuaries all the books of lore that he could find.[198] The course of his visit attests the fascination with Egyptian wisdom that we saw at the end of chapter 1, but it may also be yet another sign of Severus' essential attraction to aspects of the cultural heritage of the empire that did not stem from the purely Greco-Roman tradition.

While he was in Egypt, Severus also introduced a significant change in the way that Alexandria was governed. Augustus had abolished the ancient city council – notorious for instigating riots against the later Ptolemies – and Severus restored it. The award of a council removed an anomaly, and it was accompanied by a decree allowing Egyptians to enter the senate.[199] It may be that this was his intention, but that would seem to be out of keeping with Severus' general pattern of administration, which shows no inherent distaste for anomalies. Thus in creating Mesopotamia he had made an equestrian governor of a province with two legions, and in his use of colonial status with *ius Italicum* to reward cities he was breaking with tradition. More likely he was rewarding the Alexandrians because Egypt had deserted the cause of Niger before Issus, and the admission of Egyptians to the senate did not result in an actual senator until 212, when a former *a libellis* achieved that dignity.[200]

From Egypt, Severus returned overland to Rome, where he celebrated the tenth anniversary of the marriage between his elder son, Caracalla, and Plautianus' daughter in August 202, and his own tenth year in power (as was the custom with imperial anniversaries, the celebration marked the beginning of the tenth year rather than its end).[201] It was again a visit marked by spectacle, and by a very public display of the power that Plautianus had acquired within the regime. Sixty of the boars that fought in the amphitheater were advertised as Plautianus' own.[202] And just as it was a spectacular visit, so too it was a short one. Severus moved on to North Africa, perhaps before the end of the year.[203]

Moving on to North Africa, Severus stopped to visit his old home at Lepcis Magna, and there to observe progress that was being made on a massive building project that he had set in motion shortly after he had taken power at Rome. It involved the building of a great colonnaded street, a triumphal arch in his own honor, a new forum, and a grand nymphaeum (fountain).[204] It was also while he was here that tensions began to erupt between himself and Plautianus.

Plautianus was a relative of Severus, also from Lepcis.[205] The degree of prominence that he achieved by the time that he and Severus reached their old home was unheard of, for a public official, since the time of Sejanus. Indeed, the fact that Dio should draw this parallel is interesting, for it may tell us more about how government actually functioned under Severus than anything else. In learning about Sejanus, Dio would have learned that all the emperor's correspondence passed through him, all access to the emperor was arranged through him, and that his favor was felt to be essential among both senators and equestrians. If he drew such a parallel (which he did), Dio must have seen a similar structure of government – indeed he even goes so far as to say that Plautianus had even more power than Sejanus had had.[206] On a very basic level, the truth of his assertion is confirmed by the fact that dedications to the imperial family included Plautianus along with the immediate household.

On another level, the implications of Dio's statement are anything but obvious. The way Dio writes, it is impossible to know if he was speaking of the entire period of Severus' reign or only a portion of it. It is only because we know something about other men who held the prefecture, and have some reason to reconstruct Plautianus' career so that we can see that he only became prefect in 197, that we can refine what Dio was saying, and in refining his statement, gain a clearer view of Severus' style of administration.

The period of Plautianus' ascent mirrors exactly that of Severus' time away from Rome. Since the emperor was the ultimate arbiter of all disputes, of appointments to office, and administrative decisions, the government could not readily function in his absence. Where he went, so too went the center of administration. People who wanted a decision from him had to find him. For Severus' time in Egypt (thanks to the preservation of various documents on papyrus) we can see him handing down a series of decisions that affected people on the spot. One such text, preserving his responses over the course of three days in succession, gives some sense of his style, which appears conservative and essentially supportive of those who had issued prior decisions:

> Copies of responses published at Alexandria in the stoa of the gymnasium. Eighth Year, Phamenoth 18:
> Imperator Caesar L. Septimius Severus Pius Pertinax Arabicus Adiabenicus Parthicus Maximus Augustus and Imperator Caesar M. Aurelius Antoninus Augustus to Ulpius Heraclanus called also Callinicus: We remitted the penalties which had been imposed on Alexandrians or Egyptians but added a time limit to the benefaction.

To Artemidorus called also Achilles: It is late to complain about a decision once you have agreed to the findings.

To Aurelius Artemidorus and Aurelius Anubion and others: Obey the findings.

To Cil . . . dis called also Midas through Philocrates his son: Just as you are wrong in asking that the sale of the mortgaged properties should be rescinded, so the governor shall order that you recover possession of the properties which are held forcibly without (legal) precedent.

To [Ma]thalge daughter of Ambrelus through Abdomanchus her son: Women are not forbidden to borrow money and to pay in behalf of others.

(Oliver, *Greek Constitutions*, nn. 226–30,
trans. slightly adapted)[207]

Two days after the business reported here we find Severus ordering Plautianus himself, described as "the *clarissimus* praetorian prefect and our kinsman," to conduct an investigation into a dispute over tax collection. It is an unusual point in that here, for once, Severus appears to think that whoever had investigated the case in the past had not done a thorough job, though he is plainly unwilling to issue a wider ruling without more facts.[208] There is no reason to think that he was not fielding similar complaints from other parts of the empire at the same time. Indeed, on July 1 of 200 we have a response to a soldier named Marcellus in a dispute over inheritance, and from September and October of the same year there are responses to private individuals about their rights to slaves.[209] Although we do not know who any of the people receiving these responses were, none of them have names that suggest that they were from Egypt. The crucial point is not that the emperor did a lot of business on the road (in the text cited above he issues four decisions a day, three days in a row). Rather it is that the arrangement of his schedule may have been even more firmly planted in the hands of the praetorian prefect than usual. The best evidence that we have for the prefect's role in sorting the mail as it came in is from the year 217, when the prefect at that time received a denunciation of himself to Caracalla.[210] There seems to have been no way to get such a message to the emperor in a way that would not go through him. On the road the capital's diverse venues through which personal contact could be made with the emperor seem to have been restricted to his sessions in court, especially at times when he was not traveling in company with the army (which had its own methods of access).

The high visibility of Plautianus as both prefect and the father-in-law of the emperor's elder son (no matter that the son in question hated his wife) was confirmed by the fact that his name was included in the loyalty oath sworn each year to the emperor and his house.[211] The oath, like imperial titulature and the authorization of statue groups, was a basic way of conveying information to as many people as possible. As such, these modes of communication could have unintended results. Statues of Plautianus are said to have been torn down throughout the empire. This, in and of itself, is a remarkable statement. We have no other evidence for a praetorian prefect who was celebrated this widely since the time of Sejanus, and it is again a sign of the close attention paid by individual local hierarchies to the activities of the court. It is also evidently a sign of just how dangerous these attentions could be. Reporting an incident that took place in 204, Dio says,

> When many images of Plautianus had been made (the event is worthy of record), Severus, annoyed at their number, ordered some of them to be melted down, and a rumor arose from this and spread throughout the empire that he had been overthrown and killed, and some people destroyed statues of him, for which act they were later brought to trial.
>
> (75.16.2)

One of the people charged on this occasion was the governor of Sardinia, and Dio himself appears to have been in the emperor's council when he was tried. The accuser on this occasion said that everyone knew that the skies would fall before Severus would harm Plautianus, so people should have known that the report was untrue.[212] His statement is testimony to the way the emperor (who was listening to this) would expect his public declarations to be understood; it likewise shows some perversity in that Severus would not think that a public order to melt down some statues would also be taken as a public statement.

Severus and his entourage returned to Rome by June 10, 203, and a year later he celebrated the great games in honor of a new *saeculum*, on his reckoning the nine-hundredth anniversary of the founding of Rome.[213] Again, it appears that Severus' time at Rome was marked by a string of public events to demonstrate the stability of his regime, but, behind the scenes, tensions appear to have been building. In January 205 there was a demonstration in the Circus Maximus against Plautianus, and some people (including Dio) may have begun wondering if the recent eruption of Vesuvius portended a change in the state of affairs.[214] If Dio wondered this before January 25, the events on that evening would have confirmed him in his belief that no great event could pass without divine sanction. It was on that evening that Caracalla laid information before his father that Plautianus was plotting to kill him. Severus believed the story, and Plautianus was summoned to the palace, where Caracalla tried to kill him with his own hand (a sign of the violent temper that would erupt with devastating consequences in later years). His father stayed his hand, but stood aside as Caracalla ordered some of his attendants to cut Plautianus down.[215]

The murder of Plautianus was, predictably, accompanied by the execution of some notable supporters in the senate, and the posthumous revelation of sundry atrocious acts that had remained unnoticed while he was alive. Chief among these was the castration of numerous males of good family to serve as eunuchs for his daughter.[216] There is no point at guessing about the truth of such statements; rather they should be read in light of the pattern (illustrated as well by Pertinax's conduct with respect to Commodus' staff) of justifying a man's death because he had lived scandalously. It may be seen as a sign of an inherently puritanical streak in Roman public life that excess was always to be suspected on the part of those whom one wished to condemn.

Alternative realities

The death of Plautianus removed a buffer between the two sons of Severus, the younger named Geta, who hated each other. Little remains on record for the next three years of Severus' reign beyond the tale of their hatred, and the tale of a remarkable brigand named Bulla "the lucky" who preyed upon travelers between Rome and Brundisium (Brindisi).[217] Dio (although not having the benefit of modern social anthropology to help him) paints an ideal picture of what Eric Hobsbawm has described as a social bandit.[218] He set upon the rich, distributed gifts to artisans who supplied him, and humiliated the authorities.

Aside from contributing to the history of social brigandage, Dio's decision to include such an account reflects the flip side of the picture that has been stressed so far in this book of the extension of upper-class culture into the countryside, and the creation of a definable Roman stratum in the human geology of rural history. The brigand who put himself beyond the reach of urban society and preyed upon it was an object of fascination in upper-class society. The novels that people read, and these are, of course, upper-class people, will often oppose normalized urban society with a countryside dominated by brigands. Thus in the first book of Apuleius' splendid *Metamorphoses*, the hero, one Lucius, is greeted by a host who tells him that he is short of furniture because brigands were always attacking the city. When Lucius is transformed into an ass (literally), he falls into the hands of brigands who regale each other with tales of their attacks upon the wealthy, and are fooled by an aristocrat who penetrates their society by claiming to be an especially great one.[219] The whole action of novels like Xenophon of Ephesus' *Ephesian Tale* or Heliodorus' *Ethiopian Tale* is driven by the removal of the hero and heroine from aristocratic society when they are captured on journeys.[220] The pictures that they offer are of alternative societies with their own histories and hierarchies that are separate from those of the norm (and in these cases planted in pseudo-historical periods of the Greek past).

Alternative societies did exist, of course, even if in less glamorous forms than the novelists depicted them. The mountainous regions of southern

Turkey, for instance, were scarcely controlled through the cities on the coast, and in times of dearth their inhabitants would raid the plain to make up for shortfalls in their harvest.[221] The nomadic tribes that Severus had sought, and failed, to control in northern Mesopotamia were likewise given to preying upon the traffic of caravans that transported goods from the Tigris to the trading centers of the west. The military power of Palmyra grew in response to these tribes, and the city seems to have had some freedom to negotiate its relationship with these groups. So too the tribes of northern Arabia would raid more settled areas, demanding tribute that was necessary for their survival. They impinge upon the consciousness of Dio only in passing when he tells the story of a brigand who rode out of the desert to greet Severus while he was on campaign after the defeat of Niger.[222] But other, far more important sources carved on stone attest what is an alternative history to the master narrative of the Roman world, in one case dating an event in terms of a Roman effort to suppress brigands' activities.

Given the fact that bandits only speak for themselves when their words can be mediated through the vision of upper-class urban society, which constructed its image of the bandit as the opposite to itself, it is often hard to understand the social dynamic, region by region, that supported the brigand in the countryside. Indeed, to speak of a social dynamic, even if it is distinguished region by region, would be misleading. The villagers in upland Cilicia who became bandits under economic compulsion were very different, it would appear, from raiders who competed for local authority at all times. The sort of bandits envisioned in the Roman novel do seem to have existed, men and women who had opted out of the urban hierarchy and sought to dominate their environment. They are often described as shepherds, which is perhaps natural, as shepherds were by definition without permanent roots in civil society. But, more than that, this description reveals two levels of participant in rural disorder, the one connected with those permanently outside of society and those who might or might not join them, depending on the local balance of power.[223]

The rural balance of power was determined by the nature of policing. Italy, where Bulla roamed, seems to have lacked local police forces of the sort that are well attested for parts of Asia Minor. The people sent to capture Bulla are soldiers who seem to have been drawn from the garrison of Rome. In Asia Minor the police of the countryside were drawn from the cities, led by local magistrates who, it was feared, might exceed their authority and, being landholders themselves, use their power to coerce peasants or other landholders – the extension of urban patronage networks into the countryside could lead to precisely this sort of struggle.[224] The jurist Marcian (whose peak activity falls after the death of Caracalla in 217) wrote:

> Pius issued under his edict when he was governor of the province of Asia: that eirenarchs (local police chiefs), when they had arrested

robbers, should question them about their associates, and those who harbored them, include their interrogatories in letters, seal them, and send them for the attention of the magistrate. Therefore, those who are sent [to court] with a report [of their interrogation] must be given a hearing from the beginning although they were sent with documentary evidence or even brought in by the eirenarchs . . . [if] the judge finds that his interrogation was in any way malicious, or that he reported things that were not said as if they were said, he should impose an exemplary punishment, to prevent anyone else trying anything of this kind ever again.[225]

The converse of the bandit was the aristocrat who used his office and the ability to recruit not only men from within the city, but also strongmen from the countryside, to expand his own interests. As much of this chapter has been concerned with the intersection of imperial and local power, it is necessary also to be aware of its limitations. The role of the governor, as described here, sits at the outer edge of those limits: he cannot know for certain what is really happening, he must rely on his judgment to make a decision, and he must be aware that any individual case might derive from local interaction. Hence the stress on exemplary punishment as a deterrent to activities that could not otherwise be controlled.

The succession

Exemplary violence was not only a technique used for the control of subject peoples. It was also a crucial factor in the control of frontier zones, and it was to the application of exemplary destruction that Severus would turn during the last years of his life. The venue that he chose was Britain, where it appears that raids across walls were a cause for concern.

According to Dio, the inspiration for this action lay in Severus' perception that he needed to do something to bring his two sons together, and that the legions needed to be kept busy – an interesting pair of reasons, for they suggest that the situation in Britain was not, in and of itself, of grave concern. Dio further states that as he left Rome Severus realized that he would not return. He knew this because he knew the hour of his death from the painting on the horoscope on the ceiling of his bedroom at Rome, and because lightning had struck a statue of him near the gate through which he was leaving Rome. Three letters were erased from his name, telling him that he had only three years left to live.[226]

As so often with Dio, we may wonder who recognized the signs as he did when they occurred. But he does quote "the seers" who he says explained the omen to Severus. If that is the case, it may well explain why Severus elected to spend the rest of his life at York, though the decision to depart may also have been influenced by what we have seen to be his evident discomfort with life in the capital. He never seems to have been at ease with senatorial society, and the series of executions after Plautianus' death made him ever more an object of fear to the members of that society.

Britain was a very different place from those provinces where he had spent so much of his career. In the late second century AD, a distinctive form of urban life had developed in cities that had developed out of the old tribal capitals. These places now came to be organized on a grid pattern, and stone buildings were beginning to be built, but these changes, which looked to Mediterranean patterns of urban settlement, were accompanied by the construction in the later second century of earthen walls around the civic areas. This might be attributed to a feeling of insecurity, though it is a little hard to see why this should arise so suddenly.[227] Another explanation may be that such walls had been traditional features of tribal centers that the elite was unwilling to forgo despite the new Roman-style buildings with which they would surround city centers. That this might be the case is suggested by the art with which they adorned their dwellings, for it fuses the influence of earlier Celtic style with Mediterranean forms, and the temples in which they celebrated their gods, which developed in form from those of the Celtic world. The gods who were worshipped there, even though they were celebrated under Roman names, were those of the Celtic past. Chief among them were Mars and Mercury, names that conceal a Celtic concept of a High God, and a mounted female divinity named Epona who is at times associated with a collective female cult of the "Mothers" *(matres)*. The temples tended to be small buildings, either circular or rectangular, set within larger precincts.[228] Rural shrines continued to dot the countryside, often connected with bodies of water. The settlement pattern around them was still very much that of the pre-Roman period, though in places it was also coming to accommodate villas that were built at the rural seats of the urban aristocracy.[229] The aspirations of the Celtic elite to appear Roman, and their ability to retain their positions, is likely, as we have seen, to have stemmed from their ability to mark out a place for themselves in the imperial hierarchy through their responsibility for ensuring that the taxes were paid. These taxes went, almost certainly, to the support of the three legions that made up the local garrison.

The campaign that Severus undertook was said to have been aimed at bringing the tribes north of the Antonine wall under Roman control.[230] A legionary base has been discovered at Carpow, north of the Firth of Forth, and it is possible that some of the temporary Roman camps that have been found in the eastern Highlands date from this period.[231] Whatever the case, the new intrusion is said to have been anything but welcome. Tribes that had been free of direct Roman control rose up in 210, a year that was consumed by campaigns that appear to have resulted in hard fighting and no significant change in the situation. Severus' health declined, and, as it did so, the rivalry between his sons became ever more evident. According to one story Caracalla may actually have tried to kill his father when they were on the march, and continued to attempt to undermine the position of his brother, without success.[232] But Severus did nothing, perhaps motivated by a belief that there was nothing that he could do to alter the decrees of fate. On February 4, 211, the death that he is said to have been expecting came to him at the *praetorium* that is now below York Minster. His last words to his sons were said to have been, "Get along, make the soldiers rich, and don't give a damn for anyone else."[233]

4

THE ARMY IN POLITICS;
LAWYERS IN GOVERNMENT

The Roman army

The army that Severus advised his sons to cherish was a fossil. Its organization descended in a direct line from the sixth century BC, its tactical doctrines (when not influenced by archaizing fantasies) descended from the era of Marius and Sulla, and its size and mission had been virtually frozen since the reign of Augustus. The core of the military remained the legion, consisting of 5,400 heavy infantrymen. As a form of organization it had been sanctified by the Servian constitution in the sixth century BC. It had evolved into a dominant fighting organization against the Samnites, Etruscans, and Gauls in the fourth century, defeated the Carthaginians and Macedonians in the third and second centuries, developed again in the first century BC into an effective formation against Celtic tribes, and then ossified.

When Augustus died in AD 14, the army stood at twenty-five legions, a notional force of some 135,000 men.[1] It had recently shrunk from twenty-eight legions when the Germans had annihilated three units in the Teutoberger Wald. The number had crept back up to twenty-seven under Caligula, to twenty-nine under Vespasian (after some reorganization in the wake of the civil war and rebellions of AD 69–70), and had reached thirty under Domitian. Two of these legions had disappeared in the course of the second century to be replaced by Marcus for the German wars. The legionary establishment remained at thirty until 197, when Severus had created three new legions, in part to augment the garrison of Italy, and in part to control the new province of Mesopotamia.[2] The tale of the army was commemorated for all to see on two columns at Rome, listing the legions in geographical order. Inscribed early in the reign of Marcus, it was updated at least once, if not twice, until it gave the total number of legions, a visual testimony to the power of Rome.[3] It was also visual confirmation of the inherent conservatism of Roman military doctrine that placed the legions at the center of military thinking.

The Severan legionary forces amounted to around 165,000 men.[4] In support of the legions, and equipped to make up for their severe deficiencies in cavalry, light infantry, and missile troops, there were roughly 250 cohorts of auxiliaries, a notional total of somewhere around 125,000–150,000 more men. The reformed Praetorian Guard added some 10,000 additional troops, and roughly 40,000 men were employed in the fleets. The total peacetime establishment of the military force of Rome thus came to some 400,000 men. Given that the population of the empire may have been somewhere around 58 million in the time of Severus, it was not a particularly large army. Its size was set more by financial than strategic considerations.[5] Its training and composition were determined more by the weight of tradition than an appreciation of the threats that it would face.[6]

The legions that formed the main strike force of the army consisted, as they had in the republic, of heavy infantrymen, equipped, as in the Augustan age, with the *lorica segmentata* that protected the back, chest, and shoulders with bands of steel, and a large shield. The weapons with which these soldiers fought were, as they had been since the time of Marius, the *pilum* and the *gladius*. The *pilum* was a javelin that was specially designed to twist into the shield of an enemy. The *gladius* was a vicious weapon, equally adapted to thrusting and slashing. The choice of armament was dictated by a doctrine of battle dedicated to close combat with the enemy that was as old as the fourth century BC. The maximum effective range of the *pilum* was about one hundred feet, and it appears that soldiers carried just one in combat.[7] Standard battle tactics (well attested in the works of Caesar and showing no change in those of Tacitus) involved the movement of the front ranks into *pilum* range, after which, probably, troops would revolve through the front ranks hurling their weapons. Caesar's prose suggests that the *pilum* phase was envisioned as a series of volleys at the enemy.[8] The potential destructiveness of these volleys was sufficiently great that Caesar's opponents in Gaul tried, sometimes with success, to press home their attacks before the Romans had time to bombard them at close range.[9] Caesar himself shortened this phase of the battle at Pharsalus, where his men were heavily outnumbered, but much more skilled than their enemy at close-in fighting with the sword.[10] It appears that troops were taught to calculate the number of paces they stood from their targets to judge the effectiveness of their throws: Caesar is at one point compared to a gladiatorial trainer counting out paces for his men when they were suffering from a "long-range" missile attack in North Africa.[11] Perhaps the one significant change in the army after Caesar was the addition of more artillery to enhance the effectiveness of the opening barrage and extend its range. As neither the bow nor the javelin (as opposed to the *pilum*) was an effective long-range killer, ballistae and catapults could become significant factors in the first phase of an encounter. Tacitus describes the impact of these weapons, which appear to have been placed outside of the line, as devastating when fired into the ordered ranks of Roman legionaries at the battle of Cremona in AD 69.[12] Josephus, who was on the receiving end of a barrage from Vespasian's army at Jotopata, describes the damage that they could inflict in horrific terms:

There is no body of troops, however strong, which the force and mass of these stones cannot lay low to the last rank . . . one of the men standing on the wall beside Josephus had his head carried away by a stone and his skull was shot, as from a sling to a distance of three furlongs. . . . More alarming even than the engines was their whirring drone, more frightful than the missiles, the crash.

(BJ 3.245–46, trans. St. J. Thackery)

The horror caused by the discharge of missiles was exceeded only by the charge that followed. The *gladius* was the killing weapon par excellence of the Roman soldier. It was skill with the sword that set the veteran apart from the recruit. Thus at the battle of Mutina in 43 BC when two veteran legions encountered each other,

They raised no battle cry, since they could not expect to terrify each other, nor in the engagement did they utter any sound, either as victors or vanquished. As there could be no flanking nor charging amid marshes and ditches, they met together in close order, and since neither could dislodge the other they locked together with their swords as in a wrestling match. No blow missed its mark. There were wounds and slaughter but no cries, only groans: and when one fell he was instantly borne away and another took his place. They needed neither admonition nor encouragement, since experience made each one his own general. When they were overcome by fatigue they drew apart from each other for a brief space to take breath, as in gymnastic games, and then rushed again to the encounter. Amazement took possession of the new levies who had come up, as they beheld such deeds done with such precision and in such silence.

(App. *B. Civ.* 3.68, trans. White)

The advance of a legion, preceded by a fierce battle cry that was uttered in ordinary circumstances when the legionaries reached *pilum* range, could strike fear into the heart of an enemy as the troops moved into contact at a deliberate pace. As Appian's account of Mutina suggests, raw recruits could not be expected to stand up to an attack by veterans, and the veterans themselves understood that it would be their combat that would decide the day.

The account of Roman tactics given above presupposes that the enemy against whom the army was arrayed would be committed to a frontal assault. In an account of how a general should draw up his troops when confronted with an army that consisted primarily of mounted troops, the historian Arrian (who was also the commander of the army in question) suggests that the basic armament of the troops might be varied away from the traditional *pilum*.[13] He advises that the legionaries be drawn up eight ranks deep, and that the first four ranks be armed with pikes. He also suggests that the war machines be placed on the flanks and behind the main body of infantry, and that the flanks be covered by light troops.[14] Aside from this, his thinking about the course of the action reveals a cast of mind very similar to that of Caesar or the men at Mutina:

> When the troops have been drawn up like this there should be silence until the enemy come within weapon range. When they have come within range, everyone should utter a huge and ferocious warcry; missiles and stones should be discharged from catapults, arrows from bows, and the spearmen should throw their spears. . . . Because of the incredible weight of the missiles we may hope that the advancing Scythians will not get very close to our infantry formation. But if they do get close, then the first three ranks should lock their shields together, and, standing shoulder to shoulder, withstand the charge with all possible strength in the most concentrated formation, joined together in the strongest possible way.
>
> (Arr. *Tactica* 25–26, trans. J. B. Campbell, *The Roman Army 31 BC–AD 337: A Sourcebook* [London, 1994], 98–99)

Ideally the enemy would then flee. If not, Arrian notes that they would then charge the flanks, but that, if they were victorious in this, they would expose their flanks to the reserve cavalry. He notes hopefully that it would, however, be unlikely that, noticing that the flanks were weaker, the enemy would break up the auxiliary infantry.[15]

What is intriguing about Arrian's description of the ideal battle is the quantity of wishful thinking that goes into it. Victory depends not only on the ideal Roman tactics but also upon the ideally stupid enemy who would start a battle by charging the strongest part of the Roman line.[16] For Arrian's system to work, the enemy had to be devoted to the same style of frontal hand-to-hand combat that had remained a fundamental part of Roman doctrine since the archaic period. Some enemies may have done just this, but as time passed, the evidence suggests that they were less and less likely to do so. One reason that Marcus' wars on the northern frontier may have lasted as long as they did was that it proved difficult to force the sort of decisive battle that was central to the doctrine of frontal combat. The war with Parthia that opened Marcus' reign began with the destruction of precisely the army whose tactics Arrian describes here, the garrison of Cappadocia in eastern Turkey, by an army of cavalrymen that did not play by the rules.[17] Indeed, by the end of the second century AD the only truly ideal enemy for a Roman army in the field may have been another Roman army, and, as the evidence for Severus' struggles with Niger and Albinus suggests, these armies were ideally suited to slaughter each other.

Aside from the set battle, the other military activity at which the Roman army ought to have excelled was the siege. But this does not seem to have been the case. While Celtic hill forts, or small towns in Judaea, might be no match for the massed artillery of the legions, larger cities appear to have stood a good chance of surviving a siege. True, Jerusalem fell in AD 70, but it was scarcely the grandest city in the empire, and it had taken four legions nearly six months to reduce it, although deeply divided irregulars from the countryside defended it. The case of Byzantium, a well-fortified city defended by regular troops, is more revealing. It had held out for three years with no chance of relief. To be fair, Ctesiphon, a massive city, had fallen to Severus, as it had fallen before to Trajan and Lucius Verus, but it may well be that the Parthian defenders had been weakened by earlier failures. Hatra had withstood an attack by the full force of Severus' force when its inhabitants made a spirited response. All in all, the record suggests that the technology of Roman siegecraft had not developed to a point where major cities were automatically at risk.

If the style of legionary warfare in the third century AD appears to have failed to evolve much since the age of Caesar, the same cannot be said of the other half of the army, the *auxilia*.[18] Caesar had employed auxiliary troops to make up for the deficiencies in his heavy infantry formations: slingers had been recruited from the Balearic islands, and he had recruited particularly effective units of Germans by the time that he suppressed Vercingetorix in 52 BC.[19] The *auxilia* had developed greatly since then. In 69–70 Batavian units had proven a match for legionary forces along the Rhine, and the transformation of the auxiliary force from ad hoc tribal units into regular units of the army during the Julio-Claudian period had given able generals tactical options that were not possible with the legions.[20] Tacitus' description of Agricola's victory at Mons Graupius (somewhere in the Scottish Highlands) in AD 83 gives pride of place to six auxiliary cohorts that routed the enemy before the legions came into combat through their skill in hand-to-hand fighting.[21] A series of speeches that Hadrian delivered to units of the army in North Africa gives further insight into the diversity of their skills in AD 128. Thus he praises the cavalry of a Commagenian unit as follows:

> It is difficult for the cavalry attached to a cohort to win approval even on their own, and even more difficult still for them not to incur criticism after a manoeuver by auxiliary cavalry; they cover a greater area of the plain, there are more men throwing javelins, they wheel right in close formation, they perform the Cantabrian manoeuver in close array, the beauty of their horses and the splendor of their weapons are in keeping with their pay. But, despite the heat, you avoided boredom by doing energetically what had to be done; in addition you fired stones from slings and fought with javelins; on every occasion you mounted speedily.
>
> (*ILS* 2487, trans. Campbell, *The Roman Army
> 31 BC–AD 337*, 19–20)

The value of the *auxilia* stemmed not only from the diversity of tactical formations that it encompassed, but also from the variety of tactical formations that they brought to the battlefield. As Hadrian's comments and those of Tacitus suggest, they were in no way less well trained than their legionary colleagues, and they could quite simply do things on a battlefield that the legions could not. As will become clear in the course of the next century, it was the ability of the *auxilia* to adapt that would prove the military salvation of the empire as the weakness of the legions became clear to their non-Roman enemies.

The *auxilia* might be the future, but in the time of Severus the legions appear still to have constituted the main strike force, and their members benefited the most from his reforms. The most obvious of these was an increase in pay. Military pay had technically remained frozen since the time of Domitian, which might suggest that Severus' action was setting straight an injustice, especially as a slow but steady increase in the price of grain in Egypt amounted to about 100 percent by the end of the second century.[22] If it is correct to extrapolate from the Egyptian evidence (which is the only quantifiable evidence) to the rest of the empire, this might suggest a serious problem. As the initial theory of military pay was that it was intended to provide only a slight surplus over basic maintenance costs, this would suggest that soldiers had, in the course of the century, been reduced to virtual penury. If that was so, then it might also explain why soldiers, as we shall see, supplemented their pay by stealing from civilians. But the story is not quite that simple; the deductions from soldiers' pay to cover expenses had been reduced, effectively raising pay by those amounts.[23] The most important of these changes had been the provision of free grain, effectively insulating troops from price fluctuations.[24] One of the genuine problems that the government faced was a shortage of specie with which to mint the coins that could be used to pay soldiers, and an increase in the need for hard currency to pay other officials – senior procuratorial officials had salaries totaling over eighteen million sesterces – as well as to finance certain other activities.[25] The most obvious of these were public entertainment, which was spectacularly expensive, and required payments in cash to victors in ever greater amounts, payments for luxury goods from east Asia, and payments to foreign peoples to keep the peace.[26] Severus' decision to increase pay to soldiers by either 50 or 100 percent in 197 (the latter figure is most likely the correct one) was not, therefore, a response to a genuine need on the part of the troops, but rather a critical change in the theory of military pay.[27] The pay increase was almost certainly authorized in order to have the effect that it did: to secure the personal loyalty of the soldiers to Severus who had thereby made himself their greatest benefactor. The politicization of army pay would have serious consequences in the course of the next century, and may well only have been feasible because of the mass condemnations that had released the property of aristocrats to the treasury, and possibly a windfall that might have been expected in the event of a successful invasion of Parthia.

A second reform may have had a similar motivation, for it was likewise not actually necessary, and it too may have contributed to future difficulties. At the same time that he had raised soldiers' pay, Severus had eliminated the ban on soldiers contracting a legal marriage while on service.[28] While the tradition that soldiers could not marry is more marked by the breach than the strict observance, the fact that it should have remained on the books is an important symbol of the ideological role of the army. The army was conceived as an all-male institution, one whose members owed primary loyalty to their comrades in arms and to their emperor. In the wake of Severus' measure we begin to get evidence, for the first time in centuries, of soldiers being unhappy when they were compelled to serve far from their home bases.[29]

The independence of the army from civilian society was necessitated, in part, by its role as the agent of violent repression within the empire. Soldiers on detached duty are found throughout the empire supplementing local police forces, and engaging in a wide variety of other activities to support their units.[30] They are found attached to the governor's staff, protecting grain shipments, standing guard at various points away from their main bases, and collecting taxes. They arrest criminals, beat up peasants, and rape their women. On the march they tended to take things that did not belong to them, and to compel civilians to carry their equipment. Four edicts issued by prefects of Egypt between the reigns of Tiberius and Hadrian bemoan the seizure of property by soldiers on the move.[31] The number four is no doubt an accident of preservation: there is little reason to think that the complaint was not endemic. Outside of Egypt, we have both imperial edicts (notably of Tiberius and Domitian) on the subject of seizure, and several appeals from rural communities complaining of their treatment by soldiers.[32] The parable of the second mile involves the practice, inherited from Hellenistic armies, of soldiers compelling civilians to carry their gear for them.[33] Epictetus, the great philosopher of the later first and early second centuries, may have summed up the situation best when he remarked that you might as well give the soldier who is requisitioning your mule the mule. Otherwise you get a beating and still lose the animal.[34] Apuleius provides a version of this sort of scene that may have been played out countless times every day across the empire:

> On the road a certain large man encountered us, a soldier from the legion, as his manner and manners indicated, and he asked, in a haughty and arrogant tone, where he [a gardener] was taking the unburdened ass. My master, still confused with grief, and, furthermore, ignorant of Latin, passed him without a word. Nor was that

soldier able to restrain his innate insolence, but being offended by his silence, as if it were defiance, knocked him off my back, striking him with the vine stick that he was holding.[35]

The story becomes even more grisly when the gardener strikes back, successfully, leading to the arrival of a unit of soldiers seeking out the ass and the gardener on the false charge of having stolen some silver plate belonging to the governor. The troops, constantly invoking the "genius of the emperor," tear apart the house where the ass and gardener are hiding, despite the attempted intervention of a local magistrate who owned the property. Texts from Egypt and inscriptions from Asia Minor, recording bribes to soldiers, use the noun *diaseismos* to describe the payment. The standard English translation, "extortion," does not do full justice to the violence of the act. *Diaseismos* is connected with the verb *dieseiô*, "to shake violently," which no doubt describes the method of obtaining the payment.[36]

Those who escaped with a beating might count themselves as fortunate. A Talmudic text states explicitly that a woman who fell into the hands of brigands should not, automatically, be assumed to have been raped. If she fell into the hands of soldiers, this assumption was necessary.[37] Thus did the men who accompanied Decianus Catus in the seizure of the property of Prasutagus, king of the Iceni, rape the royal daughters. A centurion who showed up among the Frisians in the reign of Tiberius began raping the wives and children of the tribesmen. It is not unreasonable to see this conduct as a form of abuse that was, at least in part, intentionally designed to remind provincials of their vulnerability to the agents of the state.[38]

The brutality of soldiers to civilians was an extension of the brutality inherent in military life. Discipline was harsh, flogging a routine camp punishment, other penalties, left up to the creativity of a commanding officer, involved standing for long hours, a diet of inferior food, the requirement to encamp in dangerous areas, or loss of pay and rank. Penalties could be either individual or collective, and the most severe involved direct participation by the soldiers themselves. A unit guilty of gross dereliction of duty could be decimated, lots being drawn so that every tenth man was subject to a death penalty, inflicted by the members of the unit who had escaped his fate. The sentence was carried out by clubbing the unfortunates to death, and our evidence shows that this penalty, attested in accounts of the republic, was in use after Augustus.[39]

The impression of the army as an institution that lived by rules unto itself is borne out by evidence of day-to-day life, for which the city of Dura Europus on the Euphrates, garrisoned by an auxiliary cohort of Palmyrenes, offers some of the best evidence.[40] The northwest quarter of the city is divided off from the rest by a mud-brick wall, and buildings inside it were manifestly converted for use as barracks. While the wall did not cut off contact between soldiers and civilians – both groups are found making dedications in the same temple, and soldiers were quartered in the town as well – it is nonetheless an important symbol of separation. As a corporate entity, the Palmyrene garrison followed the cycle of celebrations laid down for the army everywhere (our best evidence for this calendar is, in fact, the list of observances from Dura, the *Feriale Durianum*). When not celebrating the festivals on the official calendar, it appears that many soldiers worshipped Mithras and Zeus Dolichenus, two divinities who are not attested at Dura prior to the Roman occupation, and whose worship is common at other military sites. As one scholar has put it, "while the *Feriale Durianum* provides evidence of the corporate solidarity of the army at Dura, these cults show the private solidarity of soldiers."[41] Soldiers who interacted with civilians outside of their official context do not seem to have done so as equals. In retirement they preferred each other's company, and the evidence for intermarriage with the civilian population is not such as to tell us how the women who became attached to soldiers dealt with their families. By entering into a long-term liaison with a soldier, a woman appears to have moved into a new society that was governed by its own rules, and one whose relationship with the outside world remained distinctive, even after Severus' edict.

The murder of Geta: the politics of pay and citizenship

The pay increase and other improvements in service conditions that Severus had brought about evidently endeared both himself and his sons to the soldiers. So much so that the army remained more deeply attached to Severus' ideal of the dynasty than at least one of its beneficiaries, his elder son, Caracalla.

Severus left the throne, equally, to Caracalla and Geta. The two hated each other, and to have disinherited Geta was as good as a death sentence. Severus appears, in old age, to have been unwilling to take such a radical step. He may also have had some doubts about his older son's capacity to govern. Even if one discounts the bizarre stories of Caracalla's conduct in the months prior to Severus' death, there may have been enough evidence to suggest that he had a violent temper, and, at the age of twenty-five, can scarcely have impressed anyone with his years of experience. Government divided between the two sons might de facto have become government by committee if Severus' senior advisers, and his wife, had been able to negotiate some sort of peaceful coexistence between the two brothers. For those who had lived through the reign of Commodus, that may have seemed a more palatable option than government by spoiled child and favorite *du jour*. The devotion of the army to Severus' last wishes, the support of the army for his scheme of divided government, and its affection for Geta, who is said to have looked a lot like his father (see plate 3; on coins he and his brother are virtually indistinguishable), may have given these advisers some reason to hope that they could succeed.[42]

(a)   (b)

Plate 3 Caracalla and Geta. The image of the brothers, intended to promote the notion of their equality, may also be seen as marking a "new era," as their image is quite different from that of their father (see plate 2). (a) Caracalla. *Credit: RIC* no. 191 (Rome 211); author's collection, photo courtesy of Forum Ancient Coins. (b) Geta. *Credit: RIC* Geta no. 78a (Rome 211); author's collection, photo by Ivory photo, Ann Arbor, MI.

The men charged with keeping the peace were all of long experience. The praetorian prefects, Q. Maecius Laetus and Aemilius Papinianus, had both been in office since the removal of Plautianus in 205.[43] Laetus appears to have risen through the equestrian administration to the prefecture of Egypt, which he had held from 200 to 203. Papinianus (or, as he is more usually called in the modern world, Papinian) had come through the palace ranks, rising to *a libellis*, in which office he may have served from September 194 to February 202, perhaps because of his immense judicial knowledge.[44] Caracalla's tutor, who also seems to have retained power through his long friendship with Severus, was Fabius Cilo, one of the participants in the march on Rome in 193.[45] The prefect of Rome was another man whose memory stretched back a long way. He was Julius Asper, who had risen to the consulship under Severus and who was scheduled for the extraordinary honor of assuming a second consulship as *consul ordinarius* with his son in January 212.[46]

Whatever confidence Severus may have had in these men, and others, whose names are lost to us, was not well founded. Experience of previous disasters is no guarantee of wisdom, or of an ability to keep history from repeating itself. The war in Britain was ended with exemplary speed, with the withdrawal of troops who had been based north of Hadrian's Wall to the south, and the two brothers headed back to Rome, giving every sign that they would not abide by their father's will. Although they managed to put on a public display of amity when they entered the city in triumph during the summer of 211, it is said that they had not been able to remain under the same roof the whole way back. The ceremonies that followed their return, which culminated in the official funeral of their father, did nothing to improve matters. Herodian says that the palace buildings were divided and that connecting passages were bricked up.[47] At some point it became clear that Caracalla was gaining an upper hand. He fired Papinian, who subsequent events will suggest had tried to maintain the terms of Severus' will, and dismissed Cilo as prefect of the city, replacing both with Sextus Varius Marcellus, the husband of his mother's niece, Julia Soaemias.[48] At the same time he executed his estranged wife Plautilla, who had been living in exile ever since the death of her father, Plautianus, in 205. He also executed Castor, the *cubicularius* of Severus who had tried to restrain his conduct in Britain, and his own tutor, Euodus. Finally, he ordered the death of a famous charioteer named Euprepes who had, presumably, raced for the chariot faction he opposed (and, it may be surmised, that Geta supported).[49] It appears that Caracalla drew particular support from the urban cohorts, the troops stationed in the city who fulfilled many basic police functions. These men had been under the command of Cilo, whom they seem to have disliked intensely, when he was prefect of the city, and were considerably better disposed toward Varius Marcellus.[50]

It was on December 25, 211, that Caracalla launched the coup that would result in the death of his brother, Papinian, Cilo, and, allegedly, thousands of others whom chance or inclination had joined to the cause of Geta. To achieve his end, Caracalla had to separate his brother from the strong guard of athletes and soldiers that remained loyal to him. To complete the task, Caracalla exploited the unsuspecting agency of his mother, arranging an early evening conference with Geta in her quarters, saying that both should go there alone. When Geta appeared, a group of centurions, whom Caracalla had secretly brought with him, burst into the room and killed him in their mother's arms. Caracalla then followed the by now thoroughly predictable course for the mover of a palace coup. As Geta's body was being incinerated on the palace grounds, Caracalla went to the praetorian camp, where he explained that his brother had been detected in an effort to poison him, had shown disrespect for their mother, and been killed. He then thanked the assassins and paid them a bonus.[51] The next stop was Alba, where, ever since Severus' occupation of the capital, Legion II Parthica had its base as a foil to the praetorians. The legionaries were a good deal less receptive to the news, and refused their emperor admittance on the grounds that they had sworn allegiance to both the sons of Severus.[52] It was only after a suitably lengthy harangue on the subject of Geta's manifest evil, and promise of a large donative, that the gates were opened.

The action of Legion II Parthica is a critical illustration of the emerging role of the regular army in the ritual of succession. As we have seen, it was standard practice for the emperor to wait until he was asked to take the throne. He had to appear to be the servant of the soldiers' will, for it was the army that had arrogated to itself the role of civic conscience. In this case the soldiers who had sworn to uphold Severus' will were not about to play their part until they had received assurances that their existing privileges would be secured or enhanced. The scene at Alba is thus a sort of *recusatio* in reverse: instead of an imperial display of reluctance, the soldiers of Legion II, who may well have been among those protecting Geta, would not allow the formula to be enacted until they were satisfied that their interests would be protected. The remarks that Dio quotes in the context of the prior visit to the praetorians may catch the gist of the sort of thing that he said on this occasion as well:

> Rejoice, fellow-soldiers, for now I am in a position to do you favors . . . I am one of you . . . and it is because of you alone that I care to live in order that I may confer upon you many favours; for all the treasuries are yours . . . I pray to live with you, if possible, but if not, at any rate to die with you. For I do not fear death in any form, and it is my desire to end my days in warfare. There should a man die, or nowhere.
>
> (Dio 77.3.2, trans. Cary)

With the loyalty of the army secured, it was time then to talk to the senate. A meeting was convened the next morning, which Caracalla, accompanied by a large contingent of the guard, attended in armor. The senate was not particularly receptive to the speech in which he said that Geta had plotted against him, despite the fact that he had granted his brother every indulgence. When he concluded with a demonstration of his merciful character by ordering the return of all exiles, some in the senate might have had reason to be concerned.[53] The exiles in question were members of the senate who had either been convicted of genuine wrongdoing, or at the very least had earned the hatred of Severus. The recall might have been read as a repudiation of his father's policies, and those who had supported them had reason to worry. Caracalla shared his father's admiration for Sulla, and for the ruthlessness with which Sulla had dealt with his enemies.[54]

An immense massacre of Geta's servants and supporters followed the meeting of the senate. Dio puts the number killed at twenty thousand, which may be an exaggeration, but the enormity of the number serves still to convey the extent of the process.[55] Geta certainly had a large guard, and something like half the palace servants, at his disposal. And Caracalla did not stop there. Those who might have been thought to support his father's will were killed. Papinian and one of his associates, Patruinus, another jurist, were sacrificed to the guard that asked for their death.[56] Cilo too appears to have been on the list of those who were to die, but when the detachment of the guard dragged him through the streets from a bathhouse, a public outcry forced

Caracalla to protect him, and the praetorian prefect Laenus was forced into retirement.[57] Then too perished Helvius Pertinax, the son of the emperor, the elderly Cornificia, daughter of Marcus Aurelius, and her son.[58] Caracalla was determined that there be no one left alive who could have a presumptive claim to the throne on the basis of family relationship. Dio gave a list of other members of the nobility who perished, and it seems to have been a long one. The Byzantine epitomator whose summary of Dio's history is the basis for the reconstruction of his mutilated text sums it all up with a pair of quotations from Homer.[59]

If Caracalla was determined to secure his position through the massacre of potential rivals and of those thought overly loyal to the memory of his father, he also needed money, and one way to raise it was by confiscating the estates of the very wealthy. One of the promises that he had made to the men of Legion II Parthica was that he would increase their pay, and that of all other legionaries. This move reinforced the connection between military pay and politics, and, as events would suggest, it was more than the budget of the state, even after the treasury had been reinforced through confiscations following the death of Geta, could support.[60] There is good evidence that the shortage of silver was growing.

Coinage in the Roman Empire was of three sorts. The average person used bronze coins for everyday transactions. Silver was primarily minted to cover the expenses of the central government. Gold appears to have been used for high officials. When the state could not meet its need for silver by increasing production, a problem that may have been compounded by a decline in the productivity of the Spanish mines that had supplied a great deal of the silver in the early empire, it had to take old coins out of circulation, and, as it did so, there was a consistent tendency to debase the silver through an admixture of bronze.[61] The gradual decline in silver content had been an ongoing process since the reign of Nero. By the end of the reign of Trajan, the quantity of silver in the basic silver coin, the denarius, had hovered around 90 percent. It remained at roughly that level until the later 150s, when there appears to have been a sudden decline to the vicinity of 80 percent. Under Marcus and Commodus it declined further to about 75 percent. Under Pertinax and Didius Julianus, the percentage of silver had risen somewhat to around 87 percent (Pertinax) or 81 percent (Julianus). Severus' first issues had sunk to about 78 percent silver, but in 194 it had dipped sharply to 66 percent then; in 195–96 from 61 percent to 58 percent and to between 55 percent and 58 percent for the rest of the reign. Caracalla's first issues, during 211, had been around 55 percent, but in 212 the percentage slipped again to the range of 50–51 percent.[62] At the same time it also needs to be recognized that there was no correlation between the debasement of the silver coinage and inflation. So long as the recipients of the coins were willing to accept the basic value of the coin, which was secured by an official tariff of twenty-five to one against the aureus, this would not cause a crisis in and of itself. The debasement of the coinage was not so much a sign of economic difficulty as a sign of the difficulty that the state had in meeting its expenses. The measurable decline in silver content was necessitated by the increased demand for silver resulting from the policies of Severus and Caracalla.

In the aftermath of Geta's death, the senate is said to have ordered that all coins with his image upon them be withdrawn from circulation.[63] This was part of a thoroughgoing effort to erase his memory from the public consciousness, a campaign that was so successful that its impact may also be seen on numerous inscriptions across the empire from which Geta's name was erased. But it also reflects the fact that the senate thought that it was possible to withdraw coins from general use, and it had done so as early as AD 43, when it ordered the bronze coins of Caligula, over which it had authority, to be taken out of circulation.[64] The very fact that the senate could pass such a decree suggests that there was already a mechanism in place through which coins could more generally be withdrawn from circulation. The existence of such a mechanism, which is not directly attested in a context other than that of the disgrace of a former monarch, is shown by coin hoards, which reveal that coins of certain periods were withdrawn from circulation at various points from the end of the first century onwards.[65]

The withdrawal of coinage, and the slaughter of the wealthy, could only improve the situation so far. Caracalla appears to have felt that there was need to free up hoarded wealth in other ways. This, at least, is Cassius Dio's explanation for the remarkable decree that he issued at the beginning of 212, conferring citizenship on all free inhabitants of the empire who were not *dediticii*, a status that encompassed people who had become subjects of Rome through formal surrender in war, and a category of freed slave.[66] The new citizens would be liable for the inheritance tax as well as continuing (under a system that appears to have emerged under Marcus) to be liable for existing burdens. Caracalla put the measure in a somewhat different light, inviting all to celebrate his salvation from the plot in which he claimed Geta had been engaged. The opening of the edict, preserved on a fragmentary papyrus, reads as follows:

> Imperator Caesar Marcus Aurelius Augustus Antoninus Pius says: [. . .] rather [. . .] the causes and considerations [. . .] that I give thanks to the immortal gods, because [when that conspiracy occurred] they preserved me, thus I think that I should be able [magnificently and piously] to make a suitable response to their majesty, [if] I were able to lead [all who are presently my people] and others who should join my people [to the sanctuaries] of the gods. I give to all of those [who are under my rule throughout] the whole world, Roman citizenship, [(with the provision that) the just claims of communities] should remain, with the exception of the [*ded*]*iticii*. The [whole

population] ought [. . .] already to have been included in the victory.
[. . .] my edict will expand the majesty of the Roman [people. . .].

(P. Giss. 40, col. 1.1–12)[67]

Perhaps the most interesting feature of Caracalla's statement is his explicit desire to have the whole population of the empire share in his good fortune. In the eyes of the vast majority of his subjects he was no more than a name prior to 211, the name that appeared just after that of his father and before that of his brother on countless public documents. In most practical terms his was still the name on most documents that came after that of Severus, but now his was the name that came before a name that was being chiseled out of the vast bulk of texts that were concerned with the imperial house.

Caracalla was brutal, but he was also a politician. He felt the need to get his point across as loudly and clearly as he could in the most obvious way that he could find. Unlike Pertinax, he was in no position to sell off palace property to advertise his separation from his predecessor, and he was certainly in no position to grant tax relief. By giving citizenship to the vast majority of his subjects, he joined them to himself in a most obvious way, by changing all of their names to include his own. By long tradition, new citizens always took the name of the person who sponsored their entry into the community of citizens. He also had to explain to people why they saw, again, in a very real way, a change taking place before their eyes, on every milestone that had been erected in the last fourteen years. This he plainly did in the opening lines of the text. Dio's assertion that he was only interested in money thus does not do justice to the nature of Caracalla's statement, or to his sense of the political moment. This does not mean that Dio is wrong in what he said, only that there was more to the story than he chose to tell.

It is possible to read Caracalla's act in other ways as well. By including almost all people "in the victory of the Roman people" it might also appear that he was interested in promoting a sense of Roman identity in the diverse population that he ruled. He was certainly interested in linking their fortune to his own, as he says that he would wish to lead them all to the temples of the gods to give thanks for his salvation. The grant of citizenship had the effect of reinforcing the relevance of the political fortunes of the emperor himself to all of his people. As such, Caracalla's conduct follows in the tradition of his father, who was concerned to link the welfare of the soldiers to his own welfare. The greater historical significance of the constitutio Antoniniana, as this text is known, is thus in linking, ever more closely, the survival of the empire with that of the emperor. In the emerging Severan definition of the monarchy, the emperor was becoming identified with the state itself. The entire empire was being drawn ever more into an identity with the patrimonium through the coordination of administration with dynastic politics.

139

Caracalla on the march

The massacre of Geta's supporters at Rome occurred toward the end of 211 and the beginning of 212. It was prime time for public entertainments; chariot races followed the New Year celebration when the new consuls took office, and there were numerous other days given over to games after that. Caracalla was plainly aware that he had work to do if he were to repair his relationship with the people of Rome. Those who had been killed had friends and contacts throughout the city, the elimination of a major portion of the palace staff affected people well beyond the imperial quarters, and the violence of Caracalla's troops in the street could clearly be off-putting. It was to the circus and the amphitheater that Caracalla turned, as would any emperor, to improve his standing with the people.

Both Dio and Herodian record various spectacular events that must all fall in the course of 212, some of them involving Caracalla's personal appearances as a performer. Dio says that he drove chariots in the costume of the Blue faction, and that he hunted beasts with his own hand.[68] As with Commodus, such appearances could be taken as a slap in the face of the senatorial aristocracy. But, as was also the case with Commodus, they may not have been entirely successful. The Roman people liked their heroes to be, to some degree, one with themselves. A free man who sought fame in the amphitheater was also a man who sought glory through subordinating himself to the official in charge of the games; he won his fame by inverting the social order, emerging from the lowest of the low on the social scale to the highest of the high in the eyes of those watching the games.[69] A slave who fought in the amphitheater had the potential, again, to invert the hierarchical order of society by compelling the man giving the games to recognize him as a champion. The charioteer was likewise a man who placed himself at the disposal of the crowd in the hope that he could emerge from the race on a momentary par with the man who rewarded him for his triumph. The emperor could never reduce himself to such a level. Whether he drove a chariot or killed a boar, he was still the emperor: he did not risk what another person risked by placing himself in the arena.

Various anecdotes suggest that Caracalla had trouble with the audience. According to Herodian, he lost his temper with a crowd that cheered too hard for a charioteer from the other faction and ordered troops into the stands to silence the crowd.[70] The opposition charioteer, of course, gained all the more credit by virtue of the fact that he had dared to succeed despite the favor of the emperor for others. Dio tells of an event in the amphitheater where Caracalla compelled a famous gladiator named Bato to fight three opponents in succession, until he was killed by the third.[71] The crowd was not amused, in part because the contests were simply not fair. One need not assume that Caracalla lifted his thumb to order Bato's death at the end of the day (*pollex versus*, the gesture for death, which has come into English as "thumbs down," actually means "thumb up").[72] Rather, by compelling the champion to fight repeatedly he exposed him to extreme danger through exhaustion. Accidental death stemming from the fury of the foe was far more common, it would seem, than a death sentence from the crowd. Caracalla would have known that as well as anyone, and the assaults that he launched on the leading figures of the two primary entertainments at Rome suggest quite simply that he did not like competition in the popular arena. They also suggest that he realized that his efforts to gain popular favor were not working.

By the end of 212, it would be reasonable to surmise that Caracalla had had enough of the capital, and that all orders resident there may have had their fill of him.[73] Toward the end of the year, or perhaps after waiting to assume the consulship in 213, he left the city. The ostensible reason for his departure was trouble with the newly emergent German confederation on the upper Rhine known as the Alamanni.[74] Little is known of this campaign, aside from a vague imperial pronouncement that an invasion of German territory was launched "across the boundaries of Raetia for the purpose of annihilating enemies" in August 213, and a declaration of victory in September of the same year.[75] The delay in launching the invasion may be due to a serious illness from which Caracalla suffered earlier in the year. As his point was to prove that he was a great soldier, and that he could share the hardships of his men, there was no way that strategic action could be launched until he was in a condition to take personal command. Politics, and politics of a highly personal sort, were the order of the day.

Given his failure at Rome, Caracalla seems to have had a need to find love in some other context. His mother, whom he brought with him on campaign, appears to have been no source of comfort. She had loved Geta more and never seems to have forgiven him the murder in her apartments. It was, instead, to the soldiers that he turned. Dio quotes various remarks (on what authority, we cannot know) that he is supposed to have uttered in expression of his affection for them. Herodian states that he marched with them on foot to prove that he could share their hardships, and that he ate their food. Such conduct was not, in and of itself, exceptional. Generals were expected to act this way; soldiers were, since Caesar's time at least, the *commilitones*, "comrades in arms," of the emperor. It is again a mark of the way that the emperor was expected to appeal to his various constituencies by varying his personal behavior according to the company that he kept. What sets Caracalla apart in this respect is his evident disregard for the conduct expected of an emperor in council. As Dio puts it,

> He made many mistakes because of his obstinacy; for he wished not only to know everything, but to be the only one who knew anything, and he alone wished to hold power, and because of this he

made use of no adviser, and he hated people who had useful knowledge. He never loved anyone, and he hated those who excelled in
anything.

(Dio 77.11.5)

These comments are borne out by his rescripts, which bear the mark of a
personality that was both forceful and given to self-congratulation. In
responding to a query about an amnesty he asserted that it should not have
been necessary for him to answer the question, since the previous edict was
so clear.[76] In another case, this one granting a remission of debts to people
in the North African province of Mauretania in return for a donation of
elephants, he pointed out that he granted this "magnificent indulgence"
before they had actually suggested the terms.[77] Philostratus, who was able
to pass over the excesses of Commodus without overt comment, describes
Caracalla as acting "like the gods in Homer who are portrayed as giving
things to each other not willingly, but unwillingly."[78] He persecuted the
rhetor Philiscus who had been granted the chair of rhetoric at Athens through
Julia's intervention. At a violent hearing in which he interrupted Philiscus
as he was speaking, he is said to have shouted that neither he nor any other
teacher of rhetoric could have an exemption from public service. This exemption had been a standard reward for a successful career for centuries, and it
was thus overturned in a fit of temper.[79] In a converse situation, when the
rhetor Heliodorus of Arabia stood up to him at a hearing,

> The emperor sprang from his seat and called Heliodorus "a man such
> as I have never yet known, a new phenomenon such as has appeared
> only in my own time," and other epithets of this sort, and raising his
> hand, he shook back the folds of his cloak. Now at first we felt an
> impulse to laugh because we thought that the emperor was making
> fun of him. But when he bestowed upon him the public honor
> of equestrian rank and also on all his children, men marveled at the
> goddess Fortune who showed her power by events so incredible.
>
> (Phil. V. Soph. 626, trans. Wright)

Philostratus' vignettes of Caracalla's behavior are striking in that they
confirm, from the perspective of an eyewitness, the sort of conduct that may
be surmised from documents such as those quoted above, or a text from
Dmeir in Syria, where Caracalla had two of his senior advocates argue a case
concerning who should be high priest at the local temple, interrupting them,
and cutting them short.[80]

   When not marching with his soldiers, alienating his advisers, and insulting
men of letters, Caracalla turned to intellectual pursuits.[81] He sought the
experience of the gods that others sought when they were ill (so we are told
in the case of his illness in 213) and sought to emulate Alexander. Dio says

that he recruited sixteen thousand Macedonians into a "phalanx" that was armed as had been the men of Alexander's own day, and that he collected memorabilia of the deceased king.[82] When he arrived in western Asia Minor in 214, he did so by landing near Troy and offering sacrifices to Achilles, in imitation of Alexander, and spent part of the winter touring cities through which Alexander had passed.[83]

In addition to his historical interest, Caracalla showed some concern for the gods, going to Pergamon, where he would sleep in the famous temple of Asclepius to obtain a vision of the god. He took an interest in Apollonius of Tyana, the wonder worker of the first century AD, and was delighted by an oracle that described him as an "Ausonian (Italian) beast."[84] His delight in this text was sufficiently well known that it would be quoted with great bitterness in Alexandria in the winter of 215.[85]

While Caracalla was residing in Nicomedia, there was trouble on the eastern frontier. King Abgar of Osrhoene had been summoned into Caracalla's presence a year or two earlier and deposed on the grounds that he was gaining control of the neighboring tribes and treating them with great cruelty in an effort to make them conform to Roman ways. As Dio says, this effort at Romanization, whatever that means – and it is most unclear in a context where the king governed in his native Syriac and presented himself to the world as a traditional Mesopotamian monarch – was a pretext to assert regional control.[86] Abgar indeed appears to have been using his privileged position within the Roman state to gain status locally, and this was more than Caracalla could tolerate. Sitting, as Osrhoene did, on the northern and western borders of the province of Mesopotamia, displays of independence by its king were dangerous. At the same time, it appears that Caracalla made a final peace between his family and Antioch by restoring that city's great Olympic games, and granted it the status of a *colonia* with the *ius Italicum*.[87] At the same time he elevated Emesa, his mother's home city, to the same exalted status, and he may have done the same for Palmyra.[88] But that was not all; Caracalla already had designs upon repeating the conquests of Trajan and his father while the Parthians were distracted by dynastic disputes. He would then truly be the new Alexander. But before that he wished to visit Egypt.

Caracalla reached Pelusium, the gateway to the Egypt, in November 215, and Alexandria by December, where he hoped to see the tomb of his hero, Alexander, and visit the famous temple of Serapis.[89] Herodian describes his spectacular entry into the city, where

> All kinds of musical instruments were set up everywhere and produced a variety of sounds. Clouds of perfume and incense of all sorts presented a sweet odor at the city gates, and they honored the emperor with torchlight processions and garlands of flowers.
>
> (Herod. 4.8.8, trans. Whittaker, adapted)

Caracalla proceeded to the tomb of Alexander, where he left his cloak and other gifts, and to the temple of Serapis. Then something went terribly wrong. We shall never know precisely what happened, for our sources present accounts that differ from each other on just about every point of detail, but they are clear on the one basic point: there was a massacre. Somehow the relationship between the emperor and the people broke down, the people of Alexandria took to shouting rude things about him as a fratricide, and comparing him unfavorably with Alexander.[90] Troops were ordered into the streets to slaughter the population. An edict ordering non-Alexandrians to leave the city may be connected with these events, but we cannot be sure.[91] All we do know is that Caracalla stayed in the city until March or April, at which point he returned to Syria to begin preparations for the invasion of Parthia. He arrived there in the early summer.

Before an invasion of Parthia through northern Mesopotamia could be launched, Caracalla had to ensure that the Armenians would not threaten his advance. These operations were entrusted to an officer named Theocritus, who appears to have been given general authority over the frontier in 216.[92] At the same time it appears that the administration of Rome was given over to a man named Flavius Maternianus, who held a position previously held only by Sextus Varius Marcellus. His chief qualification may have been his loyalty to the emperor (and this would cost him his life).[93]

Dio says that Theocritus was a dancer who had once been a favorite of Saoterus, the favorite of Commodus. After making a few unflattering remarks about his ability on the stage (good enough for Lyons but not Rome) Dio leaves it at that, which is unfortunate. Theocritus arguably represents the future; for hidden beneath Dio's scorn is a very long career in the palace, spanning a quarter of a century. His appointment to such a senior military command marks a stage in the movement away from senators as influential military commanders and, again, Caracalla's own tendency to place political loyalty above all other qualities in selecting his officials. We don't know how good an experiment this turned out to be. Dio says that he was defeated.[94] But if he was, it does not seem to have brought preparations to a halt, and Caracalla himself led an army as far as Arbela, the field where Alexander had won his final victory over Darius.

In 217 Caracalla was on the march once again, reaching Edessa by the end of March at the head of a large army that had consisted of detachments from all parts of the empire as well as from the eastern garrisons. His intention was to complete the work begun the previous year by advancing across Mesopotamia and into the Parthian heartland.

Death in the desert

Caracalla will remain one of the most unattractive, but in some other ways most significant, emperors of the third century. It might be possible to read the *constitutio Antoniniana* and his passion for Alexander as signs of a univer-salizing ideology that aimed at creating a "national" feeling among the diverse peoples of the empire. His presence in the east, which was marked not only by the massacre at Alexandria, but also by the introduction of a special silver coinage in the cities of the region of Syria, might be seen as separating the concept of imperial government from the capital in order to involve the diverse peoples of the empire more fully.[95]

A dossier from the temple at Dmeir, northeast of Damascus, may be taken as a sign of the benefits that direct access to the emperor, bypassing normal lines of communication, could bring to inhabitants of rural communities.[96] In this case they complained that a man named Avidius Hadrianus who had made himself high priest had usurped the control of the temple. The complaint was brought by Aurelius Carzaeus, son of Sergius, whose name and actions proclaim the complexity of intercultural relations on the eastern frontier. Although his father was named Sergius, a good Roman name, it is plain that Aurelius Carzaeus was not a citizen before he received the name Aurelius through the *constitutio Antoniniana*. Despite the fact that he was appealing to the emperor, who spoke to him in Greek, it is likewise plain that his primary interest remained the traditional operation of the temple, where there were great processions, the priest wore a golden crown, and the local population communicated with each other in Aramaic. While Caracalla held in Carzaeus' favor, he seems to have regarded the whole event as some-thing of a joke, a point lost on the people of Dmeir who recorded the hearing, verbatim, on the walls of their temple.[97] By hearing the case Caracalla was recognizing the importance of the temple less than that of himself. "You want me to hear the case," he said, "I will hear it."

Instead of advocating a universalizing ideology that recognized the import-ance of diverse parts of the empire, Caracalla might better be seen as advocating a strongly centralizing view of government, whereby the tradi-tional institutions of the state became irrelevant when they did not serve the interests of the emperor himself. As opposed to supporting the diversity of institutions that had implicitly recognized the diversity of administrative realities in the Roman world, Caracalla had suppressed those institutions insofar as they did not correspond with his need to serve his own interests above all others. He realized that he had obtained a monopoly of force through his ability to appeal to his soldiers, but in so doing he had proposed a model of autocracy from which his successors would recoil for more than a gener-ation. Nor, with the exception of his immediate successor, would these successors aspire to the office of emperor itself. That instead would pass to children who would be governed by committees of courtiers. In so doing, however, they would continue the process through which the interests of the palace would come to predominate over all others.

By the spring of 217, it would appear that the leading men in Caracalla's court had become heartily sick of him. He relied ever more heavily on astrologers for advice, and an Egyptian named Serapio had gained what, for the praetorian prefect, Macrinus, was frightening influence.[98] Serapio had told Caracalla that his days would be short, and that Macrinus would take his place, and even though Serapio was killed, Macrinus might well have thought that his own days were numbered.

There is a story that Macrinus was also influenced by the fact that a seer in Africa was reported to have predicted that he would kill his master. He is said to have learned of this prophecy because the letter sent to Caracalla informing him of this was delivered to him in the normal course of events.[99] Another version of the story has Macrinus conspire with several senior officers to find a soldier named Martialis, who hated Caracalla, and place him in the emperor's retinue when he set out from Edessa to see the famous temples of the moon around the ancient city of Carrhae, now raised to colonial status, in the province of Mesopotamia. On April 6 Caracalla participated in the rites of the moon goddess in her temple at Asagi Yarimca, two miles north of the city. On April 8 he set out to make the six-mile journey from Carrhae to the temple of the moon god at 'Ain-al-'Arus.[100] When he stopped to relieve himself, Martialis followed him into the bushes and killed him. Conveniently for those who had employed him, Martialis was then slain by Caracalla's German guards.'

The Emperor Macrinus

Cassius Dio recounted many extraordinary things that were said to have happened around the time of Caracalla's death, among them a dream in which Severus appeared to him and ordered him to write the history that has come down to us.[101] In this history he told of a daimon who had taken on the appearance of a man and led an ass up to the Capitol, and then over to the palace, saying that he was seeking his master since Caracalla was dead. After questioning by the city prefect he vanished on the road to Capua. Upon later reflection Dio decided that the ass that had been led up to the palace might be likened to Macrinus.[102]

Opellius Macrinus was from North Africa, and, indeed, from a family that traced its ancestors to the Berber tribes of the region. He had a pierced ear, as was traditional for men of his heritage.[103] The only thing wrong with him, in Dio's view, was that he dared to take the throne although he was not a senator. Macrinus was an equestrian, and his career up until the time that he ascended to the praetorian prefecture was dominated by work as an advocate and legal consultant for the palace. His knowledge of the law was so precise, and his personal integrity so strong, that Dio thought that this made up for the fact that he was born so far outside the traditional ruling classes of the empire.

He was also a cautious man. For two days after the death of Caracalla he made no move to take the throne, for fear that the soldiers would assume that he had conspired against the emperor. Herodian reports, on what authority it is not clear, that there was a suggestion that Adventus, the other prefect, take the throne, but that he refused on the grounds of his advanced age.[104] In Dio's version, Macrinus spent that time writing to the various units that were based around Mesopotamia to secure their assent for his elevation.[105] On the fourth day after Caracalla's death, on Severus' birthday, Macrinus assembled the troops to allow them to make him emperor, after a suitable show of reluctance. He then wrote to the senate explaining that he had accepted the throne from the soldiers.

Macrinus had three problems on his hands. The first was that the troops were genuinely upset about Caracalla's murder, so much so that he did all he could to distance himself from the plot. He made it clear to the soldiers that he would allow Caracalla to be deified, and commissioned pictures showing the murder in a series of panels that concluded with one of him mourning his predecessor.[106] The second was to create a government from among the men around him. Dio was to be bitterly critical of these appointments, which included the elevation of the former procurator in charge of the census, Ulpius Julianus, and Julianus Nestor, who had been in command of the imperial couriers, to the post of praetorian prefect.[107] In Dio's view they were a pair of disreputable courtiers of Caracalla. A less prejudiced account might note instead that they were precisely the sort of people to move to the fore out of the court bureaucracy in which Macrinus had spent his career. These and other appointments reinforced the centralizing tendencies of Caracalla's time. The court and the equestrian bureaucracy were the places to which a nonsenatorial emperor would look for supporters, and where he had found supporters for his conspiracy.

Macrinus' third problem was the Parthian war. When the Parthian king Artabanus learned of Caracalla's death, he gathered his army for an invasion of Roman Mesopotamia. Dio says (he might have known what he was talking about, since the army would later pass through Nicaea while he was staying there) that Artabanus even demanded that the Romans withdraw from the Severan province of Mesopotamia.[108] Macrinus, who had tried to negotiate a peace settlement, had no choice but to fight. The two armies met outside of Nisibis in the autumn of 217, and the Romans were defeated. Macrinus then bought a peace with Artabanus through an enormous subsidy; Dio puts the sum at two hundred million sesterces, a sum that amounted to something like one-eighth of the annual budget of the Roman Empire.[109]

Dio would later criticize Macrinus for keeping the army in the east throughout the winter of 217–18, but this is unjust.[110] Macrinus had no choice in the matter, for he could not leave until he had managed to make peace, and the sum that he offered to make that peace suggests that he was well aware of the problems that he was causing himself by staying in camp with an army that was devoted to the memory of his predecessor, and had little love for himself. Macrinus was the antithesis of Caracalla: a lawyer who showed little sign of enjoying the company of his men.

The genuine problems that Macrinus faced in the east caused him further problems at Rome. The Roman people expected to see their ruler, and by the end of the summer were rioting against him in the circus. The senate was displeased by a series of appointments that he had made, some of them rewarding individuals whom Marius Maximus would later identify as having been leaders in the plot against Caracalla.[111] There was little sympathy for a man who did not rush home to play the expected role of urban politician. As early as September, Dio says that there were portents that could be read as presaging Macrinus' imminent demise.[112]

Dio was no doubt assisted in recalling these portents by virtue of the fact that Macrinus indeed had a very short time left to live. The women of the house of Severus determined his fate, women whose contacts with their home at Emesa remained close, and remained strong. It may simply have been Macrinus' bad luck that Caracalla's family was as much Syrian as it was African, and that it hailed from a famous city.

At first it may not have been clear that this would be an issue. Julia Domna was at Antioch when she learned of her son's death, and it appears that she had no very great interest in going home. She is said to have feared the loss of her guards and returning to private station, and even though Macrinus treated her with respect, she heard of the hatred for Caracalla that was being expressed in Rome. She decided to kill herself – a decision that may have been hastened when the breast cancer from which she suffered had reasserted itself after a period of remission.[113] But she was not the last of her line.

Julia Domna had a younger sister named Julia Maesa who had married a man named Julius Avitus, who had, not surprisingly, obtained consular rank in the reign of his brother-in-law. While Avitus was still ascending the senatorial ladder, he and Maesa had had two daughters, Soaemias and Mamaea. These daughters had married men from the province. Soaemias' husband was the Varius Marcellus from Apamea who had played an important role in the destruction of Geta; Mamaea's husband was Gessius Marcianus from Arca. Marcellus had entered the senate as a reward for his services, while Marcianus had moved into the procuratorial service; both had died by 217, though not before each had fathered a male child.[114]

Varius Avitus, son of Soaemias and Marcellus, was the older of the two cousins, and in 217 he held the ancestral priesthood of '*lh' gbl*, or Elagabalus, as the name was rendered in Latin. Elagabalus, who manifested himself on earth as a meteorite, had, as his name, which means God Mountain, suggests, been a local form of the high god who resided on a mountain.[115] After contact with the Greeks he had changed identity somewhat, becoming instead a form of the sun god. The cult of Elagabalus appears to have been a popular one, drawing people to its celebrations at Emesa from all over Syria.[116] When

Plate 4 Severan women. (a) Julia Domna. *Credit*: *RIC* Severus no. 559 (Rome 196–211); author's collection, photo courtesy of Forum Ancient Coins. (b) Julia Maesa. *Credit*: *RIC* Elagabalus no. 268 (Rome); author's collection, photo courtesy of Forum Ancient Coins. (c) Julia Soaemias. *Credit*: *RIC* Elagabalus no. 243 (Rome); author's collection, photo courtesy of Forum Ancient Coins. (d) Julia Mamaea. *Credit*: *RIC* 343 (Rome 222); author's collection, photo courtesy of Forum Ancient Coins.

people came to behold the god, they could also behold the young Avitus, then thirteen years old, as he celebrated the cult of the god.[117]

Julia Maesa had lived with her sister throughout the reign of her nephew, and when Domna died, she went home to Emesa, and there she hatched a plot to overthrow Macrinus. The details of these events are significant, for what looks like a struggle between a fifty-five-year-old lawyer and a teenager is better described as a conflict between the two most influential wings of government: the equestrian bureaucracy and the court. The accession of Macrinus had extruded the fabulously wealthy Maesa from what she deemed her proper place, and had likewise caused discomfort to others who were used to being at the center of power: at least one disloyal *cubicularius* would play a central role in what followed.[118] The fact that these events unfolded around Emesa and Apamea in Syria cannot disguise the fact that the nature of the conflict was internal to the government as it had been shaped by Severus and his son. The key factor would be the loyalty of the army to the dynasty that had sought to identify its interests with those of the soldiers.

Maesa and those around her knew how to undermine a government, and they knew that the settlement with Parthia had done nothing to endear Macrinus to the troops, especially as Macrinus, who was strapped for cash, had altered the conditions of service for new soldiers. Complaining that Caracalla's gifts to the troops had created a deficit of seventy million sesterces a year, he had announced that the Caracallan rates of pay would not apply to new recruits.[119]

Maesa began to act as the army moved into winter quarters, making ample use of three key ingredients of a classic *coup d'état*: local connections, money, and divine intervention. It is perhaps no accident that, despite an early show of oracular support for Macrinus, the oracle of Bel at Apamea soon became ambivalent. Dio records a response in which Bel, who operated by selecting quotations from classical authors, probably by lot, came up with a couple of lines from Homer for Macrinus:

> Old man, verily do young warriors press close around you,
> Your strength is spent, harsh old age is upon you.

These words were spoken by Ajax to Nestor (who survived), but they are scarcely a ringing endorsement, and their very ambivalence suggests that when the oracle felt that Macrinus' chances were waning, it had better stake out a position for itself that was not particularly supportive.[120] The lack of support was perhaps as damning as an outright prediction of disaster, and it may be no accident that Avitus' father was a leading man of the city where the oracle operated. Other oracular responses, perhaps from Elagabalus himself, had been circulated earlier among the soldiers of Legion III, which was stationed outside Emesa, suggesting that it was time for a change of leadership.[121]

The soldiers of Legion III had witnessed the celebration of the cult and were helped by Maesa to see a striking resemblance between Avitus and the deceased Caracalla. At the same time they were told that Avitus was in fact the product of a liaison between Caracalla and his cousin. On the night of May 16, 218, Avitus was brought to the camp of the legion by Gannys, a youthful freedman of Maesa, and proclaimed emperor with the connivance of P. Valerius Comazon, the commander of the legion.[122] Maesa and Soaemias arrived later that morning and remained there to await developments.

The response to their coup was as swift as it was catastrophically ineffective. Ulpius Julianus, who was then at Apamea, ordered the execution of Soaemias' in-laws and led the troops of Legion II Parthica to Emesa. After an attack on the camp by Julianus' Mauretanian cavalry – the unit was felt to be particularly loyal to Macrinus because of the latter's North African heritage – failed, the legion approached the camp.[123] The defenders had Avitus stand on the walls, and displayed images of Caracalla as a child in support of their contention about his heritage.[124] The legionaries, who seem to have shared the general antipathy toward Macrinus, were sufficiently convinced that they killed a number of their officers before returning camp at Apamea.[125] There they received Macrinus, who asked them to proclaim his son, Diadumenianus, who had been made Caesar several months earlier, as his co-emperor. In so doing he offered the troops a huge donative, and put on a banquet for all the citizens of Apamea.[126] He plainly recognized the force of local politics that was driving the revolt and thus sought to diffuse it. He failed when he lost his nerve. At the banquet, a soldier presented him with the head of Julianus.

The new regime

The grisly denouement of the banquet at Apamea marked the beginning of the end for Macrinus. He returned to Antioch to await his adversaries, complaining that the army was disloyal because the veterans had made common cause with new recruits.[127] Both Macrinus and the supporters of Avitus, who now styled himself Marcus Aurelius Antoninus to establish his dynastic claim, wrote to the other legions around Syria for support.[128] Nothing appears to have been forthcoming for either side, perhaps because events were now moving very rapidly. The army of Antoninus, commanded by Valerius Comazon and Gannys, advanced toward Antioch, where Macrinus had with him only the Praetorian Guard and a few auxiliary cohorts. At a village some twenty-four miles from Antioch, possibly the village of Immae, the two armies met in battle on June 8.[129] Despite some initial successes on his part, Macrinus again lost his nerve just as Maesa, Soaemias, and Antoninus displayed themselves to their wavering troops. Macrinus fled while the battle was still in doubt, and it was that act that was his doom.[130] A general was supposed to be visible, and when his troops saw that he had abandoned them, they surrendered.[131]

Macrinus tried to send his son to safety in Parthia while he fled to Rome, but the agents of Antoninus moved too fast for him. Diadumenianus was arrested at Zeugma, and Macrinus, who had ridden very fast indeed in the hope of rallying support at Rome, was arrested at Chalcedon.[132] He was killed by the escort that was bringing him south.[133] At the same time, a number of his high-ranking supporters were also killed, in what might best be seen as an effort by the court to bring the equestrian bureaucracy under control. Julianus Nestor was killed while Antoninus was in Syria, as were the governor of Syria Coele, the governor of Arabia, and "the foremost equestrians among Macrinus' followers" both in Syria and at Rome.[134] Basilianus, the former prefect of Egypt whom Macrinus had elevated to praetorian prefect after the death of Julianus, was captured at Brundisium and killed later that year in Nicomedia.

The third element of government, the senate, was now also a matter of some concern to a regime that was as narrowly based as that of Antoninus. One senator, Claudius Attalus, with whom Comazon had a feud, was executed while serving as governor of Cyprus. The governor of Cappadocia, Munatius Sulla, was killed for suspicious conduct, and several others were executed at Rome, likewise for activities that could be considered treasonable. The agent of Antoninus' control in the capital was Marius Maximus, the future biographer of the Caesars, who was then urban prefect. He had served with Severus in 193 and was plainly loyal to the regime, even though his private opinions, which emerge through the later biographical tradition, appear to have been scathing.

Perhaps more striking than the killings were the promotions. Senators still held the majority of senior provincial commands, and so, rather than eliminating them, it was better policy to create new senators who could be trusted. Claudius Aelius Pollio, who had been a centurion when he killed Macrinus, was immediately elevated to senatorial rank, receiving the governorships first of Bithynia and then of Germania Superior.[135] Another former centurion, whose name is only partially preserved by Dio, was promoted to be legate of Legion III Gallica in Syria (he tried to raise a conspiracy and was killed), as was Gellius Maximus, the son of a physician, who was made a senatorial legate of Legion IV Scythica (also in Syria).[136] A complete list of such people can never be drawn up, but Dio's perception of a pattern of conduct would seem to be correct: one of his many objections to the regime of Antoninus was a lack of respect for traditional senatorial prerogative. Marius Maximus may have supported this view, as he is the source of a passage in the *Historia Augusta* biography of Antoninus in which it is stated that "he made his freedmen governors and legates, consuls and generals, and he polluted all ranks through with the disgrace of low-born men."[137]

In addition to new senators, the regime of Antoninus needed also to fill the senior ranks of the equestrian bureaucracy. In some cases they resorted to men who had occupied the middle ranks under the old regime.[138] In others they drew upon people whose administrative experience might, at best, be regarded as suspect. Marius Maximus claimed that "as prefect of the watch he appointed a charioteer named Cordius, and as prefect of the grain supply a barber named Claudius . . . as collector of the 5 percent tax on inheritances he appointed a muleteer, a courier, a cook and a locksmith."[139] Given more information, it might be possible to discover various palace services that are disguised by these terms, but the point would still remain, that the upper echelons of a suspect bureaucracy were being restocked from people who had support inside the domestic wing of the palace. As this was happening, so too were new people being recruited to join them. The cook, for instance, is plainly Aurelius Zoticus, an athlete from Smyrna.[140] There is no point in speculating about Maximus' further claim that the other common characteristic of the new appointees was a large penis.[141]

Elagabalus ascendant

After spending a few months in Antioch, Antoninus and his entourage began their journey, overland, to Rome.[142] They stopped for the winter in Nicomedia, and it is there that the personality of the young Antoninus began to manifest itself. Whatever others may have thought, he plainly regarded his position as the priest of Elagabalus as a very important feature of his identity. He brought the image of the god with him; he conducted the rites of the god in traditional fashion, and in traditional garb:

> He wore the most expensive types of clothes, woven of purple and gold, and adorned himself with necklaces and bangles. On his head he wore a crown in the shape of a tiara glittering with gold and precious stones. The effect was something between the sacred garb of the Phoenicians and the luxurious apparel of the Medes. Any Roman or Greek dress he loathed because, he claimed, it was made out of wool, which is a cheap material. Only Chinese silk was good enough for him. He appeared in public accompanied by flutes and drums, no doubt because he was honoring the god with special rites.
>
> (Herod. 5.5.3–4, trans. Whittaker)

No one seems to have been able to dissuade him from this course. While the dominant cultural matrix of the ancient world enabled local divinities to be placed in a broader context, it only did so after they had, to some degree, been domesticated within a Greco-Roman context. But just what this meant obviously varied depending upon the context. The local god '*lh*' *gbl* had become Elagabalus and was fast on his way to becoming Heliogabalus in the parlance of an observer like Marius Maximus. The new name represented the understanding that as a high god, he was a sun god. But this act of domestication was not accompanied by a significant change in the way that he was worshipped. His high priest remained very much a Syrian, and aspects of his official celebration remained Emesene.[143] In the case of the Magna Mater, also known in Rome in the form of a meteorite, the official cult had been altered so that a praetor conducted her rites at the Megalesia. Her castrate priests were not admitted to the public cult, and the wandering bands of *hierodouloi* who celebrated the cult of Atargatis throughout the empire were definite outsiders to the authorized establishment.[144] The Egyptian divinities Sarapis and Isis had their own dedicated priests, but no matter how interested members of the Roman upper class might be in them, there was no suggestion that their rites become an official part of the worship of the Roman state.[145] Antoninus' advisers had every reason to think that the response to their protégé's Syrian attire in public would not be positive; they may have tried to soften the blow that his arrival in Rome would predictably occasion by sending a picture of him, in full priestly garb, to the senate.

Fear of what would happen if Antoninus did not mend his ways may have helped slow the progress of the new emperor to Rome. Although there is some evidence to suggest that he might have reached the capital by the end of July, the source for this information is not particularly reliable. An inscription dated to September 29, 219, is probably the best evidence for the date of his arrival.[146] What follows has no parallel in Roman history.

Antoninus installed Elagabalus in the temple of Capitoline Jupiter and married Julia Cornelia Paula, a woman of senatorial rank. The marriage and the installation of the god represent the as yet unreconciled aspects of the regime: Antoninus' advisers wished somehow to integrate him into the aristocracy of Rome, while he wished to continue his career as high priest. At the beginning of 220 he declared Elagabalus the chief god of the Roman pantheon and added the title "most magnificent priest of the invincible sun Elagabalus" to his name.[147] On coins he begins to appear as "priest of the sun god Elagabalus" or as "highest priest Augustus," while the traditional title of pontifex maximus disappears from most representations.[148] His identification with the god would grow stronger in the course of the year, resulting in the tendency to refer to him by the name of his god.

The emperor "Elagabalus" celebrated the cult of the god Elagabalus in the style of Emesa. While descriptions of his activities differ somewhat in the diverse sources for his reign, it is plain that, whatever he was doing – the biggest question being whether he displayed his circumcised self in dances before the god – celebrations of the cult were offensive to basic Roman tastes.[149] This despite the fact that Herodian says that senior officials dressed in Phoenician costume as a way of currying favor with the new ruler.

Plate 5 Changing images. As Elagabalus' reign proceeded it appears that some effort was
made to improve his image, quite literally, by changing his public appearance
so that he resembled Caracalla very closely. The context is particularly interesting
as 5c commemorates Elagabalus' celebration of the cult of his god in traditional
Roman priestly garb. (a) Elagabalus. *Credit*: *RIC* Elagabalus no. 1 (Rome 218);
author's collection, photo courtesy of Forum Ancient Coins. (b) Elagabalus.
Credit: *RIC* Elagabalus no. 88 (Rome 220–22); author's collection, photo courtesy
of Classical Numismatic Group. (c) Elagabalus as *invictus sacerdos* Augustus.
Credit: *RIC* Elagabalus no. 88 (Rome 220–22); author's collection, photo courtesy
of Classical Numismatic Group. (d) Caracalla. *Credit*: *RIC* Caracalla no. 191
(Rome 211); author's collection, photo by Ivory Photo, Ann Arbor, MI.

The cult took a new turn at the end of 220 when Elagabalus (the god) was married to the form of Pallas Athena represented by the Palladium, an archaic statue of the goddess that had allegedly come from Troy and was kept in the temple of Minerva.[150] To consummate the divine marriage the Palladium was moved to the temple of Elagabalus on the Palatine.[151] At the same time, Elagabalus (the emperor) divorced Cornelia Paula and married a vestal virgin named Julia Aquila Severa.[152] The point of the marriage may have been obvious to Elagabalus – as dedicated priest of his god, he needed a wife who was a representative of her goddess on earth. That Elagabalus thought himself to be, or at least that he wished others to think that he was, in the living presence of the god, is nowhere made more clear than in a ceremony in the course of 221, described by Herodian:

> The god was set up in a chariot studded with gold and precious stones and driven from the city to the suburb. The chariot was drawn by a team of six large, pure white horses which had been decorated with lots of gold and ornamented discs. No human person ever sat in the chariot or held the reins, which were fastened to the god as if he were driving himself. Antoninus ran along in front of the chariot, but facing backwards as he ran and holding the bridles of the horses. He ran the whole way backwards like this looking up at the front of the god. But to stop him from tripping and falling while he was not looking where he was going, lots of sand gleaming like gold was put down, and his bodyguard supported him on either side to make sure that he was safe as he ran like this. Along both sides of the route, the people ran with a great array of torches showering wreaths and flowers on him. In the procession, in front of the god, went images of all the other gods and valuable or precious temple dedications and all the imperial standards or costly heirlooms. Also the cavalry and all the army joined in.
>
> (Herod 5.6.7–8, trans. Whittaker)

Elagabalus' trip down the yellow brick road to the new temple that the human Elagabalus was dedicating to him was intended to evoke a triumph. The procession of treasures and of other gods was modeled upon the display of treasures that would precede the triumphator's chariot. The gods of Rome were in the position of captives before Elagabalus, illustrating another point that the imperial version of the Wizard of Oz had allegedly made, that all gods were merely the servants of the greatest of all divinities.[153] The god took the position of the triumphator, who was, in theory, the representative of Jupiter on earth as he rode through the city. In this case, of course, the ideological message was reified as the god himself drove. Elagabalus had replaced Jupiter as the chief god at Rome, a point that outraged Dio.[154] Likewise, as the triumph was intended to end at the temple of Jupiter, it was now to end at the temple of the new chief of the Roman pantheon, Elagabalus himself. The occasion for this triumph was the arrival of yet another bride, for Athena had displeased the god as being too warlike, and was being replaced by the goddess Astarte from Carthage. Astarte, like Elagabalus, was represented by a meteorite and, like Elagabalus, was also a divinity of the heavens, having been identified with Urania.[155]

As Elagabalus divorced Athena, so too did the emperor divorce Julia Severa, replacing her with Annia Faustina, a descendant of Marcus Aurelius.[156] The purpose of his religious devotion was not, as some of his contemporaries appear to have thought, to replace the gods of the Roman people with a single cult, but rather to demonstrate the henotheistic principles that were characteristic of many Semitic cults. The high god did not eliminate other gods; rather, he ruled over them, which is why the emperor planned to have their symbols transferred to the new temple and avoided membership in traditional priestly colleges that were devoted to lesser divinities.[157]

It is fair to say that the distinction between henotheism and impiety may have been lost on many; Marius Maximus thought that he was trying to abolish the worship of all gods but his own, and his treatment of the cult of Vesta appears to have shocked Roman opinion as profoundly as did his mode of worship.[158] Even before the arrival of Urania, it appears that Maesa had had enough, and she would not have been alone.[159] On June 26 the emperor was compelled to adopt his younger cousin, Bassianus Alexianus, whose name was thereby changed to Marcus Aurelius Alexander, as Caesar.[160] Before the end of 221, relations between the cousins appear to have been strained, and there is some sign that Elagabalus was beginning to wonder about the signs he had received from his god. He divorced Annia Faustina and, allegedly after two other marriages, returned to Aquila Severa.[161] At roughly the same time he tried to rid himself of officials who he thought were favoring his cousin, including Valerius Comazon and Zoticus.[162] He was able to do this because he retained the loyalty of the praetorian prefects who were able to quell a mutiny by the guard when he agreed to put on a public display of affection for his cousin.

The situation worsened into March. Alexianus disappeared from public view, and on March 11 the guard rioted once again, demanding to see him. Elagabalus went, with his mother, to the camp to try to calm them. Instead he found himself under virtual house arrest. Maesa appeared in the camp with Alexianus, and Elagabalus tried to hide himself in a trunk.[163] Before the morning of the twelfth had dawned, members of the guard had found and decapitated him. They also killed his mother, their prefects, the prefect of the city, and two other senior associates. Elagabalus was eighteen years old. His cousin, now aged thirteen, became emperor. The god Elagabalus was sent home by decree of the senate.[164] Alexander now added Severus to his name, becoming Marcus Aurelius Alexander Severus, hoping to recall the glory of the Macedonian conqueror and the first member of the dynasty.

The age of Ulpian

The Latin biographical tradition of the fourth century represented the reign of Alexander as a sort of golden age, a decent interlude between the excesses of Caracalla and Elagabalus and the monstrosity of Maximinus, who would seize the throne in 235. To some degree interest in Alexander's reign was fed by a simple lack of information that may have given scope for invention (a characteristic of the *Historia Augusta*, the prime exemplar of this tradition). It was also fueled by an interest in jurists.[165] Within a year of the murder of Elagabalus, the greatest of all the classical Roman jurists, Gnaeus Domitius Ulpianus (better known as Ulpian), would ascend from the prefecture of the grain supply to the praetorian prefecture.[166]

Ulpian appears to have entered the emperor's *consilium* under Severus, when Papinian was praetorian prefect.[167] Taken together with Ulpian's coeval, Paul, and their slightly younger contemporaries, Aelius Marcianus and Herennius Modestinus, their works describe the culmination of the "late classical period" of Roman law. As a group, the late classical jurists provided the vast bulk of the material that was later taken up in the sixth-century AD compendium of juristic thought known as the *Digest*. Indeed, about half of the *Digest* is derived from just two of these figures, Ulpian (extracts from his writings account for a third of the whole) and Papinian (about one-sixth). The civil law, as it reemerged in twelfth-century Europe, was thus largely the result of their work. But it is not just the accident of preservation that makes these men important. They were, in their own lifetimes, a recognizable group within the court that obtained great power, at least in part, because of their legal expertise.[168]

Jurists were, to a very high degree, specialists in the arcana of the law, and they did not always function very successfully when their legal abilities had raised them to a rank that would require more generalized political skills. As we have seen, Macrinus, whom Dio thought a decent jurist, was a less than capable politician, given to fatal fits of indecision at times of crisis.[169] Papinian died as a result of his defense of Geta, and Ulpian lasted only two years as prefect before the guard lynched him. Such failures may be, to some degree, a function of legal training, which rewarded command of minutiae, and led to a mode of expression that was often oracular, and at times tinged with extreme confidence in their ability to arrive at the truth.[170] Thus Ulpian wrote "the deified Marcus has also given a rescript in accordance with our view," his point being that the logical case that he has just made in a discussion of soldiers' wills is right, and that Marcus may be congratulated for having anticipated his wisdom.[171] In another case, this one dealing with a father's ability to draft a will for children who are subject to his *potestas*, he wrote:

> However a person must first appoint an heir to himself and then a
> substitute for his son and not upset the order of the document; and

Julian takes this view, that he ought first to appoint an heir for himself and then for his son; but if he makes a will for his son before he makes one for himself, this is not valid. And this view was approved in a rescript of our emperor [Caracalla] to Virius Lupus, governor of Britain, and justifiably; for it is agreed that it is one will, although there are two inheritances.[172]

Again the logic of the case runs that the jurists have arrived at the correct solution, and the emperor has confirmed the propriety of their logic. There is a sense in the writings of all jurists, not just Ulpian, that it was their task to bring order to the law, and statements by emperors are useful insofar as they supported positions that a jurist supported. As Ulpian also wrote, "Plainly some of these (imperial decisions) are purely ad hominem and are not followed as setting precedents" (D. 1.4.1).

The role of jurists in the formation of law owes much to the decision of Augustus to give certain men the power of issuing "responses" on questions of law that magistrates were advised to follow. According to the jurist Pomponius, who wrote in the time of Hadrian,

To clarify the point in passing: before the time of Augustus the right of stating opinions at large was not granted by emperors, but the practice was that opinions were given by people who had confidence in their own studies. Nor did they always issue opinions under seal, but most commonly wrote themselves to judges, or gave the testimony of a direct answer to those who consulted them. It was the deified Augustus who, in order to enhance the authority of the law, first established that opinions might be given under his authority.
(D. 1.2.2.49)

Hadrian further refined this power by stating that, in cases where the responses of those granted the right of issuing responses with imperial authority agreed, a judge was bound to follow them. In cases where they disagreed, he should follow whichever one he thought best (but, and this is important, he was not free to act independently of them).[173] At the time that Augustus took this step, the leading jurists were members of the senatorial order. By the middle of the second century they were almost exclusively equestrians, and they had moved from outside the circle of the palace to the company of the a libellis.[174] There is no clear explanation of this process in any text, but it is a matter of great significance in the course of the gradual centralization of power within the imperial entourage.[175] And it appears that it was knowledge of the law that set the imperial entourage apart, for there is otherwise a good deal of evidence to suggest that, despite Hadrian's desire that judges be bound by what jurists had to say, ignorance of their writings was widespread in the governing class.[176]

The reason why judges might be ignorant of what the jurists had to say may be a function of the way that they said it. In addition to their responses (and these emanated only from a few, leading, figures) jurists composed a wide variety of other books. Typical productions included textbooks for beginning lawyers (tending to be called *institutiones* and *enchiridia*) or, with somewhat looser arrangement, *regulae* (rules), *definitiones* (definitions), and *sententiae* (opinions). At a more advanced level there were general books on the civil law, sometimes entitled *Books to Sabinus*, a reference to the most famous work in the early third century, and also one of the shortest (surely a coincidence), Masurius Sabinus' work in three books on the civil law. Other works offered commentaries on the praetor's edict, which was given permanent form under Hadrian to govern points of procedure, or on individual laws and senatorial decrees. For the more ambitious, there were *digesta*, which treated the whole body of law beginning with the praetor's edict, followed by the civil law, and finally by the criminal law. The final genre of legal writing included books variously entitled *quaestiones, responsa, disputationes*, and *epistulae. Responsa* tended to be collections of an individual jurist's opinions on legal matters; *quaestiones* and *disputationes* tended to record cases based on a jurist's discussions with his pupils, as did *epistulae*, though in all cases there were occasional references to cases decided in actual practice.[177]

As the foregoing list of legal genres suggests, the primary audience for juristic writing appears to have been other jurists, and there was a strong sense that a successful jurist was one who produced followers in the profession. At least at the beginning of the century there were two definable schools of thought, one entitled the Sabinian after Masurius Sabinus, the other named after the jurist Proculus.[178] A basic tenet of Sabinus' school, insofar as one can be established, is that possession depended upon the material of a thing rather than its form, as Proculus held, and, more generally, the Sabinians tended to be freer in their use of analogy than Proculians.[179] Perhaps the most significant feature of these schools (which appear not to have had a significant place in the study of the law by the time of Commodus) was that they represented the integration of some Greek philosophic concepts into Roman jurisprudence. The Sabinians appear to have been mildly Stoic, while the Proculians appealed to Aristotelian thought.[180] Equally significant is that in their self-definition mimicked Greek philosophic schools by requiring a list of leaders to help give them legitimacy (both schools in fact traced their origins some generations earlier than their eponymous founders).

More typical of the practice of jurisprudence than the study of philosophy was the study of precedent and the analysis of the interpretation of laws and procedures. Much of this involved the study of what other jurists had to say. Papinian, who was regarded as the preeminent jurist of the classical period according to the fifth-century "law of citations," which gave his opinions precedence over others, wrote thirty-seven books of *quaestiones* and nineteen books of *responsa*.[181] The *responsa*, which are partially preserved on a palimpsest of the fourth or fifth century, contain Papinian's statements on points of law, and, at least in the version that has survived, do so without preserving the sense of question and answer that the title might suggest was appropriate. A typical entry reads as follows:

> If a tutor keeps a ward from his father's inheritance, an action against the tutor should be granted to a creditor who has made a contract with the tutor himself, even though the tutor has made a profit for the ward. The curators of an adolescent offered a surety to each other in respect of a mutual risk and gave pledges for that purpose; since they were solvent on resigning their post, it was apparent that the pledge was void and the bond of the pledge was released.
>
> (Pap. *Res*. 5.6–7 [also in *D*. 26.39.4–5, trans. Lewis, adapted])

When the opinions of other jurists are cited, it tends to be in the context of justifying Papinian's response, in the form: here is a situation, here is the question that I asked, and here is the answer that the other jurist gave, or here is the imperial constitution that governs the issue.[182]

The style of the *quaestiones* is somewhat different. There Papinian would state the issue at law, and then how it affects an issue that arises from the opinion. These issues might be framed in terms of the opinions of other jurists, or simply in terms of cases with which he dealt, sometimes even correcting an earlier opinion that he had given. Thus in one case he would write:

> Sabinus and Cassius thought that a tutor who manages a tutelage, while he manages, can be liable at times on several grounds in each case. . . . From this arises the question which is commonly asked concerning a son in power who has been appointed tutor by will and emancipated after undertaking the tutelage and continued in the same office.
>
> (*D*. 26.7.37.1–2, trans. Lewis)

In another he said:

> We shall say the same in the case of two colleagues in magistracy when the state accuses one of them. But I considered these facts in the case of the magistrates, as if they were in every case two defendants for the same debt; but this is not so.
>
> (*D*. 26.7.45, trans. Lewis)

These are books written by a lawyer for other lawyers. The impression that they give is of a man who was deeply committed to the notion of the autonomy of law, of a man who worked in a context where the answer to legal questions could be found through the logical analysis of other legal questions. Ulpian's writings are of a very similar nature, though his output was far greater, exceeded in the classical period only by Paul. Ulpian had certainly served with Papinian during the period of the latter's ascendancy, and plainly shared his view of the law's autonomy, and the need for fairness. Ulpian may have taken this one step further, seeing himself as a sort of priest who was charged with ensuring that the rites of his god, the law, were carried out with propriety.[183]

The rise of jurists to high administrative position may be connected, at least to a degree, with the dependence of Commodus and Severus on the *a libellis* to answer their correspondence, and Caracalla's distinct lack of interest in detail. Perhaps the most interesting feature of the Dmeir inscription is that Caracalla clearly became bored by the proceedings, which involved two senior jurists, very quickly. Macrinus owed his position as prefect to his ability to deal with detail while Caracalla was amusing himself elsewhere. Commodus plainly played little role in the composition of his rescripts, and Severus appears to have relied very heavily on Plautianus, who in turn deferred to the lawyers on his staff, including Papinian. It may be a mark of Papinian's value to the regime that he survived his patron's fall.

Valuable though the jurists might be, it was not incumbent upon the emperor to listen to what they had to say – even when he could be bothered to allow them to make their points in full. We have ten instances in the *Digest* reporting discussions of law in the *consilium* of the emperor: one case involving Trajan, three involving Marcus, and six involving Severus.[184] In each instance, Trajan and Marcus follow the advice of a jurist. Severus ignores the advice three times. While this sample is too small to enable us to see if this is a genuine tendency, reflecting Severus' more authoritarian habits, it is nonetheless significant in that it shows that jurists did not always get their way.

It may be tempting to seek in both the rise and style of the jurists an alternative to the autocratic and, at times, irrational conduct of their rulers (when they bothered to listen). It might be tempting to see the stress on the autonomous nature of law as a desperate effort to create some stability in a world where so little may have seemed predictable. But to do this would be to stretch the evidence too far. The style of the jurists stems, in a direct and continuous line, from the jurists of the late republic, and even from pontifical commentators of earlier generations. The creation of specialized bodies of learning, to which access was granted only to initiates who devoted themselves to long years of study, was a more generalized feature of the structure of knowledge in the ancient world. The doctor Galen, for instance, transmitted the bulk of his learning through commentaries on earlier doctors; philosophers tended to attach themselves to schools whose doctrines they could command, and whose arguments against the claims of rival schools they mastered. As we shall see, important developments in Greek thought during the course of the third century would hark back to Plato, even as they transformed his philosophy in ways that he could scarcely have imagined.[185] Rhetoricians delighted in the creation of schools of students who would proclaim their glories to later generations. The inward-looking nature of all these disciplines owed more to forms of pedagogy than to any political scheme. What commanded the respect of a man like Dio was the ability of the specialist to function outside of his chosen field; and the ability of any man confronted with the temptations of power to restrain himself, and maintain faith with the discipline that had brought him into a position of influence. Dio saw Ulpian as such a man.

Alexander Severus

The age of Alexander Severus was not only (albeit briefly) the age of Ulpian, it was also, in several senses of the word, the great age of Cassius Dio himself. Although he was nearly sixty when Alexander took the throne, Dio appears to have become, quite suddenly, a man of considerable importance. When Elagabalus was emperor, Dio had been appointed curator of his home city of Nicaea, and it was there that he spent the bulk of the reign. In short order he became governor of Africa (by putting himself forward for the lottery through which governors of this province were selected), and after that, by imperial appointment, of first Dalmatia and then Pannonia Superior. In 229 he was suddenly raised to a second consulship as colleague of Alexander Severus himself, a mark of very high favor with the regime.[186]

Dio's presence in these positions appears to represent a change of direction. Julia Mamaea, who was the true power behind her youthful son's throne, appears to have tried to reverse the process of centralization by reinvigorating (if that is the right word when it comes to recording the promotion of sexagenarians) the senate's role in government. Dio was the sixth man in the last seven years who had held a first consulship under Severus to hold a second under Alexander.[187] The first of these men was Marius Maximus.[188] He was followed by Appius Claudius Julianus, about whom very little is known, and Manilius Fuscus, who appears to have been one of the first governors whom Severus appointed to the newly formed Syria Phoenice.[189] Fuscus was followed by Aufidius Marcellus, who had first held the consulship about the same time that Dio was first consul, and who had become governor of Asia in 220 or 221.[190] Dio's immediate predecessor as Alexander's colleague was Aiacius Modestus, a governor of Arabia under Severus who may have been governor of Germania Superior in 209.[191] In the era of Caracalla and Elagabalus second consulships had not gone to such men. Rather they had been given as rewards to people who had risen to prominence through the equestrian bureaucracy, or played an exceptional role in the rapid changes of government. Laetus (*consul ordinarius II* in 215) and M. Oclatinius Adventus (*consul ordinarius II* in 218) were both former praetorian prefects (Adventus' consulship was a reward for the support that he had given his colleague Macrinus). Messius Extricatus (*consul ordinarius II* in 217) had been prefect of the grain supply, and Comazon (*consul ordinarius II* in 220) was reaping the rewards for his role in the revolution of 218.[192]

The new men who rose to the consulship in Alexander's reign did so by more traditional paths than had those of earlier years. Domitius Antigonus, who had been adlected among the praetorians by Caracalla (allegedly because his name harked back to the ancient Macedonian royal house), proceeded slowly enough to the consulship that it appears that he must have followed the regular course of offices (he was consul in 225). Two other suffect consuls of equestrian descent, one the son of a former prefect of the grain supply, also reached the consulship around 230, but again, there is nothing to distinguish their promotion from that of similarly placed men a century earlier.[193] The same can be said for the career of C. Messius Q. Decius Valerianus, a man from Etruria who was suffect consul in 234.[194] Unlike the others of his era, however, he would rise to be emperor.

For once it is also possible to know that a rational supposition based on the career patterns of the people involved has some actual support from other forms of evidence. Marius Maximus' *Lives of the Twelve Caesars* was plainly completed under Alexander, as was the scathing seventy-ninth book of Dio's history.[195] In Maximus' opinion, which is preserved in the *Historia Augusta*, Caracalla was a psychopath and Elagabalus a pervert. His sentiments accord remarkably well with those of Dio, and they appear to have despised some of the same people. Valerius Comazon, who had reemerged as prefect of the city in the aftermath of Elagabalus' death, may still have been alive in the 220s when Dio and Marius described him (inaccurately) as a former dancer.[196] So too may Aurelius Zoticus have been among the living, as both Dio and Maximus described his sexual relationship with Elagabalus. Dio said that he had a very large penis, which interested Elagabalus. Maximus implied the same thing, and they both called him a cook.[197] Dio also detailed the evening when Hierocles gave Zoticus a potion so that he could not have an erection while in bed with the emperor.[198] The point of stressing Elagabalus' same-sex encounters was not, a priori, to denigrate him on the basis of his sexual proclivities (though the suggestion that he desired to have a vagina surgically added to his person goes further than usual).[199] Both Dio and Maximus were equally scathing about his marriage to Julia Severa (who likewise seems to have survived).[200] Rather it was to suggest that, as a man who could not control his lusts, he fell short of the ideals of the Roman elite; and their views extended beyond their immediate circle. An astrological text found on a papyrus from Egypt refers to "Antoninus the pervert," and at least one other gentleman produced a work in which he described Elagabalus as the "Man/Woman."[201] Dio's comment on Trajan, that he liked wine and boys, but never harmed anyone on account of either taste, is intended to be positive:

he did not conform to the pattern expected of people who behaved that way.[202] Likewise it was to imply that people who took advantage of Elagabalus' passions to promote their own careers were less than "real men." It is sometimes stated that disapproval did not attach to the active partner in a same-sex encounter between two males, but this is simply not true in the case of Elagabalus' favorites. Dio and Maximus pour scorn upon them precisely because they were the active partners of an emperor who behaved inappropriately.

That Marius and Dio should write the way that they did implies that the sentiments that they expressed were in line with those of the imperial household. Mamaea, who was taking power in a court filled with her nephew's favorites, appears to have tried to look outside the circles that had been dominant in the previous decade. As a lawyer, Ulpian might be trusted to have a very different agenda. The resort to elderly senators of Severus' era, men who hated those who had thrived under Caracalla and Elagabalus, set a tone for the administration. And this was not missed by one other interest group that now felt that it was less beloved of the regime than it deserved. Common soldiers were used to being the fellow soldiers of the emperor, but it was not so with the teenage Alexander, who was scarcely in a position to go marching with them, and whose mother was not about to pretend that she was another Caracalla.[203] Trouble with the troops began early. The praetorians complained to Ulpian that Dio was too stern a disciplinarian and plainly expected that he would hand Dio over to them.[204] Ulpian did not. Before the end of 224 discipline in the praetorian camp had broken down to such a degree that the praetorians fought a three-day battle with the people of Rome (and lost).[205] Their hatred for Ulpian was then fueled by Marcus Aurelius Epagathus, an imperial freedman who was prefect of the grain supply. At his instigation, a group of soldiers left the camp in the middle of the night at some point in the late summer of 223 and attacked Ulpian in his house. When Ulpian fled to the palace, they followed him there and murdered him before the eyes of Mamaea and Alexander, who plainly lacked the authority to stop them. Mamaea and Alexander could not then take direct action against Epagathus. Rather they promoted him to prefect of Egypt to get him away from the soldiers so that they could then remove him from office and kill him.[206]

The promotion of Dio to the consulship in 229 was another slap in the face of the praetorians, and one that does not seem to have worked all that well. The praetorians forced him to withdraw from Rome when he was consul.[207] The relationship between the emperor and his army was not improved in the next couple of years, when developments on the eastern frontier altered the politics of the region beyond redemption. Four years before Dio's consulship Artabanus had been overthrown by the head of a noble family from the area of Fars in modern Iran.[208]

Ardashir, for that was the victor's name, found that his relations with Rome were dictated, in the first instance, by the need to secure the safety of his regime. The sons of Artabanus had found protection in Armenia, and the king of Media was openly opposed to the new regime. Hatra, whose rulers appear to have had dynastic links with the Arsacids, was hostile, and appears to have become much closer to Rome. The Arab tribes of northeastern Arabia appear to have remained loyal to the Arsacids, and Vologaeses V, the onetime rival of Artabanus, seems still to have been a force with whom Ardashir would have to reckon.

Ardashir moved rapidly to strengthen his position. Although he was defeated at Hatra and was not completely successful in his initial effort to dislodge his rivals from Armenia and Media, he seems to have been able to keep them in check.[209] He may also have seen the Roman Empire as a refuge for his foes.[210]

In the later 220s Persian pressure on the Roman frontier became acute, and the sort of discipline problems that had appeared earlier in other parts of the empire are attested in the garrison of Mesopotamia.[211] Dio stated (somewhat optimistically, as it turned out) that, although Ardashir was of no great consequence himself, he could become a threat because the troops were disloyal. Some deserted to him and others mutinied, murdering the governor of Mesopotamia.[212] These events took place before Dio's retirement to Nicaea in 229. Shortly after this, Ardashir launched a massive attack across the Roman frontier. Nisibis was besieged, Cappadocia may have been raided, and Syria was threatened.[213] Ardashir may even have attempted to install a pretender on the throne of Oshroene, which had been vacant since Caracalla had removed Abgar IX in 214.[214] A usurper named Uranius is said to have been associated with the Persian invasion and to have been active around Edessa.[215]

The Persian attack appears to have come in 230, and the legions in the area were plainly incapable of handling the crisis without reinforcements. It was a scenario that would be repeated in subsequent years, and serves to illustrate the weakness of the Severan frontier system in the face of a determined adversary. It took some time to assemble an adequate force and move it to the east, and there was not much that could be done in the meantime. Alexander did not leave Rome until the spring of 231. He crossed the Balkans, collecting units from the garrisons along the way, and reached Antioch in the late summer or early autumn, where there was a further delay to rest and train the newly arrived legions.[216] There was also a mutiny among the men of Legion II Traiana from Egypt and the local garrison.[217] The mutiny appears to have been quickly suppressed, but it does suggest that the young emperor (who was accompanied in the camp by his mother) was still not doing well with his troops.

Alexander's relationship with the army would not have been improved by the inconclusive (at best) result of the campaign. The three-pronged attack on Persia enabled Alexander to win back Oshroene and the Severan province of Mesopotamia in the center, but the accompanying attacks into Armenia and Mesopotamia ended in failure. Indeed, the southern column is said to have been all but annihilated.[218] According to Herodian, both sides suffered heavy losses, though it must be admitted that his statement about Persian casualties appears to be speculation based upon the fact that the Persians did not launch a major attack on the empire for several years after Alexander's departure.[219] Loss of face before the troops would soon prove fatal. But the attentive observer might have noted something more: a severe failure of intelligence and ability to appreciate the strength of the enemy. There is evidence for Arsacid survivors in Roman service, and it may be surmised that the routes of the northern and southern columns took them respectively in the direction of Adiabene and Mesene, both areas that were not yet added to the new Sasanian state.[220] Deserters and high-ranking traitors were natural sources of intelligence, but also, quite likely, in the way of exiles, highly unreliable ones. Exiles tend to think that the people whom they left behind are in general accord with their thinking on things, and, in other periods of history, may be found contributing to gross underestimation of the abilities of their former rivals. This might have been all the more dangerous as the results of the battle of the southern column, taken together with Macrinus' defeat at Nisibis, suggest that the antiquated tactical doctrines of the Roman army were now coming back to haunt it.

As Alexander led his army back from Persia, the Alamanni launched a raid across the Upper Rhine. According to Herodian this was considered a more serious threat than that posed by the Persians because the Germans were "practically adjacent neighbors to the Italians."[221] Despite these concerns, it appears to have taken Alexander a good deal of time to reach the new front. He returned to Rome first and appears to have celebrated a triumph over the Persians. This must have taken up the greater part of 233, and suggests that he did not take the field himself until the end of that year. By the end of 234 the Alamanni were driven back across the Rhine, and a Roman army was concentrated at Mainz for an invasion of their territory.[222] By this time the rank and file of the legions appear to have been deeply hostile: the invasion of Persia had not been a success, and when the western legions had returned to their bases, they had discovered that their homes had been ravaged by the barbarians. It is not surprising, therefore, that they were unwilling to support Alexander when a distinguished warrior, C. Julius Verus Maximinus, raised the standard of revolt. The emperor and his mother were killed in late February or early March 235.[223]

Maximinus Thrax

Maximinus' name suggests that he might have been the descendant of Roman soldiers who settled in the Danubian region during the early second century;

veterans, perhaps, of Trajan's campaigns. The wild slanders reported by Herodian and other sources about his barbarous heritage are no more than that. His appearance on coins suggests that he might have been in his fifties when he assumed the throne, and, therefore, that he might have entered the service during the reign of Septimius Severus.[224] It may be surmised that he rose through a series of equestrian posts during Severus' reign and then Caracalla's, and that by the time of his revolt he had obtained a high rank in the service. Throughout his reign he advertised his military machismo in stark contrast with his predecessor, whose soldiers had called him "the cheap little girl" and "the cowardly brat tied to his mother" as they killed him.[225]

A number of serious difficulties confronted Maximinus when he took the throne, and he does not seem to have handled them with a great deal of skill. One of these problems was his background. He was not the barbarian herdsman that his enemies made him out to be, but he was still an equestrian. Senators of the Severan aristocracy were apt to sneer at him or object to his pretensions, as they had to those of so many others in recent years. Maximinus had to work to build a consensus within the aristocracy, but this would take time and diplomacy; and he does not seem to have been well suited to the task. He appears to have been more comfortable on the battle-field, and even though he continued to employ members of the Severan aristocracy in the highest positions of government, he was not inclined to go to the lengths that Macrinus had to win support among the propertied classes at the expense of the soldiers. Instead, he tried to conciliate opinion by sending pictures of himself in combat with the enemies of Rome for public display in the capital.[226] A personal visit might have been more effective; but he may have felt that this would have been more dangerous than fighting the Germans. His fiscal policies made him extremely unpopular with the people of Rome, who thought, quite rightly, that their money was being given to the soldiers. He plainly did not realize that part of his role as emperor was still to play the urban politician, and that the consequence of failure in this role could be fatal.

There is good reason to think that Maximinus had serious financial problems. The soldiers who elevated him to the throne had complained that Alexander was cheap, as well as a coward.[227] Herodian says that when he addressed the recruits who first supported the revolution, Maximinus promised to double their pay and give them a large donative.[228] He then pictures him as a tyrant who fleeced the provinces to find money for the army with which he lived "like a man in a citadel."[229]

Massive payments were the order of the day, and a new emperor would certainly have been expected to be generous.[230] More than that, he had to be able to make good on his promises, and this might mean acquiring substantial quantities of hard cash above and beyond what was ordinarily carried: when Macrinus had promised twenty thousand sesterces, he only had the money on hand to pay out four thousand sesterces.[231] It may be assumed that Maximinus' promise to the men in 238 would have been on this scale and that there was not enough money at hand to make good on this promise, especially after four years of unremunerative warfare against Persia and the Alamanni. Indeed, the policies that Maximinus implemented after his accession appear to be no more than what was necessary to raise a substantial amount of money for a large, one-time payout to the troops. They could not support a long-term pay increase. In the course of the lurid tales of judicial murder for money and the theft of temple treasures, which Herodian sketches as Maximinus' policies, there is one fact.[232] This is that Maximinus reduced the amount of money for grain and other distributions at Rome, including, it seems, the subsidy for the state cult of deified emperors. It was a move that showed an impressive ability to alienate all levels of society in the capital, for the cult of the deified emperors may still have reflected something of the traditional senatorial ability to offer post-humous judgment on an emperor's reign.[233]

Maximinus' financial problem was important. In his effort to keep his promise to his men, he had taken a step that made him deeply unpopular at Rome, and the Roman plebs would prove to be one of the most important forces behind the revolt in 238. The notion that he promised a large dona-tive, which he could not pay immediately, might also serve to explain why, despite his military virtues, Maximinus was not particularly popular in the army. Furthermore, the honorific title *Maximiniana* appears to have been restricted to units on the Rhine and Danubian frontiers before 238.[234] This would suggest that he showed particular favor to the troops under his immediate command, and it might explain why a number of eastern legions supported the revolution of 238. Indeed, the slow and uneven distribution of largess might even explain why he was not uniformly popular with the troops under his direct command. There were two serious plots against his life, the conspiracies of Magnus and Quartinus, even before the uprising in 238.[235] The problem of uniting the army behind him may also explain why Maximinus could do nothing about the Persian invasion of Mesopotamia that took place in the year of his accession and resulted in the loss of the province.[236]

Herodian describes the extraordinary events of 238 in some detail, but he does not essay any explanation other than that the oppressive tactics of a procurator in Africa Proconsularis led to a revolt by the young men in that province.[237] They murdered him and elevated the elderly governor of their province, M. Antonius Gordianus Sempronianus Romanus Africanus, to the purple. He notified friends at Rome of his rebellion; they arranged for the murder of the praetorian prefect (or acting prefect) Vitalianus, and for the senate's acclamation.[238] The future emperor Valerian, already a consular by that point, appears to have been his messenger.[239] The senate then appointed a board of twenty to assist in the defense of the republic against the "tyrant" and to rally the provinces to their cause. Several of the eastern provinces responded favorably.[240] In March, the governor of Numidia, Capelianus, who had a long-standing grudge against Gordian, led Legion III Augusta to Carthage and crushed the revolt there.[241] Gordian's son died in battle, and Gordian committed suicide. When the news of this disaster reached Rome, the senate proclaimed a pair of elderly members of the board of twenty, Pupienus and Balbinus, as rulers in his place. This led to a riot, sparked by friends of the deceased Gordian, and Gordian's thirteen-year-old grandson was proclaimed as Caesar to Pupienus and Balbinus.[242] An inscription from Aegeai in Cilicia attests well to the message that they circulated about the empire: it honors Gordian, the older Gordians, the Severi, Pupienus, and Balbinus. Maximinus is an excrescence who needed to be removed from the historical record.[243] None of this sat well with the Praetorian Guard. After an inflammatory speech by a member of the senate, and the murder of several of their men in the Forum, the guard went to war with the population of Rome for a period of several days.[244] They were driven back to their camp, after much destruction, by a force consisting of the urban plebs and gladiators from the imperial training grounds in the city. We are not told specifically how the fighting ended, though it would appear that the guard surrendered after the cutoff of its water supply.[245]

Maximinus invaded Italy at the end of March and came to a halt before the powerfully defended city of Aquileia. The siege dragged on for some time. Some people thought it was a miracle,[246] while Maximinus' troops became increasingly bored, sick, hungry, and discontented. In early May they murdered the emperor and his son.

The events of 238 are, at first glance, among the most remarkable in the entire history of Rome. A reigning emperor was overthrown by an aristocratic conspiracy, supported by the urban population of Rome, but otherwise by little available force. The Praetorian Guard, which had remained loyal to him, was besieged in its camp for the bulk of the campaign, and, although various governors declared for the rebels, none was in a position to supply immediate aid. Examined from a broader perspective, they reveal the tensions of government in the post-Severan world: deep divisions within the governing bureaucracies of the empire, and the need for the emperor to be able to juggle the demands of radically different constituencies. To some degree, of course, these divisions had always been present. The urban plebs had always disliked the Praetorian Guard, soldiers had interests that did not necessarily mesh with those of their generals, members of the senate were rarely in accord with imperial freedmen. Within the senate itself, there had long been a division between members of older families and new men. But where the emperors of the Antonine age appear to have been able to balance the interests of different groups, Severus and his sons had tended to rule by exacerbating potential points of discord. This is perhaps most notable within the senate (for which the evidence is best), as the distinction between men who pursued careers that were primarily associated with military commands and those whose careers took them into civil administration becomes stronger.[247] The notion that a senator should be competent in all areas, a long-standing feature of senatorial ideology, was increasingly occluded by the demands of specialization. There was no point in giving a person like Dio command in a garrisoned province, as his whole life experience made it very difficult indeed for him to understand his soldiers. Ulpian failed as praetorian prefect for similar reasons, and Maximinus as emperor because, it seems, he simply did not understand the whole range of the job, and he failed to realize that he needed to be able to deal with people unlike himself. The fact that careers begun under Alexander Severus tended to continue without obvious interruption is perhaps less significant than the evidence for widespread disloyalty to his regime within this class.

Shortly after the murder of Maximinus, both Pupienus and Balbinus were killed by their soldiers, and if the imperial claims of the two Gordians, as well as of Maximinus' young son, are allowed, that would mean that no fewer than six claimants to the throne were killed within five months.[248] The slaughter at the top underlines, above all else, the new relationship between the emperor and the army. Plainly no emperor had a de facto claim to the loyalty of his men. Plainly the oath of allegiance was an empty formula. The demands of soldiers, especially in the wake of Severus' politicization of military pay, had serious consequences. A Macrinus or a Maximinus had diffi-culty making good on the promises that were extracted from him as the price of his ascension to power. Even more serious was a failure to acknowledge the formula of accession, which placed acclamation by the military ahead of senatorial approval. Herodian says that Pupienus and Balbinus were doomed because

> The soldiers . . . were seething with anger inside; they disliked the
> acclaim given by the people, actually disapproved of the noble birth
> of the two men, and hated having emperors chosen by the senate.
> (Herod. 8.8.1, trans. Whittaker)

The soldiers in question were members of the Praetorian Guard, and they further feared that the emperors, who had surrounded themselves with Maximinus' former German guard, would dismiss them as Severus had dismissed the murderers of Pertinax. After they had slaughtered the two old men, they proclaimed the young Gordian as emperor, saying that they were doing what the people wanted anyway.[249] In form they were asserting their prerogative to have the first say in the succession.

The thirteen-year-old Gordian was in no position to run the empire on his own, and the administration of the state passed soon to a committee of advisers who took it upon themselves to heal the wounds caused by the civil war. Men who had remained loyal to Maximinus seem to have flourished, and leaders of the rebellious cause were either retired or, in one case, executed within a few years.[250] An effort to negotiate the divisions within the ruling classes, an effort that is now lost to us in anything but the most impressionistic way offered by study of career patterns, was not accompanied by any success in handling the problem of the army, highly politicized and increasingly inept. In addition to issues of discipline and tactical readiness, an increasing crisis in state finance was caused by the need to find, with the inelastic tools available, the hard currency to pay bills. The silver content of the denarius had slipped to around 45 percent in the time of Alexander, and it was set upon a downward course from there.[251]

Issues of finance, the military, and institutional structure are significant enough in and of themselves. But they are also, at least to some degree, features of an overall mentality of government, and of a governing class. The first half of the third century was a remarkably productive one as far as the surviving record of ancient literature goes, reflective as it may be of general attitudes. And it is thus to the culture of the Severan age that some attention must now be turned.

5

INTELLECTUAL
TRENDS IN THE EARLY
THIRD CENTURY

Fish, food, and sophists

There is a story that Severus was insulted by a philosopher named Agesilaus, who had failed to join a group that assembled to greet him when he arrived at Anazarbus in Cilicia (southern Turkey). Severus responded by exiling the philosopher to the island of Meleda in the Adriatic, where he lived in the company of his son, Oppian, a young man of poetical bent who had elected to join him. Oppian wrote poems on hunting and fishing and some time after the death of Severus ventured to Rome to recite them before Caracalla.[1] He gained a hearing, and an admirer. Caracalla asked him what he would like as a reward, and Oppian responded that his only desire was to return to Anazarbus with his father. He obtained his request, and an additional fortune; Caracalla is said to have given him one aureus for every verse of his poem.

The story is a pleasant one and may even be true; unfortunately, the Oppian who figures in it cannot be identified with either of two Oppians whose work has survived. One of these Oppians wrote *On Fishing*, a work that is plainly dedicated to Marcus Aurelius and Commodus, though it is plausible that he was from Cilicia (from Corycus rather than Anazarbus).[2] The other Oppian, who wrote a poem entitled *On Hunting*, identified himself as being from Syria. That said, the two poems have much in common. Both Oppians are remarkable for the ability to get the names of fishes and beasts to scan, and for a sort of empathy with the animal kingdom. The author of *On Fishing* declares the hunting of dolphins, whom he regards as the lords of the sea, to be immoral, denouncing those who hunt them, while showing a real knowledge of their techniques. He can tell his readers that all the denizens of the deep who bear living offspring love them, and that the cuttlefish has devised a cunning way of hunting.[3] For the author of the *On Hunting*, elephants are possessed of prophetic souls so that they will recognize the times of their own death.[4] The wild ass brays like a mother who has seen her son killed before her eyes in "grievous war," and the defeated lion evokes the image of an old boxer going down before the blows of his adversary.[5] But humans still need to hunt them, and it is the techniques of capture that occupy the fourth book of *On Hunting* and the bulk of *On Fishing*.

Taken together, these two poems are a guide to human knowledge of the natural world: the author of *On Fishing* tells his audience where to find the fish, what the character of each is, and how it may be snared. For him the sea remains a dangerous place, for fish have no sense of justice save to eat any they can, and Justice herself has withdrawn from the depths.[6] As such it is to be contrasted to the land, where justice reigns through the deeds of the emperors. The sea can be controlled only because humans have the knowledge to do so. The ability to make lists, an ability amply demonstrated by both authors, implies the ability to control. The ability to transform a list of fishes into hexameter verse implies an ability to domesticate the dangerous forces of nature. The desire to list, to control, and to order was a powerful one. Indeed, there may be no better example of this tendency than the remarkable work on dining composed by one of the readers of the Cilician Oppian.[7] This reader was Athenaeus of Naucratis; the book that he wrote, whose title may be translated *Doctors at Dinner*, gives a course-by-course survey of proper dining habits. It does so through the learned discourse of a group of intellectuals at a dinner party.

Although the actual beginning of the work is lost to us, enough is preserved to make it reasonably clear how the scene was set and how the conversations began. The story is set at the house of a wealthy Roman named Larensis, who had assembled many of the wisest men of the time, including philosophers, a jurist named Masurius, some orators, a musician, a philologist named Ulpian, and some doctors. The collection of wise men would seem to be intended to provide a list of approved academics, drawn from across much of the second century, for it includes not only Galen but also Plutarch. It is placed in the reign of Severus with glances back to the golden age of Marcus,[8] and as the story develops through endless speeches, it evolves into a sort of literary comedy of manners.[9]

The first three books, which were reconstructed, probably before the ninth century, from summaries in other authors, contained discourse on a variety of subjects ranging from other books about dining, to the eating habits of heroes in Homer, to boundaries, dancing, and drinking (among other things). When the full text begins, most of the way through book 3, the diners are at work discussing various items on the menu, beginning with a plate of liver, with the aid of countless quotations from earlier authors. The point is for the diners to show complete command of the subject, and to overtrump each other with displays of literary knowledge:

> The next dish to be brought in was fried liver wrapped in "fold-over," the so-called *epiplos*, which Philetaerus in Terus calls *epoploon*. After gazing at it Cynulcus said, "Tell us, learned Ulpian, whether liver encased is mentioned anywhere."

He answered, "Show us first in what author *epiplos* is used of the fatty caul."

Thereupon Myrtilus took up the challenge and said "The word *epiplos* for 'caul' occurs in the *Bacchants* of Epicharmus: 'the leader he hid the caul'; also in his *Envoys*: 'round the line and the caul.' So too, Ion of Chios in his *Sojournings*: 'hiding in the caul.' You are reserving the caul, my dear Ulpian, against the time when you are wrapped in it and consumed, and so rid us all of your questionings."

(Ath. *Deip.* 3.106–7, trans. Gulick)

And so on for the rest of the extant fifteen books. What is significant here is not the level of pretension, but the fact that the theoretical members of the party can control the literature on dining from memory and trace the moments of their meal to other examples in the past. As members of the dominant class, they maintain their position in their society by their ability to demonstrate their command of precedent. For them linguistic usage is as important as legal precedents in the works of jurists. They are not simply looking back in time to some golden age of fried liver, but rather creating a new age of gastronomy through their command of the past. It is the same style that can be detected in Oppian when he begins to categorize fish in terms of where they live:

Fishes differ in breed and kind and their path in the sea, and not all fishes have the same distribution: some live by the low shores, eating sand and whatever grows in the sand – the Sea-horse, the swift Cuckoo-fish, the yellow Erythinus, the Citharus, the red Mullet ... others feed in the shallows and the mud – the Skate and the monster tribes of the Ox-ray, and the terrible Sting-ray and the rightly named Cramp-fish.

(*Hal.* 1.92–97, 102–4, trans. Mair, adapted)

The similarity in technique, the assertion of command through listing, is striking. The technique in both cases echoes that of grammarians, those masters of language who determined propriety of speech and the authenticity of texts and administered the rites of passage into cultured society.

The link between culture and the right to hold power in civil society was intensified by the exclusive nature of grammatical education.[10] The dominant class could restrict membership in its ranks by demanding that its members pass the grammar test, by insisting that its members pass through the same educational curriculum. It is scarcely surprising therefore that the literature of this class should reflect the nature of teaching, with its insistence upon careful study of arcane usage and rote memorization. Those who could not pass the test were barbarians, peasants, slaves, illiterates, children, and women.[11] Within the educational structure of the Roman world, knowledge of grammar was scarcely an elementary exercise; it was rather the key to admission to the higher school of rhetoric.[12] The great intellectual was also to be a person with a prodigious memory who could recite sections from the approved texts in the curriculum. Just as Aulus Gellius would discuss a man like Favorinus, who could deliver an extemporaneous lecture on proper linguistic style, replete with specific examples, so too would Athenaeus claim that various of the people in his book possessed such skills, and then have them demonstrate it at length. The educated man was a man who commanded examples and was familiar with forms of categorization. One need not read the whole book to be familiar with the crucial lessons to be learned. Students were taught to produce brief summaries of important stories so that they could employ them as needed in an oration. A book of extracts was not simply some mindless exercise; rather it was a tool for those who sought control. Thus at the end of the first century the younger Pliny was offered a fortune for the notes of his learned uncle, and Aulus Gellius, in the middle of the second century, could produce a learned discourse on the genre into which his *Attic Nights* would fit.[13] As Aulus tells his readers, he is not putting down all that he knows (this would be boring):

> I took few items from them [his notes], confining myself to those which, by furnishing a quick and easy short-cut, might lead active and alert minds to a desire for independent learning and to the study of the useful arts, or would save those who are already fully occupied with the other duties of life from an ignorance of words and things which is assuredly shameful and boorish.
>
> (*Attic Nights*, Praef. 12, trans. Rolfe)

Lest any be mistaken, those who are too busy to keep up their researches are not aspiring members of the upper classes who are looking to Aulus as a sort of bluffer's guide to the classics. The intended readers are, in the first instance, Aulus' sons, and then others who might participate in the sort of discussions that he records. They are people who are at home in Greek and Latin and would be caught dead rather than be heard uttering words in the vernacular of the street.[14]

Aelian, who was a somewhat younger contemporary of Athenaeus, may hold pride of place in the Severan era for his production of useful books. He wrote *On the Characteristics of Animals* in seventeen books, a short book of twenty letters from farmers, one or two books on providence and/or divine signs, and a fourteen-book *Poikilê Historia*, a work that is somewhat confusingly known in English as the *Historical Miscellany*.[15] Like Aulus Gellius, who completed his *Attic Nights* around 180, Aelian does not present his material in any sort of order. The lack of order is, in a sense, its own ordering principle, for it reflects the broad range of both the author's and his reader's cultural interests. In Aelian's case, it also reflects the remarkably vague (it might be better to say nonexistent) line between things that actually happened, or could actually be observed in nature, and the stories that people told. That is the point of the title: *poikilê* does not mean "miscellany," but would be more properly translated "many-colored," "variable," or "complex." *Historia*, in his usage, is not our word "history" so much as it is used in its more general meaning of narrative, and that is what the book is, an ever-changing narrative, offering stories of every sort.[16] The very first section of book 1 concerns the stomachs of octopuses, the second is about spiders, the third about clever Egyptian frogs. In book 1, section 10, readers learn that lions heal themselves by eating monkeys, and in section 11 that the Cretans are expert archers who shoot goats. The animals then eat a plant called dittany so that the arrows fall out of their wounds. One of the longest sections in the *Poikilê Historia* is the story about Atalanta, daughter of Iasion, and what a modern reader would call her mythological life in the wild.[17] Such stories are clearly meant for amusement. But there are other comments from which any educated person might take some comfort. For Aelian will also remind his readers,

> The Divine Power does well not to prolong tyrants to the third generation; it either uproots tyrants at once like pine trees or demonstrates its strength against the children. In the whole course of Greek history the tyrannies recorded as having passed to future generations are those of Hieron of Syracuse, of the Leuconidae at the Bosporus, and the Cypselidae at Corinth.
>
> (*Misc.* 6.13, trans. Wilson)

Aelian may well have had such thoughts in his mind on the day in 222 that Philostratus of Lemnos met him,

> holding a book in his hands and reading it aloud in an indignant and emphatic voice, and asked him what he was studying. He replied, "I have composed an indictment of Gynnis, for that is the name I call the tyrant who has just been put to death, because by every sort of wanton wickedness he disgraced the Roman Empire." On which Philostratus retorted, "I should admire you for it if you had indicted him while he was alive." For he said that while it takes a real man to try to curb a living tyrant, anyone can trample on him while he is down.
>
> (Phil. *V. Soph.* 625, trans. Wright)

Despite the negative spin to this story, it would appear that our source for the incident, Philostratus the Athenian, admired Aelian. He stated that Aelian, though a Roman, had perfect command of Attic Greek and was "worthy of all praise . . . because by hard work he achieved purity of speech though he lived in a city that employed another language."[18] What Philostratus also thought admirable was that, although Aelian was called a sophist by sophists, he recognized that he was by nature unsuited to declamation and gave himself over to writing the works that have come down to us. As for his politics, we can certainly see that they were in keeping with those of a Dio or a Marius Maximus. Like Dio he seems to have enjoyed making up rude names for Elagabalus – *Gynnis* implies "a feminine man"; Dio routinely refers to Elagabalus as either "pseudo-Antoninus" or Sardanapalus, the latter being the legendary last king of Assyria who was noted for effeminate conduct.[19]

There are many senses in which Philostratus the Athenian may be seen to share Aelian's general intellectual direction. For Philostratus' two great works were one an act of cataloguing, and the other a grand fantasy about Apollonius of Tyana. The work of cataloguing is *The Lives of the Sophists*, and in it the power of the catalogue as a tool for cultural control may perhaps be seen at its most potent. *The Lives of the Sophists* stands today, as it did in antiquity, as the defining work of Greek culture in the second and third centuries AD.[20] The work was sufficiently influential that in the fourth century Eunapius of Sardis felt that it had corrupted understanding of the truly important aspects of Greek culture by concentrating on sophists rather than philosophers.[21] The theme of Philostratus' work was the nature of rhetoric in his own time, and the orators who had created the dominant style to which he was attached.

> Ancient sophistic, even when it propounded philosophical themes, used to discuss them diffusely and at length; for it discoursed on courage, it discoursed on justice, on the heroes and gods, and how the universe has been fashioned into its present shape. But the sophistic that followed it, which we must not call "new," for it is old, but rather "second," sketched the types of the poor man and the rich, of princes and tyrants, and handled arguments that are concerned with definite and special themes for which history shows the way.
>
> (*V. Soph.* 481)

With remarkable sleight of hand he thus creates a genre of classical rhetoric to authorize the significance of the practice of his own day – to be powerful, culture must be old – and justifies its concentration on themes of class and politics that dominate his own time. He then proceeds by making a list of the sophists who counted in the creation of the genre as he sees it. Aeschines is awarded pride of place as the founder of the style, and an explanation is offered as to why both Aeschines and Demosthenes used the word *sophist* as a term of abuse.[22] It is because people in an Athenian jury were suspicious of sophists, who were felt to be too eloquent for their own good. He then proceeds to point out that, as a result, the term was applied too loosely to be truly meaningful, as it was used for philosophers as well as for real declaimers. By making a list, he can then clarify his point, beginning with Eudoxus of Cnidus, who flourished in the fourth century, and stress the point that even if a person was regarded as a philosopher, he might still be called a sophist if he were truly eloquent.[23]

The tale of the philosophers who could also be called sophists then runs from Eudoxus through Leon of Byzantium and Dias of Ephesus (also active in the fourth century BC) to Carneades (second century BC) and Philostratus the Egyptian who declaimed for Cleopatra. The judgment on the sixth person whom he lists, Theomnestus of Naucratis (possibly an associate of Caesar's murderer, Brutus), is allowed to sum up the basic point: he was "by profession a philosopher, but the elaborate and rhetorical style of his speeches caused him to be classed with the sophists."[24] He then treats two of the major figures of the late first and early second centuries, Dio of Prusa and Favorinus of Arles, as the culminating examples of this category.[25]

Having completed his survey of philosophic sophists, Philostratus returns to Gorgias of Leontini, the fifth-century BC sophist whom he regards as the founder of rhetoric, and moves on through other figures of the fifth and fourth centuries, such as Protagoras, Critias, Antiphon, Isocrates, and Aeschines. Indeed, Aeschines is the last of the great sophists, in his view, to have practiced before the emergence of the Roman monarchy. The next person worthy of note is Nicetes of Smyrna, who was active in the time of Nero.[26] From this point onwards, the great sophists are men of the second and third centuries. The first book ends with a brief notice concerning the career of Secundus the Athenian. The first biography in the second book is that of Philostratus' hero, Herodes Atticus, an ancestor of Gordian I, to whom the book as a whole was dedicated some time before the extraordinary events of 238 began to unfold. The book ends with Philostratus' statement that he cannot write biographies of three close friends lest he be thought overly partial. What is perhaps even more striking is that in all of this he sees the efflorescence of Greek culture as a product of the Roman monarchy. Great sophists are treated with respect by emperors who see their attainments as being central to the government of the empire.

What Philostratus accomplished with his list of approved sophists was to define the dominant culture in terms of precisely these same practitioners. Philosophers did not matter unless, like Dio and Favorinus, they could be defined as sophists as well. Poets are certainly not part of this charmed circle, any more than are historians or satirists. If the impact of Philostratus' view was to marginalize a Dio, a Lucian, or a Herodian, it also had the impact of expanding the notion of what constituted a sophist well beyond the Greek heartland. Favorinus was, after all, a Gaul with undescended testicles, and Aelian was a Roman.[27] Heliodorus, whom, as we have seen, Philostratus did not much like, was from Arabia.[28] Philostratus' dislike did not stem from his origin, but rather from his conduct. Heraclides was a Lycian, and Marcianus, the one and only student of Apollonius of Naucratis (who aspired to the chair of rhetoric at Athens), was from Doliche in Syria.[29] Pausanias the sophist came from Caesarea in Cappadocia, and Hadrian of Tyre was a Phoenician.[30] Cilicia produced Alexander the Clay Plato, Hermogenes, and Philagrus.[31] Aspasius was, as we saw in another context, from Ravenna.[32] If Aspasius or Aelian or Favorinus could become sophists, and if emperors could be shown to be respectful of their learning, desiring them to perform, rewarding them with chairs of critical posts in government, then Philostratus' point that rhetoric was king and that it defined the nexus of culture and power must be true. This was, of course, the same point that Aulus was making about his role in Latin letters, or that a Fronto made when he gathered his correspondence with members of the imperial family for publication.

The point is not whether Philostratus exaggerates the importance of certain sophists (that is too obvious to require argument). It is rather that Philostratus constructs his exclusive image of the nature of power through manipulating the exclusive power of a list. He supports his construction through the power of defining the criteria for success, be it a chair of rhetoric, an imperial appointment, or the trouncing of a rival in a public disputation. The position of diverse emperors in his narrative obtains the same place as invocations to the emperor in the work of an Oppian; it is to set a specific work in the context of approved discourse.

The sophist and the sage

The similarity between Aelian and Philostratus does not end with their use of lists. Equally significant is their ability to move with freedom between the real and the fanciful. Philostratus' other great work was entitled *In Honor of Apollonius of Tyana*. The inspiration for his work was allegedly a man named Damis,

> by no means stupid, who formerly dwelt in the ancient city of Ninus. He resorted to Apollonius in order to study wisdom, and having shared, by his own account, his wanderings abroad, wrote an account of them . . . a certain kinsman of Damis drew the attention of the empress Julia to the documents, containing these memoirs hitherto unknown. Now I belonged to the circle of the empress, for she was a devoted admirer of all rhetorical exercises; and she commanded me to recast and edit these essays paying more attention to the style and diction of them.
>
> (Phil. *V. Apoll.* 1.3, trans. Conybeare,
> slightly adapted)

It is hard to know where the fiction here begins and ends. Damis certainly did not exist, and hence one may feel free to doubt the existence of his relatives, and the connection to the city of Ninus, known as Mespila in later ages. Indeed the mention of Ninus' city may have been intended as a signifier of the fiction, calling forth an image of the ancient rather than modern site.[33] Suspicion should also attach to the story of Julia and her orders. If there was no Damis, and thus no memoirs, then her instruction must also be false. The question of her circle of learned men, which long bedeviled modern scholarship, has now been put safely to rest, having been shown to include only people like Philostratus and Philiscus rather than the men of great influence.[34] That she, like any important person, kept learned people around her for fun is not to be doubted, but that is not the real point of this passage. Julia's position looks like another authorizing detail intended to give the work a claim to importance precisely because it has a connection with the court. An empress could be the alleged audience of works that she may or may not have ever read, but which also used her name to give them authority. The imperial dedications in the words of the two Oppians served the same function: they establish a context for the author that continues to lend authority to the work well after the point of composition, and may even have helped inspire the fictions with which later scholars surrounded their works. While it would be pleasant to think that Philostratus read his *Apollonius* to the empress, there is no necessary reason to believe that he did, and, even if he did do so, that the main reason why this section was included was to tell Julia what she had already done.[35] It was to assure readers that the highest authority supported the fictions that followed.

The tale of Apollonius' wanderings takes the reader in two directions, directions whose convergence around the figure of Apollonius enables the reader to perceive the importance of Philostratus' view of the connection between his cultural values and the structure of authority. Apollonius journeys to the east to meet the sages of India, to Egypt to meet the "naked sophists," to the centers of Greek culture and to Rome.[36] In all places, and all venues, Apollonius makes a contribution. He also encounters thought that is recognizably Greek. Thus the king of India who gives him directions to the Brahmins was reading Euripides' *Sons of Hercules* when he was given the news that he would be king.[37] The journey to India itself follows those of both Alexander and Dionysus, and, not surprisingly, the king of India can give him precise information on where Alexander stopped.[38] Apollonius too would see that point, marked by an inscription of Alexander, and close by an enormous monument of the conqueror.[39] When Apollonius reaches the castle of the sages, he finds that Dionysus had once been there and tried to storm the place. The marks of the Pans who died in the assault on the place could still be seen, and in the castle there were statues of the Greek gods, "set up by these Indians and worshipped with Greek rites."[40]

What is perhaps most impressive about the fiction is the way that Philostratus can support it with the marks of authenticity from historical accounts.[41] Autopsy and local informants of high standing prove his points. A quotation from an alleged speech of Apollonius, *To the Egyptians*, is produced to prove that he actually saw the Indian sages (whom he calls the Brahmins), and it is explicated on the basis of Damis' *Memoirs*.[42] The landscape through which he passes, the ethnographies that he includes, echo the style of Herodotus and historians who wrote about Alexander the Great. Apollonius, as they had, will record the existence of the Fish Eaters, and he will confirm an observation of Nearchus, who sailed with Alexander's fleet from India.[43] The opinions that he expresses are informed by contemporary debates. Thus, in the midst of India, Apollonius will lecture Damis on prophetic dreams, and how dreams that one has under the influence of alcohol cannot fit into this category.[44] Apollonius will then receive confirmation of his views on prophecy from the leader of the Indian sages.[45] On other occasions Philostratus has him debate true prophecy in Egypt and explain how his diet made him capable of perceiving things just before they happened.[46] He explicitly clears Apollonius of the charge that he was a wizard by saying:

> Wizards, whom for the most part I reckon to be the most unfortunate of mankind, claim to alter the course of destiny, by having recourse either to the torture of lost spirits or to barbaric sacrifices, or to certain incantations or anointings; and many of them when accused of such practices have admitted that they were adepts of such practices. But Apollonius submitted himself to the decrees of the Fates, and foretold things that must come to pass; and his foreknowledge was gained not through wizardry, but from what the gods revealed to him.
>
> (Phil. *V. Apoll.* 5.12, trans. Conybeare)

Insofar as we know anything about the historical Apollonius, the two things that he appears to have been known for were healing and prophecy. A monument was on display at Ephesus in the fourth century that commemorated his defeat of a plague demon; Dio told a story about how he described the murder of Domitian as it happened; and a Syrian tradition recorded talismans that he made against disease.[47] The two activities were not unrelated, as mortals would turn to the gods for their cures, and doctors might regard divinities as associates. Galen reported that a vision helped him perform an operation on himself.[48] Apollonius is seen as working in the same framework when he visited the temple of Asclepius at Pergamon, giving "hints to the supplicants of the god about what to do to obtain favorable dreams," and healed some of them himself.[49] Cassius Dio, as we have seen, sought order in the human world on the basis of signs that proved that what befell him and his contemporaries was part of some divine plan. He would no doubt have agreed with the tenor of sentiments that Philostratus puts into the mouth of Apollonius, "If you should kill the person who is fated to become tyrant after you, he will return to life."[50] There was no way to control such things.

In many contexts prophecy provided an alternative to acceptance of the status quo, offered an alternative mode of interpretation to those offered by the dominant classes. The question of what constituted proper divine information was just too important to ignore, and it certainly could not be left to just anyone. It was a sign that the gods cared. But the realm of prophecy was also the playground of frauds and charlatans (which is what Lucian thought that Apollonius was). At roughly the same time that Philostratus wrote, Oenomaeus the Cynic produced a book attacking the traditional oracles of the Greek world. Artemidorus of Daldis produced a different kind of book, this one setting forth a novel theory of the interpretation of prophetic dreams, and the oracle of Zeus Belus entered actively into the realm of imperial politics.[51] Septimius Severus had worried enough about various forms of Egyptian divination that he had tried to ban them when he was in Egypt. The decree that went out over his name read (in part):

> Encountering many who believed themselves to be deceived by the practices of divination, I quickly considered it necessary, in order that no danger should ensue upon their foolishness, clearly herein to enjoin all people to abstain from this hazardous inquisitiveness. Therefore let no man through oracles, that is, by means of written documents supposedly granted under divine influence, nor by the means of the parade of images or suchlike charlatanry, pretend to know things beyond human ken and profess [to know] the obscurity of things to come, neither let any man put himself at the disposal of those who inquire about this or answer in any way whatsoever. If any person is detected adhering to this profession, let him be persuaded that he will be handed over to the extreme penalty.
>
> (Trans. J. Rea, "A New Version of P. Yale Inv. 299," *ZPE* 27 (1977): 153–54)[52]

One thing that Apollonius did was to prevent the cities of Ionia from paying money to false prophets who styled themselves Egyptians and Chaldaeans.[53]

Prophecy was not the only issue of contemporary importance that Philostratus' Apollonius would take a position on. He decried departures from traditional Greek practice when he visited Greece, commented upon the evils of animal sacrifice (a significant theme in some polytheist circles), criticized Greeks who took Latin names, and lectured on civic patriotism.[54] He also dealt with emperors. Philostratus has him excite the enmity of Nero and Domitian. He has him predict Vespasian's rise to power and discuss good government with him. He tells Titus how he will die. In the dialogue with Vespasian, and in the defense that Philostratus writes for Apollonius before Domitian, the philosopher is made to say various things about good government. In the speech to Domitian he clearly distinguishes the people within the empire from those without, suggesting that he identified all subjects of the empire as being equally valued subjects. But in the dialogue with Vespasian he suggests that Greek speakers be made governors of Greek-speaking provinces. There are various ways to take this statement; one would be in the context of his criticisms of Greeks who did not respect their past. In this sense the predominant message might be that Greek culture ought to have a special place that is free from Roman interference. But Greek culture can be found anywhere – at Cadiz in Spain, as in India.[55] Another reading would be that Apollonius recommended that every people remain true to its traditions. Philostratus was interested in Greek culture and Greek traditions. He honored emperors who also respected those traditions, and he claimed authority for his sentiments through claiming association with the court. It might be easier to read his view as being that the Roman Empire was compatible with the preservation of local traditions, and that it was up to people in each part of the empire to protect the purity of whatever traditions they had. As important as the role of the gods on earth might be, the issue of how to maintain the past in the face of an ever-changing present may have seemed every bit as crucial.

The war at Troy

In the course of his journeys, the Philostratean Apollonius has the opportunity to visit Troy, and there he spends the night on the tomb of Achilles. While we do not now know where this tomb was, it is very likely to have been one of the man-made tumuli that are in the Trojan plain and, in the later part of the nineteenth century, had attracted the attention of antiquarians like Frank Calvert.[56] These tumuli are substantial and, as Calvert showed when he dug one of them, do indeed contain burials of the archaic period.[57] As Philostratus correctly suggests in his narrative, they are at some distance from the site of Troy, and they are very large.

According to Philostratus' story, Apollonius obtained a vision of Achilles, who commanded him to rid himself of a sophistic companion named Antisthenes, who claimed descent from Priam, and to carry a message to the Thessalians.[58] This was to find an image of Palamedes, the legendary inventor of Greek letters, and establish a shrine to him. Philostratus' interest in Palamedes had also manifested itself while Apollonius was in India, for it was there that he is said to have met a boy who had in him the soul of the hero (which, of course, also confirmed the Pythagorean doctrine of the transmigration of souls). The leader of the sages had told him that Palamedes had found that his two bitterest enemies at Troy were Odysseus, who arranged his death, and Homer, who left him out of his epic. Philostratus himself claims to have seen the image that Apollonius erected, which was a statue whose base was inscribed "to the Divine Palamedes," by the side of an archaic tomb. He also records what he says to have been Apollonius' prayer:

> O Palamedes, forget the wrath, through which you once raged at the Achaeans, and grant that mortals may grow more numerous and wise. Verily Palamedes, on account of whom there is eloquence, on account of whom there are Muses, on account of whom there is myself.
>
> (Phil. *V. Apoll.* 4.13, trans. Conybeare)

The appearance of Palamedes in this context, as a sort of patron of sophists, underlines the importance of the Homeric cycle in the era of Philostratus, and the very practical way that it was expressed.

Homeric archaeology did not begin with Calvert or Schliemann. It was a feature of life in the second and third centuries AD, when ancient monuments were recognized as such and attached to the world of the poems. There is no reason to doubt that the scepter of Agamemnon that Pausanias reported as being the most revered object at Chaeronea in Boeotia was still there in the time of Philostratus, or that the spear of Achilles had departed from its privileged position at Phaselis in Lycia.[59] So too we may well suppose that the letter that Sarpedon sent from Troy to Xanthus and Lycia was just as readily available for inspection by famous people as it had been in the first century AD, when Vespasian's associate, Mucianus, saw it.[60]

The truth of the stories was vouchsafed by the fact that a person could go see where they took place, could see treasures taken from Troy, could meet descendants of the heroes, and even go to visit the heroes themselves. The spear that was at Phaselis was of bronze, and so was the sword of Memnon that was in the temple of Asclepius at Nicomedia, proving that Homer was correct to say that the heroes fought with bronze weapons.[61] The tomb of Ajax in the Troad was huge, as befitted the hero, and the tomb of Agamemnon said to be within the ruined walls of Mycenae was said to be rich in gold (which makes it all the more interesting that the gold was still there when Schliemann found it).[62] While the Homeric poems were the foundational texts of Greek culture, the story of Troy and its value in the second century went well beyond anything that Homer had to say. The people of Phrygia, for instance, could point to the road that Memnon took through their country on his way to battle, and the career of Memnon had been massively embellished by the identification of the monument of Amenhotep near Thebes as being his. Although there were dissenting voices (Pausanias notes that the locals called him Phamenopha, and others claimed that he was Sesostris), the identification of the monument was an important addition to the story.[63] Memnon had conquered the Persians prior to his journey to Troy, making him a model for the ambitions of Roman emperors in his own right.[64] Even more important was the notion that Homer, who, it was generally conceded, had lived well after the event, could get things wrong. He was biased in favor of characters like Odysseus, whom later tradition portrayed in a much less favorable light than he had. And he had told only part of the story. Both Palamedes and Memnon, who figured heavily in the imagination of the third century, were not characters in his work.

According to the *Cypria*, the oldest poem that described the early years of the war, Palamedes was killed by Diomedes and Odysseus while he was fishing.[65] This story was transformed and embellished by later tradition, according to which Odysseus forged a letter to him from Priam, promising him gold, and then buried the promised sum in his tent.[66] This tale of Palamedes figures heavily in a third work composed by Philostratus, the remarkable dialogue on Homeric heroes, the *Heroicus*.[67] This work is cast as a dialogue between the owner of a vineyard on the Gallipoli peninsula and a Phoenician merchant who had wandered inland while his ship was held up in harbor, and was worried by a dream.[68] In this dream he had appeared to be reading the catalogue of Greek heroes in book 2 of the *Iliad* and calling them onto a ship. His initial (false) reading of the dream was that he would be delayed further because encounters with the dead portended such a fate. He soon learned the truth: that he was to hear many stories about the heroes, stories that were supported on the highest authority.[69] This authority was none other than Protesilaus, the first man killed in the Trojan War, and who routinely visited the vinegrower. It transpired that the vinegrower owned the land around the massive tumulus believed to be that of the hero outside the city of Elaious.[70] In Philostratus' lifetime this tumulus was adorned with a statue of the hero standing on the prow of a ship.[71]

The Palamedes to whom Protesilaus introduces the vinegrower is a figure remarkably like Apollonius. He is able to avert a plague by advising the Greeks at Troy on how to improve their diet (like Apollonius he recommended a vegetarian regime), and he was able to explain the causes of an eclipse, establishing himself as a founder of astronomy. This claim, like those that Apollonius could find traces of Greek learning as far as the land of India, reflects a certain desire to support the claims of Greek learning against those who attributed the discovery of wisdom to peoples of the East. It is a tendency that is further reflected in his correction of the tradition that the Memnon of the *Aethiopis*, the poem in the epic cycle that narrated events after the death of Hector, was the same as the Egyptian king. In Protesilaus' version the Memnon at Troy was a Trojan who only became significant after Hector was killed.[72]

The literary form of the dialogue was a popular way of exploring issues of all sorts, having developed from its Platonic past as a vehicle for philosophic thought to a more generalized form of communication. Its value was to draw the reader (or auditor, since most participants in literary life either read aloud to themselves or were read to by slaves) directly into an issue, making that reader an implicit partner in the discourse. In this case the discussion moves from proofs of the existence first of the heroes and then of Protesilaus on the basis of externally verifiable statements. Once the author had proved his credentials, it was possible to draw the audience on to further stages of the argument. As he moved further from the known to the novel, the assumption would have to be made that the vintner was telling the truth because he had been shown to be a truthful person in cases where he could be checked. As a literary form the dialogue existed on the fringes of the *plasma*, or fiction that was like life, but there is a sense in which it was intended to create its own reality by enabling the audience to decide what position to take on what was being said. It deliberately obscured the dividing line between truth and fiction. Thus if one believed the ideas that the fictional Socrates propounded, they became true statements. If one wanted to believe what the vintner said about the Homeric heroes, they too could become true. Whether or not the heroes of Homer actually convened in the company of Protesilaus, whether one could hope to see them in person, is thus less important than that one could feel that they were still a vibrant part of the world.

The vinegrower's Protesilaus, who gave oracles (including advice on the best pancration techniques to contemporary athletes) and performed cures for various ailments, was the ideal character for the early third century.[73] He was, in a sense, a localized Apollonius who protected the good people of his region and took vengeance upon those who violated the norms of decent society. The vinegrower reported that Protesilaus had blinded the man who had despoiled him of his inherited estate, and repeated Herodotus' story of the revenge on Xerxes, who had violated his shrine.[74] The proofs that the vinegrower offered about the truth of his proposition that Protesilaus and other Homeric heroes were much larger than the mortals of his own time stemmed from the remains of giant beasts that could be found throughout the Troad and Thessaly.[75] The modern reader might recognize in these stories the report of dinosaur fossils, but for the classical reader, they reinforced the point that they lived in close contiguity with the past. It was this contiguity that gave the stories of attacks by Trojan shepherds upon the tomb of Ajax, or Hector's revenge on the arrogant youth who had dishonored him at Troy, a place in the spectrum of believable events.[76] But perhaps most interesting was the way that Protesilaus could correct misperceptions that could be attributed to the prejudice of Homer, or other errors in the tradition.[77] Thus the failure to mention Palamedes was due to the partisanship of Odysseus. It transpired that Homer had journeyed to Ithaca, where he had evoked the soul of Odysseus from the dead and had agreed, in return for learning of the war from him, to say nothing bad about him in his poems. Odysseus had told him the truth (souls cannot lie when brought forth by the rites described in the eleventh book of the *Odyssey*) and then revealed that he was being punished in Hades for what he had done to Palamedes. Homer changed the facts so as to honor his agreement.[78] But when it came to the crucial question of the day, the question of where Homer was born, he would say nothing, for that would ruin his relationship with the Fates and the Muses.[79] Protesilaus could also correct Homer in the matter of Aeneas, who was shown to be second only to Hector among the Trojans, and he could describe Euphorbus, whose soul was reincarnated in Pythagoras.[80] There is no question in this account but that Homer was wrong to say that Helen was at Troy rather than in Egypt during the war.[81]

Protesilaus could not only correct the tradition; he could confirm various details that had arisen alongside of it. He explained how the baths of Agamemnon came to be at Smyrna (in the wake of a spectacular battle that had preceded the arrival of the Greeks at Troy).[82] He confirmed with many further details the tradition that Achilles could now be found with his great love, Helen, if one visited their shrine on the White Island at the mouth of the Sea of Azov.[83] He could offer details of the rites with which the Lemnians expiated the slaughter of their men, and he could sort out the chronology of Homer and Hesiod.[84]

The *Heroicus* stands as part of a literary program that was consciously intended, in the context of works like *The Lives of the Sophists* and the *In Honor of Apollonius*, to assert the continuing value of Greek traditions. These works are not set in conscious opposition to any perceived threat from the culture of the Latin West (it is the barbarian East that is arguably more problematic). They are designed, like works listing amazing events of the past, the habits of fishes, or the culinary habits of antiquity, to assert the ongoing vitality of traditions inherited from the past. The choice of Troy is particularly significant because of its place in the heritage of both Rome and the Greek world.

The *Heroicus* is but the tip of a Homeric iceberg, and a somewhat eccentric one at that. As might be expected of a text that was central to the educational curriculum, and a cycle of myths that was among the most important sources of Greek identity, responses to both Homer and the tale of Troy were immensely varied. At the most basic level of comprehension, there are a number of glossaries preserved on papyri from the Hellenistic period onwards to explain epic language that was obscure to the classical reader.[85] These texts could range in complexity from simple word lists where an epic term was glossed by a word in common usage, to a remarkable text of *Iliad* 4.349–63 where each line of hexameter is transformed on the next line into prose.[86] Another text, this one of *Iliad* book 2, offers an interlinear gloss in which each line of Homer is followed by an "updated" hexameter that replaces difficult Homeric words while keeping as close to the Homeric word order as possible.[87] In some cases these glosses are joined to a summary of the book, ordinarily ranging in length from nineteen to about a hundred words, ending (and at times beginning) with the first line of the book in question.[88] These summaries, known as hypotheses (to distinguish them from a type of text to which we shall turn in a moment), were, like the glosses, usually intended to help readers through Homer rather than act as a substitute for the text itself. But there are cases when it appears that they were intended to be used without the text. Three fragments from one papyrus (now at Michigan) offer summaries of books with no glossary in between, suggesting that this text might have been intended to act as a substitute for the original. If so, it is of even more interest in that it leaves out references to the divine actions that take place in these books.[89]

If the Michigan papyri are indeed a portion of a book that collected individual hypotheses as a substitute for reading the whole, that book sits upon the generic boundary between the commentary and the cribs represented by a number of papyri that may be described as Homeric summaries. This generic gray zone is also occupied by a work that has come down through the manuscript tradition as the accomplishment of Pseudo-Dositheus, a grammarian who composed three books of interpretations in 207 AD.[90] His first book was on grammar, his second a glossary, and the third a summary of *Iliad* 7–24. The territory on the other side of this generic boundary is most clearly mapped out in the fourth book of the mythological epitome of Pseudo-Apollodorus (also, probably, of third-century date), who says quite explicitly that his version of the *Iliad* can be used as a substitute for reading the poem itself.[91] The use to which a book like Pseudo-Apollodorus' could be put is well illustrated by a remarkable series of objects that are known, collectively, as the *Tabulae Iliacae*.[92] These objects, which are carved on stone, and are all found between Rome and Campania, date from the first and second centuries AD. They contain illustrations of scenes from Homer with captions in Greek, and the most complete of them includes a Greek summary of the poem that has clear points of contact with Pseudo-Apollodorus. Both, for instance, play down the role of the gods, and both severely truncate the contents of books 13 to 15, in which the Trojans drive the Greeks back to their ships.

The rationale for the reduction of the role of the gods in Apollodorus, the *Tabulae Iliacae*, and in the summaries preserved on the Michigan papyri is not self-evident. One explanation that has some plausibility is that the authors who contributed to these traditions thought that Homer's portrayal of the gods was inappropriate. In this they would share in a tradition that stretched back through Plato to the sixth-century BC Ionian philosopher Xenophanes.[93] Another possibility is that these authors were concerned to treat the Trojan War as if it were a historical event, which would mean that the epic machinery of divine intervention needed to be removed. This view may receive support from the literature that was arguably shaped in response to the historicizing form of the Homeric narratives, books that sought to rewrite the Trojan saga with the developed claims of self-conscious classical historiography. For this it was necessary to claim the authority of an eyewitness who could be placed at Troy during the war. Two such books have

189

survived through the Latin manuscript tradition, one of them also attested by two Greek papyri.

The books in question are Dictys of Crete's *Commentary on the Trojan War*, and Dares of Phrygia's *History of the Destruction of Troy*. Dictys is presented as a companion of Idomeneus of Crete, Dares as a fighter on the side of the Trojans. The date of the composition attributed to Dares (no later than the early third century) is fixed by Aelian's mention of his work.[94] We are on firmer ground with Dictys, as one of the Greek papyri attesting his work is written on the back of a tax register from 207, and the other is written in a hand that was current in the early third century AD.[95] Both are presented as recent discoveries of long-lost texts (a form similar to that of much Egyptian wisdom, or the *Phoenician Tale* of Philo), and the Latin translations of both are prefaced by letters explaining their existence.[96] In the case of Dictys, the parallel with Philo is even closer, since it is said that he wrote in Phoenician characters. The story of the discovery of the text and the details that are used to lend it an air of authenticity are as follows:

> Dictys, a native of Crete from the city of Knossos, who lived at the same time as the sons of Atreus, knew the language and letters of the Phoenicians, which had been brought to Greece by Cadmus. He was a comrade of Idomeneus, the son of Deucalion, and of Meriones, the son of Molus, who were generals in the army that went to Troy, and he was instructed by them to write the history of the Trojan War.[97]

When he returned from Troy as an old man, he ordered that his book, written on wooden tablets, be buried with him in a tin box. In the thirteenth year of Nero, some shepherds found the box in his tomb, which had been revealed by an earthquake. They opened it, thinking that it contained treasure, but when they found that it contained only the tablets, they brought it to their master, who recognized the book for what it was and gave it to the governor, who in turn presented it to Nero. It was translated into Greek on Nero's orders and placed in the Greek library at Rome. The authority of Dictys is thus supported by his antiquity (and the use of an alphabet felt to be more ancient than the Greek) as well as by imperial authority (the benign picture of Nero reflects memory of his love of things Greek).[98]

Dictys' narrative proceeds without any sign of divine intervention. The cause of the war is not the apple of discord hurled by Envy at the marriage of Peleus and Thetis. The rape of Helen is not the act of Aphrodite, but rather of Paris, who was smitten with desire for her.[99] The death of Hector comes as a result of an ambush laid by Achilles to catch him on his return from negotiating with Penthesilea, queen of the Amazons. He does not drag his body behind his chariot, and he returns it to Priam, not in the middle of the night, but rather at a public conference, compelled to do so by the other leaders of the Greeks.[100] When the plague strikes the Greek camp after Agamemnon's refusal to return the captive Chryseis (who is called Astynome), Dictys says, "Whether this was due to the wrath of Apollo, as everyone thought, or to some other cause, was uncertain."[101]

More generally, Dictys turns the tale of Troy into a morality play. At the beginning, the Greeks are united, the Trojans treacherous. The evil machinations of the sons of Priam drive the Trojan people, unwillingly, into war, while the Greeks try to arrive at a peaceful solution. But, with the passing of time, the Greeks are gradually corrupted. Achilles is an isolated character, brutal and less than heroic. It is from him that the rot begins to spread, until, by the time of the capture of the city, the Greeks are divided among themselves, and behaving as badly as ever did the Trojans.[102] The final collapse of their society comes in a quarrel about booty: who will carry home the Palladium? When Ajax claims it as a reward for his valor, Agamemnon and Menelaus award it instead to Odysseus, who, along with Diomedes, had captured it. Ajax swears revenge, dividing the army into two factions, a division that is deepened when Ajax is found dead the next morning.[103] Agamemnon and Menelaus never regain their authority and are the first to leave, "like exiles or outcasts."[104]

In the case of Dares, the preface appears in the form of a letter (from Nepos to Sallust in the manuscript tradition) explaining that Nepos had found the book of Dictys in Athens and translated it into Latin. If there was ever a preface in the original Greek, we do not know, but there may not have been. "Nepos" refers only to the title of the book, and Dares is allowed to identify himself twice in the course of the text, once prior to a physical description of the Greek heroes (whom he says that he saw in the course of the war) and once at the end of the book.[105] He too leaves out any reference to the gods, explaining that the theft of Helen occurred on an expedition that Priam had sent to Greece to seek reparations for Hercules' sack of the city, and the return of his sister, Hesione, whom Hercules had carried away.[106] Achilles' killing of Hector, in open battle, has nothing to do with the prior death of Patroclus. Palamedes is elevated to the role of the leader of the Greeks during much of the war (after Agamemnon is voted out as leader), and he is killed not through a conspiracy of Odysseus, but rather by the Trojans in battle.[107] The fall of Troy is engineered by a cabal of Trojan nobles, including Aeneas, who open the Scaean gate (which is said to have been carved in the form of a horse).[108]

If "Dares" and "Dictys" may be seen as responses to the historicizing trends of Homeric summaries, they must also be seen as representative of a tendency toward the internalization of literary discourse that is quite distinct from the process of a Philostratus or even of an Aelian. Their works sought to define what was valuable, while those of the "internalizing sort" sought to undermine the authority of tradition by subverting its formulae of authority. The "internalizing" subversion of authority is perhaps a natural reaction to, and against, other forms of scholarly discourse against which they were reacting. But theirs was not the only form of reaction that was either natural or possible.

Poetic traditions of all sorts remained vital in the cultural world of the third century, supported by traditions of entertainment that continued competitions between artists for status, prizes, and, quite frankly, amusement. New tragedies continued to be written, as did new comedies.[109] Indeed, one play that has come to light from third-century (probably) Egypt depicts the theft of the Palladium from Troy. The preserved section includes portions of speeches by Athena, Odysseus, and Antenor (in his role as betrayer of the city), looking to the tradition adumbrated by Dares.[110] Mythological themes were also the subject of countless productions of pantomime, and melic poetry, performed to the accompaniment of the cithara, remained a popular genre.[111] The vibrant tradition of performance and the importance of poetry in the curriculum of the educated person supported yet more forms of inter- action with the Homeric poems. Students of rhetoric were expected to practice through fictional debates and other forms of performance in which they took on the character of some hypothetical speaker. Crucial performa- tive techniques included *prosopopoia*, in which the speaker imitated the voice and mannerisms of the character whose role he was taking. At the same time, as an author, he was expected to create speeches that were appropriate to the characters that he created (the vast majority of authors were, as always in antiquity, male). The exercise of creating an appropriate character, or *ethopoesis*, lies behind several works on Homeric themes that have survived on papyri. Thus in a text from Oxyrhynchus – written in a fourth-century hand, but still illustrative of the way that the tradition worked – the author took the eight-line speech in which Athena restrained Achilles after Agamemnon had ordered him to surrender Briseis, and turned it into twenty- six-line speech of his own. Athena appears here as an adviser, counseling restraint, rather than as a goddess instructing a mortal. She opens her address in the *Iliad* with the words:

> I have come from heaven to restrain you, but will you obey me? The white-armed goddess Hera sent me, for she loves you both in her heart and cares for you.
>
> (*Il.* 1.207–8)

Here she says:

> if it had been the Trojans against whom you were arming your hands, Achilles, and raging with your invincible sword drawn, I would will- ingly have drawn sword along with you. But if it is against your own people, the Greeks, that you armed yourself, Athena no longer agrees with you, nor does queenly Hera.
>
> (*P. Oxy.* 3002.1–5, trans. Parsons)

The scene reflects the view that the Homeric poems were a guide, among other things, to political life, and to make the point more plainly, the divinity is placed on a par with the human, rather revealed than as a character who can give him orders.

Other variations on Homeric themes ran in a different direction. In these cases, authors rewrite sections of the Homeric poems or, more generally, of the epic cycle. Some poets took it upon themselves to update various other portions of the Homeric cycle, the most important of whom may have been a character named Pisander of Laranda whose account of the sack of Troy appears to have been the source of the account of the fall of Troy in Virgil's *Aeneid*.[112] A papyrus fragment from the third or fourth century AD preserves a scrap of another such poem in which the returned Odysseus is evidently giving proofs of his identity to people on Ithaca.[113] Another fragment, in a third-century hand, offers a new version of the story of the Greeks' encounter with Telephus of Mysia on their way to Troy (a scene also described at length by Philostratus' Protesilaus).[114] More thorough forms of rewriting had also been a feature of literary life since at least the fifth century BC. Pigres of Halicarnassus, a brother of the Artemisia who played a significant role in Xerxes' invasion of Greece, rewrote the *Iliad* in elegaics, adding a pentameter of his own after each Homeric hexameter.[115] A poet named Idaeus of Rhodes later appears to have done something similar, inserting one line of his own after each line of Homer. Nestor of Laranda, who was active between the reigns of Severus and Alexander, produced a version of the *Iliad* in which he avoided words beginning with the same letter as the book number, a style known as lipogramatic.[116] Thus in book 1 of the *Iliad* (alpha, in Greek numeration) he did not admit any word that began with the letter alpha, and so forth. It was this style that was adopted by a close contemporary, an Egyptian poet named Triphiodorus, who may either have inspired or supplemented Nestor's production with a lipogrammatic *Odyssey*. He also wrote a paraphrase of Homeric similes, and three poems on epic themes, one of which, *The Capture of Troy*, has survived.[117]

Triphiodorus is explicit that his *Capture of Troy* will be brief (it is only 691 lines) – asking the Muse Calliope to "put an end to the constant hatred of the heroes in a brief song."[118] In so doing he may be inscribing himself into the tradition of Callimachus, whose doctrine of short, learned poetry remained a significant alternative to the grand style of epic. He succeeds in his task through astute allusion to the Trojan cycle as a whole. Thus he links the death of Priam at the hands of Neoptolemus to his ransom of Hector's body in the twenty-fourth book of the *Iliad*, saying:

> Neoptolemus, the descendant of Aeacus, slew the old king, worn out by suffering, beside the altar of Zeus of the Court-yard, putting aside his father's pity; he did not listen to his prayers, nor did he show pity seeing grey hair like that of Peleus, that hair which had

once caused Achilles to soften his heart and spare the old man despite his fierce wrath.[119]

In another instance, this one the building of the horse, he links the beginning and end of the war by pointing out that the wood for the horse came from the same slope that had provided the wood for the ship of Paris.[120]

While linking the beginning of the war to the end, and his poem to the older elements of the Homeric tradition, Triphiodorus had a number of points to make about what constituted the story. It seems to be the case that he preferred Lesches' *Sack of Troy* (a poem in the archaic cycle) to later accretions, such (it may be argued) as Pisander's poem. But he also needed to solve problems inherent in that story. Thus, with respect to the credibility of Sinon's account of why the Greeks had left the wooden horse (which the poet says had wheels under each hoof, again in accord with the oldest traditions), he offers a new reading of the character.[121] Sinon, it transpires, volunteered for the task and had himself subjected to what is plainly a Roman-style *fustigatio*, or beating with rods.[122] The welts all across his naked back convince the Trojans that he must be telling the truth. In this Triphiodorus echoes a theme that inspired the discourse of Christian martyr acts, in which the display of courage under torture was a sign of moral strength.[123] Cassandra is produced, with many allusions to Lycophron's inexplicably popular *Alexandra*, to predict the fate of the Trojans when the horse is brought into Troy, occluding the role of Laocoon, as a late invention.[124] The problem of Helen's conduct, in that she both tried to expose the Greeks in the horse and signaled to them that all was clear, is explained through the intervention of Aphrodite, who drove her to treason before Athena straightened her out.[125]

Triphiodorus' program was then to impose Callimachean poetic ideals upon the epic tale, and in so doing to present a story that was closer to the earliest versions, stripped of later accretion. There was, however, one critical exception, the fate of Aeneas. Here he says, "Aphrodite snatched away Aeneas and Anchises, pitying the old man and his son, and he ruled Ausonia, far from his fatherland; the counsel of the gods was fulfilled with the approval of Zeus, so that there would be unceasing power for the sons and grandsons of Aphrodite, beloved of Ares."[126]

If Triphiodorus represents the Callimachean end of the poetic spectrum, and is making a statement about what constituted proper poetry as well as the proper story, a rough contemporary, Quintus of Smyrna, stands at the other. His great work, the *Events after Homer*, is in fourteen books, beginning with the arrival of Penthesilea and ending with the sack of the city. Quintus prefers Hellenistic versions of the tale to archaic and subsumes tragic tellings of the story into his own.[127] Euripides is arguably of more interest to him than Lesches is, and his knowledge of local traditions connected with the war is on full display. Quintus' Memnon is unquestionably an Ethiopian, and upon his death he is transformed into the Aesopus River, which ran red once a year and gave forth a stench as of an unhealed wound, while Memnon's army is metamorphosed into birds that surround it. This tale, which has been traced, in part, to a Hellenistic book on birds, is representative of Quintus' approach to the story.[128] Likewise representative is Quintus' version of the contest between Odysseus and Ajax over the arms of Achilles. As an exercise in (extended) *ethopoesis* it is impressive. Ajax makes his case through abuse of Odysseus and praise of himself, Odysseus through praise of the power of the mind, and thus argues for his greater value to the Achaeans. The characters are as distinct as their qualities.

Quintus' interest in *ethopoesis* is matched by his delight in local geography and spectacle. The treatment of Sinon is grotesque (his nose and ears are cut off, and his body is tortured by fire), and the fate of Laocoon goes well beyond what is attested elsewhere in the tradition: he is struck blind by Athena, and his sons are eaten by the serpents that she sends. When Scylaceus returns home (to be stoned by his people), he is laid out in a tomb at Tlos next to that of Bellerophon, by the "crag of the Titenis." As Quintus knew, Titenis was a local cult title of Leto, and Scylaceus was later worshipped near her spot on the order of Apollo.[129] He knows that the tomb of Glaucus is on the border of Lycia, and that the stream of the Glaucus River that flows out from Mount Telandrus is, despite its importance to the Lycians, in Caria.[130] In another exercise of local history (of a sort) he knows the story of how Aeneas escaped from Troy with his father on his shoulders, but he needs also to invoke the seer Chalcas to make his point about what will happen in the future:

> Stop hurling your cruel arrows and destructive spears at mighty Aeneas. It is decreed for him by the splendid plan of the gods to go from Xanthus to the broad stream of Tiber. There he will fashion a sacred city, a wonder for future generations, and he shall be lord of a widespread people. The stock born from him shall thereafter rule all the way from the rising to the setting sun.
>
> (Q.S. *Post.* 13.334–41, trans. Combellack)

The tale of Troy was, of course, not the only story that interested people during the age of the Severan dynasts. Nor was epic, as we have briefly seen, the only genre of poetry that interested people. Hercules and Dionysus, who brought unity to the world through their wanderings, were likewise powerful figures, and so too was Alexander. What all of these characters have in common is that their stories, like the story of Troy, are symbols of the unity of classical culture. It is simply the survival of so many texts from this period that makes the Trojan cycle emblematic of the diverse uses to which the traditions of culture could be exposed. These traditions are not prescriptive in that they allow only one sort of response; rather, their existence offers a starting point for a wide range of diverse intellectual endeavors. But at the heart of the matter there are still text-based questions of authority: which version is "true" or "better," what local story is "right" or "wrong"? Just how far can a person go in correcting existing accounts? If an Aelian, an Athenaeus, or a Philostratus could define propriety through his control of a list (and it should be noted that, among other things, Philostratus was not interested in poets), a Homeric commentator had earlier narratives as a touchstone of authority in his realm. It may be the inherent stress on "demonstrable" authority in these realms of intellectual life that opened completely different doors into realms where neither the power of the list, nor that of the text, much mattered.

Reacting and inventing

Success in *ethopoesis* depended upon the ability to provide a coherent response to a situation. The aim of the rhetorical education that dominated the upper end of the educational curriculum was persuasion, and the evocation of emotive responses to situations created by the orator. The very same period that saw Aelian making his lists of events was also one of spectacular display. The pantomime artist, who danced mythological scenes to the accompaniment of an orchestra and singers, sought to stir the emotions of his audiences through the power of his mimesis. The interaction of the emperor with his subjects took place through massive public spectacles such as the ceremonial entry into a city, games, or the use of pictures that ideally evoked a suitable response from their viewers. The art of the period ranged (as it had for centuries) from extraordinarily stylized portraits that were intended to demonstrate attachment to a common ideal of culture, to pictures that were intended to draw the viewer into an emotional state. The figure of Philoctetes, for instance, who suffered intense pain resulting from the bite of a serpent, was a favorite theme for artists who sought to catch the idea of dignity in suffering.[131]

It is the work attributed to Philostratus of Lemnos entitled the *Imagines* (or *Pictures*) that reveals, as well as anything, the profoundly visual aspects of efforts to summon up powerful emotion. In this book Philostratus claims that he is describing the paintings that adorn the porticoes of the house of a wealthy man who lived at Naples. Philostratus says that he had decided not to give a standard oration, but, as he observed the paintings, he had decided to discuss them for the ten-year-old son of his host.[132] "Painting," says Philostratus, "is imitation by the use of colors; and not only does it employ color . . . it both reproduces light and shade and also permits the observer to recognize the look now of the man who is mad, now of the man who is sorrowing or rejoicing."[133] His descriptions are extraordinarily vivid, seeking to catch the feelings inherent to a scene, and the marvel of distant places. For instance, a description of a painting of islands begins by inviting the readers to imagine that they are on a boat, "sailing in and out among them in the springtime, when Zephyrus makes the sea glad by breathing his own breeze on it."[134] As the journey continues, one begins to perceive that the islands are not as they might seem: "the painting, following the account given by the poets, goes further and ascribes a myth" to one of them. This island holds down a giant, and you "will imagine that you have not been left out of the contest, when you look at the peak of the mountain," for you will see Zeus hurling his thunderbolts.[135] To see a myth is to experience it. A good painter could also enable one to understand a character from literature, as did a man "very good at painting" who created a picture of Pantheia (a character in Xenophon's *The Education of Cyrus*) "as from her soul he divined her to be."[136] An artist who could depict the calm of Severus, his dignity as he addressed his troops, the discipline of his troops, the terror of his foes, and their high-walled city, could enable the viewer to gain an impression of the war. Likewise, on an object like the Ludovisi sarcophagus, the viewer is brought into the chaos that is a battle, the mass of bodies churning, as the victorious Romans massacre their despairing foes.

Philostratus' description of the painting of the islands may be taken as a thematic introduction to another form of literature that was popular in his day: the novel.[137] Indeed, the connection may be said to be more than just thematic, for works of art might play a role in defining or forwarding the plot of a novel. Achilles Tatius' *Leucippe and Clitophon* opens with the narrator describing an astonishing painting of Europa's rape at Tyre, and later, Clitophon, when searching for words to describe his beloved, says,

> Such beauty I had seen only once before, and that was in a painting
> of Selene on a bull: delightfully animated eyes; light blond hair –
> blond and curly; black eyebrows – jet black; white cheeks – a white
> that glowed to red in the center like the crimson laid on ivory by
> Lydian craftswomen.[138]

Likewise a famous painting lies behind the complex description of Photis in Apuleius' *Metamorphoses*:

> With joyous wantonness she beautifully transformed herself into the
> picture of Venus rising from the ocean waves. For a time she even
> held one rosy little hand in front of her smoothly shaven pubes,
> purposely shadowing it rather than modestly hiding it.
>
> (Apul. *Met.* 2.17, trans. Hanson)

It is the image that Photis conjures up that deceives the easily confused Lucius into thinking of her as Venus, concealing her very much more real role as a modern Circe. The novel partakes fully of the world of mimesis, a role that is perhaps all the more striking at a time when effective mimesis was expected to arouse very real passions. It was not just an official prude like the Christian Tertullian who could argue that the love stories seen on the stage could inspire people to lust, or Augustine who would suggest that a trip to the theater was all it took to get him thinking (again) about sex.[139] These same themes appear in Ovid's great denunciation of Augustan hypocrisy. How could anyone, he argues, think that his *Art of Love* was a threat to public morality when they could see far more any day in the theater? The theater could be packed with "ten thousand pathetic scenes, with emotions tumbling over each other – tears, joy, astonishment, pity, disbelief and prayers."[140]

Insofar as the novel expresses the values of the dominant class, with its ideal landscapes of the city or countryside, with its beautiful heroes and their struggles with the loss of status that separation from home entailed, it also expresses a passionate side of life that was at odds with the ideology of aristocratic self-restraint. There are no more erotic passages in extant ancient literature than Apuleius' description of Lucius' encounters with Photis, or the encounter in Lucius of Patras' *Lucius or the Ass*, upon which it is modeled. Although medical theory could proclaim that sexual indulgence was bad for a person, so too could Achilles Tatius counter this view by describing the male perspective on the joys of heterosexual sex with extraordinary detail:

> When the sensations named for Aphrodite are mounting to their peak, a woman goes frantic with pleasure; she kisses with mouth wide open and thrashes like a mad woman. Tongues all the while overlap and caress, their touch is like passionate kisses within kisses. Your part in heightening the pleasure is simply to open your mouth.
>
> When the woman reaches the very goal of Aphrodite's action, she instinctively gasps with that burning delight, and her gasp rises quickly to the lips with a love breath, and there it meets a lost kiss, wandering about and looking for a way down: this kiss mingles with the love breath and returns with it to strike the heart.
>
> (*Leuc.* 2.37, trans. Winkler)

It is perhaps the very explicit description of passion, the literal description of private moments, that set the novel at odds with the canons of dignity that theoretically adhered to a member of the ruling order. It was plainly a genre that Philostratus the Athenian did not approve of, suggesting that what appears to have been a love story written by one of his subjects was unworthy of a true sophist.[141] And it is the case that, with a group of novels that survive, the interest in romance might be taken as unworthy of a gentleman, and the fictionalized past in which the action takes place might be taken as a slight to the sophist's proper concern with tradition.

Philostratus' disapproval is all the more striking, as the developed novel is perhaps the literary form most characteristic of the second and third centuries AD. Its appearance opens a window into the collective consciousness of the upper class; its relationship to other forms of prose fiction is a paradigm for the evolution of literary forms akin to those evident in the brave new world of Homeric reinterpretation.

Characteristic of the developed novel (as opposed to shorter fictions) is the tale of two lovers: these lovers are young and beautiful members of the upper classes, who might either be wandering far from home into exotic landscapes, or located in some past period of history.[142] The theme of monogamous love sets the developed novel apart from other forms of prose fiction that dealt with passion, of which there were a wide variety. Cornelius Sisenna, a noted Roman historian of the first century BC, translated a book of love stories, the *Milesian Tales*, that were allegedly so racy that copies found in the baggage of Roman officers killed at Carrhae in 53 BC were displayed by the Parthians as proof of Roman degeneracy.[143] Plutarch said that this was unfair since "so many of the Arsacids who had ruled were born from Milesian and Ionian courtesans." Another source, a book called the *Lovers*, attributed to Lucian, suggests that Aristides presented himself as the recorder of stories told by others.[144] We know less about three other works, one by a man named Eubius, who appears to have written about adulterous affairs, and two that were contemporary with Augustus, one entitled the *Sybaritic Tales*, and another that purported to be one man's account of his sex life.[145] Martial clarifies the point about a book *Sybaritic Tales* by suggesting that a man who read them without his girlfriend present would "make himself a husband without a wife."[146]

In addition to the collections of explicit stories mentioned above, and completely unrelated to them, there were long Egyptian prose narratives (one of them resembling a novel, and existing in both Demotic and Greek versions).[147] These may have given rise to the form of narrative that is best attested by the immensely popular *Alexander Romance*, which narrated the deeds of the great Macedonian conqueror with many fantastic additions. Indeed, the *Alexander Romance* may bridge the gap between narratives with a Near Eastern pedigree and travel literature with a philosophical bent that may be traced back, possibly, as far as the sixth century BC. By the second and third centuries BC these works may have been particularly well known in the form of Euhemerus' novel about the birth of the gods (popular reading among Christian intellectuals) and Antonius Diogenes' *Incredible Things beyond Thule*. This later work, which espouses Pythagoreanism, may be, at least in part, a model for the journeys of Apollonius in Philostratus' *In Honor of Apollonius*. These books stand quite apart as well from other prose narratives that were, at least to some degree, satirical, like Lucius of Patras' book, or, in Latin, the first-century novel of Petronius, the *Satyricon*. There is no obvious way to relate Petronius' book to the Greek novel (which was yet to emerge as a genre in the age of Nero), but later readers would place it in a generic connection with Apuleius' *Metamorphoses*, a book whose extraordinary complexity, mingling tales of magic and love with a serious avowal of faith in the goddess Isis, is, in detail, unlike anything else that has survived.[148] Still, the Latin term for a book like those of Petronius and Apuleius was *fabula*, and that looks very much like a translation of the Greek term *dramatikon* that the ninth-century Byzantine patriarch Photius used to categorize what I have been calling the "developed novel." In both cases the terminology suggests a theoretical connection with drama that dealt with the problems of everyday life and of ordinary people.

The fact that Philostratus should compose *In Honor of Apollonius* and yet still disapprove of a book entitled *Araspes the Lover of Pantheia* is perhaps the most important indication that the novels were perceived as being categorically different from other forms of prose fiction. The notion that they should deal with ordinary people, as suggested by the terminology of Photius, is initially more problematic, as some of the characters that we meet are of royal status. Thus, for instance, there are fragments of a novel whose lead male character is an Assyrian king named Ninus (probably the famous Ninus who was thought to be the first man to establish a world power) that have come down to us outside the manuscript tradition, on a battered papyrus.[149] Another group of papyri treats the adventures of the great Egyptian king Sesonchosis and like the *Ninus* explores his crises as an adolescent, trying to reconcile his exalted state with the passion that he feels for a young woman.[150] The existence of works like these makes it better to suggest that the novel treated the problems of humanity against an extraordinary background, for these royal figures are presented as young people dealing with the problems of young people rather than as omnipotent beings who are learning to rule an empire.[151]

Another feature of these novels is the fantastic background of imagined eastern kingdoms. This is also the case with a novel preserved only in summary form by Photius, entitled the *Babyloniaca* (*The Babylonian Tale*), which tells of two lovers, Rhodanes and Sinonis, and the travails of their love at the hands of the evil king Garmus of Babylon (whom Rhodanes replaces as king at the end of the novel).[152] The longest and most spectacular of all extant novels, Heliodorus' *Ethiopian Tale*, is set up and down the Nile valley, beginning with the discovery of a wrecked ship at the mouth of the Nile and moving as far south as Meroe. Two more papyri offer fragments of novels that explore the travails (insofar as they are preserved) of women named Calligone and Chione. The preserved portion of the story of Calligone involves her reaction to what appears to be the reported loss of her lover in battle against the Scythians, while Chione is worried about how she can escape marriage to a tyrant named Mesomedes (a good eastern-sounding name). Chione is plainly in love with someone else.[153]

Not all novels depend on the tincture of Mesopotamia, Egypt, or Ethiopia for their interest. *Daphnis and Chloe* is set in the area around Mytilene, and the leading characters are two young shepherds (though it will turn out that both were originally of good birth). Here the sense of travel into a foreign environment is provided by the vision of the countryside, a life in the groves of the hills chasing sheep. It is a lifestyle that was arguably as foreign to the urban readers of these books as the Mesopotamia of Rhodanes and Sinonis.[154] Chariton's *Chaereas and Callirhoe*, by way of contrast, is set firmly in the Greek world, as is Xenophon of Ephesus' *Ephesian Tale*, though in these cases there are some substantial differences. The Greek world of Xenophon is timeless: the heroes, Habrocomes and Anthia, are captured by Phoenician pirates, enslaved in Syria, and wander throughout Egypt and even to southern Italy without any suggestion as to who is supposed to be in charge. The magistrate who sentences Habrocomes to be crucified by the banks of the Nile is described as the *archon*, "ruler," of Egypt, which may allude to a Roman prefect, and the Perilaus who rescues Anthia from being sacrificed by brigands is called an *eirenarch*, also an office of the Roman period.[155] But none of the other mechanisms of Roman government are present: there is, most importantly, no suggestion that a single power holds sway over all the regions that the heroes visit. The vocabulary does no more than to suggest that the author lived in the second or third century AD, and we cannot even be certain that a classical audience would have been as attuned to the peculiarities of administrative terms as the modern scholar looking for evidence of a date. This classical audience would rather be alert to the perils of lost status that resulted from the journeys of the lovers, the threat inherent in departure from the safe urban environment. We might well also wonder to what extent the classical audience would be attuned to the mishmash of fourth-century BC history that pops up in Chariton's novel. The protagonists begin in Syracuse of the late fifth century – Callirhoe is the daughter of the Hermocrates who defeated the Athenians in 413 – and have their adventures in the Persia of Artaxerxes II (404–358 BC). Most likely, readers would have recognized two names from books that they had read and would not have bothered much about the fact that Miletus is described as a city subject to Persia, which it was not for much of Artaxerxes' reign.[156] The same sort of historical pastiche occurs in the fragments of a novel about Parthenope, the lover of Metiochus, a son of Miltiades, who is placed in the court of Polycrates of Samos, a generation before any reasonable historical date for Metiochus.[157]

If members of the audience could recognize the names that gave historical flavoring, they would also recognize the institutions of urban life and the scenes associated with it. The scene where Chariclea is taken to be burned at the stake in Heliodorus would have evoked the sense of mob action that often accompanied a Roman execution:

> At once she was seized by the executioners to be taken to a place just outside the city wall. All the time a crier was proclaiming that she was being led to the stake as a poisoner, and a large crowd of other people had joined the procession: some had actually seen her

being led away, others had heard the story that raced through the town, and hurried to watch.

(Hel. *Eth*. 8.9, trans. Morgan)

They would also have recognized the emotion as the crowd demanded her release on the grounds that she was innocent, moved by the miracle that occurred as she stood in the circle of flames that was to have killed her.[158] Similarly, they would have seen prisoners hung on crosses in places where many people would pass, as Habrocomes was hung by the banks of the Nile, his hands and feet tied by ropes, "the way Egyptians crucify" (Xen. *Eph*. 4.2). They might even have tortured a slave the way that Habrocomes was tortured by his master when he (wrongly) thought that Habrocomes had seduced his daughter, saying that his torment would serve as an example for other slaves.[159]

Away from the immediate environment, readers who knew of war through accounts of imperial campaigns might well recognize some themes from imperial panegyric in novelistic descriptions of battle. Heliodorus' account of the Ethiopian siege of Syene has points of contact with accounts of a Persian attack on Nisibis (of a later date, but possibly reflecting a tradition of imperial rhetoric), and his description of armored cavalry likewise shares points of contact with traditions of imperial battle description.[160] So too might the description of Ninus' deployment of his elephants in the *Ninus*.[161] These same readers might also recognize the marvels of their own cities, be they processions like that at Ephesus where Habrocomes fell in love with Anthia, or the wondrous canals of Mytilene.[162] The traveling lovers are often shown as tourists who know how to appreciate the marvels of the civilized landscape.[163]

For all that the novel may stand in opposition to the values espoused by Philostratus, it does so from within the same ideological construct of the world's order. In a sense it was the discourse of respectability, of local tradition, self-control and calm that authorized a discourse of romantic adventure in what is often very close to a never-never land full of the bogeymen that haunted the corners of aristocratic life. As with developments in the Homeric tradition, the theme and variation are defined by the parameters of an existing tradition. And what this shows is that within those traditions there is immense room for variation, immense scope for creativity. But it may be that this very strength was a weakness. There are signs of a solipsistic cultural mood, inward-looking and self-celebratory.

Plato's new world

In proclaiming sophists as the preeminent intellectuals of his day, Philostratus was downplaying the importance of philosophy as a branch of human wisdom. Unable to let it go altogether, he would concede importance only to those philosophers who, in his view, were also qualified sophists. In doing so he was consciously reversing a feature of Platonic thought whereby the philosopher represented true wisdom as opposed to the sophist, who was filled with empty blather.

As so often with Philostratus, what he tries to establish as a rule is perhaps better described as a tendency. People did tend to think of themselves as one or the other, but this is not a hard-and-fast rule. Inscriptions reveal people who would happily have themselves described as both at the same time.[164] What is more important, in actual practice it is often very hard to distinguish the philosopher's performance from that of the sophist in form if not in content. Public performance and debate appear to have been very important features of philosophy in the second and third centuries AD, as rival teachers contended for students and sought to downplay the claims of their rivals. Two inscriptions, one from Ephesus, the other from Athens, reveal the performance of a Platonic philosopher named Ofellius Laetus, sometime in the last two decades of the first century AD. His accomplishment was a verse hymn about heaven and what lay beyond.[165] By offering public declamation of his poem, Laetus was participating in both the revival of verse exposition of philosophy and the ongoing tradition of public display. It was this same tradition that Paul sought (with rather less success) to join when he tried to explain Christianity to the Council of the Areopagus at Athens in a debate with representatives of established schools.[166] And it is the tradition that Lucian pillories in various of his satires. In Lucian's wry view, philosophers were more interested in advancing their mundane comforts than in exploring the limits of human knowledge.

The inscriptions honoring Laetus quote or echo the opening lines of his hymn, a nice gesture. But the epigraphic commemoration of Laetus' thought must pale into insignificance compared to the extraordinary effort of Diogenes of Oenoanda in Lycia, who commissioned an epigraphic exposition of the philosophy of Epicurus, engraved on the walls of a large stoa in his own city. Among the many fascinating features of this text is the fact that the documents that proclaim themselves to be the authentic words of the late fourth-century BC sage are in fact very much more recent compositions, possibly (though not certainly) written by Diogenes himself.[167] What is more, if, as was often the case, those who viewed Diogenes' stoa read it out loud to themselves, they might have filled that part of the town with a low buzz of modern Epicurean thought.[168]

Diogenes' text was in a sense a sophistic exercise in publication. Unlike many authors, he could control an authoritative text of his discourse and ensure that it got publicity where it mattered most to himself: his hometown. At roughly the same time that he erected his stoa, someone else from Oenoanda went off to the great oracular center of Claros to obtain instructions from the god on how to honor the rising sun. Whoever this person was, he or she was well enough pleased with the response, which came complete with a three-line tag to mark the authenticity of the divine, that he or she carved it on the old city wall in the best place to view the sun as it rose.[169] What makes this text so interesting (aside from the spot where it was carved) is the way that the god is described:

> Self-nourished, taught by none, unmothered, unshakeable,
> Having no name, many-named, dwelling in fire.
> This is God. We messengers (are) a small part of God.[170]

This description echoes contemporary Platonic thought about the nature of God and reflects the broad influence of philosophy on upper-class religious thought, not just in the refined circles of the dominant classes, but arguably as well in the public discourse of religion. It is hard to be more public in the ancient world than to be part of a discourse that ends up inscribed on stone or declaimed in front of a crowd.

The significant doctrinal point that is made in this oracle is that communication with mortals is conducted by divinities other than the one great god. Just as it was the daimon that spoke to Socrates, so too daimones of all sorts carried on the discourse between divinities and the average person, for they participated in both a human and a divine nature:

> Everything that has a soul must show a combination of two properties drawn from this list: it must be either emotionless and immortal, or immortal and emotional, or emotional and mortal, or irrational and capable of perception, or ensouled but incapable of emotion. It is in this way that Nature contrives a gradual and systematic descent from the most precious to the least. If you remove any of the stages you will cut nature into two. . . . You must believe that the same situation obtains in nature as does in the most perfect of scales, taking God to occupy the position marked "emotionless and immortal," *daimones* that marked as "immortal and emotional," men that marked "mortal and emotional."
>
> (Max. Tyr. *Or.* 9.1–2, trans. Trapp)

The author of this explanation, which is perhaps the clearest exposition of the critical link between human and divine that would become central to discourse of all sorts, reforming pagan practice and Christian doctrine, is a gentleman named Maximus of Tyre. He further allowed that both Asclepius and Hercules were to be classified among the daimones, and says that he had seen both of them, "not in a dream."[171] By way of contrast, the one God, "Father and Creator of all that exists, is greater than the sun and the heavens, mightier than time and eternity and the whole flux of Nature; legislators cannot name him, tongues cannot speak of him, and eyes cannot see him."[172] The similarity between his formulation of God's identity and that of the

204

oracle received by the people of Oenoanda is no accident. It was a feature of polytheist cult that oracles were continuously updating knowledge about the divine to conform with current intellectual trends.[173]

We do not really know who Maximus was, but a late biographical tradition records that he visited Rome in the reign of Commodus. His writings reveal a man who was concerned to make philosophy easy for an audience that he describes as consisting of young men.[174] The first speech in the extant corpus of his writings is suffused with the air of intellectual combat, advertisement of the virtue of philosophy against other forms of intellectual pursuit. In a passage that he admits may be somewhat out of keeping with the claims that he is making for the contemplative life, he writes,

> Behold young men this treasury of eloquence – prolific, complex, abundant – that stands before you, such as to appeal to all ears and all characters, proficient in all styles of speech and all forms of training, lavish and bountiful, unhesitating, unbegrudged, freely available to all who can receive it.
>
> (*Diss.* 1.7, trans. Trapp)

The style of Maximus, filled with quotations from Homer and replete with examples drawn only from the classical age of Greece, is plainly intended to establish the philosopher in his public role as the guardian of knowledge. As with other intellectuals of his age, learning is also seen as something of a zero-sum game. The gain of the philosopher comes at the expense of others. He is in control of past traditions, and it is with these that he seeks his place in the present. What is perhaps most significant about these past traditions is that they include those of peoples whom one might not, at first glance, think of as being Greek. But for Maximus, Persian representations of God, for instance, show that they are "similarly conscious of him," and the Assyrian king Sardanapallus is just as sound an example of failure as Smindyrides of Sybaris.[175] In one particularly telling passage, Maximus makes it clear that barbarism is a state of mind rather than a product of ethnicity. If one should hear that the philosopher and the wicked man are in love, one should realize that the philosopher's love produces friendship,

> the other hatred, the one love needs no fee, the other is mercenary. The one is praiseworthy, the other is reprehensible. The one is Greek, the other is barbarian.
>
> (Max. Tyr. *Or.* 19.4, trans. Trapp)

The philosopher's role as the guardian of what is Greek, or civilized, against what is barbarous, or opposed to the tradition of civilization, is the subject of one of the odder works composed by any philosopher in the course of the second century AD.[176] The book is by a man named Celsus; its title, *Alêthês*

Logos, may variously be translated *The True Account* or *The True Doctrine*; its theme is the barbarism of Christianity. It appears that Celsus opened with a general statement of the problem, followed by a fictitious address by a Jew, first to Christians generally, and then to Jews who have abandoned their faith to become Christians. He concludes with a lengthy discussion of the folly of Christianity from the perspective of a traditional believer.

For Celsus, it matters not "if one calls God 'Zeus,' the name that he bears from the Greeks, or by that used among the Indians or that used by the Egyptians."[177] The critical point is that many nations hold views about God that are similar to those of the Christians, which led some to think that there was an original source for all the traditions that purport to be true religion. This doctrine, which Celsus clearly believes to be correct, existed from the beginning and is shared by the wise men of all countries. These wise men, of whatever origin, are plainly those who can see through the prejudices of national histories.[178] The objection that Celsus raises to Judaism is that it attempts to separate itself from the tradition by claiming unique inspiration for Moses. He points out that while the Jews have their picture of Moses, the Egyptians also have theirs, which is very different. The reasonable person takes this as a given and thus continues to look for that which binds them all together without seeking to assert that one account must be better than others. In his view, the fact that Moses performed miracles, and that Christians claim the same for Christ, must be read in light of the fact that people perform miracles in other traditions as well. Moses is really no more than a superior sort of magician, and Jesus an inferior sort. The prophecies of Jesus, the miracles that he performed, are those of common street-corner practitioners. Perhaps the most objectionable thing about Christians is that they insist on blind faith in God as opposed to rational skepticism and inquiry.[179] It is a complaint that had been made by others, including Galen, who commented that Christians drew "their faith from parables [and miracles]," though, unlike Celsus, he admired "their self-discipline and keen pursuit of justice," which he felt was "not inferior to that of genuine philosphers."[180]

Celsus stands for a universalizing vision of classical culture, one that draws into itself the traditions of all peoples and homogenizes them. The problem with this view is quite simple. It deprives the sundry peoples whom he asserts are linked with the traditions of the classical world of their own voices. If, like Maximus and his rough contemporary, the Pythagorean Numenius, he can find a place for Moses, Zoroaster, and the Brahmins in the same world as Pythagoras and Plato, he is not listening at all closely to what they had to say.[181] What stood out about Christian and Jewish traditions was that, unlike Brahmins, they had their own representatives in the Roman world. These representatives were not ones who would necessarily force their doctrines to conform with the picture drawn for them by others, as seems to have happened with the Zoroastrian thought that emerged within the empire, as opposed to that which was continuing to evolve within the Persian heartland and would soon burst like a torrent across the eastern frontiers of the empire. Celsus himself was answered, at what date we cannot know for certain, by a Christian who was himself a great scholar and imbued with Platonic philosophy: Origen.

Origen and Hippolytus: classical thought and Christianity

Origen was probably born in AD 185 or 186; he would live until 254 or 255. He spent the bulk of his life in Alexandria, which he only departed in 233, though much of what we know about him comes from the last period of his life.[182] It is from this period that there survives an account of his teaching from the pen of Gregory of Neocaesarea in Pontus, who had left home to become a lawyer and was to return a Christian as a result of Origen's teaching. And it would appear to be from this period that the information that appears as a sort of minibiography in the sixth book of Eusebius' *History of the Church* stems.[183] The vision of Origen as the complete Christian obscures somewhat the complexity of his early life. There can be no doubt but that Origen was born a Christian of wealthy Christian parents. His father, Leonidas, oversaw his early education in both Christianity and philosophy; when Origen was around seventeen years old, his father was arrested and decapitated.[184] The coincidental confiscation of Leonidas' property would have then thrown Origen into poverty, had not a wealthy woman of Alexandria taken him under her care and enabled him to continue his education.[185] He rose rapidly to a position of prominence in the church, becoming chief of the Catechical School by the age of eighteen, and indulging in a severely ascetic lifestyle, a sort of substitute for the suffering of martyrdom, endured by a number of his pupils. It was at this point that he castrated himself.[186]

It appears to have been at the same time that he was head of the Catechical School that Origen attended the lectures of Ammonius Saccas. The connection with Ammonius is of considerable importance both for the career of Origen and for the more general issue of the relationship between Christians and the classical tradition. Ammonius had, at one point, been a Christian, before turning away from the church and devoting himself to the exploration of traditional philosophy. We cannot now know what made him change his mind, though from the second century there is a parallel in the case of Proteus Peregrinus who went through a Christian phase (attaining for himself the status of a martyr by getting himself imprisoned by the governor of Syria) before devoting himself to the Cynic school.[187] He ended his career with a spectacular autoimmolation at Olympia. It may be that for a man like Ammonius or Peregrinus, as would later be the case with Augustine, a sense of intellectual adventure carried them away from mainstream thought. Indeed, what little we know about Ammonius suggests that he was an iconoclastic teacher, seeking to assert a unity between Plato and Aristotle, as well as to join them with the Pythagorean tradition.[188] It may be that he stressed the power of the free intellect to make connections and to explicate texts independently of received wisdom. This at least might explain the odd statement that Plotinus, the great Neoplatonic philosopher of the middle third century, used Ammonius' *nous* (mind) rather than normal methods.[189]

Origen's asceticism (if not his self-castration) likewise falls somewhere between pagan and Christian tradition. The ascetic lifestyle was well established in philosophic tradition long before there were Christians at all, the point being that the control of one's body reflected the control over one's mind. The ideal is perhaps most fluently expressed in a papyrus letter urging a man to continue his asceticism.[190] So too in the pages of the Hermetic corpus (texts that again exist on the fringes of Platonism) readers are told that those who want to know God need to free themselves of human desires:

> These people have sensations much like those of unreasoning animals, and, since their temperament is willful and angry, they feel no awe of things that deserve to be admired; they divert their attention to the pleasures and appetites of their bodies; and they believe that mankind came to be for such purposes. But those who participate in the gift that comes from god, O Tat, are immortal rather than mortal if one compares their deeds, for in a mind of their own they have comprehended all – things on earth, things in heaven and even what lies beyond heaven. Having raised themselves so far, they have seen the good and, having seen it, they have come to regard the wasting of time here below as a calamity. They have scorned every corporeal and incorporeal thing, and hasten towards the one and only.
>
> (*CH* 4.5, trans. Copenhaver)[191]

In Origen are thus combined two central features of the emergent Christianity of the second and third centuries AD. The one is an ability to deal with the polytheist world on its own terms; the other is a tendency to create a Christian life as an alternative to that world. Celsus was correct to see a profound separatism as a feature of Christian life. For Celsus, and many others, the avoidance of communal activities, the shunning of sacrifice, and, occasionally, a tendency to launch a physical assault on other people's holy places, merged into a general disrespect for the all-encompassing tradition. For Origen, this was, to some degree, the point. Why, if the world was corrupt, should the virtuous person be involved with it? What good was philosophy if true understanding of it was so time-consuming an operation that only a few could truly understand? How could Christians be criticized for believing what they believed when what they were doing was no more than the average person did by deciding to attach him- or herself to one school of philosophy or another without knowing them all? His was perhaps a natural response to the sort of sugarcoating that men like Maximus of Tyre applied. But Origen did not just withdraw. Like some other of his contemporaries, Origen set himself up as a public figure. When writing for the community, Origen tended to avoid references to classical texts even as he employed Platonic ideals to explain Christian scripture (he was too smart to miss the point that there were genuine interpretative problems in the texts that formed the basis of his faith). When addressing the broader world he showed himself in command of the classical tradition, as did other Christians who could use the tradition to support the point that what they were saying was not simple barbaric nonsense.

As a representative of his faith, Origen came to be well known outside his immediate community. Porphyry, a younger contemporary who despised Christians, still linked Origen with Ammonius Saccas (though deploring the fact that he had not changed his ways) and noted that Origen knew his texts. Indeed, another student of Ammonius was Porphyry's own revered teacher, Plotinus. Although there is no good reason to think the two men had any real contact, it is the case that both Plotinus and Origen despised people whom they termed Gnostics, as intellectual frauds who appropriated traditions that they willfully or otherwise, could not understand.[192] Even when Origen was a young man, a governor of Arabia asked him to visit Bostra and explain his faith.[193] In the winter of 232–33 he was invited to Antioch by Julia Mamaea to explain his faith to her, and, probably in 244, he wrote letters explaining Christianity to the emperor Philip and his wife, Otacilia Severa.[194] It may have been the letter to Philip, as much as anything, that sealed Origen's fate in 250, when Decius, who despised the memory of Philip, issued an edict commanding all the inhabitants of the empire to sacrifice, which coincidentally led to the imprisonment and death of many Christians.[195] Origen was arrested in Caesarea, where he had settled in 233, and tortured so badly that he may never have recovered his health.[196] Too smart to see martyrdom as a glorious end in itself – perhaps touched too closely by the deaths of those close to him in youth – his own book on the subject, composed about fifteen years before his arrest, presents persecution as something to be endured rather than sought out.[197] In his response to Celsus he wrote:

> Even if a Christian were to run away, he would not do so for cowardice, but because he was keeping the commandment of his Master and preserving himself free from harm that others might be helped to gain salvation.[198]

Origen was more than a preacher, an orator, or a theologian. He was also a textual critic. His edition of the Old Testament in which he laid out the evidence for different recensions of the text, in both Hebrew and Greek, in parallel columns (eight in all) showed not only an enormous capacity for detailed work, but also that he had moved beyond the limited mind-set that characterized so many of his contemporaries, and actually learned to deal with the language of an indigenous people not his own. A prolific author himself, he knew what could go wrong with a text; an honest man, he recognized that there were genuine inconsistencies in his sacred books; a man of passion, he needed to promote what he saw to be the truth. The significance of his belief that Christ was begotten by the one God, that Christ combined humanity with divinity, was the agent of the Father and acted only with respect to rational beings, a form of theology known as "subordinationist" since it implied that the power of the Son was less than that of the Father (the Logos itself was limited to action with those who were being sanctified), would lie close to the surface of disputes that would dominate the history of the church in later centuries.[199] For now, what is significant is that one of the driving forces behind his work was to combat what he saw to be heresy – ironic, perhaps, in light of his later condemnation as one of the most offensive of heretics. He was especially concerned with ideas that stemmed from the misapplication of classical philosophy to Christian texts – again somewhat ironic, as his classic formulation of the Son, "There was not a time in which he was not," was borrowed from Platonism.[200] In the *Against Celsus*, he confronts the accusation that Christians are hostile to one another, and that there are a lot of very strange ideas passing as forms of Christianity. Just so, he admits

> that *there are some too who profess to be Gnostics*, like the Epicureans who call themselves philosophers. But neither can those who abolish providence really be philosophers, nor can those be Christians who introduce strange ideas which do not harmonize with the traditional doctrines received from Jesus.
>
> (*Contra Cels.* 5.61, trans. Chadwick; the italics indicate a presumed quotation from Celsus)

The problem that Origen and Celsus faced, as did Hippolytus of Rome and, later, Plotinus, was that it was impossible to control what people did with ideas. The range of ideas that pass under the general heading of Gnosticism is so vast that the title is almost meaningless. In theory, at least, a Gnostic was a person who possessed a special *gnosis*, or wisdom. The ultimate source of that wisdom could usually be traced back to some inspired person whose special insight proved that the conventional tradition was somehow flawed, and tended to involve a belief in the corruption of the world.[201] The existence of such groups is also, of course, testimony to the very basic problem that, while a centralizing tradition, be it Platonism, Christianity, or Judaism, could provide a vehicle for expression, it did not necessarily guarantee that localized forms of expression were either acceptable or comprehensible.

We cannot now know how exceptional a figure was Hippolytus of Rome, whose *Against All Heresies* was written in the early 220s AD. What we can say is that there is some reason to think that he knew Origen, and that like Origen and like Tertullian in North Africa, he knew the philosophic traditions of the polytheist world.[202] Indeed, Tertullian had adopted the same strategy as Hippolytus would later, in attributing what he regarded as aberrant Christian teaching to the influence of philosophy. It was Tertullian who asked, "What then has Athens to do with Jerusalem, the Academy with the Church, the heretics with the Christians?"[203] But while Tertullian ultimately rejected both traditions to embrace the extreme form of new wisdom promulgated by the followers of Montanus, Hippolytus set himself strongly against all outside traditions that he regarded as corrupting the message of the gospels. At the same time he adopted a formulation of the Trinity that made the Logos both the creation of the one God and one with him, a significant development in western theology, since it allowed that the Father was always the Father and that the Son also existed in community of being with him.[204]

The *Against All Heresies* is a truly astonishing book, even in its current mutilated state (books 2 and 3 having been lost in the course of transmission). The task that Hippolytus set himself was to refute all heresies. His method was to reveal that they owed their inspiration not to Christian scripture, but rather to the thinking of other groups. They descend, in Hippolytus' view, from the philosophy of the Greeks, the mysteries of the Egyptians, and the theories of astrologers. The essence of the argument is that the "heretics" claim new knowledge, but what they are really doing is repeating old Greek philosophy, now superseded, which means that the claims of "heretics" to novelty and divine wisdom are false.[205]

In order to illustrate his point, Hippolytus sets about explaining these different systems, beginning with the Greeks. He offers a tour of pre-Socratic philosophy, starting with Thales, and running through a large number of other thinkers (often briefly and with considerable idiosyncrasy), before reaching Socrates, who he says can only be known through Plato. The main Greek thinkers, to judge from the space that he allots them (and the knowledge that he shows of their works) are Pythagoras, Plato, and Aristotle, whose thought he attempts to reconcile with that of Plato in a rather unconvincing way.[206] He admits that the Stoics contributed something to philosophy through advances in the art of syllogism, and says that Epicurus differs from all others with his theory of the atoms and the void.[207] He has almost nothing to say about Pyrrhonism. In light of the fact that he genuinely seems to have known his Plato and Aristotle, and had at least the sort of knowledge of others that could be gleaned from a glance through some handbook, it is astonishing that the last two groups he includes are the Brahmins and the Druids. The last author he treats in this section is Hesiod.

Book 2 was devoted to the mysteries of the Egyptians, and book 3 to the wisdom of the Chaldeans. In light of what Hippolytus has to say about the Brahmins and the Druids, the loss of these books is undoubtedly a serious blow to our understanding of the way that eastern systems of thought were constructed for a Greek-speaking audience. All that we can say now is that Hippolytus must have felt that he had so demolished them that he did not need to return to them in his summary of the arguments informing heresy in his tenth book. The fourth book, whose contents he likewise did not feel the need to repeat later, offers a summary of "Chaldean" astrology and of magic. In the latter case it appears that he had an actual book in front of him, since he can tell his readers precisely how one can perform some of the "miracles" that he feels are effective. Books 5 to 9 outline a wide range of different heresies, ranging from the Naasenes, through the followers of Simon Magus to the Montanists. The culmination of all heresy was probably then to be the doctrine promulgated by his rival for the leadership of the church at Rome, Callistus, bishop from 217 to 222.

Gross misrepresentations sprinkle Hippolytus' work from beginning to end, as badly with most Greek philosophers as with the heretics who are his main concern, but that is less significant than the way that he approaches the whole subject.[208] Just as he sets himself, and all "true" Christians, apart from the classical tradition, he shows himself bound by these very forces. It is inconceivable to him that ideas (other than his version of the orthodox Christian) could exist that were independent of the classics, and, indeed, as we have seen, his own ideas about what the gospels said are helped by his reading of Plato. That he should include Egyptians, Chaldeans, and magicians among his threatening intellectuals reveals an understanding of the contemporary intellectual scene as one in which all forms of human activity could fall under one very large tent. The philosopher could intimate, as Apuleius did, that he might be a magician.[209] Plotinus himself was to accompany a Roman invasion of Persia in the hope that he could converse with the sages of the east, and his teachings, as we shall see, could inspire a brand of Platonism that embraced magical practice.[210] Plotinus' pupil Porphyry would likewise explore the eastern wisdom to incorporate his understanding of it into the practice of Platonism.[211] It is through the lens of all-embracing classicism that Hippolytus took on one last heresy that came up on his screen just as he appears to have been completing the *Against All Heresy*. The "heresy" in question involved the thought of Elchasai, as made known to the Roman public through the work of a man named Alcibiades, who lived in Apamea in Syria.

Just about everything to do with Elchasite revelation runs counter to the tendency of Hippolytus (and others) to treat translated eastern wisdom as if it were authentic. This is because the revelation of Elchasai was actual eastern wisdom. The Alcibiades who brought his Greek version to Rome had actually translated it from the original Syriac. The point of the revelation was to restore a true Jewish form of Christianity, to rescue Christianity from what the followers of Elchasai's book regarded as the contamination of Hellenism. The ultimate "heretic" for the Elchasites was none other than the apostle Paul.[212] In light of this there can be little in Hippolytus' book that is more absurd than his effort to show that it was all a debased form of Pythagoreanism.[213] Indeed, the revelation of Elchasai (he reported what he had been told by a gigantic angel in the reign of Trajan) was the foundational text for a community that was, even then, thriving on the Lower Euphrates, in the territory of the Persian Empire.[214] There it too was about to undergo a remarkable transformation at the hands of another man who would be cast from the community and form his own faith, Mani, the "Apostle of Light."[215] The thought of Mani, derived from visions, and influenced by the Zoroastrianism that was then reemergent as the dominant religion of the new Sassanid dynasty, would begin to traverse the Roman Empire a generation after Hippolytus wrote. That would be a time when the balance of power between the two empires had shifted for good.

The power of tradition

Cultural attitudes do not move with the speed of political events. The literature of the Severan era, and later (for some of the works that we cannot date firmly are probably post-Severan), was in many ways a culmination of the classical tradition. The evolution of the Homeric tradition, or of Platonism, the emergence of new forms of prose fiction, and the respect accorded to intellectuals of all sorts bespeak an era of immense confidence, even as the political structure of the state became ever more troubled.

For all its strength, the classical tradition was also a source of great weakness. The assumption that foreign wisdom was essentially Greek did not help people understand the world at large. The imposition of Greek paradigms upon Celts, Egyptians, Ethiopians, and Persians may also have led to difficulty in hearing what was actually being said. These traditions remained beneath the veneer of Hellenism that was laid over them, and the cast of mind that enabled people to comprehend these ideas by revising them transcended the world of the writer to inform the decision-making of those who formed the imperial government. It inhibited an ability to realize that situations that had been static for centuries were on the verge of change, and perhaps to see clearly what was happening within the empire itself.

Part III

THE ROMAN EMPIRE
AND ITS NEIGHBORS:
225–99

6

THE FAILURE OF THE
SEVERAN EMPIRE

The impact of the Sasanids

Philostratus' vision, which he appears to have shared with many of the people whose lives he described, was very much a vision of the second century AD. It was increasingly in disaccord with events in his lifetime. Philostratus' intellectual framework could no more absorb a Syrian god who remained very much a Syrian god, even though his name had been Hellenized, than he could imagine that intellectual movements outside of the Roman Empire did not depend on Greek thought. Although he had to admit that a man like Bassaeus Rufus could hold high office without appreciating the virtues of great sophists, his stress on imperial offices held by sophists suggests that he felt that government was still an activity for gentlemen.[1] His is an Antonine vision of a government, and the Antonine style was giving way to a government in which diverse groups of professionals were coming to dominate; the values that they brought with them were those of the bureaucrat or soldier rather than those of the urban aristocrat. A new threat from the east, and new threats from the north, were to make the army ever more influential in government. This would, in turn, bring about an increasing centralization of authority around the palace that would transform the Antonine administration, wherein senators or urban aristocrats might feel that their traditions were important, into a poorly oiled machine devoted to the emperor's service.

It was already clear, in the time of Severus Alexander, that the long-standing relationship between Rome and Iran was changing. For centuries this relationship might best be described as a watchful peace, interrupted by periodic outbursts of hostility. Aside from Trajan's short-lived effort to create a province of Mesopotamia, the boundaries of the Roman and Parthian empires had remained reasonably stable; Rome had acquired some territory along the Middle Euphrates in the wake of Marcus' victories in the 160s, but that was it. The border states of Oshroene, Hatra, and Armenia to the north had kept the two powers from direct confrontation. Severus' absorption of Oshroene had critically changed this relationship by bringing Roman garrisons within striking range of the Tigris, but nothing was to change it so much as the overthrow of the Arsacid dynasty at Ctesiphon, and the rise of Persia.[2] Armenia went from being a neutral power with leanings toward Parthia to a staunch ally of Rome, and Hatra passed from Parthian ally to Roman fortress. These changes had nothing to do with any Roman planning or initiative. They were determined by the actions of Ardashir, the first king of the Persian Sasanid line.

Ardashir brought with him a very powerful sense of Iranian tradition, centered on Zoroastrianism. The difficulty that Roman officials might have in understanding a person like this may, perhaps, best be gleaned from the way that Zoroaster and his thought had been transformed into a Hellenized fairy tale in the consciousness of educated members of the elite. There had, of course, been a time when there was a living tradition of genuine Zoroastrian thought within the territories that Rome now controlled. Not only in the period of Achaemenid control prior to the time of Alexander the Great, but even well after that in territories controlled by Iranian dynasts of northern Turkey, the tradition of Zoroaster appears to have survived from the Persian past. By the second and third centuries AD, accurate information concerning the life and teachings of Zoroaster was apparently unavailable. When Plutarch wanted to provide an account of the thinking of Zoroaster, he turned to Theopompus, an author of the fourth century BC who provided a garbled account of Zoroastrian ideas on the basis of what seems to have been a confused (or, more probably, heterodox) personal informant.[3] Other writers were less conscientious, and Zoroaster entered the intellectual demimonde. Historians of philosophy like Diogenes Laertius tried to find a place for him among the founders of Greek philosophy, while others simply made things up and attributed them to him. Pliny, for instance, describes him as the inventor of magic, and records a variety of opinions about when he lived. Apuleius, who argued that his activities were respectable, says that he was the son of a sage named Oromazus, a view that he derived from Plato.[4] The longest of the works contained in the Coptic library that began to emerge from Nag Hammadi in Upper Egypt during the late 1940s and early 1950s presents itself as "Zostrianos; words of truth of Zostrianos. God of Truth, Words of Zoroast[er}" and describes a series of visions that have nothing whatsoever to do with Zoroastrianism.[5] The situation is summed up by Porphyry, who says that he wrote

> a considerable number of refutations of the book of Zoroaster, which
> I showed to be entirely spurious and modern, made up by the sectar-
> ians to convey the impression that the doctrines which they had
> chosen to hold in honor were those of the ancient Zoroaster.
>
> (V. Plot. 16.15, trans. Armstrong)

There was, naturally, a comparable lack of knowledge about the teachers of Zoroastrian lore, the magi, who were, properly speaking, priests of the

Persian pantheon who espoused the beliefs of Zoroastrianism. Despite the fact that they were at home in southern Iran, it is clear that educated Romans thought that the magi could be encountered in Mesopotamia. For example, Philostratus begins the travels of Apollonius of Tyana with a visit to Babylon, where he discusses philosophy with the local magi. Babylon is described as a great city with massive fortifications and numerous great works of art, a vision that is borrowed from Herodotus, while the notion that it was home to authentic magi is nonsense.[6] In the second and third centuries AD, the word *magus* seems to have meant no more than "eastern wise man" when it did not carry the more negative connotation of "magician."[7]

The history of Zoroastrianism in the Persian homeland is largely a matter of conjecture in the centuries before the rise of Ardashir. The most important text expounding its doctrines is the grand Behistun inscription of Darius I, where he identifies himself as the agent of Ahura Mazda against those who represent the forces of the "lie," or Ahriman. Ahura Mazda himself is not represented, but a winged disc with a human head that appears above Darius appears to be a sort of guardian spirit associated with the gods.[8] These two facts, the nonanthropomorphic image of God and the clear sense of dualism – the struggle between the earthly agents of Truth and those of the Lie paralleling the struggle in the immortal sphere – offer points of reference against which to measure later developments. Beyond this, it is plain that a number of the *Gathas*, or poems of Zoroaster, that recount his visions and struggles were likely already to have been in existence, and Herodotus' account of various Persian actions may be reconciled with doctrines contained therein.[9] Taken with texts of much later date that may, nonetheless, reflect emerging doctrines of the fifth through third centuries BC, it is possible to detect the outlines of Zoroastrian cosmology, and of a Zoroastrian doctrine of time. Plainly, too, Zoroastrian elements such as the use of fire altars, and the doctrine that dead bodies should be prevented from corrupting the living through close contact, were also prevalent. These were demonstrated most strikingly at Naqsh-i-Rustam, a mountain between Persepolis and Sivan in the modern Iranian province of Fars. Although excavations at the site were never completed, it does seem clear that Naqsh-i-Rustam had some significance in the pre-Achaemenid, Elamite, period and that, for the Achaemenids, it was the most sacred place in the realm.[10] There it was that kings from Darius I onwards had their tombs cut into the side of the mountain facing out toward a great fire altar.

Zoroastrianism diffused across the territory of the former Achaemenid kingdom, but in a way that makes it very hard to detect any "mainstream" tradition. Rather, as in the case of the kings of Commagene, or the royal house of the Mithridatids in northern Anatolia, there appear to have been many local variations.[11] So too in the Iranian homeland there appear to have been traditions descending from the Zoroastrianism of the Achaemenids mixed with a wide variety of local and, at times, Greek influences.[12] While we know little about the religious life at the Arsacid court, it does not appear that it was (with some possible exceptions) dominated by any sort of doctrinaire Zoroastrianism. Insofar as the worship of Ahura Mazda according to Zoroaster's visions continued to be supported by any official body, it would only seem to have done so in southern Iran. There can be no doubt but that Ardashir was himself a committed Zoroastrian, and according to one tradition his family had some link to the cult of Anahita at Istakhr.[13]

Any effort to understand Ardashir's rise to power depends upon a combination of the extensive account offered by the Arab historian al-Tabarī, who wrote between AD 870 and 923, and the monuments of Ardashir himself. Comparison of these two sources suggests that Tabarī had access to materials that were informed by third-century Persian sources. This material, as Tabarī preserves it, seems to have presented the revolt as beginning with a local squabble in the area around Istakr. Papak, the father of Ardashir, was the first to declare some degree of independence, and to seek the title of king of a neighboring district (probably Persepolis) for his eldest son, Sapor, to whom it appears to have been refused by Artabanus. Sapor died suddenly, and the execution of Papak's plans fell to his younger son, Ardashir.[14] After Ardashir had defeated a number of local dynasts, he too asked Artabanus to confirm his disposition of the areas that he had taken over. Artabanus refused, and Ardashir extended his operations into the delta region of the Tigris and Euphrates, defeating, in turn, the Parthian rulers of a kingdom called Ahwaz (probably Elam) and Mesene, the latter by 221–22.[15] Artabanus then attempted to take matters into his own hands but was defeated and killed on the plain of Hormizdagan. Tabarī's tradition, which is reflected in contemporary Sasanian art, has Ardashir kill Artabanus with his own hand, while his son, Sapor, kills one of Artabanus' chief courtiers.[16]

Although there is no reason to think that religion played any role in the disputes that lie at the heart of Ardashir's rebellion, there can be no doubt but that Ardashir attributed to the god Ahura Mazda his extraordinary success in rising from a petty chieftain to the ruler of the empire. It was Ardashir who commissioned reliefs depicting his victory over Artabanus V in Zoroastrian terms, and his own investiture as king as coming at the hands of Ahura Mazda himself, with his horse stepping upon the head of Artabanus as his god's stepped upon that of Ahriman.[17] But here there is a significant change, and one that may be explained by the influence of anthropomorphic forms of religious depiction stemming from the Greek world. In the art of Ardashir and his descendants in the Sasanian line, Ahura Mazda and Ahriman are depicted in human form, drawing the parallel between their struggle and that of the Sasanian house ever more clearly. What may be even more significant is that the depiction of this sort of relationship with a god was such a complete break with the iconography of the previous regime that it is difficult to believe that it represents anything other than the passion of Ardashir himself. Indeed, looking back over the centuries, a writer of the Byzantine

Plate 6 Ardashir's victory over Artabanus V from Naqsh-i-Rustam. Ardashir is on the left with Artabanus beneath the feet of his horse; he is receiving a crown from Ahura Mazda, whose horse trampled Ahriman, the god who represented the forces of evil. *Credit*: photo courtesy of the Oriental Institute at the University of Chicago.

period wrote, "He was a Magian (Zoroastrian), and because of him the Magians became powerful in amongst the Persians."[18] A much later Persian document that appears to preserve portions of a letter written by Tansar, the chief priest of Ardashir, includes the words:

> Do not marvel at my zeal and ardor for promoting order in the world, that the foundations of the laws of the faith may be made firm. For Church and State were born of one womb, joined together and never to be abandoned.
>
> (Trans. M. Boyce, *Textual Sources for the History of Zoroastrianism* [Manchester, 1984], 109)

That these sentiments are conceivable in a third-century context is confirmed by the massive inscription of Ardashir's son Sapor on the structure known in modern times as the Ka'bah of Zoroaster at Naqsh-i-Rustam (one of the most important sources for early Sasanian history), where it is reported,

> And because with the help of the yazads (good spirits) we sought out and conquered these so many lands, there we have founded in

221

each region many Vahram Fires, and have acted benevolently towards
many priests, and have exalted the affairs of the yazads.

(*RGDS* 17, trans. Boyce, *Textual Sources*, 111)

The ideological drive of Zoroastrianism, the sense that one was doing the
will of Ahura Mazda in combating the forces of evil, is arguably the most
significant new factor with the Sasanian dynasty. At least through the public
proclamations of Sapor and the reliefs that both he and his father commissioned, it provides a coherent rationale for what they saw to be their purpose.
But there was more to establishing the new regime than that. Ardashir established a pattern of royal conduct that required the king to be a successful
general, to be visible in battle. Success in war became one of the central
features of Sasanian kingship, and the king himself was required to play a
central role in the business of government.[19]

The regime that Ardashir installed was also, very much, a family affair.
While we do not know enough about the structure of the Arsacid regime to
say with certainty how much of a change this was, it is clear that many
members of the royal family held the title of king in various parts of the
empire. The Vologeses who had held the throne at Ctesiphon in the reign
of Caracalla appears to have been driven from it by Artabanus, but still to
have retained a kingdom of his own. The ruler of Media was also a member
of the Arsacid clan, as was that of Armenia. Arsacid marriages are evident
in the nomenclature of the royal houses of Oshroene and of Hatra, while the
royal line of Mesene almost certainly had similar connections.[20] The establishment of the new regime involved a restructuring of family relationships
in the diverse kingdoms that had made up the Arsacid state, and a centralization of authority in the family of Ardashir. In the great inscription of
Sapor at Naqsh-i-Rustam, three Ardashirs appear as kings of principalities
in central Asia (all three are presumably relatives of Ardashir himself).
A high official (the king's deputy), the *bidakhsh*, is also named Ardashir, and
a person who appears to be a military official who is senior even to a man
identified as the "army chief" is named Papak, while the Suren, another high
officer, is named Sasan, as is the lord of Andegan. A man named Abursam
is given the further title of "glory of Ardashir."

Omissions are almost as important as inclusions on Sapor's list of courtiers
under his father. For while the central bureaucracy appears to have been filled
with close members of the family, there is no mention made of Mesene,
which would later be governed by a son of Sapor, nor of many territories in
the eastern part of the realm, and there is no mention of the important state
of Adiabene on the eastern bank of the Upper Tigris, which was also to be
governed by an Ardashir under Sapor. The most economical explanation of
these omissions is that they represent regions that were not yet under the
control of Ardashir by the time he passed power on to his son in 241.[21]
Likewise the expansion of territories indicated by Sapor's much longer list

of subordinates, and of places where they ruled, suggests that the central secular concern of the regime was to expand its power throughout the former Arsacid realm, and to protect itself from any threat of an Arsacid resurgence. The kingdom that emerges is a sort of federal state, made up of diverse subkingdoms stretching from Mesopotamia in the west to Afghanistan in the east, from the Persian Gulf in the south to central Asia in the north. The individual kings were treated in this system as subject allies of the King of Kings, who had, in turn, to respect their opinions when making decisions that affected the state as a whole. The succession had to be agreed upon by an assembly of subject kings, and it is quite likely that other major decisions had to be put before an assembly of kings. An injury done to one of these kings was something that the King of Kings had to take very seriously indeed.[22] Thus when, in 359, the son of King Grumbates of the Chiniotae was killed by a missile from the walls of Amida, King Sapor II had to abandon his plan to bypass the place and lay siege to it instead.[23] An observer of the army that was drawn up before the walls of the place could also identify the different national units that made up the Sasanian force, suggesting that they fought as distinct units under their own leaders.[24]

The internal concerns of Ardashir were lost upon the Roman state. Although Dio noted that Ardashir pursued Arsacid survivors, he also wrote that Ardashir sought to reestablish the ancient realm of the Achaemenids, even claiming that he wrote a letter to this effect to Alexander.[25] How he would have known the content of the letter in any detail is a bit hard to fathom, since he had, by the early 230s, retired to Nicaea. Herodian claims to give a text of the document, and this should be enough to arouse some concern.[26] Herodian tended to know what was in the public domain and not much else unless he was close to the scene of the action, as he appears to have been in the time of Maximinus. There was a long history of associating campaigns against the Parthians with the great struggles of the classical Greek past.[27] Even if the emperor was not a devoted imitator of Alexander, like Caracalla, emperors who commanded in the east tended to promote a view of their actions in light either of Alexander or of Themistocles. Trajan, for instance, is said to have lamented that he could not follow Alexander all the way to India when he watched a ship departing for the east from Mesene.[28] The wars of Marcus Aurelius inspired histories in imitation of Herodotus and Thucydides, and festivals connected with the classical past appear to have gotten a boost whenever war with the east threatened. There is some evidence that by the fourth century the Sasanian monarchs, quite possibly as a result of having been bombarded with propaganda from their Roman neighbors, began to play on this themselves. Sapor II, when he invaded the Roman Empire in the 350s, is said, by a reliable source, to have demanded the Achaemenid realm back.[29] But there is no reason to think that this had anything to do with the outbreak of war in the third century. While it is

Plate 7 Naqsh-i-Rustam. This appears to have been a center for Zoroastrian cult. On the cliffs opposite the so-called Ka'bah of Zoroaster (the building in the foreground), rock-cut monuments to the Sasanian kings join the tombs of the Achaemenids. *Credit*: photo courtesy of the Oriental Institute at the University of Chicago.

true that the site of Naqsh-i-Rustam was embellished with monuments in the context of those of the Achaemenid monarchs, these reliefs owe nothing in their style or inspiration to their Achaemenid predecessors, and, unlike the Achaemenids, the Sasanian kings were not buried there.

The Sasanian return to Naqsh-i-Rustam seems to have been governed by the belief that this was a most sacred Zoroastrian spot. The grand inscription of Sapor I on the Ka'bah of Zoroaster makes no reference to the Achaemenids, and the fact that his chief priest, Kirdir, chose the same monument for one of his own inscriptions, commemorating his efforts to strengthen the faith, suggests very strongly that both men chose the Ka'bah because they believed that the spot had a strong connection with Zoroaster. In Sapor's case, it is striking that he nowhere questions the right of the Roman Empire to exist where it does. He calls their land that of the non-Aryans in contrast with that of the Aryans that he rules. Sapor's primary interest in the land of the "non-Aryans" appears to have been as a source of prisoners who could be employed in the massive building projects that he, like his father before him, undertook throughout Persia in the cause of glory for himself.[30] The new regime was plainly concerned to make a physical mark upon the landscape, and it employed large quantities of captive labor to do so. Sapor sums up the result of his victorious campaign of 260 (in which he captured the emperor Valerian) with the words:

224

And men of the Roman Empire, Non-Aryans, we deported. We settled them in the empire of Iran in Persis, Parthia, Khuzistan, in Babylonia and in other lands where there were domains of our father, grandfathers, and our ancestors. We searched out for conquest many other lands, and we acquired fame for heroism.

(RDGS 16)

Tabarī gives a vast list of cities that the two kings built or refounded in their own names, and he records the memory of westerners who were engaged in some of the projects, saying that Valerian himself directed the construction of the massive dam of Shustar on the Karun River in Susiana.[31] The *Chronicle of Sé'ert*, compiled in AD 1034, also remembers the arrival of prisoners:

Sapor left the territories of the Romans, taking with him prisoners whom he settled in the countries of Iraq, Susiana, Persia and in the towns his father had founded. He also built three towns and gave them names derived from his own name. One was in the land of Mesene and was called Sod Sapor. The second, in Persia, is still called Sapor today. He rebuilt Gundeshapuhr which had fallen into disrepair and named it Anti-Sapor, a word half-Greek and half-Persian meaning: "You are Sapor's equal." He constructed a third town on the banks of the Tigris called Marw Harbor (which is 'Ukbara and its environs). These towns were populated by his prisoners who were provided with homes and land to till.

(Trans. Dodgeon and Lieu, *The Roman Eastern Frontier*, 297, slightly modified)

The remains of Gundeshapuhr, in northern Khuzistan, confirm the tradition that western engineers constructed it. It appears to have been laid out on a Hippodamian street plan, and it was later called "(the) better (is the) Antioch of Sapor" in memory of Sapor's capture of Antioch in 252.[32] The city of Bishapur, in Persia, also a foundation of Sapor's, likewise shows a Hippodamian street plan; and three more bridges, at Ahwaz, Pai-Pul, and Dizful, appear to show Roman workmanship.[33]

From the evidence of Sapor's words and deeds, it looks very much as if Dio, Herodian, and very probably Alexander and his advisers were attributing to the Sasanians a mode of thought that was very much their own. The failure to understand the dynamic behind Sasanian policy toward their empire was perhaps every bit as serious as the failure of their army to meet those of Ardashir and Sapor with a modern tactical doctrine.

The Sasanian army, like that of the Parthians, but much more efficiently so, was based on a powerful force of heavy cavalry, or cataphracts, who were armored from head to toe and rode armored horses. To these were added another body of heavy cavalry, armed with lances and bows, but with less extensive armor (chain mail extending only to the waist) and a force of horse archers. Sasanian infantry appears to have been lightly armed and to have consisted primarily of archers. Detailed evidence of Sasanian operations in the fourth century, coming from the historian Ammianus Marcellinus, who was caught up in the assault of 359, suggests that the main body of the army advanced behind a fast-moving screen of cavalry that served to disrupt Roman communications. Ammianus and his general, Ursicinus, the supreme commander of the eastern frontier, were almost captured by Sasanian patrols as they tried to reach Nisibis.[34] The frontier that they were defending was, however, a very different one from that of the third century, for in the fourth century the defense relied on a series of well-garrisoned fortress cities to slow a Persian advance. In the third century the bulk of the legions appear to have still been concentrated in their camps in Syria. Only Nisibis (probably) and Singara (definitely) had legionary garrisons. That of Singara was of strategically limited value: Ammianus noted that the city was too far forward to be reinforced, having fallen several times, with its garrison being taken into captivity.[35] And, in light of the fact that there were no other concentrations of Roman forces east of the Euphrates, the same could be said of Nisibis in the 230s. Indeed, Nisibis could not withstand the invasion of northern Mesopotamia that Ardashir launched in 236, possibly inspired by rumor of events unfolding in the west. Both Nisibis and Carrhae fell under Persian domination for the next several years, making even more tenuous any communication with the garrison at Singara and the troops garrisoned at Hatra.[36] Hatra itself was captured in 240.[37]

The Roman view

When Ardashir struck, there was plainly little that the Roman army in the east could do about it, but even if there had been political stability, the administrative apparatus of the army was not well suited to handing sudden threats. Important decisions relating to dealings with foreign peoples were ordinarily made at court. From the time of Augustus onwards, the governors of garrisoned provinces departed for their provinces (as indeed did all governors) with a set of instructions, or *mandata*, that prescribed general policies that they were to follow.[38] Unless, as was sometimes the case, a governor's *mandata* had given him great latitude with which to act, he was well advised to seek advice from the emperor before proceeding. Our more detailed sources for the first century AD are littered with references to the exchange of letters between governors and the emperor on matters of policy.[39] It is this tendency that makes it legitimate to ask if there was something that can reasonably be defined as a "grand strategy" of the Roman Empire and, if so, what it was.

The fact that important decisions were generally left up to the emperor makes it theoretically possible for there to have been an overarching vision that controlled Rome's relationship with the states on its borders. Indeed, at various periods, we are told that different emperors enunciated general principles. Augustus left advice that the empire not expand beyond the borders that were in place at the time of his death. Hadrian is said to have built physical barriers (of which the most famous is his wall in the north of England) to divide what was Roman from the land of the barbarians.[40] Antoninus Pius refused to annex peoples who offered to place themselves under Roman control on the grounds that they were too poor to repay the cost of garrisoning them.[41] Cassius Dio says that Marcus intended to add two large new provinces to the empire as a result of his northern wars.[42] The evidence that he provides of Marcus' dealings with these peoples shows something quite different, but what is perhaps more significant, he shows that Marcus pursued a coherent policy in settling Rome's relationships with these peoples. The detailed reports of treaties that Dio includes in his history show that Marcus intended to control tribal access to the empire through a series of fixed points, that he sought to control their freedom of assembly in the absence of Roman observers, and that he established advance guard posts across the river, maintaining as well zones in which settlement was forbidden.[43] Dio himself says that Severus' annexation of Mesopotamia was ill advised because it was too expensive.[44] Roman emperors, and the inhabitants of the empire, who came in time to see the empire as a fortified camp, had a clear sense that there were definable frontiers, a notion that may have descended from the importance of the idea of the *pomerium*, or sacred boundary, of the city of Rome itself.[45]

There were, of course, some practical difficulties with these ideas. A line such as Hadrian's Wall was obvious to all, as were the fortified lines of the German frontier, or the Danube River. Rather less obvious were the lines of control that could be defined in regions such as North Africa or the province of Arabia. But that may not matter on the grand scale, since Roman ideas of the way that space should be defined evolved prior to the acquisition of Arabia or the northern edge of the Sahara. There was, in any event, a tendency to view the world in terms of lists of peoples, with the accompanying notion that where one people's territory stopped, that of another began. The fact that this could be virtually irrelevant in dealing with nomadic tribes who followed cycles of annual migration would matter less than whether at some point the tribe could be said to be a Roman ally or foe, and whether it was possible to control the routes along which it traveled.

In the broadest possible terms it may be fair to say that the grand strategy of the Roman Empire consisted of the belief that what was Roman should stay Roman, that a place that had entered into a formal relationship with Rome was entitled to protection if it was outside the border of a province. The overall military posture of the Roman state was passive. The empire was as large as could reasonably be defended with the limited resources available. The ideology of world domination that was an important feature of

Rome's makeup since the days of the late republic could accommodate the notion that all the world that was worth ruling was already under Roman control.[46] Beyond that, the principal factors governing Roman strategy cannot be said to have been very detailed. It has been very well observed that forts in Judaea and Arabia were rarely sited in ways to optimize their defensive capabilities, and that overall understanding of world geography was deeply imprecise.[47] The perspective gained from studying Roman foreign policy on the basis of remains surviving in the provinces, from analyzing its impact on the peoples it encountered, is perforce radically different from that which can be gained by looking at the ideals of the central government.[48] A further problem with this dichotomy is that we are often looking at Roman policy at very different moments. The provincial view is informed, in Braudelian terms, by the study of social structures; the "central view" by the history of events. While the history of events could (and did) shape long-term structures – there can be no doubt but that the evolution of northern Mesopotamia would have been very different if Severus had not expanded the frontier – the policies of the central government were only one factor in that development.

When examining the making of Roman policy it is often worth considering the ways that a Roman might be able to gain a view of the world, and the fundamental disconnection between small- and large-scale mapping exercises. Roman surveyors had the ability to draw very detailed maps of small areas.[49] They did not have the capacity to draw accurate large-scale maps; rather they could measure the empire in terms of how far places were from each other along a road.[50] Local maps represent the ability to obtain immensely detailed local knowledge, large-scale maps the impossibility of projecting that knowledge into a useful format for central decision-making.

There is no evidence to suggest that a Roman emperor could have thought in terms of the relative advantages of a linear forward defense as opposed to a defense in depth. When Augustus said that the empire should be limited to the area within existing borders, that seems to have been the extent of what he was proposing; he could provide a list of what legions and auxiliary cohorts were where, a list of revenues and of citizens.[51] But there was no broad strategic vision on the order of plans drawn up by a European general staff in the nineteenth century. Indeed the Greek word *stratêgêma* meant only a trick or device to be used on the battlefield (the Latin *strategema* is obviously a loan word, and it means the same thing). Works on generalship entitled *Stratêgêmata*, in Greek or Latin, are no more than lists of clever battlefield maneuvers culled, ordinarily, from literature. *Taktikos*, a word connected with the verb *tassô*, is closer to the modern sense of tactics in that it denotes the ordering of troops on the battlefield. As with mapping, so too with conceptions of planning: there is a vocabulary for small-scale maneuvers, and, indeed, there survive some works such as Arrian's that give substantial practical advice, but no independent vocabulary or capacity for detailed long-range planning. The word for something like Augustus' advice that the empire be kept within existing borders was simply *consilium*, in the sense of "advice."[52]

The thinking that governed Roman relations with the outside world was of a very different sort. This thinking involved terms such as *gloria*, the glory that was won in battle, the ability to compel a foreign people to do something. That which was to be preserved was *decus*, or "face," *fastigium*, "dignity," or the *maiestas*, "majesty," of the empire. Foreign peoples who challenged the *gloria* or *decus* of Rome suffered from *superbia*, or arrogance, which led them to do *iniuriae*, injuries, to Rome, which needed, above all, to be avenged.[53]

There can be no doubt but that Ardashir had done an injury to Rome through his seizure of Carrhae and Nisibis in 235–36.[54] And so it was that the advisers of the young Gordian III, of whom the chief and most important was Gaius Furius Sabinius Timesitheus, the praetorian prefect, determined that they must take vengeance upon him. War was declared on Persia with due pomp and ceremony, accompanied by the celebration of a festival of Minerva with Greek-style games, intended, no doubt, to evoke memory of her role, in the guise of Pallas Athena, in the defeat of Xerxes' invasion of Greece in 480–479 BC.[55]

The government of Gordian III

The declaration of war in 241, and the arrival of Roman forces in the east in the course of 242, marks a significant delay in response to Ardashir's annexation of Mesopotamia six years earlier. It should ordinarily have taken no more than a year to gather an army and send it east, for such was the timetable of Lucius Verus' war in the 160s (in response to an invasion of Syria) and of Alexander's war, likewise in response to a perceived threat.[56] Part of the delay may be attributed to Maximinus' concentration on northern affairs, but that cannot explain why it took three years for the government of Gordian III to react. The explanation in this case may be sought in the problems of creating a unified government around a ruler who, in his early teens, cannot have exercised any influence over the process.

There are two events that might serve as markers of serious contention within the governing class. The first is another revolt in Africa Proconsularis, this one led by the governor Sabinianus.[57] Whatever Sabinianus, who had been consul in 225, thought he was doing, the fact of his allocation to the prestigious province at a difficult time suggests that he was seen as an ally of Maximinus' foes. It would appear that something had happened very quickly to make him unhappy, and he does not appear to have had much support on the ground. His rebellion was crushed by the equestrian governor of Mauretania, one Faltonius Restitutianus, the provincial procurator who was holding office "in place of the governor."[58] The second event of significance is the execution, in 241, of Tullus Menophilus, who had commanded the garrison of Aquileia against Maximinus. At the same time it is possible to trace numerous senatorial careers that continue without interruption. L. Caesonius Lucillus Macer Rufinianus, who was a member of the board of twenty senators in 238, appears to have replaced Sabinianus.[59] L. Domitius Gallicanus Papinianus, who had roused the people against the Praetorian Guard in 238, went on to important posts under Gordian and his successor, as did Rutilius Pudens Crispinus, another leading figure on the senatorial side against Maximinus.[60] The evidence of these careers may suggest that there were disgruntled individuals who felt insufficiently rewarded in the wake of 238, but that others who had been notable for their role found it best to go along with the regime that they had created. As such, it may be reasonable to conclude that there was no simple "senatorial" position other than a desire for reasonable government. This is all the more significant in that power was passing into the hands of a group of equestrians with strong backgrounds in the fiscal service.[61]

The most prominent of these equestrians was Timesitheus, whose preeminence was marked by Gordian's marriage to his daughter, Furia Sabinia Tranquillina, in 241 (possibly on May 12).[62] He had begun his career under Elagabalus as prefect of an auxiliary cohort in Spain, before moving into the administration of the *ratio privata* in the provinces of the Rhine frontier. This office was sandwiched between two stints as governor of Arabia in 218 and 222. In 224 he was procurator for the collection of the inheritance tax and oversight of the funds connected with Greek-style games. In 232 he was in charge of finances for the Persian expedition of Alexander in the east, before taking up four more fiscal posts, the last of which was as procurator for the provinces of Aquitania and Lugdunensis in central and southern France.[63] His career, up until his elevation to the praetorian prefecture, is quite similar to that of another equestrian officer, C. Attius Alcimus Felicianus, whose first known office is as a legal representative of the *fiscus* under Elagabalus. He passed on from there to a variety of fiscal procuratorships in the provinces before returning to Rome, where he was in charge of the mint around 233, and procurator in charge of the inheritance tax at Rome in 235. Under Maximinus his career arguably suffered something of a setback when he was placed in charge of the amphitheater, before returning to the center of power as the head of the *ratio privata* in 239. It would appear that the administration of Rome was handed over to him when the emperor went east in 241, as he then held two extraordinary posts as prefect of the *vigiles* and of the grain supply "in place of the praetorian prefects."[64]

The description of Felicianus' post bespeaks an unusual concentration of power in the office of the praetorian prefects. It was repeated, without the addition of the prefecture of the grain supply, in 242–44, when Valerius Valens was promoted from command of the fleet at Misenum to the post of prefect of the *vigiles* "in place of the praetorian prefects."[65] The repetition of the combination of the title and the clear implication that the *vigiles* had been taken under the direct control of the praetorian prefects in 241 lend the unification of the command of the guard and of the watch the air of deliberation. It ensured that there could not be a potential rival, in Rome, commanding a force of armed men. The temporary connection with the prefecture of the grain supply may have been a result of some trouble connected with the rebellion of Saturninus, and ongoing trouble in Numidia resulting from the discharge of Legion III Augusta for its role in the slaughter of the elder Gordians. Felicianus' position would thus appear to have been designed as an effort to forestall a repeat of the rebellion of 238 while the emperor and his prefects were out of town, and while the regime, as yet, had no great success to its credit. The subordination of the prefecture of the *vigiles* only ended in 243 (possibly after the death of Timesitheus), when the post was passed to Fultonius Restitutianus, the proven loyalist who had suppressed the revolt of Saturninus.[66] At the same time as the prefecture of the *vigiles* was undergoing its transformation, the last man to hold it as an independent office, Gnaeus Domitius Philippus, was moved to Egypt as "*dux* acting in place of the Prefect of Egypt."[67] This combination of offices and the fact that the independence of the prefecture of the *vigiles* was suspended at the end of his term suggest that he was closely associated with Timesitheus. Alongside of this group, and sitting in its councils, there was Marcus Gnaeus Licinius Rufinus, whose career is a virtual paradigm for the rise of equestrians to these positions. An inscription erected in the reign of Gordian III in his home city of Thyateira in western Turkey underscores the importance of being a member of the equestrian order rather than the senate.[68] It reads as follows:

> To Good Fortune
>
> To M(arcus) Gn(aeus) Licin(ius) Rufinus, of equestrian rank, *consiliarius* of the Emperor, having handled Greek letters, *a studiis Augusti*, in charge of the accounts (*a rationibus?*), in charge of the *apokrimata* (*a libellis?*), praetor of the Romans, governor of the province of Noricum, priest of the *sacerdotium* of Titus Tatius, in the *consilium* of the Twenty Men, chosen as *amicus Caesaris*, having acted often as ambassador to the Emperors, and having secured all the rights for his native city, the *clarissimus consularis*, and, on account of the generosity of his provision and his construction of many major works, both a communal and individual benefactor, the gardeners (gave honor).
>
> (*SEG* 47, no. 1656, trans. F. Millar,
> *JRS* 89 [1999]: 95)

Perhaps the single most striking feature of this text, the information for which must have been provided by the honorand or someone close to him, is that, despite being an important member of the senatorial order, he is identified first as an equestrian.[69] This is not simply a reflection of the fact that he had left his equestrian career behind him when he entered the senate. Rather, as is the case with another inscription that was erected in his honor, wherein he is described as both equestrian and senatorial as if the two statuses were equivalent, it reflects the importance of being recognized as a member of the equestrian elite at the center of government.

The "power set" in Rome thus appears to have become, by 241, a group of equestrian officers, most, if not all, from the eastern provinces, with experience in the *ratio privata*. These officials were joined by two brothers from Chahba in Arabia, Iulius Priscus and Philippus (or Philip as he is more commonly known in modern parlance). We know nothing about Philip's career prior to his accession to the praetorian prefecture in 243, but we do know that Priscus, who ascended to the prefecture while Timesitheus was still alive, had also occupied a series of provincial procuratorships prior to his rise to that office.[70]

Historiography and the war with Persia

Dio completed his history with the events surrounding his second consulship and Alexander's war with Persia. Marius Maximus' last biography was that of Elagabalus, and Herodian stopped writing with the accession of Gordian III as sole emperor. Mixed blessing though his history may be, Herodian at least offered the perspective of an interested contemporary and a reasonable chronological sense. With the end of Herodian's history, we lose all contemporary chronological narratives of Roman history until the beginning of the fourth century, whence have survived the narratives of Lactantius and Eusebius, both from a Christian perspective. The narrative of the intervening years must be pieced together from Byzantine sources that had access to contemporary Greek accounts, from the *Historia Augusta*, and from a group of short Latin histories, all written in the last quarter of the fourth century. Additionally, for the period from Gordian to roughly 263, there is the text of an oracle, known now as the *Thirteenth Sibylline Oracle*, which collects a series of earlier texts in a rough chronological order.[71] The *Thirteenth Sibylline Oracle* is invaluable as a view of the period from the eastern provinces (mostly from Syria), while the later Byzantine accounts offer a broader perspective, probably derived primarily from two books by an Athenian named Dexippus, with some additional material from another Athenian historian named Philostratus.[72] Dexippus' history is also known from quotations that appear in the *Historia Augusta*, and some extensive extracts from one of his two books, preserved by several ninth-century Byzantine collections of excerpts from earlier writers. These may all be supplemented, for the period from 244 to 260, by Sapor's trilingual inscription at Naqsh-i-Rustam and, at the end of the century, by the battered inscription of the Persian king Narses from Paikuli in northern Iraq, which is critical for internal events after Sapor's death.[73]

The main Byzantine sources are four in number. The most extensive, written in the sixth century, is Zosimus' *New History*. Zosimus despised the Christian church (an issue in evaluating what he has to say on the fourth century), using as his sources the works of two writers of the late fourth and early fifth centuries, Eunapius of Sardis and Olympiodorus of Thebes in Egypt.[74] Eunapius began his history about where one of Dexippus' works, the *Chronicle* (which concluded in 272), left off. We do not know what sources Eunapius used for his third-century history after 272, and we cannot know for certain what books Zosimus had available to him for the period prior to the point that Eunapius began.[75] It is likely, however, that he used Dexippus' *Chronicle*, and it is possible that he also read Dexippus' account of the German wars from, probably, the 250s to the early 270s. John Zonaras, the second of our Byzantine sources in terms of length and quantity of detail, wrote in the twelfth century. A man of considerable importance in his own time, Zonaras wrote numerous ecclesiastical works and composed a lexicon before he retired (or was exiled) to the monastery of Hagia Glycera, where he wrote his *Epitome of the Histories* from the Creation to 1118. For the third century he had access, it seems, to a work that offered an account based on a combination of Dexippus' *Chronicle* and excerpts from Philostratus.[76] For the fourth century he appears to have used a source informed by Eunapius as well as various later church historians. The third source is George's *Ekloge Chronographias* (*Selection of Chronography*) from Adam to the accession of Diocletian, which he finished around AD 810.[77] He too appears to have used, for secular history, a work that employed Dexippus' *Chronicle*. Finally there is John Malalas' *Chronicle of Antioch*. Malalas' work, which is primarily concerned with events in Syria, is less informative than the others for the empire as a whole, but contains material that the others do not have, some of it very interesting, much of it odd.[78]

Despite the multiplicity of books, the perspective on third-century history that has survived is largely that of one man, Publius Herennius Dexippus. His works inform much of the *Historia Augusta*, albeit through the medium of an earlier Latin historian, and provide the vast bulk of the information available through the Byzantine sources.[79] What sort of historian was he? Did he have access to good information? Was he astute and critical in his evaluation of the evidence that he had? The answers to these three questions are, unfortunately, "poor," "no," and "no."[80] The extant fragments of his history of the Gothic wars – and they are extensive enough to permit such judgments – betray a writer very much like Herodian. He liked rhetorical set pieces (which is why so much of his history has survived), and he appears to have been motivated by a desire to flatter Aurelian, who ruled from 270 to 275, and under whose reign the tribes north of the Danube were defeated. The history that comes out through Zosimus leaves much to be desired, and it is no good blaming this on Zosimus' personal ineptitude. Zosimus may not have been one of the great minds of antiquity, and indeed, it may be said that one of his virtues is that he is only as good as his sources for any period. His ability to reflect the prejudices of those sources is precisely the quality that makes it possible to reconstruct the attitudes of earlier historians to the events that they described. The same can be said of Dexippus, and, indeed, his own qualities as an historian can be tested through the fragments of a book that he wrote about the successors of Alexander. The kindest thing that can be said about it is that, if we did not also have extensive fragments of Arrian's history of the same period, we would still have Arrian, because all Dexippus did was summarize his history.[81]

Zosimus knew that Gordian had married the daughter of Timesitheus, whose name Zosimus gives, wrongly, as Timesicles, and that the Persians had invaded the empire while Ardashir was still on the throne.[82] It is through George's *Chronicle* and Zonaras that we learn that Dexippus had also recorded the capture of Nisibis and Carrhae under Maximinus.[83] Zosimus states that Sapor had succeeded his father before Gordian moved east and knows that the Romans had won an initial victory over the Persians, and that Timesitheus had then died.[84] What follows is nonsense. Zosimus and Zonaras both say that the praetorian prefecture then passed to Philip, and that Philip arranged to send the supplies that had been gathered for the army, which was in the area of Carrhae and Nisibis, too far ahead of the troops so that they began to starve.[85] When they ran short of provisions, the troops mutinied and killed Gordian.

The point of this account is to maintain the picture of Gordian as a successful ruler who died only because of a treacherous subordinate. It omits some rather important details. Sapor says that Gordian invaded his empire, and that he reached the city of Misiche on the Middle Euphrates, where, Sapor also says, he defeated and killed the emperor.[86] This too is less than accurate, for we know that Gordian died nowhere near Misiche. Rather, he

---

Plate 8 The diverse images of Alexander Severus, Maximinus, and Gordian III. Just as the image of Alexander marks a sharp break from that of Elagabalus and Caracalla (see plate 5 above), so too does that of Maximinus mark a sharp break from that of Alexander, while that of Gordian recalls that of Alexander. As significant are the changes in the imperial image within the reign. The emergence of the bearded versions of Alexander and Gordian (8b and 8e) are close in time to the beginning of their respective Persian campaigns. (a) Alexander Severus. *Credit*: KM 1991.2.693. Photo courtesy of the Kelsey Museum of Archaeology, University of Michigan. (b) Alexander Severus. *Credit*: KM 1991.2.696. Photo courtesy of the Kelsey Museum of Archaeology, University of Michigan. (c) Maximinus. *Credit*: KM 1991.2.711. Photo courtesy of the Kelsey Museum of Archaeology, University of Michigan. (d) Gordian III. *Credit*: *RIC* Gordian III no. 5 (Rome 238–40); author's collection, photo courtesy of Forum Ancient Coins. (e) Gordian III. *Credit*: *RIC* Gordian III 151 (Rome 243–44); author's collection, photo courtesy of Forum Ancient Coins.

(a)

(b)

(c)

(d)

(e)

died in Zaitha, the region near the confluence of the Khabur and the Euphrates in northern Mesopotamia. The spot was marked by a massive tumulus in which the body of Gordian was, at least temporarily, buried after he had been killed by his own men. Plotinus had accompanied the expedition in the hope of meeting the sages of the east, and his biographer says that he escaped the camp only with difficulty, which again suggests that there was serious trouble in the camp at the time that Gordian perished.[87] The date was sometime between January 13 and March 14, 244, a very odd time of year to be attempting to campaign in Mesopotamia, as it was then the height of the rainy season.[88]

Insofar as anything like the truth can be extracted from these diverse accounts, it appears that Gordian's army invaded Mesopotamia in the winter of 244, and that it reached Misiche at the northwestern end of the Naarmalcha, the grand canal that traverses Mesopotamia at that point. There Sapor defeated the Romans, who withdrew back up the Euphrates to Zaitha, where the army, possibly in frustration, murdered its teenage emperor. The Roman tradition never seems to have admitted to the defeat, for even the contemporary author of some lines contained in the *Thirteenth Sibylline Oracle* did not know of it.[89] What role, if any, Philip played in these transactions cannot now be known, but it is interesting that even the hostile accounts of Zosimus and Zonaras do not suggest that he was with the army when the emperor died.

Philip, Rome, and the millennium

The depth of confusion in the sources for the death of Gordian and the accession of Philip is such that we can say very little about what was happening. The one curious fact that we do have is that Philip's brother, Priscus, had been elevated to the prefecture before Philip and was still prefect when Philip also received that post.[90] They were, as far as we know, the first pair of brothers to hold that office. Priscus' priority in the prefecture would suggest that, in the last year of Gordian's life, he had acceded to Timesitheus' dominant position within court circles. This raises the perhaps unanswerable question of why Philip rather than Priscus or any other person should have become emperor. The most obvious answer, albeit speculative, is that Philip had a son. If Priscus did not (we have no information on this point), it would suggest that Philip's appointment was aided by the hope that he could establish a dynasty that might guarantee stability. Like Macrinus, and like Maximinus as well, Philip was not the most important man in the state when he took the throne.

The job of the emperor was, when he was capable of performing it, to balance the interests of the different groups that contributed to the government of the empire. In a sense, then, it may have been desirable that, lacking an intrinsic claim to the office, he be in a position where he would have to respect those different interests. The pattern of selecting an individual who would have to negotiate between the interests of those who had appointed him would be repeated on many occasions in the next century and a half and, in the later fourth century, result in emperors who were largely subordinate to factions within the government. But that is to anticipate much, and to anticipate changes in the structure of the state in the first half of that century; the state that Philip took over was one that he was expected to rule in his own right.

Philip's most pressing concerns were to end what was turning into a spectacularly unsuccessful war with Persia and heed the examples of both Macrinus and Maximinus, which showed what happened to men with local support who failed to solidify their positions at Rome with sufficient alacrity. His first significant act, after elevating his son to the rank of Caesar (heir designate), was to make peace with Persia, and he did so on terms that would cause a great deal of trouble.[91] Sapor still appears to have been most interested in rooting out survivors of the Arsacid regime, and at that time their most powerful kingdom in the west was Armenia. According to the Byzantine historian Evagrius of Pontus, Philip gave up Armenia to Persia. His source here is a third-century historian named Nicostratus of Trebizond, whose history covered the period from Philip's treaty to the victory of Odaenathus of Palmyra in the 260s.[92]

The problem with what Evagrius has to say is that Philip was not able to "give up" Armenia, which was an independent kingdom. What Philip could do was simply to say that he recognized the primacy of Persian interests in the area.[93] Such an agreement would be in keeping with a long history of Roman relations with Persia, in which the status of Armenia was often at the center. Under Augustus it had been agreed that the king should receive his crown from Rome while being the nominee of the Arsacid king. This arrangement was reasserted under Nero, and there is no reason to think that its principle had been abandoned in subsequent centuries, until the Arsacid rulers no longer saw themselves in any sort of dependent relationship with Persia.

The centrality of Armenia to the treaty that Philip made with Sapor is confirmed, indirectly, by Sapor himself. It is Sapor who says that the reason for his second campaign against the Roman east was occasioned by the fact that "Caesar lied about Armenia." He also reports that Philip paid him an immense indemnity, of 500,000 aurei.[94] The details here all seem to have been lost on Dexippus, who is most likely to be responsible for Zosimus' narrative of these same events:

> He made a treaty under oath with Sapor, ending the war and returned to Rome, taking care of the soldiers with abundant gifts of money, sending ahead to Rome the report that Gordian had died of disease. When he came to Rome, he seduced the most important

senators with moderate discourses. He judged it necessary to give
the most important positions to those who were closest to him. He
appointed his brother, Priscus, to the command of the legions in
Syria and entrusted his brother-in-law, Severianus, with the forces
in Moesia and Macedonia.

(Zos. 1.19.1–2)

The policies that Zosimus describes are immensely revealing. Philip in
fact went well beyond an announcement that Gordian had died of disease.
He transferred the boy's body to Rome and arranged for his deification as a
way of declaring his own legitimacy by asserting a connection with his predecessor (though he stopped short of Severus' autoadoption into the line of that
predecessor).[95] The appointments of Priscus and Severianus point very much
in the direction of dynastic ambitions on his part, and a reconstitution of
authority so that it resided less with groups within the bureaucracy than
within his family.[96] This was accompanied by a massive building project at
his hometown of Chahba, which was elevated to civic status and given the
name of Philippopolis. The architecture of the new city was stunning, being
very much in a western and, particularly, Italian style, while employing the
black basalt of the region. The effect was to create a city unlike any other
in the region (or anywhere else, given the nature of the building material)
that proclaimed by its very appearance – not to mention the statues honoring
Philip and his family members, including his father, who appears there
as "divine" – that it was the home of a Roman emperor.[97] The project at
Philippopolis recalls, to some degree, that of Severus at Lepcis, though in
this region it was a far more extraordinary departure from the local style.
As with both Severus and Elagabalus, it also represents the tension between
an emperor's avowedly non-Roman, non-Greek background and the office
that he now held. While Elagabalus had tried to bring Emesa with him to
Rome, Philip and Severus reconstructed their home cities so as to make them
appropriate to a Roman. Interestingly, Philippopolis appears to have been
no more welcome in the Arabian environment than the Emesene god had
been at Rome. Some lines in the *Thirteenth Sibylline Oracle* predict all manner
of ruination for the place.[98]

New cities cost money, a lot of it, and so too do expensive treaties with
Persia and donatives to secure the loyalty of the army. The tale of the imperial
silver coinage does not show any dramatic change that could be associated
with these needs: the maximum silver content of the *antoninianus* ranged
between 44 and 31 percent, as compared to between 47 and 37 percent under
Gordian, and the mean weight of the coin remained about the same. In any
event, the treaty with Persia was not paid with silver coin, and we do not
know how Philippopolis was paid for. Where definite changes can be seen
under Philip would appear to be in patterns of expenditure and collection.
Philip stopped paying the subsidies to tribal chieftains north of the Danube

that had helped keep the peace, and there appear to have been substantial changes in the way that taxes were collected in Egypt.[99] These changes appear to have been initiated earlier than Philip, in the time of Gordian III. At the village level, they involved the replacement of individual comarchs with boards of ten, the *dekaprôtoi*, who were responsible for ensuring that the full tax assessment of the village was met each year. Oversight of the collection process appears to have been detached from the office of the prefect of Egypt and placed in the hands of an official named Marcellus, who was given the title of *rationalis*.[100] We do not know anything about similar changes in other parts of the empire, but there is some evidence that stricter fiscal administration was the order of the day elsewhere, and possibly too that the burden fell more heavily on local aristocracies than before. A revolt that broke out in Syria during 248, led by a man named Iotapianus, is said to have been caused by the exactions of Iulius Priscus.[101]

Zosimus' statement that Philip placed Syria under Priscus while Severianus governed Moesia and Macedonia, a statement that, in Priscus' case, requires some emendation, points to an important dimension of Philip's style of government. The enormous size of the empire meant, as we have seen, that it divided naturally into a series of economic zones. Priscus' actual position, as emerges from inscriptions and a crucial papyrus that appears to contain his signature, was governor of Mesopotamia and *corrector*.[102] As *corrector* he exercised control over the governors of the individual provinces of the east, meaning, at the very least, the Syrian provinces, Oshroene, Palestine, and Arabia. He was, in effect, a deputy emperor, as would Severianus have been for the Balkans. Such arrangements had been made, as we have seen, in the past to ensure the more efficient disposition of local resources, by placing the power of ultimate decision-making closer to hand. Priscus' signature occurs on a petition from a village near Dura that came to him at Antioch. In the case of Severianus we have a rescript from Philip to a woman named Aeliana telling her that she could not appeal to a provincial governor against a ruling of "the man who then gave judgment in place of the emperor."[103]

Greater efficiency does not necessarily mean better government. The inherent inefficiency of Antonine government allowed plenty of space for local initiative, while the diverse bureaus of government allowed space for different individuals to find a niche within the administrative apparatus. Diversity of governmental styles, and distance, allowed for a government that possessed the flexibility needed to govern areas that were ecologically, ethnically, and culturally different. It may even have allowed people to create their own versions of the dominant culture of the ruling power without having to confront the consequences of their own misunderstandings. The centralizing tendencies of Severan and post-Severan government, driven above all by a need for cash to pay an ever more demanding military apparatus and to fend off new enemies from outside, threatened to upset the balance of power between the central and local governments, the balance of local and imperial cultures. It is not a process that can or should be traced to any specific individual, but rather to bureaucratic tendencies. There was a reason why men like Philip were at the center of power in ways that they were not in the past: they had skills that were needed, and Philip would appear to be very much a product of the time of Gordian III with its collection of powerful servants of the *fiscus*. His display of respect for Gordian's memory was a demonstration of his desire to continue patterns of government that were dominant after 238.

There were consequences, some of them predictable, to Philip's actions. The withdrawal of subsidies to the northern tribes led to war along the Danube, and the Arsacids of Armenia were not willing to submit to Sapor. War with Persia appears to have been renewed along the eastern frontier within a year of the peace treaty, and the prominent positions occupied by Philip's relatives made it very difficult for the emperor to dodge responsibility for anything that seemed like less than a total success.[104] At the same time Philip appears to have understood that he needed to spend money at Rome; he had, after all, emerged from a regime that was deeply interested in avoiding a repeat of the revolt of 238. The most spectacular of Philip's performances in Rome came in 248 with the celebration of the millennium of the city's foundation on April 21. It was perhaps unfortunate for Philip that the year 1000 was one pregnant with meanings that he could not control. That year also saw the outbreak of rioting in Alexandria connected with the activity of a prophet who stirred up a pogrom against the local Christian population, and some lines that came into the *Thirteenth Sibylline Oracle* appear to have been written with a view to disproving notions that the year 1000 should portend some other great change.[105] It may not be accidental that the same year saw the outbreak of a serious military rebellion on the Danube, where the garrison of Moesia proclaimed a man named Pacatianus emperor, while Iotapianus was active in the east.[106] Not all of this need be associated directly with the proclamation of the millennium. Nonetheless, it all does occur against a background, in some quarters, of speculation about the coming of radical change.

The revolt of Pacatianus was not long-lived. Coins that he issued from Viminacium suggest that his revolt began toward the end of 248, and they cease to be minted before the end of April. The agent of his destruction was a senator of Danubian background, named Decius.[107] Decius had begun his career under Severus Alexander and had been a loyal supporter of Maximinus in 238, when he held the province of Hispania Citerior for his emperor. He proved much less loyal to Philip. No sooner had the revolt of Pacatianus collapsed than Decius allowed himself to be proclaimed emperor by the troops who, according to Zosimus, saw this as a way to avoid punishment for their support of the failed rebellion. It may be that Philip had sensed that the legions in that area would not have responded to his entreaties when he sent Decius out, but now he had no choice but to move against the rebels himself. There is no reason to think that he had much experience as an operational commander, and he failed miserably on this occasion. The two armies appear to have met around Verona in northern Italy. Philip was defeated and killed.[108] The date appears to be sometime in September 249. Philip's son may have perished with him, and Priscus disappears without a trace.

Decius, history, historiography, and the "Skythai"

As a usurper who had betrayed his emperor, Decius seems to have felt that he had an image problem. He also seems to have had an interest in history, and it was to history that, in different ways, he turned to solve his problem. The most obvious sign of this was in his own name. Born C. Messius Quintus Decius Valerinus and styling himself either Q. L. Decius or Q. L. Decius Valerinus at earlier points in his life, he had, by the end of 249, taken a new name, C. Messius Quintus Traianus Decius.[109] The name Traianus (or, more commonly, Trajan) was used prominently enough that the *Thirteenth Sibylline Oracle* introduced him as follows:

> After him another king will rule mighty flourishing Rome, skilled
> in war, emerging from the Dacians, of the number 300.
> (Orac. Sib. 13.81–83)

The number 300 is the numerical value of the Greek letter tau, the first letter in Traianos, while reference to the Dacians, which is mildly inaccurate since he was in fact born at Budelia near Sirmium (and thus technically speaking a Pannonian), probably stems from the author's association of the name Trajan with the land of the Dacians that he had conquered. The point might have been reinforced by the prevalence of reverses on Decius' early silver coinage commemorating Dacia.[110] The author also seems to have read the appearance of the name Trajan as Decius intended, as a reference to his military capacity. So too the author would have caught the gist of Decius' proclamation of the state of the empire, something that appears to have been publicized by one of the most remarkable edicts hitherto issued by any Roman emperor. This was an order that all his subjects sacrifice to the gods for the well-being of the state.[111]

The text of the edict appears to have been relatively detailed. The consistency evident in the numerous texts that have survived from Egypt recording the act of sacrifice suggests that precise forms of observance were laid out.[112] The Egyptian texts, collectively known as *libelli*, a term that contemporary Christians used for them (probably because the word was used in the edict), consist of a record of the act of sacrifice, the names of the officials in charge of overseeing the sacrifice, and a statement by the sacrificant testifying to his or her loyalty to the "ancestral gods" and to the consumption of sacrificial

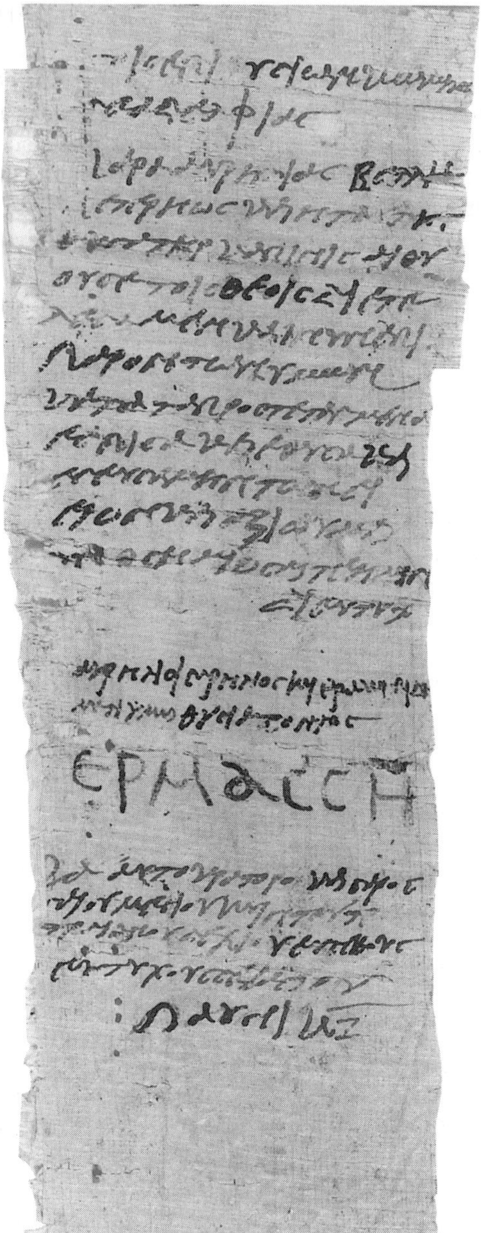

Plate 9 A Decian libellus. The text reads: "To those in charge of the sacrifices of the village Theadelphia, from Aurelia Bellias, daughter of Peteres, and her daughter, Kapinis. We have always been constant in sacrificing to the gods, and now too, in your presence, in accordance with the regulations, I have poured libations and sacrificed and tasted the offerings, and I ask you to certify this for us below. May you continue to prosper. (2nd hand) We, Aurelius Serenus and Aurelius Hermas, saw you sacrificing. (3rd hand) I, Hermas, certify. (1st hand) The 1st year if the Emperor Caesar Gaius Messius Quintus Traianus Decius Pius Felix Augustus, Pauni 27 (June 21, 250)." P.Mich. inv. 263. *Credit*: photo and translation courtesy of Special Collections, the University of Michigan Library.

food and drink. It appears from Christian texts that all the inhabitants of a province were required to perform this act by a specified day or be liable to serious penalties. The parallel with the systems of census registration and tax collection are obvious.[113] In both cases it was up to the individual taxpayer to make the proper declaration or payment by a specific time, and it was possible to check if a person had done this because of the tax registers.

The language of the oath is of interest, precisely because it is so vague. A simple reference to the "ancestral gods" did not force any individual to sacrifice to any god in particular, though it had the coincidental, and probably unintentional, effect of forcing Christians to decide if they could sacrifice under such circumstances. Decius was not trying to assert the superiority of a specifically Roman pantheon over any other gods; rather it appears that he was stressing consistency in the practice of worship. Whatever else people did, they were expected, at least once, to perform the same action before the gods as everyone else.[114] He sought to have all people declare their affinity with the gods who had preserved the empire. In all likelihood Decius was seeking to legitimize his position through a most public act of devotion and, quite possibly, to respond to the undercurrent of unease caused by the passing of the millennium. The response that Decius may have been looking for may be best illustrated by a letter he wrote to the people of Aphrodisias thanking them for their display of piety in response to his order:

> It was to be expected that you, because of the goddess for whom your city is named, and because of your relationship and loyalty to the Romans, that you would have rejoiced at the establishment of our rule and made the appropriate prayers and sacrifices.
> (*Aphrodisias and Rome*, n. 25.8–11)

Decius had been born in the reign of Severus and could remember the *constitutio antoniniana*, which may be the model for his action.[115] Emperors in the past had used decrees about taxation early in their reigns to get people's attention, but what makes the parallel between the acts of Decius and Caracalla relevant is that in both cases they asked for something more than a passive response from their subjects. It is also significant that in both cases they invoked the need to celebrate the gods along with the emperor. Just as the use of the prophetic apparatus of the ancient world had long been a standard feature of the shaping of opinion, so now was the notion that one could shape opinion by joining the emperor in worship. If nothing else these efforts underline the importance of local cult as a focal point for the expression of community identity. The impulse to join local cult to the imperial government, on the imperial government's own terms, was a substantial reversal of the ordinary practice of religion in the classical world. Cities that made particular displays of loyalty were well rewarded: Thessalonica received recognition for three imperial festivals (exalting it above its rival, Beroea),

Anazarbus in Cilicia received recognition for an additional festival, giving it one more than its rival, Tarsus, while the citizens of Mopsuestia were allowed to proclaim themselves "Decians."[116]

In addition to issuing his edict on sacrifices, which was among the very first things that he did, Decius also caused a remarkable series of *antoniniani* to be issued by the mint at Rome, commemorating his deified predecessors.[117] The list of deified emperors does not reflect a standard list that was used in sacrifices to the deified emperors through standard celebrations of the imperial cult. Rather it looks like a deliberate selection of emperors who might truly be thought to deserve the honor. The series begins with Augustus and includes Vespasian, Titus, Nerva, Trajan, Hadrian, Pius, Marcus, Commodus, Severus, and Alexander. While people might not note or miss Claudius or Pertinax in this line, the omission of the three Gordians would clearly have drawn attention to what was going on. Decius was rewriting Roman history. It was not just, of course, the history of the more distant past that he was interested in rewriting. Something also had to be done about the circumstances of his own revolt against Philip. Zosimus and Zonaras both tell a remarkable story, which they must have had from Dexippus, in which Philip, upon hearing of the revolt of Pacatianus, summons a meeting of the senate to ask its advice about how he should respond.[118] After a period of silence, Decius alone responds, telling Philip that he need do nothing, that the revolt would collapse of its own accord. Philip then ordered Decius to take up the command in the Balkans, and it was the soldiers there who forced Decius to lead them against Philip as a way of avoiding punishment. It was clear that Decius despised the memory of Philip, whose name was erased from inscriptions around the empire. Cities had been rewarded with marks of imperial favor by Philip, and one observer thought (not without good reason) that the edict on sacrifices was issued "because of the previous king."[119] This same observer connected it with the persecution of Christians who refused to sacrifice, perhaps in connection with what may have been a widely held belief in some parts of the empire that Philip had a soft spot in his heart for them.[120]

The point of the story about Decius and Philip was that Decius had done nothing wrong, unworthy though Philip was to reign. It may be that the peculiar story about Philip's role in Gordian's death, which bears little, if any, relation to the actual event, also dates to this period. But try as he might to rewrite the past, Decius could not produce a decent script for the present. He was an incompetent soldier, and his conduct on campaign in the next two years was as inept as any in the long annals of Roman military history.

In 250, Decius sent a detachment of troops to the Crimea, where the Greek kingdom of the Bosphorus offered a vantage point from which to observe the movements of peoples across the Ukraine.[121] There was good reason to do so, as a new people had been moving into the region since the time of Severus Alexander, and Philip's withdrawal of subsidies to the northern tribes had led to trouble. But it appears not to have been so serious that the available forces could not deal with it. The sudden change in the situation during 250 is thus not likely to be a function of a sudden change in the balance of power, but rather the result of Decius' assertion of personal command. The string of disasters that followed his assumption of command did change the balance of power on the frontiers, both east and west, it seems, and led to a near collapse of the prestige of the central government.

The people causing the trouble for Decius may have been called the Goths, ancestors in some way of the tribes that would reconfigure themselves in the fourth and fifth centuries to form two of the main successor states to Rome in the west. Our knowledge of early Gothic history at this point is so vague, its traditions so much the product of later invention, that it is difficult to know what it was, except perhaps language, that distinguished this group from the other Germanic tribes north of the Danube. The earliest occurrence of the word *Goth* in Latin is on an inscription from Arabia that dates to the reign of Severus. The text in question mentions a unit of auxiliaries that are part of the garrison.[122] In Greek, the situation is complicated by the fact that Dexippus wrote in a highly classicizing mode whereby tribes occupying what is now the Ukraine tended to be called "Scythians" after the people who had inhabited that region in the time of Herodotus.[123] Indeed, Dexippus' history of Rome's wars with these people is entitled the *Skythika*, and the enemies of Rome are simply called the "Skythai" in those sections of the work that precede the reign of Aurelian, when he identifies two subgroups of "Skythai" with whom Aurelian negotiates as the Juthungi and the Vandals.[124] A list of tribes that Zosimus provides, based, it would seem, upon Dexippus, lists the constituent elements of the "Skythai" who invade the empire in 253 and 259 as being the Borani, Goths, Carpi, and Ourougoundoi.[125] The Carpi are mentioned, in the context of a raid in 253, by the author of the *Thirteenth Sibylline Oracle*, which would suggest that this group made something of an impression on the author of these lines, and another group, the Herulians, makes a significant impact on the record in 268.[126] Our only reason to think that the agent of Decius' destruction was a Goth rather than a Vandal, Carp, or other sort of Scythian is that the sixth-century author of a history of the Goths identified the leader of the barbarians at this point as Cniva.[127] This name is Gothic and, since he does not appear in the fictionalized genealogy of the Gothic kings of post-Roman Italy that this author also adumbrates, it is reasonable to believe that this was a name that he found in a third-century source.

The structure of tribal organization north of the Danube was so fluid that it is dangerous to press the identity of Decius' foes too far. One thing we can know is that the archaeologically homogeneous culture that begins to appear in the southwestern Ukraine, and gives rise to groups that were the ancestors of the later Visigoths and Ostrogoths, is apparently a fourth-century development.[128] It was at this time that these diverse tribes had coalesced into two confederacies, the Greuthungi and the Thervingi, while the memory of the earlier tribes, especially the Carpi, remained strong enough for a spot on the Danube to be identified as a *vicus Carporum* (district of the Carpi).[129] By that time two other groups who were united with the "Skythai" in the 250s had moved further west, retaining an identity as the Burgundians (the Uorougoundoi of Dexippus) and the Vandals.[130] In light of the uncertainty over who these peoples actually would become in later years, it is probably best to continue to refer to the trans-Danubian tribes that assailed the Roman Empire as "Skythai." The term is less than precise and reflects the usage of inhabitants of the Roman Empire rather than of the tribesmen themselves – but it will at least avoid the implication that we actually know what the relationship was between these groups and those that appear in the fourth century.

The course of Decius' war is not recoverable with any great clarity, but it does appear that it took place in the Roman province of Moesia Inferior, in what is now Bulgaria. We also know that Decius suffered a massive defeat at the hands of his enemies near Beroea/Augusta Traiana in 250.[131] Dexippus includes an account of a siege of Marcianopolis in this context, about which we can only say that the place did not fall.[132] Dexippus also includes a very long (fictionalized) letter from Decius to a man named Priscus at Philippopolis, a city well south and west of Marcianopolis, on the Hebros River. We also know that Philippopolis subsequently fell to the Goths, in part through the treachery of a man named Priscus (probably to be identified with the recipient of Decius' "letter"), who went on to proclaim himself, albeit briefly, as emperor.[133] To explain these observations, it is best to postulate a large band of "Skythai" breaking through the Roman frontier north of Marcianopolis in 250, failing to capture the city, but then moving south to defeat Decius at Beroea. In the next summer they captured Philippopolis and began to withdraw north to their homeland, taking their booty and their captives with them. Decius caught up with them at a place called Abritus, just over forty miles northwest of Marcianopolis.[134] The account of what follows, from Zosimus and Zonaras, as well as a few lines in George's *Chronicle*, is clear enough. The "Skythai" divided their forces into three lines, the third of which was behind a swamp. Decius defeated the forces in front of him and was then foolish enough to order his troops, whom he appears to have been leading from the front, into the swamp. He, and those with him, were slaughtered.[135]

The aftermath of Abritus: Gallus and Sapor

The political situation that followed upon Decius' demise was deeply confused. Decius had two sons, Herennius Etruscus and Hostilianus. Herennius Etruscus is depicted on coins as a young man, Hostilianus as a child. Both were elevated to the rank of Caesar, but Hostilianus appears to

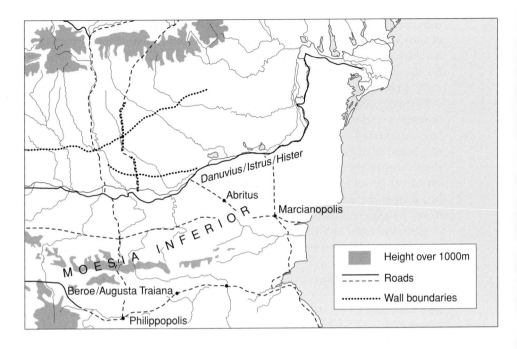

Map 3 The Balkans showing the principal area of Decius' Gothic war

Source: *Barrington Atlas of the Classical World*, courtesy of the Princeton University Press.

have remained in Rome with his mother, Herennia Cupressinia Etruscilla, while Herennius Etruscus accompanied his father on campaign. According to the confused traditions surrounding the final months of Decius' life, Herennius was either killed in an action that was fought just before the battle at Abritus, or died with his father.[136] The remnants of the army on the Danube immediately proclaimed the governor of Moesia Inferior, Trebonianus Gallus, emperor, a fact that makes improbable a nasty allegation asserted by Dexippus (also alluded to by the author of the *Thirteenth Sibylline Oracle*), that Gallus had conspired with the Goths to deliver Decius into their trap.[137] It is beyond belief that the army would have supported a man who could have been thought to have been complicit in the deaths of their comrades.

Gallus accepted the offer of imperial power from his troops and immediately negotiated a treaty with the "Skythai" so that they would leave the territory of the empire. He then appears to have returned to Rome, where he accepted Hostilianus as Caesar along with his own son, Volusianus.[138] It may have been important, in light of what were plainly some very nasty rumors, that he seem to be on good terms with the family of his predecessor, at least initially. What happened next is utterly obscure. Gallus saw to the deification of Decius on June 24, 251, and Hostilianus disappears from the historical record by July 15. It is possible that Zosimus' statement that he died of the plague is correct.[139]

Despite Decius' admission to the college of divine emperors in which he seemed so interested (and Gallus' continuation of the coin types), Decius' name was erased from a number of inscriptions, and privileges that he granted to a number of cities were canceled.[140] We have no idea why, though it is possible that the erasures were spontaneous acts when news of his defeat spread. It is also possible that these erasures (or some of them) are very much later events, as Christians, who regarded him as a persecutor, recognized his name on inscriptions. Whatever the case, it is hard to believe that it stemmed from any decision on the part of Gallus, especially as there is no consistency to the removal of Decian privileges. He had a lot more to worry about.

The situation in the east was chaotic. At some point in the reign of Decius an Antiochene nobleman by the name of Mariades had begun ravaging Syria and Cappadocia.[141] His actions may be a continuation of the revolt of Jotapianus, who was decapitated under Decius, though this is not certain. What is reasonably certain is that he led a substantial enough force to cause a lot of damage. Imperial troops proved incapable of catching him, and he fled, probably in 251, to Sapor. The state of war between Rome and Persia that had begun under Philip still obtained, and Gallus appears to have decided that some resolution of the situation was needed. In 252 he appears to have been ready to launch some sort of attack against the Persians, and to have sent Volusianus to the east. Volusianus may never have reached Antioch, for before he could arrive, an immense catastrophe had befallen Roman arms.[142] Sapor records the events as follows:

> And Caesar lied again and did wrong with respect to Armenia. Then we attacked the Roman Empire and annihilated, at Barbalissos, a Roman army of 60,000, and Syria and the environs of Syria we burned, ruined and pillaged all. In this one campaign we conquered of the Roman Empire fortresses and towns: the town of Anatha with surroundings, Birtha of Arupan with surroundings, Birtha of Asporakan, the town of Sura, Barbalissos, Hieropolis, Aleppo, Chalcis, Apamea, Rhephainia, Zeugma, Urmia, Gindaros, Arzemaza, Seleucia, Antioch, Cyrrhe, another town of Seleucia, Alexandria, Nicopolis, Sinzara, Hama, Rastan, Dikhor, Doliche, Dura, Circesium, Germanicia, Batna, Khanar, and in Cappadocia the towns of Satala, Domana, Artangil, Suisa, Sinda, Phreata, a total of thirty-seven towns and their surrounding territory.
>
> (RDGS 4–9)

The vast list of places that Sapor captured includes all of the legionary posts in Syria, suggesting that the army that had been mustered at Barbalissos had been thoroughly defeated.[143] The very presence of this concentration of troops at one place on the Euphrates suggests that Sapor had struck the Romans as they were themselves concentrating their forces for an attack.[144] The route that he took up the Euphrates may have been a surprise in and of itself. The Romans used the route for their invasions of Persia because it was relatively easy to ship supplies down the river, with the current. It was not so easy to ship supplies back up the river, and the Persians had hitherto preferred the route across northern Mesopotamia (and would ordinarily prefer that route in the future). It may well be that the choice of route was determined by the advice of Mariades, who, in the eyes of a Syrian observer, played all too prominent a part in the operations:

> Now for you, wretched Syria, I have lately been piteously lamenting; a blow will befall you from the arrow-shooting men, terrible, which you never thought would come to you. The fugitive of Rome will come, waving a great spear; crossing the Euphrates with many myriads, he will burn you, he will dispose all things evilly. Alas, Antioch, they will never call you a city when you have fallen under the spear in your folly; he will leave you entirely ruined and naked, houseless, uninhabited; anyone seeing you will suddenly break out weeping; and you will be the prize of war.
>
> (*Orac. Sib.* 13.119–29)

Just what role Mariades actually played is a bit obscure, despite the author of these lines, who equated his coming with the mythical return of Nero. Another story connected with this invasion has Antioch being betrayed by "friends of Mariades" within its walls, and that may well be true.[145] Loyalty to Rome had plainly not been at a premium among all members of the influential classes in Syria during the last few years. Questions may well have arisen, given the record of failure against Persia, increased collections of revenue, and tales of chaos from other parts of the empire, as to what sort of future there was. These questions may have been reinforced the next year when Persian troops once again invaded the region. Then the only effective resistance that could be offered to them came not from the Roman army, but rather from a descendant of the royal house of Emesa, a man named Uranius Antoninus, who, placing his faith in *'lh' gbl*, succeeded in defeating a force of Persians.[146]

We know about Uranius' victory against the Persians because it is reported in some lines of the *Thirteenth Sibylline Oracle* and is the basis of a fantasy contained in Malalas' *Chronicle*, wherein the priest Sampsigeramus went out at the head of the local militia to meet Sapor.[147] His attire convinced Sapor that he must be an important person, and so Sapor decided to parley with him. As they spoke a slinger from within the ranks of Sampsigeramus' force killed the Persian king. While this story may be false, the fact of a military confrontation may be confirmed by a curious inscription dating to 252–53 at Qual'at al Halwâys that records that a "hero" called upon Kronos to defeat the barbarians.[148]

As interesting as his effort to fight the Persians was, so too was his decision to mint a series of coins with his image upon them, an act ordinarily associated with the emperor himself. Jotapianus made a similar decision, and so did a pair of characters named Silbannicus and Sponsianus in the Balkans at the time that Decius overthrew Philip. Silbannicus appears to have been active in France (a coin with his image was found there), while Sponsianus is known from an aureus found in Transylvania.[149] By way of contrast with a man like Pacatianus (who minted coins in support of his bid for the throne), none of these characters appears to have been claiming anything other than local authority, and it is possible that they did so in the hope of securing their positions with support from the tribes along the border, as Priscus appears to have done in the last days of Decius. In doing so it may not have occurred to them that the act of minting in their own name constituted high treason under Roman law. Rather it would appear that they were asserting local authority by mimicking the outward forms of imperial power, a reflection again of confusion between what a symbol might mean in a local as opposed to an imperial context. Likewise, as may also have been the case with the group of "usurpers" who appear on the eastern frontier under Alexander, they may well have been doing so at points when the central government appeared to have failed.[150] The centralizing tendencies of emperors from Severus onwards had yet to create a common understanding of shared symbols.

There was more here, though, than a dissonance in the understanding of symbols. Far more important is the evidence for the increasing reliance of provincials upon their own resources. True, Marcus Aurelius had recruited policemen, *diôgmitai*, from Asia Minor, along with gladiators and, allegedly, brigands, in a desperate push to fill up his army with experienced fighters in the early 170s. This at least reflects the availability of such people, but it is also significant that Marcus was bringing them under the direct command of Roman officers.[151] The crucial phenomenon that accompanied the rise of individuals like Uranius Antoninus was the local availability of weapons and large enough bodies of men willing to use them outside of the legionary structure.[152] The fortification of cities, which may be seen throughout Asia Minor, mainland Greece, and in parts of Anatolia during the 250s and 260s, appears to have been locally financed.[153] Provinces appear to have been capable of creating a unified command structure, like Greece in 268, when the Greeks elected to build a wall across the Isthmus of Corinth to resist a potential barbarian attack.[154] At Athens in 268, when the city was sacked by raiders from the sea, there was a force of two thousand armed men available to harass the enemy if it moved into the countryside.[155] These men seem to have seen themselves as acting in conjunction with Roman forces rather than as being under their control. A critically important inscription from Augsburg dating to the year 260 lists the forces that intercepted a band of the Juthungi, returning from a raid in Italy, as the soldiers of the Raetian and German legions as well as the "militia."[156] In this case the militia was under the control of a governor. In Syria, the army of Palmyra appears to have been a truly significant force. Built, probably, upon local units that had long been in existence to protect caravans across the desert, it was strong enough both to defeat the main force of Sapor's army, and then to defeat the remnants of the Roman army. It was this army that would prove to be the base for the power of Odaenathus and later his wife Zenobia, as they asserted control over the eastern provinces.[157]

One cause of the sudden rise of these militia forces must have been the staggering losses of trained troops during the years between 251 and 260. The casualties in Decius' two defeats must have been substantial, as must have been those at Barbalissos and in Valerian's defeat during 260 (even if we discount Sapor's figures of sixty thousand and seventy thousand men on the two occasions). The desperate shortage of manpower is reflected in an extraordinary measure taken by the senate in the course of 259, which enrolled members of the urban plebs and sent them to reinforce Gallienus in the north of Italy.[158] The size of the army had long been restricted by the ability of the state to pay it, and now it seems that it was proving incapable of fulfilling its basic function of defending the empire because, quite simply, its members were being killed off at an unprecedented rate. This too would serve to shift the balance of power between the central and local governments.

The fall of the Severan empire

The author of *the Thirteenth Sibylline Oracle* regarded Gallus as a catastrophe, introducing him with the lines:

> When another king of Rome will rule, then ruinous Ares with his bastard son will bring the disorderly races against the Romans, against the walls of Rome.
>
> (*Orac. Sib.* 13.103–5)

In Greek the introduction of Gallus, *g' allos*, is a pun on the meaning of his name: a *gallos* was a castrated priest of the Magna Mater. The ruinous Ares of these lines would appear to be none other than Gallus himself, reflecting the rumor that he had betrayed Decius, while the walls of Rome are the figurative walls of the empire, at this time imagined as a fortress of civilization against the barbarian world.[159] The author is not a priori "anti-Roman" so much as he (presumably he) is pro-Antiochene. He detests the Persians and despises Mariades as a traitor, but he appears to feel that Gallus was responsible for the breach of an implied contract whereby loyalty to Rome was recompensed by protection from one's enemies.[160] He praises Uranius as a savior, and in so doing he recalls again the words of Hippolytus in his commentary upon Daniel. For Hippolytus the empire was an agglomeration of races held together only by the military power of Rome.[161] When that power failed, Hippolytus suggested, the empire would shatter into its constituent parts. He may have been a better prophet than even the author of the *Sibylline Oracle*.

Gallus had no time to respond to Sapor's devastation of the Syrian provinces, and Sapor's invasion was not his only problem. Bands of "Skythai" had taken to the sea in the summer of 252, penetrated the Bosphorus, and raided along the coast of Asia Minor, burning the great temple of Artemis at Ephesus.[162] The process of refortification in Asia Minor was only beginning, and the militarization of the population was perhaps less advanced here than in other provinces. What resistance could be offered was offered by local police forces. More significantly, though, the fact of this raid revealed a glaring hole in Rome's maritime defenses. There was a fleet on the Rhine that was charged with preventing raiders crossing the North Sea, and there appears to have been a fleet on the Danube, though how well organized it was after the disasters of 250–51 is a matter for conjecture (the ability of the "Skythai" to sail past it may be the best indication). Otherwise the two main fleets of the Roman Empire were those of Misenum and Ravenna.[163] Their primary duties had long been the protection of lines of communication from Italy to the provinces and, probably, the suppression of piracy. The great battle fleets of the late republic, in the absence of enemies, had long since disappeared, and there is no reason to think that there were any substantial forces available to patrol the coasts of the Aegean. It would appear that the "Skythai" went home when they felt that they had acquired enough plunder.

The raid of 252 was followed up by some sort of military action in Lower Moesia during the first part of 253. Roman forces were directed by a man named Aemilianus, who was successful enough that his troops proclaimed him emperor. He marched immediately upon Italy, catching Gallus before the reinforcements that he had ordered from Gaul, under the command of Publius Licinius Valerianus, could reach him.[164] Gallus was defeated and killed at Interamna. A few weeks later, Valerian (as Valerianus is more commonly known in modern texts) arrived and encountered Aemilianus at Spoletium. Valerian won and in September 253 became emperor.

Valerian was an elderly man. He had been consul for the first time prior to 238, when he had served as a legate to Gordian as governor of North Africa. Descended from the Italian aristocracy, he appears to have been a man of considerable energy with a passionate desire to preserve the empire as he had known it in his youth. To the extent that the coinage that was

(a)

(b)

(c)

(d)

Plate 10 Imperial images. One notable feature of the years after the death of Gordian is the lack of a coherent imperial image, reflecting, perhaps, the fact that three of the emperors depicted here were responsible for the death of an immediate predecessor, while Gallus' relationship with the house of Decius was decidedly ambivalent. (a) Philip I. *Credit*: *RIC* Philip I 44b (Rome 244–47); author's collection, photo courtesy of Guy Clark's Roman Coins. (b) Decius. *Credit*: *RIC* Decius 29c (Rome 249–51); author's collection, photo courtesy of Guy Clark's Roman Coins. (c) Trebonianus Gallus. *Credit*: *RIC* 69 Trebonianus Gallus (Milan 251–53); author's collection, photo by Ivory Photo, Ann Arbor, MI. (d) Valerian. *Credit*: *RIC* Valerian 46 (Rome 253–60); author's collection, photo courtesy of Guy Clark's Roman Coins.

issued from his mints is an indicator of his views, they appear deeply entrenched in the past. The reverse types on his coins are largely those of the Severan age, many of them unused by emperors after 235, even though the silver content of the coins upon which these reverses were stamped had slipped to between 10 and 15 percent, reflecting what appears to be an ever-increasing demand for coin on the part of his government.[165] He also recognized that the problems of the empire were more than he could manage on his own and that he needed help, if his rule was not to be precarious. To solve this problem, he immediately elevated his son Gallienus to the rank of co-emperor and would appoint Gallienus' son Valerian as Caesar in 256. When the younger Valerian died in 258, another son of Gallienus, Saloninus, replaced him.[166]

A dated inscription places Valerian at Antioch on January 18, 255; another inscription of 255 places him at Tisa near Sirmium; a third puts him at Cologne in August 256, and a dated rescript has him at Rome on October 10.[167] Issues of coins from Anazarbus in Cilicia suggest that he visited the place no later than 254, while another issue, from Mopsus on the Pyramus, suggests that he oversaw the construction of a bridge there in 255–56.[168] The most reasonable reconstruction of events is thus that Valerian went to the east as soon as he could, and it may be with his arrival that Dura Europus passed, for the last time as an inhabited spot, back under Roman rule. He would then have returned, overland, to the west, where he joined Gallienus at Cologne in the late summer of 256 before returning to Rome, where Gallienus assumed the consulship on January 1, 257.[169]

The journeys of Valerian suggest a sudden change in the pattern of administration, a change necessitated by events on the frontiers. While all his predecessors since Maximinus had hastened to the capital and remained there for as long as they could, Valerian went only briefly to Rome in 253 and left the city again soon afterwards. His son and co-emperor appears to have spent 254 and 255 in the area around Viminacium, before moving on to Cologne in 256, and then to Rome with his father. Valerian was drawn back to the east in the course of 257, possibly by news of the Persian assault that had resulted in the capture of Dura Europus, while Gallienus himself went on campaign against the Alamanni who lived above the headwaters of the Rhine.

What, it may well be asked, of the role of the emperor as urban politician? The answer is that we simply do not know. But there is some evidence from the next decade to suggest that major changes were under way in the structure of the ruling classes. Senators were becoming scarce in command of legions, and in provincial commands. The Praetorian Guard may have had little presence in the city, as three emperors (if one includes the younger Valerian) were in the provinces, and their officers may have been more closely connected with units of the regular army.[170] A background in command of legions had empowered men like Balbinus and Tullus Menophilus, but there were perhaps fewer such men in Rome. Those with military experience may well have found themselves in demand elsewhere, and their place in command was increasingly being taken by equestrian officers, in a process that would be completed in the next decade with the virtual extrusion of senators from all legionary commands.[171] Legions, in operational terms, were increasingly being replaced by combined forces of infantry and cavalry drawn from several units, commanded by equestrians.[172] The balance of power in the city between the people, the senate, palace, and guard may have been disrupted by the effective removal of the guard and the court from the capital and the diminished role that senators were playing in government.

Valerian, who was well into his sixties, was plainly putting himself under great pressure through his constant travels. He was again in Antioch in 258.[173] And he was clearly away from Rome in the later part of 257, when the senate wrote to him asking what it should do in the aftermath of an edict that was issued when he was there at the beginning of the year. This edict attempted to force Christians to conform to the religion of Rome. According to this order, high-ranking members of the church were to be arrested and asked to sacrifice. If they did so, they would be set free; if not, they would be imprisoned or exiled. Meetings of Christian congregations would be banned, and Christians were deprived of the use of their cemeteries.[174] This order went beyond Decius' edict on sacrifices in that it singled out Christians. It differs from numerous bans on various cults throughout Roman history (including Christianity) in that it does not order a halt to the practices of the cult altogether. Rather it seeks to force the adherents of the cult to offer token conformity with the rites of the state. In so doing it represents the ongoing tendency toward centralization of all activity around the will of the palace, and an insistence upon conformity among members of the ruling class. People were clearly puzzled by it, and that is why the senate asked Valerian what they should do with people who had been imprisoned. Valerian's response was brutal. Leading Christians who persevered in their habits (he notes that there were senators among their number) were to have their property confiscated, and if they still maintained their faith, they would be executed. Women of high standing were to have their property confiscated, and members of the palace bureaucracy were to be sent as slaves to the mines.[175]

As he issued this rescript, Valerian was soon to be confronted with more trouble. Another band of "Skythai" had taken to ships, and this time they had landed in northern Turkey. They ravaged Pontus and moved south into Cappadocia. Valerian led troops north from Antioch to intercept them but failed to do so.[176] Zosimus says that his army caught the plague and in this weakened condition had to deal with a new invasion of northern Mesopotamia by Sapor, probably in the early spring of 260.[177]

Sapor's account is clear. He says that he met the Romans in battle between Carrhae and Edessa, and there he captured Valerian.[178] Western accounts are much less so, but it looks as if they too told of a battle in which the Romans were defeated and besieged. Valerian, fearing for his safety in the camp near Edessa, tried to negotiate with Sapor, who took him prisoner in the course of the negotiation. It is likely that the forces that were with him then surrendered, as Sapor says, and there is no reason to doubt his claim that the captives also included a praetorian prefect. The prisoners were taken off to building projects in Persia, and it was there that Valerian ended his days, Tabarī says, after completing the structure that even now is called the "dam of Caesar."[179] According to what may be a less well informed, but certainly more dramatic, western version, Sapor would step on Valerian while mounting his horse, and, when the emperor died, Sapor had his skin flayed, dyed crimson, and hung in a temple.

After capturing Valerian, Sapor continued his operations by raiding Cilicia, but then things began to unravel. Some Roman forces were rallied by a fiscal official named Macrianus and an officer named Callistus.[180] They were joined by Odaenathus of Palmyra, holding the extraordinary position of "Lord of Palmyra," who may have been motivated to take action against the Persians by the destruction of the last Palmyrene trading stations on the Euphrates in the 250s.[181] The Persians were driven back, and Macrianus proclaimed his sons, Macrianus and Quietus, as emperors toward the end of the summer.[182] Upon the news of Valerian's capture, two governors in the Balkans, Ingenuus and Regalianus, also rose, successively, in revolt, only to be defeated by a man named Aureolus who was sent against them by Gallienus. Gallienus could not go himself because, it appears, he was dealing with a raid of the Juthungi that had swept south into Italy and was to return north, with "many thousands of Italian prisoners," despite having been defeated by Gallienus at Milan.[183]

The raid of the Juthungi led directly to the last of Gallienus' problems: the revolt of the army in Gaul. The immediate circumstances of this rebellion have recently been illuminated by the discovery of the inscription at Augsburg, already mentioned in a number of other contexts, so is now worth quoting in full:

> In honor of the divine house, (and) to the blessed goddess Victoria, because the barbarians of the race of the Semnones or Juthungi were slaughtered and routed on the eighth and seventh days before the Kalends of May by soldiers of the province of Rhaetia, by soldiers from Germany, and by the militia, after freeing many thousands of Italian prisoners, (and) in the realization of his vow, Marcus Simplicinius Genialis, *vir perfectissimus*, acting in place of the governor, with the same army, (and) with proper gratitude, erected and dedicated this altar on the third day before the Ides of September when our emperor Postumus Augustus and Honoratianus were consuls.
>
> (*AE* 1993, no. 1231)

Zosimus says that, after the defeat of the barbarians (whom he, characteristically, calls "Skythai"), Postumus, the governor of Lower Germany, who must in some way have been superior to Genialis, distributed all the booty to the soldiers. Just what this means is a bit unclear, but it is surely significant that the text of the Augsburg inscription says that the Italian prisoners were set free.[184] What remained was then the object of controversy; whatever had been distributed was reclaimed by Saloninus, acting on the advice of Silvanus, the praetorian prefect, from his headquarters at Cologne. The army then rebelled and besieged Cologne, capturing the place and killing both Saloninus and Silvanus.[185] At the same time it proclaimed Postumus emperor. The location of the army at the time of this dedication (Genialis is explicit that it was with him at Augsburg) is best explained by the fact that it was needed there to resist a counterattack from Gallienus. The revolt of Postumus may thus be placed between May and July 260.[186] By the end of the summer Postumus controlled not only the provinces of the Rhineland, but also the inland provinces of Gaul (excepting Narbonensis in the south) and Britain. The Severan empire had come to an end; the army that had supported it was in ruins.

The empire of Gallienus

The empire of which Gallienus retained control made a certain amount of geographical sense. He held Egypt, southern Spain, and North Africa, guaranteeing that Rome would not run short of food, and that his empire was the dominant economic force in the Mediterranean. He controlled the Balkans and Turkey north of the Taurus rim.

The Danubian region would provide the nucleus of a new army, organized on different principles from the old. Before the capture of Valerian, Gallienus appears to have disposed of a substantial body of cavalry that could be deployed independently of the legions, and to have had a body of troops attached to his person called the *comitatus*.[187] Well might one wonder what was the difference between the comitatus and the old Praetorian Guard, and the ad hoc formations that accompanied the emperor on the march in earlier years? The guard retained its old structure, its old privileges, and its old quarters, and that may be the point of the new entity. Neither Valerian nor Gallienus was in any position to disturb that powerful force, nor could either of them easily do without the trained manpower within its ranks. But it was a conservative institution, deeply attached to its past, and not a likely vehicle for operational innovation. The new comitatus appears to have evolved from a cavalry force into one that mingled infantry and cavalry, and it does not seem to have been wedded to the legionary system. It was a force that appears to have been designed to move quickly, and not to have been attached to any one specific location. Most importantly, it had its own, independent, command structure.

Along with the creation of the comitatus came the culmination of a tendency to employ nonsenators in virtually all significant roles of government. A much later historian, Aurelius Victor, even claimed that there was an edict of Gallienus through which it was effected that no senator could hold a military command.[188] There is no reason to think that this was, strictly speaking, true, for consular governorships continued to exist.[189] Nonetheless, the years of Gallienus saw an end to praetorian governorships and to senatorial appointments as legionary legates. The transfer of all praetorian provinces to equestrian legates profoundly affected the senatorial career by removing what had previously been the key position on the road to the consulship.[190] The senatorial career in the imperial service would now begin with the consulship, burying the last vestiges of the republican system of government. This change cannot be attributed only to the exigencies of warfare, or a gradual increase in the number of provinces, as old provinces were being subdivided in the interests of efficiency. It is a process that began well before Gallienus, and, indeed, well before the military crises of the 250s. Some role in this transition must also be allowed to the centralizing habits of government that had been taking firmer hold in the course of the last half century: the point at issue is not so much that equestrians were being preferred to senators, but that people with greater experience of necessary tasks were being promoted. The men who were taking these positions were not men whose experience lay in the fiscal world; rather they were men with long years of military service behind them.[191] As with the creation of the comitatus, the expanded role of military equestrians was a response to new challenges. And it needs to be seen as part of the process that also saw the grouping of provinces into larger divisions for military purposes; hence the dispositions of Philip, as well as the younger Valerian's place on the Danube and Saloninus' on the Rhine. The effect was to concentrate power in the hands of the few officials who held these expanded positions.

Changes in governmental structure were accompanied by systemization in the titulature of officials. Senators held the rank of *clarissimus*, while officials closely connected with the court became *perfectissimi*. The use of these titles had been going on for some time. As early as the reign of Marcus, the praetorian prefects had been set above other equestrians, with the rank of *viri eminentissimi*, and they, as well as those whose ranks were held to be those of the *perfectissimi*, had been granted immunity from torture for themselves and their descendants as far as their grandchildren.[192] But then, and even more so under the Severans, there had been no clear way of delimiting the authority of an equestrian official as opposed to a senatorial. As Ulpian put it, a governor was the representative of the emperor in the province, but he ought to respect the authority of the procurator.[193] Under the new system, respective rank was indicated by the possession of the status *perfectissimus* or *clarissimus* rather than specific office, thus equating senatorial with equestrian ranks.

Whatever else may be said of him, and he is a deeply controversial figure in the historiographic tradition, Gallienus was not wedded to his father's vision. One of his first acts was to issue a rescript to the bishops granting them freedom of worship and restoring control of their places of worship.[194] Likewise he had the sense to negotiate rather than fight when it suited his interests. It was through negotiation that he solved what may have been as pressing a problem in the east as he faced in the west. Macrianus, allied with Callistus, freed from further Persian threats by their success in routing various Persian columns as they returned from ravaging Cilicia, decided, in 262, to invade the western empire. Macrianus accompanied his elder son to the Balkans, while Callistus remained in the east with Quietus. The two Macriani were routed by Aureolus, commander of the cavalry, and killed. Gallienus then wrote to Odaenathus inviting him to complete the victory and assume the role of *corrector totius orientis*, a position that appears to have given him some capacity to give orders to governors in, at the very least, Syria and Mesopotamia. Odaenathus accepted the offer and turned on his former associates. Callistus and Quietus were killed by their men at Emesa as Odaenathus moved against them.[195]

Odaenathus appears to have taken his new role seriously, and to have used it to forge a remarkable position for himself. He appears variously on inscriptions as *rš dy tdmwr*, "Lord of Tadmor" (Tadmor being the Semitic name of Palmyra); *snqltyq' 'nhyr' wrš dy tdmwr*, "most famous senator and Lord of Tadmor"; *nhyr' hptyq'*, "most famous consular"; and, finally as *mlk mlk' wmtqnn' dy mdnh'*, "King of Kings and *corrector* of the whole region."[196] The array of titles that Odaenathus took may be arranged chronologically in the order that they appear in the previous sentence. The title Lord of Tadmor, which is rendered in Greek as *exarchos Palmyrênôn*, indicates his dominance within the city. The titles evocative of senatorial dignity appear a bit later, and parallel those of Abgar IX, the last king of Edessa, indicating that both men had received the *ornamenta consularia*, or consular ornaments, which were, at times, awarded to client rulers.[197] They may reflect a development of the time of Valerian. The title *mtqnn' dy mdnh'* is that awarded by Gallienus after 262, rendered in a Palmyrene version that seeks to translate the meaning of the title into a form comprehensible in the native language, while *mlk mlk'* (King of Kings) appears to have been taken to commemorate victories over Sapor, probably also in 262. An extraordinary inscription discovered at Palmyra in 1895, and brilliantly elucidated by the French scholar Daniel Schlumberger in an article that appeared during World War II, reveals that Odaenathus went even further and awarded the title King of Kings to his eldest son, in a ceremony outside of Antioch in the same year.[198] The choice of Antioch for this celebration is surely significant, for by that choice Odaenathus was recognizing Antioch's traditional position as the center of government in the east, and asserting his place as the supreme power in the region.[199] Just as remarkable as the choice of Antioch for this ceremony is the garb assumed by his son. A single lead tessera, discovered at Antioch and published in 1937, reveals that this son, whose name was Herodian, wore a crown shaped like that of an Arsacid king.[200] So too must have Odaenathus.

Odaenathus made no claim with regard to Rome that could not be supported by Gallienus' award of the title *corrector totius orientis*, and he clearly allowed Gallienus to appoint the governors under him.[201] But he was making a further claim in the eyes of all who were also participants in Semitic culture in that the claim of the title King of Kings appears to have been a direct challenge to the other holder of that title, Sapor, and the style of crown used at Palmyra might be taken to imply that Sapor was not a legitimate king. In this way he was proclaiming both his opposition to the Persian king and his loyalty to Rome in terms that were meaningful, first and foremost, in a Palmyrene context.[202] The one catch appears to be that he, or those around him, came to regard the Roman aspects of the title as hereditary. This was to cause immense difficulty after his death and led to some very complicated situations with regard to Roman officials, and a war with the central government, initiated by his wife Zenobia, who was the power behind his successor.

In the time of Gallienus, however, it is significant that the emperor was willing to negotiate power, and the ability to command Roman troops, with a local potentate who agreed to recognize his authority. The situation was very different in the west, where Gallienus remained in a state of war with Postumus throughout his reign.

After the mutiny in which Silvanus and Saloninus were slain, Postumus had claimed the consulship for himself and one of his associates, Honoratianus, taking as well a series of titles ordinarily associated with Roman emperors. He styled himself imperator Caesar Marcus Cassianus Latinius Postumus pius felix Augustus, pontifex maximus, Germanicus maximus, and holder of the tribunician power.[203] The entity that he ruled was not, however, the empire of the Romans, but rather that of the Gauls, the *imperium Galliarum*, and his capital was Cologne. The area that comprised the empire of the Gauls included the German and Gallic provinces, Britain, and Spain (after 261).[204] At no point does it seem that he tried to invade Italy, or to unseat Gallienus, even though Gallienus made a couple of attempts to unseat him.[205] Like Odaenathus in the east, his power rested upon the support of the local aristocracies.

In expressing his conception of the imperial office, Postumus borrowed the titulature of the central government. He is not only consul, but also a holder of the tribunician power and pontifex maximus. Officers under him held standard imperial titles, and his coins resemble those of Rome.

The parallel between Postumus and Odaenathus may be extended further, albeit tentatively (there is not a lot of information with which to take this further step), through examination of the upper echelons of their governments. In Odaenathus' case, it is plain that the interests of Gallienus were respected insofar as governors and other imperial officials were appointed from Rome. But these men do not seem to have had a place in the Palmyrene power structure, which appears to have been staffed entirely with Palmyrenes and other easterners. The two generals who led Palmyra's armies after Odaenathus was murdered in 268 were named Zabdas and Zabdai. Both were given the Roman gentilician name of Septimius by Odaenathus, a move that may be yet another parallel with Sasanian practice, for, as we have seen, there was very much a tendency to make government appear to be a family affair.[206] A third character of importance was a man named Vorodes, possibly of Persian descent. He too became a Septimius.[207] One final figure who may have begun to play an important role in court was Cassius Longinus, a rhetor born at Emesa who had studied with Plotinus in the school of Ammonius Saccas.[208] Plotinus felt that he had a great mind, and Porphyry was a student of his at Athens.[209] An oration that he delivered on Odaenathus was still current in the late fourth century, when a copy was requested from a distant descendant of the former King of Kings who was living at Rome in 391.[210] The presence of Longinus at court, and the existence of this oration, may point to efforts on Odaenathus' part to enhance his image among the elites of the more Hellenized parts of Syria.

The upper echelons of Postumus' administration appear to have been rapidly Gallicized. The (admittedly scanty, if uncontradicted) evidence of inscriptions suggests that the Rhine legions upon which he based his power were already recruited heavily from the region in which they were based.[211] This may have been a natural result of the long-term establishment of the legions in these areas, and the tendency for the legions to form their own "total institutions." In Postumus' case, however, recruitment from within the empire was supplemented by substantial recruitment from beyond the frontier. Substantial finds of his (gold) coinage in graves between the Weser and Vistula likely reflect diplomatic efforts in that area.[212] What is more significant, given the fact that the officers who commanded the legions at the time of their rebellion are likely to have conformed with the standard imperial pattern of recruitment from the entire imperial aristocracy, is that major figures under Postumus appear largely to have been of northern Gallic origin. The chief official under him at the end of his reign was Marcus Piavonius Victorinus, a man of Gallic origin.[213] Another man of importance, who would, like Victorinus, rise to become emperor of the Gauls, was Gaius Esuvius Tetricus, whose name likewise betrays a Celtic origin.[214] In both the empire of the Gauls and what might best be termed the protectorate of Odaenathus, we may see writ large the pattern of local reaction to generalizing cultural tendencies that we have seen in so many other areas of imperial life. The language of Roman imperial power provided a vocabulary for the expression of ideas about power, but it did not prescribe the exact form that these local responses would take. Unlike the situation in late fourth- and early fifth-century Britain with which we began this book, local institutions in the third century retained the vitality to shape a vigorous destiny for themselves, responding to Rome, but not reduced to such dependency upon it that they could not function in the absence of the imperial power. This was the product of the tendencies in Roman government during the first and second centuries, and a sign that the centralizing tendencies that were in evidence from the Severan period onward had yet to choke the life out of those institutions. The process of reuniting the empire, which would begin with the passing of Gallienus in 268, would hasten the tendency toward administrative homogenization and, perhaps even more significantly, toward the creation of intellectual institutions that would seek to control the nature of local response to centralizing cultural influences.

7

THE EMERGENCE
OF A NEW ORDER

Claudius Gothicus

The tripartite Roman Empire that came into being during the years 261–62 was inherently unstable, resting on Gallienus' inability to defeat Postumus, and Odaenathus' willingness to live with the arrangement that he had with Gallienus. By the end of 268 both situations ceased to obtain. Odaenathus was dead, the result of court intrigue, probably in the spring of 268, and Gallienus fell victim to a mutiny within his ranks. In the case of Odaenathus the trouble allegedly had to do with the conduct of one of his relatives on a lion hunt. Chastised for his poor conduct, this relative arranged the assassination of both Odaenathus and his heir apparent, Herodianus.[1] Power then passed to a younger son, Vaballathus, who was dominated by one of the remarkable figures of the age: his mother Zenobia.

Gallienus' troubles stemmed from a combination of Postumus and the "Skythai." Gallienus had done little about Postumus for several years. He had been unable to attack him in 260, and, possibly because of his ongoing problem with Macrianus, in the next year either. The result was that Postumus had more than four years to establish his power before Gallienus attempted a serious move against him. This came in 265 when Gallienus crossed the Alps, defeated Postumus, and began to besiege him in an (unnamed) Gallic city.[2] But then Gallienus approached the walls of the city too closely, suffered a serious wound, and was compelled to withdraw. In 268 Gallienus' situation deteriorated. The "Skythai" appear to have invaded the Balkans in the first part of the year, and Aureolus, once commander of the cavalry, declared himself emperor at Milan, proclaiming himself an ally of Postumus.[3]

The invasion, which this time appears to have been driven by a group called the Herulians, seems to have begun as yet another naval expedition into Asia Minor and then into Greece.[4] The precise details are almost impossible to reconstruct with any certainty since the chain of conflicts initiated by the Herulians in 268 continued on into the next year, creating confusion in the sources that report them. We can probably assume that the Herulian invasion was still going on when Aureolus rebelled, that Gallienus chose to concentrate his efforts against the officer who had betrayed him, and that it was left to his successor to finally defeat the Herulians.

The siege of Aureolus in Milan proved fatal to both principals, and while the sources are less than clear about the precise chain of events, they are explicit on a single issue: that most of Gallienus' senior officials wanted him dead. According to one account, the prime mover of events was the praetorian prefect, Heraclianus, and he brought in Claudius, "who, after the emperors, appeared to govern the empire."[5] In this version, Gallienus was told at dinner-time that Aureolus was advancing. He rushed from his tent to place himself at the head of his men and was killed by the commander of the cavalry. A related account, this one in the *Historia Augusta*, again makes Heraclianus the prime mover, though this time the author expressly exculpates Claudius, adds Marcianus, another prominent general, to the plot, and identifies the killer as a man named Cecropius, commander of the Dalmatian cavalry.[6] The removal of Claudius from the conspiracy is due to his later role as the progenitor of the house of Constantine – a fiction of Constantine's time – and may serve to guarantee that the original version from which these two accounts spring was current prior to the reign of Constantine. We can be less certain about a rather different story, told this time by Zonaras and Aurelius Victor. In this one, Aureolus arranges for a forged document, in which Gallienus appears to be plotting against his generals, to fall into the hands of the senior staff. The leading actor in the plot is now Aurelian, and Gallienus is once again killed as he rushes from his dinner. This story too had points of interest for later events, for, as we shall see, Aurelian, the most successful ruler in the next decade, was to become a deeply controversial man. The tale of his involvement in the conspiracy might be seen as at least partial justification for the murder of Aurelian himself under circumstances that seem remarkably similar to those in this story.

Whatever the truth, Gallienus was killed in the summer of 268, and Marcus Aurelius Claudius was chosen by the army outside of Milan as his successor.[7] Crowds at Rome are said to have reacted by murdering members of the deceased emperor's family in the street, until Claudius made it clear that he was going to respect the memory of his predecessor. Gallienus was buried in a family tomb on the Appian Way, and deified.[8] Aureolus was less fortunate. He appears to have tried to surrender and, when that attempt failed, gave battle to his besiegers and was killed. Another general leading from the front.

Claudius was one of a number of men of equestrian status from the Balkans who had achieved high office by the end of Gallienus' life. It is hard not to see this as a result of the truncation of the empire, and that the truncation had a major impact on the structure of government for decades to come. Prior to Claudius there had been two emperors from the Balkans. After Claudius, there would be only one Roman emperor who was not from a

Balkan family until the year 378, when Theodosius I, from Spain, took the throne. This one exception is Carus, who ruled for all of two years, and he was from Narbonensis. In the case of Claudius, four inscriptions help deepen our understanding of the structure of his government. One is a dedication by Traianus Mucianus to Aurelius Heraclianus, the praetorian prefect who played a central role in the conspiracy against Gallienus, at his home city of Augusta Traiana (modern Stara Zagora).[9] The second is a dedication from the same place to Heraclianus' brother, M. Aurelius Apollinarius, the governor of Thrace.[10] The fact that all these men had the family name (Marcus Aurelius) that was bestowed upon those made citizens by the *constitutio Antoniniana* suggests that they were not descended from families that had been long in the imperial elite. The third inscription reveals the career of Marcianus, another leading general by the time that Gallienus died.[11] The fourth is from Grenoble, honoring Julius Placidianus, who is described as being prefect of the *vigiles*.[12] Its location and circumstance (it commemorates an invasion of Narbonenis led by Placidianus in 269) show that he was no simple police chief. Rather he appears to have been charged with the defense of Italy. While we cannot prove that Heraclianus, his brother, Placidianus, or Marcianus were of Danubian origin themselves, it is clear that none of them were members of the Severan aristocracy, and all of them appear to owe their prominence to their military roles. To these men must be added Marcus Aurelius Aurelianus (the future emperor Aurelian) and Marcus Aurelius Probus (another emperor in waiting), both men of Balkan background, and from families enfranchised in the time of Caracalla.

A list of Balkan marshals should not obscure the fact that government without help from the traditional classes was impractical. Weakened though their influence had been in the previous decades, there were still men of importance who descended from the older aristocracy. It is possible, though by no means certain, that Claudius assumed the consulship in 269 with Aspasius Paternus, who had been *consul ordinarius* in both 267 and 268. Paternus had been governor of Africa in 257, and prefect of Rome in 264–65. His repeated ordinary consulships with Gallienus mark him as a man of great influence.[13] One of the consuls of 270 was Flavius Antiochianus, who had been appointed urban prefect in the previous year, and who would continue to hold the office during this, his second consulship. Antiochianus' colleague was Virius Orfitus, also the scion of a powerful family (his father would be prefect of the city in 273–74).[14] Aurelian's colleague as consul was another such man, Pomponius Bassus, a member of one of the oldest senatorial families, as was one of the consuls in 272, Junius Veldumnianus.[15]

The sudden implosion of the *imperium Galliarum* greatly assisted Claudius in his first full year of power. In the spring of 269 Ulpius Cornelius Laelianus, a high official under Postumus, declared himself emperor in Germania Superior. Postumus defeated him, but upon doing so, he refused to allow his men to sack Mainz, which had served as Laelianus' headquarters.[16] The army mutinied and murdered their emperor. A man named Marcus Aurelius Marius was selected by the troops as their ruler. He did not last long before Victorinus, who had evidently been Postumus' praetorian prefect, defeated him. Victorinus was now emperor of the Gauls, and he was soon in a good deal of trouble himself. The Spanish provinces deserted the Gallic Empire and declared their loyalty to Claudius, while Placidianus invaded southern France, capturing Grenoble. But there he stopped, and Victorinus' position stabilized. When Autun revolted in the next year, declaring itself for Claudius, the central government made no move to support it. The city was captured and sacked by Victorinus after a siege of many weeks.[17]

We cannot know why Claudius did nothing to help the city of Autun, but we do know that his relations with Palymra were deteriorating in the course of 270. An obscure passage in the *Historia Augusta* life of Gallienus, at precisely the point that events under Claudius and Gallienus were combined, either by the author's source, or his own inability to sort out what was in this source, says that Gallienus had sent an army under Heraclianus to the east that had been annihilated by Zenobia.[18] Since Heraclianus was plainly not in the east in 268 (he was busy arranging the murder of Gallienus in the late summer), this cannot be correct. But the confusion evident in this passage, which also places the bulk of "Skythian" activity during 269 a year earlier, under Gallienus, may stem from a later effort to pile all possible disasters in this year into the reign of the former emperor. This would help preserve the record of Claudius as ancestor of Constantine from blemish. If this understanding of the sources is correct, then it might also be correct to see the expedition of Heraclianus to the east as an event of Claudius' time.

Claudius would be remembered in the Latin tradition as a great hero because of his victory over the Goths in 269, and it was this that made him an admirable choice as an ancestor for Constantine, who was born at Naissus, the site of that victory. He is an equally noble figure in Zonaras, whose Greek tradition appears to have been influenced at this point by the Latin. For Zosimus he is less grand, and that may reflect a more reasoned contemporary view.

After the successes of 269, the year 270 was not a happy one. While the "Skythai" starved in their mountains or surrendered, an epidemic began to spread to the legions that were pursuing them. Claudius did nothing to aid Autun and may have provoked a quarrel with Zenobia.

Even if Claudius was not responsible for the break with Zenobia, or not wholly so, it came nonetheless. The point at issue was surely the position that Odaenathus had held as *corrector totius orientis*. Zenobia claimed this title, as if it were hereditary, for her son, Vaballathus.[19] Indeed, the arrival of so senior an officer as Heraclianus in the east might well have been part of an effort to reassert central control after Odaenathus' demise. If so, of course, it failed, and coins, which Odaenathus had never presumed to mint with his image upon them, began to appear with that of his son.[20] In the late summer, a Palmyrene army under Zabdas invaded Arabia and moved into Egypt. The prefect of Egypt was a man named Tenagino Probus, an able soldier who had defeated an invasion of Cyrenaica by the nomadic tribes to the south in 269 and had played some role at the beginning of 270 in hunting down "Skythian" ships in the Mediterranean.[21] His efforts at defending Egypt were, however, undermined by a Palmyrene underground, led by a man named Timagenes. Probus was defeated and killed in a battle near the modern city of Cairo in the late summer of 270.[22]

What follows is most interesting. The slaughter of a Roman commander might ordinarily be taken as a sign that a state of war existed; and, indeed, if it is right to associate the defeat of Heraclianus with the year 270, as well as an inscription from Bostra that records the later rebuilding of a temple that had been destroyed by the "Palmyrene enemy," these several acts of violence might be taken the same way.[23] But they do not seem to have been. The coins of Vaballathus avoid claims to imperial power: he remains *vir consularis, rex, imperator, dux Romanorum*, a range of titles that did not mimic those of the central government.[24] The status *vir consularis* was, as we have seen, conferred upon Odaenathus; the title *rex*, or king, is simply a Latin translation of *mlk*, or king; *imperator* in this context simply means "victorious general"; and *dux Romanorum* looks like yet another version of *corrector totius orientis*. These titles proclaim a very simple principle: that the position of Odaenathus was, like that of a king in the Semitic world, inheritable. For a Roman the status conferred by the holding of an office might be passed on, but not the office itself. It might, perhaps, not be too much to imagine that the subtle distinction between the office and the status that accompanied it would be lost at the Palmyrene court, especially in a circumstance that worked against the interests of a regime that had been able to do what a series of Roman emperors had not: defeat the Persians. The titles taken by Odaenathus plainly meant a great deal in the Palmyrene context, which is why Vaballathus stressed them.[25]

Any confusion, willful or genuine, on the part of the Palmyrene regime might be further enhanced by the fact that there were Roman officials in Egypt who were willing to serve them. Tenagino Probus appears to have been succeeded as prefect by the man who had served under him as deputy prefect, Julius Marcellinus.[26] Marcellinus was in turn succeeded by Statilius Ammianus, who, it appears, would later arrange the peaceful restoration of Egypt to the direct control of the central government.[27]

Roman officials who served under Zenobia may also have noted something that looks very much like an alternative to the grand narrative of classical history, as they knew it, taking shape. A rhetor from Petra named Callinicus addressed a ten-book history of Alexandria to Zenobia in the guise of Cleopatra.[28] In addition to suggesting a link between herself and Cleopatra, it appears that Zenobia also sought to restore some other pre-Roman institutions. In one case she appears to have restored the immunity granted to a synagogue by one of the early Ptolemies.[29] It was an interesting move that may be associated with Zenobia's interest in peoples and religions that existed on the fringes of the Roman world. Perhaps the most remarkable evidence for the impression she made appears on a Palmyrene graffito from northern Jordan that depicts a woman on a camel with the words, "May God remember her (for) good." It is hard to resist the notion that this camel-riding woman is meant to be Zenobia herself, even though the assumption cannot be proved beyond the shadow of a doubt.[30] Beyond this, and more certainly, she was a patron of Paul of Samosata, who asserted a claim to the see of Antioch under her husband's rule, and she may have received missionaries from the prophet of a new faith in Persia.[31] This prophet was Mani, and his new revelation was brought west at precisely this period.[32] One text records her personal reception of the missionary Mar Addas, another the reception of missionaries by a woman who is described as "Nafsha, the sister of the Queen of Tadmor, the wife of Caesar."[33] While this may be overstated (the fact that Nafsha is the Aramaic word for "soul" does not make it more credible), it is not unreasonable to think that there was some contact.[34] Finally, it is not impossible that the new Cleopatra attempted to do something for the old Memnon. The statue of Amenophis III that had long been identified as that of Memnon, which uttered sounds at dawn as the cool air admitted to its inner parts through cracks in the surface warmed with the coming of dawn, appears to have undergone a facelift.[35] Her efforts effectively silenced the statue.

The restoration of the central government

The summer of 270 ended on a very different note from that of 269. Success in Gaul was followed by inactivity, and by failure in the east. The resources of the state appear to have been stretched to the limit, for the silver content of the *antoninianus*, now much reduced in weight, was down to a mere 2–3 percent (1.55 percent in six coins from the mint at Cyzicus).[36] The death of Tenagino Probus was virtually coincidental with that of his emperor, who died of disease in September.[37]

Claudius had won a great victory, but little else, and his authority was not sufficient to guarantee his plans for the succession, which involved his brother, Quintillus. When news of the emperor's demise reached him at Aquileia, Quintillus duly assumed the purple.[38] But that was not the will of the army, and the messenger who brought him the news arrived little more than two weeks ahead of the army under its candidate for the throne. Quintillus died (he committed suicide or was murdered) seventeen days after assuming power. Aurelian, the candidate of the army, was now sole emperor.

It is arguable that no man since the time of Augustus was to accomplish more, in less time, for the central government than did Aurelian, and few would leave a legacy more deeply contested. Aurelian was plainly smart, and he combined intelligence with a great energy. He would restore the central government to control over all the empire, and he would do so while recognizing that it was no longer possible to retain control over everything. And in his restoration of power, he would behave with a moderation that was both as sensitive as it was wise. It was that moderation that would, in the end, prove his undoing, and the undoing of his reputation.

It is, for once, to the actual words of Dexippus that recourse may be had to form a picture of the way that Aurelian wanted to be perceived. Dexippus brought his *Skythika* to an end in 272, and it may be that the two long passages preserved in the ninth-century compendium of extracts from earlier authors known as the *Excerpts concerning Embassies from Foreign Peoples to the Romans* were among the last things in his work. This may be even more significant because there are no accounts of embassies from any other reign. Dexippan set pieces include a letter from Decius to Philippopolis, accounts of two sieges, and long extracts from two speeches given by Athenians to rally the spirits of his people after the sack of Athens in 269.[39] The excerptors tended to read through entire books copying out passages that concerned them in the order that they found them.[40] That there should be no embassies preserved from earlier books of Dexippus suggests very strongly that there were none to be preserved. In that case, his history began with tales of woe and ended, not with tales of conquest, but rather of victory followed by negotiation, the establishment of safe frontiers, and the integration of northern tribesmen into the Roman army. This was surely the message that Aurelian wanted people to get, and it was the policy that he pursued in bringing the disparate regions of the empire back together.

But first, Aurelian had to get himself into a position where he could do that. It was not an easy task, for the northern tribes appear not to have been so distraught at their defeat in 269 that they would not come again. In the autumn of 270, the Juthungi invaded northern Italy, where Aurelian defeated them. Their assault was followed, in the winter, by an attack by the Vandals, also driven back by Aurelian. The negotiations with these two tribes form the material for the two fragments of Dexippus mentioned above. But as Aurelian was finishing his business with the Vandals, Dexippus records yet another attack by the Juthungi, and this would prove far more serious. It appears that there would be three battles in northern Italy, the first, near Placentia, a thorough disaster for Aurelian, who appears to have been surprised by enemies who had been concealed in a wood.[41] The next two battles were victories at Fanum in Umbria and again at Ticinum, ending the threat.[42]

The events of 270 were not without political consequences for Aurelian. It would appear that there were two, albeit short-lived, military insurrections in other armies after the defeat at Placentia, and there would soon be extraordinary trouble in Rome itself. In the late summer of 271, the mint workers at Rome rose in rebellion, leading to bloody fighting and several thousand deaths in the capital itself.[43] Tradition had it that the suppression of the mint workers was accompanied by a massacre of leading men in the city. This is stated most fully in the *Historia Augusta*, whose author delights in the image of the emperor as a bloodthirsty tyrant, and is known to Ammianus, who includes the memorable observation that Aurelian "fell upon the rich like a torrent."[44] The existence of such a tradition in the late fourth century is not, however, the best of evidence for the third century. It is absent from the third-century Greek traditions represented by Zosimus, and it would seem to be contradicted by what appears to have been an effort to consiliate the population of Rome. Before departing for the east, Aurelian added pork to the distributions of grain and oil that formed the imperial *annona*[45] and began the construction of a massive new wall surrounding Rome.

One point of the new wall was plainly to offer security in the face of any possible repetition of the invasion that summer.[46] But there may have been more to it than that. The erection of walls suggests both that Aurelian was making a statement that he trusted the people of Rome to remain loyal, and, perhaps equally significantly, that he was capable of such a grand building project as a sign of his own power.[47] As such, the walls of Rome now came to stand for hope that the empire would long endure. It may have helped that Aurelian had aligned several representatives of the high Roman aristocracy with himself, as he shared the consulship in 271 with one of them, and allowed two other members of the Roman aristocracy to hold office in 272.[48]

With Italy pacified, Aurelian began to move east before the winter of 271–72 ended. A further "Skythian" assault upon the Balkans was repulsed, and the Dacian provinces were abandoned.[49] It was a sensible move, reflecting Aurelian's priorities. Unlike Valerian he was not devoted to the world of the early third century, but rather to rationalizing the empire that he now ruled. The reunification of the empire would not be helped if resources were wasted in defending the indefensible. But still, it was a dangerous move, and one that Aurelian attempted to obscure by carving two new provinces of "Dacia" out of Upper Moesia. The last emperor to surrender Roman territory had been Hadrian, and, necessary though Hadrian's action had been, it had many critics. So too, it may be surmised from Aurelian's creation of the new provinces, did the move concerning Dacia.

Aurelian's campaign in the east is far more complex than the straightforward tale of war and conquest that has come down through the narrative sources. First and foremost, there was the recovery of Egypt, seemingly as the result of negotiation with the prefect whom Zenobia had left in charge. This man was Statilius Aemilianus, who was appointed prefect in 270 and would remain in office until at least July or August 272, if not, indeed, until May 273.[50] He had previously been governor of Arabia (in 264–65), and he is one of a number of figures who appear to have been able to move between the two camps. Another such figure was Virius Lupus, governor of Asia in

271–72 (an ambiguous position, as Zenobia claimed that region), who had been governor of Syria Coele under Gallienus. His appointment in Syria would have placed him under the authority of Odaenathus, who, as we have seen, used Antioch as the site for the elevation of his eldest son to the dignity of King of Kings.[51]

Aided perhaps by confusion in the Palmyrene government as officials changed sides, Aurelian's march east appears to have been uncontested until he reached Tyana in Cappadocia, which seems to have refused to admit him immediately. According to legend he only decided to spare the place because he had had a vision of the sage Apollonius, who convinced him not to slaughter the inhabitants. The truth of the story is impossible now to determine, but it plainly entered the Latin tradition prior to the composition of the *Historia Augusta*, and it may reflect propaganda on Aurelian's part that showed him in contact with the divine, and respectful of local traditions.[52] Zenobia was having less luck. It appears that she attempted a highly public consultation of the Sarpedonion, a shrine commemorating Sarpedon in the Cilician city of Seleucia, a choice of shrine that is interesting in light of her evident taste for other than mainstream figures in the classical tradition. The oracle's response was, at best, unhelpful:

> Get out of my sanctuary, deceitful and evil men who offend against
> the glorious race of the immortals.

Others, who consulted the oracle about the coming of Aurelian, received a different message:

> A falcon brings an icy grief[53] to doves, all alone to many, while they
> tremble before their killer.[54]

These texts may well have been circulated by the temple itself and have found their way thence into some collection of "true oracles," whence they came to Eunapius' knowledge, and thus into Zosimus' history. They reflect the sort of "oracular propaganda" of which Dio was so conscious in an earlier age and point to a sort of fifth column of people who had guessed that Aurelian would prevail and now sought to ease his path.[55] One such person may even have been a member of the Palmyrene aristocracy: a Septimius Addoudanes appears as a supporter of Aurelian, a choice that earned him a place in the Roman senate.[56]

The Palmyrene army did not attempt serious resistance until Aurelian reached the area around Antioch. The emperor won a victory near Daphne, just outside the city, and a second battle near Emesa.[57] In a remarkable development, Aurelian appears to have attributed this victory to the sun god, to whom he would later build a magnificent temple at Rome. There he was called Sol Invictus, or Invincible Sun, and on coins commemorating Aurelian's triumph Sol regularly appears between two seated captives dressed in the traditional garb of the Parthians, or trampling a similarly attired foe.[58] In the immediate context Sol was plainly someone different: none other than the god *'lh' gbl*.[59] Once again Aurelian may be seen exploiting local traditions to support his claim to supremacy, and he even may have suggested that he was the real successor to Odaenathus. A milestone found near Emesa gives him the remarkable title of *imperator orientis*, or "victorious general of the East," yet another way of understanding the Palmyrene title of *mtqnn' dy mdnh'*.[60]

Palmyra would fall to Aurelian before the end of the summer. Zenobia denounced some of her supporters (including Longinus, who was executed) and was sent back to Rome in captivity.[61] Others appear to have been able to make their own peace with the restored regime. Paul of Samosata, assailed by his fellow Christians, was left in place, pending judgment by the bishops of Italy.[62] Callinicus of Petra followed up his book for Zenobia with a book *On the Restoration*, presumably that of the Roman Empire by Aurelian. He appears to have had a friend at court in Varius Lupus, who may have helped smooth his way.[63] Perhaps even more revealing is a text of 293 in which Diocletian ordered the restoration of free status to a man enslaved in the period of Palmyrene domination.[64] This would suggest that Aurelian left property rights as he found them, just as, it appears, the city council of Alexandria was left in office after the restoration of central control.[65]

Aurelian began his return to the west and reached Byzantium, where he is attested on January 13, before it became apparent that the reconquest of the east had been all too easy.[66] Serious rioting broke out in Alexandria, which was suppressed with much destruction, probably by the *corrector* Firmus, who had been placed in overall charge of the province (over Statilius Ammianus) in the wake of the reconquest. He was an experienced officer who had previously been prefect of Egypt.[67] Then Palmyra itself rebelled, and this time Aurelian was less merciful. The city was sacked, and though it was to become a garrison town by the end of the century, its long years of prosperity were brought to an end.

In 274 Aurelian moved at last against the empire of the Gauls. The ruler he now faced was Gaius Esuvius Tetricus, who had replaced Victorinus, the victim of conspiracy at Cologne in the first part of 271. Here again diplomacy was to play a major part. Tetricus appears to have realized that he had little chance, and so negotiated his personal surrender to Aurelian while, at the same time, placing his army in an exposed position on the Catalaunian plain.[68] The army was destroyed in a bloody action, later remembered as the Catalaunian catastrophe. Tetricus did better: after appearing in Aurelian's triumph, he was employed in the government of Italy.[69] Zenobia, still evidently a woman of childbearing age, remarried, this time to a Roman senator, and ended her days as a member of the Roman aristocracy.[70]

The legacy of Aurelian

With his authority restored over the whole empire, Aurelian set himself the task of restructuring the finances of the central government. The silver content of the basic silver coinage had, as we have seen, slipped to around 2 percent in the course of the previous decade. There is no evidence that this had a direct impact on prices. The great surge in Egyptian prices at the end of the second century AD was not matched by a continuing, upward cycle in the course of the third.[71] It is not clear why this should have been so, but it may help to explain why the central government was content to continue the debasement of its coinage throughout the century, for it does not appear to have had a significant impact on the population as a whole. The one thing that had remained constant was that the standard gold coin, the aureus, had remained in a notional 1:25 ratio to the standard silver coin, the denarius. While there is some evidence to suggest that it did trade at a higher rate, and that it was considered an advantage for a high official to be paid in gold rather than silver, the working of the open market still kept the aureus within a reasonable proximity to its official value.[72] Indeed, it may be that the official relationship between the gold and silver coinage acted as a sort of guarantee that, although the actual silver content was declining, the effective value of the coin was not. If that is so, then what Aurelian did in 274 was to throw the whole logic of the system into chaos.[73] The actual weight of the gold coin had declined in the course of the previous two decades, so that there cannot be said to have been an official weight. Nonetheless, it appears to have satisfied the demand for a benchmark against which to measure the value of the silver. Aurelian's response was to mint a new gold coin, of extreme purity, and to eliminate the formal link with the value of the silver. He also ordered the minting of a new silver coin, consisting of 5 percent silver and marked XXI, indicating a 1:20 ratio of silver to copper. The result was disastrous; prices in Egypt increased, almost overnight, eightfold, and there is no reason to think that the same effect did not occur in other parts of the empire where Aurelian's coins drove earlier ones from circulation.[74]

The question of why Aurelian did what he did is important, and it is, perhaps, answerable. The first issue is whether his currency reform should be seen as primarily a political or an economic act. The evidence suggests that the traditional currency of the state had successfully been transformed into a token coinage, or a coinage in which a greater face value is attributed to a coin than its actual value as a commodity. It had done so, quite probably without any firm understanding of what was happening on the part of the central government, because people remained willing to accept the fact that imperial silver was backed by gold at a rate that was acceptable to the holders of silver coins. The decline in silver content that we have traced in previous chapters may be attributable both to greater need for coin and, quite possibly, to a decline in available specie with which to mint it. What matters was not what the coin was made of but, rather, the fact that its usefulness as a medium of exchange was guaranteed by the imperial government and some may have glimpsed the truth. A telling order issued by the prefect of Egypt in 262, ordering people to accept coins with the image of the emperors upon them, is a case in point. The coins in question appear to have been those of Macrianus and Quietus, and people seem to have been unwilling to accept them precisely because they did not trust the authority of those who minted them.[75] The coins of Macrianus and Quietus were useless, not because they were worse than those of Gallienus, but rather because they did not have Gallienus' portrait on them. By way of contrast, right up until the moment that open war broke out, those of Vaballathus had retained the image of Aurelian, along with that of Vaballathus. By doing so they served as an advertisement for Vaballathus' authority, while the image of Aurelian may have made them more secure as usable coins.[76]

That the system worked, and had worked for Aurelian, makes it unlikely that the primary concern with the coinage reform was to stabilize a system that was badly in need of overhaul. It was not. Rather, it would appear that the primary motivation was political. By creating a new system of coinage, Aurelian was taking all the coinage that circulated with the images of his rivals, and his immediate predecessors, out of circulation. It was a striking way of advertising his claim to have renewed the empire: the coincidence between the reconquest of Gaul and the initiation of the monetary reform is surely no accident. The system of taxation had long provided a way for emperors to send messages to their subjects, and with the originality of mind that characterized some of his other deeds, Aurelian had selected another area that would have vast impact. In some places his success was immediate (and catastrophic); in others the system of circulation had broken down sufficiently that old stocks continued in use well after 274. But the fact that, in practice, he could not eliminate all earlier coinages from use, is less significant than that he should have done what he did. By so doing, he may have done more harm to his subjects than he did good through all of the rest of his actions.

The year 275 found Aurelian once more on the march. He visited Gaul in the first part of the year, repelled yet another incursion by the Juthungi in Raetia during the spring, and was in the Danubian lands by the late summer. In August or September, at a spot between Perinthos and Byzantium, a cabal of his senior officers murdered him. Confusion followed. According to Zosimus, the army buried Aurelian at the very spot where he had been killed, because of his great achievements and the dangers that he had encountered to safeguard the empire.[77] There seems to have been genuine regret among the rank and file for their deceased commander, and this may have made it impossible for any member of the general staff to be selected emperor in his place. It took some six weeks before Tacitus, an aging general who was then in Campania, could be confirmed. The choice of Tacitus as emperor may have been influenced by the fact that he was not with the army when Aurelian was killed, but it may also have been regarded as a victory for those who regarded the assassination as an outrage. The hunt for Aurelian's killers, who fled to the eastern frontier, would be the central issue in the reign of Tacitus.

Tacitus moved on into Asia Minor, where he had, briefly, and successfully, to contend with yet another "Skythian" invasion from across the Black Sea. At that point his control began to unravel. He had appointed a relative named Maximinus as governor of Syria. This Maximinus behaved atrociously to the notables of Syria,

> which filled them with fear and hate. The final consequence was the formation of a conspiracy. After they had allied themselves with those who had assassinated Aurelian, they took Maximinus and killed him, then they pursued Tacitus, who was returning to Europe, and killed him.[78]

The reign of Tacitus was little more than an appendix to the reign of Aurelian and was dominated by the question of Aurelian's legacy. The hard line taken by Tacitus was amended by Probus, whom the army selected to replace him, and that may have been necessary because the army that had been with Tacitus accepted Tacitus' half-brother, Florian, as its emperor. Probus needed to unite the army of the eastern provinces, in which he may have been placed in control as *dux* (or *corrector*) *totius orientis* after the murder of Maximinus, if he were to have a chance.[79]

The war between the rival emperors appeared, at first, to be a mismatch in Florian's favor.[80] Probus withdrew south of the Taurus, and Florian had the resources of the bulk of the empire upon which to draw. But as he passed the Taurus, his army was struck by an epidemic, and he set up camp at Tarsus. It was there that, after an inconclusive skirmish, his men betrayed him to Probus, and he surrendered his claim to the throne. A few days later, charged with trying to retake the throne, Florian was murdered.[81] In the wake of this victory, Probus turned at once to the issue of Aurelian's murderers. According to Zosimus he invited them to a banquet, for they appear again to have been too strong a group to act against openly, and had them slaughtered.[82] It may be a sign of Probus' adhesion to Aurelian's cause that Virius Lupus, a man much involved in the restructuring of post-Zenobian Syria, shared the consulship with him in 278 and served as prefect of Rome for three years, from 278 to 280.[83] The prominence of Lupus is yet another reminder that the Danubian emperors did not rule without reference to the older aristocracy.

Aurelian remains one of the most compelling figures of the third century. The restoration of a centralized empire was by no means a forgone conclusion after a decade in which it had been effectively divided, and forms of coexistence between the rival powers had begun to emerge. It was due to Aurelian's diplomatic and military ability that the empire was reformed as it was. But he was not, as we have seen, an unmixed blessing. One legacy of his reign was severe inflation, and a whole series of other problems that he appears to have ignored remained to vex his successors. The interior provinces of the Roman Empire remained highly militarized, and there was much work to be done if the central government was to regain the monopoly of internal force that it had enjoyed prior to the disasters of the 250s.

The search for stability

The decade after the death of Aurelian is one of the most obscure in the annals of the Roman Empire. For every other portion of the third century there are contemporary sources against which to measure later traditions, and that serve to flesh out, or cast a different perspective on, the basic narrative preserved in the later sources. What has come down to us in those sources is, however, deeply suggestive. It is a tale of invasion and revolt, of what appears to be a continuing struggle on the part of the central government to assert that it was the only power capable of determining the course of events on a local level. The central government would ultimately win this struggle when Diocletian and his colleagues suppressed the last heirs to the tradition of local insurrection in the 290s, but it was not easy. It was in these years that the issues raised by the failure of government that culminated in the years after the capture of Valerian were finally resolved. And they were resolved in a way that would ultimately reshape the relationship between the imperial government and its subjects, leading to the creation of a more highly bureaucratized state that was centered exclusively on an emergent group of palace offices.

Aurelian's restoration of the power of a single emperor had involved extensive negotiation with existing local power structures, be it the government of Postumus or the city council at Alexandria. In doing so, he had not established the central government as the sole arbiter of local power. If he had tried to do so, his effort would have run counter to the habits of previous centuries: the government of the empire had been based upon the devolution of local power to local elites whose job it had been to maintain order for the central government, which would only intervene if they failed to do their job. To succeed, the system depended upon the assumption that the imperial government was essentially just, and that it was, in the last analysis, all-powerful. The failure of government to retain its monopoly of force had undermined the second of these assumptions, and it also undermined the effectiveness of the former. Certainly the author of the *Thirteenth Sibylline*

276

Oracle had betrayed a sense that men like Uranius Antoninus and Odaenathus were preferable to the distant figures of the emperors, and events in the reign of Probus would suggest that the same attitude may have begun to permeate the middle ranks of the army. If the emperor was not present to be a source of rewards, then, perhaps, the emperor was not relevant.

It is just after his account of the execution of Aurelian's murderers that Zosimus tells of two rebels from within the ranks of the high command. One, Saturninus, was governor of Syria; another, who is unnamed, was governor of a British province. The Latin tradition adds two more, both on the Rhine, named Proculus and Bonosus.[84] Despite the impression that Zosimus gives of the revolts being at the beginning of the reign, there is reason to believe that the revolt of Saturninus occurred in 280, as did that of Bonosus. All three rebellions followed upon Probus' suppression of a civil war in Egypt in which the inhabitants of one part of the province, the Thebais, assaulted the region around Coptos with the aid of the nomadic Blemmyes, who dominated what is now the northern Sudan.[85] A year earlier, Terentius Marcianus, governor of Lycia–Pamphylia, had to besiege the city of Cremna in Pisidia to quell the ambitions of a local notable whose name has come down through Zosimus' history as Lydios.[86] Zosimus' account is dramatic enough, with Lydios seizing the city, massacring those inhabitants who would be of no use in the defense, and holding out with the aid of supplies brought in through an underground tunnel, until he was killed by shot from a war machine aimed by a man who had deserted him. The ruins of Cremna today tell a story that, while perhaps less dramatic in point of detail, is all the more terrible in that it is one of catastrophe unfolding, day by day, before the eyes of the defenders.[87] The Roman siege-works include two walls surrounding the plateau upon which the city sits. A huge mound was constructed in front of their main position from which artillery could be trained down upon the defenders; twenty-five-kilo catapult balls have been found within the defenses, revealing the effectiveness of their work.[88] On the inside there is a mound constructed opposite the one outside, one that only equals the height of the Roman one, despite having been started from a fifty-meter elevation above that where the imperial troops began. It bespeaks resources that could not match those of the besiegers, and growing despair as the Romans completed one wall, then the other, less than two hundred meters away from the city defenses, and then the artillery mound in front of it. The summit of the artillery mound was less than one hundred meters from the wall of the city, and what appears to be a trench to undermine one of the two towers in front of it was begun.[89] How the siege ended we do not know for certain, but it is likely, given that Cremna's walls were not breached, that, as Zosimus says, it surrendered.

In addition to internal disorders, the sundry sources for Probus' reign produce an impressive list of encounters with various barbarian peoples. We are told by the author of the *Historia Augusta* (here using a source that appears to have been decently informed) that the provinces of Gaul "had been in distress since the murder of Postumus, and had been occupied by the Germans after the death of Aurelian."[90] Zosimus reports three battles that Probus won, Zonaras one in which the Roman army was saved by a miracle in which it rained bread and water upon a starving Roman camp.[91] Yet further campaigns on the Danube are recorded prior to 280, in which it is claimed that Probus annihilated the Sarmatians and compelled the surrender of the Goths.[92] These claims are exaggerated, and the totality of the situation reflects an ongoing failure by the Roman government to control its own frontiers. Likewise they reflect the enormous personal pressure that the business of governing placed upon the emperor. Aurelian, as we have seen, was often moving from place to place in the dead of winter, and so too must have Probus. But even more serious is the evidence provided by these operations of the lack of faith in Rome's military capacity. The notion that one portion of a province would ally itself with tribes from beyond the frontier in order to go to war with another part of the same region is inconceivable in the pre-Decian empire. It had become a fact of life in the post-Valerianic empire. In each area the reasons might differ. The revolt around Cremna has plausibly been associated with the vastly enhanced presence of imperial troops in southern Anatolia as a whole, a result of the wars with Persia and Palmyra, and, it may be added, the civil war that ended in Probus' victory. After centuries of relative neglect, these places were now confronted with the often brutal day-to-day conduct of Roman soldiers, and it was this that bred resentment. No number of new festivals, and there were a number in this region, blessed by emperors whose longevity was suspect, could ameliorate the circumstances.[93] In Gaul, the militarization of the countryside stemming from garrisons planted in the heart of the Gallic provinces under Postumus, followed by repeated breakdowns of frontier defenses, would have continued the trend toward self-help and self-reliance that had been growing since the 250s. This may have been compounded by an ever-growing reliance upon war bands recruited from beyond the frontiers. Probus himself rewarded a surrendered Frankish chieftain with a command in Britain, just as Gallienus (or Claudius) had rewarded a leader of the "Skythai."[94] Such men might indeed be excellent fighters, but they were also men who were brought into relatively high commands without a background in imperial service, and they brought their own men with them. They would not always abide by the terms of the treaties that brought them into imperial service. One band of Franks, who appear to have been settled in proximity to the Black Sea, revolted and raided Greece, Sicily, and North Africa, before sailing out into the Atlantic and back to their homeland on the Rhine.[95]

We cannot now begin to guess at the stress that constant movement and constant fighting placed upon a man like Probus. But there is one suggestive piece of evidence for his reign and the entire period from 260 to 282. This is that there are only seventeen imperial rescripts preserved in the *Codex*

Justinianus from these years. Among these there is but a single rescript of Claudius, and a mere four from the six years of Probus. While it would be excessive to take this as an indication that the mechanisms of civil jurisdiction were ceasing to function, it is, at the very least, a sign that the jurists who collected material from this period for Diocletian found little of interest. At the same time it is also suggestive that Probus created a new court, the *iudicium magnum*, to hear appeals on cases involving private individuals and the treasury, and financial actions between individuals in Italy and Africa.[96] The tribunal was specifically described as being *vice Caesaris sine appellatione*, or "in place of Caesar without appeal." The use of senatorial judges to hear fiscal cases *vice Caesaris* did have a long history, stretching back, at least, as far as Severus, in cases involving the imperial properties, but in these cases it appears that only a single *iudex* was appointed.[97] There is no suggestion of a board of judges, or of the extension of their duties beyond cases involving the imperial treasuries either before or after Probus, and it does look like a solution for imperial overwork.

In 281, Probus returned to Rome, where he celebrated a triumph and then planned an expedition against the Persians, who were, as we shall see, in the throes of a civil war of their own. He advanced, in 282, as far as Sirmium, when he received news that his praetorian prefect, Carus, had proclaimed himself emperor. It appears to have been a well-engineered coup. Probus was murdered by his men just after he got the news.[98]

War with Persia may have been popular, as well, at this point, as being relatively risk-free. There remained a need to avenge Valerian, and a victory might so vastly enhance the status of the emperor who achieved it that he might regain some of the aura that the office appears to have lost. So it was that Carus placed himself at the head of Probus' army, and, in the summer of 283, he invaded Mesopotamia. The *Historia Augusta* and other Latin texts record that he advanced as far as Ctesiphon, while Zonaras, George, and Eutropius (breaking with the Latin tradition) say that he took the place.[99] It is likely that the story of the capture of Ctesiphon is an exaggeration.[100] The story that he died when his tent was struck by lightning may be no better.[101] Those who wish to believe this story may do so. Those who do not may wish to believe that Carus' success did not garner him the love and affection of his senior officers and that the "lightning" may have come in the form of torches hurled into his tent.

Carus had been accompanied on the expedition by his younger son, Numerian, and his brother-in-law, Aper, who had been appointed one of the two praetorian prefects. The elder son, Carinus, had remained behind in Italy, and the two sons duly succeeded their father upon his death. The army then withdrew from Persia, taking the body of Carus along with Numerian. The boy was probably still alive in March 284, the date of his extant rescript, issued at Emesa.[102] Coins attest the arrival of the emperor at Cyzicus at some point in the year, but by then it is hard to know if the emperor was able to appear in public.[103] There is a grisly tale that he was murdered well before his death was revealed, and that his body was carted about on a litter with the explanation that he was suffering from an eye ailment and so could not be seen in public.[104] The agent of his assassination was (possibly) Aper, who finally broke official news of the emperor's demise at Nicomedia in November. Aper then appears to have tried to garner enough support from the generals of the army to be proclaimed emperor, and failed. They selected instead a relatively junior officer of the imperial guard named Gaius Aurelius Valerius Diocles, who assumed the throne on November 20. His first act was to summon a meeting with the army, and, with his own hand, to kill Aper before the assembled multitude.[105] He would then change his name to Gaius Aurelius Valerius Diocletianus, as a way of placing himself in the succession of legitimite emperors after Gallienus.[106] The reign of Diocletian had begun.

The creation of the Tetrarchy: 284–93

Diocletian was in a relatively strong position in November 284. He had, at his back, a powerful army, and one that had recently been successful in the field. He had with him in the camp at least one senior member of the senatorial aristocracy at Rome, L. Caesonius Bassus, whom he associated with himself in the consulship that he claimed as he was proclaimed, thereby advertising a willingness to continue the collaboration between the new aristocracy and the old.[107] Bassus had served as president of Probus' *iudicium vice Caesaris* and was a man of vast experience in those areas of government where Diocletian presumably had no experience. In fact, we know nothing at all of Diocletian's career prior to 284, save that he was born (possibly) around Salonae on December 22 between 243 and 245, and was commander of Numerian's bodyguard at the time of his elevation.[108] Any further speculation about his earlier career and deeds would be pointless. It is the man who emerges in the next few years that matters.

Diocletian's first concern was to deal with Carinus, who appears, in the view of his subordinates, to have been a human being of, at best, secondary value. As he marched east to take on Diocletian, he had to contend with a revolt by his praetorian prefect, Marcus Aurelius Julianus (whom he suppressed), and increasing disaffection among his senior staff. It is quite possible that, just before the fateful battle on the River Margus in the early spring of 285, Flavius Constantius, the governor of Dalmatia, changed sides. When the battle itself was joined, before the end of May, Carinus' new praetorian prefect, Tiberius Claudius Aurelius Aristobulus, betrayed him as well.[109] Carinus died at the hands of his own men. Diocletian was now sole ruler of the Roman world, and as such he was in an interesting position. He had a daughter, but no son. He could not rule through his family, and he plainly recognized that he could not rule alone, as Aurelian and Probus had. So it was that on July 25, 285, he took the unprecedented step of elevating an old friend, Marcus Aurelius Maximianus (henceforth Maximian for clarity's sake), to the rank of Caesar.[110] The likely place of the proclamation was Milan, and Diocletian's visit to northern Italy was one of only three that he would make in his reign. It is possible that he went on from Milan to visit Rome, but, if he did, it was only a very short appearance, for he is attested back in the Balkans by November 2, on campaign against the Sarmatians.[111] It is likely that Maximian was already in Gaul. Without any fanfare – and perhaps any deliberation (at least at this point) – Rome had just ceased to be an imperial residence.

The situation that called Maximian to Gaul was portrayed by the author of a panegyric that was delivered to honor Maximian in 289 as a peasant revolt. This author, identified as a prominent Gallic rhetorician named Mamertinus by the manuscripts that preserve the work, wrote,

> Inexperienced farmers sought military garb; the plowman imitated the infantryman, the shepherd the cavalryman, the rustic ravager of his own crops the barbarian enemy.
>
> (*Pan.* 10 [2] 4.3, trans. Nixon)

Aurelius Victor would later add the detail:

> When Diocletian learned that, on the death of Carinus, Aelianus and Amandus had gathered a band of farmers and brigands, whom the Gauls called Bagaudae, and, ravaging the countryside far and wide, assailed many cities, he gave the title of emperor to Maximian.
>
> (*De Caes.* 39.17)[112]

Neither of these accounts rings wholly true. Aside from the minor error about the date at which Maximian became emperor (he would not become Augustus until a year later), it ignores the fact that Amandus claimed imperial dignity for himself, appearing on coins as Imperator Caesar Gaius Amandus Pius Felix Augustus.[113] It is more than a little bit hard to see how a group of peasants and brigands would be impressed by such pretensions, all the more so as it is quite uncharacteristic of other peasant revolts. Rather it would seem as if Amandus was asserting some degree of local autonomy, as had the inhabitants of Ptolemais when they attacked Coptos, or the people of Cremna when they defied Marcianus. Carus had been from Narbonensis, and it may well be that Amandus was a remaining supporter. While it may be the case that he derived no support from the Rhine legions, Gaul was otherwise an armed province. Its cities had walls, and it is most unlikely that the militias that had existed in the time of Gallienus had been suppressed. Amandus' pretensions to power make more sense in this context. His claim of imperial status might mean something to organized bodies of soldiers, and his very existence is yet another reminder of the fact that the imperial government had yet to reestablish its monopoly on power. It fell to Maximian to reestablish this point.

Maximian succeeded in his task and repelled an invasion from across the Rhine in the course of the next year. He was rewarded for his efforts by promotion to the rank of Augustus on April 1, 286.[114] The elevation of Maximian was an extraordinary event, made all the more extraordinary by the fact that there is no way that Diocletian himself could have been with him at the time.[115] A rescript dated to March 3 of that year places him at Nicomedia, and another, of March 22, at Byzantium, and he went on from there to Judaea, where he is attested on May 31.[116] Diocletian had clearly intended that Maximian should be able to act in his own right. But the fact that he should have been permitted to present himself as Augustus is testimony to Diocletian's faith in Maximian, and, perhaps, to the significance of a new ideology of government that was enunciated at the very same time. Maximian would be emperor in his own right, and he would also be associated with Hercules at the same moment that Diocletian identified himself as Jupiter. His job as emperor would be to assist the senior emperor, just as Hercules assisted Jupiter. Mamertinus expressed the implication of this ideology with singular clarity in his panegyric of 289:

> Nor did you put your helping hand to the tiller when a favoring breeze impelled the ship of state from the stern, but when only divine help was sufficient for its restoration after its collapse in former times, and not even the help of one god sufficed; you came to the aid of the Roman name, as it faltered, at the side of the leaders, with that timely assistance as your Hercules once lent to your Jupiter, when he was beset with difficulties in his war with the Earthborn. Hercules then gained a great part of the victory, and proved that he had not so much received heaven from the gods as restored it to them.
>
> (*Pan.* 10 [2] 4.2, trans. Nixon)

In this scheme Maximian is to appear in the west as every bit as magnificent a character as Diocletian. As Hercules he may look up to the authority of his "father," but he is just as much a god. It would appear that Diocletian had decided that if he were to have a co-ruler, that ruler must be given sufficient standing that those under his immediate command would not be looking over his head to Diocletian himself. In practical terms this also involved equipping Maximian with a court on the same scale as Diocletian's own. And, like the court of Diocletian, the court of Maximian traveled with him. The only times that his court would be established at Rome were those when he visited the city. In the 280s his primary location would be in northern Gaul, possibly at Trier (or Mainz or Cologne; our inability to fix the spot with certainty suggests that he may have spent much of his time on the move between the three). Diocletian's court would have been with him in the Balkans for much of the same time (the exceptions being portions of 286 and 287 when he went to Syria).[117]

Through all their wanderings, the two emperors still formed one government; there was no firm territorial division between the two, and officials could move back and forth between their courts. In Mamertinus' words,

> So it is that this great empire is a communal possession for both of you, without any discord, nor would we endure there to be any dispute between you, but plainly you hold the state in equal measure as once those two Heracleidae, the Spartan Kings, had done.
>
> *(Pan.* 10 [2] 9.4)

In practical terms, while the vast bulk of legislation after the promotion of Maximian emanated from Diocletian, it is clear that Maximian could issue edicts and rescripts in his own right.[118] In fact it appears that he had even been able to do so as Caesar – there is a rescript from February 285, posted at Milan, which must be on the authority of Maximian.[119] Diocletian gave instructions to officials in North Africa, and, in principle there seems no reason to doubt that Maximian could give instructions to officials in the Balkans. The choice of emperor to whom an official might refer some business is likely to have been dictated by proximity rather than anything else. Again, in the words of Mamertinus,

> Above all else may you illuminate more frequently these, your provinces (I believe that the East asks Diocletian the same thing), and may you, as it is possible, render them, flourishing though they be with the most profound peace, even more fortunate through the appearance of your divinity.
>
> *(Pan.* 10 (2) 14.4)[120]

The provinces of the west are Maximian's simply because he is there, just as those of the east are Diocletian's because that was where he spent his time. This ode to the virtues of imperial proximity is perhaps the clearest expression of the practical theory behind Diocletian's reformation of government.

Mamertinus' oration may be an excellent guide to the theory of government. It is less useful (as one might expect) as a guide to what was really happening. Mamertinus had duly celebrated Maximian's victories over a variety of Germanic barbarians who had crossed the Rhine in 285, his own crossing of the Rhine, and his establishment of a client king named Gennoboudes among the Franks, probably in 287.[121] But he also alludes archly to a pirate, and to that pirate's imminent demise as soon as the fleet that had been prepared could set sail.[122] The pirate in question is a man named Carausius, a senior officer who had been in revolt since 286.[123]

The revolt of Carausius was the most significant political event of Maximian's first decade as Augustus, and, despite Mamertinus' confidence, it was not about to end in 289. Indeed, it would continue for another seven years, and end only after another significant change in the government, for which it may be the proximate cause. The outbreak of the revolt, which allegedly stemmed from a dispute over treasure, bespeaks the weakness of central government control, both practically and morally. Carausius appears to have been in command of the fleet that was intended to protect the coasts of Britain and Gaul from sea-borne pirates, in these years identified primarily as Saxons and Franks.[124] It is alleged that he would allow the raiders to pillage the coast and attack them as they returned home, seizing their plunder for himself and his men. When Maximian learned what he was doing, he ordered him to be killed. According to the literary sources Carausius then fled to Britain, which surrendered to him, and proclaimed himself emperor. Victors write the history of events, and rulers, ancient and modern, can live happily without full disclosure of their embarrassments. This does not begin to tell the story of Carausius' revolt, for a coin hoard at Rouen reveals that Carausius retained control of that area and he may well have maintained his base at Boulogne until 293. Other coins reveal that at as many as six major units took his side on the mainland, which makes it clear that there was more to the story than the tale of stolen plunder: what was really at stake was the legitimacy of the central government.[125]

Maximian was a relative newcomer to the Gallic scene, and he had plainly arrived with a mandate to govern. Carausius' fleet and the substantial garrison of Britain were not willing to submit on Maximian's terms, and it is a mark of the ongoing inability of the central government to instill a sense of its own overwhelming power in the frontier regions. Indeed, it is notable that the region where Carausius held power was one significant area where the reformed coinage of Aurelian had not circulated with any success, and it is interesting that the author of the *Panegyric* to Constantius I of 297 or 298 says that he had the support of Gallic merchants.[126] Evidence from Dover and Boulogne suggests that neither place had remained a base for naval operations in the decade and a half before Carausius, which would suggest that his effort to control raiders from the north was a relatively new initiative.[127] He may have appeared as a person who would provide the security that the central government had not.

In 288 Maximian defeated Carausius' troops on the Lower Rhine and captured Rouen. In the next year he thought that he could produce a fleet of his own that could wrest control of the English Channel. In this, like so many men after him whose experience was of land warfare, he was wrong. It seems to have taken a year to build the fleet, and much less time to lose it – possibly in a storm during the spring of 290.[128] The failure encouraged

Carausius, who regained several cities on the mainland, including Boulogne, Amiens, and Rouen.[129] The result of the summer's campaign in 290 plainly led to some difficulty. Diocletian appears to have broken off a tour of the eastern provinces in which he seems to have attempted to win control of the desert lands that separated Rome from Persia in southeastern Syria, Jordan, and northern Saudi Arabia. The Palmyrenes had previously controlled the tribes in this area, and it may be that, while establishing a new military camp at Palmyra, Diocletian felt it necessary to win back control of former zones of influence. Indeed, the movements of Diocletian may provide the best evidence for events in Gaul: he was at Emesa on May 10 and at Sirmium on the Danube by July 1.[130] The haste with which he moved may suggest that he had received news of a crisis in the west stemming from an ill-timed naval effort in the early spring.

Maximian appears to have spent the summer shoring up support in Gaul, before crossing the Alps in the dead of winter to meet with Diocletian at Milan.[131] The importance of this meeting for the future of their government cannot be over-estimated. Members of the senate came to see the emperors, who evidently spent a good deal of time making public appearances together:

> But when you passed through the gate and rode together through the middle of the city, the very buildings, I hear, almost moved themselves when every man, woman, little child and aged person either ran out through the doors into the open or hung out of the upper thresholds of the houses. All cried out for joy, then openly, without fear of you, they pointed with their hands: "Do you see Diocletian? Do you see Maximian? Both are here! They are together! How closely they sit! How amicably they converse! How quickly they pass by!"
>
> (*Pan.* 11 [3] 11.3–4, trans. Rodgers, slightly adapted)[132]

The panegyrist who wrote these lines in a speech delivered on Maximian's birthday during the summer of 291 surely caught the main point of this display.[133] The regime was under threat, and Diocletian was doing his utmost to show his full support for his troubled colleague. At the same time it may be that they arrived at a new plan of action. Henceforth someone other than Maximian would undertake action against Carausius, and it may be the case that it was then that Diocletian resolved that he too would stand back from direct command in risky situations. Both men may have felt that the regime could ill afford another blow such as that suffered in the summer of the previous year. The fact that this was the last time that Maximian and Diocletian would see each other before 303, when they were to celebrate the twentieth anniversary of their joint rule at Rome, may suggest that they had resolved at this point that they should acquire new colleagues. The final

(a)

(b)

(c)

(d)

Plate 11 The Illyrian look. The image of Claudius marked a significant break from that of Gallienus and set a style that was followed by emperors down to the monetary reform of Diocletian. The one exception to the uniform image was Tacitus, who may have needed to distance himself somewhat from Aurelian. (a) Claudius II. *Credit: RIC* Claudius 32 (Rome 268–70); author's collection, photo courtesy of Forum Ancient Coins. (b) Aurelian. *Credit: RIC* Aurelian 152 (Ticinum 270–74); author's collection, photo courtesy of Forum Ancient Coins. (c) Tacitus. *Credit: RIC* Tacitus 207 (Siscia 275–76); author's collection, photo courtesy of Forum Ancient Coins. (d) Probus. *Credit: RIC* Probus 104 (Lugdunum 276–82); author's collection, photo courtesy of Forum Ancient Coins.

(e)

(f)

(g)

(h)

Plate 11 (*continued*) (e) Carus. *Credit*: *RIC* Carus 12 (Lugdunum 282–83); author's collection, photo by Ivory Photo, Ann Arbor, MI. (f) Carinus. *Credit*: *RIC* 5 Carinus 327 (Rome 283–85); author's collection, photo courtesy of Forum Ancient Coins. (g) Diocletian. *Credit*: *RIC* 5 Diocletian 181 (Rome 285); author's collection, photo courtesy of Forum Ancient Coins. (h) Maximian. *Credit*: *RIC* 5 Maximian 559 (Ticinum 288); author's collection, photo courtesy of Forum Ancient Coins.

proclamation of these new colleagues was still more than two years away, and the question of how far in advance Diocletian and Maximian could or did plan the future is often difficult to answer. But in this case, the fact that the radical transformation of government that would occur in 293 should have taken place without another one-on-one meeting between the two must suggest that detailed plans had been laid at this point.[134] It might appear precipitate to change the nature of government immediately in the wake of a disaster, so a decent interval was left until the groundwork could be laid to inaugurate the new regime with a signal triumph.

When we again get evidence (in 293) for the conduct of operations against Carausius, the command had been passed from Maximian to Constantius Chlorus, the former governor of Dalmatia, who had married Maximian's daughter, Theodora, in 289.[135] He was a man of vast military experience, stretching back, on the most probable reconstruction, to Aurelian's campaign against Zenobia.[136] On March 1 Constantius was promoted to Caesar and sent against Carausius, whom he defeated and drove from mainland Gaul, allegedly after a siege of Boulogne that was of near epic proportions.

Carausius did not long survive his defeat. Shortly after the capture of Boulogne a man named Allectus murdered him and took over his imperial insignia.[137] As these events were unfolding in the west, equally dramatic events were taking place in the east. Some weeks later, possibly on May 21, 293 at Philippopolis, Diocletian proclaimed Maximianus Galerius (henceforth Galerius for clarity's sake) Caesar as well.[138] In late June, after divorcing his first wife, Galerius married Valeria, the daughter of Diocletian.[139] The government of the tetrarchs had begun: none of the members of this group had assumed their imperial dignity at Rome.

The new government set itself before its subjects with increasingly novel forms of imagery, ceremony, and architecture. Early coins of Diocletian and Maximian depict both rulers as being almost identical, but in the style of imperial portraits that had been prevalent from Claudius through Carinus.[140] Around 290, the image began to change, as the emperors began to be shown with rounder features. In 293, when the silver coinage was reformed, perhaps in connection with the creation of the tetrarchy, all four rulers appear with full-featured busts, with very little to distinguish between them.[141] At the same time, new residences were under construction. As the third century turned into the fourth, palaces were being built at Milan and Nicomedia, the official residences of the Augusti; as well as at Aquileia and Sirmium.[142] These were buildings that made a statement: public receptions were held in a huge basilica attached to the large building that housed the day-to-day workings of government, and joined closely to a circus. At Sirmium, in particular, where Philostratus had mentioned a building that he called the *palation* in the time of Marcus Aurelius, the change seems to have been striking.[143] There was no circus prior to the early fourth century, and the large, new, apsidal basilica, located on one of the two most prominent spots

Plate 12 The Tetrarchic look: Diocletian, Maximian, Constantius, and Galerius. A significant change in the representation of the imperial image accompanied the introduction of the Diocletianic reform coinage in 293. (a) Diocletian. *Credit*: *RIC* 6, Diocletian, Siscia 79a (294); author's collection, photo courtesy of Forum Ancient Coins. (b) Maximian. *Credit*: KM 1991.2.816. Photo courtesy of the Kelsey Museum of Archaeology, Univeristy of Michigan. (c) Constantius I. *Credit*: *RIC* 6, Constantius I, Ticinum 32a (296–7); author's collection, photo courtesy of Classical Numismatic Group. (d) Galerius. *Credit*: *RIC* 6, Galerius, Aquileia 24b (295); author's collection, photo courtesy of Classical Numismatic Group.

within the city walls, was clearly intended to make a statement. Although Roman government had always divided points of contact with the emperor among those areas where private discourse was possible into areas for public displays of governmental activity for members of the ruling class, and the massive buildings where the mass of people could see their ruler as they watched some performance, this was different. The elevation of the circus as a virtual part of the palace was new, as was the use of a purpose-built basilica as opposed to a temple, bathhouse, or other large building. The new architecture of power was designed to accompany a new form of ceremonial. Diocletian limited the use of purple cloth to members of the imperial group; he wore a gold crown and spectacular jewels.[144] The style of government so memorably described by Marcus, whereby the emperor sought to show himself as a model of correct aristocratic deportment, had given way to a style in which the emperor was seen to be distinct from all other mortals.[145] His house could no longer be a grander version of houses that other people might live in: it, like him, had to be different.

Rome and Persia

The slow and awkward process by which the central government was able to gain a semblance of control over the bulk of the territory once ruled by the Severans had been greatly aided by the chaos that had enveloped the Persian Empire in the years after 260. Sapor had failed to follow up his success against Valerian with any comparable operations. The victories celebrated by Odaenathus had not only led to the recapture of cities that had fallen to the Persians in the year of Valerian's failure. Odaenathus had advanced into the Sasanian homeland, appearing at least once in the vicinity of Ctesiphon.[146] Carus' invasion more than a decade after the time of Odaenathus likewise appears to have meet with little coherent resistance, and one story suggests that the Sasanians had been forced to breach the dikes that were crucial to the irrigation system of Mesopotamia in an effort to slow him. Why were they suddenly so ineffective?

It appears that when Sapor died in 270, his son Hormizd-Ardashir succeeded him. All that is known of his reign, which seems to have lasted only a year, is that he founded the city of Ramuz and engaged in a war with the nomads of Central Asia. He was in turn succeeded by his son Bahram, under whom great power devolved upon Kirdir, a Zoroastrian priest who now came to occupy the position of mobad of Ahura Mazda.[147] This position represents not only a striking advance in status for a man who was not related to the royal family, but also a remarkable effort to provide central control of what had become the state religion. Kirdir's status is reflected by the fact that he inscribed an account of his career in what were plainly royal contexts. Two of these inscriptions were at Naqsh-i-Rustam, one next to the relief depicting Valerian's surrender, the other (an abbreviated version of the first) on the Ka'bah itself. The two other inscriptions were at Sar Meshed above a relief of Bahram II (who succeeded his father in 276) killing a lion, and the other next to a bust of himself at Naqsh-i Rajab. There can be little doubt but that he was the crucial figure in Sasanian politics during the 270s, and there is strong reason to think that his interests in the enhancement of his power turned Sasanian interests away from the west. Some sense of these developments emerges from his own statement:

> I was made more authoritative and independent than formerly over religious matters (in the reign of Bahram II). And I was made Mobad and Judge of the whole empire, and I was made master of ceremonials and warden of the Fires of Anahita–Ardashir and Anahita the Lady at Iastakr. And I was styled "Kirdir by whom Bahram's soul is saved, Mobad of Ahura-Mazda." And in every province and place of the whole empire the service of Ahura-Mazda and the yazads (good spirits) was exalted, and the Mazda-worshipping religion and its priests received much honor in the land. And the yazads, and the water and fire and cattle, were greatly contented, and Ahriman and the devs suffered great blows and harm. And the creed of Ahriman and the devs was driven out of the land and deprived of credence. And Jews and Buddhists and Brahmans and Aramaic- and Greek-speaking Christians and Baptisers and Manichaeans were assailed in the land.
>
> (Trans. M. Boyce, *Textual Sources for the History of Zoroastrianism* [Manchester, 1984], 112, with orthography adapted)

The sufferings of the Manichaeans and, indeed, of Mani himself, are well enough documented to give some sense of the seriousness with which the persecution Kirdir describes was carried out.[148] But in a later section of the text, where he describes his efforts to reform Zoroastrian practice, he mentions no campaign abroad after the time of Sapor, which would tend to confirm the impression that there was a major change in focus within the regime. This may have been accompanied by a decline in the actual power of the King of Kings.

The power of Ardashir and Sapor may have been founded in large measure upon their personal abilities as war leaders, something that is characteristic of kings in the better-attested Sasanian regimes of later centuries.[149] Neither Bahram I nor Bahram II, who were very young when they took the throne, was in a position to do this. Additionally, it is possible that the centralizing intellectual impulse of Kirdir was at odds with the federal political structure of the state as a whole. The result may have been the need for concession. Thus while Bahram II appears with his courtiers on four rock reliefs, two others, for the only time in Sasanian history, appear to depict only nobles.[150]

This tension may also help explain why civil war was raging in the time of Carus between Bahram and a cousin named Hormizd and would break out again as Diocletian was establishing his authority in the west.

In 287 Diocletian may have been able to take advantage of the weakness of the central government in Ctesiphon to negotiate a treaty that resulted in the return of a portion of Armenia to a ruler of Arsacid descent. Mamertinus knew of these negotiations, and later Armenian sources suggest that this was the occasion upon which Tiridates, son of the Chosroes who had been driven from the throne in 252, was returned to control of a portion of Armenia.[151] The king most affected by these developments would have been Narses, a son of Sapor who had been moved from the kingdom of Seistan to that of Armenia a few years before.[152] Tiridates was astute enough to deal with Narses, who listed him among the minor kings who supported the coup d'état that he launched in 293. Bahram II had died in that year, and a noble named Vahunam had seized the opportunity to place the young Bahram III on the throne. At this point, according to Narses' own account, a group of nobles approached him, urging him to take the throne for himself. This he did at a place called Paikuli, where he later dedicated an enormous monument that includes the inscription detailing his struggles.[153] Narses then invaded Mesopotamia, defeated Vahunam (who was executed), and took the throne for himself (and probably killed Bahram III as well). A damaged passage at the end of his inscription suggests that Diocletian sent an embassy to congratulate him on his accomplishment.[154] Relations between the two powers would soon turn less friendly.

In 296 Narses declared war on Rome. It was a significant year in the west as well, for it was then that Constantius launched the fleet that he had been preparing in northern France for the invasion of Britain.[155] He divided his forces in two, placing one fleet under the command of the extraordinarily long-serving praetorian prefect, Asclepiodotus, and taking personal control of the other. The fleet under Asclepiodotus landed somewhere in the vicinity of the Isle of Wight, and his army met that of Allectus sometime after that, winning what is said to have been an easy victory. Allectus' body was found on the field. Constantius then occupied London and set about the reorganization of the province.

Matters were anything but so simple in the east. Narses appears to have begun the war with an invasion of Armenia, and it was Galerius who took the direct command against him. At first disaster struck. Narses appears to have occupied the kingdom of Armenia and then moved south to catch Galerius' army in the vicinity of Carrhae, inflicting a severe defeat upon it in 297.[156] Diocletian appears to have blamed Galerius personally for the failure, and came in person to Antioch, where he arranged a remarkable display in front of the assembled army. Diocletian rode in the cart that was now the official conveyance of the emperor and made Galerius walk before him for a mile, clad in his imperial robes.[157] The message was clear to all:

military failure would not be tolerated, and no excuses would be made. Responsibility was placed squarely on the shoulders of the commander. It was an important gesture, for the emperor was not blaming the soldiers when something had gone wrong. It signaled his public belief in the valor of his own men, and they would repay his trust. Narses had failed to press his advantage, enabling Galerius to take the offensive in 298 by invading northern Mesopotamia through Armenia, where the mountainous terrain would cause more difficulties for the cavalry forces that were the strength of the Sasanian army. Narses was defeated in two battles, losing his camp in the second of these encounters, along with the women of the court. The wife of Narses, treated with exemplary discretion by the Romans (perhaps in an effort to evoke Alexander's similar treatment of the family of Darius III after the battle of Issus), went to live in Daphne, a suburb of Antioch, where her well-advertised presence was an ongoing reminder of the Roman victory until peace could be made.[158]

The terms of the treaty, which was finally concluded at Nisibis in 299, imposed heavy sanctions on Persia. The agent of the settlement on the Roman side was an imperial secretary, Sicorius Probus, who held the new position of *magister memoriae*. His role here is a reminder of the fact that Diocletian and his colleagues depended heavily upon their senior civil officials and allows an all too tantalizingly brief glance at the evolution of a new court bureaucracy.[159]

Probus' mission was to make a treaty that would complete Roman control of the main access route from Mesopotamia into southern Armenia: there was no effort here to reconstruct the old Severan frontier in Lower Mesopotamia.[160] The terms of this treaty would reflect current realities. From now on the Romans would control access to the passage of the Tigris through the anti-Taurus range, while the five provinces that the Persians surrendered were Ingilene (centered on the city of Egil); Sophanene, bounded to the west by the Tigris and in the south by the Batman River; Arzanene; Corduene; and Zabdicene.[161] Taken together, the three provinces of Sophanene, Arzanene, and Corduene also secured access to the Bitlis pass, the easiest route into Persian Armenia from the south, and access to the great plateau of the Tur Abdin, which was defended in the south by Nisibis.[162] It would be impossible for a Persian army to move unobserved or swiftly through a region now controlled by strongly fortified cities, while Rome retained an advance base to the north of Ctesiphon. The longer-term impact of this treaty on the culture of the region was to take on a significance that Diocletian could not have imagined. It would provide the framework within which the emergent, and soon to be (if it was not already) heavily Christian, Syriac culture would be enabled to stretch out its roots on both sides of the Tigris. The king Tiridates (probably a relative of the Tiridates who was on the throne in 293) who was placed on the throne of Armenia as a result of the Roman victory would prove susceptible to these influences.[163]

The restorers of the whole world

A fragment from the work of the sixth-century historian Petrus Patricius gives an account of the negotiations between Galerius and an ambassador from Narses. The Persian ambassador opens with a request that the Romans recall that the Romans and Persians are the two great powers in the world, and that it did not behoove either to seek the utter destruction of the other. The Romans, he continues, should be mindful of the changing fortunes of the world and not seek to press their advantage too far. Galerius

> seemed to grow angry at this, shaking his body. In reply he said that he did not deem the Persians very worthy to remind others of the variation in human affairs, since they themselves, when they got the opportunity, did not cease to impose misfortunes on men. "Indeed you observed the rule of victory towards Valerian in a fine way, when you deceived him through stratagems and took him, and did not release him until his extreme old age and dishonorable death. Then after his death, by some loathsome art you preserved his skin and brought an immortal outrage to the mortal body."
>
> (Pet. Patr. fr. 13 *FGH* 4, 189, trans. J. M. Lieu,
> in Dodgeon and Lieu, *The Roman Eastern
> Frontier and the Persian Wars*, 132)

While we cannot be certain just how much of this reflects anything said in the third century, the tale of Valerian's skin is, at least, a tetrarchic theme. It was picked up a few years later by Lactantius, in his *On the Deaths of the Persecutors*, a diatribe against Diocletian and Galerius for their persecution of the Christians after 303.[164] Lactantius' point was to illustrate the hideous fate that would befall those who persecuted the church. In the context of Galerius' speech, the story points in a somewhat different direction, to the rewriting of the contribution of the tetrarchs to Roman history. The essential point of this rewriting may emerge most fully in the tortured syntax of the preface to the *Edict on Maximum Prices*, issued in 301:

> The memory of the wars that we have fought successfully rightly gives thanks to the Fortuna of our *Res publica*, together with the immortal gods, for the tranquil state of the world placed in the embrace of the most profound peace, and for the goods of peace, on account of that which was striven for with great sweat; decent public opinion as well as Roman majesty and dignity demand that it be stabilized faithfully and ordained decently so that we who, by the benign favor of the gods, have stifled the seething ravages of barbarian nations in previous years by the slaughter of those nations,

will surround the peace founded for eternity with the proper foundations of justice.

(*Price Edict*, Praef., 5–6)[165]

The key concepts in this outburst are *memoria*, the memory of the emperors' deeds, the profound peace that they have given to the world, the suppression of barbarian activity that was not halted prior to their accession, and the foundations of justice upon which the new peace would rest. The story of Valerian, in this context, is just one more example of how bad things were before Diocletian and his colleagues came along.

The full significance of the stress upon justice in the *Edict on Maximum Prices* lies in the remarkable effort at legal codification carried out in the 290s. The old secretariats of *ab epistulis* and *a libellis* were retitled (probably prior to Diocletian), so that their holders now became known as the *magister epistularum* and *magister libellorum*. Both offices were dominated in the 290s by a trio of extraordinary lawyers. The first of these men, Gregorius, had held office under Carinus as *magister libellorum*, before moving over to Diocletian's court, where he served in the same post for five years. In 291 he appears to have accompanied Diocletian to Milan, and moved on from there to Rome, where he completed his effort at collecting the rescripts of previous emperors that he regarded as being useful precedents for law in 291.[166] The second jurist was Aurelius Arcadius Charisius, who moved from the post of *magister libellorum* under Maximian from 286 to 287 to *magister libellorum* under Diocletian in 290–91 and then served as *magister epistularum Latinarum*, again with Diocletian, from 292 to 294.[167] An experienced jurist before he took up high office, he couched his opinions in moralizing rhetoric that colored later Latin legal writing for a long time to come. Hermogenianus, the third of these lawyers, first appears as Diocletian's *magister libellorum* from 293 to 294; in 295 he produced a supplement to Gregorius' code, collecting relevant imperial rulings from the intervening years. In 295–98 he served as *magister libellorum* for Maximian before being promoted to praetorian prefect in 298, an office that he appears to have held for the next six years.[168] Behind the activity of these men lies an impulse from Diocletian to set the record of Roman law straight. One of the significant administrative processes that appears to have accelerated under Diocletian was the subdivision of existing provinces into smaller units. The increase in the number of governors arguably required a new way of disseminating legal information so as to reduce the stress upon the imperial secretariat. But there was more to the process than that. The creation of official books of precedent had the same effect as lists of relevant cultural events that were so much a feature of the broader intellectual world. It was by definition an exclusive process. And law was no longer to be made on a case-by-case basis; rather it was to be dictated proactively from the center.[169] The fact that the existence of the codes did not solve the problem, as is suggested by the language of various later rescripts, does not mean that the symbolic importance of the attempt did not matter both to those who undertook it and to those who might later have tried to evade its purpose.[170]

The lawyers who created the codes tend to be described as inherently conservative figures. In one sense this is correct, for like their predecessors in the age of Severus, they were deeply concerned with precedent. But, in a more profound sense, they were radicals, seeking to bring a new order to the system of justice. It is under Diocletian, as well, that the old form of the imperial edict, a general statement of policy addressed either to the empire as a whole or to a specific group within it, becomes far more common than it had been in previous ages.[171] Diocletian plainly saw the administration of justice as a zone in which the emperor should function to create a new order in society. The attempted transformation of societal norms through imperial fiat was a process that gained in speed as the reign went on.

The other theme in the preface to the *Edict on Maximum Prices* is that of Diocletian's *memoria*. It is the word *memoria* that is the subject of the convoluted sentence with which the text opens, and it is for the sake of that *memoria* that Diocletian must bring justice to the Roman world. The reference to the "seething ravages" of barbarian peoples in previous reigns does not allow much of a role in their suppression to earlier emperors. The effective erasure of emperors between Gallienus and Diocletian is underlined both in the way that members of the imperial group are described on public dedications and in panegyrics delivered in their honor. The early phases of the process may be seen in dedications such as that of a Lusitanian cohort in Egypt during 288, which calls Maximian and Diocletian "the invincible emperors, restorers of the whole world," and a text from Augsburg dating to 290 honoring "the most foresightful emperor, ruler and lord of the world, founder of eternal peace."[172] A text from Rome, dating to the years 293–96, is even more pointed, calling Maximian "great, invincible and bravest of all previous emperors," while one from a newly established fort in the Balkans, dating to the period 298–300, reads:

> The Imperatores Caesares Gaius Aur(elius) Val(erius) Diocletianus and M(arcus) Aur(elius) Val(erius) Maximianus and Fl(avius) Val(erius) Constantius and Gal(erius) Val(erius) Maximianus the most noble Caesars, Greatest Victors over the Germans five times, Greatest Victors over the Sarmatians four times, Greatest Victors over the Persians twice, Greatest Victors over the Britains, after defeating the nations of the barbarians, and confirming the tranquility of their world, established this camp.[173]

The language of inscriptions, when expanded beyond mere titles (something that was at the discretion of those responsible for the text), does no more than echo the tenor of panegyrists who derived the imperial portraits for their orations from within the palace itself.[174] In 289 Mamertinus had asked,

> Indeed could there have eventuated a greater one than that famous crossing of yours into Germany, by which you first of all, Emperor, proved that there were no bounds to the Roman empire except those of your arms?
>
> (*Pan.* 10 [2] 7.2, trans. Nixon)

He had gone on to assert that the Rhine had once seemed to have been made by nature to be the protection of the Gallic provinces (and no very secure one at that). The Euphrates had likewise been a protection for Syria, but one that was much less secure than the arms of Diocletian, before whom the Persian Empire had submitted itself (a reference to the restoration of Tiridates to Armenia).[175] In both formulations, of course, the Roman presence beyond these rivers has been wiped away. The author of the panegyric of 291 told Maximian,

> I do not, therefore, bring to mind the State liberated by your valor from savage despotism, I do not speak of the provinces liberated by the injustices of the preceding era, returned to obedience by your clemency.
>
> (*Pan.* 11 [3] 5.3, trans. Rodgers)[176]

He goes on to say that the emperors have "transplanted civil wars to races worthy of that madness" (*Pan.* 11 [3] 16.2), and the author of the panegyric for Constantius on March 1, 297 or 298, completes the collapse of the decades between the 260s and 290s by saying:

> The defection of these provinces from the light of Rome, although distressing, was less honorable in the Principate of Gallienus. For then, whether through neglect of affairs or through a certain deterioration in our fortune, the State was dismembered of almost all its limbs. At that time both the Parthian had too lofty pretensions and the Palmyrene claimed equality, all of Egypt and the Syrias had seceded, Raetia was lost and Noricum and the Pannonias devastated. Italy herself, mistress of nations, lamented the destruction of very many of its cities. There was not so much distress over individual losses when the empire was deprived of almost everything. But now the whole world has been reclaimed through your courage.
>
> (*Pan.* 8 [4] 10.1–4, trans. Nixon)[177]

The scope of the rewriting of history is breathtakingly thorough. The revolt of Carausius is backdated to the time of Gallienus, and it is implied that the tetrarchs had dealt with the Palmyrenes. Elsewhere the achievement of Aurelian is noted only through a veiled reference to the slaughter on the Catalaunian plain; Probus is recalled as being on the throne during the Frankish raids in the Mediterranean.[178] The theme of the restoration of the empire may go back to Aurelian, but here it has evolved in a new way, becoming a statement of the uniqueness of the tetrarchic regime.

The ideology of restoration was a concomitant of the practice of centralization that was coming to the fore in these years. The codices of Gregorius and Hermogenianus were two signs of it, as was the increasing frequency of the use of verbose edicts to communicate an imperial value system to the inhabitants of the empire. In the next five years Diocletian and his colleagues would turn to ever more radical efforts at reforming the conduct of their subjects in order to make them worthy of life in this brave new world. There is a sense in which Diocletian may have been losing sight of what was possible in place of what was ideal. The Roman Empire was still as vast and culturally diverse at it had ever been. The fact remained that even though the provinces were smaller and governors more numerous, the emperor's pronouncements could (and did) fall on deaf ears if they could not be reconciled with local realities. Indeed, in what may be the last edict issued in the spirit of tetrarchic government, an edict of Maximinus Daia in 313, the emperor states,

> We addressed a letter to the governors in each province last year laying it down that if any should wish to follow such a custom or the same religious observances, such a one should adhere to his purpose without hindrance. . . . it cannot escape our notice even now that some of the judges misinterpreted our injunctions, and caused our people to have doubts with regard to our commands.
> (Euseb. *Hist. eccl.* 9.7.9, trans. Oulton)

The disintegration of traditional methods of negotiating authority between the palace and its subjects in the years after Decius' disaster may have made the urge to greater centralization of power around the office of the emperor predictable. A new dynamic may have seemed necessary. The further actions that were being taken to reform state finance and the structures of administration in these years will be discussed in chapter 9, but there too attention must turn away from the palace and into the broader reaches of the realm. Diocletian might now possess a monopoly of force, but he would find that he could not compel agreement. The increasing disjuncture between the policies of centralization and the realities of diversity would mold the evolution of the Roman state through the next century.

Part IV

THE
CONSTANTINIAN
EMPIRE

8

ALTERNATIVE
NARRATIVES

Manichaeans, Christians, and
Neoplatonists

Alternative narratives: 260–303

As Diocletian and his colleagues rose to prominence and reshaped the history
of the recent past, there were other groups that were shaping their own histories in quite different ways. Alternatives to the grand narrative of imperial
history had always existed, and did not necessarily clash in theme with the
one that emanated from the central government or was composed by aristocratic historians who chose to write imperial history. Through media such
as public buildings, coins, or inscriptions, cities could create a narrative of
their relationship with the imperial power, and with the more distant past.
The local traditions that informed works such as Quintus of Smyrna's poem,
recorded by men like Philostratus or Pausanias or presented to local publics
through countless orations over time, were one sort of alternative narrative.
John Malalas' sixth-century *Chronicle* derives some of its confused history of
the third century from local traditions. Thus he is alone of the traditional
sources for this period in preserving the memory of Uranius Antoninus, albeit
a distorted one. Likewise Malalas was able to extract information about the
sack of Antioch, about Mariades, and about Odaenathus, while ignoring the
fate of Decius, from broader narratives composed elsewhere. While Malalas
could err by placing the revolt of the *monetales* under Aurelian at Antioch,
he could also note what no other historian noted, that the wife of Narses
was kept at Daphne.[1] The compiler of the *Thirteenth Sibylline Oracle* likewise
was able to create a sort of prophetic history that culminated in eastern
events, with little interest, as the narrative came closer to the victory of
Odaenathus, in anything happening outside of Syria.[2] Narratives of local
focus stand alongside very personal chronicles in the private archives of
individuals who retained their tax records, records of sale, copies of imperial
edicts, and such like as they needed them. Institutions such as the Synod
of International Victors would produce documents admitting new members
that quoted individual imperial documents that guaranteed the privileges of
their members.[3] The significance of these records is that they reverse the flow

of the grand narrative, reflecting parochial concerns above the concerns of the imperial government.

It is within the context of local or group history that we need to see two very different types of history that helped stabilize identities for two groups that would soon come into conflict with the government of Diocletian: the Manichaeans and the Christians. These narratives reflect the extent to which history as defined by the imperial government often strove in vain to establish its preeminence over alternatives that were often far closer to home for its subjects. The imperial government might (and did) establish the vocabulary with which power was described, but it could not determine how the language of power would be used. A third sort of narrative that we will consider in this chapter was produced by men with a somewhat closer connection to the center of imperial power. These are narratives constructed by philosophers as a way of validating their original contributions in light of a tradition that would remain as powerful a force in the early fourth century as it had been in the early third. There is perhaps no more eloquent illustration of this point than the writing of the philosophers Plotinus and Porphyry, who justified their innovation by claiming that they represented the learning of the ancients. Their renown would, in turn, be absorbed into a narrative of the history of philosophy that involved them in practices that they would have found, at the very least, distasteful.

The revelations of Mani

Mani, the founder of a sect that was welcomed by Zenobia and persecuted by Kirdir, has been alluded to at various points in the preceding chapters.[4] He was the founder and prophet of an extraordinary religion, who laid the foundation of a remarkably coherent community that extended from Europe to India, the Persian Gulf, and ultimately into Central Asia, where it would enjoy its greatest success centuries after Mani had died. Mani, and the group of close associates who saw it as their duty to extend knowledge of his visions across the known world, did so in large measure because they understood how they might re-create the power and passion of the original teachings through ritual and the written word.

A result of Mani's interest in the written record is that our knowledge of what he taught expanded enormously in the course of the twentieth century by discoveries of texts in Central Asia and Egypt. These books are written in a mind-boggling array of languages ranging from Parthian, Middle Persian, and Syriac (the primary languages of Mani himself) to Coptic, Sogdian, Uighur, and Chinese.[5] From these diverse texts, all fragmentary, emerges a picture of a group of core documents that were used by Manichaean teachers to spread the news of the master's revelation. The array of material that is found within the expositions of Manichaean doctrine is powerful testimony to the fact that Lower Mesopotamia, principally the kingdom of Mesene, was a true intellectual crossroads where the doctrines of Asia encountered those of the Mediterranean world to form a new idiom.

Mani himself was born on April 16, AD 216, in the vicinity of Ctesiphon. When he was four, his father, Pattikos, joined the Elchesaite Baptist community in Lower Mesopotamia.[6] The Baptists appear to have maintained doctrines associated with a form of Jewish Christianity that had largely been extinguished within the territory of the Roman Empire by the emergent centrality of the gospels and the Pauline epistles in the formation of Christian doctrine.[7] The apostle Paul appears to have been regarded as the great enemy by this group, the man who had hijacked the true message of Christianity and turned it in the direction of the Greek world. One sign of the importance of the Jewish background of the Baptist community is the adaptation of an apocryphal Jewish work, *The Book of Giants* (known only from fragments found among the Dead Sea Scrolls), by Mani as a vehicle for his own revelation.[8] But the Jewish and Christian background mingled in the southern Mesopotamian environment with other forces, among them Zoroastrianism and Buddhism. For Mani himself, India was as logical a destination in his wanderings as Armenia, and he would never personally enter the territory of the Roman Empire. Sapor I would receive the dedication of a work explaining his revelation, but no Roman emperor, as far as we know, ever received a similar gift.

It was eight years after his father joined the Baptists that Mani had the first of the visions around which the narrative of his life is structured in the book *On the Genesis of His Body* that was later composed by his followers. For Manichaeans, the dates of the visions were the important ones; significant events in the world at large, such as the accession of Ardashir (probably) and the year that Sapor assumed the throne, intrude only because they correspond to important moments in Mani's visionary existence.[9] Other reference points are simply mentions of the names of kings who ruled while Mani lived, and of Kirdir, who was responsible for his death.[10]

The crucial character in the story, the agent of Mani's vision, was his heavenly twin, who taught him

> who I am, what my body is, in what way I have come, how my arrival into the world took place, who I am of the ones most renowned for their eminence, how I was begotten into this fleshly body, by what woman I was delivered and born according to the flesh, and by whose passion I was engendered . . . and who my Father on high is, or in what way severed from him, I was sent out according to his purpose; what sort of commission and counsel he gave to me before I clothed myself in this instrument, and before I was led astray in this detestable flesh, and before I clothed myself with

its drunkenness and habits, and that one is, who is himself my ever-vigilant Twin.

(CMC 21–22)

It was the Twin who told Mani about his father and his soul, "which exists as the soul of both worlds," who showed him "the boundless heights and unfathomable depths" (*CMC* 22–23).

Mani's vision and his decision, supported strongly by his father, to confront the Baptists with the error of their ways, led to his expulsion from their community and the beginning of a series of long journeys. At the end of the reign of Ardashir he took ship for India, where he preached his new revelation in the land of Turan, probably eastern Pakistan, and, as Sapor took the throne, he returned overland to the Sasanian heartland, preaching in Persis.[11] From there he went to the area around Ctesiphon (called Babylonia in the text that preserves the record of this trip) before traveling down the Tigris to Mesene, where he converted the ruling king Ormizd I, a son of Sapor.[12] Leaving Lower Mesopotamia, Mani went up to Susiane, where he was received by Sapor, who gave him a place in his entourage.[13] In the years that followed, while Sapor won his victories over the Romans, Mani spent time again in Persis, and then moved north to Parthia, Adiabene, and what he calls the borderland with Rome.[14] This may be the period in which he wrote the *Letter to Edessa*, which is quoted in *On the Genesis of His Body*, and also the period in which he dispatched missionaries who traveled as far into Roman territory as Egypt.[15] It is impossible to know if these activities corresponded in any way to the campaigns of Sapor, though the parallel with Kirdir, who accompanied the king on these expeditions to establish approved Zoroastrian places of worship, is a very tempting one indeed. Certainly the work of his missionaries may have been facilitated by the interest of Zenobia.[16]

The religion that Mani created in the course of his journeys was one that he saw as replacing all that had gone before. A Middle Persian text records this assertion:

> The religion that I have chosen is in ten things above and better than the other, previous religions. Firstly the primeval religions were in one country and one language. But my religion is of that kind that it will be manifest in every country and in all languages, and it will be taught in far away countries.
>
> Secondly: the former religions (existed) as long as they had the pure leaders, but when the leaders had been led upwards, then their religions fell into disorder and became negligent in commandments and works. And in ... [But my religion, because of] the living [books?], of the teachers, the Bishops, the Elect and the Hearers, and of wisdom and works will stay until the End.

Thirdly: those previous souls that in their own religion have not accomplished the works will come to my religion, which will certainly be the door of redemption for them.

Fourthly: this revelation of mine of the two principles and my living books, my wisdom and knowledge are above and better than those of the previous religions.

(M 5797, trans. J. P. Asmussen, *Manichaean Literature* [New York, 1975], 12)

As he sought to improve understanding, it appears that he gained supporters through what seemed to be his ability to live on two planes – human and divine – at one time. It is this that contributes to the redefinition of time in terms of the moments of revelation. More than that, his cosmopolitan worldview and his understanding of literature as a medium of communication set this vision apart. Thus his followers later sought to make the master reappear through their own versions of his teachings. The urge to re-create these moments of the sage's personal revelation emerges perhaps most clearly in the introduction to the book of his teachings known as the *Kephalaia*, where the master is made to say:

My beloved ones: at the time that [Jesus tr]od . . . the land of the west [. . . proc]laimed his hope . . . his disciples . . . which Jesus uttered [. . . a]fter him they wrote . . . his parables . . . and the signs and wonders . . . they wrote a book concerning his . . .

[The Apostle of] Light, the splendrous enlightener . . . [he came to] Persia, up to Hystaspes the king [. . . he chose d]isciples, righteous men of trut[h . . . he proclaimed hi]s hope in Persia; but . . . Zarathustra (did not) write books. Rather hi[s] disciples who came a]fter him, they remembered; they wrote . . . that they read today . . .

Again from his part, when Buddha came . . . about him, fo[r] he too proclaimed [his hope and] great wisdom. He cho[se] his chur[ches, and] perfected his churches. He unveiled to them [his hop]e. Yet, there is only this: that he d[id not] write his wis[dom in bo]oks. His disciples, who came afte[r] him, are the ones who re[membered] somewhat the wisdom that they had heard from Buddha. They [wrote it in sc]riptures.

(*Kephalaia* 7.22–8.7, trans. I. Gardiner, *The Kephalaia of the Teacher* [Leiden, 1995], 13)

The Coptic text from which these lines have been recovered becomes even more fragmentary after the discussion of Buddha, but it is notable that the word for "error" is used repeatedly (three times in fourteen lines), suggesting that Mani returned to the theme enunciated in the Middle Persian text quoted above. The fact that he was the author of his own revelation ensured its correctness.

The visions and teachings are remarkable in terms of both their imaginative breadth and the thoroughness with which Mani equipped his followers with the tools they needed to continue his work. The works that are listed as his own in the preface to the *Kephalaia* include seven books, *The Great Gospel, The Treasury of Life,* the *Pragmateia, On the Mysteries, To the Parthians* (or *At the Request of the Parthians*), *The Letters,* and the *Psalms.*[17] Other lists of his works replace *To the Parthians* with the *Book of Giants,* leading to the reasonable conclusion that the full title of the book may have been something along the lines of *To* (or *At the Request of*) *the Parthians concerning the Book of Giants.*[18] Additionally, Mani wrote a book on the nature of his revelations to Sapor (a book that, perhaps for political reasons, was never cited in the west).

Taken as a group, Mani's seven books represent several kinds of instruction. The *Psalms* would appear to have been composed as a way to simplify Mani's teaching for a larger audience. *The Treasury of Life, Pragmateia,* and *On the Mysteries* are cited as group providing the essential components of Mani's thought, perhaps for a more limited audience of exegetes who could explain their contents to others, something that may also be true of the work on the *Book of the Giants. The Great Gospel* would appear to have been a foundational account that included details of Mani's life, and the *Letters* might have been modeled on the Pauline epistles as a way of explaining points of doctrine to a group. The *Kephalaia* itself is organized in a way that is evocative of rabbinic writings where the teacher is shown explaining points of dogma to his pupils. Thus, in a section on fasting, members of the community are told:

Once more the enlightener speaks to his disciples: the fasting of the saints is profit[able] for [four] great works.

The first work; S[hall] the holy man punish his body by fasting, [he sub]dues the entire ruling-power that exists in him.

The second: This soul that comes in [to] him in the adm[ini]stration of his food, day by day; it shall be made holy, [cl]eansed, purified, and w[ash]ed from the adulteration [of] the darkness that is mixed with it.

The third: Th[at] person shall make the holy one; the mystery of [the children] of light [i]n whom there is neither corruption nor [. . .] the food, nor wound it. [Rat]her, they are holy, [there is nothing] in them that defiles, as they li[ve] in peace.

The fourth: they make a[. . . 25 . . .] the Cross, they restrain their hands from the hand [. . . not] destroy the living soul.

(*Kephalaia* 191, 9–25, trans. Gardiner,
The Kephalaia, 200)

In whatever form they were delivered, the teachings were based upon the notion of an eternal struggle between the forces of Light and Darkness that Mani alone seems to have been able to describe.[19] There were, in his vision, three creations. In the first creation there was the Paradise of Light, which occupied the north, east, and west, ruled by the Father of Greatness, who had with him two eternals, Earth and Light, each divided into five worlds. The Darkness, which occupied the south, was also divided into five regions, and gave rise to the Devil. The Devil "coveted the upper regions. Seeing the flashings of the Light and contesting them."[20] The Light World (one of the five worlds of the earth) told the Father of Greatness about the Devil and the attacks that had revealed the nature of the earthly realms to him. The Father of Greatness responded by creating the Mother of Life, who bore the Primal Man. The Primal Man descended into Hell and was defeated by the Devil, who consumed the elements of Light with which he was armed.[21] When the Father of Greatness learned of the defeat of the Primal Man, he evoked the second creation of the Gods: The Friend of Light, the Great Builder, and the Living Spirit. The Living Spirit summoned the Primal Man back from Hell and, along with the Mother of Light, escorted him back to Paradise.[22]

The Second Creation was the work of the Living Spirit, who joined the Mother of Life in attacking the powers of Darkness.[23] Victorious, he created eight worlds and ten skies from the bodies of the demons that he had killed. Captured demons, or archons, were bound in the heavens, while eight worlds and ten skies were created out of the bodies of demons that had been killed. The eight worlds appear to have been stacked one upon the other, with five of them being below Atlas (a creation of the Father of Greatness), who lifted the other three on his shoulders up to the heavens, which were supported by another of the Father's creations, the Keeper of Splendor.[24] It remained, however, to recover the light that remained within the material mass, and it was for this that the third act of creation was undertaken. This much is reasonably clear, as is Mani's notion that the rescue of light particles was facilitated by three wheels (of fire, wind, and water) that raised particles of light up to the sun and moon, which acted as filters of darkness to purify the light before it ascended to the New Paradise.[25]

The primary agent in the third creation was the Third Messenger, who evoked, as his assistant, the Virgin of Light.[26] They displayed themselves naked before the archons in the sky, who were moved to ejaculate by the beauty of the Maiden, while female devils, excited by the form of the Third Messenger, aborted the fetus that each bore within her. The semen of the archons fell to earth, where it formed trees and plants on the dry land and gave rise to a sea monster when it fell into water.[27] The sea monster was duly dispatched by the Adamas of Light (an agent of the second creation).[28] The offspring of the "abortions" were five varieties of beasts that inhabited the earth and sea. It would appear that the logic of this act of creation was to release the imprisoned Light from the bodies of devils and place it in creations that, although themselves of darkness, might still release it more readily through the Column of Glory, who was both a divinity and the path through which Light could ascend into heaven. To receive the escaping Light, the Great Builder constructed the New Paradise, ruled by the Primal Man. The New Paradise was identical to the Paradise of Light, but kept separate from it so that the rescued Light would have a home while the Paradise of Light remained undisturbed by the struggle for redemption.

The physical world appears to have been the fifth of the stacked worlds upon which Atlas stood. Its shaping was the act of the Living Spirit, and it was upon this plane that the powers of darkness struck back. As the abortions landed, creating all animal life, two archons, one male, the other female, engulfed all the male and female monsters and had sex, creating Adam and Eve in the forms in which they had beheld the Third Messenger and the Virgin of Light.[29] When the angels whom the Living Spirit had made guardians of the world realized what had happened, they called upon the Third Messenger, the Virgin of Light, Primal Man, and the Living Spirit to send a messenger to reveal the truth to Adam and Eve. This messenger was Jesus, who taught Adam his true nature so that he abstained from sex with Eve. Eve then made love to her father, engendering Cain and Abel. Cain in turn fathered two daughters by his mother and, after murdering Abel, took one of his daughters as his wife. Eve was then taught the magical arts by the archons and seduced Adam, giving birth to a son, Shem. Adam then sought to avoid Eve, but was again seduced and expelled from the garden that he had created to protect his child from the forces of darkness by his son.[30]

All creation was thus an act of evil, committed with the express purpose of preventing the particles of Light that had been imprisoned after the defeat of the Primal Man from returning to the New Paradise. Mani's own mission was to reveal the truth to all mortals so that they could free themselves of the darkness that was inherent to their bodies, and enable the light within them to be reunited with the forces of goodness. It was only when most of the imprisoned particles of Light had been released that the final battle between good and evil would come to pass, which would end with the final overthrow of Darkness.

The power of Mani's vision lay in its ability to involve all of his followers in a struggle that reached beyond the confines of ordinary time. The visions that he described were linked to a variety of traditions, as the summary of other prophets in the *Kephalaia* reveals. If there is one thing that does stand out, it is that the books that resonated most deeply with his own were often non-canonical books from other sects, be it the *Book of Giants*, or that of Enoch from contemporary Judaism, to Marcionite doctrines from the fringes of contemporary Christianity.[31] The sense of the eternal struggle between the forces of Darkness and Light was, of course, a major feature of Zoroastrian thought, and Middle Persian texts tend to refer to the Devil as Ahriman, the Primal Man as Ormizd (i.e., Ahura Mazda), and the Third Messenger as Mihryazd (i.e., Mithras in Iranian cosmology).[32] Contemporary Buddhism may have influenced the general structure of the community in that, among the Buddhists as well as the Manichaeans, there was a clear bipartite division between the monks and laypeople who supported them.[33] People who felt themselves on the fringes of any of these groups might feel themselves united with others through Mani.

The community of followers was divided into two groups: the Elect, chosen in the first instance by Mani himself, who devoted themselves entirely to the struggle with darkness, and the Hearers who still lived in the world.[34] Among the Elect there were three ranks above that of the regular member – priest, bishop, and magistrate. All in all there were to be twelve magistrates, seventy-two bishops, and three hundred and sixty priests.[35] After his death the community chose an overall leader *(archegos)* who would "be the one that directs us in love and sends us to that joy and life of the fortunate" (M 36, trans. Asmussen, *Manichaean Literature*, 29), though the first of these leaders, Sisinnos, may have been appointed by Mani himself.[36]

Diet was an important feature of the life of the Elect: meat was out of the question, for animals contained little light, and their consumption would fill a person with dark matter. Vegetables could be consumed, but even here one needed to be frugal since the act of consuming even a vegetable would cause pain to the Light that was imprisoned within it.[37] The Elect would therefore take only a single meal of vegetables after dark five days a week (they were expected to fast on Sunday and Monday). As a sign that they were not of this world they might possess food only for one day, and clothes for only a year. The duty of the Hearers was to supply the Elect with what they needed and, quite literally, to listen to their exposition of Mani's teachings, while confessing their sins to the Elect once a week. It would appear that this would take place on a Sunday, and that the Elect would meet, perhaps to hear confessions from each other, on a Monday; on other days the Elect were expected to pray seven times, the Hearers four. In the time corresponding to the Iranian month of Shahrever each year, all members of the community would join in extensive fasting for twenty-six days leading up to the Feast of the Bema, the celebration of the day that Mani died (the period of fasting corresponding to the number of days that he was imprisoned before he perished). On that day the community would face an empty chair that represented Mani's presence among them, listen to his last letter from prison, and sing hymns containing the essence of his teaching and commemorating his death.[38]

Mani himself was plainly a man of prodigious energy. The tale of his life involved a series of long journeys and meetings with the powerful that ensured that his revelation would take hold across the territory of the Persian Empire and beyond. There is much here that recalls the relentless activity of Kirdir (who would ultimately be the agent of his destruction) and of the first two monarchs of the Sasanian dynasty, suggesting that the political transformation of the Persian Empire may have, in some sense, created an atmosphere in which change for its own sake was valued.

It is in the course of the diverse narratives of these journeys that it becomes clear that Mani and his most significant followers were not simply offering tonic for the soul. In the Middle Persian account of his final confrontation with Kirdir and his associates at the court of Bahram II Mani states,

> Always I have done good to you and your family. And many and numerous were your servants whom I have [freed] of demons and witches. And many were those whom I have caused to rise from their illness. And many were those from whom I have averted the numerous kinds of fever. And many were those who came unto death, and I have [revived] them.
>
> (M 3 in Asmussen, *Manichaean Literature*, 54–55,
> quoting the translation of W. B. Henning)

In another fragment, this one from a text written in Parthian, Mani is quoted as saying:

> "I have come before the King! Peace be upon you from the Gods!" The King said: "Whence are you?" I said: "I am a physician from the land of Babylon." . . . and the whole body of the girl became healthy, (and in) great joy she said to me: "Whence are you, my God and Vivifier and my . . ."
>
> (M 566, trans. Asmussen, *Manichaean Literature*, 9)

An account of the Manichaean contact with Palmyra, preserved in a Sogdian translation, has Mani himself in Palmyra, where he heals a sister of Zenobia (called here Queen Tadi):

> [The Lord Man]i, the apostle openly descended into the presence of Nafsa, and he laid his hand upon her, and straight away Nafsa was healed, and became wholly without pain. Everyone was astonished at this great miracle. And <there were> many people who accepted the truth anew. Also Queen Tadi, the sister of Nafsa, wife of the Caesar with great [. . .] came before Mar Adda and from him [. . .] received the truth.
>
> (T.M. 389c, trans. S. N. C. Lieu, *Manichaeism in Mesopotamia and the Roman East* [Leiden, 1994], 28)[39]

As with many holy men, the proof of a divine connection was offered through the ability to heal. But that was not all that Mani could do. In another

310

passage, Mani is shown to be disputing before Sapor I against a sage named Gwdnys who was in the king's retinue, and converting him through the force of his arguments. Here Mani appears as a man in full command of the rhetorical tools of his time, and an astute observer of Sasanian political language. Even in his final defense against Kirdir, he stresses that his patron was Sapor himself, language that would resonate a decade after his death in the proclamations of Narses on his inscription at Paikuli.[40]

The ability to heal was also a feature of Mani's chosen missionaries, as is plain from the tale of Manichaean contact with Palmyra preserved in a Coptic text:

> [He (Abiesou)] again went in before queen Thamador (Zenobia), and she looked favorably on him. Abiesou the teacher had confidence [in her and settled] there with other brothers. She became a [great protectress] of the church in that place; [after which Abiesou] the teacher sent Sethel the deacon of Ta[. . . with] Abizakhias to the fort of Abiran [so that they might build up] the church in that place. [They healed numerous people]. The matter came before Amoroà the king [who was the son of] Lahim, so as to enable the brothers to go to his house for a cause of healing.
>
> (Trans. I. M. F. Gardiner and S. N. C. Lieu, "From Narmouthis (Medinet Madi) to Kellis (Ismant El-Kharab): Manichaean Documents from Roman Egypt," *JRS* 86 [1996]: 153)

The missionaries who healed followed Mani in that they also preached the error of existing customs, engaging in public disputations with believers of all other sorts to make their points. Although coming from beyond the boundaries of the Roman Empire, they appear to have been at home in the polyglot world of the eastern provinces, and they knew well enough how to hold an audience. They may have benefited not only from the fervor of Mani's own teaching, but also from a predisposition within the Roman audience to believe that interesting new wisdom came from the east.

In some ways Mani's career will also help bring into focus one of the questions with which this book opened: what did it mean to be Roman? Mani himself knew Sapor, who gave him permission to preach his revelation throughout the Persian Empire; he converted one of Sapor's most important subordinates, the king of Mesene, into a believer.[41] He was a thoroughly Mesopotamian man. In his vision of the world there were four kingdoms that appear in the *Kephalaia* as follows:

> Once again the apostle speaks: There are f[our great kingdoms] in the world.
> The first is the kingdom of] the land of Babylon and of Persia.

The [seco]nd is the kingdom of the Romans.
The thir[d is the k]ingdom of the Aksumites.
The fourth is the kin[g]dom of Silis.

> (*Kephalaia* 188, 30–190, 10, trans. Gardiner, *The Kephalaia*, 197, with orthography slightly adapted)

The kingdoms of Aksum, Ethiopia, and Silis, which was, presumably, in India, were linked with Lower Mesopotamia by trade, while it is notable as well that Rome is second to the realm of Sapor. Mesopotamian as his vision was, the faith that Mani invented was unthinkable without a religion, Christianity, that was formed within the Roman Empire. The faith that he spread to India in the 240s, that his followers took to Central Asia after his death, was as much an epiphenomenon of the Roman Near East as it was of the Sasanian.

In the early years, it seems that Mani's faith enjoyed the active support of the very powerful, but with Sapor's death and Kirdir's rise to power, persecution threatened. After Mani's death, persecution became a reality within the lands of the Persian Empire. There is no reason to think that Mani himself was much concerned to create a theology of martyrdom in his own lifetime, but with the rise of persecution in Persia, one lay ready to hand that could be borrowed. Mani's death was presented to the faithful as a crucifixion, and a remarkable hymn, preserved in a Coptic text, offers a theology of martyrdom that looks very much as if it was borrowed from the Christian church in the immediate aftermath of Mani's demise.[42] The list of martyrs begins before Jesus and ends with Mani himself. Soon, however, a theology of martyrdom would not have to be borrowed. Kirdir sought to drive the Manichaeans out of the territory of the Persian Empire, and in 302 they would fall foul of Diocletian. The irony here is that as Kirdir assaulted Mani's faith as an un-Persian activity, Diocletian would attack it as being all too Persian. The Diocletianic letter to the proconsul of Egypt, recommending persecution, begins as follows:

> Excessive idleness, my dear Julianus, sometimes drives people to join with others in devising certain superstitious doctrines of the most worthless and depraved kind. In so doing, they overstep the bounds imposed on humans. Moreover, they lure on many to accept the authority of their erroneous doctrine.
>
> But the immortal gods in their providence have deigned to dispose and arrange matters so that good and true principles should be approved and fixed by the wisdom and constant deliberation of many good, eminent, and very wise men. These principles it is not right to oppose or resist, nor ought the age-old religion be disparaged by a new one. For it is the height of criminality to reexamine doctrines

once and for all settled and fixed by the ancients, doctrines which hold and possess their recognized place and course. Wherefore it is our vigorous determination to punish the stubborn depraved minds of these most worthless people.

We take note that those men concerning whom Your Sagacity has reported to our Serenity, namely the Manichaeans, have set up new and unheard-of sects in opposition to the older creeds, with the intent of driving out to the benefit of their depraved doctrine what was formerly granted to us by divine favor. We have heard that these men have but recently sprung up and advanced, like strange and unexpected portents, from the Persian people, our enemy, to this part of the world, where they are perpetrating many outrages, disturbing the tranquillity of the peoples and also introducing the gravest harm to the communities. And it is to be feared, peradventure, as usually happens, that they may try, with the accursed customs and perverse laws of the Persians, to infect men of more innocent nature, namely the temperate and tranquil Roman people, as well as our entire empire with what one may call their malevolent poisons.

> (*Coll.* 15.3, trans. M. Reinhold and N. Lewis, *Roman Civilization*, 3rd edn. [New York, 1990], 548–49)

Diocletian knew enough about the Manichaeans to divide the community between the priests, other Elect, and the Hearers, and to know that their faith did indeed originate in Persia. Christians, who found the Manichaeans dangerous rivals, may have rejoiced in the rhetoric of their ruler, numbering themselves among those of "more innocent nature."[43] Interestingly enough, the point at issue between the emperors and the Manichaeans is not actually religion so much as it is a constructed view of *romanitas*, which is threatened by concepts from abroad. It was precisely this point that would soon be at issue between Christians and a government whose brave new Roman world had no place for a cult that took a man who had been executed by a Roman magistrate as the Son of God.

As for those Manichaeans who survived the initial persecutory impulse of the central government (which would have been the vast majority, if it is right to draw an analogy with the fate of Christians in time of persecution), there is reason to think that some of them may have turned away from the Nile valley. Persecution may have suggested that it would be a good idea to have places to hide that were off the beaten track, as Dionysius of Alexandria had used various villages as places of refuge when pursued by the imperial authorities in 257.[44] Two of these places may well have been Medinet-Madi and Kellis, in which precious Manichaean libraries were discovered in the twentieth century.[45] In these places too, the Manichaean communities may have imitated the Buddhist monasteries that Mani would have known from the east.

Christians and the imperial government

The narrative of Christianity in the later third century, or, rather, the narratives of Christianity, were rather more complex than those of their Manichaean rivals, as befitted a more established community. On a reasonable estimate, their numbers expanded between the capture of Valerian and the year 300 to around six million, leading to substantial changes in the way that Christian communities interacted with their neighbors.[46]

Ever since Gallienus' edict of restitution, Christians had been able to practice their faith openly. Large churches were constructed in the major cities of the empire: that in Nicomedia was evidently on a hill overlooking the palace, while those in Carthage, Antioch, and Alexandria appear to have been big enough to hold very large crowds.[47] In Oxyrhynchus, a list of streets assembled in 295 identifies one as the site of the northern church, and another as the site of the southern.[48] Polytheists were aware enough of what a church might hold that an imperial official in 303 would send a list of items to a church that he thought a church would have.[49] It was easy enough for him to do so, as local Christians were identified by their position in the church on public documents: various lists of landholders from late third-century Egypt identify Christian officials in the same way that they identify other professionals.[50] Although few Christians can be found in senatorial families (which may be a problem of the quality of the evidence rather than a reflection of the actual situation) before 312, it is plain that the leadership of the church was attracting men of considerable wealth and experience.[51] For at least the last half century the bishops in major cities were well-known public figures: Cyprian was well enough known that a crowd demanded his arrest in 249; Dionysius of Alexandria seems to have been thoroughly recognizable at the same period; while Paul of Samosata made a show of himself in the early 270s.[52] The reluctance of the Christian community to name a bishop at Rome after the execution of Xystus in 258 may have been caused, at least in part, by knowledge of the fact that to assume such a position was tantamount to putting one's head on the chopping block, since people outside of the church would know who he was.[53] Valerian evidently felt that there were Christians in the senate, as well as in the imperial household, and one of the men arrested as a result of his persecution edict in North Africa is specifically identified as an equestrian.[54] In the early fourth century, a church council, meeting at Elvira in Spain, stated that bishops and priests should not leave

> their places in order to engage in trade; nor are they to go the round
> of the provinces in search of profitable markets. To gain their living,

let them send a son, a freedman, an agent or some other person; and, if they want to trade, let them trade within their province.

(*Can. Elv.* 19, trans. J. Stevenson, *A New Eusebius: Documents Illustrating the History of the Church to* AD 337 [London, 1987], 291)

Another canon of the same council forbids priests from acting as money lenders.[55] The implication of both restrictions is that priests and bishops ought to live the way that members of the urban aristocracy lived, deriving money from rents rather than direct involvement in commerce. A letter that Constantine would send to an official investigating ecclesiastical controversy in North Africa in 313 granted immunity from civic liturgies to all priests who supported the bishop whom he had decided to favor.[56] The fact that Constantine should write such a letter suggests that he felt that there would be a sufficient number of priests who were drawn from the liturgical class to make a difference. There is good reason to think that he was correct in his assessment of the situation. The leaders on both sides of the controversy appear to have been people of good education who were able to deal with imperial officials as people of standing within the community as a whole.[57] The same is true of the leaders on both sides of another schism that would occupy a great deal of Constantine's attention in the east.[58]

As Christianity moved further into the mainstream of imperial intellectual life, the question arises as to how Christians might tell their own story. What traditions would have supported a man like Eusebius of Caesarea if he had decided to write his *History of the Church* in 300 rather than after the overthrow of the tetrarchic system of government in 313?[59] There were essentially two traditions to which he might turn, one being apologetic, the other perhaps best termed catastrophic, in that it would have to be based on accounts of martyrdoms. Indeed, the two most notable works of Christian fiction that were composed in the course of the third century may be seen as representing these two essential strains in Christian thought. These two works are the Pseudo-Clementine *Recognitions*, which tell of Peter's ongoing battle with Simon Magus, whom he defeats in public disputation after public disputation across the empire, and the *Acts of Paul and Thecla*, which adapts the form of a martyrology to make its point.

The apologetic tradition took as its starting point that the church was a wholly respectable institution, recognized by the best emperors, persecuted only by the worst – a theme that was first enunciated by Melito of Sardis in the second century – and nourished by a string of brilliant teachers.[60] It is significant that none of these brilliant teachers was possessed to any significant degree of supernatural power. It is also significant that certain unpleasant facts about these teachers could be smoothed over by the tradition. Eusebius, for instance, regarded Tertullian of Carthage as an important figure; he knew a version of Tertullian's *Apologeticus* that had been translated

315

into Greek, and ignored completely the fact that in his later years Tertullian was a Montanist.[61] He was not alone in his ability to ignore unpleasant facts. Divisions within the church were not always as obvious as later imperial legislation, which condemned the descendants of second-century heretical groups, would make them seem. Disputes within local Christian groups often appear to have been settled locally, making it possible for Tertullian and others whose views did not conform to post-Constantinian notions of ortho-doxy to remain important figures in church history.

For the later part of the third century, the preeminent source for the history of the church is Eusebius of Caesarea. From 260 to 303, Eusebius offers a vision of the church at peace with the empire, and untroubled by the outbreak of major new heretical movements. After recording Aurelian's settlement of the matter of Paul of Samosata, he says that the emperor was plotting to persecute the church,

> But as he was just on the point of so doing and was putting, one might almost say, his signature to the decrees against us, Divine Justice visited him, and pinioned his arms, so to speak, to prevent his undertaking.
>
> (*Hist. eccl.* 7.30.21, trans. Oulton)

Despite Eusebius' claim that rumor of the persecution was commonplace at the time that Aurelian died, there is no real reason to believe that his state-ment reflects anything more than the general contestation of Aurelian's memory after his death.[62] Otherwise the bulk of his treatment is concerned with the succession of bishops in major Christian cities, the letter of Anatolius on the date of Easter, and certain other Christian notables. Among these is a man who would reappear in his narrative of events after February 23, 303,

> Dorotheus, a learned man, who had been deemed worthy of the pres-byterate at Antioch. In his zeal for all that is beautiful in divine things, he made so careful a study of the Hebrew tongue that he read with understanding the original Hebrew Scriptures. And he was by no means unacquainted with the most liberal studies and Greek primary education; but withal he was by very nature a eunuch, having been one from his very birth, so that the emperor, accounting this a sort of miracle, took him into his friendship and honored him with the charge of the purple dye-works at Tyre.
>
> (*Hist. eccl.* 7.32.2–4)

For Eusebius, one of the most important developments is the movement of clergy from Alexandria to high positions in the province of Syria. Anatolius, for instance, was from Alexandria, and he succeeded another Alexandrian, also named Eusebius, as bishop of Laodicea.[63] It would be the bishops of

Syria who would lend crucial support to the priest Arius when he challenged the Alexandrian hierarchy over the nature of God in 318. Although Arius was himself from Cyrenaica, and his doctrines were formed within the Alexandrian church, they descended from those of Dionysius of Alexandria, who had supported the Syrian bishops in their fight against Paul of Samosata.[64] Dionysius did this because he appears to have recognized a link between Paul's views and those of a teacher named Sabellius, whose efforts to show that the three persons of the Trinity were identical Dionysius had refuted when they had surfaced in Egypt.[65] The theology of Dionysius was similar to that of Origen, in that he too taught that God was represented through three *hypostaseis*, or substances, and that God the Father created the Son and the Logos from himself. These views were also very much a part of the Syrian tradition of exegesis, having been honed in the case that was brought against Paul of Samosata in 268.[66]

It is possible that the key to understanding the position of Syrian bishops on the Trinity was Lucian of Antioch, who allegedly adopted an Origenist position in the early fourth century. He seems to have influenced another Syrian bishop, Eusebius of Beirut, who would, at some point prior to 318, become bishop of Nicomedia.[67] Eusebius of Caesarea shared a similar view of the relationship between God and the Son, and it is of considerable interest that he singles out men like Anatolius, two Alexandrian priests, Pierius and Achillas, and his countryman Pamphilus for praise precisely because of their command of Greek philosophy.[68] He notes that both Anatolius and Eusebius were treated with respect by Roman officers during the troubles that engulfed Alexandria in the reign of Aurelian.[69] If he had been inclined to cast his net wider, he might also have noted that the professor of Latin at Nicomedia was a North African Christian named Lactantius. In terms of the point that he is trying to make – that the Christian church was now accepted on the intellectual landscape of the polytheist empire – this may be reasonable. But in terms of what Eusebius knew at the time that he completed his history, it is utterly tendentious. There was no need for him to observe the existence of Lactantius, because Lactantius had no interest in the brand of theology that Eusebius espoused. Eusebius had placed in the most favorable light possible the nexus of relationships that would provide the underpinnings for the Christological controversy that split the church in the 320s.

Eusebius did not, of course, see himself as working in the tradition of classical narrative historians for whom the display of impartiality was important (even if unobtainable) and the document was a source to be used, but never quoted verbatim.[70] Eusebius' background was in the writing of apologetic works, commentaries, and what was to become an enormously important chronicle in which he sought to reconcile pagan and Christian world history from the Creation down to the present. All of these forms of writing involved the direct quotation of documents, and so it was that when he turned to the writing of a new style of Christian narrative history, Eusebius adopted the style of direct quotation that was characteristic of his earlier efforts. In addition to the direct quotation of earlier apologetic, and in anticipation, perhaps, of his own devotion to this style of writing in the last three books of his history, Eusebius also included significant sections that were derived from firsthand accounts of persecution.

Accounts of persecution formed a second branch of Christian communal thinking, even though they came in many different forms. Descriptions of martyrdom range from letters to diaries, from transcripts of actual trials to complex confections derived from multiple perspectives, including diaries composed by martyrs in prison and firsthand descriptions (by third parties) of death, to works of outright fiction. The variety of ways in which martyrdom could be described is mirrored in the range of opinions concerning martyrdom within the diverse Christian communities. Origen took the view that persecution came from God as punishment for the sins of a Christian community, a view that he shared with Cyprian, Tertullian, and Eusebius.[71] Dionysius of Alexandria, whose letters describing events in Alexandria in the wake of Decius' edict and under Valerian, thought it the act of evil men, while Lactantius thought it was the act of the Devil.[72] Whatever the cause of persecution, all these men felt that it was wrong for Christians to seek martyrdom of their own accord. Others took the view that the greatest proof that they could offer of their devotion was to seek it openly, a practice that may be described as "voluntary martyrdom" to distinguish the act of attracting attention to oneself in order to be arrested from simple refusal to obey the order of a magistrate after having been arrested.[73] That the mainstream tradition of the church evolved a strong condemnation of those who turned themselves over to the authorities as suicides must conceal what was once a tradition suggesting that, under some circumstances, provoking the authorities was the right thing to do. Vestiges of this tradition appear in works such as the *Passion of Perpetua and Felicitas* (an openly Montanist work), where the dreams that appear in the prison diaries of Perpetua and one of her companions, Satyrus, suggest that they felt that they were driven by God to do what they did.[74] In cases that were somewhat less flagrant than Satyrus', such as those of Polycarp and Pionius of Smyrna, dreams are again described that could be taken as showing that conduct that was very far along the spectrum in the direction of voluntary martyrdom were also authorized by God.[75] In other cases, and there are a number of these recorded in the time of Diocletian, voluntary martyrdom is presented as a form of protest against earthly tyranny.[76]

As problematic as the issue of voluntary martyrdom was the treatment of those who had lapsed when confronted by the threat of execution. In the wake of the Decian edict, a priest named Novatian had enunciated the strong line that a person who had done such a thing could never be readmitted to the community, and had himself been consecrated bishop at Rome in opposition to the less rigorist bishop Cornelius.[77] His views had been roundly condemned by Cyprian, and by a synod of bishops convened by Cornelius at Rome in 251.[78] Their condemnation of Novatian had been received in the east, where Eusebius took it as doctrine.[79] As will become clear in the wake of the persecution edicts of Diocletian, this point too remained open to question.[80]

The questions surrounding martyrdom, the strong polarization of opinions, indicate the importance of the issue to the church itself, an importance that is confirmed by the growth of a historiography of persecution that stands in stark contrast to the apologetic tradition. For while the apologetic tradition stressed the possibility that Christianity could coexist with other forms of worship, the tradition of martyrdom presented the church as being at odds with temporal authority. The earliest extant text of this sort, the *Martyrdom of Polycarp*, states that Polycarp was the twelfth in the line of the martyrs of Smyrna, and offers an excellent example of the way that this sort of text could be used.[81] One version of the *Martyrdom of Polycarp* was copied by Pionius of Smyrna, who was himself a man determined to seek martyrdom for himself (successfully) at the time of the Decian edict on sacrifices. The account of Pionius' death was later included with that of Polycarp and a number of other texts that Eusebius collected into a book *On the Martyrdoms of the Ancients* as a sort of history of the Christian community's sufferings at the hands of its enemies prior to 303, when Eusebius may have had reason to think that this period of church history was coming to an end.[82] In North Africa, the *Passion of Perpetua and Felicitas*, although an openly Montanist composition, was so popular that by the end of the fourth century Augustine says that it was regularly read in church.[83] The events of Valerian's persecution gave rise to a series of further texts including an account of the martyrdom of Cyprian, the *Passion of Marian and James*, and the *Passion of Montanus and Lucius*. The authors of the last two works were likely influenced by the tale of Perpetua in that they too stressed the dreams of the martyrs in prison, and they appear to have been the work of one community within the North African church.[84]

While the collection of Eusebius may be dated to the end of the third century, the value of martyr literature as an exposition of Christian faith in an oppositional setting had plainly been realized much earlier. The crucial text here is a complete fiction, *The Acts of Paul and Thecla*. The earliest mention of Thecla's story appears in a work of Tertullian, *On Baptism*, composed at the very end of the second century, in which he professes outrage that Thecla should dare perform baptisms.[85] Tertullian's complaint and a Manichaean text of around 340 (see below) confirm that key elements of the story were already well established prior to the fifth-century recension of the story that survives in the manuscript tradition. These would include Thecla's conversion by Paul, and her immediate decision to break off her engagement to a local polytheist, her flight from Iconium, where she was born, and her ordeal in the amphitheater at Pisidian Antioch, where she overcame a variety of beasts loosed against her through the force of her piety. It is likely that the story ended, as it did in the fifth century, with her departure from the earth at Seleucia in Cilicia, the site of her shrine in later generations. It is a tale filled with the reversal of conventional roles: Thecla's refusal to marry, her adoption of a celibate lifestyle, and her role as a heroine for the women of Pisidian Antioch, who applaud her successful defeat of the openly male hierarchy in their city.[86] Indeed, along with the *Passion of Perpetua and Felicitas*, it is one of the truly feminist texts of the developing church, one that carves out a place for women as positive role models for other women against the force of conventional society.[87] The stress on Thecla's performance in the amphitheater – which culminates when she casts herself into a reservoir filled with what are described as androphagous seals – illustrates the power of the tradition of martyrdom for authorizing behaviors that set members of the Christian community apart.[88] As such, the *Acts of Paul and Thecla* underline the tension within the Christian community between those who saw in the faith a vehicle for the rejection of the norms of urban life, and those who sought to reconcile the beliefs of the church with contemporary society. This tension would continue for a long time to come.

There is perhaps no better example of the way that the Christian tradition of martyrdom could work to form its own Christian historiography than a Manichaean hymn included in a Coptic hymnal. The relevant section of what is altogether a very long text opens with reference to Old Testament catastrophe before describing the Passion of Christ and then the tale of subsequent persecution:

> All the Apostles that endured their pains
> Peter the Apostle who was crucified upside down,
> How many tortures did he suffer . . . with this purity (?)
> Andrew the Apostle – they set fire to the house beneath him.
> He and his disciples – all hail to them, they were crucified.
> The two sons of Zebebee were made to drink the cup of . . .
> John the virgin, he also was made to drink the cup,
> Fourteen days imprisoned that he might die of [hunger].
> And James also, he was stoned and killed
> They all threw their stone at him that he might die beneath the
> storm.
> The same things also did Thomas endure in his cross.
> Four soldiers at once pierced him with the point of a lance
> They surrounded him on four sides and made his blood
> flow . . .
> How many mysteries did he perform. Many a sign did he fulfil.
> Paul the Apostle, – they went against him that they might kill
> him.
> How great was their wrath, he expired, he did not escape.

I therefore too have endured (?) the things which he suffered
 before today.
He was thrown into a basket and hung outside the wall.
All these things he suffered, he did not weary, he did not flinch.
He left the open court (?) of the Lord, knowing that . . .
Thecla, the lover of God, who was made to go up to the fire.
She received the sign of the cross, she walked into the fire
 rejoicing.
Yet she was not ashamed, naked in the midst of the crowd.
She was thrown to the bears, the lions were let loose to her.
All these things that she suffered, she did not flinch, she did
 not . . . them.
A garland it is that she desires, it is purity for which she fights.
The blessed Drusiane also, she suffered the same,
Fourteen days imprisoned like her master, her Apostle.
Maximilla and Aristobula – on them was great torture inflicted.
What need for them to suffer these things? It is purity for which
 they fight.
All the godly [that] there have been, male and female, – all have
 suffered,
Down to the glorious one, the Apostle Mani.

> (Trans. Allberry, *A Manichaean Psalm-Book*,
> 142, 17–143, 16)

There can be little doubt but that the Manichaean author of this hymn derived the bulk of the narrative from a Christian text onto which the fate of Mani was grafted. As it stands this text is the most striking testimony for the evolution of a community history based upon a history of persecution for the fourth-century church.

The Manichaean hymn on persecution, like Eusebius' book on the ancient martyrdoms, looks to universalize the experience of martyrs as part of a general community history. But here too there was room for dispute, for, as the notice about Polycarp's place in the succession of martyrs shows, each city could also evolve its own, special history based on the fate of the members of its community. *The Acts of Paul and Thecla* were not composed simply to let people know what a wonderful person Thecla was, nor simply to validate tradition that exalted female leadership within the church. They were also intended, and this is surely true even before the fifth-century redaction, which is explicit on this point, as an advertisement for a local shrine of Thecla at Seleucia.[89] Indeed the martyrology may often best be seen as an extension of the place, a sort of advertisement to the Christian world as a whole of the connection between the community and great figures of the past. The memorial was often a guarantee of an individual community's place in the broader Christian community. The connection with community identity is made clear by what is our earliest reference to the shrine of a martyr, in an anti-Montanist work composed by a priest at Rome named Gaius who said, "I can point to the relics *(tropaia)* of the Apostles. If you should wish to go to the Vatican or to the Ostian way, you will find the relics *(tropaia)* of those who founded this church."[90] In the same work Gaius appears to be constructing a pro-Montanist argument for an interlocutor who may be making a claim for the authority of Montanist prophecy by claiming that the bodies of the apostle Philip and his four prophetic daughters were at Hierapolis in Phrygia, the Montanist homeland.[91] His comments, though, may also point to the fact that local traditions could become areas of genuine conflict between members of individual communities and outsiders. In this case it might be agreed that Philip was buried at Hierapolis. What could not be agreed was the relevance, if any, to the Montanist tradition of inspired prophecy and the important place of women within that tradition.

The critical aspect of the *martyrion*, or martyr shrine, was the presence of the actual remains of the deceased. Polytheists had noted the tendency of Christians to venerate the remains of those who had died a martyr's death at least as early as the second century AD, when those responsible for the slaughter of Christians at Lyons had burned their bodies so that other Christians, who made real efforts to recover them, could not have them.[92]

The buildings in which the celebrations of the martyrs took place were not any different from the standard funerary buildings of the Roman world. They could scarcely be otherwise when the veneration of martyrs began, as there was as yet nothing that could be described as a definably Christian form of architecture. The church was still an aggregation of constructs based on books, people, and behaviors. In Rome, for example, the tomb of Saint Peter was in the style of a simple family mausoleum surrounded by a wall and a garden.[93] At Bonn, the oldest form of the *martyrion* was an area contained within a rectangular wall. Within this space there were two tables for the celebration of rites in honor of the martyrs and, one may surmise, sarcophagi containing the corpses themselves.[94] Near Alexandria in Egypt, the *martyrion* of Saint Menas was located in a subterranean tomb in which the body of the martyr was laid out at the foot of one of the lateral walls of the chamber. The placement of the body appears to have been designed to allow the maximum number of worshippers to enter the room.[95] The habit of moving the remains of martyrs in later years ordinarily makes it impossible to know what other original *martyria* might have looked like, something that is particularly unfortunate in the case of a plaque found in the Basilica Maiorum at Carthage. It looks very much as if this plaque is a late copy of an original tomb inscription for Perpetua and her companions, suggesting that they were interred together – but we cannot now know where or how.[96]

In the cases mentioned above it does at least appear that the remains of the martyrs were kept from physical contact with their votaries. But this was not always the case, for, as we shall see, scandal followed upon the habit of a distinguished woman of the Carthaginian community in the fourth century who had the habit of kissing a relic in church.[97] What is perhaps most significant about this tale, as well as about the diversity of physical layout within *martyria*, is that it underlines the point that the veneration of martyrs was essentially a local phenomenon. The rules were set by the local community, and it was up to the local community to advertise, or not, the tale of individual martyrdoms. Efforts such as those of Eusebius, and the author of the hymn that likely lies behind the Manichaean text quoted above, to create a generalized history of persecution were in potential conflict with the traditions of each community. This conflict inhered especially to efforts by leaders at the provincial level who might seek to define doctrine for all Christians by defining what constituted authentic martyrdom. It was an issue that would become all the more contentious in the wake of Diocletian's edict of February 23, 303, that initiated the longest and most thorough persecution that the Christian community would endure at the hands of the polytheist regime. But that persecution, which would fail, will also seem to be at odds with what was coming to be the style of debate between Christians and others, as will appear when we turn to the most significant figures of late third-century polytheist thought, Plotinus and Porphyry. Here too we shall see the importance of narrative in defining place.

Plotinus and Porphyry

In the late fourth century, Eunapius of Sardis wrote a book entitled *The Lives of the Philosophers*, in which he traced the succession of philosophers whom he felt were important in his own time. These philosophers he saw as a "third group" succeeding, first, the philosophers that had flourished in the time of Plato, and then those who had flourished in the early empire from the reign of Claudius until the time of Severus, noting "this is part of the good fortune of the emperors, that according to history, the apogee of virtue is the same as that of fortune."[98] The third group of philosophers were those of his own time, men who preserved classical learning in the face of Christian emperors. He traces the succession of these philosophers to Plotinus, about whom he says that he need say little, since his life was recorded by Porphyry. And indeed it was, revealing a man of great complexity, as do the works that Porphyry edited in six groups of nine discourses each, the *Enneads*.

The problem with Eunapius' historical vision of Plotinus and Porphyry is that, by placing them at the head of a succession of philosophers that ends in his own time, he misrepresents them in their context. Porphyry makes it very clear that Plotinus saw himself as working within the contemporary limits of Platonism even as he introduced ideas derived from other philosophic schools, notably the Pythagoreans, into his analysis of Platonic topics.[99] The bulk of Porphyry's *Life of Plotinus* is concerned with the problem of editing Plotinus' works – the master had poor eyesight, so he could not copyedit texts produced by his scribes – Plotinus' relationship with his students, with other intellectuals (including Porphyry's other mentor, Longinus), and his ascetic lifestyle.[100] Although Porphyry observes that Plotinus' teaching was often quite original, Plotinus himself tended to stress his place within the tradition, portraying himself as a simple exegete of the tradition.[101] In this Plotinus was very much a product of his time, and he had therefore to forge a narrative of his own attachment to the past in order to gain authority for his thoughts. And, of course, so too was Porphyry, who made sure that the life that he composed for his master included all the appropriate themes of a philosophic life.[102]

One of the most significant contributions of Plotinus appears in his discussion of cognition. In the modern, western, tradition of thought, it was René Descartes who arguably developed the modern understanding of the mind as the locus of subjective truth.[103] In taking this view, Descartes was influenced by Augustine, who appears in turn to have been influenced by Plotinus, who advanced the view that the body had no life without the soul.[104] The soul, however, did have a life that was independent of the body. In taking this stand he was developing the Platonic notion of the soul through a dialogue with the view in contemporary Stoicism that thought was the product of a soul that was of a bodily nature.[105]

For Plotinus subjective truth, the possession of the Intellect, existed outside the soul.[106] It was possible for a person to perceive the truth by joining the soul with the Intellect, which was itself a product of the One.[107] The philosophic ideal was knowledge of the One, which would enable a person to return to the true self as soul, to attain the divine intellect, and achieve union with the One.[108] According to Porphyry, Plotinus was able to attain complete unity with the One on four occasions in his life,[109] and it is plain that Plotinus recognized that such an ascent was not possible for everyone, for he wrote that

> The man of real dignity must ascend in due measure, with an absence
> of boorish arrogance, going only so far as our nature is able to go,
> and consider that there is room for others at God's side . . .
> (*Enn.* 2.9.9.47–51, trans. Armstrong)

The key to this ability for a human to join his or her mind with the One lay, in Plotinus' thinking, to the distinction between body and soul, and the unity of the three *hypostaseis*, or substances.[110] According to Plotinus, the One

> is the productive power of all things. The things, then, of which it
> is the productive power are those which Intellect observes, in a
> way cutting itself off from the power; otherwise it would not be
> Intellect. For Intellect also has a kind of intimate perception of its

power to produce substantial reality. Intellect certainly, by its own means even defines its being for itself by the power that comes from the One . . .

(*Enn.* 5.1.7.9–15, trans. Armstrong)

Intellect itself then

generates soul, since it is perfect Intellect. For since it is perfect it had to generate, and not be without offspring when it was so great a power.

(*Enn.* 5.1.7.36–8, trans. Armstrong)

In defense of this highly original formulation, which was central to his belief that it was possible for the soul to ascend, and to his understanding of perception, he said:

This is the reason why Plato says that all things are threefold "about the king of all" – he means the primary realities – and "the second about the second and the third about the third." But he also says that there is a "father of the cause," meaning "Intellect" by "the cause": for Intellect is his craftsman; and he says that it makes Soul in that "mixing-bowl" he speaks of . . . And [it follows] that these statements of ours are not new; they do not belong to the present time, but were made long ago, not explicitly, and what we have said in this discussion has been an interpretation of them, relying on Plato's own writings for evidence that these views are ancient.

(*Enn.* 5.1.8.1–7; 9–14, trans. Armstrong)

The defensive tone suggests that Plotinus was fully aware of the originality of what he was saying, and that, consequently, he needed to create a narrative of the history of thought in which his views could be submerged in those of Plato to gain authority. The path along which he trod was plainly a winding one, enabling him to speak his mind, while at the same time exalting antiquity against what he saw as the weaker products of modern times. He resented deeply the suggestion that he was plagiarizing the philosopher Numenius, whom he described as intellectually vapid.[111]

If it was the task of the philosopher to be the best possible exegete of tradition, so too it was his task to defend truth against what he considered light-weight speculation. It is in this context – remaining mindful of the fact that Plotinus could be scathing about fellow exegetes of the Platonic tradition – that his attack on the Gnostics must be read. In this case he states that he is worried about friends of his who were "falling for" the Gnostic line that held (as did Mani) that the material world was tinged with

325

evil. His response to such arguments was that those who made them made "arbitrary and arrogant assertions" and it would require

> Another type of writing . . . to repel those who have the insolence to pull to pieces what god-like men of antiquity have said nobly and in accordance with the truth.
>
> (*Enn.* 2.9.10.12–14, trans. Armstrong)

It is notable that this is not a plea for persecution. His response to those who thought otherwise than he did was to write about their folly. So too, it appears, did Porphyry, who says that

> There were in his time many Christians and others, schismatics of the schools of Adelphius and Aculinus who abandoned ancient philosophy, possessing many books of Alexander the Libyan, Philocomus, Demostratus and Lydus, bringing forth apocalypses of Zoroaster and Zostrianos and Nicotheus and Allogenes and Messus and many other people of this sort, deceiving themselves and others as if Plato had not penetrated the depths of intelligible reality.
>
> (*V. Plot.* 16.1–9, trans. Armstrong, adapted)

His response was to write books explaining why their books were fakes. By the time that he wrote this passage, Porphyry had also written several works in which he specifically attacked Christian modes of exegesis and their use of scripture. These books fit with part of a defined intellectual program that sought to defend the teachings of "the ancients" against the folly of "the moderns."[112] The real problem was that "the moderns" denied the viability of the narrative to which men like Plotinus and Porphyry had attached themselves, and the only way to deal with such people was to undermine their own narrative. There is no suggestion here that either Plotinus or Porphyry would encourage persecution as a way to deal with the problem, or that they were concerned with that narrative of Christianity that stressed the history of persecution.[113] It was a man like Eusebius whom they would have despised.

The one area where Porphyry, whose own intellectual production was truly staggering, may have differed from his master was in the area of religion. Plotinus' belief that one could know the gods through contemplation stands in stark contrast with Porphyry's evident need to seek assistance. It is perhaps significant that the oracle of Apollo that Porphyry quotes as a sign that the gods recognized Plotinus' divine nature is posthumous.[114] Although, according to Porphyry, Plotinus gave a demonstration of his divine nature when challenged by a magical attack, he plainly had no interest in anything that smacked of what he regarded as folly.[115] In his attack on the Gnostics, Plotinus had said:

But they themselves most of all impair the inviolate purity of the higher powers in another way too. For when they write magic chants, intending to address them to those powers, not only to the soul but to those above it as well, what are they doing except making the powers obey the word and follow the lead of people who say spells and conjurations, any one of us who is well skilled in the art of saying precisely the right things in the right way, songs and cries and aspirated and hissing sounds and everything else which their writings say has magic power in the Higher World? But even if they do not want to say this, how are incorporeal beings affected by sounds? So by the sort of statement with which they give an appearance of majesty to their own words, they, without realizing it, take away the majesty of the higher powers.

(Enn. 2.9.14.1–11, trans. Armstrong)

Plotinus believed that true Platonic doctrine involved the freedom of rational and virtuous action, that "the best actions come from ourselves."[116] Porphyry, however, was of a somewhat more traditional orientation, and his picture of Plotinus as a semi-divine being clashes with Plotinus' own thought in a significant way. In his own attack on the narratives of non-traditionalists – Christians and others – he would look to the divine for guidance.

Porphyry's desire for divine guidance, his belief that the gods could provide direction for humans, surfaced in one of his earliest works, *On Philosophy from Oracles*.[117] In it he appears to have made use of existing collections of oracles from the main oracular sites in Asia Minor, which he equipped with a commentary to show how the gods were teaching humans about their nature. In the preface to this book he stated his belief that a person who drew hope of salvation from oracles could be confident – especially as Porphyry had recorded the oracles accurately (he emended texts that he thought were incorrect). The collection itself "contains the record of many philosophic doctrines that the gods themselves contain the truth," and will give some instructions on proper methods of obtaining information.[118] He then proceeds, as he does in his many exegetical works, by citing a text, commenting upon points that he thinks are significant, and moving on to the next, at times reading into it his own views. His technique in this regard is perhaps most obvious in a commentary upon Homer, selections from which are preserved in a Byzantine collection, where he explains, for instance, how Circe's prescription for summoning spirits of the dead in the *Odyssey* is connected with the doctrines of Plato and Pythagoras on the soul.[119]

Perhaps the most interesting aspect of the text, and one that bears upon his later works attacking what he regarded as bogus books of Zoroastrian revelation, as well as Christian folly, is that he admitted oracles that discussed the wisdom of non-Greek peoples. His approach may thus be seen to be remarkably inclusive. One text that he quotes validates the revelation of the gods of Egypt, Assyria, Lydia, and the Jews.[120] In another place, Apollo is quoted as saying that "only the Chaldaeans and the Hebrews have wisdom, worshipping properly the self-generated ruler God."[121] When it comes to the Christians, Porphyry produces an oracle in which Hecate proclaimed that Christ was a pious man, and that his soul was immortal, as were the souls of all pious persons. Where he erred was in suggesting that his soul had any special connection with wisdom. Christians, however, were regarded as blasphemers for worshipping Christ as a god, and not recognizing true doctrines concerning the soul.[122] These chiefly involved the possibility of the physical resurrection, which Porphyry thought was nonsense. It may also be presumed that he recognized a certain obduracy in Christians, whom he (along with Apollo) felt were not amenable to rational argument.[123]

Porphyry's views in this work show considerable development from those of Celsus. While Celsus regarded Christians as a group that might as well be persecuted, Porphyry seems to regard them as a regular feature of the intellectual landscape. They may be misguided with respect to the doctrine of the Resurrection, but they are to be corrected rather than eliminated. And it was to the correction of the Christians that Porphyry turned on at least three occasions in his life.[124]

The style of Porphyry's attack can be reconstructed, in the first instance through direct quotations or summaries of various statements in later Christian writers, primarily Jerome and Augustine.[125] Jerome makes it clear that Porphyry compared Jesus unfavorably to Apollonius of Tyana, and to Apuleius, whose reputation as a magician stemmed from the knowledge of magical practices reflected in his works.[126] He stated that people who believed the apostles were fools, and that the authors of the gospels were ignoramuses.[127] In the latter case he showed that their quotations from Jewish scripture were incorrect.[128] Elsewhere he assailed Christian understandings of world history, taking firm aim at the Book of Daniel, which he showed (correctly) to have been concerned with the Hasmonean revolt.[129] He also seems to have found the story of Jonah and the whale rather amusing in no very polite way, and raised the critical issue of what happened to all those souls of humans who existed before Christ; could God be truly merciful if there could be no salvation for them?[130]

The direct quotations and summaries of Porphyry's work make it look very much as if Porphyry's arguments may be reconstructed in greater detail with the aid of a work by a fourth-century Christian, Macarius of Magnesia.[131] Macarius produced a dialogue in which a Christian is depicted as defending the faith against attacks by a "pagan philosopher" whose arguments sound very much like those that can definitely be associated with Porphyry. Thus Macarius' philosopher attacks the saying of Jesus:

> In a short saying attributed to him, Christ says to his disciples, "You will always have the poor among you, but me you will not always

have." The occasion for the sermon is this: A certain woman takes an alabaster container filled with ointment and pours it over Jesus' head. When [his disciples] complain about the inappropriateness of the action Jesus replies, "Why trouble the woman when she has done something good for me?"

The disciples caused quite a stir, wondering why the ointment, expensive as it was, had not been sold for profit and distributed to the poor to ease their hunger. Thus Jesus' nonsensical response: Poor people there will always be; but he will not always be with them. [Odd, therefore], that elsewhere he can say with confidence, "I shall be with you until the end of the world."

(Trans. R. J. Hoffmann, *Porphyry's Against the Christians: The Literary Remains* [Amherst, NY, 1994], 48)[132]

In attacking the imagery of the gospels – for example, the statement at Matthew. 13:31 that the kingdom of heaven is like a mustard seed – the "pagan philosopher" will complain that these images are not those of the wise, or even of sibyls, as they are "degraded and unintelligible."[133] In a complaint that rings very true to the Plotinian vision of the world, the "philosopher" objects to Christian eschatological notions (involving, as they do, the coming of God and the ruin of the physical world) on the grounds that God does not work contrary to nature.[134] Why, the philosopher says, did Jesus not do as did Apollonius of Tyana, if he were truly a man possessed of divine power, and vanish at his trial – or at the very least speak words of power?[135]

It is not clear that Celsus knew much of anything about Christian scripture, but that is perhaps not too surprising, as the notion of an actual canon was relatively new in the second century: a hundred or so years later, for Porphyry, the canon of the New Testament provides the base narrative that he attacks in trying to show that Christians were deeply misguided. The technique is very much in accord with that employed in the *Life of Plotinus*, where the assertion that Plotinus had plagiarized Numenius needed to be refuted with abuse, since it would otherwise undermine the narrative of Plotinian originality and superiority.

Alternative polytheisms

One thing that is significant about Porphyry's attack on Christianity is that it was produced by a man who was himself stepping outside the mainstream of polytheist conduct. His move away from traditional cult behaviors may be traced from the *Philosophy from Oracles*, where he quotes oracles that provide instructions for animal sacrifice and applauds the wisdom of the gods who gave them, to the manifest hostility to the practice in *On Abstinence from Killing Animals*. In *On Abstinence* he once again introduced his case with an appeal to tradition reaching back into deepest antiquity – the teachings of Pythagoras and Empedocles.[136] At the same time he admits that a vegetarian life is not for everyone – that soldiers, sailors, craftsmen, athletes, and people engaging in public rather than philosophic pursuits need not be bound by the same rules.[137] Reliance on animal sacrifice deceived ignorant people, for these people believed that piety consisted of these outward forms of cult practice, which were at odds with the philosophic path to salvation.[138] For Porphyry, sacrificial rituals came into being among primitive peoples who were unenlightened by any philosophy and were as willing to sacrifice humans as animals. They failed to realize that the earliest and most pure forms of worship involved burnt offerings that were not of animals.[139]

People needed to realize that animals were linked with them by their rationality and were in contact with the divine. He could quote a story about Apollonius of Tyana, who said that he had learned about an accident that had befallen a donkey from a swallow, and, even more astonishingly,

> A friend of mine used to relate how he was lucky enough to have a slave-boy who understood the speech of birds, and everything they said was a prophecy announcing what would happen shortly; but he lost his understanding because his mother feared that he would be sent to the emperor as a gift and urinated in his ear.
>
> (Porph. *On Abstinence* 3.3.7, trans. G. Clark, *Porphyry: On Abstinence from Killing Animals* [London, 2000], 116)[140]

If people were not convinced by the examples of daily life, and of tradition, they might do well to reflect on the habits of ancient peoples – in this case Egyptians, Jews, Syrians, Persians, and Indians – who avoided pollution by avoiding animal flesh.[141] In Greek terms,

> Purity in everything is rejection of and abstaining from multiple and opposite things; it is singling out and taking that which is natural and appropriate. This is also the reason why sex pollutes, for it is the coming together of female and male. Moreover, if the seed is retained, it makes a stain on the soul by its association with the body; and if it is not retained, it makes a stain by the dying of the deposited seed. The intercourse of male with male also pollutes, both because the seed will die and because it is against nature. In short, both sex and seminal emissions pollute, because soul is mixed with body and dragged down into pleasure. And the passions of the soul pollute by their involvement with unreason, as the inner male becomes feminised.
>
> (Porph. *On Abstinence* 4.20.2–3, trans. G. Clark, *Porphyry*, 116)

The philosopher, whom we describe as standing aloof from external things, will not trouble demons nor have need of soothsayers nor of the entrails of animals; for he has made it his care to stand apart from the very things for which divination exists. Despite the astonishing display of learning from all periods of antiquity, and the appeals throughout to tradition, *On Abstinence* was, in its own way, as radical a critique of traditional cult as anything that the Christians had to offer.

If *On Abstinence* shows Porphyry moving to one extreme of contemporary polytheism in the tradition of Plotinus, his views in another area appear to have developed away from the teachings of the master. As the oracle that he quotes at the end of his *Life of Plotinus* shows, Porphyry retained a strong interest in divine revelation (which he disassociates from mundane questions asked about quotidian concerns).[142] One reason why he may have been such a fierce critic of the books of Zoroaster and Zostrianus was that he placed such importance in his own life on properly obtained oracles from the gods, and because he was genuinely interested in the traditions of eastern peoples. In the *Life of Plotinus*, he admits that he had on but one occasion come close to union with the One.[143] He seems to have felt that he needed the help of the gods to get him there, and so it appears that he turned to other sources of wisdom. We do not know what he said in a commentary that he wrote on a book attributed to a person called Julianus the Theurgist entitled the *Chaldaean Oracles*, but it is not unlikely that his comments were unfavorable.[144] The *Chaldaean Oracles*, whose importance was exalted by a student of his named Iamblichus, purported to be visions reported by Julianus of various gods that could be used as guides to spiritual ascent without animal sacrifice.[145] In a very late work, *The Letter to Anebo*, Porphyry admits that Chaldaean wisdom may be of some use as a form of philosophy.[146] This may reveal a continuing taste in works of eastern provenience that appeared as well in the oracles that he had collected in the *Philosophy from Oracles*, and in his evident respect for Jewish tradition. But it also reveals that he regarded the wisdom of other cultures as something that could be subsumed within the Greek philosophic tradition. When it stepped outside the bounds of that tradition, it was folly. In one of his very last works, he tried to put theurgy in its place by allowing that it might achieve the purification of the soul, but it could not enable the soul to achieve union with the One. The sage achieved happiness without it.[147]

The point that Iamblichus made was very different. He argued that theurgy, as explicated through the Chaldaean tradition, was superior to philosophy.[148] For Iamblichus, theurgy was a science; its practice could allow a person to succeed in ways that traditional practices could not. The distinction between his approach and that of Porphyry is genuinely important, and it is this that may bring us back to the point from which we departed. Eunapius saw a link among Plotinus, Porphyry, and Iamblichus that was simply not there in the way that he suggests. By including Plotinus and

Porphyry in his work, he sought to establish a link between the great figures of the pre-Constantinian empire and those who later stood upon the theurgic fringe of post-Plotinian thought. We shall examine the significance of his claims when we come to the emperor Julian in chapter 13. For now, however, it may stand as yet another example of the importance of narrative in constructing authority outside the ambit of the imperial government.

Aside from an interest in the divine, the common thread that draws the three groups that we have examined in this chapter together is the centrality of narrative to the definition of their positions within the Roman Empire. It is plain that there was not a great deal of sympathy between them, and that is all the more significant, as they nonetheless contended for authority using analogous presuppositions. As we return to the imperial government, we shall see how the narrative of Roman history that was constructed by Diocletian to lend authority to the new regime was undermined and replaced by a new one that would exalt a new ruler: the emperor Constantine.

9

REWRITINGS
OF THE TETRARCHY:
300–13

Reconstruction: 300–3

Diocletian's letter about the Manichaeans falls in the midst of a series of actions that appear to have been designed to stabilize the moral fabric of the Roman state. By 300, the Persians had been thoroughly defeated for the first time since Severus' capture of Ctesiphon, Britain was recovered, and the Rhenish and Danubian frontiers were secured. On other fronts, the *Hermogenian Code* was complete, the new style of government could be seen to be taking hold with its new coins, palaces, and imperial attire, and the history of the third century was being rewritten to accommodate the ideology of Diocletian's regime.

Imperial finance had occupied the attention of Diocletian since 296–97, when he issued an edict reforming the census procedures, instituting a uniform five-year census for all provinces to replace the periodic censuses that were characteristic of earlier centuries.[1] The actual edict appears to have been issued in 296, but to have taken some time to implement. In Egypt, the fourteen-year cycle fell due in 297, and there is evidence to suggest that the new registration was carried out in this context. As significant as the new regularity of assessment was the evident effort to impose coherent units of extraction across all provinces in the form of coherent definitions of what constituted a *iugum* and a *caput*. The essence of the reform is summed up in a letter from Aurelius Optatus, the prefect of Egypt in 297, as follows:

> Our most provident emperors, the eternal Diocletian and Maximian, Augusti, and Constantius and Maximian, the most noble Caesars, having learned that it has come about that the levies of the public taxes are being made haphazardly, so that some persons are let off lightly and others overburdened, have decided to root out this most evil and baneful practice for the benefit of their provincials and to issue a deliverance-bringing rule to which the taxes shall conform. Accordingly, the levy on each *aurora* according to the classification of the land, and the levy on each head of the peasantry, and from

which age to which, may be accurately known to all from the [recently] issued divine edict and schedule annexed thereto, copies of which I have prefaced for promulgation with this edict of mine. Accordingly, seeing that in this, too, they have received the greatest benefaction, the provincials should make it their business in conformity with the divinely issued regulations to pay their taxes with all speed and by no means wait for the compulsion of the collector; for it is proper to fulfill most zealously and scrupulously all the loyal obligation, and if anyone should be revealed to have done otherwise after such bounty, he will risk punishment.

(P. *Cairo Isidore* 1, trans. Lewis and Reinhold, *Roman Civilization* 2: 419)

The joy with which the Egyptian provincials received this news may be judged from the almost immediate outbreak of the revolts of Domitius Domitianus and Aurelius Achilleus, who succeeded him late in 297.[2]

The language of Optatus' letter, probably echoing that of the preamble of Diocletian's edict, in the same way that another gubernatorial letter would explain that of the *Edict on Coinage*, is consistent with the self-righteous tone of the letter concerning the Manichaeans quoted in the last chapter. The parallel between these documents and the persecution edict issued against the Christian church in 303 suggest that the tone of Diocletian's chancery was more than mere rhetoric. It reflects a tendency to believe that the emperor genuinely did know what was best for his subjects, whether they were inclined to realize it or not.

The alteration of census procedure is an indication that Diocletian's desire to restructure the Roman state on new, more logical principles, extended beyond the immediate vicinity of the court. It may have been the case that he could produce new law codes without being able to ensure that they would be used, or that he could issue edicts without ensuring that they would be uniformly enforced, but this did not mean that he did not think that the effort at standardization was important. As the war with Persia resolved itself in his favor, he took two other steps, perhaps necessitated by what appears to have been a sudden outbreak of rampant inflation, to restructure the economy of the empire. The first of these was an edict retariffing the coinage of the realm; the second was the *Edict on Maximum Prices*.[3]

A portion of the edict on currency is preserved on an inscription from the city of Aphrodisias in Caria. This inscription contains two documents, one being an edict, the other an explanatory letter to or from the local governor.[4] The sum total of these documents is to state that the imperial coinage was to be retariffed so that it would have double its face value. Debts contracted to the *fiscus* or private individuals prior to September 1, 301, were still to be repaid in accord with the old standards, while those contracted on or after September 1 were to be paid in accord with the new regulations.[5] It is more than likely that this edict was seen as a prelude to the *Edict on Maximum Prices* that was issued between November 20 and December 10 of the same year.[6] Taken together, the two edicts look like a prescription for a new fiscal order based on what Diocletian conceived as a fair dispensation across the entire empire. The edict on coinage appears to have been a reasonable response to the problem of inflation, but the price edict was not. It is perhaps significant that Lactantius, in the course of lambasting Diocletian for all manner of woes suffered by the Romans, mentions the latter, but not the former.[7]

The justification for the *Edict on Maximum Prices* is derived from the "excesses perpetrated by persons of unlimited and frenzied avarice" that could not be checked by self-restraint. It is this action by individuals whose "only desire . . . is to have no thought for the common need."[8] The emperors act with their subjects, who can no longer ignore what is happening; hence "we hasten to apply these remedies long demanded by the situation, satisfied that no one can complain that our intervention against evil-doers is untimely or unnecessary, trivial or unimportant." In so doing they "exhort the loyalty of all, so that the regulation for the common good may be observed with willing obedience and due scruple."[9] The particular victims of high prices were the very agents through whose efforts the security of the state had been won, the soldiers.

In practical terms, the *Edict on Maximum Prices* was an act of economic lunacy. Price controls had long been part of civic life, and it may be that Diocletian did not recognize that a policy that might have short-term benefits in times of food shortage could not be translated to an empirewide level with any hope of success.[10] In simplest possible terms, the edict ignored the law of supply and demand, the fact that prices were set by the availability of goods, and that the cost of goods was effected by the cost of transport. It could be objected to this view that the prices in the edict (and prices were set for an enormous range of goods and services) were intended as maximums and thus that the numbers that appear in the edict are in fact unrealistically high for many parts of the empire. But this does not seem to be the case. The driving force behind the edict was a desire to set maximum prices that the state would have to pay for the goods and services listed, and to that end it is inconceivable that the *fiscus* would willingly overcharge itself across the bulk of the empire. Indeed, with the exception of the price of wheat, which does appear to be set near a maximum rate of one hundred denarii per *modius*, prices generally appear to be below the going rate in Egypt at the time that the edict was issued.[11] Moreover, while the edict gives differential prices for some goods in different stages of production, and transport costs, it does not appear to recognize the fact that transport costs needed to be added to production costs in the computation of a fair price. This failure cannot be taken as evidence that every community in the empire was essentially self-supporting, for in the computation of transport costs it is recognized that all manner of transport needed to be factored into the structure of the economy. It simply factored these costs in badly. Although it is true that Lactantius is un-reservedly hostile to Diocletian, his comments on the impact of the *Edict on Maximum Prices* are still significant precisely because they are offered as proof that the government was out of control prior to the beginning of the persecution:

> Since he had created an immense increase in prices by his various iniquities, he tried to enforce a law on the prices of goods for sale: then was much blood shed over small and cheap things, nor did anything go on sale, and the price increase flamed all the worse, until the law was dissolved through its own necessity after many deaths.
>
> (*DMP* 7.6–7)

Despite the vehemence of Lactantius' utterance, it is of some interest that the impact of the law cannot be traced in any other source. This would suggest that the law was in fact repealed within a year of its issuance, quite possibly because it was seen to be a massive failure.[12] If so, then it is an interesting commentary on the nature of our sources for the fourth century that one notably unsuccessful imperial edict, of limited duration, is the best-preserved Latin inscription from the Greek east. The several copies of the text, a number from quite insignificant places, are testimony to the symbolic importance of public inscription as a symbol of government, but poor testimony to the actual significance of the measure that they record.

The next act of the central government that we can trace across the empire is the persecution edict of 303. In general historical terms, the persecution edict is perhaps of greater significance as evidence for the activist stance of tetrarchic government, a stance that was inherited by the governments that succeeded it. This belief in the power of central government to effect sweeping change stands in stark contrast to the style of government in the first two centuries AD, where, for instance, one emperor's decision about the definition of colonial status would not change preexisting statuses. There are obviously precedents in the course of the third century, ranging from the *constitutio Antoniniana*, to Decius' edict on sacrifices, to Valerian's persecution edicts, to the currency reform of Aurelian, but no period in the history of Roman government offers so many examples in short order as occur in the reign of Diocletian. Unlike previous emperors who might work within existing structures, amending certain practices in, for instance, the collection of taxes, Diocletian often appears to be trying to sweep all these earlier practices away. The language that his government used was usually deeply traditional in form, but outward form is not the same thing as intent.[13] The ideology of reconstruction that informed tetrarchic reshaping of the historical level was not empty. The rhetoric offered a justification for major efforts at actual change. As such, Diocletian's tone reflects perhaps the most significant single change from the style of government current at the end of the second century and throughout the third. Then each community was encouraged to create a narrative of its own affairs that could be tied, where relevant, to the grand narrative of imperial history, but still remain fundamentally independent. In the language of Diocletian's edicts all provincials are thought to share the same interests as the imperial government. This is not simply a desire such as that manifested in the *constitutio Antoniniana* or Decius' edict on sacrifices that provincials share in the joy of the emperor while retaining their own traditions. It is qualitatively different to presume that all provincials will share the emperor's concern over tax policy, prices, or currency.

Persecution and politics: 303–5

There are no acts of government so useful for the historian of Roman imperial government as the persecution edict of 303, for we can trace the speed, contents, and style of its implementation with a remarkable degree of accuracy. We know exactly where and when it was promulgated (at Nicomedia on February 24, 303), how long it took before it was promulgated in Palestine (March), and how long after that it was dictating the action of local officials in North Africa (June 5).[14] The terms of the edict were these:

1 Churches should be destroyed.
2 Christian scriptures were to be burned.
3 Christian officials were to lose the privileges of their rank.
4 Christians were deprived of the right to answer legal actions against them.
5 Christians could not file actions against those who assaulted them.
6 Imperial freedmen who were Christians should be reduced again to slavery.[15]

The last two provisions of the edict are of particular interest, as they were an open invitation for the inhabitants of the empire to join with the emperors in purifying Roman society of what Diocletian took to be the evil of Christianity. In this way the edict participated in the ideology of the central government that suggested that Roman citizens shared with the court a basic interest in defending society as a whole against those who were regarded as malefactors.

What is far from clear is why Diocletian should have suddenly woken up to the fact that Christians were such a threat to the empire, especially as he had himself appointed Christians to very high positions, and his own wife and daughter may have been sympathetic to the church.[16] Lactantius suggests, possibly with good reason, that the origins of the persecution lay in an odd incident that occurred at some point after the war with Persia had ended, in which some Christians in the imperial entourage had been accused by the *haruspex* inspecting the entrails of a sacrificial animal of interfering with the sacrifice.[17] His view may be confirmed by Eusebius' statement that a purge of Christians within the army had preceded the issuance of the edict.[18] The point at issue was the refusal of Christian soldiers to sacrifice, something that had led to trouble prior to the reign of Diocletian in the case of a man named Marinus.[19] Insofar as the army, and its loyalty, were particular concerns of Diocletian's, it is reasonable to agree with Lactantius that the change of imperial policy arose out of some incidents connected with military discipline. It would not have helped that one of these incidents occurred in the presence of Diocletian himself. There is no reason to think that Diocletian was any less susceptible to viewing his personal experiences as being of universal application than other leaders had or have been.

Lactantius does not, however, limit the cause of the persecution to Diocletian's own experience. He adds to this factor a significant series of interventions by Galerius.[20] And in this case there may be more to it than simple dislike of Christians. If Diocletian were to die, Maximian would be promoted to senior Augustus with Constantius as his junior, while Galerius would remain in the rank of Caesar. Lactantius suggests that Galerius saw the persecution in the context of his desire to arrange the succession in his own interests. As Lactantius purports to give the content of conversations between the two men on this subject at which no one else was present, there is some reason to reject everything that he has to say as the result of prejudice ungrounded in reality.[21] But this might be going too far. Conversations between important men, even in camera, have a way of becoming public knowledge, and there is no question but that the events of the next couple of years worked entirely to the advantage of Galerius and to the disadvantage of Constantius.[22] It was Galerius' aim that he not be disadvantaged if Diocletian should predecease Maximian. It may well be that he had a particularly strong dislike of Christians, and that he sensed that Constantius was, if anything, well disposed to them.[23] By supporting Diocletian's new antipathy, he could convince the aging emperor that his interests needed to be protected if the system of the tetrarchy was to endure. Still, Diocletian may have hesitated; both Lactantius and Constantine himself (who was at court at the time) report that he made no final decision about what to do until he had consulted the oracle of Apollo at Didyma.[24] The decision would rest with Diocletian alone, and it appears that he made the final decision without a great deal of outside intervention.

Events were to move very fast in the course of the twelve months after Diocletian's consultation, in respect to both the Christians and the succession. Shortly after the promulgation of the edict a fire broke out in the palace that could be blamed on the Christians (resulting in numerous executions), and rebellions occurred in Commagene and Syria.[25] Nor could Diocletian have been pleased by the open defiance of his edict in Nicomedia itself:

on the day the edict was posted, a Christian who had then assailed the emperors as barbarians had torn it down.[26] The first edict was followed by a second ordering that leaders of the church should be arrested.[27]

The flow of the edicts down the chain of command is illustrated by a declaration made by a lector to the civil authorities at Oxyrhynchus:

> Whereas you gave me orders in accordance with what was written by Aurelius Athanasius, *procurator privatae*, in virtue of a command of the most illustrious *magister privatae*, Neratius Apollonides, concerning the surrender of all the goods in the said former church and whereas I reported that the said church had neither gold nor silver nor money nor clothes nor beasts nor slaves nor lands nor property either from grants or bequests, excepting only the unworked bronze which was found and delivered to the *logistes* to be carried down to the most glorious Alexandria in accordance with what was written by our most illustrious prefect Clodius Culcianus, I also swear by the genius of our lords the emperors Diocletian and Maximian, the Augusti, and Constantius and Galerius, the most noble Caesars, that these things are so and that I have falsified nothing, or may I be liable to the divine oath.
>
> (*P. Oxy.* 2673, trans. Rea)[28]

Despite the references here to senior imperial officials, the final responsibility for making sure that the edict was observed lay with the local authorities. The reason that the lector was making his declaration to them is that they were responsible for ensuring that he delivered the unworked bronze to the *logistes*. In the record of the persecuting activities of a man named Munatius Felix, the *flamen perpetuus* and curator of Cirta on May 19, 303, we see the official, who plainly knows several leading Christians by sight, traveling about the town trying to find someone who has a copy of the scriptures that he can confiscate, a process that speeds up after he arrests a pair of the more recalcitrant members of the community. In the end, Munatius seems a most unwilling persecutor, and he takes it on faith that whatever book he is given is a book of scripture.[29] An even more unwilling persecutor seems to have been the Caesar Constantius, who appears to have taken little effort to see to the promulgation of the edict in the western provinces, a sign that the issue of persecution was indeed dividing the tetrarchs.

Within a year of the issuance of the edict, in preparation for the celebration of the twentieth anniversary of Diocletian's accession (and now of Maximian's, as by historical sleight of hand his regnal years had been equated with Diocletian's), a third edict was issued that was related to the fate of the Christians who had been imprisoned in the course of the summer.[30] This was a general amnesty, and the first act of the "great persecution" was over, perhaps some eight months after it had begun. In some parts of the empire little had happened. In other parts, the repercussions of these few months would continue to haunt the church for more than a century.[31] And less than a year later, in the eastern part of the empire a fourth edict was issued, ordering all the subjects of Rome to sacrifice. This edict would only ever be enforced in the west.[32] The split over its enforcement may be connected with a split that may have developed as a result of events in Rome during the fall of 303.

The succession

Diocletian had decided to open the celebration of his twentieth year in power at Rome, and to meet with Maximian in person for the first time in a decade. The meeting would be a symbolic moment of significance, as the two self-proclaimed saviors of the Roman world appeared together before the people of the city, which, although no longer an imperial capital, was still very much the symbolic heart of the empire. And so it might also have been a suitable place, deep inside the territory of Maximian, for Diocletian to manage one last, overwhelming, demonstration of his superior authority. Diocletian had come not only to celebrate twenty years of rule, but also to gain Maximian's agreement to a change in what had appeared, for some years now, to be the plan for the succession. At least tacitly, it appears to have been agreed that Constantius' eldest son, Constantine, and Maximian's son Maxentius would be promoted to the rank of Caesar when Maximian and Diocletian ceased to rule.

As he went west to meet Maximian, Diocletian knew that he had a crucial card to play if Maximian demurred. Constantius' eldest son, born around 275, had been sent to Nicomedia for his education, had served in the Persian war and appeared on Diocletian's staff when the latter had traveled to Egypt in the course of 300–1.[33] If Constantine had been summoned to Nicomedia as a guarantee of his father's continued adhesion to the tetrarchy, then there may well have been an unintended consequence that may have had crucial implications. In his time at Nicomedia, Constantine was of an age to have studied Latin rhetoric. One of his teachers would have been Lactantius. One of his schoolmates was Maxentius, the oldest son of Maximian.[34]

All that remained was to arrange the timing of the transfer of power. According to Lactantius, Galerius pressured Diocletian to arrange the coincidental retirement of the Augusti in the wake of the celebration of the *vicennalia*.[35] According to the panegyrist of 307, the plan to abdicate had been agreed long ago. The two rulers confirmed the agreement at a meeting in the temple of Capitoline Jupiter during the celebration, quite possibly setting the date as May 1, 305, which would enable Maximian to enjoy a final blaze of glory when he presided over the *ludi saeculares* scheduled for 304.[36] While there is some evidence to corroborate the notion that abdication had long been in view, there is more to corroborate the notion of a sudden change in the way that it would work.[37] While Lactantius plainly detested Galerius, this does not necessarily mean that he was making things up; and the one tradition that appears to be independent of either Constantinian propaganda, or that of the panegyrics, is that of Eutropius, and his version would tend to support Lactantius. He says that the decision to abdicate, and to force Maximian's abdication, was a relatively sudden development as Diocletian felt his strength fading.[38] It is striking as well that in 303 the count of Maximian's regnal years was changed so that they suddenly became equal to those of Diocletian – this too points to a change of plan. There was no point to the move unless it was to eliminate the grounds for the sort of complaint that makes its way into a later source: that he had held power for one year less than his colleague.[39]

The crucial evidence that something disagreeable to Maximian had happened, both in the timing of the abdication and the choice of successors, lies in the events of the next few years. While we cannot know if the new Caesars who would succeed Constantius and Galerius were selected in 303, we do know that neither of the two new Caesars was close to Maximian and Constantius, and that there is some reason to think that this was a late change of plan. Severus and Maximinus Daia were friends of Galerius.[40] We also know that Maximian would be sufficiently opposed to the succession that he would support a rebellion by his son against the new dispensation in little more than a year after his abdication.[41] Likewise, Constantius seems to have been no friend to the new system. It cannot have escaped his notice, as he lay dying at York in July 306, that the son whom he had recovered from the court of Galerius would seize the throne. Both of their sons had earlier been presented as potential heirs, and the two men who had been appointed Caesars were indeed virtual unknowns at the time of their appointment.[42] While Severus had held a senior command in the army, he does not appear to have played any role as significant as Constantius had before his proclamation. Maximinus Daia's claim to fame, if any, was that he was Galerius' nephew. He was perhaps a few years older than Constantine and unlikely to have held any empirewide administrative role prior to 305.[43]

We have little information about the period between December 20, 303, when Diocletian left Rome for the last time, evidently suffering from a serious illness, and May 1, 305. What little evidence there is suggests that after spending some time at Ravenna, he returned to the Danube, where he took command, probably in Galerius' company, of a campaign against the Carpi. He reached Nicomedia by August 28 of that year and appears to have remained in the vicinity of his capital thereafter. Maximian appears to have left Rome almost immediately after Diocletian did, and he may have journeyed to Sirmium, where Lactantius claims that he had a stormy meeting with Galerius sometime after Diocletian had returned to Nicomedia.[44]

May 1, 305 dawned with Constantius and Maximian at Milan, Galerius and Diocletian at Nicomedia. The parallelism between the rulers of east and west is less significant, than the lack of symmetrical dedication to what was about to happen. Lactantius describes the events of that day at Nicomedia as follows:

> There was a high point about three miles distant from the city, on the top of which he himself had assumed the purple, and there a column had been erected with an image of Jupiter.[45] There was a procession to that place. An assembly of the soldiers was convened, in which the old man spoke, with tears in his eyes, to the soldiers. He said that he was weak, that he sought a respite from his labors, that he would hand power over to others, that he would appoint new Caesars. . . . Then, suddenly, he proclaimed Severus and Maximinus Caesars. . . . In plain view of everyone, Galerius, extending his hand behind him, brought Maximinus forward, and placed him, having removed his civilian garb, between himself and Diocletian. . . . Diocletian put his own purple cloak, which he had taken from his shoulders, on Maximinus, and was made again Diocles. Then he descended. The old king was carried through the city on a cart, and sent back to his homeland.
>
> (Lact. *DMP* 19.2–6)

In translating this passage I have omitted commentary from Lactantius to the effect that everyone there assembled had thought to see Constantine, who was standing on the tribunal and of an age – about thirty – when he might be expected to be a candidate for promotion, proclaimed instead.[46] Constantinian propaganda aside, these lines evoke splendidly the most extraordinary moment in Roman history. Never before had a man at the height of his power voluntarily laid power aside, exploiting the very symbols that he had made those of the imperial office. In so doing it is significant that he should have chosen the army as his audience, for it was the army that he hoped would guarantee the new order. On the very same day, Maximian took off his purple cloak at Milan and handed it to Severus, while proclaiming Constantius Augustus in his place.[47] Diocletian's hopes for the army would prove ill founded. The army would prove not to be united behind the college of Caesars, but divided in its loyalties among the generals that it knew.

Constantinian historiography and the collapse of the Tetrarchy: 305–7

The tale of Diocletian and his colleagues must be pieced together from a few panegyrics, some short accounts in later historians, the documentary record, and the words of their enemies. Constantine, who was to win out in the struggle for succession, was just as conscious of the value of the historical record as a tool for legitimizing his reign as had been Diocletian. He was also far more successful than Diocletian would prove to be in controlling how that record would be formed. He is the further beneficiary of the fact that the faith that he chose in 312 was a very bookish one. The Christian tradition of historiography, especially in its apologetic aspect, was highly conducive to triumphalist narratives of the sort that would be formed by Constantine and his supporters. It was also inherently hostile to those who were to be Constantine's foes as a result of the persecution of 303, and its renewal under Galerius from 305 to 311. It was under Constantine that the traditions of confessional narrative could be joined with the grand narrative of imperial politics; it was a hard combination to beat, and efforts to recover alternative versions from the rivals of Constantine must perforce be conjectural. The one genuinely hostile tradition that does survive is that of Eunapius, as preserved by Zosimus and brief passages in later ecclesiastical historians. But this tradition was itself shaped by the historiography of the Constantinian age rather than by that of Constantine's foes. Eunapius' method in treating the first Christian emperor was, it seems, primarily to embellish a pro-Constantinian narrative with negative comment and innuendo.[48]

Because a number of Latin panegyrics have been preserved from the early period of Constantine's career, it is possible to trace to a greater degree than is possible for any emperor since the death of Nero the way that the story developed. For all this, it is a story filled with significant gaps. The alternative to the Constantinian account of the years from 305 to 311 would be one asserting the right of Galerius to be treated with the same respect that Diocletian had received. We can but guess at what such a narrative would look like, aided, perhaps, by surviving decorations from the palace of Rumaliana, where it appears that Galerius gazed upon idealized representations of the state of affairs in 305. If that was so, there is every reason to think that Galerius' story was as problematic, if not more so, than the Constantinian one.

The chief problem that would beset a Galerian narrative of the year 306 would be to explain how, as junior Augustus, he seems to have been able to enact significant legislation that impacted on the whole of the empire. Under the Diocletianic dispensation, of which he set himself as the champion, the senior Augustus alone could issue edicts that would establish policy for the empire as a whole.[49] The junior Augustus and the Caesars had the power to respond to petitions, and they might use their discretion in enforcing edicts of their superior, but no more than that. Yet it was in 306 that Galerius issued an edict that included Italy within the general imperial census, eliminating the exemption from the head and land taxes that its inhabitants had enjoyed since the beginning of the monarchy, and, indeed, more than a century before that.[50] Lactantius' statement that responsibility for this decision rested squarely upon the shoulders of Galerius is likely correct, for the inclusion of Italy in the census represents the reversal of a long-standing policy with which Maximian and Constantius had been comfortable. As such it lends some credence to the notion that he was trying to assert illegitimate authority within the new tetrarchy, and quite possibly to the notion that he saw the new government as divided three against one to the detriment of Constantius.[51]

The story of Constantine's own rise to power must be set against the background of this edict. The theme of this account was Galerius' desire to seize power from Constantius, and, in light of the edict mentioned above, this was not an unreasonable position to take. The precise details of Galerius' plan were, according to Lactantius, that he would force Constantius to resign by uniting with the two Caesars against him. He would then replace Constantius with his old friend Licinius, whom he wished to reward for his years of friendship with the title of Augustus, and then, when he had ruled for twenty years, he would abdicate, leaving the rank of junior Caesar open for his own son, Candidianus, who would then be twenty-nine years old.[52] Some of this tale is perhaps grounded in observable reality: Galerius did promote Licinius to the rank of Augustus over the head of Maximinus, and he constructed a great palace for himself at Gamzigrad in Serbia on the model of Diocletian's at Split. The palace was named Felix Romuliana, after Galerius' mother, Romula, and was, or would be, overlooked by two great mausolea, one for Romula, the other for Galerius himself.[53] But a crucial feature, Galerius' hope for his son, reads a great deal like a justification for Constantine's own assertion of a dynastic claim to the throne after his father's death in 306. The critical point was that Constantine was not the first person to break what appears to have been Diocletian's "rule" of 305 that sons should not succeed their fathers in power, since Galerius already intended to break that rule. And, what is more, evidence that Constantine was already being groomed to take up the position of senior Caesar, only to be replaced through the machinations of Galerius, was further proof that "Diocletian's rule" was no rule at all.[54]

Constantine's effort to place Galerius in the wrong began at a very early stage in his career. According to a story that was current by at least 310, Galerius wished to kill Constantine before he could rejoin his father, who, in 305, was preparing to go on campaign in Britain.[55] According to the version promulgated by Lactantius when he composed *On the Deaths of the Persecutors* between 313 and 315, Constantius wrote to Galerius asking for the return of Constantine:

> After having been asked repeatedly, and being no longer able to deny the request, he gave him (Constantine) his seal as the day was ending, and ordered him to set out the next morning after he had received his orders, for he wished either to delay him on some pretext, or to send letters ahead so that he would be arrested by Severus. When Constantine realized what was happening, and when

the emperor was sleeping after dinner, he hastened to leave, and he flew away, taking all the public horses from many post stations. The next day the emperor, having slept as he had intended, until around noon, ordered Constantine to be brought before him. He was told that he had set out after dinner. He began to rage and fume. He asked for the horses of the public post so that he could bring him back. He was told that the public post had been stripped. He could scarcely restrain his tears. But Constantine came, with incredible speed, to his father, who was already upon his deathbed, and who, having commended him to the soldiers, passed on the imperial authority with his own hand.

(*DMP* 24.5–8)

A slightly different, and almost certainly earlier, version of this story is retained in a short work known as the *Rise of the Emperor Constantine*, where it is said:

Then Galerius sent him back to his father. He evaded Severus as he was passing through Italy, crossing the Alps with great speed and killing all the post horses as he passed, and came to his father, Constantius, at Boulogne, which the Gauls once called Gesoriacum. Constantius then died at York after victories over the Picts, and Constantine was made Caesar through the consensus of the troops.

(*Origo* 2.4)

Slight though they are, the differences between these two accounts are significant and reflect the way that Constantinian propaganda progressed over the years. That the account in the *Rise* reflects an earlier version of the story is guaranteed by the fact that the author of the panegyric of 310 also has Constantine come to Constantius before his departure for Britain. Since we know that Constantius celebrated a victory over his enemies in Britain on or before January 6, 306, this would mean that father and son were together for a considerable length of time before Constantius died.[56] A second feature of the "early" account is that it stresses the role of the army, something also stressed in a panegyric delivered in 307, in determining the succession. This too looks like a reference to Diocletianic forms of legitimacy since Diocletian had asked the army to recognize his dispensations for the succession in the ceremony of May 1, 305.[57] The thrust of the later version is that, as senior Augustus, Constantius had the right to choose his successor, and in doing so, he was merely returning to the version of the succession that Diocletian had once envisioned. The difference between the two stories reflects Constantine's redefinition of his claim to be a legitimate monarch, burying his past as a usurper when he accepted the acclamation of the soldiers on the day that his father died, July 25, 306, and claiming that the succession was solely the will of his father.[58] In both cases, however, Constantine demonstrated respect for the tetrarchic style by claiming, at first, only the rank of Caesar.

The problem with these accounts is, however, that the stress on Galerius' plotting obscures the role of Constantius himself in determining the course of events. It was Constantius who chose to have his eldest son associated with him in a public way during the British campaign, and, as both Lactantius and the author of the aforementioned panegyric make clear, it was Constantius who recommended Constantine to the army.[59] It was thus Constantius who was responsible for changing the "rule" of succession by promoting his own son to the fourth place in the college as he lay dying. From this point of view, there could be no question of Constantine's legitimacy since the senior Augustus was responsible for making him the junior member of the college upon his death. Lactantius says that Galerius grudgingly accepted the portrait that Constantine sent claiming the position.[60] He may have been grudging, but the fact remains that he accepted the constitutional arrangement as legitimate.

Constantius' decision sparked a revolt on October 28, 306.[61] According to Zosimus, Maxentius could not bear to remain a private citizen in the wake of Constantine's seizure of power.

> Taking as assistants in his enterprise Marcellianus and Marcellus, two tribunes, Lucianus, who was in charge of the pork that the government distributed to the people, and the soldiers of the court, who are called praetorians, was placed upon the imperial throne by these men, announcing that he would reward those who gave this to him with great gifts; the first thing they did was kill Abellius, who was *vicarius* of the urban prefecture and who was opposed to their undertaking.
>
> (Zos. 2.9.3)

The revolt of Maxentius recalls earlier urban revolts in that it began with the effective seizure of the praetorian camp, and, it would appear, some effort to assure the loyalty of the urban plebs.[62] More than that, it appears as if another major player in this conspiracy was Annius Anullinus, the *praefectus urbi* (wrongly identified as the praetorian prefect in Zosimus), then a leading figure of the urban aristocracy.[63] In addition to the support of a man well established in the urban hierarchy, Maxentius may also have believed that his father's soldiers would be loath to march against him under the leadership of a man whom they may not have known prior to May of the previous year. In this he would be proved correct. As for Abellius, it is possible that he was appointed by Severus precisely because he felt the need of his own representative in the city, filling a role analogous to that filled by Vitalianus in 238 (with like results).

The inhabitants of Italy were ready to rebel, as a result of their inclusion in the census.[64] The actual agent who would have overseen the implementation of the new policy was Severus, and he would pay a heavy price for it. As soon as he learned of Maxentius' rebellion, Severus led his army south to Rome, but there he stopped. Maximian returned to the capital from his villa in Lucania, and Severus feared (quite reasonably as it turned out) that his soldiers would not fight against their former general.[65] As he withdrew into northern Italy, his army deserted him, and he sought refuge at Ravenna. It was no refuge, and he turned himself over to Maximian on promise of his life. He was taken thence to a *villa publica* on the Appian Way where he was imprisoned.[66] In those parts of the empire ruled by Galerius he continued to be recognized as Caesar until at least September 307.

Shortly after the defeat and imprisonment of Severus, Maximian moved to cement another relationship that had been crucial to his years in power. This was with the house of Constantius. In 293, Constantius had married his daughter, Theodora.[67] She had borne him six children, three sons (Dalmatius, Constantius, and Hannibalianus) and three daughters (Constantia, Anastasia, and Eutropia), and, to judge from the absence of any reference to her in the earliest Constantinian panegyric (that of 307) had quite possibly predeceased her husband. Maximian now sought to renew the link by arranging with Constantine that he should marry his younger daughter, Fausta. There is some question as to just how old she was at this point. Since she was born in Rome while her father was there, there are three possible years: 289, 294, and 299. Of these the third is the most likely.[68] If she were only eight years old at the time of her marriage, it would perhaps explain why she bore Constantine no child earlier than 316.

The marriage of Constantine and Fausta, now hastily arranged, was a moment of great political importance. Maximian himself traveled to Trier with his daughter, and it was there that a panegyric was delivered on the occasion of the marriage in August or early September of 307.[69] There is no document more revealing of the ideological chaos into which the Diocletianic system had been thrown. The author begins by addressing Maximian as *imperator aeternus*, and Constantine as *imperator oriens*: the eternal emperor and the rising emperor.[70] Some lines later he includes the critical words: *et te quidem sentio, senior Auguste, maiestate praecedere, te sequi, iunior imperator* ("I sense that you, senior Augustus, take precedence in majesty, and that you, junior imperator, follow.")[71] Between these two statements he tells Maximian that replicating the marriage of Theodora and Constantius with that of Constantine and Fausta has renewed his youth. Constantine's maturity is seen to be

> so great that although your father left you imperial power, nevertheless you were content with the title of Caesar and preferred to

347

wait for the same man to declare you Augustus who so declared
him. Thus indeed you judged that this imperial power would be
finer not if you had acquired it as an inheritance by right of succession, but if you earned it from the supreme emperor as due reward
for your merits.

(*Pan.* 7 [6] 5.3, trans. Nixon)

It is as if Maximian had never abdicated, while Diocletian had. Maximian
has now succeeded to Diocletian's position as the leader of the state, and
it is by his authority that Constantine may now lay claim to the title of
Caesar. Forgotten is that Constantine had sent a picture of himself to Galerius
decorated with laurel, signifying his claim to the rank of Caesar, and that
Galerius had acquiesced.[72]

The crucial feature of this union is that

the Roman state, once shaken by disparate characters and fates of
its rulers, may at last be made strong through the everlasting roots
of your house, and its Empire may be as immortal as the offspring
of its emperors is perpetual.

(*Pan.* 7 [6] 2.2, trans. Nixon)

The inconcinnity in the author's language, slipping between the ideology of
adoption and that of imperial authority as the source of legitimacy, describes
the underlying principle in the struggle between Galerius and the house of
Maximian. At the abdication of Diocletian, the point that only an Augustus
could, with the agreement of the army, make an emperor had been asserted.
Now it is joined to its polar opposite, the notion that heredity determined
a ruler, and that notion is used to assert the irrelevance of events two
years earlier.

Oriens Augustus: the ascent of Constantine: 307–11

Maximian's journey to Trier was necessitated by the threat of an invasion of
Italy by Galerius.[73] Galerius' recognition of Constantine's claim to be Caesar
at the same time that he had raised Severus to the rank of Augustus made
it possible to assert control over the government by allowing the fiction
that Constantine was his appointee to go unchallenged, and raised the possibility that Constantine would actually support him. Maximian's action in
reasserting the family connection with Constantine and raising him to the
rank of Augustus gave Constantine every reason to sit on the fence, which
is exactly what he did.

Galerius invaded Italy himself in September 307, with no greater success
than Severus had enjoyed.[74] Maximian avoided battle and drew Galerius south
as far as Rome, which, defended as it was by Aurelian's wall, was impossible

to besiege without an overwhelming superiority of force. That Galerius did not have, so he halted at Interamnae and tried, in vain, to negotiate. As he did so, he sensed that he was losing control of his army and felt compelled to withdraw, ravaging Italy as he went.

So far there had been no major battle, and, so far, the major actors in this drama had treated each other with remarkable circumspection. This state of affairs changed suddenly when Maxentius had Severus murdered.[75] Of all the players on this crowded stage, Maxentius was in many ways the most dangerous. That he lacked his father's scruples was made plain enough by his murder of Severus, which displayed also an impatience with the diplomatic game that others thought crucial if they were to avoid open warfare. The death of Severus exposed the fictions upon which Galerius depended to assert that he still had some control over the situation, and a new crisis loomed.

As the year 308 opened, it did so with two sets of consuls, one named by Constantine in Gaul as a way of asserting his power as Augustus, the other established by Galerius, who proclaimed that he and Diocletian would be consuls. The sudden reappearance of Diocletian proved to be a diplomatic triumph for Galerius, and it raised a new threat to the regimes in both Gaul and Italy. In September, Constantine had ceased to recognize the consulship of Galerius, replacing him with Maximian in the *fasti*.[76] Galerius had responded by removing Constantine as Caesar on documents from those parts of the empire that he controlled.[77] More important, however, was the presence of Diocletian. Maximian had accomplished much through the prestige of his name in 306 and 307, delivering the army of Severus to his son, and an alliance with Constantine. But who would fight if Diocletian took the field?

Constantine was saved by the impatience of Maxentius. While Maximian tried to negotiate a way out of the impasse that now threatened, he seems to have encountered resistance from his son. In April Maximian attempted the overthrow of Maxentius. He failed and was forced to seek refuge with Constantine in Gaul.[78] His arrival there opened up a new chance for peace, for his eviction from Italy made him, at least briefly, acceptable as a reigning Augustus in the east.[79]

For both Galerius and Constantine, there were things that could be gained through negotiation. Constantine would benefit from external recognition of his legitimacy, while Galerius, who appears to have distrusted the abilities of Maximinus, needed a way to acquire a new colleague that would avoid an open break with the one colleague who still recognized his authority. Maximian offered a solution to the problems of both when he arranged to meet with Galerius and Diocletian at Carnuntum on the Danube.[80] On November 11, 308, in the presence of both Diocletian and Maximian, Galerius proclaimed an old friend of his, Valerius Licinianus Licinius, as Augustus in place of Severus; Constantine was recognized as Caesar and,

along with Maximinus, assumed the title "son of the Augusti."[81] The result
of this meeting reasserted the Diocletianic principle that only an emperor
could select an emperor, and that collegial government was best for the
empire. Diocletian returned to his palace at Split, where he was allegedly
devoted to the cultivation of cabbages, and Maximian retired to Gaul as a
former Augustus.[82]

The structure of this settlement reveals, as does the language of the
panegyric of 307 and of Lactantius, the importance of a sort of "constitutional theory" to the politics of these years. While it might be possible, from
the vantage point of nearly seventeen hundred years, to cavil at the flexibility of this theory (suggesting that a theory that permitted so many
permutations of authority was a sham), that would be to misrepresent the
very real effort of Diocletian to create a new form of legitimacy. In 308 both
sides were able to use Diocletian's principle that Augusti, who were, after
all, representatives of the unified mind of the provincials and army, should
determine the structure of power among themselves. It is a sign of how the
centralization of power had proceeded in the century after the revolutions
of 192, and indeed of 238, when the voice of the senate still had a place in
government, at least formally, before a person could claim legitimacy. It is
also a sign of deep discomfort with the instability inherent in the procedures
of 275 and, indeed, of 284, when the general staff had acted without reference to outside bodies other than the soldiers present at the moment. The
role of the soldiers in formalizing an agreement was still there, but it now
required the authority of an emperor to enable the soldiers to act. In 305,
the cloaks had been passed before the soldiers had shouted their acceptance.
So too in 308, the Augusti acted before others were formally involved.
Diocletian had created a system that was a genuine break with the past, and
in 308 it was strong enough to keep the peace.

Diocletian's theory would fail in the next decade, when confronted with
the ambitions of Constantine for a different kind of authority that hearkened
back to monarchic traditions of the second century, but even then the institutions of the republic were nowhere to be seen. Although collegiate government would prove to be too frail a notion to withstand the force of heredity
– Diocletian's effort to eliminate that factor after having tacitly accepted it
for the bulk of his reign would prove a gross miscalculation – the revised
narrative of imperial history that made imperial authority the product of
consensus among the provincials, the army, and the imperial house would
remain the basis of government in the next century, and beyond.

The inherent problem with collegiate government was that it depended
upon the actual success of the members of the college and their ability to
agree, to make the images of fraternal emperors embracing each other
the basis of government. Despite the fact that victory titles might still be
shared, that would no longer restrain the desires of men for unfettered control.
Nor could it occlude genuine differences of policy that were coming to be

increasingly important. At this point it may well be that the question of what to do about the Christians was becoming significant.

Diocletian had issued an edict ordering all his subjects to sacrifice in 304.[83] It may have been little more than a rhetorical gesture (depending, as always, upon the attitude of the governor), since there was no provision, as in the case of the Decian edict, for people to obtain a certificate. The edict appears also to have stated that people who did not sacrifice would have their property confiscated. There is some possible evidence for its enforcement in Egypt, but it seems otherwise to have been rather easy to evade – so easy, in fact, that Constantius never enforced it, and neither, it appears, did Maximian.[84] But there were still residual issues stemming from the first edict, the most significant, perhaps, being that the imperial government retained substantial quantities of church property. Even in Gaul, Constantius had allowed some confiscations, and it was this that enabled Constantine to take a clear stand, breaking with his colleagues on the "Christian issue." In 307 he issued an edict of restoration.[85] There is some reason to think that there were already Christians in his entourage, for one of his half-sisters bore the overtly Christian name Anastasia (Resurrection).[86] His mother, Helena, who would later be an active champion of the church, may already have converted, and a Spanish bishop, Ossius of Cordoba, appears to have become a confidant by 312. The issue of the place of Christians in the empire would reassert itself in 311, but by that time there had been another major change. Perhaps as a sign that he too recognized that a stand on the Christians would set him apart from Galerius, Maxentius appears to have issued his own edict of toleration (although he did not go so far as to restore property already confiscated).[87]

While there may have been issues that divided the emperors, they all shared a need to demonstrate that they had the ability to rule, and this meant, above all else, that they demonstrate the ability to command in battle. Constantine had begun early, smashing a raid across the Lower Rhine by a band of Franks in early 307, and giving their kings to the beasts in the amphitheater at Trier, an unusual act of savagery in the case of leaders who might otherwise be employed in Roman service or sent back to their people bound by promises to support Roman interests.[88] In 308 he launched an invasion across the Rhine.[89] Galerius had spent the early part of 308 on similar enterprises, seeking to restore confidence in his abilities as a general by slaughtering the Carpi along the Danube. Licinius would do the same in 309 and 310.[90] Maxentius had to confront a revolt by the governor of Numidia, L. Domitius Alexander, which broke out toward the end of 308. He defeated Alexander in the course of 309 and appears to have gone on to engage in some sort of campaign against the tribes to the south.[91]

The year 310 opened with yet another campaign against the Franks by Constantine, who had constructed a large bridge at Cologne as a symbol of his confidence that Roman power could successfully be projected into barbarian territory.[92] While he was engaged in this operation, Maximian, who had been left in command of the troops in southern Gaul, attempted to seize power for himself. Maximian told his troops that Constantine had died in battle, and then repaired to Marseilles, where he prepared to defend himself against his son-in-law. It was a futile effort. When Constantine appeared before the walls of the city, the garrison surrendered.[93] Maximian's own fate is obscure. According to a panegyric composed in the immediate aftermath of the revolt, Maximian had killed himself rather than experience the humiliation of facing Constantine.[94] According to Lactantius, writing a few years later, he had surrendered, and Constantine had placed him under house arrest in the palace. One night he crept out of his quarters and tried to stab Constantine in his sleep. Constantine was alerted to his design and had him apprehended, sword in hand, in the imperial bedchamber. Maximian was so distraught that he hanged himself.[95] Aside from the fact that Maximian died in the immediate aftermath of his surrender, it is impossible to be certain of much else, though the evolution of the story of his final moments might suggest that Constantine had ordered him to commit suicide when he entered Marseilles and then needed a better story to obscure his role in the destruction of the man to whom he had once owed so much.

The death of Maximian necessitated a transformation in Constantine's tale of legitimacy. He could no longer claim the throne on the basis of his connection with the elder Augustus, and it was the explanation of new facts about the emperor that fell to the orator who delivered a panegyric at Trier toward the end of the year.[96] The author wasted no time in getting to the point:

> And so I shall begin with the divinity who is the origin of your family, of whom most people, perhaps, are still unaware, but whom those who love you know full well. For an ancestral relationship links you with the deified Claudius, who was the first to restore the discipline of the Roman Empire when it was disordered and in ruins, and destroyed on land and sea huge numbers of Goths who had burst forth from the straits of the Black Sea and the mouth of the Black Sea. Oh, that he had been a longer-lived restorer of mankind, rather than too premature a companion of the gods! . . . Furthermore, that ancient prerogative of your imperial house advanced your father himself, so that that you now take your place on the highest rung, above the destinies of human affairs, as the third ruler after two rulers of your line. Among all who share your majesty, I aver you have this distinction, Constantine, that you were <born> an emperor, and so great is the nobility of your lineage that the attainment of imperial power has added nothing to your honor, nor can Fortune claim credit for your divinity, which is rightfully yours without campaigning and canvassing.
>
> (*Pan.* 6 [7] 2.1–3, 4–5, trans. Rogers)

Maximian is effectively eliminated from any role in the rise of the family. Claudius II is made, through a sleight of hand no less remarkable than the tetrarchic demotion of Aurelian, the savior of Rome and the founder of the line.[97] Constantius was emperor because he now can be proclaimed the descendant of an emperor, and Constantine is emperor because he is the son of Constantius:

> You entered this sacred palace, not as a candidate for supreme power, but as one designated to hold it, and the ancestral spirits of the household recognized you as his legitimate successor.
>
> (*Pan.* 6 [7] 1)

There is perhaps no stronger testimony to the importance of fictive historiography in forming the discourse of the tetrarchy than the deployment of this equally fictional creation of family and third-century history to overthrow it. The claims of the tetrarchs to authority granted to them by the gods and the goodwill of the provincials are rejected outright. As the panegyrist also observed, "No chance agreement of men, nor some unexpected consequence of favor, made you emperor."[98] The reference in this sentence is plainly to the conference at Carnuntum, just as the reference to campaigning and canvassing is a reference both to the torrent of tetrarchic proclamations of imperial accord with their subjects and the favor of the gods who had granted them victory. Through the invented link with Claudius, Constantine now asserts the sole principle of inheritance as ground for the holding of power. In the rest of the speech, the author repeats the gist of earlier panegyrics on Constantius, his victories over Germanic tribes and the recovery of Britain. Constantine's career is made out, as it had been in the past, to be a parallel to that of his father. The victories of Constantius in Britain make it the place most suitable for Constantine to have failed in his avoidance of the proclamation of his army. His victories on the Rhine equal and then exceed those of his father, thanks to the bridge at Cologne.[99] When Diocletian appears, he is a godlike man who both shared and resigned the imperial power, pleased to reside in an empire where Constantine exists, a far cry from the language of 307, when Constantine's legitimacy was guaranteed by Maximian.[100] In describing Maximian's revolt, the author's language strains the limits of obscurity with the phrase: "repente inter parietes consideret purpuratus et bis depositum tertio usurparet imperium" (suddenly he sat within the walls dressed in purple, and usurped for the third time the imperial power that he had laid down twice).[101] The coordination *bis* and *tertio* is scarcely accidental, not the implication that Maximian was never a true emperor. For Constantine the history of Rome according to Diocletian had passed.

After Constantine had dealt with Marseilles and Maximian, he received word that the Franks had launched yet another raid across the Rhine.

On the way north he stopped at a shrine of Apollo, possibly at Grand on the border of Belgica. There the god himself appeared to the emperor, so the panegyrist says,

> accompanied by Victory, offering you laurel wreaths, each one of which carries a portent of thirty years. For this is the number of human ages which are owed to you without fail – beyond the old age of Nestor. And – now why do I say "I believe"? – you saw and recognized yourself in the likeness of him to whom the divine song of the bards had prophesied that rule over the whole world was due.
>
> (*Pan.* 6 [7] 4–5, trans. Rodgers)

In a genre that is scarcely given to originality of expression, this scene is remarkable, and there can be little doubt but that the source for the author was the same as that for the wondrous information about the emperor's ancestry, for this vision is connected with a claim to rule the entire empire.[102] Despite overtones of a returning golden age with which the author embellishes the account, it is entirely likely that Constantine had experienced a vision of the god, quite possibly having sought it by sleeping in the sanctuary. A shrine of any divinity had multiple meanings, both local and universal, and if indeed the speaker was tempted to remind Constantine of his connection with a local shrine, this would in no way contradict the universalizing message with which he adorns the vision.[103] Accounts of such visions are not the stock-in-trade of the extant panegyrics, and that should mean that the author is suggesting something unusual about Constantine's connection with the god. It is something that others around Constantine might also have been suggesting, as his mints now begin to celebrate Sol Invictus, "Invincible Sun," who might readily be identified with Apollo, no matter what the nature of the Apollo at the shrine that Constantine visited.[104] It would be a feature of Constantine that he would shape his gods, whatever and whoever they might be, to suit his particular need. The search for visions is anything but extraordinary, and, as the tale of Mani shows more powerfully, perhaps, than any other from the third century, humans in search of guidance could well seek it from the divine plane. Constantine was not only charting a new path for the imperial office but, supported by the notion that he was himself under the special protection of Apollo, for himself as well.

Constantine may well have been encouraged not only by the gods, but also by the declining health of Galerius, and by an evident olive branch that the senior Augustus would shortly extend in his direction involving the Christians. Despite sporadic outbursts of persecution in the territory of Maximinus, especially in 305–6 and again in 309–10, when Maximinus appears to have sent out specific orders that existing laws actually be enforced, the church had been left very much to its own devices in the years since the death of Constantius.[105] Even Maximinus appears to have spent more energy reorganizing pagan cults than he did eliminating those that he did not like:

> He ordered temples built in every city, and the shrines that had been destroyed by the passage of time to be rebuilt with the greatest enthusiasm; and he appointed priests of the images in every place, and a high priest in every province over them, a man particularly experienced in public affairs, who had already filled every compulsory office, with an escort of soldiers and guardsmen.
>
> (Euseb. *Hist. eccl.* 8.14.9)

Maximinus' conduct with regard to local cults, not just the imperial cult, is in many ways the culmination of tetrarchic efforts to join local interests with those of the court.[106] There was perhaps no area of urban life that was more closely connected with an individual community's history than its religious structure. In this regard he shows himself to be the most extreme of the tetrarchs and to some degree out of touch with the spirit of compromise that had governed Galerius' actions since 308.

Galerius would go much further down the road to compromise in the week before he died. It was then that he issued an edict of toleration for Christians. His language is redolent, as always, of Diocletianic ideology, stating:

> Among all the other arrangements that we are always making for the benefit and utility of the state, we have heretofore wished to repair all things in accordance with the laws and the public discipline of the Romans, and to ensure that even the Christians, who abandoned the practice of their ancestors, should return to good sense. Indeed, for some reason or other, such self-indulgence assailed and idiocy possessed those Christians, that they did not follow the practices of the ancients, which their own ancestors had, perhaps, instituted, but according to their own will and as it pleased them, they made laws for themselves that they observed, and gathered various peoples in diverse areas. Then when our order was issued stating that they should return themselves to the practices of the ancients, many were subjected to peril, and many were even killed. Many more persevered in their way of life, and we saw that they neither offered proper worship and cult to the gods, or to the god of the Christians. Considering the observation of our own mild clemency and eternal custom, by which we are accustomed to grant clemency to all people, we have decided to extend our most speedy indulgence to these people as well, so that Christians may once more establish their own meeting places, so long as they do not act in a disorderly way. We are about to send another letter to our officials

355

detailing the conditions they ought to observe. Consequently, in accord with our indulgence, they ought to pray to their god for our health and the safety of the state, so that the state may be kept safe on all sides, and they may be able to live safely and securely in their own homes.

(Lact. *DMP* 34.1–5)

He is, to the very end, at one with his version of ancestral tradition and the well-being of his subjects. The persecution edicts were nothing more than acts to ensure that tradition be preserved (no matter how untraditional such action might be), intended to protect the average person from the menace of aberrant behavior. Now that they are released from fear of persecution, Christians may join with everyone else in praying for his good. Even if they persist in their ill-advised nonconformity, Christians will at least be praying for the right things. Nor could it ever be suggested that he had done something wrong: his logic is intact even as he allows the Christians to continue to be foolish. Nonetheless, it is an important moment in the expanding political morass of the period, for, by rescinding the persecution edict, Galerius would make it easier for Licinius to deal with Constantine and the Christians who were already, quite possibly, in his court and family.

The conversion of Constantine and the end of the Tetrarchy: 311–13

Galerius died in April or May 311.[107] At the time of his death there were three claimants to the title of Augustus, Constantine in the west, now claiming that his title applied to the whole empire, Licinius in the Balkans, and Maximinus, who had arrogated the rank to himself in 310, in the east. Despite the obloquy hurled upon him by the Constantinian tradition, Galerius had at least been able to keep the peace. As Diocletian looked out from his palace at Split, he might have taken some comfort from the fact that his most trusted lieutenant had understood his mind so that negotiation had restrained the urge to violence, and that the Roman state still stood strong against its neighbors. If he did take such comfort, it was but brief. War could no longer be avoided, and it may be a sign of the tenuous nature of Diocletian's own position that his own daughter, Valeria, the widow of Galerius, felt that she had to flee, along with her son Candidianus, to the court of Maximinus. And there the retired Augustus could not protect her from what appears to have been scandalous treatment by her erstwhile protector.[108] Leaving Candidianus at court, where he joined Severianus, the son of Severus, Valeria fled into exile.[109] The last recorded acts of Diocletian are requests to Maximinus asking that she be returned to him. It is a sign of the sudden change in Diocletian's own fortunes that the moment of his death, in either 311 or 313, was not marked with any celebration by his successors. The man who had tried so hard to reform the historical record of the Roman Empire simply dropped out of it.

It was Licinius who was in the most danger. His appointment as Augustus had been directed against Maxentius every bit as much as it had been resented by Maximinus, who had spent the year 310 engaged in some sort of border war with the Persians, perhaps in an effort to prove his credentials to the army in the likely event of war as soon as Galerius should die.[110] We do not know if it was Licinius then who initiated negotiations with Constantine in the course of 311 or the early part of 312 – but some sort of agreement was clearly reached.[111] The terms, insofar as they can be reconstructed from later events, appear to have involved some sort of military demonstration by Licinius that would tie some of Maxentius' forces down in northeastern Italy, followed by a pledge of support from Constantine for Licinius' subsequent war on Maximinus.

We do not know when Constantine crossed the Alps to begin the invasion of Italy, but it would appear that he caught Maxentius somewhat by surprise. His invasion force crossed the Alps by the pass at Mont Cenis, descending upon an army that had been set to watch the pass at Susa, which fell to his assault, before moving on to defeat a second army that had been stationed at Turin.[112] Speed was plainly of the essence, for it would enable Constantine to destroy Maxentius' northern armies in detail. And that is what happened. The garrison of Turin appears to have tried to give battle in front of the city, where it was crushed, enabling Constantine to avoid a siege and move east against the third Maxentian army in the Po valley, that which had been stationed at Aquileia under the command of Ruricius Pompeianus, the praetorian prefect.[113] Pompeianus was defeated as he moved west, just outside the city of Verona in the vicinity of the River Adige.[114] Constantine's success in these operations is remarkable, for if he had been compelled to besiege Milan or Aquileia, that might very well have prevented him from any further advance. It may be that he was assisted by the incompetence of his rivals, but it may also be that he simply moved so fast that they were incapable of reacting to him. His success in these operations compares well with the campaigns led by no less a figure than Napoleon in 1796 and 1800, in which the aspiring French emperor made full use of his highly mobile army to baffle and outmaneuver the forces of the Austro-Hungarian Empire.

With northern Italy secured, Constantine proceeded to march on Rome, probably around the end of September. His overwhelming success, and the aura of divine intervention that surrounds it, occludes the genuine difficulty of his accomplishment. To put his campaign in perspective, it is worth recalling that three men with arguably greater advantages than he began with, Maximinus Thrax, Severus, and Galerius, had all failed utterly to do what he did. On October 28, 312, Maxentius felt compelled to give battle to Constantine.[115] Pro-Constantinian accounts would stress his dependence upon a Sibylline oracle in making his decision, and while this may be true, it is hard to imagine that he could have been anything other than desperate to give battle with the river behind him.[116] Later tradition would also record enmity between him and the senate, attributed entirely to his repulsive personal habits, which ranged from rape to human sacrifice.[117] A less spectacular interpretation might suggest the presence of a very strong Constantinian sentiment in Rome that convinced Maxentius that he stood no chance of withstanding a siege. Whatever the case may be, the decisive battle at the Milvian Bridge ended in a spectacular victory for Constantine. Maxentius was drowned in the Tiber as he attempted to flee.[118]

If the victory at the Milvian Bridge left Constantine master of the western half of the empire, it also left him convinced that he was aided in his victory by the Christian god. The importance of this transformation underscores the importance of the new style of imperial government. It is quite simply inconceivable that the personal choice or experience of an emperor would have had the impact that Constantine's did if it were not for the highly developed sense that what was good for the emperor was good for his subjects, that emperor and subject shared a community of interest, that emerged under Diocletian. Aurelian's vision of Sol, Elagabalus' devotion to his eponymous divinity, resulted in changes in the cult structure of the city of Rome, but not of the empire as a whole. Constantine's decision to become a Christian not only implicated him in a cult that was unusual (though not unparalleled) in its empirewide reach, but also implicated the tetrarchic style of top-down government in the spread of the emperor's new faith.

What happened? We will perhaps never know for certain, but we can know how the story changed over time.[119] Even as the story changed, there is little doubt but that Constantine converted to Christianity because he felt that he was in direct contact with the Christian divinity. This is the one constant in the two main Christian narratives, one from the early years after the defeat of Maxentius, the other from the end of his reign. The most extensive of these is the one that Eusebius composed for the *Life of Constantine* that he completed after Constantine's death in 337:[120]

> If someone else reported it, it would perhaps not be easy to accept; but since the victorious Emperor himself told the story to the present writer a long while after, when I was privileged with his acquaintance and company, and confirmed it with oaths, who could hesitate to believe the account. Especially when the time that followed provided evidence for the truth of what he said? About the time of the midday sun, when day was just turning, he said he saw with his own eyes, up in the sky and resting over the sun, a cross-shaped trophy formed from light, and a text attached to it which said, "By this conquer." Amazement at the spectacle seized both him and the whole company of soldiers which was then accompanying

him on a campaign he was conducting somewhere and witnessed
the miracle.

He was, he said, wondering to himself what the manifestation
might mean; then, while he meditated, and thought long and hard,
night overtook him. Thereupon, as he slept, the Christ of God
appeared to him with the sign which had appeared to him in the
sky, and urged him to make himself a copy of the sign which had
appeared in the sky, and to use this as protection against the attacks
of the enemy.

(Euseb. *Vit. Const.* 1.28–29, trans. Hall)

The introduction to the passage quoted here is as significant as the story
itself, for in it Eusebius says that Constantine was deeply troubled by the
prospect of the campaign and wondered to what god he should pray, given
that previous emperors who had attacked Rome, accompanied by a variety
of gods, had failed.[121] He opted then to pray "to the God of his father,"
whom Eusebius implies was the Christian God. The vision is thus a confirmation of his decision to pray to the Christian God rather than the cause of
his conversion. There is a lot here to disbelieve. Not least in the notion that
Constantius was a closet Christian. While Constantius was plainly less interested in the persecution edicts of Diocletian than the other tetrarchs, he still
enforced the first one, and even Eusebius admits that Constantine did not
know who the god of his father was until after the events of 312.[122] On the
other hand, Eusebius' story does correspond more closely to other accounts
of Constantine's religious experience in the course of the campaign than does
the earlier story of the conversion, told by Lactantius. He says simply that
"Constantine was advised in the night that he should mark the heavenly sign
of God on the shields and then engage in battle."[123] In this case the vision
comes not at some unspecified time before the invasion, but at the decisive
moment itself. It does perhaps imply that Constantine was already prepared
to believe that he would receive a vision from the Christian God, and perhaps
that he was already praying to him, possibly in the hope that he would prove
stronger than the various divinities to whom Maxentius was praying.

Despite the late date of his account, the chronology implied by Eusebius
for Constantine's spiritual odyssey in 312 is confirmed to a remarkable degree
by the rhetoric of an orator who presented the official version of events in
the winter of 313. It is through his words that Constantine's subjects are
introduced to the *mens divina*, a character that first seems to have been making
its presence felt in the spring of 312 when it appears in a speech given in
thanks to Constantine for his reduction in the tax assessment of Arles.[124]
At the very beginning of the campaign, the audience of 313 is told, some
god had given confidence in his designs even though the signs augured
against his success.[125] This god was indeed *mens divina*, who entrusted
care of lesser mortals to lesser gods.[126] The critical point here is that the

Plate 13 The Arch of Constantine, facing toward the Via San Gregorio. Photo taken by George R. Swain in 1925. *Credit*: Photo courtesy of the Kelsey Museum of Archaeology, University of Michigan, Kelsey Museum Archives 11.2.

"authorized version" of the campaign in 313 already had Constantine seeking new divine advice prior to his crossing of the Alps. It was this version too that the Roman senate authorized with its dedicatory inscription on the arch that was erected at Rome in honor of Constantine's victory:

> The senate and people of Rome dedicated this arch, decorated with images of his triumph, to the imperator Caesar Constantine Augustus, pious and fortunate, because, at the prompting of the divinity, by the greatness of his mind, he, with his army, avenged the Res Publica upon the tyrant and his whole faction at the same instant with a just victory.
>
> (*ILS* 694)

The sculptural pattern of the Arch of Constantine, as a whole, is a serious problem, for the reliefs of fourth-century date that appear on the north and south sides above the side arches, and upon the east and west flanks of the arch, are dwarfed by sculptural tondi and other reliefs imported onto the arch, chiefly from monuments of Hadrian, Marcus Aurelius, and Trajan.[127] Images of Trajan triumphant on the battlefield over the Dacians and at his triumph adorn the inside of the main arch underneath, respectively, the inscriptions *liberator urbis* and *fundator quietis* ("liberator of the city" and "founder of peace"). Directly above the relief of Constantine's address to the people of Rome after his entry into the city are images of Hadrian's Egyptian lion hunt and of the same emperor sacrificing to Hercules, with the heads recarved so that Constantine replaces Hadrian in the lion hunt, and Constantius appears in the sacrifice scene. Images of Hadrian hunting a boar and sacrificing to the sun, with the imperial heads recarved again so that Constantine appears as the hunter and Constantius as the sacrificer, are positioned above the relief of Constantine's distributions to the Roman people.[128] On the south side, above the relief illustrating the capture of Verona on the western arch, tondi of Hadrian depict the emperor sacrificing to Silvanus and dedicating a bearskin (in this case with both heads recarved to represent Constantine). On the east side, above the relief depicting the battle of the Milvian Bridge, Hadrian hunts a bear and sacrifices to Diana on the two tondi (in this case with both heads recarved to represent Constantius). On the west side, above a relief illustrating Constantine's departure from Milan, is the image of the moon descending from the sky, while on the east, an image of Apollo ascending into the sky sits above the image of Constantine's entry into Rome. The uppermost register of the arch contains four reliefs on both the north and south sides of Marcus Aurelius engaging in various acts of government, with images of Trajan at war on the east and west – again with the imperial images recarved.

This amalgam of relief sculpture is perhaps best explained through the image of Constantine's speech to the people of Rome, depicted as having taken place upon the imperial rostra. Constantine stands front and center, surrounded by his court, but on either end of the rostra are shown the statues of Hadrian and Marcus that adorned them. Behind Constantine are visible the four columns erected in honor of the first tetrarchy in 303, flanking a statue of Jupiter. The triumphal arch of Septimius Severus is visible off to the left of the tetrarchic columns. In a very real sense the image here is that which Constantine himself wished to create and advertise: the tetrarchic background, albeit one limited to the members of the first tetrarchy, was there for all to see, but the empire that they had worked to restore was not, in the end, that of their own devising, but rather that of the Antonine age. The vigorous combination of styles, the placement of the story of Constantine's march on Rome, carved as it was in a style that was evocative of the art of Diocletian's time, illustrated the unity of past with present, and the way that the new government was now devoted to the traditions of the past. For those with good enough eyes to pick Constantine out in the battle scenes before Verona and at the Milvian Bridge, the emperor was depicted with images of Victoria by his side. The astral symmetry of the sun and moon on the east and west, rising or setting in their assigned quarters, represented the fact that the new ruler was a man in accord with the natural order.[129]

The message of conservatism that is enshrined upon the Arch of Constantine was repeated by the rhetor Nazarius in the panegyric that he delivered to celebrate the opening of the fifth year in which Constantine's sons, Crispus and Constantine, held the rank of Caesar (AD 321). In this version, Constantine had waged a great war on behalf of the city of Rome, summoned by the wretched state of the city as it suffered under the tyranny of Maxentius.[130] In this endeavor, Constantine had been aided by "God, the arbiter of all things who looks upon our affairs from on high," just as he is moved by the singular divinity in the inscription on the arch.[131] Just as on the arch he is seen to be aided by winged victories, in this version,

> It is upon the lips of all the Gauls that armies were seen that let it be known that they were divinely sent. Although heavenly objects are not accustomed to come before the eyes of mortals, because that unmixed and insubstantial essence of subtle nature eludes heavy and darkened vision, your assistants allowed themselves, nonetheless, to be seen and heard there, where they testified to your merit, and fled the contagion of mortal sight.
>
> (*Pan.* 4 [10] 14.2, trans. Rodgers adapted)

They were led by no less a divinity than Constantius, who "sensed himself to become greater through your piety."[132] After reviewing Constantine's victories over the Germanic tribes of the north, Nazarius returns to the invasion of Italy, reciting the tale of the battle at Susa, followed by the victory of Turin, stressing once again the frightening appearance of the mailed cavalry that formed the strength of Maxentius' forces (and whose demise in the Tiber is illustrated in the depiction of the battle of the Milvian Bridge upon the arch).[133] Then he turns to the victory at Brescia outside of Verona and the capture of that city itself, again recalling themes upon the arch.[134] Finally, he comes to the last battle:

> I shall not mention here the banks covered with an unbroken line of carnage, nor the Tiber filled with heaps of bodies, moving along with weakened effort among the high-piled cadavers, its waters barely forcing their way through, that not a manly death but a shameful flight betrayed the tyrant himself when the bloody billows slew him in a demise worthy of his cowardice and cruelty.
>
> (*Pan.* 4 [10] 30.1, trans. Rodgers)

From the scene of victory Nazarius moves, along with the arch, to Constantine's arrival in the city, and the joy of the city at the restoration of its liberty, and the defeat of Maxentius' surviving supporters in Africa.[135] Unconstrained by the requirements of brevity, Nazarius need not restrict his

362

account to a few crucial moments as did the sculptors upon the arch, but his themes are their themes. His is the tale, as was theirs, of the liberation of Rome.

The multiple versions of Constantine's victorious campaign reflect the progressive collapse of the Diocletianic effort to create a single central narrative for Roman government. Constantine's story needed to be told from many different perspectives and to reflect the needs of different audiences, especially those who would have noticed some novel behaviors such as the appearance of the chi–rho symbol (symbolizing either good luck, or the name of Christ, since the letters are the first two both of the Greek word *chrestos* and of *Christos*) that he seems to have ordered his men to place on their shields before the battle of the Milvian Bridge, or his failure to sacrifice at the temple of Capitoline Jupiter after his triumphant entry into Rome on October 28.[136] For Eusebius, as he wrote of Constantine's victory in later years, the defeat of Maxentius was the act of a new Moses come to lead his people to a promised land; for Lactantius it was an act of vengeance upon the impious; while for the senate it was an act of divinely inspired liberation. For the orator who composed the panegyric of 313, celebrating the emperor's return to Trier, it was a new phase in the evolution of an emperor whose form was ever changing. For Nazarius, it was the restoration of Rome to supremacy. The imperial city could feel again that it was "the citadel of all nations and the queen of all lands."[137] The polyvalent messages with which the events of 312 were encoded were to be paradigmatic of Constantine's reign as a whole. He would continue to reveal himself as an emperor with an abiding attachment to the traditions of past emperors while, at the same time, creating space within which a new, Christian, interpretation of the office could grow. In his formulation, however, and this is the most important point, the two visions of imperial power were not to be contrasting, but complementary. The one thing that all Constantine's subjects would know was that their emperor had received special assistance from a new god as he campaigned against Maxentius.

10

RESTRUCTURING
THE STATE: 313–37

Licinius in the east

In the immediate aftermath of his victory over Maxentius, Constantine traveled to Milan, where he met Licinius. There the two men cemented their alliance with the betrothal of Constantine's oldest half-sister, Constantia, to the Augustus of the Balkans, and, it seems, Constantine introduced his prospective brother-in-law to the mysteries that he had discovered on the campaign just passed.[1] As Constantia herself was a Christian, it may have been desirable that Licinius make some sort of pro-Christian demonstration in the coming year, and he could derive benefit from it that went beyond making his wife and her family happy. Although Galerius had ended the persecution, he had not restored confiscated property to Christian ownership, and the lot of the Christian community was especially harsh in the portion of Maximinus. Generosity to Christians enabled Licinius to draw a distinction between himself and his rival.

Maximinus had resuscitated in a most original way the persecution of the Christian church in the months after Galerius died. As Eusebius tells it, he had fallen under the influence of a man named Theotecnus, a member of the city council at Antioch in Syria, who attracted the emperor's attention by erecting

> a statue of Zeus Philios with some trickery and sorcery. Devising some unspeakable rites, ill-omened mysteries, and unspeakable purifications for it, he put on a display of this marvel through which he gave oracles, even to the emperor. This man stirred up a demon against the Christians out of flattery and to give pleasure to the ruler saying that the God ordered that the Christians be driven from the territory of the city and the fields around it, as they were his enemy.
>
> (Euseb. *Hist. eccl.* 9.3)

Theotecnus' activity inspired civic officials throughout the east, who, with the advice of provincial governors, sent messages to Maximinus asking him to initiate a persecution. At the same time, it appears as if someone in the court forged the *Acts of Pilate*, which contained a denunciation of the Christians and which were circulated among the provincial high priests, one of whom may have been the author.[2] The Greek title of this composition, *Hypomnêmata tou Pilatou*, suggests that it may have been in a form similar to a particular form of Christian martyrology that included a transcript of the encounter between a magistrate and a prospective martyr.

The result of Maximinus' communication was that he never issued an actual edict of persecution. Rather, he initiated a series of persecutions at the local level by responding favorably to petitions that appear to have been worded very similarly to the message of Theotecnus' god, requesting that Christians be expelled from civic territory. Three examples of these petitions have survived, one directly in Eusebius' *Ecclesiastical History*, and two, less directly on inscriptions from Asia Minor, that contain Maximinus' responses to them. These same inscriptions and other documents also reveal that, in 312, he was still wary of provoking open war with Licinius; he recognized the claim of the two western Augusti to be consuls for the year.[3]

The actions of Maximinus attest to the success that he had achieved through his appointment of priests of the imperial cult.[4] In the events of 312 we see, for the first time in Roman history, an orchestration of the petition-and-response style of government so that it could be used as a vehicle for making general policy. The use of petitions in this case may reflect Maximinus' own sense that government by edict was less effective than might be desired; that what was needed in order genuinely to effect a policy that would be observed on the local level was the reification of the tetrarchic image of the harmony between the will of the people and the court.

Given the local initiative in organizing persecution, the year 311/12 proved a very difficult one for a number of Christian communities. In Alexandria, the bishop, Peter, was arrested and executed.[5] At Ancyra in Turkey, where Theotecnus had been sent as governor, the arrival of an imperial response authorizing persecution led to the arrest of seven virgins who were leaders of the local Montanist community, and their execution by drowning.[6] After recovering their bodies in the middle of the night, another member of the community, Theodotus, launched a verbal assault upon Theotecnus in the agora, resulting in his public incineration.[7] At Pedachthoe in Armenia, anonymous letters attacking the emperor's policy led to the arrest and execution of a man named Athenogenes, a leader of the community.[8] Marcus Julius Eugenius, an official on the staff of Diogenes, governor of Pisidia, was tortured repeatedly, but survived to become bishop of Laodicea.[9] But there was still no all-encompassing edict, and, as 312 drew to a close, Maximinus appears to have recognized that he needed to step back in the face of growing tensions between himself and Licinius. He refused permission to the people of Nicomedia when they asked to expel the Christians from their community and, at the very end of the year, reversed course completely by issuing an edict of toleration.[10] The history of conflict between the tetrarchy and the

Christian church thus ended not with any grand act by Constantine, but through the actions of Maximinus.

Maximinus' edict of toleration did nothing to ease his relationship with the Augusti of the west, and it appears to have become clear to him that if he were to have any chance of survival, he would need to strike first. In the spring of 313 Maximinus sent an army across the Hellespont.[11] Licinius was well prepared and very likely was already on the march, since he was able to meet Maximinus in full strength at Adrianople. That Lactantius should say that Licinius had a dream in which an angel of God told him to pray to the Supreme God if he wished to have victory, suggests that Licinius had religious values very similar to those of his brother-in-law: he was willing to pray to a new god if he thought that it would help him win.[12] Though this point has attracted very much less attention in subsequent history than the tales of Constantine's vision, Licinius' has left a clearer mark upon the contemporary record. Rather than simply placing a symbol on the shield of his soldiers, Licinius wrote out a prayer to the Supreme God, which was recited by his army before it entered battle the next day:

> Supreme God, we pray to you, Holy God, we pray to you. We commend all justice to you. We commend our safety to you. We commend our empire to you. Through you we live, through you we emerge victorious and fortunate. Highest, Holy God, hear our prayers. We lift up our arms to you. Hear us, Holy, Highest God.
>
> (Lact. *DMP* 46.6)

The two armies drew up for battle on the morning of April 30, a date that Lactantius says was chosen by Maximinus so that he could celebrate the anniversary of his accession on May 1 as a victor.[13] After Licinius' soldiers three times uttered the prayer that had been distributed to them by their officers, the two emperors met briefly to see if they could resolve their differences; when that failed, battle was joined.[14] Licinius was completely victorious, and Maximinus fled rapidly to the east, pausing briefly at Nicomedia to gather up his family. It appears as if he planned to make a final stand at Tarsus, and in this he was no more successful than Florian had been. At the approach of Licinius' army, he committed suicide.[15]

On his way east, Maximinus had issued one final edict with regard to the Christians, and in its wording he offered a remarkable testimony to the problems with the centralized edictal style of government that was so much a feature of the tetrarchic period:

> The emperor Caesar Gaius Valerius Maximinus Germanicus, Sarmaticus, Pius Felix Invincible Augustus. We believe that no one, nay that every person who has recourse to the facts knows and is conscious that it is manifest that in every way we take unceasing

thought for the good of our provincials, and desire to grant them such things as are best calculated to secure the advantage of all, and whatsoever things are advantageous and useful to their common weal, and such as are suitable to the public advantage and agreeable to every mind. Since, therefore, before this it has been evident to our knowledge that, on the plea that the most divine Diocletian and Maximian, our fathers, had given orders for the abolition of the Christian assemblies, many extortions and robberies have been practiced by the officials, and that this increased as time went on to the detriment of our provincials. . . . we addressed a letter to the governors in each province last year laying it down that if any should wish to follow such a custom or the same religious observances, such a one should adhere to his purpose without hindrance.

(Euseb. *Hist. eccl.* 9.10.7–8, trans. Oulton,
slightly adapted)

He goes on to state that he is publishing this edict to make it clear what his intentions are, and goes a step further in ordering the restoration of all Christian property. The period of persecution could not have been more explicitly ended.

Although the edict of Maximinus obviated the need for any action on the part of Licinius, a statement on the place of the church plainly offered a vehicle through which the new regime could distance itself from the past. So it was that on June 13, 313, Licinius issued his own restoration edict at Nicomedia, saying that it represented the gist of his discussions with Constantine at Milan in the previous year.[16] It is this document, redundant and enormously long, that stands in the Christian tradition as the official beginning of a new era in the relationship between church and state. On an ideological note, it perhaps was, for it expresses a message of inclusion that goes far beyond the language of the edicts issued earlier by Galerius or Maximinus. While they stated that they would no longer persecute the Christians for the good of the state as a whole, in this edict it was made clear that the emperors were under the protection of the Highest God, who had aided them in their victories.[17] All who worshipped the gods were therefore to be treated equally.[18] It is perhaps somewhat ironic that Constantine's efforts to sort out the implications of his own edict of restoration in North Africa at the very time that Licinius was campaigning against Maximinus would truly usher in this new era.[19] Under this dispensation certain groups of Christians would again be persecuted.

The government of the empire

Licinius moved swiftly to establish his own power throughout the east, issuing an edict of his own that ordered the destruction of Maximinus' monuments, and executing a number of Maximinus' senior officials, including Theotecnus, Clodius Culcianus, a vigorous enemy of the Christian church, and Peucetius, who had been Maximinus' *praepositus summae rei*.[20] In addition to these men, Licinius had Candidianus and Severianus, the sons of Severus and Galerius, executed, the latter on the charge of plotting to seize the throne.[21] It is alleged that he had Maximinus' wife drowned in the Orontes.[22] Maximinus' two young children, a boy and a girl, were killed, and Valeria, the long-suffering daughter of Diocletian, who had made her way back into his territory, was arrested; she was executed at Thessalonica.[23]

It is in the joint reign of Constantine and Licinius that the first irrefutable evidence for the organization of Diocletian's new provinces into a series of larger units known as dioceses and prefectures occurs. Despite Lactantius' assertion that Diocletian had divided the empire into four parts, each with its own emperor, the system of the tetrarchy was in fact a good deal less formal than Lactantius makes it out to be.[24] The diverse imperial capitals that emerged under the tetrarchy did not reflect formal allocations of provinces: it just so happened that Maximian tended to stay south of the Alps and Constantius north of them. In the east, it is clear that Galerius was no more limited to the Danubian provinces than Diocletian was to the Anatolian, Semitic, or Egyptian provinces. Any formal division of authority within the empire would have run counter to the ideology of the tetrarchy and Diocletian's own inclination to see members of the college as a group rather than as men holding bits of the empire on their own.

The situation changed with the abdication of the two senior Augusti, for while Constantius retained the first rank, it appears as if he did not retain the power to be the sole source of legislation.[25] It would also appear that it became proper to speak of different portions of the empire as being in the "territory" of one or the other members of the college. This division of territory was continued at the moment that Galerius recognized that Constantine could be Caesar in the west. By doing so, he allowed that Constantine had legislative authority over a group of provinces that was independent of his own. Constantine's edict of restoration to the Christians provides our first unequivocal evidence for a member of the college issuing legislation that was restricted to one part of the empire.[26] Likewise, Constantine's refusal to enforce Galerius' persecution edict shows that he could deny authority to a piece of legislation issued by the senior Augustus.[27] It is likely that the formal division of territory was made possible by the division of the empire into twelve dioceses, each one governed by a *vicarius*.

The evidence for the administrative division of the empire into dioceses comes, in the first instance, from a list of provinces, the Verona List, that gives a register of the provinces of the empire and the dioceses in which they were placed during the joint reign of Constantine and Licinius.[28] The date at which these divisions were first made may emerge from the way that *vicarii* are described. In the later part of the reign of Diocletian, there appear men

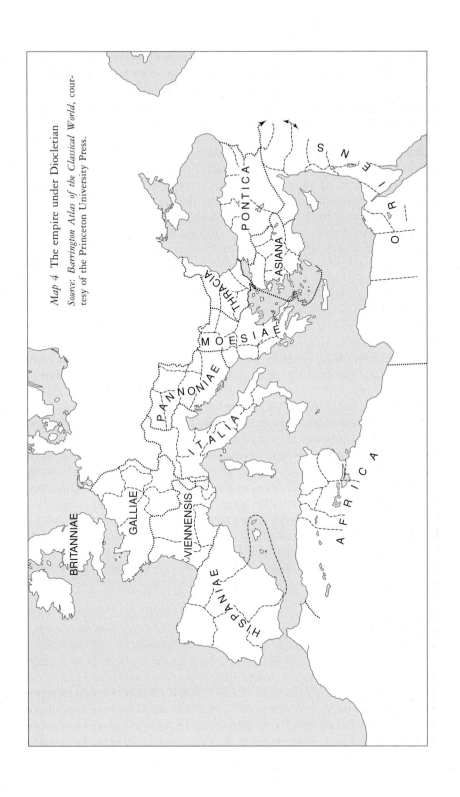

Map 4 The empire under Diocletian
Source: Barrington Atlas of the Classical World, courtesy of the Princeton University Press.

whose authority is described as *agens vicem prefectorum praetorio* (acting in place of the praetorian prefects).[29] The title implies that the praetorian prefects as a group had been given general oversight of the civil administration of the provinces, but, and this is important, they were given this authority as a group, just as the tetrarchs held their authority as a group.

After Diocletian's abdication, the situation becomes more complicated. Although it is clear that laws continued to be issued in the name of the college, with Constantius listed as senior Augustus, and that the prefects were also referred to as a college, there is some evidence to suggest that people perceived a difference.[30] Lactantius thought that it was possible to blame Galerius for the law that included Italy in the census.[31] It would be easy enough to dismiss this as empty rhetoric were it not also for the fact that, in 306, an official previously described as *agens vicem prefectorum praetorio* appears as *agens vicem prefecti praetorio* (acting in place of the praetorian prefect).[32] The change from singular to plural is surely significant, and it looks as if, for a time at least, specific prefects were seen as having particular authority in one portion of the empire, and, quite possibly, that they were seen as serving a particular member of the college. This change reflects the propriety of language such as that of Eusebius, who could speak of "his father's portion" with reference to the realm inherited by Constantine and of "those who governed the other parts" with reference to Galerius and his colleagues.[33]

The reform in the nature of the prefecture and the formalization of the diocesan structure of the empire reflects the strained relationship between Constantius and Galerius; it may be a concession on Constantius' part in that it would have given Severus more day-to-day control over a portion of the western empire than he would otherwise have had. After July 306, it may also have proved useful as defining the area in which Constantine could exercise his authority, for after his accession he controlled Britain, Gaul, and Spain, an area that may have been essentially constituted as the group of provinces controlled by his father's praetorian prefect. This area is later clearly attested as being constituted as a group of four dioceses, the provinces of Britain, the Gauls (northern and western France as well as the Rhineland), Viennensis (southern France), and the Spains, each one of which was governed by a *vicarius* who reported to the praetorian prefect

With the death of Severus, Maxentius took over control of Italy and North Africa. This area later constituted two dioceses, Italy and the Africas. Maximinus' realm was defined as three further dioceses, Oriens (comprising the territory from Libya to Cilicia and Isauria on the south coast of Turkey), Asia (running from Lycia and Pamphylia north to the Hellespont, comprising the western rim of the Anatolian plateau), and Pontica (the northern rim of the Anatolian plateau and the inland areas). The Balkans were divided into three dioceses: Thrace, Moesia, and Pannonia. Licinius was given control over this region after he was promoted to Augustus, while Galerius had claimed

370

general control over both this region and that of Maximinus. After their victories in 312 and 313, Constantine and Licinius divided the twelve dioceses of the empire equally between them.

At some point in these years it is also likely that a strict division between civil and military authority was created. It may well be that Diocletian had set the stage for this by creating a mass of provinces where there was no garrison, but governors in his reign can be seen exercising both military and civil authority where they had both to exercise. By the end of the reign of Constantine this had ceased to be the case, and it is probable (if not provable) that it was the result of changes in the military structure instituted by Diocletian that were extended by Constantine.[34]

While we cannot trace the evolution of the empire's administrative structures with any great certainty, it appears that Diocletian was a major innovator. His successors down to 324 were impeded from any significant reform by the division of government. Constantine worked within the structures established by Diocletian, only making significant changes in the last few years of his reign in the context of his succession.

Diocletian was responsible for creating four palatine ministries that broke with the traditions of republican government for good. The first was that of the praetorian prefects, who, with the exception of the period between 306 and 312, formed a college. Their number varied according to the number of emperors. Thus, during the time that Constantine and Licinius shared power, there would be two prefects, one for each emperor.[35] The *vicarii* of the twelve dioceses would report to the prefect (the western six to Constantine's prefect, the eastern six to that of Licinius). The provincial governors would report to the *vicarii*. The two most important functions of this branch of government were to oversee the administration of existing laws and the collection of the two main taxes, the head tax and the land tax.

The second branch of government was the *res privata*. There is no evidence that Diocletian ever envisaged a structure for the *res privata* that involved the appointment of officials between the provincial and imperial levels. Under Constantine and Licinius, we find diocesan *rationales* of the *res privata* who would report to the *comes summae rei* (as he was called by 319), one for each reigning emperor.[36] The management of the *patrimonium* had expanded under Diocletian to include the administration of mines, mints, taxes paid in coin, the distribution of imperial largesse, and some judicial responsibilities as needed.

The evidence for the third great bureau of government places its inception firmly in the reign of Diocletian. This is the branch that included the various imperial secretaries under the master of the offices, the *magister officiorum*.[37] There were three basic divisions of the secretariat under the *magister officiorum*: those of the *magister memoriae*, the *magister libellorum*, and the *magister epistularum*. The second and third of these offices are the direct descendants of the *a libellis* and *ab epistulis* of the earlier empire, and were concerned with communications between the palace and its subjects. The *magister memoriae* appears to have been concerned with the empire's dealings with foreign peoples. It is no accident that the second attested holder of this office was Sicorius Probus, who negotiated Diocletian's treaty with Persia.[38]

Finally, there was the palace staff. The leading figures of the staff were still the "servants of the bedchamber," the *cubicularii*, and there is no reason to think that their duties were placed under the control of any authority other than that of the emperor himself.[39] The multiplication of imperial residences would have required an increase in the number of such officials, and it appears likely (though again it is unprovable) that the office of *praepositus sacri cubiculi*, or "head of the sacred bedchamber," was created by Diocletian, even though the first person who we can identify as holding this post is a man named Festus who served Constantine.[40]

The government, based now as it was on the offices of the palace, would retain roughly the shape that it had when Constantine took the throne, until the 330s. It was then (if at all) that he created the office of the quaestor of the sacred palace to draft proactive legislation, while leaving responses to petitions in the hands of the secretaries *(notarii)* who served in the office of the *magister officiorum*.[41] The significance of this change (whether it be due to Constantine, as reported by Zosimus, or to Constantius II, as Zosimus' text could be emended to say) is the recognition that the government had a proactive role in preaching to its subjects, and that the eloquence needed for this task was of a special sort. Likewise it is significant in that, despite the title, quaestor, this official had nothing to do with the senatorial career. For the most part, imperial quaestors of the sacred palace would be drawn from the ranks of the imperial secretariat. The second change was the removal of military authority from the praetorian prefects, and the transfer of that authority to officials called the *magistri militum*. This reform may be dated to the very last years of Constantine's life, and it may be connected with his plans both for the succession and for war with Persia.[42]

While we will examine the army in more detail in chapter 12, it is, for now, worth noting that the creation of the imperial *comitatus* under Gallienus and his successors necessitated new command structures. In the nascent period of this unit, it appears that the senior official was the commander of the cavalry.[43] In the wake of Aureolus' revolt we hear nothing more of this post, and nothing of any comparable position. This is perhaps not surprising, as the comitatus was intended to follow the emperor himself, and it appears, under Diocletian, that the senior officer commanding large bodies of troops, if the emperor was not present, was the praetorian prefect, though this was not an absolute rule. Constantius had never been a praetorian prefect, even though he had a large command in Gaul prior to his elevation to the imperial college.[44] The only other title that emerges from the documentation for the early fourth century is that of *dux*, and it is likely (though unprovable) that men with widely different responsibilities, ranging from the oversight of provincial units to that of entire groups of provinces, held this title.[45]

The most significant change in government after the death of Galerius was that there was no longer a senior Augustus. Despite later assertions on the part of Constantine that Licinius had not respected him as the senior Augustus, there is no reason to think that the two men were anything but equals under the new dispensation.[46] One reason why Licinius may have felt it necessary to issue his own edict of restitution after the defeat of Maximinus was that he had both to invalidate Maximinus' actions as being those of a "tyrant," and to assert that earlier legislation by Constantine would not, de facto, have effect in his realm. Constantine's later attempt to eliminate all record of Licinius as a legitimate emperor has buried texts that were issued on Licinius' initiative deeply within the pages of the Theodosian and Justinianic Codes[47] – but not so thoroughly that they cannot be recovered. In technical terms, it may be that these were preserved because they were recognized by Constantine as having force in his own domains prior to the final overthrow of his erstwhile colleague, and it is likely that each emperor was able to decide whether or not to allow the legislation of his colleague to stand. Thus the Theodosian Code preserves a rescript addressed to a person named Mygdonius stating that if someone who had received a gift from the emperor died intestate and without children, the gift should pass to a partner. As the text is dated to 315 and was issued at Antioch, and as Mygdonius was an official of the palace, it is plain that Licinius must be the author.[48] There are several other such documents whose preservation may stem from the fact that they had become useful precedents in areas that were not of pressing interest, or did not contradict opinions expressed by Constantine's officials.[49] Thus, on February 13, 325, Constantine would promulgate an edict stating,

> Although the acts of the tyrant and his judges have been overthrown, no one should wish to alter though fraud that which he did himself of his own free will, nor what was done legitimately.
>
> (*C. Th*. 15.14.2)

Constantine's administration had shown similar restraint in dealing with the legislative record of Maxentius (who was likewise condemned as a tyrant):

> We order that whatever the tyrant ordained through rescripts that was against custom shall not have force, but his legitimate responses should not be impugned.
>
> (*C. Th*. 15.14.3)[50]

The range of the imperial chancery's activity was so vast that it was simply impractical to try and chase down every rescript to declare it invalid, or to invalidate measures if they were introduced into a pleading on the grounds that they were issued by a "tyrant." On the other hand, it was more than possible that a series of actions taken in response to appeals in some area of the law would differ in spirit if they were issued from the court of Constantine rather than that of Licinius.

The possibility that agents of the two imperial administrations would take different views as to what constituted a proper response, and that one emperor was not bound by the decisions of another, raises a question about the validity of referring to the Roman Empire in the singular. There is no easy way out of this conundrum, and it appears that the only time it was addressed was when one member of the imperial college was defeated by another. At other times the empire was theoretically a singular entity; the administrative structures were sufficiently well united that *vicarii* are once again referred to as *agens vicem prefectorum praetorio*, showing that the prefects were notionally colleagues despite serving directly under one Augustus or the other.[51] Likewise, it appears that a jurist updated the Hermogenian Code around 320, including rescripts from both emperors, suggesting again that the theory of united government held.[52] So too, it appears that an edict issued by one emperor might form the basis of an opinion by another. An inscription found at the city of Lyttus on Crete records a series of measures to be taken against people who bring false accusations against others in the hope of having them subjected to torture.[53] The text is described as a "copy of the sacred edict" and opens with a statement that the emperors "taking care for the security of our provincials" have decided that accusers must show up in court with clear evidence of wrongdoing on the part of the accused. If they should not do so (relying, by implication, on the judge to extract a confession under torture), they should themselves be subjected to torture. In the first instance, the emperors decree that, in cases where a charge of treason is involved, not only the accuser, but any who seem to have supported him, should be subjected to this penalty. In the third section of the edict they extend this penalty outwards from the charge of treason to malicious prosecutions of all sorts. In the fourth section they decree that

> in the case of slaves and freedmen who should dare accuse or report their masters or patrons, the assertion of such atrocious audacity shall be suppressed immediately at the inception of the act by the action of the judges, and, being denied a hearing, those who proceed to desperate acts of this sort should offer an example to others, so that no person in the future should attempt such audacity.
>
> (*FIRA*[7] 94.28–35)

Finally, they order that judges should not admit anonymous accusations, and that they should take action against those who adduce them. The text is plainly dated to the year 314, and copies of it have been found in a number of other places, including Tlos, Sinope, and Pergamum, as well as at Padua and in both the Theodosian and Justinianic Codes. In the case of the codes, however, only the sections dealing with accusations of treason and slaves (or freedmen) who attack their masters/patrons are included, in the form of a letter to a man named Maximus who is described as being the *praefectus urbi* (and who is thus presumably to be identified with Valerius Maximus Basilius, who held the office from 319 to 323).[54] Unfortunately, in both cases, the original dating formula, giving the consuls of 314, is also preserved, leading to some confusion. Some would emend Maximus' title to praetorian prefect and identify him as an official of Licinius, supporting this identification by pointing to the use of crucifixion as a penalty on the grounds that Aurelius Victor says that Constantine abolished it. Others object to the emendation and point to the fact that we do not know when Constantine abolished the use of crucifixion. What is really at issue is, of course, not to whom the text was sent (it was plainly an *edictum ad provinciales* that was widely circulated in the east, making it more than likely that Licinius was the author) but that Constantine (or one of his officials) should be sending a copy of it to Maximus. The most likely explanation for this is that Maximus had asked what the law governing cases where an accusation seemed frivolous was, and he duly received a copy of the edict that took precedence.[55] The reason that only the sections dealing with treason and accusations by slaves/freedmen survive in the extant codes is that these sections contained material that the compilers of the code thought relevant to treason. As for the issue of crucifixion, Constantine did not change imperial practice overnight, and there is no reason to think that he had taken this action before the reunification of the empire in 324, since most of what Eusebius knows about his legislation dates from after that point.[56]

The Edict on Accusations stands as a useful example of imperial cooperation and the continuing ability of imperial legal staffs to work in tandem even while the emperors who governed them were increasingly at odds. And it is fair to say that the relationship between the two emperors became problematic very soon after the defeat of Maximinus. There is perhaps no clearer indication of the problem than the very different styles adopted by the two men. In the years prior to the defeat of Maxentius, Constantine, who had justified his position through various claims to descent from his versions of the "legitimate" tetrarchy, had projected an image of himself that resembled that of other members of the imperial colleges. He appears on coins as a generously proportioned individual, looking very much like his father, who in turn had been portrayed as a man who looked remarkably like his colleagues. In the aftermath of his victory in 312, Constantine moved very quickly to a new style, evoking, as did the idiom of the arch at Rome, the heritage of earlier emperors. On statues and coins, as well, it may be presumed, as in painted images, it appears as if the ruler placed himself on a sort of long-term propagandistic diet program that lasted several years

(a)

(b)

(c)

Plate 14 Constantine and Licinius. While Licinius maintained a very strong tetrarchic image, that of Constantine moved slowly but definitely in new directions, as may be seen from these examples. (a) Constantine I, 310–13. *Credit*: *RIC* 6, Constantine I, Trier no. 871 (310–313); author's collection, photo courtesy of Classical Numismatic Group. (b) Constantine I in 323. *Credit*: *RIC* 7, Constantine I, Trier no. 389 (323); author's collection, photo courtesy of Classical Numismatic Group. (c) Licinius I. *Credit*: *RIC* 7, Licinius, Thessalonica no. 60 (312–13); author's collection, photo courtesy of Classical Numismatic Group.

until he emerged with an idealized form that might elicit comparisons with Trajan.[57] The first thing to go, in his case, was the tetrarchic beard with which he was usually, though not invariably, equipped prior to 313.[58] The beard was followed after 313 (he is still quite chubby on coins of that year) by the tetrarchic jowls, until all that remained were the large tetrarchic eyes in the form that predominated in the aftermath of his victory over Licinius in the first of their two civil wars.[59] Licinius began his tetrarchic life as a bulky gentleman with a beard and big eyes in the style of his colleagues. With the passing of time he got, if anything, fatter and more jovial in appearance, with a thicker beard.[60] The contrast in style was plainly a matter of deliberate choice on Constantine's part – he represented a new, youthful, order in art, just as he was presented in panegyrics as being about ten years younger than he actually was.[61] Licinius' move in the other direction may likewise be seen as deliberate: he represented the old order that had brought peace and salvation to the Roman Empire.

The theory of unified government, and the appearance of different regimes, perhaps did not matter all that much on a day-to-day basis. Provincials dealt with the power structure that was in place where they lived, and people were able to deal with the notion that there were portions of the empire that ran differently from the one that they lived in, as far as we can tell. There had always been more than one style of administration in the empire, as we saw in chapter 2, but the divisions of style in the early fourth century serve as an important reminder that what constituted the Roman Empire remained open to multiple interpretations.

The victory of Constantine

It is significant that Constantine and Licinius chose to rule without Caesars. There can be little doubt but that the reason for this was that each man harbored ambitions for the re-creation of dynastic as opposed to collegiate government. According to what may be the most reliable account (all leave something to be desired) the failure of an effort to reconcile these ambitions led to war in 316.[62] In 315 Constantia had borne Licinius a son, and Constantine appears to have sought to prevent any attempt on Licinius' part to name him Caesar by proposing that they should name Bassianus, the husband of Constantine's half-sister Anastasia, as Caesar with authority over Italy.[63] On August 7, 316, however, Fausta produced her first child, and Constantine suddenly accused Bassianus of plotting against him.[64] Bassianus was executed, and Constantine demanded that Licinius hand over Bassianus's brother, Senicio, for punishment as an accessory to his brother's crime. Licinius refused and allegedly had the statues and images of Constantine destroyed at Emona, an act that constituted a declaration of war.[65] Constantine immediately led a large expeditionary force deep into the Balkans.

The circumstances of the campaign leave little doubt but that Constantine was better prepared than Licinius and support the tradition in Zosimus that Constantine's ambitions were the true cause of the conflict.[66] Likewise, the dynastic maneuvering of the previous year gives the lie to Eusebius' assertion that the crucial issue was one of religion, and that Constantine had been moved to intervene in Licinius' territory by the latter's secret persecution of the church.[67] There is no real evidence that Licinius was ever hostile to the church: his wife was a devout Christian, and her spiritual adviser, Eusebius, bishop of Nicomedia, appears to have remained a powerful figure throughout the reign of her husband.[68]

Constantine was the aggressor from the start, though Licinius had clearly been aware that war was imminent, and had gathered a strong force of his own. Battle was joined at Cibalae, a little way east of Sirmium, on October 8, 316, and Constantine was victorious, driving Licinius back into Thrace, where he had collected a second army under the command of an officer named Valens, whom he raised to the rank of Augustus.[69] A second major battle was joined at Adrianople, where Constantine was again victorious.[70] It was then that Constantine's aggressive nature appears to have betrayed him. He had thought that Licinius would withdraw back toward the Hellespont, but he was wrong. Instead, Licinius retreated southwest in the direction of Beroea, placing him astride Constantine's lines of communication with the west.[71]

The two emperors now chose to negotiate, and it may be a sign of the fear that Constantine's unbroken string of military successes, extending from his early campaigns on the Rhine through his conquest of Italy to the Balkan blitzkrieg, instilled in Licinius that he was willing to agree to terms that were highly favorable to Constantine, despite holding the strategic advantage. According to the treaty, finalized at Serdica on March 1, 317, Licinius ceded all his European territories, aside from Thrace, to Constantine, and agreed to execute Valens.[72] New Caesars were appointed, confirming the principle of biological succession, as Constantine's two sons, Crispus and Constantine II, received the office along with Licinius' young son, Licinius II.[73]

The peace of 317 lasted for six years. We have no idea why it broke down when it did, though it would appear that the control of tribes north of the Danube was the proximate cause. Eusebius may reflect official Constantinian propaganda when he says that Licinius "called barbarian men to his support," while the *Rise of the Emperor Constantine* says

> When Constantine was at Thessalonica, the Goths broke through the neglected frontiers and, laying Thrace and Moesia to waste, began to collect booty. Then, overwhelmed by fear and the arrival of Constantine, they returned the captives to him and asked for

peace. But Licinius complained that he had broken the treaty because parts of his own territory had been secured by another.

(Or. 21)[74]

Another perspective on what is surely the same incident is offered by the Anonymous Continuator of Dio, who reports that

> Licinius refused to receive the gold coins on which Constantine had stamped the image of his victory over the Sarmatians, but melted them down and put the gold to other uses. Nor did he respond otherwise to those who came to him with complaints than that he did not wish barbarian products used in the commerce of his empire.

(Anon. post Dionem, FHG 4.199)

Taken together, these various comments suggest that Constantine charged Licinius with failure to maintain the security of the frontier, while Licinius complained that Constantine was violating the area of his sovereignty. If this was so, and that is plainly the claim that both the author of the *Rise of the Emperor Constantine* and the Anonymous Continuator of Dio put into his mouth, then it would seem to contradict the evidence examined above for interlocking legal administration. But to worry about such dissonance is perhaps to ignore the novelty of the situation as a whole, and to assume that there were hard and fast rules to which either could appeal. In Constantine's later version, Licinius was a disobedient junior Augustus.[75] In more general terms it may be easiest to see a single Roman Empire that supported two emperors: if they could get along, all was well and good. If not, then they would decide the matter on the battlefield, which is precisely what happened.

Both rulers appear to have been ready to fight in the summer of 324, with Constantine again taking the initiative. In the winter of that year he moved his court from Sirmium to Thessalonica so that he could lead an offensive along the route traversed by the Via Egnatia to the Dardanelles in the summer. The course of the subsequent maneuvers are lost to us, so that all we know is that on July 3, Constantine was north of the Via Egnatia in the valley of the Hebrus. Licinius had once again deployed his army at Adrianople, where, once again, he was defeated.[76] As Constantine proceeded to the siege of Byzantium, where Licinius had retired with the remains of his army, a large fleet under the nominal command of the Caesar Crispus won control of the sea.[77] At that point Licinius took flight, with his garrison, across the straits.[78] Byzantium could not hold out for long after that, and, in late August or early September, Constantine took advantage of his command of the sea to transport his army to Chalcedon on the Turkish side of the Bosphorus.[79] Licinius tried one last battle, at Chrysopolis, with what had by now become predictable results. His defeated army fled to

Nicomedia, and it was there that Constantia negotiated his surrender. Licinius was promised that he and his son would be allowed to live and was transported with that son into internal exile at Thessalonica. A year later he was charged with conspiracy and was executed, along with his son.[80]

Crispus emerged from the war with a mighty reputation as a soldier, and returned from the scene of his recent glory to Rome. What happened next is one of the great mysteries of the reign of Constantine. According to Zosimus, our most extensive source for these events,

> When he [Constantine] came to Rome, he was filled with arrogance, and thought fit to begin his impiety at home. Without any consideration for natural law he killed his son, Crispus, who, as I related before, had been considered worthy of the rank of Caesar, on suspicion of having had intercourse with his stepmother, Fausta. When Constantine's mother, Helena, was saddened by this atrocity and was inconsolable at the young man's death, Constantine as if to comfort her, applied a worse remedy than the disease: he ordered a bath to be overheated, and shut Fausta up in it until she was dead.
>
> (Zos. 2.29.1–2, trans. Ridley, adapted)[81]

This, according to Zosimus, led Constantine to feelings of such guilt that he sought a person who could purge him of his guilt, and so became a Christian. There is some reason to be skeptical about virtually everything, aside from the execution of Crispus, that he has to say. First and foremost is that Zosimus' source, here Eunapius, was not particularly well informed about the precise course of events: Crispus was not executed at Rome, but rather at Pola, where he had been summoned to answer whatever the charges were against him (which we cannot now know any better than did Aurelius Victor, who admits ignorance).[82] Gibbon long ago pointed to the discussion of Fausta in a panegyric delivered by the young Julian in honor of his uncle Constantius II: Rome is honored as her birthplace, and Fausta herself as the worthy mother of emperors.[83] There was no doubt a restoration of her memory under Constantius as a way of solidifying his claim to the throne. Still, the fact that she should appear at all makes it possible that she did not die in an overheated bathhouse, but rather that she disappeared into some sort of internal exile shortly after Crispus' demise. There she may have died, as Jerome put it, some three or four years later.[84] What people could know was simply that she had disappeared very suddenly from public life shortly after the death of Crispus was announced. Indeed, it is in a chronicle, composed as a continuation of that of Eusebius, that we may catch a glimpse of what it was that people were told (minus, it may be surmised, the identification of his faith): Crispus, the son of the emperor, died a Christian.[85]

Whatever happened, the destruction of Crispus does not look as if it can be put up to the dynastic ambitions of Fausta, who wanted him out of the way so that her own children could succeed to the throne: they were already Caesars and of the same rank as their half-brother. A sexual scandal is no more implausible than a political disagreement. What is perhaps more interesting is the statement by Eutropius that Constantine, "assailing his kin, killed his son, an outstanding man, and the son of his sister, a young man of pleasant nature, then his wife and, after that, numerous friends."[86] Both Fausta and Crispus had remained in the west while Constantine had based himself in the Balkans for virtually the entire period between the wars with Licinius. For them, the center of power remained in the west. For Constantine it was elsewhere: just after the defeat of Licinius, Constantine had founded a new city for himself at Byzantium, which he called Constantinople. The process was begun on November 8, 324.

The effect of his execution of Crispus and the removal of Fausta was to eliminate two figures who might have been powerful in the west after the center of government had shifted to the east. As for the scandal that surrounded their departures from the public stage, Gibbon may have seen the truth most clearly when he observed that "knowledge will appear gradually to encrease, as . . . means of information must have diminished."[87] As for Zosimus' story that Constantine sought the church as the only place where he could find forgiveness for the crimes he committed against his family, that at least is proven false by numerous documents that were produced in the previous decade. Constantine's intervention in an ecclesiastical controversy that had been raging in North Africa for years prior to his victory over Maxentius had already set the stage for an unprecedented involvement of the imperial government in religion. As acts of government, Constantine's interventions reveal him to be a ruler who masked caution behind the inflated rhetoric of the imperial chancery style. Despite much sound and fury, he does appear cautious in practice, and, insofar as that is true of the man as well as the ruler, he is not likely to have given way to a sudden outburst of misguided passion in assailing his wife and child. The political and personal demises of Crispus and Fausta are most likely acts of policy similar to those that resulted in the deaths of Maximian and Licinius.

The circumstances surrounding the deaths of Crispus and Fausta are significant for another reason as well. It has been surmised that Constantine was under considerable psychological pressure in the summer of 326, and that this is manifested in the rhetoric of a law banning a particular form of marriage that may have been employed to avoid the need to provide women with dowries.[88] The scheme tended to involve a faked abduction of the bride by her lover. In denouncing this practice Constantine stated,

> Since the watchfulness of parents is often frustrated by the stories and wicked persuasions of nurses, punishment shall threaten first such nurses whose care is proved to have been detestable and their discourses bribed, and the penalty shall be that the mouth and throat

381

of those who offered incitement to evil shall be closed by pouring in molten lead.

(*C. Th.* 9.24.1, trans. Pharr)

By looking at a text like this one, and ignoring the broader context of Constantine's behavior, it is possible to make him out to be a man of passions that he could not always control. But to look at a text like this one and to assume that Constantine composed it himself is a dangerous assumption. Constantine may have been moved by divine visions, but this was not, for a person of his age, a sign of irrationality. He emerges in other aspects of his administration as a careful planner, well able to work within institutions that already existed, and able to create space for his personal views within those institutions. He could be ruthless when crossed, as Maximian and Licinius found to their peril. So too, I think, did Crispus and Fausta. Their fates are an indication not that Constantine was becoming unbalanced (a view that would have serious consequences for any understanding of his reign), but rather that he remained very much the ruler he had been.

The New Rome

Even if the foundation of Constantinople was not the issue that led to the ruin of Crispus and Fausta, there can be little doubt that it marked a significant departure in the government of the empire. Although the empire had long been ruled from elsewhere, with the center of power residing at Nicomedia under Diocletian or at Sirmium under Galerius, Rome had remained a special place. Diocletian had recognized its importance through the celebration of his *vicennalia* there, and, in the years of Maxentius, it had been a true capital in its own right. Constantine had recognized this, at least implicitly, by taking over so many of Maxentius' buildings for himself. Thus the basilica of Maxentius had been transformed into one of Constantine, adorned with a colossal statue of the emperor. Constantine had added seats to the Circus Maximus, built new baths in a space between the Forum of Trajan and the baths of Diocletian, built a portico on the Campus Martius, and reworked Maxentius' shrine to Romulus, in a pattern that continued that of the arch. Through his building, Constantine dominated the city center.[89] What is striking in all of this, however, is that very little of it is new: only the baths and the portico represent new construction in the traditional mode, and all of this activity was concentrated in a very short period of time following Maxentius' defeat. After this period, in which Constantine also built two churches, his only significant building at Rome was St Peter's Basilica. When he left the city in 313, he did not return until the fateful year 326, and never again after that.

The construction of Constantinople was later taken as an act of enormous significance, marking a break with the past through the creation of an alternative capital. It is, however, difficult to reconcile such a substantial challenge to the past with Constantine's other policies, which aimed at reconciliation, and it is fair to say that the later tradition somewhat overstates what Constantine appears to have intended.[90] In the wake of the defeat of Licinius, Constantine had decided to found a new city to commemorate his victory. In doing so he had contemplated a number of possible sites: Serdica, where he had spent most of the previous decade, Ilium, Chalcedon, Thessalonica, and, finally, Byzantium.[91] It appears that he was on the verge of deciding upon Ilium when he was moved by a divine vision, which appears to have convinced him that it would be wrong to found a new Rome on the site of a city so closely linked with the old.[92] The result was that he chose Byzantium instead. With a man like Constantine, who plainly believed that he was in direct communication with the divinity at crucial moments in his life, it is perhaps best not to discount such stories, especially when he himself seems to have advertised the point in public.[93] If a vision sent him from Ilium to Byzantium, then too, we are told, he was guided by another vision in laying out the new limits of his city, which again is not an implausible scenario.[94] Constantine felt that his victories came from his God, and so then should his new city. The connection with the Divinity, and with victory, are such that it is difficult to see how rivalry with Rome could have been in view. The city was about Constantine, it was not about Rome.

Confusion about the relative position of Constantinople and Rome stems from a remark in the fifth-century ecclesiastical historian Socrates. He states that Constantine

> embellished the city that was once called Byzantium, surrounding it with great walls, decorating it with diverse monuments; and put it on an equal footing with Rome, the royal city, and gave it the new name of Constantinople, and ordained by a law, that the city should call itself the "New Rome." That law was inscribed on a stone stele, and Constantine placed it, during a public ceremony, in the place of the Strategeion beside an equestrian statue.
>
> (*Hist. eccl.* 1.16)

The problem with this statement is that it confuses rhetoric with reality. In 324 Constantine had written to Alexander of Alexandria, calling him the "bishop of the New Rome," by which he did not mean that Alexandria was now to be called Rome, but rather that Alexandria was an important city.[95] The only contemporary who says anything else of the sort is Publius Optatianus Porphyrius, an African senator, and a Christian, who would rise to high office within the next few years, but in his words Constantinople is "another Rome."[96] The rhetoric of these two statements represents a tendency to associate cities with the dignity of the old capital. It does not suggest that these cities actually bore that name. Constantinople was inaugurated as Constantinople on May 11, 330, not as the "New Rome." Later tradition might assert otherwise, but that is a matter that could perhaps not be fore-seen in 330.[97]

It was to dignify his new city as worthy of his dynasty, and to link it with the traditions of the earlier empire, that Constantine collected art with which to make it more splendid. Eusebius claimed that the collection of these artworks represented an effort to denigrate the polytheist gods of the past, but that statement, like so many others in his work, represents only one possible reading of what was going on, and a rather eccentric one at that.[98] If Constantine had intended to insult the gods, it is hardly likely that he would have placed the statues that he removed from their temples in the most prominent public places in the new city. Indeed, Constantine himself may not have played a particularly active role in selecting the art that arrived: a statue of Theophanes of Mytilene that was erected in the Hippodrome was most likely selected by the people of Mytilene themselves as a way of advertising their connection with the new city, and it may well be that cities were invited to send representative works for precisely this purpose.[99] Other works of art that arrived and were placed at significant locations included the Serpent Column from Delphi, erected in 479 BC to commemorate the Greek defeat of the Persians at the battle of Plataea, and an Augustan victory monument from Nicopolis.[100] From Rome itself came the famous statue of the wolf suckling Romulus and Remus, the image of the sow suckling piglets, and the statue of Hercules that Fabius Maximus had taken from Tarentum in the course of the Second Punic War.[101] Perhaps the most spectacular monument of all came from Egypt.

The story of Constantine's involvement in the removal of a porphyry column to his new city, and planned removal of an obelisk to the same place, may perhaps give the final lie to Eusebius' notion that the collection of antique art was intended as an insult to the gods. Constantine sent no less a figure than Nicagoras of Athens, the hierophant of the Eleusinian mysteries, in search of appropriate objects.[102] In the course of his trip, Nicagoras visited the Valley of the Kings, where he left two graffiti in the tomb of Ramses VI. On one he said:

> The Hierophant of the most holy mysteries at Eleusis, the son of Minucianus, an Athenian, examined the burial vaults many years after the divine Plato from Athens, admired them and gave thanks to the gods and to the most pious emperor Constantine for giving me the opportunity.
>
> (J. Baillet, *Inscriptions grecques et latines des Tombeaux des Rois ou Syringes à Thèbes* [Cairo, 1920–26], 1265)

On the wall opposite this text, Nicagoras also wrote:

384

In the seventh consulship of Constantine Augustus and the first consulship of Constantius Caesar. The Hierophant of the Eleusinian (Mysteries), Nicagoras, the son of Minucianus, an Athenian, examined the divine burial vaults, and admired them.

(Baillet, *Inscriptions grecques et latines des Tombeaux des Rois*, 1889)

There can be little doubt but that this most devout polytheist saw himself as the agent of an emperor whose bidding he was glad to be doing: there is nothing here to suggest that he saw Constantinople as a Christian capital. He must rather have seen the city as another imperial capital. So too may have the philosopher Sopater whom Eunapius says Constantine summoned to the city's inauguration, before the two men fell out, with fatal consequences for Sopater.[103] To return, however, to Nicagoras, he found his obelisk, at Karnak. In light of what happened next, it is perhaps ironic that the object in question was commissioned by Thutmoses III and erected by his successor. It took a long time to move an obelisk, and in this case it was more than a decade before it reached Alexandria, at which point Constantine had changed his mind about what should be done with it, and ordered instead that it be sent to Rome on a specially constructed boat. In all likelihood, he intended to offer this monument as a sign of his continuing appreciation of the old capital when it became clear that he would not be there himself to join the celebration of the beginning of his thirtieth year in power.[104] As that year opened, Constantine was preparing for a war with Persia, which made it advisable for him to stay in the east. He would die a few months into 337, and the obelisk would remain in Alexandria for another twenty years until his son, Constantius, saw to the fulfillment of his design.[105] At that time, as Ammianus Marcellinus remarked,

Constantine thought it a matter of little importance if he tore it from its seat, rightly thinking that he committed no impiety if he dedicated the marvel that he had removed from one temple at Rome, which is a temple for the whole world.

(Amm. Marc. 17.4.13)

Ammianus' comment reflects what was no doubt the sentiment of men like Nicagoras as well: no impiety was committed if a sacred object were taken to an imperial capital where it could be appreciated by all. It was a sign of respect for the object. In Constantine's case, the dedication at Rome could be seen as balancing his construction of the great church of Saint Peter in the later years of his reign.[106]

A further appeal of the obelisk as a decoration for either capital would have been its connection with the sun god. In 324, Constantine would declare that the "Sacred Day of the Sun" should be free of public business throughout the empire, and he would continue to advertise his special relationship with the sun god in other works of art (reflected also in the imagery of his coins).[107] This same devotion to the sun would be enshrined atop a massive porphyry column that was erected in the forum that Constantine dedicated in the heart of the new city.[108] In this case the pillar of the monument came to Rome, where it may have been commissioned for a Diocletianic monument that was never completed.[109] By way of contrast with the monument that Nicagoras had discovered at Karnak, it appears that there was a special need for the object. The porphyry column would be the centerpiece of an area on display when the city was dedicated, and so it was shipped out in what may have been near record time – three years – to be adorned with a statue of the emperor in the guise of Apollo. The issue of speed also comes up in the context of the statue. Eusebius said it was a new one; others say that it was an old one (from Troy) in a new place.[110] In all likelihood it did not much matter at the time. What mattered is that the monument in the heart of Constantinople could be read either way.[111] The decorative pattern of the new capital shows that, while the city was intended to commemorate the supremacy of Constantine, it was not intended to do so to the obvious detriment of Rome, whose symbols were joined to those of other cities as a sign of respect for tradition. Nor was it designed as a city that was intended as an advertisement for the emperor's Christianity.

The imperial aristocracy

The foundation of Constantinople represents the culmination of the process that we have traced throughout the third century: the transfer of power from the traditional aristocracy of the Antonine age to a new aristocracy that owed its power to positions at court. Unlike the situation that obtained in the later years of the third century, whereby new groups coming to power allied themselves with the traditional aristocracy of the capital, the traditional aristocracy was now cut off from direct access to the emperor.[112] Members of this aristocracy could still be included in the ranks of the grandees of the new empire, but it was only through imperial patronage. Members of the traditional aristocracy could advance into the charmed circle of imperial power if they showed the emperor that they could be of service; there is no longer a suggestion that he might seek alliances with these people because he needed their help in solidifying his position. What is more, the upper echelons of the senatorial aristocracy came to be filled with men whose origins lay outside the traditional senatorial order. This later development was a feature of the gradual restructuring of the governing class during the fourth century. The senatorial order far outgrew the bounds imposed by the old republican magistracies, and those magistracies, with the exception of the consulship, now became little more than civic offices at Rome. Provincial governors were now referred to as *praesides* or *iudices*, leaving behind the old titles of republican government save in the case of a few select provinces where very senior members of the senate could serve as proconsuls. To be a senator was to be recognized as a member of a group that stood at the pinnacle of the socioeconomic and political hierarchy.[113] Entrance into this group was governed by imperial recognition of status, doing away with the now antiquated distinction between senator and equestrian. Thus a man could become a senator if he had been a *vicarius*; he did not have to be a senator to become a *vicarius*.

The Constantinian system made sense in that it formalized a structure of offices to link those that had arisen through the patrimonial system with those descended from the republican. As such it is another symbol of the triumph of the patrimonial style over the republican, as the offices of the latter were subsumed within the new system and placed on a par with offices held by palace officials. The results of these changes were illustrated most clearly at Constantine's funeral in 337, where we are told that

> The commanders of the whole army, the *comites*, and all the ruling class, who were bound by law to pay homage to the emperor first, making no change in their usual routine, filed past at the required times and saluted the emperor on the bier with genuflections after his death in the same way as when he was alive. After these chief persons the members of the Senate and all those of official rank came and did the same, and after them crowds of people of all ranks with their wives and children came to look.
>
> (Euseb. *Vit. Const.* 67.1, trans. Hall)

The order of adoration plainly illustrates the relationship outwards from the palace to the senate and other officeholders, and it was now clearly possible to equate those with senatorial rank and other officeholders. In the new system, praetorian prefects retained the rank of *vir eminentissimus*.[114] Senior equestrian officials of the next rank, such as the *praefectus annonae* at Rome and *vicarii*, attain the title of *vir clarissimus*, once reserved for senators.[115] Provincial governors, provincial military commanders, diocesan and provincial fiscal officials, and the like retain the rank of *vir perfectissimus*.

Perhaps the most significant step that Constantine took, in addition to his award of a rank for equestrians that was superior to that of senators, was his regularization of the position of imperial "companions" or *comites*, whose significance is so well illustrated in the passage quoted above. The title of *comes* has, of course, a very long history prior to Constantine, with all manner of person claiming, or being awarded, that title, as a mark of status equivalent to the equally loosely applied title of imperial "friend" (*amicus*). In an act that has rightly been seen as an effort to fuse the court aristocracy with the senate, he formalized the order of imperial *comites*, dividing the order into three grades depending on the level of service that a person had performed.[116] This distinction, which was ultimately (if not immediately) reflected in the transformation of certain senior titles such as that of *magister rei privatae* to *comes rei privatae*, served again to indicate that the actual power structure of the empire was that of the court.[117] Birth still mattered, but it now became only one of a number of factors that could lead to great distinction.

The transformation of the bureaucracy, which was an ongoing process throughout Constantine's reign rather than the product of a sudden program of reform, had a human side in that Constantine was also reshaping the membership of the governing class, perhaps not so radically as his later critics would have it, but still noticeably. To gain some impression of just what was happening, it is worth looking again at the holders of the office of *praefectus urbi* at Rome. This group offers a useful indication of the direction of imperial policy, if for no other reason than that the holders of this office are unusually well attested members of the aristocracy. The first three *praefecti urbi* were all men who had held the office under Maxentius. Indeed, the man holding office when Constantine entered the city was the Annius Anullinus whom Maxentius had appointed as a good-luck charm on the day that he gave battle at the Milvian Bridge. Anullinus remained in office for just over a month, which was perhaps just long enough to make the point that allies of Maxentius were not automatically considered enemies of the new regime.[118] Perhaps as a way of making this point even more forcefully, Anullinus' successor was Aradius Rufinus, his immediate predecessor, and a man whose senatorial ancestors could be traced back at least as far as the reign of Gallienus.[119] He was in turn succeeded by the man who had preceded him as *praefectus urbi* under Maxentius, C. Caeonius Rufius Volusianus, a man of great age, having begun his career under Carus and won distinction under Maxentius as commander of the army that had suppressed the revolt of Alexander in North Africa in 311.[120]

If the first three prefects represent an effort on Constantine's part to reconcile the Roman aristocracy, those appointed subsequently are distinguished in a very different way. Vettius Rufinus, who was elevated to the prefecture in 315, was sufficiently trusted by Constantine that he was sent east to serve as a provincial governor under Licinius. Other concerns appear significant with later prefects. Thus the Acilius Severus who was consul in 323 and *praefectus urbi* in 325–26 may be identified with the Severus who may have been Constantine's praetorian prefect in the Balkans in 322–23. Even if that identification must remain conjectural, it is no conjecture that he was from Spain, and a Christian.[121] His predecessor in office, Lucerius Verinus, arrived at that position through adlection among the consulars after a term as *vicarius* of North Africa. He was also Christian.[122] Among the members of the traditional aristocracy who became *praefecti urbi*, three of them, Anicius Julianus,

Anicius Paulinus, and Petronius Probianus, who held office from 326 to 333, were Christian, as was another man (from North Africa), Publius Optatianus Porphyrianus (in 329 and 333).[123] Two further prefects, Caeionius Julianus Camenius and Amnius Manius Caesonius Nicomachus Anicius Paulinus (333–35), had both served in the east in the wake of Licinius' defeat, the former being proconsul of Asia in 325–27, the later being proconsul of Asia and the Hellespont a year earlier, posts that suggest that ability to serve Constantine in challenging times was more important than family connection.[124] One man who does not immediately fit this pattern is Valerius Maximus Basilius, descendant of the *praefectus urbi* of 255 and consul of 256.[125] But he served for six years in this post, years when Constantine was in the Balkans and Crispus was at Trier (319–23). The abnormal length of his service marks him as a special favorite of the regime, as does the strong possibility that his son was the Valerius Maximus who, having been consul in 327, went on to be praetorian prefect for nearly a decade after his consulship. This too is a sign of a truly significant change in the way that a senatorial career was perceived.[126] In the first three centuries AD a successful equestrian official might be adlected into the senate as a mark of distinction at the end of his career, and then, perhaps, move into some senatorial offices. It would then have been unthinkable for a senator who had achieved the consulship to hold an equestrian office. Again, in Constantinian terms, the career of Maximus is perhaps a logical development in light of other trends – and that is the true mark of Constantine's style: he made what had once been unthinkable, possible. Prior to his reign it is likewise unthinkable that a practicing Christian could have risen to the rank that the four Christian *praefecti urbi* did. So too it is the case that in the 330s, two of the four praetorian prefects were also Christian.[127]

As he restructured the aristocracy, breaking down the old division between senatorial and equestrian offices, he was faced with yet another problem: what to do about Constantinople. To leave the city with no senate would be to treat it as no more than another imperial seat, a grander version of Trier, Antioch, or Nicomedia. Such was not Constantine's plan. The very name of the new city proclaimed greater pretensions to majesty for it. His solution to the problem was very much in line with his other policies: he would avoid direct insult, while at the same time making a change that would serve his main end: the exaltation of himself, and what, by the mid-320s, he had come to see as his dynasty. The city would become a residence for senators who were closely linked with himself.

The point of Constantine's action, to create a center for his dynasty without infringing the rights of Rome, was lost on many later historians. Sozomen, an ecclesiastical historian of the fifth century, wrote that "he founded another *bouleutêrion*, which he called a senate (*synklêtos*), and assigned to it the same offices and festivals as the old one at Rome."[128] This statement is repeated in a variety of later Byzantine chroniclers and is, strictly speaking, false. The author of a description of the world, who composed under Constantine, contrasted the old capital with the new city on the grounds that Rome "has a very great senate, composed of rich men," and the *Rise of the Divine Constantine* states that "he even created a senate of the second rank there, and called its members the *clari*."[129] The body of which the author of the *Rise* speaks appears to be the amplified city council of Byzantium, whose members received a new title by virtue of their connection with the emperor's city, and who were eligible to hold a praetorship that was reserved for them so that they might join the *clarissimi*.[130] In addition, Constantine rewarded members of the senate who chose to live in his city with houses and other privileges, as he also rewarded important members of the court who resided in his company. The result was a body that could develop into something more splendid (as it did), but which was kept from offering a direct challenge to the ancient body at Rome. It was his son, Constantius, seeking to amplify his position after his accession in 337, who first appears to have addressed this group as being on a par with the senate at Rome, and then, some seventeen years after his father's death, formally elevated members of this senate to the rank of *clarissimus*.[131]

The technical aspects of the creation of the Constantinopolitan senate, while significant as an illustration of the way that Constantine behaved, are perhaps less significant than the social aspects. Thus the existence of the new imperial residence continued what must already have been a well-established pattern of shipping various foodstuffs that had once been sent to Rome to other imperial seats – it is inconceivable that regular grain shipments from Egypt to Rome continued in the time of Maxentius. So too the creation of new centers of power in the east must have kept eastern dignitaries closer to home.[132] This was not so much a new pattern (it had certainly been the case for two decades) but rather a continuation of an existing pattern that would otherwise have changed if Constantinople, or another capital, had not been built in the east.[133] The comments of Eusebius upon Constantine's conduct must be read in light of Eusebius' general lack of concern for events in the west, for when he describes the emperor's behavior, he does so from the perspective of an easterner:

> One who sought favor of the Emperor could not fail to obtain his request, nor was anyone who hoped for generous treatment disappointed in his expectations. Some received money in abundance, others goods; some acquired posts as prefects, others senatorial rank, others that of consuls; very many were designated governors; some were appointed *comites* of the first order, others of the second, others of the third. Similarly many thousands more shared honors as *clarissimi* or with a wide range of other titles; for in order to promote more persons the Emperor contrived different distinctions.
>
> (*Vit. Const.* 4.1.1–2, trans. Hall)

Those who later despised Constantine told a very similar tale. Zosimus notes the houses that he built for senators who accompanied him, and others would complain of his prodigious spending on his supporters.[134] Constantine saw clearly enough that the security of his regime depended upon the willing acquiescence of those who had served his rivals. It may have taken a divine vision to show him just where he should center this policy, but the policy itself was part and parcel of the settlement with Licinius' part of the empire. The centrality of Constantine's beneficence to the regime perhaps has no better witness than the young Julian's panegyric on the subject of his uncle Constantius. Although Julian would later be harshly critical of Constantine on precisely these grounds, his statement in this context must be taken as a statement of official policy:

> He showed such goodwill to his subjects that the soldiers remember his gifts and great-hearted generosity so that they worship him like a god. . . . When he became lord of the whole empire, when, stemming from the greed of the tyrant, like a drought, there was a great lack of money, and there was an enormous quantity of wealth collected in the corners of the palace, he ordered the doors unlocked, flooding the land with wealth.
>
> (*Or.* 1.8 a–b)

Urban elites

It may seem logical to assume that the progressive reformation of the central government under Diocletian and his successors must have had a direct impact upon the cities of the Roman Empire, and that the foundation of Constantinople had some direct impact upon the urban ruling classes of the empire. It is, however, impossible to demonstrate what may seem, at first glance, to be an obvious postulate. Like many obvious postulates, it over-simplifies the complexities of urban life, and the complex interactions between different orders of society. To move from the court to the cities of the empire is to encounter one of the classic issues of Braudelian historiography: how to relate the history of short-term developments to those of the long term. The foundation of Constantinople did nothing to alter the basic parameters of life in the cities of the west, or, indeed, in the west as a whole.

Wealth was still essentially a matter of landholding and the ability to get peasants to pay their rent. New wealth could still be created through long-distance trade both throughout the Mediterranean and with Asia, or through government service. If there was a single radical change that can be associated with any political act, it was the collapse of local currencies in the Greek east around AD 275. Aurelian's monetary policy was probably the result of his desire to have his coinage, and only his coinage, circulated throughout his empire.[135] As opposed to an economic cause for the disappearance of these coinages, we may instead be faced with the possibility that the imperial mints that supported them rapidly ceased to do so after the introduction of the new coinage, that it was a political rather than an economic act. The effect of the Aurelianic hyperinflation was probably felt throughout the empire, and it may well have ruined the foundations that endowed local festivals throughout the empire. In Egypt, where it is possible to trace the relationship between town and country in more detail than elsewhere, there do seem to have been significant changes in the way that urban elites spent their time, withdrawing from the villages and concentrating their activities in larger towns.[136] A consequence of this move was that villages lost much of their independence and were more closely integrated into the economic life of cities. Was this true elsewhere in the empire? The villages in Anatolia, Syria, and North Africa that we saw in chapter 1 were still there. Some, like Orcistus in Phrygia, were able to become cities; others might still aspire to the status of *metrokomai*.[137] One thing that we do know is that many of these villages were producing large marketable surpluses of crops and were more heavily implicated in the monetary economy than ever before.[138] Perhaps the withdrawal of aristocrats into larger towns was a sign of the strength rather than the weakness of the rural economy.

Prices appear to have stabilized in the wake of the Aurelianic reform by the early 280s, and market forces appear to have brought about a relatively stable relationship between gold and the bullion *antoninianus* (a copper coin with a silver wash) that was the basic medium of exchange, so that a pound of gold was valued at roughly sixty thousand *antoniniani*; or, since gold coins were struck at the rate of sixty to the pound, one gold coin was worth one thousand of the bullion coins. In 293, possibly as a way of promoting the authority of the new tetrarchy, Diocletian had introduced a new system of coinage that included five coins, the aureus/solidus, a gold coin that continued to weigh one-sixtieth of a pound, the *argenteus*, a silver coin, struck at 96 to the pound, *laureatus* A (in modern parlance; it was also known as the *follis*), a copper coin with a silver wash struck at the rate of 32 to the pound, the *radiatus*, a small copper coin struck at the rate of 108 to the pound without a silver wash, and a smaller copper coin, known in modern parlance as the *laureatus* B, struck at the theoretical weight of 192 to the pound.[139] This system was complicated because the coins tended to be struck at less than their nominal weight, and values were still measured in denarii, with the result that the Diocletianic coins were tariffed as follows:

1 *aureus/solidus* = 1,000 denarii
1 *argenteus* = 100 denarii
1 *laureatus* A = 25 denarii
1 *radiatus* = 4 denarii
1 *laureatus* B = 2 denarii[140]

By 301, as we have seen, Diocletian's monetary system was in serious trouble, leading to the rather arbitrary edict in which he halved the denarius values of his silver coinage, while, it appears, attempting to support the price of gold at the official rate. The official rate that he was supporting appears to have been about 20 percent below the market rate. Beneath all of this, the driving principle of Diocletianic policy appears to have been to reestablish a silver currency – the silver content of the *argenteus* was 95 percent – which was not in fact needed. The rationale behind the policy may simply have been that silver coinage was traditional and should therefore exist in his restored empire.

In the years after Diocletian's retirement, there were various changes in the coinage system.[141] Production of the smaller coins in his system – the *radiatus* and *laureatus* B – appears to have ceased around the time of his abdication, and there was a gradual reduction in the weight of the *laureatus* A. In Constantine's part of the empire it was struck at the rate of 40 to the pound in early 307, at 48 to the pound by the end of the year, in 310 at 72 to the pound, and in 313 at 96 to the pound. Maxentius' mints produced the coin at the same rates at did those of Constantine, while Galerius maintained the weight of the *laureatus* at 48 to the pound. In 313, Licinius joined Constantine in using the standard of 96 to the pound. In 330, Constantine reduced the weight of the *laureatus*, or *nummus*, as it was now called, to 132 to the pound. The reduction in the weight of this coin would continue, in stages, for the rest of the century.

What difference did all these changes in the style of coinage make? We simply do not know, and that may be significant in and of itself. Our knowledge of the transformation of ancient coinage is based upon the coins themselves, and our ability to trace price fluctuations is largely based upon the evidence of Egyptian papyri. Historians of the time did not comment on such things, and it is interesting that this includes people like Lactantius and Eusebius, who might be counted upon to denounce any practice that was regarded as harmful. Aside from three references on papyri – in one of which a person with advance warning that a retariffing by Licinius, to make his coinage conform to that of Constantine, was imminent, decides to spend the old money that he has – we cannot watch people reacting.[142] The one person whom we do see reacting is seeking a short-term advantage rather than trying to escape personal ruin. It therefore seems likely that the changes in coinage were not, in and of themselves, signs of economic trauma.

Rather than looking at changes in the system of coinage in simple economic terms, it might be better to follow the lead of a later fourth-century author, who placed them in the context of broader social change, writing that

> In the time of Constantine extravagant expenditure assigned gold
> in place of bronze, which was previously considered of great value,

to petty commercial transactions. The growth of this avarice is thought to stem from this: when the great quantity of gold, silver and precious stones that was deposited in temples in ancient times was released to the public, it excited the desire of all for spending and acquiring. While the expenditure of bronze, which, as I have said, was stamped with the imperial image, was already vast and heavy, yet from some sort of blind folly there ensued an even greater desire for spending gold, which was thought to be more valuable. From this store of gold the houses of the powerful were filled, and their splendor was enhanced to the ruin of the poor, the poorer classes, of course, were held down by violence.

(Anon. De rebus bellicis 2.1–2, trans.
Thompson, adapted)

What lies behind this statement is the fact that, in the course of the fourth century, values ceased to be expressed in terms of denarii and came to be expressed, exclusively, in terms of gold.[143] This is reasonably connected with the expanding class of imperial administrators, who were paid in gold and who tended to convert payments that they owed (and were collected from their tenants) from kind to cash.

The switch over in the expression of value from silver to gold is a sign of a new relationship between civic and imperial aristocracies.[144] The expansion of government made it possible for more people to achieve positions away from their cities, to build connections at court, to bring the values of the court closer to home. Was this a problem, and did it contribute to the decline of ancient civilization, as the author whose words are quoted here suggests?[145]

The view that increased access of local elites to imperial office harmed cities assumes that the relative stability of the government in the first and second centuries AD was the normative state in Mediterranean history. This is a very dubious proposition indeed. Governments in the pre-Augustan age were inherently unstable. The dependence of early imperial government on a relatively small governing class (albeit one that was highly permeable) may have turned pent-up ambitions for advancement back onto the local level, an almost unnatural situation in which local preeminence could make up for the small number of offices open outside of the civic context. The one thing that appears to be true of the expansion of government under Diocletian and Constantine is that it depended upon the desire of local notables to play a greater role on the imperial stage. There seems to have been no shortage of people who had the wealth that would enable them to aspire to higher rank. Indeed, as the church would also open up a wide variety of new avenues to power, both among members of the upper classes and in the countryside, it appears that the Diocletianic–Constantinian state was more socially fluid than had been the Antonine. The ability of local notables to take advantage of these opportunities may, however, be not so much the result of the short-term changes in government, as of long-term trends that had concentrated property in the hands of the curial class. The novel feature of the policy of fourth-century emperors was that a man who obtained the rank of *perfectissimus* was permanently exempt from performing the civic services *(munera)* that were required of members of the curial classes in their hometowns (this was not true in the earlier empire, where only senators and members of certain professions had immunity).

Although we do not know exactly when more extensive grants of immunity from civic *munera* were introduced, there is enough evidence to make it clear that it took place in the last decade of the third century. The earliest explicit, dated reference is on a papyrus from Oxyrhynchus dating to AD 299. The text is an appeal by one Aurelius Plutarchus, who is trying to protect his immunity from the town council that was trying to appoint him one of the *dekaprôtoi*, the group that was directly responsible for ensuring the payment of the city's tax assessment.[146] The fact that the town council should attempt such a thing might suggest that Plutarchus' exemption was a relatively new innovation, and we can be certain, at the very least, that Diocletian was responsible, since there exists a rescript of Carus that states that his equestrian officials are responsible for their civic *munera*.[147] It might be possible to suggest a somewhat earlier date than 299 (or thereabouts) if it is correct to date prior to 293 a rescript in which Diocletian writes that a man who, although having immunity from civic *munera*, nonetheless agrees to hold one, does not thereby lose his immunity.[148] But the case for such an early date is not compelling, and there is another text dating to either 299 or 300 that preserves the record of a hearing at Antioch at which Diocletian told members of the town council that

> Immunity from personal and civic *munera* has been granted by us to certain ranks, which includes those who are either former *protectores* or former *praepositi*. They may not, therefore, be summoned to personal or civic *munera*.
>
> (*CJ* 10.48.2)[149]

The nature of this inquiry, as is also the case with Plutarchus, makes it look as if town councils were trying to press the limits of the new policy. That being the case, it would appear that the exemption fits in with other Diocletianic reforms in the wake of his victory over Persia. Why did he do it? We cannot know for certain, but it is most unlikely that it was a step that was designed to offend town councils or to weaken their financial well-being.

As we have seen, Diocletian's monetary system appears to have been victimized by a bout of hyperinflation in the late 290s, to which he responded in 301 with the decree setting new values for imperial coins and the *Edict on Maximum Prices*.[150] The combination of currency reform and the edicts of 301 suggests not only that Diocletian was concerned about the health of the imperial system of coinage, but also, as the *Edict on Maximum Prices* makes abundantly clear, the connection between his system of coinage and the viability of the wages paid to his servants. In this context, it is perhaps best to see immunity from a civic *munus* as a way of enhancing compensation for imperial officials. It may well be doubted that Diocletian foresaw that his decision might mean that people would abandon their cities for the imperial service, or that he was opening up a whole new area of potential corruption as people sought to purchase these offices in order to escape local responsibilities.

A letter that Licinius wrote to the provincial assembly of Bithynia in 317 shows that Diocletian's action had precisely the effect suggested above.

> Persons who have performed imperial service in the palace and those to whom provinces have been entrusted and those who deservedly obtained the rank of *perfectissimus* or *egregiatus* by merit of the service in the most august administrative offices, and also those persons who have been established as decurions or chief decurions *(principales)* and have performed all the compulsory public services of their municipality, shall enjoy that rank which is granted them. But if a decurion should obtain the rank of *perfectissimus*, of *ducenarius*, of *centenarius*, or *egregriatus* by use of venal patronage, because he desires to evade the duties of his own municipal council, he shall surrender the imperial *codicilli* and be returned to his own status.
>
> (CTh. 12.1.5, trans. Pharr, adapted)[151]

This extract is part of what appears to have been a much longer text in which Licinius spelled out eligibility for imperial ranks according to time and location of service, showing that he did not regard the movement of decurions into higher ranks as a special problem in and of itself. Indeed, his language appears to cover three categories of former decurions: men who had entered imperial office after having "performed all the compulsory public services of their municipality," men who had enrolled in the imperial service legitimately, and men who had had themselves enrolled through bribery so as to avoid compulsory public services. The last category could only exist if imperial service were seen as offering some sort of advantage to compensate for the cost.

With the defeat of Licinius, Constantine appears to have recognized that the exemption from *munera* had the potential to be a major problem for the cities of the empire, and began to move as rapidly as he could away from it. In a section of a long letter on the privileges of soldiers that he wrote to Maximus, the *vicarius* of Oriens, in 325 he stated,

Since we have granted to different persons the privilege of being assigned to the legions or cohorts or of being restored to the imperial service, if any person should produce in court such a special grant of this sort, inquiry should be made as to whether he is of a decurial family or whether he has been previously nominated to the municipal council, and if any such thing should be proved, he shall be returned to his own municipal council and municipality. This general rule must be observed with reference to all men who have been previously approved and are holding office in the imperial service, or who have been restored and are protected by the oath of imperial service, or shall be approved henceforth through the use of patronage.

(*CTh.* 12.10, trans. Pharr, adapted)[152]

The crucial phrases here relate to people who have been "restored" to the imperial service. Constantine's letter appears to have been written in response to an inquiry by Maximus about people returning to the government who had not fulfilled the municipal duties to which they would have been liable had they not entered the imperial service under the less restrictive rules of Licinius. At the same time he extends his ruling to cover all who were currently in his service. Nor was this just the case in the area ruled by Licinius, for a few months later Constantine wrote to Constantius, his son, who was then holding the praetorian prefecture, telling him that he should likewise remove men from the imperial service who were not of a rank that required a further service of them, the burdensome *primipili pastus*.[153] The *pastus*, which is first attested in the reign of Caracalla, was the requirement that men who retired with the rank of *primuspilus* should be personally responsible for the delivery of rations to the nearest garrison.[154] This provision was enforced with extraordinary rigor throughout the third century – Carus stated that a widow's dowry could be attached to this service if all other resources were exhausted – and it appears to have been an even more onerous duty than any compulsory service required by a city, especially when the expense was compounded by the requirement that a substantial gift be given to the official who received the rations.[155]

The *pastus* is but one of a number of imposts that were levied upon rank or occupation, several of them new with Constantine. The old *aurum coronarium*, the "gold for crowns," was sent by cities to the emperor on his accession or in response to important news from the palace.[156] It was now joined by a special tax for members of the senate at Rome, the *follis*, a regular impost that fell upon their estates.[157] The order as a whole was further assessed a special tax on the model of the *aurum coronarium*, the *aurum oblaticium*.[158] Inhabitants of cities who practiced trades where fees were collected in money were assessed, as of 314 (probably), for the *auri lustralis collatio*.[159] Two of these three taxes – the *aurum oblaticium* and the *auri lustralis collatio*

– were, in theory, to be paid to commemorate imperial successes and anniversaries, but were, in effect, taxes on status, which is what, quite explicitly, the *follis* was as well. Persons freed from one sort of tax, civic *munera*, were thus taxed more heavily by the central government. Ability to pay these fees acted as a guarantee that a person had the wealth to justify his status, for it would appear that the burden of taxes to the central government, which were continuous, was greater than the burden of *munera*.

On the practical side, these various money taxes reflect a central government that needed to find a way to raise specie after having made the taxes on land and capita payable in kind. They also repair the inelasticity of the earlier imperial tax structure in that the palace could (and did) set the level at which the *aurum oblaticium*, and, it seems, the *aurum coronarium*, was paid.[160] But on an ideological level they reflect a notion that the urban elites of the empire had a direct interest in the success of the emperor – a further reification of the tetrarchic formulation of the relationship between the emperor and provincials. When the emperor was successful, his people should reward him; when people advanced to greater dignity within his service, they should show their gratitude by paying him. So long as people did not, by virtue of advancing in status, try to avoid their previous obligations, this was fine with him.

It appears that the exchange of money for status remained acceptable to the emperor's subjects, who were willing either to bribe their way into a new status or follow the approved route of serving, and paying, at the same time. The substantial increase in offices that began with Diocletian and continued throughout his reign gave far greater opportunity to those who wished some rank outside of their community. So long as the aspiring decurion was of good moral character, he was welcome in the imperial administration.[161] For Constantine, as for Diocletian, there was no a priori reason why a person should not aspire to the highest possible rank. It was Constantius II, in 354 (probably), who would state that "a decurion should not aspire to the senate," though he allowed that those who had already obtained that honor should retain it.[162] Constantius II appears to have been somewhat more snobbish than his father – there was no reason to object to these men entering the senate except that they were not born to the order – but it is his observation that those who had already obtained senatorial rank should keep it that really matters. Again it is a statement that a reasonable person who had completed his curial duties might aspire to the senate at the end of a subsequent career in the imperial service.

The association of money and status might also lead in other directions. There is some reason, as the anonymous author quoted above says, to think that the government of the fourth century was more readily corrupted than was the government of the second century. Did the association between status and the ability to pay for it make officials more venal? It is hard to tell, for, of course, we do not have the sort of evidence that enables genuine comparison between the second and fourth centuries.[163] On the other hand, even if one assumes that there was no actual change in the register of official greed and corruption between the second and fourth centuries, the fact that there was simply more government in the fourth century means that the impact of official corruption was felt more keenly, more of the time. Certainly there had been enough trouble prior to the reign of Diocletian with people obtaining rescripts to support their case from an official in the palace, thus effectively corrupting the petition-and-response system, to suggest the need for the work of Hermogenianus and Gregorius. Equally certainly, not much time passed before emperors were again deploring the fact that the system was open to abuse: for instance there is a Constantinian edict of 315 stating that rescripts that are against the law shall not be valid.[164] He would later write that people could not cite annotations on their petitions in the absence of an actual rescript.[165] Failure to change corrupt behavior in the past does not mean that there was an increase in it. What does appear to be significant, at least at a first glance, is a great increase in the number of cases where a person could be tortured, no matter what his status.[166] On one view, it is possible that this would reflect greater brutality, and thus greater possibility for corruption. This is not improbable, but it is not a necessary conclusion. The increase in the size of government, and the closure of the social gap between municipal magistrates and governors, may have meant that officials needed harsher penalties so that they could get people to listen to them. There are some cases where a governor's career was set back by excessive use of force.[167] At the end of 329 Constantine wrote to the praetorian prefect, Maximus,

> It is fitting that governors of provinces, if a powerful and insolent person should arise, and they are able neither to punish, examine, nor sentence that person, should refer his name either to me or to your gravity. In this way it will be provided that care will be taken for public discipline and the oppressed.
>
> (*CTh.* 1.16.4)

Two years later, Constantine issued an edict forbidding governors from hearing legal cases in private and stating that he would pay attention to public acclamations so that he would know whether or not an official was behaving justly.[168] These two effusions, like others deploring the fact that people bought imperial office, do not necessarily reflect greater corruption; rather they illustrate the complexities of imperial administration.[169]

The expansion of government that led to the opening up of new places had the coincidental effect of narrowing the gap between local and imperial officials. Combined with the fact that the provinces that governors ruled were much smaller than in the past, this meant that there was a greater tendency for governors to become more deeply involved in the minutiae of local affairs.

The governor was no longer a grand figure who visited but once a year and, as a senator, commanded personal resources that were off the scale of the typical magnate. Governors now found themselves more likely to be confronted with men of equal rank within the cities that they governed and more likely to stumble into situations that were more complex than they seemed. Government may or may not, as a consequence, have become more or less corrupt, and, given the prevalence of charges of corruption at all periods of Roman history, to adopt such a line may be to ask the wrong question. The real question may perhaps be this: Did the way that the imperial government did business with its subjects change in any significant way in the early fourth century? Here the answer may be yes, for the closer the governor came to the governed, the more personal the relationship became. As the gap closed, the lower levels of government got further and further from the palace, and more opportunities opened for ambitious officials to create patronage networks for themselves within their various areas of government.[170] In time the emperor appears to be less in charge of the government of the empire, which, in turn, appears to have become liable to control by various interest groups with whom he had to negotiate.

11

CONSTRUCTING CHRISTIANITY IN AN IMPERIAL CONTEXT

Constantine reformed the government of the empire through a combination of progressive developments within existing institutions and one radical step, the foundation of Constantinople. So too it was through a combination of small, progressive steps within traditional institutions, and increasingly radical steps within a new one – the Christian church – that Constantine reshaped the intellectual landscape of his realm.

Just as the tale of his conversion could change over time, so too did Constantine. His devotion to Christianity was undoubtedly sincere, for he would not otherwise have raised his children to be Christians.[1] But sincerity and comprehension are not the same thing. There can be little doubt but that Constantine's understanding of what it meant to be a Christian evolved between the moment that he decided that the Christian God had sent him a vision portending victory in 312, the termination of coin issues in the 320s equating himself with Sol, and his assertion that he could define the terms of worship for all Christians in 325.[2] So too there can be little doubt that his understanding of what it meant to be Christian evolved between 321, when he advised that haruspices be consulted about lightning striking the palace, and 337, when he forbade sacrifice in a temple erected in honor of himself and his family.[3] What did not change quite so radically was his sense of audience. A polytheist writing in the west after his death could still portray him in traditional terms, but his addresses to Christian groups, in which he openly espoused their faith, and his addresses to the rest of the empire showed that he felt that he should not treat non-Christians to the same sort of discourse that he offered Christians.[4] Most importantly, the ambivalence of address to a polytheist audience, his use of language that could be construed in a form that was acceptable to their systems of thought, shows that he did not convert because he felt that becoming a Christian was a politically simple act, or even one that was politically wise. His conversion remains a profoundly emotional act in response to a vision. But, for all of that, his conduct toward those who did not share his newfound faith would show caution and restraint. What emerged was a special relationship between the emperor and the church that paralleled the relationship between the emperor and his government.

As much as possible the two spheres would be kept separate up until the day that Constantine died and, indeed, well beyond it, for Constantine intended that he be interred, as had been other emperors, in a mausoleum.[5] He would be consecrated after his death. It would only be many years later that he would be demoted from divinity to apostle and interred in a church, first that of Saint Acacius, in 359, and finally, in 370, in the Church of the Twelve Apostles.

Constantine's administrative behavior was driven by a pragmatic understanding of institutional dynamics rather than a grand plan to revolutionize government. It will appear that his conduct toward the church was also not the product of any grand design, but consisted instead of a series of actions, often taken in response to immensely complicated relationships within various Christian communities. By the end of his life, the imperial government assumed a new role in shaping the Christian community, but how that new role came about was largely shaped by two controversies whose roots lay in the last years of the reign of Diocletian. One is the so-called Donatist controversy in North Africa, while the other is the dispute over the nature of the Christian God that takes its name from the heterodox preacher Arius of Alexandria. In the end, Constantine sought a unified church and supported those who worked to the same goal that he did. His vision of Christianity was not an exclusive one and did not involve outright conflict with polytheism except in those cases where any emperor might have seen fit to take action. He disapproved of extremists and extreme behavior on either side.

Donatists

The North African dispute into which Constantine was drawn takes its name from the bishop who refused to submit to his authority. This bishop, Donatus, came late to the center of a stage from which all but one of the main players, whose actions so enflamed passions to a degree that it had become impossible to forgive and forget, had already departed. The tale of Constantine's involvement in this dispute will reveal the limits of imperial authority when confronted by history it could neither rewrite nor control.

According to the version of events promulgated by the enemies of Donatus, the trouble began with a dispute between the then archdeacon (later bishop) Caecilian and a woman named Lucilla.[6] It is alleged that Lucilla was in the habit of kissing a bone, which she said was that of a martyr, before taking communion. When Caecilian remonstrated with her, he made of her an inveterate enemy.[7] The situation had not yet resolved itself when Diocletian's persecution edict was promulgated, and was complicated when Mensurius, the bishop of Carthage, gave shelter to a man named Felix who was accused of writing an insulting tract about the emperor. The governor demanded that Mensurius surrender Felix, and Mensurius refused, leading to his own arrest and transportation to Rome.

We do not know for certain what happened next, but it is possible that Mensurius was spared by Severus – what we do know is that, although he was not executed, he died before he could return home.[8] At this point the bishops of Numidia attempted an ecclesiastical *coup d'état*, something for which their corrupt behavior at home had well prepared them. Shortly before news of Mensurius' death reached Carthage, a group of bishops, acting in concert with Secundus of Tigisis, the senior bishop of Numidia, had overthrown the election of a man named Donatus (not to be confused with their later candidate to be bishop of Carthage) in favor of a character named Silvanus, in return for a large bribe.[9] Given the fact – alleged by his rivals in later years – that Silvanus was an avowed traditor (someone who had handed over scripture in the persecution), his election undermined any moral force that the Donatists might claim as a result of their strong stand against the edict. Their stand was already undermined by the fact that it could be claimed that Mensurius had suffered a martyrdom of sorts in a way that was consonant with his principles.[10]

When news came of the accession of Maxentius, two senior members of the Carthaginian church named Botrus and Celestius (who were allegedly withholding church plate that had been placed in their care by Mensurius) summoned a synod of the neighboring bishops in the hope that they might secure the election of one or the other of themselves. They were thwarted in their desires by the will of the people, who proclaimed Caecilian as their bishop. Caecilian was then consecrated by the bishop, Felix of Abthungi.[11] Summoned to produce an accounting of the treasures that had been left with them, Bostrus and Celestius broke communion with the church and allied themselves with Lucilla, summoning Secundus with his collection of corrupt Numidian bishops to their aid. The Numidians tried to invalidate the election of Caecilian, and, when they failed, they met to elect Majorian as bishop in opposition to Caecilian, "and that was the cause of the schism."[12] To further damage Caecilian's claim to the episcopal seat, they charged Felix of Abthungi with having been a traditor. And so the situation remained until Constantine ordered the return of church property after his defeat of Maxentius. At that point representatives of the two sides appeared before Anullinus, both claiming possession of the church that had been seized under Maximian.

The position of Caecilian's party appears to be unassailable in the narrative that Optatus of Milevis composed in the third quarter of the fourth century. Aside from the skillful weaving of tales within it, the story is of vast interest as an example of the importance of historical narrative for granting legitimacy, revealing a strong parallel to the use of history for the same purpose on the imperial level and, indeed, as we have seen, in many other areas of Roman life. The main problem here is that the use of documents by Optatus and others was highly selective and completely ignored the position of their rivals. Instead of trying to refute the powerful claims against them, the supporters of the Caecilianist position simply tried to bury them in silence.

The Donatist position had virtually nothing to do with the issues that the Caecilianist party raised to support its stand. Their position reveals a very much more sinister pattern of behavior. The thrust of the case against Caecilian was not simply that he associated with a traditor named Felix. It was rather that he was a collaborator with the persecuting authorities, and a murderer. It was also, sad to say, from the Donatist point of view, a case that it was rhetorically impossible to present before a Roman court. As we shall see, Donatist arguments before Constantine would perforce follow a script that was set by Caecilian, one in which only the issue of handing over books could be raised, and one that Donatist advocates would be unwise enough to strengthen with their own forgeries.[13] The real story, from their point of view, involved a level of brutality on Caecilian's part that may explain the dogged determination on the part of the Donatists to have nothing whatsoever to do with him.

The essence of the Donatist position emerges from an exchange of letters that they produced at a council held at Carthage in 411 that was intended to reconcile the feuding factions, and a text known as the *Acts of the Abitinian Martyrs*. According to the Donatists, Secundus wrote to Mensurius accusing him of heresy, in that he had cooperated with the authorities by handing over books when they were demanded, while he, having refused to cooperate, had gone to prison.[14] Mensurius responded that he had not handed over books of scripture, but rather books by heretics, and suggested that people who had resisted had done so not because of the strength of their faith, but rather the weight of their debts, which they had sought to escape by obtaining the crown of martyrdom. The thrust of this exchange is obviously that Mensurius was unsympathetic to martyrs. It might also be read as a confession to the acts with which he would be charged in the *Acts of the Abitinian Martyrs*.

The Abitinian martyrs were a group of Christians whom the local authorities arrested for openly defying the first edict of Diocletian as they were celebrating the Eucharist.[15] The Christians were brought before Anullinus – possibly the same man who would serve as Maxentius' praetorian prefect – on February 12, 302. Anullinus subjected them to severe tortures in order to make them recant, and, when they refused, he ordered them to be incarcerated under harsh conditions. The origins of the schism follow upon this incarceration, according to a passage that is retained in only one of the six manuscripts that preserves a copy of the text:

> Mensurius, then bishop of Carthage, polluted by his recent handing over of the Scriptures, after repenting the madness of his crime, undertook to commit greater crimes in public. Indeed that very man who ought to have implored forgiveness from the martyrs for having

burned books, instead increased his crimes with even worse deeds, and raged against the martyrs with that same spirit with which he had handed over the divine Scriptures. Verily this man, more savage than a tyrant, crueler than an executioner, chose his deacon Caecilian as a suitable agent for his crime, and placed him, armed with whips and lashes, before the doors of the prison, so that he would drive away from entrance and access all those who were bringing food and drink to the martyrs, smitten with serious injury, in prison. Those who came to feed the martyrs were struck down by Caecilian on all sides; they broke the cups, that were brought to the martyrs who were suffering from thirst in their chains, before the doors of the prison, food was scattered hither and thither to be torn apart by dogs. The fathers and mothers of the martyrs were smitten before the doors of the sacred prison and cut off from a last sight of their children, and strong guards were posted, night and day, at the entrance to the jail. There was dreadful weeping and fierce lamentation on the part of all who came, kept from the embrace of the martyrs, and the pious Christians were torn from the duty of piety by Caecilian the savage tyrant and cruel executioner . . . for this reason the holy Church follows the martyrs and detests the treason of Mensurius.

(*Act. Ab.* 20.881–917, 21.957–60 [also in
Maier, *Le dossier*, no. 4, pp. 86–87, 89])

The fact that the Caecilianist faction avoided the issue of Mensurius' conduct toward the martyrs in their tale of the event should lend credence to the tale told by his adversaries.[16] Unfortunately for the Donatists, Mensurius' conduct, as they described it, also made it very difficult to assail him before a Roman magistrate: few if any imperial officials would choose to hold that a man who had supported the action of an imperial official had acted incorrectly. That the Donatist case against Caecilian himself would begin from the fact that he had been elected illegally according to the laws of the church rather than that he was a murderer, stems from the fact that the imperial government appears to have been willing to allow the church to establish its own rules for episcopal succession so long as it did not contradict other actions by members of the imperial government. That this was the way the imperial government acted, in making a series of decisions that would lay the foundation for later imperial interaction with the church, is made abundantly clear by documents preserved both by members of the Caecilianist faction and by Eusebius.[17] Caecilianists would come to depend upon the favorable utterances of the imperial government every bit as much as the Donatists appear to have depended upon the narratives of resistance. In a sense, the division between the Caecilianist and Donatist factions would become as much a split between two styles of church historiography, the apologetic and the matyrological, as it would be a split over the propriety of the conduct of Mensurius and Caecilian.

The course of events through which Constantine held in favor of Caecilian began with a letter that Constantine sent to Anullinus – possibly the son of the persecutor of the Abitinian martyrs and now governor of Africa – at the end of 312, or the beginning of 313:

> It is the custom of our benevolence, that we wish that whatsoever rightfully belongs to another should not suffer harm, and even be restored, most honored Anullinus. Therefore, we desire that, whenever you should receive this letter, if any of those things that belonged to the Universal Church of the Christians, in any city or other place, are now held by either the citizens or by any others, we wish that you restore them immediately to those churches, since we have decided that the churches that previously owned them should, rightly, recover them. Since Your Devotion perceives that the instruction of this order is most explicit, show zeal that whatever gardens or houses or anything else that rightly belonged to those churches, be restored in their entirety to them as quickly as possible, so that we may know that you have given your most careful obedience to this command.
>
> (Euseb. *Hist. eccl.* 10.5.15–17 [also in
> Maier, *Le dossier*, no. 11])[18]

Caecilian seems to have stolen a march on his adversaries by contacting Ossius of Cordoba, who appears to have been the most influential Christian in Constantine's entourage at this point, asking him to represent his cause at court. This Ossius plainly did, for in a separate letter to Caecilian, dispatched at about the same time as the letter to Anullinus, Constantine ordered the *rationalis* of Africa to give some money to priests who were loyal to Caecilian. In doing so, Constantine refers to a prior memorandum that Caecilian had received from Ossius and makes reference to some dangerous malcontents who are seeking to turn the faithful away from the practice of the true religion.[19]

The letter to Caecilian was followed shortly thereafter by another letter to Anullinus in which Constantine ordered that all priests who were loyal to Caecilian should receive immunity from civic liturgies.[20] As reported by Eusebius, this document is not without its difficulties. A section of the letter parallels a more general statement by Constantine, to an unknown official, ordering him to ensure that priests of the true religion are not troubled by heretics, and a second letter of Constantine, dating to 319, telling the *corrector* of Lucania that clerics should be freed from civic liturgies.[21] The first letter of Constantine is dated to October 31, 313, which is far too late for it to be the same letter as was sent to Anullinus. In this case it looks as if we have here a parallel to the *Edict on Accusations*, in which an earlier document was dispatched to answer a question that had arisen someplace else. The letter of 319 preserves the restatement of a policy that had been enacted several years earlier.[22] From an administrative point of view these letters reveal just how important the dispute between Caecilian and his rivals proved to be in the making of policy, for we can see here how ad hoc responses to the North African situation in 312 were taken as precedents in the later relationship between the government and the church.

The evolution of administrative practice did not end with the letters to Anullinus. In April 313, Majorian presented what must have seemed to the governor a powerful refutation of Caecilian's position. Majorian's case was based upon two documents, one being a sealed denunciation of Caecilian's person, the other being an open statement that he was not the legal bishop in terms of the custom of the church.[23] Majorian petitioned Constantine directly, asking him to appoint a church council in Gaul to decide the case, and naming the bishops whom he would like to hear the case.[24] Constantine granted the appeal but appointed a very different council, one to be assembled at Rome, consisting of fifteen Italian bishops in addition to the three bishops requested by Majorian, and presided over by the bishop of Rome, Miltiades.[25] Here Constantine was adhering to imperial precedent, his action recalling, for instance, that of Aurelian, when he referred the complaint against Paul of Samosata to a council of Italian bishops.[26] In the months leading up to the council, Majorian appears to have died. So it was that on September 30, 313, the Donatus who would give his name to the anti-Caecilianist movement presented the case.[27]

The Council of Rome held in Caecilian's favor and condemned his opponents on the grounds that they insisted on the rebaptism of people who had been communicants of Caecilian, an act that recalled the conduct of earlier African schismatics who had been condemned in the wake of the Decian edict on sacrifices.[28] Donatus promptly accused Miltiades himself of having been a traditor and communicated his desire that members of his party resist Miltiades' attempt to unify the church by suggesting to Caecilian that he recognize all the bishops who had been appointed by Majorian.[29] It is perhaps not surprising that Constantine accepted the advice of the council and forbade Donatus' return to Carthage.[30]

Given the strength of his support for the decision of the Council of Rome, it is more than surprising that Constantine allowed a second council to be convened a year later to hear further charges against the Caecilianist faction. It is possible that he recognized that there might be some truth to the Donatist claim that Miltiades had changed the rules on them without warning when he had insisted that they present actual evidence in accord with Roman legal procedure.[31] Otherwise it is possible that Constantine was sufficiently bothered by what may have seemed to him to be the unreasonable persistence of the Donatists that he felt that another council was needed in order to convince them to see reason. One constant in his behavior was unwillingness to use force: it may be no accident that Constantine's restraint is roughly coincidental with the appearance of Lactantius' *On the Deaths of the Persecutors*. If he was to be God's agent on earth, he could scarcely be putting fellow Christians to death.

The new council was duly convened at Arles without either Ossius or Miltiades in attendance. Instead, it convened with Constantine himself, sitting as a layman, in the audience. The council opened on August 1, 314, and issued a number of rules, only three of which directly concerned the controversy in Africa. These include the statement that

> those who are said to have surrendered the Holy Scriptures or communion vessels, or the names of their brethren, we decree that whoever of them has been proved from public documents, rather than by words alone, to have done these things shall be removed from the clergy. If, however, the same persons are found to have carried out ordinations, and if the reason for the ordination remains, such ordination shall not be prejudicial to them. And seeing that there are many who seem to oppose the church, and through bribed witnesses think that they should be allowed to bring accusations, their plea is absolutely disallowed, unless, as we have said above, they produced evidence from written documents.
>
> (*Arles can.* 14 [also in Maier, *Le dossier*, no. 20])

Implicit in this canon is the view that random accusations of being a traditor should not be admitted – that witnesses were simply not to be trusted in the absence of the documentary record – and, further, that the status of a person making an ordination should not be the determining factor in deciding the legitimacy of the ordination. This decision undermined the basic Donatist tactic of claiming that people they did not like had been ordained by traditors, and paralleled their decision in the case of rebaptism, where they asserted that it did not matter who had baptized someone so long as that person proved that he or she was an orthodox believer.[32] In the same spirit the bishops also held that "those who falsely accuse their brethren . . . are not to communicate until the day of their death," the reiteration of a view that had earlier been taken by the bishops who had convened at Elvira in or around 305.[33]

The Council of Arles decided, therefore, that there was no merit in the Donatist case.[34] What is equally important is that the matter remains entirely within the church. Constantine was present, but, in the formal record, he affects nothing. The independence of the church from imperial control was formally maintained, a point that was underscored by a letter that the council formally wrote to the emperor informing him of its decision, a letter to which

Constantine formally responded at length, supporting the conclusion of the bishops against the appeal that the Donatists had immediately lodged with him.[35] The language with which he describes them is notable not only for ferocity of expression, but also for the openness with which the emperor asserts his own faith:

> For in very truth it was not without good cause that the mercy of Christ withdrew from these, in whom it is clear as day that their madness is of such a kind that we find them abhorrent even to the heavenly dispensation; so great a madness persists in them when, with incredible arrogance, they persuade themselves of things that it is not right either to say or hear, repudiating the equitable judgement that had been given by the will of heaven. . . . They demand my judgement, when I myself await the judgement of heaven.
>
> (Optatus, *Tract.* App. 5 [also in Maier, *Le dossier*, no. 21, trans. Edwards])

Such conduct would become increasingly characteristic of Constantine, who would tend to address mixed audiences with words that could be read as confessionally neutral, while addressing Christians as a member of their community.

In his own right, Constantine had a good deal to say about the results of the council, writing letters, of which two have been preserved, condemning the Donatists.[36] And so the matter would have remained if the Donatists had not returned with fresh complaints at the beginning of 315, producing documents, as the bishops assembled at Arles said they had to, to prove that Felix of Abthungi, the man who had ordained Caecilian, was a traditor. The governor of Africa heard the case and found that the evidence against Felix was forged.[37] This did not stop the Donatists, who lodged a fresh complaint with Constantine, who equivocated, first allowing the Donatist bishops who had been held in Gaul to return to Africa, then canceling this permission and summoning them to a fresh hearing at which Caecilian would be present. The business dragged on into the fall of 315, when Constantine, now at Milan, and with much else to concern him (not least being the birth of Licinius' son), held again in favor of Caecilian. The Donatists accepted this decision with no better grace than they had accepted all those that had previously been handed down, and continued to spark riots at Carthage, as they had throughout the year. Constantine finally lost patience. On November 10, 316, while pursuing Licinius' army from Cibalae, he wrote to the *vicarius* of Africa summing up the history of the dispute and, possibly, ordering the confiscation of Donatist churches.[38] The line between ecclesiastical and imperial government that Constantine had tried to maintain was finally breached. A Donatist text asserts that imperial troops burst into a basilica at Carthage on March 12, 317, slaughtering those in attendance.[39]

The persecution of the Donatists lasted until 321, when Constantine suddenly relented, ordering the *vicarius* of Africa to restore Donatist exiles, and writing to the bishops of Africa that "when vengeance is left to God, a harsher penalty is exacted from one's enemies."[40] It may be that with war again brewing with Licinius, Constantine took this action so as to be seen as the leader of a Christian crusade against the polytheists.[41] But that, perhaps, would be to attribute too much planning to the emperor. It is enough to see that Constantine had moved a very great distance in the years after 313, when he began by trying to allow the church to solve its own problems and ended by accepting a role, thrust upon him by the church, as the enforcer of church discipline.

As for the Donatists, and Donatus in particular, they appear to have learned that direct provocation of the imperial government would not work. After the return of exiled bishops signaled that Constantine, if not bothered again, might be content to live and let live, Donatus flourished. By 337 Caecilian appears to have become an insignificant figure on the North African scene, while Donatus assembled a council at Carthage that included no fewer than 270 bishops.[42] Indeed, the success of Donatus toward the end of Constantine's reign may have had significant consequences for the development of the western church in the next quarter century. It appears that Donatus had learned to listen rather better to the sounds of imperial politics, and, insofar as he gave much thought at all to more elevated issues of church doctrine (e.g. the nature of the Trinity), he appears to have been drawn toward the bishops who were ascendant at Constantinople in the 330s.[43]

The Arians

Epiphanius of Salamis, who collected information about heresies in the late fourth century, says that Arius came from Libya, by which he meant one of the two provinces that emerged from the old province of Cyrenaica before the year 320, probably Libya Inferior, the home of the ancient Greek cities of the Cyrenaican pentapolis. Arius himself appears to have been born to a wealthy Christian family around AD 280.[44] Although we know nothing for certain about Arius' education, it is plain that he had a background in Platonic philosophy. There is some possibility that he also journeyed as far as Antioch to study with Bishop Lucian, in whose church a tradition of explicating Christian doctrine with the aid of Platonic thought was perhaps strongest. But the evidence for this view, Arius' reference to the powerful bishop Eusebius of Nicomedia as a "fellow disciple of Lucian," is less straightforward than it may seem.[45] In the letter he is seeking Eusebius' support against the bishop of Alexandria, and so may be exaggerating the degree of connection between his thought and that of Lucian. Eusebius, who would support him, certainly thought so when he denied a central tenet of Arius' theology.[46] Nonetheless, the point remains that Arius argued for the significance of the humanity of Christ, and felt that a clergyman trained in Syria might find the point attractive. There was no need for him to have set foot in Syria to take this view – the real background to Arius' thought seems to have been purely Alexandrian: the teaching of Dionysius.[47]

Because he was such a controversial figure, we know very little about Arius himself. The one physical description that we get comes from Epiphanius, who may have been using an early fourth-century source that described him as

> ... very tall in stature, with a stooping figure – counterfeited like a guileful serpent, and well able to deceive any unsuspecting heart through its cleverly designed appearance. For he was always clad in a short cloak and sleeveless tunic; he spoke gently, and people found him persuasive and flattering.[48]

Arius' enemy, Bishop Alexander of Alexandria, denounces his skill as a debater and his arrogance. At the same time he suggests that Arius was an extraordinarily active preacher who moved from group to group within the city seeking to convince people of his views. It seems he was capable of inspiring great loyalty.[49] The attire that Epiphanius says Arius adopted was that of an ascetic Greek philosopher, and it is alleged that he maintained his ascetic reputation despite his responsibility for a group of seven hundred holy virgins. Indeed, it would appear that these virgins, who seem to have constituted an urban monastic community, were to prove a significant base of support for Arius when he began to come into conflict with church authorities.[50] The controversy that would surround Arius' teaching would not simply encompass the nature of God's relationship to humanity, but also basic questions about what constituted a proper Christian life. And, once again, these issues seem to lead back to the question of what counted as martyrdom, and forms of existence that may have gained strength within the church in the sixty or so years prior to Diocletian's persecution edict, when actual martyrdom seemed more a theoretical than real possibility. The lifestyle that Arius affected was, in a sense, the tip of an ascetic iceberg that was, even then, giving rise to a recognizably new form of Christian: the monk. Monastic self-mortification could replace the agony of martyrdom as a way of defining a place within the Christian hierarchy that lay outside the control of the bishops.[51] The battle over Arius' teaching would also become a struggle to control this increasingly important movement within the church.[52]

Before Arius began his fight with the ecclesiastical hierarchy at Alexandria, another controversy had torn deeply at the fabric from which the community was woven. Like the Donatist controversy, the quarrel between Peter of Alexandria and Melitius of Lycopolis was a direct consequence of Diocletian's persecution edict of 303. Simply put, when news of the edict came, Peter had fled, returning in 306 to take up his duties as the primate of Egypt, and to issue an official letter on how to treat members of the faith who might be thought to have lapsed in some way.[53] Not surprisingly, those Christians who had fled had done the right thing. Those who had handed over scripture in obedience to the edict had done no wrong. Only those who had publicly sacrificed were to punished. Unfortunately for Peter, one person who fell into this latter category was allegedly Colluthus, bishop of Lycopolis, whose place had been taken by a man named Melitius. Melitius took a very different line. In his view those who had lapsed and performed sacrifice would have to seek forgiveness from those who had suffered. If a priest had lapsed, he could never regain his position and would only be readmitted to communion after a period of penance.[54] Melitius' definition of what constituted a lapse was rather more rigorous as well – it encompassed people who had handed over scripture.

Peter's position was more closely aligned with what appears to have been mainstream thought in the church, to judge from the canons of the Council of Ancyra, probably convened in 314:

> Priests who sacrificed, and then renewed the fight, not through some deceit, but in truth, neither arranging in advance or with deliberate purpose or persuading (some official) so that they should appear to be subjected to torture, which is applied in appearance and form, shall partake of the honor of their position, but they shall neither make the offering, nor preach, nor perform any of the functions of priestly offices.
>
> (Ancyra can. 1)[55]

In the case of those who offered sacrifice under duress, having tried unsuccessfully to flee, no action at all was to be taken. In the case of people who were not priests when they sacrificed under such circumstances, "It was decided that they can be ordained as having committed no fault in the persecution."[56] The key factor that should be considered was intent: if a person had been distraught when participating in a sacrifice, then that person would be treated leniently; one who had participated willingly would suffer penance.[57] The aim of the bishops in using intent as the key factor in determining guilt was plainly an effort to defuse controversies such as Melitius had enflamed. Unfortunately for those who thought this way, the issue could not simply be shoved under the ecclesiastical carpet. In Egypt, the division between the two camps was aggravated by what seems to have been a particularly thorough enforcement of the edicts. Faced with local enthusiasm for persecution, many Christians had either fled or compromised themselves. But there were also many who had suffered for their faith. Eusebius claims that the actions of the imperial authorities in the Thebais led to many voluntary martyrdoms.[58]

When Galerius' edict of persecution arrived in 306, Peter again took flight, and remained in hiding for some time. Melitius took the opportunity offered by his flight to assume his duties as primate of Alexandria. Peter was outraged and sent a letter to the congregation ordering it to have nothing to do with Melitius until he could return and examine him – which he did, and determined that he should be excommunicated, a decision that must scarcely have surprised anyone.[59] This decision may have been made easier to enforce as Melitius himself had been arrested at about this time and sent off to the mines of Palestine.[60] That even some of Peter's own supporters could have regarded his conduct as somewhat equivocal may be reflected in a story told by Epiphanius of Salamis according to which the schism between Peter and Melitius broke out when the two of them were in prison together![61] Indeed, as Peter denounced Melitius' harsh policy toward the lapsed,

> He hung a curtain in the middle of the prison, stretching out a garment which was a kind of cloak and announcing <through> a deacon: Those who are of my mind come to me and those of Melitius' mind are with Melitius.
>
> (Epiph. *Pan.* 3.3, trans. Amidon)

Fiction though this may be, it is still an instructive fiction, as its very existence points out a perceived weakness in Peter's own case, at least up until the time that he himself could gain the authority of martyrdom for his doctrines. And become a martyr he did, when he was arrested and killed on the night of November 25–26, 311.[62] Peter's death may have taken some of the wind out of the Melitian sails; one tradition has it that Arius had broken with Peter over his treatment of Melitius and had asked forgiveness of Peter's successor, Achillas.[63] Achillas did not long survive Peter and was succeeded in turn by the Alexander who licensed Arius to preach in the church at Baucalis.[64]

Alexander appears to have tried to reconcile the different Christian groups in the city, arriving at what seems to have been a watchful truce with the Melitians and permitting considerable debate over doctrine.[65] Alexander himself may have, at least at the beginning, been willing to countenance a range of discussion at the seminars that he held on the nature of the Christian God. It was only when the Melitians complained that Alexander was harboring a heretic in Arius, that Alexander tried to silence him.[66] In response to the Melitian complaint Alexander took a strong line in advocating that the Father and the Son were *homoousios*, "consubstantial." There might have been ideological reasons for doing this; it certainly answered potential pagan criticisms that Christ was a person like Apollonius of Tyana, and thus in no way exceptional. Unfortunately for Alexander, although his view had been accepted in Rome as dogma in the third century, it was hard to reconcile with Christian scripture, and with traditions within the eastern church, including his own.[67] Dionysius of Alexandria had taken a line that could be read as being in sympathy with that of Arius.[68] The official line against Paul of Samosata, according to the findings of the Council of Antioch in 268, supported by Dionysius, had made the doctrine of strict identity between the Father and the Son heretical.[69] Eusebius of Nicomedia adhered to the view that there was one member of the Trinity who was uncreated, the Father, and that the Son was generated by the Father, meaning that he could not be of the same substance, or *ousia*, as the Father. Both Arius and Eusebius objected very strongly to the use of the word *homoousios* since it implied that the uncreated Father suffered bodily diminution in the creation of the Son.[70]

Perhaps the most important aspect of the fight that would break out between Arius and Alexander in 318 is that there was so little new about it. Arius' position that the Son was a creation of the Father had a long history at Alexandria, as it did in Syria. At least at the outset, it is arguable that the controversy between Arius and Alexander had more to do with local autonomy, and the structure of the church in Alexandria, than with doctrine. According to Epiphanius of Salamis, each man licensed to preach in one of the Alexandrian churches was entitled to take his own line on questions of doctrine, and it may have been the decentralization of doctrine that caused Alexander to run the seminars where he and Arius began to fight.[71] According to the story that finally made its way to Constantine in 325, it was at one of these meetings that Arius arose to denounce Alexander, quite possibly as a heretic. According to Alexander, the debate gathered strength when Arius went around to various priests, urging them to see things his way, and took advantage of his following among the virgins of Alexandria.[72] On this version, the dispute was wholly internal to the church of Alexandria, but this is the version of Alexander, who wished to play down the legitimacy of Arius' doctrine and the strength of his support. It was the support that Arius was able to win from bishops outside of Egypt that made him such a threat. As the situation unfolded, as Arius gained support, despite reservations about some points of his theology, from Eusebius, he may have seemed an agent for a theological *coup d'état* on the part of the bishops of Syria.[73] Or, at the very least, his quarrel with Alexander was seen as a way to discredit doctrines held by Alexander that were at odds with those of the Syrian tradition.[74] Whatever the case may be, Alexander took Arius' attack very seriously, summoning a council of Egyptian bishops to condemn him. The letter that he sent to the churches of the east after the council voted to excommunicate Arius in 319 gives some sense of the two dimensions, personal and doctrinal, that the struggle had assumed. Indeed, Alexander opened not with an attack upon Arius, but rather upon Eusebius of Nicomedia, who

> thinks that the affairs of the Church are under his control because he deserted his charge at Beirut and cast longing glances at the church at Nicomedia (and he did this with impunity) and has put himself at the head of these apostates also, daring even to send

commendatory letters in all directions concerning them, if by any means he might inveigle some of the ignorant into this most base heresy which is hostile to Christ.

(Socrates, *Hist. eccl.* 1.6.5 [also in H. G. Opitz,
Urkunden, no. 4b.4, trans. Stevenson,
A New Eusebius, 323])[75]

Alexander's attack upon Eusebius was not entirely without justification; Eusebius had sent a letter supporting Arius' position to the bishops of the east, and the first thing that Arius appears to have done in the wake of this council was to write to Eusebius asking for his help.[76] Eusebius was not the only problem. In one letter, Alexander complained of numerous preachers in Alexandria and elsewhere who were won over by Arius' eloquence.[77] In another, he lists prelates – including the bishops of Libya – who asserted the distinction between the Father and Son that was central to Arius' teaching, claiming (falsely) that it was a heresy of their own devising. Alexander was thorough in his denunciation of Arius, and in this, he sought to rewrite the history of the third century – claiming among other things that Lucian of Antioch and Paul of Samosata had espoused the same views about the nature of Christ.[78] In return, Arius wrote a letter to Alexander and the clerics who supported him in 320 characterizing Alexander as being, among other things, a Manichaean, claiming that Mani had asserted that the Son was a *homoousion meros tou patros* (consubstantial part of the Father).[79] This was the crucial point at issue, for Arius held that the Son was created after the Father, and subordinate to him, created so that he could mediate between his Father and the created world. In this formulation, the Father was the "true God" and the Son was entitled to divinity because he participated in the "substance" of the Father.[80] If the Son was a creation of the Father, he could not be *homoousios*. Arius returned to his church, writing letters to Eusebius and others asking for their support.[81] Eusebius, who maintained that the members of the Trinity were three essences of God, clearly thought that Arius' teachings were closer to his own than Alexander's view that there was a single essence that had three Persons.[82]

Neither side could gain the decisive advantage in Alexandria itself, and Arius appears to have tried to support his view by explaining it in verse. The *Thalia*, for that is what he called his poem, was not, it seems, intended for an audience of the uninitiated, but rather as a way of making clear his claims to authority.[83] It opened with the statement,

According to the faith of the chosen of God and of those knowledgeable of God, of the holy children, of those who expound the word *God* correctly, receiving the Holy Spirit, I have learned these things from the participants of wisdom, from those who are pleasing (to God), and from those who are divinely taught in all things.

415

I follow in their footsteps, the famous one, proceeding with correct learning, suffering much for the glory of God, learning from God, I know wisdom and knowledge.

(Arius, *Thalia* 4–11)[84]

Arius thus combines in his person the role of the inspired prophet with overtones of persecution, a presentation not dissimilar to that of Mani himself, or a character in the Hermetic Corpus.[85] As such these verses reveal another layer to Arius' thought that resided in what is to us still the murky realm of popular culture, where ideas fused and were reshaped by teachers on street corners as well as in churches. It is this ability to catch a different tone that enabled Arius to withstand the assaults of the Alexandrian establishment and reach out to other leaders of the church.

At the same time that he resisted his opponents in the streets, Arius responded bitterly to attacks on his thinking that reverberated through the higher levels of the church. In his letter to Eusebius of 318 he had complained,

> Eusebius, your brother in Caesarea, Theodotus, Paulinus, Athanasius, Gregory, Aëtius, and all the bishops of the east, who say that God has existence without beginning prior to his Son, have been made anathema except Philogonius, Hellenicus, and Macarius, who are heretics and uncatechized, saying that the Son is a belch, or that he is a projection, or that he is unbegotten.
>
> (Theodoret *Hist. eccl.* 1.5.3 [also in
> Opitz, *Urkunden*, no. 1.3])

A quick glance at the bishops whom Arius lists as victims of Alexander reveals again the connection between his position and that of the Syrian school. Aside from Eusebius of Caesarea, who was lavish in his praise of various supporters of the Lucianic school, Theodotus was bishop of Laodicea (and the dedicatee of one of Eusebius' major apologetic works), Paulinus was bishop of Tyre (another friend of Eusebius of Caesarea), while Athanasius of Anazarbus was a pupil of Lucian.[86] Gregory was Eusebius' successor as bishop of Beirut, and Aëtius was bishop of Lydda. Their opponents were, respectively, the bishops of Antioch, Tripoli, and Jerusalem. Without recourse to direct imperial intervention (which does not appear to have been Licinius' style), there was no real way to resolve the dispute. And so the situation remained, with the bishops of Egypt opposed to the bishops of Syria (and the bishop of Nicomedia) when Constantine emerged victorious from the final struggle with Licinius.

It appears that Constantine was interested in a quick resolution to the dispute, fearing, perhaps, that it would fester as had the quarrels of the North African Christians unless he could find some compromise. Thus his first act was to send a sharply worded letter to Alexandria, apportioning blame to both parties. It is plain that he once again hoped that the church would be able to solve its problems without involving the state. In describing his involvement in the Donatist controversy (albeit in a remarkably disingenuous way) he said:

> Indeed, when an intolerable madness had seized the whole of Africa because of those who had dared with ill-considered frivolity to split the worship of the population into various factions, and when I personally desired to put right this disease, the only cure sufficient for the affair that I could think of was that . . . I might send some of you to help towards the reconciliation of those at variance with each other.
>
> (Euseb. *Vit. Const.* 2.66, trans. Hall)

In the case of the Alexandrian dispute, he urged Arius and Alexander to forgive each other, telling them that the cause of their difficulty stemmed from a dispute that would easily be put to right:

> I understand then that the first stages of the present dispute were as follows. When you, Alexander, demanded of the presbyters what view each of them took about a certain passage from what is written in the Law – or rather about some futile point of dispute – you, Arius, thoughtlessly replied with that opinion which either ought not to have been conceived in the first place, or once conceived ought to have been consigned to silence. The dispute having thus arisen between you, fellowship was repudiated, and the most holy people were divided in two and forsook the concord of the common body. Accordingly, let each of you extend pardon equally, and accept what your fellow servant in justice urges upon you.
>
> (Euseb. *Vit. Const.* 2.69.1–2, trans. Hall)

He continued by explaining that they should not act with such great certainty when debating matters that no human could fully understand and realize that verbal dispute was just that, a game "promoted by unprofitable idleness."[87] The matters over which they quarreled were "small and utterly unimportant," especially as compared to the unity of the Christian church.[88] He concludes by imploring them to "open to me now the road to the east" that had been closed by their controversy.[89]

The letter to Alexandria did not have the desired effect. Constantine then sent Ossius of Cordoba, this time a genuinely disinterested party, to find out what was going on, and to summon a council that was to meet at Antioch in the spring of 325, quite possibly with the promise that Constantine himself would attend.[90] In the end he did not, and the reason may be that

417

Ossius had uncovered the depth of the divide within the eastern church, discovering that the politics of the matter were even more complex than those of the Donatist dispute. But, deeply as they were divided, the bishops of the east also had a good deal more personal experience of the trouble that could arise from imperial intervention than did those of North Africa. Many of Arius' supporters realized that there was no point in continuing the open struggle with one another when it was clear that the ultimate decision would lie with Constantine. They may, or may not, have been dismayed by the extraordinary speech that Constantine delivered at Nicomedia on the Friday or Saturday before Easter, explaining the essence of his faith. This document is preserved in the manuscripts of Eusebius as Constantine's *Oration to the Faithful*, and it may have made those who heard it realize that the emperor, whose theology was heavily dependent upon that of Lactantius, was incapable of understanding the subtlety of the distinctions over which they fought.[91] Constantine was devoted to the notion that the world was administered by the Great God, who occupied a position on the divine plane that was very similar to that which the emperor occupied on the terrestrial. As the emperor was charged with maintaining the unity of the empire, so too did the Great God seek the unity of his people. Constantine may not have been aware that when, in the course of the speech, he used language implying the existence of a "second God," he could be heard as supporting the position of Arius, to which he was already showing signs of hostility.[92]

Constantine now summoned a new council in a more neutral spot, at first Ancyra, and then at Nicaea, saying,

> It hath seemed to us on many accounts that it would be well for a synod to assemble at Nicaea, a city of Bithynia, both because the bishops from Italy and the rest of the countries of Europe are coming, and because of the excellent temperature of the air, and in order that I may be present as a spectator and participator in those things which will be done.
>
> (Opitz, *Urkunden*, no. 20, trans. Stevenson, *A New Eusebius*, 338)

Again he is explicit in his desire that the church find its own unity, but he was not above giving the assembled bishops some added help in their deliberations. The presence of the western bishops would act to balance the two competing sides, and lend the council an aura of universality the like of which had never occurred in the past. The Council of Nicaea opened at the beginning of June under the presidency of Ossius, with Constantine, as he promised, in attendance. The Arian controversy was the first item on the agenda, and Constantine made it clear from the start that he wanted compromise. In his opening address, delivered in Latin with a simultaneous Greek translation – a remarkable nod to an audience of Greek speakers – he said:

It was the object of my prayers, my friends, to share in your company, and now that I have received this, I know I must express my gratitude to the King of all, because, in addition to everything else he has allowed me to see in this, which is better than any other good thing; I mean, to receive you all gathered together and to observe one unanimous opinion shared by all. Let no jealous enemy ruin our prosperity; now that the war of the tyrants against God has been swept away by the power of God the Savior, let not the malignant demon encompass the divine law with blasphemies by other means. For to me, internal division in the Church of God is graver than any war or fierce battle, and these things appear to cause more pain than secular affairs.

(Euseb. *Vit. Const.* 3.12.1–2, trans. Hall)[93]

He concluded his remarks with an exhortation to get on with the work of unity without delay, and it appears that this is just what happened, with what looks like some careful stage management.

It seems that the first actor to take center stage was Eusebius of Caesarea, who produced a confession of his faith that Constantine immediately declared to be in essential conformity with his own (it lacked only the word *homoousios*).[94] It was no doubt a well-arranged piece of political theater, for Eusebius of Caesarea had arrived under a ban of excommunication from the anti-Arian bishops, but as Constantine's first act was to make a public show of reconciliation, the message was clear. If any had missed the point, it was reinforced when Eustathius of Antioch read out some work of Eusebius of Nicomedia that was regarded as heretical, presumably, though it is not certain, a writing that was at odds with the developing consensus.[95] Then Constantine himself put forward his own version of the creed, composed, it is said, by a Cappadocian priest named Hermogenes, in terms that were almost identical to the confession put forward by Eusebius of Caesarea.[96] The words of this creed remain the best-known expressions of a Roman emperor in the modern world (albeit in an edited form):

We believe in one God, the Father Almighty, Maker of all things visible and invisible – and in one Lord Jesus Christ, the Son of God, the only begotten of the Father, that is of the substance of the Father; God of God, Light of Light, true God of true God; begotten not made, consubstantial with the Father; by whom all things were made both which are in heaven and on earth; who for the sake of us men, and account of our salvation, descended, became incarnate, was made man, suffered, and rose again on the third day; he ascended into the heavens, and will come to judge the living and the dead. We also believe in the Holy Ghost. But those who say "There was a time when he was not" and "Before his generation he was not," and "he came to be from nothing," or those who pretend that the Son of God is "Of other hypostasis or substance," or "created" or "alterable" or "mutable" the universal and apostolic Church anathematizes.

(Socrates, *Hist. eccl.* 1.8.4 [also in
Opitz, *Urkunden*, no. 22])

Constantine's creed was adopted on June 19, 325, and once that was done, the bishops set about other business, defining church practice, also upon the emperor's request, and setting a uniform date of Easter throughout the empire. At the same time, the council sought to resolve the Melitian controversy, creating a formula by which Melitians could be rejoined to the Egyptian church. According to this settlement, Melitius was confirmed as bishop of Lycopolis, and his ordinations were accepted as valid, though he was forbidden to ordain further priests, and his priests were to be subordinate to those ordained by Alexander. A Melitian priest who submitted to Alexander could have full clerical privileges, and, if Alexander agreed to a congregation's request that such a thing happen, he could replace one of Alexander's priests when the latter died.[97] It was a remarkably generous settlement, and underlined the point that almost all present should have taken away: Constantine wanted a peaceful reunification of the church and favored compromise as the way of achieving that end. All but two bishops (both Libyan) subscribed to the canons of the council, including the creed. The two recalcitrants were excommunicated, as were Arius and some priests who continued to support him.[98] Shortly thereafter, Eusebius of Nicomedia was convicted of remaining in contact with Arius, and removed from his see by an enraged emperor. Compromise did not involve behaviors that seemed to undermine the point that Arius' doctrine was finished. The man who would emerge as the chief foe of compromise was Athanasius of Alexandria, who succeeded his mentor, Alexander, as bishop in 328.

Athanasius

Church historians of a later era would paint the return to power of Eusebius as an unmitigated disaster resulting from his friendship with Constantia, and the return to power of the Arian faction that would doom the church to disorder until the orthodox Theodosius took the throne in 379.[99] This is a gross oversimplification. There is no reason to think that Constantine ever consciously acknowledged a belief other than that in the creed that he had established, or that his son, Constantius II, saw himself as an Arian as he rewrote the creed as part of an effort to establish what he considered church discipline and proper belief in the course of his long reign. At the very end of his life, Constantine did restore Arius from exile – though only after he was assured that he had recanted his beliefs – and took action against Athanasius. As Athanasius' extensive discourse on his woes dominates the later historiographic tradition of the church, it is now very hard to see the history of the period in any way but his.[100] To do so, however, is to gloss over legitimate concerns on the part of Constantine and, as will be argued in the next two chapters, the complexity of Constantius' own behavior.

Athanasius was not, however, the first pro-Nicene bishop to fall foul of the emperor. Shortly after the death of Crispus, the emperor's aged mother, Helena, decided to visit the Holy Land. Her arrival in Syria was coincidental with the dismissal of Eustathius of Antioch, one of the most powerful figures in the opposition to Arius.[101] He was not a particularly popular man, it seems, in the ecclesiastical community of Syria, being one of only three major bishops who had not, initially, supported Arius. In the course of 327, Athanasius says that Eustathius was the victim of a pro-Arian conspiracy, in the course of which he was accused by his rivals before Constantine of having insulted Helena and was, as a result of that insult, exiled.[102] The absurdity of this story, as it stands, is patent. Helena did not require help from anyone in dealing with her son. Rather more likely, she agreed wholeheartedly with Eustathius' enemies. The reason for this may be that in a public act of reconciliation with the defeated party at Nicaea, she had venerated the remains of the martyred bishop Lucian.[103] Eustathius may have objected, and if he did, it would merely have confirmed that he could not let drop the issues that had divided the church before Nicaea.

The charge against Eustathius is variously reported. According to one tradition he was condemned as a Sabellian heretic.[104] Sabellianism was a third-century movement that argued for the strict unity of the Trinity, and it is deeply unlikely that, two years after the Council of Nicaea, Constantine would have believed that one of the principal supporters of the creed was a heretic. The other story, which rings more true, is that he was convicted of having fathered a child out of wedlock by a church council summoned to investigate him on charges of sexual immorality.[105] What is not, however, so obvious, is why that council should have been chaired by his longtime rival, Eusebius of Caesarea, or why his colleague in anti-Arianism, Asclepas of Gaza, should be exiled at the same time. The two of them may have been joined in exile by five other bishops. The presence of Eusebius and the exile of Asclepas make it look as if the problem went beyond the bishop's sexual to his doctrinal passion. It looks very much as if the seven bishops were exiled because they had been insufficiently welcoming of their former rivals into the fold. The same issue would soon arise in the case of Athanasius.

In the year that Eustathius was exiled, a new ecclesiastical council was held at Nicomedia. Here Arius renounced his heresy, and the bishops, including Eusebius of Nicomedia, who had been deposed, admitted their faults. Constantine must have regarded this as proof that his policy of building consensus had worked, and welcomed all of them back, writing to Alexandria to say that Arius was now welcome to come home.[106]

Despite his later claim to be the victim of Arian conspiracies, Athanasius' downfall stemmed from his refusal to accommodate the Melitians. From the start, Athanasius had a problem in that it appears that he may have been too young to become a bishop according to local custom, which seems to have been ignored, as does the custom (if that is what it was) that bishops not be consecrated with the doors of the church barred shut.[107] This action, at which seven bishops were present, preempted a council, including fifty-four bishops from other parts of Egypt, that was evidently being organized with the aim of selecting a candidate who might unite the church.[108] It was not an auspicious start.

Athanasius perceived that he needed support, and this may have directed his attention to ascetics. At this point ascetics, in some numbers, were beginning to settle in the countryside, offering, to the group that could harness their passion, a vehicle to control the countryside. We will examine these groups in chapter 13, but, for now, it is worth noting that Athanasius had extensive dealings with Ammoun and Macarius, leaders of semieremetical monks, and was attempting to form a relationship with Pachomius, who was beginning to found communities of monks.[109] Indeed, Athanasius' attempts to expand his control outside of Alexandria and his willingness to ignore the settlement with the Melitians at Nicaea, would be his ultimate undoing. In 330, Athanasius withdrew from Alexandria, evidently to avoid assisting some Melitians with their tax obligations.[110] He returned to the city and then set out again on a journey through the Mareotis, where one of his colleagues assaulted a priest named Ischyras on the grounds that he was a heretic, smashing a chalice and overturning an altar.[111] This incident would prove his undoing, though it would take several years before Constantine would finally lose patience with the bishop. At the heart of it all was the fact that Athanasius refused to compromise with his rivals, and this Constantine took very seriously indeed, even after those rivals disgraced themselves on more than one occasion by bringing patently false charges against him: in 334 Athanasius proved, before the council that had assembled to try him, that a man he was accused of having murdered was alive.[112] In 335 the emperor had finally had enough, and, after Athanasius was condemned by a church council, Constantine exiled him to Gaul. Although many of the charges against Athanasius may have been questionable, there can be no question but that he did violence to his enemies in Egypt, or that he employed gangs of thugs to do so. A letter, preserved on papyrus, details the assault upon a party that included the Melitian bishop of Alexandria.[113] It was this sort of behavior that Constantine was trying to halt, and it was to prevent this sort of behavior that he had supported the Nicene Creed. Unlike many of his rivals, chief among them being Eusebius of Nicomedia, Athanasius seems to have missed the point. In a sense Arius and his former supporters who later acknowledged their error were more in keeping with the spirit of Nicaea than was Athanasius.[114]

Christianity and government

The tale of the resurrection of "Arian" fortunes is coincidental to a number of other issues connected with Constantine's espousal of his new faith, and a tendency to avoid the sort of direct confrontation at which Athanasius excelled. But, as the polemic surrounding the career of Athanasius might obscure subtleties that the bishop of Alexandria found irrelevant, so too might the hostility of a late fourth-century writer like Eunapius obscure the complexities of religious life in the earlier part of the century. Eunapius did not choose to see major distinctions between Constantine and his son Constantius, but those differences were there, and were very significant for both Christians and polytheists. To understand Constantine's conduct, to get some impression of what it was like to be a non-Christian under Christian rule, it is necessary to look at the record of his legislation. This is a path fraught with difficulties, for books of law represent a society only in very broad outlines; they will often reveal extreme circumstances and obscure the typical.[115] Although this is as true for the fourth century as for other periods of history, the record of Constantine's legislation is still revealing, not so much because of any one text, but rather because there is a certain consistency in the behavior of his government that is apparent across many areas.

In discussing such issues, another problem that is of deep importance remains the question of who is actually writing in the emperor's name. We know, of course, that most of the emperor's correspondence was drafted by *notarii* who worked under the *magister officiorum*.[116] What we can never know in each individual case is whether Constantine himself bothered to review every decision that went out in his name, or if he cared about some more than others. We may presume that edicts were created with direct imperial involvement insofar as they represented a proactive statement of his views, but we cannot know how deeply he was concerned with the composition of letters or rescripts. In a sense we are returned here to the issue of the emperor's two bodies: there is the Constantine who was a living, breathing human being, and the Constantine whose name conferred the stamp of absolute authority when invoked in an official context by a palace official. There is a sense in which the very anonymity of the legislative process may be the single most important aspect of the surviving evidence. If a relatively consistent pattern of conduct can be associated with legislation and other imperial activities that took place under the name of Constantine, if statements made by "Constantine" include language that would be unthinkable if the name at the top of the letter were "Diocletian," then it is correct to speak of a Constantinian policy. In the case of legislation, this is particularly significant in light of the tendency of Roman lawyers to exist within an autonomous cocoon of legal reasoning, and the fact that the bulk of the evidence for Constantine's conduct not offered by Eusebius comes from the Theodosian and Justinianic Codes wherein responses have been edited to make them fit the pattern of legal development desired by the editors of the codes. For this reason, when the name "Constantine" is used below, it is often in the symbolic sense rather than an assertion that the emperor himself can actually be said to have done anything more than set a tone of discourse through his control of senior officials, who, it may be presumed, set the tone for their subordinates. In cases where it is possible to be certain that Constantine had some direct input into the making of policy, it will be important to see if the policy so made diverges significantly from that which is uttered in the name of the symbolic Constantine.

The most obvious case where Constantine was influenced by Christian doctrine is in his declaration that episcopal courts could hear civil cases, even those involving non-Christians. It appears that it was in 318 that Constantine granted anyone who wished to do so the right to have a civil case heard before a bishop rather than a magistrate, and stated that this could be done if only one party wished it that way.[117] He restated this view in 333, in a letter to the praetorian prefect Ablabius.[118] The fact that Ablabius should have been unaware of Constantine's edict may suggest that few had availed themselves of this right, but it nonetheless had the effect of putting bishops on a par with civic magistrates. The reasons that he gives Ablabius are interesting, in that he states, on the one hand, that the effect of his "salutary edict" is to ease the burden on regular courts – and that "the authority of sacrosanct religion" could discover a truth hidden by legal technicalities. At the same time he orders that the testimony of bishops be given credence against any other witness.

The overt statement that bishops have greater access to truth may stand as a touchstone against which to measure other legislation that might have some doctrinal influence, for it shows that the Constantinian chancery could be astonishingly straightforward when it felt like it. In this case then it may be best to begin with legislation affecting the Jews, who, despite their history of opposition to Roman rule, enjoyed certain privileges from the Roman state. Jews were allowed, according to a rescript of Antoninus Pius, to circumcise their sons, a modification to Hadrian's empirewide ban on the practice, and they were exempted from performing actions in the course of civic liturgies that violated the tenets of their faith.[119] In Judaea itself, it appears as if the patriarch of the Jews had the authority to act as a judge in civil actions that pitted Jews against each other, or in matters of religious law.[120] Roman governors could, and did, act to support the decisions of these courts. Additionally, Jewish priests were granted exemptions from all civic liturgies, and the patriarch was entitled to receive an annual tax from the communities in the Diaspora.[121]

The one area where the imperial government imposed restrictions upon the practice of Judaism was with regard to the conversion of non-Jews. A full convert to Judaism would have to be circumcised, and this ban remained in place, possibly leading to the growth of the class of *Theosebeis* within the synagogue.[122] This ban did not, however, extend to slaves, who could be converted by owners, who were required to convert their slaves according to Jewish law.[123]

Despite a tradition in some modern scholarship, which would see in the reign of Constantine the beginning of the long history of persecution by Christian states of Jews, Constantinian legislation with respect to the Jews does not suggest a coherent plan of persecution.[124] The various pieces of legislation that emanate from Constantine's chancery fall in a fourteen-year period from 321 to 335, making them look like ad hoc measures that, taken as a whole, indicate a tendency to make things harder for non-Christians just as other laws will suggest a tendency to make things easier for Christians. His first recorded decision reflects precisely this sort of problem. In a general law of 321 Constantine held that Jews who were members of a curial class could be compelled to take up civic duties even if those duties involved violation of their ancestral customs, though he added that two or three in every group might be excluded from such nominations.[125] On the surface this is a significant change from earlier policy, and it would appear that he found that he needed to step back from its application when he issued another law stating that Jews holding office in the synagogue were excluded from nomination to any liturgy that involved manual labor.[126] The issues here plainly move far beyond the synagogue and are connected with the overall question of the health of the civic governing classes within the empire. That being the case, it is hard to say if this measure should be envisioned as, strictly speaking, anti-Jewish as opposed to pro-curial (and hence only coincidentally anti-Jewish). What it reflects is a willingness to overlook past privileges in dealing with a current situation.

The ambiguity inherent in these matters would seem, at first glance, to contrast rather starkly with a letter to the praetorian prefect Evagrius in 329:

> We wish the Jews, their elders and their patriarchs to know that if any of them, after the publication of this law, should dare attack any person who will have fled their feral sect and turned to the worship of God, with stones or any other form of madness, which we know now happens, he will be given over to the flames and burned with all of his accomplices. If indeed someone should join their nefarious sect from the public and join in their associations at large, he will sustain the just penalty along with them.
>
> (*CTh.* 16.8.1)[127]

Aside from the violently prejudicial language in which the emperor expresses himself (and is typical of the sort of language used of others of whom he disapproves, including, as we have seen, some Christians), there is in fact very little that is new. Reference to the "worship of God" obviously need not mean only the Christian God at a time when the emperor was generally espousing his subservience to the rather vaguely defined "Highest God," and at no point in Roman history can the imperial government have sanctioned the violent pursuit of Jewish apostates. Likewise, the ban on the conversion of non-Jews is long-standing policy. The main problem here is that the editors of the Theodosian Code may not have included the entire context (which is typical). It is quite possible that this statement is part of a larger text in which Constantine also forbade the circumcision and conversion of non-Jewish slaves (ordering that any such slave should be seized by the treasury) and adding additional penalties if that slave happened to be a Christian.[128] In such cases, the purchaser would be deprived of all of his slaves. Women who were previously part of an imperial weaving establishment and had been acquired by a Jew who tried to convert them are returned to the establishment; if a Jew should acquire possession of and convert Christian women in the future, he might be executed.[129] If this is the case, Constantine's letter to Evagrius represents a restatement of existing policy, with one change in favor of the Christian church, an incremental rather than a radical shift. The stress on a particular case, the fate of the women whose ownership had been transferred, makes it appear as if the letter was prompted by an inquiry about a specific problem and that Constantine took the opportunity offered by the specific instance to utter a general statement. The essence of this statement, that Christians occupy a special position, is significant: he is not taking anything away from non-Christians; he is giving greater advantages to Christians by making the traditional penalty for Jews who held non-Jewish slaves more severe.

If the treatment of the Jews reflects a tendency toward slow alteration of existing custom, another action of Constantine appears to work in a similar direction. At the same time, it also reveals how his subjects could read the emperor's actions in different ways. This is an edict on holidays:

> All magistrates, the urban plebs, and the practice of all the arts ought to rest on the sacred day of the sun. However, those who live in the countryside ought to pursue the cultivation of fields freely and whenever they wish, since it frequently happens that no day is more apt on which crops may be harvested with the scythe or vines be dug so that the bounty granted by divine foresight not be lost through accident of time.
>
> (*CJ* 3.12.2)

The language is very carefully chosen, for Constantine speaks only of the *dies solis*, which existed as part of the traditional measurement of days within a month, rather than of the *dominice* (*kuriakê* in Greek), or day of the Lord, the Christian term for the day upon which Christians celebrated their rites. Eusebius would ignore the distinction between the two terms, which was plainly deliberate, and claim that Constantine had decreed that "the truly sovereign and really first day, the day of the Lord and Savior, should be considered a regular day of prayer."[130] Assuming that Eusebius is referring to the text that we have, this is, to say the least, something of an overinterpretation, but it is perhaps not unique to Eusebius. In Egypt, for instance, it appears to have been traditional for judges to take Thursdays off. The daybook of the *logistes* at Oxyrhynchus in 313 reads:

> 12th: Nothing.
> 13th: Day of Jupiter.
> 14th: Nothing.
> 15th: Serenus son of Dioscurides requested . . . presenting . . . a loan of one (?) talent . . . to the city in the name of The-. . .-pis wife of Horion . . . to receive his property.
>   Decided: that this should be done.
> 16th: Nothing.
>
> (P. Oxy. 3741)

The singling out of the day of Jupiter indicates that it was a day upon which no hearing could be held (as opposed to the other days on which this underemployed official was idle). Twelve years later, a record of proceedings before the *logistes* of Oxyrhynchus on October 2, 325, concludes with the *logistes* saying:

> Since the hour of *vesperes* has passed, there shall be no prejudgment, the appointed day having not yet arrived. Since some part of the coming sacred Lord's Day has supervened, the case will be deferred till (the day?) after the Lord's Day.
>
> (P. Oxy. 3759, trans. Coles)[131]

Since the day ended at sundown in the Roman world, the magistrate is calling business off because Sunday arrived at sunset, and in doing so he twice uses the word *kuriakê*. The choice of language should indicate the *logistes'* understanding of what Constantine meant when he said that courts should not be in session on the *dies solis*. It also reveals that this official is a Christian and feels free to use his confessional vocabulary in the public record. This is the same sort of subtle shift that we saw in the case of the legislation with regard to the Jews: it was traditional that there be one day a week upon which the courts would not be in session. The effect of Constantine's legislation was to change that day (and perhaps to standardize the day off throughout the empire). This then made it possible for a Christian magistrate to observe that the holiday was the *hiera kuriakê*, "sacred day of the Lord," if he chose to do so. In a sense it may be precisely this ability to use Christian language in the context of official business that would be one of the most notable aspects of Constantine's reign.

Another area where it might be expected that Christian doctrine could influence public practice was public entertainment. But here too the changes, while real, were subtle. Constantine took no action with respect to chariot-racing, which seems not to have attracted the fervent denunciation to which other forms of entertainment were subject in Christian thought, perhaps because circus chariot-racing was a relatively rare phenomenon prior to the latter part of the third century.[132] Only major cities had circuses on the model of the Circus Maximus at Rome (the sine qua non for Roman-style chariot-racing) prior to the fourth century, and when they were constructed, they were often constructed in the context of imperial palaces. Where they did exist, circuses become the primary venue for an emperor's contact with his subjects, and any effort to suppress chariot-racing would have been significantly inconvenient. Athletic events had probably suffered severely in the latter part of the third century, as the transformation of the currency system by Aurelian and Diocletian appears to have ruined the private endowments that supported most civic games.[133] By the time of Constantine, evidence for independent athletic contests becomes very slight indeed, and athletes appear to have performed most often either in small-scale municipal contests that were funded by local magistrates or between races in the circus. The same cannot be said for gladiatorial combats and theatrical performances, and here it is of great interest that, despite obvious Christian hostility to both, it is only in the context of gladiatorial combat that Constantine can be seen to do anything. On October 1, 325, Constantine wrote to Maximus, the *vicarius* of the diocese of Oriens, that

> bloody spectacles in a time of civil peace and domestic tranquility displease us. Since therefore we altogether forbid those who would be accustomed to receive this status and sentence, to become gladiators, you should ensure that they are sentenced to the mines so they may pay the penalty for their crimes without blood.
>
> (*CTh.* 15.12.1)[134]

The critique of gladiatorial combat as a "bloody spectacle" is anything but new, appearing, among other places, in the decree of the senate of AD 177 in which a schedule for pricing gladiators was fixed in the senate.[135] Moreover, prisoners were never sentenced, strictly speaking, to become gladiators. Rather they were subjected to *damnatio ad ludos*, a marginally less dreadful fate than *damnatio ad bestias*, in that they were condemned to fight other humans to the death, making it possible that a person could survive. What Constantine is doing here is simply abolishing the penalty of *damnatio ad ludos*; it appears to have been possible to conflate *damnati* with gladiators when one was being hostile to the institution. Interestingly, he did not abolish the penalty of *damnatio ad bestias* at the same time, which might be expected if he were indeed reforming the penal code to eliminate all penalties that might be thought offensive to Christian sentiment. But the horror of the latter penalty had some value to Constantine himself, who had notably employed it in the case of two Frankish kings whom he had captured in 307.[136] The abolition of *damnatio ad ludos* is then a minor step and belies the force of the opening clause. Equally a minor step was the abolition of crucifixion as a penalty, reported by Aurelius Victor.[137] All who would have been sentenced to crucifixion would henceforth join those who were sentenced to burning at the stake. As it is arguable that as many or more Christians had been burned or sentenced *ad bestias* in the previous centuries than had suffered *damnatio ad ludos* or crucifixion, these two changes in the penal code might be said to have had some symbolic value, but do not represent a major alteration of existing behaviors. It is interesting as well that Eusebius omits both measures from his account of Constantine's pro-Christian legislation.

The Theodosian Code contains many utterances from Constantine's government on the subject of the family, and in this area, Eusebius does say that church doctrine influenced Constantine.[138] In this case he singles out an ordinance that repealed Augustan marriage legislation, changed the way that wills could be made, and appears to have mitigated the treatment of delinquent debtors.[139] Eusebius' assertion with regard to the law on marriage and succession would perhaps be more convincing if the item to which he plainly refers was not the same law that he criticized in the *Ecclesiastical History* as an example of the tyranny of Licinius.[140] Taking the most generous possible view of what Eusebius says in these two places, it may be conceded that the law allowed for multiple views as to its intent and is worth some examination both for that reason and because Constantine and Licinius ended more than three hundred years of imperial practice.

The law that was repealed was the Julian law on marriages, the centerpiece of Augustus' moral legislation in 18 BC. The most striking provisions of the law were the declaration that adultery was a crime punishable by the state rather than by family council, the penalties imposed upon members of the upper class if they did not marry, and the privileges given to both men and women if they were parents to three biological or adopted children.[141] A male who had three children could subtract one year for each child from the statutory interval between offices, could hold precedence over a colleague in office who had fewer children (even if that colleague was older, something that ordinarily granted precedence), and receive precedence in being considered for cooptation into a post vacated by the death of its holder. He might also receive some advantage when lots were drawn for provincial governorships. A woman who had three children was exempt from the ordinary requirement that she have a guardian if she survived her husband. Freedmen and freedwomen were granted exemption from the requirement that they work for their former masters if they had two (in the case of a freedman) or four (in the case of a freedwoman) children.[142] For the privilege to be obtained, the children had to survive (the only exception being a child that had died in war).[143] The law also had implications for a person's ability to inherit. Under the Voconian Law of 169 BC a woman who had married according to the ordinary practice, *sine manu*, by which she did not become a member of her husband's *familia* (family group, which included all persons under the authority of either the husband if he were the pater-familias, or his father, if the father still lived), could not be the heir and executor of the estate.[144] At best she could be classified in the second category of persons who were legatees of the estate, entitled to as much as half of the husband's property.[145] Under the Julian Law, a wife could be made heir to 10 percent of the estate if the couple had had one child, and an additional 10 percent for each further child, even if none had survived. Furthermore, the widow could obtain one-third of her husband's estate for her use (usufruct), and ownership of that third if she had further children either because she was pregnant when her husband died or remarried.

In addition to the advantages granted to those who had children, the law imposed penalties upon those who did not. First and foremost it set legal maximum ages by which men and women had to marry – twenty-five for men, twenty for women. An unmarried person could not be named as heir or legatee to an estate, and a childless person could only receive half of an inheritance or legacy.[146] The rest of the inheritance would pass to qualified legatees, or, if these did not exist, to the imperial treasury as *bona caduca*.[147] It was this aspect of the law that Constantine and Licinius changed:

> Those persons who were formerly considered celibates by the ancient law shall be freed from the threatening terrors of the law, and they shall live as though numbered among married men and supported by the bonds of matrimony, and all men shall have equal status in that they shall be able to accept anything to which they are entitled.
>
> (*CTh.* 8.16.1, trans. Pharr)

The same freedom was granted to women, though the statutory limit on how much a spouse could inherit from a spouse was maintained:

> The use of this benefit shall not extend to (gifts exchanged) be-tween husbands and wives, whose deceptive pleasantries cannot be restrained by rigorous opposition of the law, but let the ancient authority of law remain in the case of those persons.
>
> (*CTh.* 8.16.1.2)

The effect of these regulations was to clear the way for people to dispose of their estates as they saw fit, a point that was reinforced by other sections of the law in which the emperors ruled that intent, rather than the actual formula involved, was the key to determining the disposition of property:

> It doesn't matter if he should say "I make my heir" or "I institute,"
> or "I wish" or "I entrust," or "I wish," or "is to be," or "will be,"
> but the will shall be made with whatever words, formed with what-
> ever expression, so long as the intent of the wish is free from doubt
> through it, nor is the order of words significant that, by chance, the
> babbling tongue of a half-dead person should pour forth.
>
> $(CJ\ 9.15.1)^{148}$

The final section of the law (as it can now be reconstructed) appears to
have concerned varying forms of debt. In one case the emperors ban a form
of forfeiture known as *commissoria*, by which it appears that a creditor could
compel a debtor to give him some piece of property in payment. The point
at issue was that the property that was seized might well be undervalued in
the creditor's interest, so the emperors also rule that anyone who has lost
property through *commissoria* should be allowed to purchase it back for the
price that it was valued in payment of the debt.[149] A final portion of the law
that survives appears to deal with people who were unwilling to take up an
inheritance because they did not wish to pay the taxes that were due. The
emperors restrict the severity of the action that their magistrates can take
against people in this condition, and provide that, if the person owing the
tax on the property should persist in refusing to pay, the property should
be seized by the community, which would then see to it that the tax was
delivered to the imperial authorities.[150]

Taken as a whole, the law does not reveal any doctrinal motivation: it
appears simply to be concerned with eliminating traditional formulae that
could clog the courts or were felt to be unfair.[151] There is no reason to think
that either emperor was concerned to make it easier for people to leave money
to ascetic communities – by definition consisting of childless individuals who
would otherwise be barred from receiving an inheritance. Why then should
Eusebius read this law as an act of religious partisanship (either polytheist
or Christian)? We really cannot know, though the very fact that he should
do so is a sign of the way that Constantine had changed the terms of Christian
discourse. It would have been inconceivable that a Christian in 300 would
have read Diocletian's action against the Manichaeans as a pro-Christian act,
even though it damaged a group that he despised, or that a Christian could
read Diocletian's law banning close-kin marriage as being influenced by
Christian doctrine. But it was now conceivable for a person to do such a
thing not just in Eusebius' church, but even in a courtroom in Oxyrhynchus.

If it is difficult to find compelling reasons to think that Eusebius is correct
about the motivation of Constantine's legislation on marriage, what about
his record of Constantine's actions against traditional cults? He points to a
number of cases, in addition to the decoration of Constantinople (where he
may charitably be described as inaccurate), where representatives of traditional cult were persecuted. Thus he says that Constantine's officials were

responsible for the arrest, torture, and execution of a prophet at Didyma. Eusebius viewed this as an act of divine judgment in return for the oracle given by Apollo to Diocletian advising him to persecute the Christians.[152] Since we cannot be certain that the person arrested in 325 (if that is the right year) had been in office twenty years earlier, it is best to reserve judgment on Eusebius' accuracy.[153] More likely this unfortunate had been arrested on suspicion of supporting Licinius. Such reinterpretation of imperial actions against isolated temples occurs also in Eusebius' *Life of Constantine*, where he reports that the emperor destroyed three temples in the east, that of Apollo at Aigeai, that of Aphrodite at Aphaca in Phoenicia, and that of Aphrodite at Heliopolis.[154] The first was famous as a place where Apollonius of Tyana had spent much time, and as the site of an oracle.[155] The rites at both temples of Aphrodite included sacred prostitution, which, it appears, was the actual cause of their demolition. Action against individual temples was anything but new in Roman history, especially those temples that were thought to be dangerous to social order. There is no reason to think that the destruction of either shrine was any more an act inspired solely by Christian doctrine; likewise, Constantine's suppression of an Egyptian priesthood on the grounds of immorality owes more to imperial tradition than explicit doctrine.[156]

When we turn away from Eusebius, one of the few actions of Constantine on the subject of polytheism to survive in the Theodosian Code is a remarkably conservative letter to the *praefectus urbi* in 320, telling him to consult the haruspices (experts in divination on the basis of natural signs) about lightning that had struck the Colosseum, and stating that the same should be done if the imperial palace were to be struck. He went on to say that people should be allowed to consult with prophets so long as they did not do so at night (a long-standing provision).[157] Just a few years earlier, he had instructed another prefect of Rome that magicians who acted to harm other people were to be arrested, but that

> the remedies that are sought for human ailments or in rural districts
> in order that rains may not be feared for the mature products of the
> vineyard or that they may not be shattered by the stones of ruinous
> hail, innocently requested, should be implicated in no crime, since
> by such devices no person's safety or reputation is injured, but by
> their action they bring it about that divine gifts and the labor of
> men are not destroyed.
>
> (*CTh.* 9.16.3)

In such cases it is impossible to discern any new policy directed against traditional practices. But it is also the case that the extant rulings of Constantine on the subject of divination come from the period prior to the defeat of Licinius, raising the possibility that he became a more determined foe of traditional belief as he grew older. It is here that a passage of Eusebius, taken with a letter written by his son Constans in 341, may be suggestive. Eusebius states that after Licinius' defeat, Constantine ordered that imperial officials not participate in public sacrifices.[158] This does appear to be an action that can be directly related to church law, which forbade such activities on the part of Christians who held local or imperial office.[159] The second thing that Eusebius says that Constantine did was to ban the erection of new cult images, the practice of divination "or even to sacrifice at all."[160] The letter of Constans states,

> Superstition *(superstitio)* shall cease; the madness of sacrifice shall be abolished. For if any man in violation of the law of the divine emperor our father, and in violation of this order of our Clemency should dare offer sacrifice, he will suffer the infliction of a suitable penalty and the effect of an immediate sentence.
>
> (*CTh.* 16.10.2, trans. Pharr, adapted)

The problem with what would seem to be the unusual clarity of this situation (two separate attestations of a general ban on sacrifice by Constantine) is a letter of Constantine himself, written in 337 to the community of Hispellum in Etruria.[161] The people of Hispellum had written asking that they be permitted to build a large temple in honor of the family of Constantine and to celebrate the emperor "every other year" with "an exhibition of theatrical shows and gladiatorial games."[162] The emperor responded,

> To your petition and desire we have acceded with ready assent. For to the municipality of Hispellum we have granted an eternal title and revered name from our appellation, so that in the future the aforesaid city shall be called Flavia Constans; and in its midst, as you wish, we desire a temple of the Flavian family, that is, our family, to be constructed in magnificent style, with this restriction, that a temple dedicated to our name be not defiled by the evils of any contagious superstition *(superstitio)*. Accordingly, we have also given you permission to exhibit spectacles in the aforementioned city.
>
> (*ILS* 705, 37–49, trans. Lewis and Reinhold, no. 174)

The word *superstitio* that Constantine uses in this letter has a long history in Latin, designating foreign, unusual, or despised religious customs – Tacitus, for instance, had described Christianity as an *exitiabilis superstitio*.[163] Its usage expanded in the course of the fourth century to designate any form of polytheist behavior, but in the reign of Constantine, it does not yet seem to have acquired so sweeping a meaning. It could be taken as designating the activities of independent practitioners of the divine, activities such as those at Aegeai, Aphraca, and Heliopolis, or more broadly public sacrifice (as here).

The fact that Constantine should specify that there should be no *superstitio* connected with celebration of his family raises the question of why he had to specify this if he had already banned all forms of sacrifice. Despite what both Eusebius and Constans had to say, the most probable explanation of Constantine's language is that he had imposed a selective ban on sacrificial acts: his officials were not to sacrifice, sacrifices were not to be offered in connection with divination, and they were not to be offered in connection with the imperial cult.[164] At the end of the fourth century, the rhetor Libanius would write that "he made absolutely no change in the traditional forms of worship," and, while it is possible that Libanius could be as tendentious as Eusebius, his statement appears to conform better with the evidence outside of Eusebius than do the various statements that Eusebius offers.[165]

Constantine appears to have felt that it was sufficient to ban an activity that he disapproved of where it touched upon his person and the actions of his officials, and in situations where it had long been banned. In this he is using the government to model approved behavior, but stopping short of compelling all of his subjects to follow suit. In his letter to Arius and Alexander asking them to compose their disputes on their own, he had written:

> My first concern was that the attitude towards the Divinity of all the provinces should be united in one consistent view, and my second that I should restore and heal the body of the republic, which lay severely wounded. In making provision for these objects, I began to think out the former with the hidden eye of reason, and I tried to rectify the latter by the power of the military arm. I knew that if I were to establish a general concord among the servants of God in accordance with my prayers, the course of public affairs would also enjoy the change consonant with the pious desires of all.
>
> (Euseb. *Vit. Const.* 2.65, trans. Hall)

The policy here enunciated appears to be consistent with his many actions in the field of religion: old practices that could support his design were supported, and changes were initiated so as to allow the government to lead by example.[166] So too, in a rescript concerning the application of the city of Orcistus in Phrygia to regain civic status in 329 or 330, Christianity is explicitly presented as a sort of "plus factor" aiding an already strong case rather than a decisive point. Constantine makes it clear that his decision is made on traditional grounds – it was a nice place with appropriate amenities – adding at the end, that "in addition to all these things it is a sort of blessing that all who live there say that they are followers of the most sacred religion."[167] Constantine had learned through the failures of the tetrarchic persecutions, and his own persecution of the Donatists, that force would not

434

work. But he also had the confidence in his own powers of persuasion to think that he would make his point if he enabled others to see the benefit of thinking the way that he did.

When it came to the church itself, Constantine's conduct was different. Here he can be seen to be far more proactive: there was no place for temporal authority in the church prior to the reign of Constantine: government officials who were also Christians were expected to be under the authority of the local bishop in matters spiritual wherever they might serve.[168] This would not do in the case of the emperor. A ruler who derived his authority from the personal favor shown to him by God could scarcely admit to a lesser degree of relationship with the Lord of Hosts than a bishop. While the church already had something of a governing structure through councils of bishops, these bishops had little authority to enforce their decisions unless they could convince some local official to help, as the bishops who approached Aurelian had hoped would happen in the case of Paul of Samosata. Constantine essentially grafted imperial authority onto the government of the church through church councils. He did not presume to dictate doctrine or the conclusion to disputes without summoning bishops to council, but he could ensure that the decisions of those councils were enforced (and provide guidance on doctrinal issues). In a sense his handling of the internal controversies of the church mirrors his handling of the relationship between Christian and non-Christian, for just as he could insert some Christian doctrine into existing practice, so too could he insert imperial government into existing structures of the church. His empire was neither polytheist nor Christian. It was both.

The architecture of coexistence: Rome, Constantinople, and the Holy Land

There is perhaps no more forceful illustration of Constantine's approach to matters of religion than the way that he built, and, in some ways, Constantine's building programs remained the most powerful illustration of his policy of religious coexistence. In this he may have owed a considerable debt to the tetrarchic legacy of construction, as may be revealed by what he did at Rome in the wake of his victory over Maxentius. The decoration of his arch was designed to place him in the context of the good emperors of the past: to show him as the true heir both to the Antonines and to the tetrarchy as the son of Constantius. So too it was intended to efface the memory of the "tyrant" Maxentius, by assimilating the latter's extensive building in his own program.[169]

The architecture of legitimacy was soon supplemented by the architecture of the new faith. Constantine was responsible for the construction of three large new churches in the city. The first of these churches, allegedly built upon the suggestion of Silvester, Miltiades' predecessor as bishop of Rome, was constructed on the site of the camp of the *equites singulares* of Maxentius on the Caelian hill.[170] The choice of location is significant, for one of Constantine's first acts had been the abolition of the two bodies of troops who might be thought to have been most loyal to Maxentius: the *equites* and the praetorians.[171] He would also have been well aware of the danger of allowing Rome to have its own garrison, and by abolishing these two units he was forever changing the political dynamic of the capital. The political geography of the city was losing one of its most important fixed points in the destruction of the praetorian camp, and, although the camp of the *equites singulares* was of very much more recent date, its concurrent demise made it clear that the capital would never again have a garrison with which it could defy an emperor. The land upon which the new church was built lay in close proximity to two other imperial residences, of which one, the house of Fausta, was large enough to accommodate the council that first heard the complaints of the Donatists.[172] The other was the Sessorian palace, which Helena soon took for her own.[173] The location of the new church could thus be seen as being associated with the new dynasty without impinging upon the regions of the city where public imperial display was expected.

The second church that can definitely be associated with Constantine appears also to have been connected with the former garrison of Rome, this time because it was erected on the Via Labicana over what appears to have been the burial ground of the *equites singulares*.[174] The building, which was associated with a large mausoleum (possibly intended, at one time, to house members of Constantine's family), again linked the private side of the imperial house with the new faith. A third church, that of Saint Laurence, was constructed somewhat later, probably after the defeat of Licinius, near the site of a large Christian cemetery, on what again appears to have been an imperial property, though this time one that was just outside the city.[175] The final church that Constantine had built at Rome, well after he had taken up residence at Constantinople, was that of Saint Peter on the Vatican.[176] This was the grandest of all his Christian buildings, and one that appears to have been intended, at least in part, to advertise the success of his house under the patronage of the Christian God. In all cases there could be no mistaking the message that Constantine was sending, that he saw himself, and his family, as being devoted to their faith, while at the same time keeping it somewhat apart from the traditional regions of imperial display – he was, in a sense, driving home a point about his own two bodies. As emperor he was a leader in the tradition of great emperors of the past. As a man he was a Christian.

Eusebius' failure to mention these churches is of considerable help in visualizing the impact and intended audience of Constantine's ecclesiastical building at Rome. This failure is particularly notable because he does mention the enormous statue that Constantine erected in the basilica of Maxentius, giving it a Christian spin that may well have been lost upon many, for the statue had in its hand a cross-shaped standard, upon which

Constantine had inscribed a statement that it was a symbol of his victory.[177] A polytheist might simply have observed a standard, which, by definition, had the shape of a cross. This statue was an early victory monument and thus came to Eusebius' attention in the context of Constantine's defeat of Maxentius. That he does not mention any of the churches that Constantine subsequently built at Rome is a sign, perhaps, that they were not intended for an empirewide audience.

Eusebius was, however, part of the intended audience for another construction project, one where Constantine had to fear no competition from aristocratic monuments and the history of earlier emperors. This was in the Holy Land, and it involved an interesting complication: a visit from the emperor's septuagenarian mother.[178] It is hard not to see Helena's move as being connected with the events in Rome during 326, and her departure for the east may be seen as symbolizing the reunification of the empire. The imperial family (albeit truncated) needed to be seen as caring for all the provincials. She may have served another purpose as well, in the wake of Nicaea, which was to emphasize the imperial house's concern for the unity of the Christian community. The focal point of her journey would be an unusual one: Palestine. It was there that Constantine had undertaken a remarkable building project, constructing a new Holy Land for all Christians. He could do this in Palestine as it was removed from the main areas of polytheist geography; buildings there would not threaten the great shrines of the Greco-Roman past, or be seen to conflict directly with them. Before her departure, Constantine had given permission to Macarius, the bishop of Jerusalem, to destroy a temple of Aphrodite that appears to have been constructed over a cave that was identified as having been the tomb of Christ.[179] The contrast to his behavior at Rome, and elsewhere, could not be more striking, but Palestine was not Rome, and aggressive Christianity would not be nearly so visible. What is more, it is arguable that the site of Christ's tomb had been identified as such prior to the construction of the temple of Aphrodite, and the temple itself was, therefore, a sign of aggressive polytheism that needed to be controlled. Christian history could then be placed upon an equal footing with the history of the classical past. Constantine would do the same thing at another site, Mamre, where three angels allegedly visited Abraham. Here too there was a polytheist shrine, and here too the shrine would be destroyed to make possible the restoration of the "true" historical significance of the site.[180] This action seems to have been somewhat later, in the context of another visit to Palestine by a woman of the imperial household (Constantine's mother-in-law) who had reported that the polytheist shrine had obscured the holy site. Constantine's language in this case represents the essence of his policy:

In these circumstances it is right, so it seems to me, that by our provision this site should be kept clear of every defilement and restored to its ancient holy state, so that no other activity goes on there except the performance of the cult appropriate to God the Almighty, our savior and the Lord of the Universe.

(Euseb. *Vit. Const.* 3.53.3, trans. Hall)

As the supposed tomb of Christ was excavated, Eusebius gives a sense of its historical significance:

Thus after its descent into darkness it came forth again to the light and enabled those who came as visitors to see plainly the story of the wonders wrought there, testifying by facts louder than any voice to the resurrection of the Savior.

(Euseb. *Vit. Const.* 3.28, trans. Hall)

The letter that Constantine sent to Macarius instructing him to build symbolizes the emperor's conception of the way that the church and the imperial government could work together, offering all the material support that Macarius needed to realize his vision of the appropriate building:

For my Religious Care has ordered that craftsmen and laborers and everything they may learn from your Good Sense to be needed for the building work should forthwith be supplied by their (two previously mentioned imperial officials) provision. As to the columns of marble, you should, after a survey yourself write promptly to us about what you may consider to be of most value and use, so that whatever quantity and kind of materials we may learn from your letter to be needful may be competently supplied from all sources. It is right that the world's most miraculous place should be worthily embellished.

(Euseb. *Vit. Const.* 3.31.2–3, trans. Hall)

The church that was built was an extraordinary one, both in size and design, for within its courtyard it contained both the alleged hill of Golgotha and the tomb.[181] It is also of interest that it was the only building begun before Helena's arrival, perhaps because the site was already known and had been the object of controversy. When Helena arrived, she was to initiate work on two more churches, also connected with the life of Christ, one at Bethlehem, to mark his birthplace, the other on the Mount of Olives, to mark the place of his ascension.[182] Work seems to have proceeded more slowly at these sites, for although both were consecrated in Helena's presence, neither may have been completed before Constantine died in 337. Nonetheless, archaeological evidence points to construction programs similar to that at Jerusalem, for in both places the focal point of the shrine was the spot where an event was supposed to have taken place.[183]

The Constantinian Holy Land gave Christians a physical center for their history, but in quite a particular way. Pagan shrines were eliminated so as not to conflict with Christian history, but a Christian history that was centered in Palestine likewise did not conflict with local histories in the centers of Mediterranean civilization. They might be thought to conflict with Jewish history, of course: especially in the appropriation of Mamre. But, in a sense, Mamre had already been lost as a Jewish site by the erection of a polytheist temple, while Jerusalem had been, since the reign of Hadrian, the Roman *colonia* of Aelia Capitolina, detached from its purely Jewish history. The new church was no more a challenge than the old shrine; the status quo was maintained. There is no suggestion that Constantine sought to appropriate other biblical sites to a purely Christian audience.

The vision of Constantine

When Constantine defeated Maxentius, there may have been six million Christians in the empire.[184] His conversion cannot be seen as an effort to subvert his rivals by joining his cause to that of a major group within the state, nor can it seriously be maintained that the organization of the church, riven as it was by controversy in two of the major centers of the empire, Carthage and Alexandria, presented an apparatus for insinuating imperial control at the local level.[185] Constantine's relationship with the church evolved as a result of his experience with the Donatists, which illustrated the failure of coercion. If the imperial government were to function in the context of the church, a method needed to be worked out whereby imperial officials and bishops could cooperate. To this end Constantine used church councils to settle points of dispute within the church, and rewarded those willing to compromise.

In dealing with his non-Christian subjects, Constantine usually acted within the traditions of Roman law. Offensive cults were suppressed because they were offensive cults, not because they were non-Christian. As the treatment of the temples on the site of the tomb of Christ and Mamre suggests, cults that actively infringed upon Christian practice could now be targeted – but the qualification is important. If a cult site was not infringing, it would be left alone. In terms of broader legislation – aside from that establishing the right of bishops to hear civil cases – there is little that can be seen to be expressly Christian, and even laws such as that providing that Sunday be a holiday were capable of multiple readings. It was Constantine's purpose to make the Christian reading a valid one in public, and that was, perhaps, the most significant effect of his reign.

Part V

LOSING POWER

12

CHURCH AND STATE:
337–55

The last years of Constantine and the years in which his sons ruled the empire saw a remarkable change in the nature of the Roman Empire. This change goes well beyond the obvious, that Christianity had obtained a new status, and impacts on the problem of what it meant to be Roman. The deep involvement of Constantine and his sons made the church a symbol of attachment to Roman-ness for those who would not readily fit any definition of what it meant to be Roman in the second century. One no longer had to be under the direct authority of Roman magistrates to be, in some degree, a member of the community of the Romans. At the same time, a new style of recruitment into the Roman army created a group with links on both sides of the border different from those whose connections could be defined simply by influence, clientage, or economic activity. The bureaucratic structures connected with the army now stretched beyond the frontiers into tribal lands, creating a form of "Roman" who was brought up outside the empire and yet played a role in the defense of the state. To be in the army, and in the service of the emperor, was to be "Roman," even if one's roots were beyond the Rhine or Danube, as may have been the member of Licinius' horse guards who died fighting for his master "in the battle between the Romans and their adversaries" at Chalcedon.[1]

These changes in the nature of Roman-ness were the consequence of the centrality of the imperial office to Roman life. There were no longer alternative styles of government reaching back into the hoary antiquity of the republic. The court was the only institution of the Roman state that mattered, and a reshaped bureaucracy now administered a state centered exclusively on the palace.[2] But while the structures of palace government were now all-encompassing, they were also, to some degree, still experimental. The effects of changes in style of government may be seen in the tale of the years between the death of Constantine and the elevation of his nephew, Julian, to the rank of Caesar in 355. But before this story can be told, some attention to the impact of Christianity abroad, and to the army, will be needed.

Christianity and foreign relations

At two points in the years after his defeat of Licinius, Constantine was moved to take the field in person. One of these campaigns, which lasted from 328 to 332, was north of the Danube and ended with the institution of a new alliance with the Gothic peoples of the region that would shape their relationship with the empire for more than thirty years. The second of these campaigns was against Persia and was only beginning when Constantine suddenly took ill and died on May 22, 337. This too would shape Roman relations with Persia for nearly three decades, culminating in the catastrophic invasion of Mesopotamia in 363 by Constantine's nephew Julian. In both cases Constantine's policies had a pronounced religious element, as he sought to press his brand of Christianity on his neighbors. This aggressive assertion of religion is at first glance strikingly different from Constantine's pattern of behavior within the empire itself, where he sought to open new paths for Christian advancement without necessarily attacking the interests of his more traditionally minded subjects. The distinction is, however, rather less striking when it is viewed in the context of the building projects that we examined at the end of the last chapter. In Palestine, as at Rome and in Constantinople, he constructed a Christian environment where he would not compete with strong local interests that opposed his designs. While he was willing to respect existing traditions among his subjects, he plainly considered the traditions of the "barbarians" across Rome's frontiers as being less worthy of respect and their lands to be fertile territory for the expansion of his faith.

We do not know what prompted Constantine to build a bridge across the Danube at Oescus in 328, or to spend that summer and the next two campaigning against the Goths.[3] What is clear, however, is that at the end of three campaigning seasons the Goths elected to make peace with the emperor, and that, in addition to more traditional terms, such as a requirement that the Goths send men to serve in the Roman army, and the dispatch of gifts to Gothic chieftains who demonstrated loyalty, Constantine appears to have taken the opportunity to promote Christianity in their lands. He even appointed a man named Ulfilas to be bishop of their people, albeit in the very last year of his life.[4] The impact of Ulfilas was perhaps less grand than later Christian historians made it out to be. Nonetheless, Ulfilas did have some success, and he created a written form of the Gothic language into which he could translate scripture. In so doing, he created a link in the minds of some Goths with participation in Roman culture through religion that was distinct from service in the Roman army. It is perhaps testimony to his success that Goths who did not themselves convert recognized in Christianity a Romanizing threat to their traditional existence.[5] Ulfilas was driven into exile and ministered at the end of his life to a Gothic community within the empire, and there was at least one other period of persecution

444

within Gothic territory in the next half century (proof, of a sort, that he had been successful).[6] Despite this, it would be Christian priests who would suddenly appear as intermediaries between Goths and Romans after the massive influx of Goths that would occur in 375. The role of these priests suggests that Ulfilas had created the conditions for a new discourse, and a way of communicating outside the traditional framework of interstate relations.

In the kingdoms of Armenia, Aksum, and Iberia, Christian missionaries achieved more spectacular successes.[7] The conversion of Armenia took place even before Constantine defeated Licinius. It appears that Tiridates III decided to convert in 313 or 314, under the influence of the Cappadocian bishop, Gregory the Illuminator.[8] The kingdom of Iberia, on the west coast of the Black Sea (roughly in the area of modern Georgia), converted in the 330s. The story of its conversion, offered by Rufinus at the end of the fourth century, gives credit to a woman whose faith enabled her to conduct miraculous cures.[9] Her activities brought the church to the positive attention of the king, who decided to convert if he was rescued from a darkness that enveloped him in a forest while hunting. Constantine is then said to have lent material aid for the construction of churches. Whatever lay behind the conversion itself, it was plainly a departure for the Iberian king, whose realm appears hitherto to have contained many Zoroastrians. It may be that in this case religion provided a rather more successful vehicle for diplomacy than it did among the Goths, since the more organized society of the Iberians could be converted from the top down once the king himself had converted.

Perhaps the most spectacular conversion of all was that of the king of Aksum, in the area of modern Ethiopia. According to Rufinus, who appears to have been attracted to stories that emphasized the role of the humble in converting barbarian kings, two boys, once slaves of a philosopher named Meropius, were responsible for the conversion. One of them, Frumentarius, became the chief adviser to the king and gave Christian merchants particular trading privileges in the kingdom, aiding the conversion of the young ruler. In time he appears to have made contact with Athanasius and was himself ordained, while his companion returned to Roman territory, where he was ordained as a priest at Tyre.[10] The interest of this story lies in the way that Christianity could transform traditional trading partnerships. These links were, as we saw in chapter 1, of long standing, but they were not self-evidently vehicles for the translation of the cultural values of the Roman Empire onto foreign soil. Now, however, the possibility of creating extra-governmental institutions in foreign kingdoms was transforming existing patterns and changing the meaning of what it was to be Roman. For if we allow that a definition of Roman-ness is the transformation of behaviors through contact with the institutions of the Roman Empire, then the church was gradually creating a new category of extraimperial "Roman" in cases where the local authorities were willing to accede to the message of the church. Although polytheism could have an impact on local practice, and while Hellenism could provide a vehicle for communication between non-Roman and Roman, the creation of institutions that mirrored those within the empire, and derived authority from an institution that was centered in the empire, was genuinely new.[11]

The situation with respect to Persia was different, for there were already well-established Christian communities within Persian territory. Kirdir had included Christians among the peoples whom he had persecuted for not following his Zoroastrian dispensation, and the result of Constantine's intervention would not be a renewed persecution of his coreligionists.[12] It may be that Constantine thought that he could apply the model that had worked in his dealings with Goths, Iberians, and Armenians to Persia; if so, he was terribly wrong.

Constantine's first official contact with Persia came in the wake of his victory over Licinius, when Sapor sent an embassy to congratulate him on his triumph. Constantine responded with an extraordinary letter in which he told the Persian king what was important to him.[13] The letter opens with an interesting variation on the then standard Constantinian line that he had set out from the shores of the western ocean to free an empire groaning under the oppression of tyrants. In the very opening line, Constantine says that "protecting the divine faith, I participate in the light of truth; guided by the divine light, I gain knowledge of the divine faith."[14] The reference here to *lux divina* (Eusebius says that the letter was written in Latin) could have been taken by a polytheist reader as a glance toward the worship of the sun, still advertised on Constantine's coins, and read by a Persian as a statement that, in Persian terms, Constantine was protected by none other than Ahura Mazda.[15] After stating that he carries the symbol of this god (still unnamed) with his army, and attributing victory to it, he goes on to say,

> I call upon him on bended knee, fleeing all abominable blood, foul and disgusting smells, shunning every earthly lamp, the lawless and horrid error, polluted by these rites, that has taken root in many nations, casting the whole race into the lower depths.
>
> (Euseb. *Vit. Const.* 4.10)

Any Persian may well have thought that this confession of the error of classical polytheism brought Constantine closer to his own way of thinking, and have welcomed the statement in the next section that Valerian had been smitten with divine vengeance. It would have been a pleasant change from having been lectured on the ill treatment of that emperor by Constantine's predecessors.[16] In the last section of the letter, however, Constantine says something that could be regarded as deeply troubling, for there he reveals that the god about whom he is speaking is the Christian God, and that he expects the Persian king to look after Christian communities in his realm. The veiled threat implicit in this statement is softened by the assertion that Constantine's religiosity is not dissimilar to that of the Persian king himself, and that Constantine is willing to back away from the style of diplomacy known from his predecessors. Constantine thereby suggests that a new relationship is possible so long as the Persians respect the freedom of Christians to worship as they wish in the land of the Persian king.

Sapor may have had reason to be deeply suspicious of what Constantine was saying. According to a tradition reported by Tabarī, his father, Hormisdas II, had bequeathed him the throne while he was in his mother's womb, a story that may have developed as a way to explain his preternaturally long reign (309–79).[17] Certainly it is possible that he was younger than his brother Hormisdas, who had fled the country just as Constantine was defeating Licinius, and had been received at the Roman court.[18] Hormisdas would remain there in a position of honor for the rest of his life. If the presence of a rival to the throne was not enough, then Constantine's reference to Christianity may have been problematic in light of the Armenian conversion. Still, peace prevailed until 330, when Tiridates of Armenia died without a mature heir. Succession to the throne of Armenia was determined by the nobles who controlled the districts into which the kingdom was divided, the *nakharars*. After Tiridates' death, the *nakharars* appear to have split, some favoring Arsaces, a child, who was the son of Tiridates, while others looked to Persia. Arsaces fled to Roman territory, and chaos ensued, with, it seems, Persian troops entering some of the eastern districts in 336. This may be seen as a preemptive strike, for the troubles in Armenia had already led Constantine to decide on war. According to one tradition, the official cause of the war was not, however, the Armenian situation, but rather an affront offered to Constantine's own majesty by Sapor, who, when asked to hand over some treasure sent to Constantine by an Indian king, had refused. Later Roman tradition held that the whole business was a fabrication, and that Constantine had been misled by a merchant named Metrodorus, who had never had the treasure.[19] The "lies of Metrodorus" are a sham. Constantine plainly had his eye on Armenia and, beyond that, had decided, for dynastic reasons of his own, that he would conquer Persia.[20] In so doing he raised expectations that he would make his faith the faith of the peoples he conquered.[21]

If the war with Persia arose out of the traditional politics of Armenia, and Constantine's own ambitions, it remains the case that this war had a different aspect to it, an aspect lent by religious differences. For the first time the Christian community on both sides of the frontier would be drawn into the conflict for confessional reasons, and a Persian king would begin a persecution of the church not for internal reasons of his own, but rather in the context of his struggle with Rome.

The Roman army

In terms of tactics, recruitment, equipment, and organization, the army that Constantine planned to lead against the Persians was radically different from that which had failed in the middle of the third century.[22] The most significant changes were a shift in the balance between infantry and cavalry, with the latter gaining new tactical responsibilities, and a shift in the balance between the strategic reserve and frontier forces. The changes in tactical doctrine appear to have been progressive since the disasters of the 250s and 260s, while the new strategic organization likewise appears to have been gradual, culminating only in the last years of Constantine. It is not a great help to our understanding of this process that the Christian historians who provide the bulk of our information about Constantine were not interested in it, and that Zosimus' description (derived from Eunapius) implies that Constantine's policies marked a catastrophic break with the past. Zosimus' account is as follows:

> Constantine did something else that gave the barbarians unhindered access to the territory that was subject to the Romans; through the forethought of Diocletian, as I have said above, the frontiers of the Roman empire were everywhere covered by cities, garrisons, and towers, and the entire army had quarters in these places. Passage was impossible for the barbarians, confronted in every place by forces capable of resisting their incursions. Constantine destroyed this security, removing the great majority of the soldiers from the frontiers; he stationed them in cities that did not require assistance. He stripped those needing protection from the barbarians, and subjected the cities that they did not attack to the disorder of the soldiers, so that most of the cities became deserted; and he enervated the troops by allowing them spectacles and a comfortable life. To speak plainly, he was the beginning of and laid the seed for the present weakness of the empire.
>
> (2.34)

While it is unfortunate that Zosimus' treatment of Diocletian's military policies has disappeared, what he says here suggests that he tried to establish a distinction between an emperor who favored a forward defense on the frontiers over one who withdrew troops to the interior. The dichotomy between the two men is misleading. It is true that the reign of Diocletian had seen significant building activity in the border regions, as it had in many other areas, but Constantine did not abandon the frontiers. Looking at the archaeology of the northern frontiers, it is pointless to try and draw meaningful distinctions between the rulers of the first half of the fourth century: all emperors appear to have been equally concerned with the security of their borders. Constantine did expand upon one important Diocletianic reform in the strategic deployment of the army, but this cannot be said to have weakened the frontiers. What is most important is rather that there was a coherent departure from earlier patterns of behavior. This may been seen, in concrete terms, through styles of building, and in theoretical terms by the creation of new units.

Roman forts of the first two and a half centuries AD had tended, in the west, to be oblong with rounded corners, based on the pattern of the traditional marching camp with towers inside the wall and with a rampart of earth backing the stone facing that had replaced earlier timber. Administrative buildings were placed in the center with barracks and other buildings arranged around the rest of the interior space.[23] In the eastern provinces and in North Africa, the style had varied, with some forts built on the western pattern, others in indigenous styles with a square shape and square towers that broke the wall. In most cases, where units were based in cities, the old defense systems were taken over.[24] In the wake of Marcus' wars on the northern frontier, there is evidence, in a few places, of a change, with the addition of projecting gate towers to existing forts, but these were rare.[25] This pattern began to change in the last quarter of the third century with a group of forts built in Britain and along the coast of northern Gaul facing what would become known as the Saxon shore.[26] These buildings had fewer gates, usually only one, protected by projecting towers; they had thicker walls, and, with one possible exception, no earth rampart. Elsewhere, new structures were built inside of existing buildings, as at Eining on the Danube, where a citadel occupies a corner of the old, and the line of the walls was reinforced with towers.[27] At Ulcisia Castra, also on the Danube, all but one of the gates were closed off with projecting D-shaped towers, while projecting interval towers were added to strengthen the walls.[28] Similar changes appear at numerous other locations, albeit with enough variation in detail to suggest that local architects, responding to instructions to rebuild, had some leeway in selecting specific design features.[29] New forts were typically square, again with projecting towers and only one, strongly fortified, gate.[30] The bridgeheads across the Rhine and Danube all acquire, in the course of the fourth century, new buildings on similar patterns. Although it is impossible to date all of these forts with precision, and the reconstruction of the defensive lines of the empire was an ongoing process throughout the century, it is certainly under the tetrarchs that the pattern was established. It is difficult not to attribute the rise of this new design to anything other than a central policy in which smaller forces were expected to hold defensive positions; the variations between fourth-century sites are less significant than the differences between all fourth-century buildings and those of the earlier empire. While this should not be taken to imply that earlier fortifications were intended to fall at the drop of a hat, it does suggest some coherent rethinking as to how to make defense more effective.[31]

While there can be no debate as to the fact that the style of fortification was changed, there remains considerable debate as to which emperor saw fit to restructure the army so that significant forces would be held away from the frontier as a strategic strike force. The issue is further complicated by the question as to whether or not this new force should be directly connected with Gallienus' cavalry corps. The significance of that reform for the fourth century lay not so much in the detachment of a large enough force to form a strategic reserve from the frontier legions as in the fact that this force contained a much higher proportion of cavalry to infantry than had been the case earlier. With ten cohorts, the Praetorian Guard had formed a strong reserve in the past, and, although its primary skills may have been in the area of urban warfare and crowd control, it was still a capable battlefield unit. With the Severan encampment of Legion II Parthica at Alba, it is fair to say that the emperors possessed a genuine strategic reserve, and it appears that Legion II had at least one permanent encampment prepared for it at Apamea in Syria should it need to be deployed on the eastern frontier.[32]

The existence of the Gallienic cavalry corps implicitly recognized that the traditional styles of legionary warfare were no longer effective. If the Roman army was to be able to fight the Sasanians with a chance of success, it needed to abandon the tactical doctrines of the age of Marius and Caesar. This it seems to have done in the course of the later third century, for the army that appears in the age of Diocletian and Constantine was no longer equipped in the traditional *lorica segmentata* and rectangular *scutum* and no longer armed with the *pilum*. The foot soldier of the fourth century was equipped instead with a pike, throwing spears, leather armor, and an oval shield.[33] These were the weapons of the *auxilia* in an earlier age, and it now appears that the greater flexibility of these units provided fertile ground upon which the seeds of general reform could be planted.

If the real significance of the Gallienic cavalry corps is the fact that it represents a change in operational style, the question remains as to whether this was simply a measure of the reign of Gallienus, or whether it may reasonably be connected to a steady evolution away from frontier-based armies to armies that were based in the interior. The point at issue is the creation of a specific unit, or group of units, permanently described as the *comitatus*, and distinct from the earlier comitatus, a term that was applied on an ad hoc basis to units that accompanied the emperor.[34] To answer this question it is necessary to know whether such an institution can be seen to survive from the 260s into the time of Diocletian. In this case the answer is yes. The evidence offered by Dexippus' account of Aurelian's negotiations with the Vandals and a passage in the record of Zenophilus' investigation of the Donatist controversy in 320 shows that there was a unit known as the comitatus in the reign of Aurelian, and makes it likely that this unit already existed under Gallienus.[35] Although the next attestation of the comitatus does not come until the reign of Diocletian, there is no reason to think that the unit had been abolished and then re-created.[36] Similarly, we are told that Diocletian was a member of the *protectores domestici*, a special guard unit attached to the emperor, when he was elevated to the purple. This unit too appears to be attested under Aurelian in the same fragment of Dexippus, in this case as "the guard of the commander of the *comites*."[37] So too, various cavalry units that can be identified as having been created under Gallienus can be traced from the third century into the fourth, and they appear to be operating throughout this period as special troops of higher status than the old auxiliary cavalry, and independent of the legions.[38]

Although it is possible to trace the ancestors of the units that would form the later field armies or *comitatenses* into the third century, there is no direct evidence for the actual creation of that force until the reign of Constantine, but this evidence is quite complex and needs to be examined in some detail. The most important documentation comes from sections of the letter dispatched by Constantine to Maximus, *vicarius* of Oriens, in 325, and preserved in the Theodosian Code.[39] The first section runs as follows:

> *Comitatenses, ripenses milites*, and *protectores* shall be exempt from the capitation tax on their own persons, as well as those of their fathers, mothers, and wives, if they survive, and if they have been enrolled as *capiti*. But if they should not have one of these, or if they should have none of them, they will exempt, as their own *peculium*, only so much as they would have been able to exempt from these people if they had existed, and they shall not form agreements with other persons whereby they exempt the property of others by fraudulent ownership, but (they will only exempt) what they have.
>
> (*CTh.* 7.20.4)

The crucial feature of this section is the tripartite division of the military, implying a potential distinction in other terms of service between three groups: soldiers who are called *comitatenses, ripenses*, and the imperial guard. The *ripenses* in this text are the same units that were later called the *limitanei*, and, as their title suggests, they were stationed on the frontier.[40] The very title of this section of the army may also suggest that the impetus for the reform came from western or central Europe, where the bulk of the old legions were indeed stationed along the Rhine and Danube, rather than the east, where the bulk of the legions were stationed in camps removed somewhat from the lines of the Tigris and Euphrates.[41] The fact that it is part of a letter addressed to an official who is otherwise dealing with people who had served under Licinius suggests that this distinction must preexist the victory over Licinius. Indeed, this view is necessary if we are to understand the next clause, where Constantine writes,

> We sanction that veterans, after receiving letters of discharge for length of service, shall exempt themselves as well as their wives. If they should receive honorable discharges, they will exempt only themselves. We decree that all veterans, from whatever army, shall enjoy, together with their wives, the exemption of one *caput*.
>
> (*CTh.* 7.20.4.1)

In this case the first distinction that Constantine draws is between men who received retirement benefits with expanded benefits (the *emerita missio*) after twenty-four years of service, and those who retired when they became eligible for retirement with reduced benefits (the *honesta missio*) after twenty years. The second distinction that is apparent is between his troops and those of Licinius, who might be denied exemptions (another portion of this letter dealt with other such people).[42] Since Constantine is reducing the exemptions of people who had earned two exemptions, he must be setting a minimum condition for everyone.

The third section of the law returns us to the problem of when the distinction between different soldiers was first made. Constantine says:

> A veteran of the *ripenses* – who by a previous law if he requested an honorable discharge after twenty-four years of service, enjoyed the exemption of one person – even if he should have earned his honorable discharge after twenty years of service, shall enjoy the exemption of one person on the example of a soldier in the *comitatenses*.
>
> (*CTh.* 7.20.4.2)[43]

The reference to "a previous law" is interesting, as Constantine does not say that it was his law. The lack of specificity is all the more frustrating as the content of this "previous law" appears to have drawn specific comparisons between the rewards for service in the two units, and quite possibly extended the period of service from twenty to twenty-four years in both. Such a law may have been connected with the establishment of the two branches, and in this case it appears that Constantine needed to draw no distinction between men who had served under him and those who had served under Licinius. It may therefore be assumed that the division between these forces arose sometime prior to the defeat of Licinius. But how long before? Although it might be tempting to see the lengths of service specified in the law as being significant – placing the reform firmly in the reign of Diocletian – this is not an approach that can be taken. Units of the earlier army formed the basis of both branches of service, and troops already in the army at the time of the initial reform would presumably have had their time in service "grandfathered" under the earlier law. A useful indication does, however, come in the next section of this letter, treating yet another sort of soldier:

Alares and *cohortales*, as long as they serve, shall have the exemption of their own person, and veterans will retain the same benefit of exemption. If a soldier at any time or in any place has deserved a discharge, if he was discharged from the *comitatenses* by reason of age or disability, even though he had not served the requisite number of years, he will still have the exemption for himself and his wife. Soldiers discharged from the *ripenses*, will have the same privilege without discrimination, if they prove that they were discharged because of wounds they have suffered; if a person will leave military service after fifteen years but before twenty-four years, he will benefit only from the exemption of his own person; he will receive the benefit of the exemption for his wife as well if, as a *ripensis*, he leaves military service after twenty-four years.

(*CTh.* 7.20.4)

The *alares* and *cohortales* mentioned in the first line here are members of units that were still termed *auxilia*, and were recruited from outside the frontiers. It is of some interest that they were not formally classified as belonging to either the *ripenses* or the *comitatenses*, and in this case it appears that the distinction between these types of soldiers continued a practice of Diocletian, who drew a firm distinction between troops in the "regular army" and those recruited into the *auxilia*.[44] The existence of the distinction between the *ripenses* and *comitatenses* and the *auxilia* may also help explain the terms of a letter of Licinius to an officer named Dalmatius, written a month after the death of Galerius in 311 and preserved on a bronze tablet found at Brigetio in Hungary.[45] In this letter, Licinius grants better exemptions than Constantine does in 325, allowing a soldier to exempt five *capita* from the tax rolls while serving, and after obtaining an *emerita missio*. In the concluding lines of the text he says that this rule will affect the "legionary soldiers in Illyricum and the cavalry serving there in detachments," which can be read in one of two ways: either as proof that the distinction between *comitatenses* and *ripenses* did not yet exist, or as a restatement of the Diocletianic policy favoring the "regular army" over the *auxilia*. The answer to this question must be dictated by probability rather than any evidence that is now available. Despite the limited evidence for cooperation between Constantine and Licinius that was examined in chapter 10, I doubt very strongly that anything so significant as the reorganization of the army into the *comitatenses* and *ripenses*, which betrays a common strategic vision, was possible for these two men. As Constantine ignores Licinius' legislation granting greater exemptions for recipients of an *honesta missio*, while referring to "a previous law" for which he does not claim responsibility, I think that the institution of the *comitatenses* should be attributed to Diocletian, even though there is otherwise no unequivocal attestation for its creation.[46]

Even if it is right to conclude that Diocletian was responsible for the creation of the *comitatenses*, a significant role should still be allowed to Constantine for adjusting the command structure by creating new officials to control that formation. According to Zosimus, it was Constantine who first created the offices of *magister peditum* and *magister equitum*, officials who later appear to command sections of the *comitatenses*.[47] Although no official with this title is known prior to 343, there is no good reason to doubt this statement, and it is tempting to see this development in the context of preparations for the war with Persia. Given the limited military experience of his sons, Constantine may well have wanted senior officials in charge of his troops while a major operation was under way. One feature of these offices in the reign of Constantius was that the holders reported directly to the emperor rather than through a Caesar, and there is no reason to think that this was not also the case under Constantine.[48] It appears that the *magistri* exercised direct authority over the units of the *comitatenses* and the guards. But their authority was not limited to these forces.

Since the time of Diocletian, who had initiated the division between civil governors *(praesides)* and military commanders, the units of the field army had reported to regional officials – *comites* or *duces* – who could exercise command over troops in a single province, or, if need dictated, the forces of several provinces. Up until the time that Constantine created the offices of the *magistri equitum* and *peditum*, they appear to have reported to the praetorian prefects. After the creation of the *magistri*, the praetorian prefects ceased having any military role.

Tactics

The transformation of buildings, command structure, and equipment was accompanied by further changes in the army's tactical doctrine. To judge from Ammianus' description of Julian's campaigns in both Gaul and Persia, it appears that the infantry ordinarily formed a base to support attacks launched by the heavy cavalry upon the enemy in the west, while in the east it might be transformed into a shock force, advancing rapidly upon the heavy cavalry that formed the heart of the Sasanian army. At the battle of Strasbourg in 357, for instance, the infantry is described as being grouped into tight formations that held back the Alamannic charge.[49] In a battle outside Ctesiphon in 363, however, it was the Roman infantry that advanced, driving the Sasanian cavalry back upon its infantry and elephants in confusion.[50] In both cases, Ammianus also stresses the use of missile weapons before the hand-to-hand fighting began, and the skill of the Roman infantryman as a swordsman fighting in close formation once battle was joined at close quarters.[51] In addition to the missile weapons used by the main line infantry, Ammianus notes the use of lighter armed troops to cover the advance of the main line.[52] That Ammianus should describe distinctively different tactical operations on the two fronts suggests that one of the great strengths of the late imperial army was its ability to adapt to local conditions and diverse tactical situations. Descriptions of Constantine's battles that appear in Zosimus tend to stress the role of cavalry over infantry.[53] It is impossible to know how true this was, but these descriptions might help confirm the impression offered by Ammianus that, when not fighting the Persians, the cavalry was meant to be the main strike force.

Size and recruitment

When Severus enhanced the strategic reserve of the Roman army by placing Legion II Parthica at Alba, and created Legions I and III to garrison his new acquisitions in northern Mesopotamia, he had increased the legionary force by roughly 10 percent, and it may be surmised that he increased the number of auxiliaries by roughly the same percentage. But what of the fourth century? While there was plainly some carryover from the army of Gallienus and Aurelian, even a cursory glance at the *Notitia Dignitatum*, the list of "all offices, civil and military," composed in AD 395, reveals a host of units that must have been raised in the first part of the fourth century. While the *Notitia* is not a perfect guide, the evidence it offers for the shape of the late Roman army raises the immediate question of whether the reforms of the early fourth century exceeded those of Severus by a significant order of magnitude.[54] Thus, for instance, the list of western *legiones comitatenses* consists of thirty-five units, of which only five descend from the Severan army. This list follows a list of twelve palatine (guard) legions, of which the earliest are Diocletianic, and sixty-five units described as *auxilia*, and is followed by a list of seventeen units described as *pseudo-comitatenses* (former frontier troops that were brought into the *comitatensis* in the course of the fourth century). When units described in the *Notitia* as legions that are plainly later than the time of Diocletian are taken out, there are still no fewer than thirty-five new legions that were brought into service by Diocletian.[55] If these units were the same size as those of the Severan army, this would mean that the army doubled in size, since there is no reason to think that the proportion of nonlegionary troops to those in legions declined.

Lists, however, can be very misleading, and while the lists of the *Notitia* show that new units were raised throughout the fourth century, possibly to replace those that were lost, or possibly to respond to new demands, they do not tell us how many men actually served in any of these units. To assume that units remained the same size is unwise. There is some direct evidence to suggest that the new legions consisted of only about 1,000 men, and even though this would still suggest an increase in the size of the army of roughly 20 percent, that assumption is based upon the view that the older legions retained their original strength.[56] That assumption too is without foundation. The size of the fortifications, whose new design was surveyed above, is, on the whole, smaller than that of the earlier empire, and a record of the pay for a pre-Diocletianic legion in Egypt that is listed in five different places in the *Notitia* (presumably indicating five detachments) suggests that it may have consisted of about 2,500 to 3,000 men.[57] As with the legions, so too with auxiliary units. There is no direct evidence for their strength aside from the size of forts, which seem capable of holding between 80 and 150 men. The variation in size of fortification suggests that there was variation in the size of units with the same designation (there is no evidence that two units were brigaded together in the larger camps). The only thing that can be said for certain is that the army as a whole consisted of many small units. There is no a priori reason, therefore, to think that the increase in the number of units signifies a major increase in the size of the army

If lists of units can tell us very little about the size of the army, then the only evidence that is really of any help is the (admittedly rare) evidence for the total size of an army in the field. But the use of this evidence is problematic. On the one hand, Zosimus says that Constantine had 98,000 men when he invaded Italy in 312, and that Maxentius commanded 188,000, which, if these are total forces, would give 286,000 men for the western empire. This number is not out of line with the astonishingly precise number for men serving under Diocletian – 435,266 – given by John Lydus in the sixth century.[58] This figure would also support the notion (rejected above) that Diocletian had increased the size of the army by around 20 percent. Another number given by Zosimus points in the same direction, which is his tally of the forces that Constantine prepared for the war against Licinius, 130,000 soldiers and 10,000 sailors, while Licinius gathered 165,000 men (no figure is given for sailors, though the implication of a fleet of 350 triremes is 70,000).[59] If we allow that Constantine may have had something like the 286,000 men in the west that were available in 312, it looks as if Zosimus is saying that he brought half his army into the battle, and we may assume (for the sake of argument) that the number for Licinius represents the bulk of his army, since he was defending a smaller empire, meaning that the total number of men under arms may be placed at roughly 500,000.[60] The problem with these estimates is that the armies attributed to Constantine and Licinius are vastly larger than those attested later in the fourth century, and belied by other figures. The author of the panegyric of 313 states that Constantine invaded Italy with fewer than 40,000 men (which is said to be a quarter of all troops under his command).[61] The author of the *Rise of the Emperor Constantine* puts the forces at Cibalae at 35,000 for Licinius and 20,000 for Constantine.[62] Julian had only 18,000 men at Strasbourg, and the army of Barbatio in the same period (the bulk of the *comitatenses* in Gaul) was 25,000.[63] The army that Magnentius led to the battle of Mursa against Constantius in 351 is given by Zonaras as 36,000 men, while that of Constantius, which combined the army of Vetranio with the forces he brought from the east, is given by Zonaras as 80,000.[64] The army that Julian led into Persia was 65,000 strong.[65] The figure for Julian's army is given by Ammianus, who was part of it, and may be taken as the most reliable figure that we have. Ammianus' number may also confirm the essential accuracy of Zonaras' number for the army of Magnentius. It is worth noting that Julian, for both logistical and strategic reasons, divided his army into two parts, and that he had brought with him to the Persian campaign about 23,000 men from the west, the force that he had led against Constantius in 361.[66] In his description of Barbatio's endeavors, Ammianus notes serious logistical problems in moving 25,000 men around for the summer.[67] Indeed, an army of between 30,000 and 40,000 men was about as big a force as could be supplied under the conditions of premodern warfare for a summer. Although Caesar, by the end of his time in Gaul, maintained an army of roughly double this size, the army that he had at Pharsalus was only about 30,000 strong (after a summer of campaigning), while that of Pompey (reinforced just before the battle) was just over 50,000.[68] The armies in the field during the civil war of AD 69 were of roughly the same size.[69] It is only for the Philippi campaign that we get much larger figures (in the hundreds of thousands), and those may be explained by those who wish to believe them as stemming from the unusual nature of the combat, where both sides were committed to a fight to the death.[70] More probably, of course, the numbers were inflated (as were numbers in some traditions connected with Pharsalus) to match the importance of the event.[71]

Where does this leave us? My suspicion is that the evidence from the size of encampments, payrolls, and Ammianus points in the correct direction. The numbers given by Zosimus participate in the time-honored tradition of inflating the number of soldiers to match the importance of an event and are useless for the question of how big the Roman army actually was. If we allow that the army of Julian represents the combined force of the *comitatenses* in the east with half that of the west, and allow further that the *comitatenses* in the Balkans were roughly 40,000 men, that would give a figure of roughly 120,000 men. The reason to think that this is reasonable is that Libanius states that after defeating Magnentius, Constantius controlled the armies of three emperors, with the implication that they were roughly the same size.[72] What proportion was that of the whole? We do not know for certain, but it would not be unreasonable to assume that the *comitatenses* was no larger than the *ripenses*, and possibly only about half the size of the frontier army; these calculations would yield a figure between 240,000 and 360,000 men. In other words, the army of the fourth century was either smaller than, or about the same size as, the Severan army.

Although the fourth-century army was about the same size as the Severan, it does appear that it was recruited differently.[73] There is substantial evidence to suggest that military service was a deeply unpopular occupation for inhabitants of the empire in the fourth century. The long period of service meant that a young man would be removed from his community for the bulk of his adult life, and the army was, as we have seen, an institution that was feared, rather than loved, by the average Roman. A series of laws issued throughout the fourth century reveals that young men would mutilate themselves rather than serve, or that they would try to escape while being transported from their home districts to the legions.[74] Self-mutilation had, however, always been a tactic used by men who feared military service, and the significance of these laws should not be overstressed. What cannot be overstressed, on the other hand, is the role assigned to members of the aristocracy in the provision of recruits. In this, a rule of Diocletian appears to have been crucial. Diocletian, while ordering an annual levy of recruits, permitted landholders to substitute money for men – paying the *aurum tironicum*.[75] Large landowners appear to have been expected to provide one or more men, while lesser landholders formed associations to provide either the man (on a rotating basis) or a portion of the money. It was a system that was open to easy abuse, especially as it appears that collection of the *aurum tironicum* became a *munus*. This meant that landholders could claim that they were commuting the recruit for money, and then withhold payment. Ammianus noted, in describing Julian's government of Gallia Belgica, that the effect of nominally high tax rates resulted in little or no actual payment to the state.[76] Those responsible for paying, if they were powerful enough, would simply await the forgiveness of the community debt, while less powerful men were forced to pay up immediately – with the implication that they lacked the resources to make the full payment and were often ruined by the effort. Valens recognized the same principle in 375 when he wrote to his praetorian prefect:

> The provision of recruits ought to fall on the resources of estates rather than on the *munera* of individuals, so the *munus* of the previous sort,[77] which feasts upon the vitals of the provincials, will be torn out, as is said, by the deepest roots. Amongst other abuses, we judge these two to be particularly intolerable, that an enormous money payment is often demanded, and the purchase price for foreigners as recruits is estimated as being higher than it is. Against these abuses, we have devised an easy and advantageous remedy, so that no one will be able to be excused, as men were accustomed to be released by privilege, and so that no one who should be relieved will be consigned to a perpetual burden.
>
> (*CTh.* 7.13.7)

At the time that he wrote this, Valens was so pressed by the shortage of manpower that he was about to admit a vast number of Goths to the empire so that he could have a ready source of cheap recruits.[78] By his reign the ability to corrupt the system of payment had plainly reached such a point that the emperor could no longer afford to balance revenue against recruits. He appears to have been losing out on both counts.

The result was that emperors came, increasingly, to recruit large portions of the army from beyond the frontiers. Ammianus described a Roman army opening a battle with the *barritus*, a Germanic war cry, and suggests at various points that soldiers on leave would be tempted to visit their homelands across the frontier.[79] The progressive Germanization of the army would be reflected in the command structure by midcentury, as officers with Germanic names that they made no effort to Romanize rose to very high positions of command.[80] The presence of such officers might well raise questions about where loyalties lay, but it would be easy to oversimplify this question into one of loyalty to Rome and to the Germanic relatives. Loyalty to an emperor was perhaps not the most obvious quality of the army in the third century. But loyalty to the army as an institution was, and this does not seem to be any less true in the fourth century than in the third.[81] The problem, however, lay in the connection between the army and other institutions of government. As will become apparent in discussing the years that follow, the army remained very much a "total institution," with its own rules and priorities, and the years after Constantine would witness many periods of strife between one or another army group and the palace. The tendency to employ German officers in senior positions was a logical consequence of the increased use of Germans as rank-and-file soldiers. In the short run, it was an efficient way of acquiring officers with command experience without impairing, and perhaps even enhancing, the loyalty of the common soldier. In the longer term, it would create a military class with its own interests, and very different experiences, from those who served elsewhere in government.

The death of Constantine

Constantine could neither predict the moment of his own death nor the reception of his last will and testament by his heirs. It is inconceivable that he would have provoked the war with Persia if he had not felt that he was in good health and could win great glory for himself in bringing it to a successful conclusion. Indeed, it appears that he planned to have himself baptized in the River Jordan as he went on campaign in 337, and it is quite possible that he intended to invade Persia by launching an offensive down the Euphrates.[82] The ultimate objective of the campaign may have been nothing less than the complete overthrow of the Sasanian dynasty. Victory would serve two ends: the advancement of the emperor's faith and the stability of his plans for the future of his dynasty. In 335 Constantine had elevated Hannibalianus, the son of his half-brother Flavius Dalmatius, to the rank of "king of kings," and appointed him to rule the kingdoms of Pontus and Armenia with a view to placing him on the throne of Persia.

459

Coins celebrating his appointment to royal rank significantly have an image of the Euphrates on the reverse.[83]

The elevation of Hannibalianus was coincidental with the promotion of his brother, Dalmatius, to the rank of Caesar.[84] These two steps would seem to betray a radical view of government. No previous emperor had made plans for the succession that depended upon the occupation of new territory, or the installation of a relative upon a foreign throne. On reflection, however, Constantine may have been less radical than at first sight he seems: implicit in his action was the notion that the Roman Empire would be wherever his family ruled. In a move that harked back to Diocletian's plans, and the situation into which he had come in 306, Constantine appears to have contemplated five equal partners in control of Roman territory.[85] As soon as he had promoted Dalmatius, he seems to have divided the empire into four regions, with each of the four Caesars supported by a praetorian prefect. Constantine, his oldest son, ruled from Trier, Constans, the youngest, appears to have been established at Milan, Dalmatius in the Balkans, and Constantius at Antioch. If the Persian war had been waged to a successful conclusion, Hannibalianus would have had a realm fully as significant as those governed by his cousins.

All was not to be as Constantine had wished, and he had not secured the genuine acceptance of his vision by all involved when he suddenly took ill in the spring of 337. On May 22, after a short illness, and having allowed himself to be baptized by Eusebius of Nicomedia, Constantine died.[86]

The subsequent handling of his body, as described by Eusebius of Caesarea, reveals how even then, the two spheres of Constantine's life remained distinct. He had died a baptized Christian in his bedchamber, but his body lay in state just as had the bodies of emperors in the Antonine age, while the emperor's subjects treated the corpse as they would a living man.[87] On the day of the funeral, the body was escorted from the palace by members of the guard; it was again as if he were an emperor of the past, save that the embalmed body was not burned, but rather interred in the mausoleum that Constantine had built. It may be that Constantine had intended that, in the long run, the relics of the Twelve Apostles would surround his body, but, in 337, there were no apostolic relics. There was, however, a building that could evoke comparison with the funeral building constructed for Diocletian at Salonae or that for Galerius at Thessalonica.[88]

The imperial lying in state must have lasted for some weeks, for the funeral was only conducted after Constantius, who was at Antioch when his father died, arrived at Constantinople to preside over the final ceremony. But even then, it seems, Constantine could not really die, for there was not, as yet, a new Augustus. The four Caesars continued to govern as Caesars until September, when Constantius demolished his father's arrangements for the empire with spectacular ruthlessness. Dalmatius and Hannibalianus were

460

suddenly arrested, and executed. In a subsequent purge, all male descendants of Constantius and Theodora were put to the sword save only two young children, half-brothers and sons of Julius Constantius.[89] These boys, Gallus and Julian, were confined in the palace at Nicomedia. They may have been spared only because Constantius had married their elder sister in the previous year.

The official version of the destruction of Dalmatius, as it was later promulgated, made the army the driving force and the prime agent in the promotion of the three sons of Constantine to the rank of Augustus on September 9.[90] According to Aurelius Victor, the troops had objected to Dalmatius' proclamation in 335, and his execution might thus be seen as a logical conclusion to the desire of the troops to be ruled only by sons of Constantine.[91] Constantius is said to have been forced to allow them their way, and a rumor appears to have been spread that Dalmatius and Hannibalianus had actually poisoned Constantine.[92] Eusebius, who completely ignores the existence of these two men, states simply that Constantine had wished only ever to be succeeded by his children.[93] Eusebius' blatant lie may be the best evidence for the degree to which Constantius orchestrated the slaughter, for it reflects a rewriting of dynastic history on a point that was of primary concern to him. So too may Julian's own actions when he succeeded his uncle in 360. In what was perhaps a deliberate reprise of Constantius' behavior in 337, he ordered the trial and execution of many of Constantius' chief courtiers, saying that the army demanded it.[94] Ammianus thought it was a deplorable farce, and there is no reason to think that Constantius was any more the passive agent of troops than Julian was to be.

The unanimity of the army in the autumn of 337 is open to question. Julian mentions revolts among the garrisons of the eastern provinces that followed upon Constantine's death and a sudden shift in the allegiance of Armenia while Constantius was negotiating with his brothers in Pannonia.[95] Both revolts were occasioned, according to Julian, by the change in government, and there is reason to think that this version of events may be true. Constantine's intentions were clear in the two years before his death, and portions of the army may well have resented the overthrow of his designs, while the murder of Hannibalianus would have upset the delicate balance of political power in Armenia, where the king needed to maintain the loyalty of a fractious aristocracy in order to maintain his power. The appointment of Hannibalianus, even if it was intended as a temporary step, still symbolized a close relationship between the ruling power and the Armenians, which was shattered by the murder of the king.[96] There is some reason to think that the will of the army was represented by a pair of generals, Flavius Ursus and Flavius Polemius, who were to become the ordinary consuls of 338, perhaps as a reward for their support, and that others found their intervention difficult to take.[97]

The sons of Constantine

The three sons of Constantine met in Pannonia to divide up the empire shortly after the murder of their kin. Constantius retained all that he had held at the time that his father died, and gained the diocese of Thrace from what had been the portion of Dalmatius.[98] Constans received the rest, and Constantine retained what he already held. What was not then determined was how the three would rule: would they be a college, or would one of them have power that was superior to that of the others? Constantine II appears to have held the latter view, while his brothers were attached to the former. There is some reason to think that Constantine's view would have had the support of their father, for in a much later panegyric, delivered by Julian in honor of his uncle, it is stated,

> When he (Constantine I) was dying, passing over his eldest and youngest sons, although they were at leisure, he summoned him (Constantius), although he was busy, and entrusted him with the whole empire. Becoming ruler of the whole, he then behaved so justly and moderately to his brothers that while they, who had neither been summoned nor come themselves, quarreled and then fought with each other, they showed no resentment towards him, nor did they reproach him.
>
> (Jul. Or. 2.94c)[99]

As was the case with Eusebius' omission of Constantine I's actual dispositions, this looks like a piece of special pleading. Julian's language suggests that there was an issue of one brother being senior to the others; it is the claim he makes for the nature of that arrangement that defies logic. What really seems to have been the case is that Constantius obtained a concession from Constantine that he should have the right to issue legislation in his own name in his part of the empire. Such an arrangement allowed Constantine to claim, as the eldest brother, that he was the guardian for Constans, who was still a minor.[100] It may have been this presumption that enabled Constantine to issue orders to officials within Constans' part of the empire, and others seem to have seen him as the senior member of the group.[101] While Constantius could live with this, Constans' officials appear to have resented the notion that they could be ruled from Trier. The precipitous breakdown in the relationship between the two brothers may have been facilitated by officials who were seeking their own advantage. Ammianus mentions a man named Amphilochius whom he says played a significant role in their quarrel.[102] This quarrel came to a head in the early part of 340, when Constantine led an army into the territory of Constans, allegedly to aid Constantius in his war with Persia.[103] Constans took this as an act of war and dispatched troops to halt his brother's advance, which they did, ambushing and killing him outside of Aquileia.[104]

The empire was now divided into two parts, and it would appear that the character of the two brothers led to genuine divisions in how the two parts of the empire were ruled. Constantius had given notice of a certain ruthlessness not only through the murder of his kin in 337, but also by a series of executions the next year. The chief victim was Flavius Ablabius, who had been praetorian prefect when Constantius had arranged the downfall of Dalmatius and then been dismissed. Ablabius had a large estate in Bithynia where he had retired. Constantius is said to have suspected him of having designs upon the throne, and tricked him into claiming it moments before he was killed. Jerome adds that many other nobles were killed at the same time.[105] The murder of a man who had served as praetorian prefect for five years, a man who had risen from allegedly humble birth through his abilities and the favor of Constantine, was yet another sign, if any were needed, that Constantius saw himself as his own man. It is also support for Ammianus' assertion that he was prone to fear conspiracy and to react brutally to it.[106]

Constantius was no less forceful in matters of religion. As soon as he had asserted his primacy at Constantinople, he had exiled the newly elected, pro-Nicene bishop, Paul, to Pontus and replaced him with Eusebius of Nicomedia.[107] His authority to do so was based upon what must have been a very hastily summoned council of bishops. Paul would not be the last victim of well-orchestrated church councils, nor would his exile be the last to involve serious violence. A crowd of Paul's supporters murdered Hermogenes, the *magister equitum* who had been sent to ensure Paul's departure.[108] Constantius responded by curtailing the privileges of the population.

Constantius' next victim was Athanasius, who had returned to Alexandria in November 337, and found himself in exile again by the spring of 339.[109] It would appear that his return to his see had not been peaceful; riots are reported in the course of his return to the city.[110] The violence that he caused led his enemies to convene a council, probably within a few months of his return, which had again condemned him. Constantius then summoned Athanasius to defend himself at court, delaying the hearing until the latter part of the year because he was on campaign.[111] It appears that Athanasius had mustered enough support, in part from western bishops, to withstand the condemnation by his foes at Alexandria, and Constantius decided, after meeting Athanasius at Caesarea, that he could not act until another council had met that could hear the charges. This council duly assembled at Antioch within a few months of the emperor's meeting with the bishop, and supported the decision of the Egyptian bishops.[112] Athanasius went into exile for a second time on April 16, and again sought refuge in the lands of Constans. Here he found powerful support from western bishops who wished to maintain their independence from imperial control. In the years that followed, Athanasius appears to have become a symbol of resistance to imperial domination of the church among the westerners, and in the writing of a man like Hilary of Poitiers there appears to be a strong distinction between the bishops of the west, as a group, and those of the east. This language appeared already as early as 343 and reflects a sense that, whatever Constantius might say, the political division of the empire had opened a genuine rift between those bishops who thought in Latin, and those who thought in Greek.[113]

Constantius was undeterred, and as his reign progressed, he became ever more aggressive in his efforts to enforce both what he perceived (wrongly) as creeds that could bring the church together, and the exile of bishops who opposed his control. The key moments in his campaign to enforce his definition of Christianity would be, first, a council of eastern bishops held at Antioch in 341, a council at Serdica in 342 (which led to a break between the bishops of the east and west), a council at Sirmium in 351 (enunciating doctrine for the empire as a whole), at Arles in 353, at Milan in 355, and at Ariminum and Seleucia in 359. In all there would be three significant creeds (those of Antioch, Sirmium, and one debated in the councils of 359 that resulted in the creed of Constantinople in 360). Constantius would take a personal interest in the wording of all of them.[114]

The sheer number of councils is an indication of the importance that Constantius attached to defining his faith and enforcing agreement to that definition. There is considerable truth to Ammianus' observation that "confounding the plain and simple doctrine of the Christians with absurd superstition, in which by involved discussions rather than efforts at agreement, he aroused more controversies."[115] The result of these policies would always be to enflame debate, and possibly to strengthen interest in alternative forms of Christian lifestyle, stressing practice over ideology, that acquired fresh importance in the first half of the fourth century.[116]

Constans, who emerged from the conflict with Constantine as the more powerful of the surviving Augusti, ruling two-thirds of the empire, appears a good deal less harsh than his brother, and this need not seem merely an act of policy or, necessarily, the result of weakness. In taking over the realm of his brother he was confronted with the problem of reconciling two distinct bureaucracies. The problem was complicated by the fact that his brother's armies could not be said to have been crushed in war, the reputation of his senior commanders besmirched by defeat, or tarnished by treason. Faced with this situation, he might resort either to full-scale massacre or to reconciliation. He seems to have selected the second course. We cannot even be certain that Constantine's praetorian prefect, Ambrosius, was executed; though we know that he died soon after Constans assumed power.[117] Constans was also aware that he needed to reconcile the officials of his brother by moving, at least temporarily, to the west, and placing its administration ahead of that of his Balkan lands. To this end he appears to have journeyed to Gaul in the course of 340, and to have been present there for campaigns against the Frankish tribes in 341 and 342, using the traditional imperial capital at

Trier as his seat. In 343 he ventured briefly to Britain on what appears to have been a mission of inspection (accompanied, it seems, by some sort of military demonstration) before returning to Trier for the winter of 343. After revisiting his Pannonian lands in 344, he returned again to the west, probably through the winter of 345. Feeling, perhaps, secure in the loyalty of Gaul, he then settled back down in the Balkans for the next four years.[118] This would prove to be a fatal miscalculation.

In matters of religion he also seems to have been a moderate. Although he was responsible for a strongly worded letter to the *vicarius* of Italy, Creperius Madalianus, in 341, reasserting Constantine I's ban on some form of sacrifice, he rapidly conceded important ground to polytheists.[119] In the very next year he wrote to the prefect of Rome, Acco Catullinus Philomatius, a devout follower of the traditional gods:

> Although we wish that all *superstitio* be utterly abolished, nonetheless the buildings of the temples that are outside the walls should remain intact and undisturbed. Since the origin of many of the games, chariot races, and contests arose from many of these, it is not right that those places be destroyed, from which the celebration of ancient pleasures is provided to the Roman people.
>
> (*CTh.* 16.10.3)[120]

This statement is even more ambivalent than it appears at first, as the celebration of *ludi* should ordinarily have involved an event at the temple itself, as Constans implicitly notes in his statement that the buildings should be left undisturbed lest the festival not be held. If it is right to understand *superstitio* at this point as meaning "illicit sacrifice" as opposed to all sacrifice, he is here issuing a ruling recognizing the role of temples in the lives of polytheists.[121] In so doing he is further suggesting that he has no desire to offend the sensibilities of his subjects, and it is of no small interest that, aside from the reign of Julian, his reign saw the highest percentage of polytheists rising to high office in any period of the fourth century.[122] Unwillingness to cause controversy may likewise lie behind his evidently lenient policy toward the senior officials of his deceased brother.

Unlike his brother, Constans appears to have sought ecclesiastical peace rather than doctrinal conformity. He would have nothing to do with his brother's efforts to rewrite the Nicene Creed, whether through conviction or policy. The one time that he took decisive action in a church controversy in his own territory, the investigation of the Donatists in 347, the issues at stake were ones of discipline rather than doctrine. He acted to support one group within the church against another on a matter of priority (who would be the chief bishop of Carthage). Although this intervention turned very bloody when the Donatists resisted his commissioners, and resulted in the exile of a number of bishops, including Donatus himself (who had asked,

"What has Caesar to do with the Church?" when Caesar's emissaries held for his rival), it lacked the intellectual dimension typical of Constantius.[123]

The fact that Constans avoided issues of doctrine may have strengthened his relationship with the bishops of Constantine II's realm, who seem, at least into the 340s, to have had little interest in Trinitarian issues.[124] In the first ecumenical council of the reign (and the only one that would occur while Constans was alive), the 130 western bishops who appeared at the council of Serdica in 343 made it clear that they were acting in their own right, not as agents of their emperor. What they made less clear was the fact that they had more than one agenda of their own. Donatus was trying to enlist the support of Constantius to secure his position as bishop of Carthage against Gratus, the successor to Caecilian.[125]

Ossius was the leader of the delegation that appeared at Serdica, and it is difficult to see how there could not be a connection between the strong stand that they took and the presence of Donatus' representatives on the other side. The agenda that the western bishops set is best seen as a strong rejection of any effort on the part of Constantius to intervene in their affairs in conjunction with the Donatists. The westerners announced that they would review the "long creed" of Antioch, the justification for the exile of Athanasius and other eastern bishops, and investigate the claims that priests who subscribed to the Nicene Creed were being persecuted in the east.[126] The fact that Constans stayed at Trier, while Constantius was on campaign against the Persians, makes it look very much as if the council was intended to model Constans' approach to church affairs. Matters of doctrine and the installation of bishops were the business of the church. Constantius' interventionist approach, in which questions of doctrine were mingled with discipline, was de facto rejected.[127]

In the end (and not surprisingly) the Council of Serdica was a failure. The few eastern bishops who joined the delegation to the council refused to be seated with the western bishops since they had allowed Athanasius and others to attend. After a period of negotiation, mediated by Ossius, the eastern bishops received a letter announcing a victory of Constantius over the Persians and departed with the issues unresolved. But the bad blood stirred up by Constans' support for his brother's episcopal and doctrinal foes would poison relations between them for several years to come. In the wake of the failed council Socrates says that the western church was severed from the eastern.[128] Constans is also said to have written a threatening letter to his brother demanding the restoration of the exiled bishops. In 344 different pairs of consuls appear to have been recognized in the east and west, a sign of just how deep the split was.[129] In 345, when the two brothers might have been expected to hold the consulship together (as they had in 339 and 342), the joint consulship was not recognized in the west until the end of the year. A link between the sudden advertisement of fraternal unity at the end of the year, both through recognition of the joint consulship in the west and the issue of several series of coins announcing the "restoration of fortunate times," may be connected with the return of Athanasius to Alexandria on October 21 of that year.[130] Constantius had given in. The reason for his sudden change of heart may be sought on the eastern frontier.

Persia

The conflict of 343 that provided the excuse for the bishops of the east who were seeking to evade a meeting with their western colleagues at Serdica was not the first intervention of Persia in imperial politics, nor would the Persian invasion of 346, which may be connected with the return of Athanasius, be the last. It is very likely that one reason for the delay in naming the three sons of Constantine in 337 was that, as Constantius was conducting his father's funeral at Constantinople, a Persian army crossed the frontier.[131] Sapor II recognized the threat that was growing on his western border and had mobilized his forces for a preemptive strike against Roman positions in northern Mesopotamia. If successful, he might hope to interrupt Roman access to Armenia through the lands that Diocletian had taken as a result of the treaty with Narses, or prevent them altogether from launching an offensive if he took a city that Constantius could then be forced to retake. The obvious target was Nisibis, and it was there that he struck in the spring of 337.

Little is known of Nisibis, the modern Nusabyn in eastern Turkey, save that it was strongly walled, and that within the walls there was a fortified citadel as well, someplace, a headquarters building.[132] It had had a permanent garrison of at least one legion since the time of Septimius Severus, and it appears to have been a stronghold of the Syriac Christian church. Within the walls of the city there dwelt, in the reign of Constantius, the supremely eloquent bishop, Ephraim, whose intense hatred of the Persians may have been inflamed by the persecution of his coreligionists in Persian territory, and by the fervor of the potent brand of ascetic Christianity within the Syriac church.[133] In the course of the next thirteen years, the city would be besieged three times, and each time, the inhabitants would join with the garrison in resisting the Persian assault.

The strength of Nisibis, and of other fortified cities, would prove to be the key to Constantius' strategy against Persia throughout this period, for he would engage in few set battles with his enemies, relying instead upon his fortresses to break their strength and delay invasions so that they could not launch damaging attacks into the Roman hinterland.[134] Ammianus, who felt himself betrayed, along with other defenders of the city of Amida, which was sacked in 359, regarded Constantius' willingness to fight a war of cities as a great weakness. He felt that Julian's offensive strategy in 363 was the proper one, and that, perhaps, betrays the limit of Ammianus' strategic understanding. Julian had with him not only the eastern army that

Constantius had commanded, but also substantial drafts of men from the west that had been denied Constantius by his brothers, and later by the civil strife that had followed upon the death of Constans in 350. In fact, Constantius may have been correct in estimating that he lacked the strength for any full-scale operation against the Persian cities of Mesopotamia such as that which Julian would undertake, and after the battle of Singara in 344, he may have been correct in his estimation that major battles should be avoided in the future. There was small chance of decisive success, and a very good chance of decisive failure. Perhaps the best testimony to the essential wisdom of Constantius' strategy was the fact that Sapor himself acknowledged the folly of trying to win by taking frontier cities when he launched a large-scale invasion during 359, planning, allegedly upon the advice of a Roman traitor named Antoninus, to bypass the cities and strike deeply into northern Mesopotamia.[135] He was forestalled by the accidental death of a client king's son, slain by a ballista bolt outside of Amida, which he then had to besiege in order to assuage the angered father.[136] The nearly three months that it took for him to capture Amida ruined his plans, and at what was relatively small cost to Rome, his grand invasion force had to turn back.[137]

The basic logic of Constantius' strategy (whether adopted through choice or circumstance) is illustrated by the events of the very first year of his reign. Sapor was repulsed before Nisibis, and in 338 the emperor was able to restore Roman interests in Armenia with no resistance from Sapor.[138] The damage to Persian interests was serious, for Constantius' success appears to have convinced Saracen tribes that dwelt in the desert to ally with Rome.[139] For the next twelve years the war continued in roughly this way, with Persian attacks that accomplished little, and at least one Roman advance into Persian territory. The only encounter between the two main armies came at Singara, where Constantius appears to have been deceived by a fake retreat on the part of the Persians so that he allowed his infantry to press too far forward, into the Persian camp, where the Persians turned upon them and inflicted heavy casualties.[140] Constantius blamed the excessive zeal of his troops and could point to the death of a son of Sapor as a sign that rumors of a Roman catastrophe were exaggerated.[141] Whatever the truth may be, the Persians felt strong enough to launch another attack on Nisibis two years later, which was again repulsed, and an uneasy peace reigned on the frontier for the next several years.[142]

Expectations were, however, somewhat greater. These are reflected in a passage that appears in a short history of Rome composed later in the fourth century by a courtier named Festus, stating that Constantius had fought nine great battles against the Persians (he was present at two of them).[143] Among contemporaries, two documents cast some light on the propaganda that flowed from the Roman camp. So radically different are these documents in tone, content, and origin that they may be seen as paradigmatic not only of the disjuncture between the avowed aims of the Roman state and its actions, but also of the dual nature of the Roman monarchy in these years as both heir to the traditions of the past and representative of the new Christianity. Taken together, these texts, the *Itinerary of Alexander* and the Fifth Demonstration of Aphrahat, are yet another instance of a new form of Roman-ness. Aphrahat appears to have been the bishop of Mar Mathai in the vicinity of the modern city of Mosul, and the second-ranking bishop of the church in Persia. He is known solely through a group of twenty-three writings, the *Demonstrations*, composed between 337 and 344.[144] The Fifth Demonstration is entitled "On Wars" and takes as its subject the prospective conquest of Persia by Constantine, based upon the vision of the beast in Daniel 7:7. Here he accepts the common view that the polytheist Roman Empire is the fourth kingdom in the vision. His explication of the chronology is as follows:

> The fourth beast, it said, was dreadful, mighty and exceedingly strong; it devoured, broke in pieces and trampled with its feet anything that remained (Daniel 7.7). Now this is the kingdom of the sons of Esau. Because after Alexander the Macedonian came to the throne, the kingdom of the Greeks came into being; Alexander also being from the Greeks. But the vision of the fourth beast was fulfilled in him, because the third and fourth are one. Alexander ruled for twelve years, and there were kings of the Greeks after Alexander; the kings were seventeen and their years were two hundred and sixty-nine from Seleucus Nicanor till Ptolemy. The Caesars were from Augustus till Philip Caesar, twenty-seven kings, and their years were two hundred ninety-three years and eighteen years of Severus.
>
> (*Dem.* 5.19, trans. Valavanolickal)

While it may cheerfully be conceded that Aphrahat's understanding of Roman history is a bit vague, he seems to believe the (bogus) tradition that Philip was a Christian, to have confused Galerius with Severus, and might, perhaps, have identified the "Greeks" with the Romans because the Syriac term for polytheists within the Roman Empire was *Hellene* (Greek).[145] The stress on Philip is interesting as it may suggest that Aphrahat's reading of Daniel had a third-century ancestor, composed in the 250s, to which a later reading had been grafted (hence the appearance of Severus/Galerius).[146] But there is no question about his present meaning, which is that the fourth kingdom is now over, and thus that the Second Coming and the ultimate victory of the church are at hand:

> For after them, when Christ the King rules, then he will humble the fourth kingdom and break the whole image. For the image refers to the whole world, its head is Nebuchadnezzar and its breast and

arms the king of Media and Persia and thighs the king of the Greeks, and its legs and feet the kingdom of the sons of Esau. The stone which smote the image and broke it to pieces and by which the whole earth was filled is the kingdom of Christ the King who will make an end to the kingdom of the world and he will rule for ever and ever.

(Dem. 5.14, trans. Valavanolickal)

Even as he wrote, however, Aphrahat was aware of the picture from the Persian point of view, and their claims of victory in the summers of 336 and 337, writing in his last section,

> Even though the forces should go up and conquer, realize that it is a punishment of God. If they overcome, yet they shall be found guilty in a just judgement. But you should know this, that the beast shall be killed in its time. But you my brother, take pains in this time to seek for mercy, that there will be peace upon the people of God.

(Dem. 5.25, trans. Valavanolickal)

In the course of his reading of Daniel, Aphrahat lays great stress on the figure of Alexander the Great, who had defeated Darius. It is interesting that he separates Alexander from the other kings of the Greeks and returns to his role on more than one occasion.[147] The stress on the role of Alexander may be a reflection of something beyond the interpretation of scripture, for it was in this very period, on the other side of the frontier, that the image of Alexander was once more being aired out as a model for the house of Constantine. The comparison between Constantius and Alexander is duly trotted out by Julian to provide a context for the virtues of his uncle in the panegyric that he delivered in 355.[148] Constantius is seen by Julian as superior not only to the great Macedonian (and any number of other heroes of the past), but as waging a war that can only be compared with the invasion of Xerxes.[149] Julian's display of classical learning in this case reflects the language of the court. So too, it appears that Flavius Polemius, consul in 338, a man who had translated the *Alexander Romance* into Latin and no doubt a pillar of the regime despite his evident attachment to polytheism, was moved to produce a book that compared Constantius to both Alexander and his erstwhile imitator, Trajan, who had come, by the fourth century, to be regarded as one of the great figures in Roman history.[150]

Polemius' book is interesting for two reasons, one being the fact that he used Arrian as a source, an apt tribute to a man who was likewise a general, a courtier, and a historian. The second is that he makes a very clear reference to Roman intentions in the last year of Constantine. Persia is viewed as an ancestral territory of Rome that needs to be recovered.[151] This point may not have gone unnoticed in Persia. For, although we have seen that the

470

earliest Sasanid kings had no interest in the "Achaemenid heritage," especially the claim to the empire of Xerxes that is attributed to them by Herodian, it is precisely in the reign of Sapor II that we get unambiguous evidence, for the first time, of a Persian king making this claim. Ammianus says that in the letter that Sapor wrote to Constantius in 358 (and which he actually saw) the king had written that "your writers of ancient history also attest that my ancestors ruled as far as the Strymon River and the borders of Macedonia." While this is plainly not the original text (which was written in Greek), the language of other sections suggests that Ammianus is recalling the gist with some accuracy, and the attribution of Sapor's information to classical texts would in this case be a clever echo of the propaganda coming from the other side of the border.[152]

Dynastic catastrophes

After the reconciliation of 346, relations between Constans and Constantius appear to have been pacific.[153] Although Constans seems to have offered Constantius no substantial aid in the war with Persia, he summoned no more episcopal councils on matters connected with the east. At the same time he failed to revisit his western lands. The army of the west was still the army of Constantine II, and the absence of the emperor may have suggested that he favored the Danubian forces over the Gallic. That the most powerful figure at the court, Eugenius, the *magister officiorum*, appears to have had no strong connection in the west could also have been a problem.[154]

Resentment about Constans' years in the Balkans is suggested very strongly by the words of an ambassador who was sent subsequently to Constantius, "who hurled a thousand injurious reproaches against Constantine and his sons, attributing the ruin of the cities to their lack of interest in ruling."[155] The man who delivered this message, Fabius Titianus, had served as praetorian prefect of Gaul from 341 to 349 and supported a conspiracy that had formed under the leadership of Flavius Magnentius, a senior officer in the Gallic *comitatenses*, and included Constans' *magister rerum privatarum*, Marcellinus.[156] On January 18, 350, at a dinner party celebrating the birthday of Marcellinus' son, Magnentius suddenly appeared in the attire of an emperor and was proclaimed by the troops.[157] Constans, who was away on a hunting expedition, tried to flee when he received the news. He reached Helena in the foothills of the Pyrenees before Gaiso, the officer who had been dispatched for that purpose, captured and killed him.[158] Flavius Magnentius was now emperor of the west.

Magnentius was a man of German ancestry (it is said that his mother was a Frank), the first man to claim the throne whose recent ancestors could legitimately be said to have been born beyond the frontiers (as he may have been himself). In a sense his success is a sign of the expanding definition of Romanness. His ability to win acceptance from senior officials of impeccably Roman origins shows how membership in the governing class depended upon service rather than birth: in addition to Titianus, Marcellinus and Gaiso, we are told that he appointed a man named Anicetus as his praetorian prefect in 349, and that a man named Hermogenes, who may also have had a long history of service to the court, was his *praefectus urbi* in 349–50.[159]

In Italy, loyalty to the dynasty of Constantine did not, however, perish with Constans. News of Magnentius' usurpation was greeted with an uprising at Rome, led by a man named Julius Nepotianus, a nephew of Constantine by his half-sister Eutropia.[160] Despite his lineage, he was unable to gain sufficient support to resist the troops Magnentius sent against him, and he perished amid a massacre of his supporters less than a month after he attempted to seize power.

There was little that Constantius could do, immediately at least, to avenge his brother's death. Sapor launched yet another invasion of northern Mesopotamia in the summer of 350, and Constantius had to remain in the east to support Nisibis, which was subjected to an epic siege of four months before Sapor was finally driven off.[161] It was then that he could think about moving west, and dealing with yet another complication.

While Constantius had been concentrating on Sapor, Constans' former *magister peditum* in the Balkans was proclaimed emperor. Odd as it may seem, this rebellion may actually have been an act of loyalty. By taking the purple for himself, Vetranio was able to stave off Magnentius' attempt to seize direct control of the *comitatenses* of the Balkans, a fact that would play decisively in Constantius' favor. Indeed one account records that his messenger to Constantius was none other than Volcacius Rufinus, Constans' praetorian prefect, a member of the polytheist aristocracy of Rome and a relative by marriage of the imperial house.[162] His sister was the first wife of Julius Constantius, making him the uncle of the soon-to-be Gallus Caesar. In the official version promulgated at Constantinople, Constantia, the sister of the emperor, encouraged Vetranio, and Constantius actually sent him a diadem.[163]

The developments in the Balkans suggest that a direct imperial presence was a very strong factor in determining the loyalty of an army. This point was not lost upon Constantius (who had no son of his own) and would lead to crucial decisions in the next few years. The first of these decisions was to make use of his male cousins, the sons of Julius Constantius, in government. As soon as Constantius led an army into the Balkans in the late fall of 350, Vetranio had met him at Serdica, and on December 25 he had appeared with the emperor on a podium that had been erected before their armies at Naissus, a site no doubt chosen because of its significance to the dynasty. After Constantius gave a speech to the assembled soldiery, they responded by demanding Vetranio's abdication, a demand to which he duly acceded. On March 15, 351, Constantius took the further step of elevating the elder of his two cousins, Gallus, to the rank of Caesar and sending him to Antioch.

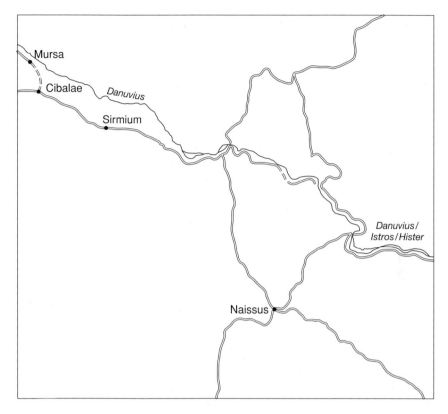

Map 5 The Balkans, showing the area around Sirmium

Source: *Barrington Atlas of the Classical World*, courtesy of the Princeton University Press.

Magnentius, in the meantime, was not content to allow his numerically superior foe to invade the western empire as was convenient to him. After his troops had repulsed an attempt by Constantius to enter northern Italy near Aquileia, he moved into Pannonia. Following complex maneuvers and some involved diplomacy (which resulted in the betrayal of Magnentius by a Frankish officer named Silvanus), the two armies met at Mursa on September 28, 351.[164] According to the official version promoted by Julian in his panegyric on Constantius, delivered a couple of years later, the victory was readily won by the heavy cavalry of the east. According to other traditions, the battle was a bloody disaster for both sides. Zonaras says that Magnentius lost two-thirds of his men, while Constantius lost nearly 40 percent of his – which, given the huge disparity in numbers, meant that Constantius' losses were worse than those of his defeated rival.[165] Zosimus, here following Eunapius, suggests that the result was the equivalent of a major disaster, leaving the army so weakened that it could no longer counter the barbarians.[166] Constantius himself seems to have let it be known to the Christian community that he received significant aid from God. This announcement may be connected with his efforts to enforce his creed at a council of bishops that he summoned at Sirmium within weeks of his victory; the agent of this announcement was a bishop named Valens, who had already established his credentials as an enemy of Athanasius. The Council of Sirmium looked ahead to what Constantius now had reason to think would be the inevitable conclusion of the civil war. The coming of Constantius to the west would mark not only a reunification of the empire, but also of the church.[167] As a sign of his willingness to compromise, he even allowed Athanasius to return to Alexandria.[168]

After a brief campaign against the Sarmatians in the first part of 352, Constantius invaded Italy, seizing control of the peninsula by the end of September. In the spring of 353, his armies crossed the Alps, defeating Magnentius in a battle at a place called Mons Seleucus. The rebellion came to a formal end on August 10, when Magnentius committed suicide. Constantius, who celebrated the thirtieth anniversary of his appointment to imperial office at Arles, started a thoroughgoing purge of Magnentius' supporters in the west, and began bullying western bishops so that they would subscribe to the version of Christianity that had been promulgated at Sirmium in 351. At the same time, he appears to have realized that he had left a serious problem behind him in the east.

Just how soon relations between the two men broke down is a bit hard to tell. Constantius clearly saw Gallus' appointment as symbolic. In his chain of command no one actually reported to the Caesar, a point that Gallus, and his new wife, Constantina, the widow of Hannibalianus, found very hard to take. In 352 he had taken credit for the suppression of a Jewish revolt in Palestine and, according to Zonaras, evaded a conspiracy launched by a supporter of Magnentius named Orphitus.[169] At roughly the same time he appears to have begun to put his own stamp on the urban landscape by constructing a martyrium for the bones of the third-century bishop, Babylas, near the temple of Apollo at Daphne.[170] While we have no description of the exhumation of the martyr's bones and their translation to the new site, we may reasonably imagine a ceremony as grand as that organized by the people of Antioch ten years later when Julian ordered the bones to be removed. By laying claim to a connection with Babylas, Gallus could also be seen as trying to upstage Constantius, who had completed Constantine's great octagonal church in the city itself in 341.[171]

The very first chapters of the surviving part of Ammianus Marcellinus' *History* are concerned with Gallus' misgovernment of the east and his removal from office, which Ammianus sees as arising in the immediate aftermath of the defeat of Magnentius. In this he is supported by Zonaras, and it seems likely that, having gained a sense of his own importance in the course of 352, Gallus was unable to revert to the completely subordinate position to which he had been destined.[172] Certainly the point at issue between Gallus and Constantius' officials appears to have been quite straightforward: who was in charge?[173] Gallus appears to have felt that he was competent to judge legal cases, and the first point of contention that Ammianus identifies is the execution of a man named Clematius, an Alexandrian, whose condemnation was secured by his mother-in-law, allegedly with the aid of a large bribe to Constantina. Gallus did not hear the actual case, but rather dispatched an order to the *comes orientis* ordering his execution.[174] The *comes orientis* reported, however, not to Gallus, but rather to the praetorian prefect, Thalassius, who appears to have protested Gallus' conduct both to Gallus and directly to Constantius.[175] Honoratus, the *comes orientis* who had obeyed Gallus' instruction with reference to Clematius, subsequently refused to obey his order to execute members of the Antiochene city council.

It appears that the sudden execution of Clematius may have inspired some members of the city council to lay charges against their political enemies in that body, hoping that Gallus would take summary action against them. These men were charged with artificially inflating the price of grain in the marketplace and arrested.[176] Despite Ammianus' claims that all Thalassius did was irritate Gallus, it appears from Libanius' narrative of these same events that Thalassius had in fact managed to reassert control over the situation. The members of the city council who had been arrested were released, and the sophist Libanius, who had returned to Antioch from Constantinople in the hope of succeeding to the chair of rhetoric in his native city, casts further light on the situation from his own experience:

> Then a lad, who had earned many a dinner by the favors of his person, was influenced by a large bribe to scurry off to this emperor with allegations that I had cut off the heads of a couple of girls and kept them for use in magic, one against him, the other against his senior colleague. . . . Gallus directed him to the courts, which was the last thing he expected, for both he and those who had hired him anticipated that my execution would follow straight upon the charge.
> (*Autobiography* 98–99, trans. Norman)

Honoratus' refusal to act seems to have driven Gallus to assert his dominance through appeal to the people of Antioch. The charge against the members of the city council appears to have stemmed from a legitimate food shortage, and when the people appealed to Gallus for aid, he told them that their fears were the result of the machinations of the provincial governor, a man named Theophilus.[177] Theophilus was murdered by a mob, and it appears that Gallus tried to build up support for himself among officials who had fallen from favor.

When Thalassius suddenly died, Gallus tried to secure his independence of Constantius' officials before a new praetorian prefect could arrive.

Whatever fears he had about his relationship with the emperor were aggravated by the arrival of Thalassius' successor, Domitianus, who had marched into Antioch at the head of some units of the guard and delivered letters from Constantius summoning him to Italy.[178] Domitianus marched straight through the city upon his arrival without pausing to salute Gallus, a clear sign that he would not submit to his authority.[179] Some time later, he appeared in the palace and ordered Gallus to depart. Gallus responded by appealing to his own guards, who murdered Domitianus and the quaestor, Montius. This was the penultimate straw.

Gallus continued to try to play factional politics in the courts while waiting on Constantius' next move, which came fast. In the summer of 354, Constantius was convinced that he had to remove Gallus from the east (although, according to Ammianus, he was not yet convinced that he needed to execute him). He first sent for his sister, who died on the journey, and then for his cousin, who appears to have realized that his position was now hopeless, especially as Constantius had summoned the senior military officer in the east, Ursicinus, to Gaul.[180] Gallus agreed to come west, but as he reached Constantinople he took a seat in the imperial box at the chariot races.[181] This was the last straw.

Gallus reached Histria, still as Caesar. It was there that the former commander of his personal guard, Barbatio, arrested him and stripped him of his imperial garb. He was conveyed thence to Pola where he was asked to explain the executions at Antioch to Constantius' *cubicularius* and two other officials. When he tried to shift the blame to Constantina, Constantius, who was informed of these proceedings, ordered him to be executed along with three of his closest associates.[182]

The government of Constantius

The career of Gallus is important for understanding the structure of government during the sole reign of Constantius. At the death of Constantine there had been four imperial courts and four military command structures. After the assassination of Dalmatius and the execution of his praetorian prefect, it appears that the number of prefects had been reduced to three. In 340 these were Ambrosius in the west, Antonius Marcellinus in Italy and Illyricum, and Septimius Acidynus in the east.[183] This basic structure remained intact until 347, when it appears that Constans created a new prefecture for Italy and Africa, entrusting it to Ulpius Limenius while retaining Vulcacius Rufinus as prefect in Illyricum.[184] This was an important step, and it solidified the division of the empire into four administrative zones in which the civil authorities would be responsible to a regional praetorian prefect.[185] The other important feature of this division was that it meant that the praetorian prefect reported only to the emperor. This was the point that Thalassius and Domitianus made to Gallus, and which Gallus found so hard to take, quite possibly because it represented a break from tradition wherein members of an imperial college each had their own prefect. The military command, divided between a group of *magistri equitum* and *magistri peditum*, probably numbering six, who likewise reported directly to the emperor, reinforced central control. As for the other major offices, it appears that both Constans and Constantius maintained their own *cubicularii, magistri memoriae, comites rei privatae, comites sacrarum largitionum*, and quaestors. While Gallus was equipped with his own quaestor, it would appear that this man, Montius Magnus, was subordinate to Flavius Taurus, who served Constantius directly. As far as the other officers go, it appears that after the defeat of Magnentius, the control of all the great bureaus of government was reunified, with a single department head for each. The import of this was very great, for it shows that Constantius viewed Gallus and later Julian as mere figureheads, whose job it was to represent the family as Constantius saw fit. They were not independent figures, and they had no power other than that granted them by Constantius.

The division of offices offers an opportunity for a description of the functions of government. The praetorian prefect was charged with oversight of the provincial governors, whose primary duties were to ensure that supplies (the *annona militaris*) reached the army, and judicial. The *comes rei privatae* oversaw the collection of revenue from the imperial estates and other public properties by provincial *rationales* and local *procuratores*. The *comes sacrarum largitionum* controlled the mints, collection of money taxes, imperial arms factories, the issuance of clothing to state employees, and the payment of cash donatives to the army. The *magister scriniorum* was charged with answering legal questions, while the composition of new laws remained the province of the quaestor. Finally, there were the *primicerius notariorum* and the *magister officiorum*. The *primicerius* was in charge of the palace secretariat, while the *magister officiorum* oversaw the collection of information, both domestic and foreign. He was, in modern parlance, the head of the secret police.

Careers in many of these offices were open to people drawn from well outside the traditional governing class of the empire. Thus, while holders of the praetorian prefecture were ordinarily members of an imperial governing glitterati, exchanging that post for the consulship and prefecture of Rome, the same could not be said of men who filled secretarial positions, or posts associated with the imperial bedchamber. Moreover, by the end of the reign of Constantius, it appears that even the glitterati were being excluded from high positions in favor of men who had risen through the ranks and proven their loyalty.[186]

Inherent distrust of traditional aristocrats and a tendency to favor new men led to complaints about the power of secretaries (*notarii*) and eunuchs. The use of eunuchs in government was not, however, a new phenomenon. Constantius was continuing a practice instituted by his father.[187]

Eunuchs were, by definition, slaves, and almost always of foreign origin, as castration was technically forbidden within Roman territory: the eunuch Eutherius was from Armenia, and Mardonius, the eunuch to whom the education of the young Julian was entrusted, was a Goth.[188] Their power arose from their access to the emperor and from the fact of their emasculation, which separated them from the ordinary social world of court life. Ammianus notes, perhaps with some truth, that retired eunuchs mixed rarely with civil society, and they appear to have felt a strong sense of class solidarity (something also true of powerful eunuchs in other societies). The eunuchs whom Ammianus says were particularly keen to see Gallus eliminated united to protect Gallus' *cubicularius* from execution.[189] Their tendency toward self-enrichment, as strong as their tendency toward self-protection, was an outward manifestation of hyperaggressive behavior characteristic of eunuchs.[190] This very aggressiveness made them especially efficient masters of the complexities of government, enabling them to outperform men drawn from the traditional aristocracy, while at the same time creating a symbiotic relationship with the ruler, who could count on them in ways that he could not count on others.

One of the most important figures in the court of Constantius was the eunuch Eusebius. He rose to prominence in the service of Constantius' first wife before being transferred to the palace as a *praepositus*, a position that gave him access to important state papers – including the will of Constantine, which he is alleged to have concealed so that Constantius could make his own arrangements.[191] Perhaps as a result of such singular service, he became *cubicularius*, and retained that office until Julian took the throne in 363. So skilled was he in this post that Ammianus observed that people thought Constantius had much influence with him.[192] If one reads behind the rhetoric of Ammianus, it becomes clear that no one was closer to the ruler on a day-to-day basis.

Another eunuch who attracts the attention of Ammianus, in a rather different light, is Eutherius. Ammianus knew him when he was living in retirement (and considerable comfort) at Rome in the 380s.[193] Eutherius had been born in Armenia, where he had been kidnapped and castrated as a child, and sold to slave-traders who brought him to Constantine's palace. There he was educated and gained the emperor's favor. In the 340s he was the *cubicularius* to Constans, and Ammianus says that if Constans had listened to him, he would have avoided many crimes. Eutherius survived the reign of Magnentius and returned to a position of influence under Constantius and Julian. It is of some interest as well that, while Eusebius was a Christian, Eutherius was a pagan.

While eunuchs were the most obvious example of a tendency to recruit for some tasks from outside the aristocracy, the case of another group that is tarred with the same brush is more complicated: these are the *notarii*. Libanius, for instance, identified skill at shorthand as a form of slave labor,

casting *notarii* into the same class as eunuchs. Under Constantius, he complained, knowledge of shorthand was enough to qualify a person for the
highest offices.[194] Philippus, the praetorian prefect who had risen through
the ranks of the secretariat (an unusual accomplishment for a prefect) was,
in his words, the son of a sausage-maker, and Datianus, one of the wealthiest men in the Antioch of his time (a status he owed to the favor of
Constantine and Constantius II) was the son of a bath attendant.[195] The
prefect Domitianus, whose death Gallus caused, was likewise, for Libanius,
the son of a manual laborer, and Dulcitius, another *notarius* who rose to high
office, was the son of a fuller.[196] Ammianus, however, who could be quite
scathing about individual *notarii* because of the way that they acted, does
not suggest that they were, by origin, members of the lower classes, and
Libanius' own correspondence gives the lie to the notion that *notarii* were
not to be found among the well-born. In writing to Bassus, the *primicerius*
of the *notarii* in 358, Libanius asks that one of his pupils, Honoratus, be
allowed not to take up a position because he is unwell. At the same time he
wrote to another *notarius*, Spectatus, asking him to intercede with Bassus.
Spectatus was his cousin, while Honoratus is elsewhere praised by Libanius
as a man who combined rhetorical skill with ability as a writer of shorthand
– as was Spectatus.[197] The approach to Bassus may have been facilitated
by the fact that his own son was one of Libanius' other pupils. Another of
Libanius' students, Hierocles, was the son of Alypius, the former *vicarius*
of the British provinces.[198] So too Libanius could praise Flavius Ablabius,
the long-serving praetorian prefect who was victimized by Constantius, as a
man who was accomplished at shorthand.[199] In 359 he recommended a man
named Maras to the *comes* of Euphratensis on the grounds that he was a skilled
shorthand writer.[200] It would therefore appear that when Libanius complains
about men who entered the senate because of their skill as shorthand writers,
he is at best disingenuous. In his most rhetorical flights of fancy he may be
drawn to attack this occupation solely because it was a new path to power
for men of standing. He was rarely a friend of change that was not of direct
benefit to himself.

While it is true that the vast majority of people who were capable of
writing in shorthand from the first three centuries AD were indeed slaves
and others of low status, Diocletian appears to have preferred having better-
born men as his secretaries. The trend continued after his death, with a *schola*
notariorum being attested under Constantine and Licinius, and it is to their
time as well that it appears the habit of giving *notarii* the title of *tribunus*
should be dated.[201] Like eunuchs, *notarii* were included at the most secret
moments and came to be trusted above others by their masters. There is
some reason to think that Athanasius owed his sudden rise to prominence
to the fact that he had been Alexander of Alexandria's secretary, and *notarii*
are often paired with eunuchs on the most sensitive missions dispatched by
Constantius.[202] Thus when Eusebius ran the trial of Gallus, he had a *notarius*

named Pentadius on the tribunal.[203] Pentadius was later appointed to the court of Julian as Constantius became suspicious of his Caesar, along with Paul and a third former *notarius*, Gaudentius. Pentadius was sent by Julian as an ambassador to Constantius after he usurped the position of Augustus.[204] When Lucillianus was sent to negotiate with Sapor in 358, he had with him Procopius, a relative of Constantius, who was also a *notarius*.[205] In 350 and again in 355, *notarii* were sent by the emperor to Alexandria to advise Athanasius that the emperor had determined that he should leave the city, while Paul was still in that office when he was charged with investigating cases against the followers of Magnentius. Athanasius identifies *notarii* among the agents sent to threaten bishops who opposed Constantius.[206] Like eunuchs, *notarii* owed their importance to the simple fact that they had direct access to the emperor. This set up a dichotomy between those whose influence stemmed from private contact and those whose influence stemmed from their abilities outside the palace.

More important, however, than the lines of reporting and bureaucratic structure, more important than the emergence of new skill-sets in the higher administration, is the question of what might be termed "corporate culture." How did the members of the diverse groups within the imperial bureaucracy get along with each other, and with their subjects, the ultimate consumers of their product? It does appear that links between members of the high command of the army could be quite strong.[207] Thus when Ursicinus was brought back from the east and sent to suppress the revolt of Silvanus the Frank in Gaul, the two men immediately had something to talk about: their mutual dislike of Constantius.[208] So too, on the civil side, Volcacius Rufinus was plainly well connected with members of the court of Constantius, which enabled him to survive the upheavals of Magnentius' reign, and Flavius Philippus, the praetorian prefect of the east from 344 to 351, appears to have had a good relationship with Eusebius the *cubicularius*.[209] C. Ceionius Rufius Volusianus, also known as Lampadius, who served as praetorian prefect in Illyricum and Gaul in 354–55, is said to have been particularly close to Eusebius Mattycopus, the *comes rei privatae* of Constans in 342, and Aedesius, the *magister memoriae* in 355.[210] The fact that Aedesius was a committed pagan, and Lampadius (as he preferred to be known) appears to have been a Christian, reveals how bureaucratic sympathy outweighed religious conviction in the formation of factions within the court.

The evidence for shared interest is, however, often overshadowed by that for interoffice conflict – and evidence that Constantius encouraged this rivalry as a way of securing his position at the top of the governmental food chain.[211] Ammianus makes it plain that men rose to high office through only one branch of government, and they would take pains to enhance the standing of their own group when they reached the palace. What is all the more striking about the conduct of high officials is the viciousness with which punishments were inflicted upon other officials. Roman government had always been brutal, but the routine use of torture against members of the bureaucracy appears to be a new feature of government in this age. In his description of Constantius' arrival in the west, Ammianus singles out the conduct of Paul "the Chain" for his abuse of officials who had served under Magnentius in Britain.[212] Gallus' search for allies of Montius led him to order the brutal torture of an officer named Eusebius, and Paul is once more on display in the history of Ammianus inflicting harsh torture upon supporters of Silvanus after the latter's murder.[213] Indeed, the so-called conspiracy of Silvanus is perhaps the best example of the way that imperial officials could and did conspire against one another.

Silvanus, the son of a Frankish chieftain who had thrived in Roman service during the reign of Constantine, had betrayed Magnentius at the battle of Mursa, earning him rapid promotion to the rank of *magister peditum* in Gaul. The appointment may have helped ease the transition to Constantius' rule among restive survivors of the defeated faction. But it also represented a plum position going to a man who was outside the ordinary avenues of patronage at the court of the emperor. Ammianus reports that Arbitio, Constantius' powerful and long-serving *magister equitum*, regarded him as a rival, and it is this that may have inspired Dynamius, who, despite being a relatively junior officer, already had access to the upper echelons of command, to plot against him.[214] What Dynamius did was to obtain a letter of recommendation from Silvanus, which he then erased and covered over with a new letter in which Silvanus appeared to be suggesting to certain colleagues that he was planning to rebel against Constantius. He passed the forged letter on to Lampadius, who was able to present it to Constantius in private. The emperor read the letter to his council, which included the commanders of guard regiments, one of whom protested bitterly against the emperor's proposal to arrest everyone named in it. This officer, Malarichus, was a Frank, and he was supported by another of the guard tribunes, Mallobaudes, also a Frank.[215] His argument was that "men devoted to the empire ought not to be entrapped by faction and conspiracy," and in this, his language is curiously similar to that of Silvanus himself, who later remarked to Ursicinus that

> unworthy men were raised to the consulship and high offices while he and Ursicinus alone, having toiled through many and constant tasks, were despised, and that he had been cruelly harassed though the interrogation of his friends in a disreputable controversy, and summoned to a trial for treason, while he had been dragged from the east by the hatred of his enemies.[216]

After the meeting of the council at which Malarichus had defended Silvanus, Dynamius dispatched another letter, again purporting to be from Silvanus, in which he sought to incriminate Malarichus, who, when he learned of it, perceived an effort to persecute the Franks as a group within government.[217] In the end, Constantius had sent an official named Apodemius to recall Silvanus, who was so frightened by his approach that he decided that he must indeed seize the throne as his only possible protection. When news of his actual revolt reached Constantius, he had then sent Ursicinus with his staff (including Ammianus) to murder him. Silvanus, as the passage quoted above clearly shows, regarded Ursicinus as a kindred spirit and let down his guard sufficiently so that Ursicinus could accomplish his mission on Easter Sunday, 355.[218]

Even before Silvanus had proclaimed himself emperor, the deception of Dynamius had been uncovered, thanks in large measure to his effort to incriminate Malarichus, which led to the appointment of a commission that uncovered the forgery of the first letter. The aftermath of this discovery, however, points to the truth of Silvanus' complaints. Lampadius was dismissed, but then "acquitted through the active conspiracy of a multitude." Aedesius denied any knowledge of the plot and was also acquitted; only Eusebius Mattycopus was tortured and dismissed. Dynamius was actually promoted![219] As we have already seen, and, as Malarichus' complaints show, factions at court were able to rally around and protect their members even when plainly guilty. They needed to do this, for all ran the risk of torture, which heightened the stakes for which they played. The unfortunate followers of Silvanus were treated much more harshly, again through the agency of Paul.[220] They were outsiders to the charmed circle of courtiers. In another case, unflattering remarks about Constantius, uttered by the governor Rufinus at Sirmium, were reported, leading to the torture and execution of those present, save for members of the guard for whom Arbitio obtained a pardon.[221] A frequent refrain in Ammianus' history is the absence of justice upon earth, and that is a fair reflection of a process of government that worked all too often through personal influence and connections.

If one ran a risk of severe prosecution within the bureaucracy, the closer linkage between government and society that resulted from the change in the scale of government in the first third of the century increased the peril that all others faced as well. Libanius' story about his peril under Gallus was a fortunate one. A philosopher named Epigonus and an orator named Eusebius were arrested by Gallus on the grounds that Montius, when attacked at the behest of Gallus, had cried out to two men (otherwise unidentified) named Epigonus and Eusebius.[222] Both men were tortured, as was a man named Apollinaris, a retired official, and his father, then serving as a provincial governor, on the charge of conspiracy because an unauthorized purple cloak was discovered to have been made at Tyre.[223] Athanasius, admittedly a biased source, observed that bishops who refused to knuckle under to Constantius did so in the knowledge that they faced imprisonment, beating, and the confiscation of their property for their acts of conscience.[224]

The effect of interdepartmental conspiracy was to secure the position of Constantius, for he was the supreme arbiter of disputes within his administration.[225] The brutality of his administration, and the violent acts of repression against officials, extended the old principle of exemplary violence in government as a method of control. The place of eunuchs and *notarii* at the heart of his administration, his willingness to move senior generals in and out of office, might frustrate a man like Ammianus – or Ursicinus – but it also ensured that men who might otherwise follow the example of Magnentius were in no position to do so.

Julian

The year 355 marked an important turning point in the reign of Constantius. He now felt that he could turn his attention to the church. Immediately after the conquest of Italy, Constantius had begun communicating with important western bishops, hoping to persuade them, and right after the death of Magnentius, he had summoned a council of bishops at Arles consisting of some eastern bishops and those of Gaul so that they could accept the definition of the faith arrived at by the Council of Sirmium. Constantius issued an edict ordering that the bishops who refused to support the removal of Athanasius from his see be exiled, and that all subscribe to the decision at Sirmium. Many bishops stayed away, and some of those who came continued to defy him.[226] Constantius dispatched messengers to individual bishops ordering them to subscribe on pain of exile. Many still continued to resist, and few attended a conference that he summoned at Milan in 355. Liberius, the bishop of Rome, was summoned to a personal interview with Constantius by Eusebius the eunuch, a sign of just how important the issue was becoming. When Liberius refused to subscribe to the acts of Sirmium, he too went into exile, and, at the same time, Athanasius was removed yet again from the see of Alexandria.[227] Constantius no longer had any need to tolerate him. At the same time western bishops joined with Athanasius in identifying Constantius as the source of all their problems – gone would be the excuse that he had been tricked by the faction of (the now deceased) Eusebius. Rather, Constantius would come to be identified, in some circles, as the Antichrist.[228] It was not a recipe for successful negotiation.

Preoccupation with the affairs of the church may have suggested that if he were to keep control of other branches of government, Constantius needed to insert a new element of uncertainty into the lives of his officials. If he was to return to the Balkans, he would need to have a figurehead in the west who could keep officials there from uniting against him, if they were so inclined. He would need another Caesar. There remained only one choice for this post, Constantius' young cousin, Julian. Julian, who had grown up as a virtual prisoner at Nicomedia, and then at an imperial estate in Cappadocia, had been freed from confinement a few years earlier when Gallus had been made Caesar. He had spent the intervening years on a spiritual odyssey that would lead to his fervent conversion from Christianity to a extreme brand of philosophic polytheism, but this seems now to have remained secret to Constantius. Julian was still in Athens, attending lectures, when he was suddenly summoned before Constantius at Milan. It was there that he was proclaimed Caesar and sent to wave the banner for the family in Gaul.

Constantius was evidently not impressed with his nephew's abilities, as he had to be convinced to make use of him by his second wife, Eusebia. When he finally did agree to use him, he seems to have learned something from the failure of Gallus: when he dispatched Julian to Gaul, he did so with a lengthy document "as if sending a stepson away to school" in his own hand that spelled out Julian's rights and privileges down to the items that he could have to dinner.[229] It was a start.

13

THE STRUGGLE FOR
CONTROL: 355–66

When he promoted his cousin to the rank of Caesar, Constantius appears to have feared that he might just have promoted an eccentric to very high office. Julian lived as an ascetic, had perhaps too great an interest in Greek philosophy, and hated the trappings of office. It is perhaps not surprising that Constantius desired that Julian be cut off from his existing friends, only one of whom was allowed to join the four servants and 360 guardsmen who made up the new Caesar's entourage.[1]

Julian may indeed have been eccentric, but his brand of eccentricity was a by-product of the centralizing urges of Constantius and his predecessors. Constantius' brand of bookish Christianity may be seen as a force inspiring others to take a simpler, more emotional approach to their faith. Constantius' effort, through the closure of the temples to stifle public polytheism, enhanced the appeal of alternative forms of worship, some of which did indeed attract the young Julian.

At the same time as he encouraged (albeit unintentionally) the rise of alternative practices in religion, Constantius failed to maintain Rome's ability to dictate the pace of events along its frontiers. As we have seen, the image of the empire as a fortress resonated in the discourse of the second century AD; by the end of the century the walls of this fortress were in nearly as serious a state of disrepair as they had been in the reign of Gallienus. Allowing himself to be distracted by his passion for imposing unity on the church, Constantius contributed to the failure of Roman hegemony through his inability to bring the Persian war to an end. The difficulties of Constantius were subsequently compounded by the ambitions of Julian. Feeling the need for a massive military success – a success on a scale that was beyond the capacity of his army to win – Julian embarked upon a catastrophic invasion of Persia. After his death in battle, his successor would surrender critical territories to Persia in an effort to save himself and his army. The result was the end of Diocletian's frontier system in the east; the collapse in the east would be compounded by the failure of Valens' effort to assimilate a large Gothic population within the empire fifteen years later. A contributing factor in Valens' activity was a perceived manpower shortage that was aggravated by difficulties in securing domestic recruits, stemming in part from a shift away from the strong central control of government that was a feature of Constantinian government to domination by vested interests that controlled the court. The disasters suffered by Julian and Valens initiated the progressive military failure of the Roman Empire, the emergence of successor states in western Europe, and the loss of Roman control over the western part of the empire in the second half of the fifth century.

The control of religion

Constantius had a deep interest in shaping the discourse of the church; it may be that he thought that the terms of the Nicene Creed were too imprecise to create the order that he sought, or that he wanted to centralize the government of the church as he did that of the imperial administration. In a world where the notion that church and state might be separate was unheard of, it was not, perhaps, an unreasonable desire, even if it was to prove an impractical one. Constantius was stuck with the problem that, however much he wanted to govern the church, he still had to rely on bishops to do the work, and he could not ignore their thoughts.[2] Hence his solution to whatever problems he saw (aside from removing bishops whom he felt to be disobedient) was to support the promulgation of longer and more detailed creeds by ecumenical councils. Unlike his father, he appears to have lacked the diplomatic skill needed to enforce these decisions. To be fair, Constantine had the advantage in that he was seen by many Christians as a savior, sent by God to preserve the church in the wake of the persecutions of the early fourth century. In no part of the empire did he have to deal with a Christian hierarchy entrenched in its position by a long period of imperial favor. Constantius may well have appeared to bishops in the west as an interloper, inserting himself into church affairs in a way that neither his father nor his brothers had done.

With the appointment of Julian to Gaul, and Sapor licking his wounds after yet another failure before the walls of Nisibis, Constantius devoted himself to the promotion of his faith. In the spring of 357 he went to Rome for the first time since he had become Augustus. Celebrating a triumph, removing both the altar and statue of Victory from the Senate House, he installed an obelisk at the Circus Maximus. The removal of the altar was a strong statement that Christians should not be forced to participate in events where sacrifices would take place. The installation of the obelisk must be taken as a repetition of the "obelisk diplomacy" of his father, this time in reverse. It was a symbol of unity between the new seat of the dynasty and the ancient capital. Constantius left after a stay of only a month for northern Italy.[3] It would be the last time that a reigning member of the dynasty visited the city.

While Constantius was in Rome, a group of western bishops assembled at Sirmium to promulgate a compromise creed that would be acceptable to bishops of both east and west.[4] The centerpiece of this document was a plea for Christians to stop using controversial terminology – especially the word *ousia* in Greek, which was rendered in Latin as *substantia* (and in English, "substance," the issue being the physical nature of Christ and whether he was of the identical – as held in the Nicene Creed – or similar "substance" to the Father).[5] Constantius would have none of it: he promulgated an edict attacking the bishops who had met at Sirmium.

Although he might condemn bishops who said things that he did not like, Constantius had learned that he could not convene the bishops of the west and east at a single council. In the thirty years since Nicaea, the number of Christians had expanded enormously, local traditions had become more firmly entrenched, and the burst of enthusiasm that had greeted Constantine had been transformed into cynical manipulation of the imperial power. Foes of Constantius like Hilary of Poitiers would complain that church doctrine was now made in the palace rather than by bishops.[6] As Hilary would put it, the *occidentes* had a true understanding of the gospels and did not require dialectic to know the faith. The Nicene Creed, supported by Ossius, was good enough.[7]

In order to defuse the controversy, Constantius summoned two councils, one for the western bishops at Ariminium, the other for eastern bishops at Seleucia on the Calycadnus in 359. In summoning the council of Ariminium he instructed the bishops to ignore the bishops of the east and to arrive at a definition of the faith that suited them.[8] He even went so far as to offer a framework for compromise, suggesting a creed that left out the dread word *ousia* that he had supported so strongly two years earlier. Valens of Mursa presented the model creed. It was not a success. Many western bishops detested Valens as a toady of the emperor; any gesture toward compromise in which he was involved would not readily be trusted. Thus, when the council – consisting of four hundred bishops – convened, it issued a statement maintaining the supremacy of the Nicene Creed while excommunicating Valens and two of his associates.[9] When the council, as it had been instructed, dispatched ambassadors to tell Constantius of their decision, they found themselves delayed at Sirmium for months. Constantius was (inconveniently) on campaign against the Sarmatians.[10] The long delay, during which time the members of the synod were forbidden to leave Ariminium, resulted in a significant change of heart. The ambassadors revoked the condemnation of the Pannonian bishops and agreed to the substance of the creed originally proposed by Valens.

The situation at Seleucia was no less fraught. In this case a faction of bishops led by Basil of Ancyra insisted upon a version of the creed that used terminology evocative of the doctrines of Arius. They were resisted by Acacius of Caesarea, who led the fight for a creed like that proposed by Valens to the Council of Sirmium. In the end, ambassadors for both parties went off to present their case to Constantius, who had moved on from the Balkans to Constantinople at the end of 359.[11] Constantius met in person with the ambassadors and, on December 31, elicited agreement to the creed agreed upon in the west. In January he convened yet another council of bishops, this time in Constantinople, to promulgate the new creed throughout the empire (and exile the recalcitrant).[12] He may well have thought that he had unified the church by careful management. If so he was very wrong: micro-managed councils arriving at predetermined solutions could not alter the fact that the Christian church was even then too large and complex an institution to be controlled by the will of a single man. Constantius simply missed the point that there were too many different kinds of Christians, too many different ways of reading scripture.

As Constantius persisted in his desire to create a unified church, he also persisted in his efforts to abolish the outward forms of traditional cult. On February 19, 356, he issued an edict that imposed a capital penalty upon those who "offered sacrifice or cultivated the images of the gods."[13] This was followed, in early December, by a sweeping edict against all manner of divination, and when, it seems, the praetorian prefect, Taurus, asked about the application of this edict he was told,

> It is our pleasure that temples in all places and in all cities be closed and that access should be forbidden to all persons so that the freedom to sin be denied to all debased mortals. We also wish everyone to abstain from sacrifice. If someone should, by chance, do something of this sort, that person is to be smitten with the avenging sword. We order that the property of those who are executed be confiscated to the treasury, and that governors of provinces be similarly punished if they neglect to prosecute these crimes.
>
> (*CTh.* 16.10.4 [also in *CJ* 1.11.1])[14]

While the buildings themselves remained intact, and while priests might still oversee the property, rites involving sacrifice, both public and private, ceased. As Libanius makes clear, the impact of this edict upon polytheists was profound. They could no longer practice their faith as they had for a millennium. This was an act more far-reaching than any that Constantine had enacted, and marked a final break with the Constantinian program. For while Constantine had enabled debate and had made it possible for Christians to act in public as never before, he had not done so by attacking the foundations of polytheist cult. As was the case with his policy toward the church, Constantius was prescribing as well as proscribing behaviors on the part of his subjects in a way that is evocative of the tetrarchs. Through his actions, he reinforced tendencies among both polytheists and Christians to find new ways to practice their faith.

Asceticism

Perhaps the single most striking development in fourth-century Christianity was the growth of extraurban asceticism.[15] Ascetic behaviors per se were anything but new. The most common varieties — avoidance of sexual relations, strict control of diet, the use of rough clothing, and (at times) the choice of an uncomfortable abode — were neither limited to Christians nor particularly unusual in the Roman world.[16] It was scarcely unusual to insist that a person who wished to approach a divinity abstain from sex for a period of time before entering a shrine.[17] There was a strong tradition of abstinence associated with a number of cults in Syria, as is perhaps most eloquently illustrated by a text in which

> Hochmaea, virgin of the God Hadaranes accomplished her vow with good will that, upon the order of the god, she would not eat bread for twenty years.[18]

An ascetic style of life was expected of people who sought to demonstrate particular attachment to a particular philosophic sect, as we saw in the case of Plotinus and his pupils. Mani made an ascetic lifestyle mandatory for the Elect, and appears to have seen work in the world as a distraction from the mission of the teacher.[19] From the non-Christian world, perhaps the most telling example is a papyrus letter in which the writer tells an aspiring philosopher named Serapion,

> Our friend Callinicus was testifying to the utmost about the way that you live under such conditions — especially in your not abandoning *askêsis*. Yes, we may congratulate ourselves not because we do these things, but because we are not diverted from them by ourselves. Courage! Carry through what remains like a man! Let not wealth distract you, nor beauty, nor anything else of the same kind: for there is no good in them, if virtue does not join their presence, no, they are vanishing and worthless.
>
> (*P. Oxy.* 3069, trans. Parsons, adapted)

Within the Christian church there were urban communities of dedicated virgins well before the fourth century, as well as women who remained dedicated virgins within their families.[20] There were also groups of males who lived together, known variously as *apotaktoi*, *surbaitae*, or *remnouth*, who lived a communal ascetic lifestyle in the cities.[21] What is exceptional is the move to the desert, and it may be no accident that this movement appears to have gained momentum in early fourth-century Egypt.[22] What is also exceptional is the degree of self-abnegation that was to become a feature of the movement. While Porphyry may have gone about as far as a polytheist philosopher might go in advocating removal from society, suggesting that the philosopher should not go to places where there were crowds, he did not suggest that the philosopher should go off into the desert.[23] While he advocated vegetarianism, he did not advocate a diet so restrictive that it was potentially harmful, nor did he advocate behaviors that were physically destructive. His abstention from sex was intended to help clear his mind; what would become the Christian style of sexual abstinence would involve an obsession with restraining any sign of human sexuality. Porphyry and others remained members of aristocratic society; the new Christian ascetics – while, as we shall see, providing services to aristocratic society – were separate from it. They went to live with the poor, and to live as the poorest among the poor – in this Christian asceticism should be seen as deriving some impulse from particularly Christian interest in the virtues of poverty.[24]

One of the striking features of village life in fourth-century Egypt was the withdrawal of urban elites from their village estates into Alexandria, opening up a power vacuum of sorts in the countryside.[25] Additionally, the spread of Christianity, while certainly not eliminating traditional agents of divine communication such as magicians, priests, and other forms of healers and seers, may have created a demand for new, specifically Christian, agents to provide basic services. The choice of an ascetic lifestyle made such practitioners seem closer to God, making them likely to be able to operate the channels of communication between immortal and mortal.

It may not be pure coincidence that the upsurge in the importance of solitary holy persons, and of communities of ascetics, took place in a region that was particularly riven with doctrinal controversy. As the sudden upsurge in the number of Christians during the fourth century turned Christianity from a religion of practice to one of ideology, people in local communities may have felt excluded.[26] Ascetics functioned primarily in local settings. They might be thought to have chosen sides because God had shown them the way, but their allegiance to ideologically determined brands of Christianity would remain, at least for a time, secondary to their niche as practitioners of a holy life. Freedom from the established hierarchy of the church, a freedom that was often maintained with considerable vigor even if a person had expressed a preference for one group over another, enabled ascetics to fill the role of mediator, a role that became their primary function in society. It was the need for mediation outside of official channels, and a fascination with the independence manifested by the ascetic lifestyle, that lent authority. The authority that accrued to such people was only enhanced by the desire of bishops to acquire their allegiance, and of members of the imperial administration to be seen to deal with them.

Our understanding of the rise of Egyptian ascetics derives from a wide variety of sources ranging from papyri to collections of sayings, to "histories" of monks and to biographies. Among the literary representations of ascetics, pride of place was awarded, in the fourth century, to a work of Athanasius. His *Life of Antony* was the first biography of a Christian holy man.[27] As it stands, the *Life of Antony* is a deceptively simple text telling of a Copt named Antony who was allegedly born in AD 251 and died in AD 356.[28] Moved by passages of scripture that he heard when entering church, Antony sold the extensive family property, entrusted his sister to the care of holy virgins, and betook himself to the fringes of Egyptian society to live as an ascetic.[29] As time passed, his spiritual power grew, and the power of God enabled him to win many victories over the Devil and demons that sought to move him from his chosen path.[30] The knowledge of demonic habit enabled him to cure the afflicted through his prayers.[31] No demon was safe, no matter how well concealed, when Antony was about – thus Athanasius tells (among other tales) of the time when

> he came down . . . to the outer hermitages, and he was invited to go onto a boat and pray with the monks. He alone perceived a dreadful and penetrating odor. The people on the boat said that they had fish and salted meat on the boat and that the odor came from them, but he said that the evil odor was of another sort. As he spoke, a young man possessed by a demon who, coming on board, had been hidden in the boat, suddenly cried out. The demon, submitting to the name of our Lord Jesus Christ, exited; the man was cured, and everyone recognized that the bad smell was from the demon.
>
> (Ath. *V. Ant.* 63)

The journey that Antony was engaged upon when he encountered this demon appears to have been to visit another community of ascetics, one of the critical activities of a monk who would travel about to ensure that his reputation remained intact.[32] In time he had become the recognized leader, or "father" of the monks who dwelt in the region of Mount Pispir.[33] It was characteristic of such people to dwell in loosely connected groups looking to a figure like Antony as a guide to spiritual perfection and the proper manner of asceticism. So great was his influence that several later "fathers" claimed Antony as their teacher.[34]

Foe that he was to demons, so too Antony stood for what Athanasius believed to be right: he was a steadfast foe to Melitians, Manichaeans, and especially Arians.[35] He confounded polytheist philosophers through the power of his arguments and was obedient to the duly constituted representatives of church authority.[36]

The *Life of Antony* was directed to audiences both within and without Egypt. Westerners would be relieved to discover that the extremely pious man of God should share their dislike of "philosophizing," and feel that Christian scripture was the ultimate guide to divine knowledge. The Egyptian audience was rather more complicated. For this audience Athanasius occluded the facts that he had only ever met Antony once in his life, and that there were separate traditions that made Antony out to be a rather less docile servant of the church hierarchy than Athanasius allowed.[37] One of Athanasius' contemporaries, Serapion of Thmuis, saw Antony as a spiritual patron, and there was a tradition of sayings that fell outside the purview of Athanasius. More significantly a group of seven letters survives in a variety of manuscript traditions that are attributed to Antony. This would appear to be the collection known to Jerome, who says that the letters were in "Egyptian" (by which he means Coptic).[38] If the extant collection is the same as that known to Jerome, and the letters are authentic, which seems likely, then Antony is revealed as a man of some education. The same conclusion may be drawn from an eighth letter, an autograph preserved on papyrus.[39] It is arguable that Antony's actual views were that the true Christian need not submit to the established hierarchy; and it is arguable that he was a forceful representative of a powerful brand of asceticism that drew its appeal from that detachment. Antony was the archetypical anchorite, a person who withdrew to the fringes of society to live in the desert where he could intercede with God on behalf of his fellow Christians.[40]

To gain a more accurate picture of the activity of Antony and other monks it is perhaps better to turn away from Athanasius and in the direction of the several archives containing letters to monks that have survived from fourth-century Egypt. Typical of these letters is one sent to an anchorite named Paphnutius, in which a man wrote,

> To the beloved and most pious and dear to God and blessed father Paphnutius, Ammonius greeting in the Lord God. I always know that by your holy prayers I shall be saved from every temptation of the Devil and from every contrivance of men, and now I beg you to remember me in your holy prayers; for after God you are my salvation. Our brother Didymus came to see me, and I met him according to your instructions in the matter. I pray for your health for many years, most sweet father; may the God of peace preserve you for a great length of time. (Addressed) To my lord the beloved father Paphnutius.
>
> (P. Lond. 1923, trans. Bell)[41]

Somewhat less typical, insofar as it reveals rather more secular actions on the part of a monk, is a letter addressed by a man of high status who sought the intervention of "abbot" John in the area of Hermoupolis:

> To my master, the beloved Apa John. I give thanks to God and whoever will assist me for your sake and through God; for all souls live through you because of your piety (towards) the Almighty.

So help me now; write a letter to Psois from Taeto, ex-tribune, that I may be released – if I have not (by then) been released. For Psois son has already demanded of me seven gold solidi and his assistant another gold solidus; for you took money from me so that I might obtain my release, and they (?) have not released me. I ask God that you either release me or hand over to me the eight gold solidi. For I am Psois, son of Cyllus from the village of Pochis in the Antaeopolite nome. Now then do not neglect this, master, for God's sake; for you have already given my children as securities to the moneylender on account of the gold. And I never go on active service, being unfit; for I have a compete excuse for this on account of my finger; it has not festered, nor has it healed either. (Address) Deliver to my master, the anchorite John.

(P. *Herm.* 7)

In this case Psois is writing despite what appears to be an earlier failure of John to intervene successfully on his behalf in a dispute over a loan. It looks as if Psois had given the money that he owed to John, who was to act as his agent in his dealings with his creditors, and that John had so far failed to deliver. In this case John seems to be acting as a patron (albeit badly) in matters that had nothing directly to do with the faith, precisely because he is able to move within elite circles. Paphnutius, as we know from another letter, was similarly well connected, for one of those who asks for his prayers appears to be a provincial governor named Ausonius.[42] Just as striking is the fact that these letters come from archives kept by the anchorites, and Psois expects that John will write on his behalf. This would suggest that both Paphnutius and John were men of good education.[43]

In church one could hear the words of the evangelists, in the desert one could witness the re-creation of the miraculous experiences of the earliest members of the faith. Perhaps the closest that Athanasius comes to the real Antony is his connection between asceticism and the ideology of martyrdom.[44] The idea was not new, but lack of originality made it no less powerful. Moreover, unlike the martyr who might conveniently be dead, the anchorite was alive, well, and residing within easy reach of his fellow Christians. As the church establishment became ever more entwined in debates over the nature of the Trinity, the ascetic came to represent God's actual concern for humanity. It might be better to see in Antony and the many others who came to live in the desert, offering their wisdom and the example of their lives to those who sought them out, the spiritual heirs of Montanus.

Athanasius realized that the rigorist passions that fed the monastic tradition could be a valuable tool in the hands of a bishop who could control them – his rivals realized the same thing, as we know from letters of Athanasius to the monks urging them to ignore the appeals of "Arians," as well as by the fact that two or three of the archives we have are Melitian.[45] In overstating the strength of his relationship with Antony, Athanasius was seeking to paint an ideal picture of the relationship between bishop and monk. He insisted that the ultimate arbiter of disputes among monks must be a bishop, and wrote at some length on concerns of the community (not the least of which appears to have been nocturnal emissions).[46] At the same time that he sought to assert episcopal control over the monks, he sought to bind monastic communities to himself by appointing leading monks as bishops. In a letter that he wrote urging a monk named Dracontius to accept the see of Hermopolis Parva, he said,

> For you are not the only one who has been elected from among the monks, nor are you the only one to have presided over a monastery, or the only one to be loved by monks. But you know that Serapion was also a monk, and presided over many monks; you were not unaware of how many monks had Apollos as their father; you know Agathon and are not ignorant of Ariston. You remember Ammonius who went abroad with Serapion. Perhaps you have also heard of Muitus in the Upper Thebaid, and can learn about Paul at Latopolis and many others.
>
> (*Ep.* 49.7, trans. Robinson)

Athanasius was not alone in this recognition, for he reports that Constantine himself had written to Antony, as did Constans and Constantius.[47] Rufinus offers further details, saying that Constantine asked that the monk pray for his rule over the empire.[48] It may have seemed a wise thing to do at the time, for with the church in crisis, Constantine and his sons may have recognized the power that independent practitioners could have over the rank and file of the church.[49] Athanasius admitted as much to himself not only in the way that he portrayed Antony, but in begging Dracontius to take up episcopal office he also wrote,

> Do not say, or believe those who say that the bishop's office is an occasion of sin, nor that it gives rise to temptations to sin. . . . For we all know both bishops who fast, and monks who eat. We know bishops who drink no wine, and monks who do. We know bishops who work wonders, as well as monks who do not. Many also of the bishops have not even married, while monks have been fathers of children; just as conversely we know bishops who are fathers of children and monks "of the completest kind." And again, we know clergy who suffer hunger, and monks who fast. . . . But let a man, wherever he is, strive earnestly; for the crown is not given according to position, but according to action.
>
> (*Ep.* 49.9, trans. Robinson)

In the long run, it was this sort of action that authorized the holy man as a source of patronage and power in the countryside. Athanasius soon realized that he had opened a dangerous can of worms – for communities throughout Egypt would turn of their own accord to the men of the desert for leadership.[50]

At roughly the same time that Antony was achieving prominence among the solitary ascetics of the desert, another form of ascetic community was taking shape along the Nile, and around the oases of the desert.[51] We cannot now know who was the first person to gather a group of other ascetics into a structured community, but we can discern two such communities as they formed in the 320s and 330s. It may be that the inspiration for this movement derived from earlier settlements of Manichaeans at sites such as Kellis – but we cannot date this community, which is known through excavation, or others, with enough precision to be sure.[52] What we can be sure of is that a structured community took shape, under Melitian influence, in the area of Hathor, and that the community was sufficiently prominent that its leader was asked to send representatives to the Council of Tyre in 335. This community appears to have been led by one who is referred to as the "father of the monastery" or abbot, and to have included people described as *presbyteroi*, *diakonoi*, a reader, and *oikonomos*, as well as monks.[53] The inclusion of men who fulfilled what appear to have been liturgical functions sets this monastery apart from another style of organization that was established at roughly the same period by a Copt named Pachomius. Pachomius, who formed his first community at Tabennesi in Upper Egypt in 323–24, favored a less hierarchical structure and a greater separation from established clergy.[54] The centerpiece of Pachomius' experiment was the effort to govern a community of "equals" who agreed to live together under a rule, each contributing what he was able to contribute to the community. While one man (Pachomius) was in charge of the distribution of the property in this ecclesiastical version of a communist collective, the property itself belonged to the monks as a group. Instead of spending their lives in ascetic meditation, members of the Pachomian community were expected to work, while maintaining an ascetic style of existence.

Throughout his career, Pachomius appears to have been the master of passive resistance to clerical control. He held that a monastery should be independent of the church hierarchy, and that while the local priest was welcome to conduct services, the day-to-day life of the monastery was conducted according to the rule of the community. In defense of his ideal he is said to have sparred with Athanasius' friend Serapion (himself a former monk), who tried to have him ordained – and, according to one story, hid in a crowd when Athanasius passed Tabennesi on a boat to avoid being seen, fearing lest Athanasius should force an office upon him.[55]

In the end Athanasius managed to reach a basic agreement with the Pachomian community – which began to expand rapidly in the 330s with the foundation of new coenobitic institutions – whereby the leaders of the movement recognized his authority, and he recognized their right to make their own rules. In a sense this was perhaps the single most important development in the middle of the fourth century, outlasting the results of church councils and other efforts to regularize the faith. For it was from these foundations that the seed of later monastic traditions in both Europe and the eastern empire grew, preserving elements of the classical tradition through the Middle Ages. But, in the immediate context of the mid-fourth century, this would not have been obvious, and there were others practicing an ascetic lifestyle, well clear of the sands of Egypt, who would garner far more immediate attention.

The imperial ascetic and apostate

Constantius lived as ascetic an life as was possible amid the grandeur of the imperial palace; he was sexually abstemious and was a frugal diner.[56] But it was Julian who would raise asceticism in public office to new heights. In 356, his frugal mode of existence may have been seen as a signal to the world that he was a man of immeasurable restraint who would not follow Gallus down the path to ruin. One of the important features of asceticism was that it defied confessional definition: to a Christian he might indeed have appeared to be especially devout, especially since he seems to have had a profound knowledge of Christian texts. Only a very few people would have known that he had very different interests, and it may not be extreme to view this very limited group as a sort of "pagan underground" that was deeply offended by the extreme policies of Constantius.[57]

How did Julian, the outwardly Christian ascetic prince, become the inwardly polytheistic potential rebel? This remains a compelling question, despite the fact that Julian's reign was marked by catastrophic failure and appears to be of little consequence for the history of economy, social structures, art, or letters. For all that the conversion of Julian was a vastly less significant historical event than the conversion of his uncle, he struck contemporaries like Ammianus and Libanius as a vital figure in their lifetimes. That he should seem so to those who knew him or observed him from no very great distance, suggests that he struck a chord in the collective consciousness of his age. The champions of lost causes may often achieve greater sympathy than the victors.[58]

The intellectual odyssey of Julian may be traced, with the aid of Julian's own voluminous writings, in some detail. After murdering the other male members of their family, Constantius had given Julian and Gallus over to the care of Eusebius of Nicomedia, who entrusted Julian's education to a eunuch named Mardonius. In later life, Julian looked back to the few years that he spent with Mardonius, who, as a *grammatistês*, was charged with teaching him his letters by following a traditional curriculum that involved reading Homer, as a golden period of childhood.[59] Mardonius taught him for four years. At the age of eleven, Julian was placed under the care of Bishop George of Cappadocia, who had him educated, along with Gallus, on his estate at Macellum near Caesarea in Cappadocia. Julian later claimed that the period was something of a nightmare, that he was cut off from learning.[60] It is a loaded comment – while there was plenty of learning to be had at Macellum, of a decidedly Christian sort, there also appears to have been plenty to read of a non-Christian variety. Although George was, in the eyes of some, a most unpleasant man (Ammianus compares his conduct to that of a snake), he appears to have had an excellent library.[61] He seems to have taken this library with him to Alexandria in 356 – and, after his murder by a mob in 361, Julian wrote saying that he knew the books well and wanted the library intact.[62] Eunapius, for what it is worth, says that Julian amazed his Christian tutor with his command of dialectic.[63]

In 348, Julian returned to the capital, where he studied with the polytheist Nicocles and the Christian Hecebolius.[64] Both men would remain close to him, with Hecebolius leaving the church after Julian became sole emperor (he rejoined after Julian's death), and the people of Antioch recognizing Nicocles as a valuable intermediary to the emperor when Julian was annoyed with them. At the same time, Julian attended lectures by another polytheist, Themistius, with whom he seems later to have quarreled, at least in part because Themistius believed that Christian and non-Christian could coexist in harmony.[65] Up to this point it is fair to say that Julian's education revealed that Themistius was right: issues other than religion were of primary importance to educated people. Quarrels between Christians were a more serious problem than quarrels between educated men of either form of belief. For Julian this would all change within three years.

In 350–51 Julian went to Pergamon, where he studied with the philosopher Aedesius, who had once been a pupil of Porphyry's former student and antagonist, Iamblichus.[66] By this point it appears to have been well known that Iamblichus' followers claimed that their master had achieved special contact with the divine. Eunapius said that the tradition was so strong that he did not wish to add to it with hearsay.[67] So it may be presumed that by 350 it was taken as fact that, although Iamblichus disclaimed the ability imputed to him by his servants of being able to float ten feet in the air while taking on a golden hue as he prayed, he had communicated with spirits that he raised from two springs before the eyes of his followers.[68] So too, Eunapius says, he saw that he was about to follow a road along which a corpse had been taken for burial (contact with a corpse being a long-standing source of pollution) and avoided it.[69]

Although Aedesius seems not to have discussed his own divine inspiration, Eunapius says that when he had sought an oracular dream, the god wrote the response on his hand in hexameter verse as follows:

On the warp of the spinning of two fates lies the thread of your life's work. If you wish the towns and cities of mortals, your fame will be deathless, shepherding the divinely given impulse of young men. If you should tend the course of sheep and bulls, then you shall have hope for yourself to be among the immortal gods. This does the woven fate ordain for you.

(Eunap. *VS* 464–65)

The result of this message was that Aedesius gave up his career and retired to a family farm in Cappadocia, until entreaties of his former pupils compelled him to take up teaching once again. Upon returning to Pergamon, Aedesius had left his farm to a relative of his named Eustathius, who would himself, after a time, acquire a great reputation and marry a woman named Sosipatra, who had a very powerful soul and communed with the gods. Sosipatra herself was a witness to the divine links of another philosopher who moved into the orbit of the family, a man named Maximus. It transpired that one of her male relatives, Philometor, was in love with her, and cast a spell upon her to win her love in return. Sosipatra confessed her conflicted emotions to Maximus, who discovered the source of her illness through his "sacrificial lore" *(sophia thutikê)*, and cast a spell upon Philometor to overcame the one that he had cast upon Sosipatra, enabling the two of them to resume friendly discourse. It proved no bad thing for Philometor; Sosipatra is said to have seen him in an accident, and to have sent servants to rescue him.[70]

The stories surrounding this group of people, who were from the wealthiest and best-connected families in Pergamon, were no doubt in the air when Julian arrived to learn from Aedesius. Aedesius recommended to Julian that he devote his attentions to Maximus and three others, a philosopher named Priscus, then at Athens, and two who had remained in Asia, Chrysanthius and Eusebius. Chrysanthius appears to have been very chary of discussing theurgy with the imperial prince, but not so Eusebius, who recommended that Julian make the acquaintance of Maximus.[71] It was through his association with Maximus that Julian became aware that he could no longer be a Christian. With Maximus as his guide, Julian was initiated into what he described as the mysteries.[72]

In the complex intellectual matrix of the 350s, the decision to follow a person who could be a personal guide to the divine was hardly unusual – the letter of Paphnutius shows us a man seeking a special unity with the Christian God that he could not find in church. The life of the ascetic, whether polytheist or Christian, promised something vital that was not to be found elsewhere. In most cases it made little difference for one's public career, if a person were so placed as to be able to pursue one, if one were Christian or not. It is, however, wrong to see Julian's experience solely in this context. He was the emperor's cousin, and, by 351, he was the half-brother of the reigning Caesar. For him to abandon the religion of his family was a major act of rebellion: he knew it, and so did those who were around him. Had it been otherwise, he would not have needed to keep his decision secret.

Constantius could not object to a person associating with non-Christians, and actually had frostier relations with many Christians than he did with many polytheists. But Constantius also regarded the safety of his throne as dependent upon the favor of the Christian God: while he could allow others to follow whatever faith their conscience called them to, he could scarcely allow such freedom to a member of his own family.[73] By converting secretly, Julian protected himself, and his friends – and he put them at risk if Constantius should learn what happened. While there may have been no active "pagan underground" opposing the Christian emperor on confessional grounds prior to 350, the conversion of Julian created a group of people who might have wished Constantius dead. It is perhaps no accident that the conversion of Julian occurred on the eve of the campaign against Magnentius, when Constantius' future may have seemed uncertain. In later years it also seems that Julian's Pergamene friends formed a sort of emotional support network.[74] Given the close family connections within this group, the tight links between teacher and student, Julian may have felt as if he was joining a family that was a good deal more supportive than his own, as well as a new religion. He may have escaped detection because the ascetic life of the pious Christian was outwardly indistinguishable from that of the pious poly-theist, save only that the one went to church while the other prayed in private to the traditional gods or, prior to 356, made offerings at the temples. So long as Julian observed Christian rites in public, his ascetic style of existence would have seemed to a mark him a very good Christian.

Julian in Gaul

Constantius appointed Julian because he felt that he needed a family member in Gaul; he otherwise had no great expectations of him. He neither knew him very well nor seems to have trusted him. At best, he might have hoped that Julian would have learned from the example of his brother that he was supposed to be a figurehead.[75] Such was not the ambition of Julian, who gradually forged for himself a place in government that seems to have been very different from anything that Constantius would have expected. Although Julian began with no reporting lines that ended in his palace, he was able, within a very few years, to so insinuate himself into the fabric of government that he was de facto ruler of one-third of the empire. If the job had been better defined, it is possible that Julian would never have been able to succeed as he did, but, as the job had no actual definition other than to be family representative in Gaul, Julian was able to use every victory by himself, every misstep by his rivals, to define a position that suited him.

The nature of Julian's responsibilities are set out by Julian himself in a remarkably tendentious letter that he addressed to "the Athenians" after his rebellion against Constantius in 361:

> Giving me 360 soldiers, he sent me into the distressed land of the Celts in the middle of the winter, not as a commander of the troops there, but rather as a subordinate of the generals in that region. It was clearly written and mandated to them that they should watch me rather than the enemy, so that I should not rebel. When these things had happened as I have described, around the time of the summer solstice, he allowed me to join the army, carrying around his dress and his image, for he had said and he had written that he did not give a ruler to the Gauls, but rather a person who would carry his image to them.
>
> (Jul. *Ep. Ath.* 277d–278a)

The plain suggestion here is that there was something inherently wrong or unusual with Constantius' arrangement. In the same letter Julian obfuscated the nature of Gallus' position and asserted that jealousy moved Constantius to murder him.[76] In point of fact, given that Constantius had equipped him with a detailed set of instructions, there is no reason to think that Julian could have misunderstood that his job was precisely to carry the dress and image of Constantius to the soldiers. In the next few years, he would convince Constantius to change the nature of his instructions, and it is arguable that he waged a massive campaign of disinformation that aimed at convincing Constantius that his own officials were inept.

Although Constantius may have intended that Julian play no more than a symbolic role in government, it was still important that he been seen to be doing something. Constantius had decided that some sort of action needed to be taken against the Alamanni, and that this would be best accomplished by a joint operation in which an army from Gaul advanced eastward into the Lower Rhine while he brought another force from what is now Switzerland.[77] As nominal commander of the Gallic army, Julian would be able to win credit for the imperial family, ensuring that no member of the general staff in Gaul could claim it for himself. If this plan would have any chance of success, it is unlikely that Julian could have had any but a minimal role in its execution. It would take time, even for a man of Julian's considerable intellectual gifts, to learn the basics of the military art. Julian had never drilled an army, he had never arranged a supply train, he had never arranged a line of march or seen a battle. These were all things that he would learn how to do in the next year or so, but they were not things that could be learned from reading the copy of Caesar's *Gallic War* that Eusebia had given him before he left Milan.[78] There can be no doubt but that the operational command of the army was left to Marcellus, who had succeeded

Silvanus the Frank, and to Ursicinus, who had some experience in dealing with imperial princes from his time under Gallus.[79]

Operations in the summer of 356 ended with some successes: the army advanced up the Rhône to its confluence with the Rhine, and then moved west to recapture Cologne, which had been seized by the Alamanni in November 355.[80] In the course of these operations, Julian's relationship with Marcellus (and, it may be surmised, Ursicinus as well) worsened. When the army went into winter quarters, deep inside Gaul, Julian selected Sens as his headquarters. It was an odd choice, for, although the city had walls, it could scarcely be regarded as the sort of place where an imperial prince should be found spending the winter. It might normally be expected that a Caesar should reside at Trier – though in this case it is just possible that Constantius' instructions included an order that the Caesar stay clear of a major admin-istrative center so as to avoid the conflicts that beset Gallus. Whatever the case may be, Sens proved most unsafe: a large band of Franks crossed the Rhine and laid siege to the place for several months. Marcellus was slow in coming to Julian's rescue, or so Julian maintained in letters to Constantius after the siege was lifted. Constantius, who could ill afford to lose another Caesar, agreed with Julian's version of the events and removed both Marcellus and Ursicinus from Gaul, replacing them with an elderly officer named Severus, who seems to have been rather more to Julian's taste.[81]

The next summer proved to be a decisive turning point in Julian's career. Constantius ordered another invasion of the land of the Alamanni, sending an army of twenty-five thousand men through Switzerland under the *magister peditum*, Barbatio, while Julian was ordered (in the company of Severus) to advance up the Rhine at the head of a force of around thirteen thousand troops.[82] The campaign got off to a bad start when Barbatio was repulsed. The reason for his failure – though the pro-Julianic account of Ammianus would never suggest such a thing – is quite possibly that Julian failed to show up on time, allowing himself to de distracted by a variety of minor targets along the Rhine.[83] When Barbatio withdrew, Chnodomarius, the king of the Alamanni, threw his entire force against Julian at Strasbourg. In Julian's version, which may not be too far from the truth, the result should have been a mismatch. There were, so Julian claims, thirty-five thousand Alamanni (twenty to twenty-five thousand is more likely the truth) to his thirteen thousand Romans.[84] Still, the Romans managed to triumph in a hard-won fight in which Julian appears to have displayed a tactical flair that might have won the approval of Julius Caesar himself. Julian chose ground that was restricted by forests on either flank, thereby negating the value of superior numbers, and deployed the available troops to take advantage of the Alamannic way of war, which appears to have involved little more than a headlong charge. The best way to negate such an attack was to force the Alamanni to launch it too early; to this end Julian deployed his cavalry well forward of the infantry.[85] By getting the Alamanni to commit their energy to an attack on the cavalry, Julian was able to engage a tired enemy with fresh troops, and create the psychological imbalance that could result in a catastrophic flight. Exhaustion is compounded under such circumstances by horror as advancing troops have to pass over the bodies of their slain comrades: Ammianus describes the walls of corpses that impeded first their movement forward, and then their retreat when the line suddenly collapsed.[86]

Strasbourg was a well-conceived battle, and the result was to give Julian fresh influence with Constantius, especially as Julian had resisted the attempt by his soldiers to proclaim him Augustus after his victory.[87] Despite the complaint of Ammianus that all Constantius did after the battle was write self-congratulatory letters to the provinces claiming the glory of the victory for himself, it is plain that Constantius felt that he should give Julian more leeway.[88] The new influence of the Caesar was manifest during the winter of 357–58, when he clashed with Florentius, the praetorian prefect, about tax policy in northern Gaul. Florentius had been present at Strasbourg, where Ammianus singles him out as a senior officer who had agreed with Julian, but, during the winter, stress appeared in the relationship.[89] According to Julian (whose account collapses several years into a sentence), Florentius was greedy.[90] The facts of the matter are rather more complex. In 356, Constantius had issued an order by which officials could not raise taxes without the consent of the praetorian prefects, who should then inform the emperor. At the end of 357, it appears that Florentius, who was worried by a shortfall in tax receipts, planned to impose an extraordinary levy to make good on the revenue.[91] Julian objected and, it appears, invoked the letter of Constantius' law, demanding that they write to the emperor before imposing an increase.[92] Although it is not clearly stated that this should be the procedure, it was a logical interpretation of the edict of 356, and it is therefore not surprising that Constantius agreed with his Caesar.

As the year 358 progressed, it would appear that Constantius had every reason to be pleased with Julian: he had won a great victory, he had rejected an invitation to usurp higher office, and he had insisted on following the instructions of the palace. Constantius' officials may also have begun to fear confrontation with the Caesar who had, by this point, established himself in a much more powerful position by public demonstration of loyalty. Julian was now well situated to do what he may well have intended to do all along: make himself emperor and restore the worship of the gods.

In the next two years he had virtually a free hand to strengthen his base in Gaul, which he did to the best of his abilities. His first step was to demand direct control of the administration of a province so as to demonstrate the propriety of his view that a lower rate of taxation would result in better collection. Florentius, who had perhaps learned that it was best not to argue with Julian, gave in to this unprecedented request.[93] The province that Julian had selected for his own – Belgica Secunda – was an interesting choice, lying, as it did, between Trier and Julian's own favored winter quarters at Paris.[94]

Away from Trier, Julian was able to construct his own links with the local aristocracy, and the resolute choice of this region as his headquarters in the years after 357 is perhaps the most obvious indication that he was planning an uprising.

The avoidance of Trier is not the only indication that Julian was beginning to think that he could succeed in unseating his cousin. In a letter to Oribasius of Pergamon, a renowned doctor and associate of the Pergamene philosophers who knew the secret of his faith, Julian wrote,

> The divine Homer says that there are two gates of dreams, and he does not accord the same faith to everything they announce. I, however, think that now you will see, if ever, the future clearly. I have myself seen this today. I saw a mighty tree, planted in a great *triclinium*, leaning towards the ground, with another one, small, young, and flourishing at its roots. I was very anxious about the smaller one, lest someone should pull this one out with the big one; then, when I drew close, I saw that the big one was lying on the ground, while the small one stood straight, suspended above the earth. As I saw this, I said in anguish, "There is a danger for this tree that its offspring will not survive." Then someone who was unknown to me said, "Look closely and reassure yourself; the root remains in the ground, the little one will survive intact, and will be established more solidly than before." So much for my dreams.
>
> (Jul. *Ep*. 14 Bidez)[95]

This was plainly not the first dream that Julian had experienced with respect to his future, or the first time that he had written to Oribasius on the topic – the second sentence of this letter implies the previous correspondence. In the previous summer he had invited another Pergamene friend, the philosopher Priscus, to come to visit him in Gaul. As he waited for his friend to set out, he wrote saying,

> Concerning the visit of your good self to me, if you intend to do so, plan now with the aid of the gods, and hurry, for shortly, I will have little time to spare. Find all the works of Iamblichus on my namesake (Julianus the Theurgist). You alone can do this, for your sister's son-in-law has a thoroughly revised copy. If I am not mistaken, a marvelous sign was given to me as I write this.
>
> (Jul. *Ep*. 12 Bidez)

Taken together, these letters provide evidence to confirm the obvious inference drawn from the selection of Belgica Secunda as his base that Julian was thinking of rebellion as early as 358.[96]

Dreams and philosophic friends are one thing, actually seizing power is quite another, and to accomplish that aim, Julian knew he needed the support of the army. His campaigns in the next two years appear to have been well calculated to achieve precisely that end. In the summer of 358 he launched an attack on the Franks, who seem to have been in no position to mount an effective resistance. In 359 he turned his attention to the Alamanni, who appear not to have recovered from the defeat at Strasbourg. Outmaneuvering a large army that had been assembled to contest the passage of the Rhône at Mainz, Julian's forces pushed well north of the Rhine and compelled the surrender of a number of the kings that constituted the leadership of the Alamannic federation.[97]

As Julian triumphed, so now did Constantius grow suspicious. For several years Julian had been served by Saturninus Secundus Salutius, himself a native of Gaul.[98] Prior to the opening of the summer campaign, Constantius recalled Salutius to court and sent out a new group of advisers to surround the Caesar. Julian resented the recall of Salutius, with whom he appears to have become close, and despised the new arrivals, Paul "the Chain," Pentadius, and Gaudentius.[99] Ammianus specifically says that Gaudentius was sent to investigate Julian – he needed to say nothing more about Paul and Pentadius. Paul had followed up his brutal pursuit of the supporters of Magnentius and Silvanus by conducting a wide-ranging investigation into people connected with an oracular shrine in Egypt.[100] Pentadius had first risen to prominence as an informer against Gallus, a fact that would hardly make him welcome to Julian. The arrival of this triumvirate of thugs may be seen as a message to Julian that Constantius was becoming concerned about his conduct. The appointments may also be connected with the fact that Constantius had a new problem on his hands.

Even as he had striven to bring unity to the church in 359, Constantius had been aware that he would soon face a new war with Persia. In 358 Sapor had sent him a letter demanding the surrender of much of the eastern empire, and as the embassy (which included the Pergamene philosopher Eustathius) that was dispatched to Persia failed to achieve peace in 359, he would have known that war was imminent.[101] A Persian army followed hard upon the heels of the ambassadors, bringing with them a recent deserter named Antoninus who had promised to show Sapor how to avoid Roman defenses and strike deeply within the empire.[102] Evidence provided by Ammianus suggests that Roman commanders in the east were ill prepared for this attack. Persian cavalry ambushed Ursicinus, recently reappointed *magister equitum*, as he rode with his staff to check the progress of the invasion.[103] Ursicinus barely escaped with his life, and Ammianus, after a hair-raising flight, found himself trapped in the city of Amida.[104] Only an accident, the lucky (for the Romans) shot from a ballista on the walls of Amida, prevented the Persians from continuing their attack. The ballista hit the son of one of Sapor's client kings, which necessitated, from Sapor's point of view, the destruction of the

Roman garrison to satisfy his ally. Amida held out for more than two months, and all Sapor could do once the city fell was to return home.[105] It was, however, clear that the Persians would be back in force the next year.

It is a weakness of Ammianus' account that he has very little interest in the affairs of the Christian church. Had he had more, he might have pointed to the fact that the summer of 359 was appointed for the councils of Ariminium and Seleucia on the Calycadnus, that Constantius had chosen to remain with the bulk of the field army in the Balkans while the bishops argued, and also that an autumn campaign against the Sarmatians had provided the interval needed to bring the delegation of the western bishops into line.[106] He might also have noted that it was in December 359 that Constantius summoned the Council of Constantinople to finalize his doctrinal desires. Although he had ample warning that trouble was brewing on the eastern frontier, Constantius had given higher priority to debates over Christian doctrine than to the safety of his provinces.

Julian Augustus

In the wake of the Persian attack, Constantius sent to Julian asking for drafts of troops to assist in the next summer's campaign against Persia.[107] Despite what Julian was later to say – suggesting that this was a plot to weaken him – it was a necessary action on Constantius' part if he hoped to be able to undertake any sort of offensive action.[108] Julian, who was once again wintering at Paris, had, however, decided that it was time to act upon his dreams. He would use the troop transfer to foment revolt among his soldiers. In February or March 360, the *notarius* Decentius arrived with Constantius' instruction that Julian should dispatch four full units of infantry and three hundred men from every other unit under his command. Julian was now ready to act; his later contention that events were driven by the enthusiasm of his soldiers is given the lie by his own impossibly convoluted account of what happened.[109] The first point that he does not address in this account (and the key to the story) is why there were any troops marching through Paris in the first place. Neither he nor Ammianus provides the crucial information that could make sense of the troop movement – that is where the men were coming from. He simply says that the two units that were to play the crucial role in his proclamation were in a town near Paris. The problem is that Paris was far south of the main areas of Roman military occupation, and the main east–west road ran well to the north of the city. There is no obvious reason why troops who were thought to be on the verge of mutiny should have been brought anywhere near his headquarters. Nor is there any obvious reason why he should have thought their acclamation of him as Augustus would have resonated with the rest of the army unless preparations had already been made to ensure its support. Julian's desire to portray events in Paris on the evening that the Celtae and Petulentes proclaimed him Augustus as the result of bungling by Constantius' officials betrays a desire to obfuscate the considerable advance planning that must have taken place.[110]

The cousins spent the next summer in very different ways. Julian campaigned again on the Rhine, this time against the Franks.[111] The Franks do not seem to have been able to muster much in the way of opposition, and as one the ostensible causes of the mutiny of the winter was that the troops feared for the safety of their families, who they claimed would be at the mercy of the barbarians if they were sent east, it gave Julian a chance to demonstrate his sympathy with their plight – perhaps no bad thing, as he must already have been planning to lead this army east the next year. By the end of the summer he was consulting the gods with the aid of Oribasius, a man named Euhemerus of Libya, and a person identified by Eunapius only as the "hierophant from Greece."[112]

Constantius' summer was less successful. Without reinforcements from the west, and, indeed, now threatened from the west, he dared not risk a decisive battle. He had reason to be thankful that Sapor had reverted to a more traditional strategy of attacking cities in the hope of drawing him out. The Persians contented themselves with the capture of the minor fortress city of Bezabde, and the destruction of Singara, a more serious blow.[113] Constantius waited for Sapor to retire before putting on a military demonstration of his own, during which he recaptured Bezabde.[114]

While these operations were under way, Julian and Constantius kept open lines of communication. Shortly after his proclamation, Julian sent Eutherius, the eunuch who was his *cubicularius*, and Pentadius, with a letter in which it appears that Julian suggested that he should keep the title of Augustus in the west, while retaining the rank of Caesar in the east.[115] This was essentially a reprise of the settlement at Carnuntum in 308, with Julian assuming the role of Constantine. Although it appears from his writings that he had no love for Constantine, he may nonetheless have had the historical imagination to see himself as a sort of reverse Constantine who would move outwards from Gaul to capture the empire, and restore the worship of the gods to its pristine form.[116] In November he issued what was no less than a direct challenge to Constantius on this matter when, openly rejecting Constantius' order that he renounce the title Augustus, he celebrated massive games in honor of the beginning of his fifth year in power at Vienne.[117] Here he took the title Augustus openly, and coins minted in Gaul would have his image on them with that title – sometimes sharing space with Constantius, sometimes not.[118]

At the same time that he challenged Constantius by using the title Augustus, Julian sought to conciliate the opinion of the bishops of Gaul, whom he allowed to meet at Paris toward the end of the year.[119] There was little affection in this group for the result of the council at Constantinople, something that is reflected in the writings of the driving force behind this

(a)   (b)

Plate 15 Constantius II and Julian. Julian's break with Constantius was marked by his abandonment of Constantius' image, in favor of a portrait with a beard on coins issued to celebrate his vicennalia at Lyons in 361; the style was adopted by the Rome mint in the summer of 361. (a) Constantius II. *Credit*: *RIC* Constantius II, Siscia 350 (332–49); author's collection, photo courtesy of Classical Numismatic Group. (b) Julian. *Credit*: *RIC* Julian, Rome 329 (361). KM 1991.2.910. Photo courtesy of the Kelsey Museum of Archaeology, University of Michigan.

meeting, Hilary of Poitiers, who had recently returned from exile in the east.[120] He had written at some length describing Constantius as the Antichrist. The most vehement section of this book appears to have been written just after the proclamation of Julian, and he continued writing in this vein after the death of Constantius, and after Julian had revealed himself as a polytheist.[121] There can be little doubt but that his experience with the bishops of Gaul in 360 would help shape Julian's policy toward the bishops of the east a year later. Julian would have every reason to think that the hatred of Christian for Christian, as it was manifested among those who had involved themselves deeply in the Trinitarian controversy, was far stronger than their latent distaste for polytheists.

As the winter of 360–61 turned into the spring, Julian began to move west. First he took an army into the land of the Alamanni, where he obtained the surrender of a king named Vadomarius (who duly entered Roman service). The capture of Vadomarius provided Julian with the opportunity to claim that he had come into possession of letters that Constantius had written the Alamannic ruler asking him to attack Gaul.[122] The campaign also placed Julian in the Black Forest, from whence he could move rapidly to the head-waters of the Danube a few months later. In the meantime, Constantius could only wait at Edessa, fearful of another invasion by the Persians.[123] Sapor had his army ready to attack, but, in the end, declined to do so (bad omens were said to be the reason).[124] By the time that the threat of invasion had evaporated, Julian had seized control of the Balkans.[125]

Julian's campaign in the late summer of 361 was a masterpiece of planning. Taking a small army down the Danube on boats, he occupied the major garrison cities as far as Sirmium without a battle.[126] At the same time, a second force, under the command of his *magister equitum*, Nevitta, had advanced out of the area of modern Switzerland into the central Balkans.[127] The second phase of the campaign saw Julian leave the Danube and march to Naissus, where his troops linked up with those of Nevitta. All seemed to be going very well until two legions that had been dispatched from Sirmium to occupy Italy from the east mutinied at Aquileia.[128] It was a dangerous moment, for if Julian allowed himself to be distracted by the failure to occupy Italy, he would lose the momentum of the eastward advance: he had to rely on a third army, which he dispatched from southern France, to eliminate opposition before he moved on. Julian thus paused for some weeks, sending letters to various cities of the east attacking Constantius for what he claimed to be faithless conduct toward himself.[129] It was then that he got very lucky. In early December he received news that Constantius had died on November 3 in Cilicia, while marching to contend for the empire. Julian was now sole Augustus.

The restoration of the gods

There is no more striking aspect of Julian's regime than his effort to reinstitute the public cult of the gods. When Julian learned of Constantius' death, he wrote a letter to his mentor, Maximus of Ephesus, that appears to have been intended for a general audience. In it he takes care to refute the basic charges of Constantius – that he had seized the throne and held high officials hostage – and then expands upon the theme of his own contact with the traditional gods, which he had already introduced into the correspondence that he had sent to various cities from Naissus. In this case he tells Maximus,

> I call as my witness Zeus, I call great Helios as my witness, I call powerful Athena as my witness, and all the gods and goddesses how, as I descended from the land of the Celts to Illyricum, I trembled for you. I asked the gods, not daring to do this myself, for I did not have the courage to see or to hear anything so terrible as one might imagine would be happening to you, but I used others. The gods revealed plainly that some troubles beset you, but nothing terrible or that any impious councils were effected.[130]
>
> As you see, I pass over many great events, that you may know most of all, how, all at once, I have perceived the presence of the gods. . . . I worship the gods openly, and the great part of the army

that follows me is full of piety. I sacrifice oxen in public; we have given thanks to the gods with numerous hecatombs. The gods command me to purify everything that I can, and I obey them with zeal. They say that they will give me great rewards if I am not remiss.

(*Ep.* 26 [Bidez], 415a–d)

To Eutherius he wrote, this time in private:

I live, having been saved by the gods. Offer sacrifice as thank-offerings on my behalf to them. You will sacrifice not for one man, but for all the true believers (Hellenes).

(*Ep.* 29 [Bidez], 382c)

Ammianus dates Julian's open avowal of devotion to the gods to the time after he arrived at Constantinople, but in this he is surely wrong.[131] Julian's *Letter to the Athenians* is an openly polytheist document, making it plain that he worships the traditional gods, and that letter was written when Julian thought that battle loomed in his future. If he were to die fighting, Julian seems to have resolved that he should do so as what he was, and his fears for Maximus suggest that the importance of his philosophic friends had become known in the east. The sudden death of Constantius after Julian had proclaimed his allegiance could have no other effect than to confirm his belief that he was chosen to restore their worship, and that by doing so he would, as he wrote to Maximus, go on to greater glory.

Ammianus' error about the date at which Julian proclaimed his faith may be explained by the fact that, to the eyes of the average inhabitant of the empire, the change would perhaps not have been so obvious until February. It was then that his image appeared on coins with a philosopher's beard.[132] The break with the clean-shaven dynasty was obvious and accompanied a new phase in Julian's activity, one in which he not only avowed his own faith, but sought to change that of his subjects. Julian would not deny that the God of the Christians existed. Nor would he deny, even when attacking the memory of Constantine, that Jesus could be found among the gods (albeit in the company of Pleasure and Incontinence).[133] It is obvious from his conduct at Antioch in 362 that he also believed in the intercessory power of martyrs, since he plainly thought that the presence of the remains of Babylas was silencing the oracle at the Castalian spring.[134] Acceptance of the fact that Christ might be divine and that the Christian God, who was, after all, the God of the Jews – whose rites Julian respected – was not extraordinary for a polytheist of the fourth century, especially one connected with Neoplatonic thinkers.[135] What would be extraordinary was Julian's effort to alter the social place of Christianity in the empire as a whole by returning the Christian God to his proper place among the divinities.[136] In doing so, his methods were the aggressive methods of Constantius rather than those of Constantine.

Although Julian felt that he had a special relationship with the gods, one stemming from his particular philosophic training, he does not appear to have thought that his way was the only way to honor the gods. It would therefore be wrong to suggest that Julian was trying to impose a specific form of worship upon his subjects.[137] The error inherent to such a supposition is demonstrated by the fact that there were at least three quite distinct features of Julian's own religious practice. One aspect was his devotion to the theurgic school of Iamblichus, another was his interest in the cult of Mithras, the third was his (large-scale) indulgence in sacrificial cult. So great was Julian's interest in Mithras that he appears to have had a Mithraeum built on the grounds of the palace at Constantinople, and the best explanation of a remarkable series of coins depicting a bull on the reverse with two stars overhead is that it was intended to be evocative of Mithraic beliefs.[138] Such was Julian's indulgence in large-scale sacrifice (even in a time of food shortage at Antioch in the winter of 362–63) that Ammianus thought it excessive.[139] Julian's interest in theurgy likewise aroused the irritation of Ammianus, who thought that the philosophers with whom he surrounded himself gave advice that was contrary to logic and custom.[140] When Julian tried to organize provincial cult with strict guidelines for the priesthood so that it might more efficiently compete with the church, at least one philosopher, Chrysanthius, who was appointed a provincial priest, did as little as humanly possible.[141] When Julian arrived in Syria several months after he began to appoint these new provincial high priests, he found that the priest who attended the great temple of Apollo was an old man who could offer a goose when the emperor arrived expecting to witness a hecatomb of cattle.[142]

Despite the evident failure of the effort, Julian's attempt to create provincial high priests who would organize the worship of the gods is perhaps the best testimony both to the eccentricity of his thought and to the difficulty inherent in organizing local institutions on an imperial scale. It was hard for Julian to ensure that the men he appointed as priests would do what he wanted them to do. It was also hard to make appointments at the local level that were congenial to all. There exists a fragment of a letter to an official who appears to have beaten a man who had been appointed to a priesthood at Miletus. Julian is not pleased and forbids the official to bother the man again for three months – but he also allows that the official, who is plainly Christian, may have had a point.[143] In another letter, Julian defends his appointment of the bishop of Troy as a provincial priest on the grounds that he had actually met the man, and was impressed by the fact that he was maintaining the local tourist attractions (including the temple of Athena).[144] In writing to a man named Theodorus, whom he appointed high priest of Asia, he stresses that men to be appointed must be of good character – and admits that people may have forgotten the rites that had been handed down

(a) (b)

Plate 16 (a) Julian's new image with a full philosopher's beard. (b) The standard reverse type of Julian was a bull. *Credit*: KM 1987.11.9. Photo courtesy of the Kelsey Museum of Archaeology, University of Michigan.

from the gods.[145] To Arsacius, whom he appointed priest of Galatia, he writes to say that the restoration of the old faith is not coming along as well as he had hoped. To help, he recommends that the priest set up benevolent foundations to help the poor: in this way he will be able to compete with the charity offered by the church.[146] He may have been surprised that there was no great upsurge of support for traditional cult; he was certainly disappointed in the results of his efforts. Thus he wrote to the philosopher Aristoxenos that he was pleased that he had greeted him at Tyana – proving that he was a Hellene (by which he means both a true believer in the old gods, as well, in this case, as a civilized person), among the Cappadocians.[147] To Arsacius he wrote saying that "Hellenism [here simply the worship of the gods] is not making the progress that I desire, because of those who profess it."[148]

There were other disappointments as well. At times it appears that people whom Julian regarded as his friends did not get on very well, and that Julian's displays of affection for these friends, especially Maximus, were thought by others to be excessive.[149] While he was at Antioch he received a letter from a woman named Theodora, a devout polytheist who was the high priestess of some divinity. She had earlier written to Maximus complaining that she thought that another of Julian's philosophic friends, Seleucus, was blackening her reputation with the emperor. Julian assured her that this was not so, but, since she had written attacking Seleucus, he would confess that he was angry with her for harboring Christians in her house. In his view people devoted to the gods ought to start by looking after their own houses if they hoped to convert others.[150] She was not the only one susceptible to such a rebuke: Julian had appointed her son, Thalassius, as high priest in Syria, and his house was filled with Christian slaves.[151] Many polytheists were unwilling to break their connections with Christian friends, and Themistius, whose lectures he had once attended, appears to have angered Julian by suggesting that polytheist and Christian could live in peace with each other.[152] It must be conceded that Julian was himself inconsistent. He invited the Christian sophist Prohaeresius of Athens, with whom he had studied, to write an account of his rise to power. Prohaeresius refused.[153] He also invited his former schoolmate, Basil, a Christian, to court. Basil also refused to come.[154]

If Julian was not satisfied with the progress of polytheism in the few months after the death of Constantius, he appears to have become even less satisfied with the response of Christians. He had no one but himself to blame for his troubles, and this may also explain why many polytheists were lukewarm at best about his espousal of the gods. In December 361, his former tutor, George of Cappadocia, had returned to Alexandria from the court of Constantius, whom he had accompanied on his final journey. Possibly laboring under the misapprehension that his former ward bore him some goodwill, he made an offensive remark about the temple of the Genius of Alexandria (he asked how long this tomb should be allowed to stand).[155] In the wake of actions taken by the *dux* of Egypt, a man named Artemius, who was immediately recalled by Julian after the death of Constantius, this seemed an open threat. Artemius had quartered soldiers in the Sarapeion, the great shrine of Serapis at Alexandria, and attacked the crowd that had gathered to protest.[156] George's comment was taken, not unreasonably, as a precursor to a similar act of impiety. A crowd of polytheists murdered him and two of his associates in the street.[157] Julian's response was to suggest that the people of Alexandria had good reason to hate George because of what Artemius had done at the Sarapeion, and that when they suspected him of planning a similar outrage, they killed him. This, he said, was wrong – they should have allowed him to punish George for his crimes.[158] The failure to do more than lecture the Alexandrians on their behavior could be read as a declaration that any who attacked Christians would be safe.

Alexandria was not the only place where people might have had the impression that it was "open season" for Christians if they wished it. Sozomen states that Julian refused to receive embassies from cities that were Christian. This included Nisibis, from whence an embassy was dispatched to ask for aid against a threatened Persian attack in 362.[159] He told them that, since they refused to reopen their temples, he would not help. This decision may provide the background for a series of poems that Ephraim wrote attacking him.[160] As for Caesarea in Cappadocia, another strongly Christian city, he expressed anger that the people had destroyed their temple of Apollo, confiscated church property, ordered priests to be enrolled in the army, registered women and children for the capitation tax, and told the city that it must rebuild its temple.[161] The language of Sozomen's description echoes a letter that Julian sent to Edessa and may well derive from the text of a letter from Julian that is now lost. In the letter to Edessa, he wrote,

> I have behaved towards the Galileans with such moderation and humanity that none of them has suffered violence, been dragged into a temple, or been constrained by ill treatment to any other action against their will. However, those of the Arian church, swollen with their wealth, have assailed the followers of Valentinian, and have dared such things in Edessa as never occur in a well-governed city. Therefore, since the most admirable of their laws enjoins them to renounce their property so that they may pass more readily into the kingdom of heaven, associating our efforts in this regard to those of their saints, we order that all the goods of the church of Edessa shall be confiscated, the money is to be given to the soldiers, and the lands are to be handed over to our domains. Thus, being poor, they will be wise, and they will not be deprived of the kingdom of heaven, for which they still hope. I order all the inhabitants of Edessa to abstain from sedition and violence, lest, troubling our clemency, you shall pay the penalty for disturbing the state and be sentenced to the sword, exile, and the flame.
>
> (Jul. *Ep.* 115 Bidez)

Aside from the blatant irony of the emperor's teachings about poverty, what is perhaps most striking about this letter is the way that he suggests that the troublemakers are Arians. In this he appears to be adopting the rhetoric of Athanasius and the western bishops, who would assert, in a most skillful and cynical way, that those who had been favored by Constantius must be Arians. Here, as in the letters that he wrote advising Arsacius, the influence of his Christian upbringing shows most clearly. Those polytheists who had trouble with Julian may have recognized the fact that his understanding of religion had a remarkably Christian flavor to it.

Julian would further defend his actions by claiming that Christians should be grateful to him for being more lenient to them than Constantius had been. In a letter to the people of Bostra he professes to be surprised that the leaders of the Christian community are not more grateful to him, since, unlike Constantius, he did not massacre communities of "heretics," which he accuses Constantius of doing in Samosata, Cyzicus, and other places.[162] In this same letter he blames internecine Christian violence (not without reason) upon the priesthood and invites the people of Bostra to expel the local bishop. His further statement that they should not then assault the rank-and-file members of the church looks, in context, less than sincere.[163]

There is little evidence to suggest that Julian's duplicitous policies fooled anyone, and a city like Constantina in Palestine, which had been transformed into a city from being a village, would not have forgiven its reduction in status to village once again, nor its attachment to the territory of strongly polytheist Gaza.[164] Nor were his efforts to sow dissension among the Christians by allowing bishops to return to their cities inevitably successful. Athanasius returned to Alexandria, claimed the episcopal seat vacated by the death of George, and began dispatching his supporters to other cities of the east. Julian, at first, ignored him, and when a Christian embassy came to Constantinople to discuss problems in the city, he had sent it to Chalcedon where he could ignore it.[165] Later he realized that Athanasius had once again become the focal point for the Christian community and challenged Julian by baptizing some women who were members of important polytheist families.[166] He ordered Athanasius to go into exile once again, asserting that when he had said that exiled bishops could return to their native cities, he did not mean that they could resume their former positions.[167] But the damage was done, and by the time that he reached Antioch on May 12, 362, the city was in the throes of heated factional disputes.[168] The one thing that seemed to unite Christians at Antioch was the presence of the polytheist emperor.

Julian's policies toward the Christians, which also included the promulgation of an edict banning them from teaching traditional literature, seem, for the most part, to have backfired. The attitude of Themistius and of people like Ammianus, who felt that Christians and polytheists could coexist, was more prevalent. Ammianus, in fact, condemned the edict banning Christians from teaching in the strongest possible terms.[169] Julian's efforts to reach out to the Jewish community, which included the reconstruction of the temple at Jerusalem, in an effort to prove that Christ, who had predicted the destruction of the place, was a false prophet, likewise failed when some sort of natural disaster halted construction.[170]

Julian's incongruity with the views of the mass of his subjects was matched by a failure to appreciate the importance attached to the ceremonial of the imperial office. When he arrived at Constantinople, he had dismissed the bulk of the palace staff.[171] He behaved in public with what seemed to people to be a lack of the appropriate dignity, and he angered people of all sorts when he tried to strengthen civic government by forcing men who had qualified for exemptions from curial duties onto town councils.[172]

Antioch, Persia, and catastrophe

When Julian came to Antioch, he planned to invade the Persian Empire the next summer. He may have felt that a striking success against the Persians would give him the authority to succeed in his religious policies; he may also have felt that he required some activity that could unite the staff that he had brought from the west with that of the eastern empire. He had a start at binding the senior military staff to his cause when he had ordered the trials of a number of Constantius' senior officials at Chalcedon very soon after he had arrived in Constantinople.[173] Many might agree that Paul "the Chain" was no loss, but a number of other officials were also killed, several of them, in Ammianus' view, unjustly.[174] Beyond this, if it is right to read between the lines of the panegyric on Julian that Libanius delivered at Antioch on January 3, 363, his appointments to various offices raised questions in people's minds. Libanius says that he employed his prophetic powers to make these appointments, with the result that people who were expected to get them did not.[175] In the west he had also cashiered a number of officials so that he could reward those loyal to himself. His approach to the bureaucracy in general appears to have been aggressive, and that, combined with years of neurosis inspired by Constantius, would contribute to a backlash that would have a dire influence on the fate of the empire in the years after his death.

Julian's time in Antioch was not happy. His aggressive polytheism led him, soon after his arrival, into making a terrible public-relations mistake when he ordered the bones of the martyred third-century bishop Babylas be removed from the resting place near the temple of Apollo at Daphne that Gallus had built for them.[176] Julian desired to resurrect the ancient oracular spring in that spot, and he seems to have believed that the bones of the martyr were suppressing the god. The result was a massive Christian procession as the bones were transferred to a new resting place.[177] When the temple of Apollo burned down shortly afterward, Julian blamed the Christian community, before it was demonstrated that the fire was an accident.[178] His relationship with the Antiochenes worsened as the result of a food shortage, which may, in part, have been aggravated by the presence of the army Julian had brought with him.[179] He responded by fixing the price of grain, releasing grain stockpiled for the campaign against Persia, and importing more grain from Egypt.[180] The result was that local landholders refused to put their grain up for sale in the city until Julian compelled them to do so.[181] In his view they were simply engaged in price-gouging. Landholders claimed that their harvests had failed and that they should be allowed to charge fair prices.

Julian's relationship with the people of Antioch was not helped by the fact that he disliked public spectacles, and made it clear that he did so.[182] While the emperor may have seen an ascetic lifestyle as crucial for a proper relationship with the gods, his subjects expected something very different. They expected a man who was both removed from them by the awesome spectacle of imperial power, and would validate their interests and desires by sharing them from his Olympian height. The ascetic was supposed to be detached from the world, to derive his power in the temporal world from the fact of this separation. The emperor derived his legitimacy from his ability

to exercise power at the heart of the temporal construct of power relationships. He was supposed to be interested in what interested his people, and
he was supposed to be dignified. He was not supposed to leap up and show
his appreciation for a panegyric as it was being delivered, as Julian had done
on January 3, when Libanius was speaking, and ignore the chariot races.[183]
There is perhaps no better evidence for the exasperation that people felt with
Julian than Libanius' defense of Julian's behavior at the circus:

> When he was compelled to sit in the circus he kept his eyes on other
> things, honoring the day through his presence, and his thoughts by
> his concentration upon them. For no struggle, no contest, diverted
> his mind from his thoughts.
>
> (*Or.* 1.170–71)

Implicit in this criticism may have been the memory of Constantius, who
had evidently been an attentive member of the audience.[184] Julian himself
responded to the criticisms of the people of Antioch at the festival of the
Kalends of January in 363 later in that month or in early February by posting
a remarkable satire on himself, in many pages, on the Tetrapylon of the
Elephants at Antioch.[185] The posting of this document would have been
preceded, as would have been the case with any imperial pronouncement, by
a public reading of the text. In this work, titled variously the *Antiochene
Oration*, or the *Beard-Hater*, he responded to his critics with a lengthy justification of his policies and his lifestyle, blaming the Antiochenes for their
troubles with him:

> No, my temperament does not allow me to look wanton, casting
> my eyes in all directions in order that in your sight I may appear
> beautiful, not indeed in soul but in face. For, in your judgement,
> true beauty of soul consists in wanton life.
>
> (*Mis.* 351a, trans. Wright)

At least in the short term, this response may have worked, in that it convinced
the Antiochene council that it needed to apologize to him, and to promise
to punish those who had insulted him in the theater.[186] In more general
terms, however, all it did was to underline the fundamental problem that
Julian was out of touch with the emotions of his people. He seems to have
felt that there would be no immediate way to repair the damage (despite the
pleas of Libanius), and so he left instructions that Tarsus be prepared to serve
as his capital after he returned from Persia.[187] For a man who knew as much
about Christianity as Julian did, the choice of the city of Saint Paul is remarkable. Did Julian plan to complete the work he had begun (albeit without
success) at Jerusalem in the previous year by appropriating important
Christian sites to new purposes? This we can never know.

As for the war with Persia, Ammianus says that Julian was motivated by the desire to add the title *Parthicus* to his name.[188] Ammianus thought that this was an entirely reasonable thing to want. Others disagreed. There seems to have been some vocal opposition to this plan on the grounds that, if the Persians were ready to make peace, Julian should do so. The war was expensive and dangerous.[189] Both Ammianus and the critics whom he cites overlook an important feature of Julian's plan that survives only in a letter that Libanius wrote after the campaign got under way, saying, "We hope that our emperor will bring the current ruler, handing the kingdom over to the one who was exiled."[190] Julian's ultimate aim, then, appears to have been "regime change," the replacement of Sapor with his brother Hormisdas, who would accompany Julian on the campaign. The most serious issue with his plan was not expense, but rather that Julian sought victory on too grand a scale, and he did so at a time when peace was possible. Julian dismissed an embassy from Sapor, offering the terms for a truce, with a show of contempt at a public hearing in Antioch at the end of 362.[191]

Julian's plan of attack was as ambitious as his design on the throne of Persia. He intended to distract Sapor by dispatching a portion of his force, commanded by his kinsman, Procopius (who he allegedly marked out as his successor if he did not return), to demonstrate against Persian positions in northern Mesopotamia with the active support of Arsaces of Armenia.[192] It was natural for Sapor to think that Julian would concentrate his attention in this area, as it had been the theater of the previous two decades of warfare, and would not put the Roman army at great risk if he should fail.[193] With the main force of the Persian army drawn away to the north, Julian hoped that, by a swift assault down the Euphrates and across Iraq where it was transected by the great canal known as the Nahrmalcha, he would be able to reach Ctesiphon and take it before its defenses could be set in order.[194]

Julian's plan, which resembles his bold move toward Sirmium in the campaign against Constantius, was initially successful. He captured a number of fortresses and encountered limited opposition. What he had not counted on was the ruthlessness with which Persian commanders would defend their heartland. As he moved east along the Nahrmalcha, the Persians opened the dikes, flooding their own country to slow him down.[195] Nor, it seems, did he have very good intelligence about the defenses of Ctesiphon itself. When he reached the city in mid-June, he found that he lacked the wherewithal to lay siege to the place.[196] He had no choice but to retreat, but the land behind him was flooded, making it impossible to go back the way that he had come.[197] To return to Roman territory, he would have to march north along the Tigris. At this point he decided to burn the ships that had been used to transport a part of the army, and the bulk of its supplies. Ammianus says that he was deceived by Persian spies who told him that there would be places where he could forage on the way north, if he took an inland route.[198] Ammianus may well be right (he was there), though more than Persian deception may have been involved. The powerful stream of the Tigris would make it difficult to keep the fleet in contact with his army, and speed was of the essence if he was going to be able to escape before the main force of the Persian army could trap him. It is with the benefit of hind-sight that Ammianus and others looked upon the destruction of the fleet as the moment at which the campaign took a turn for the worse.[199] The later surrender of the army for lack of supplies could be linked to the decision to abandon the river. In truth, the campaign was doomed before Julian left Roman territory. The failure to bring an adequate siege train meant that Julian would have to retreat once he found that Ctesiphon was too strongly defended to be taken by assault.

Sapor, who arrived with his main force as Julian began his withdrawal, was not evidently eager for a set battle. Sapor's lack of interest in direct confrontation with an army that was cut off within his territory removed any hope that Julian might still have entertained of inflicting so catastrophic a defeat upon the Persians that he could replace Sapor with Hormisdas. Realizing that he could win by slowing the pace of the Roman withdrawal, Sapor contented himself with attacks that were designed to retard the Roman column, the most serious being one launched on the rear guard of the Roman force near the ancient city of Akkad on June 20.[200] He may even have offered Julian terms of surrender.[201] The Persians continued to harry the Romans until, on the morning of June 26, Julian was mortally wounded while rallying his forces to drive off a raid. He had failed to put on his breastplate during the initial attack, and his bodyguard dispersed as he led the pursuit of the fleeing Persians, leaving him undefended. It was then that a spear pierced his back. Ammianus, who was with the army at the time, would write, many years later, that the weapon was cast by an unknown hand. Gregory of Nazianzus, a Christian bishop, wrote in 364 that there were four possible killers: a Persian, an Arab, a barbarian camp-follower, or a disgruntled Christian soldier.[202] Libanius, also writing in 364, stated that the killer was a Christian, and later Christian tradition claimed that the hand of a saint cast the spear.[203] Fourteen years later Libanius said that it was a Saracen, and this may have been confirmed by no less an authority than Oribasius, who, having examined the wound, said that it was from a spear used by a group of Saracen auxiliaries in Persian service. This evidence – which is preserved by Philostorgius – should be unimpeachable.[204]

The fact that Julian was not killed by one of his own men makes the story that he was murdered all the more significant. It reflects the uncertainty in the camp and the collapse of the army's morale when Julian died that evening. He died without naming an heir. There was really no way that he could.

The search for an emperor, whose task would be either to lead the army out of an impossible situation or to negotiate the army's surrender, was not an easy one. Ammianus says that, at first, the high command was split between those who favored a palatine official and those who favored a soldier (the division was essentially between former officials of Constantius who favored one of their own kind, and men who had followed Julian from Gaul).[205] The dispute was solved when the two groups decided to offer the throne to Salutius, the praetorian prefect, who bridged the gap between the two sides. Salutius turned the job down, and Ammianus places a good summary of the problem facing any potential candidate in the mouth of an anonymous senior officer:

> What would you do . . . if an absent emperor, as has often happened, entrusted the care of the war to you? Would you not, putting all else aside, rescue the army from the perils that surround it? Do that now, and, if it is permitted to see Mesopotamia, the joint votes of both armies will declare a legitimate emperor.
>
> (Amm. Marc. 25.5.3)

The general staff was not fully convinced and so went for another compromise candidate, Jovian, the commander of Julian's guard.[206] It was hardly to be expected that Jovian would provide dynamic leadership to a group that consisted of his former superiors. Rather he was selected to provide symbolic leadership for the duration of the crisis, and then, it might be hoped, be able to work with the senior staff to forge consensus around his leadership. His first act gave promise that he would be able to do so. Although a Christian, Jovian consulted the haruspices before ordering the army to break camp.[207]

On July 1, the army had advanced another thirty miles and had arrived at a point where it might be possible to bridge the Tigris, but the weather intervened, and the Persians continued to harry the army, which by this point was on the verge of disintegration.[208] It was only then that Sapor reopened negotiations and obtained terms from Jovian that were probably far better than anything that he could have obtained from an emperor who might have been selected within Roman territory if he had annihilated the remnants of Julian's force.[209] In return for being granted safe passage over the Tigris, Jovian agreed to surrender the five provinces that Diocletian had won from Narses, as well as the cities of Nisibis and Singara without their inhabitants.[210] The result of the treaty was that Rome lost control over the region that controlled access to northern Mesopotamia. The inclusion of Nisibis and Singara meant that the result was more than a return to the *status quo ante Diocletianum*. By surrendering cities that had been under Roman control since the foundation of the province of Mesopotamia, Jovian was delivering a fortified bridgehead into Roman territory. The population of Nisibis was transferred to Amida so that Sapor would not have to fear that they would betray the city to Rome.

When this book began, Marcus was in the process of stabilizing control over access to Rome's borders. One definition of a hegemonic power must be that it has control over the security of its borders. By surrendering Nisibis, Jovian had shattered Rome's hegemonic position in the Near East. The words of Bishop Ephraim stand as poignant testimony to the personal tragedy of the people who were losing their homes:

> A wonder! By chance the corpse of the accursed one,
> Crossing over towards the rampart met me near the city!
> And the Magus took and fastened on a tower
> The standard sent from the east,
> So that this standard-bearer would declare to the onlookers
> That the city was slave to the lords of that standard.
> Glory to the One Who wrapped the corpse in shame!
> I wondered, "Who indeed set a time for meeting
> When corpse and standard-bearer both at one moment were
>   present?"
> I knew it was a prearrangement, a miracle of justice
> That when the corpse of the fallen one crossed over,
> The fearful standard went up and was put in place to proclaim
> That the evil of his conjurors had surrendered that city.
> For thirty years Persia had made battle in every way
> But was unable to cross over the boundary of that city;
> Even when it had been broken and collapsed, the cross
>   came down and saved it.
> There I saw a disgraceful sight:
> The standard of the captor set up on the tower,
> The corpse of the persecutor laid in a coffin.
>
> (*Hymn in Jul.* 3.1–3, trans. McVey)

Valentinian and Valens

Although his position as emperor was secured by the preservation of his army, and the presence of much of the senior military staff of the empire in his train, Jovian felt the need to return to Constantinople as fast as he could. He also had to do something with the corpse of his predecessor. As Tarsus had been prepared to be Julian's capital upon his return from Persia, and Julian appears to have expressed the desire to be buried there, Jovian decided to honor his request.[211] The task of burying Julian was left to Procopius, who appears to have had no interest in contesting Jovian's election; his willingness to take the larger part of the army to accomplish this task was a powerful demonstration of his acquiescence, as was his subsequent withdrawal to an estate in Cappadocia.[212] It is also a powerful indication of Jovian's ability to reconcile diverse groups to his regime. He took further steps in this direction when he had himself portrayed without a beard, a clear sign that he rejected Julian, and declared that he wished for there to be peace in the church, a sign, perhaps, that he would eschew the interventionist policies of Constantius.[213] There too he summoned Athanasius to join him, another indication that he intended to pursue a course that would end the divisions that had racked the empire in recent decades.[214] At the same time, he reaffirmed the validity of the Nicene Creed, an act that was well designed to win him popularity in the west. While he sought to bring peace to the church, he also attempted to improve his reputation by dispatching messengers throughout the empire claiming that the Persian expedition was a success: a campaign that is echoed on coins proclaiming the "victory of the Romans."[215] Whatever happened, he had to introduce himself to his subjects as a man bringing peace where there had been chaos, and victory even where there was none.

Jovian needed to be secure in the east, as news from the west may have been disturbing. Immediately after his return to Roman territory, Jovian had recalled Lucillianus, the former *magister equitum* of Illyricum and his father-in-law – living in retirement after his defeat by Julian – to government, sending him to the west as *magister militum et peditum*.[216] Lucillianus appears to have decided that Jovinus, who had been left as *magister equitum* in Gaul by Julian, was a potential threat, and sought to replace him with the Malarichus who had, years earlier, denounced the machinations against Silvanus.[217] When Malarichus turned the job down, Lucillianus (who was accompanied by, among others, a tribune named Valentinian) had gone to Rheims himself. There he was murdered in a mutiny, and the situation was only saved when Jovinus made a timely demonstration of loyalty to the new regime.[218] It was the action of Jovinus that saved Valentinian's life, and he appears to have returned to the east to let Jovian know what had transpired. The fact of the matter was that Jovinus was the real power broker in Gaul and, despite his demonstration of loyalty, would need to be handled with care.

Leaving Antioch in the autumn, Jovian made his way toward Constantinople, reaching Ancyra by January 1, where he assumed the consulship with his young son, Varronian, who cried throughout the ceremony. Ammianus saw this as a prophetic event.[219] Jovian died six weeks later, on February 17, 364. The official story was that he had been asphyxiated by a coal fire in his bedroom at Dadastana, a place on the border between Galatia and Bithynia.[220] Ammianus thought that he had been murdered, and that it was suspicious that there was no investigation into his death.[221] Zosimus says that he killed himself.[222]

It took a few days for the general staff to agree on a successor. When Salutius, who was once again offered the job, once again rejected it, the assembled marshals, after rejecting a relative of Jovian who was too far away, decided upon another relatively junior officer, the very Valentinian who had recently escaped with his life from Gaul.[223] On February 26, 364, Valentinian, who had been in Ancyra, was presented to the army at Nicaea, which duly acclaimed him emperor, after some protest. After the formal act of acclamation, the soldiers demanded that the new Augustus select a colleague.[224] Valentinian demurred for the moment, but a month later, now at Constantinople, he rejected the advice of a senior staff officer, Dagalaifus, that he seek his colleague outside of his own family, and had his brother, Valens, declared Augustus on March 28.[225]

After recovering from a severe illness and determining that they were not the victims of a magical assault, the brothers traveled together in the summer of 364 to Naissus, where they would make division of the dioceses of the empire between them.[226] They confirmed the structure of the empire as it had been under Constantius, divided into three great prefectures, one consisting of Gaul, Britain, and Spain, the second of Italy, Illyricum, and Africa, the third of the east. Valentinian, "by whose will the business was accomplished," would retain direct control over the two western zones, Valens over the eastern.[227]

Procopius and the end of the Constantinian dynasty

The brothers were right to be concerned; the house of Constantine had held power for a very long time, and there remained, in some quarters, a deep attachment to the departed dynasty.[228] When Valentinian and Valens parted company, never to see each other again, in the late summer of 364, their regime was already at risk. Procopius had taken flight and would soon be ready to try and reassert the claims of hereditary monarchy.

It appears that the emperors, in the course of the investigation of the alleged magical assault upon their persons, had decided to take action against major supporters of Julian. Maximus of Ephesus had been arrested and sent into exile, and it is likely that this is the context of an attempt mentioned by Zosimus to arrest Procopius.[229] The soldiers sent to seize him failed, and Procopius was able to flee to the Crimea. From there he made contact with potential supporters at Constantinople. His previous connections with the bureaucracy gave him the access to disgruntled individuals that he needed, and the access to information that was necessary, if he was to succeed.

As Procopius plotted, Valens passed through Constantinople on his way to Antioch. With Valens safely clear of the city, and two regiments from Thrace in transit, Procopius made his move. It was September 28, 365, when Procopius entered the city and went to the baths named for Constantine's sister, Anastasia.[230] The spot was well chosen: the association with the house of Constantine resonated with the dynastic claims that Procopius would make, and it was a place that Procopius could use as his headquarters until the palace and senate house could be secured. Both were duly occupied without resistance, and Procopius rapidly set about forming a new government. Nebridius, the praetorian prefect, and Caesarius, prefect of the city, were arrested, being replaced by two men who had served under Julian, and the commander of the garrison of Thrace, a man named Julius, was tricked into coming to Constantinople, where he too was arrested.[231] Two of Constantius' senior officers, Gomoarius and Agilo, were placed in charge of the army that Procopius immediately set about raising. Ammianus portrayed those who joined with Procopius as desperate men, or (in the case of Gomoarius and Agilo) men moved by the winds of fortune. This is unreasonable. The fact that Procopius was able to rally men who had held senior positions in government under both Julian and Constantius suggests instead that there was deep unhappiness with the way that Valentinian and Valens had begun constructing their own regime. He had further support from Constantius' third wife, Faustina, who had given birth to a daughter just before Julian had triumphed. Procopius was seen carrying the young child about in the capital, and Ammianus admits that Faustina herself had been present when Procopius was given some of the imperial insignia.[232] The pair would later accompany Procopius on campaign.

One of Procopius' first acts as he sought to establish the legitimacy of his regime was to attempt to circulate his portrait. Agents carrying gold coins were intercepted and executed by Equitius as they entered Illyricum.[233] The image on these coins is interestingly varied, as he is shown with a beard less full than that of Julian, but still striking in an age of beardless rulers. It clearly distinguished him from Valens, and the Constantan style of portrait that he espoused.

Valens received less assistance from his dynastic connections. In a forerunner of much that was to come, Valentinian submitted to the will of his staff and decided that he could not afford to leave the Rhine open to assault by withdrawing troops for service in the east. The excuse was that he could not be sure if Valens was still alive – and he had to deal with an invasion of the Alamanni.[234] Procopius was his enemy, he would say, while the Alamanni were the enemy of the whole world.[235]

Valens was not dead, nor was he about to act decisively. He was in Cilicia when he learned of the revolt, and all that he did in the winter was move to Galatia, where he took up a position from which he could observe Procopius' activity.[236] Before moving against a regime that was filled with men who had, until the last year, been his superiors, he needed to be sure that he had sufficient support in his own ranks.

In the next few months it looked as if Procopius might succeed. He gained control of Bithynia, and he appears to have obtained the promise of further troops from the Goths by invoking their treaty with Constantine.[237] Slowly, however, Valens gathered enough strength to make his own move, greatly heartened when Constantius' old general, Arbitio, agreed to appear with him and lend his support.[238] At the same time significant forces arrived from Antioch. Although we are not told how many men arrived, these reinforcements probably gave Valens a substantial advantage in numbers if he could retain their loyalty. For this the presence of Arbitio was crucial.[239] In a scene that is reminiscent of that staged by Constantius when he received the

(a)  (b)

(c) (d)

(e)

surrender of Vetranio, Arbitio addressed troops under the command of Gomoarius, who promptly deserted.[240] They were followed, when battle was joined, by units under the personal command of Agilo.[241] Procopius was arrested as he tried to flee, and decapitated by Valens when he was brought into camp.[242] So ended the last effort to continue the dynasty of Constantine.

Procopius fell victim to the forces that he had tried to use in order to overthrow Valens. He had hoped that his ancestry and his personal friendship with many senior officers would be enough to defeat Valens. The fact that he should have come so close to succeeding is perhaps the most significant testimony to the strength of the corporate government of Constantius that was discussed at the end of chapter 12. But, in the end, it proved to be not enough; indeed, it may be that Procopius' close connection with Julian proved his ultimate undoing. The troops who remained loyal to Valens were those who had remained at Antioch; they were Constantius' men, with little reason to feel fondly toward Julian. Valens' victory might best be seen as the last act in the civil war between the two imperial cousins.

Plate 17 Procopius and the House of Valentinian. To mark a clear break with Julian, Jovian adopted an image that evoked that of Constantius II, which was, in turn, adopted by Valentinian and his house (and later by Theodosius as well as other claimants to the throne). Procopius' image, conversely, harks back to that of Julian with his beard, while at the same time displaying the overtly Christian chi–rho symbol on the reverse. (a) Jovian. *Credit*: *RIC* Jovian, Constantinople no. 179 (363–64); author's collection, photo courtesy of Classical Numismatic Group. (b) Valentinian. *Credit*: *RIC* Valentinian, Siscia 5 (a2) (364–67); author's collection, photo courtesy of Classical Numismatic Group. (c) Valens. *Credit*: *RIC* Valens, Siscia 7 (b2) (364–67); author's collection, photo courtesy of Classical Numismatic Group. (d) Gratian. *Credit*: *RIC* Gratian, Antioch 50 (a) (378–82); author's collection, photo courtesy of Classical Numismatic Group. (e) Procopius. *Credit*: *RIC* Procopius, Constantinople 17a (365–66); author's collection, photo courtesy of Forum Ancient Coins.

14

THE END
OF HEGEMONY:
367–95

Nine years before Julian died, a boy was born in the town of Thagaste in North Africa, the son of a woman named Monica and a man named Patricius. Members, barely, of the curial class, the boy's parents were resolved that their child take advantage of the best education they could afford, and advance in society.[1] Although both were Christian, they had no doubt but that the road out of Thagaste was paved with the classics of Latin literature. So it was that their son, when not stealing apples, became a devotee of the classics. He loved Virgil, he wept for the death of Dido, and scored his first competitive triumph at school with his version of the speech that Juno might have made when she watched Aeneas sail from Carthage to Italy.[2] When he was fifteen, the boy moved to another town to study with superior rhetoricians. The next year the family ran short of money, so he had to come home, where he objected so strenuously to the marriage that his parents tried to arrange for him that they dropped the idea. At the age of seventeen he was able to return to school, this time at Carthage.[3] He now received assistance from a wealthy man of Thagaste, who supported able boys who might enhance his own status by climbing the ranks of the imperial bureaucracy.[4]

At Carthage the young man fell in love with a woman of a much lower class, with whom he would live for the next fifteen years, and with whom he become a parent. He named their child, a boy, Adeodotus. The name, popular among Christians at Carthage, was a Latin translation of the Phoenician *Iatanbaal*, "gift of Baal."[5] The old ways might be passing, but they were not disappearing. Christians, who in Africa were still divided between Donatists, who held the upper hand, and the orthodox, dwelt in a world where there remained many other intellectual options; they lived in cities where open debate flourished. So it was that our young man found himself deeply attracted to Manichaeism. To the horror of his mother – his father had died – he became a "Hearer" when he was twenty.[6]

While he may have rebelled against his parent's social ambitions by living with a concubine, and against their faith by listening to the Manichaean Elect, he did not disappoint his patron (who likewise found Manichaeism attractive). Nor did his interest in Manichaeism preclude other lines of thought. He delighted in Platonic philosophy after reading Cicero's *Hortensius* and honed his rhetorical skills, becoming himself a teacher.[7] He was a classic product of his age, moving with ease between different traditions, negotiating the radical differences between systems of thought through the cultural idiom of the classics. The reign of Julian made no impact upon him at the time; and, in a very real sense, his life and upbringing underscored the folly of what Julian had tried to do.[8] This man could get ahead in the world because religion remained secondary to education in the formation of his identity. In later life he would become a Christian, a devout Christian, and would influence the evolution of the faith more powerfully than any thinker since Paul – but he did so because he was, first and foremost, a man of letters.

What he could not understand at the time was that the true legacy of the reign of Julian was not the failed effort to create a new brand of polytheism; it was rather the irreparable harm that Julian's failure in Persia did to Rome's hegemonic position in the Mediterranean world. Four years after our young man moved to Carthage, Valens would make the fatal error of admitting large numbers of Goths to the empire. Two years after that, Valens would die in battle against the same Goths, whom his officials had driven to rebellion.[9] Still, the young man from Thagaste does not seem to have understood what was happening to his world. For this man, the year 375 was more important than the year 376 because he returned to his hometown to be a teacher of rhetoric; then a friend died and he returned to Carthage. Here the ascent that his talents allowed continued. Winning a poetry competition, he was befriended by the governor, a man named Vindicianus.[10] By 382 he had contacts enough to venture to Rome, where Symmachus, the bastion of the polytheist aristocracy, recognized his talent, and perhaps rejoiced that he could recommend a person who was not a Christian to be professor of rhetoric at the imperial capital at Milan.[11] In 384, the orator from Thagaste obtained this appointment.

The glory of addressing the emperor turned out to be less exciting than the young man may have thought it would be; the fact that the emperor in question was a child may help explain why no more senior person wanted the job.[12] "I sensed," he would later write, "my misery on that day that I was to recite my panegyric to the emperor, in which I lied about many things, and was applauded in lying by those who knew better."[13] He discovered that he greatly admired the local bishop, Ambrose, who could read without moving his lips (among other things) and defy the emperor successfully.[14] The experience started him back down the path to Christianity, conversion in August 386, and his baptism at the hands of Ambrose in 387.

Jumping ahead nearly half a century, we may see this same man, now aged and dying, once again in North Africa, in the city of which he had long been bishop, Hippo Regius. It had been to introduce himself to his flock, and

answer questions about his past, that he had composed one of the most extraordinary books ever written in Latin, showing how he had grown into his
faith.[15] In this work, which was finished in 397, he still shows no sign
that he understood what was happening to the empire. The death of Valens
had seemingly made no great impact upon him, and the recent victory of
Theodosius – who had succeeded Valens – over a usurper may have seemed
to confirm the inherent strength of the imperial system. He could not have
known that Theodosius would be the last man to rule the entire empire. Nor
could he then have known that, within fifteen years of Theodosius' decisive
victory over his rivals, a Gothic chieftain would have set in motion the
creation of a people that would succeed to a portion of the territory of Rome.
In 410, this Gothic chieftain, Alaric, disappointed in his desire to become
a high Roman official himself, would sack the city of Rome.

For all the apparent normalcy of our young man's upbringing – and we
may as well admit that his name was Augustine – it is of great importance
that it was contemporary with the youth of Alaric. Although we know little
about Alaric prior to the 390s, we do know that he was in his mid-
twenties in 395, and thus that he would have been born prior to the entry
of his people into the Roman Empire.[16] Like Augustine, Alaric had his own
ambitions for advancement within the Roman imperial system. He may even
have been, like many of his people, a Christian: despite his burial in a riverbed
(not a traditional Christian thing to do) he had ordered his men not to loot
the churches of Rome in 410. To see Alaric and Augustine as two sorts of
Roman in the later half of the fourth century is to see as well the different
definitions of what it meant to be successful in the empire. For Alaric, to be
Roman was to obtain status within the imperial system: he did not have to
buy into its cultural idiom, he simply had to find an office for himself. His
models were Germans who had risen to high rank in the previous twenty
years, the bureaucratic descendants of Agilo, Dagalaifus, Nevitta, Silvanus,
Gomoarius, and the other officials whom we have already seen rising to positions of power. Alaric's rival, the man from whom he sought recognition,
was Stilicho, the *magister militum* in the western empire. Stilicho was a
Vandal. Stilicho's predecessors included three Franks, Arbogast, Bauto, and
Richomer (with whom he feuded) as well as men named Merobaudes, Vallio,
Rumoridus, and Butheric (plainly Germans, though we do not know their
tribes). That Alaric could see the world the way that he did is a reminder
of just how important it was that the Roman state be able to define the ways
that people participated in it. It would have been unthinkable for a tribal
chieftain in the age of Marcus to presume to a high command over Roman
soldiers without serving as a junior officer in the Roman army first. Alaric's
career is emblematic of just how suddenly, and dramatically, the state was
losing the ability to exercise that control. Not only could Alaric think what
he thought, he also could do so as the leader of an independent people within
the boundaries of the empire. The significance of the frontiers themselves

had now to be called into question, and before Alaric sacked Rome, the Rhine frontier was swept away by other tribes. Rome's loss of the ability to preserve the integrity of its boundaries marked the true end of its hegemonic position in the western world. By losing its hegemonic position, by losing the ability to control its own frontiers, by losing ability to control access to administration, the Roman state lost its ability to define what it meant to be Roman. It also lost its ability to defend the urban heartland of the empire. As Augustine lay dying in 430, his city was threatened by the fleet of the Vandals, who had earlier crossed the Rhine, never to be brought under the control of the government.

Julian and Valens bear much of the responsibility for what happened. While there is no reason to think that the new style of government introduced by Diocletian and Constantine would, in the long run, have threatened the health of the cities of the empire, there is every reason to think that the failure of the government to maintain the internal security of the empire led to the rapid disintegration of imperial control over much of the land that it had controlled in 180. As we saw in the first chapter, the imperial government provided the framework within which the cities of the empire could thrive. It did so not because it sought to control the hearts and minds of its subjects, but rather because its overwhelming military power enabled its subjects to create their own forms of interaction with the culture of the central government. The theme of this chapter is the demise of Roman hegemony. The demise of hegemony should not be confused with the demise of the Roman Empire. Rather it should be understood as a lessening of state power that would result in a redefinition of the Roman Empire's place in the Mediterranean world. The Roman Empire would cease to be the hegemonic power in the region, but it would continue to be a powerful state for centuries to come. At times it would retain the power to determine its own fate; at others it would be forced to redefine itself in the face of new threats that it could no longer control as its urban infrastructure declined.

Adrianople and the Frigidus

If Augustine and Alaric may be taken as representatives of two kinds of Romans in the late fourth century – we shall encounter many other kinds of Romans in the course of this chapter – two battles may be taken as illustrative of the transformation of imperial power in their lifetime. It is quite possible that Alaric was present at both. We know that he was in a command position during the second, and he may have been a toddler in the Gothic camp during the first. This first battle was fought outside of Adrianople on August 9, 378. The second took place on the banks of the River Frigidus in northern Italy on September 6, 394.[17] The issue at stake in the latter case was the survival of the regime of a man named Eugenius, who had been made emperor by the *magister militum* of the west, Arbogast, after the death of Valentinian II, the younger son of Valentinian I (see p. 552).

Although Ammianus and other writers attributed the Roman catastrophe at Adrianople to the impiety of Valens, another view might reasonably take in developments in central Asia.[18] A group of nomads known to westerners as the Huns arrived suddenly on the scene in the early 370s. Although a straightforward identification with the Xiongnu, a confederation of Turkic nomads who had made life miserable for the Chinese empire, is unlikely, a description of this people by the Chinese historian Sima Qian offers good insight into the impression that nomads made upon settled people. He described them as follows:

> They move about in search of water and pasture and have no walled cities or fixed dwellings, nor do they engage in any sort of agriculture. Their lands, however, are divided into regions under the control of various leaders. They have no writing, and even promises and agreements are only verbal. The little boys start out by learning to ride sheep and shoot birds and rats with a bow and arrow, and when they get a little older they shoot foxes and hares, which are used for food. Thus all the young men are able to use a bow and act as cavalry in time of war. It is their custom to herd their flocks in times of peace and make their living by hunting, but in periods of crisis they take up arms and go off on plundering and marauding expeditions. This seems to be their inborn nature. For long-range weapons they use bows and arrows, and swords and spears at close range. If the battle is going well for them they will advance, but if not, they will retreat, for they do not consider it a disgrace to run away. Their only concern is self-advantage, and they know nothing of propriety or righteousness.
>
> (Sima Qian, *Records of the Grand Historian*,
> trans. Burton Watson, rev. edn. [New York,
> 1993], 2, 129)

Although the Huns were not the Xiognu, there can be no doubt that the arrival of central Asian nomads in the Ukraine introduced a radically new style of fighting to the area. The speed with which the Huns moved was beyond the experience of the Goths, who were heavily defeated and despaired of being able to combat the new threat. In an effort to escape the Huns a large portion of the Gothic inhabitants of the area west of the Dniester, the Thervingi, sought refuge in Roman territory. Valens saw in the Goths a source of recruits and agreed to admit them on the understanding that they behave when in Roman territory and convert to Christianity, by which he meant a form of the faith based on the creed of Constantinople to which he subscribed.[19]

Unfortunately for Valens, his officials in Thrace were either deeply corrupt – Ammianus' version – or ill prepared to deal with the massive influx of new mouths to feed.[20] According to Ammianus, the generals in Thrace took to exchanging dogs for slaves while failing to find the Goths a place to live. The situation soon flew out of their control. A group of the Greuthingi, the Gothic inhabitants of the area east of the Dniester, crossed the Danube, this time without permission, and began to move into Thrace.[21] When Lupicinus, the *comes rei militaris* in Thrace, failed in an effort to arrest the leaders of the two groups at a dinner party, open war broke out.[22] In the course of the next year there were a series of battles, with mixed results as Valens' generals tried to regain control of the situation. Valens himself, who was at Antioch as the result of an ongoing dispute with Sapor over Armenia, could not commit either himself or the bulk of the *comitatenses*.

Peace was made with Persia by the end of 377, and in the summer of 378 the balance of numbers should have swung decisively in favor of the Romans. Gratian, the elder son of Valentinian, who had died three years earlier (see p. 541), committed to help his uncle and was leading troops from the west, while Valens could now bring his whole strike force against the invaders. If he had the bulk of the *comitatenses* with him, he commanded a force that probably numbered around forty thousand men.[23] This should have been more than sufficient, even if, as there is some reason to believe, the army could have used some additional training, to defeat a group that, while it had not been repressed by the garrison of Thrace, had still not been able to overwhelm it either.[24] Valens was led to believe that the total armed force of the Goths was no more than ten thousand men.[25] His intelligence was faulty, but there is no doubt but that the Goths were heavily outnumbered.

The biggest problem that Valens may have brought with him to the field was that he could not decide what he wanted: did he want the glory of destroying the Goths, or did he still want them in his service? It appears that his general staff was also deeply divided on this point, and that no decisions had been reached, though it may be that Valens would have preferred to have the soldiers, and that may explain his conduct.[26] The Goths were encamped some eight miles north of Adrianople on a ridge near the modern village of Muratcali.[27] Valens led his army out, and then stopped to negotiate.[28] In the meantime, the Goths aggravated the climatic conditions for the Romans – it was a very hot day – by lighting fires to the windward of them so that the smoke would blow down into their ranks.[29] Just as it looked as if an agreement might be reached, a skirmish began between units on the Roman left and the Goths who were drawn up in front of their wagon laager, and then, all of a sudden, a large force of Gothic cavalry that had been away on a foraging expedition returned, slamming into the left flank of the Roman army as it advanced toward the wagons.[30] As the left wing collapsed, the rest of the army was hemmed in by Goths who advanced from their position on the ridge to support their cavalry.[31] The strength of the late Roman army was its tactical flexibility, and it was of this flexibility that it was deprived by the nature of the Gothic assault. Ammianus says that the troops were now packed so closely together that they could not use their weapons.[32] Valens himself was killed by an arrow – his body never found, and possibly incinerated by the Goths in a house to which some said he had been brought after suffering his wound.[33] Two-thirds of the army was lost, a number that tells only part of the story, for Valens had taken the cream of the eastern army into battle – 60 percent of the best-trained troops in that army died.[34] As an effective fighting force, the eastern Roman army perished on August 9, 378. When Goths approached Constantinople after the battle, the defense of the city appears to have resided with the guards of Valens' widow, Domnica – some of them Saracens – who sallied forth to drive off the raiders.[35] Ammianus says that their savagery terrified the Goths, completing his picture of the descent of the empire into barbarism.[36]

The Goths would never be brought fully under the control of the empire. Theodosius, the western general who would take the throne of the east a few months after Adrianople, granted them their own lands within the frontiers in return for their service, under their own commanders, in his army.[37] It was thus with a large Gothic contingent that he would fight the battle of the Frigidus. His opponents on that day were Arbogast, whom he had appointed some years before as *magister militum* in the west, and a man named Eugenius, whom Arbogast had made emperor. Arbogast was a devoted polytheist, and he sought to invoke the power of the traditional gods against Theodosius. For the first and only time would an army that identi-fied its cause with that of the gods confront an army that had identified its salvation with the Christian God.

While we have no historian of the quality of Ammianus to describe the encounter that took place between the two armies in the valley of the Vipava River, enough details survive to make a reconstruction of the events possible.[38] The army of Arbogast was encamped to the south of the road that ran in antiquity from Aquileia to Emona. In this position the western army controlled the egress from the Col de Poidre, compelling Theodosius to launch a piecemeal attack from his line of march. On the first day of what would prove to be a two-day struggle, Theodosius' Gothic troops bore the brunt of the battle, losing, according to tradition, half or more of their strength.[39] On a high hill to the east of the battlefield a huge statue of Jupiter had been erected to encourage the defenders, and it must have seemed that the old gods were indeed present as the Christian Goths were slaughtered in the plain below.[40] The next day, however, a high wind arose, allegedly in response to the prayers of Theodosius, blowing down upon his foes. The wind in the region is indeed notorious, reaching more than sixty miles an hour, and on this day it proved decisive, demoralizing the army of Arbogast. The defense collapsed, Eugenius was captured and executed, Arbogast committed suicide a day later.[41] The victorious emperor would be dead within the year.

For our purposes, the significance of the battle lies in the way that it was fought. While we have no reliable evidence for the numbers involved, it is unlikely that Theodosius could have disposed more than the forty thousand or so men that made up a large field army in the late empire, while the strategy employed by Arbogast suggests that his forces were considerably weaker.[42] He probably moved into the mountains, taking up a position with the River Frigidus to his back, because he could not confront Theodosius if he reached the plains of northern Italy. The statue of Jupiter may, in retrospect, be seen as a symbol of the fact that it would have taken a miracle for him to win. Given Theodosius' heavy dependence upon Gothic allies, and the evident weakness of Arbogast's army, the battle is evidence for the progressive weakening of the empire's military forces.[43] Neither man is likely to have had as many Roman soldiers with him as Valens had led in his ill-fated assault on the Gothic laager outside Adrianople less than twenty years before.

Emperors and their courts: 364–95

Another significant feature of the battle of the Frigidus was that Arbogast had not had himself proclaimed emperor, but rather chose to place a puppet on the throne. He was in a position to do this because the reigning emperor of the west had committed suicide after failing to dismiss him from office.[44] The career of Arbogast reflects a progressive weakening of the imperial office in the decades after the death of Julian. Although Ammianus paints Valentinian as a man of fierce passions and of considerable efficiency, it appears that neither quality ensured control.[45] Time and again Valentinian appears to have been at the mercy of his generals and of courtiers who determined access to his person. Ammianus' portrait of Valens is less favorable – as is that offered by Eunapius and later Christian authors – but concentration on the personal failure of the emperor disguises the complexity of government.[46] The difficulties encountered by Valentinian and Valens stemmed, in part, from the fact that their regime came into being at the sufferance of the general staff – a point that was driven home during the revolt of Procopius by Valentinian's inability to lend aid to his brother, and by Valens' dependence on Arbitio's authority to defeat his rival. Despite the fact that both men remained on the throne for a long time – eleven years in the case of Valentinian, fourteen years in the case of Valens – they cannot be said to have been in full control of their governments. The rages that seem to have been a feature of both men's personal style seem, at times, calculated to gain the attention of subordinates who were expected to demonstrate their skill by calming the emperor down.

Valentinian came to the throne without a circle of dependants. He needed to find men who would put his interests first, and he had to deal with men who might be thought to have their own claims to power.[47] The theory of government to which Valentinian and his officials worked is summed up very well by Ammianus in his discussion of the abortive attempt to appoint Malarichus as *magister equitum* during 364:

> This was seen to have two advantages: one that a general of genuine merit, though suspect, should be removed from his situation, and that a man of lesser expectations, promoted to a higher post, would support the still uncertain status of his patron with great zeal.
>
> (Amm. Marc. 25.8.11)

Throughout his reign, Valentinian would promote a number of men who had been early supporters – some Pannonian, others from Gaul – to high positions in an effort to create a particularly loyal faction within the government.[48] When it came to dealing with the army, the events of 364 had left Valentinian with so great a debt to Jovinus that he could do no better than to continue him in his command until 369, and reward him with a consulship.[49] At the same time, he sought to build his own relationship with the soldiers through repeated campaigns against the Germanic tribes north of the Rhine.[50] In the end, he succeeded in securing neither the dominance of his early supporters in government, nor the enduring loyalty of the general staff to his dynasty. His own loyalty to the men he promoted made him unwilling to see their faults even when they were glaring; his inability to control access to his person led to scandals that did little to win the affection of those outside the charmed circle he sought to create. A decent enough soldier, Valentinian appears to have lacked the sophistication necessary to control the behavior of the officials upon whose support he depended.

Valens was no more adroit than his brother. He too tried to create a cadre of supporters, but reasonable fear that he was not beloved made him prone to actions of great viciousness that undermined his position. The seeds of the Gothic revolt were arguably planted by officials who essentially ignored Valens' intention to exploit the Goths.[51] Valens' urge to give battle at Adrianople is largely explained by his desire to win a victory that would give him the authority in the empire that he lacked.[52]

The major offices of government in the west remained very much as they had been under Constantius. On the civilian side they were the praetorian prefecture of Gaul, Britain, and Spain, the praetorian prefecture of Italy, Illyricum, and Africa, the *comes sacrarum largitionum*, the *comes rei privatae*, the *magister memoriae*, and the *quaestor sacri palatii*. With Valentinian taking an active role in command of his armies, the three senior military offices were those of the *magister peditum praesentalis*, the *magister equitum praesentalis*, and the *magister equitum et peditum in Illyricum*. About the holders of most of these offices we are not well informed. We know the name of only one *comes rei privatae* – Florianus – who appears to have held office from 364 to 369.[53] We also hear of only two *comites sacrarum largitionum*, Germanianus and Philematius, who held office respectively in 365–67 and 371–72, both of whom are known solely as the addressees of texts in the codes.[54] The only *magister memoriae* we hear about is Flavius Eupraxius, who held that office in 367 before moving over to become *quaestor sacri palatii* from that year until 370. He is one of four quaestors we know by name. Viventius held the office in 364 before rising rapidly through the ranks in the later half of the decade in recognition of his role in investigating the illness of the two brothers at Constantinople.[55] We also know that Flavius Claudius Antonius succeeded Eupraxius from 370 to 373.[56] It is likely that the poet and aspiring *éminence grise* Ausonius (the tutor to Valentinian's son, Gratian) succeeded him – he was certainly in office in 375.[57] When we turn, however, to the praetorian prefectures and to military commands, the situation is rather different, reflecting, in the end, some very deep divisions.

To begin on the military side, Jovinus remained in office until 369, when he was replaced by Theodosius, who remained *magister equitum* in Gaul until his sudden fall from favor (and execution) in 375.[58] Severus, who had been a guard officer in the previous year, replaced Dagalaifus, the *magister peditum* when Valentinian became emperor, in 366.[59] Severus remained in office until 372, at which point he may have been replaced by Flavius Merobaudes, the only other man attested in this rank under Valentinian.[60] Flavius Equitius, who had agitated for Valentinian's selection as emperor, was made *comes* in Illyricum in 364, and a year later became *magister equitum et peditum* in the same region, in which office he remained for the rest of the reign.[61] Equitius appears to have been connected with a group including a man named Remigius who would be *magister officiorum* from 367 to 371. He was related to the *comes Africae*, a man named Romanus. This personal connection may help explain how the military government of Africa would become a flash point for factional rivalry.

Romanus had several other marks in his favor. Like Valentinian, he had been dismissed by Julian, probably in 362. Like Valentinian again, he had been brought back to service by Jovian, and, as a guard officer, he appears to have supported Valentinian at the time of his acclamation. His timely support of Valentinian, taken with his connection to Equitius, enabled his rapid ascent to high command.[62] Another man who had also been in the right place at the decisive moment was Leo. As a guard officer, he too had agitated for Valentinian's appointment. He subsequently became a *notarius* and would rise through the palatine ranks until he succeeded Remigius as *magister officiorum* in 371.[63] It was through his influence that a series of court appointees to posts in, or in the vicinity of, Rome sought to impose the will of the court upon the traditional aristocracy of the city.[64] One of these men, a Pannonian named Maximinus, would occupy the praetorian prefecture of Gaul, Britain, and Spain from 371 to 375, in which office he succeeded Viventius.[65]

Viventius' predecessor as praetorian prefect of Gaul, Britain, and Spain was Sextus Petronius Probus, who had already held the praetorian prefecture of Illyricum, Italy, and Africa in 364 at the age of thirty-six.[66] Probus differed from the officials already mentioned in that he was descended from the Roman aristocracy, which may explain his rapid rise to power (he had governed Africa in his twenties). We do not know what he did after his term in Africa, but he must have been favored by Jovian to hold the office that he did in 364. With the arrival of Viventius, he would resume the prefecture of Illyricum, Italy, and Africa, an office that he held from 368 to 375.

Taken together, Jovinus, Viventius, Probus, Remigius, Aequitius, and Leo form a remarkably stable group holding the crucial positions in the court, the civil government of the provinces, and the army for the bulk of the reign of Valentinian. By the end of Valentinian's reign the influence of the court was beginning to extend to the prefecture of Rome as well. In 372 a man named Bappo, whose name proclaims a Gallic origin, is attested in this office.[67] His successor was a man named Principius, about whom nothing is known other than that he received a law on exemptions for physicians and teachers in 373.[68] Principius' successor was Flavius Eupraxius, who had previously served as quaestor of the palace.[69]

Valens got off to a somewhat slower start in assembling his governmental circle in the east, in part because of the disruption caused by the revolt of Procopius. He had to move with circumspection – allowing, for instance, the city of Constantinople to make an official apology, and suffer no punishment, for supporting the usurper.[70] Within the bureaucracy, while he distinguished between "co-conspirators" with Procopius and those who had supported them, forgiving the latter, a man's conduct during the crisis became a factor in his future success.[71] Saturninus, the praetorian prefect arrested by Procopius, did not return to government after his captivity. Instead he was succeeded by Auxonius, who owed his appointment to Clearchus, the loyal *vicarius* of Asia.[72] Clearchus himself went on to become prefect of Constantinople and appears to have remained a powerful influence throughout the reign of Valens despite the fact that he held no further office.[73] Domitius Modestus, who had been *comes orientis* and then prefect of Constantinople under Constantius, succeeded Auxonius in 369 and remained in office for the rest of Valens' reign.[74] The chief military officers were the *magister equitum praesentalis*, Victor, and the *magister peditum praesentalis*, Arintheus. Victor served from 363 to 379, Arintheus from 366 to 378.[75] The *magister officiorum* for the bulk of Valens' reign was a man named Sophronius who took office in 369 and appears to have remained there until 378.[76] These are the officials that we can trace – there were others, of course, but they only appear in Ammianus' narrative when they matter. Thus we only get a picture of the command structure in Thrace in 377–79 because of the Gothic invasion. At that time both commanding officers had long records of service with Valens. Traianus, the *magister peditum*, had served in Armenia in 371–73.[77] Saturninus, who was appointed to the post of *magister equitum*, was evidently a long-term servant of the regime – an exile as a result of Julian's trials at Chalcedon, he returned to service fairly rapidly, becoming a *comes rei militaris* in Syria as early as 373.[78]

The contrast between the government of Valentinian and Valens and that of Constantius is striking. We know of three *magistri officiorum* under Constantius between 355 and 361 – Florentius, Musonius, and Ampelius, with Florentius holding office both in 355 and in 359–61. Between 354 and 361, there were five praetorian prefects in succession in Gaul, two in Italy and Africa, four in Illyricum, and four in the east. In the top ranks of the military, there were two officials who served very long terms – Ursicinus as *magister equitum* in the east, with a brief interruption for service in the west, from 349 to 359, and Arbitio, who was *magister equitum praesentalis* from 351 to 361. On the other hand, in Gaul, Barbatio was the only *magister* to serve as long as four years – the turnover in the office of *magister equitum* was annual throughout Julian's tenure. We have less information about the east, as Ammianus, our primary source for these officials, does not mention a single *magister peditum*, perhaps as a way of enhancing the importance of Ursicinus as the guardian of the frontier.

The upper echelons of the new regimes, once formed, remained remarkably stable. Stagnant might be a better word, and it cannot be said that security of tenure was altogether a healthy thing.[79] While it must be admitted that all of our primary narratives of the reigns of Valentinian and Valens are unfavorable, either because they were composed under Theodosius, or, an additional factor in Valens' case, for religious reasons, the patterns of official behavior that are detailed in these narratives make for a depressing read. While Ammianus can be shown to inflate his accounts of the poor conduct of Valentinian's officials, it remains the case that he has stories of a particular type.[80] The consistent theme is that members of the inner circle took advantage of their access to the emperor.

In general terms the sort of problems that could arise are suggested by Ammianus in his portrait of Probus:

> Like a type of fish expelled from its element that can no longer breathe on land, thus did he wither away from prefectures, which he was driven to seek by the complaints of his vast family, on account of immense greed that was never free from guilt, so that they could accomplish much evil with impunity: although he was fortified by magnanimity so that he never, himself, ordered a client or slave to do something illegal, if he learned that any of them did something

illegal, he would defend them, resisting Justice herself, without investigation of the matter, and without regard for right and honor.

(Amm. Marc. 27.11.4)

Ammianus is describing a member of an entrenched oligarchy that defined the interests of the state in terms of its own advantage. It is a pattern that emerges clearly from Ammianus' more detailed account of incidents in Rome and North Africa.

In the reign of Jovian, a man named Stachao, a member of a tribe known as the Austoriani, was burned at the stake. His fellow tribesmen claimed that he had been unjustly treated, and raided the region around Lepcis.[81] The people of Lepcis appealed to Romanus (the relative of Remigius) for help. Romanus duly showed up with an army, but said that he could proceed no further unless he was provided with four thousand camels. After remaining in the city for forty days – and not receiving the camels, which the inhabitants said they could not provide – Romanus took his soldiers away.[82] Despite the fact that Valentinian (or someone issuing a rescript in his name) appears to have declared that the *comes rei militaris* could take possession of tax revenues to justify what Romanus had done, the people of Lepcis decided to protest.[83] Perhaps not realizing the extent to which the die had been loaded against them, the Lepcines prevailed upon the provincial assembly to bring their complaints before Valentinian. They elected to do so when they presented the emperor with the *aurum coronarium* that was to be sent on the occasion of his accession.[84]

When Romanus heard what was happening, he wrote to Remigius, asking that he ensure that the investigation be handed over to himself and Dracontius, the *vicarius Africae*.[85] The result of this action was that

> when the ambassadors reached court, they described in words, with the emperor listening, how they had been oppressed; they brought forth the decree (of the provincial assembly) containing the account of the whole matter. Having read this report, the emperor gave credence neither to the version of the *magister officiorum* exculpating the crimes of Romanus, nor to those asserting the opposite, and the promised inquiry was put off, in that way that the greatest powers are customarily deceived amidst pressing obligations.
>
> (Amm. Marc. 28.6.9)

Nothing happened for more than a year, save that the Austoriani launched another devastating raid, and the people of Lepcis sent a third ambassador to Trier. This enraged Valentinian, who sent a *notarius* named Palladius to pay off the arrears owed to the garrison and find out what was happening.[86] After a series of corrupt operations by which Romanus entrapped Palladius – he arranged for him to keep most of the money that he had brought with

538

him by having his junior officers say that they did not need it, and then threatened to use the fact that Palladius was thereby left with the bulk of the money as grounds to charge him with peculation if Palladius did not turn in a report exonerating him.[87] Palladius, who appears to have been willing to listen to the Lepcines, now capitulated, turning in a report that damned them instead.[88] Valentinian flew into yet another rage and ordered that men who had informed against Romanus have their tongues cut out (they managed to go into hiding, thereby avoiding this fate). Romanus then proceeded, with Palladius in tow, to Lepcis, where, in conjunction with a local dignitary named Caecilius, he convinced the people to blame the ambassadors and the *praeses* of the province, who had taken their side. Valentinian then ordered those responsible for the "fraudulent" accusations against Romanus to be executed.[89] The truth about these events only became known years later, when Romanus himself was condemned for corruption by the *magister equitum*, Theodosius.[90] We shall return to Theodosius' involvement in this matter, though it is worth noting here that the proximate cause of the trouble in North Africa was again that Remigius had suppressed complaints lodged against Romanus. This time he claimed that the emperor was too busy to listen to such trivial communication.[91]

It was the duty of a good courtier to assuage rather than to inflame the wrath of the emperor. As we shall see, there had evolved a pattern of communication between emperor and subject that involved the indication of imperial displeasure, followed by a period in which the emperor's subjects could apologize, and prevail upon the emperor to forgive them.[92] In the case of the unfortunate Lepcines, they were not given chance because senior officials were the source of the difficulty and cut off the expected ritual before it had run its course.

A similar pattern of behavior, pitting those who were well connected at court against a local aristocracy, is detectable at Rome in the late 360s and early 370s. In this case the person involved was Maximinus, who would later rise to the office of praetorian prefect. According to Ammianus, he was deputy prefect of the *annona* at Rome, when a complaint was lodged with Olybrius, the prefect of the city, about an attempted poisoning. Olybrius fell ill and left the investigation to Maximinus, who appears to have been aware that Valentinian, whose health was not good, would be particularly interested in learning about the rigorous investigation of such charges.

> The hellish judge went "beyond the limit," as the saying goes, and told the emperor, in a malicious report, that it would only be possible to investigate and punish the pernicious deeds that many were perpetrating at Rome with the use of harsher means. The emperor, enraged by this report – for he was a hasty rather than effective enemy of vice – ordered that cases of this sort be treated under one heading, which he arrogantly added to the charge of treason, so that all those

who had been exempted from torture by the justice of earlier laws and the judgments of the divine emperors could be tortured if the case merited it.

(Amm. Marc. 28.1.10–11)

Although Ammianus' account is not without its own challenges – mostly connected with an evident desire to portray Maximinus as the source of all manner of evil – it is plain that Valentinian was open to manipulation in his dealing with the senate.[93] A few years earlier Valentinian had responded to an inquiry as to what circumstances might justify a death sentence being imposed upon a senator by saying that such cases had to be referred to him in person.[94] The response to Maximinus' report, which is preserved as a letter to Olybrius in the Theodosian Code, does indeed, as Ammianus suggests, contradict the tenor of this earlier ruling. In the letter to Olybrius it is stated:

> No person will stripped of his rank in the imperial service or the defense of rank or birth for the sake of suffering the torment of the cords if we have not been consulted or are uninformed, except in cases of treason, in which there will be one condition only, for everyone. People may also be subjected to torture without prior consultation, who are shown by clear proofs to have forged our subscriptions, in which case we order that even the assumption of palatine rank will not exempt anyone from interrogation.
>
> (CTh. 9.35.1)[95]

The letter is all the more interesting in that when a delegation from the senate arrived at Trier in March 371 to complain about the use of torture against its members, Valentinian denied that he had ever issued such an order. After he had done so, the quaestor of the palace, Eupraxius, pointed out that he had indeed made such a decision.[96] The result was that Valentinian then did rescind the policy enunciated in the letter to Olybrius. Although in this case the ritual of rage and forgiveness did work – possibly because senior members of the Roman senate could not be ignored, the way that it worked made the emperor look foolish rather than merciful. Those who witnessed the scene may well have been left wondering just who was in charge.

Wonder at the amount of influence that the emperor retained in his court may also have been stimulated by the remarkable series of events that surrounded the proclamation of Valentinian's son Gratian as Augustus in 367, a year in which Valentinian once again fell seriously ill. Ammianus describes two groups at court, one whom he calls the "Gauls," the other whom he merely identifies as consisting of those "with better aims," who met to debate the succession if the emperor should expire. The Gauls put forward the *magister memoriae*, Rusticus Julianus, while the other group favored the *magister militum*, Severus.[97] There was no question here of consulting Valens, or of an innate loyalty to the dynasty. What is more, Valentinian seems to have accepted the point. Although he proclaimed Gratian as soon as he recovered, there is no suggestion that anyone was punished for taking part in conversations that might, in another age, have been taken as treasonous. Indeed, although Rusticus appears to have been replaced, he went on to be governor of Africa, while Severus remained in his command for another five years. A creation of the general staff and court himself, Valentinian appears to have acquiesced in the notion that they were free to consult their own interests if he did not make a prior disposition.

The obvious sense that the staff could create an emperor without reference to Valens makes it appear that the two parts of the empire were, to some degree, regarded as being independent of each other. Likewise, in 375, when Merobaudes, the *magister peditum praesentalis* in the west, decided to make the four-year-old Valentinian II co-Augustus with Gratian and Valens, he consulted neither emperor. Perhaps more telling, Ammianus says that while Merobaudes recognized that Gratian might be annoyed to find himself with a fellow Augustus about whose promotion he had not been consulted, he appears to have had no concern lest Valens be disturbed.[98] Although there is some reason to doubt the details of this account as Ammianus gives them, the important point for now is the way that he tells the story. He appears to have thought that it was reasonable to believe that Valens should not have been consulted, and, even though it appears that it took him some time to acquiesce in what had happened, Valens did, in the end, go along.[99] Thus, although the formal unity of the empire was recognized in the prefixes to laws, wherein the ruling Augusti were listed in the order in which they obtained the office – Valentinian, Valens, and Gratian gave way in 375 to Valens, Gratian, and Valentinian II – the order did not reflect formal authority over officials. Valens had no power to make appointments in the west after 375, and it appears that he previously had to acquiesce in decisions made by his brother with which he did not agree.[100] On the other hand, to judge from the contents of the Theodosian Code, laws issued in the name of any member of the college had authority throughout the empire. The effect was to further elevate the authority of the palace bureaucracies in both west and east as, first, the main unifying forces in the political structure of the realm, and, then, the main destabilizing forces. The ultimate result of this structure was to create a new form of conflict whereby dominant figures in one part of the empire would attempt to unseat leading members of the bureaucracy in the other. Although the details of struggles such as those between Stilicho and Rufinus or Eutropius after 395 lie outside the scope of this book, the roots of those struggles are set in the style of administration that arose in the 360s and 370s and would continue under Theodosius.

Turning now to Valens, we note that perhaps the most significant evidence for the potential conflict between different groups arises in the context of a series of treason trials that took place at Antioch during 371. In that year a man named Palladius, who had been charged with attempting to poison the *comes rei privatae*, Fortunatianus, revealed that three men had met in secret to inquire about the succession.[101] One of these men was a former provincial governor; another was a palatine official. They determined who the theoretical successor of Valens would be through a mode of divination that revealed the first four letters of his name – theta, epsilon, omicron, and delta. They decided that this must indicate a senior *notarius* named Theodorus, and duly informed him of what they had learned.[102] Valens flew into a fury, which, Ammianus says, was fed by Modestus, the praetorian prefect.[103] It is what Ammianus says next that is particularly significant – he says that Modestus was deeply agitated by fear for the succession.[104] As Valens had no son, Modestus must have been concerned that the eastern establishment would have the opportunity to name his successor, and that the power to do so would not fall to the west. His concern may have been heightened by the fact that Theodorus was himself a Gaul, and it appears that he retained some affinity with the western bureaucracy. His son, Icarius, would rise to the post of *comes orientis* under Theodosius.[105] Theodorus himself, and the man who had informed of the prediction, Euserius, did not think that it was unlikely that he would succeed Valens. Indeed, Euserius assured him that he need not try to unseat Valens himself, but rather await the "working of inevitable fortune."[106] Theodorus even claimed that he had thought of revealing the prophecy to Valens.

Leaving aside, for the moment, a number of the other remarkable features of this passage – for example, that a polytheist official should explain to a Christian emperor that a decidedly non-Christian form of prophecy had revealed the future to him – the story of Theodorus offers a important reading of the structure of power. The fears of Modestus, not to mention the conversations between Euserius and Theodorus, reveal both that Valens was not expected to make a "dynastic" choice of successor, and that an elderly official could imagine that he was a potential candidate for the throne. Taken together with the advice that Dagalaifus gave to Valentinian about the choice of a colleague, and the discussions in Gaul about a potential successor to Valentinian, these events reveal a distinct hostility among the senior officials of the empire to the notion of dynastic succession. It may be surmised that the emperors were aware that they needed to negotiate the acquiescence of their senior officials in determining what would happen to the throne once they died.

The emperor's need to negotiate his position with his senior officials is brought into sharper focus by a series of marriages, proclamations, and murders between 374 and 379. In 374 Valentinian appears to have decided that he could challenge inherent hostility to dynastic succession. In 369 he

THE END OF HEGEMONY

had divorced his first wife, Severa, to marry Justina, a tangential relative of Constantius who had, in her childhood, been married to Magnentius.[107] He now strengthened the family connection by arranging a marriage between Gratian and Constantia, the posthumous daughter of Constantius II, whom we last saw in the train of Procopius. She was now twelve, and Gratian now fourteen – the earliest ages at which marriage would usually be contemplated in aristocratic circles.

Constantia was duly brought to the west – barely evading capture by a raiding party of the Sarmatians and Quadi outside of Sirmium – and married. In the next year Valentinian himself moved to the Balkans to avenge the raid that had nearly netted Constantia, making Aquincum his headquarters. On November 17 he had moved about forty miles away to Brigetio, where he fell into what appears to have been an apoplectic fit while listening to an embassy from the Quadi, and died. Five days later, his younger son, Gratian's half-brother, Valentinian II, was proclaimed Augustus for Italy, Africa, and Illyricum. Ammianus says that when the elder Valentinian died, the younger was in a villa called Murocincta, one hundred Roman miles from Brigetio. On the orders of Merobaudes, he was brought to the city by his maternal uncle, Cerialis.[108] Given that it would have taken several days to retrieve Valentinian, the decision to make him emperor must have been reached within twenty-four hours of his father's death, and, on that timetable, it looks as if Ammianus has left out some very significant facts. The author of the *Epitome de Caesaribus* says that the decision was made jointly by Merobaudes and Equitius, as does Zosimus.[109] Philostorgius adds that the boy's mother, Justina, "and the army in Pannonia immediately made him emperor."[110] There is no reason to think that Justina, who had the blood of emperors in her veins, was close to her stepson, and it is of some interest that, like Valentinian's first wife, Sabina, and Valens' wife, Domnica, she had been kept very much in the background.[111] None of them had been awarded the title Augusta, a sign perhaps that the imperial brothers had not dared advertise dynastic ambitions of their own before Valentinian decided to join his family to the house of Constantine. Justina might never get the title, but it will appear that she was interested in exercising power in her own right, and that there were senior officers ready to support her.

In his version of the proclamation of Valentinian II, Zosimus adds the further observation that Equitius and Merobaudes thought that Gratian and Valentinian lived too far apart, so that a third ruler was needed. Ammianus says that Merobaudes acted to prevent a usurpation by another official, probably the *comes rei militaris*, Sebastianus.[112] In reporting his departure from the west, Zosimus says that he left because the "young emperors" could not make common cause in their own interest against their eunuchs. These versions are neither contradictory nor necessarily complementary. In fact, both look like fabrications concocted after the fact to justify a usurpation by the officials at Brigetio, and the dismissal of officers whom they could not trust – including the aforementioned Sebastianus and the younger Theodosius.[113] The agreement of Justina was important in lending authority to their action; the speed with which they moved makes it appear as if the officials who ruled Illyricum were not willing to submit their authority to that of either of the other two Augusti. Valens had been very much the junior partner to his brother, and the court of Gratian was on the verge of upheaval from which officials in Illyricum may well have wished to have some cover. For such officials a four-year-old was preferable to a teenager. Zosimus may have, for once, derived something important from Eunapius in his observation that the eunuchs (for which we may read instead senior officials) could not be governed.

The raiders who had just missed out on capturing Constantia were crushed by a young general named Theodosius, who then held the position of *dux Moesiae* at the tender age of twenty-seven.[114] His youth, as was the case years earlier when the young Probus was appointed to the first of his prefectures, indicates that he had powerful support, which he did. His father had been promoted to the rank of *magister equitum* in 369 after a successful operation in Britain during the previous two years.[115]

The elder Theodosius appears to have won the trust of Valentinian as he accompanied the emperor on campaign against the Alamanni in 372 and seems to have been publicly credited with a victory over the Alamanni the previous year, as well as over Sarmatians in the same year.[116] In 373 he was sent to Africa, where the conduct of Romanus had led to the outbreak of a revolt led by a tribal chieftain named Firmus.[117] It took Theodosius two years to suppress the revolt, and in the course of this operation he had not only removed Romanus from office, but also brought to light the correspondence that proved that Remigius had covered up his conduct toward the Lepcines.[118] When his involvement in the wrongdoing of Romanus was revealed, Remigius hanged himself in the house to which he had retired near Milan. The exposure of Remigius may not have sat well with his successor, Leo, and Maximinus, who was now praetorian prefect. The rising star of Theodosius was plainly a threat, as would have been the influence that Gratian's tutor, Ausonius, held with his pupil.

Since Ausonius was still the preeminent person in the western court when the younger Theodosius was suddenly recalled from his estates in Spain after Valens died at Adrianople, it is reasonable to assume that Ausonius had a good relationship with the elder Theodosius.[119] The elder Theodosius' attack on Romanus and the exposure of the corrupt conduct of Remigius could well have appeared to Maximinus as a threat. In this context it appears most likely that the sudden arrest and execution of the elder Theodosius in the months after Valentinian I died was a preemptive strike by Maximinus to secure his position against those linked with Ausonius. It may also appear to have been a serious miscalculation on his part. He was removed from office and executed at some point between the end of March and the middle of April

376.[120] Two of his clients who were rising in the imperial administration along the path that he had taken, through the vicariate of Rome, were executed at the same time. His death, and theirs, may be seen as retaliation for the execution of Theodosius and as a moment that cleared the way for the creation of a new, dominant, faction at court. It may be no coincidence that Petronius Probus ceased to be praetorian prefect at roughly the same time, nor accidental that the younger Theodosius and Sebastianus were both returned to high commands before the campaign of 378 opened. Sebastianus joined Valens, while Theodosius may have been restored to his previous rank.[121] Of the significant figures connected with the elevation of Valentinian II to the throne, only Merobaudes retained his post, and that looks like a concession to the old ruling group, especially as Merobaudes was made one of the two judges in the case brought against Romanus on the basis of the documents uncovered by Theodosius. The connection would seem to be confirmed by the fact that Merobaudes acquitted Romanus despite the manifest evidence of his guilt.[122] Merobaudes may simply have been too powerful a man to tangle with – even though he never seems to have been particularly close to Gratian. In 384, he would side with the rebellious general Maximus, who murdered Gratian and ruled in Gaul.

The effect of the ejection of Maximinus appears in the list of praetorian prefects under Gratian. As we have seen, Probus held office for most of Valentinian I's reign, while Viventius and Maximinus held office for eight years between them. In 377 Ausonius assumed the prefecture of Gaul, and his father assumed that of Illyricum.[123] In 378–79 Ausonius shared the prefectures of Gaul, Italy, and Illyricum with his son, Decimius Hilarianus Hesperius.[124] In 379, Ausonius stepped down from his prefecture, followed soon after by Hesperius. In 380 the prefect of Gaul was Siburius, *magister officiorum* of Gratian from 374 to 379, while the prefect of Italy was Flavius Afranius Syagrius, and that of Illyricum was Eutropius.[125] In Gaul, Siburius gave way to Manlius Theodorus in 382; Syagrius left the prefecture of Illyricum in the same year, and it was taken up by a relative, who soon gave way to Flavius Hypatius. Ausonius, Siburius, Theodorus, and one, if not both, of the Syagrii were Gauls, while Hypatius was from Thessalonica. Not all of these men were newcomers to office. Eutropius had been *magister epistularum* for Constantius, served with Julian on the Persian expedition, been *magister memoriae* for Valens in 369, and proconsul of Asia in 371, in which office he was accused of treason but acquitted. He had been out of office for a decade when he was appointed prefect. Similarly, Hypatius had been consul in 359 but had held no further office, save perhaps that of *vicarius* of Rome in 363. In 371 he had been exiled, along with his brother, by Valens for complicity in the plot of Theodorus.[126] Flavius Afranius Syagrius had been proconsul of Africa in 379 and prefect of Rome in 381. Flavius Syagrius had been a *notarius* in 369, in which year he was dismissed by Valentinian, and is not attested as holding any office (though there must have been some) until he was *magister memoriae* to Gratian in 379. Another Theodorus appears to have succeeded Syagrius as *magister memoriae* in 379, having earlier served as an advocate in the office of the praetorian prefect. Unlike the other prefects of this era, he does not seem to have been a member of the nobility.[127] Although the government of the empire may appear, at this time, to be every bit as cliquish as that of Valentinian, the least that can be said for this group is that they turned over office more rapidly, and it is arguable that the rash of appointments represents a backlog created by the long tenures of Valentinian's men. There would soon be new worlds to conquer.

There is no reason to think that if Valens had not died in battle, Gratian would have inherited any more authority with the eastern bureaucracy than Valens had done with the western. In the wake of Adrianople, however, there was a need for someone to make senior appointments for the army quickly, and that person could only be Gratian. He duly made two appointments to the high command of the army, one in Armenia, where the Persians were threatening to take advantage of the expulsion of Valens' candidate for the throne, the other in Illyricum, although that territory was nominally controlled by his younger brother.[128] The man appointed to the eastern command was plainly an easterner himself – a Persian in fact – named Sapores.[129] To Illyricum he appointed a man who was in his own train, the younger Theodosius.[130]

The appointment of two *magistri militum* may be an indication that Gratian's long-range intention was to assert personal control over the east. Control over the army might reasonably lead to control over the rest. If that was the case, the ambition of Theodosius undid his design. Theodosius won a victory over the Sarmatians and then, it appears, prepared to claim the title of Augustus for himself. A remarkable passage in an oration delivered by Themistius before Theodosius' *consilium* shows what was known about these events in Constantinople during the summer of 379. Themistius says first that "virtue made you emperor and Gratian announced it."[131] Four years later, speaking this time in the senate at Constantinople, Themistius would claim that Gratian announced the vote from above.[132] The fact that the consuls of 379 were two westerners – Ausonius and Olybrius – is perhaps another sign that Gratian had not anticipated making a new Augustus when he appointed the new consuls in the wake of the battle of Adrianople.[133]

Theodosius may have been protected to some extent by relatives at court – his uncle, Flavius Eucherius, was *comes sacrarum largitionum*, and the Syagrii were his relatives – but he could expect very little active support in the short term.[134] If he wanted to be emperor, it was up to him to make himself one. Thus it was that in the immediate aftermath of his acclamation, Theodosius appears to have remained very much the emperor of Thessalonica, which, as a city of Illyricum, was not even in the portion of the empire formerly governed by Valens.[135] The first evidence that he was winning acceptance for his claim to the throne does not come until several months after his acclamation. It was then that the senate at Constantinople sent an embassy to congratulate him at Thessalonica.[136] In June, we find him issuing a rescript when Pancrates, the *comes rei privatae* at Antioch, wrote to him inquiring about the rights of the city *alytarch* (an official charged with putting on games). Although Theodosius' response, as preserved in the Theodosian Code, is very brief, it still reads like an effort to reconcile a suspicious public.

> You should know that we have acceded to ancient custom and the rulings of our predecessors. We grant to the *alytarch* of the city of Antioch that he can plant more cypress trees, and we order that he shall have the right to cut down one cypress.
>
> (*CTh.* 10.1.12)

Theodosius had reason to be cautious. As a participant in the administrative culture of the age he knew that senior officials owed their first loyalty to the person who had appointed them. He would have understood why Julius, the *magister militum* of the east, had sought authority from the senate of Constantinople for his plan to massacre the Goths who had been transferred from the Danube to eastern units prior to the outbreak of the rebellion in 377.[137] According to Zosimus,

> He decided not to reveal his intention to the emperor Theodosius, in part because he was residing in an area of Macedonia, and in part because he had not received his appointment from him, but rather from Valens, and, finally, because he was still a virtual unknown to those whom he was ruling. He (Julius) therefore wrote to the senate at Constantinople and received an order to do what he judged advantageous.
>
> (Zos. 4.26.5–6)

In the coming months, Theodosius moved with considerable skill, not trying to push his claims too far or too fast, in order to secure the loyalty of the eastern commanders. His one advantage was that, after the destruction of the main force of *comitatenses*, there was no one else who commanded an efficient fighting force. What he needed to do was to build a body of officials who would be beholden to him. Zosimus writes scathingly of his appointment of five *magistri militum*, but he does so in terms that reveal that his source, Eunapius, understood the principle of government involved every bit as well as did Ammianus. While Eunapius accuses Theodosius' appointees of corruption, he does so in terms that suggest that he saw that Theodosius was trying to build a corps of loyal officers.[138] Furthermore, as he constructed a base for himself within his still-exiguous military establishment, Theodosius also began to reconcile members of the civil administration.

It would not be until 381 that he would enter Constantinople, by which time he had established a claim to the throne that others would recognize. One of the advertised virtues of his regime would be the friendship that the emperor extended to all and sundry. Several years later a Gallic orator named Pacatus would sum up this aspect of Theodosius' self-presentation as follows:

> Since with equal kindness you wished to confer honors on more people than the number of places allowed, and since your means were more limited than your desires, and your power, however extensive, could not match your intentions, you consoled with your esteem whomever you had not yet promoted to some rank or other. . . . And so all who in your Principate have justly had confidence in themselves have either advanced in rank or found compensation in your kindly regard.
>
> (*Pan.* 2. [12] 20.1–2, trans. Nixon)

It is perhaps a mark of the success that Theodosius achieved in the course of 379, both in ingratiating himself with the eastern establishment and in fighting the Goths, that much more help was forthcoming from the west in 380. Gratian held the consulship with him, an important sign of legitimacy, and appears to have come as far east as Sirmium.[139] In the next year he sent troops under two officers who would later have much influence over events, Bauto and Arbogast.[140] Theodosius was further aided in his task by lack of direction among the Goths.[141]

Although they had united to fight Valens, the various tribal leaders who roamed the countryside now had no positive cause to unite them. In 381, old king Athanaric of the Tervingi, who had refused to cross the Danube in 376 because of the personal hostility of Valens, crossed over and was entertained by Theodosius in the capital itself for a few days.[142] Athanaric's appearance in Constantinople marks an important diplomatic moment, not so much, as Themistius suggests, because it showed that the Goths were eager to make peace, but rather because Theodosius was on his way to making terms that even a man who was determined to maintain Gothic national identity could agree to. This could be seen as an important step toward the announced goal of driving the Goths back across the river.[143]

By the end of 382, the war had come to an end, but on very different terms from those envisaged in 381. The main provision of the treaty was that the Goths would be given their own land within the empire, and that they would live under their own chieftains, probably (though not certainly) on the provision that they would contribute troops, under their own leaders, to Theodosius if he needed them.[144]

The admission of the Goths may be seen not only as a concession to immediate necessity, but also as a concession to the interests of wealthy landowners.

They were now available to be recruited into the Roman army without detriment to existing interests. Valens, as we have seen, had issued a law in which he had tried to make the imposition of the *aurum tironicium* more fair. Historians hostile to his memory recalled that he caused the compensation money for recruits to rise as high as sixty solidi a man – this may in fact have been the situation that he was trying to correct. Theodosius issued a law in January 380 setting forth the terms under which men could be brought into the army, tightening up the standards, so that people who were regarded as being "bad stock" as soldiers should not be sent forward.[145] A few months later he wrote to Neoterius, the praetorian prefect of the east, telling him that honest men should be sent into appropriate areas to find recruits – and that governors who prevented them from doing their duty would be punished.[146] Both emperors issued strong regulations attacking people who concealed deserters on their estates.[147] What lies behind these expostulations is the unwillingness of large estate owners to give up their tenants for military service. By acquiring a new source of recruits, Theodosius, tacitly at least, conceded a point to the interests of the landed aristocracy. The fact that such actions might be considered friendly to the aristocracy is brought out perhaps most clearly in Pacatus' panegyric of 389. According to Pacatus, Theodosius had

> granted the privileged status of fellow soldiers to the barbarian peoples who promised to give you voluntary service, both to remove from the frontier forces of dubious loyalty, and to add reinforcements to your army. Attracted by your kindness, all the Scythian nations flocked to you in such great numbers that you seemed to have imposed a levy upon barbarians from which you exempted your subjects.
>
> (*Pan.* 2 [12] 32.3–4, trans. Nixon)

Seven years earlier, Themistius had made a similar point when he asked,

> Is it better to fill Thrace with corpses or with farmers? Is it better to show it filled with graves or with men? Is it better to walk through empty lands or cultivated fields? Is it better to count dead bodies or ploughmen? Is it better, if it should come to this, to resettle the Phrygians and Bithynians, or to dwell with those who have been conquered?
>
> (*Or.* 16.211a–b)[148]

The rhetoric in both cases conceals the point that dealing with the northern tribes in this way was not popular with everyone. The group in front of whom Themistius spoke, the senate at Constantinople, had, just two years earlier, given Julius permission to kill every Goth in the service of the eastern army. Zosimus, recording the sentiments of Eunapius, regards all Theodosian dealings with the tribes as a disaster. There also seems to have been strenuous opposition from some military quarters. Julius acted as he did because he was plainly suspicious of the new recruits. The story would later be spread that Gratian undermined his position as emperor because of the excessive favor that he showed a band of Alans that was newly arrived in his service. In this case Zosimus offers a description that suggests the lines of division between landholding aristocrats and soldiers:

> Convinced by those courtiers who are accustomed to corrupt the character of princes, he received some Alan refugees and incorporated them into his army, honoring them with abundant gifts and judging them to be worthy of the most important tasks, while making small account of the soldiers.
>
> (Zos. 4.35.2)[149]

As is so often the case, the fact of the story may be more significant than its actual truth – it is something that a person could think plausible. Others attributed the demise of Gratian to more general factors. Ammianus says that he lost interest in the business of government and devoted himself to the pleasures of the hunt.[150]

What were these realities of state? The answer may lie in the tale of Gratian's movements. In 383, Gratian took his court to northern Italy to confront the Alamanni more efficiently. In strategic terms, the move made sense; in political terms it was a serious mistake. Zosimus' reference to courtiers reflects a view that Gratian was easily influenced by those around him.[151] It would later be said of his court that "everything was for sale there through the greed and might of a few men," and by withdrawing from the headquarters of the Gallic armies at Trier, Gratian was cutting himself off from access by its commanders.[152] It would prove a fatal error.

In the same year that Gratian moved the court, Magnus Maximus, *comes* of Britain, rebelled and brought his army over to Gaul. In the spring of 383 the army confronted that of Gratian in the vicinity of Paris. The standoff ended after five days when the bulk of Gratian's army deserted; the figure responsible for this betrayal is said to have been Merobaudes.[153] Maximus appears to have been a tangential relative of Theodosius, to have served with Theodosius' father, and to have been acceptable to Theodosius as a co-emperor.[154] In an empire where the will of the senior administration conferred legitimacy, it was perhaps not unreasonable that Maximus would expect Theodosius' acquiescence – or that he would receive it.

Theodosius' acceptance of Maximus might reasonably raise questions about the nature of his relationship with Gratian, especially as Theodosius would later claim that he attacked Maximus, in part, because he had killed the man who was the source of his own power. Speculation on this point is pointless in an empire where the person of the emperor could be subsumed within the folds of factional dispute, and in some sense it is more remarkable that the court of Valentinian II felt that it could live with Maximus than that Theodosius could. Broadly speaking, the court of Valentinian would remain home to the interests of the landholding bureaucracy, while it is arguable that Maximus represented better the interests of the frontier army.

Maximus made no effort to cross the Alps and evict the younger Valentinian, allowing a frontier to be established along the Alps. In so doing he tacitly recognized the authority of Theodosius as the arbiter of power in the empire, the person who would maintain the balance between the two groups.[155] This would appear to have been in accord with the will of the court of Theodosius, which can be seen extending its reach in the west, expanding networks of patronage into Italy, and laying the groundwork for an effective takeover of the government of Italy.[156] Neoterius, praetorian prefect of the east in 380–81, was appointed praetorian prefect of Italy, Illyricum, and Africa in 385; Gildo, a brother of Firmus who had served the elder Theodosius, was appointed *magister utriusque militiae* in Africa, while Flavius Promotus, a close friend of Bauto, who ordinarily served in the east, would be *comes* of Africa.[157] Despite conduct on the part of Maximus that could be construed as openly provocative – his refusal to turn over the body of Gratian to his brother, who desired to create a dynastic shrine over the corpse – Theodosius formally recognized Maximus as his colleague.[158] Their names appear together on inscriptions, their images (which are strikingly similar in appearance) appear together on coins, and their statues were erected together in cities of the east. Valentinian, although nominally the senior Augustus, was left as a very junior partner in the empire: his name was now listed after that of Theodosius in the preambles to imperial letters. Maximus even offered to send troops to help Theodosius with a Gothic invasion that threatened the Balkans.[159]

Theodosius had much to occupy him in the east. He had a strong interest in promoting Nicene Christianity, reversing the policies of Valens, and he had an ongoing problem with Persia. As we have seen, Valens was delayed in his response to the Gothic revolt of 377 until he could reach an agreement with Sapor over the status of Armenia. In 370, Valens had broken Jovian's treaty with Persia by supporting the installation of Pap, son of Arsaces, on the Armenian throne.[160] Pap had, however, proved an unreliable client, developing notions of independence, which led to his murder, on Valens' orders, in 375.[161] In the next year Valens was preparing a substantial military intervention, when the arrival of the Goths put his plans on hold. The treaty that he made with Sapor so that he could attempt to deal with the situation in Thrace recognized Persian preeminence over the eastern and central portions of the kingdom, and the legitimacy of the Roman candidate, Varazdat, in the west.[162] Varazdat could not maintain his position in the face of opposition from the *nakharars*, and the Persians took control of the whole country. Sapor's death in 379 precluded further action on their part. A series of short-lived Persian kings followed – as did civil war within Persia itself – permitting the imposition of a new Roman nominee, Arsaces IV.[163] The *nakharars* again tried to upset Roman plans, attracting a nominee who was a member of the Sasanian royal house, but neither side was interested in full-scale conflict. In 386 Theodosius made peace with Sapor III, agreeing to surrender two-thirds of the country to Persian control.[164]

It was then that Maximus appears to have overplayed his hand. Toward the end of 386, he launched a sudden invasion of Italy but failed in his effort to capture Valentinian II. The young emperor fled with his family to Thessalonica, and there Justina is said to have convinced Theodosius to invade the west.[165] Given that Theodosius would marry her daughter, Galla, it is a plausible story – at least in part. Maximus' real crime may have been that his invasion interfered with Theodosius' own plans. In the summer of 388, Theodosius moved faster than Maximus expected. An army under the *magistri* Timasius and Promotus defeated advanced forces of Maximus' army at Siscia and Poetovio, seized his supply depots, and arrested Maximus, who had no time to organize an adequate defense, at Aquileia.[166] He was executed, and Valentinian, who had returned to Rome by sea while Theodosius' armies fought in the Balkans, was restored to his nominal position of Augustus in the west. Theodosius took advantage of his position to strip the western field army of a number of units for service in the east, and to arrange the government of the west to his satisfaction.[167] The new praetorian prefect of Italy and Illyricum was Trifolius, an official whose previous career had been in Theodosius' service, and effective control of the army was handed over to Bauto and Arbogast.[168] When Bauto died before the end of the year, Arbogast assumed the title of *magister militum* and went on campaign in Gaul, where he defeated Maximus' son and campaigned against the Franks.[169] Valentinian found himself transferred to Vienne, where he was held under virtual house arrest. Four years later, when Valentinian tried to serve Arbogast with a letter dismissing him, Arbogast is said to have torn it up before his eyes, telling him that he had no authority. Arbogast had been appointed by Theodosius, so Valentinian could not give him an order.[170] Whether or not this story is literally true, it is a sign of the widespread perception that imperial bureaucrats had come to occupy a very different position with respect to holders of the imperial office than had been the case a half century earlier.

Another thing that is certain is that, having failed to remove Arbogast from office, Valentinian died – probably by his own hand. After a four-month interregnum in which it appears that Arbogast tried to negotiate with Theodosius to recognize Arcadius as emperor in the west, he gave up and turned to Eugenius.[171] Although both were polytheists, the cause of their war with Theodosius lay not in the realm of religion, but rather in that of bureaucratic politics.

Emperors and bishops

One of the striking features of the Frigidus campaign was the open hostility displayed between polytheist and Christian. Arbogast is said to have told Ambrose, the bishop of Milan, that if he succeeded in fending off Theodosius, he would turn his cathedral into a stable. In order to understand how it was that the symbols of classical culture could be adopted by a Frankish general in opposition to a Christian emperor, we need first to examine the restructuring of Christianity that took place after the death of Julian. If one of the main themes that runs through the political history of the period is the growing power of officials with respect to the emperor, this is even more true in the case of certain bishops (most notably Ambrose of Milan). The contrast with the state of affairs under Constantius could not be more striking. Whether they followed his doctrinal lead or went into exile for opposing him, there was no question where the power lay in the relationship between emperor and church. By 395, the situation was much less obvious.

Valentinian and Valens pursued very different policies toward the church – Valentinian appears to have been comfortable with a church that took the Nicene Creed as its central doctrine, while Valens was attached to views that were closer to those of the deceased Constantius. Both brothers, in fact, had probably been educated in the faith by priests who were acceptable to Valens of Mursa, in whose see their hometown of Cibalae lay.[172] But this may not have mattered all that much, as neither brother seems to have been much of a theologian. Ammianus tells how a group of minor officials whom Valentinian had condemned to death at Milan were later regarded as martyrs by the local Christian community.[173] This story, and another anecdote reported by Ammianus, in which Eupraxius urges restraint on Valentinian lest he create more Christian martyrs, may suggest that the emperor was not very well informed himself on the doctrine of martyrdom.[174] Theodoret preserves a portion of a letter to an assemblage of bishops in which he tells them that, since they are the ones who have studied scripture, they are the people best able to make an episcopal appointment.[175] Sozomen simply records that Valentinian left ecclesiastical matters up to the bishops.[176]

As far as Valens is concerned, an understanding of his policies is complicated by the fact that both polytheists like Ammianus and church historians were inclined to see his death at Adrianople as an act of divine vengeance.[177] Socrates, who used Eunapius' history as the prime source for his secular history, even quotes an oracle, allegedly discovered when the walls of Chalcedon were demolished, that is used by Ammianus to demonstrate that Valens' fate was in accord with the will of the gods.[178] Socrates appears to have used this text because he, like other church historians, thought that Valens was an "Arian." A plausible explanation for the differences between Valens and Valentinian is that they were dominated by very different groups of bishops. The bishops of the west had long been hostile to anything that smacked of Nicene revisionism, while the bulk of the eastern bishops occupying major sees would have been elected under Constantius and were more likely to subscribe to the creed of Constantinople.[179] Bishops exiled by Constantius, who had been allowed to return to their native cities under Julian, would have remained in place in the wake of the general amnesty issued by Jovian. In a sense, the reputation of Valens as a foe of the Nicene Creed is perhaps as much a result of this amnesty, and Julian's earlier one, insofar as they reinforced local doctrinal tensions to which Valens felt that he had to respond.

That Valens did not arrive on the throne with a set policy, but rather evolved an antipathy toward individual Nicene bishops, appears to be confirmed by a story contained in Theodoret's history.[180] Unlike Socrates and Sozomen, who brand Valens as an "Arian" from the start, Theodoret says that he was corrupted by his wife, Domnica, and by Eudoxius, whom Constantius had appointed as bishop of Constantinople.[181] We may presume that Eudoxius had little to do with Procopius, thus ensuring Valens' favor – and, as the bishop appointed at the same time as Constantius had issued the creed of Constantinople, that he convinced the emperor that this was the right sort of Christianity. Another bishop with whom Valens would have had close connections was also an appointee of Constantius, Euzoius of Antioch. Still, Valens appears to have been willing to allow the consecration of Nicene bishops such as Basil of Caesarea, if there was no undue controversy. It was only in cases where the Nicene side tried to steal a march and appoint someone without what might be considered due process, that we can see Valens taking a particularly active hand. When Eudoxius died in 370, a Nicene faction at Constantinople rushed to elect a man named Evagrius in his place, calling upon a bishop named Eustathius (wrongly identified as Eustathius of Antioch – now deceased – in the extant sources) to consecrate him. The supporters of Eudoxius had elected a man named Demophilus; the result of the imbroglio was the exile of Evagrius and Eustathius, as well, allegedly, as the murder of a pro-Nicene delegation whose ship was said to have been set alight on the orders of Modestus.[182] Demophilus was confirmed as bishop. In Alexandria, when the supporters of Athanasius elected Paul as his successor, Valens followed the advice of Euzoius and appointed a man named Lucius in his place, exiling Paul.[183] While there is an obvious doctrinal element to these actions, what appears to have been uppermost in the mind of Valens was the need to enforce order. He never summoned an ecumenical council.

The issue of Valens' policy toward polytheists is somewhat more complicated. On the one hand, there is Theodorus' evident belief that he could tell Valens about the oracle that he had received. In and of itself this suggests that polytheists did not see Valens as a man who was an inveterate foe of the old religion. This is not unreasonable, as Valens took no action to alter the toleration proclaimed by Jovian.[184] On the other hand, Valens also appears to have been of the opinion that some polytheists, those most closely connected with Julian, were his enemies. Maximus of Ephesus was arrested during the investigation of the illness of the imperial brethren after their accession. In the course of the investigation of the Theodorus affair, Maximus was again arrested on the grounds that he was complicit in the conspiracy. It was a plausible suspicion, as he does seem to have known of the oracle prior to his arrest. He was tortured and executed.[185] Eunapius named at least four other philosophers (one also mentioned by Ammianus) who were also executed "more through jealousy than because of a just decision."[186] Ammianus adds a fifth philosopher, a man named Pasiphilus, who he says was tortured severely.[187] Given the ravages among the governing class resulting from the investigation of the Theodorus affair, the fate of these unfortunates may be attributed to their connections more reasonably than to their faith. Just under seventy years later, Socrates looked back on the Theodorus affair as if it were primarily an attack on Christians, and it is of some interest that he quotes from a speech of Themistius (now lost) as if it mollified the emperor somewhat in his attacks on Nicene Christians. Themistius' argument is an interesting one.[188] He appears to have argued that Valens should forgive the Christians their quarrels about the nature of God since they had but two views, while polytheists had more than three hundred.[189] Socrates also thought that Themistius' speech had some impact (though it is equally possible that Themistius had been summoned to Antioch to act as the mouthpiece for the enunciation of new policy). Shortly before he set out to fight the Goths, and perhaps as an effort to mend fences while confronting a new threat, Valens recalled the Nicene bishops whom he had exiled.

Whatever the precise political circumstances, Themistius' role is testimony to the capacity of Christians and non-Christians to live side by side. It serves as well as a reminder of the point with which we began this chapter, that the range of religious activity in the 370s was sufficiently fluid that a person could move between a variety of options. There might be extremists on either end of the religious spectrum, but there appears to have been a solid center that held coexistence to be both possible and preferable. Julian had rejected this view; Valens, it seems, accepted it.

That polytheists had been essentially free to indulge their beliefs in the years between the accession of Julian and the death of Valens makes the sudden transformation of the religious situation under Gratian and Theodosius all the more striking. The key figures in this transformation appear to have been a pair of extreme Nicene bishops, Acholius of Thessalonica and Ambrose of Milan. Acholius appears to have taken advantage of his proximity to Theodosius to instruct the emperor in the faith, and to offer other useful services. Ambrose says that his prayers repelled the barbarians from Macedonia and brought plague upon them.[190] When

Theodosius himself fell seriously ill in the spring of 380, Acholius was the man who baptized him. It is an important sign of the influence that he could wield, and it is to Acholius that significant movement in the imperial understanding of doctrine during 379 and 380 should probably be attributed.[191] In 378, Gratian had issued an edict of toleration, permitting all but a select few heretics to practice their faith. It looks as if this was simply an effort to ease tensions within the community in the face of the post-Adrianopolitan crisis, and, perhaps, to ensure that God would return his favor to the Roman camp.[192] An edict issued on August 20, 379, in which Gratian had canceled the freedom granted in the "edict recently issued at Sirmium," marked a sudden change of heart.[193] As such it may be seen as a prelude to the remarkable edict issued by Theodosius to the people of Constantinople on February 28, 380. It was through this edict that Theodosius profoundly altered the nature of theological discourse in the empire:

> We wish all people whom the temperance of our clemency rules, to be involved with that religion which the divine apostle Peter handed on to the Romans, as the religion instituted by him makes clear every day, which it is plain that the pope Damasus follows, and Bishop Peter of Alexandria, a man of apostolic sanctity, that is, we believe, according to apostolic discipline and evangelical doctrine, in the unitary deity of the Father, Son, and Holy Ghost, under the concept of equal majesty and the Holy Trinity.
>
> We command that those following this rule will embrace the name of Catholic Christians, judging that the rest, being mad and insane, follow the infamy of heretical doctrine; none of their meeting places will have the title of churches, and they will be smitten first with divine vengeance, and then by our animosity, which we will take up in accordance with divine judgment.
>
> (*CTh.* 16.1.2)

In the next year he would move decisively to back up the theological position taken in this edict, undermining a more moderate approach that was favored by Gratian's court.[194]

Gratian's preliminary move in the direction of the Nicene position may be linked to the work of one of the most powerful personalities of the late fourth century: Ambrose of Milan. Ambrose may have been better placed than any other western bishop to take advantage of the aristocratic bias evident at the court of Gratian. His father had been praetorian prefect to Constantine II, and, even if he was executed in the wake of Constantine's failure – something that is by no means certain – he left his two sons with reasonable expectations of high office, and his daughter with reasonable expectation of a marriage to another aristocrat.[195] Their lives did not, perhaps, work out as he may have intended. His daughter, Marcellina, never married, becoming instead a consecrated virgin, one of the leaders of a group of such women in the capital.[196] She may have been a key figure in the rise of her two brothers, the elder being named Satyrus, to their first offices in the train of Petronius Probus, when the latter began his long career as praetorian prefect of Italy, Illyricum, and Africa.[197] Both boys became lawyers, and neither married, preferring to share their property with their sister as celibates.

Ambrose's civil career was cut short in 374, when, as governor of the province of Aemilia and Liguria, he was suddenly proclaimed bishop of Milan, which lay in his territory. The congregation had been split between supporters of the recently deceased bishop Auxentius, an appointee of Constantius II, and supporters of the Nicene Creed. Probus, who was on friendly terms with Damasus, the Nicene bishop of Rome, appears to have seen the dispute as an opportunity to place a Nicene in a crucial episcopal seat. Thus, despite the fact that supporters of Ambrose were later to claim that he was elected by the sudden (and, by implication, divinely inspired) acclamation of the congregation, it is likely that Ambrose's nomination had been fixed in advance by Probus, who may have acquired Valentinian's prior agreement.[198]

In 377–78 there are two events that point to a desire on Ambrose's part to exercise influence greater than that of the average bishop. The first was his intervention to consecrate a man named Anemius as bishop at Sirmium, previously a stronghold of the anti-Nicene cause.[199] It is likely that he became involved through connections that he had made while serving Probus, and that he could count on the support of his former superior if he needed it. Some sort of support proved necessary, as he was opposed by no less a person than Justina, who would remain his enemy for years to come.[200] The other event was the funeral of his brother, who appears to have died either as the Gothic revolt began in 377, or, more plausibly, about the time of the battle of Adrianople. Ambrose had him buried in the martyrium of Saint Victor, next to the tomb of the martyr himself, on ground that would soon be covered by the massive basilica that Ambrose was then having built. It established a family link with the church that would become Ambrose's stronghold.[201] He would need it as he continued his career of spectacular self-aggrandizement and intolerance.

While leading his army to Sirmium in 378, Gratian had written to Ambrose, asking him to produce a statement of his faith. It is quite possible that he did this because complaints about Ambrose's theology had already begun to surface in anti-Nicene circles, which may have been strengthened in Milan as people fled from the expanding Gothic crisis in the east. The first two books of Ambrose's *On Faith*, his response to Gratian's request, stand as an ominous foreshadowing of actions that he would take in the rest of his career. Gratian had excluded three groups from his amnesty of 378,

Manichaeans, "Photinians," and "Eunomians."[202] Photinians were followers of Bishop Photinus of Sirmium, who had been exiled by Constantius for his fervently Nicene views (and opposition to Valens of Mursa) in 347, and replaced by the anti-Nicene Germinius, whose pro-Nicene successor Ambrose had consecrated in 377.[203] Eunomius of Cyzicus was the author of a flagrantly anti-Nicene doctrine holding that the substance of the Son was unlike that of the Father.[204] He had briefly been exiled by Valens.

By naming Photinians and Eunomians as heretics, Gratian had evidently intended to suggest that he would tolerate anything short of what could be classified as extremist views. What he surely did not intend to do was to open a theological hole through which Ambrose could charge by asserting that all anti-Nicenes were really Eunomians. Thus he states:

> Allow me, blessed emperor, if I turn my attention briefly to those people. But to whom should I best refer, to Eunomius or to Arius or to Aetius, or to their teachers? They have many names, but one heresy (*perfidia*), they do not disagree in impiety, but are discordant in communion, they are not dissimilar in fraud, but they are discreet in assemblage. Arians flee the person of Eunomius, but they assert his sin, they follow his impiety. They proclaim widely that he betrayed what Arius wrote. What a great effusion of blindness! They approve the author, but refute the follower. Thus they now divide themselves into many forms: some follow Eunomius or Aetius, others Palladius or Demophilus and Auxentius, or their heirs in heresy. Surely Christ has not been divided [1 Cor. 1:13]! Yet those who would divide him from the father are divided amongst themselves.
>
> (*De fide* 1.6.44–45)

He argues that this undifferentiated group of Arians (a term none of them would admit) were accustomed to close their ears or create a riot "in the Jewish way" when the words of salvation were uttered.[205] They were no different from polytheists who worshipped divinities distinct by gender and power when they asserted a trinity with distinctions of divinity and power; the beliefs of the Arians were foreseen by Paul when he had assailed the beliefs of the heathen.[206] The teachings of the Arians were as deadly to the empire as the Goths:

> Do we not hear from the regions of Thrace that throughout the Dacian border, Moesia, all Valeria and the whole frontier of the Pannonians tremble equally with sacrilegious voices and the movements of barbarians?
>
> (*De fide* 2.16.140)

Gratian had decided to act against extremist anti-Nicene groups as well as Donatists about the time that he received the *On the Faith*, and he may have found the oversimplification of Ambrose's approach congenial. When Palladius of Ratiaria responded, he complained that Ambrose had not been punished for his impiety – how could he get a fair hearing when a person like Ambrose was allowed to go free, having uttered the sentiments that he did?[207] Gratian may not have fully passed over to Ambrose's point of view, but he seems to have been leaning that way. Those who helped govern his thought may also have been of the opinion that, for the peace of the empire, it would be wise to do so. Theodosius' openly pro-Nicene edict of 380 came hard on the heels of Ambrose's tirade. It may be that Acholius' influence over the theologically insecure Theodosius strengthened Ambrose's hand with Gratian.

The Nicene position in the east had been transformed by Theodosius' baptism in the summer of 380, in that it was as a baptized Nicene that he prepared to enter Constantinople for the first time on November 14. On January 10 he issued another edict, worded even more strongly than his previous utterances:

> There is no place for the mysteries; there shall be no occasion for exercising the madness of a more obstinate mind for heretics. Let all men know that even if something has been obtained, elicited by a special edict, obtained by fraud by this kind of man, it will have no force. Crowds of all heretics are forbidden from illicit con-gregations. The name of the one highest God will be celebrated everywhere. The observation of the Nicene faith, handed down from our ancestors and affirmed by the testimony and declaration of the divine religion, destined to be continued forever, will be maintained. The contamination of the Photinian error, the poison of the Arian sacrilege, the crime of Eunomian heresy, and the unspeakable, from the monstrous names of their authors, prodigies of the sects will be banished from hearing. He, however, must be accepted as a defender of the Nicene faith and true adherent of the Catholic religion, who confesses the Almighty God and Christ the Son of God with one name, God from God, Light from Light, who does not violate the Holy Spirit by denial, whom we hope for and receive from the highest parent of things; for whom the undivided substance of the Holy Trinity thrives with uncorrupted faith, that substance which those who think correctly call through the use of the Greek word *ousia* (substance). These beliefs verily are acceptable to us and must be venerated.
>
> (*CTh*. 16.5.6.1–2)

Those who did not subscribe to the Nicene faith were to be banned from all churches and exiled. Theodosius put immediate force behind this edict when he exiled Demophilus, the bishop of Constantinople. On November 27, 381, he appointed the Nicene Gregory Nazianzus in his place and summoned the bishops of the east to a council at his capital from May to July, 382.[208] Nearly two hundred bishops came, reversing the outcome of the Council of Constantinople some twenty years before. At the conclusion of the council, Theodosius issued an edict specifying that only those bishops who were acceptable as followers of the Nicene faith could serve. Those dissenting from the communion of approved bishops would be adjudged heretics and denied the right to obtain priesthoods, "so that the priesthood of the true Nicene faith should remain pure."[209]

Theodosius' swift assault on the anti-Nicenes of the east undermined the more moderate approach on the part of Gratian, who had summoned an "ecumenical" council to meet at Aquileia toward the end of the summer. Not only had Theodosius taken an extreme doctrinal position, he had also proclaimed that the bishop of Constantinople should henceforth be regarded as second in primacy to the bishop of Rome. At Gratian's council there would be no assemblage of bishops from the east to hear an open debate about doctrine. Instead, Ambrose manipulated the council at Aquileia, attended by only a small number of bishops from northern Italy and other places in the west, so that it would become, in effect, a hearing on the doctrines of Palladius, well known to be anti-Nicene.[210] The records of the council reveal that the bishops assembled in a relatively small room next to the main basilica. Ambrose seated himself by the side of Valerian, the presiding bishop, with two secretaries seated behind them to keep the record.[211] When the council opened on September 3, Ambrose interrogated Palladius on his beliefs, in an effort to force him to acknowledge either that the doctrines contained in the letter of Arius to Alexander contained heresy, or that he participated in that heresy. Palladius defended himself as best he could, complaining that the secretaries were making an inadequate record, and refusing to fall for most of the traps that Ambrose set him.[212] It did no good. He was condemned as an Arian heretic on September 4, along with his supporter, Secundianus of Singidunum, and a priest named Attalus.

So far, neither Theodosius nor Gratian had taken any official measures against polytheists, but the course of events, which suggested that Christian extremists were coming to the fore at court, may well have disturbed leading proponents of traditional cult. Gratian gave them even more reason to be concerned. At the end of 382 he suddenly withdrew the traditional subsidies granted by the state to the holders of priesthoods at Rome, resigned as pontifex maximus, an office that he had held since his accession, and ordered the altar of Victory to be removed from the senate house.[213] There is no obvious explanation for his action, though it is possible that Valerius Severus, a Christian who held both the office of *praefectus urbi* and the praetorian prefecture of Italy in that year, suggested the move.[214] Such an explanation would imply that the move is simply another example of court politics, in which the emperor followed the advice of senior officials without thinking of the consequences. On no rational appraisal was it a good idea to offend powerful aristocratic interests with a symbolic gesture at the very moment that Maximus was raising the standard of revolt in Britain. Nor was it good politics to shut out without a hearing the embassy that brought the robe back to him.[215]

If Gratian's action reflects the insularity that contributed to the success of Maximus in the summer of 383, the subsequent debate over the altar of Victory in 385 further reveals the extent to which the emperor could be ruled by parochial politics. When Symmachus came to Milan pleading for the return of the altar of Victory, he had some reason to hope that he would get a better hearing from Valentinian II than the embassy to Gratian had received. Bauto took his side, as did some other Christians.[216] The motion may not even have been opposed by the bishop of Rome, Damasus, who submitted no petition of his own in the matter.[217]

For Ambrose, the question of the altar became a matter of prestige. He sent a letter to Valentinian, before the actual contents of Symmachus' pleas became known, opposing the return. This letter represents Ambrose's high controversial style, a style that would reappear at later moments of crisis. The emperor is first praised for his true devotion to the church, and then treated to a statement of the bishop's pure amazement that such a good Christian could even contemplate the erection of altars for the heathen, or could possibly forget all the wrongs done to Christians by polytheists.[218] What right have they to complain about an altar when they have, in the past, destroyed so many churches, and killed so many of the faithful? To reinstall the altar would be, in effect, to institute a persecution of the Christians by forcing them to attend meetings where sacrifices were made.[219] Surely the emperor would do better to consult Theodosius on this matter rather than to decide in favor of Symmachus.[220] How disappointed would be his brother and father, who are made to speak from beyond the grave in the final section of the letter. Gratian is made to say that the reversal of his policy on this point would be a heavier blow than that struck by his assassin.[221] Valentinian, in what reads as a virtual parody of the criticisms of his regime contained in the narrative of Ammianus, says that he had no idea that there were sacrifices going on in Rome:

> Many and diverse crimes were committed while I was emperor. I punished those I detected. If someone escaped my notice, should it be said I approved what no one had told me? You have judged me very ill if an alien superstition rather than my faith preserved the empire.
>
> (Amb. *Ep.* 72.16)

The Ambrosian strategy of lumping all his rivals together in one group, employed to such effect in *On Faith*, is deployed even more flagrantly here, where the emperor is told that he will, in effect, become a polytheist by giving into their demands. But there is also a thinly veiled suggestion that Valentinian's court is not really in control – it needs to defer to Theodosius (why risk the embarrassment of his disapproval?). Valentinian himself is only the ruler because he is the son and brother of two emperors. He dare not differ from their policies (even when the policy in question was not that of one of them). Those in the court would perhaps hear, as well, a reminder that their chief claim to office might not be worth all that much. Ammianus composed his portrait of Valentinian I as a brute while Valentinian II was still alive, suggesting that dynastic authority was none too strong.[222]

Symmachus' appeal was likewise not free of threat. He tells the emperor that people no longer think that they will gain influence with court officials if there is a difference of opinion over a petition.[223] Constantius may have removed the altar, but it was agreed by all that he had made a mistake, and even he had not gone so far as to remove state subsidies from priesthoods. For a court that had long been anxious about its relationship with the house of Constantine it was a pointed remark – Valentinian's advisers are reminded that they ought not to imitate the failed policies of the old regime.[224] Far better the policies of emperors who knew how to turn a blind eye.[225] Against pure dogmatism, Symmachus would appeal instead to the complexity of human experience:

> Man's reason moves entirely in the dark; his knowledge of divine influences can be drawn from no better source than from the recollection and evidences of good fortune received from them. If long passage of time lends validity to religious observances, we ought to keep faith with so many centuries, we ought to follow our forefathers who followed their forefathers and were blessed in so doing.
>
> (*Rel.* 3.8, trans. Barrow)

Rome itself is now called upon to speak, to defend the religious institutions of the past, to recall how Hannibal was repulsed, how the Gauls were driven from the Capitoline. Humanity is the common experience that binds all together:

> What does it matter what practical system we adopt in our search for truth? Not by one avenue only can we arrive at so tremendous a secret.
>
> (*Rel.* 3.10, trans. Barrow)

The treasury does not need the savings that would accrue from cutting off subsidies to the priests, and the emperor is not a greedy man.[226] Symmachus does not plead only the cause of religion, but of all humans – the emperor is aware that a famine struck the city after the withdrawal of the subsidies and the removal of the altar.[227] Symmachus admits that the monies were spent to support observances that were no longer part of the religion of the state, but they were still insurance against disaster.[228] The emperor should allow the gods of all people, whoever they are, to protect him, an interesting adaptation of the theme of earlier Christian apologists who had claimed that they prayed for the emperor and were not enemies of the state.[229] Valentinian, looking down from heaven, should not see that his policies had been overthrown. Gratian would be relieved to know that his inadvertent error had been corrected.[230] The similarity between the final appeals of both Symmachus and Ambrose show that the issue of the altar extended beyond the issue of religion, to the narrative that justified the existence of the regime. Was Gratian right to do what he did? Was the example of Valentinian the proper one to follow? How much freedom did the court of the younger Valentinian have to make its own policy? In the end, Ambrose's version of policy proved victorious. The sentiments of religious toleration pleaded by Symmachus were rapidly being consigned to the thesaurus for lost causes.

Ambrose's victory may not have come without cost to himself. His invocation of Theodosius was pointed, and it raised the question of what real power the court had. His manner of address suggested that he would be the sole spokesman before God for the emperor.[231] That too was a challenge, for many at the court, including Justina, were anti-Nicene, celebrating their rites in private.[232] It was not a situation that appealed to Justina, and so, once the anti-Nicene bishop Auxentius arrived in Milan toward the end of 385, she appears to have been the moving force behind a complex plot to gain a basilica from Ambrose for the coming Easter.[233]

In January 386 Valentinian had issued a law openly contravening Theodosius' edict of 381 in which it was stated that orthodoxy had been defined by the Council of Ariminium and confirmed by that of Constantinople in 361.[234] The point of the edict was to establish the right of anti-Nicenes to worship in public. All they needed now was a church, and so, as Easter approached, the court announced that it would take the basilica of San Lorenzo, which was probably the closest church to the palace, standing just outside the walls of the city, for its members. When Ambrose refused to hand the basilica over, court officials attempted to sequester it, so that priests selected by the court could hold the Easter service there.[235] Ambrose filled the church with his followers (while remaining out of the line of fire himself).[236] When imperial troops laid siege to the congregation, Ambrose convinced them that they were persecutors. They were on the brink of mutiny, before they were ordered to withdraw. When the order came, many soldiers entered the church to celebrate with the people who had been besieged within.[237] Valentinian was forced to back down on Maundy Thursday. He celebrated Easter on the road to Aquileia.

While no one would have confused Valentinian II with Constantine or Severus, his withdrawal from Milan was a symbolic moment of tremendous importance. One of the principal requirements of an emperor, in any period, was the capacity to balance the diverse interests of the capital to his advantage. The failure of Valentinian represents not so much the influence that could accrue to an urban bishop, but the weakness of the court. There was simply no one who could oppose the public influence of Ambrose. It was a humiliating situation to have to admit, and there were plainly people at court, in addition to the empress Justina – whom Ambrose would paint as the Jezebel of her time – who wanted to get back at him.[238] In the wake of the Easter fiasco, it appears that there were those at court who wished to use the January law to attack Ambrose directly. He was ordered to answer charges about his interpretation of the faith against that of Auxentius. Ambrose flatly refused to appear and took refuge in a church.[239] There he was sustained by a crowd of his pious supporters to whom he taught hymns that they could sing to keep up their morale. After some time, we do not know how long, the siege was lifted – the reason was a letter from Maximus, now recognized by Theodosius as his colleague, demanding to know why bishops were being besieged in their basilicas.[240] There can be little doubt but that Ambrose had gotten word to Maximus of his troubles, perhaps exploiting links that he had established or strengthened on his mission a couple of years earlier.[241] Valentinian had no choice but to back down again. Maximus was a staunch supporter of the Nicene Creed, leaving Valentinian the odd man out. This time he had fallen victim to Ambrose's superior command of imperial politics.

Victorious though he was, Ambrose may have appreciated that he needed additional, local, support if he were to continue to feud with the palace. It was shortly after Valentinian had given way on the matter of Ambrose's appearance to discuss doctrine that Ambrose found the help that he needed. He discovered the relics of two martyrs and moved their remains to reside by the altar of the basilica he had recently completed, so as to link himself as intimately as possible with their authority.[242] The day of the discovery was marked by high drama, as Ambrose wrote to his sister:

> I am accustomed to let nothing that is done here escape your sanc-
> tity when you are away; you should know that we have found holy
> martyrs. For, when I was dedicating the basilica here, many began
> appealing to me with one voice, "Dedicate the basilica like the one
> in Rome." I responded, "I will do it if I can find the remains of
> martyrs." Immediately the flame of some sort of prescience came
> to me.

What else is there to say? The Lord gave grace; I ordered fearful clerics to clear away the ground in the spot that is in front of the grate of Saints Felix and Nabor. I found promising signs; when some people were brought forward so that my hands would be laid upon them, the sacred martyrs began to act, so that, when I was still silent, a woman was taken and thrown down upon the place of the sacred sepulcher. We found two men of astonishing size, such as ancient times bore. All their bones were intact, full of blood. A great crowd of people was there for two days. What more? We arranged everything in an orderly way; with evening at hand, we transferred them to the basilica of Fausta. There a vigil was kept all night, with the laying on of hands. The next day we transferred them to the basilica that is called the Ambrosian.

(Amb. Ep. 77.1–2)

Moving the bones to the church most closely associated with them, Ambrose established himself as the guardian of the martyrs. Augustine says that those who were cured of demonic possession revealed the names of the martyrs to be Gervasius and Protasius.[243] The miracles that they performed, and Ambrose's own miraculous discovery of their resting place, stood as proof of his doctrinal purity. He could even point to imperial support for his action, as Theodosius had written the year before that people who found the bones of martyrs could construct a martyrium to house them.[244] It was a spectacular piece of theater, and with his position secured by the performance, Ambrose could once again assume a position of leadership with respect to the imperial court, which now sent him to Gaul to recover another body – that of Gratian. As Ambrose had bodies to grant him spiritual authority, he could allow Valentinian a chance to gain the body he desired for dynastic purposes.

Ambrose failed to gain the body of Gratian, for very good reason. Maximus had now decided to press his luck further, convinced, perhaps, that Valentinian had forfeited any claim to protection from Theodosius. He may well have been ready to march before Ambrose set out, for his invasion of Italy followed hard upon Ambrose's return to Milan. A man of staunch Nicene leanings – he had recently executed the Gallic heretic Priscillian – he appears to have had no serious issues with Ambrose.[245] Despite his faith, he also sought to reach out to the Italian aristocracy of whatever confessional stripe. A fulsome panegyric from Symmachus himself may be taken as a sign that he succeeded.[246]

The defeat of Maximus brought Theodosius to Italy in person. Ambrose needed to forge a relationship with a new ruler with whom he had had very little contact. To do so he would insert himself into the rituals of imperial government in an unparalleled fashion, exploiting patterns of violence and reconciliation in order to do so. From a theological point of view,

Valentinian's forced renunciation of his anti-Nicene preferences, one of the terms for Theodosius' assistance, made the Nicene Creed supreme in the empire for the first time since the death of Constantine.[247] The preference of Theodosius reset the nature of theological controversy for the future, reversing the efforts of Constantius, but bringing the church no closer to doctrinal peace. The Goths who had converted would remain attached to their anti-Nicene doctrines, and other forms of anti-Nicene thought would emerge later. While there was an emperor, he would remain, in theory, the final arbiter of doctrine: as it had been with Constantine and Constantius, so it would be for centuries to come.

Rituals of violence and reconciliation

In discovering the relics of Gervasius and Protasius, Ambrose had resorted to the assertion of authority through the time-honored method of an invented narrative whose significance was reified through a festival. The myth that he invented would help stabilize his position at Milan throughout a period of rapid change and civil war. Throughout these years other rituals would be enacted on a grander or lesser scale to help bind the wounds of conflicts that remained endemic between the government of Theodosius and his subjects.[248] On an individual level, rituals of apology and forgiveness would enable men who had found themselves on the wrong side, willingly or otherwise, in the conflicts of the imperial bureaucracy, to retain their place in society. Symmachus, for instance, would make his profound apology to Theodosius for supporting Maximus, and then express irritation that, despite his having apologized, the emperor would support a rival in a legal case.[249] The myth of imperial omnipotence – ever more of a myth as years passed – required that the emperor be able to forgive rather than punish. Theodosius had not the power of a Severus to massacre his opponents. He required the nexus of connections that linked local aristocracies with the court to remain substantially intact if he were to be able to govern. He might rescind all the acts of Maximus, refuse to honor promotions that he had made to high office, replace senior officials with men that he could trust, but he would rarely attempt to do more.[250] Those who would participate in government would not wish for the Theodorus affair – or even the purges that accompanied the death of Valentinian – to be repeated.

Rituals of individual repentance were accompanied by more formalized rituals that could be employed to calm the waters of discord between the central government and cities. The basic form of these rituals was already well established: people would signal their displeasure with the emperor, he would respond with a statement of his own annoyance, and an embassy would appear to apologize.[251] The emperor would then indicate the extent to which the apology would be accepted, and life would go on. Thus, upon leaving Antioch, Julian had sought to strengthen the position of Libanius by telling the people of the city that he was sure that their ambassador would do his best, even though he would have to attend him at Tarsus.[252] To do so Libanius sought to enlist the aid of a former rival, now friend, named Nicocles, who had negotiated a settlement between the people of Constantinople and the urban prefect following a riot that had occurred after Julian had left town.[253] It was often useful to collect patrons for such an appeal, as Libanius tried to do with Nicocles – when an anti-Nicene mob burnt the house of Nectarius, Theodosius' first Nicene bishop at Constantinople, the city avoided punishment by appealing through the infant Arcadius. It presumably made sense for Theodosius to avoid controversy and promote knowledge of his son's existence.[254] In other situations people might recall an anecdote about Constantine that summed up the situation. He is said to have told two brothers that when insulted by a city, the emperor ought to show mercy.[255] As a form of introduction to his new realm, it appears that the emperor or his representatives were treated to numerous orations on the importance of clemency.[256] The sense that there was a recognized scale of punishments appears perhaps most strongly in an edict that Theodosius issued after he had broken the implicit rules of the game in 390.

> If, in considering a particular case, we order a more severe penalty to be inflicted upon someone than is our custom, we do not wish that person to suffer the punishment or receive the sentence immediately, but for thirty days his fate and fortune with reference to his status will be in suspense. Of course, the accused will be arrested and bound in custody and watched by diligent guards.
>
> (*CTh.* 9.40.13)[257]

Despite the reference to an individual, the circumstance that led to the issuance of this edict involved an entire city.

In the months leading up to the attack on Maximus it appears that some of the Goths, possibly led by Alaric, may have refused to honor their treaty obligation to send troops to the war.[258] While we cannot be absolutely certain that this was the cause of the strife, we can at least be certain that there was a problem, that these Goths were settled well away from the Danube frontier in Macedonia, and that Butheric, the *magister militum* of Illyricum, was sent to compel them to obey.[259] He chose Thessalonica as his base and became embroiled in a dispute with the local population over a charioteer, whom he had arrested for making sexual advances to one of his attendants.[260] Butheric was killed in the ensuing riot. The murder of an imperial official required the imposition of a collective penalty. Thus Constantius had curtailed the privileges of the people of Constantinople after the murder of Hermogenes in 342, while Theodosius himself had canceled the distribution of bread for part of a day when the Constantinopolitan crowd had murdered one of his Gothic soldiers.[261] Three years before the murder of Butheric,

Theodosius had been faced with a similar crisis at Antioch, where a mob had torn down his statues.

The speech that Libanius delivered on the occasion of what he claims to have been his voluntary embassy to the emperor reveals that the business of apology and forgiveness was not a straightforward matter of abject surrender on the part of the local population. The people of Antioch, wrong though they may have been, had a point that the emperor needed to hear. Libanius is explicit that the people who rioted did so because their taxes were too high. They were also, he implies, largely Christian, and their riot got out of hand because neither the local bishop nor the imperial officials, who might have called out troops to quell the insurrection at an earlier stage, had done their duty. Implicit in Libanius' appeal is the notion that the immediate fault lay with Theodosius' coreligionists and with Theodosius' officials. His further claim that the characters responsible for the actual destruction of the statues were not even Antiochenes, but rather evil demons who had showed up for the occasion, might be read as yet another suggestion that the bishop was not up to his job. Libanius' explicit challenge to the Christian authorities at Antioch may be related to the journey undertaken a year earlier by the praetorian prefect Cynegius, who was sent to Alexandria to erect statues of Maximus and to close down certain rites that continued to be celebrated by local polytheists.[262] On his overland journey north, he had continued to encourage local acts of vandalism against traditional shrines, inspiring other acts of violence. Theodosius perhaps needed to be warned that it would be a good idea to keep his coreligionists under better control.

Theodosius was thus challenged on several fronts: he was being told that if he wanted to punish the city by turning loose his troops upon the population, which it was rumored that he intended to do, he would be attacking fellow Christians. This would be inevitable, since the Christian population would bear the brunt of any indiscriminate action on his part. In a particularly pointed section of his speech, Libanius noted that Diocletian had once ordered such an attack on the city, while Julian had not. Did Theodosius really want his name linked with that of the arch-persecutor, and to appear less merciful than Julian? Libanius' choice of examples could not have been better.

In the end Theodosius decided to spare the city. Libanius claimed that the city's salvation was his doing.[263] Christians may have had reason to think otherwise. When Theodosius' commissioners appeared in the city, it would seem that he had accepted Libanius' argument about the culpability of Bishop Flavian: the local clergy kissed the feet of the commissioners, and Flavian was found, shortly thereafter, at court pleading his case. Before the people of Antioch, a holy man from the Syrian desert named Macedonius attacked the commissioners and the emperor for threatening the city with destruction. The commissioners made a point of forgiving the city at his request.

Thus Theodosius was legitimizing the role of monks, and seeking to bind ascetics more closely to his regime. It is significant that he would later consult a monk of Egypt named John before setting out to do battle with Arbogast and Eugenius. That there could be two such different versions of the city's fate suggests that the ceremony of reconciliation was worked out as relevant with various groups within the city, reinforcing links between those groups and the court.

The settlement at Antioch had forwarded the emperor's agenda and enabled him to appear as a man of mercy. At Thessalonica the situation would be different. The murder of Butheric must have thrown the campaign against the Goths into disarray, and that was, the emperor seems to have thought, a more serious matter than destroying his statues. Bishop Acholius was also now several years in his grave, so the people may have lacked a man of Libanius' standing to make their case, and, in any case, Butheric was not just any imperial official. It was Eunapius' view that Theodosius had devolved the day-to-day administration of the empire onto his chief subordinates, the *magistri militum*, as he would later turn virtually "imperial" power over to Rufinus, the praetorian prefect of the east during the 390s. Butheric was thus one of the ruling circle, and it may have been that no one could have turned aside the emperor's wrath.

The emperor's wrath appears to have come with a stated number of people to be killed, and a time limit on the action, again suggesting that, despite his later suggestion that the penalty was too great, Theodosius was not acting in the heat of passion, but rather through calculation.[264] He ordered the soldiers stationed in the city to loot it for three hours. If the penalty thereby satisfied the demands of Butheric's status, the public repentance that followed was something new. Theodosius appears to have decided that he had stepped over the line, perhaps because the massacre cast a pall over his ongoing operations in the west. The law quoted above is one public sign of his repentance; another would take place in Ambrose's church at Milan, where the emperor tolerated Ambrose's public refusal to grant him communion.[265] It is quite likely that the majority of the victims at Thessalonica were Christians who followed the Nicene Creed that had been so significantly maintained there under Acholius. Had the city been a stronghold of anti-Nicene thought, it is possible that Theodosius would not have found himself under the pressure that he did to apologize to the empire as a whole, but now he was a prisoner of his own rhetoric. The victims of the massacre allegedly numbered some seven thousand, and the brutality of the troops who appeared to have known where to look for victims they wanted to attack perhaps went beyond what even Theodosius might have anticipated.[266]

For Ambrose, the massacre at Thessalonica offered an opportunity for redemption after a stunning failure to deal with the ritual of repentance a few months earlier. In the wake of Cynegius' trip to the east, the bishop at Callinicum had destroyed the local synagogue.[267] While Theodosius was willing to countenance sectarian violence under imperial control, he was plainly unhappy with the sort of initiative that the bishop had shown. He ordered the bishop to rebuild the synagogue at his own expense. Ambrose had gotten wind of this action through contacts at court and written to the emperor to condemn his action. Using arguments very similar to those he had used in his letter to Valentinian on the subject of the altar of Victory, he accused the emperor of being a persecutor, comparing him to, among others, Julian.[268] Theodosius conceded the point – and ordered that no one at court was to reveal the business of the court to Ambrose again.

The events at Callinicum and Thessalonica are both failures of the ritual of threat and reconciliation. In the case of Callinicum, Ambrose had breached protocol by taking the initiative in a matter that was simply not his concern. In the case of Thessalonica, the emperor, having failed to realize that he need not back up the threat of violence with the reality, used Ambrose as a vehicle for making his apology to the empire as a whole. In both cases, however, Theodosius was making it plain that, while he was emperor, the church must play a role in the ritual of government, and it is perhaps this point that marks the most significant change that was taking place in his time. Having settled, as far as he was concerned, the doctrinal issue by fiat, Theodosius was trying to carve out a place for his faith in long-standing forms of negotiation with his subjects.

The view from Antioch

Throughout the last three chapters, one character has emerged, from time to time, as a central figure in the negotiations between emperors and their subjects in the province of Syria. This figure is Libanius of Antioch.[269] In the early 370s he composed an autobiography, which he continued to update, with varying degrees of lucidity, to 393. His story, self-serving though it is, represents yet another perspective on the structure of power within the empire, one very different from that of Ambrose, of a member of the bureaucracy, or of an aspiring German general.

Libanius was born in 314. His family, he says, was one of the "greatest in a great city, in education, wealth, the provision of artistic and athletic events, and in the oratory that opposes itself to the passions of governors."[270] Although this family had suffered severely in the suppression of the revolt of Eugenius in 303, Libanius' father had restored something of its fortunes before dying while his son was still a boy. Raised thereafter by his mother, Libanius came relatively late to the study of oratory, but when he began to take his studies seriously, he showed immediate talent. When he was twenty, he says, he was struck by lightning, an injury that resulted in serious headaches for the rest of his life.[271] At twenty-two, he went to study rhetoric at Athens, where he again excelled while taking advantage of his situation to visit religious sites of antiquity.[272] As a result of a disturbance in the city in 340, which caused the governor to strip those holding official chairs (with the accompanying immunities) of their positions, he was offered, despite his youth, one of the vacant positions.[273] The appointment, which lasted for less than a year, did Libanius no favors, ensuring that others would regard him with hatred. Forced out by his rivals, he went to Constantinople, where his reputation enabled him to establish himself as a successful teacher. In the wake of the riots that accompanied the removal of Paul, he was accused by his professional rivals of fomenting difficulty, and withdrew from Constantinople to Nicomedia, where he would hold the chair of rhetoric from 343 to 348. He would later claim that these were the happiest years of his professional life outside of Antioch.

In 349 Libanius reached what many might have regarded as the pinnacle of his professional career. Having written a panegyric on Constans and Constantius that achieved official recognition, he was recalled to Constantinople and appointed to the chair of rhetoric. He would claim that he was never comfortable there – he felt that the senate was filled with soldiers who could not appreciate his skills. He may also have found that Constantius was not an easy master – for though he never will say this openly, there is no sense in his writings that there was any warmth between the two men. Libanius valued personal displays of admiration that may not have been forthcoming, despite the gifts that he says that he received.[274] In 353, pleading ill health, he obtained permission to return to Antioch. Surrounded by childhood friends and family, he felt welcome and appreciated. He resolved therefore to return, obtaining Constantius' permission after a visit to Constantinople in the next year. Surviving threats to his safety under Gallus, he became the official sophist of Antioch, the city's representative to outside powers.[275]

Shortly after his return to the city, Libanius fell in love with a woman of low status, with whom he would live until her death a few years before his own. They had a son named Cimon. The causes that would occupy Libanius thereafter would be those of his city. He delighted in the arrival of Julian, he grieved that the relationship between the emperor and the city should deteriorate – even though he too appears to have recognized that Julian's confessional extremism was ill-advised. He appears to have been befriended by Valens, about whom he has some nice things to say, and honored by Theodosius, who appointed him to the rank (though not the office) of praetorian prefect shortly after his accession.[276] This latter appointment may be seen as part of the new emperor's effort to win influence with the notables of his new realm.

As his career changed, so too did the causes that Libanius espoused. The experience of his youth reveals that the career of the aspiring academic had changed little over the centuries. As was also the case with the young Augustine, he was expected to be a man of many places.[277] As Augustine moved to Carthage to win the chance of a career in Rome and then at court, so did Libanius move to the hotbed of Greek academe at Athens – the Oxford or Cambridge (Massachusetts) or Paris of the time. His themes were those of the great rhetoricians of past ages. On tour through Greece he delivered a speech in praise of Athens wherever he stopped, challenging the local sophist to a contest of rhetoric.[278] In Constantinople he says that he turned to public competitions, speaking on various themes, rejoicing that "it was no detriment to winning the crown not to be supported by the imperial treasury."[279] At Nicomedia he spoke on all manner of topics, attracting students from afar. His rivals would seek to steal his work, corrupting copyists, or charge him with magic. It was scarcely a charge to be ignored in this age – though Libanius treats such events as a sign of jealousy. Augustine had turned down an offer from a magician who promised to help him to victory at Carthage.[280]

The range of topics on classical themes upon which Libanius chose to speak represents the continuing importance, for aspiring gentlemen of whatever faith, to be versed in tradition. Nor is he alone in the robust tradition of fourth-century oratory. In the corpus of Himerius of Prusias, for instance, there are six speeches that hearken back to the world of classical Athens, and among the private orations of Themistius there are declamations that evoke the world of Plutarch. In this, Themistius' speeches offer confirmation of Eunapius' point in his *Lives of the Philosophers*, that the classical world of rhetoric continued despite the Christianity of its rulers. A man who would aspire to an episcopal throne, like Gregory Nazianzus, would be educated with Julian at Antioch. A John Chrysostom had the rhetorical training to match that of Libanius, with whose career his own would overlap when he preached at Antioch from 386 to 398. The skills of the rhetoricians were transferable to the church, as their careers and that of Augustine, among others, show. Toward the end of Libanius' life, an Italian named Jerome had moved to the desert of Palestine, where he would prepare the definitive Latin translation of the Bible and help shape, through his version of Eusebius' chronicle, the nature of historiography in the west. He too was a man of liberal education and would sing the praises of his traditional upbringing even as he chose to live an ascetic, Christian life.

As a professional teacher, Libanius would remain free of attachments. He did not marry – as Augustine did not marry, only contemplating the prospect when professional success seemed assured just prior to his conversion. He retained the freedom stemming from his fame to resist invitations from government officials to take up positions that he did not want, and could even refuse the emperor when he asked him to return to Constantinople.

In later life, Libanius is more a man of one location, while retaining a vast range of associates throughout the eastern empire, and the concerns of Antioch are now his main concerns. The later portions of his autobiography read like a summary of his opinions on different governors with whom he dealt. He felt that he could use his position to bring governors into line.

He expected to be treated with respect; he expected that his pupils would be advanced in their careers, and that the emperor would listen to him. Often he was correct. Still, there were disappointments and worries. He laments the advance in the study of Latin at the expense of Greek, as he does attacks upon the worship of the gods.[281] In the first section of his auto-biography he had ridiculed a rival from his first days in Constantinople who, though a polytheist, appears to have crossed the line of what Libanius regarded as good taste by traveling the empire to deliver a panegyric on Constantine and his church at Constantinople.[282] He rejoiced in being able to celebrate the gods with Julian, spoke with respect of those who felt that they could live with the gods, fought with a governor who wished to cut cypress trees from the sacred grove at Daphne. Although he appears to have gotten along well on a personal level with Cynegius, he deplored his support for the closure of the temples – and his encouragement of monks to ruin rural sanctuaries.

The policies of Theodosius toward the temples were plainly a work in progress as Libanius delivered the oration that has come down us as number 30 in the collection of his works, with the title "On the Temples." In 381 Theodosius had issued an edict stating that people should not indulge in sacrificial acts that had been banned.[283] Libanius read this as a continuation of the policies of Valentinian and Valens, who permitted offerings of incense.[284] In the next year Theodosius had ordered that the temple at Edessa be allowed to remain open, and in 385 had issued an edict banning sacri-fices connected with divination – hardly a novel restriction.[285] The journey of Cynegius thus represented a departure from this policy, and Libanius would suggest that it had nothing to do with the emperor's real thoughts on the matter.[286] He would acknowledge that Theodosius had the right to believe that his faith was better than that of others, and to encourage people to convert by his example. Forced conversions, he pointed out, would not work.[287] Libanius expected that Theodosius would recognize that temples were inextricably linked with a city's past and with the welfare of those who dwelt in the countryside.[288] Statues of the gods were not simply objects of cult, they were great works of art that needed to be preserved out of a sense of shared cultural heritage.[289] This was presumably something that monks could not understand, for they were

> this black-robed tribe, who eat more than elephants and, by the quantities of drink they consume, weary those that accompany their drinking with the singing of hymns, who hide these excesses under an artificially contrived pallor.
>
> (Or. 30.8, trans. Norman)

This plea for tradition could not, however, halt the movement in Theodosius' court from toleration to extremism, as would be manifest in 392 by a law banning all forms of polytheist sacrifice and closing all the temples. A year earlier, the great temple of Serapis had been destroyed at Alexandria, and several members of the local polytheist aristocracy were murdered there – without penalties being imposed upon the city.[290]

The transformation of the religious landscape would trouble Libanius, who knew himself to have been guided throughout his life by the goddess Fortune. But he could still see himself as living in the grand tradition of the man of letters, a position sanctified through the centuries by the crucial importance of culture as the defining element of the governing class. Even a German officer like the praetorian prefect Richomir, also a devout polytheist, might be expected to pick up a sufficient veneer of education to be able to appreciate what Libanius had to offer. In the pages of Libanius there is a great sense of continuity with the urban culture of the past, and no sense that the state stood upon the brink. For Libanius, the Persians were always the foes of choice, and so long as they were in check, the empire would flourish. He cared nothing for the west – his Roman Empire was centered at Antioch.

From Libanius to Alaric

It is often hard to see Alaric and Libanius as men who could have shared the same world, yet they did. Perhaps the most significant aspect of their shared space was that each would have been largely blind to the interests of the other. It is the specialization of interest, group by group, during the second half of the fourth century that is perhaps the most important trend. Members of the imperial bureaucracy pursued their own ambitions, at times relegating the emperors they served to positions of impotence. The aim of each group was to secure its own space. Often there is a sense that the state lacked a central direction – despite the joint headings of their edicts, the courts of Gratian, Valentinian II, and Theodosius often seem to have little to do with each other. The emperor, behind the facade of imperial power, appears to have had less and less actual control of affairs. As with the period between the death of Caracalla and the accession of Valerian, those who occupied the principal offices of the state were content to be without a firm guiding hand. In the third century this may have been a response to the impact of a ruler or rulers with particularly forceful natures who distressed their subordinates. With the death of Julian, the army and the court again reasserted themselves to ensure that the emperors that they selected would be respectful of their interests. The presence of Alaric and other Goths on the fringes of the imperial government reflects a view of imperial power in which support for the established power structure mattered more than an ideological link to principles of government. Theodosius was content to reconstruct the eastern army on new principles, drawing people from beyond the frontiers to fill his ranks rather than refashioning the army that had been lost. In a sense this may be seen as yet another expansion of the definition of Roman-ness – that a person be content to serve for a time with the emperor. But this sort of definition left too much to the will of the individual to stake out a role on his own terms. For those around Valens, Gratian, the Valentinians, and Theodosius, the maintenance of Roman hegemony was seen as coincidental with the maintenance of their own.

CONCLUSION

Change in the Roman Empire

A villa near the ancient site of Sufetula, the modern Birel-Hafay in Tunisia, that may be dated to the "early Byzantine" period – something of a misnomer in this case since the region was under the control of the Vandal kings for much of the fifth and sixth centuries AD – is decorated with a seascape that includes scenes of fishermen, many different fish, and naked Nereids riding upon monsters of varying descriptions.[1] One has the foreparts of a stag and the hindquarters of a squid; another is composed of a bull's head and forelegs with a fish's tail, while the third might be described as a dolphin. This may not be the finest art in the history of the world, but it is remarkable that the themes are unmistakably those of the classical world. A few miles further away there is another villa, this one in the environs of the ancient site of Thagameta, the modern Henchir Errich. Here there are more mosaics, one depicting hunters releasing dogs in pursuit of antelope, another depicting a fishing scene, and a third with some naked wrestlers. A fourth mosaic is devoted to heroes of pagan antiquity – Menelaus, Theseus, Perseus, Bellerophon, and Acteon. They are shown as hunters with their mythological victims (albeit with one variation, as the Minotaur is shown as a dead bear, rather than as half-man and half-bull). As a group, these mosaics depict the idea of virtue in an idiom that began to be commonplace in the fourth and fifth centuries AD.[2] The villas in which they reside are descendants of the great rural villas that had dominated the African landscape since the Punic period.[3]

The continuity of economic and cultural life, despite the great changes in the political and intellectual landscape of the Mediterranean, suggested in these mosaics, and other works of this period, wherein classical themes are reworked in a way that would not be offensive even to Christian sensibilities may reasonably raise questions about the nature of historical change in the Roman Empire. What these mosaics, and many others like them, reveal is a process by which old forms were adapted to new realities, and great continuity in the social structure of the empire. Unlike Britain, where most traces of imperial government appear to have vanished with the withdrawal of the Roman garrison and the failure of any successor state to emerge, most areas of the Mediterranean, whether they remained subject to Roman rule or not, retained a social structure allowing for the continuity of the local governing classes. Indeed, the weaker the central government, the stronger would be the power of regional elites. A new governing group needed still to assimilate the old; the Vandal kings of North Africa, the Ostrogothic kings of Italy, the Frankish and Visigothic rulers of Spain and France needed the skills that these people possessed, and they could not simply extrude them from their estates if they hoped to rule. The failures of imperial government during the later part of the fourth century, the domination of the court by bureaucratic factions that were soon content to rule, once again, with children as the titular heads of state, would contribute to the ultimate decline of the empire's authority in the west. Members of the governing class, people like Symmachus, one of whose last letters was to a rebellious general in Africa asking that he permit ships carrying grain from his estate to sail for Italy, men who saw government as a tool to satisfy their own ends, were more concerned with immediate advantage than the long-term success of the state.

The people who commissioned the mosaics at Birel-Hafay and Henchir Errich saw in the tales of classical antiquity a symbol of their own authority rather than that of any specific state. Even if they may not have known the stories very well (or have been well educated in Greek, which may explain why a Minotaur appears as a bear), they were aware that the narratives of the past conferred authority upon themselves. Their education, even if lacking by the standards of the second century AD, was still superior to those whose rents they collected. Although narratives of the classical past might now be supplemented by narratives derived from Hebrew scripture, the tales of Christ, of martyrs and visions of Christian eschatology, the ability to attach oneself to a narrative that conferred authority was as crucial as the ability to extract produce from peasants to their self-image. One constant throughout this book has been the centrality of narrative to the definition of power, whether it be the broader cultural narrative of urban civilization, the narrative of orthodoxy triumphant over heterodoxy, the narrative that justified an emperor's hold upon power, the stories of martyrs or holy people, the tale of one's own city, or family. These narratives helped people define their own place within the Roman Empire, to attach to institutions that mattered to them, or enabled them to further their aspirations. It was Constantine, the master of revisionist narrative in his own cause, who profoundly altered the narrative structures of imperial history by allowing Christian narratives to stand on an equal footing with traditional narratives of power. No emperor could make the empire into a Christian empire; there would still be polytheists for centuries after the death of Theodosius, but the master narrative of Christianity would become so deeply implicated in the narrative of imperial power that Christianity and government would become inextricably linked. Narratives such as Athanasius' tale of his oppression by "Arian" opponents might have no greater accuracy than many spun in other quarters, but they would come to have an authority that helped shape the way that later generations would understand the world around them.

Another theme of this book has been the centralization of power around the office of the emperor. That office, as forged in the lifetime of Augustus, had tremendous potential: the control of patronage, of appointments, and of the army, when it could actually be exercised by the holder of the office, enabled effective disposition of enormous power. It was all the more potent in the decentralized system of government inherited by Marcus Aurelius, who could balance the interests of diverse groups, and draw them to support his own agenda. While Marcus may have been inherently conservative; his cause may have been little more than to maintain the status quo – Rome's control over its frontiers, the loyalty of the urban upper classes, and of the diverse groups who took service in the central government – it was nonetheless a task that required that he ensure some distance between himself and any one group. He could support a Pertinax against the complaints of traditional senators, and, in some sense, he needed to be able to do so, as a reminder of who it was that made the final decision. The diverse groups that made up the governing class in the time of Marcus appear, consciously or unconsciously, to have desired to draw the emperor away from a middle position, and associate their interests with his own as the primary determinant of affairs. Marcus ruled at the end of a century when powerful rulers had been able, in the course of their long reigns, to avoid attaching the power of the ruler too closely to any one group. It was this that gave the Antonine era its unusual aura of stability, even when compared to the Julio-Claudian period, where various groups may be seen wrestling for control around the curious figures who succeeded Augustus. Tacitus wrote, in looking back on the events of AD 69, that a great secret of empire had been revealed – that it was possible to make an emperor somewhere other than at Rome. A greater secret seems to have been recovered when Marcus died: that it was possible to reduce the emperor to a figurehead. The twelve years during which Commodus ruled alone provided an object lesson in possibilities that inhered in a weak ruler.

Terror was one way to counteract the effect of centralization. We need not look to the terrors of Stalinist Russia or Mao's China in the twentieth century, or even to the legendarily brutal tactics employed by the first emperor of the Chin dynasty, to find instances against which to measure the conduct of Severus, and to do so would be to exaggerate. Severus himself points to the examples that he followed: he seems to have seen himself as a new Sulla. In praising Sulla, while adopting himself into the Antonine house, he sought to redefine the power of the emperor. Like Sulla, his power would rest with the legions; those who supported him would flourish, those who defied him would suffer. Despite his senatorial relatives, he seems to have seen himself as an outsider; like another outsider, the emperor Hadrian, he tried to exercise power by separating himself from traditional bases of power. His long journeys had the effect of concentrating power in the hands of officials he felt he could trust, and when he no longer felt he could trust them, he had no compunction about killing them. He deliberately created insecurity and fear as a substitute for Marcus' balancing act. Caracalla learned this much from his father, but he went too far, alienating officials from the notion that the emperor could balance interests other than those that were immediately obvious. The Severan age marks an important turning point in Roman history because Severus and Caracalla changed the balance between the senatorial and equestrian aristocracies, empowering officials who governed the *patrimonium* as never before.

Constantius II, who likewise employed terror as a means of controlling his government, had no less an impact on the development of the imperial office than did Severus. After Julian's death, there appears to have been little interest in continuing a dynasty whose last two members had shown themselves immune to ready control by members of their government. It may well be true that the eunuch Eusebius was the evil genius behind Constantius, but, in structural terms, it matters little. Whether the eunuch or the emperor was the dominant partner, it was no easy thing to hold office and build one's one group of clients while Constantius lived. Valentinian and Valens, for all their rages, were very much creatures of their senior officials, as were Gratian and Valentinian II. The reign of a powerful emperor created a desire to have a much less powerful one among those closest to the palace, with the result that there were long periods during which the state was effectively run by cabals of senior officials. This was perhaps not such a bad thing in time of peace, but in time of war it could be fatal, as the bickering on Valens' staff before Adrianople may show, and, even more seriously, the failure to respond to the new challenges offered by Ardashir in the time of Alexander.

While he might change the balance of power, no emperor was capable of addressing the impact of years of deeply conservative thought on the collective consciousness of the governing class. The grand narrative of classical culture, promoting, as it did, the notion that the inhabitants of the empire were inherently superior to those who lived elsewhere, was a serious matter. The second-century army, more than ever an instrument of domestic repression and internal politics, was ill prepared to fight on the frontiers. The easy victories of Lucius Verus' armies over the Persians, and later of Severus' own, disguised the fact that the army was reliant upon outmoded doctrines. The fact that Marcus could not fully subdue the Danubian tribes was a more telling indication that something was wrong. The inability of Severus Alexander's staff to understand that there was something qualitatively different about the armies of Ardashir may perhaps be explained by their participation in a culture where the present was measured in terms of the past.

When the inhabitants of the empire looked at the world around them, they tended to do so with a profound sense of their superiority to all others, with problematic results. Another consequence is often to hide from view the great importance of outsiders in changing the way that the empire did business. Some things we can trace more easily than others. Thus we can see that the development of mailed cavalry, cataphracts, in the second and third centuries, was due to the desire to match the cavalry units available to the Sarmatians and other tribes north of the Danube; that the formation of other units, *clibinarii*, was an effort to match the Persians.[4] On the other hand, we cannot trace with any degree of accuracy the rise of Germans in the military service of the western and Balkan armies. We know, for instance, from the anonymous author of a contemporary account of Caesar's campaign in Spain during 45 BC that the *clamor*, or battle cry, was a set phase of the battle, intended to strike fear in the heart of the enemy.[5] We do not, however, know when this *clamor*, which would have been in Latin for Caesar's men, was replaced by the *barritus*, or German war cry, as the standard form of opening a battle.[6] Nor can we trace with great confidence, prior to the fourth century (when some, if not great, confidence may be allowed), the rise of men with barbarian names to positions of high command. The inclusion of German officers in the highest ranks of the army, a sign that talent may have been as important as birth in determining a man's success, shows that the Roman state remained open to outsiders, something that was always its greatest source of strength. The spread of Manichaeism in the empire was a sign of the openness of the empire (albeit not without complaint) to influence from outside, though concentration on movements of this sort, necessitated by the state of our evidence, should not hide lesser movements such as that reflected in a shrine of Mithras discovered at Huarte, near Apamea in Syria. This shrine was constructed in an artificial grotto during the fourth century, later concealed by a church; its decoration is radically different from that of earlier shrines known from the west. While we have scenes from the Mithraic myth, including a gigantomachy, the birth of Mithras, his hunt of the cosmogonic bull, and his connection with the sun, we also have the theme of the struggle between good and evil, light and shadow, in forms that show obvious Iranian influence. The style of decoration is that of the Semitic rather than the Greek world, making it appear as if the myth had perhaps been updated in response to contemporary Persian thought.[7]

For a very long time all students of the past have been intrigued by the question of why the empire fell. So too they have been aware that it is all too easy to proclaim the death of a patient who would continue to thrive.[8] To deny either perspective would be wrong: the Roman state was less powerful in 395 than it was in 180, and it was not about to disappear from the face of the Mediterranean world. The empire whose cityscapes included churches rather than temples was not the same empire that Marcus Aurelius had left; its intellectual direction was not the same, nor was its political structure. Classical culture was adopted into new forms; it became ever more a tool for the expression of Christian thought, which, at the same time, lost much that had defined it as an alternative to classicism. There were many points of continuity with the past, and conclusions about one part of the vast territory dominated by Rome in the fourth century AD, as in the second, are not necessarily going to hold for another. It may though be possible to explain how the empire changed in these years in some ways, how it lost the power to project force as effectively as it once had done, how its rulers failed to recognize the impact of changes that affected it, how that failure led them to overreach themselves with catastrophic results, and how its policies were dominated by groups with special interests that did not necessarily benefit society as a whole. As a consequence the Roman state passed from hegemonic power to regional power in the course of the third and fourth centuries, but it did not cease to be a power. Still, the change was important to people who lived at the time, and it remains important for those who seek lessons from the past. Nothing threatens a great power as much as the failure to realize that it cannot compel compliance with its wishes.

NOTES

1 CULTURE, ECOLOGY, AND POWER

1 Hipp. *Dan.* 4.5 (destructive power); 4.8 (the empire levies recruits).

2 Hipp. *Dan.* 4.9, 23. For the place of Hippolytus in the evolution of subsequent Christian chronological systems see R. Landes, "Lest the Millennium Be Fulfilled: Apocalyptic Expectations and the Pattern of Western Chronology 100–800 CE," in *The Use and Abuse of Eschatology in the Early Middle Ages,* ed. W. Verbeke, D. Verhelst, and A. Welkenhuysen (Leuven, 1988), 141–49.

3 J. A. Cerrato, *Hippolytus, Between East and West: The Commentaries and the Provenance of the Corpus* (Oxford, 2002), 242–49.

4 Hipp. *Dan.* 4.18; see also *Dan.* 4.19 for a Pontic priest who was also in error about the date.

5 Hipp. *Dan.* 4.9.

6 Hipp. *Dan.* 4.21.3 (the empire restrains the end); ten democracies see Hipp. *Dan.* 4.17; *Antichr.* 27 and, for parallels in contemporary Christian thought, Cerrato, *Hippolytus,* 239–42.

7 D. S. Potter, *Prophecy and History in the Crisis of the Roman Empire: A Historical Commentary on the Thirteenth Sibylline Oracle* (Oxford, 1990), 288–89 (references), and D. S. Potter, "Emperors, Their Borders, and Their Neighbours: The Scope of Imperial *mandata,*" in *The Roman Army in the East,* ed. D. L. Kennedy, *JRA* suppl. 18 (Ann Arbor, 1996), 54, for the chronological development of the idea.

8 I owe this formulation to Dr Nigel Pollard.

9 *ILS* 6870; the best text is now T. Hauken, *Petition and Response: An Epigraphic Study of Petitions to Roman Emperors, 181–249* (Bergen, 1998), 7–10.

10 D. P. Kehoe, *The Economics of Agriculture on Roman Imperial Estates in North Africa* (Göttingen, 1988), 22–23, 48–55.

11 Kehoe, *Economics of Agriculture,* 113, 188–97, on the organization of tenants; see also p. 21–23 below.

12 Euseb. *Hist. eccl.* 5.1.3–2.8; for the circumstances see D. S. Potter, "Performance, Power, and Justice in the High Empire," in *Roman Theater and Society,* ed. W. Slater (Ann Arbor, 1996), 155–59.

13 A. Watson, *Aurelian and the Third Century* (London, 1999), 4.

14 Tert. *Apol.* 25.5.

15 D. S. Potter, *Prophets and Emperors: Human and Divine Authority from Augustus to Theodosius* (Cambridge, Mass., 1994), 110–30.

16 C. F. Noreña, "The Communication of the Emperor's Virtues," *JRS* 91 (2001), 146–68.

17 R. P. Duncan-Jones, *Structure and Scale in the Roman Economy* (Cambridge, 1990), 48–58 (a significant study of the trade in lamps). This work and that which is

cited in the following notes effectively invalidated K. Hopkins, "Taxes and Trade in the Roman Empire (200 BC–400 AD)," *JRS* 70 (1980): 101–25, though see now the important discussions of C. Howgego, "The Supply and Uses of Money in the Roman World, 200 BC to AD 300," *JRS* 82 (1992): 1–31, and P. Temin, "A Market Economy in the Early Roman Empire," *JRS* 91 (2001): 169–201, for the clearest statement of a new understanding of the imperial economy.

18 See especially C. Howgego, "Coin Circulation and the Integration of the Roman Economy," *JRA* 7 (1994): 12–16, with extensive bibliography.

19 C. M. Kraay, "The Behaviour of Early Imperial Countermarks," in *Essays in Roman Coinage Presented to Harold Mattingly*, ed. R. A. G. Carson and C. H. V. Sutherland (Oxford, 1956), 113–36 (foundational); and C. Howgego, *Greek Imperial Countermarks: Studies in the Provincial Coinage of the Roman Empire* (London, 1985), 32–50 (clinching the case).

20 Howgego, "Supply and Uses," 28; J. Andreau, "Financiers de l'aristocratie à la fin de la République," in *Le dernier siècle de la République romaine et l'époque augustéenne*, ed. E. Frézouls (Strasbourg, 1978), 51–55; J. Andreau, *Banking and Business in the Roman World* (Cambridge, 1999), 20, 117, 132.

21 W. E. Metcalf, "Rome and Lugdunum Again," *AJN* 1 (1989): 51–70; I. Carradice and M. Crowell, "The Minting of Roman Imperial Bronze Coins for Circulation in the East: Vespasian to Trajan," *NC* 147 (1987), 26–50; Howgego, "Coin Circulation," 9, 16.

22 S. Esmonde Cleary, *The Ending of Roman Britain* (London, 1989), 131–61. See in general terms, the important discussion of C. Wickham, "The Other Transition: From the Ancient World to Feudalism," *Past and Present* 103 (1984): 3–36.

23 Esmonde Cleary, *Ending of Roman Britain*, 139–40.

24 Esmonde Cleary, *Ending of Roman Britain*, 139, 141.

25 Esmonde Cleary, *Ending of Roman Britain*, 149–59.

26 For other treatments of this theme, from very different perspectives, see C. Ando, *Imperial Ideology and Provincial Loyalty in the Roman Empire* (Berkeley, 2000), for a splendid analysis of the behaviors and institutions of consensus; and G. Woolf, *Becoming Roman: The Origins of Provincial Civilization in Gaul* (Cambridge, 1998), from a cultural perspective. What follows has links to both approaches.

27 J. D. Hughes, *Pan's Travail: Environmental Problems of the Ancient Greeks and Romans* (Baltimore, 1994), 8–23, for a good survey of the basic environmental features.

28 These are, of course, approximations; figures used here are in fact from Edinburgh and Baghdad. They are derived from G. Rumney, *Climatology and the World's Climates* (London, 1968), 217, 440, deriving from reports in 1959 and 1961 respectively, and consequently prior to the onset of significant global warming in the last thirty years of the twentieth century. See also Rumney's rainfall map for western Europe on p. 218.

29 For travel times see Duncan-Jones, *Structure and Scale*, 7–29, to be supplemented by the extraordinary papyrus published by P. Heilporn, "Registre de navires marchands," *P. Bingen* (Amsterdam, 2000), 339–59 (publishing *P. Mich. inv.* 5760a).

30 See now the invaluable discussion of the concept of the Mediterranean in P. Horden and N. Purcell, *The Corrupting Sea: A Study of Mediterranean History* (Oxford, 2000), 9–25, with discussion in the important review article by B. D. Shaw, "Challenging Braudel: A New Revision of the Mediterranean," *JRA* 14 (2001): 421–24.

31 Rumney, *Climatology*, 243; R. Meiggs, *Trees and Timber in the Ancient Mediterranean World* (Oxford, 1982), 43–44.

32 Rumney, *Climatology*, 243–44, reconstructing ancient terrain.

33 The importance of beans is stressed by P. Garnsey, *Food and Society in Classical Antiquity* (Cambridge, 1999), 15–16.

34 For the population of Egypt, somewhere in the vicinity of 4.75 million people; see R. S. Bagnall and B. W. Frier, *The Demography of Roman Egypt* (Cambridge, 1994), 56.

35 Garnsey, *Food and Society*, 16–17, 122–27.

36 What follows is dependent upon A. King, "Diet in the Roman World: A Regional Inter-Site Comparison of Mammal Bones," *JRA* 12 (1999): 168–202.

37 B. H. Slicher van Bath, *The Agrarian History of Western Europe, AD 500–1850*, trans. O. Ordish (London, 1963), 182.

38 L. Foxhall and H. A. Forbes, "*Sitometreia*: The Role of Grain as Staple Food in Classical Antiquity," *Chiron* 12 (1982): 41–90.

39 C. L. Barnes, "*Tarentum victum*: Processes of Evolution," PhD diss., University of Michigan, 1999, 30–47, on fish consumption at Tarentum, showing that J. Davidson, *Courtesans and Fishcakes* (New York, 1998) can be corrected on a regional basis, as also the important study of N. Purcell, "Eating Fish: The Paradoxes of Seafood," in *Food in Antiquity*, ed. J. Wilkins, D. Harvey, and M. Dobson (Exeter, 1996), 132–49.

40 R. I. Curtis, *Garum and Salsamenta: Production and Commerce in Materia Medica* (Leiden, 1991), with Purcell, "Eating Fish," 145.

41 D. Kyle, *Spectacles of Death in Ancient Rome* (London, 1998), 190–94.

42 For Galen see Garnsey, *Food and Society*, 15.

43 Garnsey, *Food and Society*, 118–19.

44 T. Jacobson, *Towards the Image of Tammuz and Other Essays on Mesopotamian History and Culture* (Cambridge, Mass., 1970), 74–75.

45 Garnsey, *Food and Society*, 67–68.

46 F. Braudel, *The Structures of Everyday Life*, trans. S. Reynolds (New York, 1981), 120.

47 Plin. *HN* 17.3.41, 18.21.94, with R. Sallares, *The Ecology of the Ancient Greek World* (Ithaca, NY, 1991), 497, n. 245.

48 Cic. *Verr.* 2.3.109–13, with Sallares, *Ecology*, 497, n. 243.

49 M. Aymard, "Production et productivité agricole: L'Italie du Sud à l'époque moderne," in *Prestations paysannes, dîmes, rente foncière et mouvement de la production agricole à l'époque préindustrielle*, ed. J. Le Goy and E. Le Roy Ladurie (Paris, 1982), 147–63.

50 E. Le Roy Ladurie, *The French Peasantry, 1450–1660*, trans. A. Sheridan (London, 1987), 110.

51 Slicher van Bath, *Agrarian History*, 175, with the caveats of Ladurie, *The French Peasantry*, 110.

52 Slicher van Bath, *Agrarian History*, 176.

53 For North Africa see B. D. Shaw, "Climate, Environment, and History: The Case of Roman North Africa," in *Climate and History: Studies in Past Climates and Their Effect on Man*, ed. T. M. L. Wigley, M. J. Ingram, and G. Farmer (Cambridge, 1981), 390–91.

54 Slicher van Bath, *Agrarian History*, 84; Garnsey, *Food and Society*, 43–61.

55 B. W. Frier, "Roman Demography," in *Life, Death, and Entertainment in the Roman Empire*, ed. D. S. Potter and D. J. Mattingly (Ann Arbor, 1999), 105–6.

56 Bagnall and Frier, *Demography of Roman Egypt*, 177–78.

57 Bagnall and Frier, *Demography of Roman Egypt*, 109; for their discussion of the method see pp. 40–52. For criticism of the evidence (overstated) see T. G. Parkin, *Demography and Roman Society* (Baltimore, 1992), 19–21, and (more judiciously) R. P. Saller, *Patriarchy, Property, and Death in the Roman Family* (Cambridge, 1994), 19–20.

58 Duncan Jones, *Structure and Scale*, 92–96, a study that is suggestive rather than definitive; see Parkin, *Demography and Roman Society*, 137–38, and Saller, *Patriarchy, Property, and Death*, 16–18.

59 W. Scheidel, "Roman Age Structure: Evidence and Models," *JRS* 91 (2001): 1–26, esp. 15–19.

60 M. Gleason, "Elite Male Identity in the Roman Empire," in Potter and Mattingly, *Life, Death, and Entertainment*, 68, 82–84.

61 N. Morley, *Metropolis and Hinterland: The City of Rome and the Italian Economy, 200 BC–AD 200* (Cambridge, 1996), 183; Horden and Purcell, *The Corrupting Sea*, 107.

62 D. J. Mattingly, "Oil for Export? A Comparison of Libyan, Spanish, and Tunisian Olive Oil Production in the Roman Empire," *JRA* 1 (1988): 33–56.

63 Horden and Purcell, *The Corrupting Sea*, 230.

64 L. F. Pitts, "Relations between Rome and the German 'Kings' on the Middle Danube in the First to Fourth Centuries AD," *JRS* 79 (1989): 45–58. For other areas see P. S. Wells, *The Barbarians Speak* (Princeton, 1999), 232–58.

65 Pitts, "Relations," 55; D. S. Potter, "Empty Areas and Roman Frontier Policy," *AJP* 113 (1992): 269–74.

66 Wells, *The Barbarians Speak*, 256.

67 D. Graf, "The Roman East from the Chinese Perspective," *International Colloquium on Palmyra and the Silk Road, AAS* 42 (1996): 205–13.

68 Plin. *HN* 6.84–91 with J. F. Matthews, "Hostages, Philosophers, Pilgrims, and the Diffusion of Ideas in the Late Roman Mediterranean and Near East," in *Tradition and Innovation in Late Antiquity*, ed. F. M. Clover and R. S. Humphreys (Madison, 1989), 30–31; Graf, "Chinese Perspective," 3; G. K. Young, *Rome's Eastern Trade: International Commerce and Imperial Policy, 31 BC–AD 305* (London, 2001), 32–33.

69 L. Casson, "New Light on Maritime Loans: P. Vindob. G 40822," *ZPE* 84 (1990): 195–206; for the location of the original agreement see pp. 202, 206.

70 F. G. Millar, "Looking East from the Classical World: Colonialism, Culture, and Trade from Alexander the Great to Shapur I," *International History Review* 20 (1998): 525–29.

71 Arr. *Perip. M. Eux.* 24, with Young, *Rome's Eastern Trade*, 30–31.

72 Young, *Rome's Eastern Trade*, 80–81, on the Egyptian connection, though for the date of the Dendrah text (*CIS* 2:3910), which he puts as early as 160, see M. Dijkstra and A. M. F. W. Verhoogt, "The Greek–Palmyrene Inscription," in *Report of the 1997 Excavations at Berenike and the Survey of the Egyptian Desert, including Excavations at Shenshef*, ed. S. E. Sidebotham and W. Z. Wendrich (Leiden, 1999), 215. It is, perhaps, unnecessary to postulate changes in the political situation on the Syrian frontier. For further evidence, a bilingual Greek–Palmyrene inscription from Berenice that dates from the period 180–212, see Dijkstra and Verhoogt, "The Greek–Palmyrene Inscription," 207–19. I am indebted to Professor Verhoogt for drawing this to my attention.

73 D. Graf, "Zenobia and the Arabs," in *The Eastern Frontier of the Roman Empire: Proceedings of a Colloquium Held at Ankara in September 1988*, ed. D. H. French and C. S. Lightfoot, BAR International Series 553 (Oxford, 1989), 1:147.

74 *SEG* 48, no. 1923, with G. W. Bowersock, "The New Inscription from Rāsūn in Jordan," *Syria* 76 (1999): 224–25. On Sakla and other toponyms reflecting estate ownership in the region see D. Feissel, "Remarques de toponymie syrienne d'après des inscriptions grecques chrétiennes trouvées hors de Syrie," *Syria* 59 (1982): 333–34. See also J. Gascou, "Unités administratives locales et fonctionnaires romains. Les données des papyrus du Moyen Euphrate et d'Arabie," in *Lokale Autonomie und römische Ordnungsmacht in der kaiserzeitlichen Provinzen vom 1. bis 3.*

Jahrhundert, ed. W. Eck and E. Müller-Luckner (Munich, 1999), 68–70, on cantonments in Mesopotamia and Arabia that were not attached to cities.

75 *IGR* 3, nos. 1186–87.

76 *IGR* 3, no. 1213, with F. Millar, *The Roman Near East* (Cambridge, Mass., 1993), 426–27.

77 M. Sartre, "Les *metrokomai* de Syrie du sud," *Syria* 76 (1999): 211–19.

78 *SEG* 48, no. 1585.

79 *SEG* 48, no. 1769.

80 *IGR* 4, no. 1245. See also the important discussion to which this paragraph owes a substantial debt in A. P. Gregory, "Country, Village, and Town in Central Anatolia," *JRA* 10 (1997): 547–48, and the further discussion in S. Mitchell, "The Administration of Roman Asia from 133 BC to AD 250," in Eck and Müller-Luckner, *Lokale Autonomie*, 33–36. While Mitchell is right that the appeals of villages are addressed to Roman officials by higher-status individuals, what is significant is that villages had access through these people, which shows not, as Mitchell suggests, that this is evidence for the "wide gulf in status that separated the rural and urban inhabitants of Asia" (p. 36), but rather for the methods used in bridging the gulf.

81 J. Nollé and W. Eck, "Der Brief des Asinius Rufus an die Magistrate von Sardeis. Zum Marktrechtsprivileg für die Gemeinde der Arillenoi," *Chiron* 26 (1996): 267–73. This is particularly interesting as Asinius appears at the time to have been resident in the west.

82 *SEG* 32, no. 1220, with the discussion, summarizing earlier work, of L. de Ligt, *Fairs and Markets in the Roman Empire: Economic and Social Aspects of Periodic Trade in a Pre-industrial Society* (Amsterdam, 1993), 124–25.

83 See also J. Nollé, "Marketrechte außerhalb der Stadt: Lokale Autonomie zwischen Statthalter und Zentralort," in Eck and Müller-Luckner, *Lokale Autonomie*, 93–113.

84 See J. Banaji, *Agrarian Change in Late Antiquity* (Oxford, 2001), 7–10, 13–15.

85 De Ligt, *Fairs and Markets*, 176–85.

86 Hauken, *Petition and Response*, 258–89, offers the best discussion of the formal aspects of these petitions.

87 For the problem of where petitions were composed see Hauken, *Petition and Response*, 289; for the "grammarian's complaint" see *P. Oxy.* 3366, with P. J. Parsons, "Petitions and a Letter: The Grammarian's Complaint, 253–60 AD," in *Collectanea Papyrologica: Texts Published in Honor of H. C. Youtie*, ed. A. E. Hanson (Bonn, 1976), 409–46, and R. Kaster, *Guardians of Language: The Grammarian and Society in Late Antiquity* (Berkeley, 1988), 115–16.

88 *IGBR* 4, no. 2236, with the new text in Hauken, *Petition and Response*, 85–94; for the soldier, Aurelius Pyrrus, a member of the Praetorian Guard, who transmitted the petition, see now E. I. Paunov and D. J. Dimitrov, "Die Siegelring des Aurelius Pyrrus aus Scaptopera," *Chiron* 26 (1996): 183–93, showing that he returned home after his service.

89 J. Keil and A. von Premerstein, "Bericht über eine dritte Reise in Lydien und den agrenzenden Gebieten Ioniens, ausgeführt 1911 im Auftrage der Kaiserlichen Akademie der Wissenschaften," *Denkschrift der Kaiserlichen Akademie der Wissenschaften in Wien*, philosophisch-historische Klasse 57, no. 1 (Vienna, 1914), no. 55, 10, reprinted in Hauken, *Petition and Response*, 38–40. For the size of the ransom see Hauken, *Petition and Response*, 46.

90 P. D. Garnsey, "Peasants in Ancient Roman Society," *Journal of Peasant Studies* 3 (1976): 230–31 (also in P. D. Garnsey, *Cities, Peasants, and Food in Classical Antiquity: Essays in Social and Economic History*, ed. W. Scheidel [Cambridge, 1998], 99–101).

91 See, most recently, N. Pollard, *Soldiers, Cities, and Civilians in Roman Syria* (Ann Arbor, 2000), 200–4, with earlier bibliography.

92 M. I. Rostovtzeff, *The Social and Economic History of the Roman Empire*, 2nd edn., ed. P. M. Fraser (Oxford, 1957), xii–xiii.

93 M. I. Rostovtzeff, M. L. Shine, R. H. Whitbeck, and G. B. L. Arner, *Urban Land Economics* (Ann Arbor, 1922), 18: "Now, what is my purpose in giving this short introduction to your work? It is to interpret one of the main problems of modern economic and social life. I do not know if you, being Americans, grasp entirely the importance of this problem; but I, being a Russian, grasp it fully and entirely."

94 Rostovtzeff, *Social and Economic History*, 266, 347–48, 413 (an incredibly perceptive passage), 501; G. E. M. De Ste. Croix, *The Class Struggle in the Ancient Greek World* (Oxford, 1981), 9–19.

95 E. Le Roy Ladurie, *The Territory of the Historian*, trans. B. Reynolds and S. Reynolds (Chicago, 1979), 79.

96 T. Derks, *Gods, Temples, and Ritual Practices: The Transformation of Religious Ideas and Values in Roman Gaul* (Amsterdam, 1998), 49–50.

97 *SEG* 7, no. 341. The discussion that follows is based on Millar, *The Roman Near East*, 1–23.

98 See also Derks, *Gods, Temples*, 245–46, who properly points out that the form of attachment to Rome is a complex function stemming from the level of attachment of communities to Rome. The key question, as he rightly sees, is not a division between attachment and detachment, but rather degrees of attachment and the socioeconomic factors that determine them. For a very different approach see J. Webster, "Necessary Compromises: A Post-colonial Approach to Religious Syncretism in the Roman Provinces," *W. Arch.* 28 (1996–97): 324–38, who seeks parallels from the experience of Central American peoples under Spanish domination who preserved local traditions under Christian practices. This is a less attractive model, for the interests of Spanish conquerors involved the promotion of Christianity, making the relationship between "pagan" cult and the religion of the conquerors most unlike that of indigenous cults and Roman cult. For views similar to those of Derks, on a more general model, see G. Woolf, "Beyond Romans and Natives," *W. Arch.* 28 (1996–97): 339–50, esp. 347.

99 *AE* 1996 no. 1705; see also *AE* 1942–43 no. 111; for the use of Augustus with local divinities see the numerous examples in G. Camps, "Qui sont les Dii Mauri?", *Ant. af.* 26 (1990): 133–45.

100 J. B. Rives, *Religion and Authority in Roman Carthage from Augustus to Constantine* (Oxford, 1995), 157–61. See also, possibly, *AE* 1995 no. 1656.

101 Diod. 14.70.4, 77.5.

102 For Dii Mauri see Camps, "Qui sont les Dii Mauri?", 145–53; E. W. B. Fentress, "Dii Mauri and Dii Patrii," *Latomus* 27 (1978): 507–16; for Dii Magifae Augusti see *ILS* 4493; for the Dii Macni see *CIL* 8, nos. 8023, 19981.

103 For the problem of syncretism see D. S. Potter, "Hellenistic Religion," in *The Blackwell Companion to the Hellenistic World*, ed. A. Erskine (Oxford, 1993).

104 G. W. Bowersock, *Hellenism in Late Antiquity* (Ann Arbor, 1990), 1–13.

105 Potter, *Prophets and Emperors*, 4–9.

106 A Christian community is attested later (Acts 16:1), but it is not suggested that it comprised the population.

107 L. Robert, "Documents d'Asie mineure," *BCH* 107 (1983): 529–42 (also in L. Robert, *Documents d'Asie mineure* [Paris, 1987], 373–86).

108 *AE* 1995 no. 1659, deriving from M. Le Glay, *Studia in Honorem G. Mihailov* (Sofia, 1995), 211–17.

109 *ILS* 4080, discussed by J. Aronen, "Dragon Cults and ΝΥΜΦΗ ΔΡΑΚΑΙΝΑ in IGUR 974," *ZPE* 111 (1996): 125–32.

110 *IGR* 4, no. 1498; L. Robert, *A travers l'Asie mineure: Poètes et prosateurs, monnaies grecques, voyageurs et géographie* (Paris, 1980), 405–8; C. P. Jones, *Culture and Society in Lucian* (Cambridge, Mass., 1986), 143. For Lucian on Alexander's sexual activity see *Alex.* 41–42.

111 Aronen, "Dragon Cults," 127.

112 *CIL* 8, no. 9326, with Camps, "Qui sont les Dii Mauri?", 138.

113 *CIL* 8, no. 15247.

114 J. T. Milik, *Dédicaces faites par des Dieux (Palmyre, Hatra, Tyr) et des thiases sémitiques à l'époque romaine* (Paris, 1972), 431–32, 439.

115 Lucian, *Alex.* 38–40; Potter, *Prophecy and History*, 45.

116 *SEG* 38 no. 1462 C. 70–73, trans. S. Mitchell, "Festivals, Games, and Civic Life in Roman Asia Minor," *JRS* 80 (1990): 186. For discussion of the panegyriarchs, clarified by this text, see M. Wörrle, *Stadt und Fest im kaiserzeitlichen Kleinasien* (Munich, 1988), 209–15. For contextualization of the role of Oenoanda in the region see also Horden and Purcell, *The Corrupting Sea*, 95.

117 For the date of P. Mummius Sisenna Rutilianus' governorship of Asia see *PIR²* M 711.

118 A. Birley, *Marcus Aurelius: A Biography* (New Haven, 1987), 163–64; for the renaming of the city see Jones, *Culture and Society*, 146.

119 Potter, *Prophets and Emperors*, 158–70.

120 Birley, *Marcus Aurelius*, 172.

121 *Orac. Sib.* 12.195–200 with Potter, *Prophets and Emperors*, 122, and bibliography in Potter, *Prophecy and History*, 135–37.

122 Dio 71.8.4.

123 G. Fowden, *The Egyptian Hermes* (Cambridge, 1986), 126–31.

124 Potter, *Prophets and Emperors*, 12, 183–206.

125 What follows is based very heavily on the brilliant discussion of D. Frankfurter, *Religion in Roman Egypt: Assimilation and Resistance* (Princeton, 1998), 217–37.

126 *PGM* 4.2446–55.

127 Ath. 15.677 with *P. Oxy.* 73 and Jones, *Culture and Society*, 50.

128 Dio 79.4.4–5.

129 Frankfurter, *Religion in Roman Egypt*, 225.

130 Lucian, *Philops.* 34–35; Jones, *Culture and Society*, 50.

131 A. J. Festugière, "L'expérience religeuse du médecin Thessalos," *RB* 48 (1939): 45–77; A. J. Festugière, *La Révélation d'Hermès Trismégiste* (Paris, 1950), 1:56–59; for the text see now H. V. Friedrich, *Thessalos von Tralles* (Meisenhaim am Glan, 1968). For Nectanebus, who occupied an important position in the pseudepigrapha of early Hellenistic Egypt, see especially P. M. Fraser, *Ptolemaic Alexandria* (Oxford, 1972), 1:676–80; J. G. Griffiths, "Apocalyptic in the Hellenistic Era," in *Apocalypticism in the Mediterranean World and the Near East: Proceedings of the International Colloquium on Apocalypticism, Uppsala, August 12–17 (1979),* ed. D. Hellholm (Tübingen, 1983), 273–79. Another important Nectanebus text is *The Dream of Nectanebo*, on which see L. Koenen, "The Dream of Nektanebos," *BASP* 22 (1985): 171–94.

132 On the redesign of Egyptian temples to accommodate Greek tastes see Frankfurter, *Religion in Roman Egypt*, 168–69, with discussion of this text. For underground oracular sites in the Greek world see Potter, *Prophets and Emperors*, 43–45.

133 *P. Berol.* 21243 published by W. Brasher, "Ein Berliner Zauberpapyrus," *ZPE* 33 (1979): 261–78. For similar statements *see P. Oxy.* 886, 1382; *Catalogus Codicum Astrologorum Graecorum* 7.62; *PGM* 4.885–87 with Brasher's discussion.

134 Frankfurter, *Religion of Roman Egypt*, 299–30.

135 D. Potter, "Hellenistic Religion," in *A Companion to the Hellenistic World*, ed. A. Erskine (Oxford, 2003), 425–6.

136 For Atargatis and Hadad see now J. L. Lightfoot, *Lucian: On the Syrian Goddess* (Oxford, 2003), 1–85; for Cybele see L. E. Roller, *In Search of God the Mother: The Cult of Anatolian Cybele* (Berkeley, 1999), 27–115 on the Anatolian context.

137 For the temple tax see E. Schürer, *The History of the Jewish People in the Age of Jesus Christ (175 BC–AD 135)*, ed. G. Vermes, F. Millar, and M. Black (Edinburgh, 1979), 2: 272–77, and 3: 122–23 for the history of the tax after the destruction of the temple, on which see also M. Goodman, "Nerva, the *Fiscus Judaicus*, and Jewish Identity," *JRS* 79 (1989): 40–44.

138 F. Dunand, *Le culte d'Isis dans le bassin orientale de la méditerranée* (Leiden, 1973), 1: 1–4.

139 See now the important study of S. Mitchell, "The Cult of Theos Hypsistos between Pagans, Jews, and Christians," in *Pagan Monotheism in Late Antiquity*, ed. P. Athanassiadi and M. Frede (Oxford, 1999), 81–148. What follows is a response to some of Mitchell's arguments, whom I read to be suggesting greater unity of practice than seems to me to be justified by the evidence, for which he provides an invaluable catalogue. My views approximate those of J. Ustinova, "The *Thiasoi* of Theos Hypsistos in Tanais," *History of Religions* 31 (1991): 165, who argues that Iranian traditions shaped the image of the god in the Bosphoran kingdom, but not necessarily elsewhere.

140 *I. Strat.* nos. 1306, 1110, 1112, 1113; L. Robert, "Reliefs votifs et cultes d'Anatolie," *Anadolu* 3 (1958): 115 (Zeus the Highest and the Divine) (also in Robert, *OMS* 1: 414); (Zeus the Highest and the Divine, 1117, 1307 (Zeus the Highest and the Divine Messenger), 1307 (Zeus the Highest and the Divine Heavenly Messenger), 1114 (Zeus the Highest and the Divine Good), 1115 (Zeus the Highest and the Divine Good).

141 For the Highest God Hearer see, e.g., *CIRB* 1260, 1278, 1279, 1280 (all from Tanais on the Black Sea from the mid–second century to early third century AD); for Palmyra see, e.g., *OGIS* 634 (Zeus Highest Greatest Hearer); *LW* 2572 (Zeus the Highest the Hearer), but see also *LW* 2627, 2571b, 2574 (Zeus the Highest and the Hearer); see also Robert, "Reliefs votifs," 112–14 (The Highest God and the Great Divine Epiphanes who receive a dedication of the goddess Larmênê) (also in Robert, *OMS* 1: 411). For Jewish usage see Mitchell, "Cult of Theos Hypsistos," 110–15.

142 Mitchell, "Cult of Theos Hypsistos," 114–15.

143 Ustinova, "*Thiasoi* of Theos Hypsistos," 160–63; Mitchell, "Cult of Theos Hypsistos," 115–21.

144 For origins in the Black Sea area see P. Beskow, "The Routes of Early Mithraism," *Études mithriaques: Actes du 2e Congrès International Téhéran, du 1er au 8 septembre 1975*, *Acta Iranica* 17 (1978): 7–18; for Rome see M. Clauss, *The Roman Cult of Mithras: The God and His Mysteries*, trans. R. Gordon (London, 2000), 7, 22; the case for Cappadocian origin has recently been argued with considerable conviction by R. Beck, "The Mysteries of Mithras: A New Account of the Genesis," *JRS* 88 (1998): 115–28. The parallel with Alexander is observed by Clauss, *Roman Cult of Mithras*, 7; see also Beck, "The Mysteries of Mithras," 116–21, reviewing the vast earlier bibliography and making a highly sophisticated case for the invention of the cult by a small group in the service of the kings of Commagene. This approach is of great importance for understanding the nature of religious change; see also R. Stark, *The Rise of Christianity: A Sociologist Reconsiders History* (Princeton, 1996), 33–34. The extraordinary mithraeum that was recently discovered in the vicinity

of Apamea is too late to be relevant to the study of Mithraic origins (it dates from the fourth century); for details see M. Gawlikowsky, "Un nouveau mithraeum récemment découvert à Huarté près d'Apamée," *CRAI* (2000), 161–71 and p. 580 below.

145 For the most recent catalogue of Mithraic monuments see M. J. Vermaseren, *Corpus Inscriptionum et Monumentorum Religionis Mithriacae*, vols. 1–2 (The Hague, 1956–60). For analysis of the basis elements of the myth see Clauss, *Roman Cult of Mithras*, 62–101. For a reconstruction of the rites of the Mithraeum see now R. Beck, "Ritual, Myth, Doctrine, and Initiation in the Mysteries of Mithras: New Evidence from a Cult Vessel," *JRS* 100 (2000): 145–80.

146 R. Gordon, "Mithraism and Roman Society," *Religion* 2, no. 2 (1972): 108–12 (also in R. Gordon, *Image and Value in the Graeco-Roman World: Studies in Mithraeism and Religious Art* (Brookfield, VT, 1996), ch. 3).

147 R. Gordon, "The Sacred Geography of a Mithraeum: The Example of Stette Sfere," *Journal of Mithraic Studies* 1 (1976): 119–65, esp. pp. 145–46 (also in Gordon, *Image and Value*, ch. 6); Beck, "The Mysteries of Mithras," 122–25.

148 For the Elchesaites who are referred to in the text see pp. 212–13; 304 below. For Christian groups that seem to have existed in conjunction with Jewish groups in Anatolia see P. R. Trebilco, *Jewish Communities in Asia Minor* (Cambridge, 1991), 28–29, 101–3; for Jews and Christians being buried in the same cemeteries see Mitchell, "Cult of Theos Hypsistos," 124.

149 A. von Harnack, *The Mission and Expansion of Christianity*, trans. J. Moffatt (repr. Gloucester, Mass., 1972), 1: 147–98, on the "gospel of love and charity"; R. J. Lane Fox, *Pagans and Christians* (London, 1987), 336–74, on the draw of an alternative lifestyle; and P. L. R. Brown, *Poverty and Leadership in the Later Roman Empire* (Hanover, NH, 2002), 1–26, on the Christian interest in the poor as a class (on which see also Harnack, *Mission and Expansion* 1: 153–57), distinguishing it from contemporary polytheist traditions. See also Stark, *The Rise of Christianity*, 29–47, suggesting that the movement was unlikely to have succeeded if it consisted of the poor – this is quite reasonable, since sympathy for the dispossessed is not necessarily a sign of being dispossessed oneself.

150 See now C. Trevett, *Montanism: Gender, Authority, and the New Prophecy* (Cambridge, 1996), 1–45; R. E. Heine, *The Montanist Oracles and Testimonia*, Patristic Monograph Series 14 (Macon, 1989); W. Tabbernee, *Montanist Inscriptions and Testimonia: Epigraphic Sources Illustrating the History of Montanism*, Patristic Monograph Series 16 (Macon, 1997).

151 H. von Campenhausen, *The Formation of the Christian Bible*, trans. J. A. Baker (Philadelphia, 1972), 148–67, on the significance of the Marcionite movement for the formation of the Christian canon. For a radical revision of this understanding of Marcion see R. J. Hoffmann, *Marcion: On the Restitution of Christianity: An Essay on the Development of Radical Paulinist Theology in the Second Century, AAR* Academy Series 46 (Chico, 1984). Hoffmann argues that Marcion should be seen as a first- rather than second-century figure, and that his theories need to be understood as emerging from contemporary Judaism. It is an interesting suggestion, though I remain attached to the more traditional view as it appears in Campenhausen.

2 GOVERNMENT

1 D. S. Potter, "The *Tabula Siarensis*, Tiberius, the Senate, and the Eastern Boundary of the Roman Empire," *ZPE* 69 (1987): 269–76.

2 Tac. *Hist.* 4.56–57; Joseph. *BJ* 2.361–88; Arist. *Or.* 26.72–84; *Orac. Sib.* 13.105, 14.165, 247, with Potter, *Prophecy and History*, 288–89.

3 R. R. R. Smith, "Cultural Choice and Political Identity in Honorific Portrait Statues in the Greek East in the Second Century AD," *JRS* 88 (1998): 56–93, esp. 91–92; J. Trimble, "Replicating the Body Politic: The Herculaneum Women Statue Types in Early Roman Italy," *JRA* 13 (2000): 41–68.

4 See the classic formulation of this view in C. Nicolet, "The Citizen: The Political Man," in *The Romans*, ed. A. Giardina, trans. L. Cochrane (Chicago, 1993), 16–54.

5 *D*. 1.4.1: on the history of *leges de imperio* see J. Béranger, *Recherches sur l'aspect idéologique du principat* (Basel, 1953), 6; P. A. Brunt, "*Lex de imperio Vespasiani*," *JRS* 67 (1977): 95–116.

6 For the significance of the first imperatorial acclamation see B. Campbell, *The Emperor and the Roman Army, 31 BC–AD 235* (Oxford, 1984), 127.

7 *D*. 1.18.4 (1.16.8), 1.16.9.1.

8 *D*. 1.19.1.

9 G. P. Burton, "Proconsuls, Assizes, and the Administration of Justice," *JRS* 65 (1975): 92–106.

10 See the classic statement in Dio Chrys. *Or*. 35.15, with Burton, "Proconsuls, Assizes," 94–99.

11 A. R. Birley, *Hadrian: The Restless Emperor* (London, 1997), 180.

12 Dio 69.16.1–2; Birley, *Hadrian*, 264–65; A. J. S. Spawforth and S. Walker, "The World of the Panhellenion. I. Athens and Eleusis," *JRS* 75 (1985): 78–104; A. J. S. Spawforth and S. Walker, "The World of the Panhellenion. II. Three Dorian Cities," *JRS* 76 (1986): 88–105, with the important qualifications introduced by C. P. Jones, "The Panhellenion," *Chiron* 26 (1996): 29–56, who shows that the initiative for the foundation of the league came, as Dio says, from the Greeks, responding to the encouragement of Hadrian; see also C. P. Jones, "A Decree of Thyatira in Lydia," *Chiron* 29 (1999): 1–21, showing (among other things) how the league might provide a vehicle for relations between cities and governors. A. J. S. Spawforth, "The Panhellenion Again," *Chiron* 29 (1999): 339–52, takes a somewhat different view, while playing down the importance of the Panhellenion as a Roman institution, and arguing that Hadrian's role was central, which made the appeals to Greeks seem like an imposition. Spawforth is correct, I think, to stress the ephemeral nature of the league, since it was so closely associated with a particular emperor – something that will be true of a number of other festivals that we shall see in the third century. His view should act as a corrective to more elaborate interpretations of those institutions. On the other hand, Jones' view that Greek cities did take the initiative when encouraged by the emperor seems to me to be correct and is the natural corollary to Spawforth's position. See also I. Romeo, "The Panhellenion and Ethnic Identity in Hadrianic Greece," *CPh* 97 (2001): 21–40, arguing that Hadrian was influenced by Polemo, and a desire to assert ethnic Hellenism against cultural Hellenism on the part of the inhabitants of Asia Minor, a view that may be seen as a valuable complement to both Jones and Spawforth.

13 G. W. Bowersock, "Hadrian and Metropolis," *BHAC* 17 (Bonn, 1985), 75–88.

14 For fictive kinship groups in archaic Greece see J. M. Hall, *Ethnic Identity in Greek Antiquity* (Cambridge, 1997), 36–37; C. P. Jones, *Kinship Diplomacy in the Ancient World* (Cambridge, Mass., 1999), 6–16.

15 R. Meiggs, *The Athenian Empire* (Oxford, 1972), 294–97.

16 Jones, *Kinship Diplomacy*, 50–65.

17 F. Jacques and J. Scheid, *Rome et l'intégration de l'empire (44 av j.-c–260 ap j.-c.)* (Paris, 1990), 227–30; and F. G. Millar, "*Civitates Liberae, Coloniae*, and Provincial Governors under the Empire," *Mediterraneo Antico* 2 (1999): 95–113, for an excellent summary of the issues.

18 G. P. Burton, "The *Curator Rei Publicae*: Towards a Reappraisal," *Chiron* 9 (1979): 465–87.

19 See the classic studies of A. N. Sherwin-White, *The Roman Citizenship*, 2nd edn. (Oxford, 1973), 264–74; P. D. A. Garnsey, *Social Status and Legal Privilege in the Roman Empire* (Oxford, 1970), esp. 74–76.

20 Acts 21:39.

21 See also Garnsey, *Social Status*, 261.

22 Sherwin-White, *The Roman Citizenship*, 337–52; P. A. Brunt, *Italian Manpower, 225 BC–AD 14* (Oxford, 1971), 525–35.

23 T. J. Cornell, *The Beginnings of Rome* (London, 1995), 295–98.

24 Millar, "*Civitates Liberae*," 96.

25 Millar, "*Civitates Liberae*," 100.

26 A. T. Fear, *Rome and Baetica: Urbanization in Southern Spain c. 50 BC–AD 150* (Oxford, 1996), 134.

27 Brunt, *Italian Manpower*, 246.

28 Brunt, *Italian Manpower*, 246–55; A. D. Rizakis, "*Incolae-Paroikoi*: Populations et communautés dépendantes dans les cités et les colonies romaines de l'orient," *REA* 100 (1998): 599–617.

29 Brunt, *Italian Manpower*, 259, 326–42.

30 M. H. Crawford, *Roman Statutes* (London, 1996) 1, no. 37 fragment (b) col. 1, 8: *aut colonia c(ivium) R(omanorum) aut Latinorum*.

31 Millar, "*Civitates Liberae*," 106.

32 Plin. *HN* 3.139; *ILS* 212.2.16–17 with Sherwin-White, *The Roman Citizenship*, 320; Jacques and Scheid, *Rome et l'intégration*, 244.

33 Rizakis, "*Incolae-Paroikoi*," 599–617.

34 Woolf, *Becoming Roman*, 54–60.

35 Millar, "*Civitates Liberae*," 107.

36 Millar, *The Roman Near East*, 123–24.

37 P. Brunt, "Procuratorial Jurisdiction," *Latomus* 25 (1966): 481–83 (also in P. Brunt, *Roman Imperial Themes* [Oxford, 1990], 182–83).

38 *D.* 30.38.8–10 with F. Millar, *Emperor in Roman World* (Ithaca, NY, 1992), 176; Hekster, "All in the Family: The Appointment of Emperors Designate in the Second Century AD," in *Administration, Prosopography, and Appointment Policies in the Roman Empire*, ed. L. De Blois (Amsterdam, 2001), 47–48, on the wills of Hadrian and Pius in which portions of the *patrimonium* were left to heirs other than their successors.

39 Jacques and Scheid, *Rome et l'intégration*, 187–88.

40 Mitchell, "Administration of Roman Asia," 39, and see, in general, his important discussion on pp. 37–46.

41 *FIRA* 7 122.

42 *CIL* 8, nos. 10570, 14464 ii 11–16; see ch. 1, n. 10 for further details.

43 Tac. *Ann.* 14.31.1; Plin. *Ep.* 10.27.

44 Plin. *Ep.* 10.84 (procurators as part of the *concilium*) with Brunt, "Procuratorial Jurisdiction," 481–84 (also in Brunt, *Roman Imperial Themes*, 182–84). The rule might not hold in all cases, as the conduct of Decianus Catus suggests.

45 See the *senatus consultum* of 177 ed. by J. H. Oliver and R. E. A. Palmer, "Minutes of an Act of the Roman Senate," *Hesperia* 24 (1955): 320–49.

46 Millar, *Emperor in Roman World*, 158–63.

47 *P. Dura* 12.14–16 with Millar, *Emperor in Roman World*, 160 n. 16, and, more generally, 158–60.

48 W. Eck, "The Growth of Administrative Posts," in *The Cambridge Ancient History*, 2nd edn., vol. 11, ed. A. K. Bowman, P. Garnsey, and D. Rathbone (Cambridge,

2000), 238–65, shows that the number of posts increased substantially in the course of the second century.

49 D. S. Potter, "Procurators in Asia and Dacia under Marcus Aurelius: A Case Study of Imperial Initiative in Government," *ZPE* 123 (1998): 270–74.

50 For the gladiators see the *senatus consultum* of 177, n. 45 above.

51 A. H. M. Jones, "Taxation in Antiquity," in A. H. M. Jones, *The Roman Economy*, ed. P. A. Brunt (Oxford, 1974), 164–66, for a succinct summary.

52 P. A. Brunt, "Publicans and the Principate," in Brunt, *Roman Imperial Themes*, 393–414.

53 For Egypt see R. Bagnall and B. W. Frier, *Demography of Roman Egypt*, 2–3; for the rest of the empire see L. Neesen, *Untersuchungen zu den direkten Staatsabgaben der römischen Kaiserzeit (27 v. Chr.–284 n. Chr.)* (Bonn, 1980); P. A. Brunt, "The Revenues of Rome," *JRS* 71 (1981): 161–72, reprinted with additional material in Brunt, *Roman Imperial Themes*, 329–35.

54 For the fourteen-year cycle in Egypt see Bagnall and Frier, *Demography of Roman Egypt*, 2–3; the twelve-year cycle for Syria is implied by Ulpian in *D.* 50.15.3; a regular ten-year cycle in other places is implied by Ulpian in *D.* 50.15.1. with Neesen, *Untersuchungen*, 51. For an ad hoc census ordered at Pessinus by Caracalla in 214 see *AE* 1948 no. 109.

55 Bagnall and Frier, *Demography of Roman Egypt*, 11–26. The account that follows is based upon their discussion, and the able discussion in M. Sharpe, "Shearing Sheep: Rome and the Collection of Taxes in Egypt, 30 BC–AD 200," in Eck and Müller-Luckner, *Lokale Autonomie*, 213–41.

56 *Sel. Pap.* 2.220. For discussion of the applicability of the decree, see Bagnall and Frier, *Demography of Roman Egypt*, 15.

57 See also Neesen, *Untersuchungen*, 48–53.

58 The fundamental study of these taxes is Neesen, *Untersuchungen*, supplemented by Brunt, "The Revenues of Rome," 161–72 (also in Brunt, *Roman Imperial Themes*, 324–46); Duncan-Jones, *Structure and Scale*, 187–98. The general overview by Jones, "Taxation in Antiquity," remains invaluable.

59 *Corpus Agr. Rom.* 168–69 with Neesen, *Untersuchungen*, 44–48 and Duncan-Jones, *Structure and Scale*, 187–88; for technical aspects of the process see J. B. Campbell, *The Writings of the Roman Land Surveyors: Introduction, Text, Translation, and Commentary*, Journal of Roman Studies Monograph 9 (London, 2000), 399 (some elements of the translation in the text are borrowed from Campbell's translation on pp. 161–62).

60 Duncan-Jones, *Structure and Scale*, 200–201.

61 *IGR* 4, no. 914 with D. Magie, *Roman Rule in Asia Minor* (Princeton, 1951), 1400.

62 *CIL* 8, no. 25902 ii.8: *in octonarium agru{m}* (Henchir Mettich) with Kehoe, *Economics of Agriculture*, 46, n. 28 with bibliography (including the dissenting view of M. de Dominicis, "L'apicultura e alcune questioni connesse nel regolomento di un fundo imperiale africano," *RIDA*, 3rd ser. [1960], 391–93); Dio Chrys. *Or.* 38.26 (Nicaea); Neesen, *Untersuchungen*, 54, 69.

63 For a useful list of basic measurements see J. Rowlandson, *Landowners and Tenants in Roman Egypt: The Social Relations of Agriculture in the Oxyrhynchite Nome* (Oxford, 1996), 366.

64 Details in D. Rathbone, *Economic Rationalism and Rural Society in Third-Century AD Egypt* (Cambridge, 1991), 243; Rowlandson, *Landowners and Tenants*, 247.

65 Rowlandson, *Landowners and Tenants*, 54.

66 Rowlandson, *Landowners and Tenants*, 75.

67 App. *Syr.*, 50 (Syria and Cilicia); Joseph. *AJ* 14.202–6, 18.3 with Duncan-Jones, *Structure and Scale*, 189.

68 Neesen, *Untersuchungen*, 69; Duncan-Jones, *Structure and Scale*, 192.

69 Neesen, *Untersuchungen*, 55–56 with notes on these two regions.

70 For taxes in kind see Tac. *Ann.* 2.5.3, 2.6.1, where the reference to the census is in the context of gathering materials for the upcoming campaign in Germany (AD 16). For the Rhine see Tac. *Ann.* 4.72.1: *tributum iis Drusus iusserat modicum pro angustia rerum, ut in usus militares coria boum penderent*, an explicit statement of tax assessment according to local capacities and local needs. For general agnosticism on this point see also Woolf, *Becoming Roman*, 44.

71 Neesen, *Untersuchungen*, 117–48 is particularly valuable.

72 *IG* xii 5.724. See also *IG* xii 5.946.

73 *ILS* 6960 with Neesen, *Untersuchungen*, 118.

74 J. H. Oliver, *Greek Constitutions of Early Roman Emperors from Inscriptions and Papyri*, Memoirs of the American Philosophical Society 178 (Philadelphia, 1989), no. 156. The extent of the registration must be deduced from l.3–4. For a different understanding (limiting it to all free persons) see Neesen, *Untersuchungen*, 121.

75 App. *Mith.* 83, recording that Lucullus imposed a tax on slaves, is not relevant to later practice as it was plainly an emergency measure; contra Neesen, *Untersuchungen*, 121. What is relevant is Caes. *B. Civ.* 3.32.2 (suggesting that it was a novel and indecent act of Pompey, not that he changed it later), which Neesen, *Untersuchungen*, 121, correctly sees as governing later practice.

76 Plin. *HN* 3.3.28 with Neesen, *Untersuchungen*, 252–53.

77 App. *Pun.* 135 with Neesen, *Untersuchungen*, 118. No stress should be placed on Tert. *Apol.* 13.6: *sed enim agri tributo onusti viliores, hominum capita stipendio censa ignobiliora (nam hae sunt notae captivitatis)*. His point here is not that only men paid the head tax, but rather that it fell on the poor rather than the rich. He is contrasting the head tax with the land tax, and both with charges made for sacrifice. Similarly, the records of very elderly persons from a number of provinces reported by Phlegon of Tralles *FGrH* 257 fr. 37 does not mean that they were taxed; rather it suggests that the information was available from the house-to-house register.

78 For figures see Neesen, *Untersuchungen*, 128.

79 Tert. *Apol.* 13.6.

80 For the tax law of Palmyra (*OGIS* 629) see J. F. Matthews, "The Tax Law of Palmyra: Evidence for Economic History in a City of the Roman east," *JRS* 74 (1984): 157–80; for Zarai see *CIL* 8.4508; for Anazarbus see G. Dagron and D. Feissel, *Inscriptions de Cilicie* (Paris, 1987), n. 108, with some additional remarks in D. S. Potter, "Recent Inscriptions from Flat Cilicia," *JRA* 2 (1989): 310.

81 *OGIS* 629 iiia 40–63.

82 *AE* 1989 no. 681.

83 *OGIS* 674.

84 Plin. *HN* 6.84 (Annius Plocamus); 12.65 (outflow of 100 million HS per annum in the trade with India and the east) with Brunt, "Publicans and the Principate," 409.

85 Brunt, "Publicans and the Principate," 407–8.

86 Brunt, "Publicans and the Principate," 407 (he is not to be blamed for the suggestion concerning the reason for the change).

87 See also Jones, "Taxation in Antiquity," 167.

88 Brunt, "Publicans and the Principate," 402–6, for the inheritance tax and the manumission tax; Duncan-Jones, *Structure and Scale*, 195, for the auction tax.

89 Duncan-Jones, *Structure and Scale*, 195–96.

90 App. *B. Civ.* 4.102, 124–25, 147, 5.79, 87; Dio 47.14.5, 16.2–3; Plin. *HN* 37.81–82 (the triumvirs); Suet. *Calig.* 38.1 (Caligula). For other late republican precedents see Millar, *Emperor in Roman World*, 164–67.

91 Tac. *Ann.* 1.75.4, 3.18.1.

92 Amm. Marc. 30.8: . . . *torrentis ritu ferabatur in divites*. The description is of Aurelian, when he was faced by a treasury emptied by Gallienus. Ammianus in fact suggests that his behavior was justified by the emergency of the state, unlike the cruelty of Valentinian. See also M. Hendy, *Studies in the Byzantine Monetary Economy, c. 300–1450* (Cambridge, 1985), 231.

93 *ILS* 5163.8.

94 For rewards to soldiers see Campbell, *Emperor and Roman Army*, 181–203.

95 Dio 72.34.4.

96 What follows depends upon A. S. L. Farquharson, *The Meditations of Marcus Aurelius Antoninus*, 2 vols. (Oxford, 1944), whose translation is used (with some adaptations) in the text; R. Rutherford, *The Meditations of Marcus Aurelius: A Study* (Oxford, 1989); and, especially, P. A. Brunt, "Marcus Aurelius in His *Meditations*," *JRS* 64 (1974): 1–20.

97 Rutherford, *Meditations of Marcus Aurelius*, 65 with n. 57 on the text.

98 *Med.* 3.14.

99 *Med.* 3.5; see also 7.44, 8.8 (although he cannot read, he can restrain his arrogance); but contrast 8.1, 9.26, 10.8, on his falling short of the ideal and see Rutherford, *Meditations of Marcus Aurelius*, 234.

100 *Med.* 4.16. For the sentiments see Farquharson ad loc. For the importance of listening see 4.38, 6.53, 7.4, 10.12; tolerating those who disagree see 6.20, 6.50, 7.26, 7.62, 8.17, 9.16, 9.27, 11.9; people with whom he is angry, 9.34, 42, 11.18.4; accepting help, 7.7, 8.16; people who are wrong, see 6.27; people who speak ill of him, 8.49, 11.13.

101 *Med.* 7.24; compare also 8.29.

102 *Med.* 10.10.

103 *Med.* 5.10, 9.2, 11.8 with Brunt, "Marcus Aurelius," 12.

104 Tac. *Ann.* 1.3.7 and D. S. Potter, "Political Theory in the *Senatus Consultum Pisonianum*," in "The *Senatus Consultum De Cn. Pisone Patre*: Text, Translation, Discussion," special issue of *AJP*, ed. C. Damon and S. Takács, 120 (1999): 65–88.

105 Joseph. *AJ* 19.228.

106 See F. G. Millar, "Emperors at Work," *JRS* 57 (1967): 9–19; and Millar, *Emperor in Roman World*, 644–51, restating the thesis most forcefully set out on pp. 228–59.

107 Oliver, *Greek Constitutions*, nos. 108–18 with commentary and bibliography. For the inscription of unfavorable responses to other cities, which are also inscribed on the Aphrodisias wall, see J. Reynolds, *Aphrodisias and Rome*, Journal of Roman Studies Monograph 1 (London, 1982), nos. 13, 14; no. 12 is a letter of Augustus to Ephesus ordering it to return a stolen statue of Eros that had originally been dedicated by Julius Caesar at Aphrodisias. In doing so he further notes that "Eros is not a suitable offering when given to Artemis," an interesting example of Augustus' concern for religious propriety (rather than a joke – *pace* Reynolds ad loc.).

108 Apul. *Met.* 9.39 with F. G. Millar, "The World of the *Golden Ass*," *JRS* 71 (1981): 67 (also in S. J. Harrison, *Oxford Readings in the Roman Novel* [Oxford, 1999], 255).

109 Pp. 22–23 above.

110 J. Reynolds, "New Letters from Hadrian to Aphrodisias: Trials, Taxes, Gladiators, and an Aqueduct," *JRA* 13 (2000), letter 2 (ll. 13–26). The translation offered here is adapted from Reynolds's on p. 15.

111 For a valuable discussion of Braudel's thought in the context of ancient history see now Shaw, "Challenging Braudel," 420, noting that Braudel is not at all clear how narrative and deep structures are to be related, but see too his comments on p. 427 on the problem of change.

112 Pp. 5–6 above.

113 C. Nicolet, "Augustus, Government, and the Propertied Classes," in *Caesar Augustus: Seven Aspects*, ed. F. G. Millar and E. Segal (Oxford, 1984), 92; R. J. Talbert, *The Senate of Imperial Rome* (Princeton, 1984), 10–11.

114 *D.* 24.1.42 (Gaius): *ut ecce si uxor viro lati clavii petenti gratia donet*; Ulpian, *Regulae* 7.1 with Millar, *Emperor in Roman World*, 279; Talbert, *Senate of Imperial Rome*, 11–15.

115 *D.* 23.2.44 (Paul) with *AE* 1978 n. 145 (*senatus consultum* of 19 AD) section 7 and Talbert, *Senate of Imperial Rome*, 39.

116 K. Hopkins and G. P. Burton, "Ambition and Withdrawal: The Senatorial Aristocracy under the Emperors," in *Death and Renewal: Sociological Studies in Roman History*, ed. K. Hopkins, vol. 2 (Cambridge, 1983), 145.

117 *D.* 24.1.42 (Gaius) (note 114 above).

118 Hopkins and Burton, "Ambition and Withdrawal," 184–93, for a succinct summary. For details in the second and third centuries see G. Alföldy, *Konsulat und Senatorenstand unter den Antoninen: prosopographische Untersuchungen zur senatorischen Führungsschicht* (Bonn, 1977), 61–75; P. Leunissen, *Konsuln und Konsulare in der Zeit Commodus bis Severus Alexander (180–235 n. Chr.)* (Amsterdam, 1989), 355–74.

119 E. Gabba, *Republican Rome, the Army, and the Allies*, trans. P. J. Cuff (Oxford, 1976), 142–43, is fundamental.

120 For the closure of the Roman *nobilitas* in the late republic see P. A. Brunt, "*Nobilitas* and *Novitas*," *JRS* 72 (1982): 1–17, significant for the first century BC despite the objection to the overall analysis raised by D. R. Shackleton Bailey, "Nobiles and Novi Reconsidered," *AJP* 107 (1986): 255–60 (also in D. R. Shackleton Bailey, *Selected Classical Papers* [Ann Arbor, 1997], 309–13); E. Badian, "The Consuls, 179–49 BC," *Chiron* 20 (1990): 371–413; for the dominance of consulars in the business of the senate see M. Bonnefond-Coudry, *Le sénat de la république romaine de la guerre d'Hannibal à Auguste* (Paris, 1989), 620–44, 676–82 (a nuanced presentation of a standard view).

121 H. Halfmann, *Die Senatoren aus dem östlichen Teil des Imperium Romanum bis zum Ende des 2. Jh. N. Chr.* (Göttingen, 1979), 100–1.

122 R. Syme, *The Roman Revolution* (Oxford, 1939), 490–508, remains the classic treatment.

123 Tac. *Ann.* 3.55. For the possibility that Tacitus was from Narbonensis see R. Syme, *Tacitus* (Oxford, 1958), 611–24. For discussion of an inscription that may possibly record his career see now A. R. Birley, "The Life and Death of Cornelius Tacitus," *Historia* 49 (2000): 230–47.

124 Suet. *Otho* 1; Tac. *Hist.* 2.50; *PIR* S 108–9.

125 For the legates of Pompey and Metellus Creticus in 67 see T. R. S. Broughton, *The Magistrates of the Roman Republic*, vol. 2 (New York, 1952), 147–52, showing Licinius Sacerdos (pr. 75) with Metellus and Cornelius Lentulus Clodianus (cos. 72), L. Cornelius Sisenna (pr. 78), L. Gellius Publicola (cos. 72), A. Manlius Torquatus (pr *c.* 70), and L. Manlius Torquatus (pr. 68) with Pompey. For Caesar's legates see *MRR* 2, 198–99 (58 BC, one certain ex-praetor, Labienus); p. 204–5 (again only one certain ex-praetor), but note also Q. Cicero (pr. 66) serving Pompey, Valerius Flaccus (pr. 63) and Vergilius (pr. 62) under Gabinius in Macedonia; *MRR* 2, 213 for 56 BC (same breakdown); *MRR* 2, 219–20 for 55 BC with (again) Labienus, Plaetorius (pr. 64) under Spinther, Afranius (pr. 72 ? cos. 60) and Petreius (pr. before 63) under Pompey in Spain; *MRR* 2, 225–27 for 54 BC with Labienus and Q. Cicero under Caesar, Afranius and Petreius under Pompey and MRR 2, 231–32 (same individuals in the same places) in 53 BC; in 52 BC see *MRR* 2, 238–39 (in addition to those of 54–53 BC) see L. Julius Caesar (cos. 64) with Caesar and Nigidius Figulus (pr. 58) in Asia.

126 W. Eck, "Beförderungskriterien innerhalb der senatorischen Laufbahn, dargestellt an der Zeit von 69 bis 138 n. Chr.," *ANRW* 2.1 (1974), 205 on the number of consulships compared to the number of praetorians; Alföldy, *Konsulat und Senatorenstand*, 11; A. R. Birley, *The Fasti of Roman Britain* (Oxford, 1981), 24–25.

127 Talbert, *Senate of Imperial Rome*, 202.

128 Talbert, *Senate of Imperial Rome*, 206–7.

129 For the number of consuls per year from 143 to 155 see Alföldy, *Konsulat und Senatorenstand*, 14.

130 This table is based on Birley, *Fasti of Roman Britain*, 16–17; for the proportions of all officeholders who are known, see Leunissen, *Konsuln und Konsulare*, 23.

131 This table is based on Birley, *Fasti of Roman Britain*, 26–27.

132 W. Eck, "Emperor, Senate, and Magistrates," in Bowman, Garnsey, and Rathbone, *The Cambridge Ancient History*, 11: 231 (number of provincial posts each year in the second half of the second century); 11: 232 (proportion of career spent in provincial posts).

133 Dio 52.21 trans. Cary; see also 52.33.3 on the importance of learning the character of high officials by observing the way that they act; see also Eck, "Emperor, Senate, and Magistrates," 230, on the "socialization" aspect of the career.

134 See esp. the important discussion in J. E. Lendon, *Empire of Honour: The Art of Government in the Roman World* (Oxford, 1997), 181–85.

135 For details of his career (often debated in points of detail) see Leunissen, *Konsuln und Konsulare*, 163, with bibliography; and A. M. Gowing, *The Triumviral Narratives of Appian and Cassius Dio* (Ann Arbor, 1992), 19–32.

136 See A. Andermahr, *Totus in Praediis. Senatorischer Grundbesitz in Italien in der frühen und hohen Kaiserzeit* (Bonn, 1998), 210, showing also that the *figilinae* that had connected Apronianus to Ostia were misread.

137 Dio 75.15.3, 76.2.

138 W. Eck, *Tra epigrafia prosopografia e archeologia* (Rome, 1996), 220.

139 *AE* 1975 no. 880. All known senatorial benefactors (as of 1996) to their hometowns are listed in Eck, *Tra epigrafia*, 187–203.

140 *TAM* 2.414.

141 Listed in Eck, *Tra epigrafia*, 177–87.

142 Phil. *V. Soph.* 534, noting that Antoninus was reconciled with Polemo by Hadrian.

143 Arist. *Or. Rom.* 59; for the circumstances see R. Syme, "Greeks Invading the Roman Government," in *The Seventh Stephen J. Brademas Sr. Lecture* (Brookline, Mass., 1982) (also in Syme, *Roman Papers*, ed. A. R. Birley, vol. 4 [Oxford, 1988], 8).

144 Dio 52.19.3 (no leaders of revolts); 52.15.2–3 (value of aristocratic government).

145 Dio 71.31.1; for Cassius' career see R. Syme, "Avidius Cassius: His Rank, Age, and Quality," *BHAC 1984–85* (Bonn, 1987), 207–22 (also in Syme, *Roman Papers*, ed. A. R. Birley, vol. 5 [Oxford, 1988], 689–701).

146 R. Syme, "Antonine Government and Governing Class," *Scienze dell' Antichità* 1 (1987) (n.v.) (also in Syme, *Roman Papers*, 4: 668–88).

147 D. S. Potter, "The Inscriptions on the Bronze Herakles from Mesene: Vologaeses IV's War with Rome and the Date of Tacitus' *Annales*," *ZPE* 88 (1991): 282–85.

148 For the list see Alföldy, *Konsulat und Senatorenstand*, 25. For a list of consular fathers with consular sons see Alföldy, 323–26. The connection between M. Iallus Bassus and Q. Iallus Bassus suspected in *PIR²* I 5 is possible – the latter may be the brother of the former.

149 *PIR²* I 5 for Bassus; C 874 for Fronto. For Fabianus see Andermahr, *Totus in Praediis*, 428 (two inscriptions, neither necessarily proving origin).

150 *PIR²* A 1088; for Vettius see H.-G. Pflaum, "Deux familles sénatoriales des iie et iiie siècles," *Journal des Savants* (1961): 108.

151 *PIR²* C 973.

152 The basic study of his career remains G. Alföldy, "P. Helvius Pertinax und M. Valerius Maximianus," *Situla* 14–15 (1974): 199–215 (also in Alföldy, *Römische Heeresgeschichte: Beiträge, 1962–1985* [Amsterdam, 1987], 326–67).

153 *HA V. Pert.* 1.4–5; see also Dio 74.3.1, saying that this gave him just enough money to get by. Dio's information about his earlier career is not good.

154 *PIR²* H 40, he was *consul ordinarius* in 144. The application may not have resulted in appointment as a centurion, but rather as a lower-ranking officer; see Birley, *Fasti of Roman Britain*, 143.

155 *PIR²* H 39.

156 For other possible patrons at this point see Birley, *Fasti of Roman Britain*, 144.

157 *HA V. Pert.* 2.4 with Alföldy, "P. Helvius Pertinax," 201 (also in *Römische Heeresgeschichte*, 328).

158 *HA V. Pert.* 2.4; the connection with Pompeianus clearly impressed Dio; see Dio 74.3.1–2; see also Alföldy, "P. Helvius Pertinax," 203 (also in Alföldy, *Römische Heeresgeschichte*, 330).

159 *HA V. Pert.* 2.6; see also Alföldy, "P. Helvius Pertinax," 206 (also in *Römische Heeresgeschichte*, 333, without discussion of Marcus' attitude).

160 Dio 74.3.2–3. He showed similar respect for Acilius Glabrio, *PIR²* A 69; see p. 94.

161 S. Demougin, *L'ordre équestre sous les Julio-claudiens* (Rome, 1988), 851, provides the summary upon which this account is based.

162 W. Eck, "*Ordo Equitum Romanorum, Ordo Libertorum*: Freigelassene und ihre Nachkommen im römischen Ritterstand," in *L'ordre équestre d'une aristocratie (iie siècle av. J.-C.–iiie siècle ap. J.-C.)*, ed. S. Demougin, H. Devijver, and M.-T. Rapsaet-Charlier (Paris, 1999), 5–29.

163 Demougin, *L'ordre équestre*, 855–57.

164 The full style *ab epistulis latinis* is attested on *ILS* 1453.

165 Phil. *V. Soph.* 571 with Millar, *Emperor in Roman World*, 91; G. W. Bowersock, *Greek Sophists in the Roman Empire* (Oxford, 1969), 53–54.

166 Phil. *V. Soph.* 587 (personal style), 588–89 (encounter with Marcus), 589 (the chair at Rome) with Millar, *Emperor in Roman World*, 91–92; Bowersock, *Greek Sophists*, 55, 91–92.

167 Phil. *V. Soph.* 627, saying that he visited many parts of the world in the emperor's company, a description that would seem to fit Caracalla, as would the attack on him by Philostratus of Lemnos.

168 Oliver, *Greek Constitutions*, no. 244.

169 Phil. *V. Soph.* 607.

170 See Bowersock, *Greek Sophists*, 92, for other ramifications of the quarrel.

171 Dio 71.24.2 with *Med.* 5.33; Dio 71.26.4 with *Med.* 6.2 and discussion by Farquharson xiv. See also Herod. 1.2.3.

172 Changes in secretarial prose style are crucial to the (highly controversial) argument of T. Honoré, *Emperors and Lawyers* (London, 1981).

173 *HA V. Comm.* 13.6. The assertion in the text that the ultimate source here is Marius Maximus is open to dispute; for bibliography see D. S. Potter, *Literary Texts and the Roman Historian* (London, 1999), 199 n. 80. For a coherent and powerful exposition of the opposite view, that the good information in the lives derives from an unknown biographer, see T. D. Barnes, *The Sources of the Historia Augusta* (Brussels, 1978), 98–107. For the present point the issue of the specific source is irrelevant since this passage of the *vita Commodi* plainly derives from autopsy.

174 For careers of senior prefects see now R. Sablayrolles, "Fastigium equestre: Les grands préfectures équestres," in Demougin, Devijver, and Rapsaet-Charlier, *L'ordre équestre*, 351–89.

175 *PIR²* B 69 with Birley, *Marcus Aurelius*, 156.

176 *PIR²* M 25.

177 *PIR²* F 584.

178 *PIR* T 24, the date of his promotion to the prefecture, no later than 177; see *AE* 1971 534.

179 *PIR* T 146.

180 Phil. *V. Soph.* 561; Dio suggests that he was a good man even if he was very badly educated; see esp. 61.5.2–3.

181 The key passage reflecting criteria for appointment is Fronto, *Ep. ad Marc. Caes.* 5.52: *petit nunc procurationem ex forma suo loco ac iu<st>o tempore*; see also Fronto, *Ep. ad Ant.* 9 (implying annual appointment cycle). For the view adopted here see H. Devijver, "Les relations sociales des chevaliers romains," in Demougin, Devijver, and Rapsaet-Charlier, *L'ordre équestre*, 237–69, arguing that eligibility for promotion depended on factors such as length of service and merit as well as patronage; on these points see also S. Demougin, "Considérations sur l'avancement dans les carrières procuratoriennes équestres," in De Blois, *Administration, Prosopography*, 24–34. For the view that there was no control over patronage on the grounds of performance see R. P. Saller, *Personal Patronage under the Early Empire* (Cambridge, 1982), 110. P. A. Brunt, "The Administrators of Roman Egypt," *JRS* 65 (1975): 141 (also in Brunt, *Roman Imperial Themes*, 244), offers a strong statement in favor of "amateurism."

182 Eck, "Growth of Administrative Posts," 11: 261.

183 Saller, *Personal Patronage*, 78–117.

184 P. A. Brunt, "Princeps and Equites," *JRS* 73 (1983): 42–75, demolishes the notion that senators and equestrians held different attitudes towards the government. He looks at the situation from the point of view of the equestrian order, which may somewhat skew his conclusions, as suggested in the text.

185 Lendon, *Empire of Honour*, 177–236.

3 CRISES IN GOVERNMENT

1 M. Aur. *Med.* 1.17.4 (brother and children), 1.17.8 (wife).

2 For the qualities of Lucius Verus see *HA V. Marci* 29.1; for a list of four lovers of Faustina, the information derives from Marius Maximus, and is repeated in the case of one of them at *HA V. Comm.* 8.1, assuming that the reference is to L. Tutilius Pontianus Gentianus, cos suff. 183. For Commodus see n. 7 below.

3 Dio 72.22.3 on Faustina and Cassius; for Avidius Cassius see p. 73 above.

4 Joseph. *AJ* 18.214 with Potter, *Prophets and Emperors*, 159; for the second century, pointing out the biological links between the "adoptive emperors," see now the discussion in Hekster, "All in the Family."

5 Hekster, "All in the Family," 43–44, pointing out that it was possible that Antoninus was distantly related to Hadrian.

6 For the evidence see D. Kienast, *Römische Kaisertabelle: Grundzüge einer römischen Kaiserchronologie* (Darmstadt, 1990), 147. Commodus' first imperial salutation occurred in 177, and it is only in the summer of that year that he appears with the full titulature of his father. Nonetheless, November 27 was afterwards celebrated as the *dies imperii*; see now O. Hekster, *Commodus: An Emperor at the Crossroads* (Amsterdam, 2002), 38–39.

7 Dio 72.1.1; Herod. 1.3.1–3; *HA V. Comm.* 15.4, attesting to Marius' statement concerning Commodus' inclusion of things that were foul or cruel in the *acta diurna*; *V. Comm.* 13.2 on Marius' preservation of verses referring to a conspicuous growth on Commodus' groin; *V. Comm.* 18.2 on Marius' preservation of the acclamations

against Commodus in the senate. It is not unreasonable to assume that the themes of cruelty and debauchery that run throughout the biography come from Marius.

8 H. Halfmann, *Itinera principum. Geschichte und Typologie der Kaiserreisen im römischen Reich* (Stuttgart, 1986), 213, for the chronology.

9 *HA V. Marci* 27.10; *HA V. Comm.* 3.5; Dio 71.33.4, 72.1.3 with Potter, "Emperors," 55.

10 For Trajan's ambitions see Potter, "Inscriptions on Bronze Herakles," 282–83, arguing against C. S. Lightfoot, "Trajan's Parthian War and the Fourth-Century Perspective," *JRS* 80 (1990): 115–26, the most recent and best statement of the view that Trajan did not aim to annex Iraq. For the adjustment of frontiers after 165 see Millar, *The Roman Near East*, 111–14.

11 App. *Praef.* 7 with *HA V. Ant. Pii* 7.9, 9.10 with Potter, "Emperors," 54.

12 P. Salway, *Roman Britain* (Oxford, 1984), 200–206, though some forts continued to be occupied north of the Hadrianic wall.

13 For the terms of Marcus' treaties with northern tribes see M. Stahl, "Zwischen Abgrenzung und Integration: Die Verträge der Kaiser Mark Aurel und Commodus mit den Völken jenseits der Donau," *Chiron* 19 (1989): 289–317, summarized with minor adjustment in Potter, "Emperors," 61–63. For ideological aspects of the treaties see also Potter, "Empty Areas." For a different view, which to my mind places excessive emphasis on a single medallion, see the discussion in Hekster, *Commodus*, 41–42.

14 Halfmann, *Itinera principum*, 216.

15 J. Fitz, "A Military History of Pannonia from the Marcomannic Wars to the Death of Alexander Severus (180–235)," *A. Arch. Hung.* 14 (1962): 87–89.

16 Pp. 74–76 above for issues within the senatorial aristocracy.

17 For the relationship between Saoterus and Commodus see *HA V. Comm.* 3.6: *subactore suo Saotero post se in curro locato ita triumphavit ut eum saepius cervice reflexa publice oscularetur.* The word *subactor* is rare, elsewhere appearing in *HA V. Hel.* 5.4, 31.7, passages that may also derive from Marius Maximus. For the meaning of the word in this context see J. N. Adams, *The Latin Sexual Vocabulary* (London, 1982), 155. A less sensationalizing historian has taken the chariot ride as a simple sign of imperial favor; see Millar, *Emperor in Roman World*, 81.

18 Hekster, *Commodus*, 55–59.

19 *HA V. Comm.* 4.4.1; Dio 72.4.5, saying that Lucilla was motivated by her hatred of her husband; Herod. 1.8.3–4, saying that Lucilla was motivated by her jealousy of Commodus' wife, Bruttia Crispina. Parallels between the three accounts are systematically collected in F. Kolb, *Literarische Beziehungen zwischen Cassius Dio, Herodian und der Historia Augusta* (Bonn, 1972). It is an admirable work even though I find myself at odds with the general conclusions (see p. 164 below for a discussion of the relationship between Dio and Marius Maximus, whom I take to be the basic source of the *Historia Augusta*).

20 Herod. 1.8.3–4.

21 *HA V. Comm.* 4.4 (the statement that Norbanus and Paralius were young men is an assumption based on the fact that neither appears to have been advanced in his career and the fact that they kept company with Pompeianus and Quadratus). The youth of Pompeianus is attested by Dio 72.4.5. See also H.-G. Pflaum, "La valeur de l'information historique de la vita Commodi à la lumière des personnages nommément cités par le biographe," *BHAC 1970* (Bonn, 1972), 203–5.

22 The role of Paternus would seem to be confirmed by the use of *frumentarii* to kill Saoterus at roughly the same time as the assassination attempt; see *HA V. Comm.* 4.5–6 with Hekster, *Commodus*, 53–54. Dio 72.12.2 (see also Dio 77.21.2) dates his death later in the reign, accusing Cleander of the deed. It seems to me that the

circumstantial details offered by *HA V. Comm.* 4.5–6, which place the murder of Saoterus in the immediate aftermath of the assassination attempt, are to be preferred. Dio plainly did not think that Paternus was involved in the conspiracy – and the murder of Saoterus is the best evidence that he was.

23 *HA V. Comm.* 4.3 for this version of the words; Dio 72.4.4 has *idou touto soi hê boule pepomphen;* Herod. 1.8.6 gives the gist of a similar announcement. For the location see Dio 72.4.4: *to theatron to kunêgetikon;* for its identification as the Colosseum, see R. Rea, "Amphitheatrum," in M. Steinby, ed., *Lexicon Iopographicum Urbis Romanae* (Oxford, 1995), 1: 30.

24 *HA V. Comm.* 4.4, 5.7; Dio 72.4.6 (Lucilla).

25 Dio 72.5.1–2.

26 *HA V. Comm.* 4.7–9.

27 Dio 72.5.3–6.5; *HA V. Comm.* 4.9 with Pflaum, "Valeur de l'information historique," 205–6.

28 *HA V. Comm.* 4.8 for Secundus (who appears to have been retired if it is right to press the phrase *qui epistulas imperatorias curarat* that far).

29 Leunissen, *Konsuln und Konsulare,* 399, for details.

30 Dio 72.7.

31 Hekster, *Commodus,* 55.

32 *HA V. Comm.* 4.7; Herod. 1.8.8.

33 F. G. Millar, *A Study of Cassius Dio* (Oxford, 1964), 128, objects to what he regards as the simplistic notion that Dio had received favors from Perennis.

34 For the competitive aspect of Dio's history with respect to Marius Maximus see pp. 164–65 below.

35 Millar, *Emperor in Roman World,* 80–81.

36 *PIR²* A 1481.

37 Dio 72.12.1 (Damostratia).

38 *AE* 1952 no. 6.14–16. This may be compared with the position of Saoterus, a native of Nicomedia, who was honored by the city for his services to it; see Dio 72.12.2.

39 Dio 72.12.1; see also Herod. 1.12.3.

40 Birley, *Fasti of Roman Britain,* 140–42.

41 Dio 72.9; supported, at least in principle, by *HA V. Comm.* 6.2.

42 Dio 72.9.3.

43 For the history of acclamations in ancient government see Potter, "Performance, Power, and Justice," 132–47.

44 Fronto, *Ep. ad Marc. Caes.* 1.8.

45 Joseph. *AJ* 19.24, trans. Wiseman. See also Millar, *Emperor in Roman World,* 368–75; A. D. Cameron, *Circus Factions* (Oxford, 1976), 157–92.

46 G. Aldrete and D. J. Mattingly, "Feeding the City: The Organization, Scale, and Operation of the Supply System for Rome," in Potter and Mattingly, *Life, Death, and Entertainment,* 181–204, offer the best short introduction to the subject. See also P. Garnsey, *Famine and Food Supply in the Graeco-Roman World* (Cambridge, 1988), 182–243; G. Rickman, *The Corn Supply of Ancient Rome* (Oxford, 1980); and now the splendid work of C. Virlouvet, *Tessara Frumentaria: Les procédures de la distribution du blé public à Rome à la fin de la république et au début de l'empire* (Rome, 1995).

47 Dio 72.12.4 (consuls); *HA V. Comm.* 6.10–11 (praetorian prefects); for the title *a pugione* see *HA V. Comm.* 6.13 (implying equal status with the praetorian prefects); see also *AE* 1961 no. 280.7–8: *M. Aurelius Cleander | a cubicu(lo) et a pugione;* the meaning of *a pugione* is clarified by the translation into Greek in *AE* 1952 no. 6.15: *kai epi {tên tou thalamou kai t} ou sômatos,* which in turn confirms the accuracy of

Herod. 1.12.3: *tên te tou sômatos phrouran kai tên tou thalamou* . . . On the point that he would never become praetorian prefect see Hekster, *Commodus*, 70.

48 *PIR²* B 170 with *HA V. Comm.* 5.9; Dio 72.4.6.

49 *PIR²* M 261.

50 Dio 72.4.6; Hipp. *Ref.* 9.12.12; *ILS* 406 (dedication to Marcia at Anagnina); *ILS* 1909 (statue in honor of her father as patron of Anagnina). *ILS* 406 shows that she was awarded the status of a *femina stolata*, a status ordinarily reserved for a free woman who had borne three children.

51 *PIR²* E 3.

52 J. Humphrey, *Roman Circuses: Arenas for Chariot Racing* (Berkeley, 1986), 76, with discussion of the improbability of higher numbers.

53 Dio 72.13.5; contra Herod. 1.13.1–2, who attributes this to Fadilla, Commodus' surviving sister. If Herodian is correct here, it would be the only time that he has better information about events in the palace than did Dio. For these events in the context of urban violence see C. R. Whittaker, "The Revolt of Papirius Dionysius AD 190," *Historia* 13 (1964): 348–69 (also in Whittaker, *Land, City, and Trade in the Roman Empire* [Brookfield, VT, 1993], ch. 6).

54 This is pure speculation in the absence of any evidence for another court favorite and based upon the high status that Marcia obtained; see *HA V. Comm.* 8.6, 11.9 for suggestions of Marcia's influence, and the evidence for her visibility collected in n. 50 above. Note also *HA V. Comm.* 9.2–3 for the execution of various supporters within the palace, including concubines with whom Cleander had children, actions that would work in favor of Marcia.

55 M. P. Speidel, "Commodus as God-Emperor and the Army," *JRS* 83 (1993): 109–14; Hekster, *Commodus*, 117–29 for recent summaries of the evidence.

56 Dio 72.21.1–2.

57 Dio 72.22.4–6; *HA V. Comm.* 17.1–2; Herod. 1.17.1–11; *PIR²* A 358. Herodian adds considerable details to the accounts of Dio and the *Vita Comm.*, saying that Commodus had decided on the thirty-first to execute Marcia, Laetus, and Eclectus, and that he discovered the plot when Marcia intercepted the tablets upon which Commodus had decreed their fate while greeting the boy whom Commodus kept with him. This may be true, though it may also have been a story circulated after the murder to justify the actions of the killers. Marcia is given a leading role in all three accounts. Both Dio and *HA V. Comm.* 16.8–9 suggest a less dramatic, but more probable, scenario whereby the conspirators were fed up with his erratic conduct. Herodian says that the poison was delivered in a drinking cup rather than through dinner.

58 Talbert, *Senate of Imperial Rome*, 200–1.

59 Dio 73.1.2–3; Herod. 2.2.5–10; *HA V. Pert.* 5.7.

60 Dio 73.1.1; see also Dio 73.2.5; Herod. 2.1.2–4.

61 *HA V. Pert.* 4.9, also stating that Claudius Pompeianus came to him there. If so then it suggests a much more involved conspiracy, as Pompeianus did not reside at Rome, according to Dio, and only came there after Pertinax's accession (Dio 73.2.2). Herodian is, as usual, the odd man out, as he says that the soldiers took Pertinax to the palace, and that he went from there to the senate house in the morning (Herod. 2.2.1).

62 Dio 73.1.4.

63 Béranger, *Recherches*, 159.

64 Dio 73.1.3; *HA V. Pert.* 4.7, 5.7, 6.3; Herod. 2.5.1.

65 Phil. *V. Soph.* 590, 593; for the reception of Commodus' image in the provinces see Hekster, *Commodus*, 168–86.

66 P. 79 above.

67 Potter, "Political Theory," 65–71.

68 Oliver and Palmer, "Minutes of an Act," 327–8.

69 Potter, *Prophets and Emperors*, 118–21.

70 The descriptions of Pertinax's conduct in Dio and *HA V. Pert.* read at times like a virtual reprise of Pliny's panegyric on Trajan; see esp. Plin. *Pan.* 37–43, 50.

71 Herod. 2.4.2.

72 *HA V. Pert.* 7.6–11; Dio 73.5.4–5.

73 *HA V. Pert.* 8.1; Dio 73.6.2.

74 Dio 73.5.2; *HA V. Pert.* 9.8, 10; Herod. 2.4.8; for precedents see Plin. *Pan.* 34–35; implied in Dio 66.19.3, 68.1.

75 *HA V. Pert.* 7.4.

76 Herod. 2.4.6.

77 P. 5 above.

78 Herod. 2.4.7.

79 Dio 73.13.4; *HA V. Jul.* 3.7.

80 Dio 73.8.5; *HA V. Pert.* 10.10.

81 Dio 73.10.3.

82 Dio 73.9.2; *HA V. Pert.* 11.1 gives the number as three hundred.

83 Dio 73.10.2 says that they sheathed their swords. *HA V. Pert.* 11.9 identifies the assailant as Tausius and says that he threw his spear; Dio omits the spear. An alternative account has Pertinax killed while hiding in his bedroom (*HA V. Pert.* 11.13).

84 *PIR²* F 373; Dio 73.7.1 (appointment), 11.1 (at the camp); *HA V. Jul.* 2.6; Herod. 2.6.8 (again eccentric, as it places the events two days after the assassination, though the overall account is largely in agreement with that of *HA V. Jul.* 2.6 rather than with Dio 73.2–3).

85 *HA V. Jul.* 2.4 with circumstantial detail (the initial trip to the Forum) not in Dio 73.11.2.

86 *HA V. Jul.* 2.6; echoed in Herod. 2.6.10; omitted altogether by Dio.

87 *HA V. Jul.* 2.6 with a similar account in Herod. 2.6.10–11.

88 The notion of an auction is in Dio 73.11.3. There is no auction in Herod. 2.6.10, which merely records that he promised more money than any man had thought possible; *HA V. Jul.* 2.7 does not mention the donative at all, and says that the guard insisted that he not avenge himself on Sulpicianus.

89 *HA V. Jul.* 2.7, 2.6.11–12.

90 *HA V. Jul.* 3.3; Dio 12.1–5 giving details of the speech at which he says he was present; Herod. 2.6.12–13, without mention of the meeting of the senate.

91 Suet. *Jul.* 37.2; see also Plin. *Pan.* 17.2; Plin. *HN* 9.118; Stat. *Theb.* 6.126, 12.524; Val. Flacc. 3.529; in all cases they carried pictures of conquered peoples as well. See also *Acta Pauli et Theclae* 19 for placards identifying criminals at executions giving their crimes, and, perhaps most famously, John 19:19–22.

92 Potter, "Performance, Power, and Justice," 142–44.

93 Joseph. *AJ* 19.237–66.

94 Suet. *Ner.* 48.2.

95 Tac. *Hist.* 1.31–47.

96 Dio 73.13.2–4; *HA V. Jul.* 4.1–6.

97 Dio 73.13.5; *HA V. Jul.* 4.7; Herod. 2.7.3.

98 J. C. Edmondson, "Dynamic Arenas: Gladiatorial Presentations in the City of Rome and the Construction of Roman Society during the Early Empire," in Slater, *Roman Theater and Society*, 109–10.

99 *HA V. Jul.* 5.1.

100 Herod. 2.8–9; at 2.9.4 Herodian identifies Severus as his source. J. Hasebroek, *Untersuchungen zur Geschichte des Kaisers Septimius Severus* (Heidelberg, 1921), 21. Hasebroek's analysis of these events remains fundamental. See also pp. 101–02.

101 For the possibility that the plan to invade Italy was originally devised as a response to the plot of Falco see A. R. Birley, *Septimius Severus: The African Emperor* (New Haven, 1989), 97.

102 Birley, *Septimius Severus*, 35.

103 Birley, *Septimius Severus*, 24.

104 What follows is based on Birley, *Septimius Severus*, 46–58.

105 *HA V. Sev.* 3.2 (8.1 by implication); *IRT* 410–11; *CIL* 8, no. 19494 with M. T. Rapsaet-Charlier, *Prosopographie des femmes de l'ordre sénatorial (Ier–IIe siècles)* (Louvain, 1987), no. 590; Birley, *Septimius Severus*, 225, n. 56.

106 *HA V. Pert.* 3.3–4 with Birley, *Septimius Severus*, 62.

107 *HA V. Sev.* 3.2; recall *HA V. Sev.* 3.8 (by implication; see Birley, *Septimius Severus*, 73, 75).

108 *HA V. Sev.* 3.9.

109 *HA V. Sev.* 4.4; Dio 72.12.4 (Cleander and the consuls); Birley, *Septimius Severus*, 68–78.

110 For Julianus' mother see *HA V. Jul.* 1.2 with *PIR²* D 7; for Clodius see *HA V. Clod.* 5.1 with *PIR²* C 1186.

111 *HA V. Jul.* 1.5 (origin) with Andermahr, *Totus in Praediis*, 84–85; Leunissen, *Konsuln und Konsularen*, 213, 241, for his provincial commands and, in general *PIR²* D 77; for Albinus see *PIR²* C 1186, and Birley, *Fasti of Roman Britain*, 146–49.

112 *PIR²* P 254.

113 Herod. 2.9.7.

114 Kienast, *Römische Kaisertabelle*, 156, for the date, and n. 119 below.

115 Campbell, *Emperor and Roman Army*, 69–88, 106–7.

116 B. Thomasson, *Laterculi Praesidum*, vol. 1 (Göteborg, 1984), 138, n. 104.

117 Thomasson, *Laterculi Praesidum*, vol. 1, 155, n. 44.

118 Herod. 2.9.12, 10.1 says that Severus approached other governors after his proclamation. This would be Severus' version of events (see p. 99, n. 100 above). For the people involved see Birley, *Septimius Severus*, 97.

119 *HA V. Sev.* 5.1. It is significant that there is no reference here to a prior proclamation of Niger that appears in Herod. 2.8–9. *HA V. Sev.* 5.1 does give the wrong date, *idibus Augustis* (the correct date is given by *P. Dura* 54 ii.3), and incorrectly states that he was proclaimed in Germany. Dio's account of the actual proclamation is lost.

120 Herod. 2.15.4, placing the letter after Severus' arrival at Rome, which is incorrect, but the error may stem from his use of the memoirs of Severus, which makes it possible that he is reporting what Severus said that he had written.

121 Herod. 3.24.

122 Dio 75.16.2–3; Herod. 2.11.9; for the elephant farm see P. Sabbatini Tumolesi, *Epigrafia anfiteatrale dell' Occidente Romano* (Rome, 1988), no. 8.

123 For the letter concerning the arrest of the assassins of Pertinax see *HA V. Jul.* 8.5; Dio 73.17.3; Dio 74.17.3–4; Herod. 2.12.6–7. Herodian places Julianus' proposal to make Severus co-emperor three days before the final meeting. Dio mentions the call to the meeting but does not say that it took place, and he was at the final meeting. This may be the same meeting that is reported at *HA V. Jul.* 7.2, in which it is said that Julianus convened a meeting of the senate asking for advice that he did not receive. For his death see also *HA V. Jul.* 8.7.

124 Dio 74.1; *HA V. Sev.* 6.11; Herod. 2.13.1–12.

125 *HA V. Sev.* 6.6 with *PIR²* F 300 (Flavius Juvenalis); *HA V. Jul.* 7.5 (Veturius Macrinus, allegedly appointed as a gesture by Julianus to appease Severus); for the fates of Julianus' previous prefects Flavius Genialis and Tullius Crispinus see *HA V. Jul.* 8.6 (death of Genialis with Julianus) and *HA V. Jul.* 8.1 (death of Crispinus, who was sent as an ambassador to Severus); see also L. L. Howe, *The Praetorian Prefect from Commodus to Diocletian (AD 180–305)* (Chicago, 1942), 68–69.

126 *HA V. Sev.* 6.10; *HA V. Nig.* 5.2.

127 Dio 74.4.2–5; *HA V. Sev.* 7.8–9.

128 He actually seems to have added the cognomen of Pertinax as an additional cognomen at the time of his proclamation; see Herod. 2.10.1; contra, *HA V. Pert.* 15.2; *HA V. Sev.* 7.9 with Hasebroek, *Untersuchungen*, 42–43, showing that the evidence of coins confirms Herodian's statement. Herodian was using Severus' *Memoirs*, which should have been accurate on this point as opposed to Marius Maximus, who appears to have been relying on his memory.

129 See E. Ritterling, "Legio," *RE* 12 (1925): 1366, for the distribution of legions in the second and third centuries.

130 *HA V. Sev.* 8.13; Dio 74.6.3; *ILS* 1141 with Hasebroek, *Untersuchungen*, 54–55.

131 Dio 74.6.5–6; *ILS* 1140 with Hasebroek, *Untersuchungen*, 57.

132 *HA V. Sev.* 8.13; Dio 74.6.3.

133 For the sloth of Niger see esp. Herod. 2.8.9–10 with Z. Rubin, *Civil War Propaganda and Historiography* (Brussels, 1980), 92–96; Dio 74.6.3 offers a different view, saying that he was disturbed by omens and it was this that kept him from advancing further. For the theme of the degenerate qualities of the eastern legions see E. L. Wheeler, "The Laxity of Syrian Legions," in Kennedy, *Roman Army*, 229–76.

134 For Anullinus see *PIR²* C 1322; Birley, *Septimius Severus*, 112.

135 A date in May is inferred from *P. Dura* 54.2.10–11, recording an imperatorial salutation for Severus on May 11. This may be the date of the final surrender of Niger's forces; see Birley, *Septimius Severus*, 113, n. 13 for this point and other views that would put the defeat later in the year. For Severus' triumphal arch see Hasebroek, *Untersuchungen*, 61.

136 For the defection of Arabia, deduced from the fact that P. Aelius Severianus Maximus was retained by Severus, see M. Sartre, *Trois études sur l'Arabie romaine et byzantine* (Brussels, 1982), 85; for the defection of Legion VI Ferrata, deduced from the fact that it received the title *constans* from Severus, see Ritterling, "Legio," 1593, with Birley, *Septimius Severus*, 112. For other defections see below.

137 Dio 74.5.7–8.1 (and p. 000 below); Herod. 3.4.5–6.

138 Herod. 3.4.6.

139 Herod. 3.2.9, trans. Whittaker. The classic account of the rivalry between these two cities is L. Robert, "La titulature de Nicée et de Nicomédie: La gloire et la haine," *HSCP* 81 (1977): 1–39 (also in Robert, *OMS* 6: 211–49), esp. pp. 22–27 (*OMS* 6: 232–37). In light of this there is no need to speculate that Nicaea may have been motivated by the fact that Claudius Candidus had been *curator* there in the past (for which view see Whittaker n. ad Herod. 3.9), though it may have helped.

140 See also Mal. 12.293.

141 Herod. 3.6.9; *HA V. Sev.* 9.4; *D.* 50.15.1.3 (Ulpian); *D.* 50.15.8.3 (Paul); *IGR* 3, no. 1012, Mal. 12.294. See also G. Downey, "Malalas on the History of Antioch under Severus and Caracalla," *TAPA* 68 (1937): 141–56.

142 F. G. Millar, "The Roman *coloniae* of the Near East: A Study of Cultural Relations," in *Roman Eastern Policy and Other Studies in Roman History: Proceedings of a Colloquium at Tvärminne, 2–3 October 1987*, ed. H. Solin and M. Kajeva, Commentationes Humanarum Litterarum 91 (Helsinki, 1990), 10–18.

NOTES TO PAGES 105–112

143 For more detail see the excellent discussion in Millar, *The Roman Near East*, 274–95.
144 *FGrH* 790 fr. 1.29, trans. A. L. Baumgarten, *The Phoenician History of Philo of Byblos: A Commentary* (Leiden, 1981) (slightly adapted).
145 Dio 74.8.4.
146 Millar, "The Roman *coloniae*," 31–34; Millar, *The Roman Near East*, 121–22.
147 *D.* 50.15.1.3–4 with Millar, *The Roman Near East*, 124.
148 Millar, "The Roman *coloniae*," 35–38.
149 Astonishing coincidences connected him with Pertinax; see Dio 73.4. Dio, who disliked Julianus, seems to have provided no such information concerning him, but Marius Maximus did offer the incident reported in the text; see *HA V. Jul.* 2.3.
150 Potter, *Prophets and Emperors*, 147–70.
151 Potter, *Prophets and Emperors*, 173.
152 See, in general, the excellent study of Rubin, *Civil War Propaganda*, 66–74, 117–20.
153 *HA V. Sev.* 2.9; Suet. *Aug.* 94.12; the similarity is noted by F. H. Cramer, *Astrology in Roman Law and Politics* (Philadelphia, 1954), 209; for Severus as the source for this event see Birley, *Septimius Severus*, 41.
154 *HA V. Sev.* 3.9.
155 Dio 78.8 with Potter, *Prophets and Emperors*, 170.
156 Dio 72.23.1; for the occasion in 193 see Millar, *Study of Cassius Dio*, 29.
157 Dio 76.11.1.
158 Potter, *Prophets and Emperors*, 158–62.
159 Herod. 2.9.4.
160 Potter, *Literary Texts*, 87–88.
161 Gowing, *Triumviral Narratives*, 29–30, on Dio's belief in divine action.
162 The assertion that Herodian had been to Issus is based on his description of the place in 3.4.3, which is accurate. Dio's description, at 74.7.3, is not of the plain of Issus.
163 Rubin, *Civil War Propaganda*, 66–68.
164 For the version including Pertinax see Jer. *Chron.* ad 2189 with Birley, *Marcus Aurelius*, 173; Rubin, *Civil War Propaganda*, 74, on the connection between Marcus and Severus.
165 Millar, *The Roman Near East*, 125; S. K. Ross, *Roman Edessa: Politics and Culture on the Eastern Fringes of the Roman Empire* (London, 2001), 47–53.
166 For the date see Halfmann, *Itinera principum*, 220.
167 *HA V. Sev.* 10.6 with Hasebroek, *Untersuchungen*, 89; for context see Hekster, "All in the Family," 48–49. For a reflection of Severus' attitude toward Caracalla in a contemporary author – Athenaeus – see D. Braund, "Learning, Luxury, and Empire: Athenaeus's Roman Patron," in *Athenaeus and His World: Reading Greek Culture in the Roman Empire*, ed. D. Braund and J. Wilkins (Exeter, 2000), 16–17.
168 I. Gradel, *Emperor Worship and Roman Religion* (Oxford, 2002), 350.
169 Dio 75.5.1 with Birley, *Septimius Severus*, 123.
170 For the date see Hasebroek, *Untersuchungen*, 85. He thinks that the year is given incorrectly as 195 by Dio. This is unnecessary, as what Dio says (as reported by Xiphilinus) is that Severus had not yet had time to catch his breath after the war with the barbarians, which merely means that it was a short time later. This is not unreasonable, as Severus had only been in Rome for about six months.
171 For the structure of acclamations see Potter, "Performance, Power, and Justice," 140–41.
172 The utterly ingenious interpretation of this event in Rubin, *Civil War Propaganda*, 82–83, depends, unfortunately, on the acceptance of 195 as the date for the outbreak of the war. In his view the silver rain signifies Albinus, as the Greek word for silver

606

is etymologically connected with that for the color white, and the three days equals three years in power for Albinus.

173 Dio 75.7.3; Herod. 3.7.3. The Laetus in question is identified with the Julius Laetus who led the advance guard of Severus' army against Julianus and the Laetus who was executed for excessive popularity during the siege of Hatra in 198; see Chastagnol ad *HA V. Sev.* 15.6.

174 Dio 75.8.3–4.

175 Dio 75.7.4–8.3.

176 Tert. *Apol.* 35.11.

177 For Severus' movements see Halfmann, *Itinera principum*, 217.

178 Dio 75.9.1; Birley, *Septimius Severus*, 117, 129.

179 *HA V. Sev.* 15.1; Herod. 3.9.1 with Hasebroek, *Untersuchungen*, 110; Birley, *Septimius Severus*, 129–30.

180 Dio 75.9.3. His name is nowhere recorded.

181 For Commagene see the excellent discussion in Millar, *The Roman Near East*, 452–55.

182 Lucian, *Syr. D.* 1 with Millar, *The Roman Near East*, 227, 454; compare Tatian, *Oratio ad Graecos* 42.

183 Millar, *The Roman Near East*, 457–67, 472–81.

184 H. J. W. Drijvers, *The Book of the Laws of Countries: Dialogue on Fate of Bardaisan of Edessa* (Leiden, 1965); see also Millar, *The Roman Near East*, 474–75.

185 Ross, *Roman Edessa*, 87–90.

186 The crucial discussion of the topography of Carrhae and the extraurban temples remains S. Lloyd and W. Brice, "Harran," *Anatolian Studies* 1 (1951): 77–112. See also W. Cramer, s.v. "Harran," *RAC* 634–50.

187 H. J. W. Drijvers, "Hatra Palmyra und Edessa: Die Städte der syrisch–mesopotamischen Wüste in politischer kulturgeschichtlicher und religions–geschtlicher Beleuchtung," *ANRW* 2.8 (1997): 803–37, remains the basic treatment. See also D. Kennedy and D. Riley, *Rome's Desert Frontier from the Air* (Austin, 1990), 106–7.

188 W. Ball, *Rome in the East: The Transformation of Empire* (London, 2000), 343–44.

189 Dio 75.9.1–3.

190 Dio 75.9.4; *HA V. Sev.* 16.1–2; Herod. 3.9.9–11. The date was probably January 28, 198, the occasion upon which Severus took the title Parthicus; see Birley, *Septimius Severus*, 130.

191 Dio 75.10–12; Herod. 3.9.4–7.

192 For the creation of the province see D. L. Kennedy, "Ti. Claudius Subatianus Aquila, 'First Prefect of Mesopotamia,'" *ZPE* 36 (1979): 255; D. L. Kennedy, "The Garrisoning of Mesopotamia in the Late Antonine Period," *Antichthon* 21 (1987): 57–66; Millar, *The Roman Near East*, 125–26; Ross, *Roman Edessa*, 54–57.

193 B. Isaac, *The Limits of Empire: The Roman Army in the East* (Oxford, 1990), 255–57, for a sensible discussion.

194 For the extent of the province of Mesopotamia under Severus see the map at E. Winter, *Die sasanidisch–römischen Friedensverträge des 3. Jahrhunderts n. Chr. – ein Beitrag zum Verständnis der aussenpolitischen Beziehungen zwischen den beiden Gross-mächten* (Frankfurt am Main, 1988), 172.

195 Downey, "Malalas on History of Antioch," 142.

196 Dio 75.13.1 for the sacrifice to Pompey; *HA V. Hadr.* 14.4 for the rebuilding of the tomb; Birley, *Septimius Severus*, 136, for the notion that he was expiating a curse, a notion that is strengthened by the fact that Dio 42.3.3 stresses it.

197 Dio 75.8.1.

198 *HA V. Sev.* 16.4; Dio 75.13.1–2.

199 *HA V. Sev.* 17.2 with Birley, *Septimius Severus*, 137.

200 Dio 76.5.7, though the connection may be less correct than Dio would suggest since he did not enter the senate until 212; *PIR²* A 161.
201 Dio 76.1 with Hasebroek, *Untersuchungen*, 117; Birley, *Septimius Severus*, 140–41.
202 Dio 76.1.3.
203 Halfmann, *Itinera Principum*, 218.
204 For details see J. B. Ward-Perkins, *The Severan Buildings of Lepcis Magna*, Society for Libyan Studies Monograph 2 (London, 1993), 104–7.
205 *PIR²* F 554, suggesting that he was related through Severus' mother.
206 Dio 58.14.1 with Millar, *Study of Cassius Dio*, 145. For Sejanus see also p. 79 above.
207 For a thorough analysis of these texts and others see W. Williams, "The *Libellus* Procedure and the Severan Papyri," *JRS* 64 (1974): 86–103.
208 Oliver, *Greek Constitutions*, no. 236.
209 *CJ* 2.3.1, 4.55.1, 4.55.2.
210 Dio 78.4 with p. 146 below.
211 Dio 75.14.7; see also *AE* 1914 no. 178.2–3: *necessario dominorum nnn | Auggg. Socero et consocero Auggg.*; *ILS* 1366.8–9: *adfinis domin[orum | nostr]orum Augustorum* (a dedication by an imperial slave at Ephesus); *ILS* 2185, listed third after Severus and Caracalla; *ILS* 2186, listed either before or after Julia Domna; *AE* 1944 no. 74. See also Dio 75.15.2a for someone (unnamed) writing to him as a fourth Caesar.
212 Dio 75.16.4.
213 G. B. Pighi, *De ludis saecularibus populi Romani Quiritum* (Rome, 1941), 140–75.
214 Dio 76.2.1–2.
215 For this version of events see Dio 76.2–4. Herod. 3.11–12 gives a radically different account, asserting that Plautianus actually plotted against Severus. See the judicious discussions in Millar, *Study of Cassius Dio*, 146; Birley, *Septimius Severus*, 161–62.
216 Dio 75.14.4 (eunuchs), 75.15.7 (gluttony); Herod. 3.10.6–7.
217 Dio 76.10.1–7.
218 E. Hobsbawm, *Bandits*, 4th edn. (New York, 2000), 19–33.
219 Apul. *Met.* 7.5–9.
220 See further pp. 200–02 below.
221 B. D. Shaw, "Bandits in the Roman Empire," *Past and Present* 105 (1984): 3–52.
222 Dio 74.2.4.
223 See the important discussion by K. Hopwood, "Bandits between Grandees and the State: The Structure of Order in Roman Rough Cilicia," in K. Hopwood, *Organized Crime in Antiquity* (London, 1999), 179–84.
224 K. Hopwood, "Bandits, Elites, and Rural Order," in *Patronage in Ancient Society*, ed. A. Wallace-Hadrill (London, 1990), 171–87.
225 *D.* 48.3.6.1 (the text that is omitted here is concerned with accurate reports). For the context see Hopwood, "Bandits, Elites," 177–85; for an up-to-date list of eirenarchs see now J. L. Rife, "Officials of the Roman Provinces in Xenophon's *Ephesiaca*," *ZPE* 138 (2002): 107–8, and a list of attested *diogmitae* on p. 108.
226 Dio 76.11.2.
227 M. Fulford, "Britain," in Bowman, Garnsey, and Rathbone, *The Cambridge Ancient History*, 11: 570.
228 Salway, *Roman Britain*, 668–69.
229 M. Millett, *The Romanization of Britain: An Essay in Archaeological Interpretation* (Cambridge, 1990), 117–23.
230 Dio 76.13.1.
231 Salway, *Roman Britain*, 229–30, for details of the campaign.
232 Dio 76.14.4.
233 Dio 76.15.2.

4 THE ARMY IN POLITICS; LAWYERS IN GOVERNMENT

1 The starting point for the study of the legionary army is now Y. Le Bohec and C. Wolff, *Les légions de Rome sous le Haut-Empire. Actes du Congrès de Lyon (17–19 septembre 1998)* (Lyons, 2000), replacing Ritterling, "Legio," *RE* 12 (1925), 1211–1829 (though not for Legion XVI Flavia Firma).

2 For these legions see C. Wolff, "Legio I Parthica," in Le Bohec and Wolff, *Les légions de Rome*, 247–49; C. Wolff, "Legio III Parthica," in Le Bohec and Wolff, *Les légions de Rome*, 251–52; C. Ricci, "Legio II Parthica. Una messa a punto," in Le Bohec and Wolff, *Les légions de Rome*, 397–406 (concentrating on the west); and W. Van Rengen, "La IIe Légion Parthique à Apamée," in Le Bohec and Wolff, *Les légions de Rome*, 407–10 (concentrating on the evidence from the east).

3 *ILS* 2288, with discussion in J. B. Campbell, *The Roman Army, 31 BC–AD 337: A Sourcebook* (London, 1994), no. 144.

4 R. Alston, "Roman Military Pay from Caesar to Diocletian," *JRS* 84 (1994): 115, though, as he points out, this number represents the paper strength of the army.

5 For financial concerns limiting the size of the army see p. 227 below.

6 For a more generous estimation of the legion, and a good account of its structure, see M. P. Speidel, *The Framework of an Imperial Legion*, Fifth Annual Caerleon Lecture (Cardiff, 1992).

7 A. Goldsworthy, *The Roman Army at War* (Oxford, 1996), 198.

8 Contra Goldsworthy, *Roman Army at War*, 198–99. The key passage is Caes. *B. Gall.* 1.25, where it appears that the *pilum* phase goes on long enough for the Helvetians to be seen waving their arms to get rid of their shields. As Goldsworthy points out, rear ranks would have difficulty reaching the front of the enemy, which is why I suggest that the troops rotated through the front. Note also Tac. *Agr.* 36, where auxiliary cohorts are described bombarding the Britons with javelins; in this case the individual soldier seems to have carried two into combat, meaning that if there were to be an extended period of assault, they would have to be rotating through the front ranks.

9 Caes. *B. Gall.* 1.52.3; implied in the account of the battle with the Nervii, which stresses the speed of the attack (*B. Gall.* 2.2.21–23), although it failed (see *B. Gall.* 2.23.1); see also *B. Gall.* 5.34.3–4 on the tactics employed by Ambiorix in the defeat of Sabinus and Cotta.

10 Caes. *B. Civ.* 3.93.1.

11 [Caes.] *B. Afr.* 71.1.

12 Tac. *Hist.* 3.23.2, evidently custom made for the legion. Caesar does not mention the use of war engines on the battlefield, and the use of one at Lepcis in 46 caused a panic, suggesting that they were unfamiliar (*B. Afr.* 29). They do not feature in accounts of the major battles of 43 and 42 BC, suggesting that their introduction in this context may have been one of the few tactical innovations of the Julio-Claudian period. They are present in Tacitus' account of Germanicus' campaign in AD 16 (*Ann.* 2.20).

13 Arr. *Tactica* 16. For various aspects of this work see A. B. Bosworth, "Arrian and the Alani," *HSCP* 81 (1977): 237–42; E. L. Wheeler, "The Roman Legion as Phalanx," *Chiron* 9 (1979): 303, 307–14; J. B. Campbell, "Teach Yourself to Be a Roman General," *JRS* 77 (1987): 26.

14 Arr. *Tactica* 19.

15 Arr. *Tactica* 30–31.

16 For a more generous view see Campbell, "Teach Yourself," 27, though he too notes that the tendency evident in all of these works is to plan for the future on the basis

of the past. There is no suggestion of reforms guided by proactive uses of intelligence. Such study of enemy techniques in advance of a campaign appears to have had no place in classical intelligence gathering. For the sort of information that was collected – chiefly about strategic movements and more general "background" intelligence – see A. D. Lee, *Information and Frontiers: Roman Foreign Relations in Late Antiquity* (Cambridge, 1993), 81–142.

17 For the defeat of Severianus see Birley, *Marcus Aurelius*, 121–22.

18 G. L. Cheesman, *The Auxilia of the Roman Imperial Army* (Oxford, 1914) remains valuable; for the earlier period see also D. B. Saddington, *The Development of the Roman Auxiliary Forces from Caesar to Vespasian* (Harare, 1982).

19 Caes. *B. Gall.* 2.7.1, 7.67.5.

20 Goldsworthy, *Roman Army at War*, 20, suggests that the chief value of the *auxilia* was to provide more flexible forces that would fulfill the same basic tasks as the legions. This is true of the infantry cohorts. But, as he himself shows on pp. 135, 137 (through a good reading of Arrian), the *auxilia* offered significant forces that were not traditional heavy infantry and performed different functions on the battlefield.

21 Tac. *Agr.* 36.

22 R. P. Duncan-Jones, "The Price of Wheat in Roman Egypt," *Chiron* 6 (1976): 241–62 (also in Duncan-Jones, *Structure and Scale*, 143–55). The one piece of comparative data, the price of bread at Ephesus in the late second century, does not contradict his conclusions (as he points out).

23 M. A. Speidel, "Roman Army Pay Scales," *JRS* 82 (1992): 97.

24 Speidel, "Roman Army Pay Scales," 98; Alston, "Roman Military Pay," 122.

25 For the number of officials drawing salaries of 60,000 HS and above in the reign of Severus (a total of 174) see H. G. Pflaum, *Les procurateurs équestres sous le haut-empire romain* (Paris, 1950), 96.

26 Howgego, "Supply and Uses," 5–6, for expenditures on barbarians and luxury goods. The cost of public entertainments at Rome (funded at least in part by the palace) would have amounted to hundreds of millions of sesterces. The charioteer Diocles won 35,863,120 HS in the course of a twenty-four-year career (*ILS* 5287). This merely suggests the scale of expenditure, for which an accurate estimate is impossible given that we do not know how many individual races were run on any given day. We do know that money prizes were awarded to the top three finishers. For the cost of imports (significant because they had to be paid in specie) see Strabo 16.4.20; Plin. *HN* 6.101, 12.84 with J. I. Miller, *The Spice Trade of the Roman Empire, 29 BC–AD 641* (Oxford, 1969), 222–23. There are no figures that begin to quantify the scale of subsidies to Germanic tribes, though the nature of Dio's complaints at 77.14.3 suggests that the sums were significant enough to be noticed. See, in general, R. P. Duncan-Jones, *Money and Government in the Roman Empire* (Cambridge, 1994), 33–46 and esp. 43–45 on subsidies.

27 Pay increase: Herod. 3.8.4; *HA V. Sev.* 12.2; relationship between pay and expenses: Alston, "Roman Military Pay," 122; on inflation see the suggestive study by Duncan-Jones, *Structure and Scale*, 150, and p. 137 below.

28 J. B. Campbell, "The Marriage of Soldiers under the Empire," *JRS* 68 (1978): 165; S. E. Phang, *The Marriage of Roman Soldiers (13 BC–AD 235): Law and Family in the Roman Imperial Army* (Leiden, 2001), 387.

29 Herod. 6.7.3; there were complaints as early as the time of Tiberius, but these appear to be from troops who were newly raised; see Tac. *Ann.* 1.17, 4.46; Campbell, *Emperor and Roman Army*, 12.

30 See the classic study of O. Hirschfeld, "Die Sicherheitspolizei im römischen Kaiser-reich," *Sitzungsberichte der Berliner Akademie* (1891), 845–77 (also in Hirschfeld,

Kleine Schriften [Berlin, 1913], 576–612), esp. 859–69 (Kleine Schriften, 591–600);
R. Alston, Soldier and Society in Roman Egypt: A Social History (London, 1995), 81–96,
for an updated examination of the Egyptian evidence.

31 Campbell, Emperor and Roman Army, 249–50.

32 Keil and von Premerstein, "Bericht," no. 55, 10, reprinted in Hauken, Petition and
Response, 38–40; Syll.³ 888, reprinted with an improved text in Hauken, Petition
and Response, 85–94; OGIS 519, reprinted in Hauken, Petition and Response, 145–48;
OGIS 609, reprinted in Hauken, Petition and Response, 183; Hauken, Petition and
Response, 189 (publishing a text from Kilter from the time of Commodus); SEG
43, no. 870, reprinted in Hauken, Petition and Response, 204–5; L. Robert, "La ville
d'Euhippè en Carie," CRAI (1952): 589–99, reprinted in Hauken, Petition and
Response, 215; SEG 37, no. 1186, reprinted in Hauken, Petition and Response, 220–24.

33 Matt. 5:41 with De Ste. Croix, Class Struggle; 14–16 and Campbell, Emperor and
Roman Army, 249–50.

34 Epict. 4.1.79.

35 Apul. Met. 9.39 with ch. 2, n. 108 above.

36 P. Oxy. 240; Keil and von Premerstein, "Bericht," no. 55 (Hauken, Petition and
Response, no. 4) with L. Robert, "Sur un papyrus de Bruxelles," Revue de Philologie,
3rd ser., 17 (1943): 111–19 (also in Robert, OMS 1: 364–72) and Campbell, Emperor
and Roman Army, 248–49.

37 Isaac, The Limits of Empire, 86.

38 For the evidence see Isaac, The Limits of Empire, 86; Phang, Marriage of Roman
Soldiers, 251–61, noting as well that soldiers were punished for rape if they assaulted
a woman of good standing (pp. 259–60), which makes other instances that are
attested look like deliberate terror tactics; see esp. Tac. Ann. 4.72.2, 14.31.1.

39 Suet. Aug. 24; Tac. Ann. 3.21; Y. Le Bohec, The Imperial Roman Army (London,
1994), 60–61; Campbell, Emperor and Roman Army, 303–14.

40 What follows is wholly indebted to N. Pollard, "The Roman Army as 'Total
Institution' in the Near East? Dura-Europus as a Case Study," in Kennedy, Roman
Army, 212–27. For a very different picture of the interaction between soldiers and
society see Alston, Soldier and Society, 96–101.

41 Pollard, "The Roman Army," 222.

42 For soldiers' affection for Geta see Dio 77.1.3.

43 Howe, Praetorian Prefect, 71–72.

44 Honoré, Emperors and Lawyers, 56–58.

45 PIR² F 27.

46 PIR² I 182.

47 Herod. 4.1.5.

48 CIL 6, no. 1641; ILS 478 with H. Halfmann, "Zwei syrische Verwandte des
severischen Kaiserhauses," Chiron 12 (1982): 230–33.

49 Dio 77.1.1–2. For the previous relationship between Castor and Caracalla see Dio
76.14.1–2.

50 K. Dietz, "Caracalla, Fabius Cilo und die Urbaniciani: Unerkannt gebliebene
Suffektkonsuln des Jahres 212 n. Chr.," Chiron 13 (1983): 381–404, esp. 397.

51 Dio 77.3.1–2; Herod. 4.4.4–8; HA V. Car. 2.5–6.

52 HA V. Car. 2.7–8; the incident is omitted in other accounts.

53 Dio 77.3.3; HA V. Car. 2.9–3.1. Herod. 4.5.2–5 gives a version of the speech that
is based on this theme but omits the recall of exiles. Oliver, Greek Constitutions, no.
261a, quotes a portion of this edict.

54 Severus and Sulla: see Dio 75.8.1 (praising Sulla, among others, for knowing how
to deal with enemies); Caracalla's praise of Sulla: HA V. Car. 2.2, 5.5; Herod. 4.8.5
confirmed by Dio 77.13.7, who says that he restored Sulla's tomb.

55   Dio 77.4.1; Herod. 4.6.1–2.
56   Dio 77.4.1a.
57   Dio 77.4.2–5.1, 4.
58   Herod. 4.6.3.
59   Dio 77.6.1. The *Excerpta Valesiana* perserves only one name, that of Thrasea Priscus, presumably L. Valerius Messalla Thrasea Priscus, *consul ordinarius* in 196, who may actually have been a descendant of the ancient republican aristocracy; see Leunissen, *Konsuln und Konsulare*, 109.
60   The precise percentage of the increase is unclear; see Alston, "Roman Military Pay," 115.
61   J. C. Edmondson, "Mining in the Later Roman Empire and Beyond: Continuity or Disruption," *JRS* 79 (1989): 91; G. D. B. Jones, "The Roman Mines at Riotinto," *JRS* 70 (1980): 163.
62   D. R. Walker, *The Metrology of the Roman Silver Coinage*, 3 BAR Supplementary Series 40 (Oxford, 1978), 106–43 for the decline in silver; for the lack of a link between debasement and inflation see p. 237 below.
63   Dio 77.12.6.
64   Dio 60.22.3 with F. Vittinghof, *Der Stattsfeind in der römischen Kaiserzeit* (Berlin, 1936), 34–35.
65   Duncan-Jones, *Money and Government*, 194–200.
66   Sherwin-White, *The Roman Citizenship*, 381, and, in general, pp. 281–89, with Jacques and Scheid, *Rome et l'intégration*, 284–85.
67   The text translated here is taken from Oliver, *Greek Constitutions*, no. 260. For a survey of the extensive bibliography on individual points see Oliver's notes ad loc. It should be obvious that I accept the text here as being that of the *Constitutio Antoniniana*, even though that position has been challenged with great vigor (see esp. E. Bickermann, *Das Edikt des Kaisers Caracalla in P. Geiss 40* [Berlin, 1926]; H. Wolff, *Die Constitutio Antoniniana und Papyrus Gissensis 40*, vol. 1 [Cologne, 1976]).
68   Dio 77.10.1–2.
69   D. S. Potter, "Entertainers in the Roman Empire," in Potter and Mattingly, *Life, Death, and Entertainment*, 324–25.
70   Herod. 4.6.4.
71   Dio 77.6.2, noting that he gave Bato a great funeral. For the duration of gladiatorial fights and the ideology of death see Potter, "Entertainers," 313–14.
72   For the gesture, see A. Corbeill, "Thumbs in Ancient Rome: Pollex as Index," *MAAR* 42 (1997): 1–21.
73   Herod. 4.7.1. *CJ* 7.16.2 was given *(data)* at Rome on February 7, 214. This reflects the posting of the rescript there rather than Caracalla's presence; see Halfmann, *Itinera principum*, 226.
74   Dio 77.13.4. For the transformation of German society north of the Rhine see Wells, *The Barbarians Speak*, 224–58; the statement that the Alamanni are first attested in 231 (Wells, 259) is a misprint.
75   *ILS* 451 with Halfmann, *Itinera principum*, 223–26.
76   Oliver, *Greek Constitutions*, no. 261.6–10.
77   *AE* 1948, no. 109. For another odd expression, showing lack of enthusiasm while granting a request, see Oliver, *Greek Constitutions*, no. 266, with discussion of the text of lines 18–19 in C. P. Jones, "Imperial Letters at Ephesus," *EA* 33 (2001): 43, and the curious expression in Oliver, *Greek Constitutions*, no. 267, 11.
78   Phil. *V. Soph.* 622.
79   Phil. *V. Soph.* 623 with Bowersock, *Greek Sophists*, 40–41.

80 *SEG* 17, no. 749 with W. Williams, "Caracalla and the Rhetoricians: A Note on the *cognitio de Gohariensis,*" *Latomus* 33 (1974): 663–67.

81 See more generally the splendid exposition in M. Meckler, "Caracalla the Intellectual," in *Gli imperatori Severi: Storia archeologia religione,* ed. E. dal Covolo and G. Rinaldi (Rome,1999), 39–46.

82 Dio 77.7.1. For Caracalla's military activity along the Danube see J. Fitz, "A Military History of Pannonia from the Marcomannic Wars to the Death of Alexander Severus (180–235)," *A. Arch. Hung.* 14 (1962): 99–106.

83 B. M. Levick, "Caracalla's Path," in *Hommages à Marcel Renard* (Brussels, 1969), 426–46, whose point stands despite corrections in points of detail by A. Johnston, "Caracalla's Path," *Historia* 32 (1983): 58–76.

84 Dio 77.16.7.

85 Dio 77.23.4.

86 Dio 77.12.1 with Ross, *Roman Edessa,* 57–64.

87 Downey, "Malalas on History of Antioch," 142, n. 6, on *D.* 50.15.8 (Paul); and p. 152 for the games.

88 For Emesa see *D.* 50.15.1.4 (Ulpian); *D.* 50.15.8.6 (Paul) with Millar, "The Roman *coloniae,*" 40–42; for Palmyra see *D.* 50.15.1.5 (Ulpian); the syntax makes it unclear whether Severus or Caracalla was responsible, but Caracalla is more likely; see Millar, "The Roman *coloniae,*" 42; Millar, *The Roman Near East,* 143.

89 Herod. 4.8.6–7.

90 Herod. 4.9.3 (interestingly asserting that Alexander was tall while Caracalla was short – Alexander was not tall); Dio 77.22.1 (mentioning only the criticism of the murder of Geta).

91 Oliver, *Greek Constitutions,* no. 262.

92 He appears to have accompanied Caracalla to Alexandria, which would place the Armenian operations in 216.

93 *PIR²* F 317 with M. Peachin, *Iudex vice Caesaris: Deputy Emperors and the Administration of Justice during the Principate* (Stuttgart, 1996), 236.

94 Dio 77.21.

95 Millar, *The Roman Near East,* 143.

96 *SEG* 17, no. 7591.8–17. The positive view of this document is offered by Millar, *The Roman Near East,* 143.

97 Williams, "Caracalla and the Rhetoricians," 663–67.

98 Dio 78.4.4; see also Herod 4.12.3 for Caracalla's increasing interest in astrology and other forms of prognostication.

99 Dio 78.4.1–3; Herod. 4.12.5–7.

100 For the date see Dio 78.5.4, contra *HA V. Car.* 6.6 for the date of his death. For details of the geography see Lloyd and Brice, "Harran," 89, 96. The date in the *Historia Augusta* account may be explained by confusion over which temple he visited on which day. Herodian 4.13.1 states that he was on his way to visit the temple of Selene when he was killed. No single source shows knowledge of more than one temple. April 6 is otherwise attested as the main festival day for the moon goddess, and, if he visited the goddess then, it would explain how a date for a visit to a temple in the area made it into the *Historia Augusta* account.

101 Dio 78.10.2.

102 Dio 78.7.4, 11.1.

103 Dio 78.11.1.

104 Herod. 4.14.2.

105 Dio 78.11.4–6.

106 Herod. 4.13.3–7 with Potter, *Literary Texts,* 87.

107 *PIR²* I 99 (Julianus Nestor); *PIR* U 555 (Ulpius Julianus).

108 Dio 78.26.4.
109 Dio 78.27.1 with Duncan-Jones, *Money and Government*, 45.
110 Dio 78.29.1–2.
111 Dio 78.13.2–3 with *HA V. Car.* 6.7.
112 Dio 78.30.1.
113 Dio 78.23.
114 Dio 78.2.1–4.
115 M. Frey, *Untersuchungen zur Religion und zur Religionspolitik des Kaisers Elagabal* (Stuttgart, 1989), 45–49.
116 For the nature of the rites see Frey, *Untersuchungen*, 14–42.
117 Herod. 5.3.6; *HA V. Macrin.* 9.3. For Herodian's information on these points see G. W. Bowersock, "Herodian and Elagabalus," *YCS* 24 (1975): 229–36.
118 Herod. 5.3.9 on clients of Julia Maesa who had fled to her for protection. For the disloyal *cubicularius*, Festus, see Dio 78.32.4.
119 Dio 78.33.1 (awareness of the dislike for Macrinus), 28.1–2 (reasons for military discontent). See also Dio 78.34.3 for Macrinus' restoration of the Caracallan pay rates for new recruits after the revolt of Elagabalus.
120 Dio 78.40.4.
121 Dio 78.33.1 says the oracular utterances encouraged the conspirators, but it is hard to believe that they were not circulated more widely.
122 Dio 78.33.1. The text here is deeply corrupt. The identification of the main actor here as Gannys depends on Dio 79.6.1–2, which, as Boissevain points out, alludes to this passage. Herodian and the *Historia Augusta* make no reference to Gannys and suggest that Maesa was the primary mover of the action. Dio's explicit statement that Maesa did not know in advance that Avitus was being brought to the camp looks like a response to the tradition known to the author of the *Historia Augusta* through Marius Maximus.
123 Dio 78.32.1.
124 Dio 78.32.2; Herodian 5.4.3 replaces the images of Caracalla with purses full of money that were shown off as a reward for changing sides.
125 Dio 78.32.3, explicitly excluding Julianus; Herod. 5.4.4 places his death here, but he also knows that the head was given to Macrinus. *HA V. Macrin.* 10.2 also places the death of Julianus at Emesa. I suspect that Dio is consciously correcting what he knew to be a false story at 78.34.4, where he says that Julianus had been found hiding somewhere.
126 Dio 78.34.3.
127 Dio 78.36.1.
128 Dio 78.34.6.
129 Dio 78.37.3. For the precise location see Honigmann, *RE* 1692. For the date see Dio 78.39.1.
130 Dio 78.38.3–4; Herod. 5.4.7–9 and *HA V. Macrin.* 10.3 both say that he fled after he saw his army deserting him. Again Dio looks like he is trying to correct what he thought to be a false tradition, and, as in the case of the death of Julianus, he appears to have circumstantial detail that the other two accounts lack.
131 On this point, at least, there is agreement between Dio 78.38.4 and Herod. 5.4.9.
132 Dio 78.39.5; Herod. 5.4.11.
133 Dio 78.40.2.
134 Dio 78.3.4.
135 Leunissen, *Konsuln und Konsulare*, 31.
136 Dio 78.7.1–2.
137 *HA V. Elag.* 11.1.

138 B. Salway, "A Fragment of Severan History: The Unusual Case of . . . atus, Praetorian Prefect of Elagabalus," *Chiron* 27 (1997): 148–53, distinguishing the career of . . . atus from that of T. Messius Extricatus, who likewise continued (albeit with an interruption) to ascend.

139 *HA V. Hel.* 12.1–2.

140 *PIR²* A 1641.

141 *HA V. Elag.* 12.2: *ad honores reliquos promovit commendatos sibi pudibilium enormitate membrorum.*

142 See also *CIL* 3, no. 6764 with M. Christol and T. Drew-Bear, "Un inscription d'Ancyre relative au *sacer comitatus,*" in Le Bohec and Wolff, *Les légions de Rome,* 529–39.

143 Dio 79.11.1, saying that Elagabalus' true offense was not in celebrating his god with strange rites, but exalting him over Jupiter, but the tone suggests that he did not much care for the "strange rites" either, esp. in light of 79.11–12.

144 L. R. Roller, *In Search of God the Mother: The Cult of Anatolian Cybele* (Berkeley, 1999), 287–325, esp. 318–19.

145 For the cult of Sarapis at Rome see S. Takács, *Isis and Sarapis in the Roman World* (Leiden, 1995), 71–129.

146 July–August is favored by Halfmann, *Itinera principum,* 231, on the basis of Eutrop. *Brev.* 8.22: *biennioque post et octo mensibus tumultu interfectus est.* Eutropius' numbers should not be pressed so closely in the light of *ILS* 2188.

147 Dio 79.11.1 with *ILS* 2008 and *CIL* 16, no. 141 with Frey, *Untersuchungen,* 80. The use of the title is inconsistent; compare e.g. *AE* 1993 no. 1565 (June–December 221) on a milestone from Cappadocia and *AE* 1991 no. 1441, a statue base for a group honoring Elagabalus, Alexander, their mothers, Julia Mamaea and Annia Faustina from Sparta dating to 221; *AE* 1990 no. 469, a milestone from Sardinia dating to 220; and *AE* 1989 no. 731, a milestone from Caesarea in Cappadocia dating to 221–22. For the use of the title see also *AE* 1990 no. 654, a dedicatory inscription from the amphitheater at Tarragona in Nearer Spain dating to 218; *AE* 1995 no. 1565, a military diploma for a soldier of Arabian birth who had served in the fleet at Misenum, dating to November 29, 221; and *AE* 1995 no. 1641 (January 222) from Bou Njem in Tripolitania.

148 Frey, *Untersuchungen,* 81; numerous inscriptions use the title as early as 218; see Frey *Untersuchungen,* 86 (to which *AE* 1990 no. 654 may now be added), confirming the restoration of *archiereus* at Dio 79.2.4.

149 Note 143 above.

150 Herod. 5.6.3 with Frey, *Untersuchungen,* 52, 87, suggesting that he was identifying the Palladium as an image of Athena with Athena–Allat in Emesa.

151 *HA V. Hel.* 6.9; contra Herod. 5.6.3, who says that he placed the image in the palace. See also Bowersock, "Herodian and Elagabalus," 234–35.

152 Herod. 5.6.2; Dio 79.9.3–4; *HA V. Hel.* 6.6, 11.1, 12.1–2; and Frey, *Untersuchungen,* 87–93.

153 *HA V. Hel.* 7.4. Frey, *Untersuchungen,* 48–49, offers another interpretation of the festival, suggesting a connection with the New Year festival at Babylon. This is not impossible, but the symbolism here seems to me to owe more to the Roman triumph, which, I suspect, was the way that it was read by the Roman audience.

154 Dio 79.11.1.

155 Dio 79.9.4, 12.1.

156 Dio 79.5.4 with Frey, *Untersuchungen,* 96.

157 See Gradel, *Emperor Worship,* 361, on *CIL* 6, no. 1984, suggesting that Elagabalus may have refused membership in the *sodales Augustales Claudiales.*

158 Dio 79.9.3; *HA V. Hel.* 6.7–8.

159 Herod. 5.6.7; contra Dio 79.17.2–3, who says that Elagabalus did this because, as he said in the senate, he had received an omen from his god.

160 Herod. 5.7.1 for Maesa's role; Dio 79.17.2, saying that Elagabalus announced that he was adopting Alexianus because his god told him to.

161 Frey, *Untersuchungen*, 97, for the chronology.

162 Dio 79.16.6 (exile of Zoticus), 79.21.2 for the restoration of Comazon.

163 Dio 79.20.

164 Dio 79.21.2.

165 R. Syme, "Fiction about Roman Jurists," *Zeitschrift der Savigny-Stiftung für Rechtsgeschichte* 97 (1980): 78–104 (also in Syme, *Roman Papers*, vol. 3, ed. A. R. Birley [Oxford, 1984], 1393–1414).

166 R. Syme, "Lawyers in Government: The Case of Ulpian," *PAPS* 116 (1972): 408 (also Syme, *Roman Papers* 3: 867).

167 T. Honoré, *Ulpian* (Oxford, 1982), 16.

168 Doubts on this point are expressed by Syme, "Lawyers in Government," 407 (also in *Roman Papers* 3: 866). He also demolishes the notion that Paul was ever praetorian prefect in "Three Jurists," *BHAC 1968–69* (Bonn, 1970), 314–17 (also in Syme, *Roman Papers*, vol. 2, ed. E. Badian [Oxford, 1979], 794–98), supporting Howe, *Praetorian Prefect*, 105–6. But on Syme's estimation, Ulpian lacked political skills, which might argue that he was useful because he was a lawyer.

169 Dio 78.11.2.

170 D. Johnston, *Roman Law in Context* (Cambridge, 1999), 6–7; Syme, "Lawyers in Government," 409 (also in Syme, *Roman Papers* 3: 868); M. Peachin, "Jurists and the Law in the Early Roman Empire," in De Blois, *Administration, Prosopography*, 109–120.

171 *D.* 29.1.3.

172 *D.* 28.2.4.

173 Gai. *Inst.* 1.7.

174 W. Kunkel, *An Introduction to Roman Legal and Constitutional History*, trans. J. M. Kelly (Oxford, 1973), 108–9.

175 Syme, "Lawyers in Government," 406 (also in Syme, *Roman Papers* 3: 863).

176 Peachin, *Iudex vice Caesaris*, 33–65.

177 H. Jolowicz, *Historical Introduction to the Study of Roman Law* (Cambridge, 1954), 386–87.

178 B. W. Frier, "Early Classical Private Law," in *The Cambridge Ancient History*, 2nd edn., vol. 10, ed. A. K. Bowman, E. Champlin, and A. Lintott (Cambridge, 1996), 969–70.

179 Gai. *Inst.* 3.141; *D.* 18.1.1.1, 19.4.1 pr (Paul) with Jolowicz, *Historical Introduction*, 389–90; and Frier, "Early Classical Private Law," 971.

180 Jolowicz, *Historical Introduction*, 388–91.

181 *C. Th.* 1.4.3: *ubi autem diversae sententiae proferuntur, potior numerus vincat auctorum, vel, si numerus aequalis sit, eius partis praecedat auctoritas in qua excellentis ingenii vir Papinianus emineat, qui, ut singulos vincat, ita cedit duobus.*

182 *D.* 26.7.46; Pap. *Resp.* 5.9.

183 Honoré, *Ulpian*, 32.

184 *D.* 37.12.5 (Trajan agrees with an opinion advocated by the jurists Neratius Priscus and Titius Aristo reported in Papinian 11 *quaestionum*), *D.* 28.4.3 (Marcus supports Marcellus reported in Marcellus 29 *digestorum*), *D.* 35.1.48 (Marcus agrees with Marcellus on a matter concerning a trust reported in Marcellus 1 *digestorum*), *D.* 37.14.17 (Marcus agrees with an opinion expressed by Salvius Julianus against Maecianus, overturning an opinion of Proculus reported in Ulpian 11 *ad legem Juliam et Papiam*), *D* 4.4.38 pr (Severus overrules Paul, reported in Paul 1

decretorum), *D.* 14.5.8 (Severus supports the *prefaectus annonae*'s opinion against Paul reported in Paul 1 *decretorum*), *D* 29.2.97 (Severus supports a view of Papinian reported in Paul 1 *decretorum*), *D.* 32.27 pr–1 (Severus holds against Paul in a matter of a will reported in Paul 2 *decretorum*), *D.* 49.14.50 (Severus agrees with Papinian and Messius on a matter concerning an estate reported in Paul 3 *decretorum*), *D.* 50.16.240 (Severus disagrees with legal advisers on a matter concerning a divorce reported in Paul 3 *decretorum*). For a full discussion of these cases see Peachin, "Jurists and the Law," 113–20.

185   Chapter 5, p. 213 below and the important discussion in R. MacMullen, *The Roman Government's Response to Crisis, AD 233–337* (New Haven, 1976), 196–203, whose work anticipates the discussion offered here and in that chapter.

186   Dio 81.1.2–3, 5.1; for the dates of these offices see Leunissen, *Konsuln und Konsulare,* 163, 219 (Africa), 241 (Dalmatia), 259 (Pannonia inferior).

187   Leunissen, *Konsuln und Konsulare,* 113, 136–37.

188   Leunissen, *Konsuln und Konsulare,* 217; see also Syme, *Emperors and Biography: Studies in the Historia Augusta* (Oxford, 1971), 135–43.

189   Leunissen, *Konsuln und Konsulare,* 154; *PIR²* M 137.

190   Leunissen, *Konsuln und Konsulare,* 162; *PIR²* A 1389.

191   Leunissen, *Konsuln und Konsulare,* 157–58; *PIR²* A 470.

192   Leunissen, *Konsuln und Konsulare,* 98, 100.

193   Leunissen, *Konsuln und Konsulare,* 99.

194   K. Dietz, *Senatus contra principem: Untersuchungen zur senatorischen Opposition gegen Kaiser Maximinus Thrax* (Munich, 1980), 190, and A. R. Birley, "Decius Reconsidered," in *Les empereurs illyriens: Actes du colloque de Strasbourg (11–13 octobre 1990) organisé par le Centre de Recherche sur l'Europe centrale et sud-orientale,* ed. E. Frézouls and H. Jouffroy (Strasbourg, 1998), 59–68.

195   For the date of Marius' book see Barnes, *Sources of Historia Augusta,* 101; R. Syme, *Ammianus and the Historia Augusta* (Oxford, 1968), 90.

196   *HA V. Hel.* 12.1 and Dio 78.31.1; Herod. 5.7.6. For the issue of his connection with the dancer Eutychianus see Leunissen, *Konsuln und Konsulare,* 31.

197   For Zoticus' survival see Dio 79.16.1; for his equipment see Dio 79.16.2, and for the issue in general see *HA V. Hel.* 12.2, and comments in Salway, "Fragment of Severan History," 132.

198   Dio 79.16.6.

199   Dio 79.16.7.

200   Dio 79.9.3–4; *HA V. Hel.* 6.5.

201   *P. Oxy.* 3298i.2 for Aelian (the person in question) see chapter 5, n. 15 below.

202   Dio 78.7.5.

203   Campbell, *Emperor and Roman Army,* 54–55, 197.

204   Dio 81.4.5.

205   Dio 81.2.3.

206   Dio 81.2.2, 4; for the date see *P. Oxy.* 2565, attesting Epagathus as prefect of Egypt in 224, and, in general, Syme, "Fiction about Roman Jurists," 91 (also in Syme, *Roman Papers* 3: 1403).

207   Dio 81.5.1.

208   For details see E. Kettenhoffen, "Die Einforderung des Achämeniderbes durch Ardasir: Eine Interpretatio Romana," *Orientalia Lovaniensa Periodica* 15 (1984): 177–90.

209   Dio 81.3.2–3.

210   Herod. 6.7.8.

211   Dio 81.3.4.

212 Dio 81.3.4; *PIR²* F 283 (nothing is known about him aside from this passage of Dio).

213 Herod. 6.2.1; George, p. 674 (Mosshammer, p. 437); Zon. 12.15. For further details see Potter, *Prophecy and History*, 376–80, also pointing out that the historian generally known as Syncellus was in fact George the Syncellus. I have therefore referred to him throughout by his proper name.

214 The notion appears in Drijvers, "Hatra Palmyra und Edessa," 879–80, but is implicitly dismissed in Ross, *Roman Edessa*, 67.

215 George, 674 (Mosshammer, 437); George, 675 (Mosshammer, 439); Zos. 1.12.2; Pol. Silv. *Chron.*, p. 521; [Aur. Vict.] *Epit. de Caes.* 24.2; with discussion in Potter, *Prophecy and History*, 20, n. 55.

216 For discussion of the date see Whittaker, *Herodian* 2: 102–3, n. 2.

217 Herod. 6.4.7. This may be the revolt of Taurinus; see n. 215 above.

218 Herod. 6.5–6.6.3.

219 Herod. 6.6.5–6.

220 Herod 7.2.2 with D. S. Potter, "Gaining Information on Rome's Neighbours," *JRA* 9 (1996): 530–31. See also p. 222 below on the status of Adiabene and Mesene under Ardashir.

221 Herod. 6.7.4.

222 Halfmann, *Itinera principum*, 232.

223 M. Peachin, *Roman Imperial Titulature and Chronology AD 235–284* (Amsterdam, 1990), 26–27.

224 Syme, *Emperors and Biography*, 179–93.

225 Herod. 6.9.5; Campbell, *Emperor and Roman Army*, 68–69, on the image of Maximinus.

226 Herod. 7.2.8.

227 Herod. 6.9.4, 8.4.

228 Herod. 6.8.8.

229 Herod. 7.1.3.

230 Campbell, *Emperor and Roman Army*, 170–71; J.-P. Callu, *La politique monétaire des empereurs romains de 238 à 311* (Paris, 1969), 310–11.

231 Dio 78.34.2–3.

232 Herod. 7.3.5.

233 Gradel, *Emperor Worship*, 357–59.

234 X. Loriot, "Les premières années de la grande crise du IIIᵉ siècle: De l'avènement de Maximin le Thrace (235) à la mort de Gordien III (244)," *ANRW* 2.2 (1975): 673, with n. 131.

235 For discussion cf. Loriot, "Les premières années," 672–73. See esp. Herod. 7.1.4; 9.

236 For the date of the Persian invasion see now E. Kettenhoffen, "Die Eroberung von Nisibis und Karrhai durch die Sāsāniden in der Zeit Kaiser Maximins (235/236 n. Chr.)," *Iranica Antiqua* 30 (1995): 159–77.

237 What follows relies heavily on Herodian. The *Historia Augusta* lives of the Maximini and of Pupienus and Balbinus have little independent value, though they are both now well served by commentaries. See A Lippold, *Maximini duo. Kommentar zur Historia Augusta*, vol. 1 (Bonn, 1991); and H. Brandt, *Maximi et Balbini. Kommentar zur Historia Augusta*, vol. 2 (Bonn, 1996).

238 Herod. 7.6.4–8.

239 Zos. 1.14.1 with K. Dietz, *Senatus contra principem*, 177–81; Syme, *Emperors and Biography*, 165.

240 Loriot, "Les premières années," 699–700.

241 Herod. 7.9.1–11. For discussion of these events and the identity of Capelianus, see Dietz, *Senatus contra principem*, 109–20.

242 Herod. 7.10.5–6.

243 *AE* 1982 no. 897; *SEG* 32, no. 1312.

244 Herod. 7.11.2–5.

245 Herod. 7.11.5–9.

246 Herod. 8.3.8–9.

247 Dietz, *Senatus contra principem*, 279–80; Leunissen, *Konsuln und Konsulare*, 123–24.

248 For the date of their assassination see M. Sartre, "Le Dies Imperii de Gordien III: Une inscription inédite de Syrie," *Syria* 61 (1984): 49–61. For a very different chronology, based on papyrological evidence, see M. Peachin, "Once More AD 238," *Athenaeum* 67 (1989): 594–604, who would place the death of Maximinus in early June, and the murder of Pupienus and Balbinus in early August. I prefer Sartre's chronology because I think that it would be impossible to honor Gordian in advance of his proclamation, while papyri in a time of considerable confusion may be slow to pick up changes in administration. Still, Peachin's objection to the compression of events implied by the chronology accepted here is not unreasonable, and new evidence may confirm his view.

249 Herod. 8.8.7.

250 Dietz, *Senatus contra principem*, 103–9, 197–99, 210–45. See also p. 229–232 below for more details.

251 Walker, *Metrology*, 3–51.

5 INTELLECTUAL TRENDS IN THE EARLY THIRD CENTURY

1 Vita A. For a brief discussion of this and other biographical traditions concerning the Oppians see M. Drury, "Appendix of Authors and Works," in *The Cambridge History of Classical Literature*, ed. P. E. Easterling and B. M. W. Knox, vol. 1, pt. 4 (Cambridge, 1985), 228.

2 The invocation of book 1 is to Marcus, while the address to the rulers at the end of book 2 is plainly to Marcus and Commodus (*Hal.* 2.681–83). The invocation of book 5 and the conclusion are both to a singular ruler (5.1, 675–80). The invocation at *Hal.* 4.4 is to "Antoninus" and son. The invocation at *Cyn.* 1.1–15 is also to Caracalla. The origin of the author of *On Fishing* is shown to be Cilicia by *Hal.* 3.7–10, 205–10. As for the author of *On Hunting*, he states that Apamea in Syria is his fatherland at *Cyn.* 2.127. Note also that he asserts that the tomb of Memnon was on the Orontes at *Cyn.* 2.150–55. For a summary of the problem see G. W. Bowersock, "The Hexameter Poems Ascribed to Oppian," in Easterling and Knox, *Cambridge History of Classical Literature*, vol. 1, pt. 4, 93–94.

3 Opp. *Hal.* 1.646–47, 2.12–7.

4 Opp. *Cyn.* 540–46.

5 Opp. *Cyn.* 4.210–16, 4.200–5.

6 Opp. *Hal.* 2.43–47 echoing Hes. *Op.* 276–78, which became a commonplace; see Plut. *Mor.* 964b, 970b; Ael. *NA* 6.50.

7 Ath. *Deip.* 1.13b.

8 Ath. *Deip.* 1.1–2. For the identity of Larensis, and the time of writing, see now Braund, "Learning, Luxury, and Empire"; see also J. Davidson, "Pleasure and Pedantry in Athenaeus," in Braund and Wilkins, *Athenaeus and His World*, 292–303, esp. 298.

9 G. Anderson, "Athenaeus: The Sophistic Environment," *ANRW* 34.3 (1997): 2183–84; G. Anderson, "The Banquet of Belles-Lettres: Athenaeus and the Comic

Symposium," in Braund and Wilkins, *Athenaeus and His World*, 316–26; Davidson, "Pleasure and Pedantry," 299–303; L. Romeri, "The λογόδειπνον: Athenaeus between Banquet and Anti-Banquet," in Braund and Wilkins, *Athenaeus and His World*, 256–71, with the discussion of the tradition of reading Archestratus of Gela, on which see S. D. Olsen and A. Sens, *Archestratus of Gela: Greek Culture and Cuisine in the Fifth Century BCE* (Oxford, 2000), xliii–xlvi.

10 Kaster, *Guardians of Language*, 18.
11 T. Morgan, *Literate Education in the Hellenistic and Roman Worlds* (Cambridge, 1998), 235.
12 Morgan, *Literate Education*, 162–63.
13 Plin. *Ep.* 3.5.17; A. G. *NA* Praef. 3–10.
14 A. G. *NA* 1.22.2; see also Kaster, *Guardians of Language*, 21, for later examples.
15 The best discussion of his life and works is N. G. Wilson's introduction to his Loeb edition of the *Historical Miscellany* (Cambridge, Mass., 1997).
16 Potter, *Literary Texts*, 9–10.
17 *VH* 13.1; see also Apoll. *Bib.* 3.9.2.
18 Phil. *V. Soph.* 624.
19 P. 164 above.
20 G. Anderson, "The Second Sophistic: Some Problems of Perspective," in *Antonine Literature*, ed. D. A. Russell (Oxford, 1990), 94–96, on the decision to refer to the phenomenon as the "second" rather than "new" in order to strengthen the link with Aeschines. P. A. Brunt, "The Bubble of the Second Sophistic," *BICS* 39 (1994): 25–52, rightly stresses the fact that Philostratus' view is idiosyncratic, but that does not mean that it was not influential. See the sensible comments in Bowersock, "Philostratus and the Second Sophistic," in Easterling and Knox, *Cambridge History of Classical Literature*, vol. 1, pt. 4, 96. For a particular case in point, the novel, see n. 141 below.
21 Eunap. *VS* 424.
22 Phil. *V. Soph.* 483.
23 Phil. *V. Soph.* 484.
24 Phil. *V. Soph.* 486.
25 Phil. *V. Soph.* 487–92.
26 Phil. *V. Soph.* 511–12.
27 For Favorinus see Phil. *V. Soph.* 489 with M. Gleason, *Making Men: Sophists and Self-Presentation in Ancient Rome* (Princeton, 1995), 3, n. 2; for Aelian see p. 177 above.
28 P. 142 above.
29 Phil. *V. Soph.* 613 for Heracleides and Marcianus.
30 Phil. *V. Soph.* 585 (Hadrian), 594 (Pausanias).
31 Phil. *V. Soph.* 570–76 (Alexander), 577–78 (Hermogenes), 578–81 (Philagrus).
32 Phil. *V. Soph.* 627 and p. 78 above. For Julia's role in handling appeals see Dio 78.18.2; Oliver, *Greek Constitutions*, no. 265, with Jones, "Imperial Letters at Ephesus," 44.
33 For Nineveh as Mespila see Xen. *An.* 3.10 (badly informed as to the nature of the site; see Dillery's note to the Loeb edition). Ammianus calls it *Nineue*, an *ingens civitas Adiabenae* at 18.7.1; see also J. F. Matthews, *The Roman Empire of Ammianus* (London, 1989), 50.
34 For the demise of the circle of Julia see Bowersock, *Greek Sophists*, 103–9.
35 S. Swain, *Hellenism and Empire: Language, Classicism, and Power in the Greek World, AD 50–250* (Oxford, 1996), 381, accepts the content of chapter 3 at face value, dating the work to the period after her death. In this he follows E. L. Bowie, "Apollonius of Tyana: Tradition and Reality," *ANRW* 2.16.2 (1978): 1670, n. 71, who observes, properly, that Julia is spoken of in the past tense.

36 Phil. *V. Apoll*. See also Heliod. *Aeth*. 10.2, 6, 10; for another version of the "naked sophists" here rather than in India, in what may be a roughly contemporary work, see also J. R. Morgan, "Heliodorus," in *The Novel in the Ancient World*, ed. G. Schmeling, Mnemosyne Supplement 159 (Leiden, 1996), 434, though it is likely that this book should be dated to the fourth century instead. For the problem of the date of Heliodorus' *Ethiopian Tale*, see n. 160 below. For the placing of the naked sophists in India see Hippol. *Haer*. 1.21.

37 Phil. *V. Apoll*. 2.32.

38 Phil. *V. Apoll*. 2.33.

39 Phil. *V. Apoll*. 2.42–43.

40 Phil. *V. Apoll*. 3.13 (Pans), 14 (statues).

41 Potter, *Literary Texts*, 144–50, on imitation of historiographic style in fiction.

42 Phil. *V. Apoll*. 3.15.

43 Phil. *V. Apoll*. 3.52, 55.

44 Phil. *V. Apoll*. 2.26–27.

45 Phil. *V. Apoll*. 3.42.

46 Phil. *V. Apoll*. 6.11.

47 Potter, *Prophets and Emperors*, 32–34.

48 Bowersock, *Greek Sophists*, 74.

49 Phil. *V. Apoll*. 4.1.

50 Phil. *V. Apoll*. 7.9.

51 For Oenomaeus see the excellent edition of J. Hammerstaedt, *Die Orakelkritik des Kynikers Oenomaeus* (Frankfurt am Main, 1988); for the nature of Artemidorus' work see G. W. Bowersock, *Fiction as History: Nero to Julian* (Berkeley, 1994), 77–98.

52 For a good discussion see the original publication of G. M. Parássoglou, "Circular from a Prefect: Dileat Omnibus Perpetuo Divinandi Curiositas," in Hanson, *Collectanea Papyrologica*, pt. 1, pp. 261–74.

53 Phil. *V. Apoll*. 6.41.

54 Failure of the Spartans to maintain their traditions: Phil. *V. Apoll*. 4.27; animal sacrifice: Phil. *V. Apoll*. 4.19; Greeks taking Latin names: Phil. *V. Apoll*. 4.5; civic patriotism: Phil. *V. Apoll*. 4.7.

55 Phil. *V. Apoll*. 5.4.

56 D. F. Easton, "Troy before Schliemann," *Studia Troica* 1 (1991): 111–29, for the history of the area in general; S. Allen, *Finding the Walls of Troy: Frank Calvert and Heinrich Schliemann at Hisarlik* (Berkeley, 1999), 36, 63, for specific sites. See also Erskine, *Troy*, 98–112.

57 F. Calvert, "The Tumulus of Hanai Tepe in the Troad," *Archaeological Journal* 16 (1859): 1–6, with Allen, *Walls of Troy*, 59–63.

58 F. I. Zeitlin, "Visions and Revisions of Homer," in *Being Greek under Rome: Cultural Identity, the Second Sophistic, and the Development of Empire*, ed. S. Goldhill (Cambridge, 2001), 253–55, on the vision.

59 Paus. 9.40.10–12 (scepter of Agamemnon), 3.3.8 (spear of Achilles).

60 Plin. *HN* 13.88 (letter of Sarpedon).

61 Paus. 3.3.8 (spear of Achilles and sword of Memnon).

62 Paus. 1.35.4–5 (Ajax's tomb), 2.16.6 (tomb of Agamemnon).

63 Paus. 1.42.2–3, 10.31.7 (road); G. W. Bowersock, "The Miracle of Memnon," *BASP* 21 (1984): 21–32 (also in G. W. Bowersock, *Studies on the Eastern Roman Empire* [Goldbach, 1994], 253–64).

64 Paus. 10.31.7 (conquest of Persia).

65 Paus. 10.31.2 (*Cyp*. fr. 21 Allen).

66 Apoll. *Epit*. 3.8; Hyg. *Fab*. 105; Phil. *Her*. 33.31.

67 For the evidence see de Lannoy, *Flavii Philostrati Heroicus* (Leipzig, 1977), 1. The Suda identifies the author of the *Heroicus* with that of the Lives; Ps. Menander the author of the *Heroicus* with that of the *Imagines*. While agnosticism on the question of authorship may be possible (see G. Anderson, *Philostratus: Biography and Belles Lettres in the Third Century A.D.* [London, 1986], 77–96), L. de Lannoy, "Le problème des Philostrate (État de la question)," *ANRW* 34.3 (1997): 2431–36, makes a powerful case for identifying the author of the *Heroicus* with that of *In Honor of Apollonius*. This is accepted by C. P. Jones, "Time and Place in Philostratus' Heroikos," *JHS* 121 (2001): 143.

68 Zeitlin, "Visions and Revisions," 264–66, for discussion of the selection of a Phoenician as the interlocutor.

69 Phil. *Her.* 6.3–6.

70 Jones, "Time and Place," 144–46, for discussion of the site.

71 See L. Robert, *Études de numismatique grecque* (Paris, 1951), 75; and J. Babelon, "Protésilas à Scioné," *Revue numismatique*, 5th ser., 13 (1951): 7–8.

72 Phil. *Her.* 26.16–17.

73 For the importance of the reference to recognizable athletes see Jones, "Time and Place," 141–49.

74 Phil. *Her.* 4.2, 9.5–7 (the Persian); see Hdt. 9.116, 120.

75 Phil. *Her.* 8.

76 Phil. *Her.* 18.2–6. According to a tradition reported in Max. Tyr. *Or.* 9.7, Hector could be seen "flashing with light" on the Trojan plain. For sacrifices to Hector at Troy see Lucian *Conc. Deorum* 12.

77 In two places he appears to be correcting another version of the story, this one being that of Dictys; see *Her.* 26, stating that the use of writing was unknown, contra Dict. *Eph.* Praef. 5.17 (saying that he wrote in Phoenician characters) and *Her.* 30, stating that Idomeneus did not take part in the war. On these points see S. Merkle, "Telling the True Story of the Trojan War: The Eyewitness Account of Dictys of Crete," in *The Search for the Ancient Novel*, ed. J. Tatum (Baltimore, 1994), 193–94; and S. Merkle, "The Truth and Nothing but the Truth: Dictys and Dares," in Schmeling, *Novel in Ancient World*, 579.

78 Phil. *Her.* 43.13–16.

79 Phil. *Her.* 44.2–4.

80 Phil. *Her.* 38 (Aeneas), 42.1–2 (Euphorbus).

81 Phil. *Her.* 25.12.

82 Phil. *Her.* 23.30.

83 Phil. *Her.* 54–57; Paus. 3.19.11–13; Max. Tyr. *Or.* 9.7; Arr. *Peripl. M. Eux.* 21–33; see also Zeitlin, "Visions and Revisions," 258–62.

84 Phil. *Her.* 53.5–6 (Lemnos), 43.7–9 (Hesiod and Homer), 7.5 (other opinions about the date of Homer).

85 J. Spooner, *Nine Homeric Papyri from Oxyrhynchus*, Studi e Testi di Papirologia n.s. 1 (Florence, 2002), 1–42.

86 *Bodl. Gr. Inscr.* 3017 with P. J. Parsons, "A School-Book from the Sayce Collection," *ZPE* 6 (1970): 141.

87 *PSI* 12.1276, with Parsons, "School-Book," 141.

88 M. van Rossum-Steenbeck, *Greek Reader's Digests? Studies on a Selection of Subliterary Papyri* (Leiden, 1998). I am grateful to Dr. Robert Caldwell for bringing this excellent book to my attention.

89 J. J. O'Hara, "Fragment of a Homer-Hypothesis with No Gods," *ZPE* 56 (1984): 2–4.

90 Van Rossum-Steenbeck, *Greek Reader's Digests*, 69.

91 Van Rossum-Steenbeck, *Greek Reader's Digests*, 108–9. For a list of these texts see also Parson's introduction to *P. Oxy.* 3830; F. Montanari, "Revisione di P. Berol. 13282 le *Historiae Fabulares* omeriche su papirio," *Atti del xvii Congresso internatazionale di Papirologia (Napoli 19–26 maggio 1983)* (Naples, 1984), 241–42.

92 N. Horsfall, "Stesichorus in Bovillae," *JHS* 99 (1979): 26–48, and N. Horsfall, "Tabulae Iliacae in the Collection Froehner, Paris," *JHS* 103 (1983): 144–47, are basic discussions of the material; see van Rossum-Steenbeck, *Greek Reader's Digests*, 83–84, for connections with the papyrus summaries.

93 O'Hara, "Fragment of a Homer-Hypothesis," 2.

94 Ael. *VH* 11.2. See also Dares, *Exc.* 25 with Dict. *Eph.* 1.19 (Agamemnon replaced by Palamedes as leader of the Greeks); Dares, *Exc.* 14 with Dict. *Eph.* 1.17 (list of Greek leaders, some points of contact); Dares, *Exc.* 18 has points of contact with Dict. *Eph.* 2.35 (list of Trojan leaders, though the parallels are not overwhelming). For the possible connection between Dictys' account and Philostratus' *Heroicus* see n. 77 above.

95 See the notes on *P. Teb.* 268 and *P. Oxy.* 2539. See also Merkle, "Telling the True Story," 192 (also discussing the date of the Latin version, placing it in the later fourth century); Merkle, "Truth and Nothing but Truth," 577–78 (dating the Latin version of Dares to the fifth century).

96 Pp. 32–33 above (Egyptian texts) and p. 106 above (Philo).

97 Dict. *Eph.* Praef.; see also Dict. *Eph.* 5.17.

98 D. A. Russell, *Plutarch* (London, 1973), 2–3.

99 Dict. *Eph.* 1.3.

100 Dict. *Eph.* 3.15, 20–21.

101 Dict. *Eph.* 2.30.

102 Merkle, "Telling the True Story," 186–91; Merkle, "Truth and Nothing but Truth," 568–71.

103 Dict. *Eph.* 5.14–15.

104 Dict. *Eph.* 5.16.

105 Dares, *Exc.* 12, 44.

106 Dares, *Exc.* 3–4, 9–10.

107 Dares, *Exc.* 25, 28.

108 Dares, *Exc.* 39–40.

109 E. L. Bowie, "Greek Poetry in the Antonine Age," in Russell, *Antonine Literature*, 90; C. P. Jones, "Greek Drama in the Roman Empire," in *Theater and Society in the Classical World*, ed. R. Scodel (Ann Arbor, 1993), 39–52.

110 M. Parca, *Ptocheia or Odysseus in Disguise at Troy (P. Köln VI 245)* (Atlanta, 1991), 8 (date).

111 For pantomime see E. Csapo and W. J. Slater, *The Context of Ancient Drama* (Ann Arbor, 1995), 377–85.

112 Macrob. *Sat.* 5.4–5 with F. Vian, *Recherches sur les Posthomerica de Quintus de Smyrne* (Paris, 1959), 89–90, separating him from Pisander of Laranda, who wrote in the time of Alexander Severus. That Pisander was the son of Nestor of Laranda, on whom see n. 116 below.

113 E. Heitsch, *Die griechischen Dichterfragmente der römischen Kaiserzeit* (Göttingen, 1961), no. 21; D. L. Page, *Select Papyri*, vol. 3 (Cambridge, Mass., 1941), no. 137.

114 Heitsch, *Die griechischen Dichterfragmente*, no. 18; Page, *Select Papyri*, vol. 3, no. 133.

115 M. L. West, *Iambi et Elegi Graeci* (Oxford, 1972), 93–94.

116 For Idaeus of Rhodes see *Suppl. Hell.* 501–2. For Nestor of Laranda see A. Barbieri, "Settimio Nestore," *Athenaeum* 31 (1953): 158–69.

117 The tradition that he wrote in the time of Severus is essentially confirmed by *P. Oxy.* 2946, written in a hand characteristic of the second to early fourth centuries;

see also the discussion in B. Gerlaud, *Triphiodore, La prise d'Ilion* (Paris, 1982), 7–8. For the form of the name see Gerlaud's discussion on pp. 1–2. For characteristics of his style see A. Cameron, *Claudian: Poetry and Propaganda at the Court of Honorius* (Oxford, 1970), 478–82. Gerlaud's interpretation of lines 653–55 as a reference to the foundation of Constantinople (p. 9) is, in my view, an overreading of a standard phrase that means no more than that Aeneas' descendants will have an eternal empire. If one wanted to press the interpretation of *paisi kai huiônoisin* in line 655 further, it might simply be seen as a reference to the foundation of Alba Longa and then of Rome by later descendants.

118 Tryph. 4–5, and ll. 636–37. For the "Callimacheanism" of his program see Gerlaud's note ad loc. (p. 103).

119 Tryph. 634–39 with M. J. Anderson, *The Tale of Troy in Early Greek Poetry and Art* (Oxford, 1997), 46, and Gerlaud's notes ad loc.

120 Tryph. 59–61 with Anderson, *Tale of Troy*, 26.

121 Tryph. 99–102; Anderson, *Tale of Troy*, 183–84.

122 Tryph. 219–21, 227–29, 258–61.

123 D. S. Potter, "Martyrdom as Spectacle," in Scodel, *Theater and Society*, 66–70.

124 Tryph. 376–438; the connection with Lycophron is explored by Gerlaud, pp. 29–30.

125 Tryph. 455–64, 487–97 with the discussion of Gerlaud, pp. 30–35.

126 Tryph. 651–55; for the interpretation of these lines see n. 117 above.

127 Vian, *Recherches sur les Posthomerica*, 87–95, 101–9.

128 Q.S. *Post.* 2.558–92 with Vian, *Recherches sur les Posthomerica*, 28–29.

129 Q.S. *Post.* 10.147–66 with Vian, *Recherches sur les Posthomerica*, 138–39.

130 Q.S. *Post.* 4.6–12 with Vian, *Recherches sur les Posthomerica*, 136–37.

131 Plin. *HN* 34.8 with Bowersock, *Fiction as History*, 69.

132 Phil. *Imag.* 1 Praef. 4.

133 Phil. *Imag.* 1 Praef. 2.

134 Phil. *Imag.* 2.17.1.

135 Phil. *Imag.* 2.17.5.

136 Phil. *Imag.* 2.9.1.

137 I think that I can say, without fear of contradiction, that I have nothing here to add to the debate on the origins of this literary form. For useful and balanced introductions to the issue see N. Holzberg, "The Genre: Novels Proper and the Fringe," in Schmeling, *Novel in Ancient World*, 11–28; S. Swain, "A Century and More of the Greek Novel," in *Oxford Readings in the Greek Novel*, ed. S. Swain (Oxford, 1999), 3–35. For the novels themselves, see E. L. Bowie, "The Greek Novel," in Easterling and Knox, *Cambridge History of Classical Literature*, vol. 1, pt. 4, 123–39 (also in Swain, *Oxford Readings*, 39–59).

138 *Leuc.* 1.4, trans. Winkler.

139 Tert. *De spect.* 10, 17 (on the theater) and passim; Aug. *Conf.* 3.2.3 with J. J. O'Donnell, *Augustine: Confessions* (Oxford, 1992), 2: 151–52.

140 Char. *Leuc.* 5.8.2 with S. Said, "The City in the Greek Novel," in Tatum, *Search for Ancient Novel*, 221.

141 Phil. *V. Soph.* 524 with B. E. Perry, *The Ancient Romances: A Literary Historical Account of Their Origins* (Berkeley, 1967), 169, with the caveat of E. L. Bowie, "The Readership of Greek Novels in the Ancient World," in Tatum, *Search for Ancient Novel*, 445.

142 See the excellent summary in J. R. Morgan, "On the Fringes of the Canon: Work on the Fragments of Ancient Greek Fiction," *ANRW* 34.4 (1998): 3295.

143 For Sisenna's translation see Ov. *Tr.* 2.443–44. Ten fragments of Sisenna's translation are printed in F. Buecheler, *Petronii Saturae* (Berlin, 1862), 239–40. Of these fr. 1: *nocte vagatrix* suggests a prostitute and fr. 10: *ut eum penitus utero suo recepit* is plainly an explicit description of a sexual act.

144 Plut. *Crass.* 32.6; [Lucian] *Amores* 1. The date of the Greek works, which were evidently the ones found in the Roman baggage since the Parthians could read them, should be no later than the beginning of the first century BC. For Aristides of Miletus see P. G. Walsh, *The Roman Novel* (Cambridge, 1970), 10–18. Walsh includes tales involving magic in his discussion of the *Milesiaca*. This does not seem to be relevant to the content of Aristides' book. There is a sensible discussion in Perry, *The Ancient Romances*, 92–95, and the OCD³ article by E. L. Bowie.

145 Ov. *Tr.* 2.415–18.

146 Mart. 12.95. The OLD entry under *thalassio* is inadequate on this point, as is the LSJ entry (with supplement) under *thalassios*. Mart. 12.95.5–7: . . . *ne thalassionem | indicas manibus libidinosis | et fias sine femina maritus* indicates the meaning of "the purple part," or penis. The use of a Greek noun here may indicate the Greek context of the *Sybaritici libelli*.

147 S. Stephens and J. Winkler, *Ancient Greek Novels: The Fragments* (Princeton, 1999), 14–15.

148 The very close connections between some episodes in Apuleius, ones that are not derived from Lucius of Patras' work, with the *Phoenicica* of Lollianus, suggest that there may be a direct connection between the two works. We are not now in a position to be absolutely certain of the direction of borrowing; see Stephens and Winkler, *Ancient Greek Novels*, 324.

149 The work is conventionally called *Ninos*, but there is no direct evidence for the title. If it is correct to think that the female love interest is Semiramis, it might be tempting to think that the title of the book was the *Babyloniaca*, possibly the work of that title attributed to Xenophon of Antioch. For discussion of the problem see Stephens and Winkler, *Ancient Greek Novels*, 24–27.

150 Stephens and Winkler, *Ancient Greek Novels*, 249–50, showing that these two novels should not be read as being part of the same genre as the *Alexander Romance* and Xenophon's *Cyropaedeia* because those two works do not seem to have the same interest in the youth of their respective heroes.

151 Morgan, "Fragments," 3295, with a sound caveat against assuming that Photius and texts preserved in the Byzantine manuscript tradition are representative of the tradition as a whole. On the other hand, the evidence that emerges from the fragments does not seem to alter the picture much from that suggested here.

152 Stephens and Winkler, *Ancient Greek Novels*, 185–88.

153 Stephens and Winkler, *Ancient Greek Novels*, 267–70, 289–91.

154 For the countryside in the Greek novel see the perceptive comments of S. Said, "Rural Society in the Greek Novel; or, The Country Seen from the Town," in Swain, *Oxford Readings*, 85, and, on Longus' novel, pp. 97–107. See also L. Cresci, "The Novel of Longus the Sophist and the Pastoral Tradition," in Swain, *Oxford Readings*, 214.

155 Xen. *Eph.* 4.2 *(archon tês Aigyptou),* 2.13 *(eirenarch)* with B. Kytzler, "Xenophon of Ephesus," in Schmeling, *Novel in Ancient World*, 346–48; and Rife, "Officials of Roman Provinces."

156 T. Hägg, "*Callirhoe* and *Parthenope*: The Beginnings of the Historical Novel," in *Cl. Ant.* 6 (1987): 184–204 (also in Swain, *Oxford Readings*, 150–51); B. P. Reardon, "Chariton," in Schmeling, *Novel in Ancient World*, 326–27; C. P. Jones, "Hellenistic History in Chariton of Aphrodisias," *Chiron* 22 (1992): 91–102.

157 Hägg, "*Callirhoe* and *Parthenope*," 154.

158 Potter, "Performance, Power, and Justice," 147–59, for public involvement in trials and executions.

159 Xen. *Eph.* 2.6; for the exemplary value of punishment see Potter, "Martyrdom as Spectacle."

160 Hel. *Eth.* 9.2–9, 15, with Julian *Or.* 1.22–23, 3.11–13 and Ephraim of Nisibis, *Carm. Nis.* 2.9–10 (*Des heiligen Ephraem des Syrers Carmina Nisibena*, tr. E. Beck, *Corpus Scriptorum Christianorum Orientalium Scriptores Syri* 93 [Louvain, 1961], 8–9). The points of contact here have been used to propose a date in the later fourth century. For different perspectives see T. Szepessy, "La siège de Nisibe et la chronologie d'Héliodore," *Acta Antiqua* 24 (1976): 247–76; C. S. Lightfoot, "Facts and Fiction – the Third Siege of Nisibis (AD 350)," *Historia* 38 (1988): 105–25; Bowersock, *Fiction as History*, 153–55, correcting errors in the reading of Ephraim by others (the wall in question is plainly an earth wall in 2.10) and restating the case for a date of Heliodorus after 350. Bowersock is absolutely correct in stating that it is absurd to think that Julian would have modeled his account of the siege of Nisibis on Heliodorus, though it is also hard to think that he would have been influenced by a Syriac text, which makes it possible that all three authors are drawing from a common tradition, even though Ephraim was an eyewitness to the actual siege.

161 *Ninus* fr. B iii, 1–27.

162 Xen. *Eph.* 1.2; Long. *Daph.* 1.1.1 with Said, "City in Greek Novel," 229.

163 Said, "City in Greek Novel," 228–31.

164 J. Keil, "Vertreter der zweiten Sophistik in Ephesus," *JÖAI* 40 (1953): 5–22.

165 *BÉ* 1981 no. 481; *IG* ii² 3816 with J. Nollé, "Ofellius Laetus, platonischer Philosoph," *ZPE* 41 (1981): 197–206; G. W. Bowersock, "Plutarch and the Sublime Hymn of Ofellius Laetus," *GRBS* 22 (1982): 275–79 (also in Bowersock, *Eastern Roman Empire*, 61–65) for the date and context.

166 Acts 17:16–34.

167 P. Gordon, *Epicurus in Lycia: The Second-Century World of Diogenes of Oenoanda* (Ann Arbor, 1996), 44, 66–93.

168 Gordon, *Epicurus in Lycia*, 33–36, on the dedication of the stoa; see also Potter, *Literary Texts*, 107–9, for bibliography on reading styles (silent and otherwise) in the ancient world.

169 For this view of the text see Potter, *Prophecy and History*, 351–55, based on autopsy in 1981, and some experience of the extreme repetitiveness of oracular language. There are alternative views, seeking to attach this specific response to one in *T. Theos.* 13; for a survey see now the attack on my views (with reference to other discussions) in Mitchell, "Cult of Theos Hypsistos," 81–92. It should be noted that two of his objections to the views expressed in *Prophecy and History* are incorrect. The fact that Oenomaeus criticizes oracles for repeating themselves is not, as Mitchell suggests, a point in favor of separating the Oenoanda text from other, similar texts, but a point in favor of identifying it with these texts. If oracular texts did not repeat each other, then Oenomaeus' point would not hold. He is observing a tendency within the genre. Mitchell might also consult *Prophecy and History*, 125–32, on the repetitive nature of prophetic language. As for the fact that the text is carved on one stone, which I take as a sign that the people receiving it knew that they had a text of a certain length rather than that they had, as Mitchell (following others) supposes, shortened a longer text, my point is precisely that the text fits the space chosen. The people who inscribed this text did not need to select a space carved on an altar; they could have selected two blocks, or more, if they had had a longer text. My point is precisely that the choice of the particular mode of inscription is the result of their having a short text, since it is my feeling that what was most important to them was the text rather than the space.

170 For the content of this text and other inscriptions of philosophical oracles see L. Robert, "Trois oracles de la Théosophie et un prophète d'Apollon," *CRAI* (1968), 568–99 (also in Robert, *OMS* 5: 584–616); L. Robert, "Un oracle gravé à Oinoanda," *CRAI* (1971), 597–619 (also in Robert, *OMS* 5: 617–39).

171 Max. *Or.* 9.7.
172 Max. Tyr. *Or.* 2.10; compare Max. Tyr. *Or.* 11.9, 41.2 with other parallels noted by Trapp ad *Or.* 2.10.
173 Potter, *Prophets and Emperors*, 1–57.
174 What follows is dependent on the excellent discussion in M. B. Trapp, *Maximus of Tyre: The Philosophical Discussions* (Oxford, 1997), xi–lv, and M. B. Trapp, "Philosophical Sermons: The 'Dialexeis' of Maximus of Tyre," *ANRW* 34.3 (1997): 1945–76.
175 Max. Tyr. *Or.* 2.4, 14.2; see also M. Frede, "Celsus Philosophus Platonicus," *ANRW* 36.7 (1994): 1584; F. G. Millar, "Porphyry: Ethnicity, Language, and Alien Wisdom," in *Philosophia Togata II. Plato and Aristotle at Rome*, ed. J. Barnes and M. Griffin (Oxford, 1997), 257–58.
176 For the problem of Celsus' identity see R. J. Hoffmann, *Celsus: On the True Doctrine* (Oxford, 1987), 30–33; Frede, "Celsus Philosophus Platonicus," 5188–91; H. Chadwick, *Origen, Contra Celsum*, rev. edn. (Cambridge, 1965), xxiv–xxvii.
177 Origen, *C. Cels.* 1.24. For the status of Origen's quotations of Celsus see Chadwick, *Origen, Contra Celsum*, xxii–xxiv; M. Frede, "Origen's Treatise, Against Celsus," in M. Edwards, M. Goodman, and S. Price, *Apologetics in the Roman Empire: Pagans, Jews, and Christians* (Oxford, 1999), 140–41. For attempts to reconstruct Celsus' text out of Origen see O. Glockner, *Celsi ΑΛΗΘΗΣ ΛΟΓΟΣ* (Bonn, 1924), who lists passages in the order that they appear in Origen's text, and R. Bader, *Der ΑΛΗΘΗΣ ΛΟΓΟΣ des Kelsos* (Stuttgart, 1940). Hoffman, *Celsus*, offers a good translation, but without including reference to the placement of fragments in Origen, which he mixes up to create a more logical argument for Celsus. I refer to Celsus only through passages where he is quoted by Origen.
178 Origen, *C. Cels.* 1.14, 16, 17.
179 Origen, *C. Cels.* 1.9, 12, 13.
180 R. Walzer, *Galen on Jews and Christians* (Oxford, 1949), 15, quoting from an Arabic translation of Galen's lost summary of Plato's *Republic*.
181 Num. Fr 1, 1b (Des Places).
182 What follows here depends upon H. Crouzel, *Origène* (Paris, 1985), 17–61.
183 P. Cox, *Biography in Late Antiquity: A Quest for the Holy Man* (Berkeley, 1983), 69–101.
184 Euseb. *Hist. eccl.* 6.2.6.
185 Euseb. *Hist. eccl.* 6.2.13–15.
186 Euseb. *Hist. eccl.* 6.8.1–3 with Origen, *Comm. In Matt.* 15.1–5 and Crouzel, *Origène*, 27, n. 32.
187 For the career of Peregrinus see Jones, *Culture and Society*, 117–32. For Augustine see pp. 526–28 below.
188 J. Dillon, *The Middle Platonists: A Study of Platonism, 80 BC to AD 220* (London, 1977), 380–83; see also G. Fowden, "The Pagan Holy Man in Late Antique Society," *JHS* 102 (1982): 36.
189 Porph. *Plot.* 14; the statement in the text goes somewhat beyond Dillon's observation (*The Middle Platonists*, 381) that "this tells us something, but it is not quite clear what." For more on Plotinus see pp. 323–26 below.
190 *P. Oxy.* 3069; see also p. 489 below, where the text is quoted.
191 See also B. P. Copenhaver, *Hermetica: The Greek Corpus Hermeticum and the Latin Asclepius in a New English Translation, with Notes and Introduction* (Cambridge, 1992), 112 (ad *CH* 1.18–19), 128 (ad *CH* 2.17), 136 (ad *CH* 4.6), 157 (ad *CH* 10.5); see also further passages in Fowden, *The Egyptian Hermes*, 107, n. 60.
192 The identification of Origen the Christian with Origen the Platonist (also a student of Ammonius) is supported by Crouzel, *Origène*, 30–31. For a clear statement of

the case against the identification see A. H. Armstrong's note in the Loeb edition of Porphyry's *Life of Plotinus* (*Plotinus*, vol. 1 [Cambridge, Mass., 1966], 11, n. 10).

193 Euseb. *Hist. eccl.* 6.19.15. It would appear that this took place shortly before Caracalla's bloody visit to the city in 215–16. For discussion of the date see Crouzel, *Origène*, 34.

194 Euseb. *Hist. eccl.* 6.21.3–4, 26.3. The date of the letter to Philip presumes that it was composed while Philip was in Antioch, which he left in the spring of 244.

195 See pp. 241–43 below.

196 For the circumstances of his death and the divergent traditions connected with it see Crouzel, *Origène*, 57–61.

197 See esp. Origen, *Exhort.* 4, 9, 14, 35–36, 49.

198 Origen, *C. Cels.* 8.22, trans. Chadwick; see also *C. Cels.* 8.41, 55, 65 and p. 318 below.

199 *Princ.* 4 with Crouzel, *Origène*, 243 and *C. Cels.* 6.64, quoting Plato, *Rep.* 509b, distinguishing between God and the Logos, and *C. Cels.* 7.38; *Comm. in Joann.* 19.6. The notion also appears in Clem. Al. *Strom.* 6.25, suggesting an Alexandrian background. See also Origen, *C. Cels.* 1.60, 66, 2.9 and *C. Cels.* 6.63, 7.24, 8.23 for his view that humans were composed of Soul and Body. See also J.N.D. Kelly, *Early Christian Doctrines*, 5th edn. (London, 1977), 126–32.

200 *Princ.* 1.2.9, 4.4.1; *Comm. In Rom.* 1.5; Greg. Thaum. *Or.* 4.37 with Crouzel, *Origène*, 244–46.

201 K. Rudolph, *Gnosis: The Nature and History of Gnosticism*, trans. R. Wilson (San Francisco, 1987) is fundamental for the analysis of these groups. See also, on the connection with Platonism, Dillon, *The Middle Platonists*, 384–96.

202 For the connection with Origen see Jer. *Vir. Ill.* 61 with Crouzel, *Origène*, 34 and, at length, Cerrato, *Hippolytus*, 33–38. I accept his argument that this is not the same person as the author of the Commentary on Daniel discussed in chapter 1. For Tertullian, who plainly exists in a different milieu, see Barnes, *Tertullian*, 211–32.

203 Tert. *De praescr. haeret.* 7.9; see also the extensive discussion of this passage in E. Osborn, *Tertullian, First Theologian of the West* (Oxford, 1997), 27–47, who shows that at this point in his career Tertullian's views were similar to those of Hippolytus in that he saw "the perfection of Christ" as "the climax of a history which includes Greek philosophy" (p. 45).

204 Hipp. *Ref.* 10.29; see also Kelly, *Early Christian Doctrines*, 124.

205 C. Osborne, *Rethinking Early Greek Philosophy: Hippolytus of Rome and the Presocratics* (London, 1987), 16.

206 Hipp. *Ref.* 1.17. In this he was similar to Ammonius Saccas; see Dillon, *The Middle Platonists*, 382. For a generous reading of Hippolytus' handling of Aristotle see Osborne, *Rethinking Early Greek Philosophy*, 66–67.

207 Hipp. *Ref.* 1.18–19.

208 It should be noted that his readings of Greek philosophers may be defended as an idiosyncratic reading of the texts, as shown by Osborne, *Rethinking Early Greek Philosophy*, passim. For the problem of Hippolytus as a source for Gnosticism see Rudolph, *Gnosis*, 12–14.

209 G. B. Conte, *Latin Literature: A History*, trans. J. Solodow (Baltimore, 1994), 558.

210 Porph. *Plot.* 3.

211 For Porphyry see pp. 327–28 below.

212 See S. N. C. Lieu, *Manichaeism in the Later Roman Empire and Medieval China: A Historical Survey* (Manchester, 1985), 41–42.

213 Hipp. *Ref.* 9.9.

214 For Elchasai's book see the excellent study of G. P. Luttikhuizen, *The Revelation of Elchasai: Investigation into the Evidence for a Mesopotamian Jewish Apocalypse of the Second Century and Its Reception by Judaeo-Christian Propagandists* (Tübingen, 1985).

215 Chapter 6, pp. 302–14 below.

6 THE FAILURE OF THE SEVERAN EMPIRE

1 Phil. *V. Soph.* 561 with p. 80, n. 180 above.

2 Pp. 165–67 above.

3 *FGrH* 115 fr. 65. For the connection between this and Zurvanite thought see G. Widengren, "Leitende Ideen und Quellen der iranischer Apokalyptik," in Hellholm, *Apocalypticism*, 127–33. See also Millar, "Looking East," 521–53.

4 Plin. *HN* 30.3–5; Apul. *Apol.* 26; Plato *Alc.* 1.121e.

5 For this material see now the thorough discussion by R. Beck, "Thus Spake Not Zarathustra: Zoroastrian Pseudepigrapha of the Greco-Roman World," in *A History of Zoroastrianism*, ed. M. Boyce and F. Grenet, vol. 3, *Zoroastrianism under Macedonian and Roman Rule* (Leiden, 1991), 491–565.

6 Phil. *V. Apoll.* 1.25.1 with. Hdt. 1.178.1.

7 Beck, "Thus Spake Not Zarathustra," 511–21; A. D. Nock, "Paul and the Magus," in *The Beginnings of Christianity: The Acts of the Apostles*, ed. F. J. Foakes-Jackson and K. Lake (London, 1920–33), 5: 164–82 (also in Nock, *Essays on Religion and the Ancient World*, ed. Zeph Stewart, vol. 1 [Oxford, 1986], 308–24).

8 For discussion of the symbolism see M. Boyce, *A History of Zoroastrianism*, vol. 2 (Leiden, 1982), 103–5, who rejects other views, including that it is Ahura Mazda.

9 See especially Boyce, *History of Zoroastrianism*, 2: 165–71, 179–83. There are, however, some points upon which Boyce's interpretations are excessive, as e.g. in the case of the monuments of the rulers of Xanthus, on which see (with bibliography) D. S. Potter, "The Identities of Lycia," forthcoming.

10 For the Elamite background see D. T. Potts, *The Archaeology of Elam: Formation and Transformation of an Ancient Iranian State* (Cambridge, 1999), 182, 186; on the place of Naqsh-i-Rustam under the Achaemenids see Boyce, *History of Zoroastrianism*, 2: 110–12.

11 For the evidence of Zoroastrian practice in Commagene see now Boyce and Grenet, *History of Zoroastrianism*, 3: 309–52; H. Waldmann, *Der kommagenische Mazdaismus, Istanbuler Mitteilungen* Beiheft 37 (Tübingen, 1991); for Cappadocia see Boyce and Grenet, *History of Zoroastrianism*, 3: 262–81, and for Pontus see Boyce and Grenet, *History of Zoroastrianism*, 3: 281–304.

12 Boyce and Grenet, *History of Zoroastrianism*, 3: 34–124, with the cautions scattered through J. Duchesne-Guillemin, "Zoroastrian Religion," in *The Cambridge History of Iran*, ed. E. Yarshater, vol. 3, pt. 2 (Cambridge, 1983), 866–74, and the clear statement of the alternative view that it is "less likely that 'Parthian religion' derived from an endogenous revival of Zoroastrianism" in C. Colpe, "Development of Religious Thought," in Yarshater, *Cambridge History of Iran*, vol. 3, pt. 2, 834.

13 C. E. Bosworth, *The History of al-Ṭabarī: The Sāsānids, the Byzantines, the Lakmids, and Yemen* (Albany, NY, 1999), 4 with n. 10. One classical tradition concerning his origin, Agath. 2.27.1–5 and George, 677–78 (Mosshammer, 440–41), stating that Papak was an astrologer who had a wandering soldier named Sasan sleep with his wife, having foreseen that his son would be a king, is late and useless, as is George of Pisidia, *Heraclias* 2.173–77, which states that he was a slave. Dio says simply that he was "*tis Persês*" (80.3.2), which is expanded upon by Zonaras at 12.15.7 to say that he was of obscure lineage; see Boissevain's notes in his edition of Dio, 3: 477. For doubts that Sasan was a real person see n. 14 below. Despite

this, the connection with Istakr and with his cult there may still point to the original base of Sasanian power.

14 The role of the elder Sapor in all of this is most obscure. In Tabarī's account he seizes the title of king against Ardashir's wishes, but is killed by a falling piece of masonry before the two brothers can come into conflict. But he is listed by Sapor as a legitimate holder of the title of king after Papak, who is also styled "king," in contrast to his father Sasan, who is called "lord," and before Ardashir. See T. Nöldeke, *Geschichte der Perser und Araber zur Zeit der Sasaniden. Aus der arabischen Chronik des Tabari übersetzt und mit ausführlichen Erläuterungen und Ergänzungen versehen* (Leiden, 1879), 8; M. H. Dodgeon and S. N. C. Lieu, *The Roman Eastern Frontier and the Persian Wars: A Documentary History* (London, 1991), 276–77; for the elder Sapor's place in the royal lineage see *RDGS* 20 and Göbl, *Antike Münzen* 2106; there may be only three coins of Sapor, who describes himself as "the divine Sapor, the king" and "son of the divine Papak, the king." The third known coin of Sapor is illustrated in the auction catalogue for Triton VI (n. 519). There is a good chance that Sasan is not a real person, but rather a minor divinity who was adopted as the progenitor of the line; see R. N. Frye, *The History of Ancient Iran* (Munich, 1984), 291.

15 The chronology of these events is clarified, to some degree, by the record of Mani's journey to India; see now the excellent discussion in C. Römer, *Manis frühe Missionsreisen nach der Kölner Manibiographie*, Papyrologica Coloniensia 24 (Cologne, 1994), 106.

16 Bosworth, *The History of al-Tabarī*, 13–14. It is tempting to associate defeats of the rulers of Ahwaz and Mesene with the first two battles mentioned by Dio, and the battle of Hormizdagan with the third. For the identification of Ahwaz with Elam see Potts, *The Archaeology of Elam*, 412. For the artistic evidence see the next note.

17 This seems to have been picked up by Bosworth, *The History of al-Tabarī*, 14, as is the description of the battle with Artabanus that appears in the two Firzabad reliefs, on which see W. Hinz, *Altiranische Funde und Forschungen* (Berlin, 1969), 115.

18 George, 677 (Mosshammer, 440). Direct authorial intervention at this point is to be suspected because George observes that he was the ancestor of Chosroes. The parallel passage from Agath. 2.27.1–5 omits reference to his Zoroastrianism.

19 See now the important discussion of M. Whitby, "The Persian King at War," in *The Roman and Byzantine Army in the East: Proceedings of a Colloquium Held at the Jagiellonian University, Kraków in September 1992*, ed. E. Dąbrowa (Cracow, 1994), 227–63.

20 Potter, *Prophecy and History*, 377.

21 Frye, *History of Ancient Iran*, 295.

22 See p. 292 below on the Paikuli inscription that illustrates this process.

23 Amm. Marc. 19.1.7, 2.2.

24 Amm. Marc. 19.2.3, identifying the placement of the Chiniotae, the Cuseni, the Segestani, and the Albani.

25 Dio 80.4.1. The argument here is developed in more detail in Potter, *Prophecy and History*, 370–72; see also E. Kettenhofen, "Einige Überlegungen zur sasanidischen Politik gegenüber Rom im 3. Jh. n. Chr.," in Dąbrowa, *Roman and Byzantine Army*, 99–108. For an interesting critique of my position see Whitby, "Persian King at War," 234–35, suggesting that Sapor's ambition to rule the west was omitted in the Naqsh-i-Rustam inscription because Sapor had not in fact realized this ambition. My feeling is that the text betrays such a consistent attitude toward the division of the world between the Romans and Persians that this is unlikely, but I concede that it remains a possibility.

26 Herod. 6.6.6. The view of Herodian's qualities here, which is implicit in earlier discussions, is argued for at greater length in Potter, *Literary Texts*, 99–100.

27 L. Robert, "Deux concours grecs à Rome," *CRAI* (1970), 14–17 (also in Robert, *OMS* 5: 655–58) remains fundamental. For an excellent extension of this point see A. J. Spawforth, "Symbol of Unity? The Persian-Wars Tradition in the Roman Empire," in *Greek Historiography*, ed. S. Hornblower (Oxford, 1994), 233–47.

28 Dio 68.29.

29 Amm. Marc. 17.5.5; see also the discussion on p. 471 and n. 152 below.

30 E. Kurshudian, *Die Parthischen und Sasanidischen Verwaltungsinstitutionen nach den literarischen und epigraphischen Quellen 3. Jh. v. Chr.–7. Jh. n. Chr.* (Jerewan, 1998), 17, noting the difference between this and later conceptualizations of the world.

31 Bosworth, *The History of al-Ṭabarī*, 29–31 with nn. 93–94; Potts, *The Archaeology of Elam*, 418; Ball, *Rome in the East*, 117–18.

32 Potts, *The Archaeology of Elam*, 419–21; Ball, *Rome in the East*, 117.

33 Ball, *Rome in the East*, 117–18, with plate 24 depicting the modern bridge at Ahwaz.

34 Amm. Marc. 18.6.8–16.

35 Amm. Marc. 20.6.9.

36 Zon. 12.18; George, 681 (Mosshammer, 443); *HA V. Gord.* 26.5–6 (with discussion in Potter, *Prophecy and History*, 191, n. 5).

37 Loriot, "Les premières années," 760–63; Potter, *Prophecy and History*, 192; Millar, *Roman Near East*, 15–51.

38 Discussed at length in Potter, "Emperors," 49–60.

39 Potter, "Emperors," 56–60.

40 *HA V. Hadr.* 12.6.

41 Arr. *Praef.* 7 with *HA V. Ant. Pii* 7.9.

42 Dio 71.32.4, 72.13; see also *HA V. Marci* 27.10; Herod. 1.5.6, 1.6.8; *HA V. Comm.* 3.5 with Potter, "Emperors," 55.

43 Stahl, "Zwischen Abgrenzung und Integration," 289–317.

44 Dio 76.3.3; compare 77.19, 77.1, and p. 86 above.

45 E. Lo Cascio, "Imperio e confini nell' età principato," in *L' ecumenismo politico nella coscienza dell' occidente*, ed. L. A. Foresti, A. Barzanò, C. Bearzot, L. Prandi, and G. Zecchini (Rome, 1988), 340–45.

46 Potter, "Emperors," 54–55, 60–61.

47 See the classic study of Isaac, *The Limits of Empire*, 130–40 and 186–208 (primarily fourth century).

48 B. Isaac, "An Open Frontier," in *Frontières d'empire: Nature et signification des frontières romains*, ed. P. Brun, S. van der Leeuw, and C. R. Whittaker (Nemours, 1993), 106–7 (also in Isaac, *The Near East under Roman Rule: Selected Papers* [Leiden, 1998], 405–6).

49 C. Nicolet, *Space, Geography, and Politics in the Early Roman Empire* (Ann Arbor, 1991), 149–69, is fundamental on small-scale maps. See also C. Gallazi and B. Kramer, "Artemidorus im Zeichensaal. Eine Papyrusrolle mit Text, Landkarte und Skizzenbüchern aus späthellenistischer Zeit," *Archiv für Papryusforschung* 44 (1998): 189–207.

50 See e.g. Plin. *HN* 3.16–17 with Nicolet, *Space, Geography, and Politics*, 98–99; S. Mattern, *Rome and the Enemy: Imperial Strategy in the Principate* (Berkeley, 1999), 40–41.

51 Tac. *Ann.* 1.11.4; Suet. *Aug.* 101.4 (showing that it was for public display).

52 Tac. *Ann.* 1.11.4.

53 See the superb treatment in Mattern, *Rome and the Enemy*, 162–94.

54 See p. 236 above, depending on the analysis of Kettenhoffen, "Die Eroberung von Nisibis," 159–77.

55 Robert, "Deux concours grecs à Rome," 14–17 (also in Robert, *OMS* 5: 655–58).
56 For Verus' eastern campaign see Birley, *Marcus Aurelius*, 121–26; for Alexander Severus see p. 166 above.
57 *HA V. Gord.* 23.4; Zos. 1.17.1 with Dietz, *Senatus contra principem*, 90–93.
58 *PIR²* F 109.
59 Dietz, *Senatus contra principem*, 103–9.
60 Dietz, *Senatus contra principem*, 140–43 (Domitius), 210–26 (Crispinus).
61 A. Chastagnol, "L'évolution de l'ordre sénatorial aux iiiᵉ et ivᵉ siècles de notre ère," *Revue historique* 244 (1970): 307–8.
62 Loriot, "Les premières années," 738.
63 Dietz, *Senatus contra principem*, 294–95; Loriot, "Les premières années," 735.
64 Dietz, *Senatus contra principem*, 294–95, 292–93; Loriot, "Les premières années," 737; Peachin, *Iudex vice Caesaris*, 237, on this and the appointment of Valens.
65 Loriot, "Les premières années," 742.
66 Loriot, "Les premières années," 742.
67 *PIR²* D 157.
68 P. Hermann, "Die Karriere eines prominenten Juristen aus Thyateira," *Tyche* 12 (1997): 111–25, for the editio princeps and F. Millar, "The Greek East and Roman Law: The Dossier of M. Cn. Licinius Rufinus," *JRS* 89 (1999): 90–108, for a discussion of this text in the context of the five previously known texts (*IGR* 4, nos. 1214, 1215, 1216; *IG* x.2 (1), 142; *AE* 1949 n. 341), honoring this man.
69 Hermann, "Die Karriere," adduced *BÉ* 1971 n. 531; *AE* 1983 to explicate *hippikos* in the text; Robert (*BÉ* 1971 n. 531) drew attention to Dittenberger's valuable note on *OGIS* 495. This explains the term, but not the fact that Rufinus does not refer to himself as *synkletikos*, or as *ho lamprotatos hupatikos* immediately after his name as on *IGR* 4, nos. 1214, 1215, 1216 and *AE* 1949 no. 341, which would be expected in this context. It is significant, perhaps, that he does appear as *kratistos* (the equivalent of the equestrian designation *egregius*) and *lamprotatos* (the equivalent for the senatorial designation of *clarissimus*) on *IG* 10.2 (1), no. 142, which also stresses his legal knowledge. The suggestion that the placement of *hippikos* reflects the chronology of his career is made by Millar, "Greek East," 98, who rightly notes the oddity of the expression.
70 Potter, *Prophecy and History*, 213–15, with earlier bibliography.
71 For a summary of the sources see Potter, *Prophecy and History*, 70–94, and 141–54 for the *Thirteenth Sibylline Oracle*.
72 The case for Philostratus is made in Potter, *Prophecy and History*, 72–73, 90–93, 341, 361; see also, though attributing him less significance, B. Bleckmann, *Die Reichskrise des III. Jahrhunderts in der spätantiken und byzantinischen Geschichtsschreibung: Untersuchungen zu den nachdionischen Quellen der Chronik des Johannes Zonaras* (Munich, 1992), 16, 54, 118, and 121, n. 240 (not wishing to extend his influence on the tradition beyond the single fragment that appears in Mal. p. 297), on which see also A. Schenk Graf von Stauffenberg, *Die römische Kaisergeschichte bei Malalas* (Stuttgart, 1931), 374–76, who sees Philostratus as a chronographer.
73 H. Humbach and P. O. Skjærvø, *The Sasanian Inscription of Paikuli*, pt. 3.1 (Wiesbaden, 1983).
74 R. C. Blockley, *The Fragmentary Classicising Historians of the Later Roman Empire: Eunapius, Olympiodorus, Priscus and Malchus* (Liverpool, 1981), 1, 2, 28.
75 The best treatment of the Byzantine sources for this period is now Bleckmann, *Die Reichskrise*, 20. Eunapius may have begun his history in 270, and Zosimus began using his history from that point.
76 Potter, *Prophecy and History*, 361. The probability is that Zonaras derived information from the Dexippan tradition from the same source that was used by George,

a source that was used in the eleventh century by the chronicler Leo; for this see Bleckmann, *Die Reichskrise*, 43–53.

77 There is now a good treatment of the chronicle and its place in the Christian tradition, by W. Adler and P. Tuffin, *The Chronography of George Synkellos: A Byzantine Chronicle of Universal History from the Creation* (Oxford, 2002), xxix–lxxxiii, which replaces earlier discussions.

78 For this period there is a valuable edition of the text with commentary in Schenk Graf von Stauffenberg, *Die römische Kaisergeschichte;* for studies of Malalas see also E. Jeffreys with B. Croke and R. Scott, *Studies in John Malalas* (Sydney, 1990), supporting the useful translation with notes by E. Jeffreys, B. Croke, and R. Scott, *The Chronicle of John Malalas* (Sydney, 1986). J. Thurn, *Ioannis Malalae Chronographia* (Berlin, 2000), the first modern critical edition, is a significant event and places the study of Malalas on a new footing.

79 The case for the transmission of Dexippan material into the *Historia Augusta* through a Latin source is made by Potter, *Prophecy and History*, 365–69, and Potter, *Literary Texts*, 199–200, n. 82 (in both cases basing the argument on the treatment of Herodian). It has been attacked by T. D. Barnes, "The Sources of the *Historia Augusta*," in *Historiae Augustae Colloquium Parisinum: Atti dei Convegni sulla Historia Augusta*, n.s. 1, ed. G. Bonamente and N. Duval (Macerata, 1991), 1–28. A very different case, based on the belief that Eunapius used the *Annales* of Nichomachus Flavianus, has been made by F. Paschoud, *Cinq études sur Zosime* (Paris, 1975), 93–99, 154–55, 217–18, accepted by Bleckmann, *Die Reichskrise*, 23–24, 414.

80 This view is argued at greater length in Potter, *Prophecy and History*, 73–94; see also p. 244 below. For a much more positive assessment see F. Millar, "P. Herennius Dexippus: The Greek World and the Third Century Invasions," *JRS* 59 (1969): 12–29.

81 Potter, *Prophecy and History*, 77.

82 Zos. 17.2, 18.2; see also Eutrop. *Brev.* 9.2.2–3. For the form of the name see Bleckmann, *Die Reichskrise*, 61, n. 29, adducing the suggestion of A. von. Domaszewski, "Die Personennamen bei den Scriptores Historiae Augustae," *Sitzungsberichte der heidelberger Akademie der Wissenschaften. Philosophisch-historische Klasse, Jahrgang 1918*, vol. 13 (Heidelberg, 1918), 85, that the name was altered by Dexippus to suggest that Timesitheus was playing the role of Themistocles. It is an attractive suggestion, though it should be noted that the name Timesitheus was Attic (see Loriot, "Les premières années," 736). The harshly worded criticism in F. Kolb, *Untersuchungen zur Historia Augusta* (Bonn, 1987), 134, seems excessive; on the other hand, his derivation of the Misitheus of the *HA* (a corruption in the manuscript tradition) seems reasonable (p. 137).

83 George, 681 (Mosshammer, 443) with Kettenhoffen, "Die Eroberung von Nisibis," 161, 170, properly stressing Herod. 6.6.6; and *HA Max. et Balb.* 13.5.

84 Amm. Marc. 23.5.17; there is a recollection of the battle in Zos. 1.18.2.

85 Zos. 1.18.3; Zon. 12.18 with Bleckmann, *Die Reichskrise*, 62, on the source for the coincidence. The fantasies of *HA V. Gord.* 26.3–27.3, 28.1, 29–30 do not require discussion, but see Potter, *Prophecy and History*, 207–8.

86 *RGDS* 1.

87 Amm. Marc. 23.5.17; Zos. 3.14.2 (deriving from Eunapius); Porph. *V. Plot.* 3 with Potter, *Prophecy and History*, 202–3, 207–10.

88 Potter, *Prophecy and History*, 201.

89 *Orac. Sib.* 13.13–20.

90 P. 232 above.

91 Zos. 1.19.1, 3.24.4; Zon. 12.19; Evag. *Hist. eccl.* 5.7 and other texts commented upon in W. Felix, *Antike literarische Quellen zur Aussenpolitik des Sasanidenstaates,*

vol. 1, Österreichische Akademie der Wissenschaften, Phil.-Hist. Klasse, Sitzungs-berichte 456 (Vienna, 1985), 51–54; Winter, *Die sāsānidisch–römischen Friedens-verträge*, 97–107.

92 *FGrH* 98 T 1 with Potter, *Prophecy and History*, 70–72, 222; Bleckmann, *Die Reichskrise*, 16, 102, n. 170; Winter, *Die sāsānidisch–römischen Friedensverträge*, 106–7.

93 Potter, *Prophecy and History*, 221–24.

94 For the identification of the *denarioi* of *RGDS* 9 as aurei see J. Guey, "Deniers (d'or) et deniers d'or (de compte anciens)," *Syria* 38 (1961): 261–74; T. Pékary, "Le Tribut aux Perses et les finances de Philippe l'Arab," *Syria* 38 (1961): 275–83.

95 *HA V. Gord.* 31.3; Eutrop. *Brev.* 9.2.3; *ILS* 1331 (a dedication by Julius Priscus), 6–7: *item a Divo] Gordiano*; the restoration of *divus* may now be confirmed from *AE* 1964, no. 231 (also in *BÉ* 1963, no. 223, 23): *touto kai theou Gordianou*; D. MacDonald, "The Death of Gordian III – Another Tradition," *Historia* 30 (1981): 507.

96 F. Hartmann, *Herrscherwechsel und Reichskrise: Untersuchungen zu den Ursachen und Konsequenzen der Herrscherwechsel im Imperium Romanum der Soldatenkaiserzeit (3. Jahrhundert n. Chr.)* (Frankfurt am Main, 1982), 67–68, is immensely percep-tive on the dynamics of "family politics."

97 For the "palace" see H. C. Butler, *Architecture and Other Arts: Publications of the American Archeological Expedition to Syria in 1899–1900*, vol. 2 (New York, 1903), 382–84; R. E. Brünnow and A. von Domaszewski, *Die Provincia Arabia*, vol. 3 (Strasbourg, 1909), 164–67; the "Philippeion": G. Amer and M. Gawlikowski, "Le sanctuaire impérial de Philoppopolis," *Damaszener Mitt.* 2 (1985): 1–14; the baths: Butler, *Architecture and Other Arts*, 384–90; Brünnow and von Domaszewski, *Provincia Arabia*, 3: 155–60; theater: P. Coupel and E. Frézouls, *Le théâtre de Philippopolis en Arabie* (Paris, 1956); Millar, *The Roman Near East*, 156.

98 *Orac. Sib.* 13. 64–73 with Potter, *Prophecy and History*, 249–53.

99 Jord. *Get.* 89 explaining the outbreak of the war recorded at Zos. 1.20.1; *Orac. Sib.* 13.36. Jordanes mingles a third-century tradition with a much later one that includes the fabricated Amal genealogy (invoked with no regard to chronology in the next sentence). For the structure of the account here see P. Heather, *Goths and Romans, 332–489* (Oxford, 1991), 37. For Egypt see P. J. Parsons, "Philippus Arabs and Egypt," *JRS* 57 (1967): 134–41; J. D. Thomas, "The Introduction of the Dekaprotoi and Comarchs into Egypt in the Third Century AD," *ZPE* 19 (1975): 111–19, showing that the *dekaprotoi* replaced *sitologoi* ca. 242–46 and that the *comarch* replaced the *comogrammateus* ca. 245 to 247–48.

100 Parsons, "Philippus Arabs and Egypt," 134–37.

101 Aur. Vict. *De Caes.* 29.2; Zos. 1.20.2; Pol. Silv. *Chron.* 37–38 with Potter, *Prophecy and History*, 248.

102 *ILS* 9006; *P. Euphr.* 1 with Potter, *Prophecy and History*, 245, n. 116.

103 *CJ* 2.26.3 with Peachin, *Iudex vice Caesaris*, 119–20. The use of the perfect tense in this case may indicate that Severianus had left office by the time that Philip issued the rescript on October 15, 245, and was probably in the Danubian provinces at that time.

104 For the outbreak of war with Persia see Zon. 12.19 with Potter, *Prophecy and History*, 229; for a reasoned exposition of the view that there was no continuation of the war see J. Eadie, "One Hundred Years of Rebellion: The Eastern Army in Politics, AD 175–272," in Kennedy, *Roman Army*, 146.

105 Euseb. *Hist. eccl.* 6.41.1 with Potter, *Prophecy and History*, 236–41, 252–53.

106 Zos. 1.20.2–21; Zon. 12.19 with the perceptive discussion in Hartmann, *Herrscherwechsel und Reichskrise*, 160–61, 180–81, who sees this in the context of emergent Balkan separatism. He may be correct, and it may be significant that it

occurred in the wake of a dynastic assertion of the special role of the Balkan armies in the form of Severianus's command there.

107 For his early career see now X. Loriot, "Un sénateur illyrien élevé à la pourpre: Trajan Dèce," in Frézouls and Jouffroy, *Les empereurs illyriens*, 43–55; Birley, "Decius Reconsidered," 59–68.

108 Aur. Vict. *De Caes.* 28.10; [Aur. Vict.] *Epit. de Caes.* 28.2; Eutrop. *Brev.* 9.3. An alternative tradition has him killed at Beroea; see John of Antioch fr. 148 (*FHG* 4.597–98), which may be a mistake, as the confusion of Beroea and Verona is elsewhere attested; see J. F. Matthews, *Western Aristocracies and the Imperial Court, AD 364–425* (Oxford, 1975), 312, n. 1; and T. D. Barnes, "Emperors on the Move," *JRA* 2 (1989): 257. The reconstruction followed here is that in Potter, *Prophecy and History*, 254–58. For earlier treatments see J. M. York, "The Image of Philip the Arab," *Historia* 21 (1972): 320–32; S. Dušanić, "The End of the Philippi," *Chiron* 6 (1976): 427–39; H. A. Pohlsander, "Did Decius Kill the Philippi?" *Historia* 31 (1982): 214–22. More recently, a case has been made for Beroea in Macedonia; see R. Ziegler, "Thessalonike in der Politik des Traianus Decius und der Tod des Philippus Arabs," in *Roma Renascens. Ilona Opelt von ihren Freunden und Schülern gewidmet*, ed. M. Wissemann (Frankfurt am Main, 1988), 385–414. I will allow that the evidence that he adduces for a special connection between Decius and Thessalonica is strong, but not so strong as to permit the assertion that John of Antioch is dependent upon Dexippus (398–99). The story known to Zosimus and Zonaras has Philip appoint Decius at a meeting of the senate. After the defeat of Pacatianus, Zonaras has Decius send Philip a letter letting him know what he has done: none of this involves an unsuspecting Philip marching to Perinthus. In order to make the case that John is using Dexippus, Ziegler needs to show that Zonaras and Zosimus do not.

109 For his origin and nomenclature see Wittig, *RE* 15, col. 1247; Syme, *Emperors and Biography*, 220; and, in greater detail, Birley, "Decius Reconsidered," 68–73.

110 *RIC* 4.3 Decius, nos. 2, 12, 14, 36, 101, 112–14.

111 The crucial treatment of the Decian *libelli* remains J. Knipfing, "The *libelli* of the Decian Persecution," *HTR* 16 (1923): 345–90 (to which may be added *PSI* 778); J. Schwartz, "Une déclaration de sacrifice du temps de Dèce," *RB* 54 (1947): 365–67; *P. Oxy.* 3565. The views expressed here, which obscure points of genuine contention, are those argued in Potter, *Prophecy and History*, 261–67. For a more recent treatment see J. B. Rives, "The Decree of Decius and the Religion of Empire," *JRS* 89 (1999): 135–54, who, after a balanced discussion, favors (p. 151) the view that the edict was intended as an anti-Christian measure; the issue as to whether or not the purpose of the edict was anti-Christian is not "oddly academic," as viewed by Gradel, *Emperor Worship*, 368. It is central to understanding what Decius was doing. He might rather have noted that the introduction of the *constitutio antoniniana*, wherein Caracalla expresses his hope that his subjects will join with him in sacrifice, is very close to what appears to have been the point of the Decian edict (see pp. 138–39 above for the text). If one were to follow Gradel's approach, that too would have to be read as a persecution edict. For a different view see Birley, "Decius Reconsidered," 75, who suggests that Decius was influenced by Cassius Dio, whom Birley supposes that Decius knew, and wanted to bring Christians into line.

112 *P. Pion* 8 with Potter, *Prophets and Emperors*, 263.

113 Potter, *Prophecy and History*, 262, n. 174; and Rives, "The Decree of Decius," 149.

114 Rives, "The Decree of Decius," 153: "Decius was in effect establishing a kind of orthopraxy."

115 Rives, "The Decree of Decius," 153, draws the parallel.

116 For these and other cities, see R. Ziegler, *Städisches Prestige und kaiserliche Politik: Studien zum Festwesen in Ostkilikien im 2. und 3. Jahrhundert n. Chr.* (Düsseldorf, 1985), 99–108; for more detail on Thessalonika see Ziegler, "Thessalonike in der Politik," 386–91, where his argument that the honors for Thessalonica are Decian rather than from Philip depends upon dating the four neocorates and colonial status of the place on *IG* 10, 2, n. 162, depends upon acceptance of his view that the text reflects the status of the city when the inscription was erected rather than when Marcus Dioscurides held office, which was in 246–47. The problem with this view is that it assumes that he was not honored immediately upon leaving office, as were the officeholders honored in *IG* 10, 2, n. 163–65. This is not impossible, and the case may be strengthened by the fact that two of the neocorates were canceled under Gallus. What is not obvious is that these honors must be connected with these cities siding with Decius in the war against Philip rather than reaction to something like the edict on sacrifices.

117 *RIC* 4.3 Decius, nos. 77–98; for the attribution of these coins to Rome see K. J. J. Elks, "Reattribution of the Milan Coins of Trajan Decius to the Rome Mint," *NC* 12 (1972): 111–15. The historiographic significance of this issue is recognized by Rives, "The Decree of Decius," 142–43, contra K. E. T. Butcher, "Imagined Emperors: Personalities and Failure in the Third Century," *JRA* 9 (1996): 522. The eccentricity of the list is commented upon by Gradel, *Emperor Worship*, 368, n. 167.

118 Zon. 12.19; Zos. 1.21.1–2. See also Bleckmann, *Die Reichskrise*, 278–83, for the path by which the story was transmitted to Zonaras. He notes that, in the pagan tradition of historiography, Decius remained a good emperor, which would suggest the need for such a story. But the story does not appear in the Latin tradition, which in Bleckmann's view had some influence upon the tradition known to Zonaras and should thus be seen as stemming from a third-century account.

119 *Orac. Sib.* 13.88 with Potter, *Prophecy and History*, 267–68.

120 Euseb. *Hist. eccl.* 6.41.9 with Potter, *Prophecy and History*, 267–68.

121 *AE* 1996, no. 1358. For the history of the region (insofar as it is recoverable) in these years see N. A. Frolova, *The Coinage of the Kingdom of Bosphoros, AD 242–341/342*, trans. H. B. Wells, BAR International Series 166 (Oxford, 1983).

122 *AE* 1911, no. 244 (*BÉ* 1943, no. 76) with M. P. Speidel, "The Roman Army in Arabia," *ANRW* 2.8 (1977): 712–14 (also in Speidel, *Roman Army Studies*, vol. 1 [Amsterdam, 1984], 254–56) (the date is 208), contra H. Wolfram, *History of the Goths*, trans. T. J. Dunlap (Berkeley, 1987), 20, who states that the first appearance of the name is in *RDGS* 3. For the use of the word to describe enemies under Caracalla see Fitz, "A Military History of Pannonia," 105.

123 Wolfram, *History of the Goths*, 19.

124 *FGrH* 100, fr. 6, 7.

125 Zos. 1.27.1, 31.1.

126 *Orac. Sib.* 13.141.

127 Jord. *Get.* 101–2 with Wolfram, *History of the Goths*, 35, on the form of the name; for the Amal genealogy see P. Heather, "Cassiodorus and the Rise of the Amals: Genealogy and the Goths under Hun Domination," *JRS* 79 (1989): 103–28.

128 P. Heather and J. F. Matthews, *The Goths in the Fourth Century* (Liverpool, 1991), 51–101, for discussion of the archaeological evidence, noting that the distinctive Sîntana de Mureş/Černjachov cultures that are associated with the fourth-century Gothic peoples are not evident before the fourth century.

129 Amm. Marc. 27.5.5 with Matthews, *Roman Empire of Ammianus*, 319, and, more generally, Heather, *Goths and Romans*, 84–89; Wolfram, *History of the Goths*, 57–116; H. Wolfram, *The Roman Empire and Its Germanic Peoples*, trans. T. J. Dunlap (Berkeley, 1997) 67–79.

130 Wolfram, *Roman Empire*, 42–43.
131 Jord. *Get.* 101 with Potter, *Prophecy and History*, 280; Bleckmann, *Die Reichskrise*, 161–67; for the geography of the campaign see now R. J. A. Talbert, *Barrington Atlas of the Greek and Roman World* (Princeton, 2000), map 22.
132 *FGrH* 100, fr. 25.
133 *FGrH* 100, fr. 26 with Potter, *Prophecy and History*, 280; Hartmann, *Herrscherwechsel und Reichskrise*, 111–12. The siege of Philippopolis in *FGrH* 100, fr. 27 plainly refers to a later event; contra Jacoby ad loc.
134 Potter, *Prophecy and History*, 278; Bleckmann, *Die Reichskrise*, 157–60; for the spelling of the place see Talbert, *Barrington Atlas*, map 22; for the location, correcting various misstatements in Potter, *Prophecy and History*, 14, 278, see Birley, "Decius Reconsidered," 77.
135 Zos. 1.23.2–3; Zon. 12.20 with Potter, *Prophecy and History*, 286–87, on various problematic details.
136 Amm. Marc. 31.5.16; *FGrH* 100, fr. 22; Zon. 12.20 (death at Abritus); Aur. Vict. *De Caes.* 29.5; Jord. *Get.* 103 (death in an earlier engagement) with Potter, *Prophecy and History*, 283.
137 *Orac. Sib.* 13.104; Zos. 1.23.3; Zon. 12.20.
138 The evidence is laid out with clarity in Peachin, *Roman Imperial Titulature*, 69–74.
139 Zos. 1.25.2; *FGrH* 100, fr. 22 with Potter, *Prophecy and History*, 314–19.
140 *ILS* 518; *AE* 1996, no. 1358; for the possible cancellation of Decian privileges see Ziegler, "Thessalonike in der Politik," 391, for Thessalonica (though he concedes that Valerian is possible); however, see Ziegler, *Städisches Prestige und kaiserliche Politik*, 113, reasonably explaining games at Anazarbus under Gallus as stemming from the importance of the place for troop movements to the east.
141 *Orac. Sib.* 13.89–100, 111, 122–28; Mal. 12.26; Anon. post Dionem fr. 1 (*FHG* 4.192); *HA Tyr. Trig.* 2 and the text discussed in S. Lieberman, "Palestine in the Third and Fourth Centuries," *JQR* 37 (1947): 37–38. See also Potter, *Prophecy and History*, 268–77.
142 Potter, *Prophecy and History*, 290–97, for the events of this campaign with earlier bibliography (which is extensive). The conclusions there are supported by J.-C. Balty, "Nouvelles données sur l'armée romaine d'orient et les raids Sasanides du milieu du IIIe siècle," *CRAI* (1987), 213–42; see esp. pp. 229–31. For a reasoned exposition of a different view, suggesting that there was a Roman offensive into northern Mesopotamia in 252 (reflected in the inscriptions collected by Balty) while the main Persian attack came in 253, see Hartmann, *Das palmyrenische Teilreich*, 73, with references. I stand by my earlier view that the sack of Antioch took place in 252, because it seems to me to make best sense of the text of the *Thirteenth Sibylline Oracle*.
143 E. Kettenhoffen, *Die römischen–persischen Kriege des 3. Jahrhunderts n. Chr. nach der Inschrift Šahpuhrs I an der Ka 'be-ye Zartost (skz)* (Wiesbaden, 1982), 50–76, offers a detailed study of the geography of the campaign.
144 Potter, *Prophecy and History*, 294.
145 Anon. post Dionem fr. 1 *FHG* 4.192; *Orac. Sib.* 13.122–28.
146 *Orac. Sib.* 13.147–54; Mal. p. 296; A. T. Olmstead, "The Mid-Third Century of the Christian Era," *CPh* 37 (1942): 407–8, is the crucial contribution on the place of Uranius Antoninus in the *Thirteenth Sibylline Oracle*. H. R. Baldus, *Uranius Antoninus* (Bonn, 1971) is fundamental for the coinage and offers a good analysis of the texts.
147 Mal. p. 296.
148 *IGLS* 1799 with Baldus, *Uranius Antoninus*, 250–52.

149 See, for competent summaries of the relevant evidence, Kienast, *Römische Kaisertabelle*, 201; Peachin, *Roman Imperial Titulature*, 268–69. For the significance of these two characters see Hartmann, *Herrscherwechsel und Reichskrise*, 82, 93–94, 161–62, on Silbannicus as an example of a rebel who allies with the tribes across the border (a highly speculative, but characteristically astute, proposal).

150 Potter, *Prophecy and History*, 20–21; Potter, "Palmyra and Rome: Odaenathus' Titulature and the Use of the *Imperium Maius*," *ZPE* 113 (1996): 282.

151 *HA V. Marci* 21.7.

152 P. A. Brunt, "Did Imperial Rome Disarm Her Subjects?" *Phoenix* 29 (1975): 260–70 (also in Brunt, *Roman Imperial Themes*, 255–66, esp. 260–66).

153 For Asia Minor see Magie, *Roman Rule*, 1567. For Greece see next notes.

154 George, 715 (Mosshammer, 466); Zon. 12.23; Zos. 1.29.2–3 with *IG* 5.1, no. 1188 (epitaph for the Spartan Epaphrys who died "repulsing the enemies of the Athenians at this time").

155 *FGrH* 100, fr. 28.1, 4. For the problem of the speaker here see Potter, *Prophecy and History*, 73, n. 18.

156 *AE* 1993, no. 1231, 6–8; see also *CIL* 12, no. 149 with the comments of I. König, "Die Postumus-Inschrift aus Augsburg," *Historia* 46 (1997): 341–54.

157 The evidence for Palmyrene forces prior to the time of Odaenathus is discussed well in Hartmann, *Das palmyrenische Teilreich*, 55–57.

158 Zos. 1.37.2.

159 Potter, *Prophecy and History*, 283–88.

160 Potter, *Prophecy and History*, 151–54.

161 *Orac. Sib.* 13.150–54; Hipp. *Dan.* 4.5, quoted p. 3 above.

162 Potter, *Prophecy and History*, 312.

163 D. Kienast, *Untersuchungen zu den Kriegsflotten der römischen Kaiserzeit* (Bonn, 1976), 79–81.

164 Zos. 1.28.1–3; Zon. 12.21; Aur. Vict. *De Caes.* 31.1; Eutrop. *Brev.* 9.5.1; Jord. *Get.* 105 with Potter, *Prophecy and History*, 319–21; Bleckmann, *Die Reichskrise*, 178–80 (with valuable comments on the ideology inherent to the accounts of Zosimus and Zonaras); Hartmann, *Herrscherwechsel und Reichskrise*, 82, on the importance of "military qualities"; and M. Christol, "A propos de la politique extérieure de Trébonien Galle," *Rev. Num.* (1980): 73, on the role of Valerian.

165 Walker, *Metrology*, 49–51. I am indebted to Dr. Paul Legutko for discussion of the point; for a full tabulation see P. Legutko, "Roman Imperial Ideology in the Mid-Third Century AD: Negotiation, Usurpation, and Crisis in the Imperial Center," PhD diss., University of Michigan, 2000, 87–88.

166 For details see, most conveniently, Kienast, *Römische Kaisertabelle*, 217–18; Peachin, *Roman Imperial Titulature*, 353–63.

167 *AE* 1965, no. 304; Halfmann, *Itinera principum*, 237, notes that *BÉ* 1951, no. 124, which places Gallienus at Sirmium, may date to this period, though the date of 260, which he also canvasses, is more likely.

168 Halfmann, *Itinera principum*, 237.

169 For details see Halfmann, *Itinera principum*, 236–37, with the addition of C. Roueché, *Aphrodisias in Late Antiquity*, Journal of Roman Studies Monograph 5 (London, 1989), no. 1.

170 M. Christol, *Essai sur l'évolution des carrières sénatoriales dans la seconde moitié du III*ᵉ *siècle ap. J.C.* (Paris, 1986), 38, n. 9.

171 Christol, *Essai sur l'évolution*, 35–44.

172 Christol, *Essai sur l'évolution*, 38.

173 *CJ* 5.3.5, 9.9.18 with Halfmann, *Itinera principum*, 237.

174 *Acta Proc.* 1.1: *sacratissimi imperatores Valerianus et Gallienus literas ad me dare digni-tati sunt quibus praeceperunt eos, qui Romanam religionem non colunt, debere Romanas caeremonias recognoscere* is crucial for understanding the edict. For the other terms see *Acta Proc.* 1.4, 7; Euseb. *Hist. eccl.* 7.11.10.

175 Cyp. *Ep.* 80.1.2.

176 Zos. 1.35.4–36.1 with Potter, *Prophecy and History*, 313–14, citing earlier dis-cussions.

177 The date of Valerian's capture may now be refined by *AE* 1993, no. 1231. Zos. 1.37.2 places Gallienus near the Alps when Valerian was captured; Zon. 12.24 says that this was in the context of a raid by the Alamanni, which this inscription shows to have been in late March (assuming that it took some time for the Juthungi to recross the Alps so that they could be defeated again on April 24–25). The usually reliable guide to chronology offered by the prescripts of Egyptian papyri does not help in this case, as they appear to have continued the reign of Valerian up to the point that Egypt fell under the control of Macrianus and Quietus. D. König, *Die gallischen Usurpatoren von Postumus bis Tetricus* (Munich, 1981), 20–31, had already made the astute observation that the election of Dionysius as bishop of Rome on July 12 (the position had been open since the execution of Xystus on August 6, 258) must have followed news of Valerian's capture. The difficulty of dating the coinage of Ingenuus and Regalianus on the basis of the coinage of Viminacium to 259 or 260 may be explained if it is allowed that the Danubian rebellion that is said to have been sparked by news of Valerian's capture was early in the year. For the problem with this evidence see J. F. Drinkwater, *The Gallic Empire: Separatism and Community in the North-Western Provinces of the Roman Empire, AD 260–274*, Historia Einzelschriften 52 (Stuttgart, 1987), 101–2.

178 *RGDS* 9–11.

179 Bosworth, *The History of al-Ṭabarī*, 30, n. 94. Ṭabarī allows that Sapor either freed him after cutting off his nose, for a large ransom, or killed him.

180 For Macrianus' career prior to 260 see *PIR²* F 549. For Callistus see Potter, *Prophecy and History*, 340–41, 343–46.

181 Potter, *Prophecy and History*, 389, and Hartmann, *Das palmyrenische Teilreich*, 91–96, suggesting that the title reflected his command of the Palmyrene militia. On the fate of Palmyrene trading stations see now the perceptive discussion in Hartmann, *Das palmyrenische Teilreich*, 76–81.

182 The circumstances are completely obscure; see A. Alföldi, "The Numbering of the Victories of the Emperor Gallienus and the Loyalty of His Legions," *Num. Chron.*, 5th ser., 9 (1929): 258 (German version in A. Alföldi, *Studien zur Geschichte der Weltkrise des 3. Jahrhunderts nach Christus* [Darmstadt, 1967], 103); J. Fitz, *Ingenuus et Régalien* (Brussels, 1976), 38–71; M. Christol, "Les règnes de Valérien et de Gallien (253–268), travaux d'ensemble, questions chronologiques," *ANRW* 2.2 (1975): 820–21; Drinkwater, *The Gallic Empire*, 105.

183 Zon. 12.24; Zos. 1.37.2. For the date see next notes.

184 Contra H. Lavagne, "Une nouvelle inscription d'Augsbourg et les causes de l'usurpation de Postume," *CRAI* (1994): 440–41, who sees the prisoners as the object of the controversy, noting that under the Roman law of *postliminium*, they ought to have been returned to their former status. Lavagne is correct in his view of the law of *postliminium*, but the explicit stress on the freedom of the prisoners here ought to show that their fate was not at issue.

185 Zos. 1.38.2.

186 König, "Die Postumus-Inschrift aus Augsburg," 341–54, would, perhaps correctly, extend the interval to July; see also the chronological discussion in M. Christol and X. Loriot, "À propos de l'inscription d'Augsbourg: remarques liminaires," *Cahiers Glotz* 8 (1997): 223–27.

187 The origin of the comitatus under Gallienus or Valerian rather than Aurelian (under whom the first clear attestation appears in *FGrH* 100, fr. 6.2 and *FGrH* 100, fr. 7.4) may be conjectured from the fact that the events narrated in those two fragments must be dated to 271, before there was any time for a significant reorganization of the army, and from *Gesta apud Zenophilum* 1 (Optatus, *Tract.* App. 1), see Potter, *Prophecy and History*, 83, n. 49. There is clear evidence for an independent cavalry corps under Gallienus at Zon. 12.25, Zos. 40.1, and the same language is used at *HA V. Aurel.* 18.1 (based, ultimately, on a third-century source; see F. Paschoud, *Histoire Auguste. Vies d'Aurélien et Tacite* [Paris, 1996], 113), suggesting that the comitatus was based on the cavalry corps of Gallienus even it had come to contain the other elements suggested in *FGrH* 100, fr. 6.2; see also p. 450 below.

188 Aur. Vict. *De Caes.* 33.34. For a useful summary of scholarship on the problem (into the mid-1970s) and sensible discussion see L. de Blois, *The Policy of the Emperor Gallienus* (Leiden, 1976), 57–83. The crucial study is now M. Christol, "Les réformes de Gallien et la carrière sénatoriale," *Epigrafia e ordine senatorio*, 1, *Tituli*, 4 (Rome, 1982), 143–66; Christol, *Essai*, 45–54.

189 Christol, *Essai*, 48–52.

190 Christol, *Essai*, 47.

191 M. Christol, "L'ascension de l'ordre équestre: Un thème historiographique et sa réalité," in Demougin, Devijver, and Rapsaet-Charlier, *L'ordre équestre d'une aristocratie*, 625–27.

192 *CJ* 9.41.11 with O. Hirschfeld, "Die Rangtitel der römischen Kaiserzeit," *Sitzungsberichte der Berliner Akademie* (1901), 584–85 (also in Hirschfeld, *Kleine Schriften*, 652).

193 See p. 39 above.

194 Euseb. *Hist. eccl.* 7.13.1; for discussion see De Blois, *Policy of Gallienus*, 177–85, though for very different conclusions see p. 263 below.

195 Zon. 12.24; *HA V. Gall.* 3.1, 4 with Potter, *Prophecy and History*, 343–46.

196 The relevant inscriptions are *CIS* 2: 3945, 3946, 4202. The view asserted here is controversial; for various opinions, and a defense of the position taken in the text, see Potter, "Palmyra and Rome," 272–74.

197 Potter, *Prophecy and History*, 389–90.

198 D. Schlumberger, "L'inscription d'Hérodien: Remarques sur l'histoire des princes de Palmyre," *Bulletin des études orientales* 11 (1942–43): 36–50.

199 Potter, "Palmyra and Rome," 273–74.

200 First published (with a very poorly reproduced photograph) by H. Seyrig, "Note sur Hérodien, prince de Palmyre," *Syria* 18 (1937): 1–4; there is an excellent photograph in E. Equini Schneider, *Septimia Zenobia Sebaste* (Rome, 1993), 98. The anti-Persian implication of the title is amply discussed by Hartmann, *Das palmyrenische Teilreich*, 179–83.

201 H.-G. Pflaum, "La fortification de la ville d'Adraha d'Arabie," *Syria* 29 (1952): 322–24.

202 Long, "Two Sides of a Coin," 63–64.

203 *ILS* 561 with König, *Die gallischen Usurpatoren*, 57.

204 See Drinkwater, *The Gallic Empire*, 118, arguing that, despite the lack of epigraphic evidence, Narbonensis was under Postumus' control. See also König, *Die gallischen Usurpatoren*, 56, on the numismatic evidence.

205 Drinkwater, *The Gallic Empire*, 241–42.

206 D. Schlumberger, "Les gentilices romains des Palmyréniens," *Bulletin d'études orientales* 11 (1942–43): 53–64.

207 D. Schlumberger, "Vorod l'agoronome," *Syria* 49 (1972): 339–41, and now the balanced discussion of his career in Hartmann, *Das palmyrenische Teilreich*, 203–11, who is especially good on the mixture of local and imperial offices that appears in inscriptions relating to this man's career.

208 *PIR²* C 500.

209 Porph. *V. Plot.* 14.19–20; Eunap. *VS* 456.

210 Lib. *Ep.* 1078.

211 König, *Die gallischen Usurpatoren*, 89–91.

212 Drinkwater, *The Gallic Empire*, 225, with the map on p. 216.

213 *ILS* 563 with König, *Die gallischen Usurpatoren*, 141–42; he was consul with Postumus in 267.

214 Drinkwater, *The Gallic Empire*, 125–26, on both names.

7 THE EMERGENCE OF A NEW ORDER

1 The version of the assassination accepted here is that given in Zon. 12.24. Anon. Post Dionem fr. 7 has Odaenathus put to death by the governor of Syria on the instigation of Gallienus, and shares with George, 717 (also in Mosshammer, 467) the invention of another Odaenathus. For what it is worth, *HA. V. Gall.* 13.1; *Ha.V. Tyr. Trig.* 15.5 give a version of the story that might agree with that in Zonaras, and has the correct detail that Odaenathus had raised his eldest son to share power with him (on which see p. 259 n. 198 above) and gives the name as Herodes, an easy corruption for Herodianus. Zos. 1.39.2 says that he was killed at "some annual festival" at Emesa. It is tempting to see this as being the annual new year festival of *'lh' gbl*, which may have fallen in April; see, for the date, Frey, *Untersuchungen*, 48–49. There remains a problem as to the relationship between a son of Odaenathus named Hairan and Herodianus. For the view that Herodianus is the name in Greek see Hartmann, *Das palmyrenische Teilreich*, 114–15. This is possible, though, for another view, that there were two sons of Odaenathus named Hairan, both named for Odaenathus' father (the elder dying before the birth of the younger, who appears to have been born after Vaballathus), see Potter, *Prophecy and History*, 387–88. On balance I think that the separation of Herodianus from the elder Hairan is preferable since it will explain why it appears that Zenobia also had a son named Hairan, who appears with Vaballathus on a seal impression from Palmyra, as argued by H. Seyrig, "Les fils du roi Odainat," *AAS* 13 (1963): 171–72 (also in Seyrig, *Scripta Varia: Mélanges d'archéologie et d'histoire* [Paris, 1985], 277–78).

2 Zon. 12.24; Anon. Post Dionem fr. 6; for the date see Drinkwater, *The Gallic Empire*, 31, 106; König, *Die gallischen Usurpatoren*, 106–7. The date is based on coin reverses that have been read to indicate a conflict in that year; see G. Elmer, "Die Münzprägung der gallischen Kaiser in Köln, Trier und Mailand," *Bonner Jahrbücher* 146 (1941): 1–106. It is supported by *AE* 1950 no. 208 (*IRT* 456), which records his twelfth imperatorial salutation in 265. Gallienus' salutations 6–10 took place between 262–63 and 265; some of these may reflect victories by Odaenathus in the east (see Kienast, *Römische Kaisertabelle*, 216), but the evidence is sufficiently erratic that it cannot be pressed. Coinage from Siscia has been used to suggest that Gallienus was in the Balkans in 262, which would remove this year, at least, from consideration, if correct (which is not without its own complexities; see, for this argument, R. Göbl, "Gallienus als Alleinherrscher," *NZ* 75 [1953]: 23). For the literary sources see Bleckmann, *Die Reichskrise*, 248–51.

3 König, *Die gallischen Usurpatoren*, 125–31.

4 Our understanding of its course is greatly complicated by the fact that Zon. 12.26 and Anon. Post Dionem fr. 9.1 date the sack of Athens under Claudius. Zos. 1.40.1

places one invasion under Gallienus in 268, and a second one under Claudius in 269 (1.42–43). George, 717 (Mosshammer, 467) places the capture of Athens under Gallienus and a second invasion under Claudius (p. 720) (Mosshammer, 469). *HA V. Gall* 11.1–3 places one invasion, reaching Cappadocia, in 267 (dated by reference to Gallienus' archonship at Athens in that year), and a second, which includes the capture of Athens, in 268, at *V. Gall.* 13.6–10. The author has another invasion under Claudius at *V. Claud.* 9.3–9. The confusion is amplified by the record of a battle in which three thousand Goths were killed, placed under Gallienus at George, 717 (Mosshammer, 467), which may be the same battle reported at *V. Gall.* 13.10 and under Claudius at Zos. 1.43.2. The problem with George's account is well handled by Bleckmann, *Die Reichskrise*, 198–200, who shows that events of two years were conflated in the tradition and placed under different emperors. For further problems in the sources stemming from the placement of events under the emperor ruling either when a chain of events began or ended, see below, p. 266. For a different approach, noting that the events as narrated by George parallel those in *HA V. Gall.* 13, see T. Forgiarini, "A propos de Claude II: Les invasions gothiques de 269–270 et le rôle de l'empereur," in Frézouls and Jouffroy, *Les empereurs illyriens*, 81–86. If he is right, then the significance of Claudius' victory is greatly diminished, making it no more than a mopping-up operation after Gallienus' victory. On the other hand, as he also notes, there is a high degree of correlation between Zosimus' account and that of the *HA V. Claud.*, and I do not think that it is correct to ignore the date given by the Anonymous for the fall of Athens, for I think that it is the date in the Anonymous and Zonaras that acts as a control on the deformation of the Dexippan tradition in George and the *HA V. Gall.*

5   Zos. 1.40.2.

6   *HA V. Gall.* 14.1–9, 15.2 for Marcianus' role in reconciling the troops to the regime of Claudius.

7   For the date see Christol, "Les règnes de Valérien," 824–25; König, *Die gallischen Usurpatoren*, 130; Kienast, *Römische Kaisertabelle*, 215, 228; Peachin, *Roman Imperial Titulature*, 40. This has been challenged by H. Huvelin, "Le début du règne de Claude II, empereur illyrien apport de la numismatique," in Frézouls and Jouffroy, *Les empereurs illyriens*, 87–95, who argues that the accession of Claudius took place in the spring of 268 on the basis of hoard evidence and *AE* 1944 no. 85. She makes an interesting case and may be correct, though the chronology of 268 would thereby become desperately compressed, and for that reason I think that the later date, based on papyrological evidence, is to be preferred.

8   Aur. Vict. *De Caes.* 33.31 (reaction at Rome), 33.27 (deification); [Aur. Vict.] *Epit. de Caes.* 40.3 (tomb).

9   *IGBR* 3.2.1568 (Heraclianus); *IGBR* 3.2.1570 for Mucianus, with M. Christol, "La carrière de Traianus Mucianus et l'origine des *protectores,*" *Chiron* 7 (1977): 393–408.

10 *IGBR* 3.2.1569.

11 *AE* 1965 no. 114 with B. Gerov, "La carriera di Marciano generale di Gallieno," *Athenaeum* 43 (1965): 333–54.

12 *ILS* 569 with *PIR²* I 468. Placidianus would become consul in 273.

13 Christol, *Essai sur l'évolution*, 109–10, is cautiously agnostic on the identification of the Paternus of 269 with the consul of 267 and 268.

14 Christol, *Essai sur l'évolution*, 110.

15 Christol, *Essai sur l'évolution*, 111.

16 König, *Die gallischen Usurpatoren*, 131–36.

17 *Pan.* 8 (5) 2.5, 4.2–4 with König, *Die gallischen Usurpatoren*, 148–52.

18 *HA V. Gall.* 13.4–5; see also Chastagnol's observation on this passage in his edition of the *Historia Augusta*, at 824, n. 1.

19 *CIS* 2: 3971; see also Eadie, "One Hundred Years," 148–49.

20 *RIC* 5.1 Aurelian no. 381; see also n. 24 below.

21 *HA V. Claud.* 11.2 (with the wrong form of the name, calling him Probatus); his career is confused with that of the emperor Probus at *HA V. Prob.* 9.1–5; the correct form appears in George, 721 (also in Mosshammer, 470); Zon. 12.27; and Zos. 1.44.2. The details of the career of Tenagino Probus are attested on *AE* 1934 no. 257, 1936 no. 58, and 1941 no. 33 with R. Hanslik, "Tenagino Probus," *RE* 23 (1927), cols. 5–8. For the confusion of the two men, which is the work of the *Historia Augusta*'s sources, see also Barnes, *Sources of Historia Augusta*, 70–71.

22 For the date (summer rather than autumn) see Hartmann, *Das palmyrenische Teilreich*, 286, n. 116. Palmyrene control of Alexandria is not attested prior to November; see *P. Oxy.* 40, 15–20. For a thorough study of the papyri see now G. Kruecher, "Die Regierungszeit Aurelians und die griechischen Papyri aus Ägypten," *Archiv für Papyrusforschung* 44 (1998): 255–64, with a useful chart on p. 264 summarizing the problem.

23 *IGLS* 9107 with G. W. Bowersock, *Roman Arabia* (Cambridge, Mass., 1983), 136, n. 55. For further evidence see the important discussion by Graf, "Zenobia and the Arabs," 149–50. See also Mal. 12.29 (p. 299 Dittenberger), saying that Zenobia attacked Arabia, killing the *"dux"* Trassos and all those with him, with Hartmann, *Das palmyrenische Teilreich*, 279–81. The date is confirmed by milestones of Vaballathus in Arabia; see T. Bauzou, "Deux milliaires inédits de Vaballath en Jordanie du Nord," in *The Defense of the Roman and Byzantine East*, ed. P. Freeman and D. L. Kennedy, BAR International Series 297 (Oxford, 1986), 1–8.

24 For this expansion of the abbreviation *VCRIMDR*, which appears on coins, see C. Gallazzi, "La titolatura di Vaballato come riflesso della politica di Palmira," *NAC* 4 (1975): 249–65, confirming the earlier suggestion of U. Wilcken, "Die Titulatur des Vaballathus," *ZfN* 15 (1887): 330–32; see also Long, "Two Sides of a Coin," 65. Galazzo's reading is supported by *P. Oxy.* 2898, 23–28; 2904, 15–23; 2906, 1.21–26; 2908, 2.20–25, 3.29–33; 2916, 12–13; 2921, 6–11; 2922, 1–5; 2936, 25–28; 3294, 14–19; 3367, 1.14–16, 2.14–15; P. Bureth, *Les titulatures impériales dans les papyrus, les ostraca et les inscriptions d'Égypte (30 a.C.–284 p.C.)* (Brussels, 1964), 122, nn. 1, 5.

25 Long, "Two Sides of a Coin," 64–65.

26 *PIR²* I 403. He is presumably the same man who was placed in charge of rebuilding the walls of Verona in 265 (*ILS* 544).

27 J. Rea, "The Date of the Prefecture of Statilius Aemilianus," *Chronique d'Égypte* 44 (1969): 134–38, and his discussion on *P. Oxy.* 2612. See p. 270 below.

28 *FGrH* 281 T 1 with E. Stein, "Kallinikos von Petra," *Hermes* 58 (1923): 448–56; Bowersock, *Roman Arabia*, 134–36. See also G. Gaggero, "Memorie del passato nella propaganda politica di Zenobia," in *Un incontro con la storia nel centenario della nascita di Luca de Regibus*, ed. A. F. Bellezza, Atti del pomeriggio di storia a Vogogna d'Pasola 1° luglio 1995 (Genoa, 1996), 211–22, who attempts to show that *V. Tyr. Trig.* 27.1: *Didonem et Samiramidem et Cleopatram sui generis principem inter cetera praedicans* is not simply the result of the author's imagination. In addition to the evidence for Cleopatra, he draws attention to *BMC Phoenicia* 277 no. 409, 284 nos. 439–41, 290 no. 470, coins of Tyre representing Dido. It is not impossible that such traditions could have survived in late fourth-century Rome, given the fact that Longinus' panegyric on Odaenathus was still extant in Rome at that time; see Lib. *Ep.* 1078.

29 Bowersock, "The Miracle of Memnon," 31–32 (also in Bowersock, *Eastern Roman Empire*, 263–64).

30 F. Winnett and G. L. Harding, *Inscriptions from Fifty Safaitic Cairns* (Toronto, 1978), nos. 353–55 with Graf, "Zenobia and the Arabs," 151–52.

31 Euseb. *Hist. eccl.* 7.30 (implying but not stating a connection with Zenobia); Ath. *Hist. Ar. ad mon.* 71.1 (calling Zenobia a Jew and the patron of Paul); Filastrius, *Diversarium haereseon liber* 36/64 (*CSEL* 38, p. 33); John Chrys. *Hom 8 in Ioannem* (*PG* 69, col. 66); Theodoret, *Haereticarum fabularum compendium* 2.8 (all three stating the connection). It is significant that the sources later than Eusebius are clearest on this point, suggesting that there was significant information that Eusebius did not have, not unlikely in any case, but particularly significant with regard to John Chrysostom and Theodoret, who were working with local knowledge. For acceptance of the connection see D. S. Potter, "Palmyra and Rome," 284. For a negative view see F. Millar, "Paul of Samosata, Zenobia, and Aurelian: The Church, Local Culture, and Political Allegiance in Third-Century Syria," *JRS* 61 (1971): 12–13. There are, however, fragments of what appears to be correspondence between Paul and Zenobia after 268; see A. Baldini, "Il ruolo di Paolo di Samosata nella politica culturale di Zenobia e la decisione di Aureliano ad Antiochia," *Riv. Stor. Ant.* 5 (1975): 59–78; J. H. Declerck, "Deux nouveaux fragments attribués à Paul de Samosate," *Byzantion* 54 (1984): 116–40.

32 See p. 302 below for a discussion of Mani's beliefs, which defy simple description.

33 I. M. F. Gardiner and S. C. Lieu, "From Narmouthis (Medinet Madi) to Kellis (Ismant El-Kharab): Manichaean Documents from Roman Egypt," *JRS* 86 (1996): 153, where Zenobia is indicated as Queen Thanador. See also W. Sundermann, *Mitteliranische manichäische Texte kirchengeschichtlichen Inhalts*, Schriften zur Geschichte und Kultur des alten Orients: Berliner Turfantexte 11 (Berlin, 1981), 41–42. The other text is Sundermann, nos. 3.3, 10–11 (p. 42).

34 For the problem of whether or not Nafsha was a real person see Hartmann, *Das palmyrenische Teilreich*, 312–13. Although Hartmann's skepticism about the whole tradition is not unreasonable, I find it hard to believe that the story would have been invented to the advantage of the Manichaean community if there were not some contact with the court – if the story was complete invention (as opposed to exaggerated), we might expect that a more successful person than Zenobia would have been its object.

35 Bowersock, "The Miracle of Memnon," 31–32 (also in Bowersock, *Eastern Roman Empire*, 263–64). For other observations of the statue see p. 185 with n. 63 above.

36 L. H. Cope, "The Nadir of the Imperial Antoninianus in the Reign of Claudius II Gothicus, AD 268–70," *NC* 9 (1969): 145–61.

37 Kienast, *Römische Kaisertabelle*, 228; Peachin, *Roman Imperial Titulature*, 43.

38 Eutrop. *Brev.* 9.12; Zon. 12.26; Zos. 1.47.1; [Aur. Vict.] *Epit. de Caes.* 34.5; *HA V. Aurel.* 16.1 with Kienast, *Römische Kaisertabelle*, 230; Peachin, *Roman Imperial Titulature*, 43.

39 *FGrH* 100, fr. 24 (preface); fr. 26 (letter of Decius) (immediately following fr. 24 in the mss); fr. 28 (speech of Athenian) (fr. 28 b should be printed as fr. 29, as it opens with *hoti*, as also do fr. 28b–e, which might otherwise be fr. 30–33). Fr. 28d suggests that Dexippus began speaking at this point rather than earlier. For the problem of the identity see De Ste. Croix, *Class Struggle*, 654–55, n. 42 (not Dexippus). G. Fowden, "City and Mountain in Late Roman Attica," *JHS* 108 (1988): 51, n. 13, defends the identity, but a cardinal point of his defense, that *HA V. Gall.* 13.8 is derived directly from Dexippus, is debatable; see works cited in n. 4 above; *FGrH* 100 fr. 25, 27, 29.

40 Potter, *Literary Texts*, 73.

41 *HA V. Aurel.* 18.3, placing the battle near Milan, and 21.1, placing it at Placentia. [Aur. Vict.] *Epit. de Caes.* 35.2 has the first battle at Placentia, erroneously calling it a victory. See also Anon. Post Dionem 10.3, which has Aurelian, upon learning that a part of the "barbarian" force had occupied Placentia, send them a message telling them that they would be well advised to surrender, and their refusing to do so.

42 *HA V. Aurel.* 21.4 (vague reference to victory with divine aid); *Epit. de Caes.* 35.2 for the two locations, and, Paschoud, *Vies d'Aurélien et Tacite*, 118–20. Paschoud's excellent notes to his Budé edition are arranged in so complex a fashion that it seems best to cite his views according to the relevant pages.

43 *HA V. Aurel.* 18.4, 21.5–6, 38.2–3; Aur. Vict. *De Caes.* 35.6; [Aur. Vict.] *Epit. de Caes.* 35.6; Eutrop. *Brev.* 9.14 with R. Turcan, "Le délit des monétaires rebellés contre Aurélien," *Latomus* 28 (1969): 948–59.

44 *HA V. Aurel.* 21.5–6, 40.1–2, 44.2 (invented; see Paschoud, *Vies d'Aurélien et Tacite*, 205); Amm. Marc. 30.8.8.

45 *HA V. Aurel.* 35.2, placing the beginning of the distribution before Aurelian left for the east (see also Paschoud, *Vies d'Aurélien et Tacite*, 171) in a section that elsewhere contains correct chronological detail; Aur. Vict. *De Caes.* 35.7; [Aur. Vict.] *Epit. de Caes.* 35.6. There is no reason to believe that the distribution of wine attested at *HA V. Aurel.* 48.1 is anything other than an invention of the author; see Paschoud, *Vies d'Aurélien et Tacite*, 215.

46 *HA V. Aurel.* 21.9–11; Aur. Vict. *De Caes.* 35.7; [Aur. Vict.] *Epit. de Caes.* 35.5; Eutrop. *Brev.* 9.15. The author of the *Historia Augusta* alone records an expansion of the *pomerium*, probably a fantasy; see R. Syme, "The *Pomerium* in the *Historia Augusta*," *BHAC 1975–76* (Bonn, 1978) (also in R. Syme, *Historia Augusta Papers* [Oxford, 1983], 136–38) and Paschoud, *Vies d'Aurélien et Tacite*, 131–33.

47 T. Kotula, *Aurélien et Zénobie: L'unité ou la division de l'empire* (Warsaw, 1997), 80.

48 Christol, *Essai sur l'évolution*, 110–11 with p. 265 above.

49 Eutrop. *Brev.* 9.15; *HA V. Aurel.* 39.7 with Paschoud, *Vies d'Aurélien et Tacite*, 188–89; Kotula, *Aurélien et Zénobie*, 34–35; L. Okamura, "Roman Withdrawals from Three Transfluvial Frontiers," in *Shifting Frontiers in Late Antiquity*, ed. R. W. Mathisen and H. S. Sivan (Brookfield, Vt., 1996), 17–19. V. Velkov, "Aurélien et sa politique en Mésie et Thrace," in Frézouls and Jouffroy, *Les empereurs illyriens*, 155–69, makes a case for 275, but the epigraphic evidence that he adduces does not necessitate the later date, though it must also be admitted that the evidence for the early date in Eutrop. *Brev.* 15.1 and *HA V. Aurel.* 39.7 (deriving from the same source) is impressionistic, suggesting that the decision was made when the northern tribes were undefeated, while Aur. Vict. *De Caes.* 33.4 puts the loss of the region under Gallienus. What does necessitate this conclusion is the astute observation of K. Tausend, "Bemerkungen zum Wandaleneinfall des Jahres 271," *Historia* 48 (1999): 126–7 who shows that the terms of Aurelian's settlement with the Vandals specify that the border with the Vandals will be the Danube in Pannonia, which presupposes that Dacia will be abandoned.

50 N. Lewis, "ΝΟΗΜΑΤΑ ΛΕΓΟΝΤΟΣ," *BASP* 4 (1967): 34, establishing the presence of Statilius Aemilianus in the text and reading Aurelian as emperor; Rea, "The Date of the Prefecture of Statilius Aemilianus," 134–38, and his discussion on *P. Oxy.* 2612. For Aemilianus' governorship of Arabia see Sartre, *Trois études*, 97–98.

51 *ILS* 1210 with the reconstruction of the text; see Christol, *Essai sur l'évolution*, 263–70.

52 *HA V. Aurel.* 24.2–5.

53 For the text see Paschoud ad loc. in his edition of Zosimus. The mss. reading, *hieron*, is accepted in LSJ s.v. *hêgêlazô*, uncorrected in the latest supplement. *Krueron*, which is read here, is supported by *Il.* 24.524; *Od.* 4.103, 11.212.

54 Zos. 57.4 with Paschoud's excellent note in Zosime, *Histoire nouvelle*, vol. 1 (Paris, 1971), 166–67.

55 See pp. 000 and 000 above.

56 G. W. Bowersock, "Roman Senators from the Greek East: Syria, Judaea, Arabia, Mesopotamia," *Epigrafia e ordine senatorio*, 2, Tituli 5 (Rome, 1982), 665 (also in Bowersock, *Eastern Roman Empire*, 157).

57 Zos. 50.2–51.1 (battle at Antioch); Festus, *Brev.* 24, placing the battle at Immae; *HA V. Aurel.* 25.1, specifying Daphne as the location of the battle; Zos. 1.52–53 (battle at Emesa); *HA V. Aurel* 25.2–4; see also Hoffmann, *Das palmyrenische Teilreich*, 365–75.

58 *RIC* 5.1 Aurelian nos. 17, 61–64, 134, 137, 150–51, 187, 246–55, 278–81, 307, 309–17, 360–65, 367, 413–17; see also nos. 154, 185, 257, 353, 390, 397.

59 *HA V. Aurel.* 25.4–6 making the point explicitly.

60 *AE* 1936 no. 129.

61 Zos. 1.56.3; for Longinus see p. 261 above.

62 Euseb. *Hist. eccl.* 7.30. For the nature of the charge see Potter, "Palmyra and Rome," 284.

63 *FGrH* 281 T 1 with Sartre, *Trois études*, 93.

64 *CJ* 7.14.4.

65 *P. Oxy.* 3613.3–4. The specification that members of the boule who were responsible for the payment plainly refers to people who were on the boule in the period of Palmyrene control and who are here blamed for failing to keep the peace after the restoration.

66 *HA V. Aurel.* 30.4; Zos. 1.60.1; *CJ* 5.72.2 with Halfmann, *Itinera principum*, 240.

67 T. Gagos and R. Caldwell, "The Emperor Aurelian and the Corrector Firmus in a Private Context," *P. Bingen* (Amsterdam, 2000), 451–70, publishing *P. Mich inv.* 5457 from Karanis.

68 König, *Die gallischen Usurpatoren*, 177–79.

69 *HA V. Aurel.* 39.1 with König, *Die gallischen Usurpatoren*, 179.

70 *V. Tyr. Trig.* 27.2 confirmed by *CIL* 6, no. 1516 with Milik, *Dédicaces faites par des Dieux*, 320.

71 D. Rathbone, "Monetisation, Not Price-Inflation, in Third-Century AD Egypt," in *Coin Finds and Coin Use in the Roman World: The Thirteenth Oxford Symposium on Coinage and Monetary History, 25–27.3.1993*, ed. C. E. King and D. G. Wigg (Berlin, 1996), 329–33; M. Corbier, "Dévaluations et évolution des prix (Ier–IIIe siècles)," *Rev. Num.* 27 (1985): 69–106, esp. p. 105.

72 For the tariffing of gold above the official rate see Rathbone, "Monetisation, Not Price-Inflation," 324, 337, n. 43; C. Howgego, *Ancient History from Coins* (London, 1995), 142, n. 2.

73 For an excellent, brief summary see Howgego, *Ancient History from Coins*, 126; for a more generous view of the reform see K. Harl, *Coinage in the Roman Economy, 300 BC–AD 700* (Baltimore, 1996), 145–48. Harl bases his assessment on the fact that the new system of coinage remained in use for the next twenty years. It seems to me that the evidence of inflation (which he notes) is more important than the stability of the coinage system.

74 The new imperial coinage did not go into circulation with the same speed in every part of the empire; see C. E. King, "The Circulation of Coin in the Western Provinces AD 260–95," in *The Roman West in the Third Century: Contributions from Archaeology and History*, ed. A. King and M. Henig (Oxford, 1981), 89–126.

75 *P. Oxy.* 1411 with Rathbone, "Monetisation, Not Price-Inflation," 335–36.

76 For issues connected with the coinage of Vaballathus see in general Long, "Two Sides of a Coin," 59–71.

77 Zos. 1.62.3.

78 Zos. 1.63.3; compare Zon. 12.28.

79 E. Sauer, "M. Annius Florianus: Ein Drei-Monate-Kaiser und die ihm zu Ehren aufgestellten Steinmonument (276 n. Chr.)," *Historia* 47 (1998): 181.

80 Sauer, "M. Annius Florianus," 174–203, collects the evidence for his support.

81 Zos. 1.64.4 with Sauer, "M. Annius Florianus," 187.

82 Zos. 1.65.2; Zon. 12.29 (without details); Cedr. 1.464 (Bonn) places the banquet at Perinthus; *HA V. Prob.* 13.2–3 merely says that he killed them, and then distinguishes the killers of Tacitus from those of Aurelian.

83 Christol, *Essai sur l'évolution*, 262–70. Christol (p. 270) notes that one reconstruction of his stemma would make him a patrician, descended from L. Virius Lupus, *consul ordinarius* in 232, and wonders if it is possible for such a man to have a career such as that attested on *ILS* 1210. On any reckoning his career under Gallienus is unusual, but so is his three-year tenure of the urban prefecture, which suggests that he was a man of unusual importance. For his role in Syria after the defeat of Palmyra see Peachin, *Iudex vice Caesaris*, 128–29.

84 Zos. 1.66.1–2 (introduced, unfortunately, with the words *tauta diapraxamenô tô Probô*, a reference backward to the execution of Aurelian's murderers). The same collocation of events occurs in Zon. 12.29 (manifestly deriving from a common source, on which see Bleckmann, *Die Reichskrise*, 49–50); see also George, 723 (Mosshammer, 471) (on Saturninus alone, saying that he was killed by his men at Apamea). The proper context appears in *HA V. Prob.* 18.5–8; Eutrop. *Brev.* 9.17.2; Aur. Vict. *De Caes.* 37.3; [Aur. Vict.] *Epit. de Caes.* 37.2. Victor leaves Proculus out, which is an oversight given his appearance in the similar passage in [Aurelius Victor]. The coincidence between the dates of the revolts at Cologne and in Syria is suggested by Victor's *simul caesis Saturnino per Orientem, Agrippinae Bonoso exercitu*. The dates are established by G. Vitucci, *L'imperatore Probo* (Rome, 1952). Nothing is gained from *HA Quadr. Tyr.* 7–14, fictional biographies of all three men, on which see A. Chastagnol, "Sources, thèmes et procédés de composition dans les Quadrigae Tyrannorum," in A. Chastagnol, *Recherches sur l'Histoire Auguste avec un rapport sur les progrès de la Historia Augusta Forschung depuis 1963* (Bonn, 1970), 69–98.

85 Zos. 1.71.1; a slightly different view is offered by *HA V. Prob.* 17.3: *Copten praeterea et Ptolomaidem urbis ereptas barbarico servitio Romano reddidit iuri.* The *Historia Augusta* account appears to have confused Probus' action with Diocletian's campaign in 293; see Bleckmann, *Die Reichskrise*, 141, and Chastagnol, *Histoire Auguste*, 1067.

86 Zos. 1.69.1–70.5; *HA V. Prob.* 16.4, giving the name as Palfurius and giving Probus personal credit for the operation. *HA V. Tyr. Trig.* 26 creates a man named Trebellianus as a usurper in Isauria under Gallienus, which may be a further reflection of this episode (if not, more generally of the constant struggles between the hill peoples of the Taurus and those of the surrounding plains).

87 S. Mitchell, *Cremna in Pisidia: An Ancient City in Peace and War* (London, 1995), 177–217.

88 Mitchell, *Cremna in Pisidia*, 183–84.

89 Mitchell, *Cremna in Pisidia*, 186–88, noting the local tradition that the "sap" was in fact a trench dug in 1969–70 to remove stones from the wall, which he reasonably discounts.

90 *HA V. Aurel.* 13.5; compare Zos. 1.67.1 and Zon. 12.29. The Latin *his gestis* (the reference is to the execution of the murderers of Aurelian and Tacitus) *cum ingenti exercitu Gallias petit, quae omnes occiso Postumo turbatae fuerant, interfecto Aureliano a Germanis possessae* may be an expansion on passages in an original source that are also reflected in Zos. 1.67.1 and Zon. 12.29.

91 Zos. 1.67.1–3; Zon. 12.29.

92 *HA V. Prob.* 16.1–2.

93 Mitchell, *Cremna in Pisidia*, 216.

94 Zos. 1.68.3 (Iggilus), for Gallienus (or Claudius, a caveat stemming from the chronological confusion in the sources at this point); see George, 717 (Mosshammer, 467) on Naulobates.

95 Zos. 1.71.2 with *Pan.* 4.18.3.

96 *HA V. Prob.* 13.1 mentions the existence of the court in a context that appears otherwise fanciful (designed to offer a paradigm of the conduct for an emperor who knew how to respect the senate, an interest of the author). The existence of the *iudicium magnum* is, however, attested epigraphically under Probus; see *AE* 1964 no. 223 with discussion by A. Chastagnol, "A propos du 'judicium magnum' de l'empereur Probus," *BHAC 1966–67* (Bonn, 1968), 67–69; Christol, *Essai sur l'évolution*, 165, n. 34; and Peachin, *Iudex vice principis*, 129–32, who suggests that the office reflects the preoccupation of Probus with other matters.

97 For a list see Christol, *Essai sur l'évolution*, 265–67; Peachin, *Iudex vice principis*, 93–153.

98 Zos. 1.71.4–5; Zon. 12.29; Anon. Post Dionem fr. 11 (*FHG* 4.198).

99 Zon. 12.30, saying that he captured Seleuceia and Ctesiphon: *kai katesche Ktêsiphônta kai Seleukeian* (see also George, 724 [Mosshammer, 472]: *parelabe Ktêsiphônta*); Eutrop. *Brev.* 9.14.1 offers *Cochen et Ctesiphontem, urbes nobilissimas, cepit,* and Festus, *Brev.* 24 gives *Cochen et Ctesiphontem, urbes Persarum nobilissimas, cepit.* The *HA V. Cari, Carini et Num.* 8.1 reports instead: *Mesopotamiam Carus cepit et Ctesifontem usque pervenit.* See also Aur. Vict. *De Caes.* 38.3; [Aur. Vict.] *Epit. de Caes.* 38.2, both asserting (as they would on the basis of their shared source) that he did not take Ctesiphon. For other sources see the useful compilation in Dodgeon and Lieu, *Roman Eastern Frontier,* 112–16.

100 Contra Bleckmann, *Die Reichskrise*, 133–35.

101 Dodgeon and Lieu, *The Roman Eastern Frontier*, 116–19, for the sources.

102 *CJ* 5.52.2 with Halfmann, *Itinera principum*, 242.

103 *RIC* 5.2 Numerian no. 462. The issue may be prospective, and its meaning is complicated by a similar issue of *adventus* coins for Carinus; see *RIC* 5.2 Carinus no. 317.

104 *HA V. Cari, Carini et Num.* 12.1–2; Aur. Vict. *De Caes.* 38.7–8; [Aur. Vict.] *Epit. de Caes.* 38.4–5; Eutrop. *Brev.* 18.2.

105 Eutrop. *Brev.* 9.20.1; Aur. Vict. *De Caes.* 39.1 (without the detail concerning Aper); *HA V. Cari, Carini et Num.* 13.2–4.

106 *AE* 1973 no. 540 calls him Marcus Aurelius Gaius Valerius Diocletianus, which is probably a mistake (compare *Insc. Did.* 89; 90), but Aur. Vict. *De Caes.* 39.1 says that his original nomen was Valerius.

107 For Bassus see T. D. Barnes, *Constantine and Eusebius* (Cambridge, Mass., 1981), 5; Christol, *Essai sur l'évolution*, 166–67.

108 T. D. Barnes, *The New Empire of Diocletian and Constantine* (Cambridge, Mass., 1981), 31 on the basis of [Aur. Vict.] *Epit. de Caes.* 39.7 (making him sixty-eight at the time of his death) and Mal. 12.44 (p. 311 Dindorf), which says that he was seventy-two when he died. The epitome has him survive for "almost nine years" after his abdication, which would place his death in 312, probably a year late. For a more extreme estimate of his age, dictated by the need to make him older than Maximian, see O. Seeck, *Geschichte des Untergangs der antiken Welt* (Berlin, 1895–1920), 1: 437, who argued that he was eighty when he died.

109 For the date see T. D. Barnes, "Emperors, Panegyrics, Prefects, Provinces, and Palaces (284–317)," *JRA* 9 (1996): 535–37.

110 Barnes, *New Empire*, 32–33, for what is known of his earlier career. For a different chronology see F. Kolb, *Diocletian und dei erste Tetrarchie. Improvisation oder Experiment in der Organisation monarchischer Herrschaft?* (Berlin, 1987), 23–32; B. Leadbetter, "'*Patrimonium Indivisum*'? The Empire of Diocletian and Maximian, 285–289," *Chiron* 28 (1998): 212 (adducing the poverty of evidence for Maximian as Caesar as the reason for an early date). The early date is refuted by Barnes, "Emperors, Panegyrics," 537, though the crucial argument against the later date is that Diocletian was back in the Balkans by December, and it looks as if Maximian was already on his way to Gaul. Although Maximian was raised to the rank of Augustus in the absence of Diocletian, it is inconceivable that Diocletian would not have been present to confer initial promotion.

111 Zon. 12.31 for the visit to Rome, which he places prior to the proclamation of Maximian; *RIC* 5.2, 241 no. 203 (*adventus* Augusti at Ticinum); *CJ* 4.48.5: *PP. iii non. Nov. Atubino Diocletiano A II et Aristobulo conss.*; *Frag. Vat.* 297 (dated *iii non. Nov. Suneata Diocletiano Aug. II et Aristobulo conss.*, though Maximian's name is replaced by that of Constantius in the address) with Barnes, *New Empire*, 50, for the return to the Balkans and n. 23 for the Sarmatian campaign.

112 For similar accounts see Eutrop. *Brev.* 9.20.3, who has Maximian's title correct, but also places the revolt in the context of Diocletian's ascension (*ita rerum Romanarum potitus, cum tumultum rusticani in Gallia concitassent*) and Oros. *Contra Paganos* 7.25.2; Zon. 12.31.

113 *RIC* 5.2.595, no.1. The legend on *RIC* 5.2.595, nos. 2–3, reads *imp. S* (an error for C.) *Amandus p.f. Augustus*. See also the discussion by Z. Rubin, "Mass Movements in Late Antiquity: Appearances and Realities," in *Leaders and Masses in the Roman World: Studies in Honor of Zvi Yavetz*, ed. I. Malkin and Z. W. Rubinsohn (Leiden, 1994), 137–56, and esp. 146–48 on this point. See also the discussion of the evidence in A. Pasqualini, *Massimiano Herculius: Per un'interpretazione della figura e dell' opera* (Rome, 1979), 30–41.

114 Barnes, *New Empire*, 4, n. 6; S. Corcoran, *The Empire of the Tetrarchs: Imperial Pronouncements and Government, AD 284–324*, revised edition (Oxford, 2000), 273–74; Barnes, "Emperors, Panegyrics," 539; contra Kolb, *Diocletian*, 23–32.

115 So extraordinary, in fact, that it has been suspected that it was a usurpation of the title, tacitly recognized by Diocletian to avoid civil war; see Seeck, *Geschichte des Untergangs*, 1: 25–26; for a recent, and convincing, refutation see Leadbetter, "*Imperium Indivisum*," 218–28.

116 *Frag. Vat.* 275 (March 3); *Frag. Vat.* 281; *CJ* 4.10.3 (Tiberias; the place is given only in one ms L (eleventh century); the date is given as January in an early printed edition, which is impossible); see also Barnes, *New Empire*, 50.

117 For the movements of the two emperors in these years see Barnes, *New Empire*, 50–51, 57–58.

118 For known letters of the tetrarchic period, all but one (and that one may be a fiction), see Corcoran, *Empire of the Tetrarchs*, 125–39.

119 *Frag. Vat.* 282 (also in *CJ* 3.29.4, 8.53.6) with Kolb, *Diocletian*, 42–43; Corcoran, *Empire of the Tetrarchs*, 78, 273.

120 This passage has been taken as indicating the possibility that there was a formal division of provinces (see, with proper caution, Barnes, *New Empire*, 196). The text of *Pan.* 10 (2) 11.6: *Diocletianus + facit, tu tribuis effectum*, while clearly corrupt (*facit* requires an object), cannot sensibly be restored in a way that would not suggest Maximian's formal subordination to Diocletian.

121 *Pan.* 10 (2) 5; 10.3 with Barnes, *New Empire*, 57; for an alternative view see Kolb, *Diocletian*, 42–43, which depends on accepting Mommsen's emendation of the subscription to *Frag. Vat.* 282, which is based upon the notion that Maximian

could not issue a rescript as Caesar, a view that is generally rejected and is, on technical grounds, dubious, as it is repeated in all three citations of the edict; see n. 118 above.

122 *Pan.* 10 (2) 11.7–12.

123 For these events, see in general the valuable study of P. J. Casey, *The British Usurpers: Carausius and Allectus* (New Haven, 1994), 89–105.

124 Eutrop. *Brev.* 9.21; Aur. Vict. *De Caes.* 39 (manifestly drawing from the same source, but leaving out details concerning the identity of the raiders).

125 Casey, *The British Usurpers*, 92–94, noting *Pan.* 8 [4] 12.1, which admits one continental legion joining him (probably *legio XXX Ulpia Victrix*), though it is not impossible that the other units of continental origin were stationed in Gaul as well.

126 *Pan.* 8 (5) 12.1 with the interesting discussion of Casey, *The British Usurpers*, 99, on the sort of people involved.

127 Casey, *The British Usurpers*, 103.

128 The disaster involving a storm is deduced from *Pan.* 8 (5) 12.2; for a cautious appraisal of the validity of this conclusion see R. Rees, *Layers of Loyalty in Latin Panegyric AD 289–307* (Oxford, 2002), 68, n. 1.

129 Casey, *The British Usurpers*, 106 (on the basis of coin finds).

130 *CJ* 9.41.9 (Emesa); *CJ* 6.30.6 (Sirmium).

131 *Pan.* 11 (3) 9–10; the meeting ended in time for Maximian to return to northern Gaul by February 18, 291; see *Frag. Vat.* 315 with Barnes, *New Empire*, 58, n. 51.

132 For the arrival of a senatorial embassy see *Pan.* 11 (3) 12.2.

133 For a summary of the problem with the date see now Rees, *Layers of Loyalty*, 70–1; for discussion of the orator, identified in the manuscripts as Mamertinus, see the judicious discussion in Rees, *Layers of Loyalty*, 193–204, who shows that the panegyrics of 289 and 291 are sufficiently close in style and theme that, if the author of the panegyric in 291 was not Mamertinus, he was, at the very least, writing in the knowledge of the panegyric of 289.

134 Kolb, *Diocletian*, 70–71, contra Barnes, *Constantine and Eusebius*, 8, who has Diocletian plan the restructuring of government in the course of the next two years. See also Pasqualini, *Massimiano Herculius*, 50–51. For a very different view, suggesting that the proclamation of Constantius was an act of Maximian, taken without prior consultation, see I. König, "Die Berufung des Constantius Chlorus und des Galerius zu Caesaren: Gedanken zur entstehung der Ersten Tetrarchie," *Chiron* 4 (1974): 567–76 (esp. 575–76), on the basis of the earlier date for the promotion of Constantius. This is too much to build upon that point (tempting though it might be).

135 For the date of Constantius' marriage to Theodora see Barnes, *New Empire*, 37, on the basis of *Pan.* 10 (2) 11.4: *tu quidem certe, imperator, tantum esse in concordia bonum statuis, ut etiam eos qui circa te potissimo funguntur officio necessitudine tibi et adfinitate devinxeras.* The *potissimum officium* is now known to be a military command, not the praetorian prefecture as had been previous supposed; see Barnes, "Emperors, Panegyrics," 547; for exposition of the view that the prefecture is alluded to see Seeck, *Geschichte des Untergangs*, 1: 29 with pp. 452–53, n. to l. 13. For the question of his relationship with Helena, see p. 342, n. 46 below.

136 *Pan.* 6 (7) 4.2 with Barnes, *New Empire*, 36–37, on the text.

137 Aur. Vict. *De Caes.* 39.40–42; Casey, *The British Usurpers*, 127–39.

138 For arguments in favour of May 21 see Kolb, *Diocletian*, 73, contra Barnes, *New Empire*, 62, n. 73. Although Barnes is correct about the passage from Lactantius, which has been used to place the proclamation of Galerius at Nicomedia (wrongly, see also p. 342), he cannot so easily explain away the other evidence suggesting that there was a temporal lag between the two proclamations. That Constantius was proclaimed first should explain why he is given priority in the tetrarchy.

139 Lact. *DMP* 50.2 with Barnes, *New Empire*, 38.

140 For portraits of this period see H. Mattingly and E. A. Sydenham, *The Roman Imperial Coinage*, vol. 5, pt. 2 (London, 1933), 208–9.

141 C. H. V. Sutherland and R. A. G. Carson, *The Roman Imperial Coinage*, vol. 6 (London, 1967), 93 (coinage reform; see also p. 392 below); p. 109 on portraits.

142 For Nicomedia see N. Duval, "Les résidences impériales: Leur rapport avec les problèmes de légitimité, les partages de l'Empire et les combinaisons dynastiques," in *Usurpation in der Spätantike*, ed. F. Paschoud and J. Szidat, Historia Einzelschriften 111 (Stuttgart, 1997), 137; for Milan and Aquileia see N. Duval, "Les palais impériaux de Milan et d'Aquilée, réalité et mythe," *Antichità alto-adriatiche* 4 (1973): 158; for Sirmium see E. L. Ochsenschlager and V. Popovic, "Excavations at Sirmium, Yugoslavia," *Archaeology* 26 (1973): 85–93; D. Boskovic, N. Duval, P. Gros and V. Popovic, "Recherches archéologiques à Sirmium: Campagne Franco-Yugoslave de 1973," *MEFR* 86 (1974): 616–19. The imperial palace at Trier appears to date to the reign of Constantine. If so, Constantius would appear to have maintained himself in a style quite different from his colleagues; for the buildings see E. M. Wightman, *Roman Trier and the Treviri* (New York, 1971), 103–10. For a general summary of issues connected with imperial building activities, see Duval, "Les résidences impériales," 127–54.

143 Phil. *V. Soph.* 560 with Boskovic *et al.*, "Recherches archéologiques," 605.

144 Aur. Vict. *De Caes.* 39.2; 4; Eutrop. *Brev.* 9.26 with A. H. M. Jones, *The Later Roman Empire, 284–602: A Social, Economic, and Administrative Study* (Oxford, 1964), 1: 40.

145 P. 61 above.

146 For these events see Zos. 1.39.2; *HA V. Gall.* 10.1–8, 12.1; Zon. 12.24 (without details); George, 716–17 (Mosshammer, 466–67) and the commentary in Felix, *Antike literarische Quellen*, 82–89; Bleckmann, *Die Reichskrise*, 122–29.

147 M.-L. Chaumont, "Conquêtes Sassanides et propagande mazdéene," *Historia* 22 (1973): 664–709 for detailed discussion of the range of his activities.

148 P. 311 below.

149 Whitby, "Persian King at War," 243–48.

150 Frye, *History of Ancient Iran*, 303–4.

151 *Pan.* 10 (2) 10.6, 7.5, 9.2, in all cases correlating the submission of the Persians with Maximian's actions on the Rhine in 287. For the Armenian sources see Felix, *Antike literarische Quellen*, 106–7, though see the extremely reductionist discussion in E. Kettenhoffen, *Tirdād und die Inschrift von Paikuli: Kritik der Quellen zur Geschichte Armeniens im späten 3. und frühen 4. Jh. n. Chr.* (Wiesbaden, 1995), 156–59, who questions this assumption. Kettenhoffen is obviously correct that we do not know for certain that this happened, but we do know that at some point prior to 293 a king Tiridates was on the throne of Armenia. While Kettenhoffen is right to be skeptical of many reconstructions, this one seems plausible, as one has to explain how an Arsacid ended up on the throne of Armenia. In my view it is unlikely to have happened without Roman intervention, and this seems the best opportunity, as it appears that Carus campaigned in Mesopotamia.

152 Frye, *History of Ancient Iran*, 304–5.

153 Humbach and Skjærvø, *Sasanian Inscription of Paikuli*, 42–43, translating sect. 32.

154 Humbach and Skjærvø, *Sasanian Inscription of Paikuli*, 70–71, translating sects. 91–92.

155 The reconstruction of events here is derived from Casey, *The British Usurpers*, 137–39.

156 The initial invasion of Armenia is attested solely by Amm. Marc. 23.5.11; for Galerius' defeat see Zon. 12.31 (not specifying the location); Festus, *Brev.* 25

(without location); Eutrop. *Brev.* 9.24.5 (with location); Oros. *Contra Paganos* 7.25.9 (deriving from Eutropius); Aur. Vict. *De Caes.* 39.34 (without location) and the discussions in Bleckmann, *Die Reichskrise*, 137–41; Felix, *Antike literarische Quellen*, 112–16. T. D. Barnes, "Imperial Campaigns, A.D 285–311," *Phoenix* 30 (1976), 183, maintains that both Diocletian and Galerius were present at the battle on the basis of *Sel. Pap.* 135; a more conservative reading of the passage would take this only to mean that Diocletian was in the east. I do not think that this can be taken as proving that other statements attributing the defeat to Galerius alone are incorrect. It seems to have been Diocletian's practise to avoid taking the field in person.

157 Amm. Marc. 14.11.10; Eutrop. *Brev.* 9.24; Oros. *Contra Paganos* 7.25.9; Festus, *Brev.* 25.

158 Mal. p. 306.

159 Petrus Patricius fr. 14 (*FHG* 4.189); for what is known of Probus' career see M. Peachin, "The Office of the Memory," in *Studien zur Geschichte der römischen Spätantike: Festgabe für Professor Johannes Straub* (Athens, 1989), 168–208. For a detailed account of the negotiations see Winter, *Die sasanidisch–römischen Friedensverträge*, 173–84.

160 On this point see J. Eadie, "The Transformation of the Eastern Frontier, 260–305," in Mathisen and Sivan, *Shifting Frontiers*, 74–75.

161 Petrus Patricius fr. 14 (*FHG* 4.189).

162 Winter, *Die sāsānidisch–römischen Friedensverträge*, 171–82.

163 For the settlement of Armenia see Kettenhoffen, *Tirdād*, 56–73.

164 Potter, *Prophecy and History*, 336, on Valerian's skin.

165 For the text see S. Lauffer, *Diokletians Preisedikt* (Berlin, 1971).

166 Corcoran, *Empire of the Tetrarchs*, 90, and pp. 29–32 on the compilation of his code.

167 Corcoran, *Empire of the Tetrarchs*, 83–84 (on his style), 90–91. For his distinctive prose style see Honoré, *Emperors and Lawyers*, 116–19.

168 Corcoran, *Empire of the Tetrarchs*, 89–90; Barnes, "Emperors, Panegyrics," 547, for the tenure in office.

169 Corcoran, *Empire of the Tetrarchs*, 294–95.

170 Corcoran, *Empire of the Tetrarchs*, 169.

171 Corcoran, *Empire of the Tetrarchs*, 198–203, 294–97; D. Feissel, "Les constitutions des tétrarques connues par l'épigraphie: inventaire et notes critiques," *L'Antiquité Tardive* 3 (1995): 33–34, noting the sudden upsurge in the inscription of edicts and rescripts as characteristic of the period.

172 *ILS* 617, 618.

173 *ILS* 641; the text from Rome is *ILS* 619.

174 For the problem of the relationship between the speakers and the court see B. H. Warmington, "Aspects of Constantinian Propaganda in the *Panegyrici Latini*," *TAPA* 104 (1974): 371–84 (an extreme view); C. E. V. Nixon, "Constantinus Oriens Imperator: Propaganda and Panegyric: On Reading Panegyric 7 (307)," *Historia* 42 (1993): 230–33 (a more nuanced approach). Both discuss earlier views that imply a closer connection between speakers and the court than they argue for.

175 *Pan.* 10 (2) 7.3–6.

176 Rodgers suggests that the reference is to the time of Carinus, which appears to be rather too specific for the context. See esp. the generalizing comments at *Pan.* 11 (3) 16.2, quoted from Rodgers's translation in the text above.

177 For the date, see conclusively Barnes, "Emperors, Panegyrics," 540.

178 *Pan.* 9 (4) 18.3 (Franks), 8 (5) 4.3 (clades Catalaunica).

8 ALTERNATIVE NARRATIVES: MANICHAEANS, CHRISTIANS, AND NEOPLATONISTS

1 Pp. 249, 266, and 293 above for the various contributions of Malalas.

2 Potter, *Prophecy and History*, 141–57.

3 See the useful collection in P. Frisch, *Zehn agonistische Papyri* (Opladen, 1986).

4 P. 268 and 291 above.

5 For the recovery of Manichaean texts see S. N. C. Lieu, *Manichaeism in Central Asia and China* (Leiden, 1998), 1–58 on Central Asian finds; Lieu, *Manichaeism*, 62–88 for Egypt. In what follows passages from the *Kephalaia* will be cited by page and line from the original followed by the page in the translation of I. Gardiner, *The Kephalaia of the Teacher: The Edited Coptic Manichaean Texts in Translation with Commentary* (Leiden, 1995); passages from the *Cologne Mani Codex* [*CMC*] will be cited by page number in the codex from the edition of L Koenen and C. Römer, *Der Kölner Mani-Kodex. Über das Werden seines Leibes* (Opladen, 1988).

6 *CMC* 11.

7 But see p. 36 above for evidence of mixed Christian and Jewish communities in Asia Minor into the third century.

8 J. C. Reeves, *Jewish Lore in Manichaean Cosmogony: Studies in the Book of Giants Tradition* (Cincinnati, 1992), 185–98.

9 *Kephalaia*, 14.31–15.1 [Gardiner, *The Kephalaia*, 20]; see also al-Nadīm, *The Fihrist*, ed. and trans. B. Dodge (New York, 1970), 775. *Kephalaia*, 15.24–6 [Gardiner, *The Kephalaia*, 21] appears to give the date of Mani's departure to India as Ardashir's last year; see also *CMC* 18.

10 See *Kephalaia*, 14.24, 28, 31 [Gardiner, *The Kephalaia*, 20].

11 *Kephalaia*, 15.28–30 [Gardiner, *The Kephalaia*, 21]; M 8286, translated in J. P. Asmussen, *Manichaean Literature* (New York, 1975), 19; *CMC* 144–45 with Römer, *Manis frühe Missionsreisen*, 132–52.

12 M 216 translated in Asmussen, *Manichaean Literature*, 20–21.

13 *Kephalaia*, 15.31–34 [Gardiner, *The Kephalaia*, 21].

14 *Kephalaia*, 16.2 [Gardiner, *The Kephalaia*, 21].

15 *CMC* 64 (letter to Edessa); for the date of the Manichaean missions to Egypt see L. Koenen, "Manichäische Mission und Klöster in Ägypten," in *Das römisch–byzantinische Ägypten* (Mainz, 1983), 93–108.

16 P. 268 above and p. 310 below.

17 *Prag.* 5.25–26; C. R. C. Allbery, *A Manichaean Psalm-Book* (Stuttgart, 1938), nos. 21–30.

18 M. Tardieu, *Le manichéisme* (Paris, 1981), 59.

19 What follows is heavily indebted to M. Boyce, *A Reader in Manichaean Middle Persian and Parthian Acta Iranica*, Textes et Mémoires 9 (Leiden, 1975), 4–8.

20 al-Nadīm, *Fihrist*, 778, trans. Dodge.

21 al-Nadīm, *Fihrist*, 779, trans. Dodge; for descriptions see M 10, R 11–V 22, 710, 5877 (Parthian); M 819 (Middle Persian); M 316, 801, 1001, 1012, 1013, 1015 (Middle Persian) in Asmussen, *Manichaean Literature*, 120–22.

22 Al-Nadīm, *Fihrist*, 780, trans. Dodge; see also *Kephalaia*, 50.26–51.25 [Gardiner, *The Kephalaia*, 55–56]; *Kephalaia*, 38.21 [Gardiner, *The Kephalaia*, 43]; *Kephalaia*, 39.20–25 [Gardiner, *The Kephalaia*, 44].

23 Al-Nadīm, *Fihrist*, 781–82, trans. Dodge.

24 Gardiner, *The Kephalaia*, xxviii.

25 *Kephalaia*, 35.15–17 [Gardiner, *The Kephalaia*, 39]; *Kephalaia*, 76.15–25 [Gardiner, *The Kephalaia*, 77].

26 *Kephalaia*, 87.14–29 [Gardiner, *The Kephalaia*, 91]; *Kephalaia*, 113.26–115.31 [Gardiner, *The Kephalaia*, 119–22].

27 Gardiner, *The Kephalaia*, xxix–xxx.

28 Gardiner, *The Kephalaia*, xxx.

29 Al-Nadīm, *Fihrist*, 783, trans. Dodge; *Kephalaia*, 157.1–158.23 [Gardiner, *The Kephalaia*, 165–67].

30 Al-Nadīm, *Fihrist*, 784–86, trans. Dodge.

31 For the influence of Marcionite thought on Mani see M 28 I with I. Gardiner, *Kellis Literary Texts* (Oxford, 1996), 86, 88. For the teachings of Marcion see p. 36 above.

32 Asmussen, *Manichaean Literature*, 122–23; Boyce, *Reader*, 9.

33 G. Widengren, *Mani and Manichaeism*, trans. Charles Kessler (London, 1965), 95.

34 For the selection of the Elect see *CMC* 67; *Kephalaia*, 42.3–10 [Gardiner, *The Kephalaia*, 47]; *Kephalaia*, 193, 31–194, 12 [Gardiner, *The Kephalaia*, 203]

35 See Allbery, *A Manichaean Psalm-Book*, no. 241, 9 for the twelve teachers and seventy-two bishops; M 36 (Middle Persian) translated in Asmussen, *Manichaean Literature*, 29–31 for the bishops and priests.

36 Allbery, *A Manichaean Psalm-Book*, no. 241, 10.

37 Boyce, *A Reader*, 11.

38 See esp. Allbery, *A Manichaean Psalm-Book*, nos. 219–41. See esp. hymn no. 227 for the notion of Mani's presence on the *bema* during the ceremony through the agency of his divine twin; hymn no. 226 is written as if it is Mani himself who is speaking.

39 See p. 268 above.

40 H. J. Polotsky, *Manichäische Homilien* (Stuttgart, 1934), 48; compare e.g. Paikuli sects. 68, 70 (Humbach and P. O. Skjærvø. *The Sassanian Inscription of Paikuli*).

41 *Kephalaia*, 15.27–16.2 [Gardiner, *The Kephalaia*, 21]; *Kephalaia*, 183.10–25 (Gardiner, *The Kephalaia*, 193); al-Nadîm, *Fihrist*, 776, trans. Dodge.

42 Allberry, *A Manichaean Psalm-Book*, p. 142; see also p. 320 below.

43 Euseb. *Hist. eccl.* 7.31.

44 Euseb. *Hist. eccl.* 7.11.12 (Cephro, chosen as a place of exile by Aemilianus for Dionysius, who says that a number of Christians followed him); 7.24.6, goes to the Arsinoite nome to correct heretics.

45 See also p. 489 below.

46 K. Hopkins, "Christian Number and Its Implication," *JECS* 6 (1998): 198.

47 For the church at Nicomedia see Lact. *DMP* 12.3.

48 *P. Oxy.* 1357 with E. A. Judge and S. R. Pickering, "Papyrus Documentation of Church and Community in Egypt," *JAC* 20 (1977): 60–61.

49 *P. Oxy.* 2673 with Judge and Pickering, "Papyrus Documentation," 59–60 and p. 339 below, where the text is quoted in full.

50 P. J. Sijpesteijn and K. A. Worp, *Zwei Landlisten aus dem Hermopolites (P. Landlisten). Studia Amstelodamensia ad epigraphicum, ius antiquum et papyrologicum pertinentia* 7 (Zutphen, 1978), 18 show that *P. Flor.* 171, which lists a number of people described as *episcopoi* or bishops in common Christian parlance (lines 298; 305; 510; 512; 519; 731) must be dated between 307/8 and 325 (preferably before 316). See also Judge and Pickering, "Papyrus Documentation," 60–62 and *P. Oxy.* 1357.

51 W. Eck, "Das Eindringen des Christentums in den Senatorenstand bis zu Konstantin d. Gr.," *Chiron* 1 (1971): 381–406, a characteristically admirable analysis of the available evidence. The problem is that the available evidence is seriously deficient, all known from Christian sources with which, with the exception of Tert. *Ad Scap.* 3.5 and Hipp. *Dan.* 4.18.3 (mentioning the "wives" of the governor of Cappadocia), every other reference comes in the context of martyrdom: Euseb. *Hist. eccl.* 7.16 (a senator who buries a martyr); *ILCV* 56, 57 (commemoration of a consul who was martyred); a relative of Ambrose (Ambrose *De virgin.*

3.7.38; *Exhort. virgin.* 12.82); and the wife of the *praefectus urbi* under Maxentius (Euseb. *Hist. eccl.* 8.14.16–17). Given that members of the senatorial order might be expected to be underrepresented among the victims of persecution, the shortage of identifiable Christians may not be particularly significant. Four more Christian women of senatorial standing were turned up by M.-T. Rapsaet-Charlier, "Les femmes sénatoriales du iiiᵉ siècle. Étude préliminaire," *Prosopographie und Sozialgeschichte. Studien zur Methodik und Erkenntnismöglichkeit der kaizerzeitlichen Prosopographie. Kolloquium Köln* (Cologne, 1993), 147–63. For the significance of these studies as serving to place the rise of Christians into the families of the highest aristocracy, see T. D. Barnes, "Statistics and the Conversion of the Roman Aristocracy," *JRS* 85 (1995): 134–38. Note also Flavius Julianus *PLRE* 478.

52 Cyp. *Ep.* 20.1 with G. W. Clarke, *The Letters of St. Cyprian of Carthage*, vol. 1 (New York, 1984), 196–97; Euseb. *Hist. eccl.* 6.40.1 (a *frumentarius* sent in search of Dionysius when the Decian edict was promulgated); 7.11 (suggesting that the governor knew who Dionysius and his leading priests were); 7.30.8 (with p. 272 above) on Paul.

53 P. 255, n. 177 above on the chronology of the election of his successor.

54 Cyp. *Ep.* 80.1.2; *Pas. Mar. et Iac.* 8.1.

55 Elvira can. 20; see also Arles can. 13; Nicaea can. 17.

56 Euseb. *Hist. eccl.* 10.7.1–2.

57 See pp. 402–10 below.

58 See pp. 410–20 below.

59 The date accepted here is the traditional one, for which see the discussion of E. Schwartz, defended by Lane Fox, *Pagans and Christians*, 607–8; A. Louth, "The Date of Eusebius' *Historia Ecclesiastica*," *JTS* 41 (1990): 111–23; H. A. Drake, *Constantine and the Bishops: The Politics of Intolerance* (Baltimore, 2000), 356–58. An earlier date for books 1–7 (ca. 295) was proposed by T. D. Barnes, "The Editions of Eusebius' *Ecclesiastical History*," *GRBS* 21 (1980), 191–201. Barnes accepts the notion that Eusebius' *Onomasticon* predates the *Historia Ecclesiastica*, but would back-date a putative first edition of the *Onomasticon* on the basis of its treatment of Arabia Petraea (T. D. Barnes, "The Composition of Eusebius' *Onomasticon*," *JTS* 26 [1975]: 412–15). This was shown to be unnecessary by P. *Oxy.* 3574 (with Rea's note ad loc. and P. J. Mayerson, "Palaestina vs. Arabia in the Byzantine Sources," *ZPE* 56 (1984): 223–30). If there is no reason to backdate the *Onomasticon*, there is no posi-tive reason to assume an early edition of books 1–7. For a different approach see W. Tabbernee, "Eusebius' 'Theology of Persecution' As Seen in the Various Editions of His Church History," *JECS* 5 (1997): 319–34, which suggests that books 1–7 were completed in draft prior to 303, which explains why he takes a "scholar's view" of persecution and does not exploit the pattern of persecutor/victim of divine anger in those books. I find this an intriguing notion, though it leaves open the question of why, if Eusebius was so attached to the pattern of divine vengeance for persecution, later he did not rewrite more substantially.

60 T. D. Barnes, *Tertullian: A Historical and Literary Study* (Oxford, 1971), 102–14, for a clear summary of the tradition and Tertullian's contribution.

61 For the Greek version of the *Apologeticus* see Euseb. *Hist. eccl.* 2.2.4, 3.33.2, 5.5.5. He also quotes it at 2.25.4, 3.20.7 (both citations are from *Apol.* 5, as is that at 2.2.4).

62 Though it may have helped spawn a large, and bogus, group of martyr acts; see A. von Harnack, *Geschichte der Altchristlichen Literatur*, 2nd edn. (Berlin, 1893), vol. 1, pt. 2, 828, for details.

63 Euseb. *Hist. eccl.* 7.32.5, 21.

64 Kelly, *Early Christian Doctrines*, 133–36 and p. 414 below.

65 Euseb. *Hist. eccl.* 7.26.

66 U. M. Lang, "The Christological Controversy at the Synod of Antioch in 268/9," *JTS* 51 (2000): 54–80.

67 P. 416 below; the position of Lucian in all of this is somewhat ambivalent, see Kelly, *Early Christian Doctrines*, 230; R. P. C. Hanson, *The Search for the Christian Doctrine of God: The Arian Controversy 318–381* (Edinburgh, 1988), 79–83.

68 For Eusebius' theology see esp. Theodoret, *Hist. eccl.* 1.5.2 (also in H. G. Opitz, *Urkunden zur Geschichte des arianischen Streites 318–328* [Berlin, 1934], no. 1).

69 Euseb. *Hist. eccl.* 7.32.7–8 (Eusebius and Anatolius during the troubles at Alexandria), 7.32.25 (Pamphilus), 7.32.26 (Pierius), 7.32.30 (Achillas).

70 See Potter, *Literary Texts*, 88–9.

71 For Origen see *Exhort.* 49; 50–1; for Cyprian see part. *De lapsis* 7; for Tertullian see esp. *De fuga in persecutione* passim; for Eusebius see *Hist. eccl.* 8.1.7–9.

72 Euseb. *Hist. eccl.* 6.40.1 (showing that he was protected in hiding by God), 41.1–2; 7.10.3–8.

73 G. E. M. De Ste. Croix, "Why Were the Early Christians Persecuted?" *Past and Present* 26 (1963): 6–38.

74 *P. Perp.* 4.5 (stating that Satyrus turned himself over). The case of Perpetua is less clear. It is said at *P. Perp.* 2.1 that she was arrested, without any details. Satyrus' vision is given at *P. Perp.* 11–13.

75 *M. Pol.* 5.2, 7.1; his behavior is contrasted with Quintus, who gave himself up voluntarily: *M. Pol.* 4; *P. Pionii* 2.2.

76 *Acta Marcelli* 1.1, 2.1 (recension A); *Acta Marcelli* 1.1 (recension N); *Acta Eupli* 1.1 (recension A); *Acta Eupli* 1.1 (recension B).

77 Euseb. *Hist. eccl.* 6.48.7–20 (quoting a letter of Cornelius); Cyp. *Ep.* 44–45. See also M. Bévenot, "Cyprian and His Recognition of Cornelius," *JTS* 28 (1977): 346–59.

78 For the chronology see G. W. Clarke, *The Letters of St. Cyprian of Carthage*, vol. 3 (New York, 1986), 21–22.

79 Euseb. *Hist. eccl.* 6.43.1–2.

80 Pp. 411–12 below.

81 *M. Pol.* 19.1.

82 A. von Harnack, *Geschichte der altchristlichen Literatur*, 2nd edn. (Berlin, 1904), vol. 2, pt. 2, 111–12. The texts that he included appear to have been the martyrdoms of Polycarp, Pionius, Carpus, Papylus, and Agathonice, of the Martyrs of Lyons, and of Apollonius.

83 B. D. Shaw, "The Passion of Perpetua," *Past and Present* 139 (1993): 37–41; J. E. Salisbury, *Perpetua's Passion: The Death and Memory of a Young Roman Woman* (London, 2000), 170–79.

84 H. Musurillo, *The Acts of the Christian Martyrs* (Oxford, 1972), xxxiii–xxxvi.

85 Tert. *De bapt.* 17.4. For Thecla's baptismal activities see *Acta Pauli et Theclae* 24, 28 with G. Dagron, *Vie et miracles de sainte Thècle: Texte grec, traduction et commentaire*, Subsidia Hagiographica 62 (Brussels, 1978), 40–44; for the issue of Thecla's baptisms see also S. J. Davis, *The Cult of Saint Thecla: A Tradition of Women's Piety in Late Antiquity* (Oxford, 2001), 8–9.

86 *Acta Pauli et Theclae* 19; for the problems with the text see Dagron, *Vie et miracles de sainte Thècle*, 38; see also Davis, *The Cult of Saint Thecla*, 9–13.

87 K. Cooper, *The Virgin and the Bride: Idealized Womanhood in Late Antiquity* (Cambridge, Mass., 1996), 53–55.

88 *Acta Pauli et Theclae* 19–21.

89 Dagron, *Vie et miracles de sainte Thècle*, 13–54.

90 Euseb. *Hist. eccl.* 2.25.7. For Gaius' dates, in the early third century, see Eusebius *Hist. eccl.* 2.25.7, 6.20.3. What follows is heavily indebted to A. Grabar, *Martyrium: Recherches sur le culte des reliques et l'art chrétien antique* (Paris, 1946), 47–75.

91 Euseb. *Hist. eccl.* 3.31.4; for the four prophetic daughters see Acts 21:8–9. For a disparate tradition, also connected with Hierapolis, which has a tomb there for Philip and three daughters, two who were dedicated virgins and the third who was a prophetess, see Euseb. *Hist. eccl.* 3.31.2.

92 Euseb. *Hist. eccl.* 5.1.60–62.

93 Grabar, *Martyrium*, 63.

94 Grabar, *Martyrium*, 51.

95 Grabar, *Martyrium*, 64–65.

96 Y. Duval, *Loca Sanctorum Africae: Le culte des martyrs en Afrique du ive au viie siècle*, Collection de l'École Française de Rome 58 (Rome, 1982), 13–16, 471.

97 Below, p. 402.

98 Eunap. *VS* 456 with P. Cox Miller, "Strategies of Representation in Collective Biography: Constructing the Subject as Holy," in *Greek Biography and Panegyric in Late Antiquity*, ed. T. Hägg and P. Rousseau (Berkeley, 2000), 238.

99 Porph. *V. Plot.* 20.72–74; 21.6–7; but see also *V. Plot.* 14.4–6 with discussion in M.-O. Goulet-Cazé, "Plotin, professeur de philosophie," in *Porphyre: La vie de Plotin*, ed. L. Brisson, M.-O. Goulet-Cazé, R. Goulet, and D. O'Brien (Paris, 1982), 1: 257–76.

100 Porph. *V. Plot.* 8.16–19 (eyesight); 7–12 (associates); 17–20 (other intellectuals); on the lifestyle and its implications see Clark, "Philosophic Lives and the Philosophic Life: Porphyry and Iamblichus," in Hägg and Rousseau, *Greek Biography and Panegyric*, 45–46.

101 Porph. *V. Plot.* 14.

102 Clark, "Philosophic Lives and the Philosophic Life: Porphyry and Iamblichus," 29–51; M. Edwards, "Birth, Death and Divinity in Porphyry's *Life of Plotinus*," in Hägg and Rousseau, *Greek Biography and Panegyric*, 52–71.

103 See the valuable discussion in S. Rappe, "Self-Knowledge and Subjectivity in the Enneads," in *The Cambridge Companion to Plotinus*, ed. L. P. Gerson (Cambridge, 1996), 250–2.

104 D. J. O' Meara, *Plotinus: An Introduction to the "Enneads"* (Oxford, 1993), 19–21. I am grateful to Professor Sara Rappe for calling this book to my attention (and trusting me with her copy).

105 O'Meara, *Plotinus*, 16–17.

106 Porph. *V. Plot.* 18.10–11 with Rappe, "Self-Knowledge,"266–67.

107 Plot. *Enn.* 5.1.5.3; Porph. *V. Plot.* 23.16.

108 O'Meara, *Plotinus*, 103.

109 Porph. *V. Plot.* 17–21.

110 H. J. Blumenthal, "On Soul and Intellect," in Gerson, *The Cambridge Companion to Plotinus*, 82–83.

111 Porph. *V. Plot.* 17–18.

112 See n. 131 below defending a date in the 270s.

113 It could be objected to this view that Porph. *In Christ.* fr. 1 (Harnack) advocates the persecution of Christians. Its attribution to Porphyry might be defended because of the similarity of the sentiments expressed therein with those attributed to the philosopher identified as Porphyry at Lact *DI* 5.2, but this identification has been decisively refuted by T. D. Barnes, "Monotheists All?," *Phoenix* 55 (2001): 158. The failure of this identification decisively undermines part of the argument of E. Digeser, "Lactantius, Porphyry and the Debate over Religious Toleration," *JRS* 88 (1998): 128–9 and M. B. Simmons, *Arnobius of Sicca: Religious Conflict and*

Competition in the Age of Diocletian (Oxford, 1995), 77–78, though the thrust of Simmons's case that Arnobius is responding to Porphyry does not require that Porphyry's book be written ca. 300. All that is required is that Porphyry's book was significant enough in 300 for a Christian to feel the need to respond, which may indeed indicate a rather earlier date. On the other hand, T. D. Barnes, "Scholarship or Propaganda? Porphyry *Against the Christians* and its Historical Setting," *BICS* 39 (1994): 65 suggests that rather than being a fragment, it is in fact Eusebius' summary of the thesis of the *Against the Christians*, and therefore suggests that a date ca. 300 is more probable. While Barnes is absolutely correct in stating that it is hard to reconstruct a work from fragments, this view does not seem to me to fit with what we have, or with Porphyry's overall approach to intellectual controversy. For the date of the work see n. 131 below.

114 Porph. *V. Plot.* 22.9–10. See now the excellent discussion in R. Goulet, "L'oracle d'Apollon dans la *vie de Plotin*," in Brisson *et al.*, *Porphyre: la vie de Plotin*, 2: 372–412.

115 Porph. *V. Plot.* 10.15–25.

116 Plot. *Enn.* 3.1.10.10–11; see also *Enn.* 6.8.5–6 and *Enn.* 3.4 passim.

117 J. Bidez, *Vie de Porphyre le philosophe néo-platonicien* (Leipzig, 1913), 17–28. His view is challenged by J. J. O'Meara, *Porphyry's Philosophy from Oracles in Augustine* (Paris, 1959), 34–37, who argues that the work should date to 268. The core of his argument is that Porphyry shows knowledge of the Chaldaean oracles in the *De philosophia ex oraculis*, as well as in the *De regressu animae* – something denied by Bidez. O'Meara bases his case, in turn, on H. Lewy, *The Chaldaean Oracles and Theurgy*, rev. edn., ed. M. Tardieu (Paris, 1978). Lewy's case is overstated, and O'Meara ignores the crucial evidence for the date (exploited at great length by Eusebius in the *Praeparatio Evangelica*), which is the flat contradiction between the contents of the *De philosophia ex oraculis* and the *De abstinentia*. For the early date see now A. Smith, *Porphyry's Place in the Neoplatonic Tradition* (The Hague, 1974), 134–37, accepted by Barnes, "Scholarship or Propaganda?" 59.

118 Porph. fr. 303 (Smith).

119 Porph. fr. 382 (Smith).

120 Porph. fr. 323 (Smith); this may be explained by Porphyry's consciousness of his Phoenician background, on which see Millar, "Porphyry," 241–62.

121 Porph. fr. 324 (Smith); see also fr. 344 (Smith).

122 Porph. fr. 345 (Smith) with O'Meara, *Porphyry's Philosophy*, 53, 72–83.

123 Porph. fr. 343 (Smith).

124 Euseb. *Hist. eccl.* 6.19.1–5; a date ca. 300 for at least one of his works against the Christians could be defended on the basis of Macarius, *Apocr.* 4.1–7 (also in Porph. *In Christ.* 34 (Harnack)), but see n. 131 below.

125 On this point see the reconstruction of Porphyry's argument minus the fragments from Macarius in A. Meredith, "Porphyry and Julian against the Christians," *ANRW* 2.23.2 (1980): 1125–37.

126 Porph. *In Christ.* fr. 4, 46, 63 (Harnack); the comparison was made also by Celsus and Hierocles (Lact. *DI* 5.2.12) and noted in Aug. *Ep.* 102.32, 136.1, 138.18. For Apuleius see also Lact. *DI* 5.3. See n. 131 below for discussion of Harnack's editorial principles, which have been challenged with respect to Macarius Magnes, but not with respect to Jerome (who says that he is quoting Porphyry in the fragment quoted here and others that are adduced in the text).

127 Fools: see Porph. *In Christ.* fr. 5 and 6 (Harnack). Evangelists: Porph. *In Christ.* fr. 9, 55 (Harnack).

128 Incorrect citations: Porph. *In Christ.* fr. 9, 10, 12, 14, 21, 22 (Harnack).

129 Porph. *In Christ.* 43, 47 (Harnack); see also P. M. Casey, "Porphyry and the Origin of the Book of Daniel," *JTS* 27 (1976): 15–33, showing that Porphyry may have had access to a Syrian Christian tradition of interpretation.

130 Porph. *In Christ.* fr. 46, 81, 82 (Harnack).
131 A. von Harnack, *Porphyrius "Gegen die Christen," 15 Bücher: Zeugnisse, Fragmente und Referate,* Abhandlungen *der königlich preussischen Akademie der Wissenschaften*, Phil-Hist. Kl. 1916, vol. 1 (Berlin, 1916), 6–7, 19–21, contra the view that Macarius used the work of Sossianus Hierocles (which was arguably based on Porphyry). See also A. von Harnack, *Kritik des Neuen Testament von einem griechischen Philosophen des 3. Jahrhunderts*, Texte und Untersuchungen zur Geschichte der altchristlichen Literatur 37, pt. 4 (Leipzig, 1911), 137–44, arguing that Macarius used a summary of Porphyry's work. I see no reason to question Harnack's analysis of the relationship between Macarius and Porphyry. For the contrary view see T. D. Barnes, "Porphyry Against the Christians: Date and Attribution of the Fragments," *JTS* 24 (1973): 424–42, with a valuable discussion of fragments attributed to Porphyry after Harnack's edition. He is correct that the attribution of the opinions in Macarius to Porphyry is conjecture, but does not do justice to the point that the non-Macarian fragments bear out the Porphyrian nature of the Macarian fragments, which seems to me to be decisive. For another reconstruction of Porphyry's thought, based on Arnobius, *Adversus Nationes*, see Simmons, *Arnobius of Sicca*, which remains useful despite the failure of the identification of Lactantius' philosopher as Porphyry (n. 113 above). Barnes (who is followed in this by Simmons) also argues for a relatively late date (just prior to the outbreak of persecution in 303) for Porphyry's work. Harnack favored a date ca. 270 on the grounds that Eusebius says that Porphyry wrote the book while he was in Sicily. Barnes is correct in pointing out that quotation of Callinicus' book on Alexandria may indicate a date later than 270 (in fact it must indicate a date ca. 270–72 at the earliest) (see p. 267 above). On the other hand, Eusebius cites the book in the context of the 270s, and that seems to me to be preferable to assuming that the work was connected with the persecution of 303; see also B. Croke, "The Era of Porphyry's Anti-Christian Polemic," *Journal of Religious History* 13 (1984): 1–14, who restates arguments for a date in the early 270s.
132 Macarius, *Apocr.* 3.7 (also in Porph. *In Christ.* fr. 61 [Harnack]).
133 Macarius, *Apocr.* 4.8 (also in Porph. *In Christ.* fr. 90a [Harnack]).
134 Macarius, *Apocr.* 4.1 (also in Porph. *In Christ.* fr. 34 [Harnack]).
135 Macarius, *Apocr.* 3.1 (also in Porph. *In Christ.* fr. 63 [Harnack]).
136 Porph. *Abst.* 1.4.3–4, 4.22.1–5.
137 Porph. *Abst.* 1.27.1, 56.1.
138 Porph. *Abst.* 2.9–12, 60, 4.22.6.
139 Porph. *Abst.* 2.5–7.
140 For the story about Apollonius see Porph. *Abst.* 3.3.6.
141 Porph. *Abst.* 4.6–18.
142 Compare Plut. *Mor.* 408c.
143 Porph. *Plot.* 23.12–14.
144 Porph. fr. 362–68 (Smith) (esp. fr. 365; 366; 368).
145 For the text see É. Des Places, *Oracles Chaldaïques avec un choix de commentaires anciens* (Paris, 1971) and the commentary of R. Majercik, *The Chaldean Oracles: Text, translation and Commentary* (Leiden, 1989) with further discussion of the date in D. S. Potter, *Prophets and Emperors: Human and Divine Authority from Augustus to Theodosius* (Cambridge, Mass.), 203–4. Goulet, "L'oracle d'Apollon," 404–5 argues for a connection with Apamea for the oracle concerning the soul of Plotinus, an interesting case, but perhaps not a necessary one. See also J. Bouffartigue and M. Patillon, *Porphyre: De l'abstinence*, vol. 2 (Paris, 1979), 42–47 for an admirably cautious approach to potential parallels between *Chaldaean Oracles* and Porphyry, noting that parallels are not the same thing as quotations. P. Athanassiadi, "The Chaldaean

Oracles: Theology and Theurgy," in *Pagan Monotheism in Late Antiquity*, ed. P. Athanassiadi and M. Frede (Oxford, 1999), 152–55 argues for the second-century date on the basis of the reference to the oracle of Zeus Belos at Apamea referred to at *IG* 14, no. 2482. I think that these are political oracles of the sort discussed on pp. 108, 150 above. It is tempting to see such a book as a source for Dio's knowledge of the texts. I would concede, however, that her notion that there was an "early core" of texts that formed the basis of the collection known in the late third century may well be correct.

146 Iam. *De myst.* 1.2; 2.11 with Smith, *Porphyry's Place in the Neoplatonic Tradition*, 82.

147 Porph. *De regressu animae* fr. 2, 7, 11 with G. Luck, "Theurgy and Forms of Worship in Neoplatonism," in *Religion, Science, and Magic*, ed. J. Neusner, E. S. Frerichs, and P. V. McCracken Flesher (Oxford, 1989) (also in Luck, *Ancient Pathways and Hidden Pursuits: Religion, Morals, and Magic in the Ancient World* [Ann Arbor, 2000], 140–41).

148 Iam. *De myst.* 2.11.

9 REWRITINGS OF THE TETRARCHY: 300–13

1 E. Stein, *Histoire du Bas-Empire*, vol. 1 (Paris, 1959), 74–75; and Barnes, *New Empire*, 226. Barnes, *New Empire*, 228–30, is correct in stating that there were earlier censuses on a regular basis, but the evidence for an "empirewide" census is refuted by that adduced on pp. 51–57 above.

2 See Barnes, *Constantine and Eusebius*, 17; Barnes, *New Empire*, 11–12.

3 See p. 392 below for more on Diocletian's coinage; p. 294 above for the preface to the price edict.

4 First published in K. T. Erim, J. Reynolds, and M. H. Crawford, "Diocletian's Currency Reform: A New Inscription," *JRS* 61 (1971): 171–77 (with p. 175 on the nature of the text); see now C. Roueché, *Aphrodisias in Late Antiquity*, no. 230.

5 Roueché, *Aphrodisias in Late Antiquity*, no. 230, fr. i; see also *PSI* 965; *P. Ryl.* 4, no. 607; *P. Oslo* 83 with E. Ruschenbusch, "Diokletians Währungsreform vom 1.9.301," *ZPE* 26 (1977): 193–210, reconciling the epigraphic and papyrological evidence; on the impact, Harl, *Coinage*, 152–53. For details of the coinage see p. 392 below.

6 J. Lauferie "Remarques sur des dates de quelques inscriptions du début du ive siècle," *CRAI* (1965), 197–98; for doubts as to the precision he attempted, see Reynolds's note in Roueché, *Aphrodisias in Late Antiquity*, no. 231 (p. 268).

7 Lact. *DMP* 7.6–7.

8 *PE praef.* 7 (Lauffer).

9 *PE praef.* 9, 19 (Lauffer).

10 See Pliny *HN* 14.95 (price of wine in Italy in 89 BC); for local controls on the price of grain outside of Rome see Garnsey, *Famine and Food Supply*, 238–39. See in general the excellent discussion in Corcoran, *Empire of the Tetrarchs*, 225–33.

11 For the price of wheat in Carthage in the 370s, ranging between ten and thirty *modii* per solidus (equal to one thousand denarii in the edict) see Amm. Marc. 28.1.18 with Corcoran, *Empire of the Tetrarchs*, 226. For a survey of Egyptian prices versus those in the edict see *P. Oxy.* vol. 54, 233.

12 Corcoran, *Empire of the Tetrarchs*, 232–33; contra I. F. Finhman, "State and Prices in Byzantine Egypt," *Scripta Classica Israelica* 11 (1991–92): 139–48, with references to earlier works that argue that the edict was enforced, at least in the eastern part of the empire until the victory of Licinius in 313.

13 Corcoran, *Empire of the Tetrarchs*, 292–97, adopts a minimalist view. The view adopted here is in concord with earlier arguments, as in S. Williams, *Diocletian and the Roman Recovery* (London, 1985), 140–50; R. MacMullen, *Roman Government's*

Response to Crisis (New Haven, 1976), 195–213; Jones, *Later Roman Empire*, 40–70, stressing change over continuity, as does Barnes, *Constantine and Eusebius*, 8–12; see also Rostovtzeff, *Social and Economic History*, 505–32; Seeck, *Geschichte des Untergangs*, 1: 8.

14 Lact. *DMP* 12.1; Euseb. *Hist. eccl.* 8.2.4; *Mart. Pal.* 1.1; *Acta Felicis* 1 with R. P. Duncan-Jones, "An African Saint and his Interrogator," *JTS* 25 (1974): 106–110.

15 See Lact. *DMP* 13.1, giving items 2, 3, and 4; Euseb. *Hist. eccl.* 8.2.3–4, giving items 1, 2, 3, and 6. For brief discussion see Corcoran, *Empire of the Tetrarchs*, 179–81, though he gives only the items from Eusebius; Barnes, *Constantine and Eusebius*, 22–23. G. E. M De Ste. Croix, "Aspects of the 'Great' Persecution," *HTR* 47 (1954): 73–113, remains fundamental.

16 See Euseb. *Hist. eccl.* 7.32.3, 8.1.4 (Dorotheus); Euseb. *Hist. eccl.* 8.1.4 (Gorgonius); Euseb. *Hist. eccl.* 8.6.2–4 (Peter, one of a number of subordinates of Dorotheus who were said to be Christians); Euseb. *Hist. eccl.* 8.9.7 (Philoromus); Euseb. *Hist. eccl.* 8.11.2 (Adauctus, possibly *rationalis summae rei?* see *PLRE* Adauctus [pp. 12–13]; and Lactantius). Eusebius' evidence simply reflects people whom he knew personally; he does not mention Lactantius, and it may be reasonable to assume that there were other high officials who were Christian. For Valeria, his daughter, and Prisca, his wife, see Lact. *DMP* 15.2; for doubts see W. Seston, *Dioclétien et la tétrarchie* (Paris, 1946), 43–44.

17 Lact. *DMP* 10.2–4; Lact. *DI* 4.27. Barnes gives the date of this purge as 299 (*Constantine and Eusebius*, 18–19). His date privileges the plural in *DI* 4.27 over the account in *DMP*, which yields a date of 302 since Diocletian is alone in that version: *cum ageret in partibus orientis, ut erat pro timore scrutator rerum futurarum, immolabat pecudes et in iecoribus earum ventura quaerebat*. I take the plural in *DI* to be rhetorical in light of the emphasis on Diocletian alone in this passage and the fact that Lactantius is otherwise anything but loath to impute responsibility to Galerius. For Diocletian's presence in Syria (indicated by *in partibus orientis*) see Barnes, *New Empire*, 55. For an effort to reconcile Lactantius' date for the persecution of the Christians in the army with Eusebius, see D. Woods, "Two Notes on the Great Persecution," *JTS* 43 (1992): 128–34; but this is shown to be incorrect by R. Burgess, "The Date of the Persecution of Christians in the Army," *JTS* 47 (1996): 157–58, who shows that Eusebius appears to have placed the persecution in 300. It might be possible to be more precise if there were independent evidence for the tenure of Veturius (probably a praetorian prefect) mentioned by Eusebius as the mover of the persecution. But there is not. The version given in the text assumes that the account in *DMP* gives the best evidence, and that the time from the beginning of the "persecution in the army" was relatively short. See also p. 328 above, where the view that there was a well-orchestrated campaign against the Christians involving Hierocles and Porphyry is disputed. It is possible to obtain some support for the date of 302 for the purge of the army from T. Drew-Bear, "Les voyages d'Aurélius Gaius, soldat de Dioclétien," in *La géographie administrative et politique d'Alexandre à Mahomet: Actes du Colloque de Strasbourg 14–16 juin 1979*, ed. T. Fahd (Strasbourg, 1979), 135, who argues that Gaius served under Galerius in 302 and Maximian in 303; in 299 he would have been under the command of Diocletian in Egypt, which would provide further evidence against Barnes's early date, if Drew-Bear's reconstruction can be accepted.

18 Euseb. *Hist. eccl.* 8.4.2–4.

19 Euseb. *Hist. eccl.* 7.15.1–5, datable through the involvement of Theotecnus, the bishop of Caesarea.

20 The belief that Lactantius' picture, while obviously inflated by rhetoric, is substantially correct is central to the analysis in Barnes, *Constantine and Eusebius*, 14, 19;

see also Seeck, *Geschichte des Untergangs*, 3: 311, likewise following Lactantius, as does Stein, *Histoire du Bas-Empire*, 80–81, and, with circumspection, Jones, *Later Roman Empire*, 71.

21 Lact. *DMP* 11.3–8, 18.

22 One need look no further in the past than the conversation between President Bill Clinton and Vice-President Al Gore on who was to blame for George W. Bush's victory in the 2000 presidential campaign; see e.g. M. Williams, "Scenes from a Marriage," *Vanity Fair*, July 2001, 86–89, 132–37.

23 See p. 351 below. We do not know whether Anastasia was given this name at birth.

24 Lact. *DMP* 11.7; Euseb. *Vit. Const.* 2.51 with H. Grégoire, "Les chrétiens et l'oracle de Didymes," in *Mélanges Holleaux* (Paris, 1913), 81–91.

25 For the fire see Lact. *DMP* 14.2; Euseb. *Hist. eccl.* 8.6.6; for the revolts see Euseb. *Hist. eccl.* 8.6.8.

26 Lact. *DMP* 13.2. It cannot have helped that the person in question mocked the victory titles of the emperors in so doing; see also Euseb. *Hist. eccl.* 8.5.1, who appears to have regarded it as an especially noteworthy act, as both Diocletian and Galerius were present.

27 Euseb. *Hist. eccl.* 8.6.9 with Corcoran, *Empire of the Tetrarchs*, 181, noting that the second edict does not appear to have been enforced in the west.

28 For the text see J. Rea, "P. Oxy. XXXIII 2673.2: πύλη το ὕλην," *ZPE* 35 (1979): 128.

29 Optatus, *Tract.* App. 1.3–5 (also in J.-L. Maier, *Le dossier du donatisme*, vol. 1, *Des origines à la mort de Constance II (303–361)*, Texte und Untersuchungen zur Geschichte der altchristlichen Literatur 134 [Berlin, 1987], no. 29).

30 Euseb. *Hist. eccl.* 8.2.5, 6.10; Euseb. *MP* 2.

31 Pp. 402–05, 411–13 below.

32 Corcoran, *Empire of the Tetrarchs*, 182.

33 Euseb. *Vit. Const.* 1.19; Constantine, *Oratio* 16.2; Barnes, *New Empire*, 41–42.

34 His presence at Diocletian's court is implied by Lact. *DMP* 18.9; see also Barnes, *Constantine and Eusebius*, 9.

35 Lact. *DMP* 18.1–7.

36 *Pan.* 7 (6) 9.2: . . . *non quidem tu rei publicae neglegentia aut laboris fuga aut desidiae cupiditate ductus, sed consilii olim, ut res est, inter vos placiti constantia et pietate fraterna ne, quem totius vitae summarumque rerum socium semper habuisses, in alicuius facti communitate desereres neve illius, viderit quali, certe novae laudi cederes.* For support of this view see C. E. V. Nixon and B. S. Rodgers, *In Praise of Later Roman Emperors: The Panegyrici Latini* (Berkeley, 1994), 188–90, pointing to the evidence of palatial construction as a sign that abdication was planned well in advance. Stein, *Histoire du Bas-Empire*, 68; on p. 82 Stein suggests that abdication was always planned, but that the final decision was only made by Diocletian in 303. Seeck, *Geschichte des Untergangs*, 1: 34–36, likewise argues that abdication was long planned, but that Constantine and Maxentius were the designated heirs until 303. For the argument that Galerius launched a thinly veiled coup see G. S. R. Thomas, "L'Abdication de Dioclétien," *Byzantion* 43 (1973): 229–47; Barnes, *Constantine and Eusebius*, 25. For the *ludi saeculares* see Zos. 2.7 and Pasqualini, *Massimiano Herculius*, 76–77. For a very different view, see Seston, *Dioclétien et la tétrarchie*, 210–21, who suggests that the ideology of the regime bespoke opposition to biological succession, though noting that Maximian may still have had hopes for Maxentius.

37 See also Aur. Vict. *De Caes.* 40.48, which can be read as supporting Lactantius' view that the decision to abdicate was a sudden one. It is, however, unfortunate that Victor's tradition, which in this case depends upon a Latin history written at

the end of Constantine's reign, can be shown to have been contaminated by Constantinian propaganda (see esp. *De Caes.* 40.2 and p. 344 below) and thus not representative of an independent polytheist tradition.

38 Eutrop. *Brev.* 9.27.1: *cum tamen ingravescente aevo parum se idoneum Diocletianus moderando imperio esse sentiret, auctor Herculio fuit, ut in vitam privatam concederent et stationem tuendae rei publicae viridioribus iunioribusque mandarent.*

39 Aur. Vict. *De Caes.* 39.48; for the chronological manipulation see A. Chastagnol, "Les années régnales de Maximien Hercule en Égypte et les fêtes vicennales du 20 Novembre 303," *Rev. Num.*, 6th ser. 9 (1967): 54–81.

40 Lact. *DMP* 18.12–13.

41 P. 346 below.

42 *Pan.* 10 (2) 14.1, 8 (5) 20.1 (see also *ILS* 629) with Seeck, *Geschichte des Untergangs*, 1: 34, and pp. 456–57, n. on line 9. This evidence is more cogent than Lact. *DMP* 18.8. Seeck, *Geschichte des Untergangs*, 1: 40, is entirely correct in stressing the fact that both Caesars were not in the top echelon of government at the time of their appointment. For what is known of their earlier careers see Barnes, *New Empire*, 38–39.

43 Barnes, *New Empire*, 39, on the year of his birth, favoring a date ca. 270.

44 Barnes, *New Empire*, 56, for Diocletian's movements, and p. 60 for those of Maximian (Lact. *DMP* 18.1 for the meeting with Galerius).

45 For the problem with the text here see Barnes, *New Empire*, 72, n. 73, arguing that Maximianus in Lact. *DMP* 19.2: *in cuius summo Maximianus ipse purpuram sumperserat* is a gloss. He is surely correct that the reference is in fact to Diocletian, whom we know assumed the purple here.

46 The date of Constantine's birth is highly contentious. For the view that he was born ca. 285 see the excellent exposition in I. König, *Origo Constantini* (Trier, 1987), 64. The case for putting the year of his birth around a decade earlier is summarized by Barnes, *New Empire*, 39–41. Despite the evidence of contemporary panegyrics, which make Constantine out to be a youth in 307 (for which see *Pan.* 7 (6) 4.1 with Nixon's note ad loc.), Barnes' view is surely correct. The crucial point is the date at which his eldest son, Crispus, was born, between 295 and 300. Since Constantine was married to Crispus' mother, Minervina, it is inconceivable that he was only fifteen years old in 300; for the nature of their relationship see X. Lucien-Brun, "Minervine, épouse ou concubine?" *Bulletin de l'Association Guillaume Budé* (1970), 391–406. For the nature of Constantius' relationship with Helena, arguing that she was a concubine (contra Barnes), see J. H. W. Drijvers, *Helena Augusta: The Mother of Constantine the Great and the Legend of Her Finding of the True Cross* (Leiden, 1992), 16–19; B. Leadbetter, "The Illegitimacy of Constantine and the Birth of the Tetrarchy," in *Constantine: History, Historiography, and Legend*, ed. S. Lieu and D. Montserrat (London, 1998), 74–85. In light of the fact that sources generally favorable say that she was a concubine, he is probably right – epigraphic evidence for her marriage to Constantius from the 320s (e.g. *CIL* 10, nos. 678, 517 [*ILS* 708]) may be discounted.

47 Eutrop. *Brev.* 9.27.2; Lact. *DMP* 26.10. Constantius' role in this ceremony is confirmed by *Pan.* 7(6) 5.3: *cuius tanta maturitas est ut, cum tibi pater imperium reliquisset, Caesaris tamen appellatione contentus exspectare malueris ut idem te qui illum declararet Augustum.*

48 Blockley, *Fragmentary Classicising Historians*, 20, on the general nature of the critique. The view that Eunapius used a basically pro-Constantinian source emerges from the discussion that follows.

49 Corcoran, *Empire of the Tetrarchs*, 270; see also *CIL* 3, no. 12134; *IG* ii/iii² 1121, which looks like an edict on public debtors issued by Galerius – for discussion see

Corcoran, *Empire of the Tetrarchs*, 183–84, 347–48 and p. 368 below. For a perceptive reading of three medallions, one above the other, carved on a surviving pilaster representing the retired Augusti, Diocletian and Maximian on the upper one, Constantius and Severus in the middle, Galerius and Maximinus on the bottom, see D. Srejović, "The Representations of Tetrarchs," *Au Tard* 2 (1994): 145–46. (I am indebted to Mr Robert Chenault for calling this to my attention.)

50 See p. 370 below.

51 Stein, *Histoire du Bas-Empire*, 82, on the weakness of Constantius.

52 Lact. *DMP* 20.2–4.

53 Duval, "Les résidences impériales," 148–51; D. Srejović, ed., *Roman Imperial Towns and Palaces in Serbia* (Belgrade, 1993), 31–53.

54 P. 341 above.

55 For the view that *Pan.* 6 (7) 7.5: *ut non advectus cursu publico sed divino quodam advolasse curriculo videris* is a reference to the story of the escape, see Nixon and Rodgers, *Praise*, 228, n. 32.

56 *AE* 1961 no. 240 and König, *Origo Constantini*, 71–74.

57 The role of the army is stressed, reasonably, by Seeck, *Geschichte des Untergangs*, 1: 39–40.

58 Barnes, *New Empire*, 61; König, *Origo Constantini*, 75–76, for the date.

59 *Pan.* 7 (6) 5.3: *cum tibi pater imperium reliquisset.*

60 Lact. *DMP* 25.3–5.

61 Barnes, *New Empire*, 12 and for the date.

62 For the role of the praetorians see also *Origo* 6, Lact. *DMP* 26.3, saying that they had been alienated by Galerius' reduction in their number; see also Aur. Vict. *De Caes.* 41.5, Eutrop. *Brev.* 10.2.3, and König, *Origo Constantini*, 84–85. For the logic see Seeck, *Geschichte des Untergangs*, 1: 78, suggesting that Galerius believed that soldiers should serve on the frontier. See also Stein, *Histoire du Bas-Empire*, 83.

63 A. Chastagnol, *Les Fastes de la Préfecture de Rome au Bas-Empire* (Paris, 1962), 46–47. For a different view see Barnes, *New Empire*, 117, who accepts the existence of the Anullinus whom Zosimus makes praetorian prefect, separating him from the governor of North Africa who he allows was the prefect of the city in 306–7. He would also identify that Anullinus as *praefectus urbi* in 312, but that man seems to be identical to the *praefectus urbi* of 306–7, which makes the assumption that Zosimus was in error the most economical hypothesis.

64 Lact. *DMP* 23.5–6, 26.2; for the date of this action see Stein, *Histoire du Bas-Empire*, 89.

65 Zos. 2.10.1, saying that the first troops to betray Severus were from North Africa; see also *Origo* 6 with König, *Origo Constantini*, 86–87; Eutrop. *Brev.* 10.2.4; Aur. Vict. *De Caes.* 40.6–7.

66 *Origo* 10 with Barnes, *Constantine and Eusebius*, 30–31.

67 P. 288 above.

68 Jul. *Or.* 1.5d states that Fausta was born in Rome, where we know Maximian to have been in 298–99 (see Seeck, *Geschichte des Untergangs*, 1: 34 with p. 462n on p. 34, n. 18). The view is contested by X. Lucien-Brun, "Minervine, épouse ou concubine," 393; Barnes, *New Empire*, 34, 58, n. 49; Nixon and Rodgers, *Praise*, 198, n. 19, observing that the fact that Fausta was born in Rome does not need to imply that Maximian was there. The issue of her age arises from *Pan.* 7 (6) 2, in which a picture of a young girl handing the young Constantine a helmet at the palace at Aquileia is taken to be a picture of Fausta, a view that may be supported by Jul. *Or.* 1.7d, where it is stated that Constantine's parents arranged the marriage. To my mind there is no proof that the girl in the picture was intended to be seen as Fausta when the picture was painted, and the view that the older age postulated

for Fausta is vitiated by the fact that Constantine's marriage to Minervina appears to have ended before the abdication of Diocletian and Maximian, meaning that, if Fausta was thirteen by 303 (or fifteen by 305) there is no reason why they could not have been married unless the marriage was prevented by Diocletian, for which there is no evidence.

69 For the date see Nixon and Rodgers, *Praise*, 179–85.

70 See also C. E. V. Nixon, "The Panegyric of 307 and Maximian's Visits to Rome," *Phoenix* 35 (1981): 72, showing that the presumption of this language (esp. at 7 [6].12.6, 1.1 and 7.6) was that the abdication was illegal rather than the resumption of power. For the issue of the connection between the author and the palace see also Warmington, "Aspects of Constantinian Propaganda," *TAPA* 104 (1974): 371–84; Nixon, "Constantinus Oriens Imperator"; contra T. Grünewald, *Constantinus Maximus Augustus: Heerschaftspropaganda in der zeitgenössischen Über-lieferung*, Historia Einzelschiften 64 (Stuttgart, 1990), 26. In both cases the crucial point made by S. G. MacCormack, *Art and Ceremony in Late Antiquity* (Berkeley, 1981), 177–79, tends to be missed, which is not whether the speech was being vetted in the palace – as Grünewald would imply – or not. The point is rather that the idiom was so familiar by this point that an orator could play with the themes so as to produce a speech that would conform with the situation, which is crucial since it means that the value of an individual speech extends beyond the moment to reflect the tenor of discourse at the time that it was delivered. There may be specific points in some speeches, however, that adjust previous discourse (see below, pp. 352 and 354), and these should be taken as reflecting a different relationship between a specific speaker and the palace, one in which the speaker is, in fact, proclaiming something that he was told he should proclaim. There are plainly substantial differences in this regard between *Pan.* 6 (7) and 12 (9) and *Pan.* 5 (8) in this regard. *Pan.* 7 (6) falls between these two poles, in that, while there are no obviously new ideas, the existing idiom is handled with considerable care.

71 *Pan.* 7 (6) 3.2.

72 Lact. *DMP* 25.1, 3.

73 Barnes, *Constantine and Eusebius*, 31.

74 Lact. *DMP* 27.2–4; Zos. 2.10.3.

75 Zos. 2.10.2; *Origo* 10 (giving the proper date); see also Barnes, *New Empire*, 39.

76 Barnes, *Constantine and Eusebius*, 31.

77 Barnes, *Constantine and Eusebius*, 31, and the coin evidence discussed by Sutherland and Carson, *The Roman Imperial Coinage*, 6: 488–89.

78 Lact. *DMP* 28.2; Zos. 2.11; Eutrop. *Brev.* 10.3.1; for the date see Sutherland and Carson, *The Roman Imperial Coinage*, 6: 29–30.

79 See *P. Cairo Isid.* 8 with discussion by Youtie and Boak ad loc. and *P. Strassburg* 42.

80 Lact. *DMP* 29.1–2; Zos. 2.10.4–7; Aur. Vict. *De Caes.* 40.8; [Aur. Vict.] *Epit. de Caes.* 39.6; Eutrop. *Brev.* 10.4.1–2; Stein, *Histoire du Bas-Empire*, 85–86; Barnes, *Constantine and Eusebius*, 32.

81 Eutrop. *Brev.* 10.4.2.

82 Eutrop. *Brev.* 9.28; [Aur. Vict.] *Epit. de Caes.* 39.6 (Diocletian); Lact. *DMP* 29.3.

83 Euseb. *MP* 3.1; Lact. *DMP* 15.4 with Corcoran, *Empire of the Tetrarchs*, 182.

84 *P. Oxy.* 2665 with Corcoran, *Empire of the Tetrarchs*, 184.

85 Lact. *DMP* 24.9.

86 M. D. Smith, "The Religion of Constantius I," *GRBS* 38 (1997): 200–1.

87 Euseb. *Hist. eccl.* 8.14.1; Optatus, *Tract.* 18.1. The fact that he did not issue an edict of restoration is plain from quarrels in North Africa after 312 when

Constantine's officials began returning property; see p. 406 below. The evidence of Optatus is unequivocal on the fact of the edict of toleration: *iubente Deo indulgentiam mittente Maxentio christianis libertas est restituta.*

88 *Pan.* 7 (6) 4.2, 6 (7) 10.2, 11.3, 5, 4 (10) 16.5; Barnes, *New Empire*, 257 (table 7).

89 *Pan.* 6 (7) 12.1 with Barnes, *New Empire*, 70 (not to be confused with the bridge-building campaign of 310; see n. 92 below).

90 For these campaigns see T. D. Barnes, "Imperial Victories, AD 285–311," *Phoenix* 30 (1976): 192.

91 Zos. 2.12.1–3; Aur. Vict. *De Caes.* 40.17; for other evidence about Alexander see Barnes, *New Empire*, 14–15.

92 *Pan.* 6 (7) 11.3, 13.1.

93 Lact. *DMP* 29.8; *Pan.* 6 (7) 19.4–20.4 has Constantine call off an assault on the walls, after which the city surrendered.

94 *Pan.* 6 (7) 14.5.

95 Lact. *DMP* 30.1–6.

96 For the circumstances see Nixon and Rodgers, *Praise*, 212–17. The political significance of the speech has been questioned by Warmington, "Aspects of Constantinian Propaganda," 377 (with reference to Claudius), but that is too skeptical. Claudius was not dredged up by the author. For later reflections see A. Lippold, "Constantinus Caesar, Sieger über die Germanen – Nachfahre des Claudius Gothicus? Der Panegyricus von 297 und die Vita Claudii der HA," *Chiron* 11 (1981): 347–69 (also in Lippold, *Die Historia Augusta*, ed. G. H. Waldherr [Stuttgart, 1998], 160–82), who reviews the literature for the forgery while suggesting that the choice of Claudius for an ancestor may have been influenced by an early fourth-century work (for which there is no evidence, though Grünewald, *Constantinus Maximus Augustus*, 48–49, is correct in observing that if such a work existed, it could equally well be Constantinian). For the standard – and to my mind, correct – view see Syme, *Emperors and Biography*, 203–7; for discussion of the epigraphic evidence (*ILS* 699, 705, 256) see Grünewald, *Constantinus Maximus Augustus*, 123. For the issue of the connection between the authors of this and other panegyrics and the palace see n. 70 above.

97 See MacCormack, *Art and Ceremony*, 180.

98 *Pan.* 6 (7) 1.

99 *Pan.* 6 (7) 5–7.3 (Constantius), 9–13 (Constantine).

100 *Pan.* 6 (7) 15.4 contrasts with the view taken of abdication in *Pan.* 7 (6); see n. 36 above.

101 *Pan.* 6 (7) 16.1.

102 This reading of the vision is essentially in concord with B. S. Rodgers, "Constantine's Pagan Vision," *Byzantion* 50 (1980): 259–78, who offers a thorough survey of other opinions concerning the divinity seen in the vision (including the possibility that it was Sol or a Celtic version of Apollo).

103 The position taken here is on the extreme end of views connected with this passage in asserting that the emperor did actually have a vision. For a survey of opinion, see Grünewald, *Constantinus Maximus Augustus*, 52–53, who does not insist on the vision. I cannot agree with P. Weiss, "The Vision of Constantine," *JRA* 16 (2003), 248–50, that this is the vision connected with the conversion.

104 Sutherland and Carson, *The Roman Imperial Coinage*, 6: 42–43.

105 *P. Oxy.* 2665; Euseb. *Hist. eccl.* 8.14.9, MP 9.2; Lact. *DMP* 36.4–5; *P. Cairo Isid.* 8 with Corcoran, *Empire of the Tetrarchs*, 184–86, and p. 364 below.

106 See p. 365 below for more on his actions.

107 Lact. *DMP* 35.4; [Aur. Vict.] *Epit. de Caes.* 40.16 with Barnes, *New Empire*, 64.

108 Lact. *DMP* 39–41.

109 Lact. *DMP* 41.2–3 (requests for the return of Valeria), 50.2–4 (Candidianus and Severianus).

110 Barnes, *New Empire*, 66.

111 Zos. 2.14.1, 17.2; Lact. *DMP* 43.2–3; Seeck, *Geschichte des Untergangs*, 1: 114–16; Stein, *Histoire du Bas-Empire*, 90; Barnes, *Constantine and Eusebius*, 41. It is hard to tell if an account in Zosimus of a projected alliance between Maxentius and Licinius against Constantine may be a reflection of these negotiations, a tale leaked by Licinius to encourage Constantine.

112 *Pan.* 12 (9) 5.4, 4 (10) 3 (Susa); *Pan.* 12 (9) 6.2–5; *Pan.* 4 (10) 22.2–24.7 (Turin).

113 For Ruricius Pompeianus see *PLRE* Pompeianus 8, p. 713.

114 *Pan.* 12 (9) 8.1–11.1; *Pan.* 4 (10) 25.1–27.1; *Origo* 12; Aur. Vict. *De Caes.* 40.20.

115 For the date see *CIL* 1², no. 274; contra Lact. *DMP* 44.4.

116 Lact. *DMP* 44.8; Zos. 2.16.1; see also *Pan.* 12 (9) 16.2; *Pan.* 4 (10) 27.5, 28.1 (unspecified divine intervention); Euseb. *Vit. Const.* 1.38.1 (also reporting divine intervention, but this time that of the Christian God in helping form Maxentius' decision).

117 Euseb. *Hist. eccl.* 8.14.2–5, 17, *Vit. Const.* 1.33.1–36.2; Eutrop. *Brev.* 10.4.4.

118 *Pan.* 12 (9) 16.3–18.3; *Pan.* 4 (10) 28.4–30.3; Lact. *DMP* 44.9; Euseb. *Hist. eccl.* 9.9.2–8, *Vit. Const.* 1.38.4; Aur. Vict. *De Caes.* 40.23 (placing the battle at Saxa Rubra, an error); [Aur. Vict.] *Epit. de Caes.* 40.7; Eutrop. *Brev.* 10.4.4; *Origo* 12; for details of the battle see Barnes, *Constantine and Eusebius*, 43 with n. 144 and König, *Origo Constantini*, 103–8.

119 This is a matter upon which the range of opinion is vast, extending from those who would prefer that Constantine actually saw something like what Eusebius says he saw to those who think the whole thing is an invention (only representative opinions are cited). For the argument that he saw something in the sky see N. H. Baynes, *Constantine the Great and the Christian Church* (London, 1972) (reprint of lecture first published in *The Proceedings of the British Academy* 15 [1931]: 341–42, with an introduction by H. Chadwick), 9 with n. 31; A. H. M. Jones, *Constantine and the Conversion of Europe* (London, 1949), 96; Lane Fox, *Pagans and Christians*, 616; J. H. W. G. Liebeschuetz, *Continuity and Change in Roman Religion* (Oxford, 1979), 178–79; Weiss "The Vision of Constantine," 237–59, concurs with Barnes that Constantine saw a solar halo; T. D. Barnes, "The Conversion of Constantine," *Échos du Monde Classique* 4 (1985): 381–87 (also in Barnes, *From Eusebius to Augustine* [Brookfield, VT, 1994], ch. 3) argues that Eusebius should be preferred to Lactantius; contra Seeck, *Geschichte des Untergangs*, 1: 495, n. on p. 127, l. 27. Seeck, however, is correct in distinguishing the tradition of the dream from that of the vision of the cross. His view (*Geschichte des Untergangs* 1: 128) and that of R. MacMullen, "Constantine and the Miraculous," *GRBS* 9 (1969): 81–96 (also in MacMullen, *Changes in the Roman Empire* [Princeton, 1990], 107–16); Lane Fox, *Pagans and Christians*, 613; and A. Alföldi, *The Conversion of Constantine and Pagan Rome* (Oxford, 1948), 19–23, that Constantine might have wished the Christian God to have power over polytheist divinities and thus been attracted to that view, is adopted here. Likewise, Baynes, *Constantine the Great*, 60–62 (n. 33 to p. 10) properly distinguishes between vision and dream and canvasses a wide range of opinions. Lane Fox (p. 616) argues, conversely, that Lactantius and Eusebius are reporting the same story from different perspectives. I cannot accept this, as the vision of the cross is nowhere mentioned by Constantine in any account for Christians, while a further version of a vision had been produced in a non-Christian context, but only one vision (which I think is important); see *Pan.* 4 (10) 14.1–7. The problem of Nazarius' description is noted by Alföldi, *Conversion of Constantine*, 72, though he suggests that the heavenly army sent by Constantius to aid his son

was intended to obscure a Christianizing version. Since, however, Nazarius' version is earlier than that of Eusebius, it might rather be seen as a reflection of a tradition concerning a vision for which there was, as yet, no fixed text.

120 For the *Vit. Const.* as a free-standing biographical work, in some ways foreshadowing later hagiographic writing, see A. Cameron, "Eusebius' *Vita Constantini* and the Construction of Constantine," in *Portraits: Biographical Representation in the Greek and Latin Literature of the Roman Empire*, ed. M. Edwards and S. Swain (Oxford, 1997), 145–74; for a different approach see T. D. Barnes, "Panegyric, History, and Historiography in Eusebius' *Life of Constantine*," in *The Making of Orthodoxy: Essays in Honor of Henry Chadwick*, ed. R. Williams (Cambridge, 1989), 94–123; T. D. Barnes, "Two Drafts of Eusebius' *Vita Constantini*," in Barnes, *From Eusebius to Augustine*. For the crucial issue of the composition of book 4 see H. Drake, "What Eusebius Knew: The Genesis of the *Vita Constantini*," *CPh* 83 (1988): 20–38; B. H. Warmington, "The Sources of Some Constantinian Documents in Eusebius' *Ecclesiastical History* and the *Life of Constantine*," *Studia Patristica* 18 (1986): 83–98. See also the translation with commentary by A. Cameron and S. G. Hall, *Eusebius: The Life of Constantine* (Oxford, 1999).

121 Euseb. *Vit. Const.* 27.3.

122 Euseb. *Vit. Const.* 1.32 with Hall and Cameron's note ad *Vit. Const.* 1.27.1, 32.1.

123 Lact. *DMP* 44.5.

124 *Pan.* 5 (8) 10.2–3.

125 *Pan.* 12 (9) 2.4; Euseb. *Vit. Const.* 1.27.

126 *Pan.* 12 (9) 2.3–5.

127 What follows is dependent upon the analysis of the sculpture in A. Giuliano, *Arco di Costantino* (Milan, 1955), and the superb pictures therein. For a summary of scholarship on the arch, see A. Capodiferro, "Arcus Constantini," in Steinby, ed., *Lexicon Topographicum Urbis Romae*, 1: 85–91.

128 For appearance of Constantine and Constantius here see R. Calza, "Un problema di iconografia imperiale sull' arco di Costantino," *APARA*, Rendiconti 32 (1960): 131–61; J. Ruysschaert, "Essai d'interprétation synthétique de l'Arc de Constantin," *APARA*, Rendiconti 35 (1962–63): 79–105; J. Curran, *Pagan City and Christian Capital: Rome in the Fourth Century* (Oxford, 2000), 88.

129 The interpretation offered here expands somewhat on C. Panella, "Techniche costruttive e modalità di inserimiento dell' apparato decorativo," in *Arco di Costantino: Tra archeologia e archeometria*, ed. P. Pensabene and C. Panella (Rome, 1999), 43–73.

130 *Pan.* 4 (10) 6.3–6.

131 *Pan.* 4 (10) 7.3.

132 *Pan.* 4 (10) 14.6.

133 *Pan.* 4 (10) 21–24.

134 *Pan.* 4 (10) 25–26.

135 *Pan.* 4 (10) 30.4–33.

136 *Pan.* 12 (9) 19.3; but he may subsequently have sacrificed; see Zos. 2.29.5 with F. Paschoud, "Zosime 2, 29 et la version païenne de la conversion de Constantin," *Historia* 20 (1971): 334–53.

137 *Pan.* 4 (10) 35.2.

10 RESTRUCTURING THE STATE: 313–37

1 Lact. *DMP* 45.1. It is likely that Licinius issued a restitution edict for Christians in his territory; see Lact. *DMP* 48.1; Euseb. *Hist. eccl.* 10.5.4 with Barnes, *Constantine and Eusebius*, 62, n. 4; see also Stein, *Histoire du Bas-Empire*, 92.

2 Euseb. *Hist. eccl.* 9.5.1.

3 *TAM* 2.3.785; *AE* 1989 no. 1046 with S. Mitchell, "Maximinus and the Christians in AD 312: A New Latin Inscription," *JRS* 78 (1988): 108.

4 P. 355 above.

5 See also p. 413 below.

6 For the historical value of the text see H. Grégoire and P. Orgels, "La passion de S. Théodote d'Ancyre, œuvre du pseudo-Nil, et son noyau montaniste," *BzZ* 44 (1951): 165–84; S. Mitchell, "The Life of Saint Theodotus of Ancyra," *AS* 35 (1982): 93–113. For the nature of the community see S. Elm, *Virgins of God: The Making of Asceticism in Late Antiquity* (Oxford, 1994), 54–59; Trevett, *Montanism*, 125–26. See also Tabbernee, *Montanist Inscriptions*, nos. 88–89.

7 M. *Theod.* 20–31.

8 For the text see P. Maraval, *La passion inédite de S. Athénogène de Pédachthoé en Cappadoce (BHG 197b),* Subsidia Hagiographica 75 (Brussels, 1990), 15–19. For the arrest see *P. Ath.* 22–26, 31–36.

9 *MAMA* 1.270 with discussion in W. Tabbernee, *Montanist Inscriptions*, no. 69 with p. 436 on possible Montanist associations, suggested on the basis of *SEG* 1, no. 448 (Tabbernee's no. 70).

10 Euseb. *Hist. eccl.* 9.9a. 1–12; Lact. *DMP* 37.1 with S. Mitchell, "Maximinus and the Christians," 114–15.

11 Lact. *DMP* 45; Seeck, *Geschichte des Untergangs*, 1: 149–52; Stein, *Histoire du Bas-Empire*, 93; Barnes, *Constantine and Eusebius*, 63.

12 Lact. *DMP* 46.3–5; see, on Licinius' religiosity, Seeck, *Geschichte des Untergangs*, 1: 139, "Der alte Landsknecht verehrte die Götter in erster Linie als Schlachtenhelfer und Siegbringer."

13 Lact. *DMP* 46.7.

14 Lact. *DMP* 46.12.

15 Lact. *DMP* 49.1–7; Euseb. *Hist. eccl.* 9.10.14–15 (giving an alternative version in which Maximinus dies of disease).

16 Euseb. *Hist. eccl.* 10.5.1–14; Lact. *DMP* 48. For bibliography on the so-called Edict of Milan see Corcoran, *Empire of the Tetrarchs*, 158–60.

17 Lact. *DMP* 48.2–3, 11; Euseb. *Hist. eccl.* 10.5.4–5.

18 Drake, *Constantine and the Bishops*, 193–98.

19 P. 409 below.

20 Euseb. *Hist. eccl.* 9.11.2–6, 13; see also *PLRE* Culcianus, pp. 233–34, Peucetius, p. 692. For Culcianus' activities as a persecutor see p. 339 above. For Peucetius' office see p. 371 below.

21 Lact. *DMP* 50.3–4.

22 Lact. *DMP* 50.6.

23 Lact. *DMP* 51 (Valeria); Lact. *DMP* 50.6; Euseb. *Hist. eccl.* 9.9.7 (children of Maximinus).

24 Lact. *DMP* 7.2.

25 P. 343 above.

26 Lact. *DMP* 24.9, *DI* 1.1.13 with Barnes, *Constantine and Eusebius*, 28.

27 Constantius gave token attention to the edicts of Diocletian; see Euseb. *Vit. Const.* 1.16.1–17.2; Lact. *DMP* 8.7 (by implication). It is Constantine's refusal to enforce them at all that is the most significant change.

28 Barnes, *New Empire*, 203–5, with corrections in Barnes, "Emperors, Panegyrics," 548–50, restating the view of A. H. M. Jones, "The Date and Value of the Verona List," *JRS* 44 (1954): 21–29 (also in *The Roman Economy*, ed. P. A. Brunt, 263–79), that the text represents the divisions of the empire c. 314.

29 *AE* 1942–43 no. 81. For the terminology compare Lact. *DMP* 7.4: *vicarii praefectorum* and the discussion of Cledonius (*GL* v.13): *saepe quaesitum est, utrum vicarius debeat etiam is cui magnificentissimi praefecti vices suas in speciali causa mandaverunt; nam vicarius dicitur is qui ordine codicillorum vices ait amplissimae praefecturae. Ille vero mandatur propter absentiam praefectorum, non vicarius, sed vice agens, non praefecturae, sed praefectorum dicitur tantum*, which appears to be attempting to draw a linguistic distinction that is fanciful.

30 *AE* 1995 no. 1478 d, where the restoration of the plural is secured by the Greek translation of the text in *IG* ii/iii² 1121.42 for further discussion see D. Fiessel, "Deux constitutions tétrarchiques inscrits à Ephèse," *L'Antiquité Tardive* 4 (1996): 273–89.

31 Lact. *DMP* 23.1–9; 24.2.

32 *IRT* 464. For different views see K. L. Noethlichs, "Zur Entstehung der Diözesen als Mittelinstanz des spätrömischen Verwaltungssystems," *Historia* 31 (1982): 72–75, who would place the development later, and M. T. W. Arnheim, "Vicars in the Later Roman Empire," *Historia* 19 (1970): 595, who sees *vicarii* as deputy prefects assigned to rule groups of provinces under Diocletian. He is obviously right on the first point, but the nature of the job appears to change under Constantius as suggested above.

33 Euseb. *Vit. Const.* 1.25.1, 26.

34 For details of military administration under Constantine see pp. 451–54 below.

35 *Inschr. V. Eph.* 312 (317); *ILS* 8938 (317), mentioning the prefects of Constantine and Licinius as if they were members of a college, as were their emperors, showing that the prefects were seen as serving an emperor rather than as specifically territorial officials; see Barnes, *New Empire*, 139, contra Stein, *Histoire du Bas-Empire*, 117, showing that the creation of territorial prefectures postdates the death of Constantine.

36 *CTh.* 10.8.2 for the title *comes* with a *rationalis* reporting to him on issues connected with *bona vacantia* (319). For the duties of the *comes summae rei* see *CJ* 10.10.1 (*bona caduca*) (292); *CTh.* 10.8.1 (*CJ* 10.10.2), terms relating to grants of property (313); *CJ* 10.1.5 (rights of individuals against the *fiscus*) (undated, but Diocletianic); Roueché, *Aphrodisias in Late Antiquity*, no. 230 (mints); *CJ* 10.10.2 (imperial gifts of property from the *patrimonium*) (313); *CJ* 3.22.5 (cases of disputes with the *fiscus* involving freedmen and slaves will be heard by the provincial *rationalis*, those involving free persons by the governor) (294); *SEG* 39, no. 1698, 3–5, the responsibility of a *praepositus* (in this case probably a *rationalis*) to ensure action be taken in response to a rescript concerning possession of a piece of land, in this case perhaps not part of the *patrimonium*, as the governor is also involved (297–98); Euseb. *Hist. eccl.* 10.6.1–5 (restoration of confiscated property to Caecilian; see also p. 406 below for the circumstances) (312–13). See also Stein, *Histoire du Bas-Empire*, 114, and Barnes, *Constantine and Eusebius*, 395, n. 105.

37 Stein, *Histoire du Bas-Empire*, 113–14, and Jones, *Later Roman Empire*, 103, place the creation of the office under Constantine on the reasonable grounds that the first attestation is in *CTh.* 16.10.1 (320) followed by *CTh.* 11.9.1 (323). In my view the position is more likely to be Diocletianic, as the *magister memoriae* was a Diocletianic innovation, as were the *agentes in rebus*, who also reported to the *magister* in the fourth century (on whom see Aur. Vict. *De Caes.* 39.44–45 with Stein, *Histoire du Bas-Empire*, 114). Since it is obvious that the *magister officiorum* was not a new official in 320, I find it hard to imagine that major new offices or functions were created under Diocletian without having a person to report to. On technical grounds it is worth noting that the actual title of this official in

320 was *tribunus et magister officiorum*; the combination of a military rank with a palatine title is something that appears to have been characteristic of Diocletian; see Seeck, *Geschichte des Untergangs*, 2: 92. See also *CTh*. 6.35.1, where the bureaus that are later attested under the *magister* are listed together, suggesting that they were already united under a single administrative head; and *CTh*. 6.35.2, where they are collectively called *memoriales*.

38 P. 293 above.

39 For *cubicularii*, many of them eunuchs, see D. Schlinkert, *Ordo senatorius und nobilitas: Die Konstitution des Senatsadels in der Spätantike, Hermes* Einzelschriften 72 (Stuttgart, 1996), 244–45 and p. 000 below.

40 *PLRE*, p. 334; see also *PLRE*, p. 434 for Hilarion, who may also have held this post under Constantine.

41 J. Harries, "The Roman Imperial Quaestor from Constantine to Theodosius II," *JRS* 78 (1988): 153. The sole evidence for a Constantinian date is Zos. 5.32.6, a passage otherwise corrupt in two places. It is as well to be honest here: the common assumption (repeated in the text) that this is a late development in the reign of Constantine stems from the fact that we know no holder of the office prior to 354. It remains possible that *Konstantiou* should be read in place of *Konstantinou* in Zosimus. Harries is quite right in noting that the title is somewhat inconsistent; I have retained the appellation Quaestor of the Sacred Palace for the sake of clarity (so as not to confuse this position with the senatorial office).

42 See pp. 459–60 below.

43 For details see p. 450 below.

44 P. 288 above.

45 Jones, *Later Roman Empire*, 1: 43–44.

46 Euseb. *Hist. eccl.* 10.8.12–13; Euseb. *Vit. Const.* 1.55.1–3.

47 S. Corcoran, "Hidden from History: The Legislation of Licinius," in *The Theodosian Code*, ed. J. Harries and I. Wood (Ithaca, NY, 1993), 97–119, offers a superior analysis of the problem. For the invalidation of Licinius' acts see *CTh*. 15.14.1 with Seeck, *Regesten der Kaiser und Päpste* (Stuttgart, 1919), 99, who argues that the date should be December rather than May, postdating the final victory over Licinius. This is unnecessary, as there is no reason why Constantine could not invalidate measures by his rival as a propaganda measure early in a campaign that was initiated by his circulation of his own coinage in Licinius' territory.

48 *CTh*. 10.14.1 with Corcoran, "Hidden from History," 108–9.

49 See esp. *CTh*. 12.1.5 (a portion of the same letter to the Bithynians as *CTh*. 8.4.3, 10.7.1, 20.1) with Corcoran, "Hidden from History," 110; contra Seeck, *Regesten*, 54, 165. For the significance of this text see p. 396 below.

50 The text is dated to July 8, 326, in the manuscripts. The recipient, however, is Antiochus, who is attested as the *praefectus vigilum* at Rome in 314 and 319 (*CTh*. 1.1, 2.10.1.2), and Seeck is almost certainly correct in redating the text to 313; see Seeck, *Regesten*, 64–65. It is just possible that the law may refer to an action of Licinius, though this is unlikely.

51 See e.g. *CJ* 7.22.3; *FIRA*[7] no. 94, 46 and note 32 above.

52 Rescripts of Licinius in the *Codex Justinianus*, deriving from the updated *Codex Hermogenianus*, include *CJ* 3.1.8, 6.1.3, 7.16.41, 7.22.3; see also Corcoran, *Empire of the Tetrarchs*, 280.

53 For a thorough discussion of the scholarship on this text see J. F. Matthews, *Laying Down the Law: A Study of the Theodosian Code* (New Haven, 2000), 254–70.

54 For Maximus see Chastagnol, *Les fastes*, 72–74.

55 For parallels see p. 407 below.

56 For theoretical Christian influence on Constantine's legislation see p. 423 below.

57 I find it hard to understand how P. Bruun, *RIC* 7.32 can state that "the Constantinian portrait was basically realistic" while at the same time accepting the demonstration by M. R. Alföldi, *Die constantinische Goldprägung* (Mainz, 1963), 57–69, that Constantine's portraits were designed to evoke those of Trajan.

58 See e.g. *RIC* 6 London no. 79 (bronze, no beard, 307); Trier nos. 634a (gold, beard, 307), 638 (silver, no beard, 307); Lyons nos. 213b (silver, no beard, 307), 220b (bronze, beard, 307), 302 (bronze, beard, 307); *RIC* 7 London nos. 1 (bronze, no beard, 313–14), 4 (bronze, beard, 313–14) but none thereafter, though see Arles no. 6 (gold, 313), where the strong line of the jaw may reflect an engraver correcting for an intended beard as also on Arles 8 (bronze, 313), 13 (bronze, 313), 31 (bronze, 313–15), 33 (bronze, 313–15), 65 (bronze 315–16), 70 (bronze, 315–16).

59 The best guides here are the Italian mints, where there was no vestigial tradition of a bearded Constantine – for heavy jowls see *RIC* 7 Rome nos. 2 (bronze, 313), 33 (bronze 314–16), 40 (bronze, 314–16), 45 (bronze, 316); Ticinum nos. 28 (gold, 315), 30 (gold, 315), 31 (gold, 315; in this case it looks as if a beard may have been intended), 316 (silver, 315) (frontal portrait with what looks very much like a beard); Aquileia no. 37 (gold, 320); the "Trajanic" portrait predominates after 320, though it begins earlier; see e.g. Rome no. 237 (bronze, 321); Ticinum nos. 60 (gold, 316), 61 (gold, 316), 108 (gold, 320–21; big eyes but pronounced jowls), 110 (gold, 320–21); Aquileia nos. 33 (gold, 320), 37 (gold, 320).

60 For the iconography of Licinius and its implications see R. R. R. Smith, "The Public Image of Licinius I: Portrait Sculpture and Imperial Ideology in the Early Fourth Century," *JRS* 87 (1997): 187–94.

61 Ch. 9, n. 46 above.

62 The date is established by C. Habicht, "Zur Geschichte des Kaisers Konstantin," *Hermes* 86 (1958): 360–78, on the basis of the movements of Constantine in 315–16; see esp. *CTh* 8.7.1 and 2.30.1, the elimination of Licinius from coins minted in Constantine's part of the empire (on which see now *RIC* 7, 65–66). It conforms with chronological indications in Aur. Vict. *De Caes.* 41.7. Another chronology may be obtained from the *Fast. Hydat.* s.a. 314: *Volusiano II et Anniano | HIS CONSSulibus bellum Cibalense fuit die VIII id. Oct* (for the text see R. W. Burgess, *The Chronicle of Hydatius and the Consularia Constantinopolitana: Two Contemporary Accounts of the Final Years of the Roman Empire* [Oxford, 1993], 235) and Aur. Vict. *De Caes.* 41.2 (a date that contradicts the chronology in 41.7), while Zos. 2.18.1 also implies a short period of peace. It is impossible for Constantine to have been fighting Licinius in 314–15 since he is known to have been at Trier at precisely the time that the *Fast. Hydat.* put Cibalae (see *CTh.* 6.35.1, 1.2.1). For an effort to revive the chronology that places the war in 314 see D. Kienast, "Das Bellum Cibalense und die Morde des Licinius," in Wissemann, *Roma Renascens*, 149–71. This dating is also found in standard works prior to 1958.

63 Barnes, *Constantine and Eusebius*, 66.

64 *Origo* 15 with Barnes, *Constantine and Eusebius*, 66; König, *Origo Constantini*, 116–17.

65 *Origo* 15 with König, *Origo Constantini*, 118.

66 Zos. 2.18.1.

67 Euseb. *Vit. Const.* 2.3.1.

68 P. 414 below.

69 *Origo* 17; Zos. 2.19.2; for the rank of Augustus see Barnes, *New Empire*, 19; König, *Origo Constantini*, 126–27.

70 *Origo* 17 (for the location with König, *Origo Constantini*, 128–29, on the text); Zos. 2.19.2–3.

71 *Origo* 18 with Barnes, *Constantine and Eusebius*, 67.

72 *Origo* 18 (removal of Valens); Zos. 2.20.1; [Aur. Vict.] *Epit. de Caes*. 40.9 (execution).

73 *Origo* 19; Zos. 2.20.2; see also *RIC* 7, 67 for details of the settlement.

74 For the problem of the Gothic war of 323 see also König, *Origo Constantini*, 144, and p. 147 on the passage quoted here. See also *CTh*. 7.1.1, 7.12.1, which may also reflect these circumstances. For the coins celebrating the victory see *RIC* 7, 115 nos. 289–90 (London, 323–24), 135 nos. 209, 212, 214, 219, 222 (Lyons, 323–24), 201–2 nos. 429, 435–38 (Trier, 323–24), 262 nos. 257–8 (Arles, 323–24), 475 no. 48 (Sirmium, 324).

75 Euseb. *Hist. eccl.* 10.8.2–6, *Vit. Const*. 1.49.1–50.2.

76 *Origo* 24; Zos. 2.22.3–7; König, *Origo Constantini*, 151–52.

77 *Origo* 25–26; Zos. 2.24.1–3. For the date see *CTh*. 7.20.1; Seeck, *Regesten*, 173.

78 Zos. 2.24.3–25.2.

79 Zos. 2.23.3, 26.2.

80 *Origo* 28–29; [Aur. Vict.] *Epit. de Caes*. 41.7 (attributing responsibility for the negotiations to Constantia); Zos. 2.28.1–2; Eutrop. *Brev*. 6.1.

81 Compare [Aur. Vict.] *Epit. de Caes*. 41.11–12; *Chron. Pasch*., p. 525; Phil. *Hist eccl.* 2.4 (derivative from Eunapius for the death of Crispus, but not Fausta); Soz. *Hist. eccl.* 1.5.1–2 on the origin of the story in polytheist circles. For a broader analysis of the historiographic tradition that lies behind this account see G. Fowden, "The Last Days of Constantine: Oppositional Versions and Their Influence," *JRS* 84 (1994): 163–68. See also Drijvers, *Helena Augusta*, 60–62, who surveys a variety of options.

82 Amm. Marc. 14.11; see also Aur. Vict. *De Caes*. 41.11: *quorum {filii Constantini} cum natu grandior, incertum qua causa, patris iudicio occidisset*.

83 Jul. *Or*. 1.5d, 9d and E. Gibbon, *The Decline and Fall of the Roman Empire*, ed. D. Womersley, vol. 1 (London, 1994), 652; see also Jul. *Or*. 2.51c. Maximian's favorable presentation in this passage stems from his restoration as a "divine ancestor" in 318; see Barnes, *Constantine and Eusebius*, 47.

84 Jer. *Chron*. s.a. 328; see also Phil. *Hist. eccl.* 2.4a, saying that she was executed on a charge of adultery with a *cursor*, which might suggest that it was possible to separate her story from that of Crispus since there is no direct chronological connection between the two. This cannot, however, be pressed too far, as the source for this fragment of Philostorgius is a life of Constantine that dates to some point between the ninth and eleventh centuries and has other eccentric details; for the Byzantine lives of Constantine see the valuable discussion in S. Lieu and D. Montserrat, eds., *From Constantine to Julian: Pagan and Byzantine Views* (London, 1996), 101–6.

85 Theoph. *Chron*. 22.12–13 (also in *Continuatio Antiochiensis Eusebii* 21, ed. Burgess). For the reconstruction of this chronicle, which is due to the efforts of Richard Burgess, see R. W. Burgess, *Studies in Eusebian and Post-Eusebian Chronography, Historia* Einzelschriften 135 (Stuttgart, 1999), 113–22.

86 Eutrop. *Brev*. 10.6.3.

87 Gibbon, *Decline and Fall*, 1: 650, n. 16.

88 For expositions of this view see Jones, *Constantine and Conversion*, 199; Barnes, *Constantine and Eusebius*, 220.

89 Curran, *Pagan City*, 76–86.

90 What follows depends upon G. Dagron, *Naissance d'une capitale: Constantinople et ses institutions de 330 à 451* (Paris, 1974), 29.

91 Serdica: Anon. post Dionem, *FHG* 4.199; Zon. 13.3.1–4; Ilium: Soz. *Hist. eccl.* 2.3; Zos. 2.30; Zon. 13.3; Chalcedon: Zon. 13.3; Kedrenos, p. 496; Thessalonica:

Kedrenos, p. 496 with Dagron, *Naissance d'une capitale*, 29, n. 3, who gives further references.

92 *Anth. Gr.* 14.115; Soz. *Hist. eccl.* 2.3.3 with Dagron, *Naissance d'une capitale*, 31–32.

93 *CTh.* 13.5.7: *pro commoditate urbis, quam aeterno nomine iubente deo donavimus* . . .

94 Phil. *Hist. eccl.* 2.3.

95 E. Schwartz, "Die Dokumente des arianischen Streits bis 325," *Nachrichten von der k. Gesellschaft der Wissenschaften zu Göttingen, phil.-hist. Klasse* (1905), 272 (also in E. Schwartz, *Gesammelte Schriften*, vol. 3 [Berlin, 1959], 117).

96 Porph. 4.5–6; see p. 389 below for his later career. But see also the Syriac Acts of the Council of Antioch in 325, where Byzantium is also described as the "New Rome," in E. Schwartz, "Das antiochenische Synodalschreiben von 325," *Nachrichten von der k. Gesellschaft der Wissenschaften zu Göttingen, Phil.-hist. Klasse* (1908), 272, 79 (also in E. Schwartz, *Gesammelte Schriften*, vol. 3 [Berlin, 1959], 136, 143), but this is a later redaction of the acts, and we cannot know when Byzantium was replaced in the text by the "New Rome," which is glossed in the second reference as Constantinople.

97 Dagron, *Naissance d'une capitale*, 45–47.

98 Euseb. *Vit. Const.* 3.54.2; for the eccentricity of Eusebius' view (or at least the point that it was not shared by all) see J. Curran, "Moving Statues in Late Antique Rome: Problems of Perspective," *Art History* 17 (1994): 46–58.

99 L. Robert, "Théophane de Mytilène à Constantinople," *CRAI* (1969), 52–57 (also in Robert, *OMS* 5: 571–76).

100 S. Bassett, "The Antiquities in the Hippodrome at Constantinople," *DOP* 45 (1991): 90 (much of what follows in the text is influenced by Bassett's work).

101 For the date of the arrival of the statue of Hercules, which is dated only to the consulship of a Julianus, see Bassett, "Antiquities in the Hippodrome," 90, n. 35; for the other two statues see p. 93.

102 G. Fowden, "Nicagoras of Athens and the Lateran Obelisk," *JHS* 107 (1987): 51–52.

103 Eunap. *VS* 6.2.

104 Fowden, "Nicagoras of Athens," 55.

105 Fowden, "Nicagoras of Athens," 53–54.

106 Fowden, "Nicagoras of Athens," 55. For the date of the construction of St Peter's see p. 436 below.

107 See p. 426 below on Sunday; for the use of solar imagery on coins see the discussion in P. M. Bruun, *The Roman Imperial Coinage 7: Constantine and Licinius AD 313–337* (London, 1966), 48 – the Sol coinage lasted until at least 324.

108 G. Fowden, "Constantine's Porphyry Column: The Earliest Literary Allusion," *JRS* 81 (1991): 122.

109 Fowden, "Constantine's Porphyry Column," 124.

110 Mal. 13.320, Euseb. *Vit. Const.* 4.16; for other references see Fowden, "Constantine's Porphyry Column," 125–26.

111 Fowden, "Constantine's Porphyry Column," 130–31.

112 P. 265 above.

113 Schlinkert, *Ordo senatorius und nobilitas*, 68.

114 Hirschfeld, "Die Rangtitel," 588 (also in Hirschfeld, *Kleine Schriften*, 656).

115 Hirschfeld, "Die Rangtitel," 591–92 (also in Hirschfeld, *Kleine Schriften*, 659–60).

116 Jones, *Later Roman Empire*, 104–6.

117 For the functions of these officials see p. 371 above; for the issue of the title of the *comes rei privatae* see n. 36 above.

118 Chastagnol, *Les fastes*, 45–48.

119 Chastagnol, *Les fastes*, 59–62.
120 Chastagnol, *Les fastes*, 52–58.
121 Chastagnol, *Les fastes*, 77–78; R. von Haehling, *Die Religionszugehörigkeit der hohen Amtsträger des Römischen Reiches seit Constantins I. Alleinherrschaft bis zum Ende der Theodosianischen Zeit* (Bonn, 1978), 364–65.
122 Chastagnol, *Les fastes*, 75–76.
123 For the religious affiliations of Porphyrius and Paulinus see von Haehling, *Die Religionszugehörigkeit*, 365–66. Von Haehling considers the affiliations of Petronius Probianus and Amnius Anicius Julianus as questionable.
124 Chastagnol, *Les fastes*, 86–92.
125 Chastagnol, *Les fastes*, 72.
126 Jones, *Later Roman Empire*, 106.
127 Von Haehling, *Die Religionszugehörigkeit*, 57, 355 (Flavius Ablabius and Gregorius).
128 Soz. *Hist. eccl.* 2.3.6. For similar statements in post-Constantinian sources see Dagron, *Naissance d'une capitale*, 120, n. 1.
129 *Expositio totius mundi* 50; *Origo* 30: *ibi etiam senatum constituit secundi ordinis: claros vocavit*; see also Zos. 2.38.3–4.
130 Dagron, *Naissance d'une capitale*, 123, with correction with regard to the praetorship by A. Chastagnol, "Remarques sur les sénateurs orientaux au IVe siècle," *Acta Antiqua* 24 (1976): 346–47; P. Heather, "Senators and Senates," in *The Cambridge Ancient History*, 2nd edn, vol. 13, ed. A. Cameron and P. Garnsey (Cambridge, 1998), 185–86.
131 *CTh.* 4.5, 4.6; Them. *Epist. Constantii ad senatum* 19b, 23b with Dagron, *Naissance d'une capitale*, 124–25.
132 *Chron. Pasch.* 531; Eunap. *V. Phil.* p. 462; *CTh.* 13.5.7.
133 P. Heather, "New Men for New Constantines," in *New Constantines*, ed. P. Magdalino (Aldershot, 1994), 11–33.
134 Zos. 2.31.3 with Paschoud's note ad loc. See also Aur. Vict. *De Caes.* 41.15; [Aur. Vict.] *Epit. de Caes.* 41.16; Amm. Marc. 16.8.12; Jul. *Caes.* 335b.
135 P. 273 above.
136 R. Bagnall, *Egypt in Late Antiquity* (Princeton, 1993), 314–19.
137 For *metrokomai* see p. 21 above; for Orcistus in Phrygia, which lost civic status under Maximian, allegedly because its inhabitants were Christian, and regained it, in part because its inhabitants were Christian and because of the amenities it claimed, see A. Chastagnol, "L'inscription constantinienne d'Orcistus," *MEFR* 93 (1981): 381–416.
138 Banaji, *Agrarian Change*, 81–88.
139 Sutherland and Carson, *The Roman Imperial Coinage*, 6: 93–100; Harl, *Coinage*, 149.
140 Ruschenbusch, "Diokletians Währungsreform," 201.
141 For what follows see C. E. King, "The Fourth Century Coinage," in *L' "inflazione" nel quarto secolo d.c. Atti dell'incontro di studio Roma 1988* (Rome, 1993), 21–26.
142 *P. Ryl.* 607; see also *P. Oslo* 83; *PSI* 965.
143 Banaji, *Agrarian Change*, 40.
144 P. Brown, *Power and Persuasion in Late Antiquity: Towards a Christian Empire* (Madison, 1992), 3–34.
145 Jones, *Later Roman Empire*, 1: 740–57 (with some reservations).
146 *P. Oxy.* 1204 with F. G. Millar, "Empire and City, Augustus to Julian: Obligations, Excuses, and Status," *JRS* 73 (1983): 92. For the institution of the *dekaprôtoi* see p. 239 above.
147 *CJ* 10.48.1; see also *CJ* 10.42.1, 10.43.1, all laying down strong rules against exemptions from *munera*.

148 *CJ* 10.44.2. The prescript omits mention of the Caesars, but this cannot be decisive; see next note.

149 For the date see Barnes, *New Empire*, 55, for evidence that Diocletian was at Antioch in February 299 and 300. The year 290 is impossible since Diocletian was at Adrianople on February 27 (*CJ* 6.5.2) and only arrived in Syria in May (*Frag. Vat.* 276). The heading of this extract reads: *pars actorum Diocletiani et Maximiani AA id Febr . . . Inductis Firmino et Apollinario et ceteris principalibus Antiochensium adstantibus Sabinus dixit . . .* The Greek that follows is too corrupt to be read. What is interesting is that Diocletian replied to this Greek speech in Latin.

150 P. 334 above.

151 For the origin of this law see note 49 above.

152 See also *CTh.* 7.20.4 with Seeck, *Regesten*, 118. The text, identifying Maximus as the *praefectus urbi*, is incorrect. For discussion of *CTh.* 7.20.4 see p. 451 below.

153 *CTh.* 12.1.11 for the *pastus*; see Jones, *Later Roman Empire*, 459 with n. 117.

154 *CJ* 7.73.1, restoring the liquid assets of widows whose property was committed to paying for the *pastus* to which their husbands were liable.

155 *CJ* 8.14.4; see also *CJ* 12.62.3: a woman could claim property for her dowry only after it was established that it was not needed to pay the *pastus*, and this was a ruling by Diocletian, who alone appears to have been inclined to mitigate the burden when he stated that a man who had been reduced to the money needed to pay for his funeral could transfer the remainder of his obligation to the governor of his province (*CJ* 4.8.1) (294). We do not know when the mandatory gift to governors was instituted, but Julian issued a ruling to the effect that such gifts were limited to fifty pounds of silver from all of those responsible for the *pastus* (*CTh.* 8.4.9) (369).

156 For a thorough discussion see Ando, *Imperial Ideology*, 175–90.

157 Zos. 2.38.4 (placing the beginning of the tax under Constantine); Jones, *Later Roman Empire* 1: 431; for the burden of the tax see S. J. B. Barnish, "A Note on the *Collatio Glebalis*," *Historia* 38 (1989): 254–56.

158 Stein, *Histoire du Bas-Empire*, 115; Jones, *Later Roman Empire* 1: 430–31.

159 Zos. 2.38.1–2 (placing the beginning of the tax under Constantine); Jones, *Later Roman Empire*, 1: 431–32.

160 Jones, *Later Roman Empire*, 2: 1176, nn. 49–50, collecting evidence connected to setting the rates.

161 See *CTh.* 12.1.6 on decurions who married other people's slaves.

162 *CTh.* 12.1.18; for the date see Matthews, *Laying Down the Law*, 232–36, contra Seeck, *Regesten*, 43, who had dated the text to 326.

163 R. MacMullen, *Corruption and the Decline of Rome* (New Haven, 1988), 148–67.

164 *CTh.* 1.2.2 with Seeck, *Regesten*, 54.

165 *CTh.* 1.2.1 with Seeck, *Regesten*, 162.

166 R. MacMullen, "Judicial Savagery in the Roman Empire," *Chiron* 16 (1986): 43–62 (also in MacMullen, *Changes in Roman Empire*, 204–17).

167 Brown, *Power and Persuasion*, 29–30.

168 *CTh.* 1.16.6 with MacMullen, *Corruption and Decline*, 157.

169 For purchase of office see MacMullen, *Corruption and Decline*, 161–67.

170 See esp. the well-documented case of Abinnaeus, who had to appeal to Constantius II to uphold his appointment to the command of a military unit in Egypt against rival claimants, on which see H. I. Bell, V. Martin, E. G. Turner, and D. van Berchem, *The Abinnaeus Archive* (Oxford, 1962), 6–12.

11 CONSTRUCTING CHRISTIANITY IN AN IMPERIAL CONTEXT

1 For an excellent survey of the literature on the "sincerity" of Constantine, a debate that was in many ways defined by J. Burckhardt, *Die Zeit des Konstantins des Grossen* (1853) (for an English translation see J. Burckhardt, *The Age of Constantine the Great*, trans. M. Hadas [New York, 1949], 292–93), see Baynes, *Constantine the Great*, 4–6; Drake, *Constantine and the Bishops*, 12–19.

2 The view adopted here is essentially in accord with the views promulgated by Baynes, *Constantine the Great*, 3, 30; Lane Fox, *Pagans and Christians*, 609; and Drake, *Constantine and the Bishops*, xv.

3 Pp. 432, 433 below.

4 Firm. Mat. *Math.* 1.13 is obviously written prior to the author's conversion to Christianity.

5 For the problem of the Church of the Twelve Apostles and the burial of Constantine see G. Downey, "The Builder of the Original Church of the Apostles at Constantinople: A Contribution to the Criticism of the Vita Constantini Attributed to Eusebius," *DOP* 6 (1951): 53–80; C. Mango, "Constantine's Mausoleum and the Translation of Relics," *BzZ* 83 (1990): 51–60, contra Dagron, *Naissance d'une capitale*, 401–9.

6 M. Labrousse, *Optat de Milève, Traité contre les Donatistes*, vol. 1, Sources Chrétiennes, vol. 412 (Paris, 1995), 12–14, 32–56, on the two editions of the work. See also the lucid summary in M. J. Edwards, *Optatus: Against the Donatists* (Liverpool, 1997), xi–xxix.

7 Optatus, *Tract.* 16.1.

8 Optatus, *Tract.* 17.

9 Optatus, *Tract.* App. 1.13–16.

10 Optatus, *Tract.* App. 1.3–6.

11 Optatus, *Tract.* 1.18.1–2.

12 Optatus, *Tract.* 1.18.2–19.4 and App 5.6 (for the words quoted here).

13 See p. 409 below.

14 Aug., *Breviculus*, 3.13 (25) (S. Lancel, *Gesta conlationis Carthaginiensis anno 411*, Corpus Christianorum series Latina, vol. 149a [Turnholt, 1974]). Optatus, *Tract.* 14.2 implies that it was well known that Secundus had been released from jail because he had agreed to hand over books of scripture. For the situation in Numidia see W. H. C. Frend, *The Donatist Church: A Movement of Protest in Roman North Africa* (Oxford, 1952), 8. In what follows I follow Barnes's "early chronology;" for arguments in favor of a "late" chronology see S. Lancel, *Actes de la conférence de Carthage en 411*, vol. 4 (Paris, 1991), Sources Chrétiennes, no. 373, 1553–57, who places the election of Secundus in 309. Since the *tyrannus imperator* of Optatus, *Tract.* 1.17 must be an emperor on the throne during the persecution, this can only be Maximian. The most likely explanation for Mensurius' release is that Severus had succeeded Maximian in the interim, meaning that the election of Caecilian cannot reasonably be pushed back further than early 307.

15 *Act. Ab.* 3. For another martyrology that would appear to derive from the Donatist tradition see now P. Chiesa, "Un testo agiografico africano ad Aquileia: gli Acta di Gallonio e dei martiri di Timida Regia," *Analecta Bollandiana* 114 (1996): 241–68. I am grateful to Professor T. D. Barnes for calling this text to my attention.

16 The point was taken by Seeck, *Geschichte des Untergangs*, 3: 509n on p. 322, l. 12. Frend, *The Donatist Church*, 17, doubts the charges, but the essence of the case seems to be admitted in Mensurius' denunciation of the martyrs. The crucial

difference between Frend's approach, which places great stress on the history of division in North Africa over the subject of martyrdom (*The Donatist Church*, 125–40), and that which is taken here, is that I believe that the opposition to Caecilian stems from specific behaviors on his part rather than from a generalized tradition of discord, a point that emerges from the summary of the Donatist case in *Gesta. con. Carth.* 3.343. The severity of the charge would appear to be confirmed by the fact that Augustine's account of efforts to prove that the account of Caecilian's conduct is a forgery (*Breviculus* 3.14.26). On this point see also Drake, *Constantine and the Bishops*, 214.

17 Drake, *Constantine and the Bishops*, 212–13.

18 For the relationship between the two Anullini see *PLRE* Anullinus 2 and C. Annius Anullinus 3, pp. 78–79.

19 Euseb. *Hist. eccl.* 10.6.1–5 (also in J.-L. Maier, *Le dossier du donatisme*, vol. 1, *Des origines à la mort de Constance II (303–361),* Texte und Untersuchungen zur Geschichte der altchristlichen Literatur 134 [Berlin, 1987], no. 12, pp. 140–42, with her discussion of the date on p. 140).

20 Euseb. *Hist. eccl.* 10.7.1–2.

21 *CTh.* 16.2.1, 2 with Corcoran, *Empire of the Tetrarchs*, 155, 162.

22 Matthews, *Laying Down the Law*, 272–73.

23 Aug. *Ep.* 88.2.

24 Optatus, *Tract.* 1.22.2 (giving a faulty text); see also Aug. *Ep.* 88.2; *Brev. coll.* 3.12.4; *Gesta con. Carth.* 3.315 with Labrousse's no. 3 ad Optatus, *Tract.* 1.22.2 (pp. 222–23 of her edition).

25 Optatus, *Tract.* 23–24. For the significance of the appeal as calling into question Ossius' standing as a reliable guide to Christian affairs see Drake, *Constantine and the Bishops*, 217. For Donatist attacks on Ossius see Aug. *C. litt. Petil.* 1.4.7, 1.5.10, 1.8.13.

26 Euseb. *Hist. eccl.* 7.30.19.

27 Aug. *Ep.* 43.2.4; *Contra partem Don.* 17.21; *Breviculus* 3.12.24, identifying Donatus as being from Casa Nigra; see J. S. Alexander, "The Motive for a Distinction between Donatus of Carthage and Donatus of Casa Nigra," *JTS* 31 (1980): 540–47: Donatus of Casa Nigra was Donatus of Carthage; contra T. D. Barnes, "The Beginnings of Donatism," *JTS* 26 (1975): 16–17. On the date of Majorian's death see Frend, *The Donatist Church*, 148.

28 Optatus, *Tract.* 24.1. For the earlier controversy see Cypr. *Ep.* 69.7, 71.1.1–2, 4, 73.1, 3, 75.5–6, 17, 22–25.

29 For Miltiades' initiative see Aug. *Ep.* 43.7, 16; for Donatus' charge against Miltiades see Aug. *C. Parm.* 1.5.10.

30 Optatus, *Tract.* App. 3 (also in Maier, *Le dossier*, no. 18, ll. 34–36).

31 The procedural issue is well made by Drake, *Constantine and the Bishops*, 218–19.

32 Arles can. 9; for the parallel see Maier's note (*Le dossier*, 166, no. 23).

33 Arles can. 15; compare Elvira can. 73.

34 See also Optatus, *Tract.* App. 4 (also in Maier, *Le dossier*, no. 20), a letter from the council to Silvester, the bishop of Rome.

35 Optatus, *Tract.* App. n. 5 (also in Maier, *Le dossier*, no. 21).

36 Optatus, *Tract.* App. n. 3 (also in Maier, *Le dossier*, no. 18); Euseb. *Hist. eccl.* 10.5.21–24 (also in Maier, *Le dossier*, no. 19).

37 Optatus, *Tract.* App. n. 2 (also in Maier, *Le dossier*, no. 22).

38 Aug. *Contra Cresc.* 3.71.82 (also in Maier, *Le dossier*, no. 27); see also Barnes, *Constantine and Eusebius*, 60.

39 Maier, *Le Dossier*, no. 28. There is an English translation in M. A. Tilley, *Donatist Martyr Stories: The Church in Conflict in Roman North Africa* (Liverpool, 1996), 51–60.

40 For the letter to Verinus see Aug. *Contra partem Donati post gesta* 31.54, 33.56; for the letter to the bishops see Optatus, *Tract.* App. n. 10 (also in Maier, *Le dossier*, no. 30).

41 Barnes, *Constantine and Eusebius*, 60.

42 Aug. *Ep.* 93.43 with Frend, *The Donatist Church*, 167–68.

43 Aug. *Ep.* 44.3.6; *Contra Cresc.* 3.34.38, 4.44.52 with Frend, *The Donatist Church*, 170.

44 R. Williams, *Arius: Heresy and Tradition* (London, 1987), 30.

45 Theod. *Hist. eccl.* 1.5.4 (also in H. G. Opitz, *Urkunden zur Geschichte des arianischen Streites 318–328* [Berlin, 1934], no. 1.1–3).

46 For Eusebius' objection to some of Arius' teaching see Theod. *Hist. eccl.* 1.6.3; see also the important review of all issues connected with Arius by C. Kannengiesser, "Arius and the Arians," *Theological Studies* 44 (1983): 456–75 (also in Kannengiesser, *Arius and Athanasius: Two Alexandrian Theologians* [Brookfield, VT, 1991], ch. 2); Kannengiesser, "Athanasius of Alexandria vs. Arius: The Alexandrian Crisis," in *The Roots of Egyptian Christianity*, ed. B. A. Pearson and J. E. Goehring (Philadelphia, 1986), 208 (also in *Arius and Athanasius*, ch. 12); M. Slusser, "Traditional Views of Late Arianism," in *Arianism after Arius: Essays on the Development of the Fourth Century Trinitarian Conflicts*, ed. M. R. Barnes and D. H. Williams (Edinburgh, 1993), 3–30, on the later historiography of the dispute. See also n. 100 below.

47 For the Alexandrian background, see esp. M. Wiles, "In Defense of Arius," *JTS* 13 (1962): 344; C. Kannengiesser, "Alexander and Arius of Alexandria: The Last Ante-Nicene Theologians," in *Miscelánea En Homenaje Al P. Antonio. Orbe Compostellanum* 34, nos. 1–2 (Santiago de Compestella, 1990), 392, 398, 401–2 (also in Kannengiesser, *Arius and Athanasius*, ch. 4).

48 For the appointment of Arius as a preacher by Alexander see Soz. *Hist. eccl.* 1.15.2; Epiph. *Pan.* 68.4.2, 69.1.2 with Seeck, *Geschichte des Untergangs*, 3: 542n on p. 386, l. 8; Barnes, *Constantine and Eusebius*, 202; A. M. Ritter, "Arianismus," *Theologische Realenzyklopädie*, vol. 3 (Berlin, 1978), 698–99. The sources for the outbreak of the conflict had an unusually strong documentary background, as later accounts were based upon collections of documents made by both sides from a very early date; see Socrates, *Hist. eccl.* 1.6.41; Ath. *De synod.* 18 with the valuable discussion of E. Schwartz, "Die Dokumente des arianischen Streits bis 325," 257–99 (also in Schwartz, *Gesammelte Schriften*, 3: 117–68); see now L. Parmentier's discussion in the introduction to his edition of Theodoret (Theodoret, *Kirchengeschichte*, *GCS* n.f. 5 [Berlin, 1997], lxxiii–lxxvi). On Epiphanius see Schwartz's comments in "Dokumente des arianischen Streit," 258 (also in Schwartz, *Gesammelte Schriften*, 3: 117). See also D. Brakke, *Athanasius and the Politics of Asceticism* (Oxford, 1995), 64–65, on the significance of his role as an ascetic.

49 Theod. *Hist. eccl.* 1.4.7–9 (also in Opitz, *Urkunden*, no. 14).

50 Elm, *Virgins of God*, 350–53; Brakke, *Athanasius*, 16–22.

51 See p. 489 below.

52 Brakke, *Athanasius*, 9–11.

53 E. Schwartz, "Die Quellen über den melitianischen Streit," *Nachrichten von der k. Gesellschaft der Wissenschaften zu Göttingen, phil.-hist. Klasse* (1905), 166–75 (also in Schwartz, *Gesammelte Schriften*, 3: 89–100); F. H. Kettler, "Die melitianische Streit in Ägypten," *Zeitschrift für die neutestamentliche Wissenschaft* 35 (1936): 155–93; Barnes, *Constantine and Eusebius*, 201.

54 Epiph. *Pan.* 68.2.1, 4; Ath. *Apol. contra Ar.* 71; Soz. *Hist. eccl.* 1.24.1; Seeck, *Geschichte des Untergangs*, 3: 382.

55 For the text see E. J. Jonkers, *Acta et symbola conciliorum quae saeculo quarto habita sunt* (Leiden, 1954), 28; for details of the acts and discussion of the date, see

S. Parvis, "The Canons of Ancyra and Caesarea (314): Lebon's Thesis Revisited," *JTS* 52 (2000): 625–36.

56 Ancyra can. 3; Jonkers, *Acta et symbola conciliorum*, 29. Canon 2 relates to deacons in the same situation as priests with the provision that they might receive absolution from a bishop.

57 Ancyra can. 4–5; Jonkers, *Acta et symbola conciliorum*, 30.

58 Euseb. *Hist. eccl.* 8.9.5–8 (8.10.1–10 is a version of the *Acts of Phileas*, a voluntary martyr, for which see also Musurillo, *Acts of the Christian Martyrs*, no. 26), MP 8.1, including ninety-seven from Palestine who attract Eusebius' particular attention.

59 A Latin translation of the letter is preserved in *Codex Vaticanus* lx, discussed by Schwartz, "Die Quellen," 177–79 (also in Schwartz, *Gesammelte Schriften*, 3: 103–5); see also the text printed in Turner, *EOMIA* 1: 635–56; see also *Symbolae Osloenses* 38 (1963): 80. This was later regarded as the beginning of the schism, which Athanasius dated to the nineteenth year before the Council of Nicaea; see Ath. *Ep. ad ep. Aeg. et Lib.* 22 with Seeck, *Geschichte des Untergangs*, 3: 540n on p. 383, l. 24.

60 Epiph. *Pan.* 68.3; Ath. *Hist. Ar. ad mon.* 60; Seeck, *Geschichte des Untergangs*, 3: 383; Barnes, *Constantine and Eusebius*, 202.

61 Epiph. *Pan.* 68.1.4.

62 Barnes, *Constantine and Eusebius*, 202, with the evidence for the date collected in his n. 112.

63 Soz. *Hist. eccl.* 1.15.2 with Schwartz, "Die Quellen," 186–87 (also in Schwartz, *Gesammelte Schriften*, 3: 114–15), correcting the tendentious picture of Ath. *Ap.* 11, 59, *Ep. ad ep. Aeg. et Lib.* 22.

64 See note 48 above.

65 Schwartz, "Die Quellen," 187–88 (also in Schwartz, *Gesammelte Schriften* 3: 115–16).

66 Soz. *Hist. eccl.* 1.15.4; Epiph. *Pan.* 68.4, 69.5.

67 Seeck, *Geschichte des Untergangs*, 3: 388; Ritter, "Arianismus," 696.

68 H. Chadwick, "Faith and Order at the Council of Nicaea: A Note on the Background of the Sixth Canon," *HTR* 53 (1960): 179 (also in Chadwick, *History and Thought of the Early Church* [London, 1982], ch. 12).

69 Lang, "Christological Controversy," 79–80.

70 J. C. Stead, "'Eusebius' and the Council of Nicaea," *JTS* 24 (1973): 86–87.

71 Epiph. *Pan.* 69.2.3–6.

72 Theod. *Hist. eccl.* 1.4.5–7 (also in Opitz, *Urkunden*, no. 14).

73 See n. 46 above and p. 415 below for discussion of the differences between Arius' teaching and that of the Syrian school.

74 For Arius as the agent of Eusebius see C. Kannengiesser, "Où et quand Arius composa-t-il la Thalie," *Kyriakon: Festschrift J. Quasten* 1 (1971), 350; for the view that Arius' attack on Alexander was convenient to Eusebius and others but not directly instigated by them see R. D. Williams, "The Quest of the Historical *Thalia*," in *Arianism: Historical and Theological Reassessments. Papers from the Ninth International Conference on Patristic Studies, September 5–10, 1983*, ed. R. C. Gregg (Philadelphia, 1985), 19–21.

75 For the chronology see H. G. Opitz, "Die Zeitfolge des arianischen Streites von den Anfängen bis zum Jahre 328," *Zeitschrift für die neutestamentliche Wissenschaft* 33 (1934): 147–48.

76 Theod. *Hist. eccl.* 1.5 (also in Opitz, *Urkunden*, no. 1); for the chronology see also H. G. Opitz, "Zeitfolge des arianischen Streites," 147.

77 Theod. *Hist. eccl.* 1.4.

78 Theod. *Hist. eccl.* 1.4.35–36 (also in Opitz, *Urkunden*, no. 14).

79 Ath. *De synod.* 16.3 (also in Opitz, *Urkunden*, no. 6). He also compares Alexander's thinking with that of the Valentians and Sabellians. In the case of Mani, the

statement is utterly preposterous: he did not write in Greek (and see p. 309 above for Mani's contact with Christian thought).

80 Ritter, "Arianismus," 701; H. Chadwick, "Orthodoxy and Heresy from the Death of Constantine to the Eve of the First Council of Ephesus," in Cameron and Garnsey, *The Cambridge Ancient History*, 13: 565.

81 Opitz, *Urkunden*, nos. 4b, 5, 14.

82 Ritter, "Arianismus," 695; Chadwick, "Orthodoxy and Heresy," 565; see also n. 46 above.

83 For this view of the *Thalia* see Williams, "Quest," 1–35.

84 For the text see K. Metzler and F. Simon, *Ariana et Athanasiana: Studien zur Überlieferung und zu philologische Problemen der Werke des Athanasius von Alexandrien*, Abhandlungen der Rheinisch–Westfälischen Akademie der Wissenschaften 83 (Opladen, 1991), 37. For analysis of the meter see their discussion on pp. 20–22 and M. L. West, "The Meter of Arius' *Thalia*," *JTS* 33 (1982): 98–105. For the accuracy of Athanasius' quotation of these lines see also S. G. Hall, "The *Thalia* in Athanasius' Accounts," in Gregg, *Arianism*, 37–58.

85 Brakke, *Athanasius*, 64–65.

86 For Theodotus see Euset. *Hist. eccl.* 7.32.23 with Barnes, *Constantine and Eusebius*, 178; for Paulinus see Euseb. *Hist. eccl.* 10.4.1; for Athanasius see Phil. *Hist. eccl.* 3.15.

87 Euseb. *Vit. Const.* 2.69.2.

88 Euseb. *Vit. Const.* 2.70.3.

89 Euseb. *Vit. Const.* 2.72.3.

90 For the decision of the council, which held strongly against Arius, see Opitz, *Urkunden*, no. 18. For the chronology see Opitz, "Zeitfolge des arianischen Streites," 151–52. What survives of the acts is discussed (with a Greek translation of the Syriac text by Schwartz) in E. Schwartz, "Das antiochenische Synoldalschreiben von 325," *Nachrichten von der k. Gesellschaft der Wissenschaften zu Göttingen, phil.-hist. Klasse* (1908), 305–79 (also in Schwartz, *Gesammelte Schriften*, 3: 169–87 [reprinting pp. 354–59, 365–74]); see also E. Abramowski, "Die Synod von Antioch 324/25 und ihr Symbol," *Zeitschrift für Kirchengeschichte* 86 (1975): 356–66 for corrections.

91 See now T. D. Barnes, "Constantine's *Speech to the Assembly of the Saints*: Place and Date of Delivery," *JTS* 52 (2001): 26–36.

92 Barnes, "Constantine's *Speech*," 34–36.

93 Drake, *Constantine and the Bishops*, 253, for stress on this point.

94 Theod. *Hist. eccl.* 1.12.1 For a sympathetic discussion of the position of the bishops previously opposed to Alexander of Alexandria see Chadwick, "Faith and Order," 170–79.

95 Theod. *Hist. eccl.* 1.8.2 with Stead, "'Eusebius' and the Council of Nicaea," 98.

96 Basil, *Ep.* 81 with Barnes, *Constantine and Eusebius*, 216.

97 Opitz, *Urkunden*, no. 23, 6–10.

98 Phil. *Hist. eccl.* 1.9.

99 For the crucial break with previous traditions of scholarship, which took Athanasius at his word in describing his foes as Arians, see Wiles, "In Defense of Arius"; see also the important discussion in T. D. Barnes, *Athanasius and Constantine: Theology and Politics in the Constantinian Empire* (Cambridge, Mass., 1993), 14–15.

100 For Athanasius' impact on later ecclesiastical historians see H. Leppin, *Von Constantin dem Grossen zu Theodosius II. Das christliche Kaisertum bei den Kirchenhistorikern Socrates, Sozomenus und Theodoret* (Göttingen, 1996), 49–51.

101 What follows is heavily derivative from H. Chadwick, "The Fall of Eustathius of Antioch," *JTS* 49 (1948): 27–35 (also in Chadwick, *History and Thought*, ch. 13). See also Drijvers, *Helena Augusta*, 71–72, noting that Helena may also have had some sympathy for Arius' thought (Phil. *Hist. eccl.* 2.12).

102 Ath. *Hist. Ar. ad mon.* 4.

103 Phil. *Hist. eccl.* 2.12 with E. D. Hunt, *Holy Land Pilgrimage in the Later Roman Empire, AD 312–460* (Oxford, 1982), 36.

104 Socrates, *Hist. eccl.* 1.23.8–24.1.

105 Theod. *Hist. eccl.* 1.21 (a woman, allegedly a bribed prostitute, produces her child by him in court, allegedly lying); Soz. *Hist. eccl.* 2.19 (claims he disgraced the priesthood); Phil. *Hist. eccl.* 2.7 (sexual immorality).

106 Barnes, *Athanasius and Constantius*, 17–18.

107 Ath. *Apol. contra Ar.* 6.5.6, denying the charge; but see also Soz. *Hist. eccl.* 2.17. Sozomen quotes a document by Apolinarius the Syrian that models the election of Athanasius on an imperial acclamation, stressing the *recusatio*.

108 Soz. *Hist. eccl.* 2.17.

109 Brakke, *Athanasius*, 80–82, 113.

110 Ath. *Apol. contra Ar.* 60.1–2 with Barnes, *Athanasius and Constantius*, 21.

111 Ath. *Apol. contra Ar.* 63.1–4.

112 Ath. *Apol. contra Ar.* 66–70 with Barnes, *Athanasius and Constantius*, 28.

113 *P. London* 1914.

114 Drake, *Constantine and the Bishops*, 261–68.

115 See the important discussion by B. Shaw in a review of J. Evans Grubbs, *Law and Family in Late Antiquity: The Emperor Constantine's Marriage Legislation* in *BMCR* (1996) 8.12.

116 P. 371 above.

117 *CTh.* 1.27 with Seeck, *Regesten*, 57. An early date may be confirmed by *SC* 1, for Ablabius is unaware of Constantine's earlier edict, suggesting that it was some time in the past.

118 *SC* 1.

119 For a summary of the legal evidence see A. Lindner, *The Jews in Roman Imperial Legislation* (Detroit, 1987), 68–71; Schürer, *History of Jewish People*, vol. 3, pt. 1, 107–37.

120 A. Oppenheimer, "Jewish Penal Authority in Roman Judaea," in *Jews in a Greco-Roman World*, ed. M. Goodman, vol. 3, pt. 1 (Oxford, 1998), 181–91.

121 Lindner, *Jews in Roman Imperial Legislation*, 71–73; Schürer, *History of Jewish People*, vol. 3, pt. 1, 124–25.

122 See p. 35 above.

123 Lindner, *Jews in Roman Imperial Legislation*, 82.

124 It is asserted, for instance, that there was a direct line that can be traced from the conversion of Constantine to much harsher legislation against the Jews in the early fifth century (and, by implication to modern anti-Semitism) in J. Carroll, *Constantine's Sword: The Church and the Jews* (New York, 2001), 176, 185, etc. See, however, the balanced discussion in F. Millar, "The Jews of the Greco-Roman Diaspora between Paganism and Christianity," in *The Jews among Pagans and Christians in the Roman Empire*, ed. J. Lieu, J. North, and T. Rajak (London, 1992), 102–5, 112–21, showing that the treatment of Judaism by Christians cannot be separated from that of polytheism.

125 *CTh.* 16.8.2 with Lindner, *Jews in Roman Imperial Legislation*, 120–21.

126 *CTh.* 16.8.3.

127 For the date see Lindner, *Jews in Roman Imperial Legislation*, 125.

128 Euseb. *Vit. Const.* 4.27.1, with Lindner, *Jews in Roman Imperial Legislation*, 126. The textual issue is, however, more complicated than Lindner allows, as *CTh.* 16.9.2, 16.8.6 may be part of the same letter; see Barnes, *Constantine and Eusebius*, 392, n. 74.

129 *CTh.* 16.8.6; see previous note on the date.

130 Euseb. *Vit. Const.* 4.18.1.

131 See also *P. Oxy.* 3758, 119–20; though not stated explicitly, it is clear that a court holiday will take place the next day, which happened to be a Sunday.

132 Potter, "Entertainers," 302–3.

133 P. 392 above.

134 This was certainly not a law banning gladiators (see *CTh.* 15.12.2, 3, and the letter to Hispellum, where permission to hold a biennial festival, including gladiatorial exhibitions, is granted; see p. 433 below). See also *CTh.* 9.18.1: *ad ludum gladiatorium* for *damnati ad ludum* (in 315). Assuming that this is the law referred to in Euseb. *Vit. Const.* 4.25.1, his reading of it is an overstatement. For another place where *damnati* are called gladiators see *P. Pion.* 18.8; these passages show that *monomachous* in the text need not be a gloss.

135 T. Wiedemann, *Emperors and Gladiators* (London, 1992), 128–46.

136 P. 351 above.

137 Aur. Vict. *De Caes.* 41.4.

138 See in general, J. Evans Grubbs, "Constantine and Imperial legislation on the Family," in *The Theodosian Code*, ed. J. Harries and I. Wood (Ithaca, NY, 1993), 120–42, summarizing J. Evans Grubbs, *Law and Family in Late Antiquity: The Emperor Constantine's Marriage Legislation* (Oxford, 1995).

139 Euseb. *Vit. Const.* 4.26.1–5; *CTh.* 8.16.1; *CJ* 6.9.9, 6.23.15, 6.37.21; *CTh.* 3.2.1, 11.7.3 (all sections of the same law) with Seeck, *Regesten*, 59–60; Matthews, *Laying Down the Law*, 236–40. Matthews's doubts as to whether this law was promulgated in the east as a cooperative measure between the two emperors would seem to be answered by Eusebius' evident reference to it as a law of Licinius; see the next note. Evans Grubbs, *Law and Family*, 130, likewise assumes that the law was originally promulgated in the west, but rightly questions the authority for Eusebius' statement that the text was motivated by Christianity.

140 Euseb. *Hist. eccl.* 10.8.12 with Corcoran, "Hidden from History," 102.

141 This was altered by a law of AD 62 whereby adoptive children were counted for their biological parents; see S. Treggiari, *Roman Marriage: "Iusti coniuges" from the Time of Cicero to the Time of Ulpian* (Oxford, 1991), 72.

142 Treggiari, *Roman Marriage*, 68–69.

143 The standard account is Treggiari, *Roman Marriage*, 66–68.

144 For the concept of the *familia*, see A. E. Hanson, "The Roman Family," in Potter and Mattingly, *Life, Death, and Entertainment*, 20–21.

145 Treggiari, *Roman Marriage*, 69.

146 Treggiari, *Roman Marriage*, 72.

147 P. 49 above and Treggiari, *Roman Marriage*, 73–76.

148 For other excerpts from this section of the law see *CJ* 6.9.9, 6.37.21.

149 *CTh.* 3.2.1 with Evans Grubbs, *Law and Family*, 120, on the date.

150 *CTh.* 11.7.3.

151 Evans Grubbs, *Law and Family*, 112–23, placing the law within the context of imperial practice.

152 P. 338 above.

153 Euseb. *Praep. evang.* 4.135c–136a with Drake, *Constantine and the Bishops*, 144–45. For the structure of the oracle see Potter, *Prophets and Emperors*, 43.

154 Euseb. *Vit. Const.* 3.55–56; 58.

155 Lane Fox, *Pagans and Christians*, 671; Potter, "Recent Inscriptions," 309–10.

156 Euseb. *Vit. Const.* 4.25.2–3.

157 *CTh.* 16.10.1 with Potter, *Prophets and Emperors*, 178.

158 Euseb. *Vit. Const.* 2.44.
159 See e.g. Elvira can. 1, 2.
160 Euseb. *Vit. Const.* 2.45.1.
161 *ILS* 705 with a new text and discussion in J. Gascou, "Le rescript d' Hispellum," *MEFR* 79 (1967): 600–59.
162 *ILS* 705, 19–20; see also ll. 32–33.
163 Tac. *Ann.* 15.44; for the meaning of *superstitio* in late imperial legislation see M. R. Salzman, "*Superstitio* in the Codex Theodosianus and the Persecution of Pagans," *Vigiliae Christianae* 41 (1987): 172–88; E. D. Hunt, "Christianizing the Roman Empire: The Evidence of the Code," in Harries and Wood, *The Theodosian Code*, 145–46.
164 For the view that *CTh*. 16.10 cannot be taken as evidence for a general ban on pagan practice see the discussion in P. Cuneo, *La legislazione di Constantino II, Constanzo II e Constante (337–361)* (Milan, 1997), 89, with extensive bibliography. On Euseb. *Vit. Const.* 2.45.1 see also R. M. Errington, "Constantine and the Pagans," *GRBS* 29 (1988), esp. 313; on p. 315 he does allow the possibility that a broader ban was enunciated briefly in 324. S. Bradbury, "Constantine and the Problem of Anti-Pagan Legislation in the Fourth Century," *CPh* 89 (1994): 120–39, argues in favor of a ban, but suggests that it was intended as an admonition. He supports his case for a Constantinian ban with Lib. *Or.* 1.27, but that passage could be read as having to do with behaviors other than sacrifice – "living with the Gods" may involve indulgence in magical practices – and needs to be read in light of other statements. For general discussions of antipagan legislation, which likewise suggest that the reign of Constantine was not a period of radical change, see Hunt, "Christianizing the Roman Empire," 143–58; M. R. Salzman, *The Making of a Christian Aristocracy: Social and Religious Change in the Western Roman Empire* (Cambridge, Mass., 2002), 194–97.
165 Lib. *Or.* 30.6; see also p. 573 below.
166 Drake, *Constantine and the Bishops*, 244–50.
167 *MAMA* no. 305, panel 1, lines 39–43; for the date see Chastagnol, "L'inscription constantinienne d'Orcistus," 398.
168 P. 315 above on the council of Elvira.
169 Curran, *Pagan City*, 76–90.
170 Curran, *Pagan City*, 93–96.
171 Aur. Vict. *De Caes.* 40.25.
172 P. 407 above.
173 Drijvers, *Helena Augusta*, 45–54.
174 Curran, *Pagan City*, 99–102.
175 Curran, *Pagan City*, 102–5.
176 Curran, *Pagan City*, 105–9.
177 Euseb. *Hist. eccl.* 9.9.10, *Vit. Const.* 1.40.1–2.
178 The only evidence for her age is Euseb. *Vit. Const.* 3.46.1.
179 Euseb. *Vit. Const.* 3.26.4–6, 30.3.
180 Hunt, *Holy Land Pilgrimage*, 13–15.
181 Hunt, *Holy Land Pilgrimage*, 12.
182 Euseb. *Vit. Const.* 3.43.1–3.
183 Hunt, *Holy Land Pilgrimage*, 12–13, noting that Eusebius describes neither.
184 Hopkins, "Christian Number," 193.
185 For a very different view see Barnes, *Constantine and Eusebius*, 191; Barnes, "Christians and Pagans under Constantius," in *L'église et l'empire au ive siècle*, Entretiens Fondation Hardt 36 (Geneva, 1987), 308–12.

12 CHURCH AND STATE: 337–55

1   M. P. Speidel, "A Horse Guardsman in the War between Licinius and Constantine," *Chiron* 25 (1995): 183–87.

2   See also P. Brennan, "The *Notitia Dignitatum,*" in *Les littératures techniques dans l'antiquité romaine: Status, public et destination, tradition,* ed. C. Nicolet, Entretiens Fondation Hardt 42 (Geneva, 1995), 152–53.

3   For Constantine's dealings with the Goths see Heather, *Goths and Romans,* 107–15.

4   T. D. Barnes, "The Consecration of Ulfila," *JTS* 41 (1990): 541–55 (also in Barnes, *From Eusebius to Augustine* [Brookfield, VT, 1994], ch. 10).

5   Heather, *Goths and Romans,* 104–5.

6   Socrates, *Hist. eccl.* 4.33.7; Soz. *Hist. eccl.* 6.37.12; Epiph. *Pan.* 70.

7   See in general G. Fowden, *Empire to Commonwealth: Consequences of Monotheism in Late Antiquity* (Princeton, 1993), 101–16.

8   Soz. *Hist. eccl.* 2.8; for a Christian community there in the mid–third century see Euseb. *Hist. eccl.* 6.46; for the date see now the exhaustive analysis in Kettenhoffen, *Tīrdād,* 120–35.

9   Ruf. *Hist. eccl.* 1.10–11; Soz. *Hist. eccl.* 2.7 with D. Braund, *Georgia in Antiquity: A History of Colchis and Transcaucasian Iberia, 550 BC–AD 562* (Oxford, 1994), 251–52.

10   Ruf. *Hist. eccl.* 10.9–10; Socrates, *Hist. eccl.* 1.19; Soz. *Hist. eccl.* 2.24; Theod. *Hist. eccl.* 1.23 (the last three all depend on Rufinus).

11   On the cultural role of Hellenism see esp. Bowersock, *Hellenism in Late Antiquity,* 71–82.

12   For Kirdir see p. 290 above.

13   For the date of the letter contained in Euseb. *Vit. Const.* 4.8–13 see T. D. Barnes, "Constantine and the Christians of Persia," *JRS* 75 (1985): 131; R. C. Blockley, *East Roman Foreign Policy: Formation and Conduct from Diocletian to Anastasius* (Leeds, 1992), 11.

14   Euseb. *Vit. Const.* 4.9.

15   See p. 354 above on the solar coinage of Constantine.

16   Euseb. *Vit. Const.* 4.11; for the use of the exemplum of Valerian by Diocletian see p. 244 above.

17   Bosworth, *The History of al-Ṭabarī,* 51.

18   *PLRE* Hormisdas 2, p. 443; Blockley, *East Roman Foreign Policy,* 10.

19   Amm. Marc. 25.4.23; Cedrenus, 1, 516–17 with B. H. Warmington, "Ammianus Marcellinus and the Lies of Metrodorus," *CQ* 32 (1981): 464–68. It is unlikely that this Metrodorus should be identified with the "philosopher" Metrodorus who Rufinus says visited India Ulterior, as it appears that he means Aksum. See P. R. Amidon, *The Church History of Rufinus of Aquileia* (Oxford, 1997), 19, n. 18, on Rufinus' geographical terms.

20   P. 459 below.

21   Barnes, "Constantine and Christians," 132.

22   There are excellent recent discussions of the army in H. Elton, *Warfare in Roman Europe, AD 350–425* (Oxford, 1996); P. Southern and K. R. Dixon, *The Late Roman Army* (New Haven, 1996); and A. D. Lee, "The Army," in *The Cambridge Ancient History,* vol. 13, ed. Cameron and Garnsey, 211–37.

23   For earlier styles see J. Lander, *Roman Stone Fortifications: Variation and Change from the First Century AD to the Fourth,* BAR International Series 206 (Oxford, 1984), 20–30.

24   Lander, *Roman Stone Fortifications,* 18–19; Pollard, *Soldiers, Cities, and Civilians,* 43.

25   Lander, *Roman Stone Fortifications,* 102–5.

26 Lander, *Roman Stone Fortifications*, 172–80; S. Johnson, "Introduction to the Saxon Shore," in *Roman Frontier Studies, 1989: Proceedings of the XVth International Congress of Roman Frontier Studies*, ed. V. A. Maxfield and M. J. Dobson (Exeter, 1991), 94–95.

27 Lander, *Roman Stone Fortifications*, 181; see also Southern and Dixon, *The Late Roman Army*, 133, suggesting that what Lander identifies as the citadel is the whole fort.

28 Lander, *Roman Stone Fortifications*, 217 and p. 200, fig. 197 (the fortification probably dates to the reign of Constantius II but stands as a good example of the style).

29 H. von Petrikovits, "Fortifications in the North-Western Roman Empire from the Third to the Fifth Centuries AD," *JRS* 61 (1971): 204 (also in von Petrikovits, *Beiträge zur römischen Geschichte und Archäologie 1931 bis 1974* [Bonn, 1976], 577).

30 Elton, *Warfare in Roman Europe*, 155–67; Southern and Dixon, *The Late Roman Army*, 142–45.

31 Von Petrikovits, "Fortifications," 179–81 (also in von Petrikovits, *Beiträge*, 548).

32 For the significance of Severus' actions see Birley, *Septimius Severus*, 196; for the use of Apamea see Pollard, *Soldiers, Cities, and Civilians*, 263–66; Van Rengen, "La IIe Légion Parthique," 407–10.

33 For late Roman military equipment see Elton, *Warfare in Roman Europe*, 108–16; Southern and Dixon, *The Late Roman Army*, 89–126.

34 For this usage see Christol and Drew-Bear, "Un inscription d'Ancyre."

35 P. 257 above.

36 *ILS* 2781, 664.

37 *FGrH* 100, fr. 7.4.

38 The crucial study is that of D. Hoffmann, *Das spätrömische Bewegungsheer und die Notitia Dignitatum*, Epigraphische Studien 7 (Düsseldorf, 1969), 243–78.

39 For another section of this letter see p. 396 above.

40 B. Isaac, "The Meaning of *Limes* and *Limitanei* in Ancient Sources," *JRS* 78 (1988): 139–46 (also in Isaac, *The Near East under Roman Rule* [Leiden, 1998], 366–78); see also G. A. Crump, "Ammianus and the Late Roman Army," *Historia* 22 (1973): 91–103, showing that the distinction between *comitatenses* and *ripenses* did not imply that the latter were not a "militia."

41 Pollard, *Soldiers, Cities, and Civilians*, 35–67.

42 P. 396 above.

43 The final sentence of this clause is not translated as being spurious. I see no justification for the exclusion of the first two sentences of *CTh.* 7.20.4.1.

44 *CJ* 7.64.9, 10.55.3.

45 *AE* 1937, no. 232, read correctly by M. Amelotti, "Da Diocleziano a Costantino: Note in tema di costituzioni imperiali," *SDHI* 27: 270; see also the discussion of the style of the document in Corcoran, *Empire of the Tetrarchs*, 145–48.

46 If this argument is acceptable, it would confirm the propriety of the expansion of *ILS* 664.9–10 as eqq. Dalm. *Aq/uesinis comit(atensibus) laetus libens merito* as argued in Seeck, *Geschichte des Untergangs*, 2: 491–92 (n. on p. 35, l. 27) and Hoffmann, *Das spätrömische Bewegungsheer*, 1: 258 with his note at 2: 106, n. 530 (see also *ILS* 2792.3–4 for eqq. *Dalm. Comit. Ancial\itana*); contra D. van Berchem, *L'armée de Dioclétien et la réforme constantinienne* (Paris, 1952), 108, who expanded the crucial word as *comit(ibus)*. See also Seston, *Dioclétien et la tétrarchie*, 304, who further adduces Jul. *Or.* 1.34c, observing that Diocletian's role is omitted as he was not an ancestor of Constantius, but it is not directly relevant to the question at hand. More significant may be *AE* 1981, no. 777.7–8 on *optio comitum* with the important discussion in Drew-Bear, "Les voyages," 112–13, showing that there is still no unambiguous attestation of the *comitatenses* under Diocletian.

47 Zos. 2.33.3.

48 P. 481 below.
49 Amm. Marc. 16.12.36–37 and p. 501 below.
50 Amm. Marc. 24.6.9–11; see also 25.1.17.
51 Amm. Marc. 16.12.26, 43–44, 24.6.10–11.
52 Amm. Marc. 24.6.10; Zos. 2.19.2 with Elton, *Warfare in Roman Europe*, 250–53.
53 Zos. 2.16.2, 18.3.
54 See Brennan, "The *Notitia Dignitatum*," 147–69, on the ideology behind the text; and M. Kulikowski, "The *Notitia Dignitatum* as a Historical Source," *Historia* 49 (2000): 360, on the dates of the lists.
55 Jones, *Later Roman Empire*, 55–60.
56 Seston, *Dioclétien et la tétrarchie*, 299.
57 R. P. Duncan Jones, "Pay and Numbers in Diocletian's Army," in *Structure and Scale*, 117, 215.
58 Zos. 2.15.1–2; John Lydus, *De Mens.* 1.27.
59 Zos. 2.22.1–2.
60 For acceptance of these figures as roughly correct see Jones, *Later Roman Empire*, 679–83; Elton, *Warfare in Roman Europe*, 120.
61 *Pan.* 12 (9) 3.3; 5.1.
62 *Or.* 5.16 with Hoffmann, *Das spätrömische Bewegungsheer*, 1: 209.
63 Amm. Marc. 16.12.2; for discussion of specific units see Hoffmann, *Das spätrömische Bewegungsheer*, 1: 203.
64 Zon. 13.8 with discussion in Hoffmann, *Das spätrömische Bewegungsheer*, 1: 201, 209.
65 Amm. Marc. 16.11.2.
66 Zos. 3.10.2. At this point in his narrative Eunapius, Zosimus' source, was using the notebooks of Oribasius, which would appear to have been rather more accurate than whatever source was used by Eunapius for the wars of Constantine.
67 Amm. Marc. 16.11.
68 Caes. *B. Civ.* 3.84.4, 88.3–5, 89.2 followed by Plut. *Caes.* 42.3–4 for these numbers; another tradition (probably Livian) makes the numbers closer; see Oros. 6.15.3; Eutrop. *Brev.* 6.20.4; see M. Gelzer, *Caesar: Politician and Statesman*, 6th edn., trans. P. Needham (Oxford, 1969), 238, n. 1.
69 For details of troop strengths see J. Nicols, *Vespasian and the Partes Flavianae*, Historia Einzelschriften 28 (Stuttgart, 1978), 73–9.
70 App. *B. Civ* 4.454.
71 App. *B. Civ.* 2.290; Flor. 2.13.44.
72 Lib. *Or.* 18.37; though in *Or.* 1.31a Julian says that Vetranio's force was larger.
73 For a good summary see Southern and Dixon, *The Late Roman Army*, 67–70.
74 Amm. Marc. 15.12.3 on the practice of self-mutilation to avoid service; *CTh.* 7.22.1 (313), 7.13.5 (368), 7.13.10 (381), decreeing increasingly harsh penalties for the practice; *CTh.* 7.18.4 (380), 7.18.6 (382), 7.18.9 (396), 7.18.14 (403) on desertion.
75 Jones, *Later Roman Empire*, 615–16.
76 Amm. Marc. 17.3.1–5.
77 For the text see Mommsen ad loc. The mss offer only *proto . . . munus*, which he would restore as *prototypiae*.
78 See p. 53 below.
79 Amm. Marc. 16.12.43, 26.7.17, 31.7.11 with Matthews, *Roman Empire of Ammianus*, 296, on the *barritus*; Amm. Marc. 16.12.2, 31.10.3 for communications with Matthews, *Roman Empire of Ammianus*, 316–17.
80 Matthews, *Roman Empire of Ammianus*, 317, but see Elton, *Warfare in Roman Europe*, 145–52, suggesting that the number of Germans is less than commonly assumed. He suggests that two-thirds of the army was still raised within the empire. This

view is based on the number of attested German names, but this is not a particularly reliable indicator, as Germans might take Roman names, as he concedes on
pp. 146–47.

81 Elton, *Warfare in Roman Europe*, 138–45, for a good discussion of the "loyalty"
issue.

82 See the very interesting suggestions in W. E. Kaegi, "Constantine's and Julian's
Strategies of Strategic Surprise against the Persians," *Athenaeum* 59 (1981): 209–13,
who notes that writings of Constantine on how to fight the Persians were extant
in the sixth century.

83 Seeck, *Geschichte des Untergangs*, 4: 25; Barnes, *Constantine and Eusebius*, 259,
adducing *RIC* 7, 584, no. 100 (silver from the mint at Constantinople), 589–90,
nos. 145–48 (bronze from Constantinople). For his appointment to Pontus and
Armenia see *Origo* 35: *Ponticarum regionum*; [Aur. Vict.] *Epit. de Caes.* 41.20:
Armeniam nationesque circumsocias.

84 Barnes, *New Empire*, 8 and *PLRE* Dalmatius 7, p. 241, for details.

85 Seeck, *Geschichte des Untergangs*, 4: 25.

86 Euseb. *Vit. Const.* 4.61.3 with R. Burgess, "ΑΧΥΡΩΝ or ΠΡΟΑΣΤΕΙΟΝ: The
Location and Circumstances of Constantine's Death," *JTS* 50 (1999): 153–61.

87 MacCormack, *Art and Ceremony*, 117–19.

88 Mango, "Constantine's Mausoleum," 51–60.

89 For the chronology of the massacre see Seeck, *Geschichte des Untergangs*, 4: 391–92,
n. 34. The crucial point is whether Julian was eight or in the eighth year of life,
as correctly given by Soz. *Hist. eccl.* 5.2.9. Since Julian was born in November or
December 331, the massacre of his family needs to be placed at the very end of
337 or early in 338.

90 Zos. 2.40.3; Euseb. *Vit. Const.* 61.3 on the role of the army.

91 Aur. Vict. *De Caes.* 41.15.

92 Zos. 2.40.2, referring to a plot; Phil. *HE* 2.16, reporting the poisoning; see also
Eutrop. *Brev.* 10.9.1; [Aur. Vict.] *Epit. de Caes.* 41.18 and the lucid discussion by
E. D. Hunt, "The Successors of Constantine," in *The Cambridge Ancient History*, vol.
13, ed. Cameron and Garnsey, 4.

93 Euseb. *Vit. Const.* 51.

94 Amm. Marc. 22.3.10.

95 Jul. *Or.* 1.18d–19a.

96 Seeck, *Geschichte des Untergangs*, 4: 65 rightly adduces Jul. *Or.* 1.18d as evidence
that the Armenian revolt resumed while the brothers were meeting at Viminacium.
He is incorrect, however, in seeing this as a prelude to Sapor's first attack on Nisibis,
on which see n. 131 below.

97 R. J. Lane Fox, "The Itinerary of Alexander: Constantius to Julian," *CQ* 47 (1995):
247; T. D. Barnes, "Two Senators under Constantine," *JRS* 65 (1975): 49.

98 See also Seeck, *Geschichte des Untergangs*, 4: 40, noting that the diocese of Thrace
was "naturally" attached to the east as under Licinius.

99 See also the similar treatment in Jul. *Or.* 2.94a–95a.

100 Seeck, *Geschichte des Untergangs*, 4: 45; the view of the inferiority of Constans was
expanded by J. R. Palanque, "Collégialité et partages dans l'émpire romain," *REA*
46 (1944): 58; and Stein, *Histoire du Bas-Empire*, 132 (Constans in a subordinate
position), based on Zos. 2.29.2 (not actually what Zosimus says anyway); the
extreme view is rejected, correctly, by T. D. Barnes, "Imperial Chronology, AD
337–350," *Phoenix* (1980): 160; and Cuneo, *La legislazione*, xl–xliii.

101 Aur. Vict. *De Caes.* 41.21; Zos. 2.41.1 with *CTh.* 12.1.27 and Seeck, *Geschichte des
Untergangs*, 4: 399–400 (nn. to p. 46, ll. 7, 16).

102 Amm. Marc. 20.6.2.

103 Zos. 2.41.1, a confused passage.
104 [Aur. Vict.] *Epit. de Caes.* 41.21; Zon. 13.5.7–14.
105 Zos. 2.40.3; Eunap. *VS* 464; Jer. *Chron.* 338 with *PLRE*, p. 4.
106 Amm. Marc. 21.16.8–9.
107 Socrates, *Hist. eccl.* 2.7–8; Ath. *Hist. Ar.* 7.1, 3 with Barnes, *Athanasius and Constantius*, 212–13, for the date, and Dagron, *Naissance d'une capitale*, 423–24, 427–28, on the circumstances and significance.
108 Socrates, *Hist. eccl.* 2.13; Soz. *Hist. eccl.* 3.7; Amm. Marc. 14.10.2; *PLRE* Hermogenes 1, pp. 422–23.
109 Ath. *Encyc. ep.* 6.3 with Barnes, *Athanasius and Constantius*, 42–43; at this stage Athanasius still blamed his troubles on Eusebius and other ecclesiastical enemies; see M. Humphries, "*In Nomine Patris*: Constantine the Great and Constantius II," *Historia* 46 (1997): 455.
110 Ath. *Apol. contra Ar.* 3.5–7, defending Athanasius on the charge of murder after his return. For the date of the council attacking him see Barnes, *Athanasius and Constantius*, 36.
111 Ath. *Apol. ad Const.* 41, *Apol. contra Ar.* 5 with Barnes, *Athanasius and Constantius*, 41–45.
112 Ath. *Encyc. ep.* 2.1 with Barnes, *Athanasius and Constantius*, 45–46.
113 *Collectanea Antiariana Parisina*, ser. A iv 1, 26 (*CSEL* vol. 65, 65).
114 See Kelly, *Early Christian Doctrines*, 248–49 for a succinct summary; in more detail see Hanson, *The Search*, 284–92 (Antioch in 341); 293–306 (Serdica); 325–29 (Sirmium in 351); 329–34 (Arles and Milan); 357–86 (Ariminium, Seleucia and Constantinople).
115 Amm. Marc. 21.16.18.
116 P. 489 below.
117 Paulinus, *V. Amb.* 2.4, merely stating that Ambrose lost his father.
118 Barnes, *Athanasius and Constantius*, 224–25; Hunt, "The Successors of Constantine," 8–9.
119 *CTh.* 16.10.2 with p. 433 above.
120 Chastagnol, *Les fastes*, 121–23.
121 Cuneo, *La legislazione*, 104.
122 Barnes, "Statistics and the Conversion," 144.
123 Frend, *The Donatist Church*, 177–82; Hunt, "The Successors of Constantine," 9–10.
124 D. H. Williams, "Defining Orthodoxy in Hilary of Poitiers' Commentarium in Matthaeum," *JECS* 9 (2001): 151–71, argues that western bishops may not even have been very familiar with the Nicene Creed at this point.
125 Frend, *The Donatist Church*, 170.
126 Socrates, *Hist. eccl.* 2.20.
127 Williams, "Defining Orthodoxy," 167.
128 *Collectanea Antiariana Parisina*, 128–29 (synodial letter of Julius); Socrates, *Hist. eccl.* 2.22 with H. Hess, *The Canons of the Council of Sardica, AD 343: A Landmark in the Early Development of Canon Law* (Oxford, 1958), 7–18; for the rhetoric of western bishops, who, like Athanasius at this period, blamed Eusebius and his supporters so as to avoid a direct attack on Constantius, see Humphries, "*In Nomine Patris*," 458–59.
129 See now W. Portmann, "Die politische Krise zwischen den Kaisern Constantius II. und Constans," *Historia* 48 (1999): 300–29, esp. 305–7.
130 Portmann, "Die politische Krise," 307–10.
131 See Lib. *Or.* 49.2, 59.73–76; Zon. 13.5.6 with Burgess, *Eusebian and Post-Eusebian Chronography*, 233–38, with reference to earlier bibliography, the bulk of which followed Seeck, *Geschichte des Untergangs*, 4: 65 and 411, n. 26, in placing the invasion in 338.

132 Amm. Marc. 25.8.17 with Lightfoot, "Facts and Fiction," 107; Pollard, *Soldiers, Cities, and Civilians*, 286–87.

133 For Ephraim's background see R. Murray, "The Characteristics of Earliest Syriac Christianity," in *East of Byzantium: Syria and Armenia in the Formative Period*, ed. N. G. Garsoïan, T. F. Matthews, and R. W. Thomson, Dumbarton Oaks Symposium, 1980 (Washington, 1982), 6–9; and S. Brock, "From Antagonism to Assimilation: Syriac Attitudes to Greek Learning," in Garsoïan, Matthews, and Thomson, *East of Byzantium*, 19–20.

134 For the essentially defensive posture of Constantius as depicted in contemporary accounts see R. Seager, "Perceptions of Eastern Frontier Policy in Ammianus, Libanius, and Julian (337–363)," *CQ* 47 (1997): 253–62.

135 Amm. Marc. 18.6.3, 19.1.3 with Matthews, *Roman Empire of Ammianus*, 58.

136 Amm. Marc. 19.1.7, 2.1–2.

137 See Matthews, *Roman Empire of Ammianus*, 58.

138 For the Armenian revolt see Jul. *Or.* 1.19a with note 131 above; for the restoration and the course of Constantius' operations in 338 see Jul. *Or.* 1.20d–21a and Seeck, *Geschichte des Untergangs*, 4: 65–66 with p. 412 (n. to p. 65, l. 31).

139 Jul. *Or.* 1.21b.

140 The date of the battle is in dispute (and there have been suggestions that there were two, based upon the different dates implied in the sources). The evidence is set out and discussed with brevity in Seeck, *Geschichte des Untergangs*, 4: 424 (n. to p. 92, l. 2), suggesting that the text of Jul. *Or* 1.26b, where it is stated that the battle took place six years before the revolt of Magnentius, is corrupt. His view is supported by R. C. Blockley, "Constantius II and Persia," in *Studies in Latin Literature and Roman History*, ed. C. Deroux, vol. 5 (Brussels, 1989), 465–90 (see esp. 475–77). The case for two battles is made by W. Portmann, "Die 59. Rede des Libanios und das datum der Schlacht von Singara," *BzZ* 82 (1989): 1–18. J. Vanderspoel demonstrates that Themistius *Or.* 1 should be dated to 347 (*Themistius and the Imperial Court: Oratory, Civic Duty, and Paideia from Constantius to Theodosius* [Ann Arbor, 1995], 74). For discussion (and rejection) of 348, a date obtained from the chronicle tradition, see Burgess, *Eusebian and Post-Eusebian Chronography*, 270–71. The case for 344 is now stated with an exhaustive review of the evidence by K. Mosig-Walburg, "Zur Schlacht bei Singara," *Historia* 48 (1999): 330–84, showing, conclusively, that there was one battle and tracing the evolution of errors in the tradition.

141 Jul. *Or.* 1.24a–25b.

142 Lightfoot, "Facts and Fiction," 111.

143 Festus, *Brev.* 27 with Portmann, "Die 59. Rede des Libanios," 14–18.

144 For the chronology of his works, with reference to earlier literature, see Barnes, "Constantine and Christians," 127–30; K. Valavanolickal, *Aphrahat: Demonstrations* (Changanassery, 1999), 1–8.

145 For the confusion of Severus with Galerius see Barnes, "Constantine and Christians," 134.

146 For the belief that Philip was a Christian see Potter, *Prophecy and History*, 267–68.

147 *Dem.* 5.5, 12, 18, 19.

148 Jul. *Or.* 1.10b, 17c–d, 41c–d, 43c–d, 45d–46a, 2.96b.

149 Jul. *Or.* 1.28b–d, 29a–b, 42c (Xerxes); note also 32b (Odysseus and Nestor), 32c (Scipio Aemilianus), 32a, 33b–c, 44a (the younger Cyrus), 41c (Cyrus the Great), 44a (Agesilaus).

150 For the identification see Lane Fox, "The Itinerary of Alexander," 242–45.

151 *It. Alex.* 2.

152 Amm. Marc. 17.5.5 with Matthews, *Roman Empire of Ammianus*, 39–40. The preface, *rex regum Sapor, particeps siderum, frater Solis et Lunae*, has a ring of authenticity; see G. Widengren, "Iran, der grosse Gegner Roms: Königsgewalt, Feudalismus, Militärwesen," *ANRW* 2.9.1 (1976): 231; Whitby, "Persian King at War," 245. For the earlier Sasanids see p. 223 above.

153 P. 467 above.

154 *PLRE*, p. 292. His influence under Constans is stated by Libanius at *Or.* 14.10 and implied in Ath. *Ap. ad Const.* 3. The extremely negative picture offered by Libanius must reflect Constantius' attitude and is no basis upon which to judge his career.

155 Zos. 2.49.1; see also Jul. *Or.* 2.96a.

156 *PLRE* 546 (Marcellinus); for his role see esp. Zos. 2.42.2; *PLRE* 918 (Titianus); Chastagnol, *Les fastes*, 107–11.

157 Zos. 2.42.2–4.

158 Zos. 2.42.5; [Aur. Vict.] *Epit. de Caes.* 41.23. Gaiso (*PLRE*, p. 380) would be elevated to the consulship with Magnentius in 351. There is no evidence to support the suggestion in *PLRE* that he was Magnentius' *magister militum*.

159 For Anicetus see *PLRE*, pp. 66–67; for Hermogenes see Chastagnol, *Les fastes*, 130 (*PLRE* 423 Hermogenes 3). Chastagnol identifies him with the Hermogenes who is *PLRE* 423 Hermogenes 4) and *PLRE* Hermogenes 9 (pp. 424–45), a pagan official who served under Licinius and Constantine, following J.-R. Palanque, *Essai sur la préfecture du prétoire du Bas-Empire* (Paris, 1933), 29, n. 92.

160 *PLRE*, p. 624. For the events of his rebellion see Aur. Vict. *De Caes.* 42.6–9 (including the information that he used gladiators as his armed force); Eutrop. *Brev.* 10.11 (also with gladiators); [Aur. Vict.] *Epit. de Caes.* 42.3; Zos. 2.43.2–4 (stating that Nepotianus began his revolt outside the city); Socrates, *Hist. eccl.* 2.25; Soz. *Hist. eccl.* 4.1 (both also with gladiators).

161 Lightfoot, "Facts and Fiction," 112–25.

162 *PLRE* Volcacius Rufinus 23, pp. 782–83; for the significance of this see Hunt, "The Successors of Constantine," 16.

163 *Chron. Pasch.*, p. 539 (Dindorf). For the view accepted in the text, see B. Croke, *Count Marcellinus and His Chronicle* (Oxford, 2001), 183–84, answering the critique of his earlier exposition of this view (B. Croke, "City Chronicles in Late Antiquity," in *Reading the Past in Late Antiquity*, ed. G. Clarke, B. Croke, R. Mortley, and A. E. Nobbs [Sydney, 1990]), rejected in Burgess, *Chronicle of Hydatius*, though he would agree that there is material shared between the *Chronicon* and *Consularia*. See also Phil. *HE* 3.22 and Barnes, *Athanasius and Constantius*, 101.

164 Zon. 13.8, p. 197 (Dindorf) (Silvanus).

165 Zon. 13. 8b, p. 198 (Dindorf).

166 Zos. 2.51.1.

167 Barnes, *Athanasius and Constantius*, 109–10 and p. 487 below.

168 Seeck, *Geschichte des Untergangs*, 4: 142–43.

169 Zon. 13.9, p. 201 (Dindorf).

170 For the shrine of Babylas see G. Downey, *A History of Antioch in Syria from Seleucus to the Arab Conquest* (Princeton, 1961), 364. For Julian's removal of the relics see p. 515 below. For Gallus' intervention in other controversies involving the church, possibly connected with a patronage struggle in connection with the recently converted kingdom of Aksum, see D. Woods, "Three Notes on Aspects of the Arian Controversy c. 354–367 CE," *JTS* 44 (1993): 604–10.

171 Downey, *History of Antioch*, 358–59.

172 Amm. Marc. 14.1.1; Zon. 13.9, pp. 200–1 (Dindorf). Zosimus reflects a very different tradition in which Gallus was the victim of a conspiracy of the eunuchs at Constantius' court (2.55.2).

173 For a different view see E. A. Thompson, *The Historical Work of Ammianus Marcellinus* (Cambridge, 1947), 60–62; and C. Vogler, *Constance II et l'administration impériale* (Strasbourg, 1979), 85, who see the struggle as being between Gallus and the curial class of Antioch supported by members of the civil bureaucracy. This is obviously a feature of what follows, but, I think, secondary to the issue of control.

174 Amm. Marc. 14.1.3.

175 Amm. Marc. 14.1.10.

176 Amm. Marc. 14.7.2.

177 Amm. Marc. 14.7.5.

178 Amm. Marc. 14.7.8–9; *PLRE* Domitianus 3, p. 262.

179 Amm. Marc. 14.7.10; Phil. *HE* 3.28; Zon. 13.9, p. 200.

180 Amm. Marc. 14.11.6–10.

181 Amm. Marc. 14.11.12.

182 Amm. Marc. 14.11.23.

183 *PLRE* Ambrosius 1, p. 51; Marcellinus 16, pp. 548–49; Acindynus 2, p. 11.

184 *PLRE* Limenius 2, p. 510; Rufinus 25, pp. 782–83.

185 Vogler, *Constance II*, 110–44, for a detailed discussion of the reduction in the effective power of the prefects by making them into regional rather than "ministerial" officials.

186 Vogler, *Constance II*, 144.

187 It is possible that the tendency can be traced to the reign of Diocletian and the capture of the harem of Narses, but it is only with Constantine that we get clear attestation of large numbers in the palace. For the suggestion of Diocletian's role see K. Hopkins, "The Political Power of Eunuchs," in *Conquerors and Slaves*, Sociological Studies in Roman History 1 (Cambridge, 1978), 193, though Diocletian's ban on castration within the empire (Amm. Marc. 18.4.5) would suggest that he was not a major user. For the power of eunuchs under Constantine see Socrates, *Hist. eccl.* 2.2 and Soz. *Hist. eccl.* 3.1, who backdate the rise of eunuchs to the reign of Constantius II, but the context (the return of Eusebius of Nicomedia to power) shows that he is in fact writing about the court of Constantine.

188 For Eutherius (*PLRE* Eutherius 1, pp. 314–15) see Amm. Marc. 16.7.5 with Matthews, *Roman Empire of Ammianus*, 275; for Mardonius (*PLRE* Mardonius 1, p. 558) see Julian, *Misop.* 352a–b.

189 Amm. Marc. 15.2.10.

190 Hopkins, "Political Power of Eunuchs," 193, n. 59.

191 There is no clear date for his appointment, and the passages cited in *PLRE* Eusebius 11, p. 302 do not prove that he was *cubicularius*. For a detailed discussion of his career see Vogler, *Constance II*, 212–16.

192 Amm. Marc. 18.4.3.

193 Matthews, *Roman Empire of Ammianus*, 275–76.

194 Lib. *Or.* 62.11.

195 Lib. *Or.* 42.24–25, 62.10 with *PLRE* Datianus 1, p. 243; for Philippus see n. 209 below. See in general Jones, *Later Roman Empire*, 128; H. C. Teitler, *Notarii and Exceptores: An Inquiry into the Role and Significance of Shorthand Writers in the Imperial and Ecclesiastical Bureaucracy of the Roman Empire (from the Early Principate to c. 450 AD)* (Amsterdam, 1985), 34; Vogler, *Constance II*, 192–97.

196 Lib. *Or.* 42.24–25 for both; on the career of Aelius Claudius Dulcitius see *PLRE* Dulcitius 5, p. 274; for Domitianus see n. 178 above.

197 Lib. *Ep.* 359.7, 358.4, 300.2; Amm. Marc. 17.5.15; Lib. *Ep.* 331, 545 (on Spectatus' oratorical skill) with Teitler, *Notarii and Exceptores*, 118–19; *PLRE* Bassus 5 (p. 151) Honoratus 3 (p. 439); Spectatus 1 (p. 850).

198 Lib. *Ep*. 324.2 with Teitler, *Notarii and Exceptores*, 66, 139; *PLRE* Alypius 4, pp. 46–47; Hierocles 1 (p. 431).
199 Lib. *Or*. 42.25 and p. 463 above.
200 Lib. *Ep*. 136 with Teitler, *Notarii and Exceptores*, 148.
201 Teitler, *Notarii and Exceptores*, 49–56.
202 For Athanasius see Teitler, *Notarii and Exceptores*, 116.
203 Amm. Marc. 14.11.21, 23; *PLRE* Pentadius 2, p. 687.
204 Amm. Marc. 17.9.7; *PLRE* Gaudentius 3, p. 386; Amm. Marc. 20.9.1 (Pentadius); Amm. Marc. 20.4.2; *PLRE* Decentius 1, p. 244.
205 Amm. Marc. 17.14.3; for Procopius' attainments see Teitler, *Notarii and Exceptores*, 162.
206 Ath. *Hist. Ar. ad. mon*. 31.2.
207 R. C. Blockley, "Constantius II and His Generals," in *Studies in Latin Literature and Roman History*, ed. C. Deroux, vol. 2 (Brussels, 1980), 472–75.
208 Amm. Marc. 15.5.28.
209 *PLRE* Philippus 7, pp. 696–97 with Lib. *Or*. 52.11. For Rufinus see n. 162 above.
210 Amm. Marc. 15.5.4 with *PLRE* Volusianus 5, pp. 978–79; Eusebius 6, p. 302; Aedesius 7, pp. 15–16.
211 Blockley, "Constantius II and His Generals," 471, is important on structural issues leading to conflict.
212 Amm. Marc. 14.5.6–9.
213 Amm. Marc. 14.9.5–6, 15.6.1–2.
214 Amm. Marc. 15.5.2–3; for Dynamius' earlier contact with Constantius see Zos. 2.55.2 and *PLRE* Dynamius 2, p. 275.
215 Amm. Marc. 15.5.6; for the ethnic origins of the two men see *PLRE* Malarichus, p. 538, and *PLRE* Mallobaudes, p. 539.
216 Amm. Marc. 15.5.6.
217 Amm. Marc. 15.5.11.
218 Amm. Marc. 15.5.31.
219 Amm. Marc. 15.5.12–14.
220 Amm. Marc. 15.6.1–4.
221 Amm. Marc. 15.3.7–11.
222 Amm. Marc. 14.7.18, 9.5–6.
223 Amm. Marc. 14.7.19–20, 9.7–9.
224 Ath. *Hist. Ar. ad. mon*. 31.3.
225 See also Vogler, *Constance II*, 281–87.
226 For details see Barnes, *Athanasius and Constantius*, 118.
227 Barnes, *Athanasius and Constantius*, 117–20.
228 Humphries, "*In Nomine Patris*," 455–62.
229 Amm. Marc. 16.5.3; Vogler, *Constance II*, 96.

13 THE STRUGGLE FOR CONTROL: 355–66

1 Jul. *Ep. Ath*. 277d.
2 See the important discussion of E. D. Hunt, "Did Constantius II Have 'Court Bishops'?" *Studia Patristica* 19 (1989): 86–90, who shows that even people closely associated with Constantine like Ursacius and Valens were advisers rather than functionaries.
3 Amm. Marc. 16.10.20.
4 Barnes, *Athanasius and Constantius*, 231–32.
5 Ath. *De synod*. 28.
6 Hil. *In Constant*. 15.

7 Hil. *Liber ad Constantium* 8.2: *memento eam non in quaestione philosophiae esse, sed in evangelii doctrina* (*CSEL* 65, 203).

8 Hil. *Collectanea Antiariana Parisina*, ser. A viii, 2 (*CSEL* 65, 94).

9 Ath. *De synod.* 8–9; Socrates, *Hist. eccl.* 2.37; Soz. *Hist. eccl.* 17.2–18.15; Hil. *Collectanea Antiariana Parisina* ser. A v, 1 (*CSEL* 65, 79–85).

10 Hil. *Collectanea Antiariana Parisina*, ser. A v, 2–3, vi, 2 (*CSEL* 65, 85–90). For Constantius' movements see Barnes, *Athanasius and Constantius*, 223.

11 Barnes, *Athanasius and Constantius*, 146–49, for analysis of the sources.

12 *Chron. Pasch.* a. 360; Socrates, *Hist. eccl.* 2.41.5–7; Phil. *Hist. eccl.* 4.12; Soz. *Hist. eccl.* 4.24.1; Theod. *Hist. eccl.* 2.26.11.

13 *CTh.* 16.10.6 with Cuneo, *La legislazione*, 288.

14 For the ban on divination see *CTh.* 9.16.4–5; *CJ* 9.18.5–6 with Cuneo, *La legislazione*, 308–10 and Lib. *Or.* 30.7.

15 J. E. Goehring, "The Origins of Monasticism," in *Eusebius, Christianity, and Judaism*, ed. H. W. Attridge and G. Hata (Detroit, 1992) (also in Goehring, *Ascetics, Society, and the Desert: Studies in Early Egyptian Monasticism* [Harrisburg, 1999]), 35, correctly observes that there is no single source for monasticism; see also Hopkins, "Christian Number," suggesting that the vast increase in the number of Christians made it harder to define a single form of Christian conduct. That said, it remains significant that the movement drew its strength from one area of the Roman Empire.

16 A. Meredith, "Asceticism – Christian and Greek," *JTS* 27 (1976): 313–32, esp. 331; P. Brown, "Asceticism: Pagan and Christian," in Cameron and Garnsey, *The Cambridge Ancient History*, 13: 601–5.

17 R. Parker, *Miasma: Pollution and Purification in Early Greek Religion* (Oxford, 1983), 85–86.

18 *IGLS* 2928; the text is in Latin, and Hochmaea may not have understood the implication of the standard formula *v.l.a.s.* that she had fulfilled her vow, which would explain the text inscribed along with this one stating that she had fulfilled the vow. Hochmaea may also be the individual commemorated on the funeral stele that is *IGLS* 2929, which identifies her as the virgin prophet of Dea Syria Nihatena (rendered Atargatis in an accompanying Greek text, which states that she lived to be one hundred years old). See also Milik, *Dédicaces faites par des dieux*, 374–75; Lightfoot, *Lucian: On the Syrian Goddess*, 82–83.

19 For the possible influence of Manichaean communities on the development of Christian ascetic communities see Koenen, "Manichäische Mission"; G. Stroumsa, "The Manichaean Challenge to Egyptian Christianity," in Pearson and Goehring, *Roots of Egyptian Christianity*, 307–19.

20 Elm, *Virgins of God*, 25–59; E. A. Wipszycka, "Le monachisme égyptien et les villes," in *Travaux et Mémoires*, Collège de France Centre de researche d'histoire et civilization de Byzance 12 (Paris, 1994), 1–44 (also in Wipszycka, *Études sur le christianisme dans l'Égypte de l'antiquité tardive* [Rome, 1996], 241–42).

21 Jer. *Ep.* 22.34; John Cass. *Conlationes* 18.4–7 and papyrological evidence gathered in E. A. Judge, "The Earliest Use of Monachos for 'Monk' (P. Coll. Youtie 77) and the Origins of Monasticism," *JAC* 20 (1977): 77–89; E. A. Judge, "Fourth Century Monasticism in the Papyri," in *Proceedings of the Sixteenth International Congress of Papyrology, New York, 24–31 July 1980*, ed. R. Bagnall, G. M. Browne, A. E. Hanson, and L. Koenen (Chico, Calif., 1981), 616–17; A. Emmett, "Female Ascetics in the Greek Papyri," in *Akten: XVI Internationaler Byzantinistenkongress Wien 4–9. Oktober 1981*, ed. W. Hörander, *JÖB* 23.2 (Vienna, 1982), 507–15; J. E. Goehring, "Through a Glass Darkly: Images of the Ἀποτακτοί (αἱ) in early Egyptian Monastacism," in *Discursive Formations, Ascetic Piety, and the Interpretation of Early*

Christian Literature, ed. V. L. Wimbush, pt. 2 (also in *Semeia* 58 [1992]: 25–45; also in Goehring, *Ascetics, Society, and the Desert: Studies in Early Egyptian Monasticism* [Harrisburg, 1999], 53–72). See also E. Wipszycka, "P. Coll. Youtie 77 = P. Coll. 171 Revisited," in *Essays in Honor of J. David Thomas*, ed. T. Gagos and R. Bagnall (Exeter, 2001), 45–50, arguing that Isaac the monk was not an *apotaktos*. For what may be earlier, polytheistic, uses of the term monk, see G. Clark, "Philosophic Lives and the Philosophic Life: Porphyry and Iamblichus," in Hägg and Rousseau, *Greek Biography and Panegyric*, 45.

22 P. Brown, "The Rise and Function of the Holy Man in Late Antiquity," *JRS* 61 (1971): 80–101 (also in Brown, *Society and the Holy in Late Antiquity* [London, 1982], 103–52) remains a classic, but see also the significant afterthoughts in P. Brown, *Authority and the Sacred: Aspects of the Christianization of the Roman World* (Cambridge, 1995), 57–78.

23 See Porph. *Abstin.* 1.32–39; for the contrast between polytheistic and monastic forms of asceticism offered here see Clark, "Philosophic Lives," 46–47, upon which what follows here is derivative.

24 P. 36 above.

25 Bagnall, *Egypt in Late Antiquity*, 268.

26 Hopkins, "Christian Number," 217–21, on the importance of the switch from definition by practice to definition by ideology.

27 See now the excellent discussion of the text in G. J. M. Bartelink's edition (Athanase d'Alexandrie, *Vie d'Antoine, SC* no. 400 [Paris, 1994]). Bartelink provides an excellent review of scholarship on pp. 27–37 defending Athanasian authorship and showing that the Syriac version of the life does not, as has been argued, go back to an earlier Coptic life. There is no need to repeat the arguments on either side here, though see the fresh case for skepticism advanced in P. Rousseau, "Antony as Teacher in the Greek *Life*," in Hägg and Rousseau, *Greek Biography and Panegyric*, 100–4.

28 Ath. *V. Ant.* 89.3.

29 Ath. *V. Ant.* 2.1–5, 3.1. For the significance of the story that he was "illiterate" and moved by hearing scripture see S. Rubenson, *The Letters of St. Anthony: Monasticism and the Making of a Saint* (Minneapolis, 1995), 142, and Rousseau, "Antony as Teacher," 91–92.

30 Ath. *V. Ant.* 5–6, 16.8, 17.2, 22.2 (on the nature of demons), 35–43.

31 For the cures see, e.g., Ath. *V. Ant.* 48.2, 56.1–2, 57.1, 58.5, 61.1, 71.2.

32 See, in general, M. W. Gleason, "Visiting and News: Gossip and Reputation Management in the Desert," *JECS* 6 (1998): 501–21.

33 Bartelink, *Vie d'Antoine*, 61–62.

34 A. Veilleux, *La liturgie dans le cénobitisme pachômien du quatrième siècle, Studia Anselmiana* 57 (Rome, 1968), 174.

35 Ath. *V. Ant.* 68–69; Ath. *V. Ant.* 69–71 (visit to Alexandria), 82, 86 (Balacius). For the visit to Alexandria contrast *Chron. Ath.* 10 showing that Antony stayed in Alexandria for two days in 337 and left before Athanasius returned from exile. For Balacius and Antony see the rather different narrative in Ath. *Hist Ar. ad mon.* 14 with Brakke, *Athanasius*, 204–7.

36 Ath. *V. Ant.* 72–73 (philosophers), 67.1 (bows to leaders of the church).

37 See also D. H. Raynor, "Non-Christian Attitudes to Monasticism," *Studia Patristica* 18, no. 2 (1983): 270, on the context for Athanasius' need to present a "tame" Antony.

38 Jer. *De vir. Ill.* 88; the collection is edited with a good introduction by Rubenson, *Letters of St. Anthony*.

39 Rubenson, *Letters of St. Anthony*, 4; Brakke, *Athanasius*, 208–13, and, for the letter, *P. London* 1658 (also in M. Naldini, *Cristianesimo in Egitto: Lettere private nei Papiri dei Secoli ii–iv* [Fiesole, 1998], no. 42; I am grateful to Professor Traianos Gagos for bringing this book to my attention).

40 Brakke, *Athanasius*, 215–16.

41 H. I. Bell, *Jews and Christians in Egypt: The Jewish Troubles in Alexandria and the Athanasian Controversy Illustrated by Texts from Greek Papyri in the British Museum* (London, 1924) (also in *P. London* 6, 101). Bell identified Paphnutius as a pro-Athanasian monk; the case that he was in fact a Melitian is argued in B. Kramer and J. C. Skelton (with G. M. Browne), *Das Archiv des Nepheros und verwandte Texte* (Mainz, 1987), 23, n. 7, suggesting that the language associated with him is also that associated with Nepheros, whom the editors view as Melitian. It is not clear to me that the evidence cited proves the case either way. R. Bagnall, "Count Ausonius," *Tyche* 7 (1992): 9–13, identifies the Ausonius of *P. London* 1924 as the *praeses*. The question of whether or not Paphnutius was a Melitian does not impact on the prosopographical point.

42 *P. London* 1924.

43 For Paphnutius see n. 41 above; for Psois see Bell, *Jews and Christians*, 43–44.

44 Brakke, *Athanasius*, 223–24; and Bartelink, *Vie d'Antoine*, 58–59.

45 See e.g. Ath. *Ep.* 53, 54.

46 See Ath. *Ep.* 48.65.9–23J, 66.21–67.1J with Brakke, *Athanasius*, 90–91.

47 Ath. *V. Ant.* 81.1.

48 Ruf. *HE* 10.8. I cannot agree with Bartelink (n. ad loc.) that this passage was inspired by Ath. *V. Ant.* 81.1, as it offers details not present in Athanasius.

49 *P. London* 1913.

50 Brakke, *Athanasius*, 101.

51 See also Goehring, "The Origins of Monasticism" (also in Goehring, *Ascetics, Society, and the Desert*).

52 Gardiner and Lieu, "From Narmouthis (Medinet Madi) to Kellis (Ismant El-Kharab)," 161–68 on the excavations.

53 Kramer and Skelton, *Das Archiv des Nepheros*, 15–16, on the organization of the monastery, which is also unusual in that it is located at a site that retained an obviously non-Christian name (this too may be an indication of a very early date). The significance of this evidence was recognized in J. E. Goehring, "Melitian Monastic Organization: A Challenge to Pachomian Originality," *Studia Patristica* 25 (1993): 388–95 (also in Goehring, *Ascetics, Society, and the Desert*, 187–95).

54 P. Rousseau, *Pachomius: The Making of a Community in Fourth Century Egypt* (Berkeley, 1985), 59–70, for an excellent analysis of the sources.

55 For Serapion see Rousseau, *Pachomius*, 72; for the issue between them see also J. E. Goehring, "New Frontiers in Pachomian Studies," in Pearson and Goehring, *Roots of Egyptian Christianity*, 246–47.

56 Amm. Marc. 21.15.5, 6.

57 For the notion of a "pagan underground" see Lib. *Or.* 18.20, 22; 13.13; 15.45, 47; 14.41 with the discussion of P. Petit, *Libanius et la vie municipale à Antioche au ive siècle après J.-C.* (Paris, 1955), 204, who fleshes the notion out as a more generalized dislike among polytheist municipal aristocrats for Constantius; for a more limited application of the notion see G. W. Bowersock, *Julian the Apostate* (London, 1978), 30–31. The notion is challenged by J. F. Drinkwater, "The 'Pagan Underground,' Constantius II's 'Secret Service' and the Survival, and the Usurpation of Julian the Apostate," in *Studies in Latin Literature and Roman History*, ed. C. Deroux, vol. 3 (Brussels, 1983), 348–87. I retain the notion for the reasons given in the text despite Drinkwater's impressive discussion, and my agreement with him that Libanius' statements are not helpful.

58 For polytheist recollections of Julian see R. B. E. Smith, *Julian's Gods: Religion and Philosophy in the Thought of Julian the Apostate* (London, 1995), 23; for Julian and Ammianus see Matthews, *Roman Empire of Ammianus*, 469–70; T. D. Barnes, *Ammianus Marcellinus and the Representation of Historical Reality* (Ithaca, NY, 1998), 143–65.
59 Jul. *Mis.* 351b–352b.
60 Jul. *Ep. Ath.* 271b–c.
61 Amm. Marc. 22.11.3.
62 Jul. *Ep.* 106, 107 (Bidez) with Smith, *Julian's Gods*, 25.
63 Eunap. *VS* 473.
64 Socrates, *Hist. eccl.* 3.1.10 with P. Athanassiadi-Fowden, *Julian and Hellenism: An Intellectual Biography* (Oxford, 1981), 26–27; for Nicocles' relationship with Julian see also Lib. *Ep.* 1368.4 with Kaster, *Guardians of Language*, 203. For a more generous (and convincing) picture of Hecebolius than is the norm see Smith, *Julian's Gods*, 26–27, with a defense of the authenticity of Jul. *Ep.* 194 (Bidez) on p. 27, n. 23.
65 For the contact with Themistius at this point see Smith, *Julian's Gods*, 27; Vanderspoel, *Themistius and Imperial Court*, 118–19. For Julian's subsequent letter to Themistius (written while he was in Gaul) see S. Bradbury, "The Date of Julian's Letter to Themistius," *GRBS* 28 (1987): 235–51.
66 Eunap. *VS* 461; see also Smith, *Julian's Gods*, 38, on Aedesius' continuation of Iamblichus' teaching based on Aristotle; the point is an important one, for Aedesius' interests complemented those of Themistius.
67 Eunap. *VS* 460.
68 Eunap. *VS* 458 (golden hue), 459 (spirits).
69 Eunap. *VS* 459; for corpses as a cause of ritual impurity see R. Parker, *Miasma*, 32–48.
70 Eunap. *VS* 469–70. For family groups of philosophers (especially this one) see Smith, *Julian's Gods*, 44 with n. 155.
71 Eunap. *VS* 474–75 with Athanassiadi-Fowden, *Julian and Hellenism*, 33–37, and Smith, *Julian's Gods*, 38, pointing out that Maximus was the author of a work on Aristotle's *Categories*, and thus the continuation of Julian's interest in Aristotelian thought at the same time as he was initiated.
72 Jul. *Ep.* 111 (Bidez) 434d; Smith, *Julian's Gods*, 180–89, for a nuanced discussion.
73 Lib. *Or.* 12.34; contra Drinkwater, "Pagan Underground," 357.
74 P. 503 below.
75 The point is well made by D. Hunt, "Julian," in *The Cambridge Ancient History*, vol. 13, ed. Cameron and Garnsey, 50.
76 Jul. *Ep. Ath.* 272a.
77 Bowersock, *Julian the Apostate*, 39.
78 Jul. *Or.* 3.124b–c; *Ep.* 26 (Bidez) 414c referring to Caes. *B. Gall.* 1.38 (as shown by Bidez); see also Bowersock, *Julian the Apostate*, 36.
79 Amm. Marc. 16.1.8 with Hunt, "Julian," 49; Blockley, "Constantius II and His Generals," 478; Matthews, *Roman Empire of Ammianus*, 88–89.
80 Amm. Marc. 16.2.10–13; for the recapture of Cologne see Bowersock, *Julian the Apostate*, 36.
81 Amm. Marc. 16.10.21.
82 For Severus see Amm. Marc. 16.12.27.
83 For the plan of campaign see Amm. Marc. 16.11.3; for the failure of cooperation see Amm. Marc. 16.11.8–12 with Matthews, *Roman Empire of Ammianus*, 299.
84 Amm. Marc. 16.12.2 (Roman numbers), 16.12.26 (number of Alamanni); for a cogent discussion of the number given by Ammianus for the Alamanni and the

figure used in the text see N. J. E. Austin, "In Support of Ammianus' Veracity," *Historia* 22 (1973): 334–35.

85 For dispositions see Amm. Marc. 16.12.36, 37 (cavalry rally), 42 (Alamanni reach the infantry line after engaging the cavalry – *proinde Alamanni pulsis disiectisque equitibus nostris primam aciem peditum incesserunt*). Although Ammianus says that the cavalry who fled were protecting the right wing, it looks as if they were doing so in advance of the infantry line. For a different reconstruction of the battle see Elton, *Warfare in Roman Europe*, 255–56.

86 Amm. Marc. 16.12.54; on the heaps of bodies see J. Keegan, *The Face of Battle* (Harmondsworth, 1976), 75.

87 Amm. Marc. 16.12.64.

88 Amm. Marc. 16.12.68–70 and Jul. *Ep. Ath.* 279c.

89 Amm. Marc. 16.12.14 and *PLRE* Florentius 10, p. 365.

90 Jul. *Ep. Ath.* 282c with Hunt, "Julian," 54; Matthews, *Roman Empire of Ammianus*, 89.

91 *CTh.* 11.16.7–8.

92 Amm. Marc. 17.3.2–5.

93 Amm. Marc. 17.3.6.

94 See E. M. Wightman, *Gallia Belgica* (Berkeley, 1985), 214.

95 J. Bidez, *L'empereur Julien: Lettres* (Paris, 1924), 7, dates the letter to 359. An earlier date is preferable, as the recall of Salutius is still in prospect when the letter was written.

96 Libanius tells us that this visit took place as the light of Julian's brilliance was beginning to shine (*Or.* 12.55), while Eunapius makes it clear that Priscus had returned to the east before Julian's proclamation (*VS* 471).

97 Amm. Marc. 18.2.15–19.

98 *PLRE* Secundus 3, pp. 814–15.

99 Jul. *Ep. Ath.* 282b; Amm. Marc. 17.9.7 with 21.7.2 and Matthews, *Roman Empire of Ammianus*, 92, for Gaudentius.

100 Amm. Marc. 19.12.13.

101 Amm. Marc. 17.5.3–8; for the authenticity of the language used in this letter, as reported by Ammianus, see E. Winter, *Die sasanidisch–römischen Friedensverträge*, 39–40. For the embassy of Eustathius see Amm. Marc. 17.5.7–15, 17.14, 18.6.17–18.

102 Amm. Marc. 18.5.1–3, 7, 6.3, 19.

103 Amm. Marc. 18.6.6–7.

104 Amm. Marc. 18.6.10–15.

105 Amm. Marc. 19.9.9; for Ammianus' account of the siege see Matthews, *Roman Empire of Ammianus*, 57–65.

106 P. 487 above.

107 Jul. *Ep. Ath.* 282c–d; and Matthews, *Roman Empire of Ammianus*, 94–95.

108 For relative troop strengths see p. 467 above and Amm. Marc. 19.11.17.

109 For Julian's version see Jul. *Ep. Ath.* 282d–285d; Amm. Marc. 20.4; Zos. 3.9 with Bowersock, *Julian the Apostate*, 49–52.

110 Jul. *Ep. Ath.* 283c–284a.

111 Amm. Marc. 21.10.

112 Eunap. *VS* 476 (also in Eunap fr. 21 (Blockley)); Amm. Marc. 21.1.6; for the chronology see Potter, *Prophets and Emperors*, 179 with n. 71. For the identity of the hierophant as Nestorius, whom Eunapius had advised Julian to visit (*VS* 475), see Smith, *Julian's Gods*, 30 with n. 51. See also Jul. *Ep.* 26 (Bidez) 415a for another reference to helpers in consulting the gods.

113 Amm. Marc. 20.6–7.

114 Amm. Marc. 20.11.

115 Amm. Marc. 20.8.19; Zos. 3.9.3; Lib. *Or.* 18.106; the possibility that one purpose of this embassy was to introduce Julian to the cities along the route is canvassed by Ando, *Imperial Ideology*, 195–99. The notion remains attractive despite the fact that this embassy cannot have had anything to do with spreading the notion that Constantius was in communication with the Alamanni, information that only became available (or was only invented) after the surrender of Vadomarius in 361, as is clear even from Julian's own account (*Ep. Ath.* 286b).

116 See esp. Jul. *Caes.* 328d–329d, 335b, 336a–b; but see esp. *ILS* 754, which echoes specifically Constantinian language; see also Firm. Mat. *Math.* 1.13. See also Amm. Marc. 21.10.8, noting an open attack by Julian on the memory of Constantine; see also *CTh.* 2.5.2 (September 3, 362), 3.1.3 (December 6, 362), both specifying that he is rescinding legislation of Constantine; see also Hunt, "Julian," 64. It also looks as if he modeled some of his titulature on that of Magnentius, advertising the title *Romani orbis liberator*, which was picked up on a dedication by the *koinon* of Phoenicia as well as in *ILS* 9465; see now the excellent discussion in K. Dietz, "Kaiser Julian in Phönizien," *Chiron* 30 (2000): 814–15.

117 Amm. Marc. 20.9.4; Jul. *Ep. Ath.* 286c. Zos. 3.9.4 offers an interesting misrepresentation of Constantius' response, saying that Constantius ordered him to lay down all power, a version clearly intended to exculpate Julian, and it backdates Julian's espousal of polytheist cult.

118 Amm. Marc. 21.1.4, 21.2.2; Zon. 13.11; Zos. 3.9.6 reports a dream in which Julian foresees the death of Constantius, on which see F. Paschoud, ed., Zosime, *Histoire nouvelle* 2.1 (Paris, 1979), 89, showing that the position of the stars is accurate for November 361, suggesting that the text was produced shortly after the death of Constantius. For the coinage see F. D. Gilliard, "Notes on the Coinage of Julian the Apostate," *JRS* 54 (1964): 136–38, showing that the images are ambiguous – Julian is beardless – but employ symbolism that suggests his authority is derived from the divine rather than his cousin.

119 *Collectanea Antiariana Parisina* A I (*CSEL* 65, 43–46), letter of the Gallic bishops at Paris to the bishops of the east; *Collectanea Antiariana Parisina* A II (*CSEL* 65, 46–47), letter of Eusebius of Vercellae to Gregory of Spain.

120 *Collectanea Antiariana Parisina* A I.4 (*CSEL* 65, 45); for his movements see Barnes, *Athanasius and Constantius*, 153–54, and for his language, Humphries, "*In Nomine Patris*," 458–62.

121 A. Rocher, *Hilaire de Poitiers, Contre Constance, SC*, vol. 334 (Paris, 1987), 36.

122 Amm. Marc. 21.3.4–6. Much was made of these alleged letters, whose authenticity Ammianus doubts – see Jul. *Ep. Ath.* 286b–c; Lib. *Or.* 18.107, 113; Socrates, *Hist. eccl.* 3.1.38; Soz. *Hist. eccl.* 5.2.23; *Pan.* 11 (3) 6.1; Zos. 3.9.7 with Paschoud in Zosime, *Histoire nouvelle*, 90, showing that Zosimus' displacement of Julian's worship of the gods is used to explain Constantius' actions, thus piling distortion upon distortion in Eunapius' account.

123 Amm. Marc. 21.7.1 (Constantius moves as far as Edessa).

124 Amm. Marc. 21.13.1–5.

125 Amm. Marc. 21.13.7 clarifies the chronology.

126 Amm. Marc. 21.8.1–3, 9.5–8; Zos. 3.10.2–3.

127 Amm. Marc. 21.8.3.

128 Amm. Marc. 21.11.1–12, 21.

129 Amm. Marc. 21.10.2–5; Zos. 3.10.4, 11.1, again introducing the theme of divine intervention, suggesting that Julian remained where he was as a result of divine monition.

130 See Jul. *Ep.* 19 (Bidez), telling him that he had arranged for a ship to carry him to safety; the letter was written when Julian was openly at war with Constantius.

131 Amm. Marc. 22.5.1–3.

132 Gilliard, "Notes on Coinage," 136.

133 Jul. *Caes.* 336a–b.

134 P. 515 below.

135 P. 328 above for Porphyry's treatment of Jesus. For Julian's dealings with the Jews see Smith, *Julian's Gods*, 200–2; F. Millar, "Greco-Roman Diaspora," 106–7, pointing out that Julian resisted the claim that the God of Moses was the Lord of All Things, while respecting Jewish sacrificial cult.

136 Smith, *Julian's Gods*, 202–3.

137 See esp. Smith, *Julian's Gods*, 111–12, for a nuanced discussion; for a different approach see Athanassiadi-Fowden, *Julian and Hellenism*, 161–91, who stresses Julian's philosophic side more heavily.

138 For the Mithraeum see Lib. *Or.* 18.127 and Him. *Or.* 41.1 with T. D. Barnes, "Himerius and the Fourth Century," *CPh* 82 (1987): 221–22 (also in Barnes, *From Eusebius to Augustine*, chap. 16); for this explanation of Julian's "bull coinage" see Barnes, *Ammianus Marcellinus*, 159–60. For another view see Gilliard, "Notes on Coinage," 148–51.

139 Amm. Marc. 22.12.6.

140 Amm. Marc. 23.5.10, 13, 25.2.7–8 with Matthews, *Roman Empire of Ammianus*, 126–27. But see n. 122 above for Eunapius' version, which exalted the opinions of the philosophers. Ammianus may, in part, be responding to this form of historiography; it may be significant that Libanius does not mention the philosophers who accompanied Julian until he describes his death (*Or.* 17.26, 18.272–73), perhaps because he too was aware of complaints like those voiced by Ammianus.

141 Eunap. *VS* 478.

142 Jul. *Mis.* 361d–362c.

143 Jul. *Ep.* 88 (Bidez) 450b.

144 Jul. *Ep.* 79 (Bidez) with Bowersock, *Julian the Apostate*, 85.

145 Jul. *Ep.* 89a (Bidez) 452d–453c; for the prior relationship between Julian and Theodorus (also an associate of Maximus) see Athanassiadi-Fowden, *Julian and Hellenism*, 185, n. 95; Smith, *Julian's Gods*, 36.

146 Jul. *Ep.* 84 (Bidez) 430a–d; Bowersock, *Julian the Apostate*, 87; Smith, *Julian's Gods*, 111.

147 Jul. *Ep.* 78 (Bidez) 375c.

148 Jul. *Ep.* 84 (Bidez) 429c with Bowersock, *Julian the Apostate*, 87.

149 Amm. Marc. 22.73 (his greeting of Maximus). For Maximus' display on the way to join Julian see Eunap. *VS* 477. Compare also his conduct with reference to Libanius (Lib. *Or* 1.129) and n. 183 below.

150 Jul. *Ep.* 86 (Bidez).

151 Phil. *Hist. eccl.* p. 235 (Bidez) (extract from Theophanes).

152 Vanderspoel, *Themistius and Imperial Court*, 125–26, though see the contrary view of Smith, *Julian's Gods*, 28–29, suggesting that there was not a serious split, and T. Brauch, "Themistius and the Emperor Julian," *Byzantion* 63 (1993): 79–115, who is correct in seeing that Themistius' ability to compromise was not atypical, though I think that this was in fact the essence of his problem with Julian. See also R. M. Errington, "Themistius and His Emperors," *Chiron* 30 (2000): 901–2, for a plausible suggestion as to how the tradition could have arisen later that Themistius held office under Julian.

153 Jul. *Ep.* 31 and Eunap. *VS* 493.

154 Jul. *Ep.* 32 with Bowersock, *Julian the Apostate*, 64.

155 Amm. Marc. 22.6.7.

156 Jul. *Ep.* 60 (Bidez) 379a–b.

157 Amm. Marc. 22.6.9–11.

158 Jul. *Ep.* 60 (Bidez), 379d–380b with Bowersock, *Julian the Apostate*, 83.

159 Soz. *Hist. eccl.* 5.3.5.

160 For Ephraim's poems against Julian see now K. McVey, *Ephraim the Syrian: Hymns* (Mahwah, 1989), 221–57 and p. 520 below.

161 Soz. *Hist. eccl.* 5.4.2–5.

162 Jul. *Ep.* 114 (Bidez) 436b.

163 Jul. *Ep.* 114 (Bidez) 437c–438c.

164 Soz. *Hist. eccl.* 5.3.6–9.

165 Amm. Marc. 22.6.

166 Jul. *Ep.* 112 (Bidez) 376b–c (written in the emperor's own hand).

167 Jul. *Ep.* 110 (Bidez) 398d.

168 Theod. *HE* 3.4.1–5; Socrates, *Hist. eccl.* 3.9; with the admirably clear summary in Downey, *History of Antioch*, 396–97.

169 Amm. Marc. 22.10.7, 25.4.20–21.

170 Amm. Marc. 23.1.2–3 (placing events five months too early); the point was taken by Cyril of Jerusalem, and picked up by Socrates, *Hist. eccl.* 3.20.7–8, whence also Soz. *Hist. eccl.* 5.22.4–6; see also Phil. *Hist. eccl.* 7.9, 14. For the Gospel prophecies see Matt. 24:2, Mark 13:2, Luke 19:44, 21:6, as well as Dan. 9:27 with Smith, *Julian's Gods*, 217. S. Brock, "The Rebuilding of the Temple under Julian: A New Source," *PEQ* 108 (1976): 103–7, is crucial for the chronology and what may actually have happened (an earthquake). The text is printed in S. Brock, "A Letter Attributed to Cyril of Jerusalem on the Rebuilding of the Temple," *BSOAS* 40 (1977): 267–86. See also F. Blanchetière, "Julien philhellène, philosémite, antichrétien," *Journal of Jewish Studies* 31 (1980), 61–81, who argues that the reconstruction of the temple should not simply be seen as an anti-Christian measure, but as one taken because Julian saw the restoration of the sacrificial cult as beneficial to the empire as a whole.

171 Amm. Marc. 22.4.1–10; Lib. *Or.* 18.130–39; but see also Lib. *Or.* 18.155–56, praising Julian for his reception of Maximus.

172 Amm. Marc. 22.7.1–4; contrast Lib. *Or.* 18.146–49, praising Julian's edict concerning town councils; Jul. *Mis.* 368a, justifying it; 370d, admitting that it was unpopular.

173 Amm. Marc. 22.3 with Thompson, *Historical work of Ammianus*, 73–79, for the view accepted in the text.

174 Amm. Marc. 22.3.3–8.

175 Lib. *Or.* 18.180.

176 For Gallus' activity see p. 474 above.

177 Amm. Marc. 22.12.8 obscures the significance of Julian's action; see otherwise Socrates, *Hist. eccl.* 3.18; Theod. *Hist. eccl.* 3.10; Soz. *Hist. eccl.* 5.19; Ruf. *Hist. eccl.* 10.36; John Chrys. *De S. Bab.* 2–3; Lib. *Or.* 60.5–6; Zon. 13.12 with Downey, *History of Antioch*, 364, n. 217, 387; Matthews, *Roman Empire of Ammianus*, 429–31.

178 Amm. Marc. 22.13.1–3. The investigation of the incident appears to have given rise to a series of Christian martyr stories, on the significance of which see Barnes, *Ammianus Marcellinus*, 53.

179 Jul. *Mis.* 349b, 370b, admitting that the increased population had something to do with the shortage.

180 Lib. *Or.* 18.195, 16.21 (both blaming local landholders), 1.126 (a very different view), 15.20 (asking Julian to forgive local landholders in difficult circumstances); Amm. Marc. 22.14.1; Jul. *Mis.* 349d–350a, 369c–d (price-gouging).

181 Jul. *Mis.* 369c–d.

182 See esp. Lib. *Or.* 15.19, 74; Amm. Marc. 22.12.4–5 may reflect this event.

183 For Julian's response to Libanius see Lib. *Or* 1.129; for criticism of his public behavior see Greg. Naz. *Contra Jul.* 2.23.

184 See Lib. *Or.* 18.207, where Constantius' behavior is given as the reason he did not fight the Persians; but see also Amm. Marc. 21.6.2, where Constantius exploits his presence in the circus to make a public-relations point.

185 Mal. 13.19 (p. 328 Dindorf). See also the classic discussion by M. W. Gleason, "Festive Satire: Julian's Misopogon and the New Year at Antioch," *JRS* 76 (1986): 106–20.

186 Gleason, "Festive Satire," 119–20.

187 Amm. Marc. 23.3.5; Lib. *Or.* 1.132.

188 Amm. Marc. 22.12.2, 25.4.26–27.

189 Amm. Marc. 25.4.23; Lib. *Or.* 18.170, admitting that it was expensive.

190 Lib. *Ep.* 1402.2.

191 Lib. *Or.* 17.19, 18.164–65.

192 Amm. Marc. 23.2.2, 3.5; Lib. *Or.* 18.215. But see also Lib. *Or.* 18.260, claiming that Arsaces did not perform as hoped.

193 See also R. T. Ridley, "Notes on Julian's Persian Expedition (363)," *Historia* 22 (1973): 318.

194 For the geography of the campaign see Matthews, *Roman Empire of Ammianus*, 140–61. For a different view of Julian's strategy in the campaign see Barnes, *Ammianus Marcellinus*, 164–65, who suggests that Julian intended to force Sapor into a decisive battle by demonstrating in front of Ctesiphon, and that this is the reason that he brought no siege train. If that was the case, it is hard to explain why Julian should have left the area around Ctesiphon before Sapor arrived. For the planning of the campaign, noting that Constantine had evidently left detailed plans for precisely the sort of attack that Julian launched, see Kaegi, "Constantine's and Julian's Strategies," 209–13. Kaegi's suggestion gains force from the fact that both Constantine and Julian intended the same end to their campaign, the replacement of Sapor on the throne; for Constantine see p. 460 above. While Ridley, "Notes on Julian's Persian Expedition," 326, is right to see that the campaign was planned for only one year, this does not invalidate the notion that the objectives set for that year were unreasonably ambitious.

195 Lib. *Or.* 18.223–27, 232–33 with Matthews, *Roman Empire of Ammianus*, 154–55.

196 N. J. E. Austin, "Julian at Ctesiphon: A Fresh Look at Ammianus' Account," *Athenaeum* 50 (1972): 301–9.

197 Lib. *Or.* 18.250 (intends to live off land that had not been devastated).

198 Amm. Marc. 24.7.3, 5 (a corrupt passage); Zos. 3.26.2 does not mention the deserters.

199 But see Lib. *Or.* 18.262–63, justifying the burning of the ships on the grounds that they could not be taken up the Tigris.

200 Amm. Marc. 25.1.10–19; Zos 3.28.2 and Eunap. fr. 20 with Paschoud in Zosime, *Histoire nouvelle* 2.1, 198, showing that Ammianus seems to have exaggerated the nature of the conflict, which appears to have been an attack on the rear guard of the Roman army.

201 See Lib. *Or.* 18.268, 1.133, not noted in any other source. It is not impossible that he has retrojected the Persian offer of terms to Jovian onto Julian.

202 Amm. Marc. 25.3.6, 6.6; Greg. Naz. *Or.* 5.13.

203 Lib. *Or.* 18.274; see also Soz. *Hist. eccl.* 6.2.

204 Lib. *Or.* 24.6; Phil. *Hist. eccl.* 7.15 with Bowersock, *Julian the Apostate*, 117.

205 Amm. Marc. 25.5.2–3.

206 Amm. Marc. 25.5.4; Zos. 3.30.1; Eutrop. *Brev.* 10.17.1; Zon. 13.14.
207 Amm. Marc. 25.6.1.
208 Amm. Marc. 25.6.9.
209 Amm. Marc. 25.7.4–8.
210 Amm. Marc. 25.7.9; Zos. 3.31.1–2 with Matthews, *Roman Empire of Ammianus*, 185–87.
211 Amm. Marc. 23.3.5.
212 Zos. 3.35.1 (on the dispatch of Procopius to the west); 3.34.4 (burial of Julian); 4.4.3 on the role of Procopius and his retirement.
213 For the image of Jovian see plate 17a. For Jovian on religion see Socrates, *Hist. eccl.* 3.25.4. This is decidedly not a declaration that Christianity was the "official religion" of the empire, as in J. Curran, "From Jovian to Theodosius," in Cameron and Garnsey, *The Cambridge Ancient History*, 13: 79.
214 Barnes, *Athanasius and Constantius*, 159–60.
215 Amm. Marc. 25.8.12 with K. Ehling, "Das Ausgang des Perserfeldzuges in der Münzpropaganda des Jovian," *Klio* 78 (1996): 186–91.
216 Amm. Marc. 25.8.9 with *PLRE* Lucillianus 3, pp. 517–18.
217 Amm. Marc. 25.8.11, 10.6; *PLRE* Malarichus, p. 538 and p. 481 above.
218 Amm. Marc. 25.10.8–10 and *PLRE* Flavius Jovinus 6, pp. 462–63.
219 Amm. Marc. 25.10.11.
220 Amm. Marc. 25.10.12; Zos. 3.36.3.
221 Amm. Marc. 25.10.13.
222 Zos. 3.35.3.
223 For Salutius see Zos. 3.36.1.
224 Amm. Marc. 26.2.6.
225 Amm. Marc. 26.4.3; Zos. 3.36.3; see now the discussion in N. Lenski, *Failure of Empire: Valens and the Roman State in the Fourth Century AD* (Berkeley, 2002), 19–24.
226 Amm. Marc. 26.5.1–3; Phil. *Hist. eccl.* 8.8, astutely noting the parallel between the territory taken by Valens and that held by Constantius at the beginning of his reign; Zos. 4.3.1; see also Lenski, *Failure of Empire*, 26.
227 Amm. Marc. 26.5.1.
228 See also Lenski, *Failure of Empire*, 97–9.
229 Zos. 4.5.1–2, which contains circumstantial details lacking in the very different account of Ammianus (26.6.1–4). The most significant difference between the two narratives is that Ammianus places the flight of Procopius under Jovian. To omit Valens' attempt to arrest Procopius exculpates Valens, and it looks as if this might be part of an official version promulgated after the failure of the revolt. For suspicion falling upon the friends of Julian in the wake of the illness of the brothers see also Zos. 4.2.1–2; Eunap. *VS* 478–79. See now the thorough discussion in Lenski, *Failure of Empire*, 68–72.
230 Amm. Marc. 26.6.14.
231 Amm. Marc. 26.7.4; Zos. 4.6.2.
232 Amm. Marc. 26.7.10.
233 Amm. Marc. 26.7.11; see also Lenski, *Failure of Empire*, 96.
234 Amm. Marc. 26.5.9–10; see also Symm. *Or.* 1.17 and discussion in Lenski, *Failure of Empire*, 76–77.
235 Amm. Marc. 26.5.13.
236 Amm. Marc. 26.9.2.
237 Amm. Marc. 26.10.3, 27.5.1 with Matthews, *Roman Empire of Ammianus*, 208.
238 Amm. Marc. 26.8.13; Zos. 4.7.4.
239 Amm. Marc. 26.9.3.
240 Amm. Marc. 26.9.5–6; Zos. 4.8.2 (omitting Arbitio).

241 Amm. Marc. 26.9.7; Zos. 4.8.3.
242 Amm. Marc. 26.9.8–9; Zos. 4.8.3–4.

14 THE END OF HEGEMONY: 367–95

1 P. Brown, *Augustine of Hippo* (Berkeley, 1967), 31.
2 Aug. *Conf.* 1.13.21, though for the significance of the passage see S. G. MacCormack, *The Shadows of Poetry: Vergil in the Mind of Augustine* (Berkeley, 1998), 96; Aug. *Conf.* 1.17.27.
3 Brown, *Augustine of Hippo*, 38.
4 Aug. *Conf.* 3.3.6 and Brown, *Augustine of Hippo*, 21, 48.
5 Aug. *Conf.* 4.2.2 (on the marriage) with O'Donnell, *Augustine: Confessions*, 2: 207, on the chronology and the date of Adeodotus' birth, and pp. 383–85 on the legal status of the "marriage"; Brown, *Augustine of Hippo*, 62–63, on the name of Adeodotus.
6 Aug. *Conf.* 3.11.19, 4.1.1 and Brown, *Augustine of Hippo*, 46–60.
7 Aug. *Conf.* 3.4.7 with O'Donnell, *Augustine: Confessions*, 2: 162–67.
8 The one reference to Julian – a retrospective one at that – in the *Confessions* (8.5.10) is to the impact of Julian on the career of Victorinus; for Augustine's other references to Julian, principally to embarrass the Donatists, see O'Donnell, *Augustine: Confessions*, 3: 31 (note ad *imperatoris Iuliani*).
9 Amm. Marc. 31.4.10–11 with p. 531 below.
10 Aug. *Conf.* 4.3.5 and *PLRE* Vindicianus 2, p. 967.
11 Aug. *Conf.* 5.13.23 with Brown, *Augustine of Hippo*, 66–67, on the circumstances.
12 N. B. McLynn, *Ambrose of Milan: Church and Court in a Christian Capital* (Berkeley, 1994), 170.
13 Aug. *Conf.* 6.6.9; for the circumstances see O'Donnell, *Augustine: Confessions*, 2: 356–57, showing that the panegyric was delivered on Bauto's accession to the consulship in January 385.
14 Aug. *Conf.* 6.3.3, 9.7.15–16.
15 Brown, *Augustine of Hippo*, 158–64, on the circumstances of composition.
16 O. Seeck, "Alaricus," *RE* 1, col. 1286.
17 See Aug. *Civ. Dei* 5.26.
18 For the structure of Ammianus' account see Matthews, *Roman Empire of Ammianus*, 226–27; for the Christian response see Lenski, *Failure of Empire*, 261–62. For the relationship (or lack of it) between the Huns and the Xiongnu see Matthews, *Roman Empire of Ammianus*, 488, n. 26.
19 P. Heather, "The Crossing of the Danube and the Gothic Conversion," *GRBS* 27 (1986): 289–318; but see now N. Lenski, "The Gothic Civil War and the Date of the Gothic Conversion," *GRBS* 36 (1995): 51–87, who suggests, convincingly, that the conversion was a less monolithic process, and that significant members of the Gothic leadership (e.g. Fritigern) had converted before crossing the Danube.
20 Amm. Marc. 31.4.10–11.
21 Amm. Marc. 31.5.3.
22 Amm. Marc. 31.5.5–8.
23 E. Stein, *Histoire*, 1: 190 with n. 189; Hoffmann, *Das spätrömische Bewegungsheer*, 444, 455–58.
24 M. P. Speidel, "Sebastian's Strike Force at Adrianople," *Klio* 78 (1996): 434–37.
25 Amm. Marc. 31.12.3 with T. S. Burns, "The Battle of Adrianople: A Reconsideration," *Historia* 22 (1973): 341, offering a convincing explanation of the error (that only one of a number of separate bands was seen). Still, the fact that Valens could think this is enough to suggest that Eunapius' figure of 200,000 (fr. 42 [Blockley])

for the Goths who crossed the frontier is a fabrication. There seems no reason to adduce other numbers given in Roman sources for barbarian migrations to suggest it is possible given the fact that those numbers (esp. that given by Caes. *BG* 1.29 for the Helvetians) are likely to be false as well; for a different view see Lenski, *Failure of Empire*, 354–55.

26 Lenski, *Failure of Empire*, 363–64.

27 The best discussion of the location of the battle is now S. MacDowall, *Adrianople, AD 378: The Goths Crush Rome's Legions*, Osprey Campaign no. 84 (Botley, 2001), 68, who places the battle at Muratcali.

28 Amm. Marc. 31.12.11.

29 Amm. Marc. 31.12.13 with MacDowell, *Adrianople*, 71, who shows that the Goths were drawn up in front of the laager.

30 Amm. Marc. 31.12.16–17.

31 For Gothic tactics see Burns, "The Battle of Adrianople," 339, 342–43 (especially his astute observations on the nature of the Roman attack).

32 Amm. Marc. 31.13.2, 10.

33 Amm. Marc. 31.13.14–16; Zos. 4.24.2; Socrates, *Hist. eccl.* 4.37.8–10; Phil. *Hist. eccl.* 9.17; Soz. *Hist. eccl.* 6.40.3–5; Lib. *Or.* 24.4 suggests death in battle, though he may allude to the story about the burning house with a reference to fire and sword in 24.5.

34 For this calculation see Hoffmann, *Das spätrömische Bewegungsheer*, 458.

35 D. Woods, "Saracen Defenders of Constantinople in 378," *GRBS* 37 (1996): 259–79, for the identification of the Saracens as Domnica's guards.

36 Amm. Marc. 31.16.4–5; contrast, however, Zos. 4.22.1–2 who shows them to be disciplined troops.

37 P. 548 below.

38 The basic study of the battle is now F. Paschoud in *Zosime, Histoire nouvelle* 2.2 (Paris, 1979), 474–500.

39 Zos. 4.58.3; Ruf. *Hist. eccl.* 11.33; Socrates, *Hist. eccl.* 5.25.14; Theod. *Hist. eccl.* 5.24.3.

40 Aug. *Civ. Dei* 5.26; Theodoret accords them a statue of Hercules at *Hist. eccl.* 5.24.4, 17.

41 Zos. 58.5–6; John. Ant. fr. 187 (*FHG*); Ruf. *Hist. eccl.* 11.33; Phil. *Hist. eccl.* 11.2; Socrates, *Hist. eccl.* 5.25.15; Soz. *Hist. eccl.* 7.24.7; Claud. *De VI cons. Hon.* 102–5; Amb. *Ex. Ps.* 36.25.

42 See also Hoffmann, *Das spätrömische Bewegungsheer*, 46, showing that the eastern army at this point, which included the army of Illyricum, outnumbered the western by 180 units to 100.

43 For a different view see Elton, *Warfare in Roman Europe*, 265–68, who sees the Roman army as a more potent force after 378 than I do. I feel that Hoffmann's discussion of Theodosius' manipulation of troop strengths (see previous note) shows that there was a shortage of trained men.

44 P. 552 below.

45 For Ammianus' portrait of Valentinian see Matthews, *Roman Empire of Ammianus* (London, 1989), 237–38.

46 Leppin, *Von Constantin zu Theodosius II*, 102.

47 The point is well made by Seeck, *Geschichte des Untergangs*, 5: 11.

48 Matthews, *Western Aristocracies*, 32–55, remains the basic study; but see also Lenski, *Failure of Empire*, 57–60.

49 *PLRE* Flavius Jovinus 6, pp. 462–63.

50 For Valentinian's German campaigns see Matthews, *Roman Empire of Ammianus*, 283–85.

51 Amm. Marc. 31.5.1–2.

52 Amm. Marc. 31.12.1.

53 *PLRE* Florianus 3, p. 366.

54 *PLRE* Germanianus 1, p. 391, Philematius, p. 694.

55 Amm. Marc. 26.4.4 for his role in the investigation; see also *PLRE* Viventius, p. 972.

56 *PLRE* Flavius Claudius Antonius 5, p. 77.

57 *PLRE* Decimius Magnus Ausonius 7, pp. 140–41.

58 P. 544 below.

59 For Severus see *PLRE* Severus 10, p. 833.

60 For Merobaudes see *PLRE* Flavius Merobaudes 2, pp. 598–9. There is no clear attestation of him as *magister peditum* before 375, but he seems well established at that point.

61 *PLRE* Equitius 2, p. 282.

62 B. H. Warmington, "The Career of Romanus, *comes Africae*," *BzZ* 49 (1956): 63–64.

63 *PLRE* Leo 1, p. 498.

64 P. 539 below.

65 *PLRE* Maximinus 7, pp. 577–78.

66 *PLRE* Sex. Claudius Petronius Probus 5, pp. 736–40.

67 Chastagnol, *Les fastes*, 188–89. R. P. H. Green, *The Works of Ausonius* (Oxford, 1991), takes the person described in Aus. *Mos.* 405–9 to be an unknown *vicarius*, contra Chastagnol (and others), who entertain the possibility that it is Bappo. Green is correct that the rather opaque reference would seem to rule out the urban prefecture, mentioned by the figure alluded to in lines 410–14, whom he identifies as Petronius Probus.

68 Chastagnol, *Les fastes*, 189–90.

69 Chastagnol, *Les fastes*, 190–91; there appears to be no room in this sequence for the prefecture of Tanaucius Isfalangius as postulated in *PLRE* Isfalangius, pp. 464–65.

70 Lib. *Or.* 19.18.

71 Lib. *Or.* 1.171; Them. *Or.* 7.92c–93c, 99b–101a with Errington, "Themistius and His Emperors," 882, showing that the search for supporters of Procopius lasted for only four months before Valens enunciated a policy of clemency; see also Vanderspoel, *Themistius and Imperial Court*, 165–67, with less precision on the time frame; Lenski, *Failure of Empire*, 105–15 for more details.

72 *PLRE* Auxonius 1, pp. 142–43.

73 *PLRE* Clearchus 1, pp. 211–12; see also Lenski, *Failure of Empire*, 113 for other instances where Clearchus was influential.

74 *PLRE* Domitius Modestus, pp. 605–8.

75 *PLRE* Victor 4, pp. 957–59; *PLRE* Flavius Arintheus, pp. 102–3.

76 *PLRE* Sophronius 3, pp. 847–48.

77 *PLRE* Traianus 2, pp. 921–22; he had been *dux Aegypti* in 367–68 and had served in Armenia as *comes rei militaris* in 371–74.

78 *PLRE* Flavius Saturninus, pp. 807–8; for the nature of his appointment in 377 see Amm. Marc. 31.8.3.

79 The striking lack of mobility in senior offices is noted by Seeck, *Geschichte des Untergangs*, 5:426 (n. on p. 11, l. 32); Stein, *Histoire du Bas-Empire*, 178; Lenski, *Failure of Empire*, 62–3.

80 Barnes, *Ammianus Marcellinus*, 183.

81 Amm. Marc. 28.6.3–4.

82 Amm. Marc. 28.6.5–6.

83 *CTh*. 11.1.11 (also in *CJ* 1016.6, preserving a better text of a part of the rescript). In both cases the wording is obscure, stating simply *pro locis ac proximitate posses-sionum annonam ad limitem transvehi praecipimus*. By *ad limitem* the author of this text presumably means to the *comes rei militaris*. It reverses an earlier ruling of Constantius, who had forbidden the *comes rei militaris* to take direct possession of tax revenues (*CTh*. 7.4.3). For the connection of the rescript with this affair see Warmington, "The Career of Romanus," 56–57.

84 Amm. Marc. 28.6.7.

85 Amm. Marc. 28.6.8 with *PLRE* Dracontius 3, pp. 271–72.

86 Amm. Marc. 28.6.12.

87 Amm. Marc. 28.6.17.

88 Amm. Marc. 28.6.20.

89 Amm. Marc. 28.6.22–24.

90 Amm. Marc. 28.6.25–28.

91 Amm. Marc. 29.5.2 and p. 544 below.

92 P. 566 below.

93 Amm. Marc. 28.1.1 with Matthews, *Roman Empire of Ammianus*, 210, and p. 472 above for the revolt of Nepotianus.

94 *CTh*. 9.40.10.

95 The opening of this letter in the Theodosian Code reads: *nullus omnino ob fidiculas preferendas inconsultis ac nescientibus nobis vel militiae auctoramento vel generis aut digni-tatis defensione nuderetur*. The parallel passage in *CJ* 9.4 reads: *nullus omnino, cui inconsultis ac nescientibus nobis fidicularum tormenta offerentur, militiae vel generis ait digni-tatis defensione prohibeatur*.

96 For the date and location see *CTh*. 9.16.9, 38.5; *CJ* 9.43.3; for Eupraxius' inter-vention see Amm. Marc. 28.1.25; for Eupraxius see *PLRE* Eupraxius (pp. 299–300); he too served for some time at court, being *magister memoriae* by 367, and holding the quaestorship from 368 to 371 (the date 370 given in *PLRE* is incorrect since Valentinian's decree is manifestly connected with the embassy of Praetextatus).

97 Amm. Marc. 28.6.1–3. For Rusticus Julianus see *PLRE* Sextus Rusticus Julianus 37, pp. 479–80; for Severus see n. 59 above.

98 Amm. Marc. 30.10.6.

99 Errington, "Themistius and His Emperors," 891–92; Lenski, *Failure of Empire*, 357–61 stresses Valens' continuing resentment of the proclamation, with good reason.

100 Lib. *Or*. 1.145.

101 Amm. Marc. 29.1.5 with *PLRE* Fortunatianus 1, p. 369.

102 Amm. Marc. 29.1.8; for the nature of the procedure see now A. Mastrocinque, "The Divinatory Kit from Pergamon and Greek Magic in Late Antiquity," *JRA* 15 (2002): 173–87; Gordon, "Pergamon Divination Kit," JRA 15 (2002): 187–98.

103 See also Lib. *Or*. 1.177 on the rage of Valens.

104 Amm. Marc. 29.1.11.

105 *PLRE* Icarius 2, pp. 455–56.

106 Amm. Marc. 29.1.34.

107 Lenski, *Failure of Empire*, 103–4.

108 Amm. Marc. 30.10.4; for Cerialis see *PLRE* Cerialis 1, p. 197 with Lenski, *Failure of Empire*, 102–3.

109 Zos. 4.19.1.

110 Phil. *Hist. eccl.* 9.16.

111 K. Holum, *Theodosian Empresses: Women and Imperial Dominion in Late Antiquity* (Berkeley, 1982), 31; Zos. 4.19.1; John. Ant. fr. 187 (*FHG* 4, 609) for Justina's marriage to Magnentius; and Lenski, *Failure of Empire*, 103.

112 Eunap. fr. 44.3 (Blockley) and Zos. 4.22.4 with R. M. Errington, "The Accession of Theodosius I," *Klio* 78 (1996): 441–43.

113 Errington, "Accession of Theodosius II," 443–44.

114 Amm. Marc. 29.6.15.

115 Amm. Marc. 27.8.3, 6–10, 28.3.1–8; *Pan.* 2 (12).5.2; *AE* 1931 no. 53; Amm. Marc. 28.3.9 (promoted to succeed Jovinus) with *PLRE* Flavius Theodosius 3, pp. 902–3; A. Demandt, "Die Feldzüge des älteren Theodosius," *Hermes* 100 (1972): 81–113, with pp. 84–91 for details of the British expedition.

116 Amm. Marc. 28.5.15; *Pan.* 2(12).5.2 (victory in 371); Amm. Marc. 29.4.5 (with Valentinian); *AE* 1931 no. 53 (Sarmatian victory); see also Demandt, "Die Feldzüge des älteren Theodosius," 91–94.

117 Amm. Marc. 29.5 passim; Zos. 4.16.3 with Demandt, "Die Feldzüge des älteren Theodosius," 94–111.

118 For a summary of the chronology, placing Theodosius' exposure of Romanus at the beginning of the campaign, see Demandt, "Die Feldzüge des älteren Theodosius," 111.

119 While there is no direct evidence of a connection, both were among the correspondents of Symmachus. See esp. Symm. *Ep.* 10.9.4, 33 and Symm. *Or.* 6.4 celebrating the elder Theodosius prior to the accession of the younger.

120 See also Symm. *Or.* 4.11 perhaps suggesting that recent executions for which Maximinus was responsible were the proximate cause of his demise. Symm. *Ep.* 1.13 cannot refer to the removal of Maximinus, but suggests that significant change was promised in an oration of Gratian that was read to the senate on January 1, 376. For the circumstances surrounding the death of the elder Theodosius see the detailed analysis of A. Demandt, "Der Tod des älteren Theodosius," *Historia* 18 (1969): 598–626.

121 For Sebastianus, who was killed at Adrianople, see Amm. Marc. 31.11.1 with Errington, "Accession of Theodosius I," 449; for Theodosius see Errington, "Accession of Theodosius I," 445, 449, drawing the parallel.

122 Amm. Marc. 28.6.29–30.

123 See, in general, Matthews, *Western Aristocracies*, 75–78.

124 *PLRE* Decimius Hilarianus Hesperius 2, pp. 427–28.

125 For Siburius see *PLRE* Siburius 1, p. 839; for Syagrius see *PLRE* Flavius Afranius Syagrius 2 (p. 862); for Eutropius see *PLRE* Eutropius 2, p. 317, who is probably not to be identified with the historian; R. Burgess, "Eutropius *v.c. magister memoriae*," *CPh* 96 (2001): 76–81 (esp. 77, n. 2).

126 *PLRE* Flavius Hypatius 4, pp. 448–49.

127 *PLRE* Flavius Mallius Theodorus 27, pp. 900–2.

128 For the Armenian situation see p. 551 below.

129 For the appointment of Sapores see Theod. *Hist. eccl.* 5.2–3 and *PLRE* Sapores, p. 803.

130 Vanderspoel, *Themistius and Imperial Court*, 190.

131 Them. *Or.* 14.182c–d; for the circumstances of the speech see R. M. Errington, "Theodosius and the Goths," *Chiron* 26 (1996): 8–9.

132 Them. *Or.* 16.207b with Vanderspoel, *Themistius and Imperial Court*, 197–98; H. Sivan, "Was Theodosius I a Usurper," *Klio* 78 (1996): 198–211. For the view that Gratian took the initiative see S. Williams and G. Friell, *Theodosius: The Empire at Bay* (London, 1994), 26; and, in more detail, Errington, "Accession of Theodosius I," 451–52, who argues that an emperor was needed, and Theodosius was the obvious available candidate.

133 For the date see Aus. *Act. grat.* 9.42 with Seeck, *Regesten*, 250.

134 *PLRE* Eucherius 2, p. 288 with Seeck, *Geschichte des Untergangs*, 5: 124.

135 Seeck, *Geschichte des Untergangs*, 5: 125.

136 Errington, "Theodosius and the Goths," 8, on the date of the embassy.

137 For Julius see *PLRE* Julius 2, p. 481, though the date of his tenure in office given there is incorrect, and must be extended to 379 in light of the evidence of Zosimus. Amm. Marc. 31.16.8: *his diebus efficacia Julii magistri militiae trans Taurum enituit salutaris et velox* is too imprecise to date his action before 379.

138 Zos. 4.27.2–3.

139 For Gratian's movements see Seeck, *Regesten*, 254–55. For the question of whether or not he also reacquired control of the Illyrian dioceses that had been part of Theodosius' empire see n. 165 below.

140 Zos. 4.33.1; Eunap. fr. 53; John Ant. fr. 187; Phil. *Hist. eccl.* 11.6; for the chronology see Heather, *Goths and Romans*, 155.

141 Williams and Friell, *Theodosius*, 30.

142 Amm. Marc. 31.4.13.

143 Errington, "Theodosius and the Goths," 12–13.

144 Heather, *Goths and Romans*, 158–65; Errington, "Theodosius and the Goths," 22, argues that the Goths were not required to send troops to help Theodosius. He is correct that this does not appear in the direct evidence for this treaty. It is, however, difficult to understand the nature of the dispute between Theodosius and the Goths in 388/9 if there was no such requirement.

145 *CTh.* 7.13.9.

146 *CTh.* 7.13.10, 18.3.

147 *CTh.* 7.18.4, 18.5.

148 For the context see Vanderspoel, *Themistius and Imperial Court*, 207.

149 See also [Aurelius Victor], *Epit.* 47.6.

150 Amm. Marc. 31.10.18–19.

151 See the excellent discussion in McLynn, *Ambrose of Milan*, 150–55.

152 Sulp. Sev. *Chron.* 2.49.3.

153 Prosper Tiro, *Chron.* s.a. 384.

154 For Maximus' background see *Pan.* 2 (12) 24.1 and Matthews, *Western Aristocracies*, 95–96, raising the interesting possibility that he is the *dux exitiosus* of Amm. Marc. 31.4.9; see also *PLRE* Magnus Maximus 39, p. 588.

155 See the detailed analysis in D. Vera, "I rapporti fra Magno Massimo, Teodosio e Valentiniano II nel 383–384," *Athenaeum* 53 (1975): 267–301, showing that a *modus vivendi* was reached very rapidly after the death of Gratian.

156 The contact between eastern officials and western aristocrats is reflected in the correspondence of Symmachus in these years; see esp. Symm. *Ep.* 3.59, 61, 5.46; *Rel.* 9 with Matthews, *Western Aristocracies*, 179; McLynn, *Ambrose of Milan*, 168–69.

157 *PLRE* Flavius Neoterius, p. 623; *PLRE* Gildo, pp. 395–96; *PLRE* Flavius Promotus (750–51); for his connection with Bauto see Zos. 5.3.2; for Promotus' links with Symmachus see Symm. *Ep.* 3.74–80.

158 For the body of Gratian see p. 565 below.

159 Zos. 4.42–45 with *CTh.* 1.32.5, suggesting the extent of the threat; see also Matthews, *Western Aristocracies*, 181.

160 Amm. Marc. 27.12.10 (return of Pap without insignia in 369); coronation is implied for 370 at Amm. Marc. 27.12.14.

161 Amm. Marc. 27.12.14, 30.1.4–12, 2.1; in 27.12.14 Ammianus admits that Sapor tried to lure Pap from the Roman alliance. In the latter two cases, Ammianus omits the interests of the Persians; see also Blockley, *East Roman Foreign Policy*, 35, noting Armenian traditions that stress the fact that Pap was about to change sides, and now the detailed discussion in Lenski, *Failure of Empire*, 167–83.

162 Blockley, *East Roman Foreign Policy*, 35 (again relying on Armenian sources to fill gaps in Ammianus' narrative).

163 Blockley, *East Roman Foreign Policy*, 38, 42.

164 A. Piganiol, *L'empire chrétien (325-395)* (Paris, 1947), 275-76.

165 For Justina and Theodosius see Zos. 4.44.2-4. Thessalonica was presumably chosen because it was in the prefecture of Illyricum, which had been restored to Gratian, and had then passed to Valentinian. For this view see Piganiol, *L'empire chrétien*, 233; Stein, *Histoire du Bas-Empire*, 193, and, with compelling arguments, M. Kulikowski, "The *Notitia Dignitatum*," 364; Errington, "Theodosius and the Goths," 22-27, showing that the return to Gratian occurred in 382. Seeck, *Geschichte des Untergangs*, 5: 210, asserts that it had remained in the portion of Theodosius. Although Flavius Eusignius (*PLRE*, p. 307) held the praetorian prefecture of Italy and Illyricum in 386-87, the next attested prefect is Trifolius, from 388 to 389, whose previous office was that of *comes sacrarum largitionum* in the east. He was probably appointed first as prefect of Illyricum, as Italy was still under Maximus' control, and as prefect of Italy and Illyricum after the reconquest. Butheric's appointment as *magister militum* in Illyricum is best seen as reflecting Valentinian's loss of control over appointments in what was theoretically his portion of the empire, as the price for Theodosius' aid.

166 *Pan.* 2 (12). 34 (Siscia), 35-36 (Poetovio), 38.4-42 (capture of Maximus); Zos. 4.46.2; Amb. *Ep. extra coll.* 1a.22 (*CSEL* 82 pt. 3, 172) on the seizure of supplies; Phil. *Hist. eccl.* 10.8 on the commanders with Seeck, *Geschichte des Untergangs*, 5: 212 and 523 (n. on 212, l. 3). For other aspects of the campaign, which appears to have included an invasion of Africa, see Piganiol, *L'empire chétien*, 280, n. 1.

167 Hoffmann, *Das spätrömische Bewegungsheer*, 481-87.

168 For Trifolius see *PLRE* Trifolius, p. 923; for Bauto's connections with the east see esp. Phil. *Hist. eccl.* 11.6; Zos. 5.3.2 (his daughter married Arcadius); see also *PLRE* Flavius Bauto, pp. 159-60; for Arbogast see Zos. 4.53.1; Phil. *Hist. eccl.* 10.8 and *PLRE* Arbogastes, pp. 95-97.

169 Zos. 4.47.1, 53.1.

170 Zos. 4.53.3.

171 For the circumstances surrounding the death of Valentinian and the accession of Eugenius see B. Croke, "Arbogast and the Death of Valentinian II," *Historia* 25 (1976): 235-44.

172 Lenski, *Failure of Empire*, 241.

173 Amm. Marc. 27.7.5; see also McLynn, *Ambrose of Milan*, 80-81 on the absence of a strong religious presence in the court at Trier.

174 Amm. Marc. 27.7.6.

175 Theod. *Hist. eccl.* 4.6.

176 Soz. 6.21.7 with D. H. Williams, *Ambrose of Milan and the End of the Arian-Nicene Conflicts* (Oxford, 1995), 71.

177 N. 18 above.

178 Socrates, *Hist. eccl.* 4.8; Amm. Marc. 31.1.4.

179 See also Chadwick, "Orthodoxy and Heresy," 13: 575.

180 See also McLynn, *Ambrose of Milan*, 94-96, who shows that the documents quoted in Theod. *Hist. eccl.* 4.8-9 are most likely forgeries. This does not necessitate the further belief that his account of Domnica and Eudoxius as the moving forces behind Valens' actions against Nicene partisans is false.

181 Theod. *Hist. eccl.* 4.12; though see Lenski, *Failure of Empire*, 243-44 for doubts about the validity of the tradition. While Lenski is correct that Eudoxius was an important influence from early in the reign, this story would seem to reflect a perception that Valens was relatively neutral in the first part of his reign.

182 Socrates, *Hist. eccl.* 4.13–14; for a list of bishops exiled by Valens see Woods, "Three Notes," 617–18. See also Lenski, *Failure of Empire*, 250–51.

183 Socrates, *Hist. eccl.* 4.21–22; Theod. *Hist. eccl.* 4.20–22.

184 See also P. Petit, *Libanius et la vie municipale*, 199.

185 Zos. 4.15.1; Amm. Marc. 29.1.42.

186 Zos. 4.15.1; Amm. Marc. 29.1.37–38 (Simonides).

187 Amm. Marc. 29.1.36.

188 Socrates, *Hist. eccl.* 4.19 with T. Urbainczyk, *Socrates of Constantinople: Historian of Church and State* (Ann Arbor, 1997), 153.

189 Socrates, *Hist. eccl.* 4.32 with Vanderspoel, *Themistius and Imperial Court*, 178–79, on the circumstances and the state of the text. See also Urbainczyk, *Socrates of Constantinople*, 30, 153.

190 Amb. *Ep.* 51.

191 See McLynn, *Ambrose of Milan*, 106–11; Williams, *Ambrose of Milan*, 165. The importance of Acholius was noted by Seeck, *Geschichte des Untergangs*, 5: 137. See also A. Ehrhardt, "The First Two Years of the Emperor Theodosius," *JEH* 15 (1964): 1–17, who shows that there is no evidence of a theological agenda in the first two years of the reign.

192 Socrates, *Hist. eccl.* 5.2.1; Soz. *Hist. eccl.* 7.1.3; McLynn, *Ambrose of Milan*, 91 and p. 557 below. Seeck, *Geschichte des Untergangs*, 5: 122 sees it as a measure to ensure divine protection for the empire in the wake of Adrianople.

193 *CTh.* 16.5.5 with Soz. *Hist. eccl.* 6.26.7, 9; Phil. *Hist. eccl.* 10.4 and Piganiol, *L'empire chrétien*, 246–47 (suggesting the influence of Damasus); Williams, *Ambrose of Milan*, 157–60; McLynn, *Ambrose of Milan*, 102, holds that the edict was concerned only with Donatists. He was not able to take account of Williams's argument, which seems persuasive to me.

194 P. 559 below.

195 P. 464 above.

196 *PLRE* Marcellina 1, p. 544; Salzman, *Making of Christian Aristocracy*, 167–69, for the context.

197 McLynn, *Ambrose of Milan*, 39.

198 For the story of sudden acclamation see Rufinus, *Hist. eccl.* 2.11; Paulinus, *V. Amb.* 6.5–10 with Williams, *Ambrose of Milan*, 112–16; for Probus' agency see the sensible discussion in Williams, *Ambrose of Milan*, 114–16.

199 Paulinus, *V. Amb.* 11.1 with McLynn, *Ambrose of Milan*, 92.

200 McLynn, *Ambrose of Milan*, 97–98.

201 McLynn, *Ambrose of Milan*, 68–78. For other views as to the date see esp. J.-C. Picard, *Le souvenir des évêques* (Rome, 1988), 604–7; *CSEL* 73.

202 *CTh.* 16.5.6 (referring to it); Soz. *Hist. eccl.* 7.1.3; *Acta conc. Aquil. Ep.* 2.12 (*CSEL* 82.3, 324).

203 Socrates, *Hist. eccl.* 2.29.1–2; Soz. *Hist. eccl.* 6.1–4; Epiph. *Her.* 71.1.3.

204 Socrates, *Hist. eccl.* 5.24.1–6; Soz. *Hist. eccl.* 26.1–27.10; Phil. *Hist. eccl.* 10.6.

205 Amb. *De fide* 2.15.130.

206 Amb. *De fide* 1.13.85, 16.103.

207 McLynn, *Ambrose of Milan*, 113–16 for details of the dispute.

208 Socrates, *Hist. eccl.* 5.8; Soz. *Hist. eccl.* 7.7–9; Theod. *Hist. eccl.* 5.6.3; 8.1–8.

209 *CTh.* 16.1.3.

210 The prejudice of the proceedings is obvious from the cover letters sent with the *acta*; see *Gesta conc. Aquil.* (*CSEL* 82.3, 315–25 for the *epistulae*; 325–68 for the actual *acta*); Amb. *Ep.* 1.2: *quam necessarius autem conventus hic fuerit rebus ipsis patescit, quando adversarii et inimici dei, Arrianae sectae interpretes ac defensores, Palladius*

ac Secundianus, duo tantum qui ausi sunt ad concilium convenire, debitam praesentes excepere sententiam super impietate convicti; *Ep.* 2.2; see also Ambrose's opening statement at *Acta conc. Aquil.* 2, 6–7; McLynn, *Ambrose of Milan*, 125–37.

211 McLynn, *Ambrose of Milan*, 127.

212 Palladius suggested that they did not keep an accurate record, yet the record is complete enough to contain Palladius' complaints; see *Gesta* 43, 46–47, 51.

213 Zos. 4.36; Symm. *Rel.* 3.7 with A. D. E. Cameron, "Gratian's Repudiation of the Pontifical Robe," *JRS* 58 (1968): 96–99. For the statue see H. A. Pohlsander, "Victory: The Story of a Statue," *Historia* 18 (1969): 594, noting that Gratian left it in place.

214 *PLRE* Severus 29, p. 837 with McLynn, *Ambrose of Milan*, 151.

215 The absence of a hearing is attested by Symm. *Rel.* 3.1, showing that the meeting between a senatorial embassy and Gratian reported in Zos. 4.36.5 did not take place. There is also a question as to where such a meeting might have occurred.

216 Amb. *Ep.* 57.3 (Bauto), 72.8 (other Christians).

217 Noted by McLynn, *Ambrose of Milan*, 166, n. 34, taking Ambrose at his word that the embassy was a sudden development. It is nonetheless hard to imagine that an event involving highly visible members of the aristocracy could have remained invisible to Damasus. Damasus had presented a petition from Christian senators against the embassy of 283; see Amb. *Ep.* 72.

218 Amb. *Ep.* 72.3–4.

219 Amb. *Ep.* 72.9–11.

220 Amb. *Ep.* 72.12.

221 Amb. *Ep.* 72.15.

222 For the date of Ammianus' composition see Matthews, *Roman Empire of Ammianus*, 31.

223 Symm. *Rel.* 3.2.

224 Symm. *Rel.* 3.4, 6.

225 Symm. *Rel.* 3.3.

226 Symm. *Rel.* 3.12.

227 Symm. *Rel.* 3.15–16.

228 Symm. *Rel.* 3.18.

229 Symm. *Rel.* 3.19.

230 Symm. *Rel.* 3.20.

231 McLynn, *Ambrose of Milan*, 179.

232 H. O. Maier, "Private Space as the Social Context of Arianism in Ambrose's Milan," *JTS* 45 (1994): 74, showing that there was no Arian basilica.

233 Maier, "Private Space," 84–85.

234 *CTh.* 16.1.4. For the sequence of events see A. Lenox-Cunyngham, "The Topography of the Basilica Conflict of AD 385/6 in Milan," *Historia* 31 (1982): 353–56, with a review of earlier scholarship.

235 Amb. *Ep.* 76.2.

236 Amb. *Ep.* 76.4–10.

237 Amb. *Ep.* 76.26. It is particularly interesting that the troops chosen to besiege the basilica were Goths, and thus anti-Nicene; see Amb. *Ep.* 20.13 with Lenox-Cunyngham, "Topography of Basilica Conflict," 355, n. 4, making the failure of the court all the more striking.

238 For a survey of Ambrose's comments on Justina (he also compared her to Herodias) see J.-R. Palanque, *Saint Ambrose et l'empire romaine: Contribution à l'histoire des rapports de l'église et de l'état à la fin du quatrième siècle* (Paris, 1933), 140.

239 For the problem of which church see McLynn, *Ambrose of Milan*, 199, n. 142.

240 *Coll. Avell.* 39.1.

241 Williams, *Ambrose of Milan*, 216–17.
242 P. Brown, *The Cult of the Saints: Its Rise and Function in Latin Christianity* (Chicago, 1981), 36–37.
243 Aug. *Conf.* 9.7.16 with other references in O'Donnell, *Augustine: Confessions*, 3: 112–13.
244 *CTh.* 9.17.7.
245 Williams, *Ambrose of Milan*, 197–98, 227, suggesting that relations were cordial between Ambrose and Maximus.
246 Socrates, *Hist. eccl.* 5.14.
247 Theod. *Hist. eccl.* 5.16.1–2, 3 with Williams, *Ambrose of Milan*, 228.
248 What follows owes much to Brown, *Power and Persuasion*, 105; McLynn, *Ambrose of Milan*, 318–19.
249 For the apology see Symm. *Ep.* 2.13, 28, 32; complaints of ill treatment in a legal action connected with a property in Sicily, *Ep.* 2.30–31. It is unfortunate that we cannot confirm from his own writings the story of Socrates that he sought asylum in a church (Socrates, *Hist. eccl.* 5.14.6).
250 *CTh.* 15.14.6, 7, 8.
251 P. 516 above.
252 Lib. *Or.* 1.132.
253 Lib. *Ep.* 1368 with Kaster, *Guardians of Language*, 203.
254 Amb. *Ep. extra coll.* 1a.13 (*CSEL* 82.3, 168); Socrates, *Hist. eccl.* 5.13.
255 Lib. *Or.* 19.19.
256 Lib. *Or.* 1.180–81.
257 Seeck, *Regesten*, 92–93.
258 Claud. *De VI cons. Hon.* 105–9 with M. Dewar, *Claudian: Panegyricus de sexto consulatu Honorii Augusti* (Oxford, 1996), 132–37 (n. ad ll. 107ff.) and Heather, *Goths and Romans*, 183–86.
259 *PLRE* Butherichus, p. 166.
260 Soz. *Hist. eccl.* 725.3–5; Zon. 13.18d (p. 227 Dindorf) with an incorrect context and placing Theodosius at Thessalonica; Ruf. *Hist. eccl.* 11.18.
261 P. 463, n. 108 above for Hermogenes; for the soldier see Lib. *Or.* 20.14 with McLynn, *Ambrose of Milan*, 317.
262 Brown, *Power and Persuasion*, 107, notes the connection between the final form that the settlement took and the journey of Cynegius.
263 Lib. *Or.* 1.253.
264 Soz. *Hist. eccl.* 7.25.4; the point is stressed by McLynn, *Ambrose of Milan*, 321; on the possible time limit see Paul. *V. Ambr.* 24.
265 For Ambrose's communication see Amb. *Ep. extra coll.* 11 with McLynn, *Ambrose of Milan*, 323–30.
266 Theod. *Hist. eccl.* 5.17.3.
267 For Cynegius and his family see J. F. Matthews, "A Pious Supporter of Theodosius I: Maternus Cynegius and His Family," *JTS* 18 (1967): 438–46, noting that the legislation attacking heretics and polytheists associated with his term in the east is likely of his inspiration (p. 441). He was replaced, as Matthews notes, by the one polytheist (and one easterner) appointed to the praetorian prefecture by Theodosius, Flavius Eutolmius Tatianus (*PLRE* Fl. Eutolmius Tatianus 5, pp. 876–78). For influences on Cynegius see Lib. *Or.* 30.46 with Seeck, *Geschichte des Untergangs*, 5: 218, with pp. 526–28 (n. on p. 218, l. 27).
268 Amb. *Ep. extra coll.* 1a. 21 (*CSEL* 82 pt. 3, 172).
269 For an excellent short discussion of Libanius' career see W. Liebeschuetz, *Antioch, City and Imperial Administration in the Later Roman Empire* (Oxford, 1972), 1–16.
270 Lib. *Or.* 1.2.

271 Lib. *Or.* 1.9–10.
272 Lib. *Or.* 1.23; Eunap. *VS* 483.
273 Lib. *Or.* 1.48 with Kaster, *Guardians of Language*, 219.
274 Lib. *Or.* 1.80.
275 P. 475 above.
276 Lib. *Or.* 1.171 on Valens.
277 See, in general, R. Kaster, *Guardians of Language*, 230.
278 Lib. *Or.* 1.29.
279 Lib. *Or.* 1.37.
280 Lib. *Or.* 1.43; Aug. *Conf.* 4.2.3.
281 On Latin see Lib. *Or.* 1.154, 213–15, 234; 2.43, 40.5 and the evidence for the use of Latin in the east in the late fourth century collected in Dietz, "Kaiser Julian in Phönizien," 810–12.
282 Lib. *Or.* 1.39–40.
283 *CTh.* 16.10.7.
284 Lib. *Or.* 30.7.
285 *CTh.* 16.10.8, 9 with Potter, *Prophets and Emperors*, 171–82.
286 Lib. *Or.* 30.46–47.
287 Lib. *Or.* 30.27; see also *Or.* 18.121, where the same point is made to Julian in reverse.
288 Lib. *Or.* 30.9, 14–15, 35–36, 39, 42, 44.
289 Lib. *Or.* 30.22–23.
290 For a discussion of Theodosius' antipolytheist legislation see R. M. Errington, "Christian Accounts of the Religious Legislation of Theodosius I," *Klio* 79 (1997): 423–31, suggesting that it is less significant than it appears. In a sense his case is supported by the fact that Libanius feels that the matter is open to discussion. It remains the case, however, that Theodosius was loath to punish Christian extremists (and could be dissuaded, albeit with irritation, when he did).

CONCLUSION: CHANGE IN THE ROMAN EMPIRE

1 M. Fethi-Bejaoui, "Deux mosaïques tardives de la région de Sheïtla, l'antique Sufetula en Tunisie," *CRAI* (2001): 489–516.
2 Fethi-Bejaoui, "Deux mosaïques," 514–16.
3 P. 22 above.
4 J. Eadie, "The Development of Roman Mailed Cavalry," *JRS* 57 (1967): 161–73.
5 [Caes]. *Bell. Hisp.* 31.1.
6 P. 459 above.
7 M. Gawlikowsky, "Un nouveau mithraeum récemment découvert à Huarte près d'Apamée," *CRAI* (2000): 161–71.
8 For a recent perspective on the issue see J. H. W. G. Liebeschuetz, "The Uses and Abuses of the Concept of 'Decline' in later Roman History; or, Was Gibbon Politically Incorrect?" in *Recent Research in Late-Antique Urbanism*, ed. L. Lavan, *JRA* supplement 42 (Portsmouth, 2001), 232–8 and responses on pp. 238–45.

BIBLIOGRAPHY

Abramowski, E. "Die Synod von Antioch 324/25 und ihr Symbol." *Zeitschrift für Kirchengeschichte* 86 (1975): 356–66.

Adams, J. N. *The Latin Sexual Vocabulary.* London, 1982.

Adler, W., and P. Tuffin. *The Chronography of George Synkellos: A Byzantine Chronicle of Universal History from the Creation.* Oxford, 2002.

Aldrete, G., and D. J. Mattingly. "Feeding the City: The Organization, Scale, and Operation of the Supply System for Rome." In *Life, Death, and Entertainment in the Roman Empire*, ed. D. S. Potter and D. J. Mattingly, 181–204. Ann Arbor, 1999.

Alexander, J. S. "The Motive for a Distinction between Donatus of Carthage and Donatus of Casa Nigra." *JTS* 31 (1980): 540–47.

Alföldi, A. "The Numbering of the Victories of the Emperor Gallienus and the Loyalty of His Legions." *Num. Chron.*, 5th ser., 9 (1929): 218–79. Also in *Studien zur Geschichte der Weltkrise das 3. Jahrhunderts nach Christus* (Darmstadt, 1967), 73–119.

——— . *The Conversion of Constantine and Pagan Rome.* Oxford, 1948.

Alföldi, M. R. *Die constantinische Goldprägung.* Mainz, 1963.

Alföldy, G. "P. Helvius Pertinax und M. Valerius Maximianus." *Situla* 14–15 (1974): 199–215. Also in *Römische Heeresgeschichte: Beiträge 1962–1985* (Amsterdam, 1987), 326–67.

——— . *Konsulat und Senatorenstand unter den Antoninen: Prosopographische Untersuchungen zur senatorischen Führungsschicht.* Bonn, 1977.

Allbery, C. R. C. *A Manichaean Psalm-Book.* Stuttgart, 1938.

Allen, S. *Finding the Walls of Troy: Frank Calvert and Heinrich Schliemann at Hisarlik.* Berkeley, 1999.

Alston, R. "Roman Military Pay from Caesar to Diocletian." *JRS* 84 (1994): 113–23.

——— . *Soldier and Society in Roman Egypt: A Social History.* London, 1995.

Amer, G., and M. Gawlikowski. "Le sanctuaire impérial de Philoppopolis." *Damaszener Mitt.* 2 (1985): 1–14.

Amidon, P. R. *The Church History of Rufinus of Aquileia.* Oxford, 1997.

Andermahr, A. *Totus in Praediis. Senatorischer Grundbesitz in Italien in der Frühen und Hohen Kaiserzeit.* Bonn, 1998.

Anderson, G., *Philostratus: Biography and Belles Lettres in the Third Century AD* (London, 1986).

——— . "The Second Sophistic: Some Problems of Perspective." In *Antonine Literature*, ed. D. A. Russell, 91–110. Oxford, 1990.

——— . "Athenaeus: The Sophistic Environment." *ANRW* 34.3 (1997): 2173–85.

——— . "The Banquet of Belles-Lettres: Athenaeus and the Comic Symposium." In *Athenaeus and His World: Reading Greek Culture in the Roman Empire*, ed. D. Braund and J. Wilkins, 316–26. Exeter, 2000.

Anderson, M. J. *The Tale of Troy in Early Greek Poetry and Art*. Oxford, 1997.

Ando, C. "Pagan Apologetics and Christian Intolerance in the Age of Themistius and Augustine." *JECS* 4 (1996): 171–207.

——— . *Imperial Ideology and Provincial Loyalty in the Roman Empire*. Berkeley, 2000.

Andreau, J. "Financiers de l'aristocratie à la fin de la République." In *Le dernier siècle de la république romaine et l'époque augustéenne*, ed. E. Frézouls, 47–62. Strasbourg, 1978.

——— . *Banking and Business in the Roman World*. Cambridge, 1999.

Arnheim, M. T. W. "Vicars in the Later Roman Empire." *Historia* 19 (1970): 593–606.

Aronen, J. "Dragon Cults and ΝΥΜΦΗ ΔΡΑΚΑΙΝΑ in IGUR 974." *ZPE* 111 (1996): 125–32.

Athanassiadi, P. "The Chaldaean Oracles: Theology and Theurgy." In *Pagan Monotheism in Late Antiquity*, ed. P. Athanassiadi and M. Frede, 149–83. Oxford, 1999.

Athanassiadi, P., and M. Frede, eds. *Pagan Monotheism in Late Antiquity*. Oxford, 1999.

Athanassiadi-Fowden, P. *Julian and Hellenism: An Intellectual Biography*. Oxford, 1981.

Austin, N. J. E. "Julian at Ctesiphon: A Fresh Look at Ammianus' Account." *Athenaeum* 50 (1972): 301–9.

——— . "In Support of Ammianus' Veracity." *Historia* 22 (1973): 331–35.

Aymard, M. "Production et productivité agricole: L'Italie du Sud à l'époque moderne." In *Prestations paysannes, dîmes, rente foncière et mouvement de la production agricole à l'époque préindustrielle*, ed. J. Le Goy and E. Le Roy Ladurie, 147–63. Paris, 1982.

Babelon, J. "Protésilas à Scioné." *Revue numismatique*, 5th ser., 13 (1951): 1–11.

Bader, R. *Der ΑΛΗΘΗΣ ΛΟΓΟΣ des Kelsos*. Stuttgart, 1940.

Badian, E. "The Consuls, 179–49 BC." *Chiron* 20 (1990): 371–413.

Bagnall, R. S. "Count Ausonius." *Tyche* 7 (1992): 9–13.

——— . *Egypt in Late Antiquity*. Princeton, 1993.

Bagnall, R. S., and B. W. Frier. *The Demography of Roman Egypt*. Cambridge, 1994.

Baldini, A. "Il ruolo di Paolo di Samosata nella politica culturale di Zenobia e la decisione di Aureliano ad Antiochia." *Riv. Stor. Ant.* 5 (1975): 59–78.

Baldus, H. R. *Uranius Antoninus*. Bonn, 1971.

Ball, W. *Rome in the East: The Transformation of Empire*. London, 2000.

Balty, J.-C. "Nouvelles données sur l'armée romaine d'orient et les raids sassanides du milieu du IIIᵉ siècle." *CRAI* (1987): 213–42.

Banaji, J. *Agrarian Change in Late Antiquity*. Oxford, 2001.

Barbieri, A. "Settimio Nestore." *Athenaeum* 31 (1953): 158–69.

Barnes, C. L. *"Tarentum victum*: Processes of Evolution." PhD diss., University of Michigan, 1999.

Barnes, T. D. *Tertullian: A Historical and Literary Study*. Oxford, 1971.

——— . "Porphyry against the Christians: Date and Attribution of the Fragments." *JTS* 24 (1973): 424–42.

——— . "The Beginnings of Donatism." *JTS* 26 (1975): 13–22.

——— . "The Composition of Eusebius' *Onomasticon*." *JTS* 26 (1975): 412–15.

——— . "Two Senators under Constantine." *JRS* 65 (1975): 40–49.

——— . *The Sources of the Historia Augusta*. Brussels, 1978.

——— . "Imperial Chronology, AD 337–350," *Phoenix* (1980): 160–66.

——— . "The Editions of Eusebius' *Ecclesiastical History*." *GRBS* 21 (1980): 191–201.

——— . *Constantine and Eusebius*. Cambridge, Mass, 1981.

——— . *The New Empire of Diocletian and Constantine*. Cambridge, Mass., 1982.

——— . "Constantine and the Christians of Persia." *JRS* 75 (1985): 126–36.

——— . "The Conversion of Constantine." *Échos du Monde Classique* 4 (1985): 381–87. Also in *From Eusebius to Augustine: selected papers, 1982–1993* (Brookfield, VT, 1994), ch. 3.

——— . "Christians and Pagans under Constantius." In *L'église et l'empire au ive siècle*, 308–12. Entretiens Fondation Hardt 36. Geneva, 1987.

——— . "Himerius and the Fourth Century." *CPh* 82 (1987): 221–22. Also in *From Eusebius to Augustine* (Brookfield, VT, 1994).

——— . "Emperors on the Move." *JRA* 2 (1989): 247–61.

——— . "Panegyric, History, and Historiography in Eusebius' Life of Constantine." In *The Making of Orthodoxy: Essays in Honor of Henry Chadwick*, ed. R. Williams, 94–123. Cambridge, 1989.

——— . "The Consecration of Ulfila." *JTS* 41 (1990): 541–45. Also in *From Eusebius to Augustine* (Brookfield, VT, 1994), ch. 10.

——— . "The Sources of the *Historia Augusta*." In *Historiae Augustae Colloquium Parisinum*, ed. G. Bonamente and N. Duval, 1–28. Atti dei Convegni sulla Historia Augusta, n.s. 1. Macerata, 1991.

——— . *Athanasius and Constantius: Theology and Politics in the Constantinian Empire*. Cambridge, Mass., 1993.

——— . "Two Drafts of Eusebius' *Vita Constantini*." In *From Eusebius to Augustine*. Brookfield, VT, 1994.

——— . "Scholarship or Propaganda? Porphyry *Against the Christians* and Its Historical Setting." *BICS* 39 (1994): 53–65.

——— . "Statistics and the Conversion of the Roman Aristocracy." *JRS* 85 (1995): 134–38.

——— . "Emperors, Panegyrics, Prefects, Provinces, and Palaces (284–317)." *JRA* 9 (1996): 532–52.

——— . *Ammianus Marcellinus and the Representation of Historical Reality*. Ithaca, NY, 1998.

——— . "Constantine's Speech to the Assembly of the Saints: Place and Date of Delivery." *JTS* 52 (2001): 26–36.

——— . "Monotheists All?" *Phoenix* 55 (2001): 142–62.

Barnish, S. J. B. "A Note on the *Collatio Glebalis*." *Historia* 38 (1989): 254–56.

Bartelink, G. J. M. Athanase d'Alexandrie, *Vie d'Antoine. SC* no. 400. Paris, 1994.

Bassett, S. "The Antiquities in the Hippodrome at Constantinople." *DOP* 45 (1991): 87–96.

Baumgarten, A. L. *The Phoenician History of Philo of Byblos: A Commentary*. Leiden, 1981.

Bauzou, T. "Deux milliaires inédits de Vaballath en Jordanie du Nord." In *The Defense of the Roman and Byzantine East*, ed. P. Freeman and D. L. Kennedy, 1–8. BAR International Series 297. Oxford, 1986.

Baynes, N. H. *Constantine the Great and the Christian Church*. Intro. H. Chadwick. London, 1972. Reprint of lecture first published in *The Proceedings of the British Academy* 15 (1931): 341–42.

Beck, R. "Thus Spake Not Zarathustra: Zoroastrian Pseudepigrapha of the Greco-Roman World." In *A History of Zoroastrianism*, ed. M. Boyce and F. Grenet, 3: 491–565. Leiden, 1991.

——— . "The Mysteries of Mithras: A New Account of the Genesis." *JRS* 88 (1998): 115–28.

——— . "Ritual, Myth, Doctrine, and Initiation in the Mysteries of Mithras: New Evidence from a Cult Vessel." *JRS* 100 (2000): 145–80.

717

Bell, H. I. *Jews and Christians in Egypt: The Jewish Troubles in Alexandria and the Athanasian Controversy, Illustrated by Texts from Greek Papyri in the British Museum.* London, 1924.

Béranger, J. *Recherches sur l'aspect idéologique du principat.* Basel, 1953.

Berchem, D. van. *L'armée de Dioclétien et la réforme constantinienne.* Institut Français d'Archéologie de Beyrouth, Bibliothèque Archéologique et Historique, vol. 56. Paris, 1952.

Beskow, P. "The Routes of Early Mithraism." In *Études mithriaques: Actes du 2ᵉ Congrès International Téhéran, du 1ᵉʳ au 8 septembre 1975. Acta Iranica* 17 (1978): 7–18.

Bévenot, M. "Cyprian and His Recognition of Cornelius." *JTS* 28 (1977): 346–59.

Bickermann, E. *Das Edikt des Kaisers Caracalla in P. Geiss 40.* Berlin, 1926.

Bidez, J. *Vie de Porphyre le philosophe néo-platonicien.* Leipzig, 1913.

——. *L'empereur Julien: Lettres.* Paris, 1924.

Birley, A. R. *The Fasti of Roman Britain.* Oxford, 1981.

——. *Marcus Aurelius: A Biography.* New Haven, 1987.

——. *Septimius Severus: The African Emperor.* New Haven, 1988.

——. *Hadrian: The Restless Emperor.* London, 1997.

——. "Decius Reconsidered." In *Les empereurs illyriens: Actes du colloque de Strasbourg (11–13 octobre 1990) organisé par le Centre de Recherche sur l'Europe centrale et sud-orientale,* ed. E. Frézouls and H. Jouffroy, 57–80. Strasbourg, 1998.

——. "The Life and Death of Cornelius Tacitus," *Historia* 49 (2000): 230–47.

Blanchetière, F. "Julien philhellène, philosémite, antichrétien," *Journal of Jewish Studies* 31 (1980), 61–81.

Bleckmann, B. *Die Reichskrise des III. Jahrhunderts in der spätantiken und byzantinischen Geschichtsschreibung: Untersuchungen zu den nachdionischen Quellen der Chronik des Johannes Zonaras.* Munich, 1992.

Blockley, R. C. "Constantius II and His Generals." In *Studies in Latin Literature and Roman History,* ed. C. Deroux, 2: 467–86. Brussels, 1980.

——. *The Fragmentary Classicising Historians of the Later Roman Empire: Eunapius, Olympiodorus, Priscus, and Malchus.* 2 vols. Liverpool, 1981–83.

——. "Constantius II and Persia." In *Studies in Latin Literature and Roman History,* ed. C. Deroux, 5: 465–90. Brussels, 1989.

——. *East Roman Foreign Policy: Formation and Conduct from Diocletian to Anastasius.* Leeds, 1992.

Blumenthal, H. J. "On Soul and Intellect." In *The Cambridge Companion to Plotinus,* ed. L. P. Gerson, 82–104. Cambridge, 1996.

Bonnefond-Coudry, M. *Le sénat de la république romaine de la guerre d'Hannibal à Auguste.* Paris, 1989.

Boskovic, D., N. Duval, P. Gros, and V. Popovic. "Recherches archéologiques à Sirmium: Campagne Franco-Yugoslave de 1973." *MEFR* 86 (1974): 597–656.

Bosworth, A. B. "Arrian and the Alani." *HSCP* 81 (1977): 217–55.

Bosworth, C. E. *The History of al-Ṭabarī: The Sāsānids, the Byzantines, the Lakmids, and Yemen.* Albany, NY, 1999.

Bowersock, G. W. *Greek Sophists in the Roman Empire.* Oxford, 1969.

——. "Herodian and Elagabalus." *YCS* 24 (1975): 229–36.

——. *Julian the Apostate.* London, 1978.

——. "Plutarch and the Sublime Hymn of Ofellius Laetus." *GRBS* 22 (1982): 275–79. Also in Bowersock, *Studies on the Eastern Roman Empire,* 61–65.

——. "Roman Senators from the Greek East: Syria, Judaea, Arabia, Mesopotamia." *Epigrafia e ordine senatorio* 2, *Tituli,* 5, 651–68. Rome, 1982. Also in Bowersock, *Studies on the Eastern Roman Empire,* 141–59.

718

——. *Roman Arabia*. Cambridge, Mass., 1983.

——. "The Miracle of Memnon." *BASP* 21 (1984): 21–32. Also in Bowersock, *Studies on the Eastern Roman Empire*, 263–64.

——. "Hadrian and Metropolis." *BHAC* 17, 75–88. Bonn, 1985 (Also in *Studies on the Eastern Roman Empire*, 371–84).

——. "The Hexameter Poems Ascribed to Oppian." In *The Cambridge History of Classical Literature*, ed. P. Easterling and B. M. W. Knox, vol. 1, pt. 4, 93–94. Cambridge, 1989.

——. "Philostratus and the Second Sophistic." In *The Cambridge History of Classical Literature*, ed. P. Easterling and B. M. W. Knox, vol. 1, pt. 4, 95–98. Cambridge, 1989.

——. *Hellenism in Late Antiquity*. Ann Arbor, 1990.

——. *Fiction as History: Nero to Julian*. Berkeley, 1994.

——. *Studies on the Eastern Roman Empire: Social, Economic, and Administrative History, Religion, Historiography*. Goldbach, 1994.

——. "The New Inscription from Rāsūn in Jordan." *Syria* 76 (1999): 223–25.

Bowie, E. L. "Greeks and Their Past in the Second Sophistic." *Past and Present* 46 (1970): 3–41. Also in *Studies in Ancient Society*, ed. M. I. Finley (London, 1974), 166–209.

——. "Apollonius of Tyana: Tradition and Reality." *ANRW* 2.16.2 (1978): 1652–99.

——. "The Greek Novel." In *The Cambridge History of Classical Literature*, ed. P. Easterling and B. M. W. Knox, vol. 1, pt. 4, 123–39. Cambridge, 1989. Also in *Oxford Readings in the Greek Novel*, ed. S. Swain (Oxford, 1999), 39–59.

——. "Greek Poetry in the Antonine Age." In *Antonine Literature*, ed. D. A. Russell, 53–90. Oxford, 1990.

——. "The Readership of Greek Novels in the Ancient World." In *The Search for the Ancient Novel*, ed. J. Tatum, 435–59. Baltimore, 1994.

Boyce, M. *A Reader in Manichaean Middle Persian and Parthian. Acta Iranica. Textes et Mémoires* 9. Leiden, 1975.

——. *A History of Zoroastrianism*. Vol. 2, *Under the Achaemenians*. Leiden, 1982.

Boyce, M., and F. Grenet. *A History of Zoroastrianism*, vol. 3, *Zoroastrianism under Macedonian and Roman Rule*. Leiden, 1991.

Bradbury, S. "The Date of Julian's Letter to Themistius." *GRBS* 28 (1987): 235–51.

——. "Constantine and the Problem of Anti-Pagan Legislation in the Fourth Century." *CPh* 89 (1994): 120–39.

Brakke, D. *Athanasius and the Politics of Asceticism*. Oxford, 1995.

Brandt, H. *Maximi et Balbini. Kommentar zur Historia Augusta*. Vol. 2. Bonn, 1996.

Brasher, W. "Ein Berliner Zauberpapyrus." *ZPE* 33 (1979): 261–78.

Brauch, T. "Themistius and the Emperor Julian." *Byzantion* 63 (1993): 79–115.

Braudel, F. *The Structures of Everyday Life*. Trans. S. Reynolds. New York, 1981.

Braund, D. *Georgia in Antiquity: A History of Colchis and Transcaucasian Iberia, 550 BC–AD 562*. Oxford, 1994.

——. "Learning, Luxury, and Empire: Athenaeus' Roman Patron." In *Athenaeus and His World: Reading Greek Culture in the Roman Empire*, ed. D. Braund and J. Wilkins, 3–22. Exeter, 2000.

Brennan, P. "The *Notitia Dignitatum*." In *Les littératures techniques dans l'antiquité romaine: Status, public et destination, tradition*, ed. C. Nicolet, 147–71. Entretiens Fondation Hardt 42. Geneva, 1995.

Brent, A. *Hippolytus and the Roman Church in the Third Century: Communities in Tension before the Emergence of a Monarch-Bishop*. Leiden, 1995.

Brock, S. "The Rebuilding of the Temple under Julian: A New Source." *PEQ* 108 (1976): 103–7.

——— . "A Letter Attributed to Cyril of Jerusalem on the Rebuilding of the Temple." *BSOAS* 40 (1977): 267–86.

——— . "From Antagonism to Assimilation: Syriac Attitudes to Greek Learning." In *East of Byzantium: Syria and Armenia in the Formative Period*, ed. N. G. Garsoïan, T. F. Matthews, and R. W. Thomson, 17–34. Dumbarton Oaks Symposium, 1980. Washington, DC, 1982.

Broughton, T. R. S. *The Magistrates of the Roman Republic.* Vol. 2. New York, 1952.

Brown, P. *Augustine of Hippo.* Berkeley, 1967.

——— . "The Rise and Function of the Holy Man in Late Antiquity." *JRS* 61 (1971): 80–101. Also in *Society and the Holy in Late Antiquity* (London, 1982), 103–52.

——— . *The Cult of the Saints: Its Rise and Function in Latin Christianity.* Chicago, 1981.

——— . *Power and Persuasion in Late Antiquity.* Madison, 1992.

——— . *Authority and the Sacred: Aspects of the Christianization of the Roman World.* Cambridge, 1995.

——— . "Asceticism: Pagan and Christian." In *The Cambridge Ancient History*, ed. A. Cameron and P. Garnsey, 13: 601–31. 2nd. edn. Cambridge, 1998.

——— . *Poverty and Leadership in the Later Roman Empire.* Hanover, 2002.

Brünnow, R. E., and A. von Domaszewski. *Die Provincia Arabia.* Vol. 3. Strasbourg, 1909.

Brunt, P. A. "Procuratorial Jurisdiction." *Latomus* 25 (1966): 481–83. Also in Brunt, *Roman Imperial Themes* (Oxford, 1990), 182–83.

——— . *Italian Manpower, 225 BC–AD 14.* Oxford, 1971.

——— . "Marcus Aurelius in His *Meditations*." *JRS* 64 (1974): 1–20.

——— . "The Administrators of Roman Egypt." *JRS* 65 (1975): 124–47. Also in Brunt, *Roman Imperial Themes*, 215–54.

——— . "Did Imperial Rome Disarm Her Subjects?" *Phoenix* 29 (1975): 260–70. Also in Brunt, *Roman Imperial Themes*, 255–66.

——— . "*Lex de imperio Vespasiani*." *JRS* 67 (1977): 95–116.

——— . "The Revenues of Rome." *JRS* 71 (1981): 161–72. Reprinted with additional material in Brunt, *Roman Imperial Themes*, 329–35.

——— . "*Nobilitas* and *Novitas*." *JRS* 72 (1982): 1–17.

——— . "Princeps and Equites." *JRS* 73 (1983): 42–75.

——— . "Publicans and the Principate." In Brunt, *Roman Imperial Themes*, 393–414.

——— . *Roman Imperial Themes.* Oxford, 1990.

——— . "The Bubble of the Second Sophistic." *BICS* 39 (1994): 25–52.

Burckhardt, J. *Die Zeit des Konstantins des Grossen.* 1853. Trans. as *The Age of Constantine the Great* by M. Hadas (New York, 1949).

Bureth, P. *Les titulatures impériales dans les papyrus, le ostraca et les inscriptions d'Égypte (30 a.C.–284 p.C.).* Brussels, 1964.

Burgess, R. W. *The Chronicle of Hydatius and the Consularia Constantinopolitana: Two Contemporary Accounts of the Final Years of the Roman Empire.* Oxford, 1993.

——— . "The Date of the Persecution of Christians in the Army." *JTS* 47 (1996): 157–58.

——— . "ΑΧΥΡΩΝ or ΠΡΟΑΣΤΕΙΟΝ: The Location and Circumstances of Constantine's Death." *JTS* 50 (1999): 153–61.

——— . *Studies in Eusebian and Post-Eusebian Chronography. Historia* Einzelschriften 135. Stuttgart, 1999.

——— . "Eutropius *v.c. magister memoriae.*" *CPh* 96 (2001): 76–81.

Burns, T. S. "The Battle of Adrianople: A Reconsideration." *Historia* 22 (1973): 336–45.

Burton, G. P. "Proconsuls, Assizes, and the Administration of Justice." *JRS* 65 (1975): 92–106.

———. "The *Curator Rei Publicae*: Towards a Reappraisal." *Chiron* 9 (1979): 465–87.

Butcher, K. E. T. "Imagined Emperors: Personalities and Political Failure in the Third Century." *JRA* 9 (1996): 515–27.

Butler, H. C. *Architecture and Other Arts: Publications of the American Archeological Expedition to Syria in 1899–1900*. Vol. 2. New York, 1903.

Callu, J.-P. *La politique monétaire des empereurs romains de 238 à 311*. Paris, 1969.

Calvert, F. "The Tumulus of Hanai Tepe in the Troad." *Archaeological Journal* 16 (1859): 1–6.

Calza, R. "Un problema di iconografia imperiale sull' arco di Constantino." *APARA Rendiconti* 32 (1960): 131–61.

Cameron, A. "Eusebius' *Vita Constantini* and the Construction of Constantine." In *Portraits: Biographical Representation in the Greek and Latin Literature of the Roman Empire*, ed. M. Edwards and S. Swain, 145–74. Oxford, 1997.

Cameron, A., and S. G. Hall. *Eusebius: The Life of Constantine*. Oxford, 1999.

Cameron, A. D. E. "Gratian's Repudiation of the Pontifical Robe." *JRS* 58 (1968): 96–102.

———. *Claudian: Poetry and Propaganda at the Court of Honorius*. Oxford, 1970.

———. *Circus Factions*. Oxford, 1976.

Campbell, J. B. "The Marriage of Soldiers under the Empire." *JRS* 68 (1978): 153–66.

———. *The Emperor and the Roman Army, 31 BC–AD 235*. Oxford, 1984.

———. "Teach Yourself to Be a Roman General." *JRS* 77 (1987): 13–29.

———. *The Roman Army, 31 BC–AD 337: A Sourcebook*. London, 1994.

———. *The Writings of the Roman Land Surveyors: Introduction, Text, Translation, and Commentary. Journal of Roman Studies* Monograph 9. London, 2000.

Campenhausen, H. von. *The Formation of the Christian Bible*. Trans. J. A. Baker. Philadelphia, 1972.

Camps, G. "Qui sont les Dii Mauri?" *Ant. afr.* 26 (1990): 131–53.

Carradice, I., and M. Crowell. "The Minting of Roman Imperial Bronze Coins for Circulation in the East: Vespasian to Trajan." *NC* 147 (1987): 26–50.

Carroll, J. *Constantine's Sword: The Church and the Jews*. New York, 2001.

Casey, P. J. *The British Usurpers: Carausius and Allectus*. New Haven, 1994.

Casey, P. M. "Porphyry and the Origin of the Book of Daniel." *JTS* 27 (1976): 15–33.

Casson, L. "New Light on Maritime Loans: P. Vindob. G 40822." *ZPE* 84 (1990): 195–206.

Cerrato, J. A. *Hippolytus Between East and West: The Commentaries and the Provenance of the Corpus*. Oxford, 2002.

Chadwick, H. "The Fall of Eustathius of Antioch." *JTS* 49 (1948): 27–35. Also in *History and Thought of the Early Church* (London, 1982), ch. 13.

———. "Faith and Order at the Council of Nicaea: A Note on the Background of the Sixth Canon." *HTR* 53 (1960): 179. Also in *History and Thought of the Early Church* (London, 1982), ch. 12.

———, ed. *Origen, Contra Celsum*. Rev. edn. Cambridge, 1965.

———. "Orthodoxy and Heresy from the Death of Constantine to the Eve of the First Council of Ephesus." In *The Cambridge Ancient History*. 2nd edn. Vol. 13, ed. A. Cameron and P. D. Garnsey, 561–600. Cambridge, 1998.

Chastagnol, A. *Les fastes de la Préfecture de Rome au Bas-Empire.* Paris, 1962.

———. "Les années régnales de Maximien Hercule en Égypte et les fêtes vicennales du 20 Novembre 303." *Revue Numismatique*, 6th ser., 9 (1967): 54–81.

———. "À propos du 'judicium magnum' de l'empereur Probus." *BHAC 1966–67*. Bonn, 1968.

———. "L'évolution de l'ordre sénatorial aux iii et iv siècles de notre ère." *Revue Historique* 244 (1970): 305–14.

———. "Sources, thèmes et procédés de composition dans les Quadrigae Tyrannorum." In *Recherches sur l'Histoire Auguste avec un rapport sur les progrès de la Historia Augusta Forschung depuis 1963.* Bonn, 1970.

———. "Remarques sur les sénateurs orientaux au IVe siècle." *Acta Antiqua* 24 (1976): 341–56.

———. "L'inscription constantinienne d'Orcistus." *MEFRA* 93 (1981): 381–416.

Chaumont, M.-L. "Conquêtes sassanides et propagande mazdéene." *Historia* 22 (1973): 664–709.

Cheesman, G. L. *The Auxilia of the Roman Imperial Army.* Oxford, 1914.

Chiesa, P. "Un testo agiografico africano ad Aquileia: gli Acta di Gallonio e dei martiri di Timida Regia," *Analecta Bollandiana* 114 (1996): 241–68.

Christol, M. "Les règnes de Valérien et de Gallien (253–268), travaux d'ensemble, questions chronologiques." *ANRW* 2.2 (1975): 803–27.

———. "La carrière de Traianus Mucianus et l'origine des *protectores*." *Chiron* 7 (1977): 393–408.

———. "A propos de la politique extérieure de Trébonien Galle." *Rev. num.* 22 (1980): 68–74.

———. "Les réformes de Gallien et la carrière sénatoriale." *Epigraprafia e ordine senatorio* 1, *Tituli*, 4, 143–66. Rome 1982.

———. *Essai sur l'évolution des carrières sénatoriales dans la seconde moitié du IIIe siècle ap. J.C.* Paris, 1986.

———. "L'ascension de l'ordre équestre: Un thème historiographique et sa réalité." In *L'ordre équestre d'une aristocratie (iie siècle av. J.-C.–iiie siècle ap. J.-C.)*, ed. S. Demougin, H. Devijver, and M.-T. Rapsaet-Charlier, 613–28. Paris, 1999.

Christol, M., and T. Drew-Bear. "Un inscription d'Ancyre relative au *sacer comitatus*." In *Les légions de Rome sous le Haut-Empire. Actes du Congrès de Lyon (17–19 septembre 1998)*, ed. Y. Le Bohec and C. Wolff, 529–39. Lyons, 2000.

Christol, M. and X. Loriot, "À propos de l'inscription d'Augsbourg: remarques liminaires," *Cahiers Glotz* 8 (1997): 223–27.

Clark, G. *Porphyry: On Abstinence from Killing Animals.* London, 2000.

———. "Philosophic Lives and the Philosophic Life: Porphyry and Iamblichus." In *Greek Biography and Panegyric in Late Antiquity*, ed. T. Hägg and P. Rousseau, 29–51. Berkeley, 2000.

Clauss, M. *The Roman Cult of Mithras: The God and His Mysteries.* Trans. R. Gordon. London, 2000.

Colpe, C. "Development of Religious Thought." In *The Cambridge History of Iran*, ed. E. Yarshater, vol. 3, pt. 2, 834.

Conte, G. B. *Latin Literature: A History.* Trans. J. Solodow. Baltimore, 1994.

Cooper, K. *The Virgin and the Bride: Idealized Womanhood in Late Antiquity.* Cambridge, Mass., 1996.

Cope, L. H. "The Nadir of the Imperial Antoninianus in the Reign of Claudius II Gothicus, AD 268–70." *NC* 9 (1969): 145–61.

Copenhaver, B. P. *Hermetica: The Greek Corpus Hermeticum and the Latin Asclepius in a New English Translation, with Notes and Introduction.* Cambridge, 1992.

Corbeill, A. "Thumbs in Ancient Rome: Pollex as Index." *MAAR* 42 (1997): 1–21.

Corbier, M. "Dévaluations et évolution des prix (Ier–IIIe siècles)," *Revue numismatique* 27 (1985): 69–106.

Corcoran, S. "Hidden from History: The Legislation of Licinius." In *The Theodosian Code*, ed. J. Harries and I. Wood, 97–119. Ithaca, NY, 1993.

——. *The Empire of the Tetrarchs: Imperial Pronouncements and Government AD 284–324.* Rev. edn. Oxford, 2000.

Cornell, T. J. *The Beginnings of Rome.* London, 1995.

Coupel, P., and E. Frézouls. *Le théâtre de Philippopolis en Arabie.* Paris, 1956.

Cox, P. *Biography in Late Antiquity: A Quest for the Holy Man.* Berkeley, 1983.

Cox Miller, P. "Strategies of Representation in Collective Biography: Constructing the Subject as Holy." In *Greek Biography and Panegyric in Late Antiquity*, ed. T. Hägg and P. Rousseau, 209–54. Berkeley, 2000.

Cramer, F. H. *Astrology in Roman Law and Politics.* Philadelphia, 1954.

Cramer, W. "Harran." *RAC* 634–50.

Crawford, M. H. *Roman Statutes.* London, 1996.

Cresci, L. "The Novel of Longus the Sophist and the Pastoral Tradition." In *Oxford Readings in the Greek Novel*, ed. S. Swain, 210–42. Oxford, 1999.

Croke, B. "Arbogast and the Death of Valentinian II." *Historia* 25 (1976): 235–44.

——. "The Era of Porphyry's Anti-Christian Polemic." *Journal of Religious History* 13 (1984): 1–14.

——. "City Chronicles in Late Antiquity." In *Reading the Past in Late Antiquity*, ed. G. Clarke, B. Croke, R. Mortley, and A. E. Nobbs, 165–203. Sydney, 1990.

——. *Count Marcellinus and His Chronicle.* Oxford, 2001.

Crouzel, H. *Origène.* Paris, 1985.

Crump, G. A. "Ammianus and the Late Roman Army." *Historia* 22 (1973): 91–103.

Csapo, E., and W. J. Slater. *The Context of Ancient Drama.* Ann Arbor, 1995.

Cuneo, P. *La legislazione di Constantino II, Constanzo II e Constante (337–361).* Milan, 1997.

Curran, J. "Moving Statues in Late Antique Rome: Problems of Perspective." *Art History* 17 (1994): 46–58.

——. "From Jovian to Theodosius." In *The Cambridge Ancient History.* 2nd. edn. Vol. 13, ed. A. Cameron and P. D. Garnsey, 78–110. Cambridge, 1998.

——. *Pagan City and Christian Capital: Rome in the Fourth Century.* Oxford, 2000.

Curtis, R. I. *Garum and Salsamenta: Production and Commerce in Materia Medica.* Leiden, 1991.

Dagron, G. *Naissance d'une capitale: Constantinople et ses institutions de 330 à 451.* Paris, 1974.

——. *Vie et miracles de sainte Thècle: Texte grec, traduction et commentaire.* Subsidia Hagiographica 62. Brussels, 1978.

Dagron, G., and D. Feissel. *Inscriptions de Cilicie.* Paris, 1987.

Davidson, J. *Courtesans and Fishcakes.* New York, 1998.

——. "Pleasure and Pedantry in Athenaeus." In *Athenaeus and His World: Reading Greek Culture in the Roman Empire*, ed. D. Braund and J. Wilkins, 292–303. Exeter, 2000.

Davis, S. J. *The Cult of Saint Thecla: A Tradition of Women's Piety in Late Antiquity* (Oxford, 2001).

de Blois, L. *The Policy of the Emperor Gallienus.* Leiden, 1976.

Declerck, J. H. "Deux nouveaux fragments attribués à Paul de Samosate." *Byzantion* 54 (1984): 116–40.

de Dominicis, M. "L'apicultura e alcune questioni connesse nel regolomento di un fundo imperiale africano." *RIDA*, 3rd ser., 1960.

de Ligt, L. *Fairs and Markets in the Roman Empire: Economic and Social Aspects of Periodic Trade in a Pre-industrial Society.* Amsterdam, 1993.

Demandt, A. "Der Tod des älteren Theodosius." *Historia* 18 (1969): 598–626.

——. "Die Feldzüge des älteren Theodosius." *Hermes* 100 (1972): 81–113.

Demougin, S. *L'ordre équestre sous les Julio-claudiens.* Rome, 1988.

——. "Considérations sur l'avancement dans les carrières procuratoriennes équestres." In *Administration, Prosopography, and Appointment Policies in the Roman Empire*, ed. L. De Blois, 24–34. Amsterdam, 2001.

Demougin, S., H. Devijver, and M.-T. Rapsaet-Charlier, eds. *L'ordre équestre d'une aristocratie (iie siècle av. J.-C.–iiie siècle ap. J.-C.).* Paris, 1999.

Derks, T. *Gods, Temples, and Ritual Practices: The Transformation of Religious Ideas and Values in Roman Gaul.* Amsterdam, 1998.

Des Places, É. *Oracles Chaldaïques avec un choix de commentaires anciens.* Paris, 1971.

Devijver, H. "Les relations sociales des chevaliers romains." In *L'ordre équestre d'une aristocratie (iie siècle av. J.-C.–iiie siècle ap. J.-C.)*, ed. S. Demougin, H. Devijver, and M.-T. Rapsaet-Charlier, 237–69. Paris, 1999.

Dewar, M. *Claudian: Panegyricus de sexto consulatu Honorii Augusti.* Oxford, 1996.

Dietz, K. *Senatus contra principem: Untersuchungen zur senatorischen Opposition gegen Kaiser Maximinus Thrax.* Munich, 1980.

——. "Caracalla, Fabius Cilo und die Urbaniciani: Unerkannt gebliebene Suffectkonsuln des Jahres 212 n. Chr." *Chiron* 13 (1983): 381–404.

——. "Kaiser Julian in Phönizien." *Chiron* 30 (2000): 807–55.

Digeser, E. "Lactantius, Porphyry, and the Debate over Religious Toleration." *JRS* 88 (1998): 129–46.

Dijkstra, M., and A. M. F. W. Verhoogt. "The Greek–Palmyrene Inscription." In *Report of the 1997 Excavations at Berenike and the Survey of the Egyptian Desert, including Excavations at Shenshef*, ed. S. E. Sidebotham and W. Z. Wendrich, 207–19. Leiden, 1999.

Dillon, M. *The Middle Platonists: A Study of Platonism, 80 BC to AD 220.* London, 1977.

Dodgeon, M. H., and S. N. C. Lieu. *The Roman Eastern Frontier and the Persian Wars: A Documentary History.* London, 1991.

Domaszewski, A. von. "Die Personennamen bei den Scriptores Historiae Augustae," *Sitzungsberichte der Heidelberger Akademie der Wissenschaften. Philosophisch-historische Klasse, Jahrgang 1918.* Vol. 13. Heidelberg, 1918.

Downey, G. "Malalas on the History of Antioch under Severus and Caracalla." *TAPA* 68 (1937): 141–56.

——. "The Builder of the Original Church of the Apostles at Constantinople: A Contribution to the Criticism of the Vita Constantini Attributed to Eusebius." *DOP* 6 (1951): 53–80.

——. *A History of Antioch in Syria from Seleucus to the Arab Conquest.* Princeton, 1961.

Drake, H. "What Eusebius Knew: The Genesis of the *Vita Constantini*." *CPh* 83 (1988): 20–38.

——. *Constantine and the Bishops.* Baltimore, 2000.

Drew-Bear, T. "Les voyages d'Aurélius Gaius, soldat de Dioclétien," in *La géographie administrative et politique d'Alexandre à Mahomet: Actes du Colloque de Strasbourg 14–16 juin 1979*, ed. T. Fahd, 93–141. Strasbourg, 1979.

Drijvers, H. J. W. *The Book of the Laws of Countries: Dialogue on Fate of Bardaisan of Edessa*. Leiden, 1965.

———. "Hatra Palmyra und Edessa: Die Städte der syrisch–mesopotamischen Wüste in politischer kulturgeschichtlicher und religionsgeschtlicher Beleuchtung." *ANRW* 2.8 (1997): 799–906.

Drijvers, J. H. W. *Helena Augusta: The Mother of Constantine the Great and the Legend of Her Finding of the True Cross*. Leiden, 1992.

Drinkwater, J. F. "The 'Pagan Underground.' Constantius II's 'Secret Service' and the Survival, and the Usurpation of Julian the Apostate." In *Studies in Latin Literature and Roman History*, vol. 3, ed. C. Deroux, 348–87. Brussels, 1983.

———. *The Gallic Empire: Separatism and Community in the North-Western Provinces of the Roman Empire, AD 260–274. Historia* Einzelschriften 52. Stuttgart, 1987.

———. "The Revolt and Ethnic Origin of the Usurper Magnentius (350–353) and the Rebellion of Vetranio (350)." *Chiron* 30 (2000): 131–59.

Drury, M. "Appendix of Authors and Works." In *The Cambridge History of Classical Literature*, ed. P. Easterling and B. M. W. Knox, 1: 721–892 Cambridge, 1989.

Duchesne-Guillemin, J. "Zoroastrian Religion." In *The Cambridge History of Iran*, ed. E. Yarshater, vol. 3, pt. 2: 866–74. Cambridge, 1983.

Dunand, F. *Le culte d'Isis dans le bassin orientale de la méditerranée*. Leiden, 1973.

Duncan-Jones, R. P. "An African Saint and his Interrogator," *JTS* 25 (1974): 106–10.

———. "The Price of Wheat in Roman Egypt." *Chiron* 6 (1976): 241–62. Also in Duncan-Jones, *Structure and Scale in the Roman Economy*, 143–55.

———. "Pay and Numbers in Diocletian's Army." In Duncan-Jones, *Structure and Scale in the Roman Economy*, 105–17.

———. *Structure and Scale in the Roman Economy*. Cambridge, 1990.

———. *Money and Government in the Roman Empire*. Cambridge, 1994.

Dušanić, S. "The End of the Philippi." *Chiron* 6 (1976): 427–39.

Duval, N. "Les palais impériaux de Milan et d'Aquilée, réalité et mythe." *Antichità alto-adriatiche* 4 (1973): 151–58.

———. "Les résidences impériales: Leur rapport avec les problèmes de légitimité, les partages de l'Empire et les combinaisons dynastiques." In *Usurpation in der Spätantike*, ed. F. Paschoud and J. Szidat, 127–54. *Historia* Einzelschriften 111. Stuttgart, 1997.

Duval, Y. *Loca Sanctorum Africae: Le culte des martyrs en Afrique du ive au viie siècle*. Collection de l'École Française de Rome 58. Rome, 1982.

Eadie, J. "The Development of Roman Mailed Cavalry," *JRS* 57 (1967): 161–73.

———. "One Hundred Years of Rebellion: The Eastern Army in Politics, AD 175–272." In *The Roman Army in the East*, ed. D. L. Kennedy, 133–51. *JRA* Supplement 18. Ann Arbor, 1996.

———. "The Transformation of the Eastern Frontier, 260–305." In *Shifting Frontiers in Late Antiquity*, ed. R. W. Mathisen and H. S. Sivan, 72–79. Brookfield, VT, 1996.

Easterling, P., and B. M. W. Knox, eds. *The Cambridge History of Classical Literature*. Vol. 1, pt. 4. Cambridge, 1989.

Easton, D. F. "Troy before Schliemann." *Studia Troica* 1 (1991): 111–29.

Eck, W. "Das Eindringen des Christentums in den Senatorenstand bis zu Konstantin d. Gr." *Chiron* 1 (1971): 381–406.

——. "Beförderungskriterien innerhalb der senatorischen Laufbahn, dargestellt an der Zeit von 69 bis 138 n. Chr." *ANRW* 2.1 (1974): 158–228.

——. *Tra epigrafia prosopografia e archeologia.* Rome, 1996.

——. "*Ordo Equitum Romanorum, Ordo Libertorum*: Freigelassene und ihre Nachkommen im römischen Ritterstand." In *L'ordre équestre d'une aristocratie (iie siècle av. J.-C.–iiie siècle ap. J.-C.),* ed. S. Demougin, H. Devijver, and M.-T. Rapsaet-Charlier, 5–29. Paris, 1999.

——. "Emperor, Senate, and Magistrates." In *The Cambridge Ancient History.* 2nd edn. Vol. 11, ed. A. K. Bowman, P. Garnsey, and D. Rathbone, 214–37. Cambridge, 2000.

——. "The Growth of Administrative Posts." In *The Cambridge Ancient History.* 2nd edn. Vol. 11, ed. A. K. Bowman, P. Garnsey, and D. Rathbone, 238–65. Cambridge, 2000.

Edmondson, J. C. "Mining in the Later Roman Empire and Beyond: Continuity or Disruption?" *JRS* 79 (1989): 84–102.

——. "Dynamic Arenas: Gladiatorial Presentations in the City of Rome and the Construction of Roman Society during the Early Empire." In *Roman Theater and Society,* ed. W. J. Slater, 69–112. Ann Arbor, 1996.

Edwards, M. *Optatus: Against the Donatists.* Liverpool, 1997.

——. "Birth, Death and Divinity in Porphyry's *Life of Plotinus.*" In *Greek Biography and Panegyric in Late Antiquity,* ed. T. Hägg and P. Rousseau, 52–71. Berkeley, 2000.

Ehling, K. "Das Ausgang des Perserfeldzuges in der Münzpropaganda des Jovian." *Klio* 78 (1996): 186–91.

Ehrhardt, A. "The First Two Years of the Emperor Theodosius." *JEH* 15 (1964): 1–17.

Elks, K. J. J. "Reattribution of the Milan Coins of Trajan Decius to the Rome Mint." *NC* 12 (1972): 111–15.

Elm, S. *Virgins of God: The Making of Asceticism in Late Antiquity.* Oxford, 1994.

Elmer, G. "Die Münzprägung der gallischen Kaiser in Köln, Trier und Mailand." *Bonner Jahrbücher* 146 (1941): 1–106.

Elton, H. *Warfare in Roman Europe, AD 350–450.* Oxford, 1996.

Emmett, A. "Female Ascetics in the Greek Papyri." In Akten: *XVI. Internationaler Byzantinistenkongress Wien 4.–9. Oktober 1981,* ed. W. Hörander. 23.2. Vienna, 1982. 507–15.

Equini Schneider, E. *Septimia Zenobia Sebaste.* Rome, 1993.

Erim, K. T., J. Reynolds, and M. H. Crawford. "Diocletian's Currency Reform: A New Inscription." *JRS* 61 (1971): 171–77.

Errington, R. M. "Constantine and the Pagans." *GRBS* 29 (1988): 309–18.

——. "The Accession of Theodosius I." *Klio* 78 (1996): 438–53.

——. "Theodosius and the Goths." *Chiron* 26 (1996): 1–27.

——. "Christian Accounts of the Religious Legislation of Theodosius I." *Klio* 79 (1997): 398–43.

——. "Themistius and His Emperors." *Chiron* 30 (2000): 861–904.

Erskine, A. *Troy between Greece and Rome: Local Tradition and Imperial Power.* Oxford, 2001.

Esmonde Cleary, S. *The Ending of Roman Britain.* London, 1989.

Evans Grubbs, J. "Abduction Marriage in Antiquity: A Law of Constantine (CTh IX. 24.1) and Its Social Context." *JRS* 79 (1989): 59–83.

——. "Constantine and Imperial Legislation on the Family." In *The Theodosian Code,* ed. J. Harries and I. Wood, 120–42. Ithaca, NY, 1993.

——. *Law and Family in Late Antiquity: The Emperor Constantine's Marriage Legislation.* Oxford, 1995.

Fear, A. T. *Rome and Baetica: Urbanization in Southern Spain, c. 50 BC–AD 150.* Oxford, 1996.

Feissel, D. "Remarques de toponymie syrienne d'après des inscriptions grecques chrétiennes trouvées hors de Syrie." *Syria* 59 (1982): 319–41.

———. "Les constitutions des tétrarques connues par l'épigraphie: inventaire et notes
critiques," *L'Antiquité Tardive* 3 (1995): 33–53.

———. "Deux constitutions tétrarchiques inscrits à Éphèse," *L'Antiquité Tardive* 4 (1996):
273–89.

Felix, W. *Antike literarische Quellen zur Aussenpolitik des Sasanidenstaates.* Vol. 1. Österreichische Akademie der Wissenschaften, Phil.-Hist. Klasse. *Sitzungsberichte* 456.
Vienna, 1985.

Fentress, E. W. B. "Dii Mauri and Dii Patrii." *Latomus* 27 (1978): 507–16.

Festugière, A. J. "L'expérience religeuse du médecin Thessalos." *RB* 48 (1939): 45–77.

———. *La Révélation d'Hermès Trismégiste.* Vol. 1. Paris, 1950.

Fethi-Bejaoui, M. "Deux mosaïques tardives de la région de Sheïtla, l'antique Sufetula
en Tunisie," *CRAI* (2001): 489–516.

Finhman, I. F. "State and Prices in Byzantine Egypt." *Scripta Classica Israelica* 11 (1991/2):
139–48.

Fitz, J. "A Military History of Pannonia from the Marcomannic Wars to the Death of
Alexander Severus (180–235)," *A. Arch. Hung.* 14 (1962): 25–112.

———. *Ingenuus et Régalien.* Brussels, 1976.

Forgiarini, T. "À propos de Claude II: Les invasions gothiques de 269–270 et le rôle de
l'empereur." In *Les empereurs illyriens: Actes du colloque de Strasbourg (11–13 octobre 1990)
organisé par le Centre de Recherche sur l'Europe centrale et sud-orientale,* ed. E. Frézouls and
H. Jouffroy, 80–86. Strasbourg, 1998.

Fowden, G. "The Pagan Holy Man in Late Antique Society." *JHS* 102 (1982): 33–59.

———. *The Egyptian Hermes.* Cambridge, 1986.

———. "Nicagoras of Athens and the Lateran Obelisk." *JHS* 107 (1987): 51–57.

———. "City and Mountain in Late Roman Attica." *JHS* 108 (1988): 48–59.

———. "Constantine's Porphyry Column: The Earliest Literary Allusion." *JRS* 81 (1991):
119–31.

———. *Empire to Commonwealth: Consequences of Monotheism in Late Antiquity.* Princeton,
1993.

———. "The Last Days of Constantine: Oppositional Versions and Their Influence." *JRS*
84 (1994): 163–68.

Foxhall, L., and H. A. Forbes. "*Sitometreia*: The Role of Grain as Staple Food in Classical
Antiquity." *Chiron* 12 (1982): 41–90.

Frankfurter, D. *Religion in Roman Egypt: Assimilation and Resistance.* Princeton, 1998.

Fraser, P. M. *Ptolemaic Alexandria.* Oxford, 1972.

Frede, M. "Celsus Philosophus Platonicus." *ANRW* 2.36.7 (1994): 5183–5213.

———. "Origen's Treatise, *Against Celsus.*" In *Apologetics in the Roman Empire: Pagans,
Jews, and Christians,* ed. M. Edwards, M. Goodman, and S. Price, 131–55. Oxford,
1999.

Frend, W. H. C. *The Donatist Church: A Movement of Protest in Roman North Africa.* Oxford,
1952.

Frey, M. *Untersuchungen zur Religion und zur Religionspolitik des Kaisers Elagabal. Historia*
Einzelschriften 62. Stuttgart, 1989.

Frézouls, E., and H. Jouffroy, eds. *Les empereurs illyriens: Actes du colloque de Strasbourg
(11–13 octobre 1990) organisé par le Centre de Recherche sur l'Europe centrale et sud-orientale.*
Strasbourg, 1998.

Friedrich, H. V. *Thessalos von Tralles*. Meisenhaim am Glan, 1968.

Frier, B. W. "Early Classical Private Law." In *The Cambridge Ancient History*. 2nd. edn. Vol. 10, ed. A. K. Bowman, E. Champlin, and A. Lintott, 959–78. Cambridge, 1996.

——. "Roman Demography." In *Life, Death, and Entertainment in the Roman Empire*, ed. D. S. Potter and D. J. Mattingly, 85–109. Ann Arbor, 1999.

Frisch, P. *Zehn agonistische Papyri*. Opladen, 1986.

Frolova, N. A. *The Coinage of the Kingdom of Bosphoros, AD 242–341/342*. Trans. H. B. Wells. BAR International Series 166. Oxford, 1983.

Frye, R. N. *The History of Ancient Iran*. Munich, 1984.

Fulford, M. "Britain." In *The Cambridge Ancient History*. 2nd. edn. Vol. 11, ed. A. K. Bowman, P. Garnsey, and D. Rathbone, 561–76. Cambridge, 2000.

Gabba, E. *Republican Rome, the Army, and the Allies*. Trans. P. J. Cuff. Oxford, 1976.

Gaggero, G. "Memorie del passato nella propaganda politica di Zenobia." In *Un incontro con la storia nel centenario della nascita di Luca de Regibus*, ed. A. F. Bellezza, 211–22. Atti del pomeriggio si storia a Vogogna d'Pssola 1° luglio 1995. Genoa, 1996.

Gagos, T., and R. Caldwell. "The Emperor Aurelian and the Corrector Firmus in a Private Context." *P. Bingen*. Amsterdam, 2000.

Gallazzi, C. "La titolatura di Vaballato come riflesso della politica di Palmira." *NAC* 4 (1975): 249–65.

Gallazzi, C., and B. Kramer. "Artemidorus im Zeichensaal. Eine Papyrusrolle mit Text, Landkarte und Skizzenbüchern aus späthellenistischer Zeit." *Archiv für Papyrusforschung* 44 (1998): 189–207.

Gardiner, I. *The Kephalaia of the Teacher: The Edited Coptic Manichaean Texts in Translation with Commentary*. Leiden, 1995.

Gardiner, I., and S. N. C. Lieu. "From Narmouthis (Medinet Madi) to Kellis (Ismant El-Kharab): Manichaean Documents from Roman Egypt." *JRS* 86 (1996): 146–69.

Garnsey, P. D. *Social Status and Legal Privilege in the Roman Empire*. Oxford, 1970.

——. "Peasants in Ancient Roman Society." *Journal of Peasant Studies* 3 (1976): 221–35. Also in *Cities, Peasants, and Food in Classical Antiquity: Essays in Social and Economic History*, ed. W. Scheidel, 91–106 (Cambridge, 1998).

——. *Famine and Food Supply in the Greco-Roman World: Responses to Risk and Crisis*. Cambridge, 1988.

——. *Food and Society in Classical Antiquity*. Cambridge, 1999.

Gascou, J. "Le rescript d' Hispellum." *MEFR* 79 (1967): 600–59.

——. "Unités administratives locales et fonctionnaires romains. Les données des papyrus du Moyen Euphrate et d'Arabie." In *Lokale Autonomie und römische Ordnungsmacht in der kaiserzeitlichen Provinzen vom 1. bis 3. Jahrhundert*, ed. W. Eck and E. Müller-Luckner, 61–73. Munich, 1999.

Gawlikowsky, M. "Un nouveau mithraeum récemment découvert à Huarte près d'Apamée," *CRAI* (2000): 161–71.

Gelzer, M. *Caesar: Politician and Statesman*. Trans. P. Needham. 6th edn. Oxford, 1969.

Gerlaud, B. *Triphiodore, La prise d'Ilion*. Paris, 1982.

Gerov, B. "La carriera di Marciano generale di Gallieno." *Athenaeum* 43 (1965): 333–54.

Gibbon, E. *The Decline and Fall of the Roman Empire*. Ed. D. Womersley. London, 1994.

Gilliard, F. D. "Notes on the Coinage of Julian the Apostate." *JRS* 54 (1964): 135–41.

Giuliano, A. *Arco di Constantino*. Milan, 1955.

Gleason, M. W. "Festive Satire: Julian's Misopogon and the New Year at Antioch." *JRS* 76 (1986): 106–20.

———. *Making Men: Sophists and Self-Presentation in Ancient Rome.* Princeton, 1995.

———. "Visiting and News: Gossip and Reputation Management in the Desert." *JECS* 6 (1998): 501–21.

———. "Elite Male Identity in the Roman Empire." In *Life, Death, and Entertainment in the Roman Empire*, ed. D. S. Potter and D. J. Mattingly, 67–84. Ann Arbor, 1999.

Göbl, R. "Gallienus als Alleinherrscher." *NZ* 75 (1953): 5–35.

Goehring, J. E. "New Frontiers in Pachomian Studies." In *The Roots of Egyptian Christianity*, ed. B. A. Pearson and J. E. Goehring, 237–57. Philadelphia, 1986.

———. "The Origins of Monasticism." In *Eusebius, Christianity and Judaism*, ed. H. W. Attridge and G. Hata, 235–55. Detroit, 1992. Also in Goehring, *Ascetics, Society, and the Desert: Studies in Early Egyptian Monasticism* (Harrisburg, 1999), 13–35.

———. "Through a Glass Darkly: Images of the Ἀποτακτοί (αἱ) in Early Egyptian Monastacism." In *Discursive Formations, Ascetic Piety, and the Interpretation of Early Christian Literature*, ed. V. L. Wimbush. Pt. 2. Also in *Semeia* 58 (1992): 25–45. Also in Goehring, *Ascetics, Society, and the Desert: Studies in Early Egyptian Monasticism* (Harrisburg, 1999), 53–72.

———. "Melitian Monastic Organization: A Challenge to Pachomian Originality." *Studia Patristica* 25 (1993): 388–95. Also in Goehring, *Ascetics, Society and the Desert: Studies in Early Egyptian Monasticism* (Harrisburg, 1999), 187–95.

Goldsworthy, A. *The Roman Army at War.* Oxford, 1996.

Goodman, M. "Nerva, the *Fiscus Judaicus*, and Jewish Identity." *JRS* 79 (1989): 40–44.

Gordon, P. *Epicurus in Lycia: The Second-Century World of Diogenes of Oenoanda.* Ann Arbor, 1996.

Gordon, R. "Mithraism and Roman Society." *Religion* 2, no. 2 (1972): 92–121. Also in *Image and Value in the Graeco-Roman World: Studies in Mithraeism and Religious Art* (Brookfield, VT, 1996), ch. 3.

———. "The Sacred Geography of a Mithraeum: The Example of Stette Sfere." *Journal of Mithraic Studies* 1 (1976): 119–65. Also in *Image and Value in the Graeco-Roman World: Studies in Mithraeism and Religious Art* (Brookfield, VT, 1996), ch. 6.

———. "Another View of the Pergamon Divination Kit." *JRA* 15 (2002): 187–98.

Goulet, R. "L'oracle d'Apollon dans la *vie de Plotin*." In *Porphyre: La vie de Plotin*, ed. L. Brisson, M.-O. Goulet-Cazé, R. Goulet, and D. O'Brien, 1: 372–412. Paris, 1982.

Goulet-Cazé, M.-O. "Plotin, professeur de philosophie." In *Porphyre: La vie de Plotin*, ed. L. Brisson, M.-O. Goulet-Cazé, R. Goulet, and D. O'Brien, 1: 257–76. Paris, 1982.

Gowing, A. M. *The Triumviral Narratives of Appian and Cassius Dio.* Ann Arbor, 1992.

Grabar, A. *Martyrium: Recherches sur le culte des reliques et l'art chrétien antique.* Paris, 1946.

Gradel, I. *Emperor Worship and Roman Religion.* Oxford, 2002.

Graf, D. "Zenobia and the Arabs." In *The Eastern Frontier of the Roman Empire: Proceedings of a Colloquium held at Ankara in September 1988*, ed. D. H. French and C. S. Lightfoot, 143–67. BAR International Series 553, vol. 1. Oxford, 1989.

———. "The Roman East from the Chinese Perspective." In "International Colloquium on Palmyra and the Silk Road." *AAS* 42 (1996): 199–216.

Green, R. P. H. *The Works of Ausonius.* Oxford, 1991.

Grégoire, H. "Les chrétiens et l'oracle de Didymes." *Mélanges Holleaux*. Paris, 1913. 81–91.

Grégoire, H., and P. Orgels. "La passion de S. Théodote d'Ancyre, œuvre du pseudo-Nil, et son noyau montaniste." *BZ* 44 (1951): 165–84.

Gregory, A. P. "Country, Village, and Town in Central Anatolia." *JRA* 10 (1997): 545–56.

Griffiths, J. G. "Apocalyptic in the Hellenistic Era." In *Apocalypticism in the Mediterranean World and the Near East: Proceedings of the International Colloquium on Apocalypticism, Uppsala, August 12–17 (1979)*, ed. D. Hellholm, 273–79. Tübingen, 1983.

Grünewald, T. *Constantinus Maximus Augustus: Heerschaftspropaganda in der zeitgenössischen Überlieferung. Historia* Einzelschiften 64. Stuttgart, 1990.

Guey, J. "Deniers (d'or) et deniers d'or (de compte anciens)." *Syria* 38 (1961): 261–74.

Habicht, C. "Zur Geschichte des Kaisers Konstantin." *Hermes* 86 (1958): 360–78.

Hägg, T. "*Callirhoe* and *Parthenope*: The Beginnings of the Historical Novel." *Cl. Ant.* 6 (1987): 184–204. Also in *Oxford Readings in the Greek Novel*, ed. S. Swain (Oxford, 1999), 137–60.

Hägg, T., and P. Rousseau. *Greek Biography and Panegyric in Late Antiquity.* Berkeley, 2000.

Haehling, R. von. *Die religionszugehörigkeit der hohen Amtsträger des Römischen Reiches seit Constantins I. Alleinherrschaft bis zum Ende der Theodosianischen Zeit.* Bonn, 1978.

Halfmann, H. *Die Senatoren aus dem östlichen Teil des Imperium Romanum bis zum Ende des 2. Jh. N. Chr.* Göttingen, 1979.

——. "Zwei syrische Verwandte des severischen Kaiserhauses." *Chiron* 12 (1982): 217–35.

——. *Itinera principum. Geschichte und Typologie der Kaiserreisen im römischen Reich.* Stuttgart, 1986.

Hall, J. M. *Ethnic Identity in Greek Antiquity.* Cambridge, 1997.

Hall, S. G. "The *Thalia* in Athanasius' Accounts." In *Arianism: Historical and Theological Reassessments*, ed. R. C. Gregg, 37–58. Philadelphia, 1985.

Hammerstaedt, J. *Die Orakelkritik des Kynikers Oenomaeus.* Frankfurt am Main, 1988.

Hanslik, R. "Tenagino Probus." *RE* 23 (1927), 55–56.

Hanson, A. E. "The Roman Family." In *Life, Death, and Entertainment in the Roman Empire*, ed. D. S. Potter and D. J. Mattingly, 19–66. Ann Arbor, 1999.

Hanson, R. P. C. *The Search for the Christian Doctrine of God: The Arian Controversy 318–381* (Edinburgh, 1988).

Harl, K. *Coinage in the Roman Economy, 300 BC–AD 700.* Baltimore, 1996.

Harnack, A. von. *Geschichte der Altchristlichen Literatur.* 2nd edn., vol. 1, pt. 2. Berlin, 1893.

——. *The Mission and Expansion of Christianity.* Trans. J. Moffatt. Vol. 1. Reprint. Gloucester, Mass, 1972.

Harries, J. "The Roman Imperial Quaestor from Constantine to Theodosius II." *JRS* 78 (1988): 148–72.

Harries, J., and I. Wood. *The Theodosian Code.* Ithaca, NY, 1993.

Hartmann, F. *Herrscherwechsel und Reichskrise: Untersuchungen zu den Ursachen und Konsequenzen der Herrscherwechsel im Imperium Romanum der Soldatenkaiserzeit (3. Jahrhundert n. Chr.).* Frankfurt am Main, 1982.

Hartmann, U. *Das palmyrenische Teilreich.* Stuttgart, 2001.

Hasebroek, J. *Untersuchungen zur Geschichte des Kaisers Septimius Severus.* Heidelberg, 1921.

Hauken, T. *Petition and Response: An Epigraphic Study of Petitions to Roman Emperors, 181–249.* Bergen, 1998.

Heather, P. "The Crossing of the Danube and the Gothic Conversion." *GRBS* 27 (1986): 289–318.

——. "Cassiodorus and the Rise of the Amals: Genealogy and the Goths under Hun Domination." *JRS* 79 (1989): 103–28.

——. *Goths and Romans, 332–489.* Oxford, 1991.

——. "New Men for New Constantines: Creating an Imperial Elite in the Eastern Mediterranean." In *New Constantines,* ed. P. Magdalino, 11–33. Aldershot, 1994.

——. "Senators and Senates." In *The Cambridge Ancient History.* 2nd. edn. Vol. 13, ed. A. Cameron and P. Garnsey, 184–210. Cambridge, 1998.

Heather, P., and J. F. Matthews. *The Goths in the Fourth Century.* Liverpool, 1991.

Heilporn, P. "Registre de navires marchands." *P. Bingen.* Amsterdam, 2000. 339–59.

Heine, R. E. *The Montanist Oracles and Testimonia.* Patristic Monograph Series 14. Macon, GA, 1989.

Heitsch, E. *Die griechischen Dichterfragmente der römischen Kaiserzeit.* Göttingen, 1961.

Hekster, O. "All in the Family: The Appointment of Emperors Designate in the Second Century AD." In *Administration, Prosopography, and Appointment Policies in the Roman Empire,* ed. L. De Blois, 35–49. Amsterdam, 2001.

——. *Commodus: An Emperor at the Crossroads.* Amsterdam, 2002.

Hellholm, D., ed. *Apocalypticism in the Mediterranean World and the Near East: Proceedings of the International Colloquium on Apocalypticism, Uppsala, August 12–17 (1979).* Tübingen, 1983.

Hendy, M. F. *Studies in the Byzantine Monetary Economy c. 300–1450.* Cambridge, 1985.

Hermann, P. "Die Karriere eines prominenten Juristen aus Thyateira." *Tyche* 12 (1997): 111–25.

Hess, H. *The Canons of the Council of Sardica, AD 343: A Landmark in the Early Development of Canon Law.* Oxford, 1958.

Hinz, W. *Altiranische Funde und Forschungen.* Berlin, 1969.

Hirschfeld, O. "Die Sicherheitspolizei im römischen Kaiserreich." *Sitzungsberichte der Berliner Akademie* (1891): 845–77. Also in Hirschfeld, *Kleine Schriften* (Berlin, 1913), 576–612.

——. "Die Rangtitel der römischen Kaiserzeit." *Sitzungsberichte der Berliner Akademie* (1901): 569–610. Also in Hirschfeld, *Kleine Schriften* (Berlin, 1913), 646–81.

——. *Kleine Schriften.* Berlin, 1913.

Hobsbawm, E. *Bandits.* 4th edn. New York, 2000.

Hoffmann, D. *Das spätrömische Bewegungsheer und die Notitia Dignitatum.* Epigraphische Studien 7. Düsseldorf, 1969.

Hoffmann, R. J. *Marcion: On the Restitution of Christianity: An Essay on the Development of Radical Paulinist Theology in the Second Century.* AAR Academy Series 46. Chico, Calif., 1984.

——. *Celsus: On the True Doctrine.* Oxford, 1987.

Holum, K. *Theodosian Empresses: Women and Imperial Dominion in Late Antiquity.* Berkeley, 1982.

Holzberg, N. "The Genre: Novels Proper and the Fringe." In *The Novel in the Ancient World,* ed. G. Schmeling, 11–28. *Mnemosyne* Supplement 159. Leiden, 1996.

Honoré, T. *Emperors and Lawyers.* London, 1981.

——. *Ulpian.* Oxford, 1982.

Hopkins, K. "The Political Power of Eunuchs." In *Conquerors and Slaves.* Sociological Studies in Roman History 1 (Cambridge, 1978), 171–96.

——. "Taxes and Trade in the Roman Empire (200 BC–400 AD)." *JRS* 70 (1980): 101–25.

——. "Christian Number and Its Implication." *JECS* 6 (1998): 185–226.

Hopkins, K., and G. P. Burton. "Ambition and Withdrawal: The Senatorial Aristocracy under the Emperors." In *Death and Renewal.* Sociological Studies in Roman History 2 (Cambridge, 1983), 120–200.

731

Hopwood, K. "Bandits, Elites, and Rural Order." In *Patronage in Ancient Society*, ed. A. Wallace-Hadrill, 171–87. London, 1990.

———. "Bandits between Grandees and the State: The Structure of Order in Roman Rough Cilicia." In *Organized Crime in Antiquity*, 179–84. London, 1999.

Horden, P., and N. Purcell. *The Corrupting Sea: A Study of Mediterranean History*. Oxford, 2000.

Horsfall, N. "Stesichorus in Bovillae." *JHS* 99 (1979): 26–48.

———. "Tablulae Iliacae in the Collection Froehner, Paris." *JHS* 103 (1983): 144–47.

Howe, L. L. *The Praetorian Prefect from Commodus to Diocletian (AD 180–305)*. Chicago, 1942.

Howgego, C. *Greek Imperial Countermarks: Studies in the Provincial Coinage of the Roman Empire*. London, 1985.

———. "The Supply and Uses of Money in the Roman World, 200 BC to AD 300." *JRS* 82 (1992): 1–31.

———. "Coin Circulation and the Integration of the Roman Economy." *JRA* 7 (1994): 5–21.

———. *Ancient History from Coins*. London, 1995.

Hughes, J. D. *Pan's Travail: Environmental Problems of the Ancient Greeks and Romans*. Baltimore, 1994.

Humbach, H., and P. O. Skjærvø. *The Sassanian Inscription of Paikuli*. Pt. 3, no 1. Wiesbaden, 1983.

Humphrey, J. *Roman Circuses: Arenas for Chariot Racing*. Berkeley, 1986.

Humphries, M. *"In Nomine Patris*: Constantine the Great and Constantius II." *Historia* 46 (1997): 448–64.

Hunt, E. D. *Holy Land Pilgrimage in the Later Roman Empire, AD 312–460*. Oxford, 1982.

———. "Did Constantius II Have 'Court Bishops'?" *Studia Patristica* 19 (1989): 86–90.

———. "Christianizing the Roman Empire: The Evidence of the Code." In *The Theodosian Code*, ed. J. Harries and I. Wood, 143–58. Ithaca, NY, 1993.

———. "The Successors of Constantine." In *The Cambridge Ancient History*. 2nd. edn. Vol. 13, ed. A. Cameron and P. Garnsey, 1–43. Cambridge, 1998.

———. "Julian." In *The Cambridge Ancient History*. 2nd. edn. Vol. 13, ed. A. Cameron and P. Garnsey, 44–77. Cambridge, 1998.

Huvelin, H. "Le début du règne de Claude II, empereur illyrien apport de la numismatique." In *Les empereurs illyriens: Actes du colloque de Strasbourg (11–13 octobre 1990) organisé par le Centre de Recherche sur l'Europe centrale et sud-orientale*, ed. E. Frézouls and H. Jouffroy, 87–95. Strasbourg, 1998.

Isaac, B. "The Meaning of *Limes* and *Limitanei* in Ancient Sources." *JRS* 78 (1988): 139–46. Also in *The Near East under Roman Rule: Selected Papers* (Leiden, 1998), 366–78.

———. *The Limits of Empire: The Roman Army in the East*. Oxford, 1990.

———. "An Open Frontier." In *Frontières d'empire: Nature et signification des frontières romains*, ed. P. Brun, S. van der Leeuw, and C. R. Whittaker, 105–14. Nemours, 1993. Also in *The Roman Near East under Roman Rule: Selected Papers* (Leiden, 1998), 402–26.

Jacobson, T. *Towards the Image of Tammuz and Other Essays on Mesopotamian History and Culture*. Cambridge, Mass., 1970.

Jacques, F., and J. Scheid. *Rome et l'intégration de l'empire (44 av. j.-c–260 ap. j.-c.)*. Paris, 1990.

Jeffreys, E., with B. Croke and R. Scott. *Studies in John Malalas*. Sydney, 1990.

732

Johnson, S. "Introduction to the Saxon Shore." In *Roman Frontier Studies, 1989: Proceedings of the XVth International Congress of Roman Frontier Studies*, ed. V. A. Maxfield and M. J. Dobson, 94–95. Exeter, 1991.

Johnston, A. "Caracalla's Path." *Historia* 32 (1983): 58–76.

Johnston, D. *Roman Law in Context.* Cambridge, 1999.

Jolowicz, H. *Historical Introduction to the Study of Roman Law.* Cambridge, 1954.

Jones, A. H. M. *Constantine and the Conversion of Europe.* London, 1949.

——. The Date and Value of the Verona List." *JRS* 44 (1954): 21–29. Also in *The Roman Economy*, ed. P. A. Brunt, 263–79. Oxford, 1974.

——. *The Later Roman Empire, 284–602: A Social, Economic, and Administrative Study.* 3 vols. Oxford, 1964.

——. "Taxation in Antiquity." In *The Roman Economy*, ed. P. A. Brunt, 164–66. Oxford, 1974.

Jones, C. P. *Culture and Society in Lucian.* Cambridge, Mass., 1986.

——. "Hellenistic History in Chariton of Aphrodisias." *Chiron* 22 (1992): 91–102.

——. "Greek Drama in the Roman Empire." In *Theater and Society in the Classical World*, ed. R. Scodel, 39–52. Ann Arbor, 1993.

——. "The Panhellenion." *Chiron* 26 (1996): 29–56.

——. "A Decree of Thyatira in Lydia." *Chiron* 29 (1999): 1–21.

——. *Kinship Diplomacy in the Ancient World.* Cambridge, Mass., 1999.

——. "Imperial Letters at Ephesus," *EA* 33 (2001): 39–44.

——. "Time and Place in Philostratus' *Heroikos.*" *JHS* 121 (2001): 141–49.

Jones, G. D. B. "The Roman Mines at Riotinto." *JRS* 70 (1980): 146–65.

Jonkers, E.J. *Acta et symbola conciliorum quae saeculo quarto habita sunt.* Leiden, 1954.

Judge, E. A. "The Earliest Use of Monachos for 'Monk' (P. Coll. Youtie 77) and the Origins of Monasticism." *JAC* 20 (1977): 77–89.

——. "Fourth Century Monasticism in the Papyri." In *Proceedings of the Sixteenth International Congress of Papyrology, New York, 24–31 July 1980*, ed. R. Bagnall, G. M. Browne, A. E. Hanson, and L. Koenen, 613–20. Chico, Calif., 1981.

Judge, E. A., and S. R. Pickering. "Papyrus Documentation of Church and Community in Egypt." *JAC* 20 (1977): 47–71.

Kaegi, W. E. "Constantine's and Julian's Strategies of Strategic Surprise against the Persians." *Athenaeum* 59 (1981): 209–13.

Kannengiesser, C. "Où et quand Arius composa-t-il la *Thalie?*" *Kyriakon: Festschrift J. Quasten* 1 (1971).

——. "Arius and the Arians." *Theological Studies* 44 (1983): 456–75. Also in *Arius and Athanasius: Two Alexandrian Theologians* (Brookfield, VT, 1991), ch. 2.

——. "Athanasius of Alexandria vs. Arius: The Alexandrian Crisis." In *The Roots of Egyptian Christianity*, ed. B. A. Pearson and J. E. Goehring, 208. Philadelphia, 1986. Also in *Arius and Athanasius: Two Alexandrian Theologians* (Brookfield, VT, 1991), ch. 12.

——. "Alexander and Arius of Alexandria: The Last Ante-Nicene Theologians." In *Miscelánea En Homenaje Al P. Antonio Orbe Compostellanum* 34, nos. 1–2, 392, 398, 401–2. Santiago de Compestella, 1990. Also in *Arius and Athanasius* (Brookfield, VT, 1991), ch. 4.

Kaster, R. L. *Guardians of Language: The Grammarian and Society in Late Antiquity.* Berkeley, 1988.

Keegan, J. *The Face of Battle.* Harmondsworth, 1976.

Kehoe, D. P. *The Economics of Agriculture on Roman Imperial Estates in North Africa.* Göttingen, 1988.

Keil, J. "Vertreter der zweiten Sophistik in Ephesus," *JÖAI* 40 (1953), 5–22.

Keil, J. and A. von Premerstein, "Bericht über eine dritte Reise in Lydien und den angrenzenden Gebieten Ioniens, ausgeführt 1911 im Auftrage der Kaiserlichen Akademie den Wissenschaften," Denkschriften den Kaiserlichen Akademie der Wissenschaften in Wien, philosophisch-historische Klasse 57: 1 (1914).

Kelly, J. N. D. *Early Christian Doctrines.* 5th edn. London, 1977.

Kennedy, D. L. "Ti. Claudius Subatianus Aquila, 'First Prefect of Mesopotamia.'" *ZPE* 36 (1979): 255–86.

——. "The Garrisoning of Mesopotamia in the Late Antonine Period." *Antichthon* 21 (1987): 47–66.

Kennedy, D. L., and D. Riley. *Rome's Desert Frontier from the Air.* Austin, 1990.

Kettenhoffen, E. *Die römischen–persischen Kriege des 3. Jahrhunderts n. Chr. nach der Inschrift Sahpuhrs I an der Ka^c be-ye Zartost (skz).* Wiesbaden, 1982.

——. "Die Einforderung des Achämeniderbes durch Ardasir: Eine Interpretatio Romana." *Orientalia Lovaniensa Periodica* 15 (1984): 177–90.

——. "Einige Überlegungen zur sasanidischen Politik gegenüber Rom im 3. Jh. n. Chr." In *The Roman and Byzantine Army in the East: Proceedings of a Colloquium Held at the Jagiellonian University, Kraków in September 1992,* ed. E. Dąbrowa, 99–108. Cracow, 1994.

——. "Die Eroberung von Nisibis und Karrhai durch die Sāsāniden in der Zeit Kaiser Maximins (235/236 n. Chr.)." *Iranica Antiqua* 30 (1995): 159–77.

——. *Tirdād und die Inschrift von Paikuli: Kritik der Quellen zur Geschichte Armeniens im späten 3. und frühen 4. Jh. n. Chr.* Wiesbaden, 1995.

Kettler, F. H. "Die melitianische Streit in Ägypten." *Zeitschrift für die neutestamentliche Wissenschaft* 35 (1936): 155–93.

Kienast, D. *Untersuchungen zu den Kriegsflotten der römischen Kaiserzeit.* Bonn, 1976.

——. "Das Bellum Cibalense und die Morde des Licinius." In *Roma Renascens. Ilona Opelt von ihren Freunden und Schülern gewidmet,* ed. M. Wissemann, 149–71. Frankfurt am Main, 1988.

——. *Römische Kaisertabelle: Grundzüge einer römischen Kaiserchronologie.* Darmstadt, 1990.

King, A. "Diet in the Roman World: A Regional Inter-site Comparison of Mammal Bones." *JRA* 12 (1999): 168–202.

King, C. E. "The Circulation of Coin in the Western Provinces, AD 260–95." In *The Roman West in the Third Century: Contributions from Archaeology and History,* ed. A. King and M. Henig, 89–126. Oxford, 1981.

——. "The Fourth Century Coinage." In *L' "inflazione" nel quarto secolo d.c.: Atti dell' incontro di studio Roma 1988,* 1–87. Istituto Italiano di Numismatica, Studi e Materiali 3. Rome, 1993.

Knipfing, J. "The *libelli* of the Decian Persecution." *HTR* 16 (1923): 345–90.

Koenen, L. "Manichäische Mission und Klöster in Ägypten." In *Das römisch–byzantinische Ägypten,* 93–108. Mainz, 1983.

——. "The Dream of Nektanebos." *BASP* 22 (1985): 171–94.

Kolb, F. *Literarische Beziehungen zwischen Cassius Dio, Herodian und der Historia Augusta.* Bonn, 1972.

——. *Diocletian und der erste Tetrarchie. Improvisation oder Experiment in der Organisation monarchischer Herrschaft?* Berlin, 1987.

——. *Untersuchungen zur Historia Augusta.* Bonn, 1987.

König, D. *Die gallischen Usurpatoren von Postumus bis Tetricus.* Munich, 1981.

König, I. "Die Berufung des Constantius Chlorus und des Galerius zu Caesarem: Gedanken zur Entstehung der ersten Tetrarchie." *Chiron* 4 (1974): 567–76.

——. *Origo Constantini.* Trier, 1987.

——. "Die Postumus-Inschrift aus Augsburg." *Historia* 46 (1997): 341–54.

Kotula, T. *Aurélien et Zénobie: L'unité ou la division de l'empire.* Warsaw, 1997.

Kraay, C. M. "The Behavior of Early Imperial Countermarks." In *Essays in Roman Coinage Presented to Harold Mattingly*, ed. R. A. G. Carson and C. H. V. Sutherland, 113–36. Oxford, 1956.

Kramer, B., and J. C. Skelton, with G. M. Browne. *Das Archiv des Nepheros und verwandte Texte.* Mainz, 1987.

Kruecher, G. "Die Regierungszeit Aurelians und die griechischen Papyri aus Ägypten." *Archiv für Papyrusforschung* 44 (1998): 255–64.

Kulikowski, M. "The *Notitia Dignitatum* as a Historical Source." *Historia* 49 (2000): 358–77.

Kunkel, W. *An Introduction to Roman Legal and Constitutional History.* Trans. J. M. Kelly. Oxford, 1973.

Kurshudian, E. *Die Parthischen und Sasanidischen Verwaltungsinstitutionen nach den literarischen und epigraphischen Quellen, 3. Jh. v. Chr.–7. Jh. n. Chr.* Jerewan, 1998.

Kyle, D. *Spectacles of Death in Ancient Rome.* London, 1998.

Kytzler, B. "Xenophon of Ephesus." In *The Novel in the Ancient World*, ed. G. Schmeling, 336–60. *Mnemosyne* Supplement 159. Leiden, 1996.

Labrousse, M. *Optat de Milève, Traité contre les Donatistes.* Vol. 1. *SC*, vol. 412. Paris, 1995.

Ladurie, E. L. *The Territory of the Historian.* Trans. B. Reynolds and S. Reynolds. Chicago, 1979.

——. *The French Peasantry, 1450–1660.* Trans. A. Sheridan. London, 1987.

Lander, J. *Roman Stone Fortifications: Variation and Change from the First Century* AD *to the Fourth.* BAR International Series 206. Oxford, 1984.

Landes, R. "Lest the Millennium Be Fulfilled: Apocalyptic Expectations and the Pattern of Western Chronology, 100–800 CE." In *The Use and Abuse of Eschatology in the Early Middle Ages*, ed. W. Verbeke, D. Verhelst, and A. Welkenhuysen, 137–211. Leuven, 1988.

Lane Fox, R. J. *Pagans and Christians.* London, 1987.

——. "The Itinerary of Alexander: Constantius to Julian." *CQ* 47 (1997): 239–52.

Lang, U. M. "The Christological Controversy at the Synod of Antioch in 268/9." *JTS* 51 (2000): 54–80.

Lannoy, L. de *Flavii Philostrati Heroicus.* Leipzig, 1977.

——. "Le problème des Philostrate (État de la question)." *ANRW* 34.3 (1997): 2362–2449.

Lauferie, J. "Remarques sur des dates de quelques inscriptions au début du ive siècle," *CRAI* (1965): 192–21.

Lavagne, H. "Une nouvelle inscription d'Augsbourg et les causes de l'usurpation de Postume." *CRAI* (1994): 421–46.

Leadbetter, B. "'*Patrimonium Indivisum*'? The Empire of Diocletian and Maximian, 285–289." *Chiron* 28 (1998): 213–28.

——. "The Illegitimacy of Constantine and the Birth of the Tetrarchy." In *Constantine: History, Historiography, and Legend*, ed. S. N. C. Lieu and D. Montserrat, 74–85. London, 1998.

Le Bohec, Y. *The Imperial Roman Army.* London, 1994.

Le Bohec, Y., and C. Wolff. *Les légions de Rome sous le Haut-Empire. Actes du Congrès de Lyon (17–19 septembre 1998)*. Lyon, 2000.

Lee, A. D. *Information and Frontiers: Roman Foreign Relations in Late Antiquity*. Cambridge, 1993.

——— . "The Army." In *The Cambridge Ancient History*. 2nd. edn. Vol. 13, ed. A. Cameron and P. Garnsey, 211–37. Cambridge, 1998.

Le Glay, M. *Studia in Honorem G. Mihailov*. Sofia, 1995.

Legutko, P. "Roman Imperial Ideology in the Mid-Third Century AD: Negotiation, Usurpation, and Crisis in the Imperial Center." PhD diss., University of Michigan, 2000.

Lendon, J.E., *Empire of Honour: The Art of Government in the Roman World*. Oxford, 1997.

Lenox-Cunyngham, A. "The Topography of the Basilica Conflict of AD 385/6 in Milan." *Historia* 31 (1982): 353–63.

Lenski, N. "The Gothic Civil War and the Date of the Gothic Conversion." *GRBS* 36 (1995): 51–87.

——— . *Failure of Empire: Valens and the Roman State in the Fourth Century AD*. Berkeley, 2002.

Leppin, H. *Von Constantin dem Großen zu Theodosius II. Das christliche Kaisertum bei den Kirchenhistorikern Socrates, Sozomenus und Theodoret*. Göttingen, 1996.

Leunissen, P. *Konsuln und Konsulare in der Zeit Commodus bis Severus Alexander (180–235 n. Chr.)*. Amsterdam, 1989.

Levick, B. M. "Caracalla's Path." In *Hommages à Marcel Renard*, 426–46. Brussels, 1969.

Lewis, N. "NOHMATA LEGONTOS." *BASP* 4 (1967): 15–21.

Lewy, H. *The Chaldean Oracles and Theurgy*. Ed. M. Tardieu. Rev. edn. Paris, 1978.

Lieberman, S. "Palestine in the Third and Fourth Centuries." *JQR* 37 (1947): 31–54.

Liebeschuetz, J. H. W. G. *Antioch: City and Imperial Administration in the Later Roman Empire*. Oxford, 1972.

——— . *Continuity and Change in Roman Religion*. Oxford, 1979.

——— . "The Uses and Abuses of the Concept of 'Decline' in later Roman History; or, Was Gibbon Politically Incorrect?" in *Recent Research in Late-Antique Urbanism*, ed. L. Lavan, 232–38. *JRA* Supplement 42 (Portsmouth, 2001).

Lieu, S. N. C. *Manichaeism in the Later Roman Empire and Medieval China: A Historical Survey*. Manchester, 1985.

——— . *Manichaeism in Central Asia and China*. Leiden, 1998.

Lieu, S. N. C., and D. Montserrat, eds. *From Constantine to Julian: Pagan and Byzantine Views*. London, 1996.

Lightfoot, C. S. "Facts and Fiction – the Third Siege of Nisibis (AD 350)." *Historia* 37 (1988): 105–25.

——— . "Trajan's Parthian War and the Fourth-Century Perspective." *JRS* 80 (1990): 115–26.

Lightfoot, J.L., *Lucian: On the Syrian Goddess* (Oxford, 2003).

Lindner, A. *The Jews in Roman Imperial Legislation*. Detroit, 1987.

Lippold, A. "Constantinus Caesar, Sieger über die Germanen – Nachfahre des Claudius Gothicus? Der Panegyricus von 297 und die Vita Claudii der HA." *Chiron* 11 (1981): 347–69. Also in *Die Historia Augusta*, ed. G. H. Waldherr (Stuttgart, 1998), 160–82.

——— . *Maximini duo. Kommentar zur Historia Augusta*. Vol. 1. Bonn, 1991.

Lloyd, S., and W. Brice. "Harran." *Anatolian Studies* 1 (1951): 77–112.

Lo Cascio, E. "Imperio e confini nell' età principato." In *L'ecumenismo politico nella coscienza dell' occidente*, ed. L. A. Foresti, A. Barzanò, C. Bearzot, L. Prandi, and G. Zecchini, 333–47. Rome, 1988.

Long, J. "Two Sides of a Coin: Aurelian, Vaballathus, and Eastern Frontiers in the Early 270s." In *Shifting Frontiers in Late Antiquity*, ed. R. W. Mathisen and H. S. Sivan, 59–71. Brookfield, VT, 1996.

Loriot, X. "Les premières années de la grande crise du IIIe siècle: De l'avènement de Maximin le Thrace (235) à la mort de Gordien III (244)." *ANRW* 2.2 (1975): 657–787.

——. "Un sénateur illyrien élevé à la pourpre: Trajan Dèce." In *Les empereurs illyriens: Actes du colloque de Strasbourg (11–13 octobre 1990) organisé par le Centre de Recherche sur l'Europe centrale et sud-orientale*, ed. E. Frézouls and H. Jouffroy, 43–55. Strasbourg, 1998.

Louth, A. "The Date of Eusebius' *Historia Ecclesiastica*." *JTS* 41 (1990): 111–23.

Lucien-Brun, X. "Minervine, épouse ou concubine?" *Bulletin de l'Association Guillaume Budé* (1970): 391–406.

Luck, G. "Theurgy and Forms of Worship in Neoplatonism." In *Religion, Science, and Magic*, ed. J. Neusner, E. S. Frerichs, and P. V. McCracken Flesher, 185–225. Oxford, 1989. Also in *Ancient Pathways and Hidden Pursuits: Religion, Morals, and Magic in the Ancient World* (Ann Arbor, 2000), 110–52.

Luttikhuizen, G. P. *The Revelation of Elchasai: Investigation into the Evidence for a Mesopotamian Jewish Apocalypse of the Second Century and Its Reception by Judaeo-Christian Propagandists*. Tübingen, 1985.

MacCormack, S. G. *Art and Ceremony in Late Antiquity*. Berkeley, 1981.

——. *The Shadows of Poetry: Vergil in the Mind of Augustine*. Berkeley, 1998.

MacDonald, D. "The Death of Gordian III – Another Tradition." *Historia* 30 (1981): 502–8.

MacDowall, S. *Adrianople, AD 378: The Goths Crush Rome's Legions*. Osprey Campaign no. 84. Botley, 2001.

MacMullen, R. "Constantine and the Miraculous." *GRBS* 9 (1969): 81–96. Also in *Changes in the Roman Empire* (Princeton, 1990), 107–16.

——. *Roman Government's Response to Crisis*. New Haven, 1976.

——. "Judicial Savagery in the Roman Empire." *Chiron* 16 (1986): 43–62. Also in *Changes in the Roman Empire* (Princeton, 1990), 204–17.

——. *Corruption and the Decline of Rome*. New Haven, 1988.

Magie, D. *Roman Rule in Asia Minor*. Princeton, 1951.

Maier, H. O. "Private Space as the Social Context of Arianism in Ambrose's Milan." *JTS* 45 (1994): 72–93.

Majercik, R. *The Chaldean Oracles: Text, Translation, and Commentary*. Leiden, 1989.

Mango, C. "Constantine's Mausoleum and the Translation of Relics." *BzZ* 83 (1990): 51–60.

Maraval, P. *La passion inédite de S. Athénogène de Pédachthoé en Cappadoce (BHG 197b)*. Subsidia Hagiographica 75. Brussels, 1990.

Mastrocinque, A. "The Divinatory Kit from Pergamon and Greek Magic in Late Antiquity." *JRA* 15 (2002): 173–87.

Mathisen, R. W., and H. S. Sivan, eds. *Shifting Frontiers in Late Antiquity*. Brookfield, VT, 1996.

Mattern, S. *Rome and the Enemy: Imperial Strategy in the Principate*. Berkeley, 1999.

Matthews, J. F. "A Pious Supporter of Theodosius I: Maternus Cynegius and His Family." *JTS* 18 (1967): 438–46.

——. *Western Aristocracies and the Imperial Court, AD 364–425*. Oxford, 1975.

——. "The Tax Law of Palmyra: Evidence for Economic History in a City of the Roman East." *JRS* 74 (1984): 157–80.

—— . "Hostages, Philosophers, Pilgrims, and the Diffusion of Ideas in the Late Roman Mediterranean and Near East." In *Tradition and Innovation in Late Antiquity*, ed. F. M. Clover and R. S. Humphreys, 29–49. Madison, 1989.

—— . *The Roman Empire of Ammianus*. London, 1989.

—— . *Laying Down the Law: A Study of the Theodosia Code*. New Haven, 2000.

Mattingly, D. J. "Oil for Export? A Comparison of Libyan, Spanish, and Tunisian Olive Oil Production in the Roman Empire." *JRA* 1 (1988): 33–56.

Mattingly, H., and E. A. Sydenham. *The Roman Imperial Coinage*. Vol. 5, pt. 2. London, 1933.

Mayerson, P. J. "Palaestina vs. Arabia in the Byzantine Sources," *ZPE* 56 (1984): 223–30.

McLynn, N. B. *Ambrose of Milan: Church and Court in a Christian Capital*. Berkeley, 1994.

Meckler, M. "Caracalla the Intellectual." In *Gli imperatori Severi: Storia archeologia religione*, ed. E. dal Covolo and G. Rinaldi, 39–46. Rome, 1999.

Meiggs, R. *The Athenian Empire*. Oxford, 1972.

—— . *Trees and Timber in the Ancient Mediterranean World*. Oxford, 1982.

Meredith, A. "Asceticism – Christian and Greek." *JTS* 27 (1976): 313–32.

—— . "Porphyry and Julian Against the Christians." *ANRW* 2.23.2 (1980): 1119–49.

Merkle, S. "Telling the True Story of the Trojan War: The Eyewitness Account of Dictys of Crete." In *The Search for the Ancient Novel*, ed. J. Tatum, 183–96. Baltimore, 1994.

—— . "The Truth and Nothing But the Truth: Dictys and Dares." In *The Novel in the Ancient World*, ed. G. Schmeling, 563–80. *Mnemosyne* Supplement 159. Leiden, 1996.

Metcalf, W. E. "Rome and Lugdunum Again." *AJN* 1 (1989): 51–70.

Metzler, K., and F. Simon. *Ariana et Athanasiana: Studien zur Überlieferung und zu philologische Problemen der Werke des Athanasius von Alexandrien*. Abhandlungen der Rheinisch–Westfälischen Akademie der Wissenschaften 83. Opladen, 1991.

Milik, J. T. *Dédicaces faites par des dieux (Palmyre, Hatra, Tyr) et des thiases sémitiques à l'époque romaine*. Paris, 1972.

Millar, J. N. C. *A Study of Cassius Dio*. Oxford, 1964.

—— . "Emperors at Work." *JRS* 57 (1967): 9–19.

—— . "P. Herennius Dexippus: The Greek World and the Third Century Invasions." *JRS* 59 (1969): 12–29.

—— . "Paul of Samosata, Zenobia, and Aurelian: The Church, Local Culture, and Political Allegiance in Third-Century Syria." *JRS* 61 (1971): 1–17.

—— . "The World of the *Golden Ass*." *JRS* 71 (1981): 63–75. Also in *Oxford Readings in the Roman Novel*, ed. S. J. Harrison (Oxford, 1999), 247–68.

—— . "Emperors, Frontiers, and Foreign Relations, 31 BC to AD 378." *Britannia* 13 (1982): 1–23.

—— . "Empire and City, Augustus to Julian: Obligations, Excuses, and Status." *JRS* 73 (1983): 76–96.

—— . "The Roman *coloniae* of the Near East: A Study of Cultural Relations." In *Roman Eastern Policy and Other Studies in Roman History: Proceedings of a Colloquium at Tvärminne, 2–3 October 1987*, ed. H. Solin and M. Kajeva, 7–58. Commentationes Humanarum Litterarum 91. Helsinki, 1990.

—— . *The Emperor in the Roman World*. 2nd edn. Ithaca, NY, 1992.

—— . "The Jews of the Greco-Roman Diaspora between Paganism and Christianity." In *The Jews among Pagans and Christians in the Roman Empire*, ed. J. Lieu, J. North, and T. Rajak, 97–123. London, 1992.

—— . *The Roman Near East*. Cambridge, Mass., 1993.

——— . "Porphyry: Ethnicity, Language, and Alien Wisdom." In *Philosophia Togata II. Plato and Aristotle at Rome*, ed. J. Barnes and M. Griffin, 241–62. Oxford, 1997.

——— . "Looking East from the Classical World: Colonialism, Culture, and Trade from Alexander the Great to Shapur I." *International History Review* 20 (1998): 507–31.

——— . "*Civitates Liberae, Coloniae,* and Provincial Governors under the Empire." *Mediterraneo Antico* 2 (1999): 95–113.

——— . "The Greek East and Roman Law: The Dossier of M. Cn. Licinius Rufinus." *JRS* 89 (1999): 90–108.

Miller, J. I. *The Spice Trade of the Roman Empire, 29 BC–AD 641.* Oxford, 1969.

Millett, M. *The Romanization of Britain: An Essay in Archaeological Interpretation.* Cambridge, 1990.

Mitchell, S. "The Life of Saint Theodotus of Ancyra." *AS* 35 (1982): 93–113.

——— . "Maximinus and the Christians in AD 312: A New Latin Inscription." *JRS* 78 (1988): 105–24.

——— . "Festivals, Games, and Civic Life in Roman Asia Minor." *JRS* 80 (1990): 183–93.

——— . *Anatolia: Land, Men, and Gods in Asia Minor.* Oxford, 1993.

——— . *Cremna in Pisidia: An Ancient City in Peace and War.* London, 1995.

——— . "The Administration of Roman Asia from 133 BC to AD 250." In *Lokale Autonomie und römische Ordnungsmacht in der kaiserzeitlichen Provinzen vom 1. bis 3. Jahrhundert*, ed. W. Eck and E. Müller-Luckner, 17–46. Munich, 1999.

——— . "The Cult of Theos Hypsistos between Pagans, Jews, and Christians." In *Pagan Monotheism in Late Antiquity*, ed. P. Athanassiadi and M. Frede, 81–148. Oxford, 1999.

Montanari, F. "Revisione di P. Berol. 13282 le *Historiae Fabulares* omeriche su papirio." *Atti del xvii Congresso internazionale di Papirologia (Napoli 19–26 maggio 1983).* Naples, 1984. 241–42.

Morgan, J. R. "Heliodorus." In *The Novel in the Ancient World*, ed. G. Schmeling, 417–56. *Mnemosyne* Supplement 159. Leiden, 1996.

——— . "On the Fringes of the Canon: Work on the Fragments of Ancient Greek Fiction," *ANRW* 2.34.4 (1998): 3293–339.

Morgan, T. *Literate Education in the Hellenistic and Roman Worlds.* Cambridge, 1998.

Morley, N. *Metropolis and Hinterland: The City of Rome and the Italian Economy, 200 BC–AD 200.* Cambridge, 1996.

Mosig-Walburg, K. "Zur Schlacht bei Singara." *Historia* 48 (1999): 330–84.

Murray, R. "The Characteristics of Earliest Syriac Christianity." In *East of Byzantium: Syria and Armenia in the Formative Period*, ed. N. G. Garsoïan, T. F. Matthews, and R. W. Thomson, 3–16. Dumbarton Oaks Symposium, 1980. Washington, DC, 1982.

Musurillo, H. *The Acts of the Christian Martyrs.* Oxford, 1972.

Naldini, M. *Cristianesimo in Egitto: Lettere private nei Papiri dei Secoli ii–iv.* Fiesole, 1998.

Neesen, L. *Untersuchungen zu den direkten Staatsabgaben der römischen Kaiserzeit (27 v. Chr.–284 n. Chr.).* Bonn, 1980.

Nicolet, C. "Augustus, Government, and the Propertied Classes." In *Caesar Augustus: Seven Aspects*, ed. F. Millar and E. Segal, 89–128. Oxford, 1984.

——— . *Space, Geography, and Politics in the Early Roman Empire.* Ann Arbor, 1991.

——— . "The Citizen: The Political Man." In *The Romans*, ed. A. Giardina, trans. L. Cochrane, 16–54. Chicago, 1993.

Nicols, J. *Vespasian and the Partes Flavianae. Historia* Einzelschriften 28. Stuttgart, 1978.

Nixon, C. E. V. "The Panegyric of 307 and Maximian's Visits to Rome." *Phoenix* 35 (1981): 70–76.

——. "Constantinus Oriens Imperator: Propaganda and Panegyric: On Reading Panegyric 7 (307)." *Historia* 42 (1993): 229–46.

Nixon, C. E. V., and B. S. Rodgers. *In Praise of Later Roman Emperors: The Panegyrici Latini.* Berkeley, 1994.

Nock, A. D. "Paul and the Magus." In *The Beginning of Christianity,* ed. Jackson Lake, 5: 164–82. Also in *Essays on Religion and the Ancient World,* ed. Zeph Stewart (Oxford, 1986), 308–24.

Noethlichs, K. L. "Zur Entstehung der Diozesen als Mittelinstanz des spätrömischen Verwaltungssystems." *Historia* 31 (1982): 70–81.

Nöldeke, T. *Geschichte der Perser und Araber zur Zeit der Sasaniden. Aus der arabischen Chronik des Tabari übersetzt und mit ausführlichen Erläuterungen und Ergänzungen versehen.* Leiden, 1879.

Nollé, J. "Ofellius Laetus, platonischer Philosoph." *ZPE* 41 (1981): 197–206.

——. "Marketrechte außerhalb der Stadt: Lokale Autonomie zwischen Statthalter und Zentralort." In *Lokale Autonomie und römische Ordungsmacht in der kaiserzeitlichen Provinzen vom 1. bis 3. Jahrhundert,* ed. W. Eck and E. Müller-Luckner, 93–113. Munich, 1999.

Nollé, J., and W. Eck. "Der Brief des Asinius Rufus an die Magistrate von Sardeis. Zum Marktrechtsprivileg für die Gemeinde der Arillenoi." *Chiron* 26 (1996): 267–73.

Noreña, C. F., "The Communication of the Emperor's Virtues," *JRS* 91 (2001): 146–68.

Ochsenschlager, E. L. and V. Popovic, "Excavations at Sirmium, Yugoslavia." *Archaeology* 26 (1973): 85–93.

O'Donnell, J. J. *Augustine: Confessions.* 3 vols. Oxford, 1992.

O'Hara, J. J. "Fragment of a Homer-Hypothesis with No Gods." *ZPE* 56 (1984): 1–9.

Okamura, L. "Roman Withdrawals from Three Transfluvial Frontiers." In *Shifting Frontiers in Late Antiquity,* ed. R. W. Mathisen and H. S. Sivan, 11–19. Brookfield, VT, 1996.

Oliver, J. H. *Greek Constitutions of Early Roman Emperors from Inscriptions and Papyri.* Memoirs of the American Philosophical Society 178. Philadelphia, 1989.

Oliver, J. H., and R. E. A. Palmer. "Minutes of an Act of the Roman Senate." *Hesperia* 24 (1955): 320–49.

Olmstead, A. T. "The Mid-Third Century of the Christian Era." *CPh* 37 (1942): 241–62, 398–420.

Olsen, S. D., and A. Sens. *Archestratus of Gela: Greek Culture and Cuisine in the Fifth Century BCE.* Oxford, 2000.

O'Meara, J. J. *Porphyry's Philosophy from Oracles in Augustine.* Paris, 1959.

Opitz, H. G. *Urkunden zur Geschichte des arianischen Streites 318–328.* Berlin, 1934.

——. "Die Zeitfolge des arianischen Streites von den Anfängen bis zum Jahre 328." *Zeitschrift für die neutestamentliche Wissenschaft* 33 (1934): 131–59.

Oppenheimer, A. "Jewish Penal Authority in Roman Judaea." In *Jews in a Greco-Roman World,* ed. M. Goodman, vol. 3, pt. 1, 181–91. Oxford, 1998.

Osborn, E. *Tertullian, First Theologian of the West.* Oxford, 1997.

Osborne, C. *Rethinking Early Greek Philosophy: Hippolytus of Rome and the Presocratics.* London, 1987.

Page, D. L. *Select Papyri.* Vol. 3. Cambridge, Mass., 1941.

Palanque, J.-R. *Essai sur la préfecture du prétoire du Bas-Empire.* Paris, 1933.

——. *Saint Ambrose et l'empire romaine: Contribution à l'histoire des rapports de l'église et de l'état à la fin du quatrième siècle.* Paris, 1933.

——. "Collégialité et partages dans l'empire romain." *REA* 46 (1944): 280–98.

Panella, C. "Techniche costruttive e modalità di inserimiento dell' apparato decorativo." In *Arco di Costantino: Tra archeologia e archeometria*, ed. P. Pensabene and C. Panella, 43–73. Rome, 1999.

Parássoglou, G. M. "Circular from a Prefect: Dileat Omnibus Perpetuo Divinandi Curiositas." In *Collectanea Papyrologica: Texts Published in Honor of H. C. Youtie*, ed. A. E. Hanson, pt. 1, 261–74. Bonn, 1976.

Parca, M. *Ptocheia or Odysseus in Disguise at Troy (P. Köln VI 245).* Atlanta, 1991.

Parker, R. *Miasma: Pollution and Purification in Early Greek Religion.* Oxford, 1983.

Parkin, T. G. *Demography and Roman Society.* Baltimore, 1992.

Parsons, P. J. "Philippus Arabs and Egypt." *JRS* 57 (1967): 134–41.

——— . "A School-Book from the Sayce Collection." *ZPE* 6 (1970): 133–49.

——— . "Petitions and a Letter: The Grammarian's Complaint 253–60 AD." In *Collectanea Papyrologica: Texts Published in Honor of H. C. Youtie*, ed. A. E. Hanson, 409–46. Bonn, 1976.

Parvis, S. "The Canons of Ancyra and Caesarea (314): Lebon's Thesis Revisited." *JTS* 52 (2000): 625–36.

Paschoud, F. "Zosime 2, 29 et la version païenne de la conversion de Constantin." *Historia* 20 (1971): 334–53.

——— . *Cinq études sur Zosime.* Paris, 1975.

——— . *Histoire Auguste. Vies d'Aurélien et Tacite.* Paris, 1996.

Pasqualini, A. *Massimiano Herculius: Per un' interpretazione della figura e dell' opera.* Rome, 1979.

Paunov, E. I., and D. J. Dimitrov. "Die Siegelring des Aurelius Pyrrus aus Scaptopera." *Chiron* 26 (1996): 183–93.

Peachin, M. "The Office of the Memory." In *Studien zur Geschichte der römischen Spätantike: Festgabe für Professor Johannes Straub*, 168–208. Athens, 1989.

——— . "Once More AD 238," *Athenaeum* 67 (1989): 594–604.

——— . *Roman Imperial Titulature and Chronology, AD 235–284.* Amsterdam, 1990.

——— . *Iudex vice Caesaris: Deputy Emperors and the Administration of Justice during the Principate.* Stuttgart, 1996.

——— . "Jurists and the Law in the Early Roman Empire." In *Administration, Prosopography, and Appointment Policies in the Roman Empire*, ed. L. De Blois, 109–20. Amsterdam, 2001.

Pearson, B. A., and J. E. Goehring, eds. *The Roots of Egyptian Christianity.* Philadelphia, 1986.

Pékary, T. "Le Tribut aux Perses et les finances de Philippe l'Arab." *Syria* 38 (1961): 275–83.

Perry, B. E. *The Ancient Romances: A Literary Historical Account of Their Origins.* Berkeley, 1967.

Petit, P. *Libanius et la vie municipale à Antioche au iv siècle après J.-C.* Paris, 1955.

Petrikovits, H. von. "Fortifications in the North-Western Roman Empire from the Third to the Fifth Centuries AD." *JRS* 61 (1971): 178–218. Also in *Beiträge zur römischen Geschichte und Archäologie von 1931 bis 1974* (Bonn, 1976).

Pflaum, H. G. *Les procurateurs équestres sous le haut-empire romain.* Paris, 1950.

——— . "La fortification de la ville d'Adraha d'Arabie (259–260 à 274–275) d'après des inscriptions récemment découvertes." *Syria* 29 (1952): 307–30.

——— . "Deux familles sénatoriales des ii\ue et iii\ue siècles." *Journal des Savants* (1961): 108–22.

——— . "La valeur de l'information historique de la vita Commodi à la lumière des personnages nommément cités par le biographe." *BHAC 1970*, 199–247. Bonn, 1972.

Phang, S. E. *The Marriage of Roman Soldiers (13 BC–AD 235): Law and Family in the Roman Imperial Army.* Leiden, 2001.

Piganiol, A. *L'empire chrétien (325–395).* Paris, 1947.

Pighi, G. B. *De ludis saecularibus populi Romani Quiritum.* Rome, 1941.

Pitts, L. F. "Relations between Rome and the German 'Kings' on the Middle Danube in the First to Fourth Centuries AD." *JRS* 79 (1989): 45–58.

Pohlsander, H. A. "Victory: The Story of a Statue." *Historia* 18 (1969): 588–97.

——— . "Did Decius Kill the Philippi?" *Historia* 31 (1982): 214–22.

Pollard, N. "The Roman Army as 'Total Institution' in the Near East? Dura-Europus as a Case Study." In *The Roman Army in the East*, ed. D. L. Kennedy, 212–27. *JRA* Supplement 18. Ann Arbor, 1996.

——— . *Soldiers, Cities, and Civilians in Roman Syria.* Ann Arbor, 2000.

Polotsky, H. J. *Manichäische Homilien.* Stuttgart, 1934.

Portmann, W. "Die 59. Rede des Libanios und das Datum der Schlacht von Singara." *BzZ* 82 (1989): 1–18.

——— . "Die politische Krise zwischen den Kaisern Constantius II. und Constans." *Historia* 48 (1999): 300–29.

Potter, D. S. "The *Tabula Siarensis*, Tiberius, the Senate, and the Eastern Boundary of the Roman Empire." *ZPE* 69 (1987): 269–76.

——— . "Recent Inscriptions from Flat Cilicia." *JRA* 2 (1989): 309–10.

——— . *Prophecy and History in the Crisis of the Roman Empire. A Historical Commentary on the Thirteenth Sibylline Oracle.* Oxford, 1990.

——— . "The Inscriptions on the Bronze Herakles from Mesene: Vologaeses IV's War with Rome and the Date of Tacitus' *Annales*." *ZPE* 88 (1991): 277–90.

——— . "Empty Areas and Roman Frontier Policy." *AJP* 113 (1992): 269–74.

——— . "Martyrdom as Spectacle." In *Theater and Society in the Classical World*, ed. R. Scodel, 53–87. Ann Arbor, 1993.

——— . Review of M. Goodman, *Mission and Conversion: Proselytizing in the Religious History of the Roman Empire. BMCR* (1993) 5.4.

——— . *Prophets and Emperors: Human and Divine Authority from Augustus to Theodosius.* Cambridge, Mass., 1994.

——— . "Emperors, Their Borders, and Their Neighbours: The Scope of Imperial *mandata*." In *The Roman Army in the East*, ed. D. L. Kennedy, 49–66. *JRA* Supplement 18. Ann Arbor, 1996.

——— . "Gaining Information on Rome's Neighbours." *JRA* 9 (1996): 528–32.

——— . "Palmyra and Rome: Odaenathus' Titulature and the Use of the *Imperium Maius*." *ZPE* 113 (1996): 271–85.

——— . "Performance, Power, and Justice in the High Empire." In *Roman Theater and Society*, ed. W. Slater, 129–59. Ann Arbor, 1996.

——— . "Procurators in Asia and Dacia under Marcus Aurelius: A Case Study of Imperial Initiative in Government." *ZPE* 123 (1998): 270–74.

——— . "Entertainers in the Roman Empire." In *Life, Death, and Entertainment in the Roman Empire*, ed. D. S. Potter and D. J. Mattingly, 256–325. Ann Arbor, 1999.

——— . *Literary Texts and the Roman Historian.* London, 1999.

——— . "Political Theory in the *Senatus Consultum Pisonianum*." In "The *Senatus Consultum De Cn. Pisone Patre*: Text, Translation, Discussion," special issue of *AJP*, ed. C. Damon and S. Takács, 120 (1999): 65–88.

Potter, D. S., and D. J. Mattingly, eds. *Life, Death, and Entertainment in the Roman Empire.* Ann Arbor, 1999.

Potts, D. T. *The Archaeology of Elam: Formation and Transformation of an Ancient Iranian State.* Cambridge, 1999.

Purcell, N. "Eating Fish: The Paradoxes of Seafood." In *Food in Antiquity*, ed. J. Wilkins, D. Harvey, and M. Dobson, 132–49. Exeter, 1996.

Rappe, S. "Self-Knowledge and Subjectivity in the Enneads." In *The Cambridge Companion to Plotinus*, ed. L. P. Gerson, 250–74. Cambridge, 1996.

Rapsaet-Charlier, M. T. *Prosopographie des femmes de l'ordre sénatorial (Ier–IIe siècles).* Louvain, 1987.

——— . "Les femmes sénatoriales du iiie siècle. Étude préliminaire." In *Prosopographie und Sozialgeschichte. Studien zur Methodik und Erkenntnismöglichkeit der kaizerzeitlichen Prosopographie. Kolloquium Köln*, ed. W. Eck. (Cologne, 1993), 147–63.

Rathbone, D. *Economic Rationalism and Rural Society in Third-Century AD Egypt.* Cambridge, 1991.

——— . "Monetisation, Not Price-Inflation, in Third-Century AD Egypt." In *Coin Finds and Coin Use in the Roman World: The Thirteenth Oxford Symposium on Coinage and Monetary History 25.27.3.1993*, ed. C. E. King and D. G. Wigg, 329–33. Berlin, 1996.

Raynor, D. H. "Non-Christian Attitudes to Monasticism." *Studia Patristica* 18, no. 2 (1983): 267–72.

Rea, J. "The Date of the Prefecture of Statilius Aemilianus." *Chronique d'Égypte* 44 (1969): 134–38.

——— . "P.Oxy. XXXIII 2673.2: πύλη or ὕλην," *ZPE* 35 (1979): 128.

Reardon, B. P. *Aphrodisias and Rome. JRS* Monograph 1. London, 1982.

——— . "Chariton." In *The Novel in the Ancient World*, ed. G. Schmeling, 309–35. *Mnemosyne* Supplement 159. Leiden, 1996.

Rees, R. *Layers of Loyalty in Latin Panegyric AD 289–307.* Oxford, 2002.

Reeves, J. C. *Jewish Lore in Manichaean Cosmogony: Studies in the Book of Giants Tradition.* Cincinnati, 1992.

Rengen, W. van. "La IIe Légion Parthique à Apamée." In *Les légions de Rome sous le Haut-Empire. Actes du Congrès de Lyon (17–19 septembre 1998)*, ed. Y. Le Bohec and C. Wolff, 407–10. Lyons, 2000.

Reynolds, J. "New Letters from Hadrian to Aphrodisias: Trials, Taxes, Gladiators, and an Aqueduct." *JRA* 13 (2000): 5–20.

Ricci, C. "Legio II Parthica. Una messa a punto." In *Les légions de Rome sous le Haut-Empire. Actes du Congrès de Lyon (17–19 septembre 1998)*, ed. Y. Le Bohec and C. Wolff, 397–406. Lyons, 2000.

Rickman, G. *The Corn Supply of Ancient Rome.* Oxford, 1980.

Ridley, R. T. "Notes on Julian's Persian Expedition (363)." *Historia* 22 (1973): 317–30.

Rife, J. L. "Officials of the Roman Provinces in Xenophon's *Ephesiaca*." *ZPE* 138 (2002): 93–108.

Ritter, A. M. "Arianismus." *Theologische Realenzyklopädie*, 3: 698–99. Berlin, 1978.

Ritterling, E. "Legio." *RE* 12 (1925): 1211–1829.

Rives, J. B. *Religion and Authority in Roman Carthage from Augustus to Constantine.* Oxford, 1995.

——— . "The Decree of Decius and the Religion of Empire." *JRS* 89 (1999): 135–54.

Rizakis, A. D. "*Incolae-Paroikoi:* Populations et communautés dépendantes dans les cités et les colonies romaines de l'orient." *REA* 100 (1998): 599–617.

Robert, L. "Sur un papyrus de Bruxelles." *Revue de Philologie*, 3rd ser., 17 (1943): 111–19. Also in *OMS* 1 (Amsterdam, 1969): 364–72.

——. *Études de numismatique grecque.* Paris, 1951.

——. "Reliefs votifs et cultes d'Anatolie," *Anadolu* 3 (1958): 103–36. Also in *OMS* 1 (Amsterdam, 1969): 402–35.

——. "Trois oracles de la Théosophie et un prophète d'Apollon." *CRAI* (1968): 568–99. Also in *OMS* 5 (Amsterdam, 1989): 584–616.

——. "Théophane de Mytilène à Constantinople." *CRAI* (1969): 42–64. Also in *OMS* 5 (Amsterdam, 1989): 561–83.

——. "Deux concours grecs à Rome." *CRAI* (1970): 6–27. Also in *OMS* 5 (Amsterdam, 1989): 655–58.

——. "Un oracle gravé à Oinoanda." *CRAI* (1971): 597–619. Also in *OMS* 5 (Amsterdam, 1989): 617–39.

——. "La titulature de Nicée et de Nicomédie: La gloire et la haine." *HSCP* 81 (1977): 1–39. Also in *OMS* 6: 211–49.

——. *À travers l'Asie mineure: Poètes et prosateurs, monnaies grecques, voyageurs et géographie.* Paris, 1980.

——. "Documents d'Asie mineure." *BCH* 107 (1983): 529–42. Also in *Documents d'Asie mineure* (Paris, 1987), 373–86.

Rodgers, B. S. "Constantine's Pagan Vision." *Byzantion* 50 (1980): 259–78.

Roller, L. R. *In Search of God the Mother: The Cult of Anatolian Cybele.* Berkeley, 1999.

Romeo, I. "The Panhellenion and Ethnic Identity in Hadrianic Greece." *CPh* 97 (2001): 21–40.

Römer, C. *Manis frühe Missionsreisen nach der Kölner Manibiographie.* Papyrologica Coloniensia 24. Cologne, 1994.

Romeri, L. "The λογόδειπνον: Athenaeus between Banquet and Anti-Banquet." In *Athenaeus and His World: Reading Greek Culture in the Roman Empire*, ed. D. Braund and J. Wilkins, 256–71. Exeter, 2000.

Ross, S. K. *Roman Edessa: Politics and Culture on the Eastern Fringes of the Roman Empire.* London, 2001.

Rossum-Steenbeck, M. van. *Greek Reader's Digests? Studies on a Selection of Subliterary Papyri.* Leiden, 1998.

Rostovtzeff, M. I. *The Social and Economic History of the Roman Empire.* 2nd edn., ed. P. M. Fraser. 2 vols. Oxford, 1957.

Rostovtzeff, M. I., M. L. Shine, R. H. Whitbeck, and G. B. L. Arner. *Urban Land Economics.* Ann Arbor, 1922.

Roueché, C. *Aphrodisias in Late Antiquity.* *JRS* Monograph 5. London, 1989.

Rousseau, P. *Pachomius: The Making of a Community in Fourth Century Egypt.* Berkeley, 1985.

——. "Antony as Teacher in the Greek *Life*." In *Greek Biography and Panegyric in Late Antiquity*, ed. T. Hägg and P. Rousseau, 89–109. Berkeley, 2000.

Rowlandson, J. *Landowners and Tenants in Roman Egypt: The Social Relations of Agriculture in the Oxyrhyncite Nome.* Oxford, 1996.

Rubenson, S. *The Letters of St. Anthony: Monasticism and the Making of a Saint.* Minneapolis, 1995.

Rubin, Z. *Civil War Propaganda and Historiography.* Brussels, 1980.

———. "Mass Movements in Late Antiquity: Appearances and Realities." In *Leaders and Masses in the Roman World: Studies in Honor of Zvi Yavetz*, ed. I. Malkin and Z. W. Rubinsohn, 137–56. Leiden, 1994.

Rudolph, K. *Gnosis: The Nature and History of Gnosticism.* Trans. R. Wilson. San Francisco, 1987.

Rumney, G. *Climatology and the World's Climates.* London, 1968.

Ruschenbusch, E. "Diokletians Währungsreform vom 1.9.301." *ZPE* 26 (1977): 193–210.

Russell, D. A., *Plutarch.* London, 1973.

———., ed. *Antonine Literature.* Oxford, 1990.

Rutherford, R. *The Meditations of Marcus Aurelius: A Study.* Oxford, 1989.

Ruysschaert, J. "Essai d'interprétation synthétique de l'Arc de Constantin." *APARA* Rendiconti, 35 (1962–63): 79–105.

Sablayrolles, R. "Fastigium equestre: Les grands préfectures équestres." In *L'ordre équestre d'une aristocratie (iie siècle av. J.-C.–iiie siècle ap. J.-C.),* ed. S. Demougin, H. Devijver, and M.-T. Rapsaet-Charlier, 351–89. Paris, 1999.

Saddington, D. B. *The Development of the Roman Auxiliary Forces from Caesar to Vespasian.* Harare, 1982.

Said, S. "The City in the Greek Novel." In J. Tatum, *The Search for the Ancient Novel.* Baltimore, 1994.

———. "Rural Society in the Greek Novel, or the Country Seen from the Town." In *Oxford Readings in the Greek Novel,* ed. S. Swain, 83–107. Oxford, 1999.

Ste. Croix, G. E. M. de. "Aspects of the 'Great' Persecution." *HTR* 47 (1954): 73–113.

———. "Why Were the Early Christians Persecuted?" *Past and Present* 26 (1963): 6–38.

———. *The Class Struggle in the Ancient Greek World.* Oxford, 1981.

Salisbury, J. E. *Perpetua's Passion: The Death and Memory of a Young Roman Woman.* London, 1997.

Sallares, R. *The Ecology of the Ancient Greek World.* Ithaca, NY, 1991.

Saller, R. P. *Personal Patronage under the Early Empire.* Cambridge, 1982.

———. *Patriarchy, Property, and Death in the Roman Family.* Cambridge, 1994.

Salway, B. "A Fragment of Severan History: The Unusual Case of . . . atus, Praetorian Prefect of Elagabalus." *Chiron* 27 (1997): 127–53.

Salway, P. *Roman Britain.* Oxford, 1984.

Salzman, M. R. "*Superstitio* in the Codex Theodosianus and the Persecution of Pagans." *Vigiliae Christianae* 41 (1987): 172–88.

———. *The Making of a Christian Aristocracy: Social and Religious Change in the Western Roman Empire.* Cambridge, Mass., 2002.

Sartre, M. *Trois études sur l'Arabie romaine et byzantine.* Brussels, 1982.

———. "Le *Dies Imperii* de Gordien III: Une inscription inédite de Syrie." *Syria* 61 (1984): 49–61.

———. "Les *metrokomai* de Syrie du sud." *Syria* 76 (1999): 197–222.

Sauer, E. "M. Annius Florianus: Ein Drei-Monate-Kaiser und die ihm zu Ehren aufgestellten Steinmonument (276 n. Chr.)." *Historia* 47 (1998): 174–203.

Scheidel, W. "Roman Age Structure: Evidence and Models." *JRS* 91 (2001): 1–26.

Schenk Graf von Stauffenberg, A. *Die römische Kaisergeschichte bei Malalas.* Stuttgart, 1931.

Schlinkert, D. *Ordo senatorius und nobilitas: Die Konstitution des Senatsadels in der Spätantike.* *Hermes* Einzelschriften 72. Stuttgart, 1996.

Schlumberger, D. "L'inscription d'Hérodien: Remarques sur l'histoire des princes de Palmyre." *Bulletin des études orientales* 11 (1942–43): 36–50.

——. "Les gentilices romains des Palmyréniens." *Bulletin des études orientales* 11 (1942–43): 53–64.

——. "Vorod l'agoronome." *Syria* 49 (1972): 339–41.

Schmeling, G. *The Novel in the Ancient World. Mnemosyne* Supplement 159. Leiden, 1996.

Schürer, E. *The History of the Jewish People in the Age of Jesus Christ.* Rev. edn., ed. G. Vermes, F. Millar, M. Black, and M. Goodman. 3 vols. Edinburgh, 1973–87.

Schwartz, E. "Die Dokumente des arianischen Streits bis 325." *Nachrichten von der k. Gesellschaft der Wissenschaften zu Göttingen, phil.-hist. Klasse* (1905): 257–99. Also in E. Schwartz, *Gesammelte Schriften*, vol. 3 (Berlin, 1959): 117–68.

——. "Die Quellen über den melitianischen Streit." *Nachrichten von der k. Gesellschaft der Wissenschaften zu Göttingen, phil.-hist. Klasse* (1905): 166–75. Also in E. Schwartz, *Gesammelte Schriften*, vol. 3 (Berlin, 1959): 89–100.

——. "Das antiochenische Synodalschreiben von 325." *Nachrichten von der k. Gesellschaft der Wissenschaften zu Göttingen, phil.-hist. Klasse* (1908): 305–79. Also in E. Schwartz, *Gesammelte Schriften*, vol. 3 (Berlin, 1959): 169–87 (reprinting pp. 354–59 and 365–74).

Schwartz, J. "Une déclaration de sacrifice du temps de Dèce." *RB* 54 (1947): 365–67.

Scodel, R., ed. *Theater and Society in the Classical World.* Ann Arbor, 1993.

Seager, R. "Perceptions of Eastern Frontier Policy in Ammianus, Libanius, and Julian (337–363)." *CQ* 47 (1997): 253–62.

Seeck, O. *Geschichte des Untergangs der antiken Welt.* 6 vols. Berlin, 1895–1920.

——. *Regesten der Kaiser und Päpste.* Stuttgart, 1919.

——. "Alaricus." *RE* 1, cols. 1286–91.

Seston, W. *Dioclétien et la tétrarchie.* Paris, 1946.

Seyrig, H. "Note sur Hérodien, prince de Palmyre." *Syria* 18 (1937): 1–4.

——. "Les fils du roi Odainat." *AAS* 13 (1963): 159–72. Also in *Scripta Varia: Mélanges d'archéologie et d'histoire* (Paris, 1985), 265–78.

Shackleton Bailey, D. R. "Nobiles and Novi Reconsidered." *AJP* 107 (1986): 255–60. Also in *Selected Classical Papers* (Ann Arbor, 1997), 309–13.

Sharpe, M. "Shearing Sheep: Rome and the Collection of Taxes in Egypt, 30 BC–AD 200." In *Lokale Autonomie und römische Ordungsmacht in der kaiserzeitlichen Provinzen vom 1. bis 3. Jahrhundert*, ed. W. Eck and E. Müller-Luckner, 213–41. Munich, 1999.

Shaw, B. D. "Climate, Environment, and History: The Case of Roman North Africa." In *Climate and History: Studies in Past Climates and Their Effect on Man*, ed. T. M. L. Wigley, M. J. Ingram, and G. Farmer, 390–91. Cambridge, 1981.

——. "Bandits in the Roman Empire." *Past and Present* 105 (1984): 3–52.

——. "The Passion of Perpetua." *Past and Present* 139 (1993): 3–45.

——. Review of J. Evans Grubbs, *Law and Family in Late Antiquity: The Emperor Constantine's Marriage Legislation. BMCR* (1996) 8. 12.

——. "Challenging Braudel: A New Revision of the Mediterranean." *JRA* 14 (2001): 419–53.

Sherwin-White, A. N. *The Roman Citizenship.* 2nd edn. Oxford, 1973.

Sijpesteijn, P. J. and K. A. Worp. *Zwei Landlisten aus dem Hermopolites (P. Landlisten).* Studia Amstelodamensia ad epigraphicum, ius antiquum et papyrologicum pertinentia 7. Zutphen, 1978.

Simmons, M. B. *Arnobius of Sicca: Religious Conflict and Competition in the Age of Diocletian.* Oxford, 1995.

746

Sivan, H. "Was Theodosius I a Usurper?" *Klio* 78 (1996): 198–211.

Slater, W. J., ed. *Roman Theater and Society*. Ann Arbor, 1996.

Slicher van Bath, B. H. *The Agrarian History of Western Europe, AD 500–1850*. Trans. O. Ordish. London, 1963.

Slusser, M. "Traditional Views of Late Arianism." In *Arianism after Arius: Essays on the Development of the Fourth Century Trinitarian Conflicts*, ed. M. R. Barnes and D. H. Williams, 3–30. Edinburgh, 1993.

Smith, A. *Porphyry's Place in the Neoplatonic Tradition*. The Hague, 1974.

Smith, M. D. "The Religion of Constantius I." *GRBS* 38 (1997): 187–208.

Smith, R. B. E. *Julian's Gods: Religion and Philosophy in the Thought of Julian the Apostate*. London, 1995.

Smith, R. R. R. "The Public Image of Licinius I: Portrait Sculpture and Imperial Ideology in the Early Fourth Century." *JRS* 87 (1997): 187–94.

———. "Cultural Choice and Political Identity in Honorific Portrait Statues in the Greek East in the Second Century AD." *JRS* 88 (1998): 56–93.

Southern, P., and K. R. Dixon. *The Late Roman Army*. New Haven, 1996.

Spawforth, A. J. S. "Symbol of Unity? The Persian-Wars Tradition in the Roman Empire." In *Greek Historiography*, ed. S. Hornblower, 233–47. Oxford, 1994.

———. "The Panhellenion Again." *Chiron* 29 (1999): 339–52.

Spawforth, A. J. S., and S. Walker. "The World of the Panhellenion. I. Athens and Eleusis." *JRS* 75 (1985): 78–104.

———. "The World of the Panhellenion. II. Three Dorian Cities." *JRS* 76 (1986): 88–105.

Speidel, M. A. "Roman Army Pay Scales." *JRS* 82 (1992): 87–106.

Speidel, M. P. "The Roman Army in Arabia." *ANRW* 2.8 (1977): 712–14. Also in *Roman Army Studies*, vol. 1 (Amsterdam, 1984): 254–56.

———. *The Framework of an Imperial Legion*. The Fifth Annual Caerleon Lecture. Cardiff, 1992.

———. "Commodus as God-Emperor and the Army." *JRS* 83 (1993): 109–14.

———. "A Horse Guardsman in the War between Licinius and Constantine." *Chiron* 25 (1995): 183–87.

———. "Sebastian's Strike Force at Adrianople." *Klio* 78 (1996): 434–37.

Spooner, J. *Nine Homeric Papyri from Oxyrhynchus*. Studi e Testi di Papirologia, N.S. 1. Florence, 2002.

Srejović, D., ed. *Roman Imperial Towns and Palaces in Serbia*. Belgrade, 1993.

———. "The Representations of Tetrarchs in Romuliana," *An. Tard* 2 (1994): 143–52.

Stahl, M. "Zwischen Abgrenzung und Integration: Die Verträge der Kaiser Mark Aurel und Commodus mit den Völken jenseits der Donau." *Chiron* 19 (1989): 289–317.

Stark, R. *The Rise of Christianity: A Sociologist Reconsiders History*. Princeton, 1996.

Stead, J. C. "'Eusebius' and the Council of Nicaea." *JTS* 24 (1973): 83–100.

Stein, E. "Kallinikos von Petra." *Hermes* 58 (1923): 448–56.

———. *Histoire du Bas-Empire*. Vol. 1. Paris, 1959.

Stephens, S., and J. Winkler. *Ancient Greek Novels: The Fragments*. Princeton, 1999.

Stroumsa, G. "The Manichaean Challenge to Egyptian Christianity." In *The Roots of Egyptian Christianity*, ed. B. A. Pearson and J. E. Goehring, 307–19. Philadelphia, 1986.

Sundermann, W. *Mitteliranische manichäische Texte kirchengeschichtlichen Inhalts*. Schriften zur Geschichte und Kultur des alten Orients. Berliner Turfantexte 11. Berlin, 1981.

Sutherland, C. H. V., and R. A. G. Carson. *The Roman Imperial Coinage*. Vol. 6. London, 1967.

Swain, S. *Hellenism and Empire: Language, Classicism, and Power in the Greek World,* AD *50–250.* Oxford, 1996.

——— . "A Century and More of the Greek Novel." In *Oxford Readings in the Greek Novel,* ed. S. Swain, 3–35. Oxford, 1999.

Syme, R. *The Roman Revolution.* Oxford, 1939.

——— . *Tacitus.* Oxford, 1958.

——— . *Ammianus and the Historia Augusta.* Oxford, 1968.

——— . "Three Jurists." *BHAC 1968–69,* 309–23. Bonn, 1970. Also in Syme, *Roman Papers,* vol. 2, ed. E. Badian (Oxford, 1979): 790–804.

——— . *Emperors and Biography: Studies in the Historia Augusta.* Oxford, 1971.

——— . "Lawyers in Government: The Case of Ulpian." *PAPS* 116 (1972): 406–9. Also in Syme, *Roman Papers,* vol. 3, ed. A. R. Birley (Oxford, 1984): 863–68.

——— . "The *Pomerium* in the *Historia Augusta.*" *BHAC 1975–76,* 217–31. Bonn, 1978. Also in Syme, *Historia Augusta Papers* (Oxford, 1983), 131–45.

——— . "Fiction about Roman Jurists." *Zeitschrift der Savigny-Stiftung für Rechtsgeschichte* 97 (1980): 78–104. Also in Syme, *Roman Papers,* vol. 3, ed. A. R. Birley (Oxford, 1984): 1393–1414.

——— . "Greeks Invading the Roman Government." The Seventh Stephen J. Brademas Sr. Lecture, Brookline, Mass., 1982. Also in Syme, *Roman Papers,* vol. 4, ed. A. R. Birley (Oxford, 1988): 1–20.

——— . "Antonine Government and Governing Class." *Scienze dell' Antichità* 1 (1987) (n.v.). Also in Syme, *Roman Papers,* vol. 5, ed. A. R Birley (Oxford, 1988): 668–88.

——— . "Avidius Cassius: His Rank, Age, and Quality." *BHAC 1984–85,* 207–22. Bonn, 1987. Also in *Roman Papers,* vol. 5, ed. A. R. Birley (Oxford, 1988): 689–701.

Szepessy, T. "La siège de Nisibe et la chronologie d'Héliodore." *Acta Antiqua* 24 (1976): 247–76.

Tabbernee, W. "Eusebius' 'Theology of Persecution' as Seen in the Various Editions of His Church History." *JECS* 5 (1997): 319–34.

——— . *Montanist Inscriptions and Testimonia: Epigraphic Sources Illustrating the History of Montanism.* Macon, GA, 1997.

Takács, S. *Isis and Sarapis in the Roman World.* Leiden, 1995.

Talbert, R. J. A. *The Senate of Imperial Rome.* Princeton, 1984.

——— . *Barrington Atlas of the Greek and Roman World.* Princeton, 2000.

Tardieu, M. *Le manichéisme.* Paris, 1981.

Tausend, K. "Bemerkungen zum Wandaleneinfall des Jahres 271." *Historia* 48 (1999): 119–27.

Teitler, H. C. *Notarii and Exceptores: An Inquiry into the Role and Significance of Shorthand Writers in the Imperial and Ecclesiastical Bureaucracy of the Roman Empire (from the Early Principate to c. 450* AD*).* Amsterdam, 1985.

Temin, P. "A Market Economy in the Early Roman Empire." *JRS* 91 (2001): 169–201.

Thomas, G. S. R. "L'Abdication de Dioclétien." *Byzantion* 43 (1973): 229–47.

Thomas, J. D. "The Introduction of the Dekaprotoi and Comarchs into Egypt in the Third Century AD." *ZPE* 19 (1975): 111–19.

Thomasson, B. *Laterculi Praesidum.* Vol. 1. Göteborg, 1984.

Thompson, E. A. *The Historical Work of Ammianus Marcellinus.* Cambridge, 1947.

——— . *A Roman Reformer and Inventor.* Oxford, 1952.

Tilley, M. A. *Donatist Martyr Stories: The Church in Conflict in Roman North Africa.* Liverpool, 1996.

748

Trapp, M. B. *Maximus of Tyre: The Philosophical Discussions.* Oxford, 1997.
——. "Philosophical Sermons: The 'Dialexeis' of Maximus of Tyr." *ANRW* 2.34.3 (1997): 1945–76.
Trebilco, P. R. *Jewish Communities in Asia Minor.* Cambridge, 1991.
Treggiari, S. *Roman Marriage: "Iusti coniuges" from the Time of Cicero to the Time of Ulpian.* Oxford, 1991.
Trevett, C. *Montanism: Gender, Authority, and the New Prophecy.* Cambridge, 1996.
Trimble, J. "Replicating the Body Politic: The Herculaneum Women Statue Types in Early Roman Italy." *JRA* 13 (2000): 41–68.
Turcan, R. "Le délit des monétaires rebellés contre Aurélien." *Latomus* 28 (1969): 948–59.
Urbainczyk, T. *Socrates of Constantinople: Historian of Church and State.* Ann Arbor, 1997.
Ustinova, J. "The *Thiasoi* of Theos Hypsistos in Tanais." *History of Religions* 31 (1991): 150–80.
Valavanolickal, K. *Aphrahat: Demonstrations.* Changanassery, 1999.
Vanderspoel, J. *Themistius and the Imperial Court: Oratory, Civic Duty, and Paideia from Constantius to Theodosius.* Ann Arbor, 1995.
Veilleux, A. *La liturgie dans le cénobitisme pachômien du quatrième siècle.* Studia Anselmiana 57. Rome, 1968.
Velkov, V. "Aurélien et sa politique en Mésie et Thrace." In *Les empereurs illyriens: Actes du colloque de Strasbourg (11–13 octobre 1990) organisé par le Centre de Recherche sur l'Europe centrale et sud-orientale,* ed. E. Frézouls and H. Jouffroy, 155–69. Strasbourg, 1998.
Vera, D. "I rapporti fra Magno Massimo, Teodosio e Valentiniano II nel 383–384." *Athenaeum* 53 (1975): 267–301.
Vermaseren, M. J. *Corpus Inscriptionum et Monumentorum Religionis Mithriacae.* Vols. 1–2. The Hague, 1956–60.
Vian, F. *Recherches sur les Posthomerica de Quintus de Smyrne.* Paris, 1959.
Virlouvet, C. *Tessara Frumentaria: Les procédures de la distribution du blé public à Rome à la fin de la république et au début de l'empire.* Rome, 1995.
Vittinghof, F. *Der Stattsfeind in der römischen Kaiserzeit.* Berlin, 1936.
Vitucci, G. *L'imperatore Probo.* Rome, 1952.
Vogler, C. *Constance II et l'administration impériale.* Strasbourg, 1979.
Waldmann, H. *Der kommagenische Mazdaismus.* Istanbuler Mitteilungen Beiheft 37. Tübingen, 1991.
Walker, D. *The Metrology of Roman Silver Coinage.* Vol. 3: *From Pertinax to Uranius Antoninus.* BAR International Series 40. Oxford, 1978.
Walsh, P. G. *The Roman Novel.* Cambridge, 1970.
Ward-Perkins, J. B. *The Severan Buildings of Lepcis Magna.* Society for Libyan Studies Monograph 2. London, 1993.
Warmington, B. H. "The Career of Romanus, *Comes Africae.*" *BzZ* 49 (1956): 55–64.
——. "Aspects of Constantinian Propaganda in the *Panegyrici Latini.*" *TAPA* (1974): 371–84.
——. "Ammianus Marcellinus and the Lies of Metrodorus." *CQ* 32 (1981): 464–68.
——. "The Sources of Some Constantinian Documents in Eusebius' *Ecclesiastical History* and the *Life of Constantine.*" *Studia Patristica* 18 (1986): 83–98.
Watson, A. *Aurelian and the Third Century.* London, 1999.
Webster, J. "Necessary Comparisons: A Post-colonial Approach to Religious Syncretism in the Roman Provinces." *W. Arch.* 28 (1996–97): 324–38.
Weiss, P. "The Vision of Constantine." *JRA* 16 (2003): 237–59.

Wells, P. S. *The Barbarians Speak.* Princeton, 1999.

West, M. L. *Iambi et Elegi Graeci.* Oxford, 1972.

——— . "The Meter of Arius' *Thalia.*" *JTS* 33 (1982): 98–105.

Wheeler, E. L. "The Roman Legion as Phalanx." *Chiron* 9 (1979): 303–18.

——— . "The Laxity of Syrian Legions." In *The Roman Army in the East,* ed. D. L. Kennedy, 229–76. *JRA* Supplement 18. Ann Arbor, 1996.

Whitby, M. "The Persian King at War." In *The Roman and Byzantine Army in the East: Proceedings of a Colloquium Held at the Jagiellonian University, Kraków in September 1992,* ed. E. Dąbrowa, 228–63. Cracow, 1994.

Whittaker, C. R. "The Revolt of Papirius Dionysius, AD 190." *Historia* 13 (1964): 348–69. Also in *Land, City, and Trade in the Roman Empire* (Brookfield, VT, 1993), ch. 6.

Wickham, C. "The Other Transition: From the Ancient World to Feudalism." *Past and Present* 103 (1984): 3–36.

Widengren, G. *Mani and Manichaeism.* Trans. Charles Kessler. London, 1965.

——— . "Iran, der grosse Gegner Roms: Königsgewalt, Feudalismus, Militärwesen." *ANRW* 2.9.1 (1976): 219–306.

——— . "Leitende Ideen und Quellen der iranischer Apokalyptik." In *Apocalypticism in the Mediterranean World and the Near East: Proceedings of the International Colloquium on Apocalypticism, Uppsala, August 12–17 (1979),* ed. D. Hellholm, 127–33. Tübingen, 1983.

Wiedemann, T. *Emperors and Gladiators.* London, 1992.

Wightman, E. M. *Roman Trier and the Treviri.* New York, 1971.

——— . *Gallia Belgica.* Berkeley, 1985.

Wilcken, U. "Die Titulatur des Vaballathus." *ZfN* 15 (1887): 330–32.

Wiles, M. F. "In Defense of Arius." *JTS* 13 (1962): 339–47.

Williams, D. H. "The Quest of the Historical *Thalia.*" In *Arianism: Historical and Theological Reassessments,* ed. R. C. Gregg, 19–21. Philadelphia, 1985.

——— . *Arius: Heresy and Tradition.* London, 1987.

——— . *Ambrose of Milan and the End of the Arian–Nicene Conflicts.* Oxford, 1995.

——— . "Defining Orthodoxy in Hilary of Poitiers' Commentarium in Matthaeum." *JECS* 9 (2001): 151–71.

Williams, S. *Diocletian and the Roman Recovery.* London, 1985.

Williams, S., and G. Friell. *Theodosius: The Empire at Bay.* London, 1994.

Williams, W. "Caracalla and the Rhetoricians: A Note on the *cognitio de Gohariensis.*" *Latomus* 33 (1974): 663–67.

——— . "The *Libellus* Procedure and the Severan Papyri." *JRS* 64 (1974): 86–103.

Winnett, F., and G. L. Harding. *Inscriptions from Fifty Safaitic Cairns.* Toronto, 1978.

Winter, E. *Die sāsānidisch–römischen Friedensverträge des 3. Jahrhunderts n. Chr. – Ein Beitrag zum Verständnis der außenpolitischen Beziehungen zwischen den bieden Großmächten.* Frankfurt am Main, 1988.

Wipszycka, E. A. "Le monachisme égyptien et les villes." In *Travaux et Mémoires.* Collège de France Centre de researche d'histoire et civilization de Byzance 12. Paris, 1994. 1–44. Also in Wipszycka, *Études sur le christianisme dans l'Égypte de l'antiquité tardive* (Rome, 1996).

——— . "P. Coll. Youtie 77 = P. Coll. 171 Revisited." In *Essays in Honor of J. David Thomas,* ed. T. Gagos and R. Bagnall, 45–50. Exeter, 2001.

Wissemann, M. *Roma Renascens. Ilona Opelt von ihren Freunden und Schülern gewidmet.* Frankfurt am Main, 1988.

Wolff, C. "Legio I Parthica." In *Les légions de Rome sous le Haut-Empire. Actes du Congrès de Lyon (17–19 septembre 1998)*, ed. Y. Le Bohec and C. Wolff, 247–49. Lyons, 2000.

———. "Legio III Parthica." In *Les légions de Rome sous le Haut-Empire. Actes du Congrès de Lyon (17–19 septembre 1998)*, ed. Y. Le Bohec and C. Wolff, 251–52. Lyons, 2000.

Wolff, H. *Die Constitutio Antoniniana und Papyrus Gissensis 40*. Vol. 1. Cologne, 1976.

Wolfram, H. *History of the Goths*. Trans. T. J. Dunlap. Berkeley, 1987.

———. *The Roman Empire and Its Germanic Peoples*. Trans. T. J. Dunlap. Berkeley, 1997.

Woods, D. "Two Notes on the Great Persecution." *JTS* 43 (1992): 128–34.

———. "Three Notes on Aspects of the Arian Controversy, c. 354–367 CE." *JTS* 44 (1993): 604–19.

———. "Saracen Defenders of Constantinople in 378." *GRBS* 37 (1996): 259–79.

Woolf, G. "Beyond Romans and Natives." *W. Arch.* 28 (1996–97): 339–50.

———. *Becoming Roman: The Origins of Provincial Civilization in Gaul*. Cambridge, 1998.

Wörrle, M. *Stadt und Fest im kaiserzeitlichen Kleinasien*. Munich, 1988.

York, J. M. "The Image of Philip the Arab." *Historia* 21 (1972): 320–32.

Young, G. K. *Rome's Eastern Trade: International Commerce and Imperial Policy, 31 BC–AD 305*. London, 2001.

Zeitlin, F. I. "Visions and Revisions of Homer." In *Being Greek under Rome: Cultural Identity, the Second Sophistic, and the Development of Empire*, ed. S. Goldhill, 195–266. Cambridge, 2001.

Ziegler, R. *Städisches Prestige und kaiserliche Politik: Studien zum Festwesen in Ostkilikien im 2. und 3. Jahrhundert n. Chr.* Düsseldorf, 1985.

———. "Thessalonike in der Politik des Traianus Decius und der Tod des Philippus Arabs." In *Roma Renascens: Ilona Opelt von ihren Freunden und Schülern gewidmet*, ed. M. Wissemann, 385–414. Frankfurt am Main, 1988.

INDEX